A Quantitative Primer on Investments with R

Dale W.R. Rosenthal

Q36

www.q36llc.com/think/investments
Chicago

This book was typeset using Emacs and LaTeX2$_\varepsilon$. The font, Computer Modern, was created by Donald Knuth in 1986 and updated in 1992 to evoke the beauty of classical hot metal printing. No rekeying has been done of the text or equations. This choice was a top priority so as to deliver the reader the highest level of accuracy.

The Q$_{36}$ wordmark uses Josefin Sans, a modern geometric font created in 2010 by Santiago Orozco.

Q$_{36}$, Chicago
www.q36llc.com/think/

Publisher's Cataloging-in-Publication Data
      Provided by Five Rainbows Cataloging Services
Names: Rosenthal, Dale W.R., author.
Title: A quantitative primer on investments with R / Dale W.R. Rosenthal.
Description: Chicago: Q36, 2018. | Includes bibliographical references and index.
Identifiers: LCCN 2018904581 | ISBN 978-1-7322356-0-1 (hardcover)
Subjects: LCSH: Investments. | Investments–Mathematical models. | Quantitative
   research. | Portfolio management. | Financial risk management. | Derivative
   securities. | BISAC: BUSINESS & ECONOMICS / Investments & Securities /
   Analysis & Trading Strategies. | BUSINESS & ECONOMICS / Econometrics.
   | BUSINESS & ECONOMICS / Finance / General.
Classification: LCC HG4515.2 .R67 2018 (print) | DDC 332.6–dc23.

First Edition: May 2018
10 9 8 7 6 5 4 3 2

Hardcover ISBN-13: 978-1-7322356-0-1

This book is dedicated to Yuree and Sophia — and the wonderful people who have inspired me to see the delights of investments and to convey that knowledge to others.

¤¤¤

Contents

V   All Together Now   **569**

0.1   Preface

0.1.1   Audience

This book is meant to introduce financial instruments to a quantitatively intrepid audience familiar with light programming. That is most likely engineering, physics, math, and statistics students interested in finance; graduate finance and economics students with an interest in quantitative analysis; and, quantitative finance professionals who are seeking to broaden their financial knowledge. The text covers some of the terminology and culture of finance as well as valuation, risk, and modeling.

You should be familiar with an analysis language, *e.g.* basic R, Python, Octave, or that matrix laboratory language (which is like Octave). You should also be familiar with basic statistics and calculus: means, variances, standard deviations, correlations, integrals, and derivatives. If these are not familiar... you may find this tough going in places.

I have written the text I would use to teach in a masters of finance program — and what I would want to read as an engineer or statistician. Quantitatively-trained people with an interest in finance rarely take a course in investments. They get shut out because the course is full of business/MBA students; or, they get frustrated because the quantitative reasoning (which clarifies and unifies models) is omitted. That is truly unfortunate because a good introduction to investments gives a solid foundation to attack myriad problems with a set of useful perspectives and far less fear. As part of that foundation, I encourage a healthy, questioning approach to models: I do not worship models and neither should you.

I have tried to be more terse than the typical investments text; that is why most chapters are less than twenty pages in length. First, I presume your time is important. Second, once we get beyond the introductory material, we can focus on the mathematical and statistical commonalities. That means we do not need to explain all the variations of a possible idea (as is often done). That should allow us to play around more with valuation and risk models. My main deviations from brevity have been to also convey some of the culture and language of finance — since these are sometimes used as shibboleths.

I focus on the underlying economics because regulations and implementations are just ways of addressing people's economic needs. When the world changes (and it will), implementations may change but our needs will not. Knowing the theory may help you anticipate these changes and position yourself for success.

Economic theory is particularly important for engineers and scientists entering the field of finance — because the fields they were trained in are (1) far more precise than finance, and (2) lack the economic forces that make economics more than just accounting. The ignorance of economic forces like wealth creation and strategic choice surrounds us; for example: memes compare federal and household budgets with no concern about differences in wealth creation or infrastructure provision enabling competition.

To reinforce the core ideas, I have included quizzes (with answers) and longer exercises. While many of the examples are US-based, the economics are general. These get at basic concepts, quantitative theory, and data analysis. Hopefully, they will increase your intuition. Some of these exercises are unlike those covered in most investments texts. However, as the Danish mathematician Piet Hein said, "Problems worthy of attack prove their worth by fighting back."

While the first few chapters are less quantitative, they provide the foundation for later work; and, even in those early chapters we will explore the ideas with more rigor than is typical. The later chapters are more advanced: they are quantitative and focus on recent research. The final chapters step back from the focus on research and bring together the material of prior chapters to assess its meaning for investors and the macroeconomy.

Throughout the book, I have included copious references with DOIs and URLs. That way, if an idea is useful for a problem you are facing, you can easily consult the literature. The bibliographies are there to help *you* do better at your work.

0.1.2 Past Performance

This book is based on eight years of teaching Introduction to Investments and Investments to students at the University of Illinois at Chicago. My approach was inevitably shaped by my industry experience: an internship as a programmer/analyst in Listed Equities at Goldman Sachs, five years as an equity derivatives strategist at Long-Term Capital Management, and three years as a proprietary algorithmic trader in Morgan Stanley's Equity Trading Lab.

I wanted my students to walk into interviews with better preparation, quicker responses, and stronger analytical experience than candidates from more prestigious schools. Any reader of this text will see that I pushed my students hard to better prepare them for success. I dislike what President Bush called "the soft bigotry of low expectations."

One of the delightful results was that students often rose to meet expectations. It was not just the top students who grew: students who had never considered themselves intelligent asked pertinent and incisive questions. Some students surprised themselves with how much they loved analysis, programming, and just plain *thinking*.

I am proud to say that my top students beat out Ivy League students for top-tier jobs; and, complacent students woke up, took charge of their futures, and discovered a passion for finance. This book is an attempt to share the perspective and knowledge that helped them succeed.

Dale W.R. Rosenthal
Chicago, May 2018

0.2   Acknowledgements

I am greatly indebted to a number of people who were kind enough to provide feedback and suggestions on early versions of the text. Dave Sahota was incredibly thorough: He provided numerous suggestions on tone and flow and caught a number of inconsistencies and other errors. Yuree Whang offered advice on tone from the perspective of a quantitative finance newcomer in addition to being very patient with how this book affected our life together.

Erol Biceroğlu had excellent suggestions on indices and tone from an international industry perspective and also suggested adding references for those interested in certain asset classes. Kris Boudt suggested some changes to make the text more clear to a first-time reader. Mark Delgado had excellent suggestions for clarifying some mathematical jargon. Zohaad Fazal had particularly useful feedback on confusing or idiomatic English. Abhi Konduru had useful advice about motivation and feedback. Sabrina Kwan made the wise suggestion to comment my own example code. Lang Ellen Lang had many excellent suggestions on wording and tone. Jacob Morley caught a number of mistakes and encouraged me to cover some oft-neglected material. Eric Naegele suggested the section on game theoretic concerns in modeling. Kevin Noordhoff had feedback that clarified the exposition and was very helpful in discussing some accounting ratios. Rich O'Hara encouraged me to tighten the narrative in the introductory chapter. Catie Park was especially encouraging that I should write this book. Students at UIC and in Notre Dame's MSF program were helpful by testing this material over the years.

Finally, Kris Boudt, Justin Klosek, and Phil Maymin were all kind enough to offer high praise and give their imprimatur to this work.

Despite help from these people, I am sure I have made mistakes — hopefully different than those in texts which frustrated me. In my defense, this book is like a model: it offers a perspective, one not yet available from other texts. My hope, however, is captured by a Chinese saying:

> 书中自有黄金屋
> shū zhōng zì yǒu huángjīn wū
> A book contains a house of gold.

For those familiar with Chinese characters, even the characters evoke the meaning. It is a perfect sentiment in meaning, appearance, and sound. I hope you find it to be true of this book.

0.3 Abbreviations Used

Below are abbreviations used in the text multiple times and which may be unfamiliar.

ABS asset-backed security

APR annual percentage rate

APT arbitrage pricing theory

AR autoregressive

ARCH autoregressive conditional heteroskedasticity model

ATMF at-the-money-forward

ATM at-the money

AUM assets under management

B buy

BBO best bid and offer

BLUE best linear unbiased estimator

bp basis points

càdlàg *continu à droite, limite à gauche*, aka RCLL

CAL capital allocation line

CAPM capital asset pricing model

CCP central counterparty

cdf cumulative density function

CDO collateralized debt obligation

CDS credit default swap

CFTC Commodity Futures Trading Commission

CLOB consolidated limit order book

cmf cumulative mass function

CMG corporate-minus-government bonds

CMO collateralized mortgage obligation

CPI consumer price index

CTA commodity trading advisor

CVaR conditional value-at-risk, aka ES

DCF discounted cash flows

DDM dividend discount model

DMM designated market maker

DOL degree of operating leverage

DOOM deep out-of-the-money

DV01 dollar value of a 1 bp move

EAR effective annual rate

EBBO European best bid and offer

ECN electronic communication network

EFP exchange for physical

EMH efficient market hypothesis

EMU economic and monetary union

ES expected shortfall

ETF exchange-traded fund

EURIBOR Euro interbank offered rate

EVT extreme value theory

FCFE free cashflow to equity

FCFF free cashflow to the firm

FINRA Financial Industry Regulatory Authority

FOMC Federal Open Market Committee

FX foreign exchange

GARCH generalized autoregressive conditional heteroskedasticity model

GDP gross domestic product

GEE generalized estimating equations

GEV generalized extreme value distribution

GHD general Pareto distribution

GLM generalized linear model

HFT high-frequency trading

HICP harmonised index of consumer prices

HML high-minus-low book/market sort portfolio

ICAPM intertemporal capital asset pricing model

iid independent and identically-distributed

IIROC Investment Industry Regulatory Organization of Canada

IPO initial public offering

IRR internal rate of return

ITM in-the-money

KYC Know Your Customer

0.4 ISO Currency Codes

Below are the ISO 4217 currency codes for the 35 most-traded currencies as well as the currencies for some offshore financial centers (which may have larger trading volume than reported).[1] The Argentinian peso is also included since it often appears in New York Fed reports on FX volume.

AED UAE dirham
ARS Argentinian peso
AUD Australian dollar
BMD Bermudian dollar
BRL Brazilian real
BSD Bahamian dollar
CAD Canadian dollar
CHF Swiss franc
CLP Chilean peso
CNY Chinese yuan (aka RMB, renminbi)
COP Colombian peso
CZK Czech koruna
DKK Danish krone
EUR Euro
GBP Great British pound sterling
HKD Hong Kong dollar
HUF Hungarian forint
IDR Indonesian rupiah
ILS Israeli new shekel
INR Indian rupee
ISK Icelandic krona

JPY Japanese yen
KRW Korean won
KYD Cayman Islands dollar
MOP Macanese pataca
MXN Mexican peso
MYR Malaysian ringgit
NOK Norwegian krone
NZD New Zealand dollar
PAB Panamanian balboa
PEN Peruvian new sol
PHP Philippine peso
PLN Polish (new) zloty
RON Romanian new leu
RUB Russian rouble
SAR Saudi riyal
SEK Swedish krona
SGD Singapore dollar
THB Thai baht
TRY Turkish lira
TWD Taiwanese (new) dollar
USD US dollar
ZAR South African rand

---

[1]The 35 currencies are identified in: BIS, *Triennial Bank Survey*, 2016. http://www.bis.org/publ/rpfx16fx.pdf

0.5 ISO "Country" Codes

Below are the ISO 3166 codes for countries — and parts of countries with different economies — from the currencies listed on the prior page. EU, EFTA, and a few financial center economies have also been added.

AD Andorra	**IT** Italy
AE United Arab Emirates	**JP** Japan
AR Argentina	**KR** Korea
AT Austria	**KY** Cayman Islands
AU Australia	**LI** Liechtenstein
BE Belgium	**LT** Lithuania
BM Bermuda	**LU** Luxembourg
BR Brazil	**LV** Latvia
BS The Bahamas	**MC** Monaco
BU Bulgaria	**MO** Macao
CA Canada	**MT** Malta
CH Switzerland	**MX** Mexico
CL Chile	**MY** Malaysia
CN China	**NL** The Netherlands
CO Colombia	**NO** Norway
CY Cyprus	**NZ** New Zealand
CZ Czech Republic	**PA** Panama
DE Germany	**PE** Peru
DK Denmark	**PH** Philippines
EE Estonia	**PL** Poland
ES Spain	**PT** Portugal
EU Eurozone	**RO** Romania
FI Finland	**RU** Russia
FR France	**SA** Saudi Arabia
GB Great Britain	**SE** Sweden
GR Greece	**SG** Singapore
HK Hong Kong	**SI** Slovenia
HR Croatia	**SK** Slovakia
HU Hungary	**SM** San Marino
ID Indonesia	**TH** Thailand
IE Ireland	**TR** Turkey
IL Israel	**TW** Taiwan
IN India	**US** United States
IS Iceland	**ZA** South Africa

Part I

Fundamentals

❑❑✳

Chapter 1 introduces the world and ideas of finance.
Chapter 2 discusses what asset classes are and why they are useful.
Chapter 3 explains how markets work and common market features; and,
Chapter 4 shows how modern markets have evolved to better serve investors.
Chapter 5 discusses efficiency of economies, markets, and their interaction.

Chapter 1

Introduction

This book is intended to be a brisk introduction to the field of investments. We will discuss a number of topics: asset classes, markets, risk, valuation (often called "asset pricing"), portfolios, hedging, and some philosophy about markets. Then, we will put that together and look at derivatives, investment management, and crises.

To help you learn in the most efficient manner, I will do a few things that ten years of teaching have shown to be effective. First, I will be a bit formulaic in telling you what the goal is of each chapter. That helps set your perspective and understand why we are covering certain material. Second, I have quizzes at the end of each chapter. Take them seriously. Those are your chance to get quick feedback on whether or not you grasped the material. In my experience, quiz results had a correlation near 90% with students' career success. Finally, there are exercises to help you work with the ideas and data. That helps to cement the ideas into the beginnings of intuition.

The goal of this chapter is to start us on that journey: to explain what investments are, how we will look at them, and why we will take those perspectives.[1]

1.1   Why Quantify?

Studying investments is, invariably, quantitative. If you put your money into a bank or an investment fund, you would complain if your statements listed vague metrics like "Balance: $Plenty" or "Risk Level: Not Too Much." We need more information — more precision — than that to assess values and risks in our account.

Using numbers does not mean the values are perfectly precise; they rarely are. However, numbers let us consider orderings (more versus less risky) and take better guesses at values.

To do this we will often use models. All of the models we will use rest on

---

[1]Did you see that? Just like I said I would, I told you the goal of the chapter. I am shameless about helping people to learn. Lucky you!

assumptions. Those assumptions may not hold. Even the idea that money now and money later have different values — time value of money — assumes that there is a risk-free rate. When politicians say we can default for a short while on government debt because "debt holders understand that we have enough money," well...then you realize how tenuous it is to assume there is a risk-free rate.[2]

Thus we should always keep in mind George Box's well-known aphorism:

> All models are wrong; some models are useful.
> — George E.P. Box

Models are like plot summaries. Rick Polito is famous for his summary of a well-known movie: "Transported to a surreal landscape, a young girl kills the first person she meets and then teams up with three strangers to kill again." The movie is *The Wizard of Oz* and that description is correct; however, it doesn't jibe with most people's impression of the movie. If your concern is "movies which feature killing" so you do not upset impressionable toddlers, that description is a useful model for you. If you are looking for classic movies for kids (who are not toddlers), it is not a useful model.

We make models because, like movie plot summaries, they might be useful. However, models are not worthy of worship. We are not uncovering God's Truth; we are merely taking a perspective to tease out some generality about behavior. So keep in mind George Box's quote as we proceed.

Finally, we need to discuss **solution concepts**. This is where there is often a misunderstanding between economists and those not trained as economists. Sometimes, we can **derive** the answer: we use arithmetic and algebra to find an answer, like showing that 5 is a root of $x^2 - 6x + 5$. Sometimes we have to **prove** the answer: perhaps we can show that $x \leq \gamma$ and $x \geq \gamma$ so $x = \gamma$; or, maybe we can only show that $\sigma \frac{n-1}{n} \leq y \leq \sigma \frac{n+1}{n}$.

When we work with data, we often use **optimization** to minimize or maximize some objective function. We try to explain the data by finding general behavior across all observations. This often yields an **overdetermined system**: it has different solutions for each subset of the data. So we compromise: we minimize a distance metric between the data and the model — an **estimation**. Since the system is overdetermined, we do not know the true answer; however, the curvature of the objective function near the solution gives us an idea of how sharp our guess is.

Common assumptions behind optimization and estimation models are accuracy, stationarity, and ergodicity. Optimization results differ if our data are not accurate; then, we should consider the randomness of inputs. However, stochastic optimization is rarely covered in finance coursework. We often assume **ergodicity**: that with enough data we can estimate properties like the mean or variance. We even tend to

---

[2]This has become a recurring problem in the US. Politicians refuse to authorize new funding for the government to run — effectively taking the government hostage until their demands are met. This can endanger the ability to pay interest on debt. Some politicians rationalize this and claim (delusionally) that debt holders know we have enough money to pay and this will make the budget better off — so debt holders will be understanding.

assume **stationarity**: that joint distributions or the moments of a distribution are unchanging.[3] Unfortunately, these are poor assumptions: data contain randomness and the world changes. Means and variances and other moments change.

Sometimes, risk arises not from randomness but from other people. Thus we need to consider **strategic choice**: the fact that people choose actions which most benefit them. A clever person acting strategically might consider the effect of strategic choices made by others; this might then alter the action they take. We can iterate this thinking until we find an action that does not change, a **fixed point**. This solution concept is an **equilibrium** and is the heart and soul of game theory. Sometimes economists will refer to this as a **full equilibrium** while a statistical model (which only maximizes from one player's perspective) is called a **partial equilibrium**.

We often see a tension between us and others: buyers want to buy for less, sellers want to sell for more; or, more frustrating, you want to avoid traffic and other drivers also want to avoid traffic. Problems involving strategic choice often require a solution where we cannot expect to do better given what our opponents will do and they cannot do better given what we will do. Geometrically: where optimization and estimation problems find a maximum or minimum, equilibrium problems find saddlepoints — where your gains balance against the other person's losses.

We do not use equilibrium models nearly as often (nor as rigorously) as we should. However, the ideas of strategic choice are crucial. Even if we cannot formulate a game-theoretic model, these ideas can help us keep a critical mind.

Finally, we sometimes use **simulation**: creating random variables and then running them through a theoretical model (possibly even an equilibrium model) to see how the system responds dynamically. We may even measure aspects of the simulated system's performance. Simulation sometimes gives us weaker results; however, it can still be a valuable tool for exploring solutions.

1.2   Why Invest?

An **investment** commits resources now for a future benefit. You might commit time, cash, work, ideas, materials, or space... now. You do this because you expect more (money? happiness?) than you put in... later.

You, right now, are investing: you are spending time (and hopefully money) to read this book. Your goal is to become better educated. Hopefully, this will help you make better decisions — and maybe even make more money. You might also have a bank account holding cash so people do not steal it; that too is an investment. An investment does not guarantee a better outcome; it just means that we expect (in a statistical sense) a better outcome: we expect to be better-off on average.

We should always consider **opportunity costs**: the possible investments we

---

[3]Ergodicity and stationarity may seem to be the same, however they are not. If we have random variables from a Cauchy distribution, no amount of data will let us estimate the moments — even if they are unchanging.

could have made. Politicians often point out the benefits of an investment. However, you should always consider how much you could benefit by doing something else instead — "that which is unseen" as Hazlitt often calls it. While some may call this the next-best alternative, it may be superior to the choice which was made.

For example, why not work straight out of high school? You would have far less debt and more seniority at your workplace. Even if higher education is the right investment for you, why not study a subject you find easy? If the ease is because you are naturally better at a subject than others, this may be a sensible choice. Why not take classes from teachers known to be lax graders? You would certainly have less work to do. However, this ease is because you are fooling yourself: you're avoiding work and learning less. You are getting less for your money. Furthermore, not many employers are looking to hire lazy and less-knowledgeable people.

1.3   Real Assets and Wealth Creation

We generally break investments into two types of assets: real assets and financial assets. We create wealth from **real assets**, goods which are used to produce other goods. Real assets may be tangible or intangible.

Tangible assets are things we can physically grasp and include land, physical goods, commodities, and energy. Many real-estate investors swear by the value of owning land, everything from the land you live on to timberland or oil wells. Real estate is the most widely-held investment in the world. Most readers are (or will be) investors in real-estate at some point in their lives. When we talk about an entity's assets, we also often include physical goods: buildings and machinery used in the business. Finally, we might buy commodities: rice, corn, coffee, tea, copper, steel rebar, gold, oil, natgas, and electricity.[4]

Intangible assets are things we cannot physically grasp but which have value: knowledge and intellectual property. Thus these include training, experience, and formal education as well as patents, copyrights, trademarks, and trade secrets (what many finance firms call the "secret sauce").

Real assets are often hard to value. What is a barrel of kerosene worth? It's worth whatever the market says it is worth. We cannot argue what it *should* be worth unless we want to argue based on past prices or based on prices of related goods like jet or diesel fuel.

Nonetheless, wealth is created from real assets; money alone is not enough. This is why we use real assets every day. You wake up in your real estate investment, aka "home." You might consume some coffee or tea in the morning, use electricity for lighting and computing at work, and burn fuel to power your car. You run your business using knowledge and maybe even intellectual property. If you do your job well, your work benefits others — hence the wealth creation. As an extreme

---

[4]Electricity might seem intangible, but it is a physical flow of electrons and can be stored in a battery — so we will consider it tangible.

example, take Google: anyone who tried searching the internet before Google knows how frustrating that task was. Google's search engine created wealth by making knowledge much more accessible. In turn, the search engine's creators became rich.

We will not discuss real assets in-depth in this text; however, we should never forget that they are investments in their own right. Thankfully, many of the investment concepts are valid for both real and financial assets.

1.4 Financial Assets

Financial assets are different than real assets: they are claims on real assets or income. We often classify financial assets based on the source and strength of these claims. For example, all of these are financial assets:

- lease payments on land, buildings, equipment and oil wells;
- licensing payments for the use of intellectual property;
- a promise to pay your friend back on Tuesday for a hamburger today;
- your friend demanding partial payment each day prior to Tuesday;
- part-ownership of a firm paying owners a share of the profits;
- money in US, Canadian, Singaporean, and Hong Kong Dollars; and,
- agreeing with somebody else to exchange cashflows.

Fixed income investments offer a promised stream of income. The earliest fixed income investments offered small partial payments of a fixed amount before repaying the remainder of the loan. That investment is a **bond**. The promise is key: fixed income payment promises are contractual and legally-binding. Breaking the contract allows the lender to sue and (often) seize assets from the borrower.

Equity investments involve an ownership stake in a firm. There is no promise of payment; however, the equity holder may share in the profits. The equity holder gives up a fixed payment for the potential of much larger payments. If, however, the firm suspends payments to shareholders, an equity holder cannot sue the firm or seize its assets. Equity often goes by other names such as **stocks** or **shares**.

Money is also an investment, a store of value in a particular currency. That makes it less exciting unless something dreadful happens in that currency. While many currencies were once exchangeable for gold or silver, that is rarely true anymore: most currencies are now backed by the credit of the issuing government. This makes currencies related to government bonds.

Finally, what about exchanges of cashflows? That is where derivatives come in. Say you bet a buddy that the Blackhawks will beat the Blues in tonight's hockey game: If the Hawks win, you get \$1; if the Hawks lose, you pay \$1. This contract has a digital payoff: it does not matter how much the Hawks win or lose by.[5] Or maybe you bet with a neighbor on the price of a barrel of Bakken Sweet crude oil:

---

[5]Economists refer to these digital-payout contracts as "Arrow-Debreu securities" from the economists who used them in economic theory.

If the price in a month is above \$40/bbl, your neighbor pays you the difference from \$40/bbl; if the price is below \$40/bbl, you pay your neighbor the difference.

Some books claim that derivatives are their own type of asset. However, financial firms are not organized that way nor do most analysts think that way. We think of derivatives as investments in the related asset. Thus the oil bet is a commodity investment. However, derivatives are very important so I will say a few words on them at the end of this chapter before we discuss them in depth in Chapters 19–23.

1.5   Why Finance is Different

We often group firms by their industries or (more coarsely) sectors. Most economists will tell you, however, that the finance sector is different — not different like construction versus energy or retailing, but different in the sense that it has a unique role in the macroeconomy.

Finance is like blood pumping through the body of our economy. We use money as a medium of exchange — to buy and sell goods and services. Why? Bartering-based economies eventually fail: the need to find a chain of barters to match any given buyer and seller becomes harder as the number of goods and people to query grows.[6] Cash, however, is easily stored, transported, and valued.

Yoga Studio Down   In 2008, I met an entrepreneur who ran a yoga studio. She had recently added a second studio in a better area. Her long-run projections suggested the new studio would be more profitable; however, it had not yet reached a sustainable customer base. Her bank had reduced risk across the board — and was unwilling to "roll" (renew) her second studio's short-term loans. She was forced to close the new studio and layoff employees. Thus the financial crisis affected her non-financial business.

What if we do not have enough cash? Or what if there is a time mismatch: when we have money and when we need it are not the same? Maybe we will get cash soon but a deal will not be available if we wait. This is where finance comes in. Finance is a time machine that lets us move money across time to when we need it.[7] Finance lets us align when we have money and when we need it. It is more efficient (and secure) than waiting to accrue enough cash for a purchase — especially if a purchase would alter our behavior for the better. This is using the "disciplining power" of debt: we force ourselves to commit to pay back a loan which enables us to improve our life.[8]

When the finance sector has trouble, the whole economy experiences trauma: these time machines fail. People have a harder time getting loans to buy education,

---

[6]If we built a small model economy and then optimized to find these barter chains, I suspect we would find that it is an NP-hard problem.

[7]I am blatantly stealing Will Goetzmann's metaphor here; it is far too good to avoid.

[8]Jensen and Meckling (1976) claim debt changes firms' behavior, often for the better.

homes, and cars; storeowners may find their short-term credit curtailed, stopping them from buying goods to sell in their store; and, firms might be unable to get loans to complete projects or expand.

Why do those firms not turn to investors other than banks? If the banking crisis affects non-financial firms, the troubles may spread to their clients and suppliers. Investors might worry about the trouble spreading to all firms. That worry may make them unwilling to lend money to firms or to buy ownership stakes in firms. Economists say that the crisis spreads to the "real economy" when a financial crisis affects non-financial firms.

This potential for a crisis to spread is the reason governments often bail out banks in such situations: we need a healthy finance sector for other sectors to work. Furthermore, a healthy finance sector greatly increases economic growth and society's well-being. Bertrand, Schoar, and Thesmar (2007) show how French banking deregulation increased French economic growth. Anyone doubting this overall idea should read Will Goetzmann's superb book, *Money Changes Everything: How Finance Made Civilization Possible.*

So should we just accept bailouts and crises? No. Crises may be inevitable, but we can make them less likely and less severe without sacrificing the higher growth of a free-market capitalist system. We will discuss that in Chapter 26.

1.6   Markets

Markets are of central importance to finance: they are where investors exchange **instruments** (assets) among one another. Few instruments will be well-suited to an investor for their entire life. Without a place to exit that investment, few would purchase it in the first place. An investor may realize a profit when exiting the investment. This is often the goal of investing: people save money when they are younger and earning so that they will have money when they retire and are not earning. This is Goetzmann's time machine at work: what economists sometimes call consumption timing or intertemporal smoothing.

Markets also allow people to shift unwanted risk to others. This means that people who are most able to bear risk can take it from people who are less able to bear risk. That also lets business owners focus on what they do best instead of worrying about where prices will go. If a baker is an expert at creating pastries, the world is not better off if that baker has to spend some time trying to guess where grain prices will go. Markets help people focus on what they do best and not worry about risks they are not experts at analyzing.

Markets also help firms raise capital. Stocks and bonds are **securities**: instruments issued by entities to raise capital. When people talk about **capital markets**, they are discussing both the market for raising capital by initially issuing those securities (the **primary market**) as well as the market for exchanging those securities after they are issued (the **secondary market**).

Securities allow us to separate ownership from management. Imagine the difficulty if you had to stop by the offices of your investments every morning and see if they were making good decisions. Imagine the chaos as you and other investors micromanaged the employees by looking over their shoulders and offering suggestions. (Never mind the coordination problem of those employees also needing to check on their investments!) So equity holders hire agents (managers) to run the firm. That solves one problem but creates another, an **agency problem**: the managers you hire may pursue policies which benefit them but hurt you. They might party away the profits for "team building," hire paramours or lazy friends, or give themselves raises despite lackluster performance.

Finally, the most important function of markets is to produce information. Market prices tell the whole world what people think a firm or good is worth. This allows others to look at those prices and make business decisions. If it looks like there are big profits in building electric cars, that is a signal from consumers that they want more electric cars. That is how prices guide the allocation of capital across the economy to ventures society wants (and away from ventures society wants less). This is the idea of **price theory**: that prices decentralize economic planning by giving people information.

Prices also let us examine firms across time and compare across firms. They allow us to ask questions like, "Why has the value of the firm declined under the new CEO?" or, more pointedly, "Why has the value of the firm declined by 30% under the new CEO while, at the same time, other firms in the industry increased in value by an average of 20%?"

If it sounds like trust is important to markets, you are correct. Finance and markets flourish when the rule of law is stable, property rights are secure, and institutions are representative and offer a level playing field.[9] When we meddle with markets, we distort the information we send to everyone in the economy. That leads to misallocations in investments or, worse, to people not trusting the prices at all. In that case, they will exit that market and invest elsewhere. That leads to a fall-off in economic growth and, in some cases, declines in the value of a country's currency.

1.7   Competition

What if market prices are wrong? Markets come to their own rescue! Perhaps somebody is very good at understanding developments in the retail sector; or, maybe they are an accounting genius who quickly finds fraud. If that helps them predict where prices will go, they can make a lot of money by betting, via the markets, on the rise or fall in prices. If they are correct, they will profit and likely continue analyzing and trading. Their trading pushes prices in what they believe is the right direction. Thus the market rewards them for incorporating their analysis into prices. If they are often wrong, they will lose money and stop influencing the market.

---

[9]For more on the linkage between economic growth and institutions, I *highly* recommend Acemoğlu and Robinson's 2013 book *Why Nations Fail: The Origins of Power, Prosperity, and Poverty.*

People are always looking for easy ways to make money. Sometimes, they succeed — for a while. Perhaps many people want to buy advanced mobile phones (what we now call smart phones). In Act I, companies begin producing smart phones.[10] If those firms are new, they may issue stock to raise capital. Excited consumers pay handsomely for smart phones. People who spot the smart phone trend anticipate big profits and bet on those firms, pushing share prices up. Phone producers make big profits, enriching their founders and the profit-seeking investors (speculators). In Act II, people considering building smart phones see the money they can make and start making smart phones. They too may raise capital, attracting speculators. That competition brings people more phones at declining costs. In Act III, some firms use economies of scale to produce phones as cheaply as possible while inefficient firms fall by the wayside. Phones are cheaper than in Act I and widely-owned. Overall quality of life has improved.

In all these cases, people's desire for easy money attracted them: their actions made market prices more informative and helped give the public what they wanted. People who think they can make money are attracted, creating competition. Competition among profit-seekers encourages them to act quickly. That causes prices of products and investments to quickly reflect the latest information. Hence we think market prices reflect the prospects and risk of an investment — or that they will soon. Competition also means we should not expect to make money over time without taking some risk. Making money without risk or capital, **arbitrage**, is so unlikely that we often use it as a constraint in our models.

Before the mid-1900s, some people believed investors should just invest in

> **Booing Portfolio Theory**
> Boo.com was a London internet startup founded in March 1999. They quickly established offices in eight cities, including NYC. Their 400+ employees were known for spending lavishly on the three C's: Champagne, caviar, and Concorde (to fly to NYC). Some critics murmured that a fourth C, cocaine, surely fueled such idiocy. In 18 months, they burned through £100 mn of investor capital and were bankrupt. One fund, backed by a wealthy family, lost £20 mn. In retrospect, smaller investments in more startups might have been wiser.

one or two firms — and get to know them very well. So imagine: it's morning; you've stopped off at the office of the firm you invested in (again); it's still awkward; and, then you look around conspiratorially before asking *sotto voce* "Hey, Robert, level with me: Are they cooking the books here?" What are the odds that Robert will tell you if they *are* cooking the books? Pretty slim. That alone is one reason we do not "put all our eggs in one basket."

Apart from fraud, we also do not know how any one investment will perform.

---

[10]Here, I am blatantly stealing McCloskey's metaphor; it is also too good to pass up. For an introduction to her ideas, read her 2016 *New York Times* article.

Therefore, we invest in a collection of multiple instruments, aka a **portfolio**. We expect that usually the losses on some instruments will be overcome by the gains on other instruments. Furthermore, the fact that some instruments do well when others do not dampens oscillations in the portfolio's value compared to merely investing in one instrument. This **diversification** reduces the portfolio's risk. That makes returns less noisy so we are more comfortable waiting for portfolio gains.

Not all areas of finance welcomed the Promethean gift of fire that is portfolio theory. Many venture capital and private equity investors still, even now, explain that they "get to know the firms they invest in *really* well." That does not explain how they get bamboozled by firms like Boo.com.[11]

We will revisit these ideas later when we discuss how markets work, efficiency, arbitrage pricing, and portfolio theory.

1.8   Market Participants

Since markets are so important, it makes sense to consider who participates in them.

Individuals and households, also known as **retail investors** save and invest their cash; they may even use income share agreements to sell off some of their future earnings in exchange for education funding. **Institutional investors** are organizations with large amounts of money which they invest. Banks invest the cash of savers by lending it out. (In return, savers receive interest on the money.) Firms raise capital for plants and equipment.

Governments and governmental agencies borrow to fund improvements to infrastructure, they invest so they can later pay retirees, and they trade in markets to push prices to certain levels. This last action is how some countries try to manage their foreign exchange (FX) rate and how most central banks set interest rates.

Finally, finance firms participate in markets. **Investment bankers** advise and assist entities with raising capital, buying or selling a firm, and merging with another firm. **Financial intermediaries** help buyers and sellers of instruments find one another by matching buyers and sellers if both are present or by temporarily holding or owing instruments to smooth out the mismatch of times when buyers and sellers arrive to the market. This **intertemporal smoothing** is also done by retailers: they hold goods until you buy them or, sometimes, they sell them to you and then go buy them. Finally, **investment managers** advise on where to invest.

1.9   Acquire!

I typically end this introductory material by having students team up to play a board game. *Acquire!* was created by Sid Sackson in 1964 and involves players selecting from a hand of (unique) tiles for locations on the board.

---

[11]For more on Boo.com, read Doward's 2001 article in *The Guardian*. Harris documented a crowdfunding disaster in his 2016 article about Zano for *Medium.com*.

Each player places a tile on their turn. A player placing a second contiguous tile can found a hotel and receive a free share. After a placement, each player may invest in their hotel — or the hotels of other players. (In business and investing we face similar choices.) They then draw a tile to replace the one they played.

As hotels grow (in contiguous size), they increase in value. If hotels touch, a merger happens: the smaller hotel returns to the list of unfounded hotels, the top 2 shareholders in the acquired hotel get a bonus, and all shareholders in the acquired hotel choose to receive cash or shares in the acquiring hotel. Thus mergers may free up cash for minority shareholders.

One of the delightful aspects of *Acquire!* is that the winning team typically uses a few basic strategies. First, they diversify. Players who concentrate their investments lose out on most of the mergers; and, other players can easily avoid merging with their hotel to keep them at a disadvantage. Second, winning teams manage their cash well. Since mergers are the only sources of cash, many teams quickly become cash-constrained. Having cash on hand later in the game lets a team take advantage of new opportunities when other teams cannot. Finally, winning teams try to be a primary or secondary shareholder to receive a bonus payout in mergers. This mirrors how large shareholders can bend the terms of a merger to better suit them.

For a simple game, *Acquire!* touches on a lot of key concepts in investing. I highly recommend playing it with some friends!

Finally, I would be remiss if I did not note that many board games like *Acquire!* share strong similarities to economic models. In particular, the so-called **European board games** — which often feature scoring at the end of the game to account for the value of holdings and unused actions — are often equivalent to economic models. Hence why so many economists are avid players of such games. Cross (2017) (an article in *The Economist*'s lifestyle magazine) recommends other games.

1.10 Quiz

A good way to see if you grasped the material is to quiz yourself about basic questions. Quizzes should be done quickly: in an interview, nobody will wait for you to rack your brain for basic facts. Basic facts are needed just to enable conversation.

So give it a go! Try answering the following questions in five minutes.

1. An investment commits _____ now for _____ in the future.

2. We should also consider the benefits precluded by an investment. This is what economists call _____.

3. We break investments into two types of assets: _____ and _____
_____.

4. Economists believe the finance sector is uniquely different and important | T F
to the economy.

5. Investors and the managers they hire should have the same incentives. When
their incentives differ, we have a(n) _____ problem.

6. Price theory suggests market prices are crucial because they affect how _____
_____ is allocated throughout our _____.

7. Finance helps smooth out the mismatch of timing between the arrival of _____
_____ and _____ or _____ and _____.

8. How do markets help those worried about uncertainty in their business processes?

9. How do markets encourage people to find problems with publicly-traded firms?

10. Because markets are competitive, we think there is a tradeoff: you cannot
expect outsized returns without _____.

1.11   Exercises

Try to answer the following questions. These are a bit quantitative, but they help
bolster the ideas we covered.

I stated previously that barter-based economies eventually fall apart. Let's
explore that assertion with a little more rigor. We will not consider chains of trade
since that is more difficult; we will just consider finding one person to trade with.
Furthermore, if that is difficult, then we need not analyze chains since finding those
would be even harder.

Assume that you have k neighbors and that there are g goods.[12] Suppose that
you and your neighbors each have one good and want another good; these goods are
iid uniformly distributed.[13]

1. What is the probability that a given neighbor has a good and wants a good so
that you can trade?

2. What is the probability of a match, *i.e.* one or more matches among your k
neighbors?

---

[12]Statisticians can consider these to be your k-nearest neighbors. Heh.

[13]If you are rusty on statistics, **iid** stands for independent and identically-distributed.

3. What is the limit of the probability of a match as $k \to \infty$?

4. What is the limit of the probability of a match as $g \to \infty$?

5. Suppose you want the probability of finding a match to be α. How many neighbors k^* do you need to query for a match?

6. Having a number of goods that is unrelated to the population is unrealistic. Let's weaken that. Assume that the number of goods is given by ki where i is the fraction of the population who are innovators (with each innovator developing one good). Find the probability of a match and the limit of that probability as $k \to \infty$.

7. How realistic is it to assume a uniform distribution for the goods your neighbors have and want?

8. How realistic is it to assume that the goods your neighbors have and want are iid?

References

Acemoğlu, Daron and James Robinson. *Why Nations Fail: The Origins of Power, Prosperity, and Poverty*. New York: Crown Business, 2013.

Arrow, Kenneth J. and Gerard Debreu. "Existence of an Equilibrium for a Competitive Economy". *Econometrica* 22.3 (1954), pp. 265–290. DOI: 10.2307/1907353.

Bertrand, Marianne, Antoinette Schoar, and David Thesmar. "Banking Deregulation and Industry Structure: Evidence from the French Banking Reforms of 1985". *Journal of Finance* 62.2 (2007), pp. 596–628. DOI: 10.1111/j.1540-6261.2007.01218.x.

Cross, Tim. "Table-Top Generals". *1843: The Economist Unwinds* (Dec. 13, 2017). URL: https://www.1843magazine.com/features/tabletop-generals.

Doward, Jamie. "From Boo to Bust and Back Again". *The Guardian* (Aug. 26, 2001).

Goetzmann, William N. *Money Changes Everything: How Finance Made Civilization Possible*. Princeton University Press, 2016.

Harris, Mark. "How Zano Raised Millions on Kickstarter and Left Most Backers with Nothing". *Medium.com* (Jan. 18, 2016). Retrieved 11 May 2017. URL: https://medium.com/kickstarter/how-zano-raised-millions-on-kickstarter-and-left-backers-with-nearly-nothing-85c0abe4a6cb.

Hazlitt, Henry. *Economics in One Lesson*. New York: Harper & Brothers, 1946.

Jensen, Michael C. and William H. Meckling. "Theory of the Firm: Managerial Behavior, Agency Costs and Ownership Structure". *Journal of Financial Economics* 3.4 (1976), pp. 305–360. DOI: 10.1016/0304-405X(76)90026-X.

McCloskey, Deirdre N. "The Formula for a Richer World? Equality, Liberty, Justice". *New York Times* (Sept. 2, 2016).

Chapter 2

Asset Classes

When people talk about investments, they often mention various "asset classes." What are asset classes? The classic answer of "stocks and bonds" is wrong; that definition is woefully incomplete. More important is *why* we care: because an **asset class** is a set of instruments with similar characteristics.

Instruments in an asset class are often exposed to similar types of risks; their cashflows may follow similar structures or rules; they may be subject to the same laws and regulations; and, importantly, they may behave similarly in response to shocks or surprises. That means one asset class probably behaves differently from another. If we want to diversify our portfolio, we probably want to own instruments with different behaviors.

The goal of this chapter is to give you an overview of asset classes; to help you start seeing how different asset classes behave; and, to give you enough information to explore asset classes which interest you.

2.1 Overview

We can break instruments into roughly five asset classes:

1. Commodities;
2. Real Estate;
3. Money/Foreign Currency (FX);
4. Fixed Income; and,
5. Equities.

This list is a common classification but it is not canonical: it neither descended from Heaven nor was it whispered from a bush. We might add other areas like intellectual property or infrastructure. Infrastructure, in particular, looks like it may come to be an accepted asset class; or, it could just be seen as extending real estate.[1] I once heard of a hedge fund in London investing in art; however, they were not very successful.

That raises an interesting issue. You will eventually hear somebody talk about "XYZ as an asset class." Why? If a new set of investments is an asset class, investors worldwide should consider investing in those instruments. If you look at who is proposing XYZ as an asset class, you will often find (shocking revelation!) that they are in the business of selling XYZ.

Why listen to people who are probably just shills? We listen because new asset classes offer the hope of a better-diversified portfolio and, if the area truly is new, the attraction of undiscovered bargains. However, we should also consider size: how much money could this supposed asset class support? Art may behave differently than other investments, but the market is very illiquid and small compared to the size of most investment funds.[2]

Without getting into too much detail, we can look at these asset classes to see how they differ. Obviously, one could read multiple books on each of these asset classes. I will suggest a few to get you started. Then I will say a few words about derivatives and indices.

2.2 Commodities

Commodities are goods which are inputs to or outputs from industry. We often declare certain goods to be **fungible**: contractually equivalent. This is not controversial if the commodities are physically indistinguishable, such as electrons oscillating at 60 Hz in the North American Eastern Interconnect. However, when commodities are very different, fungibility is less natural. We tend to impose fungibility when different commodities are exposed to similar supply and demand factors. Furthermore, imposing fungibility gets more people trading in a market; that increases liquidity and encourages competition which lowers the cost to trade.

Commodities tend to have low correlations with equity markets. Commodities also have value because we can use them. That makes them stores of value that are resistant to inflation. When inflation is high, the purchasing power of a currency may fall and income from a stock or bond becomes less valuable; however, a barrel of diesel fuel is still just as useful.[3]

We tend to group commodities into a few large areas; again, this list is not canonical but it gives a flavor of the variety of commodities:

1. *Agriculturals*: grains, oilseeds, livestock, tropical/softs, and ethanol;

---

[1]For more on infrastructure, read Andrews and Wahba (2007) and Mercer (2016) as well as Liebman (2011) and Galitopoulou and Noya (2016) on social impact bonds.

[2]Pownall's *TEFAF Art Market Report 2017* estimates the market at $45 bn globally.

[3]Sadly, trading commodities is often the last resort of people stuck in hyperinflation as they frantically try to convert cash into physical goods. Most people are not good commodity traders so when they stop doing what they are best at and start trading commodities... we lose almost all prospects for economic growth.

2. *Metals*: base, ferrous, precious, and minor/strategic;
3. *Petroleum*: crude, gasoline and middle distillates, bunker, LPGs, natgas, LNG, and plastics;
4. *Power*: electricity (AC, baseload to peaking and non-dispatchable);
5. *Other minerals*: coal, phosphate; and,
6. *Intangibles*: emissions, shipping, and renewable fuel certificates.

Some commodities imply unit producer margins in certain industries; some are correlated with the performance of other industries.[4] For example, copper and steel rebar are used predominantly in construction (for wires, pipes, and reinforcing concrete); therefore, they are correlated with real-estate instruments. Gold is often seen as a store of value since it is a precious metal; however, osmium and silver are precious metals which are largely used for certain military and industrial purposes.

Commodities behave very differently from other assets. Since they are physical goods, they are subject to local price shocks. The short-term local supply curve can only move so much; there's no way to miracle a railcar of coal across the ocean in a day. Thus commodities prices tend to be more volatile (even on a percentage basis) when prices are high.

For those interested in commodities, I highly recommend the two texts I have used for eight years of teaching commodities: Dunsby et al. (2008) for background and Geman (2005) for a more quantitative perspective. Those interested in commodities trading should read Rubano (2016).

2.3 Real Estate

Real estate is an investment in land, buildings, or shares of these. Real estate is the most widely held investment in the world; however, it is highly illiquid. There is no fungibility: each house or lot is unique. There is no portability: you cannot easily transport real estate. Betting on price declines is very difficult. However, many people invest in real estate, often via their home; unlike most investments, you can use your home while you invest in it. Some people hold other properties and rent them out. That can be a hassle when you get called to fix a problem at 3 AM. An easier approach is to buy a share in a managed real estate investment trust (REIT).

Many REITs are focused on a particular type of property, *e.g.* class A office buildings. REITs tend to be of three types:

1. **Equity REITs** invest directly: they own and manage real estate and may earn rents and capital gains on the land;
2. **Mortgage REITs** invest indirectly: they own mortgages and construction loans and earn interest; and,
3. **Hybrid REITs** invest directly and indirectly.

---

[4]**Unit producer margin** is the revenue from selling a good less the cost of creating it.

Obviously, equity REITs tend to perform better in property booms since they have potential upside. Mortgage REITs, on the other hand, tend to behave more like a fixed income investment. Many REITs are traded on equity exchanges. However, both behave more like fixed income than most equities do which is why analysts often exclude REITs when they analyze the universe of equities: REITs really are their own sort of beast.

Those interested in real estate would do well to read whatever Sam Zell says along with Geltner et al. (2013) and Linneman (2016).

2.4 Foreign Exchange

Foreign exchange (*FX*) is the most liquid market in the world. About \$5 trillion trades in FX markets each day.[5] Most currencies are freely traded (**float**) against one another: their exchange rate is determined by supply and demand due to trade, interest rate differentials, and risk — not by government fiat. For example, if Swedish investments look bleak, investors will move money out of Sweden and convert (sell) their Swedish Kronor to (buy) another currency like the US Dollar. The Swedish Krona will then "fall" or "weaken" as it will take more and more Swedish Kronor to get 1 US Dollar. Or put the opposite way: 1 Swedish Krona will get you fewer and fewer US Dollars.

At this point, it makes sense to point out that we often refer to currencies by their ISO codes. The "dollar" is not specific in a world with US, Canadian, Australian, New Zealand, Singaporean, Hong Kong, Taiwanese, Jamaican, Grand Cayman, Namibian, and other types of dollars. To make matters worse, the "dollar sign" may even be used for currencies that are not dollars. For example, "\$" is also used to write amounts in Argentinian Pesos. Thus we instead refer to USD, CAD, AUD, NZD, SGD, HKD, TWD, JMD, KYD, and NAD.

The "Major" currencies, the US dollar (USD), Euro (EUR), Japanese yen (JPY), British pound (GBP), Australian dollar (AUD), Canadian dollar (CAD), and Swiss franc (CHF) are among the most actively-traded currencies. USD and EUR are, in particular, seen as **reserve currencies**: dependably stable currencies in well-managed economies so that money stored in that currency is seen as being in a safe haven. A large amount of trade is also done in CHF; and, in crises, CHF can spike significantly as people move money into CHF. Why? Probably because Switzerland is home to many international banks, has low taxes, and has very defensible borders. While the USD is still a reserve currency, it has fallen a bit in holdings with the rise of the Euro and some of the political nonsense of toying with default.

Other big currencies which are heavily-traded are the Chinese yuan (CNY), Swedish krona (SEK), Mexican peso (MXP), New Zealand dollar (NZD), Singapore dollar (SGD), and Hong Kong dollar (HKD). There is also one oddity with FX markets: they are not quoted one way consistently. Most USD cross rates are

---

[5]Graham's 2016 *Reuters* article has more details on the FX market.

quoted as foreign currency per USD. Traders will quote "JPY/USD" (or sometimes "USD-JPY") as 113 — assuming you know that means 113 JPY can be exchanged for 1 USD. The problem is some Commonwealth currencies (GBP, AUD, NZD) and EUR are quoted the opposite way: USD per foreign currency. Traders quoting 1.29 for "USD/GBP" (or "USD-GBP") assume you know this means 1 GBP is worth 1.29 USD. Since some computers (and journalists) do not know these conventions, it can be especially difficult when **FX** rates are near 1 to determine which way the rate was quoted.

Those interested in foreign exchange should read both Weithers (2013) and DeRosa (2013).[6]

2.5   Money Markets and Fixed Income

2.5.1   Bond Basics

Before we discuss money markets and fixed income, we should cover the salient features of most bonds. These details, spelled out in the bond **indenture** govern the features of a bond and the rights and obligations of creditors and borrowers. The amount borrowed is called the **par** (or **face**) value. Bonds are issued with a **maturity date**; at that time, the par value is repaid. Along the way, the bond may pay the lender **coupon payments** determined by dividing the **coupon rate** by the specified number of coupon payments/year.[7] Some bonds have a coupon rate of zero; we call these **zero coupon bonds**. Some bonds have a coupon rate which may vary over time; we call these **floating rate bonds**.

The bond face may increase. For example, US TIPS (Treasury Inflation-Protected Securities) have their face indexed to CPI to account for inflation. Decreasing face bonds are sometimes issued by reinsurance firms to cover expected catastrophe claims (cat bonds). **Convertible bonds** allow the holder to opt for repayment in a certain number of firm shares instead of the face value. Finally, to smooth out repayment cashflows, **sinking fund bonds** may be repaid over a period of time ending at the maturity date.

Bonds may be quoted as a percentage of par or as a yield. Between coupon payments, a bond accrues interest. If you sold a bond the day before a coupon payment, you deserve to get all but one day of the interest from the coupon payment. Bond traders often discuss yields and differences in yields in terms of **bond points** (percentage points) and **basis points** (bp), 1/100-ths of a percentage point). Finally, bonds differ from other securities both in the legal promise of coupon payments and in what happens when that promise is broken. When a borrower misses a bond payment, we say they are in **default**.

---

[6]In full disclosure: I know Tim Weithers. However, I believe his experience teaching the subject at UBS, Chicago Trading, and the University of Chicago has helped him distill a practical yet economically-driven view on the material.

[7]Yes, the coupon was once an actual piece of paper which one tore off and mailed in.

2.5.2 Money Markets

Money markets are not money but, rather, very short-term loans. For this reason, you may see money markets referred to as "STIRs," short-term interest-rate instruments. Since the times to maturity are very short (days to months), money markets are considered by many people to be very low risk. Furthermore, many firms use short-term funding so the markets are very **liquid** — it is easy and inexpensive to trade large amounts in both directions much of the time.

Money markets include short-term sovereign (government) debt and unsecured corporate loans (**commercial paper**), overnight loans from central banks (*e.g.* Fed Funds), savings accounts, certificates of deposit, and deposits in foreign banks with the best credit ratings (*e.g.* LIBOR). Many money market instruments are zero coupon bonds; it was historically not worth the fixed costs of collecting all the addresses to send out one or two payments.

While some people refer to money markets as "cash," this is a bad habit: money markets can lose money. Money market funds invest in money markets and maintain a net asset value of $1 per share. Interest is paid by granting more shares to all investors. In the 2008 financial crisis, the Reserve Fund lost enough money from money market investments that they could not maintain the $1 net asset value.

The **London Interbank Offered Rate**, **LIBOR**, is a widely-used interbank interest rate. A large amount of international trade is done in USD, and many of these dollars are held in London banks; hence their name of **Eurodollars**. (Note that they have nothing to do with Euros.) Quoting LIBOR requires specifying the currency and term. The most often-used rates, 3MUSDLIBOR and 6MUSDLIBOR, are for three- and six-month USD deposits. Often, we refer to lending rates as a "spread" of basis points above LIBOR, for example 6MUSDLIBOR+30. The worse the borrower's credit, the higher the spread is.

Billions of USD move daily based on changes in LIBOR. Eurodollar futures are based on 3MUSDLIBOR and are used by banks to hedge the effect of changing interest rates on their profitability. Eurodollar futures are so widely used that they are considered one of the most liquid instruments in the world. While some banks were found to have manipulated LIBOR on occasion, the manipulations have since been policed; the fixing process has moved on-exchange; and, it is unclear if the proposed replacement (SOFR, the **secured overnight funding rate**) will be accepted by the market.

There are also Euroyen deposits which receive 3MJPYLIBOR. Banks in the Eurozone and Tokyo also quote interbank offered rates (EURIBOR and TIBOR).

2.5.3 Fixed Income

Fixed income instruments are bonds, loans, and other debt as well as exchanges of cashflows based on interest rates. The term "fixed income" comes from the time when bonds promised the lender a fixed coupon payment before repaying the loan. What we call fixed income instruments are often longer-term than money market instruments. However, do not let the distinct terminology for money markets deceive you: money markets are merely short-term fixed income instruments.

There are a few quirks to the US government bond market. First, Treasuries may be referred to as bills (issued with maturities of 1 year or less), notes (issued with maturities from 2–10 years), or bonds (issued with maturities of more than 10 years). Bills pay out no coupon while notes and bonds pay half of their coupon twice a year. Finally, notes and bonds are quoted as a percentage of par (with a decimal and then 32-nds or 64-ths) while bills are quoted at an implied discount rate.

2.5.4   Debt Issuers

The bond market in the US (and many countries) is far bigger than the stock market. Stocks are only issued by firms. Bonds may be issued by firms as well as governments (aka sovereigns), government agencies, municipalities, and even groups of individuals.

Government agencies (and quasi-agencies) are often subsidized by the government to encourage certain behaviors; they, in turn, subsidize or guarantee certain loans financed through bonds. The most well-known of these entities include the Federal National Mortgage Association (FNMA, "Fannie Mae"), the Federal Home Loan Mortgage Corporation (FHLMC, "Freddie Mac"), and the Federal Agricultural Mortgage Corporation ("Farmer Mac"). Sometimes, the government gets out of the subsidy business: The Student Loan Marketing Association ("Sallie Mae") was privatized on 29 December 2004.

Municipal debt is issued by state and local governments and agencies. Typically in the US, the interest is paid semi-annually and is exempt from federal and issuing-state taxes. Thus "munis" must be examined on a tax-equivalent basis.[8] Munis come in two common flavors: general obligations ("GOs," backed by the municipality's credit), and revenue bonds aka revenue-anticipation notes (RANs, backed by an expected revenue stream). Since a revenue stream is uncertain but governments can always raise taxes, investors typically view RANs as more risky than GOs.

Corporate debt is issued by private corporations and typically pays semi-annual coupons; however, corporates may also pay quarterly coupons since that reduces the variation in quarterly results. Corporate bonds may also include other features to entice investors and help the firm better manage their risk.

Mortgages are loans used to purchase real-estate. In the 1980s, we created new structures to ease investing in mortgages.[9] Those structures were then expanded to handle other forms of asset-backed consumer debt. We will talk about those structures and how we organize these loans into bonds more in Chapter 23.

I mentioned that groups of individuals issue bonds. That includes, very probably, you. You might not realize that you were part of a bond issue; but, if you have a

---

[8]For a tax rate of τ, just divide muni yields by $1 - \tau$. Thus a 5% muni yield is worth $7\frac{1}{7}\%$ to somebody taxed at a 30% rate.

[9]Anybody interested in finance, and especially anyone interested in fixed income, should read Michael Lewis's hilarious *Liar's Poker: Rising through the Wreckage on Wall Street*. Consider it a part of your heritage.

credit card, car loan, or mortgage, then much of the paperwork you signed was so that money you borrow could be packaged into bonds and sold to investors. This opens up funding from more than just banks and is why mortgages have been far cheaper over the past decades than a few generations ago. These bonds are unusual in that they often have monthly coupon payments — because most borrowers make monthly payments on the underlying loans.

2.5.5 Further Reading

Obviously, fixed income is a gigantic asset class. The must-have book, for a long time, has been the latest edition of Fabozzi and Mann (2012). However, that can be a bit dry and encyclopedic. For an introduction prior to that, I would recommend Homer et al. (2013), Veronesi (2010), and then maybe Veronesi (2016).

2.6 Equities

2.6.1 Equity Types and Features

Equities, **stocks**, or **shares** are ownership stakes in a corporation. Equities often pay a cash **dividend**: a payment made regularly (anywhere from monthly to annually) which may increase over time but is made on a best-efforts basis. Dividends can be (and are) suspended in bad times. Equities almost always offer **limited liability**: you can lose your original investment but you cannot lose more than that. Without limited liability, few people would choose to invest in equities.

Imagine that you invest in a company, hire managers, and they commit fraud. If the government knocked on your door and tried to send you to prison, you would be upset: you did not commit fraud nor would you have advised it! Worse: what if the managers of the firm committed a capital offense? Now the government comes to execute you for their actions? Not only would you be unlikely to invest in a firm, you surely would not diversify your portfolio. Why invest a few dollars in many firms? You know one of those firms is likely to make mistakes and the more firms you invest in, the more likely you are to have your head cut off.[10]

Equity holders cannot seize assets when a firm defaults or goes bankrupt. Equity holders are **residual claimants**: they are last in line to divvy up a dead firm's assets and get whatever is left over after creditors are paid. Could equity holders sue, claiming that the asset sales are unfair? Perhaps. This is why equity holders sometimes get some small amount of money: creditors pay them to not delay the bankruptcy proceedings.

Common stock allows voting on corporate issues like who should sit on the board of directors and shareholder proposals. This is a check (albeit weak) on the power of the firm's managers. Sometimes, firms issue different classes of shares that

---

[10]Econometricians and statisticians might see that we are hinting at the difference between good financial risk measures and good insurance risk measures.

have different voting rights. Sometimes governments or firm founders hold a **golden share** which controls 51% of the vote. Thus they can prevent takeovers... or ignore shareholder votes. **Preferred stock** usually has no voting power, but it has a fixed dividend and preferred shareholders are just ahead of common shareholders in line for payouts: If dividends are not paid, the unpaid balance accumulates (sometimes up to some maximum) and that balance must be paid off before dividends can resume being paid out to common stockholders.

Finally, **depository receipts** (ADRs, GDRs) represent shares of a foreign company. This allows investors in one country to invest in stocks of foreign firms without opening up foreign brokerage accounts.

2.6.2   Corporate Actions

Equities are subject to **corporate actions**: payments or modifications to outstanding equities. These are made to keep shareholders happy, encourage others to buy the stock, or raise additional capital. Many equities pay cash dividends. Sometimes, they will split the stock to make shares less expensive for small investors who might buy a few shares: a "3 for 1" **split** turns one share of a $90/share stock into three shares of a $30/share stock. Splits neither create nor destroy the total value of equity. Sometimes firms reverse split the stock if the price has fallen; this attempts to make the stock price look more respectable or, in some cases, to avoid delisting from an exchange.[11] A **stock dividend** is another term for a split but typically one with only a minor effect: a "1.1" stock dividend grants 1 more share for every 10 held; the price per share falls by a factor of $1/11$. Again, value is neither created nor destroyed.

Finally, a firm might issue **rights** to shareholders: certificates allowing holders to purchase new stock which the firm will issue. Rights often allow purchasing those new shares at a discount since issuing new shares dilutes current shareholders' ownership stakes. Rights can often be separated and bought or sold.

2.6.3   Further Reading

For those interested in stocks, it is harder to give advice on further reading. This is because in large part, the first exposure to stocks is in an investments text like this one. Often, students with further interest in stocks learn about portfolio management or security analysis. Advice is also complicated by the sheer volume of books on stocks, many of them truly wastes of the paper and ink they consumed.

However, there are a few investment classics which I can recommend. For those interested in security analysis and value investing, the latest edition of Benjamin Graham's book *The Intelligent Investor*, Graham (2006), is a good introduction to his influential perspective. Malkiel (2016) is also definitely worth a read. Many

---

[11]Many exchanges will remove a stock from their exchange if the share price falls below some level.

others are fans of Bogle (2017). For those interested in portfolio management, Ang (2014) and Grinold and Kahn (1999) are both excellent. Berkin and Swedroe (2016) is a nice introduction to thinking about risk factors.

2.7 A Few Words on Derivatives

Derivatives are of critical importance to markets. Some people think of derivatives as risky bets on esoteric assets. However, derivatives are more general and more widely used than that. Specifically, **derivatives** are contracts whose values are derived from other (**underlying**) instruments. Some people think derivatives get their name from the need to use calculus to analyze them; that is not true. (However, knowing calculus can help in analyzing some derivatives.)

Options give the purchaser the right, but not the obligation, to buy or sell the underlying asset at a set (**strike**) price.[12] **Call** holders may buy the underlier at the strike price. **Put** holders may sell the underlier at the strike price. The right to buy or sell the underlier expires at a later (**expiry**) date.

Futures, swaps, and **forward contracts** allow the holder to *effectively* buy or sell the underlying asset later at a set price. Futures do this by exchanging cashflows to compensate the holder for price changes, effectively locking in a price up to the **expiry date**. Swaps also exchange cashflows regularly until the **maturity date**; however, they tend to differ from futures in how they trade, exchange cashflows, and age. Forward contracts are agreements to purchase or sell the underlier at the contract **maturity date**.

Finally, portfolio-related derivatives are also very common. In fact, most people are familiar with portfolio derivatives without even realizing it. Mutual funds and ETFs are portfolio derivatives. Basket swaps give you the return on a portfolio in exchange for interest (financing) on the capital used to buy the portfolio. Collateralized mortgage obligations (CMOs) are portfolio derivatives which shift the risk of prepayments — having somebody pay off a loan with fat interest payments leaving you to invest in loans with leaner payments (which make you sad). Collateralized debt obligations (CDOs) are portfolio derivatives which shift the risk of defaults in a bond portfolio. Finally, credit default swaps (CDSs) swap a defaulted bond for the par value. Indices can even be thought of as portfolio derivatives — if we stretch the definition of a derivative to allow for indicators which are not traded.

2.8 Indices

Indices are important indicators — so important that it makes sense to say a few words about just indices. Indices are the most frequently quoted metrics for markets. We create indices to gauge a particular market, sector, or part of an economy. An

---

[12]This phrase, "the right but not the obligation," is a bit of legalese familiar to every option trader — a shibboleth of sorts.

index is an average of prices or returns of multiple instruments. The goal is to use the Central Limit Theorem to reduce the noise of individual instruments so we can better ascertain where an economy or industry is headed.

Commonly-referenced indices are shown in Table 2.1. Many of the single-country European indices are less-used post-EMU.[13] While there has not been a clear winner in the race for a pan-European equity index, the Euro Stoxx 50 index of Eurozone stocks has futures trading on it and is far more used than the next-closest competitor, the pan-European (but less liquid) Stoxx Europe 600. That lower liquidity is why some investors synthesize a pan-European index by investing in the Euro Stoxx 50 (Eurozone), FTSE 100 (UK), and SMI (Switzerland). (Apparently, few investors feel the need to add companies from Sweden, Norway, or Denmark, all of whom are outside the Eurozone.)

Most indices are arithmetic averages. An arithmetic index at time t with N index members, would be given by:

$$I_{\text{arith},t} = \frac{\sum_{i=1}^{N} w_{it} p_{it}}{D_t \sum_{i=1}^{N} w_{it}}, \tag{2.1}$$

where w_{it} and p_{it} are the **weights** and prices for index member i at time t.[14] The **divisor** D_t is adjusted to maintain continuity after splits, and index additions or deletions. **Price-weighted indices** average prices equally (so $w_{it} = 1$). **Capitalization-weighting** weighs prices by the shares outstanding. Some "cap-weighted" indices weight prices by the **float** — the freely-trading outstanding shares. **Equally-weighted indices** are unweighted averages of index-member returns:

$$I_{\text{eqwt},t} = C_t I_{\text{eqwt},t-1} \left(1 + \sum_{i=1}^{N} r_{it}/N \right), \tag{2.2}$$

where r_{it} are the simple returns for index member i at time t and C_t scales the index value similar to the divisor for arithmetic indices. **Total return indices** incorporate past dividends as well as prices.

Geometric indices compute the geometric means of returns:

$$I_{\text{geom},t} = C_t I_{\text{geom},t-1} \sqrt[N]{\prod_{i=1}^{N} (1 + r_{it})}. \tag{2.3}$$

A geometric index is equivalent to a portfolio which is continuously rebalanced. The problem is that such indices are open to arbitrage. That makes them sub-optimal to hold and is why most indices are arithmetic.

We tend to prefer capitalization-weighted indices for equities because they are

---

[13]EMU is the term for the economic and monetary union of many EU-member states.

[14]Note that we have allowed for weights which do not sum to 1; hence why we divide all weights by the sum of weights.

Index	Locale	Comments
S&P 500	US	500 large-cap stocks
Russell 2000	US	2000 small-cap stocks
Bloomberg Aggregate Bond	US	c. 9000 bonds
Dow Jones Real Estate	US	100+ REITs/RE stocks
S&P/Case-Schiller	US	Uses repeat home sales
S&P GSCI	Global	Production-weighted futures
Bloomberg Commodity	Global	Volume-weighted futures
S&P/TSX 60	Canada	60 large-cap stocks
Ibovespa	Brazil	c. 50 large-/mid-cap stocks
IPC	Mexico	35 large-cap stocks
Nikkei 225	Japan	225 large stocks
Topix	Japan	Composite of stocks
CSI 300	China	300 large-cap stocks
Hang Seng	Hong Kong	50 large-cap stocks
Straits Times	Singapore	30 large-cap stocks
ASX All Ordinaries	Australia	500 largest stocks
KOSPI	Korea	Composite of stocks
JSE Top 40	South Africa	40 large-cap stocks
Euro Stoxx 50	Eurozone	50 mega-cap stocks
Stoxx Europe 600	Eurozone	600 large-/mid-cap stocks
FTSE 100	UK	100 large-cap stocks
SMI	Switzerland	20 large-cap stocks
DAX	Germany	30 large-cap stocks
CAC 40	France	40 large-cap stocks
MIB 30	Italy	30 large-cap stocks

Table 2.1: Commonly-referenced indices for institutional investors. All have active futures traded on them, allowing investors to hedge exposure. Most indices are large-cap indices while a few are composite indices which capture most or all of the market. The Nikkei 225 is the only price-weighted index while the Case-Shiller is the only index without pre-defined index members. The Bloomberg Aggregate Bond index is sometimes called the Barclays Aggregate Bond index.

more economically relevant: larger companies have more employees and produce more of the nation's GDP, so they should be more representative than smaller firms. However, there are some benefits to a float-weighted index since it is usually close to a cap-weighted index but better represents the investment opportunities available to investors. This is why US finance professionals do not watch the Dow Jones Industrial Average: the float-weighted S&P 500 is a much better measure of the economy's prospects.[15] Thus many indices are **large-cap indices** which

---

[15]I do not know why TV news mentions the Dow. However, asking a trader how "the Dow" is doing marks you as a clueless newbie. Don't do it!

are composed of many or all of the largest firms in a market. That said, we also think small firms are an important part of the economy and are exposed to different risks; therefore, we may also look at **small-cap indices**. **Composite indices** try to capture the behavior of most or all of the market. Obviously, these indices all exclude private firms since they do not have a stock price we can use.

Which public firms are included in an index? That may be decided behind closed doors to meet some unspecified objective or it may be determined by ranking firms by size. The latter might seem more objective, but it is very gameable: If I know which stocks will go into the index when it is reconstituted, I can buy them ahead of time and then sell when many people buy due to the index changing.[16]

This discussion neglects commodities, real-estate, FX, and bonds. How would one weight those indices: by global output, approximate value, or total bond face outstanding? Commodities indices use a variety of weighting schemes. The Thomson Reuters Core Commodity CRB index has 19 commodities with fixed weights of 1%, 5%, or 6% — except crude oil (23%); these seem designed to strike a compromise between weighting by the produced value and equal weighting. The S&P GSCI index is a production-weighted index of 24 commodity futures; and, the Bloomberg Commodity index is weighted by a constrained average of historical trading volumes for 22 commodity futures.

Many bond indices weight by total bond face outstanding. However, if the index holds sovereign bonds from many countries, weighting by the value of bonds issued might not be as informative as weighting by GDP. Do investors really want more exposure to a small country which issues a lot of debt? Probably not. On the other hand, if a country had little debt and high GDP, a GDP-weighting might put a lot of weight on one bond — allowing people to manipulate the index by trading that bond. Fixed income indices have other issues which we will discuss in Chapter 11 when we talk about fixed income.

Finally, we should prefer indices with futures contracts traded on them. The ability to shift risk exposure to a certain index makes that index far more attractive: it incentivizes people to watch that index and ensure its value is sensible. These "financial" futures were first developed in 1972 when the Chicago Mercantile Exchange created futures of FX rates. Ten years later, the Kansas City Board of Trade developed the first equity index futures. Financial futures are now some of the more liquid instruments traded globally.

2.8.1 Further Reading

While derivatives are not an asset class, they are an active area of interest. For those interested in derivatives, the supposedly must-have book is Hull (2016). While I first learned about options with an earlier version of that book, I believe now that there are better introductions. For those interested in options, I recommend McDonald (2012) and Luenberger (2013). Few books treat futures in much depth at all. For

---

[16]For more detail on this, read Bill Alpert's *Barron's* article about my trading that strategy.

those interested in futures, Kolb and Overdahl (2006) is the first book to read. I can find no decent books on the theory of indices.

2.9 Quiz

Try answering the following questions in five minutes.

1. What are the five major currencies which are traded? (Be specific![17])

2. (2 points!) You hear about a new and growing asset class. What are two reasons we might care about a new asset class?

3. What are the two main US equity indices — one focused on large firms, the other on smaller firms, and both having actively-traded futures?

4. The members of many benchmark indices are weighted by the market capitalization of firms in the index — so a larger firm has more weight. Why might we prefer that to weighting firms equally?

5. There are four asset classes for investors: stocks, bonds, real estate, and derivatives. T F

6. An index ETF is not a derivative. T F

7. What is the most widely-held asset class in the US and most countries?

8. The interest rate, set by supply and demand, for US dollars deposited in UK banks is referenced by many financial contracts. This is also the base rate for short-term lending among those banks. What is the name of this important floating interest rate?

9. A few years ago, Warren Buffett invested $5 bn in Bank of America. He bought a 6% bond with warrants which, if exercised, would give him at least $5 bn of stock instead of getting his money back. What would the coupon be without the warrants?

10. (Bonus!) In 2008, BlackRock closed their Florida Municipal Bond fund. Why?

2.10 Exercises

2.10.1 Exploring with R

We talked about how asset classes behave differently, but we can use R to illustrate

---

[17]For example, the "Crown" could refer to SEK (Swedish Krona), NOK (Norwegian Krone), DKK (Danish Krone), ISK (Icelandic Króna), or CZK (Czech Koruna). In the recent past, it might have also referred to the SKK (Slovak Koruna) or ESK (Estonian Kroon).

this point. The idea is to get you familiar with handling financial data and seeing some of the ideas we have discussed.

To start, you will need to download and install R, a free software implementation of the S statistical analysis language. Information on how to do this is in Appendix A.

R is widely used in academia and industry, so learning to use it is beneficial.[18] That's not to say that Python is not useful; however, the learning curve for R is more gentle than that for Python. Furthermore, R is the language in which academic statisticians largely develop new methodology.

Instructions

Use the code below to answer the questions. We will use the `xts` package for handling the time series since it aligns dates and makes a lot of drudgery easy. We will also use the `quantmod` package and `Quandl` package to download data.

⚠ **Beware!** *At the time of this writing, Google Finance data (a common source for stock and mutual fund prices) has been turned off and Yahoo Finance data has sometimes been limited. You can still use* `quantmod` *to access data from Yahoo (for now) as well as other sources. The* `Quandl` *package can access some stock prices updated by a community of users as well as inexpensive end-of-day closing prices. Other companies offer similar services, such as Alpha Vantage, YCharts, and* **eodhistoricaldata. com**.

Look at the data for the following instruments:

- Fixed Income: We want to look at some US Treasuries over time. Unfortunately, bonds mature; and, there may not be a bond maturing in exactly 2 years on a given day. So Fed economists kindly create pseudo-bonds to replicate the behavior of bonds for certain key maturities. Yields for these constant-maturity treasuries are often quoted as measures of the bond market. Also grab the Moody's seasoned Baa corporate bond yield index.
- Real Estate: Download near futures for the Dow Jones US Real Estate index and 3 REITs: Annally (a US mortgage REIT), Equity Residential (a US equity REIT), and Canadian Apartment Properties (a Canadian equity REIT).
- Commodities: Download settlement prices of near futures for the GSCI index, corn, soybeans, WTI crude oil, and US natgas (Chicago Mercantile Exchange contracts); and, copper, and steel rebar (Shanghai Futures Exchange contracts)
- Equity Indices: Fetch the adjusted close price for the S&P 500, Russell 2000, TSX Composite, IPC, FTSE 100, Euro Stoxx 50, SMI, Hang Seng, Straits Times, and Nikkei 225. Why not grab the TSX 60, CSI 300 or KOSPI? Permissioning on downloads made them difficult to get.

---

[18]I might be biased, having used R for over 15 years and having been a co-organizer of the R/Finance conference (http://www.rinfinance.com) since 2009.

- FX Rates: Download settlement prices of near futures for USD/JPY, US-D/EUR, USD/CAD, and AUD/NZD.

1. Using the R code, explore the above instruments. Start by creating a summary of prices (or yields). Which instruments seem to be fairly stable? Which are not so stable — and tend to drift widely? Which tend to stay in a small range but have rare outliers?

2. The R code also creates plots. Which instruments move similarly? Do they sometimes move around much more than at other times? Do they sometimes wander far away from their typical level? You may even see a couple of data errors, for example a series with an inexplicable spike in it.

3. I previously mentioned problems with geometric indices. We can see this with some simple simulation. Simulate five series r_{it} of simulated returns: random variates for $i \in \{1, \ldots, 5\}$ and $t \in \{1, \ldots, 10000\}$. The variates should be iid normal $r_{it} \overset{iid}{\sim} N(0, 0.04^2)$. You can generate a sequence of returns with R's rnorm function:
r1 <- rnorm(10000, 0, 0.04)

The geometric index return is $r_{gi,t} = \sqrt[5]{\prod_{i=1}^{5}(1 + r_{it})}$ while an equally-weighted portfolio would have return of $r_{ew,t} = \frac{1}{5}\sum_{i=1}^{5}(1 + r_{it})$. Run the simulations and compute summary statistics (using **summary**). Would you rather hold the index or the equally-weighted portfolio?

4. Can you prove the behavior you saw in the previous question is always true? Often true? Hint: An inequality might help.

R Code

```
library(xts)
library(Quandl)
library(quantmod)

# Get constant-maturity (US) Treasuries
ust.tickers <- c("FRED/DGS3MO", "FRED/DGS2", "FRED/DGS10", "FRED/DGS30")
ust.raw <- Quandl(ust.tickers, type="xts")
ust.colnames <- c("UST3M", "UST2Y", "UST10Y", "UST30Y")
colnames(ust.raw) <- ust.colnames

corpbond.raw <- Quandl("FED/RIMLPBAAR_N_B", type="xts")
colnames(corpbond.raw) <- c("USBaaCorp")

re.tickers <- c("CHRIS/CME_JR1", "NLY", "EQR", "CAR-UN.TO")
re.raw <- Quandl(re.tickers[1], type="xts")[,"Settle"]
# Sadly, there is a data error: a few days reported 10x price
re.raw[re.raw>1000] <- re.raw[re.raw>2000]/10
for (j in 2:length(re.tickers)) {
    tmp <- getSymbols(re.tickers[j], src="yahoo", env=NULL)
    adj.col <- last(colnames(tmp))
    re.raw <- cbind(re.raw, tmp[,adj.col])
}
colnames(re.raw) <- c("DJUSRE", "NLY", "EqRes", "CdnApt")
```

```
commodities.tickers <- c("CHRIS/CME_GI1", "CHRIS/CME_C1", "CHRIS/CME_S1", "CHRIS/CME_HG1",
                         "CHRIS/SHFE_RB1", "CHRIS/CME_CL1", "CHRIS/CME_NG1")
commodities.raw <- Quandl(commodities.tickers[1], type="xts")[,"Settle"]
for (j in 2:length(commodities.tickers)) {
    tmp <- Quandl(commodities.tickers[j], type="xts")[,"Settle"]
    commodities.raw <- cbind(commodities.raw, tmp)
}
colnames(commodities.raw) <- c("GSCI", "Corn", "Soybeans", "Copper", "Rebar",
                               "WTI", "USNatgas")

eqtidx.tickers <- c("^GSPC", "^RUT", "^GSPTSE", "^MXX", "^FTSE", "^STOXX50E",
                    "^SSMI", "^HSI", "^STI", "^N225")
tmp <- getSymbols(eqtidx.tickers[1], src="yahoo", env=NULL)
adj.col <- last(colnames(tmp))
eqtidx.raw <- tmp[,adj.col]
for (j in 2:length(eqtidx.tickers)) {
    tmp <- getSymbols(eqtidx.tickers[j], src="yahoo", env=NULL)
    adj.col <- last(colnames(tmp))
    eqtidx.raw <- cbind(eqtidx.raw, tmp[,adj.col])
}
colnames(eqtidx.raw) <- c("SP500", "R2000", "TSX", "IPC", "FTSE100", "ESTX50",
                          "SMI", "HangSeng", "STI", "NK225")

fx.tickers <- c("CHRIS/CME_JY1", "CHRIS/CME_EC1", "CHRIS/CME_CD1", "CHRIS/ICE_AR1")
fx.raw <- Quandl(fx.tickers[1], type="xts")[,"Settle"]
for (j in 2:length(fx.tickers)) {
    tmp <- Quandl(fx.tickers[j], type="xts")[,"Settle"]
    fx.raw <- cbind(fx.raw, tmp)
}
colnames(fx.raw) <- c("USDJPY", "USDEUR", "USDCAD", "AUDNZD")

alldata.full <- cbind(ust.raw, corpbond.raw, re.raw, commodities.raw,
                      eqtidx.raw, fx.raw)
alldata <- alldata.full["20140101/20180515"]

summary(alldata)

for (v in colnames(alldata)) {
    plot.tmp <- plot(alldata[,v], main=v)
    print(plot.tmp)
    invisible(readline(prompt="Press [enter] to continue"))
}
```

Commentary

A few comments on the preceding text is in order. What you see is computer **code**: instructions that tell a computer what to do. You will notice that the code sometimes puts the data into a name, for example: `foo <- 3`. Those are assignments to **variables**: named areas of memory which store data.

Note that I did not call the text "codes." Computer code is like water: indivisible and thus not pluralizable. I know you will eventually hear somebody use the term "codes" and it grates on the ear of anyone who has studied computer science. Don't do it. "Codes" are what spies use to communicate; code is what intelligent people use to instruct a computer.

You should enter the code into a file in a text editor, but not a word processor. Word processors often change what you type to substitute characters they think are prettier. That may be nice for a letter, but it is death to computer code. Use a text editor like TextEdit, Notepad, Notepad++, Emacs, vi, or the file editor in RStudio.

Finally, notice that the code is readable. Good code is **self-commenting**: it uses meaningful names for variables. When what is being done is unusual or puzzling, we can add a **comment**: a line that exists solely to explain. In *R*, comment lines start with #. Self-commenting code and comments are a good idea. You are unlikely to remember your train of thought when you return to your code a few months later. Self-commenting code also enables other people to fix your code if it breaks (for example: when you are on vacation).

References

Alpert, Bill. "The Trouble with Transparency". *Barron's* (May 18, 2009). URL: https://www.barrons.com/articles/SB124243913088626155.

Andrews, Anne Valentine and Sadek Wahba. *Investing in Infrastructure: A Primer.* Infrastructure Paper Series 2. Retrieved 23 May 2017 from: http://www.morganstanley.com/views/perspectives/files/infrastructure_paper2.pdf. Morgan Stanley, 2007.

Ang, Andrew. *Asset Management: A Systematic Approach to Factor Investing.* Oxford: Oxford University Press, 2014.

Berkin, Andrew L. and Larry E. Swedroe. *Your Complete Guide to Factor-Based Investing: The Way Smart Money Invests Today.* Saint Louis: Buckingham, 2016.

Bogle, John C. *The Little Book of Common Sense Investing.* New York: Wiley, 2017.

DeRosa, David F. *Foreign Exchange Operations: Master Trading Agreements, Settlement, and Collateral.* New York: Wiley, 2013.

Dunsby, Adam et al. *Commodity Investing: Maximizing Returns Through Fundamental Analysis.* New York: Wiley, 2008.

Fabozzi, Frank J. and Steven V. Mann, eds. *Handbook of Fixed Income Securities.* 8th ed. New York: McGraw-Hill, 2012.

Galitopoulou, Stellina and Antonella Noya. *Understanding Social Impact Bonds.* Working Paper. OECD, 2016. URL: http://www.oecd.org/cfe/leed/UnderstandingSIBsLux-WorkingPaper.pdf.

Geltner, David M. et al. *Commercial Real Estate Analysis and Investments.* 3rd ed. Mason, OH: OnCourse Learning, 2013.

Geman, Hélyette. *Commodities and Commodity Derivatives: Modeling and Pricing for Agriculturals, Metals and Energy.* New York: Wiley, 2005.

Graham, Benjamin. *The Intelligent Investor.* Revised. New York: Harper Business, 2006.

Graham, Patrick. "Daily FX volumes rise to $4.84 trillion in Jan - CLS". *Reuters* (May 11, 2016). Retrieved 11 May 2017 from: http://www.reuters.com/article/global-forex-volumes-idUSL8N15P2VA.

Grinold, Richard and Ronald Kahn. *Active Portfolio Management: A Quantitative Approach for Producing Superior Returns and Controlling Risk*. New York: McGraw Hill Education, 1999.

Homer, Sidney et al. "Inside the Yield Book: The Classic That Created the Science of Bond Analysis" (2013).

Hull, John C. *Fundamentals of Futures and Options Markets*. 9th ed. Upper Saddle River, NJ: Pearson, 2016.

Kolb, Robert W. and James A. Overdahl. *Understanding Futures Markets*. 6th ed. New York: Wiley-Blackwell, 2006.

Lewis, Michael. *Liar's Poker: Rising through the Wreckage on Wall Street*. New York: W. W. Norton & Company, 1989.

Liebman, Jeffrey B. *Social Impact Bonds: A Promising New Financing Model to Accelerate Social Innovation and Improve Government Performance*. Report. Center for American Progress, 2011. URL: http://cdn.americanprogress.org/wp-content/uploads/issues/2011/02/pdf/social_impact_bonds.pdf.

Linneman, Peter. *Real Estate Finance and Investments Risks and Opportunities*. 4th ed. Philadelphia: Linneman Associates, 2016.

Luenberger, David G. *Investment Science*. 2nd ed. Oxford: Oxford University Press, 2013.

Malkiel, Burton G. *A Random Walk down Wall Street: The Time-tested Strategy for Successful Investing*. 11th ed. New York: W.W. Norton & Co., 2016.

McDonald, Robert L. *Derivatives Markets*. 3rd ed. Upper Saddle River, NJ: Pearson, 2012.

McTaggart, Raymond, Gergely Daroczi, and Clement Leung. *Quandl: API Wrapper for Quandl.com*. R package version 2.8.0. 2016. URL: https://CRAN.R-project.org/package=Quandl.

Mercer. *Infrastructure: A Primer*. New York: Mercer LLC, 2016. URL: https://www.mercer.com/our-thinking/a-primer-on-infrastructure.html.

Pownall, Rachel A. J. *TEFAF Art Market Report 2017*. The European Fine Art Foundation, 2017.

Rubano, Joel. *Trader Construction Kit*. Needham, MA: Cehpalopod Publishing, 2016. URL: http://www.traderconstructionkit.com.

Ryan, Jeffrey A. *quantmod: Quantitative Financial Modelling Framework*. R package version 0.4-8. 2017. URL: https://CRAN.R-project.org/package=quantmod.

Ryan, Jeffrey A. and Joshua M. Ulrich. *xts: eXtensible Time Series*. R package version 0.9-7. 2014. URL: https://CRAN.R-project.org/package=xts.

Veronesi, Pietro. *Fixed Income Securities: Valuation, Risk, and Risk Management*. New York: Wiley, 2010.

— ed. *Handbook of Fixed Income Securities*. New York: Wiley, 2016.

Weithers, Tim. *Foreign Exchange: A Practical Guide to the FX Markets*. New York: Wiley, 2013.

Chapter 3

Markets in General

Economists and financiers often talk about **markets**: structures for exchanging goods and services that range from casual to highly formal. However, at their core, markets are about a few key ideas: exchange occurs; all involved parties must agree to the exchange; and, the price at which the exchange occurs is often what tips the scales from one side being unwilling to willing. **Market microstructure** is the field which studies the details of how markets work — or fail to work.

Markets are so important to economies that we should first think about why they are important. Most politicians do not study economics or markets so it is often up to us in finance to defend markets and what we do in them. Even many finance texts breeze through markets in a few pages. We will spend a few chapters discussing markets.

The goal of this chapter is to introduce markets and their benefits; explain the different forms they can take (and why); and, show how markets matter to the larger economy. It is good to remember that well-functioning markets are actually a force for good; a more in-depth discussion should make that clear.

3.1 Benefits of Markets

Economists are largely in favor of trade: trade allows firms, regions, and countries to expand their production possibilities and get more for their money by focusing on what they do best and trading to get the rest. This is why Illinois and Heilongjiang province in China grow corn, California grows grapes for wine, and Yunnan province in China grows tea leaves for Pu'er tea. This is almost always optimal for each state or province, but not for everyone: trade with California may put winemakers in Illinois and China out of work while trade with China may put tea growers in the US out of work. However, we still trade because that keeps more money in our pockets than trying to produce everything ourselves (**autarky**).

3.1.1   Exchange

On a local scale, trade (aka exchange) is one of the few life interactions that are **Pareto optimal**: both sides are left happier and everyone else is indifferent. When I buy a coffee, I and the vendor willingly exchange money and coffee. They make a profit and I get a warm wakening drink. When two consenting adults come together to exchange goods and services, we should probably let them do so: the world is usually a better place afterward.

This all assumes there are no negative **spillovers** (aka **externalities**): side effects on others or the community at large. Sometimes, we allow exchange despite the externalities: we let people buy fuel to power their cars even though it causes pollution which is unhealthy for the community and increases crime.[1] Sometimes, we criminalize exchange: communities ban certain drugs because they worry about crime externalities.

In exchange markets, spillovers are incredibly unlikely. When I buy or sell an instrument, the name in a ledger (often electronic) changes to keep track of my ownership stake. Unless I am acquiring a large stake in a company, it is hard to imagine how changing a name in an electronic ledger should have any effect on a community.

3.1.2   Prices

We need to remember that as valuable as exchange is, markets can also generate a positive spillover to society when they disseminate prices. Prices are the simplest expression of many people's wants and needs. Their analyses lead them to buy and sell when they believe prices offer a deal. Thus they buy and sell until they think a price is right, and the price averages all of those buys and sells into single number. We already discussed price theory; however, if we are going to mention the benefits of exchange, we need to remember the importance of prices and information dissemination which guides capital allocation in our economy. How important is it? I made a small subsection just to remind you. Right here. Prices are very important.

3.2   Primary Market

The **primary market** is the market which raises capital by selling newly-issued securities. The **secondary market** is where previously-issued securities are traded.

Securities may be issued in a number of ways. A **private placement** is issued only to "accredited" investors. Since the requirements for such an offering are lower, regulators demand that investors meet stricter criteria which (ostensibly) mean

---

[1]The link between pollution and crime is a recent discovery. Nevin's 2007 *Environmental Research* article shows that eliminating leaded gasoline explains long-term reductions in crime worldwide better than other explanations (like abortion). A recent working paper from Herrnstadt et al. shows that higher unleaded gasoline emissions may also cause (small) increases in crime.

they sufficiently understand the greater risk of such an offering. Private placements cannot be traded on public exchanges. However, in the US, Rule 144(a) allows accredited investors to trade restricted securities among themselves, for example via Nasdaq's Private Market.

An **initial public offering** (IPO) (aka "going public") is the first sale of a firm's stock to the public at large (and not just accredited investors). A **secondary** or **seasoned offering** occurs when a firm issues additional securities. Secondary equity offerings result in **dilution**: current owners have their ownership stakes reduced. Why would an owner tolerate that? If the secondary offering enables the firm to grow, a smaller stake in a larger firm may be worth more overall.

Sometimes an entity applies for **shelf registration** which allows them to issue up to a certain amount of securities over some time period. They may then issue stock when convertible bonds, warrants, or rights are exercised; or, they may offer the securities directly

> **Are You "Sophisticated?"** An **accredited investor** in the US is defined as a person who has made $200k/year for each of the past two years ($300k if married) and expects to make that this year also; or, someone whose net worth (excluding their primary residence) is $1 mn or more. Obviously, net assets or prior salary levels do not have much to do with a person's financial sophistication or knowledge. Furthermore, would "unsophisticated" investors be harmed by investing in a mutual fund of private placements?

into the secondary market (**at-the-market**). This can be a low-cost way of issuing more securities; and, for at-the-market offerings, it allows an entity to quickly raise capital in light of market conditions.

Finally, a company may turn part of their firm into a new independent firm, a **spin-off**. Spin-offs can create weird market dynamics; we will discuss some of those dynamics in Chapter 16 when we talk about limits to arbitrage.

Young "startup" firms often attract investors. Before a firm is ready for an IPO, **venture capitalists** (**VCs**) invest capital in the new firm and help guide the management toward success. In exchange, they often receive a private placement issuance of stock. While VCs would love for all their investments to quickly become large IPOs, many will fail and some will be bought by larger firms. Recent regulatory changes give young firms another source of funding: Regulation A+ allows US firms to raise capital by issuing securities that are not registered with the Securities and Exchange Commission through crowdfunding.

IPOs are Herculean efforts: banks which may not be much larger than the firm they are advising purchase the firm and then sell it to investors who become the owners. Sometimes, the banks cannot sell all of the firm — a sign of limited demand which leaves them holding an investment which is likely to sag in value. Banks temporarily join together ("form a **syndicate**") to share this risk.

How do investment bankers organize an IPO? They first circulate **offering documents** which describe the security being issued, the issuer, and possible investment risks. These risks range from the mildly worrying ("the firm would likely be wiped out if the Cascadia subduction zone generated a large earthquake and tsunami, an event experts believe is overdue") and the mundane ("we may find our business becoming less trendy") to the truly concerning ("our auditor cannot explain all historical cash flows in the financials presented here"). That last risk is not made up: similar warnings have turned out to be serious.[2] The offering documents that are circulated are often a **red herring**, preliminary documents which have not yet been approved (and are named for the red legal notice on the cover).

However, bankers are far more active than just circulating documents: they may hold a **road show**, presentations in various cities to present the issuer and gauge interest in the offering. Road shows are also for **bookbuilding**: bankers talk to large investors hoping they will express interest (or commit) to purchasing part of the new security.[3] Bankers also advertise the offering with a **tombstone**, often a quarter-page list of bank names in large type which also lists the issuer and the security being offered. Ironically, tombstones often say they are "neither an offer to sell nor a solicitation to buy" the securities. Offers of sale have typically been done via a **prospectus**, the approved offering documents. Since 2013, however, some general advertising of an offering has been permitted in the US.

3.2.1   How to IPO?

When a firm IPOs, investors must choose to participate; however, it is rarely so easy for the investors. Newly-issued securities offer access to a new investment with the potential to grow quickly given new capital. Thus potential **subscribers** for the new issue may demand more than what is being issued. As economists, we know how to solve that: increase the price until the market **clears**, *i.e.* the amount of securities being issued equals the amount demanded at that price. However, attempts to introduce such auctions into the IPO process have not met with universal success. Rumors abound that investment bankers want IPOs to be over-demanded so their price "pops" upon listing — and that this lets them reward loyal customers.[4]

So a few people make some extra cash; why do we care? We care because we want more economic growth and jobs.[5] If the IPO process is flawed, new (risky)

---

[2]Refco's offering documents included risks like: "two significant deficiencies in our internal controls over financial reporting," "We will become subject to additional financial and other reporting and corporate governance requirements that may be difficult for us to satisfy," and "We are a 'controlled company' within the meaning of the NYSE rules and, as a result, will qualify for, and intend to rely on, exemptions from certain corporate governance requirements." Refco went public 11 August 2005 and was out of business by 17 October; see Smith (2005) for more details.

[3]You might wonder what happens if investors are not impressed by the firm. Although rare, insufficient interest sometimes leads bankers to advise the firm to cancel the offering.

[4]Those interested in IPO pricing should read Ritter and Welch (2002).

[5]Brosnan and Waal (2003), about Capuchin monkeys receiving different rewards for the same tasks, suggests we also have a deep-seated desire for fairness.

firms will get less cash than they could. That may mean they cannot hire enough employees to succeed; they have insufficient cash to weather hard times; or, they offer too small a reward to their founders compared to the risk taken. In these cases, the firm is riskier than it could be and we may find innovators less willing to create new firms. Over a whole nation of employees and potential innovators, this can add up to a lot of lost economic growth.

3.3   Market Types

This text is mostly about secondary markets, however we gain a lot insights by studying markets in general. Therefore, much of what we learn about secondary security markets is also useful for thinking about commodity and FX markets.

Markets are not all the same — nor should they be. Buyers and sellers in different markets may have very different concerns and needs. Markets assume different structures to handle differences in flexibility, fungibility, legality, and liquidity. We will discuss these structures in increasing liquidity:

1. Direct Search,
2. Over-the-Counter (OTC),
3. Auctions,
4. Call Markets, and
5. Continuous Trading.

3.3.1   Direct Search Markets

Direct search markets feature buyers and sellers who must undergo significant work to find one another; therefore, these markets tend to be highly illiquid. Some people might not think of them as markets, but they are — and they are sometimes used for the most unusual or elusive of goods and services. Suppose we have a world like in Figure 3.1.

Here, we have Moe and Joe who wander the streets seeking to trade "blow," which could be some illicit good or service. They wander around until they meet each other. Then, they might look hard at one another; ask questions; and, warily assess how much they trust each other — and if this is someone they want to do business with. Joe could notice Moe's fangs or Moe could smell that Joe is stinky; either detail might lead one party to hold off on conducting business. In this market, a lack of formality is a benefit: it makes it harder to be caught by law enforcement; it eliminates incriminating records; and, it allows for individuals to personally assess if they want to do business with their potential counterparty.

Direct search markets need not be for illicit goods, however; there are many other scenarios where trust and flexibility are important. We see this when people buy used cars from online forums or even when you ask a bunch of friends if somebody can loan you $40 for drinks. Direct search markets are interesting, but they tend to

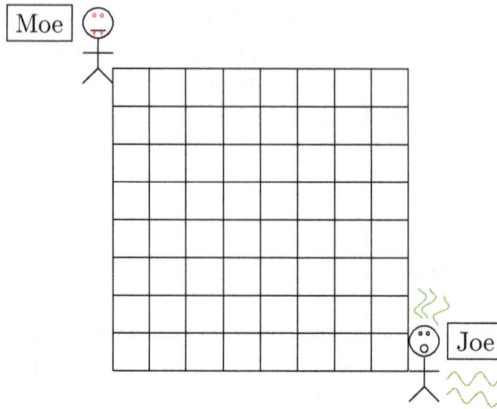

Figure 3.1: Moe and Joe wander the streets looking to trade "blow" — whatever that might be. We can imagine that trust might be a concern for many definitions of "blow." Many of those definitions also make clear why this market might not be formally organized.

lack easily gathered data and they are not where most people invest. We will not say much more about them, but Moe and Joe are useful reminders that markets take many forms.

3.3.2 Over-the-Counter Markets

Over-the-counter (OTC) markets involve buyers and sellers contacting intermediaries (or, rarely, one another) in order to trade. OTC markets are often conducted over the phone or (less often) face-to-face. When a party is interested in trading, they contact a broker-dealer to ask what prices would be to buy or sell. Most OTC markets have adopted rules that the broker-dealer must then honor those prices for some specified size.

OTC markets exist when liquidity is low or flexibility is crucial. Traders can specify more general orders, for example "I'll take $25 million up to a price of 102.55, but not above that unless you can get at least $50 million below 102.65." The low liquidity is why prices are not constantly updated; intermediaries need to assess the liquidity and how much risk they would incur by trading on a case-by-case basis.

On the other hand, there are many OTC markets which could probably move to trading on an exchange. Why do they remain off-exchange? Moving on-exchange involves increased competition. For intermediaries in an OTC market, more competition is not in their interest unless they think they can claim most of the market with the best prices. An exchange might also be unable to handle the required flexibility: some OTC markets create custom, long-term derivatives contracts. In these cases, trust is crucial because the contract is a source of counterparty risk. (We will discuss that near the end of the book when we talk about crises.)

OTC markets are used to trade everything from swaps to portfolio derivatives to municipal bonds and mortgages on homes. Most real estate transactions involving a realtor or broker take place in an OTC market.

3.3.3 Auctions

Auctions are markets where assets are sold to buyers in a singularity of time. That singularity or atomicity is what distinguishes auctions: the market does not exist before the auction; the auction is held, goods change hands, and the price is published; and, the market then ceases. Why would we use a market that only exists for a brief instant? Auctions are typically used for goods which are illiquid; thus, gathering all the buyers and sellers in an instant creates enough liquidity for the market to (hopefully) function.

Most fans of spy movies know art is sold at auctions: James Bond often first sees the villain and the *femme fatale* at an auction. However auctions are also used in the primary market to issue US Treasuries, emissions caps, and radio spectrum licenses. WR Hambrecht has also used their auction-based OpenIPO process to create IPOs which do not "pop" for Morningstar, Interactive Brokers, and (most famously) Google.

Walrasian auctions involve finding the **market clearing price** which equalizes the quantity people will sell and buy. This is done via *tâtonnement*, an iterative optimization shown in Table 3.1. While most auctions are used for illiquid goods, Walrasian auctions also excel at handling multiple buyers and sellers and high volume since many goods all clear at one price.

This is why Walrasian auctions set the opening and closing prices for US (and many other) equity exchanges.[6] Opening auctions collect pent-up supply and demand to find a relevant price to begin trading. Closing auctions anticipate supply and demand that cannot be satisfied after the market closes to find a relevant price to end trading. Auctions may also be used during the day if prices are unusually volatile or material news is released: the exchange halts the stock and notifies market participants that an auction will be held to re-open the stock for trading.

Economists study auctions using game theory and methods from analysis and operations research. Auctions are classified as one- or two-sided, if there is only one or many buyers or sellers, and may be referred to as "fixings."

3.3.4 Call Markets

Call markets consist of occasional or regular Walrasian auctions. This structure is used by the London Metal Exchange, by Euronext for some illiquid stocks, and by dark pools, off-exchange markets called "dark" because they do not publish prices at which people would buy or sell.

Frequent call markets would seem to approximate continuous trading. One

---

[6]Exchanges with an intraday break often have an auction before and after the break.

Try	Price	Brown	White	Blue	Orange	Pink	Imb.	Net
1	730	B 30	B 10	—	B 5	B 10	+55	—
2	740	B 10	—	S 5	S 5	B 10	+10	10
3	750	S 10	S 10	S 5	S 15	B 10	−30	10
4	745	—	S 5	S 5	S 10	B 10	−10	10
5	742	B 6	S 2	S 5	S 7	B 10	+2	14
6	743	B 4	S 3	S 5	S 8	B 10	−2	14
7	742.5	B 5	S 2.5	S 5	S 7.5	B 10	—	15

Table 3.1: An example of *tâtonnement* in a Walrasian auction for a good last traded at 730. Messrs. Brown, White, Blue, Orange, and Pink all give buy or sell amounts for a proposed price. The buy-sell imbalance ("Imb.") guides which way the auctioneer moves the next-proposed price.

economist has even suggested eliminating all markets as they currently exist and replacing them with a few auctions per day — or maybe many auctions.[7] However, market structure not only reflects liquidity but also influences it. Muscarella and Piwowar (2001) studied the Paris Bourse moving stocks between continuous trading and call markets. They found that the move precipitated price changes: stocks moved to continuous trading increased in price while stocks moved to call markets decreased in price. Thus moving all trading to call markets would result in firms' IPOs raising less capital and, therefore, lower economic growth.

Since call markets are rare, illiquid, and possibly suboptimal, we will not say much more about them.

3.3.5   Continuous Trading

Continuous trading is what most people imagine when they think of stock trading: markets where, at any time, multiple people may buy and sell from one another at a venue. Implicit in continuous trading is the idea of **market hours**: the time during which the market is open for trading.

In US equity markets, continuous trading accounts for about 80% of on-exchange volume with opening and closing auctions accounting for almost all the rest. A lot of financial news focuses on continuous trading: we look at how prices respond to news intraday. Trading hours vary by market: Equity markets tend to be open during business hours. Futures markets are increasingly open overnight and during the day. Bond markets are often open when equity markets are open (for corporate bonds) and overnight as well for sovereign/government bonds. FX markets are, naturally, always open.[8] US Treasuries also trade all the time although they are most active

---

[7]The proposed structure varies with the latest criticism. However, the one constant is the idea that some wise central planner knows how often the market should trade.

[8]US equity markets are open Monday–Friday, 9:30–16:00 NY time. US futures markets for

during 8:00–16:00 NY time.[9] Many markets are embracing longer hours to attract trading from around the world.

3.4 Orders and Quotes

An **order** is a request to trade an instrument. Orders express what we want: we can be attracted, repelled, or indifferent. Orders expressing these opinions can be to buy or sell (or might not exist). What if we want to bet against something we do not own? That involves making a **short sale**: something the seller does not own is sold which is (effectively) a way of holding a negative amount. Typically, this is done by borrowing the instrument and, later, repurchasing and replacing that instrument. Regulations in many countries constrain short sales for various reasons we will discuss shortly. Sometimes buyers must even specify if a buy undoes a previous short sale. Thus there are more than just two types of orders.

In US equity markets, there are four basic **order types**: Buy (B); Sell (S); Sell Short (SS); and, Sell Short Exempt (SSE).[10] Buy, sell, and sell short are self-explanatory; sell short exempt orders are used by market intermediaries to sell short without borrowing the security or (in the past) being subject to certain constraints. Sell short exempt orders were created to increase liquidity by helping market intermediaries in their intertemporal smoothing. Occasionally, you will hear the order type referred to as its **side**.

When placing orders, a trader balances immediacy with price sensitivity. **Market orders** execute immediately at the best prices available. That sounds nice, but there is no price limit: would you really be willing to trade at any price? Occasionally, traders placing market orders find the price they traded at was far from what they expected. This is why most finance professionals (and many personal investors) use **limit orders** which specify a worst-acceptable price. If a limit order is priced so that it should be filled by other outstanding orders, we call it a **marketable limit** order. Two less-used order types are the **market if touched** and **stop** orders which become market orders if their specified price is reached; a market if touched order tries to grab good prices while a stop order tries to limit losses.

Market orders do not persist: they trade and then go away.[11] However, an unsatisfied limit order does persist. **Quotes** are collections of active limit orders. Buy orders are collected by price and become **bids**; sell orders are collected by price and become **offers** or **asks**. Thus quotes are prices at which people stand ready

---

equity indices, interest rates, bonds, FX, energy, and metals are open Sunday–Friday 17:00–16:00 Chicago time (with index futures having a brief time-out from 15:15–15:30 after the stock markets close). US futures on agricultural commodities are open Sunday–Friday 19:00–13:20 Chicago time (with a timeout from 7:45–8:30).

[9]See Alloway's 2016 *Bloomberg News* article for more information on when US Treasuries trade normally versus after big events.

[10]Under US regulation Reg SHO, SSE's are merely markings.

[11]This is not exactly true. A market order encountering no other order on the far side of the market would persist until somebody traded with it.

to buy or sell. A **limit order book** ("book") lists the total amount for purchase or sale at each price for standing limit orders. Some venues even show individual orders at each price level. The book changes if a limit order is received, changed, canceled, or filled.

Because bids and offers are firm offers to buy or sell, they have economic meaning, but they may not be useful. I can place a firm bid of $1 for a new, pristine Subaru WRX (with the FA20 DIT engine); and, that is indeed a firm bid which I would honor. However, that bid is not very informative nor is it likely to get filled. Therefore, we refer to the highest bid and the lowest offer at a venue as the **best bid** and **best offer** or, together, the **best bid and offer (BBO)**. The BBO across all market centers is often called the **national best bid and offer (NBBO)**. In Europe, some venues trade stocks from multiple countries. Thus they refer to the **European best bid and offer (EBBO)**. The NBBO (or EBBO) is better known as the **spread**, **bid-ask spread**, the **inside market**, or (in the UK) the **touch**.

The spread is a term we abuse a bit. If the inside bid and ask were $20.11 for 300 shares and $20.13 for 200 shares, we might use the term "spread" to refer to the inside quotes ("$20.11–$20.13, 300 by 200"), the prices themselves ("$20.11–$20.13"), or the lowest offer minus the highest bid ("$0.02"). The spread (last meaning) is usually positive: if bids and offers overlapped, they would trade against one another until that were not the case.

The spread is also positive because of **adverse selection**, the risk of trading with people who have valuable information that you lack (aka **asymmetric information**). Imagine you had a painting which may be valuable or not; you do not know art *that* well. I ask you to set a price at which you would sell the painting — and a price at which you would buy a similar painting. You might think you have no information, but you do, conditionally. If somebody sells you a painting, you might suspect that your bid is too high. Similarly, if somebody buys your painting, you might suspect your ask was too low. Adverse selection is another reason not to quote the same bid and ask price: people trading with you gives you information.[12]

The spread is also a cost we may pay for immediacy.[13] If we were buying, we could pay the best offer to ensure purchasing the security; however, our price would be worse than entering a limit order at the best bid and hoping to save some money. The spread is like the River Styx: a price we would rather not pay. We say that a buyer paying the best offer **crosses the spread** and "lifts" the offer while a seller crossing the spread "hits" the bid. If we are buying, we refer to the best bid as the **near side** of the spread and the best offer as the **far side** of the spread.[14] For sellers, the language flips: the best offer and bid are the near and far sides of the spread.

Orders also feature modifiers which specify their **time in force** — how long they

---

[12]Those interested in exploring this idea more should read Glosten and Milgrom (1985).

[13]There are, in truth, many more reasons for spreads. That, however, is more appropriate material for a market microstructure text.

[14]This "hit" versus "lift" terminology is also a trading floor shibboleth.

will persist. **Good-til-canceled (GTC)** orders stay active until canceled by the trader.[15] **Day** orders are canceled after the market closes (after the closing auction, if there is one). **Immediate or cancel (IOC)** orders (what the London Stock Exchange calls **execute or eliminate (EOE)** orders) are like lightning strikes: they trade against the order book (if possible) and then immediately return to the sender; these orders are used by professional traders to grab liquidity while letting them quickly adapt their plans if their order was not completely filled.

Trading in the opening and closing auctions is also indicated by the time in force: a **market on open (MOO)** order (an **opening (OPG)** order on some venues) will trade in the opening auction at the market clearing price — if there is sufficient supply on the other side of the market. A **market on close (MOC)** order will trade in the closing auction. Similarly, **limit on open (LOO)** and **limit on close (LOC)** orders may participate in the auction.

Other orders can trade in the auction. Market orders sent before the open are likely to get filled in the opening auction. Similarly, limit orders which have not executed prior to the closing auction may get filled in the closing auction. Market orders sent before the closing auction are unlikely to survive long enough to participate in the auction.

An auction might have an imbalance between buyers and sellers; **imbalance only (IO)** orders are available on some markets to allow market participants to trade against auction imbalances. (Which venues offer IO orders? Hint: ones where nobody has a monopoly on balancing supply and demand. More on that shortly.)

3.5 Market Intermediaries

We mentioned before that some actors in markets are intermediaries. Intermediaries can act in two capacities: as brokers or dealers.

Brokers match buyers with sellers: either if both are present or if one side is willing to wait. Brokering involves acting as an **agent**: the broker must represent each customer's interests as they would represent their own interest in the same position (*i.e.* maintaining **fiduciary duty**). Financial market brokers are like the little old ladies who act as marriage brokers in some countries: they find someone who they think would make a suitable spouse for their first-arriving client. One hopes they use something like fiduciary duty.

Dealers, on the other hand, act when there is not a buyer and seller to match; dealers trade with the buyer or seller, temporarily holding or owing instruments. Dealers act for their own (**principal** or **proprietary**) interest: They anticipate the other side arriving soon. Thus they smooth out the asynchronous arrival of buyers and sellers. We sometimes refer to dealers as **market makers** since they always quote a bid and ask, *i.e.* **make a market**. While there are marriage brokers, I

---

[15]Some brokers will cancel GTC orders after major software upgrades or some extended time period like six months. Check the fine print to see how your broker treats GTCs.

doubt there are marriage dealers: One can imagine the concern of a young person marrying an old lady and hoping a suitable future spouse arrives soon to take over the old lady's marital duties.

Market makers are exposed to adverse selection by quoting. Suppose you learn of good news about a firm and quickly buy from the market maker. The market maker is now short; and, if the price rises, the market maker will lose money. Thus market makers constantly face a tough optimization: quoting better prices to increase revenue versus reducing their risk.

Eagles and Banners and Stars, Oh My! A major stock exchange in the US used to offer tours. The tour showed the trading floor and explained the benefits of shareholder capitalism. It concluded with a film about the exchange's workings and how specialists "maintained a fair and orderly market." The film featured lots of bald eagles, American flags, stars, and patriotic music.

Why is that? Is the specialist really some superhero who pays for their seat and then comes to work every day willing to lose money for the good of the market? And if so, why the patriotic imagery? If the specialist is doing such favors for buyers and sellers, why not make a film telling us how much money the specialist saved them? Such a film does not exist. Whenever somebody does not focus on the economics, it's probably because the economics are not in your favor.

Many market intermediaries and full-service investment firms are **broker-dealers**; they act as both. In some markets, the desire for anonymity leads to **inter-broker dealers**: dealers who will trade with another intermediary for a client.

3.5.1 *Specialists*

Many stock exchanges started as order-driven markets: they merely collected customer orders. The market acted solely as a broker. One concern quickly arose: what if orders did not always match? What if a buyer arrived to buy and nobody was there to sell? The market would then function only sporadically. The lower volume would dissuade investors from trading at that market.

The other truth is that most stock exchanges started as private clubs. The solution chosen was to hire someone to "maintain a fair and orderly market," called a **specialist**.[16] In truth, the "hired" person had to pay for the "seat" giving them the right to be a specialist. Specialists constantly quote a bid and ask (make a market). They also see all the orders and can stop trading. This makes a specialist a monopolist dealer. There are not a lot of specialists; but, for a long time they were the club that controlled trading in an exchange's stocks. While a bit harsh of a metaphor, specialists

---

[16]This phrase is also a bit of a shibboleth. But O ye of little faith [in free markets]....

are like trolls controlling their bridges, collecting tolls, and possibly stopping traders who want to cross sides.[17]

Like dealers, specialists may see an order to buy when there are no sell orders. Imagine their dilemma: a stock has been trading around \$45/share when a buy order comes in. Maybe it's a market buy, maybe it has a limit of \$50/share. There are no orders to sell shares — or not enough to fill the buy order. Unlike dealers, the specialist then stops the market; checks the news on the stock; and, if there is no positive news, **provides liquidity**: sells the shares to the buyer at \$50/share and unstops the market. If a few minutes later a seller arrives to sell at \$45/share, the specialist can make a cool \$5/share for little risk. Had the specialist instead sold the shares at \$49/share to the limit order buyer, the specialist could have trumpeted a \$1/share **price improvement**. (Imagine the troll saying "I could charge you \$50... but I'll you save \$1!") If a specialist gives you price improvement you probably did not get a good price.

This does not mean that providing liquidity is bad; it is not. Providing liquidity is a valuable service offered by intermediaries. The problem is that there is no competition to provide liquidity; the specialist gets to stop the market which cuts out potential competitors. If all dealers were on an equal footing, it's unlikely that the buyer in question would have the order filled at \$50/share — 11% above where the market had been trading.

3.5.2 Order Handling Responsibilities

Intermediaries have some responsibilities when they enter orders or handle customer orders. They must mark orders as **agency** or **principal** to reflect if they are acting as an agent (*e.g.* broker) or a principal (*e.g.* dealer). Some venues also require that orders be marked as **held** if they require "best execution" or **not held** if the intermediary has discretion in trading the order. (Agency orders default to "held.")

Best execution is a nebulous concept with good reason. For a customer with a small order, best execution is likely getting the best price at that instant. For a larger order, getting the best price right now for the whole order might be more expensive than trading the order over time. Handling the liquidity demands of that larger order changes best execution from an instantaneous price-driven decision to an overall expected price and uncertainty decision.

Order handling gets more fraught if the intermediary simultaneously has orders for themselves and clients in the same instrument. The general rules, sometimes referred to as Manning rules in the US (for the plaintiff whose legal suit led to the rules), are clear: intermediaries must fill agency before principal orders. This prevents an intermediary from buying for themselves and then the client (as the price moves upward) ending with them providing liquidity to the client at a higher price. That practice is called **front-running** and is a cardinal sin; regulators in most markets view it as a very serious offense. However, the order handling rules do

---

[17]Unfortunately, specialists stopping markets is far worse than being asked your favorite color.

have some limitations: they do not apply across different market venues nor do they apply to odd-lot orders or orders so large they require discretionary trading.

3.6   After the Trade is Made

After a trade occurs, a number of steps must occur.[18] Both sides must **confirm** the order details; this historically involved a lot of manual intervention. Then, after some amount of time, settlement and delivery take place. (Money and securities rarely transfer immediately after a trade.)

Settlement is the transfer of money from buyer to seller. In the US, Japan, and Europe, stocks and bonds settle two business days after the trade ("T+2"). That is also when FX markets settle. Chinese stocks settle T+0: you must have the money in your account before making the trade. These are all considered "regular way" settlement.[19] Payment could also be made on **margin**, a loan for part of the purchase price which uses the security as collateral. Futures markets effectively settle the same day because trades require posting money to a margin account and futures do not involve a purchase but, rather, the agreement to exchange cashflows.

Delivery is the transfer of securities from buyer to seller. Delivery almost always takes place at the same time as settlement. If you fail to deliver securities, regulators may impose penalties.

Can a trader specify settlement and delivery dates which are not "regular way?" Sure, but that consigns the order to a separate market which is highly illiquid; the order will not show up in the limit order book. One could even specify different settlement and delivery dates; however, that is like asking the market for an unsecured, no-documents, no-questions-asked loan. Obviously, that does not happen often.

Finally, when our orders are filled, they alter our **position** or holdings. Some trades increase our position, moving it away from no exposure; some reduce our position moving it closer to zero. In general, a firm's positions are among its biggest secrets because they allow an outsider to guess at the firm's profits and losses. That could allow the outsider to push markets to cause the firm enough pain to exit their positions — allowing the outsider to buy those holdings cheaply. We will see more of this bad behavior in Chapter 26.

3.7   Short Sales and Speculation

We would be avoiding an important issue if we did not discuss short sales. In derivatives markets, trades are zero-sum — so every buy is matched to a short sale. That is not the case with securities. For securities, selling short first requires

---

[18]This section title pays homage to a classic Wall Street book about post-trade order processing.

[19]As an intern, I helped prepare a firm for same-day settlement. Nearly twenty-five years later, same-day settlement is no closer to reality. However, in the Fall of 2017, the US and Japan finally moved from "T+3" to "T+2" settlement.

that you get **borrow** or **locates**: securities that you reasonably suspect you could borrow. You then sell the borrowed securities. Later, you buy the securities back and return them to the lender. If the lender sells their securities while you are short, the broker will often try to find another lender for the securities. If that fails, however, they will notify you that you need to close out your short position.

In 2008, the US Securities and Exchange Commission (SEC) got upset about a proliferation of **naked** short sales — short sales without locates. Many of those traders then covered their short positions before delivery. In one case I analyzed, naked shorting allowed a trader to greatly exceed risk limits intraday. The SEC eventually required brokers to maintain lists of clients failing to deliver from short sales and imposed penalties for long-standing delivery failures. They also required firms to implement a system to check for and document locates. However, the law had two loopholes. First, there was no requirement to commit a locate to a trader; two traders hoping to short a stock might both believe they could use the same locate. Second, while there are order handling rules, there are not locate handling rules. If a client and I wish to short a stock, I must preference their order; however, I can short-circuit that by preferencing myself for locates. If I get locates and the client does not, I can sell short while they cannot.

Short selling is often controversial. Short sellers profit when a security declines in value. Across history and many countries, politicians and populists have often seen this as unseemly, unpatriotic, or even the cause of problems. For that reason, short sales have often been restricted. In the US, short sales were restricted via price tests until 2005.[20] Prior to that, short sales were only permitted when the price had recently increased or if the sale would occur above the best bid. Sometimes, politicians ban short selling in the hope of propping up prices. We will see in Chapters 19–20 that there are many ways around such bans; bans only prevent small investors from selling short.

The demonization of short selling is related to distrust of speculators. A **speculator** takes on risk to invest in the hope of making a profit. Yet many people ascribe superhero-like powers to speculators. (Often, the blame is placed on a subset of speculators like "hedge funds.") They blame speculators for driving down bank stocks during crises and for pushing up gas prices in summer. However, maybe bank stocks declined because the banks took excessive risk and are realizing large losses? Maybe gasoline is expensive because unusually many people decided to take road trips? Furthermore, when bank stocks recover and gasoline prices decline, are speculators again to blame? Do people thank speculators then? No, they do not, because people like "heads I win, tails you lose;" they like outcomes which make them better off.

We care deeply about speculation and short selling because of price theory. One of the most important functions of markets is to digest and disseminate information. Short sales help depress prices that are too high. When prices are representative and trustworthy, we say the market is efficient. Efficient prices make more people willing

---

[20]The US also banned short selling of bank stocks during the 2008 financial crisis.

to invest. When we constrain short sales, prices remain artificially high (although they still decline), trading becomes more expensive, and we send the wrong signals to the macroeconomy.[21]

Short selling allows the market to police itself. Richard Grubman was an analyst who searched financial statements for potential issues. Firms that are up to no good do not like that; so, how did Grubman get paid? When he found a firm that seemed to have accounting irregularities, he shorted the stock and then publicized the problem. If he was right, the stock declined to a more realistic value and he made money on his short sales, rewarding him for finding problems. That led Grubman to find the biggest accounting fraud in history: Enron. Without short selling, Richard Grubman would have had far less incentive to look into Enron's books. He would never have had Enron CEO Jeff Skilling call him an "asshole" — a comment so unhinged it led others to follow up on Grubman's concerns. Without short selling, people would have continued to invest in Enron and would have lost even more money. Alpert (2018) notes how hedge fund short sellers found over twenty times more fraudulent reverse IPOs than the entire SEC. Short selling may seem strange, but it is an incredibly powerful force for good in markets.

3.8   Regulation

Regulation has long been a fact of markets. The purpose of regulation is to encourage some behaviors and punish others. **Self regulation** is common: markets create and enforce their own rules. Sometimes, governments impose additional rules. Often these rules come after a major crisis. Government regulation generally takes one of two forms: **rules-based** or **principles-based**. Rules-based regulation has clear rules and violating them is illegal. However, rules-based regulation is open to **loopholes**: omissions and oversights in the rules that can allow people to engage in unwanted behavior. Principles-based regulation is more nebulous: regulators expect adherence to certain behaviors and effects. Since this creates uncertainty, the regulators often offer guidance on what is and is not acceptable; however, this prevents regulators from having to constantly update rules whenever new technologies arise.

Self-regulatory organizations (SROs) seem to be a contradiction: how can someone regulate themself? However, this is not how an SRO works. Self-regulation is essentially regulation by your competitors; the hearing board of an SRO is typically composed of executives from major firms. This makes them effective: a judge might not notice unfair or unethical practices, but your competitors certainly will. Governments often encourage self-regulation because it lets them specify certain principles and the SRO then constantly adapts that to market practice. Thus SROs are often principles-based. That also allows the industry to meet certain behavior goals without politicians (who do not understand the business) micromanaging how to achieve those goals.

---

[21]Those interested in the economics of short selling would do well to start with Diamond and Verrecchia's 1987 *Journal of Financial Economics* article.

Markets in the US are regulated by a number of government agencies and self regulatory agencies. We will be largely concerned with just a few of these, however. Securities as well as options on securities and indices are regulated by the **Securities and Exchange Commission (SEC)** and the **Financial Industry Regulatory Authority (FINRA)** SRO.[22] Futures, swaps, retail FX, and options on commodities, futures, swaps, and FX are regulated by the **Commodity Futures Trading Commission (CFTC)** and the **National Futures Association (NFA)** SRO. Natural gas and power markets are regulated by the **Federal Energy Regulatory Commission (FERC)** and the power markets have an SRO: the **North American Electric Reliability Corporation (NERC)**.

Although the SEC is rules-based while the CFTC (and others) are largely principles-based, the differences between the effective regulation is not stark. The main difference is that the CFTC tends to employ more economists and be more proactive about studying the markets they regulate. Finally, the Federal Reserve regulates banks and monitors the stability of the financial system.

What about institutional FX? As a global market, FX is largely unregulated: firms are often regulated by a local regulator, but that regulator cannot regulate entities in other countries.

In the timeline of US financial regulation, there are a few important laws. After the stock market crash of 1929, a number of acts were passed to mandate certain behaviors. It is worth mentioning these because even outside the US, many of these laws were influential.

The most well-known of the post-1929 laws were the Securities Act, Banking Act, and the Exchange Act. The **Securities Act (1933)** required registering and disclosing relevant information in offering documents before issuing securities. The **Banking Act (1933)**, also known as "Glass-Steagall" for its authors, split the banking world into two: commercial banks were barred from investment banking and brokerage while investment banks were barred from offering standard banking products. Glass-Steagall also created the **Federal Deposit Insurance Corporation (FDIC)**. The **Securities Exchange Act (1934)** created the SEC and mandated that publicly-traded companies register with the SEC and periodically issue financial reports.

Within a few years, more regulation was added: SROs were authorized (1938); debt issues were required to have an indenture and to be accompanied by regular financial reports (1939); and, investment companies and their advisors were required to register with the SEC, issue regular financial reports, disclose conflicts of interest, and obey certain behavior standards (1940). While commodities had long been regulated, the CFTC and an SRO were authorized in 1974.

Sometimes, loopholes had to be closed. In 1956, the **Bank Holding Company Act** required holding companies to register with the Federal Reserve and prohibited

---

[22]This is slightly untrue: futures and swaps on a single security or on a "narrow" index of nine or fewer securities are classified as **security futures products** and **security-based swaps** are jointly regulated by the SEC and CFTC.

non-bank activities (like insurance or investment banking) at any of their subsidiary firms. Sometimes, there were turf wars: The SEC and CFTC could not agree on which would regulate futures on single-stocks or narrow indices. In 1982, they encoded this dispute into law by banning these futures with the **Shad-Johnson Accord**, named for the heads of the SEC and CFTC.

3.9   Quiz

Try answering the following questions in five minutes.

1. What is the difference between the primary and secondary market?

2. The NYSE and Nasdaq stock markets use continuous trading, and not auctions, to set prices. | T   F

3. Circle one for each choice:
A (limit   held   market   stop loss) order trades immediately.
A (limit   held   market   stop loss) order sacrifices immediacy to specify a worst-possible execution price.

4. What are the names for the prices at which an intermediary (*e.g.* a specialist or market maker) will buy and sell?

Intermediary buys at the _____.

Intermediary sells at the _____.

5. What are the names for the prices at which a retail investor sending a market order will buy and sell?

Retail investor's market order buys at the _____.

Retail investor's market order sells at the _____.

6. Some people think all this high-speed trading is crazy. They propose that we should just have one auction each day for trading in each stock. If we were to make this change and move to one auction/day:

   a) What effects would we likely see?

   b) Why would we see those effects?

7. A market maker collecting limit buy and sell orders is "bookbuilding." | T   F

8. Which act, over 70 years old, split commercial and investment banking? (You need not give the year for the act.)

9. Theory and data show that self regulation tends to yield greater economic growth than regulation by the government — even if both have the same goal. Why might this be?

10. Suppose I want to short shares of Motorola. It is big and in the S&P 500, so liquidity is not too much of a concern. Nonetheless: What do I need to do before I can sell those shares short?

3.10 Exercises

To flesh out a couple of the ideas we discussed, we will look at data from a couple of different types of markets and asset classes as well as some data for short selling.

Instructions

Modify the R code from Chapter 2 to answer the following questions.

Finding information about bid-ask spreads is a bit difficult in daily data; however, there is some data available. We will again use the xts and Quandl packages. Look at the data for the following instruments:

- Fixed Income: Download data from Quandl for Canadian government bond futures on the Montréal Exchange. Grab the bid and ask prices for the five- and ten-year bond futures: CHRIS/MX_CGF1 and CHRIS/MX_CGB1. Unfortunately, these data can be noisy so you will need to eliminate any days where the bid or ask is 0.
- Commodities: Download data from Quandl for metals on the London Metal Exchange. Grab the buyer and seller prices for "cash" buyer and seller (bid and ask) for copper, aluminum, and tin: LME/PR_CU, LME/PR_AL, and LME/PR_TN.
- Equity Indices: Download data from Quandl for equity index futures on the Hong Kong and Montréal Exchanges. Grab the bid and ask for the Hang Seng and TSX 60: CHRIS/HKEX_HSI1 and CHRIS/MX_SXM1
- FX Rates: Everyone is always interested in crypto-currencies. So download data from Quandl for the BitFinEx. Grab the bid and ask exchange rate between Bitcoin and USD: BITFINEX/BTCUSD.
- Equities: Finally, look at short volume versus stock price for three names: AMD, RGR, and TSLA. Download short volume from Quandl (FINRA/FNSQ_AMD, FINRA/FNSQ_RGR, and FINRA/FNSQ_TSLA) and adjusted close prices from Yahoo.

1. Using your modified R code, create a column to hold the bid-ask spread. If you name the columns for the bid and the ask correctly, you can just do this:

`alldata$CGB1.spread <- alldata$CGB1.ask - alldata$CGB1.bid`

Create a spread column for each of the fixed income, commodity, equity index, and FX instruments. Plot the spreads, all over the same time period, and comment on trends, unusual events, and commonalities.

2. Create fractional spreads, like so:

`alldata$CGB1.fracspread <- log(alldata$CGB1.ask) - log(alldata$CGB1.bid)`

and plot these spreads as in the prior question. Comment on trends, unusual events, and commonalities.

3. Look at the summaries for the spreads and fractional spreads. Which seem to be better behaved: arithmetic or log-spreads? Why?

4. Finally, plot the short volume and adjusted close for the equities, making sure all plots are for the same time scale. Do you notice any relationships between the short volume and price plots?

References

Alloway, Tracy. "Psssst. The U.S. Treasury Market Flies at Midnight". *Bloomberg News* (July 11, 2016). Retrieved 24 May 2017 from: `https://www.bloomberg.com/news/articles/2016-07-11/psssst-the-u-s-treasury-market-flies-at-midnight`.

Alpert, Bill. "When Chinese Stock Fraud Was Rampant". *Barron's* (Mar. 21, 2018). URL: `https://www.barrons.com/articles/when-chinese-stock-fraud-was-rampant-1521659454`.

Brosnan, Sarah F. and Frans B. M. de Waal. "Monkeys reject unequal pay". *Nature* 425 (2003), pp. 297–299. DOI: `10.1038/nature01963`.

Diamond, Douglas W. and Robert E. Verrecchia. "Constraints on Short-selling and Asset Price Adjustment to Private Information". *Journal of Financial Economics* 18 (1987), pp. 277–311. DOI: `10.1016/0304-405X(87)90042-0`.

Glosten, Lawrence R. and Paul R. Milgrom. "Ask and Transaction Prices in a Specialist Market with Heterogeneously Informed Traders". *Journal of Financial Economics* 14 (1985), pp. 71–100. DOI: `10.1016/0304-405X(85)90044-3`.

Herrnstadt, Evan et al. *Air Pollution as a Cause of Violent Crime: Evidence from Chicago and Los Angeles*. Working Paper. Harvard University, 2016. URL: `http://www.evanherrnstadt.com/docs/CrimePollution_JM.pdf`.

McTaggart, Raymond, Gergely Daroczi, and Clement Leung. *Quandl: API Wrapper for Quandl.com*. R package version 2.8.0. 2016. URL: `https://CRAN.R-project.org/package=Quandl`.

Muscarella, Chris J. and Michael S. Piwowar. "Market Microstructure and Securities Values: Evidence from the Paris Bourse". *Journal of Financial Markets* 4.3 (2001), pp. 209–229. DOI: 10.1016/S1386-4181(00)00022-7.

Nevin, Rick. "Understanding International Crime Trends: The Legacy of Preschool Lead Exposure". *Environmental Research* 104.3 (2007), pp. 315–336. DOI: 10.1016/j.envres.2007.02.008.

Refco. Prospectus. Retrieved 21 May 2017 from https://www.sec.gov/Archives/edgar/data/1321746/000104746905021309/a2162155z424b1.htm. Aug. 10, 2005.

Ritter, Jay and Ivo Welch. "A Review of IPO Activity, Pricing, and Allocations". *Journal of Finance* 57.4 (2002), pp. 1795–1828. DOI: 10.1111/1540-6261.00478.

Ryan, Jeffrey A. and Joshua M. Ulrich. *xts: eXtensible Time Series*. R package version 0.9-7. 2014. URL: https://CRAN.R-project.org/package=xts.

Securities Training Corporation. *Series 55: The Equity Trader Examination Study Manual*. New York, Nov. 6, 2006.

Smith, Elliot Blair. "Accounting experts: Refco prospectus offered red flags". *USA Today* (Oct. 16, 2005).

Chapter 4

Modern Markets

In the last chapter, we discussed markets in general. However, markets have recently experienced a wave of innovation. This innovation has brought benefits like cheaper trading, but it has also made trading and regulation more difficult. Some market participants could not compete under the new market structure and went out of business; and, a lot of previous assumptions about markets also changed.

The goal of this chapter is to show how technology has changed the supply of, demand for, and flexibility of market services; discuss how the building blocks of markets have been reassembled to allow for competition; and, to consider the pros and cons of these changes. It is especially worth noting that these issues have been crucial to understanding recent policy concerns and news about markets.

4.1 Electronic Markets

Almost all stock markets now allow electronic trading. Before 1971, however, stocks in the US were listed on the New York Stock Exchange (NYSE) or the American Stock Exchange (AMEX) — or they were unlisted. To be listed there were requirements on the firm: financial reporting, company size, a minimum stock price, and other constraints. If a stock was unlisted, it was traded OTC by broker-dealers overseen by an SRO: the National Association of Securities Dealers (NASD). (NASD is one of the precursors of FINRA.)

In 1969, a number of institutional investors came together to build a trading platform for OTC stocks. They believed they were paying too much to the NASD broker-dealers, so they built Instinet: an online limit order book that displayed orders and could process trades. Two years later, NASD introduced their automated quotation system: NASDAQ. While Instinet and NASDAQ were **venues** (places to trade), they were not exchanges.

The first electronic stock exchange came in 1977 when the Toronto Stock Exchange created their Computer Assisted Trading System. In the mid-1980s electronic derivatives trading was introduced. Then other exchanges began to go fully electronic: Chile in 1989, then Finland, Sweden, and Australia in 1990.

Why are electronic markets a big deal? Jain (2005) discusses a number of differences between physical ("floor-based") and electronic trading venues. These are summarized in Table 4.1. However, the brief answer is that electronic venues are more expensive to start but faster, cheaper, and fairer to operate.

Feature	Floor	Electronic
Counterparty ID	Known pre-trade	Rarely known pre-trade; often known post-trade
Order Book	Often none/fleeting	Constantly exists
Liquidity Seen	Bid-Ask	N best bid-asks or entire order book
Matching Speed	10s–minutes	Sub-second
Order/Oper. Costs	Higher	Lower
Settlement Speed	Slower	Faster
Settlement Cost	Higher	Lower

Table 4.1: Comparison of advantages and disadvantages of floor-based and electronic trading venues, based on Jain (2005).

In particular, electronic trading makes it easy to keep a history of interactions (**audit trail**). That lets us assess the performance of our orders: Did we get best execution or do well compared to other trades? Did the specialist provide liquidity to us? Electronic trading also allows machines (**trading engines**) to do the work of trading. That automation can yield economies of scale and reduces explicit costs. (If computers trade in a stupid fashion, however, implicit costs can rise.) Trading engines are also unemotional: their behavior does not change just because they lost money on the previous trade.

Putting all of these together is even more powerful. The audit trail and automation can help us reduce implicit order costs: We can use the data collected to conduct experiments and tune the behavior of our trading engines. Tunable and adaptive trading machines are the core of **algorithmic trading**. Encoding the trading logic has a couple of positive spillovers: First, it forces the market (and agent) logic to be documented (in code). Second, this creates a strong disincentive to encoding manipulative or unfair behavior: the code is subpoenable and would be direct evidence of a rule violation.

That's not to say electronic trading is without drawbacks. As with any computer program, trading engines are only as good as we program them to be. This can be very troublesome when we try to use concepts which are not very well defined. Machines also lack common sense. No human trader would try to buy a stock for $500/share if it is trading near $5/share, but a computer will do that if you tell it to. As mentioned before, the startup (and incremental) infrastructure costs may be large. This can be a barrier to entry for possible competitors. Some people also worry that this may increase the gap between unsophisticated and sophisticated investors. (In truth, this has mostly just led to unsophisticated brokers going out of business and consumers benefiting from better service from the surviving, more sophisticated brokers.)

Journalists often like to characterize this wave of innovation as an "arms race." However, that is a flawed metaphor. Every few years, there is a new record in the 100-meter dash; however, nobody ever claims that this is a mad arms race which will eventually result in humans running 100m in negative time. Nobody claims that because we intuitively know it is absurd. Instead, there is an evolution: we start to measure times more precisely and the amount of improvement decreases. Similarly, trading is going through evolution. Speed has been one area of innovation; anticipating price moves or better managing risk may be the next area of evolution.

4.2   New Venues

As innovation has increased, the number of possible trading venues has grown. Exchanges were soon challenged by other trading venues.

Early on, NASDAQ was run by market makers who all had the same rights; none of them had a monopoly on information or control. Market makers constantly quote a bid and ask and get to keep the difference because they buy low and sell high (*i.e.* they "earn the spread"). They can also provide liquidity. However, they are exposed to adverse selection. Market making is tough.

In 1969, Instinet created a new type of venue: an **electronic communication network (ECN)**. An ECN is effectively a limit order book that displays orders; matches them in some priority; tells the involved traders their orders were filled; and, then informs the outside world. Another way to think of an ECN is as an automated broker: the ECN never acts as a dealer. An ECN is very transparent: most disseminate their order book to attract order flow. That means you can see the price you are likely to get. The software is also fairly simple to optimize; so, ECNs can handle large volumes quickly. In 2000, the time from sending an order to getting a fill (the **latency**) was about 3 seconds on the NYSE compared to about 300ms on the Island ECN. By three years later, Island could match and fill an order in 20–30ms. By 2008, the BATS ECN could match an order in about 500μs and now that time is less than 150μs. (Careful readers will notice that we shifted from comparing "round trip" times to "matching" times, the time from entering to exiting the venue's "matching engine.")

In 1987, ITG developed POSIT, a system for conducting off-exchange auctions. Since the venue is an auction, there are no quotes before or after; the market takes place in a singularity of time. Thus POSIT was **dark**. In time, we developed a term for such venues: **dark pools**. Politicians and journalists seem to love this term, like telling scary stories around a campfire. (Perhaps they like the term because it makes us feel like we need them?) The very name conjures up childish fears: leeches, sharks, the creature from the black lagoon. Using the more accurate phrase "regularly-scheduled Walrasian auctions which do not publish pre-auction data" sounds much less scary.

4.3 Competition Arrives

The idea of NASDAQ and ECNs was that competition, not a specialist, would yield a fair and orderly market. However, through the mid-1990s, many investors insisted that market makers overcharged them. This was shown to be true in 1994 when Christie and Schultz published "Why do NASDAQ Market Makers Avoid Odd-Eighth Quotes?" Stocks on NASDAQ could be quoted in eighths of a dollar (the **tick size**). However, when they looked at the fractional part of over 372,000 quote prices, the evidence was damning: they did not see anything close to a uniform distribution. Instead, they saw a distribution that had roughly 21% of quotes ending in each of the even eighths and 4% of quotes ending in each of the odd eighths. Thus the spread was rarely $0.125 but often $0.25.

This led to the SEC tapping many of the NASDAQ market makers' phones. Sure enough, they heard coded (racist) phrases used to describe quotes which narrowed the spread to an eighth. In the end, the SEC charged more than 40 market makers with collusion. That, however, was just the beginning. Since the market makers had resisted competition, they were about to have it brutally forced on them through a sequence of rule changes that encouraged hyper-competition. In 1997, Rule 11Ac1-4 required market makers to reflect customer orders in their bid and ask and to quote a bid and ask if they were more than 1% of trading volume. The tick size was also ordered reduced to one-sixteenth of a dollar. In 1998, the SEC imposed settlements totaling more than $1 bn. In 2000, the tick size began (through pilot projects) to be reduced to $0.01 with **decimalization** complete in 2001.

The changes were not limited to quotes, however. Also in 2000, Rule 11Ac1-5 mandated publicly posting monthly reports of a venue's execution quality in a standardized format; and, Rule 11Ac1-6 mandated publicly posting quarterly reports of where venues routed orders they did not execute and how much they were paid for such routing. Immediately, algorithmic traders had new sources of information to tune their trading engines: they could prefer venues which offered good service and avoid venues with poor service.

The public execution quality reports and decimalization came at a propitious time: the internet bubble had just burst and programming talent was available for cheap. There were also new ways to promote new venues: **Maker-taker fees** allowed ECNs to charge marketable orders a small **access fee** and give non-marketable orders a small **rebate**: Traders were rewarded for placing limit orders into the ECN's order book. On the other hand, market makers began to **pay for order flow**: they paid a broker for marketable orders which would trade against their quote. While these seem similar, analysis reveals otherwise: Colliard and Foucault (2012) suggests that maker-taker fees are fine but Parlour and Rajan (2003) suggests that payment for order flow raises the cost of trading for customers.

The pro-competitive changes were beneficial for customers. Stoll and Schenzler (2006) found that over 1993–2001 average quoted spreads dropped from \$0.16 to \$0.01 and **effective spreads**, the average spread between buy and sell prices, dropped from \$0.12 to \$0.02. Maker-taker fees, payment for flow, and execution quality reports also led to major shifts in market share, as confirmed by Boehmer, Jennings, and Wei (2006). In some NYSE-listed stocks, the NYSE ceased to be the dominant trading venue. These reforms are largely why you can now buy stock for \$10 instead of the \$100 or more which was common in the late 1990's; and, they were so successful that they inspired the EU to pass the similar **Markets in Financial Instruments Directive (MiFID)** in 2004. (The European equivalent of ECNs were called **multilateral trading facilities**, or MTFs.)

4.4   The Effects of New Venues

How different are these new venues? Glosten (1989); Glosten (1994) analyzed the **price schedule**, the relationship between order size and the average price paid per share, using theoretical models. The theory suggested that (on average):

- market makers' average price increases linearly with order size, but they stop trading if adverse selection is too high;
- ECNs' price schedule was slightly convex in order size with a small fixed cost for any size order; and,
- specialists give large orders better prices than small orders; they lose on large orders to make money on small orders.

Are any of these necessarily good or bad? No. Rather, it suggests that the market we have now, with different intermediary types, offers a balance of services to different customer types.

What about dark pools? For a long time, dark pools did not attract significant volume: removing your orders from the continuous market was too great an opportunity cost. Recently, that has changed; evidence from Chao, Yao, and Ye (2017) suggests traders increasingly use dark pools to trade at prices finer than one cent. This suggests that maybe we need more thinking about what is an appropriate tick size for an instrument.

Competition created decentralized "fragmented" markets but it also created incentives for people to keep the prices equal at various venues. Competition also pressured exchanges to execute orders faster and cheaper; provide more pre-trade transparency (such as limit order book data); and eliminate cumbersome and anti-competitive market rules. Competition even made markets more robust to problems.

One of the first major incidents alleviated by decentralization occurred on 29 June 2001 in the Nasdaq market. On that day, the Russell 1000 and 2000 indices were undergoing their annual rebalance. The strain on the Nasdaq market led to market data slowdowns and, ultimately, Nasdaq computers crashing just before the market close — failing to generate closing prices needed for the rebalance. The

Nasdaq market was eventually revived and trading extended to 5:00 PM. Some groups (such as my group at Morgan Stanley) were able to use other venues and simply "routed around" the problem.[1]

Unfortunately, decentralization has its downsides. Decentralization fractures liquidity which is especially troublesome since liquidity tends to attract more liquidity.[2] Decentralization also increases the likelihood of having a trade occur elsewhere that should have filled your order, aka being **traded through**. From a technology perspective, decentralized markets require connecting to, monitoring, and routing among many venues. Unsophisticated customers might be unaware of these issues and negatively affected — until their broker offers that functionality to them.

Regulators were especially concerned about how customers would know where to trade. However, Reg NMS stopped short of requiring a consolidated limit order book (CLOB). The requirements to synchronize so many venues would have been onerous. Multiple venues noted that a CLOB would obscure the competitive differences between firms. However, regulators proposed another requirement: that venues route orders to other venues showing a better price. For venues that primarily attracted liquidity due to their speed, the idea of possibly being judged on an order sent to a slower competitor (with a possibly out-of-date quote) was intolerable. They argued that mandating intermarket linkages was anti-competitive and an attack on their business model by slower competitors.

However, the proposal allowed one way out: to stop publishing quotes and go "dark." One venue did just that to show the government how damaging their withdrawal would be.

Hendershott and Jones (2005) documents this unusual protest. In the early 2000's, Island (an ECN) took market share from the AMEX and NYSE by providing the market's fastest execution for S&P 500 stocks and some ETFs. In 2002, Island protested that the proposal to mandate intermarket linkages would make all venues run at the "slowest common denominator." At the time, Island was the #1 venue for the three most active ETFs. As a protest, they stopped publishing their limit order book. The effects were sudden and strong. Island's market share plummeted from 58% to 35%. Economic analysis showed that price discovery (where information first affects prices) moved to the futures market; trading costs increased overall; and, prices adjusted more slowly to information — the market became less efficient. Island later re-illuminated and execution quality then increased. In response, the government relented on the proposal.

In 2005, Reg NMS was passed with the goal of creating a national market system. Reg NMS repackaged the rules mentioned earlier and added a few others. The new law also banned quoting in increments below $0.01 and re-allocated trade fees to venues with better execution quality. Most contentiously, Reg NMS mandated intermarket linkages so that venues *could* route an order to better prices. However,

---

[1] CNNfn (2001) discusses the outage and quotes brokers who did (and did not) route around the outage.

[2] Pagano (1989) studies this clustering which creates a positive liquidity externality.

Island going dark helped convince regulators to not mandate the routing of all orders: immediate or cancel (IOC) orders were exempted so traders could make their own routing decisions. For those who wanted to use the government-mandated links, some exchanges created order types or instructions to allow routing away if the order could be traded "quickly."

4.5   From Automation to Algorithmic Trading

While many of these improvements clearly help retail investors, what about institutional investors with large orders?

An inescapable fact of trading is that orders impart a bias to the market. The extreme case is a gigantic order sitting in the order book: that order effectively chops the tail off the distribution, altering the expected return. Usually, we think about **price impact**, the bias imparted to prices by trading. Huberman and Stanzl (2004) show that the permanent part of price impact must be linear in trade size; otherwise, we could create trade sequences to probabilistically game the market. However, some price impact only temporarily affects the market and some affects only our trade.

As competition intensified and trading automation increased, managing price impact became critical. In investing, we often think about the price at which we exit the investment. Minimizing price impact allows us to enter an investment at a better price. However, it may require patience and thus can add uncertainty to the entry price we achieve. We will see more of this additional cost, with uncertainty, in Chapter 24.

Some large investors use **negotiated trades**, orders with the price negotiated in light of the liquidity challenges, expected price impact, or adverse selection risks of the trade. Most negotiated trades are one of a few types:

- **Block trades** are orders for 10,000 or more shares. In the 1960s, Goldman Sachs pioneered the idea of moving large amounts of stock among customers. Block traders had to remember clients' preferences and might call other potential clients — a bit of direct search. Block trades are declining.
- **Arrival price trades** or **prior reference price (PRP) trades** are large orders priced at a discount to the current bid or ask. Such orders are typically used when trading is urgent: the client expects the price to move soon.
- **Volume-weighted average price (VWAP) trades** are large orders traded over a predefined period of time: often a day. VWAP orders are often used when trading is less urgent and expected to move the market. Many block orders are now traded as VWAP orders.

Most negotiated trades are **program trades**: large portfolio trades. In the US, a program trade is an order for 15 or more securities ("names") totaling more than $1 mn. Program trades are not so named because they are done by computers: Program trading was initially done with a runner and a program (itinerary) of orders.

The itinerary allowed splitting orders over time and deploying the orders quickly around the exchange floor. However, all this work is why program trading was an early adopter of computers. As trading became electronic and cheaper, program traders were often the most able to adapt and attract more order flow.

Often, algorithmic trading engines are broken into a few pieces: typically an order management system which uses an execution management system. In general, the trading involves splitting larger **parent** orders into smaller **child** orders and scheduling those to reduce cost while taking some risk by not trading too quickly. An **order management system** is the strategist: it breaks parent orders into child orders across time to hit a benchmark price. This is the trading engine that targets VWAP, an arrival price, or tries to better the closing price. An **execution management system** is the tactician: it receives child orders and tries, in a shorter period of time, to achieve best execution (sometimes in light of the parent order). These both require careful thinking about how best to trade.[3]

An early program trading strategy was **index arbitrage**, trading index futures versus index stocks when the two implied different index prices. Index arbitrage pushes prices back together; that keeps index stocks, ETFs,

> **Computers Trade Better** At Morgan Stanley in 2001, human traders on the block desk charged customers $0.08/share to try to achieve VWAP. Unfortunately, they missed VWAP by $0.12/share, costing the firm $0.04/share. With a $1.50 standard deviation, however, they always had a good story about making money for the customer. What they failed to mention were the many times the customer got a terrible price. Meanwhile, the algorithmic trading engine was charging $0.02/share for VWAP and missing by $0.015/share, a $0.005/share profit. Even better: the trading engine had a standard deviation of $0.005/share. Six months later, fifty human traders had been replaced by a few computers — and customers had more money in their pockets.

and index futures all at nearly same index level. Other investors will get roughly the same price on futures, ETFs, and index stocks: they benefit from technology without having to spend on it. The index arbitrageur makes money for transmitting information between the exchanges — essentially getting paid to keep prices in line. The only problem with this is that stocks largely trade in the New York City area while futures are traded in Chicago.[4] How do we keep prices in line across a continent? In 2008, network **latency** between New York and Chicago was about 30 ms. Eventually, an entrepreneur created

---

[3]Those wanting an introduction to the theory behind order management should read through Bertsimas and Lo (1998) and Almgren and Chriss (2001).

[4]Stocks and futures often trade in different locations, for example in Canada (stocks in Toronto, futures in Montréal) and China (stocks in Shanghai and Shenzhen, futures in Shanghai).

a microwave link that reduced latency to about 5 ms. It might seem strange or spooky, but it's just traders transmitting information as quickly as possible between economic centers.

Short Sales Redux Over 1994–2001, US markets became much faster and more efficient: bid-ask spreads fell and quote changes became less predictable. Most prices adjusted quickly to new information. However, one part of the market lagged: short sales still required price tests. In other words, traders could not short a stock at price below the bid or if the last price change was a decline. In 2005, the SEC tried an experiment: Reg SHO eliminated these price tests. The idea was to bring efficiency to pricing for overvalued stocks. The result was deemed to be a success. Price tests were eliminated and rules for ensuring locates were updated.

As computers traded more and the time between Chicago and New York dropped, trading had to become very fast; the simplest decisions became highly optimized. Often, these choices had to happen so fast that they could only be true/false choices; even simple algebra was too slow. For example, if the firm buys an instrument on venue A, they then pick the other venue most likely to have an out-of-line price, to exit that position ASAP. Some high-frequency trading (HFT) makes very-short-term predictions of returns while a lot focuses on optimizing networks and connections to transmit information among markets. HFT firms may make money on only 1 in 10000 or more trades; otherwise, they use rebates and payments for flow to just break even. However, they trade very often which increases how often they make money; this is just the Law of Large Numbers at work. How do HFT firms add value? They use their speed to spread information across all venues and keep prices the same across markets. Regulators and politicians have had a lot to say on HFT — often about how absurd the level of technology is. They might do well to remember something like Arthur C. Clarke's third law: "Any sufficiently advanced technology is indistinguishable from magic [to outsiders]."

4.6 New Risks

While all of this automation was largely positive, it also created new risks. The possibility of automated problems means that glitches can be destructive quickly. Trading engines may mishandle orders or break rules and laws. In extreme cases, a logic error or mistake (**bug**) may cause trouble.

Bugs in financial markets are especially troubling because of adverse selection. If your trading engine accidentally spits out orders with random prices, the aggressively-priced orders are unlikely to be filled; however, the foolishly-priced orders will be quickly filled. (Imagine accidentally quoting a sale price on a sports car for $1;

someone will try to take advantage of your mistake before you realize it.) On 1 Aug 2012, Knight Capital ran into a particularly vicious bug. The bug resulted in mistrading and the handling of that error may have compounded the problem: Knight lost \$440 mn in 45 minutes — almost \$10 mn per minute. This led to their purchase by Chicago HFT shop Getco to create KCG (now part of Virtu).

Automation may also lack **sanity checks**, simple tests on ranges and likely values for inputs. If a person enters faulty data, trouble may then arise. The classic case of this is the **fat finger error**: when a human accidentally adds or omits an extra decimal or inadvertently enters the wrong information in a field. The most well-known fat finger error happened on 9 Dec 2005 in Japan. On that day, a company called J-Com had its IPO. A Mizuho employee entering a sell order fat-fingered the order: Instead of selling 1 share at ¥610,000, he sold 610,000 shares at ¥1.[5] The Tokyo Stock Exchange computers set to work trying to satisfy the order. Unfortunately, the computers were so busy filling orders that they stopped responding quickly; canceling the order took 10 minutes. In the end, this mistake cost Mizuho about \$330 mn.

A lack of flexibility can even cause problems. We earlier discussed the 2001 Nasdaq outage when the Russell indices rebalanced. While the Nasdaq was able to reopen the exchange and change to a 5:00 PM closing time, not everyone was able to handle that. Some computer programs had an unalterable (*hard-coded*) closing time of 4:00 PM. One clever thinker changed the computer's clock to be one hour earlier — only to have Nasdaq reject the orders for having timestamps which were too far from the current time. In the end, the rumor was that a European bank had been unable to route around or reconfigure their software for a 5:00 PM market close — and so had to guarantee prices on over \$8 bn of customer orders. Luckily, they did not lose a lot of money when they were able to finally trade those orders.

4.6.1 The Flash Crash

One of the concerns most-discussed by politicians and economists has been the "Flash Crash." On 6 May 2010, US markets opened down on concerns about riots in Greece after the country imposed the third set of austerity measures after a (first) bailout from the Eurozone. So the markets were uncertain. At 2:32 PM New York time, Kansas-based mutual fund company Waddell & Reed entered an order to sell 75,000 E-mini S&P 500 futures contracts — about \$4 bn worth of exposure. That is a large order even for the liquid S&P 500 index futures market. What complicated matters is that the order was traded via a percent-of-volume algorithm (which has no price sensitivity) and that volume begets volume.

The official report, CFTC and SEC (2010), was based in part on an early version of Kirilenko et al. (2017) and clarifies what ensued. Prices began to fall. HFT firms provided liquidity since the fall seemed like a temporary dislocation of prices. That

---

[5]Japanese shares used to trade at much higher prices than in the US. Jiji News Agency (2013) and Lewis (2015) discuss how this began to change in an effort to woo retail investors.

increased the volume, so the Waddell & Reed order sold more. By 2:41 PM, many HFT firms hit their risk limits: they decided they could not take on more risk, did not know what was happening, and sold their inventories of shares and contracts — sensible measures to reduce risk. Over 2:41–2:44 PM, S&P 500 futures and ETFs dropped 3%. During this time, index arbitrage engines traded heavily. That caused the effects to bleed into equities. As the volume continued to increase, more trading and market making engines assumed something was wrong and stopped trading.

In the fourteen seconds from 2:45:13–2:45:27 PM, *half* of that day's futures volume traded. This was too much. Computers at the Chicago Mercantile Exchange (CME) shut down the S&P 500 futures for five seconds and then sent a reset signal. To trading engines, it looked like a new day had started. The percent-of-volume order did not continue on what seemed to be a new day. Stocks and futures immediately began recovering. By 3:00 PM, most price changes that occurred after the Waddell & Reed order had reverted.

During the fastest declines, some people decided that the fall was absurd and provided liquidity. They bought stocks or futures because they did not believe that economic fundamentals had changed; and, that belief was correct. Thankfully, the market recovered and many sold as prices recovered. Then, after the market closed, Nasdaq claimed that some of those buy trades were unfair and canceled them. Traders who had bought and then sold now found they were short and had to cover their shorts (buy those stocks) at now-higher prices. Thus many traders who tried to guide prices back to sensible prices were punished for their efforts.

In the months afterward, Kerber (2010) quoted the Waddell & Reed fund manager as stating that markets were more fragile that he realized. Then, in 2015, the US had UK authorities arrest and extradite Navinder Singh Sarao. He was charged with manipulative behavior which led to the Flash Crash.[6] Sarao pled guilty to publishing quotes to make the markets appear more liquid than they were. Despite that, the exact causes and interactions that led to the crash are still unknown.

The Flash Crash raised a number of other questions that have yet to be well-answered. Was it reckless to send a large percent-of-volume order? Was it reckless to not supervise that order intensely? Should HFT firms have behaved differently? How should trading engines handle unusual/erroneous data? Should trading engines have stayed in the market? How did canceling trades affect traders the next day? How likely are those traders to provide liquidity if another flash crash arises? Finally, what are the longer term effects of such a crash?

Flash crashes seemed to reveal a previously-unknown risk of the automation revolution which had transformed the markets. However, that may not be so. Gao and Mizrach (2016) looked at the past to see if markets had previously experienced similar issues. Figure 4.1 shows the typical frequencies of how many stocks per day experience a large price increase ("breakup") or decline ("breakdown"). They found that flash crashes had happened before, were not becoming more common, and that

---

[6]Brush, Schoenberg, and Ring (2015) discusses the manipulative techniques which Sarao had previously used to make money; however, the article has nothing conclusive.

2010 was not overall a year with many such events. In fact, another such crash was documented as "The Fluctuation" in 1962 by Brooks (1969).

A few facts may explain the uproar about the 2010 crash. First, smaller, earlier crashes may not have been noticed because they occurred before journalists and retail investors had access to intraday data and charting. Second, earlier crashes that were widespread enough to be noticed without intraday data (like the 1962 crash) may have been rare and thus forgotten. Third, it may be that the overall frequency of breakdowns was not high in 2010 but that 2010 had the day with the most concurrent breakdowns.

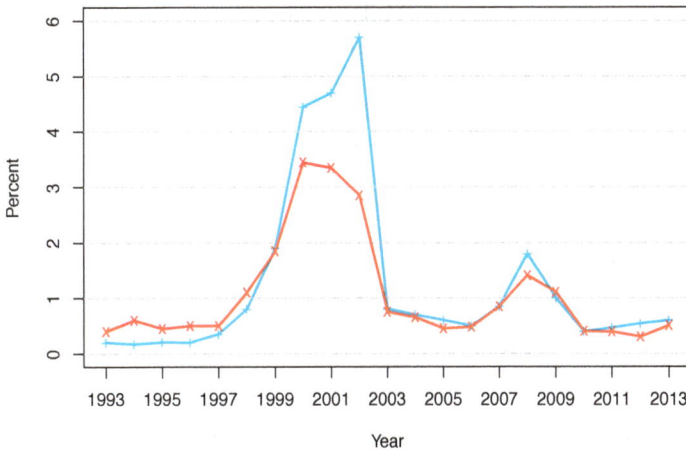

Figure 4.1: Frequency of market quality breakups (+, blue) and breakdowns (×, red). Defined as the fraction of stocks, on a given day, with an extreme price rise or fall. Note that 2010, the year of the Flash Crash, did not have an unusual number of market quality events. Plot from Gao and Mizrach (2016), recreated with R.

4.7 New Regulation

In 1998, Sandy Weill and John Reed merged Travelers Insurance and Citicorp. Since Travelers owned investment bank Salomon Brothers and Citicorp was a commercial bank, this was a direct challenge to Glass-Steagall. In 1999, Congress passed the Financial Services Modernization Act, also known as "Gramm-Leach-Bliley." The act repealed parts of the Glass-Steagall and Bank Holding Company Acts to allow mixing banking, investment banking, brokerage, and insurance in one firm.

In the 1990s, another firm had revolutionized the electricity and natural gas markets by pushing their deregulation and creating a way to finance natural gas exploration. As that firm grew, it increasingly traded energy electronically, but not on a futures market. That firm, Enron, urged Congress to pass the **Commodity**

Futures Modernization Act in 2000. The act repealed the Shad-Johnson Accord and exempted off-exchange energy trading from CFTC regulation which largely benefited Enron's online energy trading. This exemption was repealed in 2008.

Fraud at Enron led Congress to pass the **Sarbanes-Oxley Act** in 2002 which required CEOs and CFOs to personally certify reports; increased fraud and malfeasance penalties; and, created the Public Company Accounting Oversight Board.

If you thought specialists were competitive enough, you might have been surprised in 2008 when the NYSE began a pilot program to move from specialists to **designated market makers** (DMMs) who had less ability to stop the market and were not always responsible for conducting auctions. While not completely abandoning specialists, this was certainly a move toward a level playing field of competing market makers. The pilot program was adopted as permanent in 2015.

Finally, after the 2008 financial crisis, Congress passed the **Dodd-Frank Act**. Dodd-Frank was the largest change in regulation since the Great Depression, clocking in at 2,300 pages. Summarizing that is tough, but we can break the big changes into a couples of areas. Dodd-Frank created a number of entities to watch for and handle systemic crises:

- the Financial Stability Oversight Council (FSOC) and
- the Office of Financial Research to conduct research for the FSOC;
- the Orderly Liquidation Authority; and,
- gave the Federal Reserve new powers to monitor, test, and impose higher capital ratios for systemically-important financial institutions (SIFIs).

Dodd-Frank also took preventative measures to (hopefully) reduce risk and stave off systemic crises:

- Volcker Rule restricted banks' use of their capital for risk-taking (like proprietary trading or investing in hedge funds);[7]
- required securitizers to retain part of the risk of what they sold;
- moved OTC derivatives (swaps, forwards, options) under the regulation of the CFTC (some with joint oversight by the SEC);[8]
- mandated derivatives dealer registration, capital and margin requirements, segregated customer accounts, and record keeping; and,
- required central clearing, trade reporting for those derivatives.

Controversially, Dodd-Frank charged the FSOC with the ability to designate any institution which "could pose a threat to the financial stability of the United States" as a **systemically important financial institution** (SIFI). This was seen by many as enshrining "too big to fail" (and thus moral hazard) into law.

---

[7]Those wanting guidance on the Volcker Rule should consult Morrisson Foerster's guide available from their web site www.mofo.com.

[8]Careful readers of financial regulation might note that the law refers largely to "swaps." Strangely, Congress defined "swaps" to include non-swap OTC derivatives like forwards and options. One suspects they were reading Lewis Carroll and wanted their words to mean "just what they choose them to mean — neither more nor less."

Finally, the Dodd-Frank Act created the Consumer Financial Protection Bureau.

Post-Dodd-Frank, the Fed with its new powers encouraged centrally-cleared swaps to also transition to trading in swap execution facilities.

That is a lot for one piece of legislation, and we will discuss some of those changes when we talk about crises. Even now as talk swirls about repealing Dodd-Frank, some parts of the Act have been well-received. Title VII which moves swaps to central clearing has, in particular, been well-received by most of the finance community.

4.7.1 Beyond the US

Outside of the US, there were few countries with laws to repeal like Glass-Steagall. In Europe and much of Asia, commercial and investment banks had largely never separated. Canada had a similar law which was repealed; but, Canada created the Office of the Superintendent of Financial Institutions (OSFI) in 1987. The OSFI has been very aggressive at limiting leverage, preventing mergers which would create banks which are "too big," and discouraging loose lending practices.

The pro-competitive regulatory changes in the US encouraged changes in other countries. We already mentioned the EU's Markets in Financial Instruments Directive (MiFID) which brought venue competition to the EU. The Swiss were early to experiment with more efficient trading venues; in 2001, they merged their stock exchange with the UK electronic venue Tradepoint to form Virt-X. However, competition did not lead to large changes in market share until it also affected the EU via MiFID.

In 2011, Australian regulators released Market Integrity rules to introduce competition among trading venues. Canadian securities regulation is split among the provinces and SROs like the Investment Industry Regulatory Organization of Canada (IIROC). On the one hand, Canada has allowed venue competition, and Garriott et al. (2013) document that this lowered costs for Canadian investors. However, IIROC also imposed a per-message fee in 2012 to reduce high-frequency trading. Malinova, Park, and Riordan (2016) document that this increased costs for retail investors; however, neither IIROC nor other Canadian authorities has sought to remove the fees.

The post-2008 changes were more widespread. The G20 agreed at the 2009 Pittsburgh summit to encourage central clearing, centralized trading, and margining of standardized derivatives. As of mid-2017, most of those changes had been adopted (with full adoption in the US and Japan) while some economies were lagging (Hong Kong, Singapore, Canada, Korea, South Africa, and Turkey).

Many economies also added new regulatory bodies to oversee stability of the financial system. The EU created the European Systemic Risk Board to monitor systemic risk. The UK split the Financial Services Authority in 2013 into the Financial Conduct Authority to oversee market behavior and competition and the Prudential Regulation Authority (run by the Bank of England). The Prudential

Regulatory Authority is tasked with ensuring the soundness of the financial system by monitoring systemic risk and penalizing insufficient reporting or capital.

4.7.2   Whither Regulation?

Looking at a law like Dodd-Frank, it is hard for some not to feel the encroaching socialism of the nanny state. Especially lately, talk of regulation is often strongly polarized. Some insist government is the problem and that deregulation yields growth. Others insist regulation is needed to make capitalism work. It is hard to argue that a dog's breakfast like Dodd-Frank is optimal: we would have a hard time proving most of the changes were welfare-improving. However, good laws can have bad parts (Reg SHO not preferencing customers' access to locates) and bad or onerous laws can have good parts (Dodd-Frank's Title VII).

For that reason, it is helpful to note some commonalities of the best regulation we covered. The most helpful regulation encouraged more transparent and open markets. Sometimes, that was done by creating standards — a level playing field — so competition could flourish and competitors could easily police one another. Sometimes, loosening regulation (*e.g.* finer pricing grid, ECN rebates, removing short sales constraints) increased competition. And sometimes merely mandating information dissemination was effective. For those that doubt price theory, the effect of mandating execution quality reports is tough to ignore.

It also makes sense to think about how change looks to established market participants. Change may have come because established players stopped being competitive. However, a group which resists competition will accrue a lot of money. A smart move on their part is to use that money to depict change as bad. How do we combat this? Always ask three questions: Who says change is bad? How might this change affect them? And, what evidence do they have of their claims? Ultimately, our goal is to get the most economic growth over the long haul. Sometimes that requires Schumpeterian creative destruction. That is why theory and data, not anecdotes or scare stories, should guide policy.

That is also why it is important to think about *why* finance and markets are important and *how* certain regulations work: we are often the only people talking to politicians or government economists who can educate them. While many politicians like to use an anecdote in their speeches, the plural of "anecdote" is not "data."[9]

4.8   Quiz

Try answering the following questions in five minutes.

---

[9]Some econometricians derisively refer to a collection of anecdotes as "anecdata."

1. Electronic markets tend to offer more transparency before and after trading: T   F

2. Electronic markets have higher fixed/startup costs: T   F

3. What type of market venue is known for the fastest executions, shows limit orders placed by others, and matches buyers and sellers when they agree on price?

4. Give two reasons why SEC Rules 11Ac1-4–6, decimalization, and (ultimately) Reg NMS were passed.

5. How much did spreads change (indicate up/down and size of change) in response to these rule changes?

6. What is meant by *program trading*?

7. I want exposure to the S&P 500 index. I can buy ETFs (traded at the NYSE or an ECN) or index futures (traded at the CME). I am indifferent between these choices, but I worry about grossly overpaying if I don't monitor both markets in deciding where to trade.

   a) Should I be very concerned about this? (Or, put another way: am I likely to grossly overpay at one venue versus another?)

   b) Why should I or why should I not be concerned?

8. High frequency traders use high-speed optimization and complex mathematics to make money on most trades: T   F

9. The Flash Crash (2010) and the trading glitches at Knight Capital (2012) would seem to suggest that electronic mishaps have increased greatly since a decade ago. But Gao and Mizrach (2016) show this is not the case. Why do glitches *seem* to be more common?

10. (Bonus!) Which three acts have affected the split between commercial and investment banking? Hint: One act split them, another reunited them, and a third curtails their ability to take trading risks.

4.9   Exercises

Instructions

Download the 200204, 200604, 201004, 201404, and 201804 execution quality reports at `ftp://doe.chx.com`.

   You will examine the execution quality of marketable orders using field definitions at http://www.chx.com/trading-information/execution-quality/. First, however, we will look at a few applications of statistics to what we just covered.

1. If we look at Figure 3 on page 1823 of the Christie and Schultz paper, we see the histogram for 372,625 NASDAQ quotes. Assume the even eighths each have a frequency of 21% and the odd eighths each have a frequency of 4%. What is the probability of this divergence from a uniform distribution occuring randomly?

2. Assume the unconditional density for prices p has a finite expectation p_0 and a *cádlág* cdf F. A large order comes in to the order book at $p_0 + c$. Suppose this shifts some fraction γ of the probability mass between c and ∞ to a point mass at c. Show that this imparts a negative bias to the (conditional) price process.

3. Using the downloaded execution data and the R code below as a starting point, compute for each month and size group the overall average of the following metrics for marketable stock orders:

a) average realized spread for covered order executions;

b) average effective spread for covered order executions; and,

c) share-weighted average time from order receipt to execution (at the quote).

Plot each of the three average metrics across time with each size group on the same plot (so that you have three plots).

R Code

```
# The fields in an 11Ac1-5 execution quality report
field.names <- c("Participant", "MktCenter", "CCYYMM", "Symbol", "Immediacy",
                "Size", "NumCoveredOrds", "ShrsCoveredOrds", "CxldShrsCoveredOrds",
                "FillShrsCoveredOrds", "AwayShrsCoveredOrds", "Shrs0to9s",
                "Shrs10to29s", "Shrs30to59s", "Shrs60to299s", "Shrs5to30m",
                "AvgRealizedSpread", "AvgEffectiveSpread", "ShrsPriceImprove",
                "ShrWtdPriceImproved", "ShrWtdPriceImproveTime",
                "ShrsFilledAtQuote", "ShrWtdAtQuoteTime", "ShrsFilledOutsideQuote",
                "ShrWtdOutsideQuotePriceDiff", "ShrWtdOutsideQuoteTime")

# These give the meaning of coded fields in the report
field.participants <- list(A="Amex", B="BSE", M="CHX", C="CSE", T="NASD",
                          N="NYSE", P="PCX", X="Phlx")
field.sizes <- list("21"="100-499", "22"="500-1999", "23"="2000-4999", "24"="5000+")
field.immediacy <- list("11"="Market", "12"="Marketable limit", "13"="Inside limit",
                        "14"="At-quote limit", "15"="Near-quote limit")
files2grab <- c("m200204.zip","M200604.ZIP","M201004.ZIP","M201404.ZIP","M201804.ZIP")
for (zipfile in files2grab) {
  temp <- tempfile()
  download.file(paste("ftp://doe.chx.com/", zipfile, sep=""), temp)
  file.names <- unzip(temp, list=TRUE)
  exdata <- read.csv(unz(temp, file.names[1,"Name"]), header=FALSE, sep="|")
  colnames(exdata) <- field.names
  unlink(temp)

  # do some calculations across subgroups and store results
  # You can subset the data like so:
```

```
marketableorders.idx <- exdata$Immediacy == 11 | exdata$Immediacy == 12
mean(exdata$AvgRealizedSpread[marketableorders.idx])
}
```

References

Almgren, Robert and Neil Chriss. "Optimal Execution of Portfolio Transactions". *Journal of Risk* 3.3 (2001), pp. 5–40. DOI: 10.21314/jor.2001.041.

Baris, Jay G. et al. *A User's Guide to The Volcker Rule*. Retrieved 5 June 2017 from: http://media.mofo.com/files/uploads/Images/131223-A-Users-Guide-to-The-Volcker-Rule.pdf. New York: Morrison & Foerster, Feb. 18, 2014.

Bertsimas, Dimitris and Andrew W. Lo. "Optimal Control of Execution Costs". *Journal of Financial Markets* 1.1 (1998), pp. 1–50. DOI: 10.1016/S1386-4181(97)00012-8.

Boehmer, Ekkehart, Robert Jennings, and Li Wei. "Public Disclosure and Private Decisions: Equity Market Execution Quality and Order Routing". *Review of Financial Studies* 20.2 (2006), pp. 315–358. DOI: 10.1093/rfs/hhl011.

Brooks, John. *Busness Adventures*. New York: Weybright and Talley, 1969.

Brush, Silla, Tom Schoenberg, and Suzi Ring. "How a Mystery Trader with an Algorithm May Have Caused the Flash Crash". *Bloomberg News* (Apr. 21, 2015). Retrieved on 24 May 2017 from: https://www.bloomberg.com/news/articles/2015-04-22/mystery-trader-armed-with-algorithms-rewrites-flash-crash-story.

CFTC and SEC. *Findings Regarding the Market Events of May 6, 2010: Report of the Staffs of the CFTC and SEC to the Joint Advisory Committee on Emerging Regulatory Issues*. Retrieved on 24 May 2017 from: http://www.sec.gov/news/studies/2010/marketevents-report.pdf. U.S. Commodity Futures Trading Commission and U.S. Securities & Exchange Commission, Sept. 30, 2010.

Chao, Yong, Chen Yao, and Mao Ye. "Discrete Pricing and Market Fragmentation: A Tale of Two-Sided Markets". *American Economic Review: Papers and Proceedings* 107.5 (2017), pp. 196–199. DOI: 10.1257/aer.p20171046.

Christie, William G. and Paul H. Schultz. "Why do NASDAQ Market Makers Avoid Odd-Eighth Quotes?" *Journal of Finance* 49.5 (1994), pp. 1813–1840. DOI: 10.1111/j.1540-6261.1994.tb04782.x.

CNNfn. "Nasdaq Suffers Shutdown". *Cable News Network Financial News* (June 29, 2001). Retrieved on 23 May 2017 from: http://cnnfn.cnn.com/2001/06/29/markets/nasdaq/.

Colliard, Jean-Edouard and Thierry Foucault. "Trading Fees and Efficiency in Limit Order Markets". *Review of Financial Studies* 25.11 (2012), pp. 3389–3421. DOI: 10.1093/rfs/hhs089.

Gao, Cheng and Bruce Mizrach. "Market Quality Breakdowns in Equities". *Journal of Financial Markets* 28.C (2016), pp. 1–23. DOI: 10.1016/j.finmar.2016.03.002.

Garriott, Corey et al. "Fragmentation in Canadian Equity Markets". *Bank of Canada Review* Autumn (2013), pp. 20–29. URL: https://www.bankofcanada.ca/wp-content/uploads/2013/11/boc-review-autumn13-garriott.pdf.

Glosten, Lawrence R. "Insider Trading, Liquidity, and the Role of the Monopolist Specialist". *Journal of Business* 62.2 (1989), pp. 211–235. DOI: 10.1086/296460.

— "Is the Electronic Open Limit Order Book Inevitable?" *Journal of Finance* 49.4 (1994), pp. 1127–1161. DOI: 10.1111/j.1540-6261.1994.tb02450.x.

Hendershott, Terrence and Charles M. Jones. "Island Goes Dark". *Review of Financial Studies* 18.3 (2005), pp. 743–793. DOI: 10.1093/rfs/hhi013.

Huberman, Greg and Werner Stanzl. "Price Manipulation and Quasi-Arbitrage". *Econometrica* 74.4 (2004), pp. 1247–1276. DOI: 10.1111/j.1468-0262.2004.00531.x.

Jain, Pankaj K. "Financial Market Design and the Equity Premium: Electronic vs. Floor Trading". *Journal of Finance* 60.6 (2005), pp. 2955–2985. DOI: 10.1111/j.1540-6261.2005.00822.x.

Jiji News Agency. "More Listed Firms Split Stock to Make Shares Affordable". *Japan Times* (Apr. 24, 2013). Retrieved on 24 May 2017 from: http://www.japantimes.co.jp/news/2013/04/24/business/financial-markets/more-listed-firms-split-stock-to-make-shares-affordable/.

Kerber, Ross. "Manager in flash crash: markets too fragile". *Reuters* (Aug. 17, 2010). Retrieved 24 May 2017 from: http://www.reuters.com/article/us-flashcrash-avery-interview-idUSTRE67G4JC20100817.

Kirilenko, Andrei et al. "The Flash Crash: High-Frequency Trading in an Electronic Market". *Journal of Finance* 72.3 (2017), pp. 967–998. DOI: 10.1111/jofi.12498.

Lewis, Leo. "Japan does splits to woo Mrs Watanabe". *Financial Times* (June 25, 2015). Retrieved on 24 May 2017 from: https://www.ft.com/content/796fc798-1b1e-11e5-8201-cbdb03d71480.

Malinova, Katya, Andreas Park, and Ryan Riordan. *Taxing High Frequency Market Making: Who Pays the Bill?* Working Paper 2183806. SSRN, 2016. DOI: 10.2139/ssrn.2183806.

Pagano, Marco. "Trading Volume and Asset Liquidity". *Quarterly Journal of Economics* 104.2 (1989), pp. 255–274. DOI: 10.2307/2937847.

Parlour, Christine A. and Uday Rajan. "Payment for Order Flow". *Journal of Financial Economics* 68.3 (2003), pp. 379–411. DOI: 10.1016/S0304-405X(03)00071-0.

Stoll, Hans R. and Christoph Schenzler. "Trades Outside the Quotes: Reporting Delay, Trading Option, or Trade Size?" *Journal of Financial Economics* 79.3 (2006), pp. 615–653. DOI: 10.1016/j.jfineco.2005.03.006.

Chapter 5

Efficiency and the Macroeconomy

Efficiency is one of the key underlying concepts behind capitalist systems. A squishy, unrigorous definition of efficiency would be "getting the most value out of what we have." With that intuitive idea, you can imagine all sorts of ways to improve efficiency. Often, we try to create rules or policies which encourage efficiency. What we strive for is **incentive compatibility**: when individual incentives are aligned with the overall economic actions that give us the best outcomes.

The goal of this chapter is to explain how we think about efficiency; discuss different types of efficiency; and, explain some of what we know about how these relate to financial markets.

5.1   Why Markets and Efficiency Matter

Incentive compatibility is why we believe markets offer a good system for aggregating what people want. We already mentioned price theory: the idea that markets give information to the economy which helps guide production. We also briefly discussed market efficiency, the idea that prices quickly incorporate new information and its effect on a particular instrument; and, we saw how short sales and speculators could help the market police itself to root out fraud. In this chapter, we will try to flesh out different ideas on efficiency.

Ideas of efficiency are important for measuring performance. They may reveal which firms or economies are good investments. Finally, they help us explain to government officials why our actions may benefit the economy overall. Most people want greater economic growth: more jobs that pay better and improve life. We might have to make trade-offs on one of these dimensions at a given time, but more growth is always a defensible goal. If you can explain how your job furthers that goal, you are much less likely to find politicians messing up all your hard work.[1]

5.2   Terminology and Production Functions

To talk about efficiency, we need some ideas from **production functions**: functions that try to model large-scale inputs (aka production factors) to economic output. We will not actually model these functions, but they encapsulate economists' ideas about where growth comes from. When we talk about efficiency, we are often talking about where to make changes so we get more growth.

In general, production functions model economic output Y as a function of capital K and labor L, typically with a scaling constant A. Sometimes the functions include the idea of savings and capital depreciation, sometimes they use human capital H to encapsulate education, skills, on-the-job training, and other sorts of knowledge. Often, we talk about the scaling constant A as "total factor productivity." This gets at the idea that different economies have different levels of productivity. Where do these differences in total factor productivity come from? Efficiency is one answer; institutions is another; and, astute statisticians might wonder if there is an interaction term between these. (Hint: YES.)

A big question in the study of economic growth is how growth changes as an economy gets bigger. If we have **constant returns to scale**, a percent change in one input always leads to the same percent change in output. Maybe as an economy grows, there are benefits to being bigger: more innovation, attracting the hardest-working immigrants, and economies of scale that reduce costs. If these hold, an economy might have **increasing returns to scale**. In that case, we should expect rich countries to get richer and investing in emerging markets would be foolish. On the other hand, maybe larger economies are harder to manage and end up with large governments and investments in sub-optimal legacy technologies that are expensive to change.[2] If this is the case, an economy might have **decreasing returns to scale** — and we should all be investing in emerging markets.

We do not usually work with actual numbers of people or dollars; we think in terms of percent changes. For that reason, we often think about **elasticities**, the percent change in output for a percent change in an input: $\frac{\%\Delta Y}{\%\Delta L} = \frac{\Delta Y}{Y}\frac{L}{\Delta L}$. Thankfully, the derivative of $\log Y$ with respect to $\log L$ gives us this: $\frac{\partial \log Y}{\partial \log L} = \frac{L}{Y}\frac{\partial Y}{\partial L}$. If you ever encounter a production function and want to get an elasticity for factor X, take the log of both sides, differentiate, and solve for $\frac{\partial \log Y}{\partial \log X}$. This is not the last time we will see something like elasticities.

---

[1]Think of this as your first lesson in risk management. It may seem basic, but simple explanations like what follows have deflected politicians from causing economic damage many times.

[2]The slow introduction of secure chip credit cards in the US is an example of this possibility.

5.3 Market Efficiency

One of the most-discussed measures of efficiency is **market efficiency**: the idea that market prices incorporate new information as quickly as possible. We typically measure this in a few ways.

Spreads exist, in part, due to uncertainties about the value of an instrument. Thus fractional bid-ask spreads, $\log(a/b)$ for ask a and bid b, may help measure efficiency.[3] If we enact a new policy and bid-ask spreads increase, that suggests there is more uncertainty about valuations and that it is more expensive to trade — and thus more expensive for information to get into prices. The new policy would seem to reduce market efficiency.

We can also look at quote changes. In an efficient market, quotes should change instantaneously in response to information. If quotes take some time to change, that is inefficient; it also means we can predict quote changes with a simple autoregressive model (a linear regression with a y-intercept for the average quote change and a slope for the predictability of quote changes):

$$\log(a_t/a_{t-1}) = \mu + \phi \log(a_{t-1}/a_{t-2}) + \epsilon_t. \tag{5.1}$$

Finally, we can also look at a measure proposed by Durnev, Mørck, and Yeung (2004). They looked at how much variation in stock prices was explained by the local market index. In economies with healthier information production, we should see stock prices moving around more for reasons other than just the macroeconomy. They find that out of 40 economies over 1990–1992, the most efficient markets are in the US, Ireland, Canada, the UK, Australia, and New Zealand.

5.4 Allocative Efficiency

One of the biggest concerns in efficiency is if we are investing in the right balance of industries. If consumers want more electric cars, are we investing the right amount of money in that industry? **Allocative efficiency** measures to what extent we are investing in the optimal balance of industries. This is a very difficult question to answer: we never get to see the "optimal" balance of industry investments. Then how can we determine allocative efficiency?

Wurgler (2000) answers a related question: in which economies does capital move more quickly to more attractive investments? The idea is to look at a few statistics for each industry across many countries. For industry i in country c, look at investment I and the value-added for that industry V. We then build a model to see: when industry value-added increases, does investment follow?

$$\log(I_{ict}/I_{ic,t-1}) = \alpha_c + \eta_c \log(V_{ict}/V_{ic,t-1}) + \epsilon_{ict}. \tag{5.2}$$

In this model, η_c measures the allocative efficiency: economies which are more

---

[3]Finance always uses base-e natural logarithms: log means $\ln$.

efficient will have a higher estimated $\hat{\eta}_c$. Wurgler then models $\hat{\eta}_c$ on measures of the economy and financial markets. He finds that allocative efficiency is positively-correlated with legal protections for minority (*i.e.* small) investors, the amount of firm-specific information in stock prices (price theory!), and the development of financial markets. He also finds that allocative efficiency is negatively-correlated with higher fractions of state-owned firms. The most allocatively-efficient economies in his sample (65 economies, 1963–1995): Germany, Hong Kong, and New Zealand ranked 1–3. Peru and Guatemala did very well for their level of financial development while Kuwait did very poorly for its level of financial development.

Another measure comes from Durnev, Mørck, and Yeung (2004). They look at **marginal Q**, how firm valuations respond to capital shocks:

$$\dot{q}_{jt} = \frac{\text{firm value shock}}{\text{capital shock}} = \frac{V_{jt} - V_{jt-1}(1 + E_{t-1}(\text{returns+payouts}))}{A_{jt} - A_{jt-1}(1 + E_{t-1}(\text{capex+depreciation}))} \qquad (5.3)$$

where "capex" are capital expenditures and E_{t-1} is what we expected at time $t-1$.[4] Efficient industries should see capital shocks reflected quickly in their valuations; industries which are inefficient can find ways to "tighten their belt." They then aggregate this measure over industries and look at the deviation from the maximum-efficiency expectation, $|\dot{q}_{jt} - 1|$.

5.5   X-Efficiency

Anybody who has worked multiple jobs knows: there are large differences in productivity within an industry. Leibenstein (1966) looked at manufacturing plants within the same industry and noted wide variations in the productivity of those plants. These differences in efficiency seemed to arise from differences in worker incentives, motivation, workflow, and utilization. Leibenstein proposed one of the less-discussed measures of efficiency: **X-efficiency**. The idea of X-efficiency is simple: how efficiently is capital within an industry deployed to the most-efficient firms?

If the difference between allocative efficiency and X-efficiency is confusing, think of it like investing: You might choose the right balance of industries, but then pick the worst performers in those industries. Your allocative efficiency would be high but your X-efficiency would be low.

Typically, we measure efficiency at the firm level by looking at the portfolio of outputs versus the portfolio of inputs. Firms that can produce more with less inputs are said to have a higher **technical efficiency**. Note that this is not the same a **capacity utilization**: the fraction of a firm's output versus its potential output. A firm might be able to increase their capacity utilization, but if doing so requires large amounts of capital and labor, it might not be an efficient use of those inputs.

As an example of X-efficiency, Cornwell, Schmidt, and Sickles (1990) look at

---

[4]We will look more at q in Chapter 13. For now, the intuition here is sufficient.

relative efficiency within the US airline industry before and after deregulation (over 1970–1981). Specifically, they look at inputs used by a firm and what it earned as a function of those inputs. They find that deregulation not only made all of the airlines more efficient, but also that the variation in relative efficiency shrank considerably. Thus deregulation made the US airline industry more X-efficient.

Olley and Pakes (1996) look at deregulation in the US telecommunication industry. We might wonder if inefficient plants can be made more efficient. While that might be possible, they find that capital tended to be reallocated to more efficient plants. Thus it seems that X-efficiency is not just a problem of motivation but also of capital allocation.

On a broader scale, Hsieh and Klenow (2004) look at plant-level data for the US (1977–1997), China (1998–2005), and India (1987–1994). They find that the US has a higher total factor productivity and less variation in industry X-efficiency: in the US, inefficient firms die faster. They also explored what would happen if they reallocated capital within Chinese and Indian industries to be like what would be found in the US. They found that just intra-industry reallocation would increase China's total factor productivity by 30%–50% and In-

> **X-Efficiency at VAA** Gosnell, List, and Metcalfe (2016) worked with Virgin Atlantic Airways over eight months on an experiment to see how information and incentives affected employee performance. They found that performance information alone helped improve efficiency: the captains used 6.8 mn kg less fuel, saving $5.4 mn. Information especially helped post-flight performance: the captains used less fuel taxiing; and, even after incentives were removed, those gains remained. Incentives were also able to reduce excess fuel carriage and in-flight fuel consumption; however, those reductions ended when incentives ended.

dia's by 40%–60%. X-efficiency does more than just explain the performance of US airlines; it also helps explain why some economies are more productive than others.

Bartelsman, Haltiwanger, and Scarpetta (2013) take a larger perspective. They posit that in an efficient industry, more efficient firms will grow larger. To explore this, they look at the relationship between firm size and productivity. Industries with a stronger, cleaner relationship are deemed to have a higher (X-)efficiency. They also note that firms transitioning from communism have more variation in the size-efficiency relationship and that the relationship becomes stronger and less-variable as they transition to a market economy.

5.6 Dynamic Efficiency

There is another, almost meta, type of efficiency: **dynamic efficiency**. The idea of dynamic efficiency is that over time innovation occurs and pushes out less efficient ways of doing work. This is what Schumpeter (1942) called **creative destruction**:

new technologies destroy businesses reliant on old technologies, create new businesses, and thus raise productivity and living standards.

The power of dynamic efficiency is very large. Cohen, Zysman, and DeLong (2000) discuss the rise of the internet and similar large **technology shocks**. They note that the telegraph, for example, halved the capital needed to run railroads in the 1900s. Similarly, Hummels (2007) shows that innovations in transportation like jet engines and containerization have rapidly reduced the cost of shipping bulk and high-value goods over the past fifty years. Laitner and Stolyarov (2014) find that tech shocks may explain 20%–50% of the risky component of long-run returns in stocks (with market crashes perhaps explaining most of the rest). Whether the numbers are exact is not so important; what is important is that creative destruction is clearly a very powerful force. Economies which resist dynamic efficiency are turning their backs on enormous possibilities for economic growth.

Foster, Haltiwanger, and Krizan (2001) also show how industry-level productivity changes can be decomposed into X-efficiency and allocative efficiency (with implications that dynamic efficiency is part of the allocative efficiency gains). Bertrand, Schoar, and Thesmar (2007) show that the health of the finance sector increases economic productivity (interesting itself); but, they also show that a healthier finance sector increases the rate of creative destruction. The most complete research into creative destruction is likely Davis, Haltiwanger, and Schuh (1996) which looks at job creation and destruction within and across US industries.

5.7   Synthesis

Having looked at these measures of efficiency, a natural question is how they relate. Specifically: Does market efficiency lead to allocative or X-efficiency? We do not have a lot of evidence on this front, but we do have some. Wurgler (2000) shows a relationship between the two, and Durnev, Mørck, and Yeung (2004) find that market efficiency leads to allocative efficiency. They also find some mild evidence that market efficiency is related to X-efficiency. Theory in Laeven, Levine, and Michalopoulos (2015) shows that financial innovation is necessary to keep determining what innovations to finance. Finally, in some ongoing work, Brogaard, Rosenthal, and Wang (2017) find that market efficiency leads financial market development, allocative efficiency, and reductions in the cost of equity capital (which would help capital get to the right places in an economy).

5.8   Random Walks and Efficient Markets

Regnault (1863) was a successful speculator on the Paris Bourse who first proposed modeling stock price changes as a **random walk**, a process which can go up or down with random probabilities. Furthermore, he even thought that prices were what we would call a **martingale**, a process having the expected future value equal to the current value:[5]

$$X_t = X_{t-1} + \epsilon_t \qquad \epsilon_t \overset{\perp\!\!\!\perp}{\sim} (0, \sigma^2 < \infty). \tag{5.4}$$

Note that the disturbances ϵ_t are independent with mean 0 and a finite variance, but they need not be identically-distributed. Bachelier (1900) then used these ideas extensively in his academic research. Figure 5.1 shows an example of a random walk that is a martingale, started at 0.

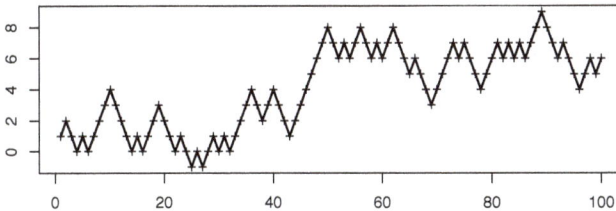

Figure 5.1: Example of a random walk, in this case a martingale which is equally likely to move +1 and -1. Processes like this were proposed by Regnault (1863) and first developed by Bachelier (1900) to model stocks on the Paris Bourse.

Why did Regnault propose this; and, why did Bachelier use such a process five years before Einstein used it to model dust particles in water? Suppose it were easy to predict prices or returns. This situation could surely not last for long: as soon as multiple people can predict prices, there will be a race to see who can capture all of that value. The price impact of trading will push the price to be near the predicted value. How quickly do prices adjust? That depends, although for simple-to-process information (*e.g.* different prices at different venues), the price gap often closes within milliseconds. Because the predictable part of prices is quickly incorporated, we should think that most prices changes are not predictable. This is why we often assume returns between different time periods are independent.

5.8.1 *The EMH*

Fama (1965) made this thinking more rigorous by proposing the **Efficient Market Hypothesis (EMH)**. In Fama (1970), he refined this to give the EMH three forms, in increasing dogmatism:[6]

1. **Weak form**: prices reflect all past trade information (prices, volumes).
2. **Semi-strong form**: prices reflect all past public information.
3. **Strong form**: prices reflect all past public and private information.

---

[5]While many people seem to think that a random walk implies a martingale, it does not.

[6]Statisticians and econometricians will note these are just statements on what is in your sigma field when you evaluate a conditional expectation.

The strong form is generally thought to be untrue and extreme; otherwise, why would anyone ever attempt insider trading? Even Fama has wavered on his support for it, sometimes saying he does not believe it (as in Fama (1970)) and other times asserting that it is true.

The semi-strong form would imply that any research is fruitless: any public information would already be incorporated in the price. Grossman and Stiglitz (1980) noted that this cannot be strictly true, however. How can the information make it into a price if it is not fruitful to trade on the information? Thus the **Grossman-Stiglitz Paradox** states that the cost of acquiring information matters: people will not conduct research and incorporate information into prices unless they (or maybe the first person) receive compensation. Thus in equilibrium, research should be fruitful.

Most academics and many industry professionals believe the weak form to be true. If you are going to do research, you need more than just past prices and volumes. You might need other data, knowledge of analysis techniques, or industry knowledge.

The EMH has other implications. For example, take technical analysis, the drawing of lines on charts to find lines of support and resistance as well as patterns that imply futures prices. All forms of the EMH would presume technical analysis to be fruitless. However, the weak form would allow for **fundamental analysis** which studies finances, cashflows, and accounting statements to make predictions.

5.8.2   The EMH Debate

The EMH can be very controversial: I have personally seen academics yelling in one another's face over differences in disbelieving the semi-strong form. However, there are a few reasons why the EMH remains a topic of debate: problems with data, the inability of proof, and risk.

The data problems are vexing. First, there is a magnitude problem: one needs only a slight predictable mispricing to be able to consistently make money. Second, our data might be censored on the upside: any investor who was making money would be wise to say nothing. Finally, it may be that the data we get are censored on the downside: we might hear about big winners but not hear from unexceptional investors.

The inability of proof, however, is the most troubling. There are scores of finance publications setting out to "prove" or "disprove" the EMH. Some papers find predictability on a given dataset; other papers then test that predictability on different datasets; and, there is then disagreement on how papers examining different datasets can come to different conclusions. (If this sounds like a lot of people who do not understand randomness well, then you are getting an accurate picture.)

The problem is simple: the EMH is not a mathematical theory; it is a hypothesis about real world data. We will never have guaranteed assumptions from real-world data; and, we cannot make proofs about data that we only see with random noise added on. Suppose we have some data y_t and we always see z_t where $z_t = x_t + \epsilon_t$ for random ϵ_t's. We can never prove that $x_t = y_t$, nor can we prove $x_t \neq y_t$. Proofs are a mathematical construct to show that a set of statements are consistent with one another or not. The EMH cannot be proven — nor can it be disproven.

Finally, there is the issue of risk. One of the subtleties of the EMH is that it says (in the semi-strong and strong forms) that public information is priced in. This suggests that public knowledge of investment risks, though uncertain, are priced in. Thus a person might earn high returns over time, but that could well be because they are taking risk and just earning the appropriate compensation for taking that risk. This is not wrong: many of the variables which seem related to future returns are often related to risk. However, it is a big out that Fama gives himself: many seeming violations of the EMH are put down to being just compensation for taking risks.

So why do people defend the EMH so vigorously? Why do they even use it? We do so for one big reason: it makes the maths easy. It gives us a nice clean argument for why we can use the current price in many models needing a later price. That saves a lot of time and hassle by not having to model the expected price. We will use this in Chapter 21 for pricing options.

5.9   Noise and the Regression Fallacy

The EMH does have some useful advice: it suggests that most people should not try to beat the market. Investments should be fairly priced for their risk; therefore, holding a diversified portfolio of everything (*i.e.* the market index) should lower the risk. This suggests a **passive investment strategy**: invest in a fund tied to the market index. (This ignores that active management might still be needed since investors differ by their tax burdens, risk factors, and investment horizons.)

If we believe that the liquidity of firms and their influence on the economy is proportional to their size, we should invest in a cap-weighted index. However, this presumes that the market capitalizations are accurate. Unfortunately, they have random noise in them. Whenever we sort on numbers with randomness, we must remember the mechanical phenomenon of **regression to the mean** (aka the **regression fallacy**).

Imagine we take a test. Some test takers know the material better, some worse. However, the top score is likely to come from somebody who knew the material and was having a very good day. The worst score is likely to come from somebody who did not know the material well and was having a very bad day. Fast forward to the next test. Suppose their level of knowledge is the same as before. However, it is very unlikely that these individuals will again have such extremely good and poor days; thus, their performance will be less extreme. The top scorer is likely to fall in the rankings and the bottom scorer is likely to rise. This has nothing to do with their preparation — and everything to do with random noise affecting the measurements.

For this reason, we should be wary of any procedures which sort investments in one period and then maintain those groupings into the next period: a mechanical "regression toward the mean" will occur and we need to correct for that to ascertain the true effect. This is especially problematic for policy interventions. If the government imposes a policy we do not like, we can just grab prices for firms with the highest market caps before the policy is implemented. Then, we show that these firms fell in value after the policy was enacted. *Presto!* the policy is bad! On the other side, somebody does the same with firm's having low market caps. Lo and behold, the policy seems to raise their market caps. Unfortunately, both arguments are utter hogwash.[7]

Regression to the mean helps explain lots of phenomena: why optimized portfolios underperform in the future, why predictions of investment returns over- and under-predict, and why market cap-weighted indices may be sub-optimal investments. This last point is tricky: investing in a passively-managed market index fund is not a bad idea; however, regression to the mean suggests we can do slightly better. This idea is what Siegel (2006) calls the **Noisy Market Hypothesis**. Because prices include random noise, we will over-invest in the highest market cap stocks and under-invest in the lowest market cap stocks.

How do we get around this issue? Arnott, Hsu, and Moore (2005) propose that they call **fundamental indexation**: weighting stocks by their fundamental values. Unfortunately, if these values were easy to find, investing would be much easier.

Statisticians, however, have proposed a different approach for this sort of problem. When estimating the true value of multiple numbers with random noise, just using those numbers is sub-optimal or **inefficient** in a statistical sense (*i.e.* we can find measures that are less noisy and more likely to be closer to the true values). The answer is to "squeeze" the values toward some average by using a **shrinkage estimator**. If we are estimating a $p \times 1$ vector θ and shrink towards α, this looks like:

$$\hat{\theta}_{\text{shrinkage}} = \alpha + (1 - w)(X - \alpha). \tag{5.5}$$

The seminal work on shrinkage estimators is James and Stein (1961) and explores a number of risk-minimizing weightings. If X are our measured market caps, and we suspect they have different variances (and possibly correlations), the **James-Stein estimator** for $X \sim N(\theta, \Sigma)$ is:

$$\hat{\theta}_{JS} = (1 - \frac{p - 2}{n - p + 3} \cdot \frac{1}{X^T \Sigma^{-1} X}) X \tag{5.6}$$

or, shrinking toward an estimated average:

$$\hat{\theta}_{JS} = \bar{X} + \left(1 - \frac{p - 2}{n - p + 3} \cdot \frac{1}{(X - \bar{X})^T \Sigma^{-1}(X - \bar{X})} \right)(X - \bar{X}). \tag{5.7}$$

---

[7]Sadly, a *Journal of Finance* article was published a few years back which had convergence of firm capital structures to the mean as one of the interesting findings of the article and tried to draw economic conclusions from that regression. The article even won a prize as one of that year's most interesting articles.

Those wanting more information on James-Stein estimators and other empirical Bayes estimates should consult Efron (2010).

5.10   The Macroeconomy

Having talked about efficiency, it makes sense to also discuss the macroeconomy. Almost all firms and organizations are affected by global economy. That makes the macroeconomy an important topic. Unfortunately, macroeconomic forecasting can be very difficult: microeconomists joke that macroeconomists have predicted eleven of the last three recessions.

5.10.1   Global Macroeconomy

Macroeconomic growth or slowdowns may help or hinder a firm's competitors and foreign operations. Changes in foreign exchange rates affect the relative purchasing power of currencies; and, currency risk may affect international revenues and costs — or even help competitors.

Currency risk may seem minor, especially when there is a temptation to ignore it. For example, high currency-adjusted interest rates may encourage investors to put on a **carry trade**: borrow money at lower rates in their home currency, convert those funds into the foreign currency, and invest them at higher foreign interest rates. However, an investor should always be watching for a **Peso problem**: a lurking risk which could cause a quick devaluation.[8]

Macroeconomic forces may even affect (or be affected by) **political risk**: the risk of governments falling or even of a political backlash against an industry.

5.10.2   Domestic Macroeconomy

Since all firms operate in at least one country, they are exposed to their domestic macroeconomy (as well as the macroeconomies of their customers). Describing the economic health of an economy is complicated and can be measured on many dimensions. Therefore, we use many metrics.

The **gross domestic product** (GDP) is all the goods and services produced in a country. We have already talked about GDP; but, it is useful to remember that the GDP, and GDP growth, are important metrics of economic health.

The **unemployment rate**, the percentage of workers who want a job and cannot get one, is a crucial measure of how much of a loss of productive efficiency the economy is taking. Most economists would say that some small level of unemployment is healthy because that results from workers reallocating their efforts to more productive uses in the economy.

---

[8]The term "Peso Problem" comes from high interest rates in Mexico during the 1970s when the Peso was pegged to the US Dollar. In 1976, Mexico could no longer support the peg and the Peso was devalued, leading to large losses for US investors with money in Mexican banks.

This is a good time to mention a measure that is *not* good. The **participation rate** is sometimes touted as a measure showing that unemployment is higher than statisticians claim. Unfortunately, the participation rate includes people who do not want a job. Thus the retirement of many "baby boomers" born after World War 2 has increased the participation rate. The participation rate has little information about how labor markets are working; and, what information it has is obscured by much larger trends unrelated to the economy.

Similarly, the **capacity utilization rate** measures actual factory output as a fraction of possible output; thus it is like an employment rate for factories. However, it also has elements of X-efficiency and maybe creative destruction as well — since we can imagine that some level of unutilized output would exist if there were creative destruction.

Inflation is the aggregate rate of increase in nominal prices. Thus if goods get 10% more expensive, then we would say that inflation had been 10%. However, this is complicated by the method used to measure inflation. Typically, the central bank has a "basket" of representative goods and services purchased by most households with weights for how much of the budget is spent on those. However, this methodology does not capture when consumers change what they buy or how much of their budget they plan to spend. Thus few consumers in 1995 purchased internet access while in 2017 most consumers in developed economies do purchase internet access.

In the US, we typically measure inflation with the **Consumer Price Index (CPI)**. However, we could also use the **Producer Price Index (PPI)**. We use the CPI to adjust income and expenditures for inflation faced by consumers, and we use the PPI is to adjust revenues and outlays for inflation faced by industrial producers.

Given that we think about inflation, it should not be surprising that we also look at interest rates since they are the prices to rent money for various periods of time. In fact, we will see in Chapter 12 that interest rates can tell us a lot about where an economy is probably headed.

Another measure often considered and debated is the **budget deficit**: the amount of government spending less government revenue. The deficit tells us if we are spending more money than we are taking in. However, a deficit is not always bad. Just as you are spending to invest by reading this book, some investments cost money now but enable greater growth later. Other investments might also be worth incurring a deficit: Duflo (2001) and Schultz (2004) show returns to education investments of about 7%–11%; and, Heller et al. (2013) shows a cost-benefit ratio of 30 or more for some violence prevention programs. Thus the deficit alone is an incomplete picture.

One way the deficit is important, however, is that having a large deficit every year is not feasible. Often, the deficit is funded by increasing debt. Again: if the debt we incur enables a higher return than the interest payments, the investment may be worthwhile. However, that means also considering what other economic actors would have done with the money.

We should clarify some confusion that is abused by politicians: the debt and the deficit are not the same. Many politicians will substitute one term for the other when answering questions or mix the terms up casually so as to be technically correct but easily misunderstood. This is a cowardly semantics game played by pusillanimous political pussyfooters pushing their position. It is not honest and you should not be so easily confused. The deficit and the debt are not the same.

The most nebulous macroeconomic indicators we have are those gauging **sentiment**: the confidence of people and businesses in a firm, industry, or the economy. These indicators tend to be of four types: equity-based, credit-based, surveys, and textual.

In equity markets, we may look at **breadth**, the difference between the number of rising and falling stocks. If we weight this by volume, we get the **trin** statistic:

$$\text{trin} = \frac{\overbrace{\text{volume declining}/\#\text{ declining}}^{\text{average declining volume}}}{\underbrace{\text{volume advancing}/\#\text{ advancing}}_{\text{average advancing volume}}}. \qquad (5.8)$$

Many people look at the **VIX**: the implied volatility index published by the Chicago Board Options Exchange. Some have even called the VIX the "fear gauge" although it is not always a good predictor of trouble. Analysts may view a an abnormally low VIX as suggesting the equity market has peaked. Shell (2016) discusses the view of a low VIX as a sign of investor complacency.

Some people also look at the **put/call ratio**: the ratio of outstanding put option contracts to outstanding call option contracts, because puts are a bet which pays off if the market falls and calls pay off if the market rises. This ratio is often around 65% because there is higher demand for puts since they provide a form of insurance against macroeconomic distress. This bias was first explored in a 2003 working paper, now published as Bondarenko (2014).

In credit markets, the measures we look at tend to have stronger predictive power. The **Barron's confidence index** is a ratio of top- and intermediate-rated corporate bond yields:

$$Barron's \text{ confidence} = \frac{\text{Avg yield(10 top-rated corporates)}}{\text{Avg yield(10 intermediate-rated corporates)}}. \qquad (5.9)$$

While a ratio, the Barron's confidence index is similar in spirit to a credit spread.

Also informative is the **TED spread**, the difference in yield between 3MUSDLIBOR and 3M T-bills. The name comes from the fact that Eurodollar futures settle to 3MUSDLIBOR; hence the "ED" in "TED." In particular, TED spreads above about 50 bp tend to signal distress, as shown in Boudt, Paulus, and Rosenthal (2017).

For more general indicators, we can also look at **consumer confidence surveys**: survey of individuals and businesses about how optimistic they are about the economy and their willingness to make large expenditures in the near future. In the US, there are two such surveys: one conducted by the Conference Board and the other by economists at the University of Michigan. The Michigan survey polls fewer people but asks more detailed questions.

In the US, many indicators, as well as anecdotal information from each Federal Reserve District, are discussed in the Summary of Commentary on Current Economic Conditions, aka the "Beige Book". The report is issued about two weeks before each Federal Open Market Committee (FOMC) meeting to determine interest rate targets.[9]

Finally, the last few years have seen the rise of text analysis algorithms that can assess the sentiment (positive versus negative) of news stories. Simple "lexicon" methods count positive less negative words. More sophisticated methods use neural networks to parse the text and identify entities being discussed. Many Reuters news stories are now tagged by a neural network with a **relevance score** and **sentiment score** for each of the entities referenced. **Relevance scores** assess the relevance of the article to an entity; sentiment scores assess the tone or positivity of the news for that entity.[10] Sinha (2016) and Heston and Sinha (2017) show that these more sophisticated methods tend to have longer-term power at predicting stock returns.

5.10.3   *Demand and Supply Shocks*

Another consideration is supply and demand shocks. **Supply shocks** affect producers and include unexpected reports of crop yields, discoveries of new oil or gas fields, and strikes by organized labor. **Demand shocks** affect consumers and include changes in tax rates, the money supply, and government spending and borrowing. Currency unions may also affect demand since they ease price comparison for consumers.

Demand-side policies are government policies which create demand shocks. The most important of these are fiscal and monetary policy. **Fiscal policy** deals with taxing and spending: government may spend to create infrastructure or inflate demand for goods or raise taxes to raise revenues and reduce consumption.

Monetary policy deals with control of the money supply: the central bank may buy or sell bonds to set yields for bonds and unsecured interbank lending; or, they may offer short-term financing of bonds held by banks. This may involve "printing" or "retiring" money. Central banks tend to announce a **policy rate** which is their target for setting yields; however, monetary policy is also affected by the **overnight rate** for unsecured interbank lending. Most central banks monitor this rate if they do not dictate it. Some of the more active policy and overnight rates are listed in Table 5.1.

---

[9]You can find the Beige Book at http : / / www . federalreserve . gov / monetarypolicy / beige-book-default.htm.

[10]In full disclosure, I know this because my ex-colleague, Nitish Sinha, wrote an early version of the Reuters engine while a graduate student at the University of Maryland. He notes in Sinha (2016) that "sentiment" does not mean emotion but, rather, the positivity or negativity of *information* in the news.

Central Bank	Policy Rate	Overnight Rate
US Federal Reserve	Fed Funds	Fed Funds
Bank of Canada	Overnight Lending Rate	Overnight Lending Rate
Banco Central do Brasil	SELIC	SELIC (Sistema Especial de Liquidação e Custodia)
Bank of England	Official Bank Rate	SONIA (Sterling Overnight Index Average)
European Central Bank	Minimum Bid Rate	EONIA (Euro Overnight Index Average)
Swiss National Bank	3MCHFLIBOR	SARON (Swiss Average Rate Overnight)
Bank of Japan	Bank Call Rate	Mutan
People's Bank of China	7-day Repo Rate	SHIBOR (Shanghai Interbank Offered Rate)
Reserve Bank of Australia	Official Cash Rate	Official Cash Rate
Reserve Bank of New Zealand	Official Cash Rate	Official Cash Rate

Table 5.1: Common policy rates used to promulgate monetary policy and unsecured overnight interbank lending rates. The minimum bid rate is from the European Central Bank's main refinancing operations.

In general, fiscal policy is more selective and targeted. Monetary policy is blunt: it merely raises or lower the price for everyone to rent money. When central banks increase the money supply, they make it cheaper for all businesses to expand and for all consumers to borrow. The idea is that the money will more easily flow to where the market wants money. Lower interest rates means cheaper funding for construction firms, automobile makers, consultancies, and retail stores — but also for pimps and prostitutes, drug dealers, and thieves. That is the unfortunate fact of monetary policy: we have no control over where the money flows.

So then why do we use monetary policy? The answer is simple: politicians. Setting fiscal policy is political and that means it takes time. Monetary policy, on the other hand is not political which enables it to be enacted quickly. Guiding the macroeconomy is like steering a speeding automobile: you cannot do it by arguing over politics. Recently, some politicians have tried to politicize central bank decisions. Most research suggests that this would be catastrophic. History is littered with the wreckage of states where monetary policy became politicized and eventually was bent to serve the whims of political leaders.

The difference between fiscal and monetary policy is not just political, however. Having one without the other can be trouble. The geographic scope of economic and monetary union (EMU) in the European Union created the **Eurozone** and gave control over the money supply to the European Central Bank. However, fiscal control was kept at the national level. This led to problems with some member states overspending or not reforming their fiscal system to, say, punish widespread tax evasion. For example, Greece's fiscal problems required large infusions from other member states lest Greece's fiscal shortfalls damage the Euro or force Greece out of the Eurozone.[11]

Supply-side policies are government policies designed to create supply shocks. Typically, supply side policies seek to reduce frictions on business such as burdensome regulations or policies which discourage innovation. Such policies were famously dismissed by George H.W. Bush as "voodoo economics" in the 1980 US Presidential debates; however, those policies later led to a long expansion under President Reagan.

Many "supply-siders" also believe that above some level, higher taxes yield less revenue. Intuition agrees with this: who would work if the tax rate were 100%? Thus at tax rates of 0% and 100%, the government receives no revenues. In between those are rates where the government would receive at least some revenues. The **Laffer curve** shows government revenues versus tax rates and also suggests some revenue-maximizing tax rate. The idea is that high taxes may remove the rewards of taking risk; less risk-taking reduces innovation; and, less risk-taking and innovation lowers tax revenues.

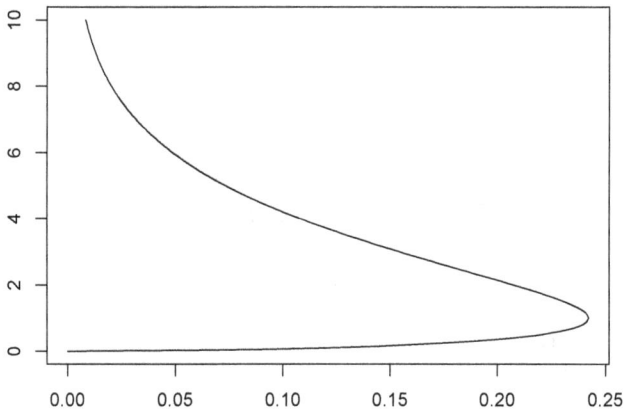

Figure 5.2: An example Laffer curve plotting tax rate versus revenues. Laffer curves typically come from theoretical economic models. In this example (for an activity or use tax), the revenue-maximizing tax rate is at about 1%.

Laffer curves often arise from theoretical models. For example, Figure 5.2 shows an example Laffer curve from a theoretical economic model. While the Laffer curve

---

[11]It is not clear, however, that a Greek exit from the Eurozone would have been damaging. Many economists suspect it might have helped Greece recover faster.

has become an accepted fact, the debate between politicians is often over where we are on the Laffer curve: are we on the bottom or top half of the curve?

5.10.4 The Business Cycle

Despite all of these efforts to understand and manage the macroeconomy, economies still experience periods of contraction and growth. The **business cycle** is the term for this irregular pattern of recession and expansion. When we talk about the business cycle, we often talk of **peaks** (local maxima) and **troughs** (local minima). The typical duration of a business cycle (*e.g.* peak-to-peak) is 6–7 years. However, there can be considerable variation: from a few years to decades.

Predicting the business cycle is difficult — so difficult that we are often unsure where we even are in the business cycle. To help assess where we are (and where we might be going), we often use a number of indicators. **Leading indicators** are correlated with later cycle movements and are the best information we have for prediction. **Coincident indicators** are correlated with current cycle dynamics and help us to establish where we are. **Lagging indicators** are correlated with past cycle movements and help us confirm where we were (and may even help us gauge where we are). Most of these indicators are released regularly by government statistical offices and are followed by the financial press.

5.11   Quiz

Try answering the following in seven minutes. Since efficiency and the macroeconomy are important topics, there is an extra question and some more detailed questions.

1. (2 points) The government worries about automobile manufacturers. To save them, the government "bails out" the car makers which are nearly bankrupt. What effect does this have on market efficiency, allocative efficiency, and X-efficiency?

2. What does the noisy market hypothesis have to say about a passive indexing approach?

3. (2 points) What are the three forms of the EMH and what do they assume?

4. You look at an industry and see three firms with the following capacities and operations:

	Mötörhaus	PowerFab	Engine & Tonic
Employees	20	12	15
Motors/Day (possible)	200	100	140
Motors/Day (actual)	180	95	110

Which firm would you prefer to invest in as a passive investor? What about as an activist investor?

5. A high-frequency trader defends what they do as making markets more efficient.

   a) What does this (efficient markets) mean and how would we measure the increase in market efficiency?

   b) Why do we care about market efficiency? Or: What do we really want?

6. Peak-to-peak, how long does the *average* business cycle last?

7. Can the EMH be proven? What if we use a better dataset?

8. Fiscal policy is more targeted than monetary policy. So why do we use monetary policy?

9. Your friend can predict the future and tells you we are about to enter a recession.

   a) Name three types of investments you should buy.

   b) Name three types of investments you should sell or sell short.

10. Country X has high political corruption, but is industrializing and will soon be privatizing some state-owned enterprises. You want to invest in a start-up with a new technology for selling tickets online — because currently tickets must be purchased from government kiosks which are slow and inefficient. What is a major risk of this investment less present in a more developed economy?

5.12   Exercises

Instructions

Download the US National Bureau of Economic Research-US Census Bureau Center for Economic Studies dataset on US industrial production from the webpage `http://www.nber.org/nberces/`. The dataset features a number of variables for each year, including the NAICS code, year, employment, payroll, production, value added, investment, and capital.

   We will fit something like the Wurgler model, except we will look at the allocative efficiency of US manufacturing since 1959. Our focus is on two variables: value added and investment to explore allocative efficiency.

1. Using the NBER-CES data, we will look at the relationship between log-ratios of investment and value added. (These log-ratios are log-returns which we will discuss in the next chapter.)

   The R code below computes log-returns of these for each industry level. For simplicity, it does not aggregate the full NAICS codes and just uses each full NAICS code as an industry. This is not the same as doing the aggregation; however, we can fix that by weighting the observations by the capital size for each level.

First fit the simple model:

$$\log\left(\frac{I_{it}}{I_{i,t-1}}\right) = \alpha + \beta \log\left(\frac{V_{it}}{V_{i,t-1}}\right) + \epsilon_{it}, \tag{5.10}$$

with weighting by cap_t. To do this use the lm function in R. You can get help on the function by typing ?lm at the command line in R.

Save the model in a variable `simple.model` and run the `summary` function on it. Plot the residuals by year (use a period for the plotting character); and, see if any observations seem unduly influential. Comment on the significance of the model terms.

2. Perhaps it takes some time to redirect investment (or to see that investment should be redirected). To investigate that possibility, we can look at a lagged value added term:

$$\log\left(\frac{I_{it}}{I_{i,t-1}}\right) = \alpha + \beta_1 \log\left(\frac{V_{it}}{V_{i,t-1}}\right) + \beta_2 \log\left(\frac{V_{i,t-1}}{V_{i,t-2}}\right) + \epsilon_{it}, \tag{5.11}$$

again weighting by cap_t. Comment on the fit, the meaning of the lag term, and examine the model residuals.

3. We can examine a slope offset to see how allocative efficiency has varied over time. To do that we will add a year (as a factor) interaction to the slope:

$$\begin{aligned}
\log\left(\frac{I_{it}}{I_{i,t-1}}\right) =& \alpha + \beta_1 \log\left(\frac{V_{it}}{V_{i,t-1}}\right) + \beta_2 \log\left(\frac{V_{i,t-1}}{V_{i,t-2}}\right) \\
&+ \gamma_{\{t\}} \log\left(\frac{V_{it}}{V_{i,t-1}}\right) \times t + \epsilon_{it},
\end{aligned} \tag{5.12}$$

again weighting by cap_t with a set of γ coefficients (one per year after the 1960 baseline). Comment on the model fit, the meaning of the year-slope interaction coefficients, and check the residuals for influential points.

4. What if we do not treat the year as a factor? Then we are estimating a model with a linear time trend. That is itself interesting, though, from an economic perspective. To assess that we will change the year to a numeric variable:

$$\begin{aligned}
\log\left(\frac{I_{it}}{I_{i,t-1}}\right) =& \alpha + \beta_1 \log\left(\frac{V_{it}}{V_{i,t-1}}\right) + \beta_2 \log\left(\frac{V_{i,t-1}}{V_{i,t-2}}\right) \\
&+ \beta_3 t \log\left(\frac{V_{it}}{V_{i,t-1}}\right) + \epsilon_{it},
\end{aligned} \tag{5.13}$$

again weighting by cap_t. Comment on the model fit, the meaning of the time trend coefficient, and check the residuals for influential points.

5. Now we turn to a more theoretical question to investigate the problems of cap-weighted indices and the Noisy Market Hypothesis with a simple simulation. Use R to simulate prices using 10,000 normal random variates for each of five instruments:

	X_1	X_2	X_3	X_4	X_5
Mean Price μ_k	18	19	20	21	22
Variance σ_k^2	1	1	1	1	1

Let each of these stock prices hang around the mean so that:

$$X_{kt} = \mu_k + \epsilon_{kt} \qquad \epsilon_{kt} \overset{iid}{\sim} N(0, \sigma_k^2). \tag{5.14}$$

Construct three indices: a cap-weighted index

$$I_{cw,t} = \sum_{k=1}^{5} X_k \tag{5.15}$$

a squeezed index,

$$I_{sq,t} = \sum_{k=1}^{5} (\bar{X}_k + \alpha(\bar{X}_k - X_k)) \quad \text{and,} \tag{5.16}$$

a μ_k-weighted (fundamental value) index

$$I_{fw,t} = \sum_{k=1}^{5} \mu_k. \tag{5.17}$$

Obviously, the mean-weighted index is not achievable, but it serves as a tool for comparison.

Invest \$1 in each index. Measure all indices' mean, standard deviation, and average squared distance from fundamental value as well as the mean and standard deviation of gains. Use a squeezing factor of $\alpha = 0.7$.

R Code

```
# Download the NBER-CES data and save it to a working directory
# Then, read in the CSV file
mfgdata <- read.csv("naics5811.csv")

# Convert columns which should be categorical variables from text
# Also pull out NAICS sectors
mfgdata$naicsind <- as.factor(mfgdata$naics)
mfgdata$naicssector <- as.factor(substr(mfgdata$naics, 1, 2))
mfgdata$yearfactor <- as.factor(mfgdata$year)

# Initialize percentage changes for value-added and investment
# Then, go through all the industries and calculate the log-return
# (percentage change) for each industry's value-added and investment.
# Also save last period's (lagged) percentage change in value-added.
mfgdata$varet <- 0
mfgdata$invret <- 0
for (ind in levels(mfgdata$naicsind)) {
```

```
temp <- mfgdata[mfgdata$naicsind == ind,]
nobs <- dim(temp)[1]
# add one into logs to guard against zeros
varet <- c(NA, log(temp$vadd[2:nobs]+1) - log(temp$vadd[1:(nobs-1)])+1)
invret <- c(NA, log(temp$invest[2:nobs]+1) - log(temp$invest[1:(nobs-1)])+1)
mfgdata[mfgdata$naicsind == ind,"varet"] <- varet
mfgdata[mfgdata$naicsind == ind,"lagvaret"] <- c(NA, varet[1:(nobs-1)])
mfgdata[mfgdata$naicsind == ind,"invret"] <- invret
}

# Some data may have been missing. Build indices to remove
# missing data for procedures which do not handle it.
usable.idx <- !is.na(mfgdata$varet)
usablear.idx <- !is.na(mfgdata$lagvaret)
```

References

Arnott, Robert D., Jason Hsu, and Philip Moore. "Fundamental Indexation". *Financial Analyst's Journal* 61.2 (2005). DOI: 10.2469/faj.v61.n2.2718.

Bachelier, Louis Jean-Baptiste Alphonse. "Théorie de la Spéculation". *Annales Scientifiques de l'École Normale Supérieure* 3.17 (1900).

Bartelsman, Eric, John C. Haltiwanger, and Stefano Scarpetta. "Cross Country Differences in Productivity: The Role of Allocation and Selection". *American Economic Review* 103.1 (2013), pp. 305–334. DOI: 10.1257/aer.103.1.305.

Bertrand, Marianne, Antoinette Schoar, and David Thesmar. "Banking Deregulation and Industry Structure: Evidence from the French Banking Reforms of 1985". *Journal of Finance* 62.2 (2007), pp. 596–628. DOI: 10.1111/j.1540-6261.2007.01218.x.

Bondarenko, Oleg. "Why Are Put Options So Expensive?" *Quarterly Journal of Finance* 4.3 (2014), pp. 1–50. DOI: 10.1142/S2010139214500153.

Boudt, Kris, Ellen C. S. Paulus, and Dale W. R. Rosenthal. "Funding Liquidity, Market Liquidity and TED Spread: A Two-Regime Model". *Journal of Empirical Finance* 43 (2017), pp. 143–158. DOI: 10.1016/j.jempfin.2017.06.002.

Brogaard, Jonathan, Dale W.R. Rosenthal, and Fan Wang. *Market Design and Cost of Capital*. Working Paper. 2017.

Cohen, Stephen S., John Zysman, and J. Bradford DeLong. *Tools for Thought: What is New and Important About the "E-conomy?"*. Working Paper 138. US Berkeley Roundtable on International Economics, 2000.

Cornwell, Christopher, Peter Schmidt, and Robin C. Sickles. "Production Frontiers with Cross-Sectional and Time-Series Variation in Efficiency Levels". *Journal of Econometrics* 46.1–2 (1990), pp. 185–200. DOI: 10.1016/0304-4076(90)90054-W.

Davis, Steven J., John C. Haltiwanger, and Scott Schuh. *Job Creation and Destruction*. Cambridge: MIT Press, 1996.

Duflo, Esther. "Schooling and Labor Market Consequences of School Construction in Indonesia: Evidence from an Unusual Policy Experiment". *American Economic Review* 91.4 (2001), pp. 795–813. DOI: 10.1257/aer.91.4.795.

Durnev, Art, Randall Mørck, and Bernard Yeung. "Value-Enhancing Capital Budgeting and Firm-Specific Stock Return Variation". *Journal of Finance* 59.1 (2004), pp. 65–105. DOI: 10.1111/j.1540-6261.2004.00627.x.

Efron, Bradley. *Large Scale Inference: Empirical Bayes Methods for Estimation, Testing, and Prediction.* Cambridge (UK): Cambridge University Press, 2010.

Fama, Eugene F. "The Behavior of Stock-Market Prices". *Journal of Business* 38.1 (1965), pp. 34–105. DOI: 10.1086/294743.

— "Efficient Capital Markets: A Review of Theory and Empirical Work". *Journal of Finance Papers and Proceedings* 25.2 (1970), pp. 383–417. DOI: 10.1111/j.1540-6261.1970.tb00518.x.

Foster, Lucia, John C. Haltiwanger, and C.J. Krizan. "Aggregate Productivity Growth: Lessons from Microeconomic Evidence". In: *New Developments in Productivity Analysis.* Ed. by Charles R. Hulten, Edwin R. Dean, and Michael J. Harper. Chicago: University of Chicago Press, 2001.

Gosnell, Greer K., John A. List, and Robert Metcalfe. *A New Approach to an Age-Old Problem: Solving Externalities by Incenting Workers Directly.* Working Paper #22316. NBER, 2016.

Grossman, Sanford J. and Joseph E. Stiglitz. "On the Impossibility of Informationally Efficient Markets". *American Economic Review* 70.3 (1980), pp. 393–408. URL: http://www.jstor.org/stable/1805228.

Heller, Sara B. et al. *Preventing Youth Violence and Dropout: A Randomized Field Experiment.* Working Paper 19104. NBER, 2013.

Heston, Steven L. and Nitish Ranjan Sinha. "News vs. Sentiment: Predicting Stock Returns from News Stories". *Financial Analyst's Journal* 73.3 (2017), pp. 67–83. DOI: 10.2469/faj.v73.n3.3.

Hsieh, Chang-Tai and Peter J. Klenow. "Misallocation and Manufacturing TFP in China and India". *Quarterly Journal of Economics* 124.4 (2004), pp. 1247–1276. DOI: 10.1162/qjec.2009.124.4.1403.

Hummels, David. "Transportation Costs and International Trade in the Second Era of Globalization". *Journal of Economic Perspectives* 21.3 (2007), pp. 131–154. DOI: 10.1257/jep.21.3.131.

James, Willard and Charles Stein. "Estimation with Quadratic Loss". *Proceedings of the 4th Berkeley Symposium on Mathematical Statistics and Probability* 1 (1961), pp. 361–379. URL: https://projecteuclid.org/euclid.bsmsp/1200512173.

Laeven, Luc, Ross Levine, and Stelios Michalopoulos. "Financial Innovation and Endogenous Growth". *Journal of Financial Intermediation* 24.1 (2015), pp. 1–24. DOI: 10.1016/j.jfi.2014.04.001.

Laitner, John P. and Dmitriy Stolyarov. *Low-Frequency Technology Shocks, Creative Destruction and the Equity Premium.* Working Paper. University of Michigan, 2014. URL: http://www-personal.umich.edu/~jlaitner/EP_PAPER2014_ISR.pdf.

Leibenstein, Harvey. "Allocative Efficiency vs. "X-Efficiency"". *American Economic*

Review 56.3 (1966), pp. 392–415. URL: http : / / www . jstor . org / stable / 1823775.

Olley, G. Steven and Ariel Pakes. "The Dynamics of Productivity in the Telecommunications Equipment Industry". *Econometrica* 64.6 (1996), pp. 1263–1297. DOI: 10.2307/2171831.

Regnault, Jules. *Calcul des Chances et Philosophie de la Bourse*. Paris: Mallet-Bachelier and Castel, 1863.

Schultz, T. Paul. "School Subsidies for the Poor: Evaluating the Mexican Progresa Poverty Program". *Journal of Development Economics* 74.1 (2004), pp. 199–250. DOI: 10.1016/j.jdeveco.2003.12.009.

Schumpeter, Joseph. *Capitalism, Socialism and Democracy*. New York: Harper & Brothers, 1942.

Shell, Adam. "Why Investors Are Ignoring Warnings About Stocks". *USA Today* (Aug. 15, 2016).

Siegel, Jeremy J. "The 'Noisy Market' Hypothesis". *Wall Street Journal* (June 14, 2006).

Sinha, Nitish Ranjan. "Underreaction to News in the US Stock Market". *Quarterly Journal of Finance* 6.2 (2016), pp. 1–46. DOI: 10.1142/S2010139216500051.

Wurgler, Jeffrey. "Financial Markets and the Allocation of Capital". *Journal of Financial Economics* 58.1–2 (2000), pp. 187–214. DOI: 10.1016/S0304-405X(00)00070-2.

Part II

Measuring

◻❋◻

Chapter 6 introduces time value of money and returns.
Chapter 7 discusses how we work with and characterize risky returns.
Chapter 8 explores, in great depth, how we measure and estimate risk.
Chapter 9 introduces diversification, our first risk alleviation technology.
Chapter 10 gives an overview of statistical modeling.

Chapter 6

Returns

Having covered the fundamentals of investments, markets, and market participants, we switch our focus to begin thinking about performance. Specifically, we need to think about **returns**, the changes in values of our investments. These changes may occur because of a schedule: money in a bank account grows at a declared rate. However, these changes may also happen because of changes in information.

The goal of this chapter is to explain the time value of money; show the different ways we look at returns; and, discuss inflation and other challenges to (ostensibly) risk-free rates of return.

6.1   Time Value of Money

The most fundamental concept in finance is **time value of money**: the idea that money now is rarely worth the same as money later. Usually, money now is worth more than money later for a few reasons: Waiting requires deferring gratification — which we would not do without the prospect of a reward. Apart from deferred gratification, having money now reduces risk: we might need the money before "later" arrives. Finally, there is opportunity cost: if I invest money now, I lose the ability to invest that money in possible (unknown) opportunities which could arise. I would not invest if I did not expect some compensation for opportunity cost. So deferred gratification, cashflow needs, and opportunity cost are all reasons money now should be worth more than money later.

Thus if you invest your money, you might expect **interest**: some promised return just for investing your cash. We often state interest in percentage terms and call it an **interest rate**, a **rate**, or a **yield**. It would be handy to have some rate we could be sure of getting. That would help us calculate equivalences between guaranteed money now and guaranteed money later. For this we use **"risk-free" interest rates**, often implied from the price of "risk-free" assets: assets we believe will surely pay out a known amount of money later.

Do we need interest or a risk-free rate to believe in time value of money? No. This is important because some parts of the world do not agree with a promised return — but are OK with an uncertain return that has a positive expectation.[1] Nonetheless, some expected rate of return on our money is necessary if we are going to calculate equivalences like "how much money would you take now in place of $100 in a month?"

The concept of a risk-free rate is useful, but as I said earlier: even this model is wrong. We are not actually *sure* we will earn the risk-free rate. Whether the risk-free rate comes from a government bond or from a bank (which might invest our money in government bonds), there is still a possibility that the government could default. Some people justify a risk-free rate by saying no government would default; they would just print money to devalue their debt. Unfortunately, the historical record is clear: governments do default, even when capable of printing currency.

For now, we will assume we have a risk-free rate — because financial analyses rest on a foundation of risk-free rates. We use risk-free rates all over the place. Sometimes, we even tack on an upcharge to the risk-free rate to account for risk. However, this means that defaulting on government bonds destroys the foundation of most financial analyses. It takes away our compass.[2] Therefore, every time you hear the words "risk free," a little bell should ring in your head to remind you to put those words in quotes because not much is risk-free.

We think risk-free rates should reflect people's aggregate preferences. The **present value** of $1 later is how much money the market would, on average, accept now in lieu of a guaranteed $1 later. That implies the risk-free rate rate which we can also express as a **discount factor** d. If $1 in 6 months is worth $0.98 now, then $d_{6M} = 0.98$. That makes computing present values easy:

$$PV(\text{money}, T) = \text{money} \times \text{discount factor for time } T = \text{money} \cdot d_T. \quad (6.1)$$

Conversely, the **future value** is what money is worth later. If we would accept $0.98 for $1 in six months, then $d = 0.98$, PV($1,6M)=$1d_{6M}=$0.98, and:

$$FV(\$1, 6M) = \$1/d_{6M} = \$1.0204. \quad (6.2)$$

By convention, we quote rates on an annualized basis. That allows us to compare the gain per unit time. If $d = 0.98$ for 1 year, the risk-free rate r_f is given by $1 + r_f = 1/d \implies r_f = 0.0204 = 2.04\%$. But what if $d = 0.98$ for six months? Or two years? We need to find what annual rate is equivalent to those rates. To get the annualized rate, we use the number of years T (0.5, 2). For the six-month rate, we can ask: what is $1 now worth in six months? And, in six months, how much

---

[1]Ghoul (2012) suggests that in Islamic finance, *qard al-hasan* (a benevolent loan) or *sadaqa* (donations to the poor) might qualify as similar to a risk-free rate.

[2]Politicians may toy with the idea of default. Our job is to smack their fingers and remind them that default would hurt real people and rain hellfire and brimstone onto their heads. Politicians need money to keep cutting ribbons and paying government workers; default brings that to a quick end.

that would be worth in a year? For the two-year rate, we can find the rate so that the future value of $1 in a year and the future value of that amount one year later would equal the two-year future value. These all imply that we reinvest money until we reach one year or we reinvest yearly until we reach time T:

$$1 + r_{f,6M} = \frac{1}{d_{6M}} \cdot \frac{1}{d_{6M}} = \frac{1}{d_{6M}^2} \iff d_{6M} = \frac{1}{(1 + r_{f,6M})^{1/2}}, \qquad (6.3)$$

$$(1 + r_{f,2Y})^2 = \frac{1}{d_{2Y}} \iff d_{2Y} = \frac{1}{(1 + r_{f,2Y})^2}. \qquad (6.4)$$

Therefore, the annualized 6M and 2Y rates are:

$$\frac{1}{0.98} = (1 + r_{f,6M})^{0.5} \implies r_{f,6M} = \frac{1}{0.98^2} - 1 = 0.0412 = 4.12\%, \qquad (6.5)$$

$$\frac{1}{0.98} = (1 + r_{f,2Y})^2 \implies r_{f,2Y} = \frac{1}{\sqrt{0.98}} - 1 = 0.01015 = 1.015\%. \qquad (6.6)$$

You might see that there is a general rule here:

$$r_{f,T} = \frac{1}{d_T^{1/T}} - 1. \qquad (6.7)$$

6.2   Interest and Compounding

In discussing interest rates, we invested and realized gains; those gains were how we we were paid interest. In computing annualized rates, we had to consider reinvesting. All of these use **compounding**: earning gains on prior gains.

Since we quote rates annualized; we may have to split the gains. Say we get 3% interest for a year on a $100 investment. This could be paid in any number of ways:

- Annually: $3 once a year;
- Semi-annually: $1.50, twice a year;
- Monthly: $0.25, each month; or
- Daily: $0.0082, each day.

Reinvesting (compounding) the interest, however, changes how much we earn from these different payment schemes. If interest is paid N times/year, the principle P grows in T years to $P(1 + r/N)^{NT}$. What if we take the limit as the compounding frequency grows? Thus we can also think about **continuous interest**. The result should be familiar to most who have taken calculus.

$$FV = \begin{cases} P\left(1 + \frac{r}{N}\right)^{NT} & N < \infty \\ \lim_{N \to \infty} P\left(1 + \frac{r}{N}\right)^{NT} = Pe^{rT} & N \to \infty. \end{cases} \qquad (6.8)$$

Thus differing interest payment and compounding schemes have differing values. For the $100 investment, the values work out to:

- Annually: $FV = \$100 \cdot 1.03^{1 \cdot 1} = \$103$;
- Semi-annually: $FV = \$100 \cdot 1.015^{2 \cdot 1} = \$103.0225$;
- Monthly: $FV = \$100 \cdot (1 + 0.03/12)^{12} = \$103.0416$; or
- Daily: $FV = \$100 \cdot (1 + 0.03/365)^{365} = \$103.0453$.
- Continuously: $FV = \$100 \cdot e^{0.03 \cdot 1} = \$103.04545$.

What if we were only earning interest for 9 months? Our future value calculations still hold; in 9 months we would have:

- Annually: $FV = \$100 \cdot 1.03^{1 \cdot 0.75} = \$102.2417$;
- Semi-annually: $FV = \$100 \cdot 1.015^{2 \cdot 0.75} = \$102.2584$;
- Monthly: $FV = \$100 \cdot (1 + 0.03/12)^{12 \cdot 0.75} = \$102.2726$;
- Daily: $FV = \$100 \cdot (1 + 0.03/365)^{365 \cdot 0.75} = \$102.2754$; or,
- Continuous: $FV = \$100 \cdot e^{0.03 \cdot 0.75} = \$102.2755$.

6.3   Comparing Rates of Return

Notice that these do not differ by much — and by very little when we compare daily to continuous compounding. Nonetheless, some banks tout that they pay a slightly lower rate than their competitors but compound interest continuously. Sadly, some customers are taken in by such misleading claims.

Lenders can be similarly misleading when they quote **annual percentage rates** (APRs): In the US, these are required by law and defined as $APR =$ Interest per payment × Payments per year. Yet lenders can game the APR by using a higher compounding frequency to make the APR farther from the compounded interest. For example, interest payments of 0.5% per month would be quoted as an APR of 6%. On the other hand, the **effective annual rate** (EAR), sometimes called the **annual percentage yield**, would be $1.005^{12} - 1 = 0.06168 = 6.168\%$.[3] If we instead reach that same EAR (6.168%) using a daily compounded rate, we can quote an APR of 5.985%. Guess which APR will attract more customers?

One of the most common failings of reason occurs when people are standing around bragging about their investments. Invariably, somebody will mention someone who "doubled their money in ABC stock." The flaw with this statement (apart from the braggadocio and the lack of adjustment for risk) is that it gives us a change without a time period. This is what we call a **holding period return**, the return for some amount of time, not normalized to ease comparison:

$$R_{\text{holding period}} = \frac{\text{End Price} - \text{Start Price} + \text{Income}}{\text{Start Price}}. \tag{6.9}$$

If someone doubled their money in six months, that is more surprising than if they did it in twelve years. So we typically compare EARs to enable comparisons of returns per unit of time. However, we need to be careful when we annualize holding

---

[3]In the EU, the APR is defined as the EAR.

period returns. If an opportunity to make 20% in three months only happens once a year, annualizing the rate to $1.2^4 - 1 = 107\%$ is dishonest; there are no reinvestment opportunities which would even make that return possible. In that case, the EAR is also 20%.

6.4 Interest Rates and Inflation

We clearly need interest rates for many financial analyses. Interest rates give us the growth rate of money. However, while interest rates give us a growth rate, there is a much simpler interpretation of them: Interest rates are simply the price to rent money. This makes it obvious that supply and demand for money affect interest rates. We infer risk-free rates from government bonds, so government actions also affect interest rates. Government borrowing can shift demand; and, the central bank (the Fed, in the US) can print money and thus shift supply.

We can also think of how interest rates relate to what we can buy with that money. **Nominal rates** give the growth rate of invested money. **Real rates** give the growth rate of that money's purchasing power. Suppose you double your money in a year but everything has become twice as expensive. We say inflation, the change in the cost of goods, was 100%. Then, your nominal rate is 100% but your real rate is 0%. Thus real rates correct for inflation.

For real and nominal interest rates of r and R with an annual rate of inflation i:

$$1 + \underbrace{r}_{\substack{\text{real} \\ \text{rate}}} = \frac{1 + \overbrace{R}^{\substack{\text{nominal} \\ \text{rate}}}}{1 + \underbrace{i}_{\text{inflation}}} = 1 + \frac{R - i}{1 + i} \approx 1 + R - i \quad \text{for small } i. \tag{6.10}$$

As we see in the above equation, however, nominal rates are not just real rates plus inflation. This is complicated further because nominal rates are the rates we see directly; we have to guess or estimate real rates. Finally, this all ignores the full equilibrium result: nominal interest rates would adjust through supply and demand to information about inflation.

The first formal thinking on incorporating inflation into interest rates was made by Fisher (1907) who proposed that nominal rates should naturally equal real rates plus anticipated inflation (what he called "appreciation"):

$$\underbrace{R}_{\substack{\text{nominal} \\ \text{rate}}} = \underbrace{r}_{\substack{\text{real} \\ \text{rate}}} + \underbrace{E(i)}_{\substack{\text{expected} \\ \text{inflation}}} . \tag{6.11}$$

Unfortunately, the data do not conclusively support this model. However, that is not to say that there is no relationship between inflation and interest rates. Since r and i are random, maybe investors demand to be compensated by some amount for the uncertainty of r and i:

$$E(R) = E(r) + E(i) + \lambda_r \operatorname{Var}(r) + \lambda_i \operatorname{Var}(i). \tag{6.12}$$

If nominal interest is taxed at a rate τ, we get to keep interest of $R(1-\tau)$. However, inflation eats away at our purchasing power, especially when taxes are involved. Let's examine a world with higher nominal rates (to compensate for inflation) and taxes:

$$\underbrace{\frac{1 + \overbrace{R(1-\tau)}^{\text{taxed interest}}}{\underbrace{1+i}_{\text{inflation deflator}}}} - 1 = \frac{R(1-\tau)-i}{1+i} = \frac{((1+r)(1+i)-1)(1-\tau)-i}{1+i} \tag{6.13}$$

$$= \frac{(r+i+ri)(1-\tau)-i}{1+i} = r(1-\tau) - \frac{i\tau}{1+i} \tag{6.14}$$

$$\approx r(1-\tau) - \underbrace{i\tau}_{\substack{\text{taxed} \\ \text{inflation}}}. \tag{6.15}$$

We can see that if nominal rates are adjusted for inflation, we still lose money compared to receiving the equivalent real interest rates and no inflation. Simply put: in a world with taxes, 7% interest with 3% inflation puts less money in your pocket than 4% interest and no inflation. Real taxes increase under inflation.

6.5   What is Risk-Free?

This discussion of inflation raises another point. We are presumably interested in a guaranteed rate of return for the value of our money, not just the numbers which happen to be printed on coins and paper notes. Many finance texts discuss inflation but neglect this risk when discussing risk-free rates. However, inflation is clearly a risk we cannot ignore if we want a true guaranteed return on the value of our money.

In many countries, there are bonds indexed to the rate of inflation. While it is true that there is still a risk of default, this is probably the closest we can get to a true risk-free rate. Why do few texts mention this approach? The reason is because the cashflows for investments are often in nominal currency and we often compute our valuations in nominal currency. Inflation is already in our frame of reference.

Sometimes, people wonder which government bond to use for the risk-free rate. We do not want to be exposed to **reinvestment risk**, the uncertainty of what rate we will get if our risk-free rate is not aligned with our investment time horizon. Therefore, the risk-free rate should come from a bond maturing at the end of our investment horizon. Thus if we expect a cashflow in two years, the two-year rate is what we should use for the risk-free rate — not the one-year rate plus some unknown one-year rate a year from now.

Another, related, risk is that of **price risk**: the risk that prices move around. "Risk-free" bonds are free of default risk but not price risk; their prices fluctuate with supply and demand for money. We are only guaranteed some rate of return if we hold the bond to maturity. If we buy and sell a bond before maturity, we can lose money. Thus we also cannot use the five-year rate as the risk-free rate for a cashflow in two years.

Finally, we assumed we have a risk-free rate. One of the most common questions asked about risk-free rates is "What is the risk-free rate in an undeveloped economy?" In other words, what is the risk-free rate if government bonds in a currency may default? What do we do if there is no risk-free asset? We could use the rates promised by the lowest-risk investments; but, that is likely to be too high since there is still some risk.

One solution proposed by Damodaran (2008) is to realize that a country's government bonds will return a higher rate if default is a possibility. If we use that country's bond rating (which assesses the likelihood of default), we can estimate how much higher the interest rate is due to the possibility of default. (This amounts to subtracting off a credit spread.) Damodaran maintains a website at `http://www.stern.nyu.edu/~adamodar/` with his current and archived estimates of these credit spreads.

Another approach to inferring a risk-free rate is to examine the relationship between risk and return and imply a rate for risk-free investments. There is more to that, and we will discuss it further in Chapter 24.

6.6   Price Returns and Log-Returns

Many financial texts incur great pains in defining returns. They introduce **simple returns** (holding period returns) as a function of the price at times t_0 and t_1:

$$r_{1,\text{simple}} = \frac{p_{t_1} - p_{t_0}}{p_{t_0}}. \tag{6.16}$$

Then they build **arithmetic** and **geometric returns** from the simple returns:

$$r_{\text{arithmetic}} = \sum_{i=1}^{n} r_{i,\text{simple}} \tag{6.17}$$

$$r_{\text{geometric}} = \prod_{i=1}^{n} (1 + r_{i,\text{simple}}) - 1. \tag{6.18}$$

Then we have to introduce arithmetic and geometric averages to get average arithmetic and geometric returns:

$$\bar{r}_{\text{arithmetic}} = \frac{1}{n} \sum_{i=1}^{n} r_{i,\text{simple}} \qquad (6.19)$$

$$\bar{r}_{\text{geometric}} = \sqrt[n]{\prod_{i=1}^{n} (1 + r_{i,\text{simple}})} - 1. \qquad (6.20)$$

Then these texts go through pages of work to reconcile these. While this is not hard, it is often not useful.

Arithmetic averages are easier to work with, but they are inaccurate. If you earned 20% over two years, that does not mean you earned 10% per year; you earned slightly less. Similarly, if you earn 10% per year for two years, you do not end up with 20% more money; you have 21% more money. Geometric averages, on the other hand, give us accurate measures of mean returns: the annual return if we earned 20% over two years is $\sqrt{1.2} - 1 = 0.0954$ or 9.54% per year. However, working with geometric returns entails a lot of multiplying and taking n-th roots — cumbersome mathematical operations that are slow and prone to inaccuracy.[4]

This runs into further trouble when we deal with returns on the value of instruments. Gains and losses due to price changes involve continuous reinvestment: Every price move for financial instruments creates returns which compound. To properly back out returns from a process which is effectively continuously compounded, we need to use **log-returns** (with base-e logarithms, aka ℓn):[5]

$$r_{1,\text{log}} = \log(p_1/p_0) = \log(p_1) - \log(p_0). \qquad (6.21)$$

⚠ **Pozor!** *Every year I taught investments, at least one student computed log-returns as the log of simple returns. This is a reasonable guess at what a log-return is, but truly wrong. Returns tend to be small and near zero so this invariably creates large negative numbers. Faced with these, many students have employed some very creative "fixes" translating values like -6.2 to -6.2%, eliminating the negative signs, or even drawing a pretty picture of a log. Avoid the drama: log-returns are just differences of log-prices.*

This fact gets to another big advantage of log-returns: they make the math simpler. We can treat them like arithmetic returns but, unlike arithmetic returns,

---
[4]These might seem like trivial matters, but when you are working with a few million returns they start to matter much more.

[5]Recall that when we found the formula for continuous compounding, it used the irrational number named for Euler, e. For that reason, we use base-e logs, aka $\log_e$ or ℓn in computing log-returns.

addition and subtraction of log-returns preserves accuracy.

$$\frac{r_{N,\log} + \cdots + r_{1,\log}}{N} = \frac{\log(\frac{p_N}{p_{N-1}}) + \cdots + \log(\frac{p_1}{p_0})}{N} \tag{6.22}$$

$$= \frac{\log\left(\frac{p_N}{p_0}\right)}{N} = \log((p_N/p_0)^{1/N}). \tag{6.23}$$

To recover the geometric mean, we just exponentiate:

$$1 + \bar{r}_{\text{geometric}} = e^{\log((p_N/p_0)^{1/N})} = (p_N/p_0)^{1/N} = \sqrt[N]{p_N/p_0}. \tag{6.24}$$

Another reason we use log-returns is because arithmetic and geometric returns have an asymmetry in them: returns can go down to -100% but up to $+\infty$%. That mechanically induces a skew to arithmetic and geometric returns. Therefore, econometricians long ago decreed that we shall work with log-returns when we are analyzing price changes.[6] There are other reasons to work with log-returns (and especially not prices), but many of those have to do with risk and will be addressed in the next chapter.

From here forward, we will use "returns" to mean log-returns.

6.7   Quiz

Try answering the following in five minutes:

1. (2 points) Suppose taxes are 30% and nominal rates (1-year T-bill) are 3% with inflation at 2%. How much does your tax bill differ versus nominal rates of 1% with no inflation?

2. Made-off Investments pays returns every six months. The six-month return is always 50%. If you reinvest, what is the effective annual rate (EAR) and annual percentage rate (APR)?

3. A good financial model reveals the truth of how markets work and is never wrong: | T   F

4. What is the future value of $1 in one year if the risk-free rate for a 1-year term is 3%?

---

[6]There are rare circumstances where we work with raw prices, but we will not get to such analyses in this text.

5. *The Economist* has long tracked the relative buying power of countries with the **Big Mac Index** — literally, the cost of a McDonald's Big Mac in various countries, converted to USD. How is this index similar to other inflation indices?

6. A stock begins the year priced at $10 and ends the year priced at $27.18. What is the annual log-return for that stock? (If you cannot get a numeric answer, write down the formula.)

6.8 Exercises

Instructions

We will download interest rates and inflation data using the `Quandl` package.

1. Using the data from Quandl, analyze government bond yields and expected inflation: are risk-free rates real rates plus inflation? What if we add a variance penalty on inflation? Or inflation surprise?

$$E(R) = E(r) + E(i) + \lambda_r \operatorname{Var}(r) + \lambda_i \operatorname{Var}(i). \tag{6.25}$$

For nominal rates R we can use constant-maturity Treasury yields, for r we can use TIPS yields, and we can also get $E(i)$ along with the CPI to measure the variance of log-returns of CPI.

While the CPI and expected inflation are monthly data series, we will need to mix them with daily data. What we will do is carry forward the last value we saw.

Try different model forms to test these various hypotheses. Use the TIPS yields, inflation (year-on-year or month-on-month annualized), expected inflation, and inflation surprise. You can also try to incorporate the uncertainty about inflation; but, that may be difficult to estimate.

Finally, consider reversing the model. Suppose we observe daily yields with some volatility σ_R but we are not sure about the volatility of inflation. What do the data imply about the volatility (*i.e.* uncertainty) of inflation?

2. We will now try to predict inflation. The Hodrick and Prescott (1997) filter solves a minimization which tries to match inflation and penalizes changes in the slope of a time trend. Unfortunately, their formulation is forward-looking: to explain inflation in a given time period, they look at the next period's inflation.

That does not work for prediction. Thus Stock and Watson (1999) proposed to predict inflation by examining a backward-looking version which penalizes a backward-difference curvature:

$$\min_{\tau_1, \dots, \tau_t} \left(\sum_{t=1}^{T} (y_t - \tau_t)^2 + \lambda \sum_{t=3}^{T} (\tau_t - 2\tau_{t-1} + \tau_{t-2})^2 \right). \tag{6.26}$$

Solving this might seem ugly, but Danthine and Girardin (1989) have an incredibly elegant way to solve this system. Realize that we can express the objective function in linear algebra:

$$(y - \tau)^T(y - \tau) + \lambda(D\tau)^T(D\tau). \tag{6.27}$$

We minimize this by differentiating with respect to τ, setting that to 0, and solving for $\hat{\tau}$:

$$-2(y - \hat{\tau}) + 2\lambda D^T D\hat{\tau} = 0, \tag{6.28}$$

$$(I + \lambda D^T D)\hat{\tau} = y, \tag{6.29}$$

$$\hat{\tau} = (I + 2\lambda D^T D)^{-1}y. \tag{6.30}$$

This is implemented in the sample code. There are only two unanswered questions. First: what curvature penalty should we use? Ravn and Uhlig (2002) suggest monthly data should use a penalty of $6.25(\# \text{ obs/year})^4 = 129{,}600$.

The second question is how do we predict inflation? Since curvature is penalized, we will predict out at the same slope as implied by $\hat{\tau}_t - \hat{\tau}_{t-1}$. Thus $\hat{\tau}_{t+1} = \hat{\tau}_t + (\tau_t - \tau_{t-1})$. Since the $\hat{\tau}$ vector changes with each data update, we need to forecast using only the data from before $t + 1$.

Write a for loop to do this prediction. Save your prediction and compare it to the actual inflation. What is the mean error and mean squared error?

3. (Basic Time Value of Money) Suppose we are going to invest in a zero coupon bond. The bond pays off $1000 risk-free. Remember that we quote yields annualized. Round to the nearest $0.001 — tenth of a cent.

a) Suppose the bond matures in one year and is yielding 0.3%. What is it worth right now?

b) Suppose the bond matures in one year and is yielding 3%. What is it worth right now?

c) Suppose the bond matures in two years and is yielding 3% (annualized). What is it worth right now?

4. (Compounding and Time Value of Money) Suppose we are going to invest in a sequence of zero-coupon-bonds so that our final payout is $1000. This means our investment gets *compounded*. Often, when we quote interest rates we fail to mention the compounding. That can make a bit of a difference.

a) Suppose we can invest in half-year zero-coupon-bonds at any time and they yield 3% (annualized). This is equivalent to semi-annual compounding. If the payoff is risk-free, what is the present value of $1000 in one year?

b) Suppose we can invest in monthly zero-coupon-bonds at any time and they yield 3% (annualized). If the payoff is risk-free, what is the present value of $1000 in one year?

c) Suppose we can invest in daily zero-coupon-bonds at any time and they yield 3% (annualized). If the payoff is risk-free, what is the present value of $1000 in one year?

d) Suppose we can invest in an instrument with continuous compounding of 3%. If the payoff is risk-free, what is the present value of $1000 in one year?

R Code

```
library(xts)
library(Quandl)

# Grab constant-maturity US Treasuries
ust.tickers <- c("FRED/DGS3MO", "FRED/DGS2", "FRED/DGS5", "FRED/DGS10", "FRED/DGS30")
ust <- Quandl(ust.tickers, type="xts")/100
ust.colnames <- c("T3M", "T2Y", "T5Y", "T10Y", "T30Y")
colnames(ust) <- ust.colnames

# Grab inflation-indexed US Treasuries
tips.yields <- c("TIPSY02", "TIPSY05", "TIPSY10")
tips <- Quandl("FED/TIPSY", type="xts")[,tips.yields]/100

# expected inflation and CPI are only available monthly...
# For expected inflation and CPI, only get the first column of data... like so:
exinfl <- Quandl("FRBC/EXIN", type="xts")[,1]
colnames(exinfl) <- c("EXINFL")
cpi <- Quandl("FRBC/USINFL", type="xts")[,1]
colnames(cpi) <- c("CPI")

# Calculate inflation and surprise by projecting CPI for one year ahead
# The surprise is how much the CPI differed from what was
# projected a year earlier
infl.yoy <- log(cpi) - log(lag(cpi, 12))
colnames(infl.yoy) <- c("INFL.YOY")
infl.mom <- (log(cpi) - log(lag(cpi)))*12
colnames(infl.mom) <- c("INFL.MOM")
excpi <- cpi*(1+exinfl)   # expected CPI in twelve months
cpi.surprise <- log(cpi) - log(lag(excpi, 12))   # % CPI surprise
colnames(cpi.surprise) <- c("INFLSURP")

# combine the data and carry monthly observations forward
inflation.tmp <- cbind(ust, tips, infl.yoy, infl.mom, exinfl, cpi, excpi, cpi.surprise)["1999/"]
inflation.data <- na.locf(inflation.tmp)

# backward Hodrick-Prescott filter function
hpbackfilter <- function(y, lambda) {
    n <- length(y)
    I <- diag(1, nrow = n)
    # build the curvature matrix
    K <- matrix(0, nrow=n-2, ncol=n)
    for (i in 1:(n-2)) {
        K[i,i:(i+2)] = c(1,-2,1)
    }
    # now invert and multiply by the data
    hat.matrix <- solve(I+2*lambda*t(K)%*%K)
    hat.matrix %*% y
}
lambda.monthly <- 129600 # for monthly data
tau <- hpbackfilter(cpi, lambda.monthly)
```

References

Damodaran, Aswath. *What is the Riskfree Rate? A Search for the Basic Building Block*. Working Paper. New York University, 2008.

Danthine, Jean-Pierre and Michel Girardin. "Business Cycles in Switzerland: A Comparative Study". *European Economic Review* 33.1 (1989), pp. 31–50. DOI: 10.1016/0014-2921(89)90035-4.

Fisher, Irving. *The Rate of Interest: Its Nature, Determination and Relation to Economic Phenomena*. New York: Macmillan, 1907.

Ghoul, Wafic Ali. *Islamic Finance and the Risk-Free Rate*. Retrieved on 9 June 2017 from http://www.islamiceconomist.com/?p=1292. Sept. 17, 2012.

Hodrick, Robert and Edward C. Prescott. "Postwar U.S. Business Cycles: An Empirical Investigation". *Journal of Money, Credit, and Banking* 29.1 (1997), pp. 1–16. DOI: 10.2307/2953682.

McTaggart, Raymond, Gergely Daroczi, and Clement Leung. *Quandl: API Wrapper for Quandl.com*. R package version 2.8.0. 2016. URL: https://CRAN.R-project.org/package=Quandl.

Ravn, Morten O. and Harald Uhlig. "On Adjusting the Hodrick-Prescott Filter for the Frequency of Observations". *Review of Economics and Statistics* 82.2 (2002), pp. 371–380. DOI: 10.1162/003465302317411604.

Stock, James H. and Mark W. Watson. "Forecasting Inflation". *Journal of Monetary Economics* 44.2 (1999), pp. 293–335. DOI: 10.1016/S0304-3932(99)00027-6.

Chapter 7

Risk versus Returns

So far, we have talked about interest rates (mostly risk-free) and a bit about returns. However, we have ignored one of the major issues in dealing with returns: risk. Risk and returns are inseparably intertwined. We believe returns may be larger to compensate us for taking risk.[1] We also believe that risk drives returns: creating them, explaining how variable they are, and even explaining "storms" of variability when prices are very jittery.

The goal of this chapter is to explain some of the theory of risky returns; discuss the economic equilibrium we expect to see between risk and returns; and, introduce some basic risk measures.

7.1 Theory

A key difference between returns and interest rates is economic interaction: returns are based on prices and prices result from a buyer and seller agreeing to trade. That makes the price economically relevant. This is why we rarely compute returns from quotes: Quotes may be prices at which nobody is willing to trade. That makes them far less economically informative.

We mentioned before the random walk time series process. This is the sort of process considered by Regnault and Bachelier — and the father of probability, Andrei Nikolaevich Kolmogorov. The random walk is also known as the "drunkard's walk" and one can imagine a young Kolmogorov in his office at night at Moscow State University, watching from overhead as a drunk man stumbles through the snow along Lomonosovský Prospekt — left and right, but always forward toward home as in Figure 7.1.[2]

---

[1]Otherwise, few would buy and the price would sag until the potential return was sufficient for the risk endured.

[2]It is a bit ironic that we use this inefficient walk home to model efficient markets.

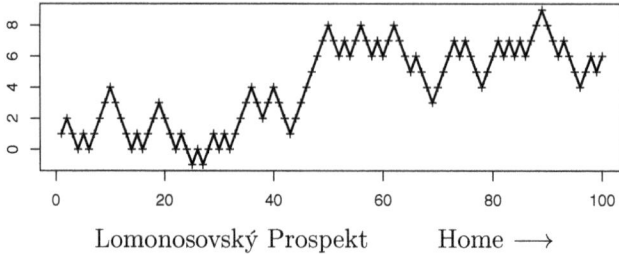

Lomonosovský Prospekt   Home $\longrightarrow$

Figure 7.1: Example of the drunkard's walk along Lomonosovský Prospekt. This is a random walk, in particular a martingale — equally likely to move +1 "left" and -1 "right."

The drunkard's walk is a basic building block of the theory behind many quantitative financial models. The process is a sum of disturbances, ϵ_t:

$$X_t = X_{t-1} + \epsilon_t \qquad \epsilon_t \overset{iid}{\sim} \begin{cases} +1 & w.p. \ p \\ -1 & w.p. \ 1-p \end{cases} \tag{7.1}$$

$$X_0 = 0 \qquad t = 0, 1, \ldots \tag{7.2}$$

If $E(X_{t+1}|X_t) = X_t$, we say X_t is a martingale. In other words: our best guess of where a price will be, say, tomorrow is where it is today. For this process, $p = 1/2$ makes X_t a martingale.[3]

However, we might see that this process is lacking. Financial instruments trade more often than every day/hour/minute; price changes tend to be more fine than $1; and, prices tend to be non-negative (due to limited liability).

However, we can take the limiting case by shrinking time by a factor of k and space by $\sqrt{k}$. If we then send $k \to \infty$, we get a **Wiener process**, often referred to as a **Brownian motion**. The stochastic differential equations below model both **arithmetic** and **geometric Brownian motion**:

$$dS_t = \mu dt + \sigma dW_t; \quad \text{(arithmetic) or,} \tag{7.3}$$

$$\frac{dS_t}{S_t} = \mu dt + \sigma dW_t \quad \text{(geometric).} \tag{7.4}$$

Note that for geometric Brownian motion, dividing by S ensures that prices remain positive.

These are the classic "drift and diffusion" equations that involve a mean return per unit of time μ and a mean-zero randomness term that adds volatility per square-root-unit of time σ.

---

[3]There are other martingales; for example, if X_t moved +2 with probability 1/3 and -1 with probability 2/3, that would also be a martingale.

Sometimes, people also invoke a probability triple $(\Omega, \{\mathcal{F}_t\}, P)$ to express that we have a well-defined probability space Ω, a filtration (sequence of increasing sigma fields) that encapsulates all events we can measure, and a probability measure P that can assign probabilities to those events. This sounds fancy (and it is), but I have never encountered an article outside of econometrics or statistics that invoked a probability triple for good reason — so do not be intimidated.

This is not to say these ideas are useless; the idea of a **sigma field** is very useful to even a general audience. A sigma field encapsulates what information we know at the time we calculate an expectation. As mentioned earlier, the different forms of the Efficient Market Hypothesis are just statements on what is in our sigma field when we claim the market is a martingale.

Why would we build such complicated probabilistic machinery? It greatly eases pricing some complicated financial instruments; and, it helps us develop better statistical estimators. There is only one small problem: these equations are a beautiful lie. (We will get to that shortly.) However, they are useful and that is why we continue to fraternize with them. We will see more of these equations when we talk about options.

> **Proof by Intimidation** A math professor was proving a theorem in a talk. At a tricky point, he exclaimed, "As any idiot can see, this leads to" the desired result. A young graduate student raised his hand and boldly said "I'm sorry, but this idiot doesn't see it." The professor struggled valiantly, but could not prove the leap in logic.
>
> If somebody makes more than a passing mention of a probability triple, they should have a good answer to how they are using something more than the standard Borel sigma field and what sort of measurability issues they foresee. Sadly, most authors seem to invoke it to intimidate.

The stochastic differential equations above have some nice features: they are continuous and the geometric Brownian motion in (7.4) is guaranteed to stay positive. Those properties let us imagine that trades are snapshots of this underlying process.[4] However, this assumes that trading does not alter the price process (*e.g.* via price impact) nor does trading tend to happen at certain times for economic reasons.

7.1.1 *Why Use Log-Returns Redux*

These processes also illuminate a few more reasons to use log-returns in analyses. These processes are not stationary. While we defined stationarity earlier, the basic intuition is that the process does not maintain the same behavior and stay living in the same space. As time goes to infinity, these processes can wander off to higher and lower prices. Thus the average price changes and the variability of the price

---

[4]A more rigorous statement of this idea is behind the Skorohod Embedding Theorem.

increases. We will have a hard time estimating properties of this process if they are not sticking around some values. This is why we do not analyze prices and we do analyze returns: prices are not stationary while returns are.

If we look at the geometric Brownian motion, we can notice that it has a $\frac{dS}{S}$ on the left hand side (LHS). Since the differential of $\log S$ is $\frac{dS}{S}$, that means the geometric Brownian motion models the log-price. If we sample from (7.4) and look at the differences $r_{t,i}$ between samples, we get:

$$r_{t_i} = \mu \Delta t_i + \sigma (W_{t_i} - W_{t_{i-1}}) \tag{7.5}$$

where $r_{t_i} = \log(S_{t_i}) - \log(S_{t_{i-1}})$.

Geometric Brownian motion has changes that are naturally log-returns. Not only that but if we sample the process at regular times, all the Δt_i's are the same and all the Wiener process differences $W_{t_i} - W_{t_{i-1}}$ are identically-distributed. That eases estimation of the parameters μ and σ. For regularly-spaced data with finite variance:

$$E(r_t | \mathcal{F}_t) = \bar{r} = \frac{1}{n} \sum_{i=1}^{n} r_{t_i} = \hat{\mu} \Delta t \overset{a.s.}{\to} \mu \Delta t \tag{7.6}$$

$$\mathrm{Var}(r_t | \mathcal{F}_t) = \frac{1}{n-1} \sum_{i=1}^{n} (r_{t_i} - \bar{r})^2 = \hat{\sigma}^2 \Delta t \overset{a.s.}{\to} \sigma^2 \Delta t \tag{7.7}$$

If you recall the EMH discussion, you might wonder, "What about risk factors?" If you know some risk factors, you might have a better guess at r_t. For example, maybe you think the average return is related to the log-return on some risk factor:

$$E(r_t^i | \mathcal{F}_t) = \alpha + \beta r_t^{\text{risk factor}}. \tag{7.8}$$

There is nothing stopping you from that modeling choice. However, for now we will just keep things simple.

7.2 Statistics Review

We need to characterize log-returns and we typically do that with statistical measures. Therefore, it makes sense to briefly recap basic statistics.

When we work with random variables, we may have a certain statistical distribution in mind. If we do, that distribution is characterized by a **probability mass function** (pmf) for discrete variables or a **probability density function** (pdf) for continuous variables. These functions apportion likelihood such that cumulated over their range of definition they sum to 1. The function which gives the partially-cumulated probability, up to a certain value, is called the **cumulative**

mass function (cmf) or **cumulative distribution function** (cdf).[5] We often use these to compute **expectations**, probability-weighted averages.[6]

7.2.1 Central Moments

Apart from the distribution parameters, we also often have use for the **central moments**: the expected values of powers of random variables (demeaned and scaled above the first and second powers).

The **expected return** is the probability-weighted average possible return:

$$\mu_r = E(r) = \int_{-\infty}^{\infty} r \underbrace{f(r)}_{\substack{\text{pdf} \\ \text{of } r}} dr \overset{or}{=} \sum_{i=1}^{N} r(i) \underbrace{p(i)}_{\substack{\text{pmf} \\ \text{of } r}} \tag{7.9}$$

Variance is the expected squared distance from the mean:

$$\sigma_r^2 = \mathrm{Var}(r) = \int_{-\infty}^{\infty} (r - \mu_r)^2 f(r) dr \overset{or}{=} \sum_{i=1}^{N} (r(i) - \mu_r)^2 p(i). \tag{7.10}$$

Skewness is the expected **standardized** (scaled to mean zero, unit variance) third moment:

$$\gamma_r = \int_{-\infty}^{\infty} \left(\frac{r - \mu_r}{\sigma_r}\right)^3 f(r) dr \overset{or}{=} \sum_{i=1}^{N} \left(\frac{r(i) - \mu_r}{\sigma_r}\right)^3 p(i). \tag{7.11}$$

Kurtosis is the expected standardized fourth moment:

$$\kappa_r = \int_{-\infty}^{\infty} \left(\frac{r - \mu_r}{\sigma_r}\right)^4 f(r) dr \overset{or}{=} \sum_{i=1}^{N} \left(\frac{r(i) - \mu_r}{\sigma_r}\right)^4 p(i). \tag{7.12}$$

We often benefit from examining expectations involving multiple variables. **Correlation** is a common measure of dependence across instruments which characterizes the strength of a linear relationship. If we scale X and Y to have the same variance and subtract their mean, correlation measures their average product: do they tend to be high or low at the same time?

$$\mathrm{Corr}(X, Y) = \rho_{XY} = E\left(\frac{X - \bar{X}}{\sigma_X} \cdot \frac{Y - \bar{Y}}{\sigma_Y}\right). \tag{7.13}$$

Covariance is correlation scaled for the typical range of X and Y:

$$\mathrm{Cov}(X, Y) = \Sigma_{XY} = E(XY) - E(X)E(Y) = E((X - \bar{X})(Y - \bar{Y})). \tag{7.14}$$

---

[5]Those wanting a review of distribution theory would do well to consult Severini (2011).
[6]We assume that these expectations are finite. That should be a reasonable assumption: data analyses do not suggest that any of the expectations we will discuss are infinite.

Note that we use a subscripted uppercase Greek letter sigma, Σ_{XY}, to denote covariance; it is not a summation.

Correlation is bounded: $-1 \leq \rho_{XY} \leq +1$, with values closer to ± 1 implying stronger dependence. If two variables have a correlation of 1, they always move proportionately together; if they have a correlation of -1, they always move opposite and proportional to one another. Since the correlation is bounded, the covariance is also bounded: $-\sigma_X \sigma_Y \leq \Sigma_{XY} \leq \sigma_X \sigma_Y$.

Covariance is also useful because it lets us find the variance of a sum of variables. So long as both variables have a finite variance, we have that:

$$\text{Var}(X + Y) = \text{Var}(X) + \text{Var}(Y) + 2\,\text{Cov}(X, Y). \tag{7.15}$$

This gets complicated as we increase the number of variables in the sum.[7] However, linear algebra was created to simplify these calculations. To handle these sums, we use a **covariance matrix**: a symmetric matrix often written as Σ (without subscripts). The off-diagonal elements hold covariances while the diagonal holds variances, since $\text{Var}(x) = \text{Cov}(x, x)$:

$$\Sigma = \begin{pmatrix} \sigma_X^2 & \Sigma_{XY} & \cdots & \Sigma_{XZ} \\ \Sigma_{XY} & \sigma_Y^2 & \cdots & \Sigma_{YZ} \\ \vdots & \vdots & \ddots & \vdots \\ \Sigma_{ZX} & \Sigma_{ZY} & \cdots & \sigma_Z^2 \end{pmatrix}. \tag{7.16}$$

To compute the variance of a sum of an arbitrary number of variables, we put the multipliers in a weight vector w and use the quadratic form $w'\Sigma w$. If your linear algebra is a little rusty, here is a refresher:

1. Write the weights along left and top borders of the covariance matrix;
2. Multiply the matrix elements by the row and column weights; and,
3. Finally, add up all the products.

We can try this for a three-asset sum $w_X X + w_Y Y + w_Z Z$:

$$\begin{array}{ccc} w_X & w_Y & w_Z \end{array}$$
$$\begin{matrix} w_X \\ w_Y \\ w_Z \end{matrix} \begin{pmatrix} \sigma_X^2 & \Sigma_{XY} & \Sigma_{XZ} \\ \Sigma_{XY} & \sigma_Y^2 & \Sigma_{YZ} \\ \Sigma_{XZ} & \Sigma_{YZ} & \sigma_Z^2 \end{pmatrix}. \tag{7.17}$$

Then multiplying leaves:

$$\begin{pmatrix} w_X^2 \sigma_X^2 & w_Y w_X \Sigma_{XY} & w_Z w_X \Sigma_{XZ} \\ w_X w_Y \Sigma_{XY} & w_Y^2 \sigma_Y^2 & w_Z w_Y \Sigma_{YZ} \\ w_X w_Z \Sigma_{XZ} & w_Y w_Z \Sigma_{YZ} & w_Z^2 \sigma_Z^2 \end{pmatrix} \tag{7.18}$$

---

[7]Unfortunately, the quantity of numbers to estimate in creating a covariance matrix can lead to them being poorly estimated. Daniels and Kass (2001) proposes a shrinkage estimate to handle such concerns.

Adding gives us the final answer: $\text{Var}(w_X X + w_Y Y + w_Z Z) = w_X^2 \sigma_X^2 + w_Y^2 \sigma_Y^2 + w_Z^2 \sigma_Z^2 + 2w_X w_Y \Sigma_{XY} + 2w_X w_Z \Sigma_{XZ} + 2w_Y w_Z \Sigma_{YZ}$.

If there is covariance, is there also **coskewness** and **cokurtosis**? There is indeed, although the definitions are more complicated:

$$\text{coskew}(X, Y, Z) = \frac{E[(X - \bar{X})(Y - \bar{Y})(Z - \bar{Z})]}{\sigma_X \sigma_Y \sigma_Z}, \tag{7.19}$$

$$\text{cokurt}(W, X, Y, Z) = \frac{E[(W - \bar{W})(X - \bar{X})(Y - \bar{Y})(Z - \bar{Z})]}{\sigma_W \sigma_X \sigma_Y \sigma_Z}. \tag{7.20}$$

We can then compute the skewness and kurtosis of a sum of random variables. Using the weight vector w, we can write these in linear algebra as:

$$\text{skewness} = w^T \Gamma (w \otimes w) \quad \text{and} \tag{7.21}$$

$$\text{kurtosis} = w^T \mathcal{K}(w \otimes w \otimes w), \text{ where} \tag{7.22}$$

$$\Gamma = E[(r - \mu)(r - \mu)^T \otimes (r - \mu)^T] = \{\gamma_{ijk}\} \quad \text{and} \tag{7.23}$$

$$\mathcal{K} = E[(r - \mu)(r - \mu)^T \otimes (r - \mu)^T \otimes (r - \mu)^T] = \{\kappa_{ijk\ell}\}. \tag{7.24}$$

This obviously gets very complicated. We will discuss this more when we talk about risky portfolios, but thankfully the `PerformanceAnalytics` package makes this much less work.

7.2.2 Notation for Random Variables

We typically write random variables with their assumed distribution and parameters, for example $\xi \sim N(\mu, \tau^2)$ or $\zeta \sim \text{Bin}(n, p)$. Sometimes, we assume only a mean and variance, written as $\upsilon \sim (\nu, \eta^2)$. We denote uncorrelated variables as $\zeta \perp \upsilon$ and independent variables as $\zeta \perp\!\!\!\perp \xi$. If a sequence of variables are uncorrelated, we write $\omega_t \overset{\perp}{\sim} (0, \theta^2)$. Finally, we may assume a sequence of variables are **iid**: independent and identically distributed.

7.2.3 Sample Distribution Metrics

For n regularly-spaced returns, we can easily estimate these metrics. We assume each observation is equally likely: $p(i) = \frac{1}{n}$. We also generally divide the sums by the **degrees of freedom**, the number of observations minus the number of parameters previously estimated. For example, estimating the mean (used in the variance) uses up one degree of freedom: knowing the mean and $n - 1$ data points implies the n-th data point. Hence we divide the variance estimate by $n - 1$.[8]

---

[8]For those wanting a more rigorous definition of where $n - 1$ comes from, it is a rank condition on the data matrix. Once we estimate the mean and subtract it from the other data (to estimate the variance), the matrix has rank $n - 1$. This is because the mean is constructed from all the rows.

Finally, we put "hats" on quantities to remind us that they are estimates.

$$\text{mean} = \hat{\mu}_r = \frac{1}{n}\sum_{i=1}^{n} r_i \tag{7.25}$$

$$\text{variance} = \hat{\sigma}_r^2 = \frac{1}{n-1}\sum_{i=1}^{n}(r_i - \hat{\mu}_r)^2 \tag{7.26}$$

$$\text{skewness} = \hat{\gamma}_r = \frac{1}{n-2}\sum_{i=1}^{n}\left(\frac{r_i - \hat{\mu}_r}{\hat{\sigma}_r}\right)^3 \tag{7.27}$$

$$\text{kurtosis} = \hat{\kappa}_r = \frac{1}{n-2}\sum_{i=1}^{n}\left(\frac{r_i - \hat{\mu}_r}{\hat{\sigma}_r}\right)^4 \tag{7.28}$$

If you research the divisors for skewness and kurtosis, some sources say to divide by n while other sources suggest dividing by the degrees of freedom. Using the degrees of freedom is intuitive since it comes from a matrix rank condition: we use an estimated mean and variance, so divide by $n-2$.

Unfortunately, both approaches are biased for small samples. An unbiased skewness estimator can be had by substituting $\frac{n}{(n-1)(n-2)}$ for $\frac{1}{n-2}$. An unbiased kurtosis estimator is more complicated. Depending on the assumptions, Cramér (1957) suggests substituting $\frac{n^2-2n+3}{(n-1)(n-2)(n-3)}$ for $\frac{1}{n-2}$ and subtracting $\frac{3(n-1)(2n-3)}{n(n-2)(n-3)}\hat{\sigma}^4$. Fisher (1973) suggests replacing $\frac{1}{n-2}$ with $\frac{n(n+1)}{(n-1)(n-2)(n-3)}$ which is unbiased under normality.[9] Thankfully, dividing by the degrees of freedom is very close for almost any dataset big enough to merit analysis.

These central moments are available in R from the mean and var functions and, using the PerformanceAnalytics package, from the skewness and kurtosis functions (pass method="sample" for unbiased skewness and the Fisher kurtosis formula).[10] For other divisors, multiply the method="moment" formulae by n and then scale by one of the preceding multipliers. Use the cor and cov functions for correlation and covariance.

In finance, we often compare instruments by looking at these metrics scaled to an annual basis. The mean, variance, and covariance (μ_r, σ_r^2) scale linearly with time. (Thus the standard deviation scales with the square root of time.) The skewness, kurtosis, and correlation require no scaling for time.

Suppose there are 250 trading days for an instrument and we calculated an average of daily returns.[11] We would then compute the annual expected return as $250\mu_{r,\text{daily}}$ and the annualized variance as $250\sigma_{r,\text{daily}}^2$. Often in finance, we also refer to the **volatility**: the standard deviation of annual log-returns. Volatility is the

---

[9]This is a poor assumption for a statistic often used with non-normal data.

[10]FYI: the kurtosis function's method=Fisher differs from the Fisher (1973) formula. Fisher was prolific, so having multiple formulae attributed to him is not surprising.

[11]Some markets, like FX and power, trade every day. So we would use 365 for those markets. On the other hand, futures on these instruments do not trade every day.

square root of the annualized variance; thus the volatility equals $\sigma_{r,\text{daily}}\sqrt{250}$. For example, a 0.04 daily volatility annualizes to $0.04 \times \sqrt{250} = 0.63$ ("63%").

7.2.4 Intuition on Moments

These higher-order moment metrics are mostly of concern for non-normal data. However, most instrument returns are not normally-distributed. Therefore, some basic intuition for these moments is useful.

The variance (or volatility) describes how variable returns are. If you have ever taken a test and asked about the mean and standard deviation, then you should already have some intuition for volatility.

Skewness measures the asymmetry of the distribution. If the skewness is negative ($\gamma < 0$), we say the distribution is **left skewed**: it has the potential for unusually large negative surprises. If the skewness is positive ($\gamma > 0$), we say the distribution is **right skewed**: it has the potential for unusually large positive surprises. Symmetric distributions have a skewness of 0.

Kurtosis measures the potential for unusually large positive and negative surprises. Specifically, kurtosis measures the bimodality of a distribution.[12] A distribution with values only at ± 1 will have the minimum kurtosis of 1. However, there is far more to kurtosis than just that.

Most financial texts, if they mention kurtosis, will say that high kurtosis ($\kappa > 3$, **leptokurtic**) distributions have "fat tails" — tails thicker than those of a normal distribution ($\kappa = 3$). That is true, but only half the story. A high kurtosis distribution also has an exaggerated central peak; statistics students used to be taught that kurtosis measured a distribution's "peakedness." This is a deadly detail. An exaggerated central peak makes the distribution seem like one with much lower variance — until we encounter a surprise from one of the tails. This can lull investors into a false sense of security and lead them to increase their exposure; then, a bad surprise comes along and causes huge losses. We can see this with some plots in R:

```
x <- seq(-5,5, 0.01)   # sequence of values to plot a standardized distribution

# Plot normal, logistic, and standardized t_5 densities; add a legend to look nice.
plot(x, dnorm(x), type='l', ylim=c(0,0.5), lty=1, lwd=2, col="cyan", xlab="", ylab="", main="")
lines(x, dlogis(x, scale=sqrt(3)/pi), lty=2, lwd=2)
lines(x, dt(x/sqrt((5-2)/5), df=5)/sqrt((5-2)/5), lty=4, lwd=2, col="red")
legend.text <- c(expression(paste('t'[5], "  ", kappa, "=9")),
                 expression(paste("logistic  ", kappa,"=4.2")),
                 expression(paste("normal  ", kappa, "=3")))
legend("topright", legend.text, lty=c(4,2,1), lwd=2, col=c("red", "black", "cyan"))


# Then plot logs of densities to show the tail behavior
plot(x, log(dnorm(x)), type='l', lty=1, lwd=2, col="cyan", xlab="", ylab="", main="")
lines(x, log(dlogis(x, scale=sqrt(3)/pi)), type='l', lty=2, lwd=2)
lines(x, log(dt(x/sqrt((5-2)/5), df=5)/sqrt((5-2)/5)), type='l', lty=4, lwd=2, col="red")
legend.text <- c(expression(paste('t'[5], "  ", kappa, "=9")),
                 expression(paste("logistic  ", kappa,"=4.2")),
                 expression(paste("normal  ", kappa, "=3")))
legend("topright", legend.text, lty=c(4,2,1), lwd=2, col=c("red", "black", "cyan"))
```

---

[12] Those interested in more on this should read Darlington (1970).

Figure 7.2 shows the result of running this code. We see three example distributions with increasing kurtoses: the normal, logistic, and a Student's t-distribution with 5 degrees of freedom. All are normalized to have unit variance so that we can properly compare their peaks and tails.

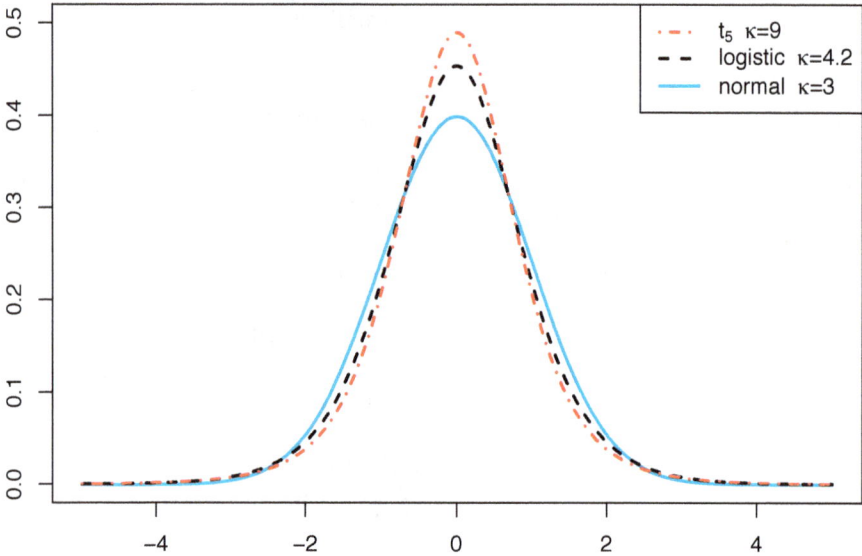

Figure 7.2: Plots of three density functions for random variables with mean zero and unit variance. The normal, logistic, and Student's t_5 densities have increasing kurtosis κ. As the kurtosis increases, the central peak becomes more exaggerated which can lull investors into a false sense of security. The tails of the distribution also become fatter, as seen more clearly in Figure 7.3.

Figure 7.3 shows a plot of the log of all three densities. We can see the difference in their tail behaviors with the normal distribution tails declining the fastest and the t_5 tails declining the slowest.

Finally, while correlation and covariance are useful measures of cross-sectional dependence, we should never forget that they characterize a *linear* relationship. Dependence, however, is a much more general idea. The plots in Figure 7.4 all have a clear dependence pattern; however, both datasets have a correlation of zero between the x and y variables.

7.2.5   Distributional Uncertainty

With a bunch of moments calculated from our data, it might seem that we know a lot about the distribution. Unfortunately, that is not so. In particular, we do

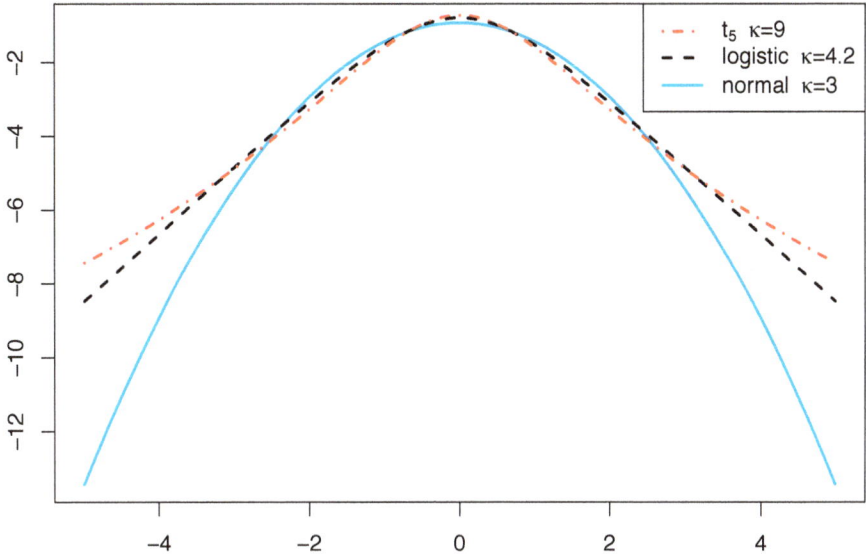

Figure 7.3: Plots of three log-density functions for normal, logistic, and Student's t_5 random variables with mean zero and unit variance. As kurtosis κ increases, the tails of the distribution become fatter and decay more slowly, as seen here.

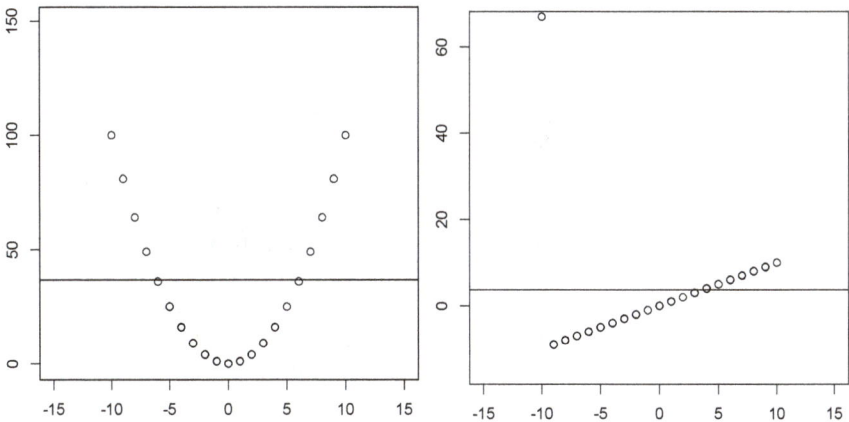

Figure 7.4: Two plots illustrating dependence yet having zero correlation. The points show a quadratic relationship (left) and a linear relationship with an influential point (right). The lines show the least squares line of best fit.

not know the distribution of log-returns. We can find a number of distributions with four or more parameters; and, many of these can be calibrated to match the observed moments. Or, we can create an Edgeworth expansion to perturb a normal distribution to match the observed moments. However, these expansions might not even be proper densities. (We will see more of these ideas in the next chapter.)

Ultimately, however, we never know which distribution generated the log-returns. Even if we impose certain characteristics like unimodality, strict positivity, and thicker tails than the normal distribution, that still does not imply a single distribution. There is also very little theory to guide us toward other distributions. The only other relevant process models are the mean-reverting Uhlenbeck and Ornstein (1930) model and the Heston (1993) stochastic volatility model. And... these models are not necessarily more accurate than the approximations or assumed forms often used.

7.2.6   Using Intraday Data

Finally, estimating the volatility and correlations with other assets can be difficult for new instruments: we would rather not wait a month or two to estimate these quantities and potentially miss a good investment opportunity. Furthermore, markets and the macroeconomy change over time so an estimate from six months or a year ago might now be a poor estimate.

One solution is to estimate these from a model considering overall and industry average volatilities and correlations. A sophisticated model might even infer these as a function of firm characteristics like debt versus total assets, size, and book value.

Another solution to this problem is to use intraday data to estimate volatilities and correlations. Over the past ten years, high-frequency volatility estimation (aka "realized variance") has been an active area of research. Much of this was driven by Zhou (1996) and Andersen et al. (2000, 2001) who noted problems with using intraday data. Specifically, they found that using log-returns removed much of the skewness, that returns using all trades had high negative autocorrelations, and that sampling periods shorter than five minutes yielded increasingly large estimates.

The problem is due to trades on alternating sides of the bid-ask spread (aka the "bid-ask bounce"). This causes returns, and thus naive volatility estimates, to be affected by the bid-ask spread.[13] Bandi and Russell (2008) show that estimates of realized variance without corrections are biased and inconsistent. The intuition is that when trading is frequent, the finite price changes of bid-ask bounce look like returns which would be very large if scaled by time. The resulting effect is that volatility estimates explode as we shrink the sampling period. The literature therefore refers to these trades as being polluted by "microstructure noise."

Aït-Sahalia, Mykland, and Zhang (2005) noted that only sampling every five minutes resulted in lost data and lower theoretical efficiency. Zhang, Mykland, and Aït-Sahalia (2005) therefore proposed an estimator to use all of the data while countering the effect of bid-ask bounce. Their approach, the two-scales realized

---

[13]This problem was first noted by Roll (1984).

variance estimator, uses the returns over a sliding window on a longer time-scale and returns over a sliding window on a short time-scale. The difference between these variances (with some scaling) yields a better estimate of the underlying variance. An example of this method is shown in Figure 7.5.

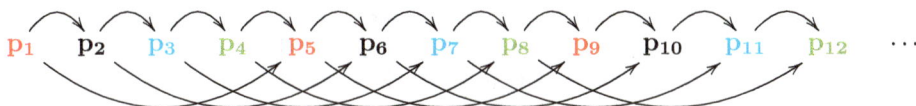

Figure 7.5: Example of two-scales realized variance estimator. In this example, the fast time scale looks at returns from $p_1 \to p_2$, $p_2 \to p_3$, ...; and, the slow time scale looks at returns from $p_1 \to p_5$, $p_5 \to p_9$, ...; $p_2 \to p_6$, $p_6 \to p_{10}$, ... The estimator takes a difference of variances computed with these different time-scale returns.

The best such estimator, proposed by Zhang (2006) uses a more complicated scheme with multiple time scales and achieves the optimal convergence rate of $n^{-1/4}$. Most variance estimators converge at rate $n^{-1/2}$ (where n is the number of observations); the $n^{-1/4}$ convergence rate shows how severely bid-ask bounce pollutes intraday returns.

Since then, other methods have been proposed. Hansen and Lunde (2006) showed that using a kernel estimator (essentially a flexible moving average) performed better than the realized variance estimators. Barndorff-Nielsen et al. (2008) showed how to design optimal kernels for such estimation which achieve the same $n^{-1/4}$ convergence rate.

The latest and best method is the pre-averaging approach developed by Podolskij and Vetter (2009) and Jacod et al. (2009). The idea is to use a moving average (often over 30 seconds to five minutes) to compute the realized variance. While a bias correction is still needed, the procedure is more intuitive, comports with pre-existing industry practice, still converges at rate $n^{-1/4}$, and can also estimate kurtosis.

The `highfrequency` R package implements many of these high-frequency inference methods.

7.3 Excess Returns and Risk Premia

Government bonds determine a currency's risk-free rate r_f. Investing in something risky should earn more than r_f, on average. Otherwise, why would one make such an investment? The **excess return** is the actual (risky) return less the risk-free return.[14] The average compensation for taking risk is the average excess return and

---

[14]Some managers define the excess return as the risky return beyond some target rate, instead of the risk-free rate.

is called the **risk premium**:

$$\overbrace{E(r_i - r_f)}^{\text{risk premium}}.\underbrace{}_{\text{excess return}} \tag{7.29}$$

Risk aversion, often denoted with λ, is a measure of how unwilling someone is to take risk. A **risk-neutral** investor would not care about risk ($\lambda = 0$) while a risk averse investor has a positive risk aversion ($\lambda > 0$). Most investors, unless they have immense capital, are risk averse. Journalists and politicians like to characterize investors as gamblers, but this is absurd: since the odds are against you in a casino, gambling only makes investment sense if you are **risk loving** ($\lambda < 0$).

The economic appeal or benefit of an investment is called the **utility**. Economic theory says that the utility should be given by a negatively-scaled cumulant generating function evaluated at the negative scaling constant:

$$\text{Utility} = U_{ij} = \frac{-1}{\lambda} \underbrace{\log(E(e^{-\lambda r_i}))}_{\text{cumulant generating function}}. \tag{7.30}$$

While that sounds fancy, crude reality intrudes; we rarely know the cumulant generating function. Worse still: for a large class of potential distributions, the cumulant generating function cannot be found in closed form. However, we do know that for members of the exponential family this formulation yields a sum of positive odd moments and negative even moments (divided by the factorial of the power). Thus we gain utility for positive expected return and skewness and we lose utility for positive variance and kurtosis.

Since we may not know the form of the cumulant generating function, we keep with the preceding idea of using expected return less powers of scaled risk measures.[15] We also believe that people have decreasing utility from risk; therefore, as risk increases, they will demand returns that increase at more than a linear rate. This also agrees with risk measures being raised to powers greater than unity. The utility of risky investment i for individual j (with risk aversion λ_j) would therefore be:

$$\text{Utility} = U_{ij} = E(r_i) - \underbrace{\lambda_j \text{Risk}_i^\omega}_{\substack{\text{risk} \\ \text{penalty}}} \quad \omega > 1, \tag{7.31}$$

where the $\omega > 1$ constraint reflects the decreasing marginal utility of risk.

If we think markets are efficient (or close to efficient), then the risk premium for an investment should compensate for the average risk penalty on the investment. This lets us create equivalences among various investments to infer the market average risk aversion. Long-run averages of excess returns over various periods

---

[15]It might seem that the sum of cumulants is a risk measure and is not raised to some power. We will see in Chapter 8 that proper risk measures scale linearly with position size. The cumulants, which scale with powers of position size, are therefore also raised to powers.

suggest US stocks have a risk premium of 6–8%. Risk premia for other industrialized nations are similar.

Does risk aversion change over time? Academic research and common sense both suggest they do. Do risk premia therefore change over time? Yes again. Over shorter time periods, the risk premium for US stocks usually ranges over 3–15% — with more variation depending on the subset ("universe") of US stocks analyzed. While risk premia seem to change, they probably do not jump suddenly: people's perception of risk rarely changes instantly. That suggests that risk premia and risk aversions are persistent or autocorrelated.

Some texts suggest using one value of the risk premium for analyses. However, given that risk premia change, that is clearly not sensible. Instead, a thorough analysis should consider various risk premia and aversions.

Finally, we might think we have a model for returns — or at least some risk factors that help explain returns. Sometimes, we look at **abnormal returns**: the difference between observed returns and what our model can explain. Typically, we use abnormal returns in an effort to assess the effect of a disturbance to the market.

7.4 The Normal Distribution

The **normal (Gaussian) distribution** is very useful in statistics and econometrics for a number of reasons. Therefore, we should be familiar with some of its properties.

Most distributions can be characterized by their parameters; and, the normal distribution is fully characterized by two parameters: the mean μ and variance σ^2. The normal probability density function is:

$$f(x) = \frac{1}{\sqrt{2\pi}\sigma} e^{-\frac{1}{2}\left(\frac{x-\mu}{\sigma}\right)^2}. \tag{7.32}$$

The normal density has points of inflection at $\pm 1\sigma$ from the mean. Furthermore, we can easily remember how much probability mass lies within a few standard deviations of the mean: 0.68 within $\pm 1\sigma$, 0.95 within $\pm 2\sigma$, and 0.997 within $\pm 3\sigma$.

If X is normally-distributed with mean μ_X and variance σ_X^2, we typically write $X \sim N(\mu_X, \sigma_X^2)$. If $Y \sim N(\mu_Y, \sigma_Y^2)$, we could then write:

$$\begin{pmatrix} X \\ Y \end{pmatrix} \sim N\left(\begin{pmatrix} \mu_X \\ \mu_Y \end{pmatrix}, \begin{pmatrix} \sigma_X^2 & \Sigma_{XY} \\ \Sigma_{XY} & \sigma_Y^2 \end{pmatrix} \right), \tag{7.33}$$

where $\Sigma_{XY} = \text{Cov}(X, Y)$.

One of the benefits of working with the normal distribution is that it is closed under addition: the sum of two normal random variables is, itself, normal. Thus for the above X and Y:

$$X + Y \sim N(\mu_X + \mu_Y, \sigma_X^2 + \sigma_Y^2 + 2\Sigma_{XY}). \tag{7.34}$$

Earlier, we discussed four central moments; however, we have characterized the normal with only two parameters. Normal random variables have 0 skewness and a kurtosis of 3.

7.4.1   A Fight is Brewing

There is a fight that has been brewing, and we have been avoiding it. It is time to confront that. The normal distribution tends to invoke heated and indignant responses from certain people, often those least informed about statistics. The normal distribution has issues, but people's anger is usually misplaced: few statisticians or econometricians posit using the normal distribution in ways that most critics get exercised about.

First, we have to acknowledge that there is truly a statistical puzzle. When we aggregate random numbers, for most variables with a finite variance and weak dependence the sum (or average) will tend toward normality.[16] This fact is known as the **Central Limit Theorem**. However, when we aggregate log-returns, we do not get a normal distribution: we sometimes get a non-zero skewness and we often get a kurtosis higher than 3.

Why financial returns do not aggregate to normality is still an unsolved mystery. However, there are some good reasons why financial returns are different from most random variables. First, returns come from prices, and prices are determined by strategic (*i.e.* game-theoretic) interactions between buyers and sellers. Thus returns can include some very non-random behaviors. Second, returns come from firms which are competing with one another. When one firm stumbles, the others will take advantage of that mistake. Bad months or quarters for one firm may be accompanied by mildly better quarters for competitors; and, that effect may persist for a few more months or quarters. Third, returns are also affected by fear: when people worry about the economy, they may sell equities and buy government bonds. As people's fear dissipates, they may change their asset allocation. Thus returns are affected by another larger source of randomness in the macroeconomy. Finally, there is the unfortunate truth that surprises in the adult world are rarely good: employees might hide losses, theft, or fraud; however, they rarely hide unexpected gains, large profits, or good behavior. Thus trouble can grow until it is too large to be hidden — at which point it bursts forth into the public eye causing large negative returns. These are just a handful of reasons why log-returns may not be normally-distributed.

Some people have been taught (incorrectly) that this means we cannot fit a linear model. That is completely false. Linear models only require a finite variance — or, in some cases, a finite $2 + \epsilon$-th moment. Non-normal data only raises the bar for determining statistical significance. You will hear again and again in your life: linear models assume normality. However, repetition does not make it any more true. Linear models do not assume normality and that lie must die.

How do we test for statistical significance, then? Often, even with non-normal

---

[16]The conditions for this to hold can get complicated quickly. However, weak dependence like that found in processes with strong mixing is sufficient.

log-returns, the Gauss-Markov Theorem still holds and so our coefficient estimates are approximately normal. If this is in doubt, however, we can use clustered standard errors or even a sampling technique like the bootstrap to estimate standard errors and assess the significance of our estimated coefficients.

There is, however, one place where the critics are correct: there are some models where we assume normality. Often we do this because assuming normality makes the math easier: a combination of normal variables is still normal; we can rely on results from the stochastic processes and probability literature; and, some problems can be solved in closed-form. Thus we sometimes willingly work with models we know are wrong. However, in those cases, we can often correct the model results to account for the wrong assumptions. We will see one such correction in Chapter 21 when we discuss options.

7.5 Historical Record of Returns

Finally, we end with some historical numbers just to give you some idea of the orders of magnitude we are discussing. Table 7.1 shows approximate historical levels of volatility, skewness, and kurtosis for a number of different assets in various classes. Note that these can vary depending on the time period analyzed. The data come from my own calculations as well as Geman (2005) and Acar and Toffel (1999).

Return Distribution	Volatility σ	Skewness γ	Kurtosis κ
Normal	N/A	0	3
Stocks	0.2–0.8	-0.5	5–7
Bonds	0.1–0.2	0.5	5–7
Currencies	0.1	-0.1	5–10
WTI Crude	0.4	0.1	6
Copper	0.2	-0.4	7.5
Electricity	0.5-1.5	0–1	7–25
Natural Gas	0.7	-1.0	31
Wheat	0.3	-0.8	60

Table 7.1: Approximate historical levels of volatility, skewness, and kurtosis for a variety of assets in different asset classes.

We should also note that the kurtosis of large indices is less than for single stocks.

7.6   Quiz

Try answering the following in five minutes:

1. (3 points) Given the following data:
  x: 2   5   1   4   -1   0   5   -3   1   3   2   5   compute (1) the mean, (2) the
variance, (3) the standard deviation, (4) the skewness, and (5) the kurtosis.

2. A stock yielded a log-return of 10% over a 7-month period, and a log-return
of 8% over the subsequent 5-month period. What is the log-return over the entire
12-month period?

3. What is a theoretical reason for using log-returns?

4. Log-returns of financial assets are effectively normal: | T   F

5. What is the term for the average excess return of an investment?

6. If the daily volatility of a stock's log-returns is 0.03, what is the annualized
volatility? (Assume 250 trading days/year. You may approximate if you show your
work.)

7. (2 points) Name two features which distinguish log-returns with large kurtosis.
(You may draw a graph and annotate the two features.)

8. Suppose $X \overset{iid}{\sim} N(0, 16)$ and $Y \overset{iid}{\sim} N(0, 1)$ with $X \perp\!\!\!\perp Y$. If $Z = X^2 + Y$, what is
the correlation of X and Z?

7.7   Exercises

You will need to download the following data using the `Quandl` and `quantmod`
packages.

- Constant maturity US Treasuries: 3M, 2Y, 10Y, and 30Y (Quandl tickers
  `FRED/DGS3MO`, `FRED/DGS2`, `FRED/DGS10`, `FRED/DGS30`)
- Eurodollar futures: near, two-years-out (Quandl tickers `CHRIS/CME_ED1` and
  `CHRIS/CME_ED8`)
- Indices: S&P 500, Russell 2000 from Yahoo via `quantmod`: `^GSPC`, `^RUT`
- "Group 1" stocks: from Yahoo via `quantmod`:
  PG, XOM, IBM, MMM, KO, GS, AXP, WMT, MRK, DIS, HD
- "Group 2" stocks: from Yahoo via `quantmod`:
  AAPL, CARB, CBRE, CZR, F, FBC, IMGN, IRDM, SBUX, SVU, SYMC,
  UPS, VLO
- Commodities near futures: WTI crude oil, US natural gas, copper, and corn
  (`CHRIS/CME_CL1`, `CHRIS/CME_NG1`, `CHRIS/CME_HG1`, `CHRIS/CME_C1`)

The bond data are yields, so they need to be rescaled to be on the same scale as log-returns (divide them by 100). The index and equity prices need to be corrected for splits and dividends (use the adjusted close field). Finally: restrict your analysis to the past three years.

R Code

Below is some *R* code to get you started.

```
library(Quandl)
library(xts)
library(quantmod)
library(PerformanceAnalytics)

# Example of reading in CMTs from Quandl
# Name columns so we know what each holds after joining them together
ust.tickers <- c("FRED/DGS3MO", "FRED/DGS2", "FRED/DGS10", "FRED/DGS30")
ust.raw <- Quandl(ust.tickers, type="xts")/100
colnames(ust.raw) <- c("T3M.yld", "T2Y.yld", "T10Y.yld", "T30Y.yld")

# This is a way to get approximate returns for these bonds.
# Later on, you will learn about duration and why we can do this.
ust.yieldchanges <- diff(ust.raw)
colnames(ust.yieldchanges) <- c("T3M", "T2Y", "T10Y", "T30Y")
ust <- ust.yieldchanges
ust$T3M  <- -0.25*ust.yieldchanges$T3M
ust$T2Y  <- -1.98*ust.yieldchanges$T2Y
ust$T10Y <- -8.72*ust.yieldchanges$T10Y
ust$T30Y <- -19.2*ust.yieldchanges$T30Y

# Get Eurodollar futures (settlement) prices and create log-returns.
ed1.raw <- Quandl("CHRIS/CME_ED1", type="xts")[,"Settle"]
ed1 <- diff(log(ed1.raw))
colnames(ed1) <- c("ED1")

# Get S&P 500 prices (just adjusted close); then create log-returns.
# Do similarly for the Russell 2000, and other stocks.
adj.close <- 6  # 6th field is adjusted close
spx.raw <- getSymbols("^GSPC", source="yahoo", auto.assign=FALSE, return.class="xts")[,adj.close]
colnames(spx.raw) <- c("SPX.prc")
spx <- diff(log(spx.raw))
colnames(spx) <- c("SPX")

# Join all of the datasets together: US Treasuries, Eurodollars,
# S&P 500, Russell 2000, and group 1 and group 2 stocks.
# Then trim them down so the dates are consistent.
alldata.full <- cbind(ust.raw, ust, ed1, ed24, spx.raw, spx,
                      rut.raw, rut, yourticker.raw, yourticker)
alldata <- alldata.full["20130513/20170516"]

# Calculate annual volatilities like so:
apply(alldata, 2, sd)*sqrt(250)

# skewness and kurtosis are independent of time; no need to scale them
skewness(alldata, method="moment")
kurtosis(alldata, method="moment")
```

1. (Risk-Free Price Risk.) When we say US Treasuries (USTs) are risk-free, we mean that their payoff is certain. (Well, as certain as can be for a USD-denominated investment.) However, you can lose money trading USTs since their prices change with interest rates. To get a handle on that capital gains risk, we will calculate some volatilities.

We want to get daily yields for some USTs at four *tenors* (times to maturity): 3M, 2Y, 10Y, and 30Y.

Since a 3M T-bill expires in three months, we obviously cannot use the same bill over a two-year period. Therefore, the Fed creates yield series called constant maturity treasuries (CMTs). CMT rates are averages of yields for instruments maturing near a certain amount of time. We use these to infer the yield for a certain maturity.

Get daily yields over the past three years for those four instruments. The yields are quoted in percentage points; thus yields of "1.23" and "0.002" are yields of 1.23% and 0.002% (*i.e.* 0.2 basis points).

We will compute six measures of returns and risk for each of these four US Treasury bonds.

a) What is the average yield for each of these instruments over the three years?

b) We cannot calculate daily log-returns for CMTs. Therefore, we must use an approximation. To do this requires two steps: First, compute the changes in yields. Then, multiply those changes by the following numbers: -0.25 (3M), -1.98 (2Y), -8.72 (10Y), and -19.20 (30Y). (These numbers are related to the average time of a bond's cashflows. We'll get to that later.) The result is a percent change for the bond price, on the same scale as the bond yields. Find the average of these approximated log-returns for each of the four maturities.

c) Using these approximated daily log-returns, calculate a standard deviation for each maturity. These are estimates of daily log-return volatilities. Scale them up to an annual basis (remembering that there are about 250 trading days/year).

d) Again using the approximated daily log-returns, calculate a skewness and kurtosis for each maturity.

2. (Short-term Credit and Price Risk.) While we say US Treasuries (USTs) are risk-free, this is not true for money deposited in a bank: That bank can fail. Eurodollar futures can be used to hedge the rate paid for large US dollar deposits in a top-credit London bank. (That rate is called LIBOR, the London Interbank Offered Rate.) Eurodollar futures are some of the most actively-traded instruments in the world. Because banks and finance firms often anticipate cashflows well into the future, Eurodollar futures are not just liquid for a few maturities but for many maturities.

For this question, you should look at "near" Eurodollars (ED1) which are used to hedge three-month rate risk and Eurodollars about two-years out (ED8). (Quandl only has continuous futures for the quarterly expiries — which are more liquid.)

a) Since Eurodollar futures trade at prices (not yields), we can easily calculate daily log-returns for them. Using these daily log-returns, calculate a standard deviation for each maturity. These are estimates of daily log-return volatilities. Scale them up to an annual basis (remembering that there are about 250 trading days/year). Report the scaled-up volatilities.

b) Again using the daily log-returns, calculate a skewness and kurtosis for each maturity. These estimates are time-independent, so they do not need to be scaled to an annual basis. Report the skewnesses and kurtoses.

c) Compare the volatilities, skewnesses, and kurtoses of these Eurodollar contracts to the volatilities of similar-term CMTs. How different are these risk measures? Why would this be?

d) Now we will examine a credit spread. The TED spread is the amount that short-term Eurodollars (the "ED" in TED) yield over a similar-term US Treasury instrument (the "T" in TED). To compute what 3M Eurodollars are yielding, just subtract their price from 100. So if 3M Eurodollars are at 99.735, that implies a yield of $100 - 99.735 = 0.265$ aka 0.265% or 26.5 basis points (bp).

The TED spread is then found by subtracting the 3M CMT yield from this number. If the 3M CMT UST is yielding 0.03% (3 bp), then the TED spread is 23.5 bp.

Calculate and report the historical average, and volatility for the TED spread.

3. (Equity Price Risk.) Stocks are not risk-free: they may be rendered worthless (or nearly so) in bankruptcy; and, dividends may be reduced or suspended. All of these possibilities affect the risk of stocks. To get a handle on that risk and how it compares to price risk for USTs, we will calculate more risk measures.

The S&P 500 and Russell 2000 are the two most relevant and widely-used indices for professional money managers. The S&P 500 is a large-cap index; the Russell 2000 is a small-cap index.

Get daily prices for the S&P 500, Russell 2000, and stocks in groups 1 and 2 from Quandl. For the equity instruments (stock indices and stocks), make sure you get prices that are adjusted for dividends and splits.

a) What is the average price of each of the equity instruments over the past sample period?

b) Calculate daily log-returns (differences in logs of daily prices) for all three equity instruments. Find the average log-return for each equity instrument.

c) Annualize each of these average daily log-returns (assuming 250 trading days/year). Compare each of the annualized average log-returns to average UST yields? What do you notice overall? Why do we see this?

d) Using the daily log-returns, calculate a standard deviation of log-returns for each equity instrument. These are estimates of daily volatility. Scale them up to an annual basis (remembering that there are about 250 trading days/year). Report each annualized volatility.

e) Again using the daily log-returns, calculate the skewness and kurtosis of log-returns for each equity instrument. Report each skewness and kurtosis.

f) Compare the volatilities, skewnesses, and kurtoses of these equity instruments to the volatilities of CMTs. How different are the risk measures? Why would this be? Are there any surprises?

4. (Commodity Price Risk.) To get a handle on commodity risk, get daily prices for the S&P 500, Russell 2000, and stocks in groups 1 and 2 from Quandl. For the equity instruments (stock indices and stocks), make sure you get prices that are adjusted for dividends and splits.

a) What is the average price of each of the commodity instruments over the past sample period?

b) Calculate daily log-returns for the commodity instruments and find the average log-return.

c) Annualize these average daily log-returns (assuming 250 trading days/year). Compare each of the annualized average log-returns to average UST yields? What do you notice overall? Why do we see this?

d) Using daily log-returns, estimate daily volatilities. Scale these up to an annual basis (remembering that there are about 250 trading days/year). Report each annualized volatility.

e) Again using the daily log-returns, calculate the skewness and kurtosis of log-returns for each equity instrument. Report each skewness and kurtosis.

f) Compare the volatilities, skewnesses, and kurtoses of these equity instruments to the volatilities of CMTs. How different are the risk measures? Why would this be? Are there any surprises?

5. (Correlation Heat Map.) Calculate the correlation matrix of all these daily log-returns. Highlight any correlations greater than 0.5 (in magnitude). Discuss any of these "large" correlations which are *not* between commodities in one of the six groups.

References

Acar, Emmanuel and Robert Toffel. "Highs and Lows: Times of Day in the Currency CME Market". In: *Financial Markets Tick by Tick*. Ed. by Pierre Lequeux. Chichester (UK): John Wiley & Sons, 1999.

Aït-Sahalia, Yacine, Per A. Mykland, and Lan Zhang. "How Often to Sample a Continuous-Time Process in the Presence of Market Microstructure Noise". *Review of Financial Studies* 18.2 (2005), pp. 351–416. DOI: 10.1093/rfs/hhi016.

Andersen, Torben G. et al. "Great Realisations". *RISK* 13.3 (2000), pp. 105–108.

— "The Distribution of Realized Exchange Rate Volatility". *Journal of the American Statistical Association* 96.453 (2001), pp. 42–55. DOI: 10.1198/016214501750332965.

Bandi, F. M. and J. R. Russell. "Microstructure Noise, Realized Variance, and Optimal Sampling". *Review of Economic Studies* 75.2 (2008), pp. 339–369. DOI: 10.1111/j.1467-937X.2008.00474.x.

Barndorff-Nielsen, Ole E. et al. "Designing Realized Kernels to Measure the ex post Variation of Equity Prices in the Presence of Noise". *Econometrica* 76.6 (2008), pp. 1481–1536. DOI: 10.3982/ECTA6495.

Boudt, Kris, Jonathan Cornelissen, and Scott Payseur. *highfrequency: Tools for Highfrequency Data Analysis*. R package version 0.5.2. 2017. URL: https://CRAN.R-project.org/package=highfrequency.

Cramér, Harald. *Mathematical Methods of Statistics*. Princeton: Princeton University Press, 1957.

Daniels, Michael J. and Robert E. Kass. "Shrinkage Estimators for Covariance Matrices". *Biometrics* 57.4 (2001), pp. 1173–1184. DOI: 10.1111/j.0006-341X.2001.01173.x.

Darlington, Richard B. "Is Kurtosis Really "Peakedness?"" *The American Statistician* 24.2 (1970), pp. 19–22. DOI: 10.2307/2681925.

Fisher, Ronald Aylmer. *Statistical Methods for Research Workers*. New York: Hafner, 1973.

Geman, Hélyette. *Commodities and Commodity Derivatives: Modeling and Pricing for Agriculturals, Metals and Energy*. New York: Wiley, 2005.

Hansen, Peter R. and Asger Lunde. "Realized Variance and Market Microstructure Noise". *Journal of Business and Economic Statistics* 24.2 (2006), pp. 127–161. DOI: 10.1198/073500106000000071.

Heston, Steven L. "A Closed-Form Solution for Options with Stochastic Volatility with Applications to Bond and Currency Options". *Review of Financial Studies* 6.2 (1993), pp. 327–343. DOI: 10.1093/rfs/6.2.327.

Jacod, Jean et al. "Microstructure Noise in the Continuous Case: The Pre-Averaging Approach". *Stochastic Processes and their Applications* 119.7 (2009), pp. 2249–2276. DOI: 10.1016/j.spa.2008.11.004.

McTaggart, Raymond, Gergely Daroczi, and Clement Leung. *Quandl: API Wrapper for Quandl.com*. R package version 2.8.0. 2016. URL: https://CRAN.R-project.org/package=Quandl.

Peterson, Brian G. and Peter Carl. *PerformanceAnalytics: Econometric tools for performance and risk analysis*. R package version 1.4.3541. 2014. URL: https://CRAN.R-project.org/package=PerformanceAnalytics.

Podolskij, Mark and Mathias Vetter. "Estimation of Volatility Functionals in the Simultaneous Presence of Microstructure Noise and Jumps". *Bernoulli* 15.3 (2009), pp. 634–658. DOI: 10.3150/08-BEJ167.

Roll, Richard. "A Simple Implicit Measure of the Effective Bid-Ask Spread in an

Efficient Market". *Journal of Finance* 39.4 (1984), pp. 1127–1139. DOI: 10.1111/j.1540-6261.1984.tb03897.x.

Ryan, Jeffrey A. *quantmod: Quantitative Financial Modelling Framework*. R package version 0.4-8. 2017. URL: https://CRAN.R-project.org/package=quantmod.

Severini, Thomas A. *Elements of Distribution Theory*. Cambridge (UK): Cambridge University Press, 2011.

Uhlenbeck, G. E. and L. S. Ornstein. "On the Theory of the Brownian Motion". *Physical Review* 36.5 (1930), pp. 823–841. DOI: 10.1103/PhysRev.36.823.

Zhang, Lan. "Efficient Estimation of Stochastic Volatility Using Noisy Observations: A Multi-Scale Approach". *Bernoulli* 12.6 (2006), pp. 1019–1043. DOI: 10.3150/bj/1165269149.

Zhang, Lan, Per Aslak Mykland, and Yacine Aït-Sahalia. "A Tale of Two Time Scales: Determining Integrated Volatility with Noisy High Frequency Data". *Journal of the American Statistical Association* 100.472 (2005), pp. 1394–1411. DOI: 10.1198/016214505000000169.

Zhou, Bin. "High-Frequency Data and Volatility in Foreign-Exchange Rates". *Journal of Business and Economic Statistics* 14.1 (1996), pp. 45–52. DOI: 10.2307/1392098.

Chapter 8

Risk Measures

> ⚠️ **Uwaga!** *This chapter is more technical than any other chapter. Sections 8.5–8.7 are not intended to be full-blown lessons on those topics. Rather, the purpose is to show what is possible in case you want to investigate these topics further. If you do not understand or are scared by these sections, do not worry: the basic ideas are more than sufficient for most people.*

Before we discuss any risks, we should consider what risk is. The study of risk and randomness usually falls under statistics. However, certain sub-branches are more relevant than others. We also need to fight some common market misconceptions. This will feed into how we analyze performance.

We have talked about statistical metrics that relate to uncertainty and risk. Most investments texts (and many finance professionals) take σ as the measure of return risk. However, as we said before, this is problematic: numerous tests show that asset log-returns are not normal. In that case, the volatility σ is not a sufficient measure of risk. Should we consider skewness γ and kurtosis κ as well? What is an appropriate measure of risk?

The goal of this chapter is to explain some theory underlying measures of risk; discuss different ways to assess risk; and, show how to conduct those assessments with real data. We will also consider how the world (and risk) may change or be difficult to qualify.

8.1 Value-at-Risk

In the mid-1990s, J.P. Morgan set out to develop risk measures they could use across the firm. Their RiskMetrics group developed a measure they called **value-at-risk** (**VaR**) and which represented a certain quantile of the return distribution. So for example, the 5%-VaR was the return such that 5% of returns were lower. These returns are typically scaled by the portfolio **notional** (value):

$$\alpha\text{-}VaR = \text{Notional} \cdot F_r^{-1}(\alpha) = \text{Notional} \cdot \{r^* | F_r(r^*) = \alpha\}, \qquad (8.1)$$

where F_r is the distribution function of r.

For the 5%-VaR, we expect our 5% worst days to lose at least the 5%-VaR. For a normal distribution, the 5%-VaR is 1.64σ below the mean. Value-at-risk quickly became a standard because it easily yielded a number which managers and regulators had wanted. The apex of this came with the Basel II banking accords which set capital standards for international banks based on VaR.

There is only one problem with all this: VaR is flawed. Deeply flawed.

We can see this through a simple example. Suppose we can invest $1 in two bonds: A and B. Each defaults independently with probability 0.04. Thus each bond has the Bernoulli payout:

$$\text{Payout}_{\{A,B\}} \overset{iid}{=} \begin{cases} \$1 & w.p.\ 0.96, \\ \$0 & w.p.\ 0.04. \end{cases} \qquad (8.2)$$

What if we put $0.50 in A and $0.50 in B? In that case, our payout would be:

$$\text{Payout}_{\frac{A+B}{2}} = \begin{cases} \$1 & w.p.\ 0.96^2 = 0.9216 & \text{(no defaults)}, \\ \$0.50 & w.p.\ 2\cdot 0.96 \cdot 0.04 = 0.0768 \text{ (1 default)}, \\ \$0 & w.p.\ 0.04^2 = 0.0016 & \text{(both default)}. \end{cases} \qquad (8.3)$$

Investing in just A, B, or half of each all have the same expected value: E(Payout of A or B) = E(Payout of $\frac{A+B}{2}$) = $0.96. However, the probability of total loss is far lower if we hold half of each. The variance of the payout for A (or B) is $0.96 \cdot 0.04 = 0.0384$. The variance of the payout for $\frac{A+B}{2}$ is $0.9216 \cdot 1^2 + 0.0768 \cdot 0.5^2 - 0.96^2 = 0.0192$. Holding half of each bond is less risky; and, that agrees with our common sense: there is less risk of a total loss; do not put all your eggs in one basket, etc.

So what insight does value-at-risk give us? The 5%-VaR for bond A equals the 5%-VaR for bond B and is... $0. At the 5-th percentile, there is no loss; we do not see a loss until the 4-th percentile. As for holding half of each bond, the 5%-VaR for that is $0.50: at the 5-th percentile we lose $0.50.

Thus VaR tells us investing in one bond is less risky and leads us into more concentrated portfolios than is wise. Consider a few facts:

- Basel II forced banks to manage their risks to a VaR target;
- VaR is poor at capturing the risks of fixed income investments;
- banks hold a lot of fixed income investments; and,
- in the financial crisis of 2008, banks found themselves holding overly concentrated and risky portfolios of fixed income investments.

I am not saying VaR caused the financial crisis of 2008; however, it may have made it worse.

8.2 Semideviation

Typically, variance has been used to characterize risk. However, when Harry Markowitz was devising modern portfolio theory, he originally wanted to use a measure that focused on downside risk. Unfortunately, the math was too tough to work out in closed-form; and, computers were still uncommon then.

One risk measure which focuses on downside risk is **semideviation**: the "standard deviation" computed with only the returns below the mean.

$$\theta_p := \sqrt{E((r_t - \mu)^2 | r_t < \mu)}; \ \hat{\theta}_p = \sqrt{\frac{\sum_{t=1}^{n}(r_t - \mu)^2 I(r_t < \mu)}{n_- - 1}} \quad (8.4)$$

$$\text{where } n_- = \sum_{t=1}^{n} I(r_t < \mu). \quad (8.5)$$

There is one tricky point with semideviation: there is disagreement on the divisor. On the one hand, some would use n or $n - 1$ so that the semideviation decomposes the standard deviation into upside and downside components which sum to the standard deviation. On the other hand, some suggest that when we compute an average we divide by the relevant degrees of freedom: the number of observations we used n_- less any numbers estimated (like the mean).

Semideviation is not the best risk measure, but it is better than volatility in many ways. It is also good, when compared to volatility, at showing whether a manager has any market timing ability: a good manager would avoid downside and thus have a more attractive semideviation.

8.3 Coherent Risk Measures

The problem with VaR is that it omits a key idea: When returns are bad, how bad are they?

Imagine you asked somebody about their year and they told you their 18-th worst day (the 5-th percentile of 365 days). Maybe on that day they tripped and hit their toe on the bed or overslept. Now consider the days worse than that 18-th worst day. If those worse days were minor (lost a few dollars, fell down when cycling) you might conclude they did not have a bad year. However, if those worse days included wrecking their car and their home burning down you might conclude they had a terrible year.

We need to know how bad other "bad" days are to form an opinion on if it was a bad year. Value-at-risk just tells us where our bad days *start*, not about all the other "bad" days. As one person has characterized it: it tells us the best of the worst; "the cream of the crap." That is not a good risk measure.

This became more clear when Artzner et al. laid out five axioms which they thought should hold for any risk measure. Artzner et al. (1997) proposed these axioms as properties of sensible risk measures and dubbed a risk measure which obeys these axioms as a **coherent risk measure**.

Suppose we have investments X and Y, cash γ which earns a risk-free rate r, and a risk measure ρ. The five axioms are:

1. **Translation Invariance**: cash lowers risk; $\rho(X + \gamma r) = \rho(X) - \gamma$.
2. **Subadditivity**: diversification may lower risk;
   $\rho(X_1 + X_2) \leq \rho(X_1) + \rho(X_2)$.
3. **Positive Homogeneity**: risk scales linearly; $\rho(\lambda X) = \lambda\rho(X)$.
4. **Monotonicity**: order preservation;
   If $r_X \leq r_Y$ stochastically (*i.e.* $F_X > F_Y$), then $\rho(X) \geq \rho(Y)$.
5. **Relevance**: no negative risk; $\rho(X) > 0$.

Thus having more cash, diversifying your holdings, and investing in instruments with higher returns should lower your risk; your risk cannot be negative; and, risk scales linearly with how much you hold.

There are certain scenarios where these may not hold. For example, positive homogeneity may not hold if liquidity is strained. The price impact incurred if one sells a large investment may be disproportionately larger than the impact from selling a small investment. This is because the larger order exhausts the limit order book. While a little patience would mitigate this greater impact, firms in distress do not always have time to be patient.

These axioms are also for financial risk measures where you cannot lose more than your initial investment. The ability to lose more than your initial investment is more like what is seen in insurance; insurance risk is much scarier. (We will see this when we discuss extreme value theory.)

As an example of an insurance-like risk, imagine a world without limited liability where participation in fraud is punished by execution. In that case, any investor in a firm which committed fraud could find themselves executed. In that sort of a world, diversification would be madness: the more firms you invest in, the greater the probability that one of the firms in your portfolio has committed fraud... and the greater the likelihood of your demise. Thus subadditivity can fail to reduce insurance-like risks.

With these axioms, we can see that VaR, semideviation, and variance all are not coherent. Another common measure, the maximum drawdown, is also not coherent even though it may govern whether a business lives or dies. Thankfully, Artzner et al. proposed a coherent risk measure. **Conditional value-at-risk** was the name of the measure they proposed; it is also known as **expected tail loss** or, most commonly, as **expected shortfall (ES)**. Expected shortfall directly answers the question, "When returns are bad, how bad are they?" Expected shortfall is simply the expected return below a given percentile. Thus the $\alpha\%$-ES is given by:

$$\alpha\text{-}ES = \text{Notional} \cdot E(r|r \leq \alpha\text{-VaR}) = \text{Notional} \cdot \frac{\int_{-\infty}^{F_r^{-1}(\alpha)} r f_r(u)du}{\alpha} \qquad (8.6)$$

We can compare the value-at-risk and expected shortfall using R and a t_5-distribution. The result of this comparison is shown in Figure 8.1. Note that the t_5 has variance $5/3$ so the VaR is 1.56 standard deviations below zero — less than the 5%-VaR for a normal distribution (1.64 standard deviations). However, the expected shortfall is greater: 2.24 standard deviations below zero for the t_5 versus 2.06 standard deviations below zero for the normal distribution.

```
alpha <- 0.05   # probability mass in the loss tail
t.df <- 5       # degrees of freedom for the t-distribution

# Calculate VaR (inverse CDF) and expected shortfall (numeric integration)
value.at.risk <- qt(alpha, df=t.df)
t5.mean.integrand <- function(x) { x*dt(x,t.df)}
ex.shortfall <- 1/alpha*integrate(t5.mean.integrand, lower=-Inf,
                              upper=value.at.risk)[["value"]]

curve(dt(x, t.df), xlim=c(-4,4), lwd=2)  # plot the t-distribution

# Setup for drawing a filled-in area under the curve
x.seq <- seq(-5, value.at.risk, 0.01)
y.seq <- dt(x.seq, t.df)
cord.x <- c(-5, x.seq, value.at.risk)
cord.y <- c(0, y.seq, 0)
polygon(cord.x, cord.y, col="plum1")  # and draw the filled-in area

abline(v=value.at.risk, lty=2, lwd=2, col="red")  # add a vertical line at the VaR
abline(v=ex.shortfall, lty=4, lwd=2, col="deepskyblue")   # add a vertical line at the ES
abline(h=0)
text(x=-2.015, y=0.05, "5%-VaR", pos=4)  # Add text notes near...
text(x=-2.890, y=0.01, "5%-ES", pos=4)   # ...the vertical lines
```

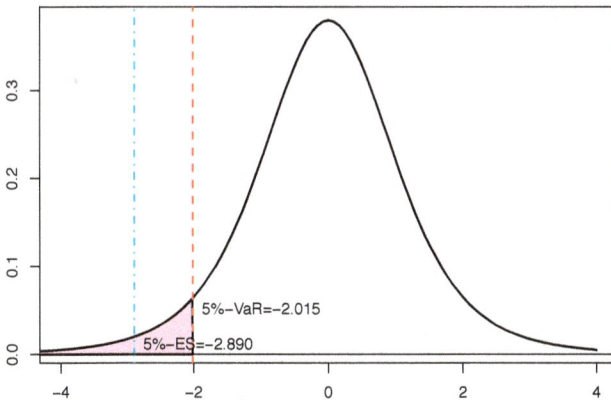

Figure 8.1: A t_5 density (not standardized to unit variance) with expected shortfall and value-at-risk. The 5%-ES is -2.890; the 5%-VaR is -2.015. Since the variance is $5/3$, the 5%-VaR and 5%-ES are -1.56 and -2.24 standard deviations from zero. For comparison, the normal distribution 5%-VaR and 5%-ES are -1.64 and -2.06 standard deviations from zero.

Expected shortfall is the best general measure of financial risk that we have: it is coherent, intuitive, and sensible. Inui and Kijima (2005) have even shown that it is the smallest-valued coherent risk measure and that other coherent risk measures are sums of expected shortfalls. Unfortunately, it is not required by regulators while VaR is. There is one other drawback which is common to expected shortfall, value-at-risk, and many other risk measures: we do not actually know the density of returns, f_r.

8.4   Risk versus Return

Now that we know a few risk measures, we can concoct metrics for risk-adjusted returns. In particular, we want to consider how much excess return we get per unit of risk. That suggests we look at ratios of risk premia to risk. Typically, we consider these metrics for a portfolio of instruments.

For a portfolio P, the **Sharpe ratio** S_p was first proposed by Sharpe (1966) and uses the volatility σ_P as the risk measure. Sortino and Price (1994) proposed the **Sortino ratio** So_P similarly, but substituting in the semideviation θ_P as the risk measure. Finally, we could also look at the **conditional Sharpe ratio** CS_P which uses expected shortfall ES_P as the risk measure. Note that all of these are calculated with annualized measurements.

$$S_p := \frac{E(r_p - r_f)}{\sigma_P}; \qquad So_p := \frac{E(r_P - r_f)}{\theta_p}; \qquad CS_p := \frac{E(r_p - r_f)}{ES_P}. \qquad (8.7)$$

Many texts will say that the Sharpe ratio and Sortino ratio are generally the same. While that may be true, it misses the point: we do not look at risk measures because they usually look good; we look at them so they can warn us about rare instances of danger.

Consider crossing a street. Most people look before they cross the street. Suppose you decide not to look because drivers will *surely* see you coming and stop so there is no difference between looking and not. This might generally be true: you might cross the street many times without injury. However, the one time you cross the street without looking and are hit by a car, you will wish you looked. Similarly, even though the Sharpe, Sortino, and conditional Sharpe ratio might *usually* give you the same message, you care about when they differ because that may signal (avoidable) danger.

We might also look at a higher threshold for adding value. The **information ratio** looks at risk-adjusted performance beyond some benchmark. The benchmark has a few common definitions as discussed in Kidd (2011): it could be some market index B or the part of returns unexplained by risk factors in a linear model, $r_P - r_f = \alpha + \beta r_{\text{risk factor}} + \epsilon$, in which case the model-excess return is α. However, the general idea of both is the average of abnormal returns per unit of uncertainty. For these definitions, the information ratio is:

$$IR_P = \frac{r_P - r_B}{\sqrt{\text{Var}(r_p - r_B)}} \qquad \text{or} \qquad IR_P = \frac{\alpha_P}{\sigma_\epsilon}, \qquad (8.8)$$

taking care to note that $\sigma_P \neq \sigma_\epsilon$. We could also substitute other risk measures in the denominator as was done above.

Finally, we could instead scale our investment down to the variability of some benchmark so as to compare the two. The **Modigliani-Modigliani** M^2 measure does just this. For a portfolio P and a benchmark B, M^2 is:

$$M_P^2 = E(r_P - r_f)\frac{\sigma_B}{\sigma_P} + r_f. \tag{8.9}$$

8.5 Density Estimation

If we do not know the density of returns f_r, how do we proceed with risk management? There are a few approaches we can take:

1. Use the empirical (*i.e.* historical) distribution;
2. Estimate a parametric distribution;
3. Approximate the density f_r with a kernel density estimator; or,
4. Use the measured moments in an asymptotic expansion.

We could also try to predict our worst loss, a topic we will explore in the following section.

8.5.1 The Empirical Distribution

If we use empirical distribution, we just use the historical returns. This is commonly done since computing the 5%-VaR is easy: sort the returns and find the maximum of the 5% lowest returns. Finding the 5%-ES is also easy: take the average of the 5% lowest returns. While common and simple, this is not the best we can do.

8.5.2 Parametric Distribution

To fit a parametric distribution, we first need to choose which distribution to use. This can be tricky since that assumption should match the data. For example, choosing the normal distribution might be a poor choice when the data display non-zero skewness or kurtosis that is not 3.

8.5.3 Kernel Density Estimation

A much better approach is to use a **kernel density estimator**: an estimate of the density function that smooths the observed data to account for the likelihood of observing values near those actually observed. A **kernel** K is a function that integrates to unity, is even, and has some adjustable **bandwidth** h: $K_h(x) = \frac{1}{h}K(x/h)$.

The most commonly-used kernel density estimator is that developed in Nadaraya (1964) and Watson (1964), the **Nadaraya-Watson estimator**:

$$\hat{Y} = E(Y|X = x) = \frac{\sum_{t=1}^{n} Y_t K_h(x - X_t)}{\sum_{t=1}^{n} K_h(x - X_t)}, \quad \text{or for a density,} \tag{8.10}$$

$$\hat{f} = E(f|X = x) = \frac{1}{nh} \sum_{t=1}^{n} K\left(\frac{x - X_t}{h}\right), \tag{8.11}$$

where X_t are the observed data having n observations. Obviously, it is easy to change the weights from $\frac{1}{n}$ if we feel certain points are more likely to be seen in the future.

There are a number of functions we can use for the kernel K. The uniform, $K(x) = I(|x| < \frac{1}{2})$, gives us a **histogram** and the Gaussian, $K(x) = \frac{1}{\sqrt{2\pi}} \exp(-x^2/2)$ gives a much smoother fit. We have neglected to specify the bandwidth h; however, we can estimate that as in Sheather and Jones (1991) or just use a value we feel is appropriate.

We can see this in Figure 8.2 using the following R code. Note that in R, the bandwidth is the standard deviation of the kernel and can be a number or, say, "SJ" for the Sheather and Jones bandwidth estimate.

```
t5.sd <- sqrt(5/3) # scaling factor to standardize t_5 distribution
desired.sd <- 0.02
scale.true <- desired.sd/t5.sd # scaling factor to get the desired sd

# left.frac of the random numbers will come from the left distribution
# the rest will come from the right distribution
left.frac <- 3/5
n.obs <- 50
x.obs <- c(rt(n.obs*left.frac, df=5)*scale.true-0.05,
           rt(n.obs*(1-left.frac), df=5)*scale.true+0.05)

# create values of the true density
x <- seq(-0.15, 0.15, by=0.001)
true.density <- left.frac*dt((x+0.05)/scale.true,df=5)/scale.true +
    (1-left.frac)*dt((x-0.05)/scale.true, df=5)/scale.true
y.max = max(true.density)

# plot the kernel density estimator; then add the true density
plot(density(x.obs, kernel="gaussian", bw="SJ"), main="",
     xlim=c(-0.15,0.15), ylim=c(0,y.max), lwd=2, col="red")
lines(x, true.density, lty=2, lwd=2)
rug(x.obs)  # show the observations as ticks at plot bottom
```

One problem with this estimator, however, is that unless we supply a kernel with heavy tails, our estimated density will still have the non-heavy tails of the normal distribution. That might be OK, but any kernel we use has an implicit assumption of the tail behavior.

8.5.4   Asymptotic Expansions

Another approach is to use an asymptotic expansion. These are approximating series

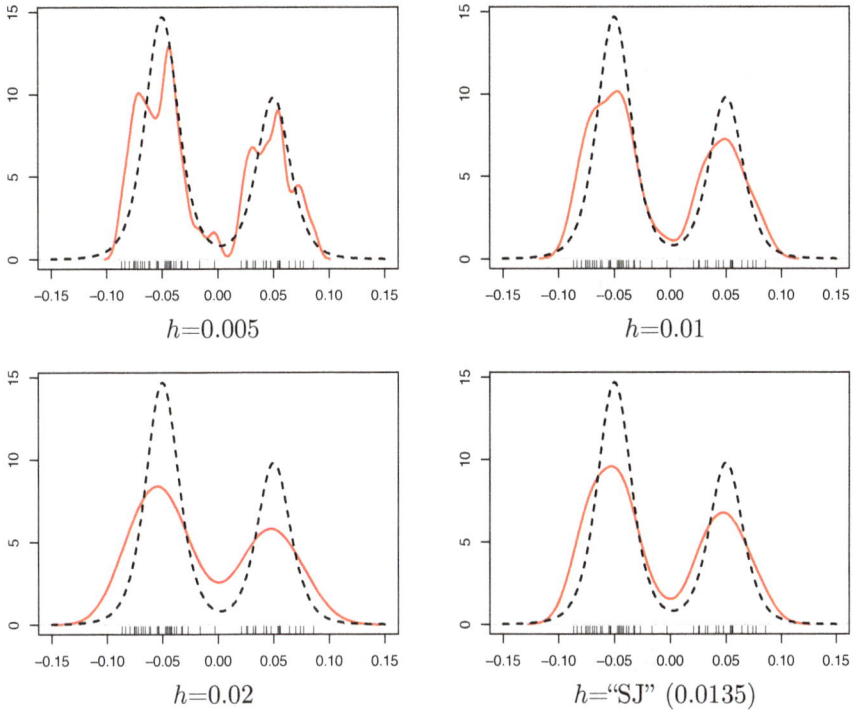

Figure 8.2: Kernel density estimates (red solid lines) for various bandwidths along with the true density (black dashed line) and the 50 simulated points, shown on the rug plot above the x-axis.

which use the moments to perturb standard densities or distribution functions to get a better-fitting density or distribution.

The **Edgeworth expansion** uses a Taylor series expansion of a density's cumulant generating function (a function which is isomorphic to the density).[1] While the expansion is typically close to the density, it can diverge. Therefore, a finite number of terms are often used — usually the $O(n^{-1/2})$ and $O(n^{-1})$ terms.[2] Most densities have cumulant generating functions which are not easy to work with; therefore, the expansion is usually done around the normal distribution. This yields

---

[1]While the original work was by Edgeworth (1883), modern readers will likely find Kolassa (2006) a more readable introduction.

[2]The n here refers to the number of summands in a sum or average. The fact that we are just using these expansions for random data might be considered slightly dodgy by conservative statisticians.

the approximation:

$$\hat{f}_r(z) = \frac{\phi(z)}{\sigma} \left[1 + \frac{\gamma(z^3 - 3z)}{6} + \frac{(\kappa - 3)(z^4 - 6z^2 + 3)}{24} \right.$$
$$\left. + \frac{\gamma^2(z^6 - 15z^4 + 45z^2 - 15)}{72} \right] + O(n^{-3/2}) \tag{8.12}$$

where $\phi(z)$ is the standard normal pdf and $z = (r - \mu)/\sigma$.

Thankfully, the EQL package implements the Edgeworth expansion. Using it to fit an Edgeworth expansion is fairly straightforward:

```
library(EQL)

# calculate moments to pass to Edgeworth expansion
mean.obs <- mean(x.obs)
var.obs <- var(x.obs)
skew.obs <- skewness(x.obs, method="moment")*n.obs/(n.obs-2)
exkurt.obs <- kurtosis(x.obs, method="moment")*n.obs/(n.obs-3)-3

# create the Edgeworth expansion. Since we have moments, we
# do this for a "sum" with 1 term.
edge.expand <- edgeworth(x, 1, rho3=skew.obs, rho4=exkurt.obs,
                    mu=mean.obs, sigma2=var.obs, type="sum")

# without EQL, we would have to do this:
dedge <- function(x) {
    z <- (x-mean.obs)/sqrt(var.obs)
    dnorm(z)*(1 + skew.obs*(z^3-3*z)/6 + exkurt.obs*(z^4-6*z^2+3)/24
            + skew.obs^2*(z^6-15*z^4+45*z^2-15)/72)/sqrt(var.obs)
}
```

One problem with Edgeworth expansions is that they are not true densities. While the expansion integrates to 1, it can take on negative values. Figure 8.3 shows Edgeworth expansions for data from the kernel density estimation example (a bimodal mixture of t-densities) and a mixture of a t- and Gamma-density. The expansion does not capture the bimodality; however, this is not surprising since we are expanding around a unimodal distribution (the normal). Unfortunately, both expansions assume some negative values.

A related asymptotic expansion is that of Cornish and Fisher (1938) for the quantile (inverse cdf) function. The **Cornish-Fisher expansion** for the inverse cdf, expanding about the normal, is given by:

$$\hat{F}_r^{-1}(p) = \mu + \sigma \left[q_N + \gamma\frac{q_N^2 - 1}{6} + (\kappa - 3)\frac{q_N^3 - 3q_N}{24} \right.$$
$$\left. - \gamma^2\frac{2q_N^3 - 5q_N}{36} \right] + O(n^{-3/2}), \tag{8.13}$$

where $q_N = \Phi^{-1}(p)$, the inverse of the standard normal cdf.

Unfortunately, the Cornish-Fisher expansion can suffer from similar issues to the Edgeworth expansion: it does not always yield a one-to-one mapping from quantiles to variable values. While there are ways to handle this, many of those

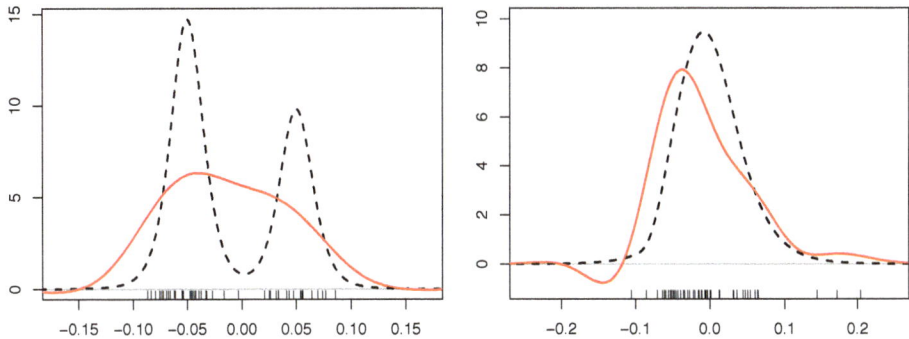

Figure 8.3: Edgeworth expansions of order $O(n^{-1})$ about the normal distribution (solid red lines) and the true density (black dashed line). The left expansion is for the t-mixture data from the kernel density estimation example. The expansion, using unimodal densities, tries hard to represent the bimodality but fails. The right expansion is for the mixture density $\frac{1}{2}t_5 + \frac{1}{2}(Gamma(5,50) - 0.1)$. For an approximation built on only four centered moments, it performs well. Unfortunately, both expansions assume negative values.

have other problems. Nonetheless, the **PerformanceAnalytics** package can use the Cornish-Fisher expansion to estimate VaR and expected shortfall based on work in Boudt, Peterson, and Croux (2008).

Asymptotic expansions might seem less attractive than kernel density estimators or parametric estimators since they can assume negative values. Furthermore, if we try to fix that by expanding about the log-density, those expansions have a tendency to explode in the tails. Nonetheless, these expansions can sometimes yield powerful results, especially considering that they only consider a handful of centered moments.

8.6 Extreme Value Theory

We have been trying to estimate densities to estimate the expected shortfall so we can ascertain our risk. However, there is a path-dependency: if we suffer a severe enough return, we are out of business. Therefore, we should probably also consider the question: What is the worst return we should expect to see?

8.6.1 The Theory Behind EVT

We can start by thinking about the maximum X, often called the **order statistic** $X_{(n)}$, of n iid random variables. If we can find the maximum of X_i, the minimum is just $-\max(-X_i)$. The maximum has a density like picking one variable x_i to be the maximum and the other $n - 1$ to be less than or equal to x_i. Since the variables are iid, they are exchangeable and so there are n possible variables (x_i's) which could be the maximum. If the variables all have pdf f and cdf F, the maximum has pdf and cdf:

$$f_{(n)}(x) = nP(x_j \leq x_i = x \forall j \neq i) f(x_i = x) = nF(x)^{n-1} f(x) \qquad (8.14)$$

$$F_{(n)}(x) = \int f_{(n)}(x) dx = P(x_i < x \forall i) = F^n(x). \qquad (8.15)$$

You can even generalize this if you think about the order statistics like coming from coin flips: $X_{(k)}$ has $k - 1$ vars below and $n - k$ above; n possibilities for which variable is the k-th order statistic; and, $\binom{n-1}{k-1}$ combinations of the other $n - 1$ variables to be lower than $X_{(k)}$. Thus:

$$f_{(k)}(x) = \binom{n-1}{k-1} nF(x)^{k-1} f(x)(1 - F(x))^{n-k}. \qquad (8.16)$$

Unfortunately, integrating over these densities can get complicated. Furthermore, we have to make some strong assumptions — like knowing the density f. To get around the need to assume the density, we can use **extreme value theory** to model the expected worst case.[3]

The **Fisher-Tippett Theorem** states that we can find a limit that converges in distribution to a maximal random variable M or (more intuitively) that the maximum cdf converges to a worst-case distribution H:

$$\lim_{n \to \infty} c_n^{-1}(X_{(n)} - d_n) \xrightarrow{D} M, \text{ or,} \qquad (8.17)$$

$$\lim_{n \to \infty} P(c_n^{-1}(X_{(n)} - d_n) < x) = \lim_{n \to \infty} F^n(c_n x - d_n) = H(x), \qquad (8.18)$$

where c_n and d_n are constants which depend on n and the distribution F. Furthermore, H falls into a **maximal domain of attraction** which is one of three families of limiting distributions. The maximal domain of attraction depends on the properties of F; thus we also say that F is in that domain.

1. Bounded/thin-tailed returns F: $H \sim$ Weibull; $H(x) = e^{-(-x)^\alpha} I_{x<0}$;
2. Moderately-tailed returns F: $H \sim$ Gumbel; $H(x) = e^{-e^{-x}}$; and,
3. Heavy-tailed returns F: $H \sim$ Fréchet; $H(x) = e^{-x^{-\alpha}} I_{x>0}$.

The normal, lognormal, and logistic distributions belong to the Gumbel domain; however, the t-distribution belongs to the Fréchet domain. How do we figure out which domain we are in and estimate the maximum? We start by generalizing these families to one distribution and then let the data suggest which domain we are in.

---

[3]This section is inspired by Jostein Paulsen's notes which were my first introduction to extreme value theory. The notation may differ a little from other sources, but the math is equivalent.

To generalize, we define the **generalized extreme value distribution**:

$$H_\xi(x) = \begin{cases} e^{-(1+\xi x)^{-1/\xi}} & \xi \neq 0, 1 + \xi x > 0 \\ e^{-e^{-x}} & \xi = 0, \end{cases} \tag{8.19}$$

where $\xi > 0$ implies a Fréchet distribution and $\xi < 0$ implies a Weibull distribution.

We can then make use of a similar distribution, the **generalized Pareto distribution**:

$$G_\xi(x) = \begin{cases} 1 - (1 + \xi x)^{-1/\xi} & \xi \neq 0, 1 + \xi x > 0 \\ 1 - e^{-x} & \xi = 0. \end{cases} \tag{8.20}$$

We also note that $G_\xi = 1 + \log(H_\xi(x)) \approx H(x)$ — except that G_ξ is simpler to work with. That eases the estimation of ξ.

There are many ways to estimate ξ: maximum likelihood and fraction of points over a threshold are two common ways. The first method uses the generalized extreme value distribution (with location and scale parameters added to shift and stretch the distribution); the second method uses the generalized Pareto distribution and also estimates a scaling parameter. Both of these are implemented in the R `evir` package. Those wanting the full details (and more) should consult Embrechts, Klüppelberg, and Mikosch (2011).

8.6.2 *EVT and Robust Optimization*

We have just used some very complicated statistics. There is a tendency after spending that much time on something to want it to work. That desire can distract us from larger issues. For example: is it realistic to think returns are all from same distribution? No, it is not. First, we know the market has certain states: volatile versus tranquil at the very least, as shown in Boudt, Paulus, and Rosenthal (2017). Second, distributions change as more people enter a trading strategy.

If somebody attempts to replicate your strategy, your trading plus their trading (possibly racing against you for better prices) will affect the market. Your trades will seem to have greater price impact because they are often accompanied by other trades in the same direction. Furthermore, you and the copycats probably have similar risk tolerances. Some days you all make money, some days you all lose money. Suppose one of those days you all lose money and the loss is enough that one of the copycats exits their positions. That will cause you and everyone else (with similar positions) to lose more money. That may trigger another exit and so on. In the worst case, these can cascade and lead to a crisis. (We will explore this idea further in Chapter 26.) Simply put: copycat traders alter the mean, volatility, and tails — the distribution — of your returns.

Worse than the above, however, is if malevolence enters the scenario. What if somebody tries to exploit your weakness or that of those copying you? They might surmise that they could cause a loss and trigger a cascade of panic selling; that could then allow them to enter your positions cheaply and make money as prices return to their prior levels. This is not hypothetical: Lefèvre (1923) details the manipulations and bear raids of the early 1900s; and, Goodwin (1987) discusses how Joseph Kennedy made his fortunes in such bear raids.

When somebody tries to exploit your weakness, you then leave the world of randomness and move into game theory. **Robust optimization** studies optimal behavior when under attack. Unfortunately, while robust optimization is an entire area of research, the findings tend to be consistent: any defense you mount will be very weak. Most results effectively say that if someone wants to hurt you, they probably can.

What this suggests is crucial. First, we should not be too reliant on extreme value theory or any other risk management methodology. Second, this implies there is a certain maximal trade size. If you grow beyond that size, you may be OK. However, in a crisis your death cannot be stopped; you will die exiting the trade, whether due to an inability to exit or due to price impact sealing your doom. Third, this is another reason to never publicize your trading strategy or positions.

8.7   From Density Measures to Risk Measures

With the above density estimates, we can try to estimate risk measures. To do this, we examine the two samples of data from above: one from a bimodal mixture of t-distributions and the other from a unimodal mixture of a t- and gamma distribution (shifted left to preserve mean 0):

$$f_X(x) = \frac{3}{5}t_5\left(\frac{x+0.05}{0.02/\sqrt{5/3}}\right)\frac{\sqrt{5/3}}{0.02} + \frac{2}{5}t_5\left(\frac{x-0.05}{0.02/\sqrt{5/3}}\right)\frac{\sqrt{5/3}}{0.02}, \qquad (8.21)$$

$$f_Y(y) = \frac{1}{2}t_5\left(\frac{y\sqrt{5/3}}{0.05}\right)\frac{\sqrt{5/3}}{0.05} + \frac{1}{2}\gamma_{k=5,\lambda=50}(y-0.1). \qquad (8.22)$$

From these we sample 50 observations (as shown above in Section 8.5.3, see Figure 8.2). The resulting central moments are listed in Table 8.1. In the following subsections, we will see how to estimate risk measures (both good and bad) for these data. In the interest of brevity, I will only show the code for estimating the bimodal X risk measures.

8.7.1   Empirical

The empirical distribution estimates are easy: find the α-quantile and the average of returns below that. For the bimodal data:

```
alpha <- 0.05  # probability mass in the loss tail
# sort the data; grab the lowest alpha fraction of the data
sorted.x.obs <- sort(x.obs)
frac.idx <- length(sorted.x.obs)*alpha
left.idx <- floor(frac.idx)
```

Distribution	Mean	Var.	Skew.	Ex. Kurt.
Bimodal t mix (f_X)	-0.0120	0.0029	0.3270	-1.3576
Unimodal t,γ mix (f_Y)	-0.0001	0.0037	1.3816	2.6460

Table 8.1: Sample central moments for observed data from the bimodal t mixture and the unimodal t+gamma mixture distributions. Note that the bimodal distribution has a negative excess kurtosis (kurtosis <3) while the unimodal distribution has positive skewness and positive excess kurtosis.

```
# VaR is linearly interpolated between points
rfrac <- 1-(frac.idx-left.idx)
VaR.emp <- sorted.x.obs[left.idx:(left.idx+1)] %*% c(1-rfrac, rfrac)

# ES is just the average of the observed data in the tail
es.emp <- mean(sorted.x.obs[1:left.idx])
```

8.7.2 Parametric

For the normal distribution, we can find the VaR using the inverse standard normal cdf; and, with a little work, we can find the expected shortfall using that and the standard normal density:

$$\alpha\text{-}VaR = \mu + \sigma\Phi^{-1}(\alpha) \tag{8.23}$$

$$\alpha\text{-}ES = \mu - \sigma\frac{\phi(\Phi^{-1}(\alpha))}{\alpha}. \tag{8.24}$$

This is easily implemented in R:

```
VaR.norm <- mean.obs + sqrt(var.obs)*qnorm(alpha)
es.norm <- mean.obs - sqrt(var.obs)*dnorm(qnorm(alpha))/alpha
```

If we want to instead use a t-distribution, we need to estimate the degrees of freedom ν and then use the formula:

$$\alpha\text{-}ES = \mu + \sigma\frac{f(F^{-1}(\alpha))}{\alpha} \cdot \frac{\nu - 2 + [F^{-1}(\alpha)]^2}{\nu - 1}. \tag{8.25}$$

Estimating the degrees of freedom for a t-distribution by maximum likelihood can run into issues: the likelihood function may be unbounded. To get around that, we can use the moment condition that the excess kurtosis for a t_ν distribution is $\frac{6}{\nu-2}$. Unfortunately, for the bimodal data, the excess kurtosis is negative — so a t-distribution fit is infeasible. For the unimodal data, we get an estimated degrees of freedom of $\hat{\nu} = 4.48$. Computing the value-at-risk and expected shortfall is easy for the unimodal mixture since the gamma contribute no mass to the left tail.

8.7.3   Kernel Density

For the kernel density estimate, we have many x values beyond those observed, so we use those to integrate numerically:

```
# create the kernel density estimate
kde <- density(x.obs, kernel="gaussian", bw="SJ")

# now create numerical CDF
int.kde <- cumsum(kde$y)/sum(kde$y)

# Find where alpha is in loss tail
left.idx <- findInterval(alpha, int.kde)

# linearly interpolate to find VaR
rfrac <- (alpha-int.kde[left.idx])/(int.kde[left.idx+1]-int.kde[left.idx])
VaR.kde <- kde$x[left.idx:(left.idx+1)] %*% c(1-rfrac, rfrac)

# numerically integrate kernel density estimate to get ES (a bit hacky)
es.kde <- kde$x[1:left.idx] %*% kde$y[1:left.idx]/sum(kde$y)/alpha
```

8.7.4   Edgeworth

For the Edgeworth expansion, we can use the properties of the Hermite polynomials to easily find the integral for the expansion previously given:

$$\int_{-\infty}^{q} \hat{f}_r(z)dz = \Phi(q) - \phi(q)\left(\gamma\frac{q^2+1}{6} + (\kappa-3)\frac{q^3-3q}{24}\right.$$
$$\left. +\gamma^2\frac{q^5-10q^3+15q}{72}\right). \tag{8.26}$$

We can also use the recursion $\int z^{n+1}\phi(z)dz = -z^n\phi(z) + n\int z^{n-1}\phi(z)dz$ to find the expectation of the Edgeworth expansion:

$$\int_{-\infty}^{q} z\hat{f}_r(z) = -\phi(q)\left(1 + \gamma\frac{q^3}{6} + (\kappa-3)\frac{q^4-2q^2-1}{24}\right.$$
$$\left. +\gamma^2\frac{q^6-9q^4+9q^2+3}{72}\right). \tag{8.27}$$

Then we can just find the point where the area "under" the left tail of the standardized expansion is α:

$$\alpha\text{-}VaR = q_\alpha = \inf\{q|\int_{-\infty}^{q}\hat{f}_r(z)dz = \alpha\}. \tag{8.28}$$

In R, we can do this (remembering to correct for the location and scale changes) with these functions and shifting the distribution down to find where it equals α:

```
# this function returns the "CDF" of the Edgeworth expansion
int.left.edge <- function(q, mu, sigma, skew=0, exkurt=0) {
  z <- (q-mu)/sigma
  pnorm(z) - dnorm(z)*(skew*(z^2+1)/6 + exkurt*(z^3-3*z)/24
```

```
                              + skew^2*(z^5-10*z^3+15*z)/72)
}

# returns the "conditional expectation" of the Edgeworth expansion
exp.left.edge <- function(q, mu, sigma, skew=0, exkurt=0) {
  z <- (q-mu)/sigma
  mu - sigma/alpha*dnorm(z)*(1 + skew*(z^3)/6 + exkurt*(z^4-2*z^2-1)/24
                             + skew^2*(z^6-9*z^4+9*z^2+3)/72)
}

# Find the point where the area under the left tail equals alpha
# Do this by shifting the integral down by alpha to find where it
# crosses zero (i.e. where the integral equals alpha)
int.left.edge.shifted <- function(q) {
  int.left.edge(q, mean.obs, sqrt(var.obs), skew.obs, exkurt.obs) - alpha
}
find.VaR <- uniroot(int.left.edge.shifted, check.conv = TRUE,
                    lower=-1, upper=mean.obs)

# The VaR is that point; the ES is the integral up to that point
VaR.edge.exact <-find.VaR$root
es.edge.exact <- exp.left.edge(VaR.edge.exact, mean.obs, sqrt(var.obs),
                               skew.obs, exkurt.obs)
```

Of course, we could also approximate that numerically with the Edgeworth expansion we created:

```
# Alternately, just use numeric integration on the Edgeworth
# expansion points we got from the moments

# create numeric "CDF"
int.edge <- cumsum(edge.expand$approx)/sum(edge.expand$approx)

# linearly interpolate to find VaR
left.idx <- which(int.edge>alpha)[1] - 1
rfrac <- (alpha-int.edge[left.idx])/(int.edge[left.idx+1]-int.edge[left.idx])
VaR.edge.num <- edge.expand$y[left.idx:(left.idx+1)] %*% c(1-rfrac, rfrac)

# numerically integrate Edgeworth expansion to get ES
es.edge.num <- edge.expand$y[1:left.idx] %*% edge.expand$approx[1:left.idx]/
    sum(edge.expand$approx)/alpha
```

8.7.5   Modified Cornish-Fisher

If we use the modified Cornish-Fisher expansion in **PerformanceAnalytics**, finding the VaR and expected shortfall is easy:

```
VaR.cornfish <- VaR(x.obs, p=0.05, method="modified", mu=mean.obs, sigma=var.obs,
                    m3=skew.obs, m4=exkurt.obs)
es.cornfish <- ES(x.obs, p=0.05, method="modified", mu=mean.obs, sigma=var.obs,
                  m3=skew.obs, m4=exkurt.obs)
```

8.7.6   Extreme Value Theory

While extreme value theory is mostly used for estimating expected worst-case returns, we can also use it to estimate VaR and expected shortfall. This is easy with the **evir** *R* package.

```
library(evir)

#evir package looks at upper tail, so flip returns
x.neg.obs <- -x.obs

# First, work with the generalized extreme value distribution
gev.model <- gev(x.neg.obs, block=23)
q.gev <- function(p) {
  -1*qgev(1-p, xi=gev.model$par.ests[["xi"]],
                mu=gev.model$par.ests[["mu"]],
                sigma=gev.model$par.ests[["sigma"]])
}
VaR.gev <- q.gev(alpha)  # use evir function
# a bit hacky: numerically integrate CDF to get ES
es.gev <- mean(q.gev(seq(0.001, alpha, 0.001)))

# Next, work with the generalized Pareto distribution
gpd.model <- gpd(x.neg.obs, nextremes=5)
riskmeasures(gpd.model, c(0.95))
```

For the bimodal data, the generalized extreme value distribution and generalized Pareto distribution calculate tail indices of $\hat{\xi}_{GEV} = -2.16$ and $\hat{\xi} = -1.26$. For the unimodal data, we get estimated tail indices of $\hat{\xi}_{GEV} = -0.04$ and $\hat{\xi} = -0.36$.

8.7.7 Comparison of Methods

We can now compare the various methods to the true VaR and expected shortfall. The true values are given by:

```
# now create the exact CDF
t.df <- 5
p.t <- function(q) {
  z1 <- (q+0.05)/desired.sd*t5.sd
  z2 <- (q-0.05)/desired.sd*t5.sd
  pt(z1, df=5)*3/5 + pt(z2, df=5)*2/5
}

# shift CDF down to find the point where alpha is in the loss tail
p.t.quantile <- uniroot(function(q) p.t(q)-alpha, check.conv=TRUE,
                        lower=-1, upper=mean.obs)
VaR.true <- p.t.quantile$root

# function finds ES for a t-distribution to left of quantile q
es.t <- function(q) {
  -dt(qt(q, df=t.df), df=t.df)/q*(t.df-2+qt(q, df=t.df)^2)/(t.df-1)
}

# ES calculation is crusty: we found point for alpha in loss tail.
# Now find ES for both t-distributions; then find average of them
q1 <- pt((VaR.true+0.05)/desired.sd*t5.sd, df=t.df)
q2 <- pt((VaR.true-0.05)/desired.sd*t5.sd, df=t.df)
es.true <- (3/5*es.t(q1) + 2/5*es.t(q2))*desired.sd/t5.sd - 0.01
```

Table 8.2 lists the various methodologies and their values for the 5%-VaR and 5%-expected shortfall. Obviously, for only 50 observations there will be a lot of noise in any estimates. Furthermore, estimating risk measures for a mixture of *t*-distributions is probably one of the more challenging tasks: while the tail behavior is fat-tailed, the kurtosis is low due to the bimodality. This is why many of the methods based on unimodal densities (all but the kernel density estimator) overestimate the risk. With most financial returns being unimodal, these methods are far less likely to overestimate the risk.

Methodology	Bimodal t mix		Unimodal $t + \gamma$ mix	
	5%-VaR	5%-ES	5%-VaR	5%-ES
True	-7.51%	-8.83%	-5.72%	-8.72%
Empirical Distribution	-8.15%	-8.50%	-7.81%	-9.56%
Parametric – Normal	-10.14%	-12.41%	-10.10%	-12.64%
Parametric – t	—	—	-9.96%	-11.32%
Kernel Density Estimate	-8.59%	-9.35%	-8.61%	-10.03%
Edgeworth – Exact	-9.40%	-12.54%	-5.82%	-22.23%
Edgeworth – Numeric	-9.96%	-10.41%	-7.85%	-6.50%
Modified Cornish-Fisher	-9.72%	-10.46%	-7.24%	-11.18%
Generalized Extreme Value	-8.65%	-8.65%	-11.34%	-13.05%
Generalized Pareto	-8.11%	-8.41%	-7.52%	-8.95%

Table 8.2: Comparison of 5%-value-at-risk and 5%-expected shortfall as computed using various methods. The data are sampled from two mixture distributions: $[\frac{3}{5}t_5(x + 0.05) + \frac{2}{5}t_5(x - 0.05)] \cdot \frac{0.01}{\sqrt{5/3}}$ and $\frac{1}{2}t_5 + \frac{1}{2}(Gamma(5, 50)(x - 0.1))$. Given that these have low kurtosis but heavy tails, they are challenging distributions to fit. We can note that the empirical and extreme value theory-based Generalized Pareto methods worked well.

If we look at these calculations, a few salient details stand out. First, the empirical distribution does not do poorly for a small dataset. The methods that are based on unimodal densities (parametric normal, Edgeworth, Cornish-Fisher) can overstate the risk when handling a bimodal distribution. The Edgeworth-based expansions can also yield very strange results like the expected shortfall being less that the value-at-risk for the numerical integration. (Since the expected shortfall is the average of returns beyond value-at-risk, this should never happen.) This is caused by the negative tail behavior in the left tail for the unimodal data. Were we to integrate over a much larger range, that would go away; however, that makes calculating expectations a manual process. The Cornish-Fisher results are much more stable, part of why they feature in the `PerformanceAnalytics` R package.

Finally, the extreme value theory-based estimates also do very well. This is a bit surprising since there are multiple levels of approximation to get at the tail behavior. However, since those methods are designed to model tail behavior, the intermediate approximations seem justified.

It also bears repeating that value-at-risk is not a good risk measure. It is shown here to get a flavor for the variation in VaR estimates; however, this should not be taken as an endorsement of VaR. If that is not crystal clear, please re-read Section 8.1 to see how badly value-at-risk can fail.

8.8   Convergence Matters

One of the topics rarely discussed, even in econometrics, is modes of statistical convergence and their practical meanings. Modes of convergence matter greatly and explain the difference between easy risk management and very difficult risk management.

As a refresher, there are a few forms of convergence we often deal with: convergence in distribution, convergence in probability, and convergence almost surely. This ordering goes from weak to strong, so convergence almost surely implies convergence in probability which implies convergence in distribution; however, the reverse are not true as we will see.

The most common mode of convergence underlies the Central Limit Theorem: **convergence in distribution**. If a sequence of variables or estimates converges in distribution, then we can find a shift and scaling so that the sequence has a stationary distribution. For example, the typical result we see for linear models like $Y = \alpha + \beta X + \eta$ with n observations used to estimate the model is:

$$\sqrt{n}(\hat{\beta}_n - \beta) \xrightarrow{\mathcal{L}} N(0, \sigma_\beta^2). \tag{8.29}$$

The $\mathcal{L}$ is sometimes written as a $\mathcal{D}$ and some will say the sequence converges in law or distribution. Both have the same meaning although "convergence in law" is an older term.

This suggests that $\hat{\beta}$ is asymptotically normal and centered around β. For linear models, this is the result of the **Gauss-Markov Theorem** and the assumptions are not very strong: the data should have a finite variance.

Convergence in probability is the mode of convergence underlying the **Weak Law of Large numbers**. Convergence in probability says that for some sequence of random variables or estimates, the probability of being far from some true value decreases to zero:

$$\lim_{n\to\infty} P(|\hat{\beta}_n - \beta| > \epsilon) = 0. \tag{8.30}$$

It is important to remember that our estimates will converge in probability for ordinary least squares (OLS); however, they may not converge in probability for some types of biased estimation like machine learning or the LASSO (if the penalty parameter is not sufficiently relaxed).[4]

Convergence almost surely is the strongest form of convergence out of these three and underlies the **Strong Law of Large Numbers**. Convergence almost surely says that the distance from the true value also decreases to zero:

$$P(\lim_{n\to\infty} \hat{\beta}_n = \beta) = 1. \tag{8.31}$$

Very little in finance converges almost surely.

The problem with these forms of convergence is that they drive how difficult risk

---

[4]If these do not mean anything to you yet, do not worry.

Moe 3%	5	-9	13	2	-10	-4	-6	1	-1	0	-4	-2	3	11	-2	1	6	-2
Joe 3%	-5	3	2	-5	2	2	1	1	-5	1	1	2	1	1	1	1	1.5	-5
Bo 3%	-5.5	2.5	1.5	-3	2.1	1.9	1	1.3	-1	1	0.8	2.2	1	1.1	1.1	1	1.1	0.

Table 8.3: Sequences of returns for Moe, Joe, and Bo showing convergence in distribution, probability, and almost surely. Note that the divergences (mostly losses) for Joe and Bo happen after increasingly long sequences of returns converging to 1% — and that Joe's divergences only get rarer and not smaller.

management is. For example, consider the three sequences of returns for Moe, Joe, and Bo in Table 8.3. Moe's returns are converging in distribution: they tend to be centered around zero, but they vary a lot and that variability does not decrease. Joe's returns are converging in probability: they are tending toward 1, but with decreasing frequency there is a return that is not converging toward 1. Big losses become rarer but they do not go away or become smaller. Bo's returns are converging almost surely: not only do they tend to 1, but the divergences are less common *and* decreasing. The "big" losses are getting rarer and smaller. We can see this graphically in Figure 8.4.

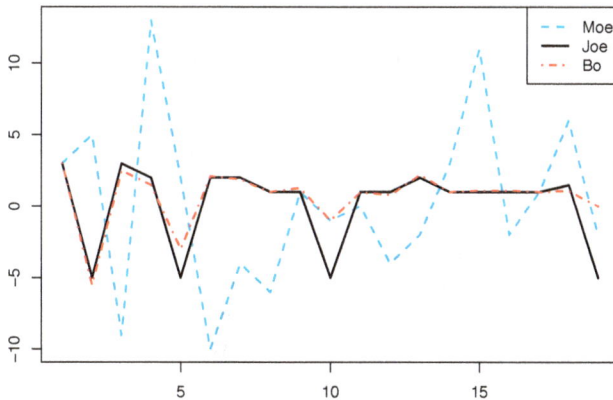

Figure 8.4: Sequences of returns for Moe, Joe, and Bo showing convergence in distribution (Moe, - -), probability (Joe, —), and almost surely (Bo, · — ·). Note that the divergences (mostly losses) for Joe and Bo happen after increasingly long sequences of returns converging to 1% — and that Joe's divergences only get rarer and not smaller.

Worse still: the world changes. Creative destruction regularly remakes industries; new technologies change costs and make price dynamics change. Thus it is hard to believe that there is "one true β" over any appreciable length of time. The truth is that these modes of convergence are our best-case scenarios over longer time frames and may be reasonable over short timeframes. This is why risk management is hard.

8.9   Other Risks

Finally, we would be remiss if we neglected to discuss other risks. Many of these are risks which are not easily quantified; however, that does not make them any less worth considering. If anything, these are areas which probably deserve more attention.

When dealing with risks, we should think about how easily they may be quantified and verified. Some risks are quantifiable and clear (*e.g.* being long 1 contract of near corn futures). Other risks are observable after a risk event occurs or time passes: for example, the losses due to defaults in a bond portfolio. These are the risks we can model and which we tend to address in finance texts.

However, other risks are more difficult to quantify. The estimates of risk may vary greatly depending on the model leading to so much uncertainty that the models (together) may add little value. The risk may be time-varying, such as for correlations across markets or between instruments. This can be especially problematic if the correlations change due to structural changes in the market, the market reassessing risk and/or risk aversion, or crisis dynamics (such as a firm reducing its risk). (We will discuss crisis dynamics in Chapter 26.)

Finally, the risks may be nearly impossible to quantify or model. This is the idea of **Knightian uncertainty**, the idea developed in Knight (1921) of uncertainty that we cannot model or know so little about that we cannot even calculate or approximate a risk measure.

Examples include the risk of models being inaccurate, operational risks (*i.e.* failures in business processes), break-ins and corporate espionage, or regulation. The best protection against model error is to never have too much faith in models in the first place (and especially not in any one model). That also means understanding the limits of a model and where it performs poorly.

The other risks fall into the category of non-market-related risks. Operational risk requires proper management and process monitoring; some firms use "Chinese walls" to separate some employees or require long vacations so that losses cannot be hidden. Physical premises and information security risks are best assessed and controlled subjectively with regular audits and sweeps. Finally, regulatory risk is probably best managed proactively by making sure self-regulation works and meeting with politicians to explain how the business works.

8.10   Quiz

Try to answer these questions in five minutes.

1. Value-at-risk is a risk measure which explains how bad extreme losses can be: T   F

2. A hedge fund manager says the strategy has a Sharpe ratio of 1.

 a) You ask for the Sortino ratio. Why?

 b) The manager says the Sortino ratio is 0.8. What does this tell you about returns?

3. Artzner, Delbaen, Eber, and Heath refer to good risk measures as being _____ _____.

4. A risk measure (as above) should show that:

 a) having more cash on hand (increases / has no effect on / decreases) the risk measure;

 b) a multiple of k times a position has _____ times the risk; and,

 c) the risk of a position in $X + Y$ is (> / ≥ / = / ≤ / <) the risk than the sum of risks of X and Y.

5. I look at the distribution of possible (expected) losses. I find the return such that 5% of my losses are worse. This number is called the _____ _____ and (is / is not) a good risk measure (as in the preceding question).

6. I then take the average of the 5% worst returns from the preceding question. This number is called the _____ and (is / is not) a good risk measure.

7. What do extreme value theory and robust optimization tell us we can do to avoid large losses if someone decides to "hunt" us?

8. How can we handle or deal with model risk?

9. I compute the standard deviation, but using only the returns which fall below the average. This is called the _____ and (is / is not) a good risk measure as above.

8.11   Exercises

You will need to download the following data from Quandl — a repository of public data. Tickers for Quandl are in parentheses. Use the code from previous chapter's exercises and the examples in this chapter.

 • Constant maturity US Treasuries: 3M, 2Y, 10Y, and 30Y (`FRED/DGS3MO`, `FRED/DGS2`, `FRED/DGS10`, `FRED/DGS30`)

- Eurodollar futures: near, two-years-out (Quandl tickers `CHRIS/CME_ED1` and `CHRIS/CME_ED8`)
- Indices: S&P 500, Russell 2000 from Yahoo via `quantmod`: `^GSPC`, `^RUT`
- "Group 1" stocks: from Yahoo via `quantmod`:
  PG, XOM, IBM, MMM, KO, GS, AXP, WMT, MRK, DIS, HD
- "Group 2" stocks: from Yahoo via `quantmod`:
  AAPL, CARB, CBRE, CZR, F, FBC, IMGN, IRDM, SBUX, SVU, SYMC, UPS, VLO
- Commodities near futures: WTI crude oil, US natural gas, copper, and corn (`CHRIS/CME_CL1`, `CHRIS/CME_NG1`, `CHRIS/CME_HG1`, `CHRIS/CME_C1`)

The bond data are yields, so they need to be rescaled to be on the same scale as log-returns (divide them by 100). The index and equity prices need to be corrected for splits and dividends (use the adjusted close field). Finally: Restrict your analysis to the past three years.

1. Re-assess the risk of these instruments as before; however, this time also compute the semideviation in addition to the first four central moments. Also compute the expected shortfall using the historical and modified Cornish-Fisher estimates.

2. Comment on the results. If you order the instruments by risk measures, which are ordered differently with different risk measures?

3. Knowing what you know now about risk, which of the instruments seem deceptively lower risk than they actually are?

References

Artzner, Philippe et al. "Thinking Coherently". *RISK* 10.November (1997), pp. 68–71.

Boudt, Kris, Ellen C. S. Paulus, and Dale W. R. Rosenthal. "Funding Liquidity, Market Liquidity and TED Spread: A Two-Regime Model". *Journal of Empirical Finance* 43 (2017), pp. 143–158. DOI: `10.1016/j.jempfin.2017.06.002`.

Boudt, Kris, Brian Peterson, and Christophe Croux. "Estimation and Decomposition of Downside Risk for Portfolios with Non-Normal Returns". *Journal of Risk* 11.2 (2008), pp. 79–103. DOI: `10.21314/jor.2008.188`.

Cornish, E. A. and R. A. Fisher. "Moments and Cumulants in the Specification of Distributions". *Revue de l'Institut International de Statistique / Review of the International Statistical Institute* 5.4 (1938), pp. 307–320. DOI: `10.2307/1400905`.

Edgeworth, Francis Ysidro. "On the Method of Ascertaining a Change in the Value of Gold". *Journal of the Statistical Society of London* 46.4 (1883), pp. 714–718. URL: `http://www.jstor.org/stable/2979314`.

Embrechts, Paul, Claudia Klüppelberg, and Thomas Mikosch. *Modelling Extremal Events: for Insurance and Finance*. Berlin: Springer-Verlag, 2011.

Goodwin, Doris Kearns. *The Fitzgeralds and the Kennedys: An American Saga*. New York: Simon & Schuster, 1987.

Inui, Koji and Masaaki Kijima. "On the Significance of Expected Shortfall as a Coherent Risk Measure". *Journal of Banking and Finance* 29.4 (2005), pp. 853–864. DOI: 10.1016/j.jbankfin.2004.08.005.

Kidd, Deborah. "The Sharpe Ratio and the Information Ratio". *Investment Performance Measurement* 2011.1 (2011), pp. 1–4. DOI: 10.2469/ipmn.v2011.n1.7.

Knight, Frank H. *Risk, Uncertainty, and Profit*. Boston: Hart, Schaffner & Marx, 1921.

Kolassa, Joe E. *Series Approximation Methods in Statistics*. 3rd ed. New York: Springer-Verlag, 2006.

Lefèvre, Edwin. *Reminiscences of a Stock Operator*. New York: Doubleday, Doran & Company, 1923.

Nadaraya, E. A. "On Estimating Regression". *Theory of Probability and its Applications* 9.1 (1964), pp. 141–142. DOI: 10.1137/1109020.

Peterson, Brian G. and Peter Carl. *PerformanceAnalytics: Econometric tools for performance and risk analysis*. R package version 1.4.3541. 2014. URL: https://CRAN.R-project.org/package=PerformanceAnalytics.

Pfaff, Bernhard and Alexander McNeil. *evir: Extreme Values in R*. R package version 1.7-3. 2012. URL: https://CRAN.R-project.org/package=evir.

Ryan, Jeffrey A. *quantmod: Quantitative Financial Modelling Framework*. R package version 0.4-8. 2017. URL: https://CRAN.R-project.org/package=quantmod.

Sharpe, William F. "Mutual Fund Performance". *Journal of Business* 39.1 (1966), pp. 119–138. DOI: 10.1086/294846.

Sheather, S. J. and M. C. Jones. "A Reliable Data-Based Bandwidth Selection Method for Kernel Density Estimation". *Journal of the Royal Statistical Society, Series B* 53.3 (1991), pp. 683–690. URL: http://www.jstor.org/stable/2345597.

Sortino, Frank A. and Lee N. Price. "Performance Measurement in a Downside Risk Framework". *Journal of Investing* 3.3 (1994), pp. 59–64. DOI: 10.3905/joi.3.3.59.

Thaler, Thorn. *EQL: Extended-Quasi-Likelihood-Function*. R package version 1.0-0. 2009. URL: https://CRAN.R-project.org/package=EQL.

Watson, Geoffrey S. "Smooth Regression Analysis". *Sankhyā: The Indian Journal of Statistics, Series A* 26.4 (1964), pp. 359–372. URL: http://www.jstor.org/stable/25049340.

Chapter 9

Diversification

> ⚠️ **Dikkat!** *This is a flawed chapter in nearly all investments texts — including this one. Balancing risk and returns is sensible, laudable even. However, the theory was developed on a flawed risk measure: volatility. We have just seen that neither volatility nor variance are coherent. While many of the qualitative insights still hold, the quantitative methods should be modified to use better risk measures. We will discuss this in Section 9.6 and in Chapter 24.*

Diversification is one of finance's two major risk-reduction technologies. Diversification also makes sense in the context of measurement: the theme of this part of the text. We know subadditivity implies that diversification may lower risk; and, Markowitz (1999) notes that diversification was long known to be beneficial. When Harry Markowitz and Andrew Roy analyzed investment returns, they realized that measures of risk should factor into most people's investment decisions. While this changed academic financial theory; Rutterford and Sotiropoulos (2016) document that UK investors hundreds of years ago diversified and considered correlations of their holdings. It is a bit surprising, therefore, to note how long there was a disconnect between practice and theory.

Nonetheless, diversification is clearly useful. Therefore, the goals of this chapter are to introduce the ideas of diversification; to determine how much of our portfolio to put at risk; and, to show the math behind why diversification works. A secondary goal of this chapter is to foreshadow how we might develop these ideas with other risk measures.

9.1 Introduction

Since risk matters, it is natural to ask how to best diversify. Markowitz (1952) and

Roy (1952) were the first works to analyze this question from a formal mathematical perspective and this led to Markowitz receiving the Nobel Prize in 1990.[1] Unfortunately, the technology available to them meant that they considered volatility as their risk measure.[2]

Mean-variance optimization uses a flawed risk measure, but this will not lead us too far astray. First, we will see that the ideas also hold for coherent risk measures. Second, the results are true for variances and covariances, regardless of the actual log-return distribution. Third, a second-order Taylor series approximation to the cumulant generating function uses the mean and squared volatility; so, we can view these results as an approximation. Finally, we explore these ideas because they are an active and important part of the heritage of quantitative finance.

Optimized portfolios are everywhere. Electricity producers own portfolios of generation technologies which adjust instantly, start quickly, or run cheaply to best meet changing demand. Petroleum refiners constantly optimize their output portfolio based on prices, volatilities, and the chemical makeup of the oil they process. Shippers optimize their portfolio of vehicles and the allocation of goods to vehicles to routes to customers. Airlines optimize the planes they use and flights offered. Even retailers optimize inventory to meet anticipated but uncertain demand.

9.2 Indifference Curves

Recall that the utility of an investment in instrument i for investor j with risk aversion λ_j was:[3]
$$\text{Utility} = U_{ij} = E(r_i) - \underbrace{\lambda_j \text{Risk}_i^\omega}_{\substack{\text{risk} \\ \text{penalty}}}. \tag{9.1}$$

We can rearrange this equation to see (for a constant utility) what expected returns investor j would demand from a portfolio P having different levels of risk. This yields an **indifference curve**:

$$E(r_P) = U + \lambda_j \text{Risk}_P^\omega \quad \omega > 1, \tag{9.2}$$

where $\omega > 1$ reflects the decreasing marginal utility of risk.

An indifference curve shows the levels of expected return and risk with which an investor would be **indifferent** (aka equally happy). The utility level U gives the **certainty equivalent** of these returns. For example, an indifference curve with

---

[1]Pedants will note that the prize is the Sveriges Riksbank Prize in Economic Sciences in Honor of Alfred Nobel and not one of Nobel's originally-endowed prizes. That is a minor quibble; Markowitz's and Roy's accomplishments are clearly worthwhile. Furthermore, even Markowitz has expressed surprise that Roy was not similarly honored.

[2]Sharpe (1964) reveals that Markowitz wanted to use a better risk measure than volatility, but it was computationally too difficult. Furthermore, coherency of risk measures would not be discovered for another 35 years.

[3]For those wondering: yes, it is likely that λ_j is related to ω.

$U = 0.04$ shows all of the combinations of expected return and risk which would be equally-valued as a guaranteed 4% return — by an investor j with risk aversion λ_j.

9.2.1   Mean-Variance Indifference Curves

Unfortunately, the risk aversion parameter λ_j varies with the risk measure used. Historically, finance has written the risk aversion as $\lambda/2$ and used volatility as the risk measure with $\omega = 2$. For now, we will continue in this historical vein to explore the ideas and results familiar to most investment professionals.

If we use variance as our risk measure, we can plot mean-variance indifference curves as a function of the volatility. Figure 9.1 shows example mean-variance indifference curves for varying levels of risk aversion and utility. Note that if our risk aversion parameter is $\lambda = 3$, we would be equally happy with any of:

- $E(r_P) = 0.04,\ \sigma_P^2 = 0$;
- $E(r_P) = 0.10,\ \sigma_P^2 = 0.04 \iff \sigma_P = 0.20$; or,
- $E(r_P) = 0.20,\ \sigma_P^2 = 0.10\bar{6} \iff \sigma_P = 0.327$.

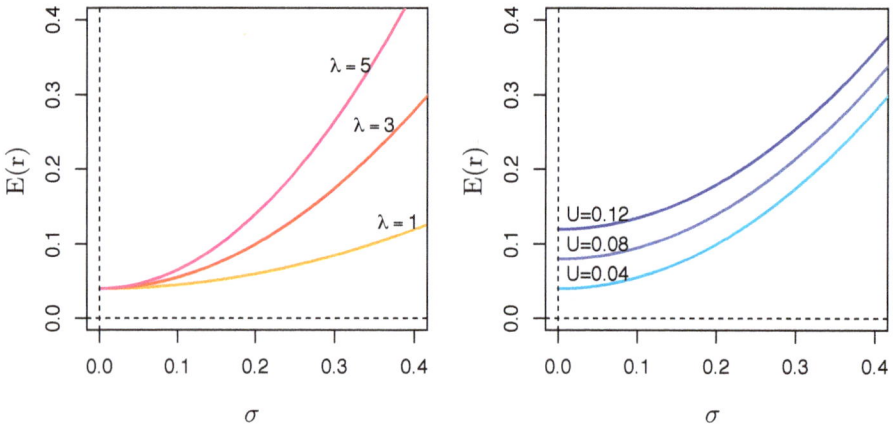

Figure 9.1: Indifference curves for mean-variance utility. The left plot shows indifference curves for a utility of 0.04 and varying levels of risk aversion: $\lambda \in \{1, 3, 5\}$. The right plot shows indifference curves for a risk aversion of $\lambda = 3$ and varying levels of utility: $U \in \{0.04, 0.08, 0.12\}$.

Whatever our λ is, we would prefer a portfolio on a higher indifference curve. However, not all combinations of expected return and risk are achievable; otherwise, everyone would pick high-return and no-risk portfolios. The benefit of utilities and indifference curves is that we can use them to choose our optimal portfolio of investments for what is feasible. We maximize our utility when choosing a portfolio by finding the indifference curve with the highest utility which is achievable with a portfolio.

Consider the three portfolios in Table 9.1: one with no risk, one with low risk, and one with high risk. As our risk aversion increases, we move from preferring the high-risk portfolio to the low-risk portfolio to, ultimately, the no-risk portfolio. This becomes more nuanced when we allow investors to split their money among portfolios — something we will explore shortly.

	Panel A:			
Risk	Risk Premium	$E(r_P)$	σ_P	
None	0%	4%	0%	
Low	2%	6%	8%	
High	8%	12%	20%	

	Panel B:		
λ	U(no-risk)	U(low-risk)	U(high-risk)
0	0.04 = 4%	6.00%	**12.00%**
2	4%	5.36%	**8.00%**
4	4%	**4.72%**	4.00%
6	4%	**4.08%**	0.00%
7	**4%**	3.76%	-2.00%

Table 9.1: Panel A shows three example portfolios with no, low, and high risk. Panel B shows the utilities of these for various risk aversions λ. The bolded entries are those preferred by an investor with that risk aversion.

9.2.2 What is Your Risk Aversion?

This raises another question: How do you know your risk aversion λ? It is difficult to know your λ precisely. Some texts claim to determine λ from simple laboratory tests using small bets and coin flips. Unfortunately, people respond differently when large amounts of their hard-earned money are at risk. Furthermore, we suspect that mean-variance risk aversions change with the level of risk in the market.[4]

What we do know is that common mean-variance λ's are in the 2–4 range. Firms with a lot of capital often invest as though they have a low or zero risk aversion; and, retail investors with little free cash often behave as thought they have a high risk aversion. Typically, people use a few values and then look at the results to determine which they prefer.

---

[4]Some might view the instability of risk aversion over time as evidence of using poor risk measures. An alternate view would be that large market moves attract enough attention from investors that they do Bayesian updating of their return assumptions.

9.3   Allocating Among Risky, Risk-Free Portfolios

We begin diversifying by splitting our portfolio into a risk-free subportfolio F and a risky subportfolio P. Putting these together yields the **complete portfolio** C.

9.3.1   Subportfolio Invariance

When we determine our allocations to portfolios, we generally assume that they are scaleable. If our analysis says to put \$X into risk-free assets, we would put \$2X into risk-free assets if we invest twice as much money.

This also holds inside each subportfolio. Suppose we hold \$100k of US T-bills, \$80k of corp bonds, and \$120k of equities. We are then invested $1/3$ in F, $2/3$ in P. If we instead allocated half of our of capital to each of F and P, we would hold \$150k of US T-bills, \$60k of corp bonds, and \$90k of equities. Note that as we change the allocation between F and P, *we do not change what is in F and P*.

9.3.2   The Capital Allocation Line

We want to allocate some fraction y of our investment to the risky portfolio P and the remainder $1 - y$ to F. The goal is to achieve a complete portfolio risk of Risk_C. Note that I have not constrained y to lie in $[0,1]$. (Many funds impose this constraint if they are prohibited from using leverage.)

Let r_P, r_f and Risk_P, Risk_f be the expected returns and risks of P and F. Then the expected return and risk of the complete portfolio C is:

$$E(r_C) = yE(r_P) + (1 - y)r_f \tag{9.3}$$

$$= r_f + y \underbrace{(E(r_P) - r_f)}_{\text{risk premium}} = r_f + yE(R_P), \tag{9.4}$$

$$\text{Risk}_C = y\text{Risk}_P. \tag{9.5}$$

Where did Risk_f go? We chose a risk-free portfolio to match our investment horizon. Therefore, there is no risk with r_f; Risk_f is zero. If the risk-free portfolio's tenor did not match our investment horizon, we would consider the price variability of the risk-free asset — and Risk_f would not be zero. This means that the preceding equations become:[5]

$$y = \frac{\text{Risk}_C}{\text{Risk}_P}, \text{ or for mean-variance utility, } y = \frac{\sigma_C}{\sigma_P}. \tag{9.6}$$

We call the line in equation (9.4) the **capital allocation line** (CAL). As we increase y, the complete portfolio transitions from the risk-free portfolio F when $y = 0$ to the risky portfolio P when $y = 1$ to a leveraged portfolio that is short F

---

[5]We will run into problems if we use an estimated volatility in equation (9.6).We will discuss that later in Chapter 24.

and long P for $y > 1$. Where we are on this line determines the allocation of capital between the risk-free and risky portfolios F and P.

9.3.3 Utility Along the Capital Allocation Line

The immediate question for a portfolio investor is "Where should I be on the capital allocation line?" We can restate this as: "What value of y makes me happiest?" While we targeted a specific amount of risk above, the optimal y maximizes utility (from equation (9.1)) along the CAL:

$$U^*_{\lambda_j} = \max_y U_\lambda(y) = E(r_C) - \lambda_j \text{Risk}^\omega_C \tag{9.7}$$

$$= r_f + y(E(r_P) - r_f) - \lambda_j y^\omega \text{Risk}^\omega_P; \text{ or, for variance,} \tag{9.8}$$

$$U^*_{\lambda_j} = \max_y U_\lambda(y) = E(r_C) - \frac{\lambda}{2}\sigma^2_C = r_f + y(E(r_P) - r_f) - \frac{\lambda}{2}y^2\sigma^2_P. \tag{9.9}$$

The function we optimize, in this case maximizing $U_{\lambda_j}(y)$, is the **objective function**. If we constrain y so that $y \in [0,1]$, then we do not allow short selling the risk-free portfolio F or the risky portfolio P.

Since U is concave, we set $\frac{dU}{dy} = 0$ and solve for the optimal y^*:

$$U' = E(r_P) - r_f - \lambda_j y^{*\omega-1}\text{Risk}^\omega_P = 0 \implies y^* = \left(\frac{E(r_P) - r_f}{\lambda_j \text{Risk}^\omega_P}\right)^{\omega-1}; \tag{9.10}$$

or, for variance,

$$U' = E(r_P) - r_f - y^*\lambda\sigma^2_P = 0 \implies y^* = \frac{E(r_P) - r_f}{\lambda\sigma^2_P}. \tag{9.11}$$

We have ignored fixed costs and truly awful (negatively-infinite) utility outcomes. However, assuming a positive risk premium and that we can pay the fixed cost of living(*e.g.* food and housing), we must be *very* risk averse to invest only in the risk-free portfolio F.[6] For a positive risk premium and finite λ_j and Risk$_P$, $y^* > 0$: we will always invest some amount in P.[7]

With this, we can restate the expected return on C. If we have a target volatility σ_C for the complete portfolio, then:

$$E(r_C) = r_f + (E(r_P) - r_f)\frac{\sigma_C}{\sigma_P} = r_f + S_P\sigma_C. \tag{9.12}$$

This defines a line relating $E(r_C)$ and σ_C with a slope equal to the Sharpe ratio. Note that if we used expected shortfall ES_C as our risk measure, this line would relate $E(r_C)$ and ES_C and have a slope equal to the conditional Sharpe ratio.

---

[6]By "very" risk averse I mean infinitely risk averse.

[7]Just as with equation (9.6), we will run into problems if we try to use an estimated risk measure in the denominator of these equations for y^*.

If, however, we do not constrain the complete portfolio volatility and maximize the Sharpe ratio, we get that:

$$E(r_C) = r_f + y^*(E(r_P) - r_f) = r_f + \frac{1}{\lambda}\left(\frac{E(r_P) - r_f}{\sigma_P}\right)^2 \qquad (9.13)$$

$$= r_f + \frac{1}{\lambda}S_P^2. \qquad (9.14)$$

9.4   Portfolio of Two Risky Assets

To explore the relationship between expected return and volatility, we will examine a two-asset risky portfolio. We will invest w_B in a risky bond subportfolio B and $w_E = 1 - w_B$ in a risky equity subportfolio E. That implies a risky portfolio return of $r_P = w_B r_B + w_E r_E$ and variance of:

$$\sigma_P^2 = w_B^2 \sigma_B^2 + w_E^2 \sigma_E^2 + 2w_B w_E \,\mathrm{Cov}(r_B, r_E) \qquad (9.15)$$

$$= w_B^2 \sigma_B^2 + w_E^2 \sigma_E^2 + 2w_B w_E \rho_{BE} \sigma_B \sigma_E. \qquad (9.16)$$

With this, we can explore the expected return and volatility of our portfolio. In particular, we will look at the S&P 500 index ETF (SPY) and the Bloomberg Barclays Aggregate Bond index ETF (AGG). These have historical returns over the past three years of 10.76% and 2.69% with volatilities of 10.27% and 2.92%. The R code to do this is easy:

```
## B = Bloomberg Barclays Aggregate Bond index ETF (AGG), from Yahoo Finance
expret.bonds <- 0.0269
vol.bonds <- 0.0292
## E = S&P 500 index ETF (SPY), from Yahoo Finance
vol.stocks <- 0.1027
expret.stocks <- 0.1076
rf <- 0.01  ## F = risk-free rate (approximately)

wt.bonds <- seq(-0.5,1.5,0.005)  ## explore bond weights: short 50% to long 150%
## create expected portfolio returns for weights
expret.port <- wt.bonds*expret.bonds + (1-wt.bonds)*expret.stocks

## plot and set up axes
plot.default(NULL, type='l', xlim=c(0,0.15), ylim=c(-0.01, 0.15))
abline(h=0, lty=2, col="gray80")
lines(c(0,0), c(0.08,-0.025), lty=2, col="gray80")

## iterate through correlations from 1 to -1 in steps of -0.25
## find the portfolio volatility and then plot the curve
line.colors <- c("purple","magenta", "red", "orange", "yellow",
                 "chartreuse", "aquamarine", "cyan", "blue")
corrs.bonds.stocks <- seq(1, -1, -0.25)
legend.keys <-   c()
for (i in 1:length(corrs.bonds.stocks)) {
    corr.bs <- corrs.bonds.stocks[i]
    var.port.tmp <- wt.bonds^2*vol.bonds^2 + (1-wt.bonds)^2*vol.stocks^2 +
        2*wt.bonds*(1-wt.bonds)*corr.bs*vol.bonds*vol.stocks
    vol.port.tmp <- sqrt(var.port.tmp)
    lines(vol.port.tmp, expret.port, lty=i, lwd=2, col=line.colors[i])
    legend.keys <- c(legend.keys, bquote(rho==~.(corr.bs)))
```

```
}
## Add a legend so we know which curves are for which correlations
legend.text <- as.expression(legend.keys)
legend("topleft", legend.text, lty=1:length(legend.text), cex=0.8, lwd=2, col=line.colors)

## show where F, B, and E are
points(0,0.01,lwd=2)
text(0.005, 0.01, "F")
points(vol.bonds, expret.bonds,lwd=2)
text(vol.bonds+0.005, expret.bonds, "B")
points(vol.stocks, expret.stocks,lwd=2)
text(vol.stocks, expret.stocks-0.01, "E")
```

This yields the plot in Figure 9.2. As the correlation decreases from 1, the hyperbola of possible portfolios built from B and E becomes more curved until it is finally V-shaped at $\rho_{BE} = -1$. Note that if $\rho_{BE} = \pm 1$, we can combine B and E to build a risk-free portfolio. If this were possible, we could arbitrage this using F: short the risk-free portfolio yielding less and invest the proceeds in the risk-free portfolio yielding more.

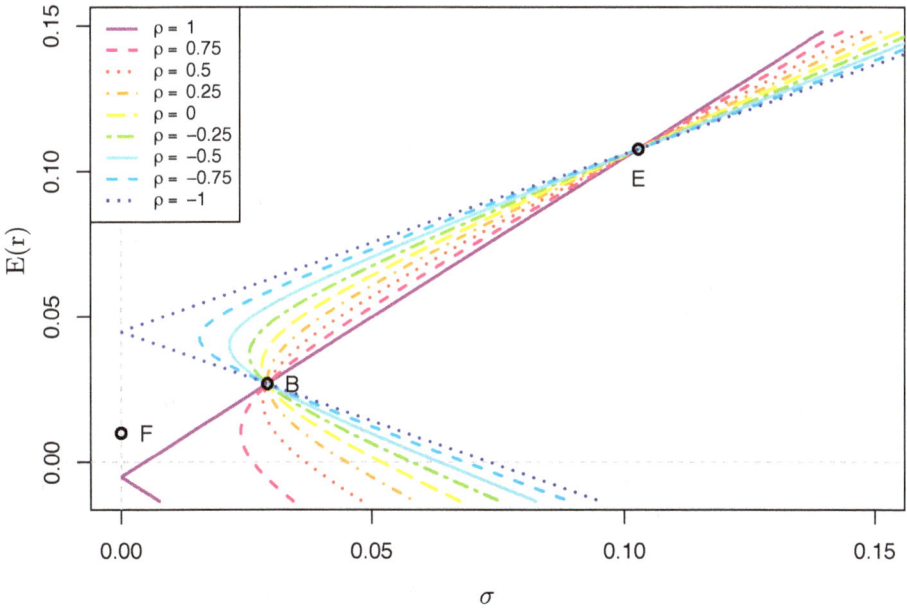

Figure 9.2: The curves show possible portfolios of stocks and bonds for correlations of stock and bond returns ranging from +1 to -1 in steps of 0.25. The stock portfolio is the S&P 500 index ETF, SPY, and bond portfolio is the Bloomberg Barclays Aggregate Bond index ETF, AGG. As the correlation becomes more extreme, the hyperbola of possible portfolios becomes more V-shaped.

9.5   Optimal Risky Portfolios

Correlation   of   Ventures?
Sixty-five years ago, Markowitz and Roy brought diversification rigor to *most* of finance. However, venture capital (VC) and private equity firms have long held (maybe) a few dozen investments, in a few industries, backed by little quantitative analysis. In 2010, Correlation Ventures posited that VC firms should use quantitative analysis and prefer investments which diversify the portfolio.

While controversial at first, firms like Correlation Ventures, Google Ventures, and Venture Science have shown that these ideas work. Rao (2013) and Miller (2013) note many VCs are now trying to copy the approach. Davis (2017) reports Correlation Ventures recently raised $200 mn more, and Geron (2017) reports quant VC SignalFire raised $330 mn. Investors obsessed with new ideas are finally coming around to an old idea.

For more info, read Farr (2012), Newlands (2015), Venture Science's Oğuz (2013,2014) on analysis, and Hunter and Zaman (2017) on increasing successful exits.

We believe diversification reduces the risk of what we hold. This is the idea behind subadditivity. Furthermore, we just saw that even for two assets, one of which had little risk, that diversification could offer more attractive portfolios. Diversification allows us to achieve more attractive combinations of expected return and risk than are possible by investing in just one instrument. We will explore optimization a bit, first graphically and then in a more mathematical form.

9.5.1   The Opportunity Set of Risky Assets

If we consider all possible combinations of risky investments, we get a convex set called the **opportunity set of risky assets** (OSRA). Figure 9.3 shows the OSRA and the capital allocation line, extended past the $F - P$ segment (typically mapped onto [0,1]). In this case, the OSRA is enveloped by a hyperbola.[8]

The top edge of the OSRA, shown as a bold line in Figure 9.3, is the **efficient frontier**: every portfolio on that curve dominates the portfolios which offer lower expected return for the same volatility. Furthermore, any combination of portfolios on the efficient frontier is also on the efficient frontier. (This is sometimes referred to as the **Two Fund Separation Theorem**.)

The bottom edge of the OSRA, shown as a dashed line, is the **inefficient frontier** because those portfolios offer the minimal expected return for a given volatility. Combinations of inefficient-frontier portfolios are also on the inefficient frontier. The left-most point of the OSRA gives

---

[8]If we use other risk measures, the OSRA is still convex but it may be a piecewise function (*i.e.* have a discontinuous derivative).

us the **minimum variance portfolio** MV. This minimum variance portfolio can often have $\sigma_{MV} < \sigma_i$ for all instruments i in the portfolio.

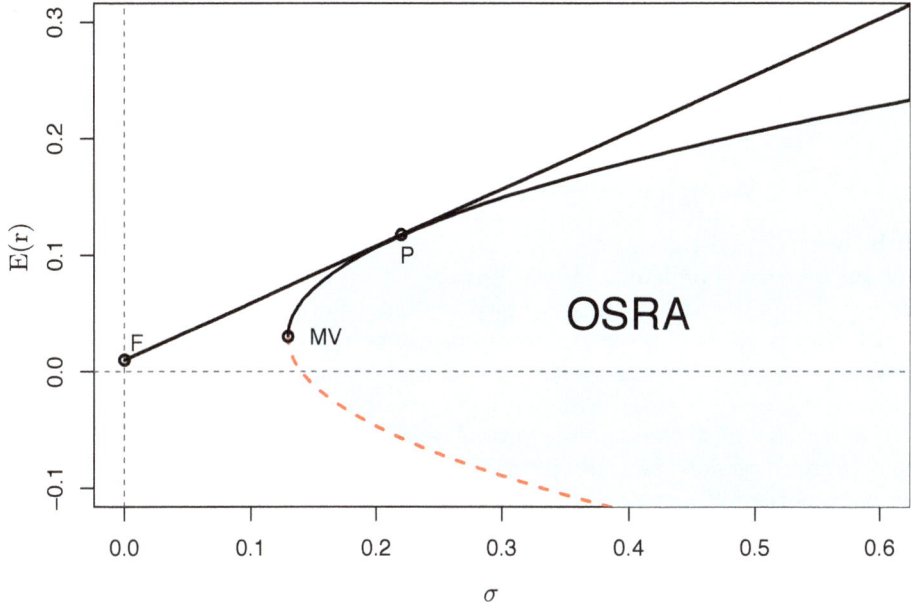

Figure 9.3: The shaded region is the mean-variance opportunity set of risky assets (OSRA) and shows the possible expected return and volatility for portfolios of solely risky assets. The capital allocation line includes the risk-free portfolio F and is tangent to the OSRA at the optimal risky portfolio P. MV is the minimum-variance portfolio and separates the OSRA envelope into the inefficient frontier (red dashed curve) and the efficient frontier (solid curve).

9.5.2 One Risky Portfolio to Rule Them All?

We next add a risk-free asset to the investment universe. That defines the risk-free portfolio F. With F and P, we have the capital allocation line. Figure 9.3 also shows the capital allocation line.

With the capital allocation line and the opportunity set of risky assets, we have enough information to find the **optimal risky portfolio**, the best possible risky portfolio. In theory, this is the risky portfolio everyone should hold in their complete portfolio — *one risky portfolio to rule them all.*

To recap, we should emphasize a few key points:

- The OSRA gives us *all possible risky portfolios.*

- *All possible complete portfolios* are on the capital allocation lines (rays) including F and a point P' in the OSRA.[9]
- Risky portfolios we invest in *should only be on the efficient frontier*.
- Combinations of efficient portfolios are *also on the efficient frontier*.
- We want CAL to *maximize excess return per unit of risk* = max slope.
- Mean-variance optimizers *maximize the CAL's Sharpe ratio*.
- The *optimal risky portfolio for all investors* is at the point of CAL tangency to the OSRA.[10]

9.5.3   From Indifference to Optimal Complete Portfolios

With the CAL and the optimal risky portfolio, we can use indifference curves to find our optimal complete portfolio. Figure 9.4 shows how we sweep indifference curves through decreasing utilities until we find a point of tangency on the CAL. That tangency point C is our **optimal complete portfolio**.

This raises a key point that many students get wrong. The *optimal risky portfolio is the same for all investors*. Different investors will have different optimal complete portfolios; however, these complete portfolios *only differ in their allocation* between the risk-free portfolio F and the optimal risky portfolio P. More risk-averse investors will hold more of F and less of P than less risk-averse investors — who will hold less of F and more of P.

9.5.4   When Borrowing Costs More Than Lending

So far, we have assumed that we earn the same excess return whether we are long F (lending money to the bond issuers) or short F (borrowing money). The only problem with this is that there usually are additional fees with short selling; and, getting a loan is also more costly.

This changes the excess return for leveraged portfolios. The capital allocation line between F and P is still tangent to the OSRA; but, the capital allocation line beyond P has a lower slope due to the borrowing rate being higher than the risk-free rate. Figure 9.5 shows what this looks like. We can see that indifference curve which would suggest a leveraged portfolio will have lower utility — reflecting the higher cost to borrow.

9.5.5   Simplifying the Optimization Process

Having seen all of this graphically, we can simplify the process. For example, we do not need the OSRA or even the efficient frontier usually. We only need to find the optimal risky portfolio.

---

[9]To be specific, CAL rays define a **cone**, a convex set in a vector space defined by combinations of positively-scaled vectors. This is why some portfolio optimization research discusses cone programming.

[10]To be fair, this is the optimal risky portfolio for all investors who share our investment horizon.

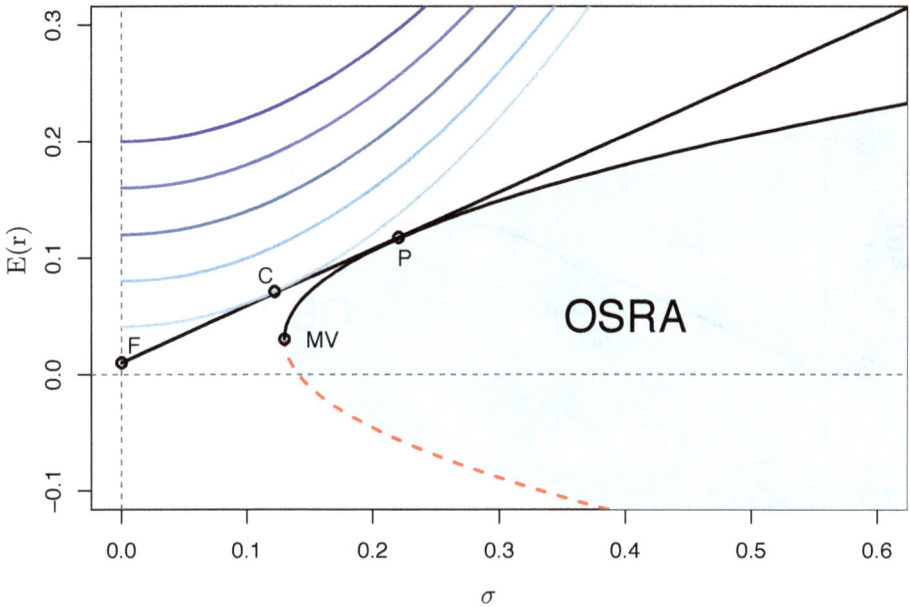

Figure 9.4: The opportunity set of risky assets and capital allocation line with mean-variance indifference curves for $\lambda = 4$ decreasing in utility until one is tangent to the capital allocation line. At the tangency point is the complete portfolio which implies a division of investment between the risk-free portfolio F and the optimal risky portfolio P.

Recall that we can write the variance as a quadratic form $w'\Sigma w$ where:

$$w = \begin{pmatrix} w_B \\ w_E \end{pmatrix}, \Sigma = \begin{pmatrix} \sigma_B^2 & \Sigma_{BE} \\ \Sigma_{BE} & \sigma_E^2 \end{pmatrix}, \quad \text{and} \tag{9.17}$$

$$\Sigma_{BE} = \text{Cov}(r_B, r_E) = \rho_{BE}\sigma_B\sigma_E. \tag{9.18}$$

The simplified process to find the optimal complete portfolio C is then:

1. Get the risk-free rate for our investment horizon, r_f. This implies F.
2. Use expected returns and risk measures to find the optimal risky portfolio P. For a mean-variance approach, this means solving the following mathematical program to find the weight vector w for instruments in the portfolio:

$$\max_{w} \frac{w^T E(r) - r_f}{\sqrt{w^T \Sigma w}} \tag{9.19}$$

$$s.t. \ \mathbf{1}^T w = 1. \tag{9.20}$$

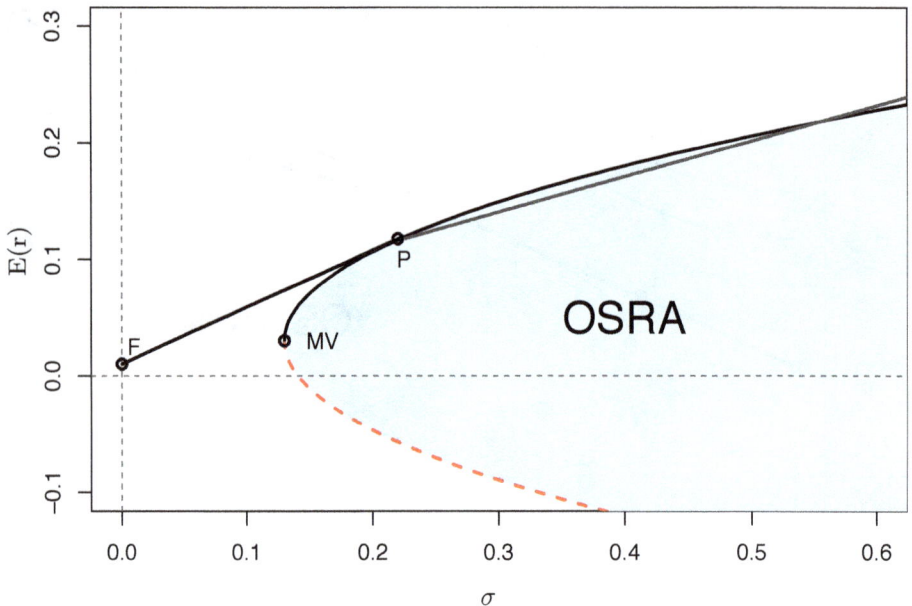

Figure 9.5: The opportunity set of risky assets and capital allocation line from F to P which is tangent to the efficient frontier. Beyond the tangency point, the investor borrows at an interest rate higher than the risk-free rate of F.

3. Determine the optimal complete portfolio C for your risk aversion λ_j:

$$y^* = \frac{E(r_P) - r_f}{\lambda_j \sigma_P^2}; \tag{9.21}$$

$$C = y^* P + (1 - y^*) F. \tag{9.22}$$

A nice aspect of this process is that these tasks have some degree of separation. We can separate determining the optimal risky portfolio P from any details about the investor. We can also separate finding the optimal complete portfolio C from knowing what is in P. This **separation property** simplifies the process and was first noted by Tobin (1958).

The gift of Markowitz and Roy was new ideas: that there is an optimal risky portfolio with the highest possible Sharpe ratio, that this portfolio is optimal for all investors, that we maximize along the capital allocation line, and that we do this all in a mean-variance framework. These ideas define **modern portfolio theory**.[11]

---

[11]Readers looking for a survey of modern portfolio theory research would do well to read the Elton and Gruber (1997) survey article.

9.6 Criticisms of Modern Portfolio Theory

Perhaps the greatest beauty of modern portfolio theory (MPT) is that it takes simple measures of risk and gives us a risky portfolio that is optimal for all investors. This is *great*; everyone can use the same risky P! We just need to have somebody figure this out and publish it for everyone to use.

There is just one problem: we do not do this. Investors do not all hold the same risky investment. Furthermore, MPT portfolios tend to underperform versus their expected return and volatility out-of-sample. This has led to a number of criticisms of modern portfolio theory.

This might seem distressing: Why learn about a criticized methodology? However, the criticisms reflect the widespread acceptance of the *general* ideas of modern portfolio theory and our attempts to improve and refine the implementation. You can think of MPT as a first-order approximation.

While there are many criticisms of MPT, we will consider the most common and most trenchant criticisms, specifically that MPT:

- "failed" in the financial crisis;
- disagrees with how people invest;
- underperforms out-of-sample;
- uses poor risk measures; and,
- does not beat simpler methods.

9.6.1 MPT "Failed" in the Financial Crisis

One of the most common criticisms of MPT (and finance in general) is that it did not predict a financial crisis; or, that people with diversified portfolios lost money in that crisis. Diversification is not magic; it does not eliminate all risk. Diversification can eliminate a lot of instrument-specific risk. However, you are still exposed to the larger macroeconomic environment.

Furthermore, the claim that MPT or finance somehow "failed" when it did not predict a financial crisis or weather the crisis unscathed is specious. Some parts of the financial ecosystem do often predict crises. For example, the USD yield curve was inverted for months well before the financial crisis of 2008. However, other indicators were not so negative. Finally, if the whole market knew a crash was coming, they would all sell — leading to the crash. So foresight does not prevent crashes.

This criticism of MPT ignores counterfactuals and imposes unrealistic (perhaps even unachievable) demands on how a well-designed portfolio behaves in a crisis. A longer refutation can be found in Statman (2013) or Pfleiderer (2012). Briefly, however: we must ignore this criticism since it is not even proposing a falsifiable test of whether or not MPT worked. Furthermore, the sentiment is just wrong-headed. When the space shuttle Challenger blew up shortly after launch, that was not proof that engineering does not work or that we needed less engineering in the space program; rather, it showed the importance of improving the analysis.

9.6.2   MPT Disagrees With How People Invest

If modern portfolio theory finds the optimal risky portfolio, then why do people not all use it? Why do people hold different investments? There are a number of answers to this question.

Prediction

One problem with a unified P is prediction: How do we create good guesses at the expected returns $E(r_i)$, volatilities σ_i, and correlations ρ_{ij}? As we will see, predicting returns is hard and predicting variances and covariances is very hard.

Estimation and Different Data

Historical estimation often performs poorly — even though it is commonly used. Furthermore, historical estimates can be inconsistent if they are combined from multiple estimations. Even estimating variances and covariances historically can be very difficult. We often must use more advanced methods of inference.

Even if our methodology is up to the task of prediction, we might all compute our predictions at different times and thus use different data. This will lead to us all computing different optimal risky portfolios. Klein and Bawa (1976) shows this can lead to investors holding different optimal risky portfolios. Duchin and Levy (2010) explores how different expected variances can lead to differences in investors' holdings and valuations of instruments.

Taxes

A common reality to intrude on financial theories is taxes — and MPT is no exception. In Hungary, India, Russia, Turkey, and the United States, for example, there is a difference in taxation between short- and long-term capital gains. Other countries, like the United Kingdom, have an annually-capped exemption from capital gains taxes. In these cases, there may sometimes be an advantage for an investor to hold on to an instrument for a little longer.

For example, suppose you had made $10,000 on a stock and wanted to now sell it since it was no longer in the optimal risky portfolio. However, if you could reduce your tax bill by a third by waiting to sell for a day, a week, or even a month. . . you might consider waiting. Thus taxation can also cause investors to hold different portfolios.

Self-Imposed Constraints and Mandates

A big reason investors hold differing portfolios is that many have self-imposed constraints on their potential investment universe. Some investors will not invest in firms which pollute or are in certain industries they consider unethical; these investors may only invest in socially responsible instruments. Some Muslim investors will not invest in instruments which pay out interest or derive income from, say, the sale of alcohol or tobacco. These investors may want a portfolio holding only shariah-compliant instruments. Finally, many mutual funds have mandates prohibiting short-selling; and, many investors impose constraints to prevent holding more than a certain amount of their portfolio in any one industry.

Total Portfolio (Life) Exposures

Another reason why investors might hold different portfolios is because of other exposures in their life. For example, if the optimal risky portfolio suggests they hold 10% in real estate and 1% in their employer, an investor who owned a home might reasonably decide to (1) count their home toward that 10% in real estate, and (2) to not invest in their employer since they already are exposed to the fate of that firm. Some investment managers refer to this as a total portfolio approach. People who ignored this at Enron, Arthur Anderson, and Lehman found themselves out of work and with decimated retirement savings. Recent research also suggests people who differ in their uncertainty about returns to skills and education may hold different portfolios.

Accessibility, Home Bias, and Local Inflation

Issues like accessibility or home bias (the tendency to prefer investments in local or national instruments) also affect what investments people hold. While the global optimal risky portfolio might involve holding German stocks, investors might not be able to easily hold those particular stocks as an investor from other countries. Furthermore, it might make sense for them to hold more investments of their home countries since those investments might increase more with local inflation which helps them hedge local inflation.

Differing Investment Horizons

Another reality is that investors have different investment horizons. Some are saving for a home, some for their next term's tuition bill, some for their children's education, and some for their retirement. Some people are even lucky enough to be saving for their grandchildren. Obviously, these people have very different abilities to recover from a temporary drop in prices.

Education

Finally, there is the issue of education. You are presumably reading this book to learn more about investing; however, not all investors read much (or anything) about investing. Given that lack of education, it is understandable why some might hold different instruments from investors who know to look at measures of return versus risk.

9.6.3   MPT Underperforms Out-of-Sample

Perhaps the most damning criticism of modern portfolio theory is that the portfolios underperform out of sample. Specifically, they have lower return and more risk than they are optimized to have. There are a number of reasons for this, many of which involve uncertainty that is ignored. Explaining and improving this is perhaps the most active area of research in portfolio management.

The Curse of Dimensionality

The first problem with MPT is the *curse of dimensionality*. MPT uses a full covariance matrix. For an investment universe of n instruments, finding the optimal risky portfolio requires us to first estimate a number of inputs:

1. $1 \times$ risk-free return r_f;
2. $n \times$ expected returns $E(r_i)$ for all instruments i;
3. $n \times$ variances σ_i^2; and,
4. $\frac{n(n-1)}{2} \times$ correlations ρ_{ij} or covariances Σ_{ij} for instruments $i \neq j$.

This means we need to estimate $\frac{n(n+1)}{2} + n + 1$ inputs to find the optimal risky portfolio. This is problematic because the number of inputs grows with the square of the size of our investment universe. This issue often results in covariance matrices which are imprecise. Bickel and Levina (2008) characterize when estimating a large covariance matrix may be particularly problematic and propose some ways to fix it. (In general, we want the number of observations to increase faster than the log-universe size, $\log(n)$.)

To the extent that there is an unusual estimate, an optimizer will be sensitive to that and may choose to avoid that instrument or to hold a lot of it.[12] Best and Grauer (1991) discuss this sensitivity, noting that in some cases a small change in expected returns eliminated half of the instruments from the optimal risky portfolio. Kondor, Pafka, and Nagy (2007) show that the sensitivity also occurs when using other risk measures.

Brown (1976) studied Bayesian approaches in an attempt to better address parameter uncertainty. Similarly, Jorion (1986) proposed to surmount this issue by using an empirical Bayes estimator which, effectively, used James-Stein estimation to get squeezed estimates. MacKinlay and Pástor (2000) suggested using information from the covariance matrix for improperly-specified pricing kernels to better estimate expected returns (with a method that also does some squeezing). Kan and Zhou

---

[12]We also have a problem with new instruments: how do we invest in an instrument if we do not know its volatility or correlation with other instruments? This conundrum is not unique to MPT, however.

(2007) showed that with parameter uncertainty, combining the risk-free portfolio F and the optimal risky portfolio P with the minimum-variance portfolio MV mitigates estimation errors and outperforms the MPT combination of only F and P.

Unfortunately, the curse of dimensionality and estimation difficulties are not unique to MPT. Other methods with skewness and kurtosis tensors have numbers of estimates which grow with the cube and quartic of universe size. Furthermore, while some might think the working with coherent risk measures will solve this, coherent measures are based on tail measures and so are also difficult to estimate.

Whence Stochastic Optimization?

The second problem with MPT is that it *ignores randomness and nonlinearity.* This might seem like a strange criticism for a methodology that uses a large covariance matrix; however, we can see this a few ways.

First, the mean and variance are not sufficient to characterize the distribution of instrument returns since we have seen that log-returns are not normal. Second, the MPT setup does not let us easily consider possible scenarios that might be of particular interest to us. Third, the output of an optimizer is not linear in the inputs; doubling any of the inputs does not clearly lead to any doubling of any output. Portfolio optimization is, simply, very non-linear. Therefore the expected return and risk of the optimal portfolio requires us to compute the expectation and risk of a nonlinear function. If we, instead, just substitute in the expected returns and risk measures and optimize, we will get a different answer.

Furthermore, the sensitivity of mean-variance, mean-expected shortfall, and other non-stochastic methods to small changes in the inputs that Kondor, Pafka, and Nagy (2007) show is another reason to use stochastic optimization. Stochastic optimization results are, by design, robust to small changes in inputs.

Some researchers, such as Almgren and Chriss (2006), have tried to develop nonparametric techniques for portfolio optimization. While this is difficult, it has some benefits. We will revisit this idea in Chapter 24.

These problems are the reason that **stochastic optimization** was developed. While a review of an entire academic field is a bit beyond this section, it is important to know that we can do better than just mean-variance or mean-expected shortfall optimization. For a flavor of how stochastic optimization can work: a common approach is to sample returns to create scenarios; to build all of these scenarios into the objective function; and, to then optimize the average scenario return less some risk penalty where both are computed from the scenarios. Interested readers should read Birge and Louveaux (2011).

Transactions Costs

Finally, there is one part of the investing process which modern portfolio theory completely ignores: transactions costs. The problem is that transactions costs add both an expected cost (lowering returns) and cost uncertainty (increasing risk).

Some explanation can clarify this. In trading a large order, we are often faced with a tradeoff. We could trade the entire order now; some of the trades would get a poor price; but, we are reasonably sure we can get this price. Alternately, we could trade a little and wait for more liquidity to arrive (hopefully!) so we get a good price for all of the trades. However, this runs the risk of prices moving for or against us. In algorithmic trading, we consider this tradeoff when planning how to trade over a period of time; and, it turns out that as in portfolio optimization, there is also an efficient frontier of trading.

Engle and Ferstenberg (2007) was the first paper to note that these optimizations have the same risk aversion and should be done together. Furthermore, they note that this additional cost and uncertainty shifts the efficient frontier for portfolio optimization down and to the right. Figure 9.6 shows this for executions having an expected round-trip cost of 1% with a standard deviation of 3%. Accounting for transactions costs reduces the Sharpe ratio from 0.49 to 0.40.

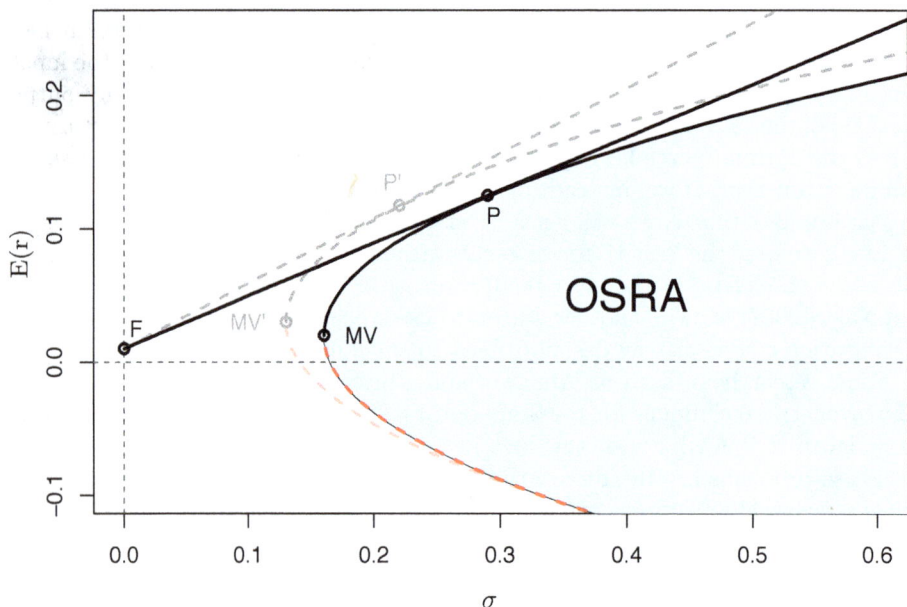

Figure 9.6: The opportunity set of risky assets and capital allocation line before (dashed lines) and after accounting for transactions costs. Note that the optimal risky portfolio is different and the Sharpe ratio is lower.

9.6.4   MPT Uses Poor Risk Measures

Another problem that causes underperformance is that MPT *uses non-coherent measures of risk.* This is a problem inherent to the formulation of the optimization problem. However, there is nothing preventing us from putting in another measure of risk. If we go back to the utility function in Chapter 7, we can use a Taylor expansion of the cumulant generating function to rewrite the utility expression:

$$\text{Utility} = U_j = \frac{-1}{\lambda_j} \underbrace{\log(E(e^{-\lambda_j r}))}_{\text{cumulant generating function}} \tag{9.23}$$

$$
\begin{aligned}
&= E(r) - \frac{\lambda_j}{2}\sigma^2 + \frac{\lambda_j^2}{6}\gamma - \frac{\lambda_j^3}{24}\kappa \\
&\quad + \sum_{k=5}^{\infty}(-1)^k \frac{\lambda_j^{k-1}}{k!} E\left(\frac{r - E(r)}{\sigma}\right)^k,
\end{aligned} \tag{9.24}
$$

where γ is the skewness and κ is the kurtosis.

Clearly, we need not stick to mean-variance optimization; and, R has a number of packages like `PerformanceAnalytics`, `PortfolioAnalytics`, and `quadprog` capable of other optimizations. One could also use the network-enabled optimization system (NEOS) via `rneos`; however, users should be aware that there is no privacy with optimization problems sent to NEOS solvers — since submitted problems may be used for development or use cases.

9.6.5 MPT Does Not Beat Simpler Methods

Finally, one of the harder-to-ignore criticisms of MPT is that it does little better than simpler alternatives such as the classic equally-weighted "$1/n$" **portfolio**.

Both Duchin and Levy (2009) and Tu and Zhou (2011) discuss the $1/n$ portfolio as derived from advice in the Babylonian Talmud. Duchin and Levy (2009) find that the $1/n$ portfolio outperforms MPT portfolios for small investment universes; but, as n grows, that MPT portfolios start to outperform the $1/n$ portfolio. Tu and Zhou (2011) find that combining the $1/n$ portfolio with one of the estimation-error-mitigating techniques of Jorion (1986), MacKinlay and Pástor (2000), or Kan and Zhou (2007) outperforms MPT and the $1/n$ portfolio. Pflug, Pichler, and Wozabal (2012) show that the $1/n$ portfolio is optimal when there is high uncertainty about the form of the pricing kernel.

Similar to the $1/n$ portfolio, Elton and Gruber (1973) study portfolios with all instruments having the same correlation or using the same correlation among instruments within an industry. They find that their equi-correlation and industry equi-correlation models outperform MPT and other methods, especially when there is little data for estimation. (Thus their approach provides some guidance for investors seeking to invest in new instruments which lack data to estimate correlations.)

If investors were to invest in instruments based on their return-risk ratio, then we should expect all instruments to (eventually) have similar return-risk ratios. Thus a portfolio of all investments — often called "the market" — should be the optimal risky portfolio. Sharpe (1963) tests a portfolio where returns are described by exposure to a single macroeconomic factor. He find that this structure, while restrictive, greatly eases the estimation of the covariance matrix and often outperforms MPT. That said, how does a market proxy look according to MPT? Strangely: not well. Asness, Frazzini, and Pedersen (2012) note the underperformance of the market portfolio versus a mean-variance efficient portfolio.

9.6.6   Coda

While there are numerous problems with MPT, it is still an improvement over eschewing diversification or uninformed diversification. Later, in Chapter 24, we will explore two approaches, the Treynor-Black and Black-Litterman approaches. These will let us extend MPT and incorporate mispricings and our own economic views.

9.7   Diversification in the Limit

Up to this point, how subadditivity (and thus diversification) works has been a bit of a mystery. We should pull back the covers on this a bit since it is informative. To do this, we will assume each instrument we invest in has exposure to a common (shared) risk factor and that the remainder of the instrument's risk is exposure to a factor specific to that instrument. We will see that the risk which is shared cannot be reduced through diversification; but, the dis-utility of the specific risks can.

Suppose we invest equal amounts in n risky assets. To simplify, we will assume that all risky assets have same expected return μ, the same shared-risk-factor $m \sim (0, \sigma^2)$, and specific-factor variance of $\eta_i \overset{\perp}{\sim} (0, \delta^2)$, $m \perp \eta_i$:

$$r_i = \mu + m + \eta_i. \tag{9.25}$$

We can then see that $\mathrm{Var}(r_i) = \sigma^2 + \delta^2$ and $\mathrm{Cov}(r_i, r_j) = \sigma^2$. This implies that all instruments have the same cross-correlation of $\frac{\sigma^2}{\sigma^2 + \delta^2}$.

The portfolio covariance matrix is then:

$$\begin{bmatrix} \sigma^2 + \delta^2 & \sigma^2 & \cdots & \sigma^2 \\ \sigma^2 & \sigma^2 + \delta^2 & \cdots & \sigma^2 \\ \vdots & \vdots & \ddots & \vdots \\ \sigma^2 & \sigma^2 & \cdots & \sigma^2 + \delta^2 \end{bmatrix} \tag{9.26}$$

With this, we can easily discern the variance of a $1/n$ portfolio:

$$\sigma_P^2 = \sum_{i=1}^{n} \frac{\sigma^2 + \delta^2}{n^2} + 2 \sum_{i=1}^{n} \sum_{j>i}^{n} \frac{1}{n^2} \sigma^2 \tag{9.27}$$

Taking the limit of this, we get that

$$\lim_{n\to\infty} \sigma_P^2 = \lim_{n\to\infty} n\frac{\sigma^2+\delta^2}{n^2} + 2\lim_{n\to\infty}\frac{n(n-1)}{2}\frac{1}{n^2}\sigma^2 = \sigma^2. \tag{9.28}$$

As we diversify our portfolio, the specific risk diminishes leaving only the shared risk. If there were risks that applied to a part of the portfolio (say, to 10% of the instruments), those would also remain after diversification. This is why we like assets that are uncorrelated with other assets: they may add some return to our portfolio but they make a vanishingly small contribution to risk.

This is also why diversification is one of our main risk-reduction technologies: with large diversified portfolios, we can largely eliminate the risk specific to certain instruments. However, we cannot eliminate risk due to risk factors shared across a non-diminishing part of the portfolio. To do that, we will need the other risk-reducing technology: hedging. We will introduce that technology in Chapter 14.

9.8 Quiz

Try to answer these questions in five minutes. For your answers, just write the equations; do not evaluate them.

1. Suppose you have mean-variance utility as in the portfolio construction lecture. What utility do you derive from *each* of the following assets? (*i.e.* You should have an answer for each asset for each of the parts below.)

	T-Bill	Stock
E(r)	2%	14%
Volatility(r)	0%	30%

   a) If your risk aversion parameter $\lambda = 4$?
      $U_{\text{T-bill}}$:

      U_{Stock}:

   b) If your risk aversion parameter $\lambda = 2$?
      $U_{\text{T-bill}}$:

      U_{Stock}:

2. What risk aversion λ would characterize a gambler?

What risk aversion λ would characterize a speculator?

3. Suppose you hold a portfolio of corporate bonds.

  a) Give an example of a systematic factor.

  b) Give an example of an idiosyncratic factor.

4. Suppose the risk-free rate is $r_f = 1\%$ and the following diagram shows expected returns and volatilities for all possible risky portfolios:

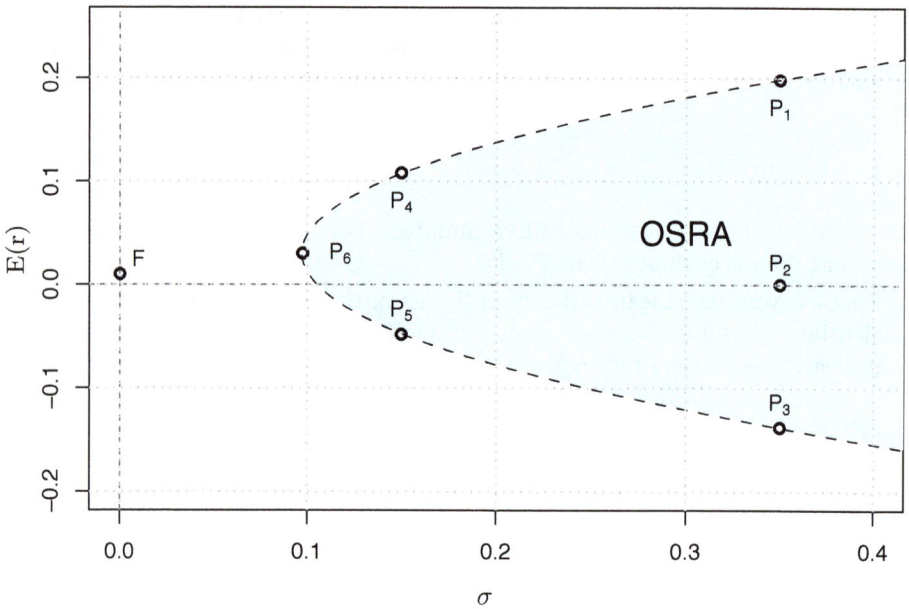

  a) Where is the optimal risky portfolio on the diagram?

  b) For portfolio P_1, what is the Sharpe ratio?

  c) Why would you be interested in portfolio P_3 instead of P_1? (Or why not?)

  d) What would happen to this diagram if we added in transactions costs?

5. You are mildly risk-averse; your friend Laszlo is very risk averse. You are rebalancing your portfolio and just figured out the optimal risky portfolio. Laszlo is lazy and wants to use the same optimal risky portfolio as you.

   a) Should Laszlo have more money than you in risk-free investments? Why or why not?

   b) Is it wise for Laszlo to hold some fraction of the same risky portfolio as you; or, should Laszlo use a different risky portfolio? Why or why not?

   c) Your friend Ellen has the same risk-aversion as you. However, Ellen decides to hold a different risky portfolio than you do. Why might Ellen do this?

9.9 Exercises

Instructions

For these exercises, we are going to try a few approaches to portfolio construction and then compare them.

To do this we will need data. Thankfully, we do not need a lot of data. Also, to keep things simple, we will grab data for some ETFs and commodities.

ETFs: SPY (S&P 500), IWM (Russell 2000), AGG (Barclays Aggregate US Bond), FEZ (Euro Stoxx 50), ACWI (MSCI All-Country World), and IYR (Dow Jones US Real Estate)

Commodities: CL (CME West Texas Intermediate crude oil), GC (CME gold), HG (CME copper), ZC (CME corn)

1. Using the code supplied, find the optimal risky portfolio and the maximized Sharpe ratio for portfolios with a possible investment universe of the preceding ETFs only, the preceding commodities only, and the preceding ETFs and commodities.

2. How do these optimal portfolios differ from most portfolios people invest in?

3. How do the optimal portfolio weights differ if you constrain them to be non-negative or between 0 and 1 (inclusive)?

4. Change the code to look at expected shortfall for risk. How do the portfolios change? Do any of the results suggest that some instruments are effectively noise, *e.g.* their weight stays near zero and could be positive or negative?

5. Are there any instruments with very large weights? Do these seem reasonable?

6. How do these statistics compare to the simple "1/n" portfolios?

R Code

```
library(MASS)
library(xts)
library(quantmod)
library(Quandl)
library(PortfolioAnalytics)
library(ROI)
library(ROI.plugin.glpk)
library(ROI.plugin.quadprog)

## risk-free rate (for example purposes)
rf <- 0.01

etf.symbols <- c("SPY", "IWM", "AGG", "FEZ", "ACWI", "IYR")
adj.close <- 6  # 6th field is adjusted close
etf.prices <- getSymbols(etf.symbols[1], source="yahoo",
                         auto.assign=FALSE, return.class="xts")[,adj.close]
for (i in 2:length(etf.symbols)) {
    etf.tmp <- getSymbols(etf.symbols[i], source="yahoo",
                          auto.assign=FALSE, return.class="xts")[,adj.close]
    etf.prices <- cbind(etf.prices, etf.tmp)
}
colnames(etf.prices) <- etf.symbols
etf.rets <- diff(log(etf.prices))["2012/"]

commodity.symbols <- c("WTI", "Natgas", "AU", "CU", "Corn")
settle <- "Settle"  # settle field is labeled
commodity.tickers <- c("CHRIS/CME_CL1", "CHRIS/CME_NG1", "CHRIS/CME_GC1",
                       "CHRIS/CME_HG1", "CHRIS/CME_C1")
commodity.prices <- Quandl(commodity.tickers[1], type="xts")[,settle]
for (i in 2:length(commodity.symbols)) {
    commodity.tmp <- Quandl(commodity.tickers[i], type="xts")[,settle]
    commodity.prices <- cbind(commodity.prices, commodity.tmp)
}
colnames(commodity.prices) <- commodity.symbols

all.returns.tmp <- diff(log(cbind(etf.prices,commodity.prices)))["2012/"]
all.returns <- na.omit(all.returns.tmp)

## set up portfolio with objective and constraints
n.assets <- length(colnames(all.returns))
port.spec <- portfolio.spec(assets = colnames(all.returns))
port.spec <- add.objective(portfolio=port.spec, type="risk", name="StdDev")
port.spec <- add.objective(portfolio=port.spec, type="return", name="mean")
port.spec <- add.constraint(portfolio=port.spec, type="full_investment")
port.spec <- add.constraint(portfolio=port.spec, type="box", min=-1, max=1)

## map out the efficient frontier (for variance risk)
eff.frontier <- create.EfficientFrontier(R=all.returns, portfolio=port.spec,
                                         n.portfolios=100, type="mean-StdDev")

## daily Sharpe ratio
sharpe.ratios <- (eff.frontier$frontier[,"mean"]-rf/250)/eff.frontier$frontier[,"StdDev"]
max.sharpe.ratio <- sharpe.ratios[sharpe.ratios == max(sharpe.ratios)]
optimal.port.name <- names(max.sharpe.ratio)
optimal.mean <- eff.frontier$frontier[optimal.port.name,"mean"]
optimal.sd <- eff.frontier$frontier[optimal.port.name,"StdDev"]

n.trading.days.per.year <- 252
print(sprintf("Optimal Sharpe Ratio: %f", max.sharpe.ratio*sqrt(n.trading.days.per.year)))
print(sprintf("Optimal E(port return): %f", optimal.mean*n.trading.days.per.year))
print(sprintf("Optimal sd(port return): %f", optimal.sd*sqrt(n.trading.days.per.year)))
print("Optimal weights")
```

```
print(eff.frontier$frontier[optimal.port.name,(1:n.assets)+3])
```

References

Almgren, Robert and Neil Chriss. "Optimal Portfolios from Ordering Information". *Journal of Risk* 9.1 (2006), pp. 1–47. DOI: 10.21314/jor.2006.143.

Asness, Clifford S., Andrea Frazzini, and Lasse H. Pedersen. "Leverage Aversion and Risk Parity". *Financial Analyst's Journal* 68.1 (2012), pp. 47–59. DOI: 10.2469/faj.v68.n1.1.

Best, Michael J. and Robert R. Grauer. "On the Sensitivity of Mean-Variance-Efficient Portfolios to Changes in Asset Means: Some Analytical and Computational Results". *Review of Financial Studies* 4.2 (1991), pp. 315–342. DOI: 10.1093/rfs/4.2.315.

Bickel, Peter J. and Elizaveta Levina. "Regularized Estimation of Large Covariance Matrices". *Annals of Statistics* 36.1 (2008), pp. 199–227. DOI: 10.1214/009053607000000758.

Birge, John R. and François Louveaux. *Introduction to Stochastic Programming*. 2nd ed. New York: Springer-Verlag, 2011.

Brown, Stephen Jeffery. "Optimal Portfolio Choice Under Uncertainty: A Bayesian Approach". PhD dissertation. Graduate School of Business: University of Chicago, 1976.

Davis, Alexander. "Venture-Capital Firms Use Big Data to Seek Out the Next Big Thing". *Wall Street Journal* (Apr. 25, 2017).

Duchin, Ran and Moshe Levy. "Markowitz Versus the Talmudic Portfolio Diversification Strategies". *Journal of Portfolio Management* 35.2 (2009), pp. 71–74. DOI: 10.3905/JPM.2009.35.2.071.

— "Disagreement, Portfolio Optimization, and Excess Volatility". *Journal of Financial and Quantitative Analysis* 45.3 (2010), pp. 623–640. DOI: 10.1017/S0022109010000189.

Elton, Edwin J. and Martin J. Gruber. "Estimating the Dependence Structure of Share Prices – Implications for Portfolio Selection". *Journal of Finance* 28.5 (1973), pp. 1203–1232. DOI: 10.1111/j.1540-6261.1973.tb01451.x.

— "Modern Portfolio Theory, 1950 to Date". *Journal of Banking and Finance* 21.11–12 (1997), pp. 1743–1759. DOI: 10.1016/S0378-4266(97)00048-4.

Engle, Robert F. and Robert Ferstenberg. "Execution Risk". *Journal of Portfolio Management* 33.2 (2007), pp. 34–44. DOI: 10.3905/jpm.2007.674792.

Farr, Christina. "Venture Capital Picks Up the Moneyball Strategy". *VentureBeat.com* (Nov. 9, 2012). URL: http://venturebeat.com/2012/11/09/startup-algorithm/.

Geron, Tomio. "SignalFire Raises $330 Million for Data-Centric Venture Capital". *Wall Street Journal* (May 10, 2017).

Hunter, David Scott and Tauhid Zaman. *Picking Winners: A Framework For Venture Capital Investment*. Working Paper. MIT, 2017. URL: https://arxiv.org/abs/1706.04229.

Jorion, Philippe. "Bayes-Stein Estimation for Portfolio Analysis". *Journal of Financial and Quantitative Analysis* 21.3 (1986), pp. 279–292. DOI: 10.2307/2331042.

Kan, Raymond and Guofu Zhou. "Optimal Portfolio Choice with Parameter Uncertainty". *Journal of Financial and Quantitative Analysis* 42.3 (2007), pp. 621–656. DOI: 10.1017/S0022109000004129.

Klein, Roger W. and Vijay S. Bawa. "The Effect of Estimation Risk on Optimal Portfolio Choice". *Journal of Financial Economics* 3.3 (1976), pp. 215–231. DOI: 10.1016/0304-405X(76)90004-0.

Kondor, Imre, Szilárd Pafka, and Gábor Nagy. "Noise Sensitivity of Portfolio Selection Under Various Risk Measures". *Journal of Banking and Finance* 31.5 (2007), pp. 1545–1573. DOI: 10.1016/j.jbankfin.2006.12.003.

MacKinlay, A. Craig and Ľuboš Pástor. "Asset Pricing Models: Implications for Expected Returns and Portfolio Selection". *Review of Financial Studies* 13.4 (2000), pp. 883–916. DOI: 10.1093/rfs/13.4.883.

Markowitz, Harry. "Portfolio Selection". *Journal of Finance* 7.1 (1952), pp. 77–91. DOI: 10.1111/j.1540-6261.1952.tb01525.x.

— "The Early History of Portfolio Theory: 1600–1960". *Financial Analyst's Journal* 55.4 (1999), pp. 5–16. DOI: 10.2469/faj.v55.n4.2281.

Miller, Claire Cain. "Google Ventures Stresses Science of Deal, Not Art of the Deal". *New York Times* (June 23, 2013). URL: http://www.nytimes.com/2013/06/24/technology/venture-capital-blends-more-data-crunching-into-choice-of-targets.html.

Newlands, Murray. "Reimagining VC Investing: How Correlation Ventures is Attracting and Keeping the Best New Startups". *Forbes* (Oct. 2, 2015). URL: http://www.forbes.com/sites/mnewlands/2015/10/02/reimagining-vc-investing-how-correlation-ventures-is-attracting-and-keeping-the-best-new-startups/.

Oğuz, Matt. "The Moneyball Strategy is the Future for Venture Capital Firms". *VentureBeat* (Jan. 10, 2013). URL: http://venturebeat.com/2013/01/10/vc-moneyball-rebuttal/.

— "A Multi-Factor Analysis Of Startups". *TechCrunch* (Apr. 12, 2014). URL: http://techcrunch.com/2014/04/12/multi-factor-analysis-of-startups/.

Peterson, Brian G. and Peter Carl. *PerformanceAnalytics: Econometric tools for performance and risk analysis*. R package version 1.4.3541. 2014. URL: https://CRAN.R-project.org/package=PerformanceAnalytics.

— *PortfolioAnalytics: Portfolio Analysis, Including Numerical Methods for Optimization of Portfolios*. R package version 1.0.3636. 2015. URL: https://CRAN.R-project.org/package=PortfolioAnalytics.

Pfaff, Bernhard. *rneos: XML-RPC Interface to NEOS*. R package version 0.3-2. 2017. URL: https://CRAN.R-project.org/package=rneos.

Pfleiderer, Paul. "Is Modern Portfolio Theory Dead? Come On." *TechCrunch* (Aug. 11, 2012). URL: http://techcrunch.com/2012/08/11/is-modern-portfolio-theory-dead-come-on/.

Pflug, Georg Ch., Alois Pichler, and David Wozabal. "The 1/N Investment Strategy is Optimal Under High Model Ambiguity". *Journal of Banking and Finance* 36.2 (2012), pp. 410–417. DOI: 10.1016/j.jbankfin.2011.07.018.

Rao, Leena. "The Quantitative VC". *TechCrunch* (June 1, 2013). URL: http://techcrunch.com/2013/06/01/the-quantitative-vc/.

Roy, A.D. "Safety First and the Holding of Assets". *Econometrica* 20.3 (1952), pp. 431–449. DOI: 10.2307/1907413.

Rutterford, Janette and Dimitris P. Sotiropoulos. "Financial Diversification Before Modern Portfolio Theory: UK Financial Advice Documents in the Late Nineteenth and the Beginning of the Twentieth Century". *European Journal of the History of Economic Thought* 23.6 (2016), pp. 919–945. DOI: 10.1080/09672567.2016.1203968.

Sharpe, William F. "A Simplified Model for Portfolio Analysis". *Management Science* 9.2 (1963), pp. 277–293. DOI: 10.1287/mnsc.9.2.277.

— "Capital Asset Prices: A Theory of Market Equilibrium under Conditions of Risk". *Journal of Finance* 19.3 (1964), pp. 425–442. DOI: 10.1111/j.1540-6261.1964.tb02865.x.

Statman, Meir. "Is Markowitz Wrong? Investment Lessons from the Financial Crisis". *Journal of Portfolio Management* 40.1 (2013), pp. 8–11. DOI: 10.2469/dig.v44.n2.12.

Tobin, James. "Liquidity Preference as Behavior Towards Risk". *Review of Economic Studies* 25.2 (1958), pp. 65–86. DOI: 10.2307/2296205.

Tu, Jun and Guofu Zhou. "Markowitz Meets Talmud: A Combination of Sophisticated and Naive Diversification Strategies". *Journal of Financial Economics* 99.1 (2011), pp. 204–215. DOI: 10.1016/j.jfineco.2010.08.013.

Turlach, Berwin A. and Andreas Weingessel. *quadprog: Functions to solve Quadratic Programming Problems.* S original by Turlach; R port by Weingessel. R package version 1.5-5. 2013. URL: https://CRAN.R-project.org/package=quadprog.

Chapter 10

Statistical Modeling

There are a few general approaches to analyzing investments. We earlier mentioned solution concepts like proofs, equilibrium models, and simulation. If we have data, we can use estimation to infer metrics like expected return and volatility as well as to value investments.

The goal of this chapter is to discuss different types of statistical analysis; consider the structure and implications of data; and, give you enough perspective to be properly critical or skeptical of analyses.

10.1 Overview

Since we want to extract as much information as possible from our data, we can also use the relationships among our data. Thus we need to measure those relationships. The measures may be cross-sectional or across time. You are likely to run into a few types of data analysis, in increasing order of control over the data environment:

1. Scenario analysis;
2. Cross-sectional analysis;
3. Time-series analysis;
4. Panel analysis;
5. Event studies; and,
6. Experiments.

While we lack the space to delve fully into any of these topics, we should become familiar enough with them to understand the basics and to know when we should investigate an area further. Furthermore, we need to talk about data issues since ignoring those is one of the most prevalent and destructive modeling mistakes.

10.2 Scenario Analysis

Scenario analysis considers likely or representative scenarios. We think of these different scenarios and guess at (or estimate) returns and other relevant data in each scenario. We then assign probabilities to the scenarios and compute the metrics we need.

The idea of a scenario analysis is to specify a few scenarios which are representative or likely, analyze what would happen in each scenario, and then specify probabilities of each scenario to determine expected metrics and valuation. Sometimes, we specify many scenarios to see how results converge as the number of scenarios increase. The idea of scenario analysis is also used in stochastic optimization.

This highlights one of the strengths of scenario analyses: they can be useful for handling difficult-to-model problems. They also allow us to consider situations not present in the data. Finally, they can be very intuitive and simple for the power of the insights they yield.

For example: suppose we buy risky bonds which promise to pay off $1000:

Estimating an EMU Before European economic and monetary union (EMU), the hedge fund Long-Term Capital Management would survey its London-based strategists on likely scenarios for Italian debt. They then used both the average and standard deviation of those guesses to guess at whether investment prospects had improved or not. While Long-Term was known for using advanced quantitative techniques, even they knew that scenario analyses could be powerful when the model form was not obvious.

specifically, a 5-year zero-coupon-bond of a small firm. We think the company could go bankrupt in year 5 with probability 0.05. However, if the firm becomes insolvent, an asset sale would incur a loss. Say, bankruptcy recovers 70% of the outstanding face; or, in other words, there is a 30% **loss given default**. If the five-year risk-free rate is 4%, the bond has value V:

$$V = [\ \underbrace{\$1000 \cdot 0.95}_{E(\text{pay}|\overline{\text{default}})P(\overline{\text{default}})} + \underbrace{\$1000 \cdot 0.70 \cdot 0.05}_{E(\text{pay}|\text{default})P(\text{default}))}\ ]\ \underbrace{\frac{1}{1.04^5}}_{\text{discount factor}} \tag{10.1}$$

$$= \$985 \cdot 0.8219\ldots = \$809.5982 \tag{10.2}$$

We can even use such models to infer more information, as we will see in the exercises.

10.3 Cross-Sectional Analysis

Cross-sectional analysis analyzes investments by comparing across instruments.

This requires looking at simultaneous returns. Cross-sectional analysis is, in many ways, natural to us: we ask "Why is Firm B doing so poorly while Firm C is doing so well?" The danger with cross-sectional analyses is, as we saw before, sorting: we need to always remember the regression fallacy and not let that pollute the analysis.

To do cross-sectional analysis, it helps to have some measures of cross-sectional relation. Correlation and covariance are the most common cross-sectional measures we work with.

One source of cross-dependence is **random effects**: shared sources of randomness which induce a common factor exposure. For example, IBM and Microsoft shares might be exposed to some common technology sector randomness, η_t^{Tech}:

$$r_t^{\text{IBM}} = \alpha^{\text{IBM}} + \eta_t^{\text{Tech}} + \epsilon_t^{\text{IBM}}, \tag{10.3}$$
$$r_t^{\text{MSFT}} = \alpha^{\text{MSFT}} + \eta_t^{\text{Tech}} + \epsilon_t^{\text{MSFT}}, \tag{10.4}$$

where $\eta_t \overset{iid}{\sim} N(0, \sigma_\eta^2)$, $\epsilon_t^{\text{IBM}} \overset{iid}{\sim} N(0, \sigma_{\epsilon,\text{IBM}}^2)$, $\epsilon_t^{\text{MSFT}} \overset{iid}{\sim} N(0, \sigma_{\epsilon,\text{MSFT}}^2)$, and $\eta_t^{\text{Tech}}, \epsilon_t^{\text{IBM}}$, and ϵ_t^{MSFT} are all independent. However, the shared randomness induces a correlation. Since the sources of randomness are all independent and mean zero, we can see by inspection that:

$$\text{Var}(r_t^{\text{IBM}}) = \sigma_\eta^2 + \sigma_{\epsilon,\text{IBM}}^2, \tag{10.5}$$
$$\text{Var}(r_t^{\text{MSFT}}) = \sigma_\eta^2 + \sigma_{\epsilon,\text{MSFT}}^2, \quad \text{and} \tag{10.6}$$
$$\text{Cov}(r_t^{\text{IBM}}, r_t^{\text{MSFT}}) = \sigma_\eta^2. \tag{10.7}$$

This means we can calculate the correlation as the covariance divided by the standard deviations:

$$\text{Corr}(r_t^{\text{IBM}}, r_t^{\text{MSFT}}) = \frac{\sigma_\eta^2}{\sqrt{\sigma_\eta^2 + \sigma_{\epsilon,\text{IBM}}^2}\sqrt{\sigma_\eta^2 + \sigma_{\epsilon,\text{MSFT}}^2}}. \tag{10.8}$$

Using random effects in modeling acknowledges that the data are not independent. One of the advantages of that is that it can greatly reduce false attributions of significance when we build models. Many economists will say that they do not use random effects but that they allow for clustering or a correlation structure in the data. The two are largely the same; random effects are just an intuitive way to imply certain correlation structures.

Random effects, like any correlation structure, do have one minor problem: they capture positive correlations better than negative correlations. That is OK though: it is very difficult to have negative correlations between all members of a group.[1]

---

[1] Could there be negative correlations between groups induced by a group random effect? Yes, especially if those groups are asset classes and we believe that trouble in one asset class might cause investors to flee to another asset class.

10.4 Time-Series Analysis

Time-series analysis is the branch of statistics that studies time-dependent, often time-ordered, data. Time series are sequences of dates and times and returns between those dates and times.[2] Time-series analysis is a direct extension of linear modeling, but also uses insights from stochastic processes and spatial statistics.[3] To talk about risk and returns, we will need a little bit of language from time-series analysis.

10.4.1 Persistence

While correlation and covariance measure cross-sectional dependence, we also care about dependence across time. In particular, we care about **persistence**, the idea that a process may be related to past values. The random walk has persistence: the value in the next time period is the current value plus a disturbance. However, the changes in the random walk (disturbances) are not persistent. Similarly, we would not expect returns to show persistence; otherwise, we could make easy money.

Another common idea of persistence is **autocorrelation**, sometimes called **serial correlation**. An autocorrelated process in one having current and past values that are correlated. We call processes with autocorrelated components **autoregressive (AR)** processes because we can regress the process on itself to infer the autocorrelations. We sometimes refer to an AR process as a mean-reverting process or an Ornstein-Uhlenbeck process in continuous time.

When we build an **autoregressive model** to capture this behavior, we often use a number indicating how many prior time periods we incorporate. An AR(1) process depends on one prior value:

$$r_{it} = \alpha + \phi r_{i,t-1} + \epsilon_{it}, \tag{10.9}$$

and an AR(p) process depends on p prior values:

$$r_{it} = \alpha + \phi_1 r_{i,t-1} + \cdots + \phi_p r_{i,t-p} + \epsilon_{it}. \tag{10.10}$$

Because we are regressing a process on itself, there is always the possibility of explosive feedback, like the whine of a microphone — except in financial markets explosive feedback looks more like bubbles. That sort of behavior complicates any inference we might hope to perform.[4] For example: $r_t = 2r_{t-1} + \epsilon_t$ explodes which means the distribution of the r_t's is not stationary.

We therefore check that estimated models imply a process with **covariance stationarity**: a finite covariance and finite autocovariances which do not vary over

---

[2]We should not assume that these dates and times are regularly-spaced. Irregularly-spaced time series are more challenging to analyze, but common in many areas of finance.

[3]Where we look for serial correlations (runs of similar returns), gold miners in the Rand looked for spatial autocorrelations (veins of gold).

[4]Phillips and Yu (2011) use tests for explosive behavior to detect bubbles.

time.[5] To do this, we check roots of the **characteristic polynomial** created from the model coefficients and lags:

$$1 - \phi_1 L - \cdots - \phi_p L^p = 0 \tag{10.11}$$

where L is the lag operator that turns r_{it} into $r_{i,t-1}$ and functions like z for z-transforms and difference equations. If there is a root inside the unit circle, the AR process is not covariance stationary.

A **moving average (MA)** process is persistent and depends on past shocks. The persistence is very short-lived which is ideal for modeling transient effects.[6] When we build a **moving average model** to capture this behavior, we use numbering as we did for AR models: an MA(1) process depends on one prior disturbance:

$$r_t = \alpha + \epsilon_t + \theta \epsilon_{t-1}, \tag{10.12}$$

and an MA(q) process depends on q prior disturbances:

$$r_t = \alpha + \epsilon_t + \theta_1 \epsilon_{t-1} + \cdots + \theta_q \epsilon_{t-q}. \tag{10.13}$$

Since the persistence in an MA process is short-lived, it is always covariance stationary (if the disturbances ϵ_t also have a finite variance). However, an MA process can be inverted to be an infinite-term AR process. Who cares? Well, you might since that is behind one of the methods of estimating MA coefficients. To find out if an MA model is invertible, we check the roots of its characteristic polynomial:

$$1 + \theta_1 L + \cdots + \theta_q L^q = 0. \tag{10.14}$$

If there is a root inside the unit circle, the MA process is not invertible.

What do AR and MA processes look like? Figure 10.1 shows example behavior for an AR(1) and an MA(1) process. The AR(1) process shows more persistence in how drifts away from 0 for longer. The MA(1) process has much shorter-lived persistence: most changes revert within two periods, causing the process to exhibit more sharp changes and stay closer to 0. AR and MA processes are not vastly different: we can write a covariance stationary AR process as an MA(∞) process and an invertible MA process as an AR(∞) process.[7] However, these plots show that their behavior is distinctive enough that we use "AR" and "MA" to describe different types of behavior.

Other models include transfer function models which relate system inputs and outputs via ratios of polynomials. Those interested in exploring time series analysis should read Box et al. (2015) and Tsay (2010). A Bayesian approach to time series analysis, state space methods, are covered by Durbin and Koopman (2012).

---

[5]Without covariance stationarity, we cannot make inferences about the mean.

[6]Estimating MA models coefficients cannot be done by ordinary least squares. Durbin (1959) and Galbraith and Zinde-Walsh (1994) offer a few easier methods which use ordinary least squares.

[7]The Wold (1938) Decomposition Theorem is what lets us make this equivalence.

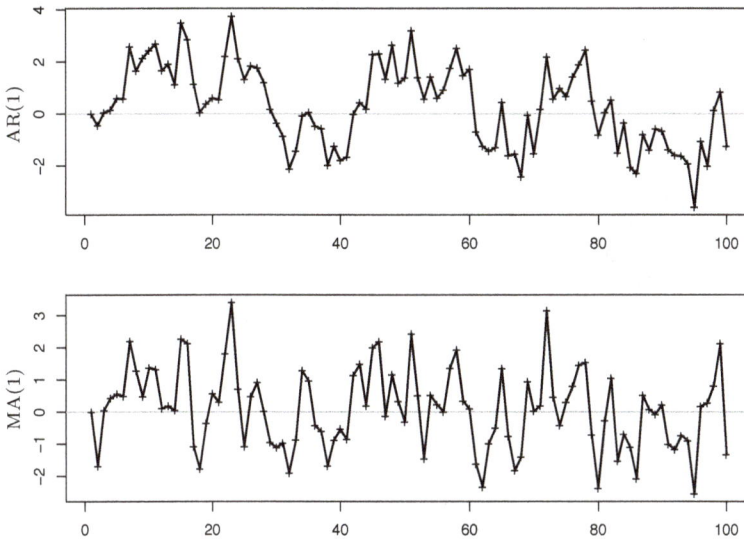

Figure 10.1: Example plots of persistent processes. The top plot shows an AR(1) process $r_t = 0.8r_{t-1} + \epsilon_t$; the bottom plot shows an MA(1) process $r_t = \epsilon_t + 0.8\epsilon_{t-1}$. The AR(1) process shows more persistence and drifts away from 0. The MA(1) process often reverts within two periods, and does not drift away from 0.

10.5 Panel Analysis

Panel analysis, also known as longitudinal analysis, uses time series of cross-sectional data. This uses the power of both time-series analysis and cross-sectional analysis and allows us to consider cross-correlations across time: for example, do stocks lead bonds? Do futures lead ETFs? There are a few ways of doing this.

One way to do panel analysis is to use the tools of cross-sectional analysis with a time component (and maybe random effects). This is common in the biological and medical literature and usually referred to as longitudinal analysis. Since those fields often predict rates or dichotomous outcomes, they tend to use generalized linear models (GLMs) and generalized estimating equations (GEEs) to model a correlation structure with a GLM. This gets far beyond the reaches of this text, however Dobson and Barnett (2008) and McCullagh and Nelder (1989) are excellent sources on GLMs; and, Diggle et al. (2013) and Fitzmaurice, Laird, and Ware (2011) are excellent sources on longitudinal analysis and GEEs.

The other way to do panel analysis is to generalize the tools of time series analysis to handle cross correlations. This leads to creating vector autoregressive models, vector moving average models, and the like. Unfortunately, the curse of dimensionality can affect these models: good performance often requires imposing constraints or structure on the matrix coefficients. If you are interested in multivariate time series models, consult the time series texts (mentioned earlier) first and then Tsay (2013) and Lütkepohl (2005) will likely prove helpful.

10.6   Event Studies

Event studies are linear models which study what happens before, during, and after an event. This is where the Efficient Market Hypothesis guides our thinking. Under the EMH, price changes are due to new information. If the event was the only new information, price changes imply the effect or relevance of the event. In assessing the effect of the event, we use abnormal returns: Typically, we compare cumulative abnormal returns before, during, and after the event.

Readers of financial news are likely familiar with less rigorous versions of event studies: one common recurring type of article plots what the market did before and after a politician made a speech about a new policy. The idea allows us to assess the market opinion of the policy/speech. However, even if we look at multiple instruments, this is (in a way) looking at just one observation; a better event study would look at multiple similar speeches or policy announcements and assess the response of a broad-based index across those events.

Other well-known event studies are those comparing cumulative abnormal returns of a firm before and after a merger announcement. Unless we believe the strong form of the Efficient Market Hypothesis, we should not see a statistically significant response before an announcement unless somebody leaks the information. Despite laws against trading on inside information, many studies show significantly positive abnormal returns for acquired firms before buyout announcements.[8] Thus it should come as no surprise that the first application of these ideas was in Fama et al. (1969).

Readers wanting more details on event studies should read that article as well as Brown and Warner (1985) and Binder (1998).

10.7   Experiments

The cleanest data analysis is of a well-defined **experiment**: a controlled environment with only one variable changed at a time. Unfortunately, we rarely get such a luxury outside of a laboratory or clinical environment. In experimental analysis, we control for the "unclean" environment with **blocking variables** — a term from how certain blocks of land in agricultural experiments are similar in terms of irrigation, sunlight,

---

[8]To be fair, this need not be due to insider trading. Strangely: while trading on inside information is illegal, deciding not to trade or canceling a trade is not illegal. So if you heard about the buyout and waited to sell your shares until after the announcement, that would be legal. The reduction in selling pressure could also explain the pre-announcement rise. More details are available at U.S. Securities and Exchange Commission (2000).

or other important factors. In financial data, we often include **controls**, variables like blocks, to account for factors which could affect our results.

Sometimes, we use a **natural experiment**: an unexpected phenomenon unrelated to what we study which allows us to compare groups. For example, consider payday lenders — the high-interest short-term lenders which many politicians have portrayed as predatory. We might wonder if payday lenders help people without a bank account weather difficult times. We could then look at communities with more and fewer such lenders and see how those communities fare, say, after an earthquake. Since earthquakes are unrelated to economic distress, this should yield a clean natural experiment.[9]

Many algorithmic traders use experiments to help optimize the performance of their trading engines. Tuning trading engines and racecars are both data-driven ways of adapting a machine for maximum performance. We will not get too into experimental analysis here; but, it is a far more useful field of study than many financiers think. Those looking for more material on design and analysis of experiments should read Oehlert (2000) and Box, Hunter, and Hunter (2005).

10.8 Data Issues

One of the greatest failings of many analysts is to not think enough about their data. Where do the data come from? How does the data get to where it is recorded? What biases are in the data? What biases affect the data we see? All of these are key questions to consider because they can bias our analysis.

10.8.1 Cleanliness

Cleanliness is always an issue. Some vendors will report trades at a zero price or quotes with a zero quantity. Obviously,

> **A Theory Too Far** Large negotiated orders often trade over a large part of the day. Once the order is done, it will be published with the total shares and average price. Since large trades are likely to have moved prices, the average price may be far from the market price when the trade is published. To prevent confusion, these trades are marked with a code indicating they are average price trades.
>
> A few years ago, a professor presented work on modeling trades occurring far outside the spread. He had spent two years creating complicated theory to model these trades. After the talk, he was asked if the large trades were marked with any codes. The professor did not know and wondered why that mattered. The questioner said nothing — because there is no nice way to say someone wasted two years modeling something untradeable.

those are not usable; however, you should check if they have some deeper meaning or indicate you should doubt other data. Once that is resolved, you can filter them out.

---

[9]This is not hypothetical: Morse (2011) explores exactly this question. The result? Payday lenders reduce post-quake foreclosures by 25%.

In intraday data, there are a number of trades or messages which are not necessarily from continuous trading. They might be trades from an auction or they might be publishing the final price and quantity for negotiated trades. Since these are not part of the continuous market, they need to be filtered out.

A common issue with stock prices is that they need to have their price history adjusted for corporate actions and their volume history adjusted for splits and stock dividends. Adjusted prices are sometimes available and are often what we should analyze to create returns; however, adjusted volumes are not always available.

Probably the two best tools for data cleaning are the `summary` and `hist` commands. Look at the minima and maxima for each variable to see if the range makes sense. Check if the mean and median make sense. A lot of data errors can be found in this way. After that, look at a histogram to see if any values are overrepresented. Many old records have "99" or "999" in fields when a previously-unencountered condition was met.

An excellent reference for data cleaning is de Jonge and van der Loo (2013).

10.8.2 Missing Data

Missing data is an under-considered data problem — in part because we usually think about problems with the data we have, not the data we *might have had*. The effect of missing data on an analysis ranges from trivial or innocuous to completely destructive. The difference comes from why the data are missing. In general, we consider missing data as being due to one of three situations: not missing at random, missing at random, or missing completely at random.

The most serious case is if the data are **not missing at random** (NMAR). This occurs when the data missingness is related to the outcome we are studying. For example, suppose we want to assess risk factors to help people live longer. We measure height and weight in the hope of relating these to the probability of death in a year. However, if we only gather these data from a doctor's current patients, we might miss those who have died. In that case we have an NMAR problem: when people die (perhaps in part due to obesity) they cease being a patient; and, we can no longer measure their height and weight (unless we quickly hustle to the morgue). This might sound unrelated to finance; however, we will see exactly this scenario when we discuss research on the equity risk premium: we often lack data for economies that go through extreme problems. Biostatisticians must always consider this when they study mortality. Hence the biostat literature talks at length about **survival analysis** (correcting for survivorship).

On the other hand, our data might be **missing at random** (MAR). This happens when the data is missing for a reason related to one of the observed variables — but not the variable we are trying to model. Consider again trying to model the probability of someone dying in a year using their height and weight. Before, death (*i.e.* the probability of dying in a year being 1) caused us to lose data. However, weight might itself make us unable to observe data. If a person were very heavy and unable to get out of bed, we might never see them and thus not get their height and weight. In this case, the mechanism for data being missing is correlated with death but not directly tied to it.

In both the NMAR and MAR cases, missing data will bias our results. The solution is to build a model that models the mechanism for missingness and thus allows us to correct for it.

Finally, the data may be **missing completely at random** (MCAR) if it is missing for no reason related to the outcome we are studying or any of the other variables of interest. This approach should certainly not be our default assumption; however, when people fail to consider or choose to ignore the possibility of missing data they are essentially choosing this approach. In this case we could ignore the missing values or try to infer them. For those looking to learn more about missing data (and handling it), de Jonge and van der Loo (2013) has a little bit; however, Little and Rubin (2002) followed by Schafer (1997) are the top texts on the subject.

10.8.3   Survivorship Bias

We mentioned survivorship above; however, it is such a pernicious source of bias that it makes sense to address it directly. **Survivorship bias** is the bias to an analysis due to ignoring people, firms, or other units which do not exist for the entire period of analysis. Even with what seems to be a well-designed, randomized experiment, we can still end up with biased data.

Suppose we decided to study the effect of having sufficient capital and business training by randomly offering these to some entrepreneurs. Entrepreneurs who do not need cash or training will decline; and, entrepreneurs may stop reporting for training if they are in arrears on the loan or do not immediately find the training useful. Alternately, we might eliminate strategic selection by forcing all entrepreneurs to take a loan and undergo training. In that case, entrepreneurs might not report for training out of protest.

In the first case, we have a form of **censoring**: we lose data for entrepreneurs who opt out or who do not succeed. Thus if we look at the performance for loans we have data on, we will be assessing a biased sample of entrepreneurs — and it might look like loans and training lead to more entrepreneurial success. (This might be true, but our bias now overstates the effect.) In the second case, we have entrepreneurs actively sabotaging the experiment and that will make it harder for us to relate their performance to taking on a loan and undergoing training.

Both of these biases are undesirable; and, the solution might seem obvious: also analyze entrepreneurs who declined or who stopped attending training. However, does that really remove the bias? Those entrepreneurs did not actually undergo the full training; ascribing an effect to the training when those entrepreneurs did not actually experience the training is incorrect. In this case, we would likely analyze the entrepreneurs who stopped reporting for training as a separate group as well as with the entrepreneurs who finished the training. In that way, we can try to see what effects might be unique to the non-finishers and see if there were any effects from the period of time they were in the training. We could then try to model the probability of entrepreneurs withdrawing from training and add that to our analysis in an attempt to eliminate the bias in our findings. This may complicate the data analysis, but it can be attempted and an honest data analysis should look at the outcomes from multiple perspectives.

For those thinking that survivorship only affects experiments: think again. Every time you select a set of traded firms and then retrieve historical data, you are opening the door to survivorship bias — because you are not choosing firms which failed. Consider the counterfactual: Suppose you went back in time, selected firms, and invested in them. Some firms would fail. Ignoring that (which is the equivalent of selecting from currently-traded firms) biases your results.

10.8.4   Endogeneity

Endogeneity is the bugbear of all non-experimental data analyses. If a variable we measure is not affected by the system we are analyzing, we say it is **exogenous**. However, if a variable is affected or determined by the system we are analyzing, we say the variable is **endogenous**.

A classic example of endogeneity could be firm risk and stock volatility. Many people would believe that a riskier firm should have a more volatile stock. However, many people might also believe that a more volatile stock presages an uptick in a firm's risk. In this case, firm risk and stock volatility are endogenous. This makes sorting out causality very difficult. However, we can use thought experiments to tease out the causality and try to figure out how to control for the endogeneity.

Suppose we were to take a firm and increase the firm's risk. We might surmise that this would make the stock more volatile. Even if the change was not immediate, eventually the increased risk would cause a missed payment or a reduced dividend and then investors would realize the stock is more risky leading to higher volatility. Thus more risk yielded more stock volatility.

However, we could instead find a way to shake up the firm's stock: perhaps a lot of buying and selling. However, this would not make the firm riskier. Thus while stock volatility seems to be caused by firm risk, firm risk is not caused by stock volatility.

This gets at one of the ways we disentangle endogeneity: by controlling for variables we think have a causal effect. In this case, we can model volatility on firm risk, but if we want to model firm risk on volatility, we need to break the causality link. (One common way to do this would be to use prior values of stock volatility so that they are not influenced by the current level of firm risk.)

Endogeneity might seem like a specialized concern; it is not. In financial markets, we see endogeneity when we look at bid-ask spreads and interest rates, spreads and volatilities, and many other variables. A good practice is to always consider how the variables in a linear model might cause or influence one another. If you can think of possible causality both ways, you have endogeneity and need to address it.[10]

10.8.5 Stationarity and Ergodicity

We should always consider if our data are stationary and ergodic (mentioned briefly before). In general, if data are generated by a process that always has the same overall behavior, we say the data (or random process) is stationary. We often write this by saying that a process is stationary if the cdf is time-invariant, *i.e.*

$$F(r_{1+k}, r_{2+k}, \ldots, r_{m+k}) = F(r_1, r_2, \ldots, r_m). \tag{10.15}$$

Sometimes, we place even weaker restrictions and say a process is covariance stationary (or wide sense stationary) if just the mean and variance are time-invariant.

However, stationarity is not sufficient for our needs; we also need the process to be ergodic. That means that if we look at a sufficient amount of data, we can estimate statistical properties like the mean, variance, and correlations.

Many systems are neither stationary nor ergodic: Financial markets are sometimes more volatile, sometimes less. Financial crises sometimes generate far more bankruptcies than is typical. A new technology may permanently change the cost of a certain industrial process. (In that case, price data from before the tech shock has little useful information for price data after the tech shock.)

How do we handle non-ergodicity? We try to control for the variables which do change; or, we try to see if the world can be described by various regimes which we then analyze separately. For example, we might use the VIX (S&P 500 volatility index) in our models to control for differing volatility across time. In Chapter 26, we will even see evidence on variables that can tell us which regime we are in.

10.8.6 Time

Since we often look at time-dependent data, time can present many issues. This becomes especially true as we increase the sampling frequency from quarters, months, or days to hours, minutes, or seconds.

One of the most obvious questions is how to deal with time? If we look at one instrument, we will notice that the times of trades and quote updates are not regularly-spaced. We might even notice that trades tend to cluster in time, a behavior that underlies the autoregressive modeling of times between trades in the ACD model of Engle and Russell (1998).

We might also notice multiple trades or quotes per timestamp. This could occur because a trade crossed the spread and traded against multiple levels in the limit order book; or, it could occur because the timestamp resolution is too coarse and obscures that those trades occurred at separate times. If the latter is an issue, one solution is to infer finer timestamps. If the timestamp resolution is Δt (*e.g.*

---

[10]A typical way to handle this is with instrumental variables. More on that later.

one second), we estimate the number of messages n_t received within a certain $t \in [t, t + \Delta t)$. (We can count messages or, if there is a sequential message ID, use the change in that.) We then assume messages are evenly-spaced within Δt. If the reported timestamp is t_{official}, the inferred timestamp for message k is then $t_{\text{official}} + \frac{k}{n_t + 1}$. An example of this inference is in Rosenthal (2012a).

Analyzing multiple instruments is even more difficult. The problem is that trading or quote updates across instruments are rarely synchronous. For example, if we try to estimate correlations with more frequent data, we can find our estimates decreasing toward zero due to the effect documented in Epps (1979). There are a number of schemes to handle this asynchronicity:

1. Omitting some data by only looking at certain observations;
2. Aggregate data into time bins;
3. Use smoothing estimators like the Nadaraya-Watson estimator;
4. Use a filtering approach (like smoothing and random effects); or,
5. Explicitly model the outcome as a function of time.

Omission, binning, and smoothing (in particular) can obscure point masses and outliers.

Omission is the most common approach, often unwittingly. Many researchers looking at intraday data will go to a database, grab trades or quotes, and then put them into a data structure. Often, one or both of these index to the minute or second. There are myriad problems with this. First, if the database is indexed by time and the index is too coarse, multiple observations in a minute or second can lose their original ordering. When multiple entries in a database sit at the same index value, the retrieval order is not defined. Second, the data structure may only store one observation per time index. Third, some research strategies effectively do this despite retrieving the complete data. Many research papers specify that they get the "last trade in each second." However, it is rare that those researchers have gone to the trouble to ensure that they get the true last observation. Finally, when trades occur as frequently as they do in some markets, grabbing the last trade in a second makes little sense.

The most common improvement over omission is to aggregate trades into time bins or, as they are commonly referred to: **bars**. Some data services will return five-minute or one-minute bars. Even daily data is often returned like a bar. Typically, a bar contains five pieces of data referred to as the OHLCV: the open, high, low, close, and volume; however, daily data often adds an "adjusted" field which may contain the closing price adjusted for corporate actions or an adjustment factor. What if an instrument does not trade during that bar? Some systems will still return values for all those fields with a zero volume being the only clue. What if there is one trade? Will the open and close be set to that trade price? Or, will the open be the preceding trade price and the close be the trade price which occurred inside the bar?

One way around this is to retrieve all trades and create your own bars. Thus we can ensure the open, high, low, and close are only set if there is a trade in that bar. On the other hand, since quotes are always active, we can set the open quote to be the prevailing quote. This also allows us to augment the bars with additional data, creating **superbars**. We can add in the observation count, time until the first observation, time until the last observation, volume-weighted average price, time-weighted average price, the volume-weighted sum of squared prices, and the time-weighted sum of squared prices. These allow us to infer weighted average prices (which are less noisy) and volatilities. Having the data in a sum-of-squares format also makes it very efficient to combine data across bars. Ultimately, bars and superbars entail some reduction in data, so there is a loss of efficiency; however, bars may make the analysis much more tractable so they are not clearly sub-optimal.

We have already demonstrated using smoothing estimators when we discussed kernel density estimation. These estimators are often used when we want to infer the time distribution of trades. These can be used for estimating a **diurnal**, the intraday pattern of volume, volatility, spreads, or other metrics.

We previously mentioned filtering when we discussed state space methods for time series. Again, Durbin and Koopman (2012) is the top reference for this approach.

Explicit modeling of time often involves changing estimations like

$$\Delta Y_t = \alpha + \beta \Delta X_t + \epsilon_t \tag{10.16}$$

to something more like

$$Y_t - Y_{t-\Delta t} = \alpha \Delta t + \beta (X_t - X_{t-\Delta t}) + \epsilon_t \Delta t \tag{10.17}$$

where $\sum_t \epsilon_t \Delta t = 0$. This becomes even more difficult if we want to model autoregressive time effects. Therefore, we will not say much more on this approach.

Obviously, none of these approaches are perfect. The solution often has to be fitted to the needs of the analysis.

Finally, we should consider the timestamps themselves. With intraday data: are the data timestamped by the trading venue at trade time, by the venue at publishing time, by a data vendor upon arrival at their server, or upon arrival to the end consumer? Are the data missing on holidays when there was no trading, on days when a data vendor's computers were busy, or on low volume days? The latter two will induce a bias to certain analyses, so the answer matters. If certain values are missing, or truncated, why did that happen? I know of one data vendor whose intraday data all have timestamps for when the data arrived at their office but do not have the timestamps from the market venue.

10.9 Estimation and Diagnostics

Another area most investments texts ignore is the process of estimation and model diagnostics. Most of the models we will consider are just a linear regression estimated by ordinary least squares (OLS). We know how to fit this in our sleep... or do we?

The truth is that many people do not know how to do this properly. They might know how to push the right buttons or give the correct commands to get numbers from a piece of software; however, they often lack insight as to which options or parameters they should set on that software. Fewer still are able to critique what they see and look for potential problems in the data.

We will briefly discuss these topics. I *strongly* recommend that any data analyst have a solid linear modeling textbook for reference. I learned linear modeling using Weisberg (1985), the latest edition of which is Weisberg (2014) (which uses R). Some analysts recommend augmenting this with Fox and Weisberg (2011) for more R examples. Finally, I have heard many good comments about Belsley, Kuh, and Welsch (1980).

10.9.1   Correcting for Non-Constant Variance

A critical assumption of OLS is that the data have constant variance. Therefore, we often plot the response against many variables to look for a clear pattern of changing variation. For example, we might see variability increasing or decreasing as another variable increases. If this is the case, we need to correct for that by either transforming the data or weighting the observations to counteract the changing variance ($w \propto \frac{1}{\sigma^2}$). Most good statistical texts discuss these two possibilities and show how transformation and reweighting achieve almost the same effect.[11]

Our data are also rarely independent. The dependence structure makes the variance differ across groups and biases standard errors to be artificially low. We can fix this with random effects (*i.e.* correlation modeling); or, we can use a clustering correction. Such "sandwich estimators" are implemented in the **sandwich** package.

10.9.2   Goodness-of-Fit Measures

How do we measure if our model fits the data well? One of the first checks is to look at the t-statistics for the covariates. If it is likely that our model is catching something, we will see t-statistics indicating statistical significance (so generally greater than 2 or 3).

What does *not* tell us if we are doing a good job is R^2. While R^2 does tell us what fraction of the variance the model explains, that ignores how much variance we should expect to be able to explain. For example: in physics, common R^2's are in the 95% to 99% range; in chemistry, R^2's may be around 60%; in biology, 30% R^2's are not unusual.

In finance, the expected R^2 varies greatly. If we are explaining past returns, we might see R^2's of 30%–50%. If we are trying to predict future returns, however, we should expect far lower R^2's — on the order of a few percent. (I know of multiple people who have made a successful career trading a model with a 5% R^2.)

A problem with both of these metrics is that they are **in-sample**: we test the

---

[11]For those looking for a quick answer, NIST/SEMATECH (2013) Section 4.4.5.2 discusses transformation and weighting and may be found at http://www.itl.nist.gov/div898/handbook/pmd/section4/pmd452.htm.

model on the same data sample used to estimate the model. This yields a model optimized to look good in test statistics. Much better is to test **out-of-sample**: assess the model on data that was not used to estimate the model. This almost always yields worse performance; however, it is far less likely to be biased.

10.9.3   Model Diagnostics

Another assessment of goodness-of-fit is to look at model diagnostics. Suppose we had T observations which we used to estimate a model with p coefficients. Many model diagnostic tests involve looking at the model's residuals $\hat{\epsilon}_t$:

$$\hat{\epsilon}_t = y_t - \hat{y}_t = y_t - \hat{\beta}_0 - \hat{\beta}_1 x_t. \tag{10.18}$$

Note that this model has $p = 2$ coefficients; we count the intercept $\hat{\beta}_0$.

Common tests to perform with the residuals are:

1. Plot residuals to check for patterns.
2. Test for autocorrelations.
3. Test for cross-correlations.
4. Check for influential points.
5. Check for multicollinearity.
6. Test alternate coefficient hypotheses.

Check Residual Plots for Patterns

Plot the residuals versus various covariates. Are there patterns of variation that seem to have been missed? If so, we should try to capture those patterns in our model. Plotting residuals is easy in R:

```
model.ibm <- lm(logret.ibm ~ logret.factor1, data=bigdataset)
res.ibm <- residuals(model.ibm)
plot(model.ibm$fitted, res.ibm)  # plot residuals vs fitted values
plot(bigdataset$date, res.ibm)   # plot residuals versus date
```

Test for Autocorrelations

Are the residuals autocorrelated? If so, we should probably add an AR term to our model. We can assess if the autocorrelation is significant with a Durbin-Watson test. In R, this is implemented by the **dwtest()** function in the **lmtest** package:

```
library{lmtest}
model.ibm <- lm(logret.ibm ~ logret.factor1, data=bigdataset)
res.ibm <- residuals(model.ibm)
dwtest(res.ibm ~ 1)
```

Test for Cross-Correlations

Are there correlations between groups of residuals? Suppose we modeled stocks with T observations each and noticed that $\text{Corr}(\hat{\epsilon}_i, \hat{\epsilon}_j) = \hat{\rho}_{ij}$ seems high. That might suggest there is an unmodeled relationship between those two stocks.

We can test the significance of the estimated correlation with the t-statistic versus the hypothesis that $\rho_{ij} = 0$ using the Student's t-test of Pearson (1895):

$$t = \hat{\rho}_{ij} \sqrt{\frac{T-2}{1-\rho_{ij}^2}}. \tag{10.19}$$

We then compare this statistic to critical values for a t-distribution with $T-2$ degrees of freedom.

Alternately, we can conduct the asymptotic z test of Fisher (1915) and Fisher (1921) versus a hypothesis that $\rho_{ij} = r$:

$$z = (\tanh^{-1}(\hat{\rho}_{ij}) - \tanh^{-1}(r))\sqrt{T-3}. \tag{10.20}$$

We can do these tests in R using the `cor.test()` function:

```
model.ibm <- lm(logret.ibm ~ logret.factor1, data=bigdataset)
res.ibm <- residuals(model.ibm)
model.aapl <- lm(logret.aapl ~ logret.factor1, data=bigdataset)
res.aapl <- residuals(model.aapl)
# Compute Pearson and Fisher tests
cor.test(res.ibm, res.aapl, method="pearson")
```

If the correlation is significant, we should examine the pair. Perhaps these stocks are in the same industry or region? If so, we should include that common effect in our model. If we are comparing multiple correlations, however, we should correct for that by requiring a higher p-value to reject the null hypothesis of no cross-correlation. One approach is to use a Bonferroni (1936) correction: If k comparisons are made, a test at the $1-\alpha$ level is then compared to a p-value of $1 - \frac{\alpha}{k}$.

Check for Influential Points

We may test for **influential points**: points which are far from the estimated model response (**outliers**) and points which may exert undue influence on the estimated coefficients (**leverage points**). There are a few tests for these.

Outliers are often found by looking at **studentized residuals**, aka **jackknifed residuals**. These are residuals scaled to incorporate the effect of omitting that observation:

$$\tilde{\epsilon}_t = \frac{\hat{\epsilon}_t}{\hat{\sigma}_\epsilon \sqrt{1 - h_{tt}}} \tag{10.21}$$

where $\hat{\sigma}_\epsilon = \frac{1}{T-p} \sum_{t=1}^{T} \hat{\epsilon}_t^2$ for a model with p coefficients (including the intercept) estimated from T observations; and, h_{tt} is the row t, column t element of the **hat matrix**: $X(X^T X)^{-1} X^T$.[12]

Leverage points may be found by looking at **Cook's distances**, discovered in Cook (1977) and Cook (1979):

$$D_t = \frac{\hat{\epsilon}_t^2 h_{tt}}{\hat{\sigma}_\epsilon^2 (1 - h_{tt})^2 p} = \tilde{\epsilon}_t^2 \frac{h_{tt}}{p(1 - h_{tt})}. \tag{10.22}$$

Typically, Cook has advised that a point with $D_t > 1$ is influential. Unfortunately, there is no distribution theory for D_i so we are often left to look at plots of values and examine relatively large values.

Finally, we can look at a sensitivity measure from Peña (2005) that is able to find outliers and leverage points, including those which may be in a cluster or missed by looking at Cook's distances. We can compute **Peña's sensitivities** as:

$$S_t = \frac{1}{p h_{tt} \hat{\sigma}_\epsilon^2} \sum_{t'=1}^{T} \frac{h_{tt'}^2 \hat{\epsilon}_{t'}^2}{(1 - h_{t't'})^2} = \frac{1}{p h_{tt}} \sum_{t'=1}^{T} \frac{h_{tt'}^2 \tilde{\epsilon}_{t'}^2}{1 - h_{t't'}} \tag{10.23}$$

$$= \sum_{t'=1}^{T} D_{t'} \underbrace{\sqrt{\frac{h_{tt'}^2}{h_{tt} h_{t't'}}}}_{<1; = \mathrm{Corr}(\hat{y}_t, \hat{y}_{t'})}. \tag{10.24}$$

A nice feature of Peña's sensitivities is that the S_t's are asymptotically normal. Furthermore, if none of the observations are influential, then $E(S_t) = 1/p$. This suggests the test statistic z_t for influential points:

$$z_t = \frac{S_t - \frac{1}{p}}{\sqrt{\mathrm{Var}(S_t)}}. \tag{10.25}$$

Peña also proposes a robust test:

$$|S_t - \mathrm{median}(S)| \overset{?}{>} 4.5 \cdot \mathrm{MAD}(S_t), \tag{10.26}$$

where MAD is the median absolute deviation which may be computed by the `mad()` function in R.

We can compute these three influence measures easily in R with the `rstudent()` and `cooks.distance()` functions:

```
model.ibm <- lm(logret.ibm ~ logret.factor1, data=bigdataset)
res.student.ibm <- rstudent(model.ibm)
plot(res.student.ibm)

cooks.distances.ibm <- cooks.distance(model.ibm)
plot(cooks.distances.ibm)
```

---

[12]The hat matrix is so named because it puts the hat on y: $\hat{y} = X(X^T X)^{-1} X^T y = Hy$.

```
# Compute Pena's sensitivities
p <- length(coef(model.ibm))
Q <- qr.Q(model.ibm$qr)   # the Q of the QR decomposition
H <- Q %*% t(Q)   # the hat matrix
h <- diag(H)
S <- H^2 %*% rstudent(model.ibm)^2/(p*h*(1-h))
```

Check for Multicollinearity

Another concern is **multicollinearity**: if our model has covariates which are strongly correlated with one another. If this is the case, interpreting the coefficients can be very difficult since multiple combinations of correlated covariates may yield roughly the same effect.

Intuitively, we see this effect in everyday life when travel navigation involves diagonal streets or autoroutes: navigation may take us past our destination and have us double back. Unfortunately the problem can be much more severe in linear models.

Mansfield and Helms (1982) outline a couple of methods to determine if we have collinearity among our covariates. Sometimes, multicollinearity manifests itself as a model with a significant F-test but no significant coefficients (except maybe the intercept). Many texts suggest looking at variance inflation factors. However, there are two even more direct ways.

First, we can look at the correlation matrix for the coefficient estimates. If there is a highly correlated pairing, we should see it there. Second: if a few coefficients are mutually collinear, then we will see that from the eigenvalues of the correlation matrix. We can also compute the **determinant** (product of all eigenvalues) or the **condition number** (ratio of the largest to smallest eigenvalue).

These can all easily be computed in R. For the above model, we can do the following:

```
cor.coeff <- cov2cor(vcov(model.ibm))
cor.coeff                         # coefficient correlation matrix
eigen(cor.coeff)                  # compute eigenvectors, eigenvalues
det(cor.coeff)                    # determinant
kappa(cor.coeff, exact=TRUE)      # condition number
```

What if multicollinearity is a problem? You have essentially projected onto a space with too many dimensions. There are a few ways to reduce the dimensions.

The most common solution is to just delete the less informative covariate(s) in a correlated group. More sophisticated approaches which effectively do this use standardized data and penalize the coefficients for these data; for example: **ridge regression**, which penalizes the sum of squared coefficients for standardized data, and the **least absolute shrinkage and selection operator** (LASSO), which penalizes the sum of absolute-valued coefficients.

Some analysts like to use **principal components analysis** (PCA) to reduce the dimension of predictors or find combinations. For data matrix X, PCA is an eigendecomposition of $X^T X$ into eigenvectors and eigenvalues. We typically use the eigenvectors for the largest eigenvalues to infer combinations of predictors. There are two major problems with PCA, however.

First, we are trying to model y, not X. We have no idea if the eigenvector-implied combinations are meaningful for the y we want to predict. True: the eigenvector with the highest eigenvalue (aka PC1) explains the most variance of the X's; PC2 explains the most variance after accounting for PC1; and so on. However, sometimes we model small effects that are present in high noise environments. We do not necessarily want predictors that align with background noise.

Second, principal components change with the data. So while we can look at the principal components and maybe derive some meaning from them, we cannot update the data and reuse PC1 or PC2 in a model; the meaning of each principal component changes over time.

Another solution is to create an **ensemble** variable (what is often called an index by econometricians): a weighted average of related variables. The weighting should relate to how relatively informative each variable is. One possible approach is to use the eigendecomposition of the coefficient correlation matrix to determine clusters of multicollinear variables. Then, for each cluster $\mathcal{K}$, run a set of univariate regressions:

$$y_t - E(y) = \underbrace{a_0}_{=0} + \beta_j x_{jt} + \epsilon_{jt}, \quad \forall j \in \mathcal{K} \tag{10.27}$$

$$RSS_j = \sum_{t=1}^{T} (y_t - E(y) - \hat{\beta}_j x_{jt})^2. \tag{10.28}$$

The RSS-minimizing ensemble variable $\tilde{x}_{\mathcal{K}}$ is then a variance-stabilizing weighted average of the coefficient effects:[13]

$$\tilde{x}_{\mathcal{K}} = \frac{\sum_{j \in \mathcal{K}} \frac{1}{\sqrt{RSS_j}} \hat{\beta}_j x_j}{\sum_{j \in \mathcal{K}} \frac{1}{\sqrt{RSS_j}}}. \tag{10.29}$$

Alternately, we could use a ensemble-minimum-variance estimator like that in Halperin (1961) based on clustering the covariates x. For a given covariate cluster $\mathcal{J}$:

$$\tilde{x}_{\mathcal{J}} = \frac{\iota \hat{\Sigma}_{X_{\mathcal{J}}}^{-1} \hat{\beta}_{\mathcal{K}} x_{\mathcal{J}}}{\iota \hat{\Sigma}_{X_{\mathcal{J}}}^{-1} \iota^T}. \tag{10.30}$$

where ι is the $1 \times |\mathcal{J}|$ vector of 1's and $\hat{\Sigma}_{X_{\mathcal{J}}}$ is the covariance matrix of the x's in cluster $\mathcal{J}$. The serious downside of this estimator is that it uses no information about prediction performance. Correlated inputs need not be informative for a given model; and, if they are not informative, their collinearity need not be problematic. This means that the covariate clusters $\mathcal{J}$ are not necessarily the same as the model-performance clusters $\mathcal{K}$.

---

[13]The proof for this is easy but we will omit it here.

Test Alternate Coefficient Hypotheses

The t-statistics for the model also typically test the estimated coefficients versus a hypothesis that the coefficients are zero. If we want to instead test, say, if $\beta_1 = 1$, we can test that with a different t-statistic:

$$t_{\beta_1=1} = \frac{\hat{\beta}_1 - 1}{\text{se}(\hat{\beta}_1)}. \tag{10.31}$$

The standard error for $\hat{\beta}_1$ (and other coefficient estimates) are reported by the summary() function in R.

10.10   Game-Theoretic Concerns

In Chapter 5 we talked about efficiency, but inherent to those concepts and (especially) to dynamic efficiency are ideas like competition, strategic choice, and market share. When General Motors or Ford makes a misstep, they know that competitors like Toyota, Subaru, and Kia are waiting to take advantage of that opportunity.

We mentioned in Section 7.4.1 how returns have skewness and kurtosis beyond what we would expect if they were completely random (with finite variances). We will see later, in Chapter 22, that limited liability explains some of the skewness; however, it does not explain it all.

We think that competition may explain some of these statistical phenomena. Competitors punish a firm's mistakes; and, that competition drives down prices which affects later profitability and revenues. Thus firms' performances are affected by game-theoretic concerns: prices and market shares result from firms finding an equilibrium with consumers and suppliers.

Even at the most atomic level of buyers and sellers, game theory is in the heart of the matter: a higher price benefits the seller and hurts the buyer; thus, they must agree — find an equilibrium — if they are going to trade. This directly affects the price of trade and we would be unwise to ignore such concerns.

This is not merely philosophical: I know of a grad student who spent years trying to build statistical models for order books. The student failed. The problem is not that such a model cannot be built; the problem is that such a model has a hard time working well if we ignore that trade (and thus order placement) is an equilibrium outcome. This might be as simple as knowing how to subset the data analyzed or as complicated as incorporating pieces of a game in a model.

That last sentence hints at one of the complicating aspects of equilibria: they are so powerful that they can distort finding a general, always-applicable linear model. Sometimes, this means we can get sharper results about one equilibrium if we restrict our analysis to a subset of data. In effect, these systems have only conditional stationarity.

Another way of seeing game-theoretic concerns is that they induce endogeneity into our data: Ford's profitability is influenced by GM's profitability and Toyota's profitability; but, their profitability is affected by Ford's and by each other's. What this means is even when we analyze investments, we may get strange, unusable results.

Suppose we wanted to see how research affects profitability at automakers. If we just grabbed data on automaker profits and research, we might see that research is associated with profitability. Unfortunately, the firms conducting research might be those with the most profits. However, research might also affect profits. Worse: when many firms invest in research, the effect on profits may be lower than if a single firm invested in research. How do we disentangle this endogeneity?

One way to disentangle cause and effect is the use of **instrumental variables**, variables which are related to the result but only through the cause we are studying. In other words: we want to find the effect of B on A; but, A also affects B; so, we need to find a C which only affects B. Since that is as clear as mud, some examples help.

For our example with automakers, we could use tax credits for research or the number of graduating engineers as a source of exogenous variation, *i.e.* variation which affects research (by making it cheaper) but not profitability (except through research). Typically, we would then use **two-stage least squares** to find the effect of research on profitability. If we denote the return on equity for firm i at time t, $\text{profits}_{it}/\text{shareholders equity}_{it}$, as ROE_{it}; the investment in research as I_{it}; and, graduating engineers as E_t, we can then write:

$$I_{it} = \alpha_{iI} + \beta_{iI} R_t + \epsilon_{it}, \tag{10.32}$$

$$ROE_{it} = \alpha_{i,ROE} + \beta_{i,ROE} \hat{I}_{iI} + u_{it}. \tag{10.33}$$

The only trick is that the standard errors have to be estimated from the endogenous equation

$$ROE_{it} = \alpha^*_{i,ROE} + \beta^*_{i,ROE} I_{iI} + u^*_{it}. \tag{10.34}$$

Obviously, this can get complicated since there might be lags to research leading to profitability. If we could find an instrument for profitability unconnected to research — say, unhedged material prices — then we could also find the effect of profitability on research. Another approach would be to do this through three-stage least squares, *i.e.* regressing ROE on $\hat{I}$ and then I on $\widehat{ROE}$; however, we need to be careful with the lag structure and this often cannot be resolved to guarantee that we are not just regressing I on I. We could also estimate the effects of ROE and research investment I on each other at the same time in a simultaneous equations model. All of these approaches are supported by the `systemfit` R package.

Finally, a very clever but rarely-applied approach would be to incorporate a small component or variable from a game-theoretic model into our statistical models. This can often yield very powerful models with new insights.

10.11   Quiz

Try to answer these questions in five minutes. For your answers, just write the
equations; do not evaluate them.

1. We are considering investing in a biotech firm's zero-coupon bonds. The firm
has one drug which is up for possible FDA approval. If the drug is approved, the
firm will pay off the bonds in full ($1000) in one year. If the drug is not approved,
the firm can only pay $800 of each bond.

    a) If we have no idea about the likelihood of approval, we might say the drug is
    equally-likely to be approved as not — so we take the probability of approval
    as 0.5. If that is the case, what is the expected payoff at bond maturity?

    b) The expected payoff factors in the risk of loss, so we can treat the expected
    payoff like it is guaranteed. (To get fancy: risk-neutral investors see them as
    identical.) If the risk-free rate is 2%, what is the present value of that payoff?

2. The concept of persistence is very general. What does it mean if a random
process has persistence?

3. What is the most often-considered form of persistence?

4. If $y_t = \phi y_{t-1} + \epsilon_t$, for which values of ϕ is the y process covariance stationary?

5. (2 points!) Log-returns for Microsoft and Apple have idiosyncratic variances
of 0.09 and share an industry variance of 0.07. What is the correlation of their
log-returns?

6. Most schemes for handling asynchronous trading involve a loss of data. | T   F

7. If log-returns Y_t follow an AR(1) process, what is you best guess of Y_{t+1} (Y
tomorrow) given Y_t (today's information)?

8. You hire a young researcher from a prestigious university. The person is learning
how markets work and reports that wheat returns Y_t behave according to the
following AR model:

$$Y_t = \alpha_0 + \phi Y_{t-1} + \epsilon_t, \tag{10.35}$$

with ϕ estimated as $\hat{\phi} = 1.03$. What does this model tell you?

10.12   Exercises

Instructions

We will download interest rates and inflation data using the **Quandl** package. The idea is to revisit the inflation prediction analysis done in Chapter 6. We will also try our hand at some simple credit modeling.

1. Hamilton (2018) suggests that the Hodrick-Prescott filter is not a good model and, instead, suggests using an AR(4) model quarterly to predict inflation. Using the downloaded data, fit an AR(4) model.

   What is the average error and average squared error for your predictions? Is that the same or worse than for the backward Hodrick-Prescott filter?

2. (Risky Business) Suppose we are considering investing in a Greek bond. The Greeks are asking for their *fourth* bailout since they still cannot pay off their bonds. If Germany, Slovakia, *et al* bail out Greece, a bond will pay off \$1000 in one year; if Greece does not get bailed out, a bond will pay off \$700.

   a) If the bond is a zero-coupon bond and the probability of a bailout is $2/3$ — and a risk-free zero-coupon bond is yielding 3% — what is the present value of the Greek bond?

   b) What is the yield of the Greek bond?

   c) Now suppose we can invest in a risky perpetuity. Each year we roll a die (1d6, if you want to be specific). If the die shows a 1 or a 2, we get \$21; otherwise, we get \$30. What is the value of this perpetuity if we can invest in risk-free zero-coupon bonds yielding 3% annualized?

3. (Ode on a Grecian Earn) With what we know so far, we can see what financial markets were saying about the situation in Greece in early 2015. (At the time of this question, the Greek government was just about to agree to a package of reforms.)

   Let p be the probability Greece defaults in a year and L be the loss given default (*i.e.* fraction of bond face not repaid). We assume defaulting in a year is independent of prior years; so, we get €1000 back in t years if there are no defaults (probability $(1 - p)^t$) and €1000×$(1 - L)$ back otherwise.

   Below are the prices of four Greek government bonds as well as EUR risk-free rates for investing over each time period. Prices are as of 23 February 2015:[14]

t	B	r_f
3 months	99.45	-0.099%
3 years	75.91	-0.196%
5 years	72.008	-0.075%
10 years	60.915	0.364%

   Find the values of p and L that best explain these bond prices. Remember that your expected bond payoff will need to be scaled to get it in percentage of bond face

---

[14]Yes, the nominal rates for the front of the EUR yield curve are *negative*. Europe was trying to get people to spend rather than save in the hope that would spur economic growth.

("1000" = "100"% of bond face); and, you need to compute the present value of the expected bond face percentage to match up with the current bond price. Finally, minimize the sum of squared differences between your predicted (modeled) bond price and the market price given.

a) Give the formula for the expected bond payoff.

b) Show how you modify that formula to get the present value of the expected percent of bond face.

c) Use that formula to find your estimated p and L. What are they?

d) Are these estimates reasonable?

e) Based on your model, which bond looks to be the most mispriced?

References

Belsley, David A., Edwin Kuh, and Roy E. Welsch. *Regression Diagnostics: Identifying Influential Data and Sources of Collinearity*. New York: Wiley, 1980.

Binder, John J. "The Event Study Methodology Since 1969". *Review of Quantitative Finance and Accounting* 11.2 (1998), pp. 111–137. DOI: 10.1023/A: 1008295500105.

Bonferroni, Carlo Emilio. *Teoria Statistica Delle Classi e Calcolo Delle Probabilità*. Florence: Pubblicazioni del Regio Istituto Superiore di Scienze Economiche e Commerciali di Firenze, 1936.

Box, George E. P., J. Stuart Hunter, and William G. Hunter. *Statistics for Experimenters: Design, Innovation, and Discovery*. 2nd ed. New York: Wiley, 2005.

Box, George E. P. et al. *Time Series Analysis: Forecasting and Control*. 5th ed. New York: Wiley, 2015.

Brown, Stephen J. and Jerold B. Warner. "Using Daily Stock Returns: The Case of Event Studies". *Journal of Financial Economics* 14.1 (1985), pp. 3–31. DOI: 10.1016/0304-405X(85)90042-X.

Cook, R. Dennis. "Detection of Influential Observations in Linear Regression". *Technometrics* 19.1 (1977), pp. 15–18. DOI: 10.2307/1268249.

— "Influential Observations in Linear Regression". *Journal of the American Statistical Association* 74.365 (1979), pp. 169–174. DOI: 10.2307/2286747.

de Jonge, Edwin and Mark van der Loo. *An Introduction to Data Cleaning with R*. Discussion Paper. The Hague: Statistics Netherlands, 2013.

Diggle, Peter J. et al. *Analysis of Longitudinal Data*. 2nd ed. Oxford: Oxford University Press, 2013.

Dobson, Annette J. and Adrian Barnett. *An Introduction to Generalized Linear Models*. 3rd ed. Boca Raton, FL: Chapman & Hall/CRC, 2008.

Durbin, James. "Efficient Estimation of Parameters in Moving-Average Models". *Biometrika* 46.3–4 (1959), pp. 306–316. DOI: 10.1093/biomet/46.3-4.306.

Durbin, James and Siem Jan Koopman. *Time Series Analysis by State Space Methods*. 2nd ed. Oxford: Oxford University Press, 2012.

Engle, Robert F. and Jeffrey R. Russell. "Autoregressive Conditional Duration: A New Model for Irregularly Spaced Transaction Data". *Econometrica* 66.5 (1998), pp. 1127–1162. DOI: 10.2307/2999632.

Epps, Thomas W. "Comovement in Stock Prices in the Very Short Run". *Journal of the American Statistical Association* 74.366 (1979), pp. 291–298. DOI: 10.2307/2286325.

Fama, Eugene F. et al. "The Adjustment of Stock Prices to New Information". *International Economic Review* 10.1 (1969), pp. 1–21. DOI: 10.2307/2525569.

Fisher, Ronald Aylmer. "Frequency Distribution of the Values of the Correlation Coefficient in Samples of an Indefinitely Large Population". *Biometrika* 10.4 (1915), pp. 507–521. DOI: 10.1093/biomet/10.4.507.

— "On the 'Probable Error' of a Coefficient of Correlation Deduced from a Small Sample". *Metron* 1 (1921), pp. 3–32.

Fitzmaurice, Garrett M., Nan M. Laird, and James H. Ware. *Applied Longitudinal Analysis*. 2nd ed. New York: Wiley, 2011.

Fox, John and Sanford Weisberg. *An R Companion to Applied Regression*. 2nd ed. Thousand Oaks, CA: SAGE Publications, 2011.

Galbraith, John W. and Victoria Zinde-Walsh. "A Simple Noniterative Estimator for Moving Average Models". *Biometrika* 81.1 (1994), pp. 143–155. DOI: 10.1093/biomet/81.1.143.

Halperin, Max. "Almost Linearly-Optimum Combination of Unbiased Estimates". *Journal of the American Statistical Association* 56.293 (1961), pp. 36–43. DOI: 10.1080/01621459.1961.10482088.

Hamilton, James D. "Why You Should Never Use the Hodrick-Prescott Filter". *Review of Economics and Statistics* Forthcoming.?? (2018), ??–?? DOI: 10.1162/REST_a_00706.

Henningsen, Arne and Jeff D. Hamann. "systemfit: A Package for Estimating Systems of Simultaneous Equations in R". *Journal of Statistical Software* 23.4 (2007). R package version 1.1-20, pp. 1–40. DOI: 10.18637/jss.v023.i04. URL: https://CRAN.R-project.org/package=systemfit.

Little, Roderick J. A. and Donald B. Rubin. *Statistical Analysis with Missing Data*. 2nd ed. New York: Wiley, 2002.

Lütkepohl, Helmut. *New Introduction to Multiple Time Series Analysis*. Berlin: Springer-Verlag, 2005.

Mansfield, Edward R. and Billy P. Helms. "Detecting Multicollinearity". *The American Statistician* 36.3, Part 1 (1982), pp. 158–160. DOI: 10.1080/00031305.1982.10482818.

McCullagh, Peter and John A. Nelder. *Generalized Linear Models*. 2nd ed. London: Chapman and Hall, 1989.

McTaggart, Raymond, Gergely Daroczi, and Clement Leung. *Quandl: API Wrapper for Quandl.com*. R package version 2.8.0. 2016. URL: https://CRAN.R-project. org/package=Quandl.

Morse, Adair. "Payday Lenders: Heroes or Villains?" *Journal of Financial Economics* 102.1 (2011), pp. 28–44. DOI: 10.1016/j.jfineco.2011.03.022.

NIST/SEMATECH. *e-Handbook of Statistical Methods*. Gaithersburg, MD: National Institute of Standards and Technology/SEMATECH, Oct. 31, 2013. URL: http://www.itl.nist.gov/div898/handbook/.

Oehlert, Gary W. *A First Course in Design and Analysis of Experiments*. New York: W.H. Freeman, 2000. URL: http://users.stat.umn.edu/~gary/Book.html.

Pearson, Karl. "Note on Regression and Inheritance in the Case of Two Parents". *Proceedings of the Royal Society of London* 58 (1895), pp. 240–242. DOI: 10. 1098/rspl.1895.0041.

Peña, Daniel. "A New Statistic for Influence in Linear Regression". *Technometrics* 47.1 (2005), pp. 1–12. DOI: 10.1198/004017004000000662.

Phillips, Peter C. B. and Jun Yu. "Dating the Timeline of Financial Bubbles During the Subprime Crisis". *Quantitative Economics* 2.3 (2011), pp. 455–491. DOI: 10.3982/QE82.

Rosenthal, Dale W.R. "Modeling Trade Direction". *Journal of Financial Econometrics* 10.2 (2012), pp. 390–415. DOI: 10.1093/jjfinec/nbr014.

Schafer, Joseph L. *Analysis of Incomplete Multivariate Data*. Boca Raton, FL: Chapman & Hall/CRC, 1997.

Tsay, Ruey S. *Analysis of Financial Time Series*. 3rd ed. New York: Wiley, 2010.

— *Multivariate Time Series Analysis: With R and Financial Applications*. New York: Wiley, 2013.

U.S. Securities and Exchange Commission. *Fourth Supplement to: Manual of Publicly Available Telephone Interpretations*. Retrieved 22 June 2017 from https://www.sec.gov/interps/telephone/phonesupplement4.htm. June 8, 2000.

Weisberg, Sanford. *Applied Linear Regression*. 2nd ed. New York: Wiley, 1985.

— *Applied Linear Regression*. 4th ed. New York: Wiley, 2014.

Wold, Herman Ole Andreas. *A Study in the Analysis of Stationary Time Series*. Uppsalla: Almqvist & Wiksell, 1938.

Zeileis, Achim. "Econometric Computing with HC and HAC Covariance Matrix Estimators". *Journal of Statistical Software* 11.10 (2004), pp. 1–17. DOI: 10. 18637/jss.v011.i10. URL: http://CRAN.R-project.org/package=sandwich.

Zeileis, Achim and Torsten Hothorn. "Diagnostic Checking in Regression Relationships". *R News* 2.3 (2002). R package lmtest: Testing Linear Regression Models, version 0.9.35, pp. 7–10. URL: https://CRAN.R-project.org/package=lmtest.

Part III

Valuation

⌑❋❋

Chapter 11

Fixed Income

The fixed income markets are vast: the market for all bonds is often far larger than equity markets. While firms may issue stock, the bond market includes firms, governments, municipalities, and even the debt of individuals. Since many institutions are restricted in how much risk they can take, they often predominantly hold bonds. We will see in later chapters that bonds are an important part of *any* portfolio.

The goal of this chapter is to introduce fixed income investments; explain their pricing; discuss their features and why those features exist; and, consider the possible risks for investors.

11.1 Overview

To see how big the bond markets are, Table 11.1 lists the size of the ten-largest sovereign bond markets according to Bank for International Settlements (2017). Table 11.2 lists those markets' most commonly-traded bonds.

Bonds now are typically related to loans; however, the earliest government bonds were sales of future revenues such as taxes, port fees, or crop assessments. These were like **revenue anticipation notes**: a loan of a fixed amount of cash which is repaid with revenues from a project or agency (for example, vehicle tolls on a road). However, revenue anticipation notes have limitations: one can only sell off a revenue stream once; and, the timing of selling off future revenue is more restricted. The introduction of bonds enabled states to raise a lot of cash quickly if needed for defense or for infrastructure which might increase taxes and thus repayment.[1]

---

[1] More on the development of sovereign bonds by the Venetians can be found in Goetzmann (2016).

Economy	Metonym	Outstanding (USD)
US	Treasuries	$17,000 bn
Canada	Bonds	$1,135 bn
Brazil	Soberanos	$2,074 bn
France	OATs	$1,921 bn
Germany	Bunds	$1,715 bn
Italy	BTPs	$1,974 bn
Spain	Bonos	$993 bn
UK	Gilts	$2,504 bn
Japan	JGBs	$8,932 bn
China	CGBs	$3,332 bn

Table 11.1: Outstanding issuance (in USD) for the top 10 (by issuance) sovereign bond markets, according to Bank for International Settlements (2017).

11.2   Bond Features

We mentioned before that a bond is a security relating to a loan. Typically, a bond is the rights to repayment of a loan with the par or face value being the amount borrowed. Often, par is repaid in one payment at the maturity date.

Before the maturity date, **coupon bonds** receive regular coupon (interest) payments. The annual interest paid is the coupon rate times par. Zero coupon bonds make only one payment: they repay par at maturity. This is common for bonds issued with maturities of one year or less; and, many bonds with maturities below two years may offer no coupon. All of these details (par, coupon, maturity, etc.) are listed in the bond indenture.

Bonds may include additional features to entice investors, help the issuer shift risk to manage funding costs, or take advantage of firm growth. Since companies face the possibility of default and cannot raise taxes, these features are much more common on corporate bonds.

11.2.1   Investor Enticements

There are many features which bonds may include to entice investors. For example, a bond might feature a **floating rate coupon** so that the interest paid varies based on current market rates. If interest rates go up, investors will receive a higher coupon. (However, if rates fall investors will receive a lower coupon.) **Indexed bonds** have a face value that increases with some measure of inflation, ensuring investors some real rate of interest.

Some bonds feature an **interest rate put**; this lets lenders force the issuer to repurchase the bond on the **put date** at the **put price** if interest rates rise above the **rate trigger**. (Bonds may have multiple put dates or a window from the first

Economy	Metonym	Maturity	Name	Full Name/Comments
US	Treasuries	$T \leq 1Y$	Bill	
		$1Y < T \leq 10Y$	Note	
		$T > 10Y$	Bond	
Canada	Bonds	$Y \leq 1Y$	Bill	aka Bons du Trésor
		$Y > 1Y$	Bond/Canada	aka Obligations
Brazil	Soberanos	$T \leq 2Y$	LTN	Letras do Tesouro Nacional
		$3Y \leq T \leq 5Y$	LFT	Letras Financeiras do Tesouro (zero coupon)
		$3Y < T \leq 5Y$	NTN-F	Notas do Tesouro Nacional - Série F
		$3Y \leq T \leq 40Y$	NTN-B	Notas do Tesouro Nacional - Série B
France	OATs	$T \leq 1Y$	BTF	Bon du Trésor à taux fixe et à intérêts précomptés
		$1 < T \leq 6Y$	BTAN	Bon à Taux Annuel Normalisé
		$6Y < T \leq 50Y$	OAT	Obligations assimilables du Trésor
		all	TEC	Taux de l'Echéance Constante n ans (const. maturity nY)
Germany	Bunds	$T \leq 1Y$	Bubill	Bundesbills
		$1Y < T \leq 2Y$	Schatz	Bundesschatzanweisungen
		$2Y < T \leq 5Y$	Bobl	Bundesobligationen
		$T > 5Y$	Bund	Bundesanleihen
Italy	BTPs	$T \leq 1Y$	BOT	Buoni Ordinari del Tesoro
		$1Y < T \leq 2Y$	CTZ	Certificati del Tesoro Zero Coupon
		$T > 2Y$	BTP	Buoni del Tesoro Poliannuali
		all	CCT	Certificati di Credito del Tesoro (float rate)
Spain	Bonos	$T \leq 1Y$	Letras del Tesoro	
		$1 < T \leq 5Y$	Bonos del Estado	
		$T > 5Y$	Obligaciones del Estado	
UK	Gilts	all	Gilt	From gilt edge of certificates.
Japan	JGBs	all	JGB	Japanese Government Bond
China	CGBs	all	CGB	Chinese Government Bond

Table 11.2: Commonly-traded fixed income securities for the top 10 (by issuance) sovereign bond markets, according to Bank for International Settlements (2017). While government issuance is often in specific maturities, those can change; therefore, the maturity regions implied by prior issuance (or specified explicitly) are given.

put date until maturity.) Similarly, **retractable** and **extendable bonds** allow holders to redeem them for par before or at some date later than the maturity date.

11.2.2   Issuer Risk Shifting

One way for an issuer to manage their risk is to issue an **inverse floating rate bond** which pays less interest when interest rates rise and more when interest rates fall. If other borrowing (often, short-term borrowing) is done at market rates, this may reduce the effect of interest rate changes on the issuer.

An issuer can also manage their risk by issuing a bond with an **interest rate call**. If interest rates are below the **rate trigger** on the **call date**, the issuer may repurchase the bond at the **call price**. (Similar to puts, some bonds have multiple call dates or a window of time.)

While many bonds feature a single repayment of par at the maturity date (sometimes called a **bullet**), the issuer might instead choose to spread the large cashflow of repayment over a few years with an **amortizing** or **sinking fund** bond. When this is done, the issuer may choose to repay some fraction of the bonds each year. The bonds to be repaid may be purchased in the market or selected randomly. If selected, the bonds are repaid at a pre-specified price. Obviously, issuers would only do this if it were advantageous. This can work similarly to an interest rate call.

Some firms which lend money repackage those loans into **asset-backed bonds**. This allows them to free up cash and lend to more customers. It also lets lenders tap into the capital of investors; and, for investors, it offers another investment which may offer an attractive return for the risk. (Or it may not offer an attractive return, as was the case with some such debt during the 2008 financial crisis.) In truth, any asset which has sufficiently predictable revenues can be turned into a bond. The most famous case is probably David Bowie's raising $55 mn selling ten years of revenues from his previously-recorded songs in 1997.

Insurance and reinsurance firms have issued **catastrophe bonds** which pay a higher coupon but a reduced face value when certain risk events happen. For example, a bond might pay one-quarter less face every time a category 5 hurricane enters a certain quadrant on a map of Florida. Obviously, if four such hurricanes enter that quadrant, investors will get no principal back. This allows those firms to tap into investors willing to take on insurance risk.

11.2.3   Taking Advantage of Firm Growth

Firms which expect to grow may monetize that expected growth by issuing **convertible bonds**, bonds which may be converted at maturity into a certain number of the firm's shares (aka the **conversion ratio**) if the share price is above the **conversion price**. The advantage for investors is potential upside: if the bond issue enables firm growth, bond investors can partake in that growth opportunistically. The advantage for the firm is twofold: the upside for investors often lets the firm offer a lower interest rate; and, if the stock rises, the firm need not make a large bond repayment when they are growing (and could use the money for more growth). These features should make clear which type of firms tend to issue convertible bonds: young growing firms.

Corporate bonds may be issued with detachable **warrants**. The warrants are issued with separate security identifiers and may be sold to investors. Similar to convertible bonds, warrants allow investors to purchase a number of shares at a certain price on the day the warrant expires. However, since the warrants may be detachable from the bond, the share purchase requires an investor to pay cash if buying the shares at the specified price. Warrants typically expire on the bond maturity date, allowing for investors share purchases to fund repayment of the bond.

Where do the shares for convertible bonds and warrants come from? They are issued by the firm. Thus convertible bonds and warrants function similar to a secondary equity offering — including dilution of existing shareholders' ownership. Strangely, some people choose to ignore this fact. See the sidebar, "Rising Sun... and Dilution" and read Ammer and Gibson (1996) for more information on government officials ignoring this issue in 1990s Japan.

Rising Sun... and Dilution

After the Japanese real estate bubble collapsed in 1991, Japan's Ministry of Finance was reluctant to let firms issue new shares to raise capital. They feared secondary offerings would dilute current shareholders and frighten them away from the equity markets. However, the Ministry of Finance did allow firms to issue convertible bonds and warrants. Thus a number of Japanese firms — even large firms — issued convertible bonds and warrants in the 1990s. Furthermore, many of these came with an unusual feature: the threshold for converting the bond to shares (or buying shares, for warrants) could reset downward. This greatly increased the likelihood that the bonds and warrants would result in new share issuance. Apparently, this indirect method of dilution was okay with the Ministry of Finance.

11.3   Bond Pricing

Bond prices may be quoted as a percentage of par or as a yield. Bond traders will refer to these in bond points (percentage points) and basis points (bp, 1/100-ths of a percentage point). We say a bond trading above 100% of par is at a **premium** and below 100% of par is at a **discount**. In general, when interest rates fall below a bond's coupon rate, the bond trades at a premium; when interest rates rise above the coupon, the bond trades at a discount. (You will get to prove this in the exercises.)

Pricing a bond is theoretically simple: we have already seen how time value of money works and a bond is just the sum of the present value of expected cash flows:

$$P_0 = \text{bond value} = E(\text{PV of par}) + E(\text{PV of coupons}). \tag{11.1}$$

11.3.1 Basic Bond Pricing

For many bills (which pay no coupon), the pricing is linear in time:

$$P = \frac{100}{1 + r\frac{T \text{ in days}}{\text{year in days}}}, \tag{11.2}$$

where T is the time to maturity and days are counted according to the daycount convention (discussed in the next section).

Other bonds are priced differently. If interest rates are constant, coupons are paid annually, and it just made a coupon payment, this is straightforward. Since we quote yields and interest rates as annualized, we need only use powers to account for compounding or partial periods. For a bond maturing in T years, this gives:

$$P_0 = \frac{\text{par}}{(1+r)^T} + \sum_{t=1}^{T} \frac{\text{coupon}}{(1+r)^t}. \tag{11.3}$$

Note that we can send $T \to \infty$ and eliminate the par payment to get a **perpetuity**, an unending sequence of cashflows. If interest rates are positive ($r > 0$), this has value P_0:

$$P_0 = PV(\text{perpetuity}) = \lim_{T \to \infty} \sum_{t=1}^{T} \frac{\text{coupon}}{(1+r)^t}, \tag{11.4}$$

$$P_1 = PV(\text{perpetuity starting at } t = 1) = \lim_{T \to \infty} \sum_{t=2}^{T} \frac{\text{coupon}}{(1+r)^t}, \tag{11.5}$$

$$P_0 - P_1 = \frac{\text{coupon}}{1+r} = P_0 \left(1 - \frac{1}{1+r}\right), \tag{11.6}$$

$$\implies P_0 = PV(\text{perpetuity}) = \frac{\text{coupon}}{r}. \tag{11.7}$$

This yields the perpetuity formula which is incredibly powerful and simple. We will make use of this more here and in Chapter 13.

We can also use this to price the coupon stream for a bond:

$$PV(\text{coupons}) = \frac{\text{coupon}}{r} - \frac{\text{coupon}}{r(1+r)^T}. \tag{11.8}$$

If the timing of the perpetuities seems strange, remember that by our derivation a perpetuity has its first cashflow one year after it starts.

This simplifies the bond formula to

$$P_0 = \frac{\text{par}}{(1+r)^T} + \frac{\text{coupon}}{r} \left(1 - \frac{1}{(1+r)^T}\right). \tag{11.9}$$

11.3.2   *Accrued Interest*

Between coupon payments, a bond accrues interest. If you sell a bond the day before a coupon payment, you deserve to get all but one day of coupon interest.

Most bonds trade **clean**: the quoted price reflects the relative value of the bond but not that partial coupon worth of accrued interest. Accrued interest is added to the clean price, but it is not quoted because there is agreement on the value of accrued interest. However, some bond markets add the accrued interest onto the clean price, quoting a **dirty price**:[2]

$$\text{Dirty Price} = \text{Clean Price} + \text{Accrued Interest}. \tag{11.10}$$

Dirty prices are harder to compare across time because there is a component of price which mechanically increases between coupon payments and drops right after coupon payments — looking like a series of saw teeth. Nonetheless, there are large bond markets which trade clean (*e.g.* US Treasuries and most corporates, most international sovereign bonds) and which trade dirty (*e.g.* distressed debt, since the next coupon payment may not be likely).

Calculating accrued interest is fairly straightforward; we only need to know the last coupon date and the **daycount convention**: the rules for how we count days.

$$AI = \frac{\text{coupon rate}}{\text{coupons/year}} \times \frac{\text{days from last coupon}}{\text{days, last to next coupon}} \tag{11.11}$$

$$= \frac{\text{coupon rate} \times \text{days from last coupon}}{\text{daycount days per year}}. \tag{11.12}$$

The daycount for most government bonds in the US is **30/360**: we count each completed month as 30 days and count a year as 360 days. Many corporate bonds and some sovereign bonds (including the UK, Canada, and Japan) use an **Actual/365** daycount: we count each completed month as its actual number of days and use 365 days for a completed year. (For those wondering, there is also an Actual/Actual daycount; and, Brazilian sovereign bonds use a business days/252 daycount.)

For example, a 6% bond which last paid a coupon on December 26 has, on May 15, $\frac{5+30\times4+15}{360} \times 6\%$ or $2\frac{1}{3}\%$ of accrued interest using a 30/360 daycount and $\frac{5+31+28+31+30+15}{365}\%$ or 2.30% of accrued interest using an Actual/365 daycount.

11.3.3   *Slightly Better Bond Pricing*

The bond pricing formulas work if the bond pays interest annually. However, many bonds pay interest more often. For a bond paying interest n times per year, the annual coupon price formula is a poor approximation. We can do better.

---

[2]In clean price markets, the dirty price may also be called the **invoice price**.

For a bond maturing in T years, constant interest rates, and just after a coupon payment, the bond price is:

$$P_0 = \frac{\text{par}}{(1 + r/n)^{nT}} + \sum_{t=1}^{nT} \frac{\text{coupon}}{(1 + r/n)^t} \tag{11.13}$$

$$= \frac{\text{par}}{(1 + r/n)^{nT}} + \frac{\text{coupon}}{r} \left(1 - \frac{1}{(1 + r/n)^{nT}}\right) \tag{11.14}$$

What if we are between coupons? We can modify this for a bond at some fraction of time $0 < \tau < 1$ between coupons. We first define τ via the daycount convention, as for accrued interest:

$$\tau = \frac{\text{days from last coupon}}{\text{days, last to next coupon}}. \tag{11.15}$$

We then modify the first discounting period to be for a fractional time to get the dirty price. In most locales, this is done like so:

$$P_\tau = \frac{\text{par}}{(1 + \frac{r}{n})^\tau (1 + \frac{r}{n})^{nT-1}} + \sum_{t=1}^{nT} \frac{\text{coupon}}{(1 + \frac{r}{n})^\tau (1 + \frac{r}{n})^{t-1}} \tag{11.16}$$

$$= \frac{\text{par}}{(1 + \frac{r}{n})^\tau (1 + \frac{r}{n})^{nT-1}} + \frac{\text{coupon}}{r(1 + \frac{r}{n})^\tau} \left(1 + \frac{r}{n} - \frac{1}{(1 + \frac{r}{n})^{nT-1}}\right). \tag{11.17}$$

In Germany, Austria, Switzerland, and some other locales, the first discounting period uses a linear calculation, aka the **Moosmüller method**:

$$P_{\tau,lin} = \frac{\text{par}}{(1 + \frac{r\tau}{n})(1 + \frac{r}{n})^{nT-1}} + \sum_{t=1}^{nT} \frac{\text{coupon}}{(1 + \frac{r\tau}{n})(1 + \frac{r}{n})^{t-1}} \tag{11.18}$$

$$= \frac{\text{par}}{(1 + \frac{r\tau}{n})(1 + \frac{r}{n})^{nT-1}} + \frac{\text{coupon}}{r(1 + \frac{r\tau}{n})} \left(1 + \frac{r}{n} - \frac{1}{(1 + \frac{r}{n})^{nT-1}}\right). \tag{11.19}$$

Finally, once we have the dirty price, we can subtract the accrued interest to get the clean price:

$$AI_\% = \tau \frac{\text{coupon rate}}{\text{coupon payments per year}}, \tag{11.20}$$

$$P_{\tau,clean} = P_\tau - AI_\%. \tag{11.21}$$

11.3.4   Bond Yields

Having derived the pricing formulas, we can now invert them. If we have a (clean) market price for a bond, we can then find the **yield to maturity**: the (risk-free) interest rate needed to reproduce the (clean) market price.

$$\text{YTM} = \{r : \text{bond market price} = P_\tau\}. \tag{11.22}$$

We can also find the **yield to call**: the yield if the bond were called for P_{call} at the first opportunity, time T_{call}:

$$\text{YTC} = \{r : \text{bond market price} = P_{T_{call}}\} \quad \text{where} \tag{11.23}$$

$$P_{T_{call}} = \frac{P_{call}}{(1 + \frac{r}{n})^{\tau}(1 + \frac{r}{n})^{nT_{call}-1}}$$
$$+ \frac{\text{coupon}}{r(1 + \frac{r}{n})^{\tau}}\left(1 + \frac{r}{n} - \frac{1}{(1 + \frac{r}{n})^{nT_{call}-1}}\right). \tag{11.24}$$

Another measure of yield is the **current yield**, the ratio of the annual coupons to the current price. For a bond trading at a premium, the coupon will be greater than the current yield; and, for a bond trading at a discount, the coupon will be less than the current yield. You might wonder if the current yield, by equilibrium, equals current interest rates. It does not, but it is close. For interest rates and coupon rates that are not "too different," the current yield is approximately the current interest rate. (You will get to quantify that in the exercises.)

11.3.5 Whence Log-Returns?

You might wonder: what happened to using log-returns? Recall that we use log-returns for, well, *returns*: changes in the price of an instrument. However, interest accumulating does not necessarily change the bond's clean price. Furthermore, if an instrument increases in price we can sell to realize that gain at any time. However, we did just discuss calculating accrued interest. Even though coupons are paid only occasionally, crediting the seller with accrued interest means that we can also realize interest at any time.

The reason we calculate bond prices this way is twofold: first, we only credit partial interest for one coupon payment at a time. That is the convention; however, it means that the dirty price of a bond exhibits a bit of a "sawtooth" pattern: accrued interest accumulates until it is paid out and falls back to zero. The second reason is philosophical: we tend to use returns to describe gains and losses. If we calculate returns based on the dirty price, the bond will seem to have lost value after it makes a coupon payment.[3] When we look at gains and losses for bonds, however, we will return to using log-returns. So take heart: our friend the log-return is here to stay.

11.3.6 Prices and Total Returns

A zero coupon bond priced at net present value will accrue capital gains when rates decline. Reinvesting funds after the bond matures will garner less interest; this capital gain offsets some lost reinvestment income.

---

[3]If you know how dividends work for stocks, you might wonder: why do we not just do similarly and adjust the prior bond prices? The answer is probably because unadjusted prices can be compared to one another across the bond's lifespan. The unsatisfying answer is because that is just how it is done.

If we have a discount and a premium bond with the same maturity, both bonds should yield the same. However, the proportion of capital gains versus coupon income will vary. This makes switching between bonds when rates change a potential tax optimization strategy.

The general intuition to have for bonds is that there is a fixed place where they will end up at maturity: they will pay out par. Therefore, when their price drops, they still have to end up at the same target; thus their yield to maturity increases. If you were holding the bond, however, an increase in yields means that your holding period returns decreased. (If yields stay the same for your holding period, your holding period return is the yield to maturity.)

Sometimes, bond holders do a **horizon analysis**: they forecast their realized returns over various holding periods. This can suggest when to switch between different bonds to maximize returns over some longer time period.

For most instruments, cashflows (*e.g.* dividends) are not a major driver of investment returns. Fixed income instruments are the opposite: capital appreciation is often not a major driver of returns while cashflows are. Therefore, it makes sense to consider **total returns**: returns which include capital gains and cashflows paid to investors. That means that for bonds we compute log-returns as:

$$r_{t \to \tau} = \log \left(\frac{P_\tau + AI_\tau + C_\tau}{P_t + AI_t} \right) \tag{11.25}$$

where C_τ captures coupons paid from time t to time τ.

11.4   Price Risk

In general, when interest rates rise, bond prices fall. There are some exceptions to this which we will discuss. But as a first-order approximation, this is worth remembering.

This raises an important point which bears emphasis since many investors forget it: *You can lose money buying and selling "risk-free" bonds.* We examined this exact idea in the data analysis done in Chapter 7. If you missed this implication, go back and look at the volatilities for long-term US Treasuries: their volatility is commensurate with that of the S&P 500. Risk-free bonds might have "negligible" default risk, but they have non-ignorable price risk. We typically characterize this as **interest rate risk**.

11.4.1   Interest Rate Sensitivity: Graphically

Can we characterize this relationship between changes in yields and changes in bond prices? Yes. We can start by plotting bond prices versus different yields to maturity using the following R code:

```
y <- seq(0.5, 8.5, by=0.01)    # range of yields
```

```
d6m <- 1/(1+y/2/100)    # 6-month discount factor
c1 <- 4.5  # annual coupon
b1 <- c1/2*(d6m+d6m^2+d6m^3+d6m^4) + 100*d6m^4    # 2Y bond
b2 <- c1/(y/100)*(1-d6m^10) + 100*d6m^10          # 5Y bond
b3 <- c1/(y/100)*(1-d6m^20) + 100*d6m^20          # 10Y bond
b4 <- c1/(y/100)*(1-d6m^40) + 100*d6m^40          # 20Y bond

plot(y,b4, type='l', xlim=c(1,8), lty=1, lwd=2, col="purple")
lines(y, b3, lty=2, lwd=2, col="magenta")
lines(y, b2, lty=3, lwd=2, col="red")
lines(y, b1, lty=4, lwd=2, col="orange")
abline(h=100, lty=1, lwd=1, col="gray")
legend.text <- c("20Y", "10Y", "5Y", "2Y")
legend("topright", legend.text, lty=1:4, lwd=2, col=c("purple","magenta","red","orange"))
```

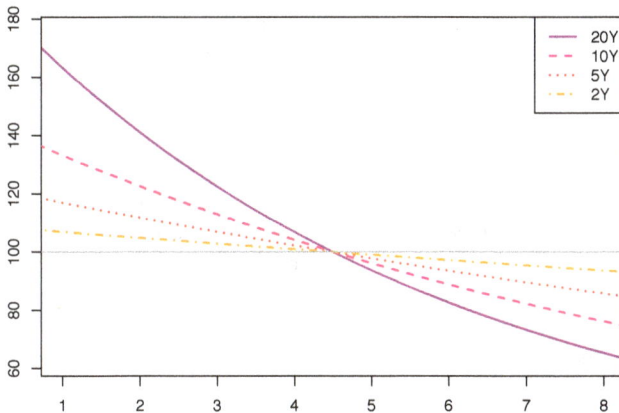

Figure 11.1: Bond prices versus yields for 4.5% coupon bonds. Note that the longer the bond maturity, the more sensitive the bond price is to changes in interest rates. Also, we can see that bonds are slightly more sensitive to interest rates at lower interest rates.

This code plots the yields and prices for 4.5% coupon bonds of differing maturities. Figure 11.1 reveals a few facts. First, as we said before, bond prices and interest rates are inversely related. More interesting is that longer-maturity bonds are more sensitive to changes in interest rates: the 20Y bond changes more than the 10Y, and similarly for the 5Y and 2Y. More subtle is that bonds are slightly more sensitive to interest rates as rates fall. Thus an increase in yields affects prices less than the same size fall in yields.

How does the coupon affect interest rate sensitivity? This is tricky because the coupon also affects the bond value at a given yield; so, comparing bond sensitivities is not so straightforward. However, we can plot the prices versus yields for bonds with differing coupons; and, we can then shift those curves or scale them to get percentage changes. Figure 11.2 shows these three plots. We can note a few details. First, the absolute price change is greater as the coupon increases. Second, the *percentage* change in a bond's value, however, decreases as the coupon increases. In other words, lower-coupon bonds should exhibit larger returns when interest rates change.

11.4.2 Interest Rate Sensitivity: Analytically

To get at the interest rate sensitivity, we can take the basic bond pricing formula (11.3) and differentiate. If we scale this, we get the **DV01**, the dollar value of a one basis point move:[4]

$$P_0 = \frac{\text{par}}{(1+r)^T} + \sum_{t=1}^{T} \frac{\text{coupon}}{(1+r)^t}, \tag{11.26}$$

$$\frac{dP_0}{dr} = -T\frac{\text{par}}{(1+r)^{T+1}} + \sum_{t=1}^{T} -t\frac{\text{coupon}}{(1+y)^{t+1}} \tag{11.27}$$

$$DV01 = \frac{dP_0}{dr} \cdot 0.0001 = \frac{-T\frac{\text{par}}{(1+r)^{T+1}} + \sum_{t=1}^{T} -t\frac{\text{coupon}}{(1+y)^{t+1}}}{10000}. \tag{11.28}$$

The DV01 formula confirms our earlier observation that the dollar value change in price was greater for larger coupon bonds. DV01 also has a simple interpretation: the change in the bond's price if interest rates for discounting all shift up one basis point. We will see later (when we consider different interest rates at different tenors) that such a move is not unusual.

On the other hand, we often think of changes in terms of returns. In that case, we need to divide $\frac{dP_0}{dr}$ by P_0:

$$\frac{1}{P_0}\frac{dP_0}{dr} = -T\frac{\text{par}}{P_0(1+r)^{T+1}} + \sum_{t=1}^{T} -t\frac{\text{coupon}}{P_0(1+r)^{t+1}} \tag{11.29}$$

$$= \frac{-T}{1+r}\frac{PV(\text{par@}T)}{P_0} + \sum_{t=1}^{T} \frac{-t}{1+r}\frac{PV(\text{coupon@}t)}{P_0}. \tag{11.30}$$

At this point, you might think this is even more confusing. Step back, however, and you may realize that P_0 is just the sum of the present value of the cashflows: $P_0 = PV(\text{par@}T) + \sum_{t=1}^{T} PV(\text{coupon@}t)$. Therefore, this percentage derivative is almost exactly -1 times the *weighted average of cashflow times* — where the weighting is the relative contribution of that cashflow to the bond value. The only difference is the division by $1+r$.

The result is that our intuition was correct: longer-maturity bonds are more sensitive to interest rates. Interest rate sensitivity is literally related to the average timing of cashflows. We also saw that lower coupon bonds were more sensitive to interest rates on a percentage basis. Sure enough, a zero coupon bond has only one cashflow at maturity: the weighted average time of that one cashflow is T. If there

---

[4]In case you are wondering, "DV01" is pronounced as "dee vee oh-one."

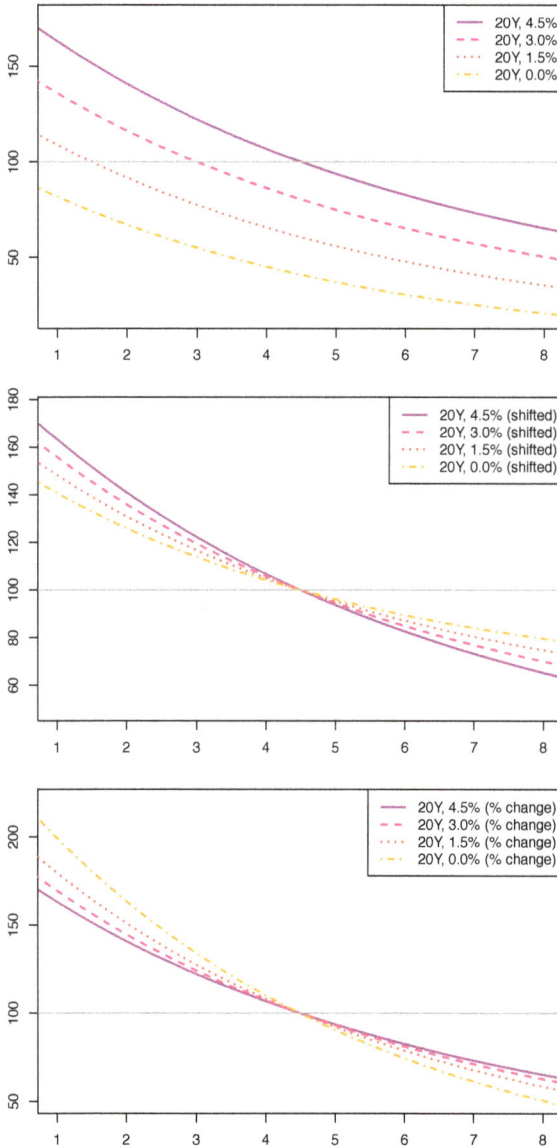

Figure 11.2: Bond prices versus yields for 20Y bonds with a range of coupons. The top plot shows the value of four 20Y bonds with a range of coupon rates. The middle plot shows those curves shifted up and down so that they all go through the (4.5%, 100) point. This allows us to compare the magnitude of changes in bond prices. The bottom plot shows those curves scaled to exhibit the percentage change versus the bond price at a yield of 4.5%. Note that the absolute price change is greater for higher coupon bonds; however, the percentage change is greater for lower coupon bonds.

were coupon payments, the weighted average timing (and interest rate sensitivity) would be less.

The flip side of this is that a T-year coupon bond has more cashflows at nearby times. These reduce the percentage sensitivity of the bond to changes in interest rates. This makes sense: \$1 tomorrow is going to be worth very close to \$1 today for a wide range of interest rates; nearby coupon payments dampen interest rate sensitivity.

This relationship between the present-value-weighted average of cashflow times and interest rate sensitivity is so useful, it has its own name: **duration** or **Macaulay duration**. In fact, we use duration to refer to the intuition average timing of cashflows and **modified duration** to refer to $\frac{1}{P_0}\frac{dP_0}{dr}$. Thus we can define the duration D and modified duration D^*:

$$D = -\frac{1+r}{P_0}\frac{dP_0}{dr} = T\frac{\text{par}}{P_0(1+r)^T} + \sum_{t=1}^{T} t\frac{\text{coupon}}{P_0(1+r)^t}, \tag{11.31}$$

$$= T\frac{PV(\text{par@}T)}{P_0} + \sum_{t=1}^{T} t\frac{PV(\text{coupon@}t)}{P_0}, \tag{11.32}$$

$$D^* = \frac{D}{1+r} = -\frac{1}{P_0}\frac{dP_0}{dr} = T\frac{\text{par}}{P_0(1+r)^{T+1}} + \sum_{t=1}^{T} t\frac{\text{coupon}}{P_0(1+r)^{t+1}}. \tag{11.33}$$

The difference between these is that we measure duration D in years and modified duration D^* as a percentage. We also note that DV01 and duration are related:

$$DV01 = -D^*P_0 \cdot 0.0001 = \frac{-D}{1+r}P_0 \cdot 0.0001. \tag{11.34}$$

Since, we have found perpetuities to be helpful, we should know the DV01 and duration of a perpetuity. Finding this is easy via calculus:

$$D^*_{\text{perp}} = -\frac{1}{c/r}\frac{d}{dr}\frac{c}{r} = -\frac{r}{c}\cdot\frac{-c}{r^2} = \frac{1}{r}, \tag{11.35}$$

$$D_{\text{perp}} = D^*_{\text{perp}}(1+r) = \frac{1+r}{r}, \tag{11.36}$$

$$DV01_{\text{perp}} = -D^*_{\text{perp}}c/r0.0001 = \frac{-c}{10000r^2}. \tag{11.37}$$

We can derive a few other insights from these equations:

- The duration of a zero coupon bond is just its maturity (in years).
- For the same maturity, a lower coupon bond has a higher duration.
- For the same coupon, a longer maturity bond has a higher duration.
- Bonds can behave like bonds with different coupons or maturities.
- Duration is like measuring the "effective maturity" of a bond (as far as interest rate sensitivity).

Finally, bond portfolio managers can buy or sell hedging instruments to cancel out their DV01. This **immunization** allows them to be more sure of achieving their target returns — even if they do not hold all bonds to maturity (*e.g.* due to portfolio rebalancing). In the extreme case, portfolio managers could hold bonds which delivered cashflows at the times they needed to disburse funds. This **cashflow matching** is an excellent hedge, but very difficult to achieve.

11.4.3   Changing Price Risk

From the plots of price versus interest rates, we know that a yield-to-maturity change that is twice as large does not have twice the effect on the bond price. Thus we know that DV01 and duration change.

This change in duration due to a nonlinear relationship between price and yield is, roughly, **convexity**. Specifically, we define convexity as related to the second derivative with respect to rates:

$$\text{Convexity} = \frac{1}{P_0}\frac{d^2P}{dr^2} = \frac{1}{P_0(1+r)^2}\sum_{t=1}^{T}(t^2+t)\frac{CF_t}{(1+r)^t}, \tag{11.38}$$

$$= \frac{(T^2+T)\frac{\text{par}}{(1+r)^T} + \sum_{t=1}^{T}(t^2+t)\frac{\text{coupon}}{(1+y)^t}}{P_0(1+r)^2}. \tag{11.39}$$

The quadratic time terms get at the curvature of the price-yield relationship.

Convexity seems like trouble: both practically and mathematically. Practically, durations must be recalculated after every yield change. Mathematically, the formula is a bit complicated and not so intuitive. And in some ways, convexity is trouble: it means that our risk exposures change and that canceling out those exposures is not trivial.

However, convexity is also informative. It tells us that interest rate cuts benefit bondholders more than interest rate hikes hurt them. This suggests that rate changes by a central bank are likely to be larger as interest rates increase. Convexity also allows us to better measure interest rate sensitivity. Specifically, we can better approximate the percentage change in bond price:

$$\frac{1}{P_0}\frac{\Delta P}{\Delta r} \approx -D^*\Delta r + \frac{\text{convexity}}{2}(\Delta r)^2. \tag{11.40}$$

Convexity is especially important for some bonds. Some bonds may be called by issuer if interest rates drop. Thus callable bonds do not usually trade above the call price. That creates **negative convexity**: as interest rates fall to become closer to the call trigger, falling interest rates may yield bond prices which tend toward the call price. Interest rate drops affect prices less and thus the duration declines. We can see this in Figure 11.3.

There is another problem with callable bonds: A called bond is extinguished before maturity. Thus calculating duration can be tricky. Instead, we often compute

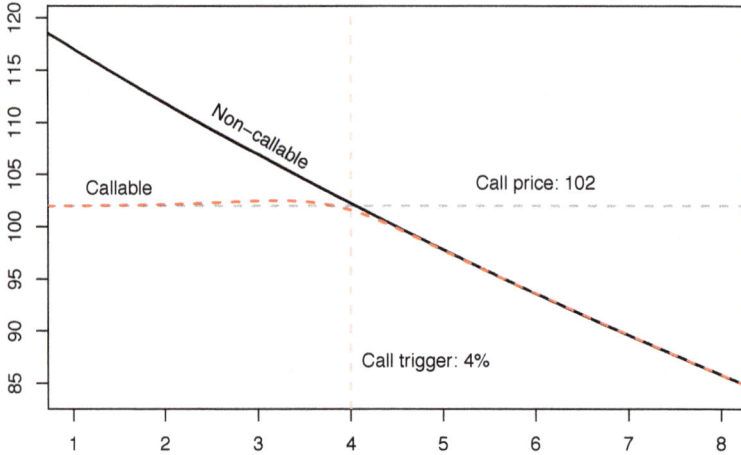

Figure 11.3: Price versus yield for a callable and non-callable bond. This illustrates the decline in duration for a callable bond as rates fall. This decline in duration yields negative convexity.

the **effective duration**: the duration implied by how the price changes for changes in yields.

$$D_{\text{eff}} = \frac{-1}{P_0} \cdot \frac{\Delta P_0}{\Delta r}. \tag{11.41}$$

These problems are not unusual. Most mortgages include an interest rate call: the ability to refinance the loan. If interest rates drop, mortgage borrowers refinance their loans. Thus mortgages also exhibit negative convexity.

Not all mortgage borrowers refinance their loans. Some people cannot afford the refinancing fees or may not even know that they can refinance. Mortgages which have been through a period of low interest rates may be largely composed of borrowers who are unlikely to refinance. The mortgage market slang for such borrowers is unkind: "dumbos." However, modeling mortgage bonds can be tricky if one tries to incorporate the "Dumbo effect."

11.5   Zero Coupon Bonds and Strippers

Bonds with zero coupon always trade at a discount; and, low coupon bonds often trade at a discount. (In the US, **original-issue discount bonds** are bonds issued with low coupons. These are much rarer than bills.)

Zero coupon bonds (and original-issue discount bonds, in the US) are often taxed based on expected implied interest. For example, consider a 10-year "zero" issued when $r = 5\%$. The bond's "fair" price is $P_0 = \frac{\$1000}{1.05^{10}} = \$613.91$. The expected fair price for the bond in one year (when it will be a nine-year bond) is $P_1 = \frac{\$1000}{1.05^9} = \$644.61$. This implies interest of $\$644.61 - \$613.91 = \$30.70$. If the bond were bought at fair value (\$613.91) and sold at \$630.00, the investor would realize a \$14.61 capital loss; if the bond were sold at \$650.00, the investor would realize a \$5.39 capital gain.

Zero coupon bonds are useful for determining discount factors. Most zero coupon bonds are issued for short-term maturities, but there is demand for longer and finer maturities than just those issued; those bonds help firms better time their cashflows to offset each other. To meet these needs, we can **strip** a bond: pull coupon and principal payments apart to turn each payment into a zero coupon bond. For example, a 4% coupon bond with $9\frac{1}{2}$ years until maturity can be turned into nineteen zero coupon bonds.

Strippers help the bond market meet demand for zero coupon bonds. The US Treasury even created a backronym for the process: **STRIPs** (Separate Trading of Registered Interest and Principal of Securities). If demand decreases, strippers also reassemble zero coupon bonds into coupon bonds.

11.6 Default and Credit

Bonds differ from other securities in the legal promise of coupon payments and in what happens when that promise is broken. A borrower who misses a bond payment is in **default**. Default can happen for a few reasons: the issuer's liabilities may exceed its assets (**balance-sheet insolvency**); the issuer may lack sufficient cash to make the payment (**cashflow insolvency**); or, the default may be strategic. If the bond is **secured**, aka **collateralized**, the creditors may seize assets pledged as **collateral**. Those assets are then sold and the money given to the bond holders. Extra money goes to other bondholders and then shareholders; insufficient money requires other asset sales. **Unsecured bonds**, aka **debentures** do not specify specific assets which may be seized but may force asset sales through legal action.[5]

Note that creditors *may* seize assets or pursue legal action. It is often cheaper to avoid legal action. Thus a default often results in a **debt workout**: creditors meet to find a way to help the borrower resume payments. Creditors may end up accepting less money but, if the loss is less than expected legal costs, less money may still be the best deal. This is where strategic default comes in; some firms will default in an effort to reduce high coupon payments. This is especially likely if a large shareholder is also a large bondholder: they may push to reduce coupon payments so the firm can grow more and increase the value of their shares.[6]

---

[5]In North America, the term "debenture" usually refers to unsecured corporate bonds.

[6]This is definitely getting into the realm of dirty tricks; however, this is not unusual behavior, especially for private equity investors.

11.6.1 Protective Covenants

While strategic default is in the realm of bad behavior, a debt workout is inherently outside the rules — so there is little to stop it. However, other forms of bad behavior by management are often precluded by bond indentures having **protective covenants**: rules governing treatment of bonds and uses of the monies raised by issuing bonds. Violating a covenant places the issuer in **technical default** and is often punished by lowering credit ratings.

> **Investor Discord** "Concord Leasing" leases and sells industrial and construction equipment. Over 2003–2007, their stock started and ended near $17 and was usually in the $20–$35 range. In 2007, the firm slightly increased debt and began its biggest share buyback in more than five years. Issuing debt was costly in 2008... but the firm increased debt from $2 bn to $3.5 bn — and bought back 30% (27 mn) of its shares. The stock price, however, sagged from $17 to $5 in early 2009.
>
> Why would a construction firm in a bursting housing bubble not conserve cash? During the 2007 buyback, data shows the CEO reduced his wealth in the firm from 80% to 70%. In 2008, while the firm nearly doubled its debt and bought back 30% of its shares, the CEO reduced his wealth invested in the firm from 70% to 30%. If the CEO sells shares or options while the firm buys shares, what should creditors think?

Covenants may require an issuer to regularly publish audited financial statements or to not engage in certain behaviors. Covenants generally protect against four categories of risks: claim dilution, asset withdrawal, asset substitution, and underinvestment.[7]

Subordination clauses state that later borrowers must be subordinated (have lower priority in liquidation). This prevents bondholders from finding more lenders ahead of them to receive payment if the issuer defaults. The hierarchy of who gets paid is referred to as seniority. **Subordinated** or **junior** debt is the last in line before shareholders.

Often, these covenants also include a clause allowing existing debt to be refinanced. For example, a ten-year senior note may, at maturity, be replaced by another ten-year note.

Cross-default clauses state default on any other of the issuer's bond is a default on this bond as well. This creates a "Three Musketeers" sort of strength in union: "all for one and one for all." This also makes strategic default more difficult and messier, if attempted.

Payout restrictions limit the amount paid out to shareholders. Often, these covenants say the firm cannot pay out more in dividends than they take in or cannot

---

[7]Bond covenants are covered in far greater depth by Jensen and Meckling (1976), Myers (1977), Smith and Warner (1979). Malitz (1986) discusses why certain firms include certain covenants; and, Stulz and Johnson (1985) discuss the pricing of certain covenants.

pay dividends until creditors have been paid. Less often, these covenants will make clear that the bond proceeds cannot be used for repurchasing shares.

Asset withdrawal restrictions state that the issuer may not sell off assets and give the money to shareholders. Even selling off an asset which generated cashflow could be deemed as violating this covenant if it increased the likelihood of default.

Asset substitution restrictions prevent changing from lower-risk to riskier projects or making the firm riskier. Thus increasing dividends or repurchasing shares could also violate an asset substitution clause.

Underinvestment clauses mandate investing in some lower risk projects and not just in higher risk projects so as to better ensure the ability to repay creditors.

Less common in bond covenants, but sometimes seen in loan covenants, is a **force majeure clause** which may temporarily or permanently exempt the borrower from making payments if certain unusual, material events occur. These are typically events which are unforeseeable, external, irresistible and affect the borrower — such as war, earthquakes, or terrorism.

11.7 Yields as a Measure of Risk

When we calculate yields to maturity, we are making the calculation as though the firm were going to pay off the bond without default. The **promised yield** is the yield to maturity based on promised cashflows. If we take into account the expected cashflows, we have the **expected yield**. While the expected yield should be similar to other yields, the promised yield may be very high if the expected cashflows are much less than the promised cashflows.

11.7.1 Credit Spreads

To measure the difference between these, we sometimes compare the promised yield to the yield for a similar (risk-free) sovereign bond. The **default premium** is defined as this difference: default premium = promised yield − similar sovereign yield. The default premium is one form of a **credit spread**. Sometimes, we measure credit spreads versus a floating rate like LIBOR instead, *e.g.* LIBOR+250 (where 250 means 250 basis points).

For example, imagine a corporate zero coupon bond maturing in one year. Suppose the bond pays $1000 in a year with probability 0.9 and $400 with probability 0.1. If a one-year T-bill yields 5%, the corporate bond is then worth:

$$P_{0,\text{corp}} = \frac{0.9 \cdot 1000 + 0.1 \cdot 400}{1.05} = \$895.24. \tag{11.42}$$

This implies a promised yield of 11.70% ($\frac{\$1000-\$895.24}{\$895.24}$) and thus a credit spread of 670 bp (11.70%-5.00%).

We will have more to say on credit spreads in Chapters 22 and 26.

11.7.2 High Yield

Obviously, promised yields are not indicators of guaranteed returns but, rather, potential return and risk. This observation is true across fixed income markets and leads to a subgroup of the fixed income universe known as high yield — bonds with substantial credit spreads. These bonds had poor **credit ratings**: assessments of bonds and issuers and their creditworthiness. Most firms would only hold investment-grade bonds: bonds with the higher credit ratings. Thus bonds below investment grade were deemed "junk." Hence high yield bonds are also sometimes referred to as **junk bonds**.

Before 1977, all junk bonds were bonds which had been downgraded due to the issuer running into trouble. These "fallen angels" often suffered because many firms would sell bonds at any price once they fell below investment grade.

However, in the mid-1970s, Drexel Burnham Lambert was trying to shake up the financial world. Drexel's Michael Milken had found an opportunity with bonds that fell below investment grade: firms dumping the bonds meant that a portfolio of high-yield bonds could deliver attractive returns at far less risk than market prices indicated.

The appetite for high-yield investments grew until the market ran out of "fallen angels" Thus in 1977, Drexel and Milken premiered the first original-issue junk bond: $30 mn of 11.5% coupon bonds issued by Texas International. This opened up a new potential funding source for early-stage firms.

High yield has now become an accepted part of the fixed-income universe — although there are still many bond holders who are prevented by mandates from holding anything below investment grade. High yield often trades somewhat like equity since its prospects are also uncertain. If assets are less than liabilities, high yield may trade very much like equities. This is why some financial firms have their high-yield and equity traders sit near one another.

11.7.3 Liquidity

Finally, yields can also reflect other risks. While it may sound strange, bonds are like puppies: they quickly find a "forever home." With bonds, insurance companies and endowments often purchase them to ensure they can meet later cashflow needs. Thus they purchase the bonds and hold them until maturity.

For this reason, government bonds are very liquid when they are newly-issued (aka **on-the-run**); however, they soon become illiquid. Once other bonds are issued at the same maturity, the old issues become **off-the-run** bonds. These bonds have a higher bid-ask spread and also trade at a slightly higher yield to reflect their lower liquidity.

Do those bonds ever become more liquid? Díaz and Escribano (2017) shows that they can when they near certain tenors. For example, a bond which has about five years remaining until maturity might become more liquid if people find it attractive compared to newly-issued five year bonds; however, this effect is slight and far outweighed by the reduced liquidity of bonds (like puppies) finding permanent holders.

11.8   A Few Words on Repos

Repurchase agreements are an important but often-overlooked part of the fixed income universe. A **repurchase agreement** (repo) is a sale linked with a (sometimes optional) repurchase at a higher price later. The higher repurchase price implies an interest rate and is often used by investors as a form of collateralized lending. This frees up cash for the investor to meet cashflow needs; however, it also increases the **leverage** — the ratio of debt to equity. If the borrowed capital is used for further speculation, losses can exceed the initial capital.

When a firm repos a security, they **hypothecate** or pledge the security for collateral.[8] They agree to a security-specific **repo rate**, the implied interest rate. That repo rate may be the **general collateral** rate used for most repos or, if there is demand to short the security, the repo rate may be a **special rate**.

The lender then takes ownership of the security and the firm receives cash. However, the firm rarely receives the full security sale price; the lender usually retains a fraction of the sale proceeds — the **haircut**. The haircut is higher for riskier securities and riskier borrowers.

Duffie (1996) discusses how special rates arise; and, Corradin and Maddaloni (2017) note how specialness of Italian government bonds increased during the European Sovereign Debt Crisis. Gorton and Metrick (2010) is an excellent reference on haircuts and how they behaved during the 2010 debt crisis.

Unfortunately, the (preceding) Great Financial Crisis revealed that repos can be used for deceptive purposes. Lehman Brothers classified certain repos as sales and then structured the repos to cover reporting periods. Thus they made their leverage look lower by having more cash and fewer assets listed in financial reports. Munyan (2017) discusses this and finds evidence that other firms are using repos in a similar way.

Finally, repo volumes have declined precipitately in recent years. The cause is largely due to regulation enacted in response to the 2008 financial crisis, specifically Basel III and the Dodd-Frank Act. Both greatly increased the regulatory capital required to hold repos. Thus many banks have exited the market; and, repo users have shifted to supplying riskier collateral. This, in turn, has caused a decline in liquidity in some markets. Duffie (2018) and Allahrakha, Cetina, and Munyan (2018) discuss these issues.

---

[8]Since the lender can in turn repo the securities (**rehypothecation**), repoed securities also have a multiplier similar to money in the Keynesian analysis of the money supply.

11.9   Quiz

Try to answer these questions in five minutes. For your answers, just write the equations; do not evaluate them.

1. A $1000 par bond pays $20 annually in semiannual coupons. The last coupon was on Jun 1; today is Aug 10. How many days of accrued interest would be owed using the following daycount methods?

   a) 30/360 daycount?

   b) Actual/365 daycount

2. An annuity starting now will pay $1 annually... *forever*. Risk-free interest rates are constant (hoo ah!) at 0.1%. How much is this annuity worth?

3. A coupon bond pays cashflows of $5 in one year, $5 in two years, and $105 in three years. The present value of these cashflows is $4.95, $4.85, and $98.70.

   a) What is the fair price of this bond?
   b) What is the duration of this bond?
   c) Are short-term rates most likely above or below 5% — and *why*?

4. A bond is trading at $105.01. Use this table for prices at different YTMs.

YTM	2.79%	2.80%	2.81%
Price	$105.05	$105.01	$104.97

   a) What is the an estimate of the bond's DV01?
   b) What is an estimate of the bond's convexity? (Think carefully.)
   c) Do you think this bond's coupon is less than 2.8%? Why or why not?
   d) Suppose this bond pays a coupon of $3 and has a face of $100. If you had to guess, would you think it matures in 3 years, 10 years, or 30 years? *Why?*

5. You are investing in an under-performing company. To limit your risk, you invest in their bonds. The company is poorly-run but in a profitable industry. A private equity firm buys the firm from shareholders and installs better management.

   a) If your bonds are paying an above-industry coupon, when might you expect the private equity firm to strategically default on your bonds?

   b) What protects you from the PE firm just defaulting on the most expensive bonds?

   c) The PE firm pays the new management largely in stock. They then propose to issue a big dividend to reward early cost cutting. What protection might you have as a bondholder to limit this action?

6. Interest rates are about to (maybe) be changed by the central bank and you hold three sovereign bonds: a 30Y zero-coupon bond, a 30Y coupon bond, and a 2Y note with the same coupon. You want to protect yourself against changes in the bond prices in case interest rates change; however, you are pressed for time. Which bond do you hedge first and second — and why?

7. A two-year bond pays semi-annual coupons of 3% annualized. If interest rates are 2%, write the formula which will give the price of this bond.

8. What is one of the big advantages of holding municipal bonds?

9. What is the highest credit rating for a bond that is still not investment grade?

10. (Bonus!) When a bond moves from speculative credit to investment grade, we expect its price to rise. What makes that jump particularly powerful?

11.10 Exercises

1. Prove: For positive rates $r > 0$, a zero coupon bond always is priced at a discount $(P < 100)$

2. Assume we have a coupon bond with a face value of 100, a coupon rate of $c/100$, and that the interest rate is r.

   a) Prove that for $r > 0$ that if the coupon rate equals the interest rate, the bond price is $P = 100$. (Hint: Use the perpetuity formula.)

   b) Prove that the above is true if we allow for $r \leq 0$.

3. For interest rates r close to the coupon rate $c/100$, show that the current yield is approximately r.

4. Show that if $r < c/100$, the current yield is greater than the market level of interest r. Then show that if $r > c/100$, $CY < r$.

5. Suppose a 3% semi-annual coupon 10Y bond has a sinking fund of 20%/year starting at the end of year 6. If interest rates are 4% and repayments are made purely by schedule (so retiring 20%/year with no strategic choice), what is the price of the bond?

6. Suppose firms default as in the example in the credit spreads section. What is the risk and expected return of a portfolio of n such bonds if they are iid? If you cannot get the answer theoretically, simulate it.

References

Allahrakha, Meraj, Jill Cetina, and Benjamin Munyan. "Do Higher Capital Standards Always Reduce Bank Risk? The Impact of the Basel Leverage Ratio on the U.S. Triparty Repo Market". *Journal of Financial Intermediation* Forthcoming.? (2018), ??–?? DOI: 10.1016/j.jfi.2018.01.008.

Ammer, John and Michael S. Gibson. *Regulation and the Cost of Capital in Japan: A Case Study.* International Finance Discussion Paper 556. Board of Governors of the Federal Reserve System, 1996. URL: https://www.federalreserve.gov/pubs/ifdp/1996/556/ifdp556.pdf.

Bank for International Settlements. *Debt Securities Statistics.* Retrieved 26 June 2017. June 6, 2017. URL: http://www.bis.org/statistics/c1.pdf.

Corradin, Stefano and Angela Maddaloni. *The Importance of Being Special: Repo Markets During the Crisis.* Working Paper 2065. European Central Bank, 2017. URL: https://www.ecb.europa.eu/pub/pdf/scpwps/ecb.wp2065.en.pdf.

Díaz, Antonio and Ana Escribano. "Liquidity Measures Throughout the Lifetime of the U.S. Treasury Bond". *Journal of Financial Markets* 33.C (2017), pp. 42–74. DOI: 10.1016/j.finmar.2017.01.002.

Duffie, Darrell. "Special Repo Rates". *Journal of Finance* 51.2 (1996), pp. 493–526. DOI: 10.1111/j.1540-6261.1996.tb02692.x.

— "Financial Regulatory Reform After the Crisis: An Assessment". *Management Science* Forthcoming.? (2018), ??–?? DOI: 10.1287/mnsc.2017.2768.

Goetzmann, William N. *Money Changes Everything: How Finance Made Civilization Possible.* Princeton University Press, 2016.

Gorton, Gary and Andrew Metrick. "Haircuts". *Federal Reserve Bank of St. Louis Review* 92.6 (2010), pp. 507–519. DOI: 10.20955/r.2010.507-519. URL: https://research.stlouisfed.org/publications/review/2010/11/01/haircuts/.

Jensen, Michael C. and William H. Meckling. "Theory of the Firm: Managerial Behavior, Agency Costs and Ownership Structure". *Journal of Financial Economics* 3.4 (1976), pp. 305–360. DOI: 10.1016/0304-405X(76)90026-X.

Malitz, Ileen. "On Financial Contracting: The Determinants of Bond Covenants". *Financial Management* 15.2 (1986), pp. 18–25. DOI: 10.2307/3664974.

Munyan, Benjamin. *Regulatory Arbitrage in Repo Markets.* Working Paper 2685592. SSRN, 2017. DOI: 10.2139/ssrn.2685592.

Myers, Stewart C. "Determinants of Corporate Borrowing". *Journal of Financial Economics* 5.2 (1977), pp. 147–175. DOI: 10.1016/0304-405X(77)90015-0.

Smith, Clifford W. and Jerold B. Warner. "On Financial Contracting: An Analysis of Bond Covenants". *Journal of Financial Economics* 7.2 (1979), pp. 117–161. DOI: 10.1016/0304-405X(79)90011-4.

Stulz, René M. and Herb Johnson. "An Analysis of Secured Debt". *Journal of Financial Economics* 14.4 (1985), pp. 501–521. DOI: 10.1016/0304-405X(85)90024-8.

Chapter 12

Yield Curves

We have been a bit naive up to this point: we talked about interest rates being set by supply and demand to rent money, but we have ignored that supply and demand vary with the length (or **tenor**) of that rent. You might not realize you ignored this, but that is the implication of assuming constant interest rates. While it is unrealistic, it is easily remedied.

Supply and demand affect prices at all maturities.[1] Thus bonds for different maturities have different yields. If we plot those yields versus the times to maturity, we get what we call the *yield curve*. We often refer to plots of financial data against times to maturity or expiry as the **term structure**. The yield curve is the term structure of interest rates.

The goal of this chapter is to introduce you to yield curves; help you identify the meaning of common yield curve shapes; classify yield curves movements; and, give you enough information to think critically about yield curve models.

12.1   Yield Curve Basics

Yield curves are probably the most informative graphic in all of finance. A two-second look at a yield curve can often tell you if an economy is doing well, floundering, or if its politicians are struggling to keep investors inside the country. Imagine suave you walking through the airport in Singapore, Shenzhen, San Francisco, Santiago, or Stellenbosch.[2] You look over at a video monitor and see a yield curve on the way to the lounge. In that instant, you can see how that economy is doing overall. Yield curves are that powerful.

---

[1]This quickly leads to questions like "Does government demand to borrow affect the quantity of loans supplied? And, if so, can government borrowing 'crowd out' other borrowers?"

[2]Well, just outside of Stellenbosch, but I have faith that you, suave dear reader, would have the good sense to stop by Stellenbosch when visiting Cape Town.

12.1.1   Plotting

Because yield curves are so informative, we discuss them in their own chapter. We often talk about the shape of yield curves: are they upward-sloping, flat, inverted, or humped? Each of these shapes has a different economic meaning. There are also a few details to remember in how we plot yield curves and their relatives.

1. We mostly *plot yields of non-indexed government bonds.* Inflation-indexed government bonds are often issued at fewer maturities. Corporate bond yields include compensation for default risk.

2. We consistently *plot yields for the same tenors* to allow us to compare curves across time. To facilitate this, many central banks produce **constant-maturity yields**: implied yields for certain benchmark tenors.[3]

3. While we plot yields versus time, *the time axis is not scaled.* Each tenor (time to maturity) is plotted in order as though they were equally-spaced.

4. We also often *abbreviate these tenors.* The overnight rate, one-, three- and six-month rates, and one-year-, two-year-, five-year-, ten-year-, twenty-year-, and thirty-year-rates are often written as O/N, 1M, 3M, 6M, 1Y, 2Y, 5Y, 10Y, 20Y, and 30Y (*e.g.* for the tenors mentioned above). You might have picked up on this convention before.

We could instead plot zero coupon bond yields to get a **zero curve**. Alternately, we might plot the **discount curve**: the curve of discount factors. These are isomorphic and are useful enough that we will discuss them more in the following sections.

If we were to plot LIBOR-based yields, we would get what is called the **swap curve**. We might also use other deposit rates like TIBOR. We will see more of these curves in Chapter 22.

12.1.2   What Yield Curves Tell Us

These yield curve movements tell us about the prices to rent money, but they also tell us where the macroeconomy is heading. In particular, they mean that the curve is moving toward or away from certain meaningful shapes. These shapes are meaningful because they tend to reflect certain macroeconomic situations. The shapes we pay the most attention to are:

- **Inverted**: the curve slopes downward;
- **Upward-sloping**: the curve slopes upward;
- **Humped**: the curve is elevated in the middle; and,
- High or low **front end**: short-term interest rates differ markedly from slightly longer-term interest rates.

We can see all of these shapes in Figures 12.1 and 12.2.

---

[3]Astute and assiduous readers will have noticed that we worked with constant-maturity Treasuries in the exercises for Chapter 2.

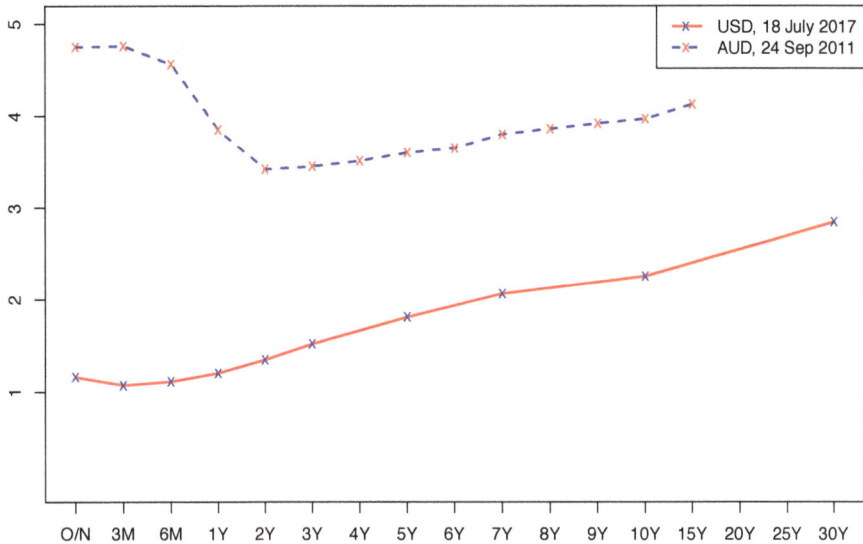

Figure 12.1: Plots of two common archetypal yield curves. The solid line is a rising yield curve for the US in September of 2011. This reflected healthy economic growth and recovery from the 2008 financial crisis. The dashed line is a rising yield curve with a sharply elevated front end for Australia in July of 2017. The elevated front end reflects the central bank trying to slow growth to avoid an overheated economy.

The most telling shape is that of an inverted yield curve. When the yield curve slopes downward, this means that investors value long-term bonds more highly than short-term bonds. Recall that small firms and individuals (which are riskier) tend to use more short-term borrowing while large firms and governments (which are less risky) tend to use more long-term borrowing. When the macroeconomy looks risky, short-term interest rates rise because there may be a greater demand to rent money to see a borrower through a possible crisis.

On the supply side, lenders are more reluctant to lend to short-term borrowers since they are riskier while they are (relatively) less reluctant to lend to long-term borrowers. However, lenders are bond investors. When the economy looks uncertain or scary, investors tend to reduce their holdings of risky investments and redeploy those funds to less-risky investments. Often, they sell stocks and buy long-term bonds, especially government bonds, since bonds are less likely to lose money. Buying long-term bonds increases their prices which reduces their yields. Thus an inverted yield curve is a strong signal that many investors believe the economy is headed for trouble. Intuitively, inverted yield curves are like dark storm clouds overhead: they signal that a storm is coming and that it may be wise to take cover.

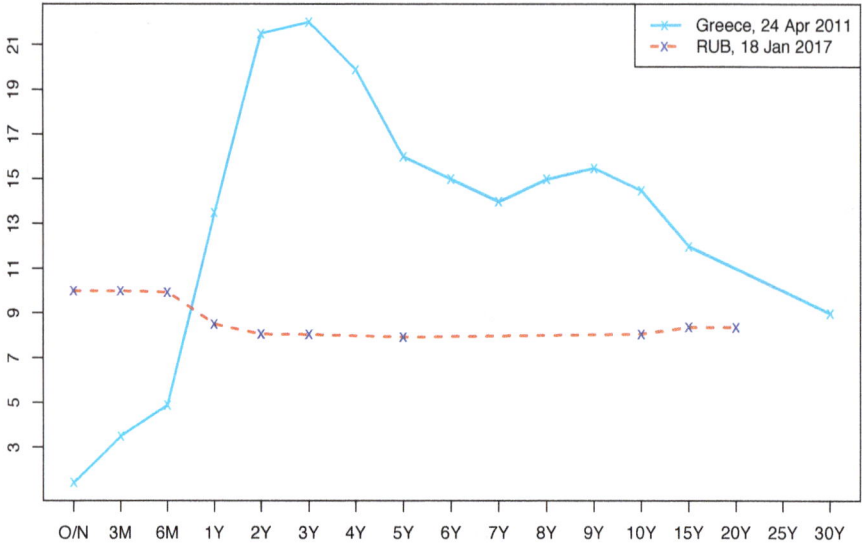

Figure 12.2: Plots of two archetypal yield curves which are less common and more troubling. The solid line is a humped yield curve for Greece in April of 2011. This curve reflected a combination of capital flight and an attempt to keep money in the economy. While Greece was in the Eurozone, this curve also reflects a possible currency defense against ejection from the Eurozone. The dashed line is an inverted yield curve for Russia in January of 2017. The inverted curve reflected Russia's continuing economic malaise due to low oil prices.

If an inverted yield curve is telling, what about an upward-sloping yield curve? That tells the opposite story: borrowers are not frantic for funds to see themselves through some crisis, and lenders are willing to lend in the short-term but would demand higher-yields to tie their money up instead of putting it into, say, stocks. To continue the analogy for intuitive sake, upward-sloping yield curves are like blue skies: they signal a pleasant day and that one should be out and active.

A humped yield curve is a bit less clear. It could suggest an economy transitioning between crisis and recovery... or it could suggest political dithering. When an economy has structural problems, investors may hope for structural reforms (*e.g.* strengthening the fairness of laws, reducing corruption and burdensome regulations, or eliminating restrictions on investment or capital flows). However, when politicians avoid the pain of structural reforms, investors may decide to invest elsewhere. That could adversely affect the currency's exchange rate (and the government's cash holdings).

What can politicians do to buy themselves more time and keep money in their economy? They can push up the yields of intermediate bonds — either through trading or by issuing more intermediate-term bonds with high coupons. This issuance may even be used to fund purchases of sovereign debt issued in foreign currencies. This makes the intermediate-term (domestic currency) bonds more attractive to investors and may entice them to keep their capital in the economy for a little longer (or even invest more). Pumping up intermediate-term yields is a **currency defense**: political meddling in an attempt to shore up a currency's value. While higher yields may be appealing, investors should consider the risk of a future devaluation if politicians continue to avoid structural reforms.

If the front end of the yield curve is much higher or lower than rates for slightly longer tenors, this suggests that monetary policy is trying to slow down or speed up the growth of the money supply (and the economy). In general, governments and central banks have a lot of money to use to set rates where they want them, so that is a risk investors should not try to fight or ignore.

What would you see if you plotted the USD yield curve along with levels of the S&P 500, the yield curve slope, and levels of two other indicators of distress or uncertainty: the TED spread and the VIX? You would notice that the yield curve was indicating, even back in mid-2006, that the US economy was headed for trouble. Figure 12.3 shows this plot for 7 September 2006. We can see that the yield curve is inverted (with a fitted slope that is negative); and, the TED spread above 50 basis points indicates a crisis, as per Boudt, Paulus, and Rosenthal (2017). For those who believe equity markets are optimistic or slow to see oncoming crises, the low level of the VIX may bolster such claims.

You can see more such plots in a movie that shows them over January 1990–April 2015. You will see how rare an inverted yield curve is; how clear the yield curve was at signaling trouble before the dot-com bust and 2001 recession (even pre-11 September) as well as the 2008 crisis; and, how government shutdowns and default threats affect the yield curve. The movie may be viewed at: `https://www.youtube.com/watch?v=6z8g9xaj3g8`.

12.2 The Types of Interest Rates

12.2.1 Spot Rates

Yield curves and zero curves are especially useful for bond pricing. The yields on zero coupon bonds are important enough that they get their own name: **spot rates**. A yield curve of spot rates is called the zero curve or the **pure yield curve**. We can relate the zero curve and discount curve easily, as in Table 12.1.

The zero curve is so useful that we often use it as the basis of pricing all bonds. Mathematically, we can easily price a bond by converting the yields to discount factors and then taking the dot product of discount factors and bond cashflows. We will discuss how to find the zero curve from a (non-pure) yield curve when we discuss bootstrapping.

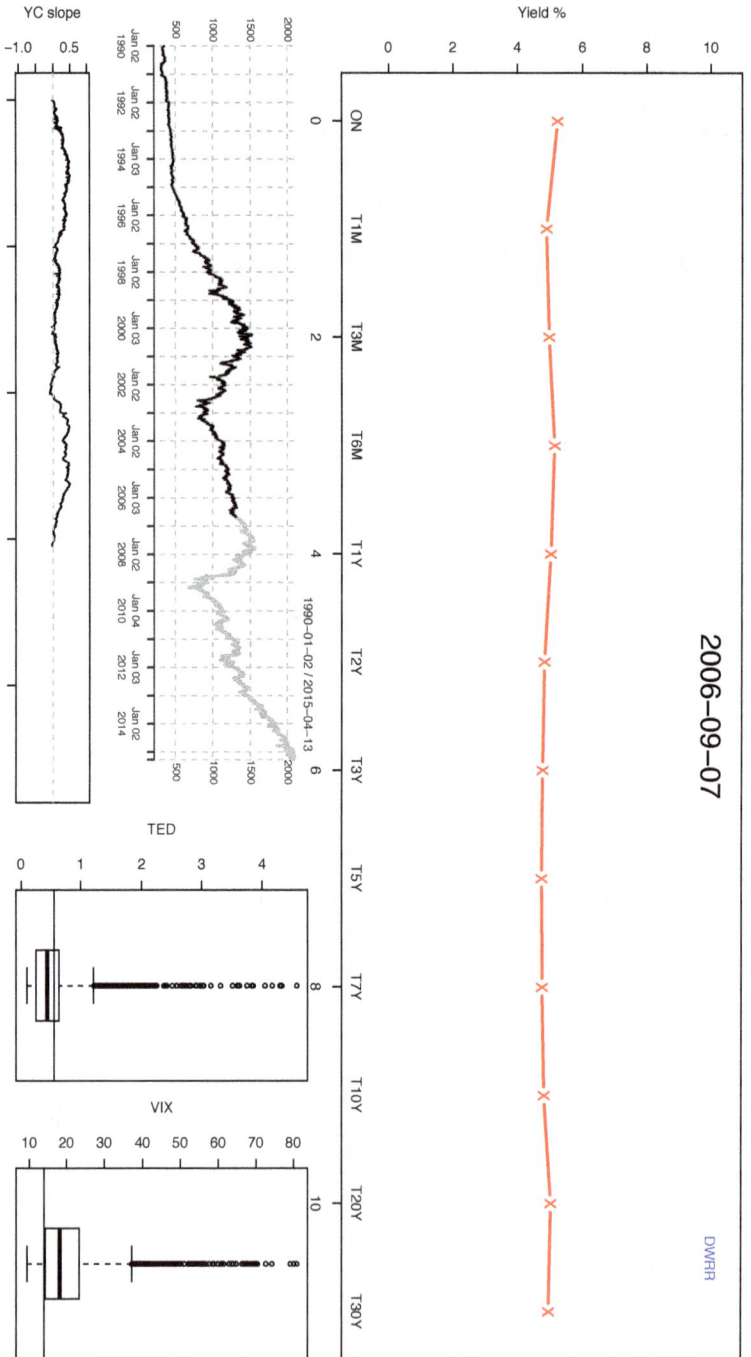

Figure 12.3: A frame from the movie showing the yield curve from January 1990–April 2015. The top plot shows the yield curve from constant-maturity Treasuries (in red, when inverted). The lower plots show the level of the S&P 500 (top right), the fitted slope of the yield curve (bottom right), and the levels of the TED spread and VIX versus their full-period boxplots. This frame shows that the yield curve was clearly inverted in September 2006, warning of looming economic trouble. The entire movie may be viewed at https://www.youtube.com/watch?v=6z8g9xaj3g8.

Maturity	YTM (%)	Price	Discount Factor
3M	0.5	$998.75	0.9988
6M	1.1	994.53	0.9945
1Y	3.0	970.87	0.9709
2Y	3.5	966.18	0.9662
3Y	4.0	961.54	0.9615
4Y	5.0	952.38	0.9524

Table 12.1: The zero curve (aka pure yield curve) is the curve of zero coupon bond yields and is in the "YTM" column. The discount curve appears in the "Discount Factor" column. Note that if the 6M yield were calculated as an EAR, instead of using the bills formula, the price would be $994.545.

12.2.2 Forward Rates

If there were no uncertainty about future interest rates, then we could use these yields to determine future interest rates. The key insight is that all bonds of the same tenor should have same yield. Otherwise, we could make easy money by selling short the bond yielding less and investing the proceeds in the bond yielding more. (This also assumes the difference is sufficient to pay the costs of this transaction.) If this sounds like one of the no-arbitrage constraints mentioned in Chapter 1, you are correct.

Thus the difference in yields for bonds of different tenors should imply the yields of bonds between those tenors in the future. For example, investing in a two-year bond and then investing in what will be a one-year bond (two years from now) should yield the same as investing in a three-year bond.

This means that the compounded rate from a bond should equal the interest we get from investing in other interest rate paths. For the example of the 3-year bond, all of these should yield the same interest:

- 1-year bond (r_1) reinvested in a 2-year 1 year from now ($f_{1 \to 3}$);
- 2-year (r_2) reinvested in a 1-year 2 years from now ($f_{2 \to 3}$); or,
- 1-year (r_1) reinvested in 1-years 1 and 2 years from now ($f_{1 \to 2}, f_{2 \to 3}$).

This implies a set of equalities (assuming semi-annual coupons):

$$(1 + \frac{r_3}{2})^{3 \times 2} = (1 + \frac{r_1}{2})^2 (1 + \frac{f_{1 \to 3}}{2})^{2 \times 2} \tag{12.1}$$

$$= (1 + \frac{r_2}{2})^{2 \times 2} (1 + \frac{f_{2 \to 3}}{2})^2 \tag{12.2}$$

$$= (1 + \frac{r_1}{2})^2 (1 + \frac{f_{1 \to 2}}{2})^2 (1 + \frac{f_{2 \to 3}}{2})^2. \tag{12.3}$$

The use of f above and this subsection should hint to you that we call these implied future interest rates **forward rates**. The terminology for them is often confusing; however, it helps to remember *at what time* are we implying these rates? What we write above as $f_{1\to3}$ is often called the "two-year, one year forward." This rate represents what yield we will get from what will be a two-year bond in one year. Similarly, $f_{2\to3}$ would be the "one-year, two years forward" and $f_{1\to2}$ would be the "one-year, one year forward." A **forward rate agreement** lets us agree on these rates right now, locking in future interest rates.

However, you might notice something from our example yield curve — something that is typical for many yield curves: the forward rates seem to be increasing. For example, the one-year yield is 3% but the implied one-year one year forward yield is about 4%. For annual coupons:

$$2\text{Y YTM} = 1\text{Y YTM} \times 1\text{Y 1-year-forward YTM, or} \qquad (12.4)$$

$$1.035^2 = 1.03(1 + f_{1\to2}) \Rightarrow f_{1\to2} = 4.00\%. \qquad (12.5)$$

Incidentally, there is a convenient approximation that we can use when interest rates are not too large. Since various interest rate paths need to return the same amount, we can think of interest rates (the growth rates of nominal money) as slopes. Thus if we only earned 3% for the first year, we need to earn 3.5% in the second year plus an additional 0.5% to "catch up" to the interest we missed out on in the first year (compared to the two-year bond). This is illustrated in Figure 12.4.

12.2.3   Short Rates

While some people refer to the one-year rate as the **short rate**, the short rate is more properly the interest rate for the shortest tenor of investment. That investment could start at any time in the future. In light of the above, you can imagine building a whole curve of short rates starting from now and increasingly later times in the future.

12.3   Yield Curve Theories

If we view future interest rates as certain, then forward rates reflect the **expectations hypothesis**: that forward rates are the expected value of future interest rates. In particular, this hypothesis looks at interest rates as expectations of current and future short rates. Thus an upward-sloping yield curve would imply that future short rates will rise even faster. The yield curve implies future rates as well as current short rates.

If there is an expectation involved, should we ignore uncertainty? Risk premia suggest we should not ignore uncertainty: if future interest rates are uncertain, investors will demand a higher rate of return to compensate them for taking on that uncertainty. In that case, forward rates will be higher than the expected value of future interest rates.

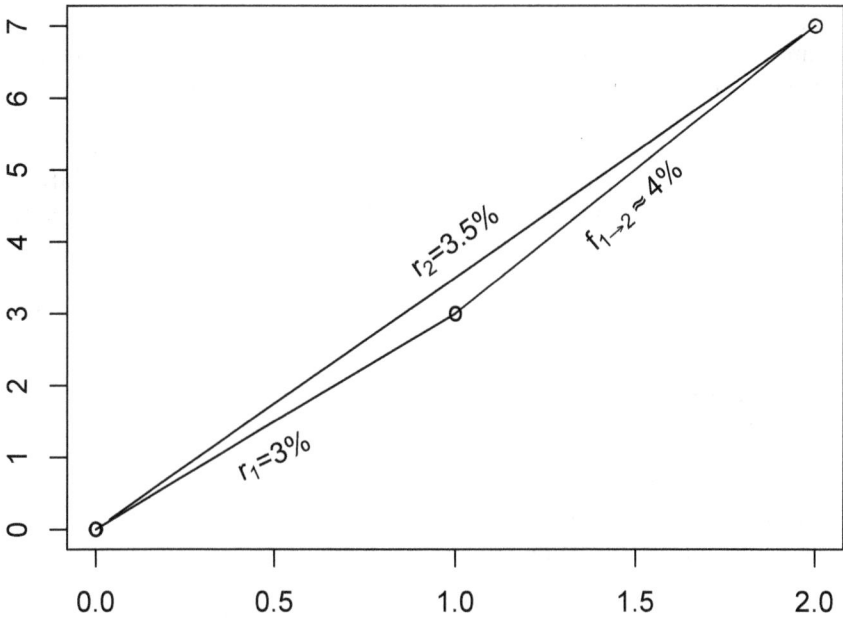

Figure 12.4: Diagram illustrating the quick approximation for finding forward rates from other yields. A more accurate diagram would show the compounding of the two-year bond with an upward kink in the line at one year.

This better reflects the world we live in: future interest rates *are* uncertain. While forward rates are often close to future short rates, forward rates tend to be above expected future short rates.

We also see that longer-term bonds tend to yield more. This reflects a **liquidity preference** demanded by lenders: Locking their money up for longer periods of time is a greater inconvenience and might cause short-term cashflow problems. Thus they demand more interest to lock their money up for longer in the future.

There is also some **market segmentation** of which type of investors borrow or lend over which tenors. Short-term borrowers include many small businesses while long-term borrowing is often done by only the most stable issuers. Short-term lenders include banks while longer-term lenders also include insurance companies and pension funds. Some lenders are even mandated to hold bonds of longer maturities.

We might suspect that this market segmentation is not so rigid for everyone, however; perhaps some investors will diverge from their **preferred habitat** to invest at tenors near to those they prefer — if the reward for doing so is sufficient.

While investors represent one part of the market, governments and central banks also trade in fixed income markets. They not only issue bonds, but they also tend to target short-term interest rates as a means of controlling their money supply and thus managing their macroeconomy. This means that we should expect to see a lot of movement at the very front of the curve when the government or central bank intervenes.[4] This means that even if we disagree with the expectations hypothesis, it probably holds for current short rates.

Finally, there is work by Litterman, Scheinkman, and Weiss (1991) which suggests that some yield curve shapes are driven by volatility. In particular, Litterman, Scheinkman, and Weiss suggest that **butterflies**, differences in yield curve slopes between adjacent pairs of instruments (which is related to curvature), are related to interest rate volatility.

Putting these ideas together gives us the economic forces driving yield curves:

- supply and demand to rent money;
- expectations of current and future short rates;
- funding liquidity premia (*i.e.* risk of locking up cash for longer);
- market liquidity premia (*i.e.* some bonds are less traded);
- equilibrium (no-arbitrage) forward rates;
- uncertainty about future short rates;
- mandated and preferred investment horizons;
- government targeting of rates; and,
- inflation (although the effect of this is not always clear).

While not precise, these theories help guide us in thinking about the willingness of lenders to alter their investment horizons and what drives interest rates at certain maturities or neighboring maturities. That may help explain some of the behavior we see in yield curves. However, we often think less about the microfoundations of interest rates and more in terms of common curve movements and the macroeconomic meanings of these movements.

12.4   Bootstrapping the Yield Curve

If we want to price a series of cashflows, we need a zero curve; however, most yield curves are composed of yields from both zero coupon bonds and coupon bonds. We can use yields and shorter-term spot rates to imply longer-term spot rates. This process of producing a zero curve is known as **bootstrapping** the yield curve.

The process is a forward iteration. Suppose we have a vector of bond yields y_t for a vector of maturities t. Some of the y_t are zero coupon bond yields — say for 3M, 6M, and 1Y.[5] Also, suppose we have coupon bond yields for later tenors. We then want to find the zero coupon bond yields $y_{z,t}$ between now (time 0) and maturity t.

We start with $y_{3M} = y_{z,3M}$, $y_{6M} = y_{z,6M}$, and $y_{1Y} = y_{z,1Y}$. Then suppose we

---

[4]Those familiar with Operation Twist, when the US Treasury targeted long-term interest rates during the 2008–2009 financial crisis, might wonder if movements in the long-end of the yield curve might be something to expect more often in the future. That remains, as of now, unclear.

[5]With no zero coupon bond yields, we would have to solve for all spot rates simultaneously.

have a bond with coupon $c_{1.5Y}$ paid semiannually, maturing in 18 months (1.5Y), and yielding $y_{1.5Y}$. We can infer the bond's price $p_{1.5Y}$. The zero coupon yield for that tenor is then found by pricing the bond cashflows using the zero coupon yields appropriate to the time of each cashflow. This suggests that:

$$p_{1.5Y} = \frac{c_{1.5Y}/2}{1 + y_{z,6M}/2} + \frac{c_{1.5Y}/2}{(1 + y_{z,1Y}/2)^2} + \frac{100 + c_{1.5Y}/2}{(1 + y_{z,1.5Y}/2)^3}. \tag{12.6}$$

To make this concrete: say that we have two spot rates $y_{z,6M} = 0.5\%$ and $y_{z,1Y} = 0.75\%$ as well as a coupon bond yield $y_{1.5Y} = 1\%$; and, suppose that the bond coupon rate is 1.25%. First, we infer the bond price:

$$p_{1.5Y} = \frac{1.25/2}{1 + 0.01/2} + \frac{1.25/2}{(1 + 0.01/2)^2} + \frac{100 + 1.25/2}{(1 + 0.01/2)^3} = 100.3713. \tag{12.7}$$

Next, we solve for the 1.5Y spot rate:

$$100.3713 = \frac{1.25/2}{1 + \frac{0.005}{2}} + \frac{1.25/2}{(1 + \frac{0.0075}{2})^2} + \frac{100 + 1.25/2}{(1 + \frac{y_{z,1.5Y}}{2})^3} \tag{12.8}$$

$$\frac{100 + 1.25/2}{(1 + \frac{y_{z,1.5Y}}{2})^3} = 100.3713 - \frac{1.25/2}{1 + \frac{0.005}{2}} - \frac{1.25/2}{(1 + \frac{0.0075}{2})^2} \tag{12.9}$$

$$(1 + \frac{y_{z,1.5Y}}{2})^3 = \frac{100 + 1.25/2}{100.3713 - \frac{1.25/2}{1+0.005/2} - \frac{1.25/2}{(1+0.0075/2)^2}} \tag{12.10}$$

$$y_{z,1.5Y} = 1.0209\% \tag{12.11}$$

We could continue this on into the future out to the 30Y tenor or longer. However, there is a complication that we often run into: we rarely have fine-grained later tenors. How do we get spot rates for far into the future when we might only have yields for 20Y, 25Y, and 30Y tenors, for example?

The answer is, unfortunately, neither precise nor satisfactory. Many texts will advise analysts to linearly interpolate spot rates. However, this creates a piecewise-linear zero curve instead of a smooth curve. That might seem like a minor concern; however, it can imply a forward curve with many "wiggles" in the areas interpolated. This is especially problematic for mortgages where interest payments are made monthly. Another approach is to average forward rates as in Fama and Bliss (1987) to get spot rates. Finally, some analysts use other techniques like cubic splines to get a smoother curve; however, even with these methods, we should impose constraints so the yields are all sensible.

12.4.1   *The Bonds That Tie Us*

We have made an implicit, but serious, assumption: we have taken these yields as perfect. We have tied our entire zero curve into the assumption that the yields we have are certain and imply the prices where bonds are trading. Unfortunately, there are two major problems with this restriction.

First, we know that trades may occur at the bid, the ask, and in between — or even outside the spread sometimes. That suggests we should take the yields as uncertain. We certainly should allow for the possibility that the observed yields might have occurred at the bid or ask; and, we should probably allow for a range of prices where trading could have occurred with respect to the bid-ask spread.

Second, we know that on-the-run bonds are more liquid than off-the-run bonds. That means that off-the-run bonds often have a higher yield and wider bid-ask spread due to their lower liquidity. Eliminating the off-the-run bonds might eliminate the liquidity factor affecting our zero curve, but it also reduces the data we have.

12.4.2   A One-Factor Model?

One solution is to assume an interest-rate model that takes the short rates as randomly-distributed around some mean. In particular, we assume that all short rates tend to revert to the same level. The reversion implies an Ornstein-Uhlenbeck process. Since there is only one governing relationship, this is a one-factor model.

This is the idea of Vašíček (1977) which builds an **Ornstein-Uhlenbeck process** for short rates r_t:

$$dr_t = \lambda(\bar{r} - r_t)dt + \sigma dW_t. \tag{12.12}$$

In this model, the drift term is positive if rates are below the equilibrium mean level $\bar{r}$ and negative if rates are above $\bar{r}$. The reversion speed is given by $\lambda > 0$ with higher values implying stronger (and faster) reversion.

We can fit this with a linear model; however, we might wonder if volatility is constant for all levels of interest rates. Cox, Ingersoll, and Ross (1985) (aka the CIR model) allows for volatility that increases with interest rates:

$$dr_t = \lambda(\bar{r} - r_t)dt + \sigma\sqrt{r_t}dW_t. \tag{12.13}$$

Some note that the Vašíček model allows for negative interest rates while the CIR model does not. Many will even state that disallowing negative interest rates is an advantage of the CIR model. Unfortunately, both Japan in the 1990s and Europe (recently) have had negative short rates.

There are reasons that we might believe in a more complicated model. In the next section, we will see that there are many forces that work on various parts of the yield curve. The multitude of forces suggests that we might need more than one factor to model a yield curve.

12.5   Yield Curve Movements

A portfolio of instruments (especially fixed income instruments) may change in value when the yield curve moves. Thus the portfolio is exposed to **curve risk**. If we wanted to insulate our portfolio from changes in interest rates, we could try to lock in all of the various interest rates for every possible cashflow from our portfolio. Obviously, that could be very onerous.

12.5.1 How Yield Curves Move

Instead, we could look at how yield curves tend to move. If we do that, we can note that certain types of movements are much more common. Instead of locking in every interest rate, we can more easily try to insulate our portfolio against these common yield curve movements.

Litterman and Scheinkman (1991) investigated yield curve movements and showed that the most common movements are (in decreasing likelihood):

1. parallel shifts up or down of the entire curve;
2. increases or decreases in the curve slope ("twists"); and,
3. increasing or decreasing curvature (aka "butterflying", "bowing", or movement in the "belly" of the curve).

This should not be surprising since these correspond to the level and first two derivatives of the curve. Some interest rate models also add a factor for government targeting of rates: a factor that focuses on the front-end of the curve

Taken together, the yield curve movements constitute risk factors in two ways. First, the economic forces driving interest rates often result in certain curve movements. Second, these curve movements will often affect the price of a fixed income instrument. In particular, the parallel shift of the yield curve corresponds to DV01, the risk measure we found in the preceding chapter. Therefore, these curve factors are a sensible form of dimension reduction: instead of hedging every cashflow, we hedge how cashflows are affected by common movements.

12.6 Modeling the Yield Curve

Having discussed how curves tend to move, it makes sense to return to our attempts to work with the yield curve. First, we might think about decomposing the yield curve into these (or similar) factors. This is the approach taken by Nelson and Siegel (1987) who fit a nonlinear model which explains 96% of the yield curve variation in their sample:

$$y_t = \beta_0 + \beta_1 \frac{1 - e^{-\lambda t}}{\lambda t} + \beta_2 \left(\frac{1 - e^{-\lambda t}}{\lambda t} - e^{-\lambda t} \right) + \epsilon_t. \tag{12.14}$$

In this model, β_0 is the coefficient for the long-term component which represents a level factor; β_1 is the coefficient for the short term component which also affects the slope, since that terms decays monotonically; and, β_2 is the coefficient for a medium-term factor which adds a hump since that term starts at zero, increases, and then decays. The speed of decay is governed by λ: higher values result in faster decay. The Svensson (1994) model adds a second humped term and is often used by central banks although it can have identifiability issues.

Is Nelson-Siegel/Svensson the only model we could fit? Surely not. We could also investigate models which featured other factors or posit a set of stochastic differential equations with factors corresponding to the drivers mentioned in the prior sections. We could also assume certain bonds are more liquid and thus have more believable prices. We could then use these as a basis and construct other yields from those basis yields. This is the approach of Duffie and Kan (1996).

As you might guess, yield curve models quickly get complicated. Furthermore, using such models to predict yield curves is an added complication, as shown in Diebold and Li (2006).

Therefore, we will likely stick with factors like those in Litterman and Scheinkman (1991). However, a full exploration of fixed income would delve into these models as well as that of Heath, Jarrow, and Morton (1992). Those looking for a brief intro to yield curve modeling would do well to start with Brousseau (2002).

For those seeking a more detailed look at yield curve modeling, you should check out the `termstrc` R package which implements a number of yield curve models. I also recommend two books. First, Brigo and Mercurio (2006) is the rare delightful, light-hearted-yet-rigorous read. To be honest, I feel like I have missed out so many models and ideas when I compare this chapter with that text; it is that good. It covers both yield curves and credit and well as fixed income volatility surface modeling. Finally, I have heard excellent opinions about Rebonato (2018) and from what I see of it before its release, it looks superb.

12.7   Yield Curve Arbitrage

After seeing how interest rates at various tenors relate to each other, we can see how to make money (assuming away the possibility of defaults). Since the yield curve should be consistent across all tenors, there is a lot of potential for arbitrage whenever any bond price changes.

Suppose, for example, the following set of US Treasury yields:

- 1Y: $y_1 = 2.0\%$
- 1Y 1 year forward: $f_{1\to2} = 2.2\%$
- 2Y: $y_2 = 2.1\%$
- 1Y 2 years forward: $f_{2\to3} = 2.2\%$
- 3Y: $y_3 = 2.3\%$.

From what we now know, something should immediately appear out-of-place: the 1Y 2 years forward short rate is less that the 3Y yield.

How would we trade this to make money? We would buy the 3Y and pay for it by short selling the 2Y and 1Y 2 years forward. Since the 2Y does not finance the 3Y for the entire time, we say that we **roll the position** in the 2Y into the 1Y 2 years forward. Thus we spend no money and pocket the difference in yields. We should make, approximately, $0.2\% \times 2 + 0.1\%$: $2.3\%-2.1\%$ for 2 years and $2.3\%-2.2\%$ for one year. A timeline shows how this plays out in detail:

$t = 0$: Arrange for buy (3Y) and short sales (2Y, 1Y 2 years forward).

- Buy 3Y bond at a cost of $\frac{\$1000}{(1+y_3/2)^6} = \frac{\$1000}{1.023^3} = \$933.369$.
- Short $933.369 of 2Y to pay for 3Y.
- Agree to short 1Y 2 years forward to pay back 2Y in 2 years.

$t = 2$: Roll short: Repay 2Y; short begins on (what was) 1Y 2 years forward.

- 2Y matures; owe 933.369\times(1 + 0.021/2)^4 = \$973.531$.
- Shorted $973.531 of 1Y 2 years forward begins; pays off 2Y.

$t = 3$: 3Y matures; repay (what was) 1Y 2 years forward.

- 3Y matures; pays off $1000.
- 1Y 2 years forward matures; owe 973.531\times(1 + 0.022/2)^2 = \$995.067$.
- Pocket $1000-$995.067=$4.933, which is close to 0.5% of $1000.

We started with $0 and ended with $1000 - $995.067 = $4.933. What are the Sharpe and Sortino ratios of this investment? We ignored the risk of default and, implicitly, the risk that someone might break their agreement with us which locked in the price of the 1Y 2 years forward. Ignoring those risks, the variance of what we might make was 0; thus the Sharpe and Sortino ratios would be infinite. However, should we ignore those risks? In many economies, the answer is clearly no. Could we use this relationship to tease out the probabilities of default and of breaking the forward contract? Perhaps.

Finally, we should consider what effect this trading will have on bond prices. Obviously, the 3Y yield will decrease and the 1Y 2 years forward short rate will increase. The 2Y yield will also increase since we short that bond. This may create an arbitrage opportunity between the 2Y and the 1Y rolled into the 1Y 1 year forward. That should pull the 1Y and 1Y 1 year forward rates up slightly.

Now that you see how to make money, you might be tempted to go apply this to all sorts of bonds. Unfortunately, the term structure of credit risk is not flat either; thus seemingly profitable trades with risky bonds could easily lose money since rates might reflect default risks.

12.8 Quiz

Try to answer these questions in five minutes. For answers with equations, just write the equations; do not evaluate them.

1. If the 6M yields 0.4% annually and the 1Y yields 0.6% annually, what is the fair annual yield for the 6M six months forward:

   a) approximately?

   b) exactly?

2. Given the following yields:

1Y	0.7%
2Y	1.2%
1Y 1 yr fwd	1.2%

   a) How would you make money with no capital?

   b) Approximately how much would you make?

3. You look at a country's yield curve and notice it is inverted.

   a) What does that suggest about the macroeconomy?

   b) (2 points) Why does it suggest that? What causes it to have that shape?

4. How does a country's yield curve usually look when the economy is doing well?

5. A country is concerned investors are going to pull money out of the country and cause the FX rate to plummet. If the country's politicians try to defend the currency through interest rate policy, what will the country's yield curve probably look like?

6. What is the most common yield curve movement? What movement is the next-most common?

12.9   Exercises

1. Show that for an upward-sloping yield curve, future short rates will always lie above the yield curve.

2. Get the USD, EUR, CHF, and SGD yield curves over the past year from Quandl. We will plot, model, and decompose movements of these curves.

   a) Plot the yield curve for now $y_{0,t}$. Then, using lines(), graph the curves from one week $y_{-1W,t}$, one month $y_{-1M,t}$, and one year ago $y_{-1Y,t}$ on the same plot.

   b) Compute a simple average level of yields for each day $\hat{\mu}_\tau$. Save those levels.

   c) Estimate the Litterman and Scheinkman (1991) model for each day. Save the fitted values $\hat{y}_{\tau,t}$.

d) Find the baseline sum of squared errors:

$$\sum_{\tau \in \{\text{days}\}} \sum_{t \in \{\text{tenors}\}} (y_{\tau,t} - \hat{\mu}_\tau)^2. \tag{12.15}$$

e) Find the sum of model squared errors:

$$\sum_{\tau \in \{\text{days}\}} \sum_{t \in \{\text{tenors}\}} (y_{\tau,t} - \hat{y}_{\tau,t})^2. \tag{12.16}$$

f) Repeat the above steps for a model including a time slope $\beta_3 t$.

3. For the preceding yield curves, compute the daily changes. Store these changes in a matrix for each currency: `yc.usd`, for example. Now, for each currency, perform a principal components analysis on the yield curve changes using the R code below. Look at the top five principle components.

a) What do the top five vectors tell you? Do they imply certain curve movements?

b) What fraction of the variance is explained by these first five PCs?

```
pca.usd <- prcomp(~ T3M + T6M + T1Y + T2Y, data=UST,
                  scale=FALSE, center=FALSE)
pca.usd <- prcomp(yc.usd, scale=FALSE, center=FALSE)
pca.usd$rotation  # eigenvectors
pca.usd$sdev^2    # eigenvalues
```

References

Boudt, Kris, Ellen C. S. Paulus, and Dale W. R. Rosenthal. "Funding Liquidity, Market Liquidity and TED Spread: A Two-Regime Model". *Journal of Empirical Finance* 43 (2017), pp. 143–158. DOI: 10.1016/j.jempfin.2017.06.002.

Brigo, Damiano and Fabio Mercurio. *Interest Rate Models – Theory and Practice: With Smile, Inflation and Credit.* 2nd ed. New York: Springer, 2006. DOI: 10.1007/978-3-540-34604-3.

Brousseau, Vincent. *The Functional Form of Yield Curves.* Working Paper 148. European Central Bank, 2002. URL: http://www.ecb.europa.eu/pub/pdf/scpwps/ecbwp148.pdf.

Cox, John C., Jonathan E. Ingersoll Jr., and Stephen A. Ross. "A Theory of the Term Structure of Interest Rates". *Econometrica* 53.2 (1985), pp. 385–407. DOI: 10.2307/1911242.

Diebold, Francis Xavier and Canlin Li. "Forecasting the Term Structure of Government Bond Yields". *Journal of Econometrics* 130.2 (2006), pp. 337–364. DOI: 10.1016/j.jeconom.2005.03.005.

Duffie, Darrell and Rui Kan. "A Yield-Factor Model of Interest Rates". *Mathematical Finance* 6.4 (1996), pp. 379–406. DOI: 10.1111/j.1467-9965.1996.tb00123.x.

Fama, Eugene F. and Robert R. Bliss. "The Information in Long-Maturity Forward Rates". *American Economic Review* 77.4 (1987), pp. 680–692. URL: http://www.jstor.org/stable/1814539.

Ferstl, Robert and Josef Hayden. *termstrc: Zero-coupon Yield Curve Estimation*. R package version 1.3.7. 2013. URL: https://CRAN.R-project.org/package=termstrc.

Heath, David, Robert Jarrow, and Andrew Morton. "Bond Pricing and the Term Structure of Interest Rates: A New Methodology for Contingent Claims Valuation". *Econometrica* 60.1 (1992), pp. 77–105. DOI: 10.2307/2951677.

Litterman, Robert and José Scheinkman. "Common Factors Affecting Bond Returns". *Journal of Fixed Income* 1.1 (1991), pp. 54–61. DOI: 10.3905/jfi.1991.692347.

Litterman, Robert, José Scheinkman, and Laurence Weiss. "Volatility and the Yield Curve". *Journal of Fixed Income* 1.1 (1991), pp. 49–53. DOI: 10.3905/jfi.1991.692346.

Nelson, Charles R. and Andrew F. Siegel. "Parsimonious Modeling of Yield Curves". *Journal of Business* 60.4 (1987), pp. 473–489. DOI: 10.1086/296409.

Rebonato, Riccardo. *Bond Pricing and Yield Curve Modeling: A Structural Approach*. Cambridge (UK): Cambridge University Press, 2018.

Svensson, Lars E.O. *Estimating and Interpreting Forward Interest Rates: Sweden 1992–1994*. Working Paper 94/114. International Monetary Fund, 1994. DOI: 10.5089/9781451853759.001.

Uhlenbeck, G. E. and L. S. Ornstein. "On the Theory of the Brownian Motion". *Physical Review* 36.5 (1930), pp. 823–841. DOI: 10.1103/PhysRev.36.823.

Vašíček, Oldřich. "An Equilibrium Characterization of the Term Structure". *Journal of Financial Economics* 5.2 (1977), pp. 177–188. DOI: 10.1016/0304-405X(77)90016-2.

Chapter 13

Equity Valuation

Now that we have seen how to price bonds, we might be curious about how to price riskier investments. Do different industries behave differently apart from making different products? Can we compare firms by looking at their financial statements? Could we apply the ideas from bond pricing to pricing stocks? The answer to all of these is yes. Furthermore, the methods we learned for pricing bonds underlie a whole class of **discounted cashflow** (DCF) models. However, because equities have so much more risk, the discount rates can be very uncertain. Thus we often consider other factors when we value equities.

The goal of this chapter is to discuss sectors and industries; consider some fundamental valuation methods; introduce some common DCF models; and, to critique these valuation methods.

13.1 Sector and Industry Analysis

Pat Dorsey, the former Director of Equity Research at Morningstar, once contrasted investing in JetBlue with investing in Microsoft. JetBlue is run by some of the sharpest business minds around, but has had trouble; Microsoft has been run by smart and not-so-smart people, but has done well across those regimes. His point in comparing these firms is that it is much easier to invest well when you invest in an industry that is doing well.

Thus it makes sense for us to consider sectors and industries. Another reason to consider them is that they may perform differently in various parts of the business cycle, perhaps due to differing cost structures or risk. Finally, we consider sectors and industries because we want to control our risk exposures.

13.1.1 Industries and the Business Cycle

Cyclical industries are industries which are sensitive to the business cycle. These typically include durable goods (like appliances) and large-expenditure items (like homes and cars). In 2008, the port of Long Beach, California was awash in miles of cars as many consumers delayed buying cars due to the financial crisis.[1]

On the other hand, **defensive industries** are the least sensitive to the business cycle, often because they produce necessities or products consumers cannot easily choose to do without. Defensive industries include utilities and healthcare. Some investors would say that alcohol, for example, is a defensive investment; after all, when a person loses their job, it is stereotypical that they go to the bar for drinks. (Indeed, this philosophy is behind the Vice Fund discussed in the sidebar "Guns, Buns, Butts, Bets, and Booze.") However, in a recession consumers might switch to *lower-cost* alcohol.

Finally, with what we know about how some industries respond to the business cycle, it makes to consider over- or under-weighting certain industries at certain parts of the business cycle. Sector or industry **rotation** is the changing of our sector or industry allocation, often because of how they respond to where we are in the business cycle. Changes in asset allocation are also sensible in response to the business cycle. For example, government bonds can be a sound investment as we enter a recession.

> **Guns, Buns, Butts, Bets, and Booze** The Vice Fund is a mutual fund which invests solely in military contractors, adult entertainment, tobacco, gaming, and alcohol stocks. The fund's founder wrote a book, *Investing in Vice: The Recession-Proof Portfolio of Booze, Bets, Bombs & Butts* and garnered publicity by talking up "socially irresponsible investing." The Vice Fund is one of my favorite examples of defensive investments. Invariably, at least one student will feverishly scrawl notes about the fund. Vice, it seems, is appealing. Read Ahrens (2004) to see if vice is your virtue.

13.1.2   Degree of Operating Leverage

Some of this difference in how industries respond to the business cycle is due to differing sensitivities to sales. The measure of that sensitivity is defined by the sales elasticity of profits and is called the **degree of operating leverage** (DOL).

$$\text{DOL} = \frac{\%\Delta \text{profits}}{\%\Delta \text{sales}} = 1 + \frac{\text{fixed costs}}{\text{profits}}. \tag{13.1}$$

Note that these two formulations may give slightly different numbers, especially since fixed costs may be difficult to estimate. (We are, after all, getting into accounting-land where numbers get "smoothed" and definitions can be arbitrary.)

---

[1] A web search on "Long Beach port cars 2008" will give you oodles of images of this inventory backlog.

However, the basic idea is what is important: some industries have different cost structures and this affects how they respond to an increase in sales. Thus we expect certain ranges of DOL for different industries.

A small firm making mobile phone apps may have to pay the fixed costs of maintaining an office and website; however, their variable costs are low: selling an additional app does not require much additional work from anyone. Contrast that with a home builder: to sell an additional home, they need to purchase all of the goods and exert almost the same amount of effort to make another home as they expended to make their first home. Thus the mobile phone app developer has a high degree of operating leverage while the homebuilder has a low degree of operating leverage.

13.1.3   Industries as Risk Factors

Another reason to consider industries and sectors is because they are exposed to similar risk factors. We often treat sectors or industries like risk factors in that we often try to avoid concentrating our investments in any one industry.

Industries may even behave differently due to their age: new industries may be highly speculative, then become very profitable and innovative as they age. As they mature, innovation may slow and price competition may dominate. Eventually, the return on investment falls below what investors could find elsewhere; in this case, firms should pay out almost all their profits in dividends so that investors can reinvest those funds elsewhere.

This fall off in profitability may be delayed by what Pat Dorsey calls **economic moats**: obstacles that make it hard for competitors to enter the market. Examples include selling applications which have become ubiquitous enough to be near-standards (Microsoft's Office Apps and Windows operating system) or having network effects that make consumers add to the product's value (like Facebook).

13.1.4   Industry Classifications

In the above discussions, we have often referred to industries and sectors. It makes sense to tighten up this language and to explain how we divide economic activity into these groups.

A **sector** is a large grouping of industries in the same general type of business: for example, energy, technology, finance, manufacturing, or agriculture. An **industry** is a refinement of a sector: a smaller subset of more related activities. For example, in the finance sector there are industries for insurance, banking, investment management, investment banking, real estate, and credit rating.

We care about these groupings because within a sector or industry, firms are often exposed to similar challenges and risks; they may respond similarly to changes in their environment (whether changes in policy or the economy); and,

Nascence versus NAICS In 2001, a proprietary trading group at Morgan Stanley was losing money in some long-short portfolios (specifically, in pharmaceuticals); but, the portfolios were long and short equivalent amounts of pharmaceutical stocks. A cluster analysis revealed biotechnology firms behaved differently than larger, more established pharmaceutical firms. The losses were often due to big, old firms being "balanced" by small, biotech firms. The losses stopped once they added an industry split to balance long and short trades in each of those groups. Industry classifications often lag market developments, so it pays to watch for emerging industries.

they are typically direct or indirect competitors. For these reasons, sectors and industries can be thought of as collecting shared risk factors. However, are industries risk factors? No, they are not; investors do not earn a risk premium just for investing in, say, oil refiners.

We often need to organize and label firms with sectors and industries so that we can group them together for research purposes. Therefore, we often use **industry classification** schemes: coding systems which tell us the primary industry of a firm. (Obviously, this breaks down for **conglomerates**: businesses engaged in many disparate industries.)

Most industry classification systems are based on the United Nations International Standard Industrial Classification of All Economic Activities (ISIC). However, national systems are often developed to overlay gradations which are more important to the local economy. Table 13.1 describes the major classification systems used by countries. Some data vendors have their own classification systems. Products and commodities also have their own coding systems which are often used for statistics on trade. The `concordance` R package helps map among some of these classification systems.

Often, these coding systems use a sequence of numbers and letters to encode a sector, and then finer gradations of industry. Sometimes people refer to these levels as sectors, sub-sectors, industries, and sub-industries; however, we will stick with how most economists treat these levels: we will call the highest level the sector and the next-highest level the industry. For example, the first character (letter) of an ISIC gives the sector and the next two characters (numbers) give the industry. For NAICS, the first two numbers give the sector (with some sectors covering a range) and the third number defines what we will call the industry. Because these codings are arbitrary, we *never* do math with NAICS or ISIC codes: we treat them as a **categorical variable** which defines dummy variables.

13.2   Fundamental Analysis

Another way to look at a firm is to compare their valuation measures of the firm's business activity or to assets which could be recoverable if the firm were dissolved.

We know that cost structures and degrees of operating leverage are similar within

Name (Abbreviation, Sponsor if unclear)	Sectors	Industries
International Standard Industrial Classification of All Economic Activities (ISIC, UN)	21	88
North American Industrial Classification System (NAICS, US/CA/MX)	20	99
Nomenclature Statistique des Activités Économiques dans la Communauté Européenne (NACE, EU)	21	88
United Kingdom Standard Industrial Classification (UKSIC)	21	88
Australian and New Zealand Standard Industrial Classification (ANZSIC)	19	96
Industrial Classification for National Economic Activities (ICNEA, China)	20	96
Japan Standard Industrial Classification (JSIC)	20	99
Korea Standard Industrial Classification (KSIC)	21	76

Table 13.1: Industry classification systems commonly used in major economies. Most of these are based on the United Nations ISIC system. Sectors refers to the highest level of variation and Industries to the next-highest level of variation.

an industry. Therefore, across an industry there should be a similar relationship between measures of a firm's business activity and firm valuation. We often look at these **comparables**, ratios of valuation and activity or assets, and compare firms. If one firm's ratios are far from their competitors, then either the firm is mispriced or it should have some competitive difference to justify the different ratio.

⚠️ **Periklu!** *We are again getting into accounting-land. This is a dangerous place: where earnings and revenues get "smoothed" or "managed," definitions may be arbitrary, and what is included or excluded in filings can be changed through tricks. Conducting statistical analysis on such numbers is fraught with danger. Proceed cautiously.*

Fundamental analysts typically compare companies using financial filings and derived measures. In the US, these filings are available for free from the SEC's EDGAR database and derived measures are often purchased from a vendor like Compustat. With these measures, we can build comparables.

13.2.1 Price Ratios

Common price ratios typically relate the firm's market capitalization ("price") to some measure of economic activity or recoverable value. The most common such ratio is the **price-to-earnings ratio**, aka P/E. (Since this uses past earnings, some analysts refer to this as "trailing P/E.") However, price-to-earnings has problems.

First, earnings is an accounting construct; the economic activity part of earnings can diverge from the accounting definition. For example, depreciation may be counted in earnings but it tells us little about if the firm is well-run. Second, many firms "manage" earnings by strategically shifting revenues before or after a quarter-end. This lets them manipulate estimates of firm riskiness and achieve forecasted earnings. Third, some firms are just cyclical or seasonal in nature; that means their earnings will not be stable over time which complicates looking at a P/E ratio. Finally, for some firms (like startups), the P/E ratio is meaningless because those firms may have no earnings — or current earnings may not be representative of future earnings. Hence why some analysts use projected earnings, aka "forward P/E."

Take a Seat... Please During the financial crisis, a number of firms were liquidated at nearly the same time. This made it harder to recover book value for the assets. Office furniture resellers were able to buy a lot of office furniture cheaply. They then greatly discounted the furniture to process the most business possible. The result was incredible deals (if you had the cash). After reading about this in Harrison (2009), I conducted some personal research by driving to one of the resellers. They told me they had been selling Aeron chairs which had never been used (and cost around $700) for $99. However, even at that price, they were barely able to store all the chairs. In a crisis, expecting to recover book value might be very optimistic.

Analysts also look at the **price-to-book ratio** (P/B, inverse of the **book-to-market ratio**) which relates firm value to what could be recovered if the firm were dissolved and its assets sold. We often think a living firm creates more value using its assets than selling them, so this ratio may indicate **value stocks**. Unfortunately, if we liquidate the firm, an equity holder is a **residual claimant**: last in line to get paid. If many firms are liquidated at the same time, the value recovered may be much lower than book value. (See the sidebar, "Take a Seat... Please" to see how correlated liquidations can drive down recovery values.)

On the other hand, a book value much greater than the market value suggests the firm is overcapitalized or cannot put money to good use. In that case, investors may demand a large payout; or, corporate raiders may come along and break up the firm to release the unneeded capital (aka "unlock value").

Another difficulty is that for some industries the assets are the employees. Valuing these intangible assets is very difficult; and, those assets are often able to leave the firm if unhappy.

Given these weaknesses, analysts may look at other price ratios. **Price-to-**

cashflow gives us a figure which avoids earnings management, but does not avoid revenue management.

Price-to-sales excludes investment income and interest and is useful for valuing firms which are not yet but soon expected to be profitable. Sales is also a measure that is only affected by active management of the firm. Therefore, it may better reveal superior management. Barbee, Mukherji, and Raines (1996) suggests price-to-sales may dominate other price measures.

For startups, analysts have even tried measures like **price-to-website-clicks** or **price-to-website-visitors**. Trueman, Wong, and Zhang (2000) suggest that these measures help in valuing new technology firms.

Once we have a number of these ratios, we can find the industry average — or create a weighted average, putting more weight on firms like the one we are valuing. That average implies a valuation for the firm. Dividing by the shares outstanding yields the implied share price.

A major problem with price ratios is that there are two noisy numbers: one in the numerator and one in the denominator. The distribution of a ratio can be tricky to determine and finding a confidence interval for it can be harder. In the extreme case, when the denominator can be close to zero, the distribution may have very fat tails and one might instead have to compute a discontiguous confidence set.[2]

13.2.2   Tobin's q

Instead of book value, we might think about the **replacement cost**: how much it would cost to replace the firm's assets, less liabilities. If that is low, we could easily build a competing firm and grab market share.[3] This possibility leads to **Tobin's** q:

$$q = \frac{\text{market price of firm}}{\text{replacement cost of assets}}. \tag{13.2}$$

In a perfectly-competitive industry, q should tend to 1 due to competition. If $q > 1$, then one of two things is true:

1. competitors can (and will) replicate firm for cheaper and the firm value will fall as competitors enter the market; or,
2. there are barriers to entry preventing competitors from entering.

13.2.3   Share Ratios

One way around this is to use share ratios. Common per-share ratios include **earnings per share**, **book per share**, **sales per share**, and **cashflow per share**. Are these necessarily better than price ratios? Perhaps slightly. They do get rid of the ratio-of-random-variables problem. We still have to model the share

---

[2]Those needing to do this would do well to consult Fieller's Method.
[3]This assumes that people trying to replicate the firm could also find funding at the same cost or better.

price as a function of these ratios; but, that is a more stable statistical problem. Furthermore, many are more interpretable. Earnings per share or earnings-to-price implies a dividend yield — which is easier to compare with fixed income investments.

So why say more about price ratios? The sad truth is that the market focuses more on price ratios. That makes them, *de facto* more important.

13.3   Discounted Cashflow (DCF) Models

Up to this point, we have sort of cheated (or bootstrapped, if you prefer a gentler criticism): we have used other stocks to price the stock we are interested in. However, this does not tell us what is a correct value if other stocks are mispriced; and, it offers no help for a stock that is unlike others. For example, how would you price Tesla stock before there are competing electric car makers?

The way around this was hinted at in the introduction: use the technology for pricing bonds and perpetuities. Equities, as residual claimants and recipients of cashflows given on a best-efforts basis, are riskier than bonds. We already saw that higher-risk investments should trade at a higher yield. In general, the riskier the cashflow we are discounting, the higher the discount rate we should use.

This is an important insight: many models we use are based on the same formula as for pricing a bond or perpetuity — except we use an uncertain cashflow and the corresponding discount rate. This (higher) discount rate goes by a couple of names: **stochastic discount factor** d for a return factor R such that $E(dR) = 1$ or the **pricing kernel** aka **required rate of return** $k = 1/d - 1$.

13.3.1   Jensen's Inequality and Valuation

> ⚠ **Опасность!** *We rarely know the inputs to DCF models at valuation time. Often, we must estimate the inputs and valuation. We put hats on estimated quantities to remind us that their value is uncertain. For example, while our models use a pricing kernel k, we will never know its value; instead, we work with its estimate $\hat{k}$. Some texts forget hats or use them indiscriminately, almost like decorations. Do not ignore hats! They remind us that we are working with uncertain quantities and that the uncertainty cannot be ignored.*

Why should we care about using estimates? If we have to infer or estimate our inputs, equality may no longer hold between the expected valuation and the formula using estimated inputs. The reason is because many valuation formulas are nonlinear in their inputs.

Jensen's Inequality tells us that for a convex function $f(k)$:

$$E(f(k)) > f(E(k)) \quad \forall f : f'' > 0. \tag{13.3}$$

The problem is that we use pricing kernels for discounting, often putting them in a denominator. Thus most DCF models are convex in the pricing kernel k — and equality breaks when we stick an estimated kernel $\hat{k}$ in the model. The typical statistical fix for this is to use a second-order Taylor expansion (since the first-order terms have zero expectation):

$$E(f(k)) \approx f(E(k)) + \frac{1}{2} f''(E(k))\sigma_k^2. \tag{13.4}$$

Furthermore, uncertainty about the pricing kernel is increasingly being realized as an important driver of valuation. In his Presidential Address to the American Finance Association, Cochrane noted that "it seems all price-dividend variation corresponds to discount-rate variation." Surprisingly, I can find no sources which mention the correction for Jensen's Inequality nor which consider the uncertainty of the pricing kernel.[4] However, that will not stop us from doing the right thing.

13.3.2 Discounting: From Finite to Infinite Horizon

Suppose we knew where the price would be in a year.[5] Then we could use the annual dividend D and price change ΔP to find the holding period return:

$$\text{HPR} = \frac{D}{P_0} + \frac{\Delta P}{P_0}, \tag{13.5}$$

$$= \text{dividend yield} + \text{capital gain yield}. \tag{13.6}$$

Is the holding period return attractive relative to the risk? Answering that requires thinking about the risk we are taking: the more risk, the higher the return should be. However, that is just the inverse of our discounting problem. For now, we will just discount by some pricing kernel k.

With this, we can turn the holding period return equation around. We use next year's dividends D_1 and ending price P_1 to get the fair value V_0, sometimes called **intrinsic value**:

$$V_0 = \frac{D_1 + P_1}{1 + k}. \tag{13.7}$$

We could also handle a price target n years in the future:

$$V_0 = \sum_{t=1}^{n} \frac{D_t}{1 + k} + \frac{P_n}{(1 + k)^n}. \tag{13.8}$$

This may seem to be just the same problem. We want to know what the stock price should be; how does deferring the unknown for a few more years help us?

---

[4] I do not know why this insight is lacking in the finance literature. The closest to this is the discussion of a Jensen correction for book-to-market in Pástor and Veronesi (2003).

[5] We ignore uncertainty for this section since it is just to motivate the following sections.

If we let our holding period tend to $t \to \infty$, we can make progress. This valuation is where we think the equilibrium level should be. That is important because in an economic system where people can infer the equilibrium, prices should quickly move toward that equilibrium; otherwise, there would be easy money to make.

In general, this perpetuity-based approach as an equilibrium outcome is a perspective we will take in many DCF models. Often, the main modeling questions are:

1. Which cashflows should be used for modeling?
2. What pricing kernel(s) should be used for discounting?
3. How will those cashflows transition to equilibrium, if not at equilibrium already?

13.4   Dividend Discount Model (DDM)

As we saw above, we could value a stock if we had a target price at some future date. If we let that future date go to infinity, the valuation is based on a perpetuity of future dividends.[6] This yields the **dividend discount model** (DDM). This result was popularized by Williams (1938) who also developed the growth version of the model which we will explore subsequently.

The perpetuity of constant dividends D yields a valuation of $V_{0,DDM}$:

$$V_{0,DDM} = \sum_{t=1}^{\infty} \frac{D}{(1+k)^t} = \frac{D}{k}. \tag{13.9}$$

While constant dividends might seem to be a poor assumption, it is exactly the situation holders of preferred shares find themselves in. Furthermore, for firms in a recession, dividends might be constant for some time — so the assumption may not be terrible in that case.

There is another problem with the formula in equation (13.9): we have to estimate D and k. From the preceding discussion of Jensen's Inequality, we know the formula in (13.9) will underestimate the value of the firm because $\hat{k}$ is a conditional expectation of k. Using the second-order Taylor expansion fix, we get the **Jensen-corrected dividend discount model**:

$$E(V_{0,DDM}) \approx \hat{V}_{0,DDM} = \frac{\hat{D}}{\hat{k}} + \frac{\hat{D}}{\hat{k}^3}\hat{\sigma}_k^2. \tag{13.10}$$

An example illustrates the degree to which this correction is needed. Suppose we estimate the pricing kernel k as $\hat{k} = 0.10$ with a standard error of 0.03. For a stock

---

[6]We should also add in the value of stock buybacks minus price impact and brokerage fees which investors would incur to get that cash out of the stock. We would treat these as single payments made at the time of the buybacks.

we expect to pay a dividend of $D = \$2$, the standard DDM gives us a valuation of $V_{0,DDM} = \$2/0.1 = \$20$ while the Jensen-corrected DDM gives us a valuation of

$$E(V_{0,DDM}) \approx \hat{V}_{0,DDM} = \frac{\$2}{0.1} + \frac{\$2}{0.1^3}0.03^2 = \$20 + \$1.8 = \$21.8. \qquad (13.11)$$

The correction increases the valuation by 9%. Furthermore, while we might estimate the uncertainty of $\hat{k}$, the truth is that there is often far more uncertainty than just that of estimation. The risk of future changes in the pricing kernel, changes in industry cost structure, and possible regulation all could increase the realized $\hat{\sigma}_k^2$.

13.5 Gordon-Shapiro Model

While the preceding model may be good for preferred stock and shares with a fixed dividend, many shares increase dividends over time. A reasonable extension, popularized by Gordon and Shapiro (1956), is to allow for dividends which grow at a rate g. This yields the **Gordon-Shapiro model**:

$$V_{0,G-S} = \frac{D_0(1+g)}{1+k} + \frac{D_0(1+g)^2}{(1+k)^2} + \cdots = \frac{D_0(1+g)}{k-g} = \frac{D_1}{k-g} \qquad (13.12)$$

Note that if the pricing kernel k and the dividend growth rate g are constant, then the stock price will also grow at a rate g. That lets us see this as a rearrangement of equation (13.5) if the stock is priced in line with the model:

$$k = \frac{D}{V_{0,G-S}} + g \quad \Longleftrightarrow \quad V_{0,G-S} = \frac{D}{k-g}. \qquad (13.13)$$

One obvious implication of this model: dividend growth g at or above k is unsustainable. Furthermore, the valuation becomes very sensitive to the inputs if g is close to k.

Yet again, however, working with estimated values means that we need to correct for underestimation due to Jensen's Inequality. Thus the **Jensen-corrected Gordon-Shapiro model** is:

$$\hat{V}_{0,G-S} = \frac{\hat{D}}{\hat{k}-\hat{g}} + \frac{\hat{D}}{(\hat{k}-\hat{g})^3}(\hat{\sigma}_k^2 + \hat{\sigma}_g^2 - 2\operatorname{Cov}(\hat{k},\hat{g})). \qquad (13.14)$$

Suppose the same stock we priced in the preceding subsection had dividends growing at an estimated rate of $\hat{g} = 0.05 = 5\%$; a standard error of that growth rate of 2%; and, a correlation between k and g of $\hat{\rho}_{k,g} = 0.7$. Then, the uncorrected model would yield a valuation of $V_{0,G-S} = \frac{\$2}{0.10-0.05} = \$40$. The Jensen-corrected model would yield a valuation of:

$$\hat{V}_{0,G-S} = \frac{\$2}{0.10-0.05} + \frac{\$2(0.03^2 + 0.02^2 - 2 \cdot 0.03 \cdot 0.02 \cdot 0.7)}{(0.10-0.05)^3} \qquad (13.15)$$

$$= \$40 + \$2 \cdot 3.68 = \$47.36. \qquad (13.16)$$

In this case, the uncorrected model is 18.4% off from the corrected model. Obviously, we cannot ignore the Jensen's Inequality correction.

13.6   Reinvestment, Gordon-Shapiro, and DuPont

We can also consider dividend policy: should the firm have some **retained earnings** to reinvest in the firm; or, should they pay out all of their profits in dividends? A modification of the Gordon-Shapiro model offers some insight if we can estimate the return on investments inside the firm.

Suppose the firm lowers their dividend payout ratio by retaining some fraction b of earnings ϵ. They then reinvest the retained earnings in the firm earning the return on equity ROE. In this case, dividends will grow at a rate of $g = b \cdot \text{ROE}$, implying:

$$V_{0,RI} = \frac{\epsilon(1-b)}{k-g} = \frac{\epsilon(1-b)}{k - b \cdot \text{ROE}} \quad \text{(or, estimating)} \tag{13.17}$$

$$\hat{V}_{0,RI} = \frac{\hat{\epsilon}(1-b)}{\hat{k} - b \cdot \widehat{\text{ROE}}} + \frac{\hat{\epsilon}(1-b)}{(\hat{k} - b \cdot \widehat{\text{ROE}})^3} \hat{\sigma}^2_{\text{denom}} \tag{13.18}$$

$$\hat{\sigma}^2_{\text{denom}} = \hat{\sigma}^2_k + b^2 \hat{\sigma}^2_{\text{ROE}} - 2b \operatorname{Cov}(\hat{k}, \widehat{\text{ROE}}). \tag{13.19}$$

Note that we assume we can know the reinvestment fraction b with certainty.

If the firm's return on equity is high enough (ROE $> k$), reinvestment will increase the value of the firm. Unfortunately, the Gordon-Shapiro model also tells us that in this case we should retain *all* earnings — which leads to a growth rate exceeding the pricing kernel $g > k$. As $g \uparrow k$, the model blows up with valuations heading to infinity. A further complication is that ROE is rarely constant.

Return on equity was first created by DuPont's Frank Donaldson Brown for a 1914 internal analysis. Most importantly, the **DuPont model** Brown devised decomposed ROE into the product of a number of important sub-ratios:

$$ROE = \text{profit margin} \times \text{asset turnover} \times \text{equity multiplier} \tag{13.20}$$

$$= \frac{\text{net profit}}{\text{sales}} \times \frac{\text{sales}}{\text{average assets}} \times \frac{\text{average assets}}{\text{average equity}}. \tag{13.21}$$

The importance of this decomposition, as explained in Meyer and Kirby (2011), is that it breaks return on equity into three tasks which can be handled by individual parts of the firm: marketers and salespeople maximize return on sales (by getting a good price); production managers maximize sales from their physical plant (by producing the most from the assets on hand); and, financial managers maximize financial efficiency (by minimizing the equity needed).

There are analysts who swear by the utility of the DuPont model and the ideas of separate task management; however, to get further into it (and related decomposition models) is more for a course in fundamental valuation. Thus we only mention the model's ideas since they are influential.

One criticism is that, as Meyer and Kirby (2011) note, thinking of these as separate tasks can encourage businesses to develop into independent (and thus less efficient) "silos."

13.7 Multi-stage Growth DDMs

A constant ROE is a simplifying assumption, but it contradicts the life cycles we see for firms: as young firms mature, the ROE typically declines. One fix is to use a life cycle model to model dividends and then discount those using the preceding models to value the firm.

Typically, a multi-stage dividend discount model is built using distinct lifecycle periods. Dividends:

1. are less certain and so are discounted individually in the near future;
2. grow rapidly during the early growth stage; and,
3. growth slows toward steady-state growth during the maturity stage.
4. We use the Gordon-Shapiro model for dividends thereafter.
5. This form can also handle one-time special dividends.

Unfortunately, we will not explore these models here. For years I tried building an example of a multi-stage model for my students. Unfortunately, the models have so many inputs — in addition to trying to guess at the time boundaries between stages — that estimating a model was an exercise in frustration. When I could get the model to work, it gave highly variable prices for small changes in the inputs. A model that suggests the share price should be between $1 and $500 is not very informative.

This does not mean such models cannot work; however, you would need to impose some constraints on the the model inputs. Furthermore, these models flirt with the warning given by Coase (1982): "If you torture the data enough, nature will always confess." In other words: an overly-flexible model lets modelers push the valuation to where they *think* it should be instead of what might better reflect the data.

13.8 Free Cashflow to the Firm

Another way to price a firm is is to discount the cashflows the firm receives. If we can replicate those cashflows, then we can replicate the firm. This is especially handy for firms which do not pay out a dividend or pay unsustainably high dividends However, we assume debt remains constant.

The **free cashflow to the firm** (FCFF) is defined as:

$$\text{FCFF} = \text{EBIT}(1 - \tau) + \text{depreciation} - \text{capex} - \Delta\text{NWC} \qquad (13.22)$$

where EBIT is the earnings before interest and taxes, τ is the effective tax rate, capex is capital expenditures, and NWC is net working capital. Here, we subtract out taxes because the firm does not get to keep the taxed part of earnings.

What discount rate should we use? The firm can issue debt and equity to raise capital and generate these cashflows. If the firm has raised capital from equity, bonds, and bank loans in fractions $w_e, w_b, w_\ell > 0$ such that $w_e + w_b + w_\ell = 1$, then the **weighted average cost of capital** (WACC) is:

$$\text{WACC} = w_e r_e + (w_b r_b + w_\ell r_\ell)(1 - \tau), \tag{13.23}$$

where r_e is the required rate of return from equity (the pricing kernel from the dividend discount model); r_b, r_ℓ are the average rates the firm pays on its bonds and bank loans; and, τ is the firm's effective tax rate, assuming interest paid is tax deductible. Here, we reduce the cost of capital by taxed interest paid because interest paid is tax deductible. If interest paid is not tax deductible, we should use $\tau = 0$ in this formula.[7]

Since the WACC is used to generate a perpetuity of free cashflows to the firm, we discount the FCFF by the WACC to get the firm's value F. Then we subtract debt and divide by the shares outstanding to get a per-share price:

$$\text{Firm value} = F_0 = \frac{\text{FCFF}}{\text{WACC} - g}, \tag{13.24}$$

$$V_0 = \frac{\text{firm value} - \text{debt}}{\text{shares outstanding}}, \tag{13.25}$$

where g is the growth rate of FCFF. Obviously, this formula also must change when we plug in estimated quantities to get an estimated firm value:

$$\hat{F}_0 = \frac{\widehat{\text{FCFF}}}{\widehat{\text{WACC}} - \hat{g}} + \frac{\widehat{\text{FCFF}}}{(\widehat{\text{WACC}} - \hat{g})^3} \hat{\sigma}^2_{\text{WACC}-g}, \tag{13.26}$$

$$\hat{\sigma}^2_{\text{WACC}-g} = \hat{\sigma}^2_{\text{WACC}} + \hat{\sigma}^2_g - 2\,\text{Cov}(\widehat{\text{WACC}}, \hat{g}). \tag{13.27}$$

$$\hat{V}_{0,FCFF} = \frac{\hat{F} - \text{debt}}{\text{shares outstanding}}. \tag{13.28}$$

For example, suppose the firm we analyzed in the preceding two sections has free cashflow to the firm of \$15 mn, which it expects to grow 4% each year. The firm was financed by one-half equity (3 mn shares outstanding) and one-half debt (\$150 mn, paying 8% interest). Finally, suppose $\hat{\sigma}_g = 0.01$ and $\rho_{\text{WACC},g} = 0.5$.

The $\widehat{\text{WACC}}$ is then $\frac{k}{2} + \frac{8\%}{2} = 9\%$ and $\hat{\sigma}_{\text{WACC}} = w_e \hat{\sigma}_k = \hat{\sigma}_k/2 = 0.015$. The

---

[7]Obviously, this is a partial equilibrium solution: corporate tax policy will also affect the required rate of return on equities demanded by investors.

uncorrected FCFF model would give us firm and equity valuations of:

$$F = \frac{\$15 \text{ mn}}{0.09 - 0.04} = \$300 \text{ mn} \tag{13.29}$$

$$V_{0,\text{FCFF}} = \frac{\$300 - \$150}{3} = \$50. \tag{13.30}$$

The Jensen-corrected formula gives us:

$$\hat{F} = \frac{\$15 \text{ mn}}{0.09 - 0.04} + \frac{\$15 \text{ mn}}{(0.09 - 0.04)^3}(0.015^2 + 0.01^2 - 0.01 \cdot 0.015) \tag{13.31}$$

$$= \$300 \text{ mn} + \$300 \cdot \frac{0.000175}{0.0025} \text{ mn} = \$321 \text{ mn}; \tag{13.32}$$

$$\hat{V}_{0,\text{FCFF}} = \frac{\$321 \text{ mn} - \$150 \text{ mn}}{3 \text{ mn}} = \frac{\$171}{3} = \$57. \tag{13.33}$$

Note that the correction adds a 7% difference to firm value — and a 14% difference to equity value.

13.9 Free Cashflow to Equity

Finally, we might choose to analyze the cashflows to equity holders. This model is also handy for firms which do not pay out a dividend or pay unsustainably high dividends. However, this model assumes the future debt-to-equity ratio remains constant.

We calculate the **free cashflow to equity** (FCFE) as:

$$\text{FCFE} = \text{FCFF} - \text{interest}(1 - \tau) + \Delta\text{net debt.} \tag{13.34}$$

Next, we need to figure out the discount rate. The pricing kernel k, if estimated from historic data, is for the past debt-equity ratio. If the firm has higher leverage, investors will demand more return. We first figure out the leverage adjustment factor ℓ_0:

$$\ell_0 = \frac{1 + \frac{\text{debt}_0(1-\tau)}{\text{equity}_0}}{1 + \frac{\text{debt}_{-1}(1-\tau)}{\text{equity}_{-1}}}, \tag{13.35}$$

where the index of "-1" refers to the period before now over which we estimated the pricing kernel.

With the leverage adjustment factor, we can compute the new levered pricing kernel $k_{E,t}$:

$$k_{E,t} = r_f + (k - r_f)\ell. \tag{13.36}$$

Finally, we discount the perpetuity of free cashflows to equity at $k_{E,t}$:

$$V_{0,FCFE} = \frac{\text{FCFE}}{(k_{E,T} - g)\text{shout}} \quad \text{(or, estimating)} \tag{13.37}$$

$$\hat{V}_{0,FCFE} = \left(\frac{\widehat{\text{FCFE}}}{\hat{k}_{E,T} - \hat{g}} + \frac{\widehat{\text{FCFE}}}{(\hat{k}_{E,T} - \hat{g})^3}\hat{\sigma}_{denom}^2 \right) \Big/ \text{shout}, \tag{13.38}$$

$$\hat{\sigma}_{denom}^2 = \ell^2\hat{\sigma}_k^2 + \hat{\sigma}_g^2 - 2\ell\,\text{Cov}(\hat{k}, \hat{g}), \tag{13.39}$$

where shout is the number of shares outstanding.

Let's revisit this hypothetical firm we have valued one last time. Suppose the risk-free rate has been constant at 3% and the firm previously had debt of $154.5 mn — during the time when we estimated $\hat{k}$. Now the firm has a debt-equity ratio of 1 which they will hold going forward.[8] Assume the FCFE will grow by 5% with a correlation of 0.6 between k and g. Finally, we will use an effective tax rate of $\tau = 20\%$.

The leverage adjustment factor is $\ell = \frac{1+1(1-0.2)}{1+1.03(1-0.2)} = 0.987$. The new-leverage pricing kernel will be $k_{E,t} = 3\% + (10\% - 3\%) \cdot 0.987 = 9.908\%$.

Recall the FCFF was $15 mn and interest is now 8% on $150 mn, yielding an FCFE of:

$$\text{FCFE} = \$15 \text{ mn} - \$150 \cdot 0.08(1 - 0.2) \text{ mn} \tag{13.40}$$

$$= \$15 \text{ mn} - \$9.6 \text{ mn} = \$5.4 \text{ mn}. \tag{13.41}$$

The typical uncorrected FCFE valuation would then price the equity at:

$$V_{0,FCFE} = \frac{\$5.4 \text{ mn}/(3 \text{ mn})}{0.09908 - 0.05} = \$36.68. \tag{13.42}$$

The Jensen correction for using an estimated pricing kernel and growth rate yields a valuation of:

$$\hat{\sigma}_{denom}^2 = 0.987^2 0.015^2 + 0.01^2 - 2 \cdot 0.987 \cdot 0.015 \cdot 0.01 \cdot 0.6 \tag{13.43}$$

$$= 0.00014 \tag{13.44}$$

$$\hat{V}_{0,FCFE} = \frac{\$5.4/3}{0.09908 - 0.05} + \frac{\$5.4/3}{(0.09908 - 0.05)^3}0.00014 \tag{13.45}$$

$$= \$36.68 + \$2.15 = \$38.83. \tag{13.46}$$

The correction adds a 5.9% increase to firm valuation.

---

[8]If you wonder how the firm will hold debt constant, debt-equity constant, and grow equity... we will get to that.

13.10 Comparing Valuation Models

In a perfect world, these valuation models should all be equivalent. The **Modigliani-Miller Theorem** says that the firm should have the same value regardless of capital structure and payout policy — if we ignore taxes, transaction costs, bankruptcy costs, agency costs, and adverse selection. That is, admittedly, a lot to ignore.

In such a perfect world, the dividend discount, Gordon-Shapiro, Gordon-Shapiro reinvestment, free cashflow to the firm, and free cashflow to equity models should all give the same valuations; and, price ratios should also all imply the same valuation.

However, these valuations differ for a number of reasons. First, there is uncertainty in many of our assumptions and inputs. Second, many of these inputs are not constant; they often do not even have a constant expectation or variance. Finally: taxes, transaction costs, bankruptcy costs, creditor rights, and even agency costs and adverse selection are the reality.

This means that when we use these models, we need to compare and critique them. We have already seen that ignoring Jensen's Inequality yields models which undervalue the firm. We examined the uncorrected models because you will run into those forms; however, we will ignore the uncorrected models from here forward.

For the example firm we considered, we can see in Table 13.2 the range of valuations from these models: from $21.80 to $57. We could just take an average and standard deviation of these valuations; and, that would be a valuable summary. However, some criticism is first in order.

Model	Value	Sustainable Value
Dividend discount model $\hat{V}_{0,DDM}$	$21.80	$17.22
Gordon-Shapiro model $\hat{V}_{0,G-S}$	$47.36	(=DDM)
Free cashflow to the firm model $\hat{V}_{0,FCFF}$	$57.00	$7.10
Free cashflow to equity model $\hat{V}_{0,FCFE}$	$38.83	$18.43
Mean	$41.25	$14.25
Standard Deviation	$14.94	$6.22

Table 13.2: Difference of valuations for the example firm discussed in each model. The table also shows valuations if the cashflows were sustainable: dividends not exceeding the free cashflow to equity and no growth in cashflows. Note that all valuations use corrections for Jensen's Inequality.

The dividend discount model seems very pessimistic. That might be because it is the only model which ignores growth in cashflows. However, there is only $1.58 of free cashflow to equity model per share. That makes a $2/share dividend look unsustainable.

This also makes the assumed growth rates look hopelessly optimistic. Unfortunately, firms like to trumpet unsustainably large growth targets in hopes of talking up their stock. Worse: if such talk were able to convince bankers to provide capital cheaply, the valuation could become self-fulfilling — a fact not missed by many CEOs (nor many bankers).

What if we revalue the firm with more sustainable cashflows: a dividend of \$1.58/share and assume no cashflow growth? (Thus $\hat{\sigma}_g = 0$.) The Gordon-Shapiro model just reverts to the dividend discount model, but the other models give:

$$\hat{V}_{sust,DDM} = \frac{\$1.58}{0.1} + \frac{\$1.58}{0.1^3}0.03^2 = \$17.22; \tag{13.47}$$

$$\hat{F}_{sust,FCFF} = \frac{\$15 \text{ mn}}{0.09} + \frac{\$15 \text{ mn}}{0.09^3}0.015^2 = \$171.30 \text{ mn}, \tag{13.48}$$

$$\hat{V}_{sust,FCFF} = (\$171.30 - \$150)/3 = \$7.10; \text{ and,} \tag{13.49}$$

$$\hat{V}_{sust,FCFE} = \frac{\$5.4/3}{0.09907} + \frac{\$5.4/3}{(0.09907)^3}0.987^2 0.015^2 \tag{13.50}$$

$$= \$18.17 + \$0.26 = \$18.43. \tag{13.51}$$

These valuations are much more consistent. Furthermore, we can still critique them. The firm benefits from the deductibility of interest paid (aka the **interest tax shield**); therefore, the free cashflow models are more credible since the dividend discount model ignores the cheaper bond funding. If the firm cannot pay out increasing dividends, then the firm's equity will not grow. It seems obvious that the firm also does not have money to retire debt. The firm can only keep two of the three promises mentioned earlier: it can maintain a fixed amount of debt and a fixed debt-equity ratio. The firm cannot grow the stock price, however.

While not so applicable here, we should always be cautious when the pricing kernel minus growth is close to zero. Under those circumstances, the model will be very sensitive. This may inflate the Jensen's Inequality correction; however, an analyst should also realize that in such a situation the valuation model is far more uncertain.

Furthermore, price and per-share ratios vary with the business cycle. Cashflows also vary with the business cycle. Therefore, inputs to the model are unlikely to remain stable over time.

13.11   Growth Opportunities and Price-to-Earnings

One nice aspect of the Gordon-Shapiro reinvestment model is that it helps us assess the value of reinvesting in firm growth. We define the **present value of growth opportunities** (PVGO) as the difference between the market price and the no-reinvestment valuation:

$$\text{PVGO} = P_0 - V_{0,DDM} = P_0 - \frac{\epsilon}{k} \quad \text{(or, estimating)}, \tag{13.52}$$

$$\widehat{\text{PVGO}} = P_0 - \hat{V}_{0,DDM} = P_0 - \frac{\hat{\epsilon}}{\hat{k}} - \frac{\hat{\epsilon}}{\hat{k}^3}\hat{\sigma}_k^2. \tag{13.53}$$

Rearranging the PVGO formulas, equations (13.52)–(13.53) gives us:

$$\frac{P_0}{\epsilon} = \frac{1}{k}\left(1 + \frac{\text{PVGO}}{\epsilon/k}\right), \quad \text{(or, estimating)} \tag{13.54}$$

$$\frac{P_0}{\hat{\epsilon}} = \frac{1}{\hat{k}}\left(1 + \frac{\hat{\sigma}_k^2}{\hat{k}^2} + \frac{\widehat{\text{PVGO}}}{\hat{\epsilon}/\hat{k}}\right). \tag{13.55}$$

If the PVGO is 0, the P/E is like that of a perpetuity. As growth opportunities become more valuable, the P/E ratio rises: if growth opportunities add, say, 50% to firm value, the P/E ratio will be 50% higher.

We can also note that the growth term $\text{PVGO}/(\epsilon/k)$ is the ratio of growth value to asset value. If the growth value is high relative to asset value, the P/E ratio will be high.

Since ROE appears in the denominator, the P/E ratio can easily be very high if ROE $> k$ and the firm reinvests a high fraction of retained earnings. We can see this by playing with the certain form of the reinvestment Gordon-Shapiro DDM.

$$P_0 = \frac{\epsilon(1-b)}{k - b \cdot \text{ROE}} \Rightarrow \frac{P_0}{\epsilon} = \frac{1-b}{k - b \cdot \text{ROE}}. \tag{13.56}$$

Table 13.3 shows how a firm with attractive internal investments can have a very high P/E ratio.

ROE	\multicolumn{4}{c}{Retained earnings b}			
	0%	25%	50%	75%
7%	10.0	9.1	7.7	5.3
10%	10.0	10.0	10.0	10.0
13%	10.0	11.1	14.3	100.0

Table 13.3: P/E ratio for various levels of ROE and retained earnings b with dividend growth driven by reinvesting retained earnings based on the Gordon-Shapiro dividend discount model. In this example, we use a pricing kernel of $k = 10\%$.

This suggests that the price-to-earnings ratio may not be stationary in some situations or for some industries. That should make us more skeptical of analyses which focus solely on P/E ratios — or news stories which try to make too much out of high P/E ratios.

13.12 The Discount Rate

In the above, we waved our hands a bit on what the pricing kernel was. I claimed that we should use the required rate of return. What is this required rate of return?

We have not yet covered the capital asset pricing model or factor models. However,

I will do a little foreshadowing: the expected return should be the risk-free rate plus some multiples of the risk premia on risk factors.

The idea is that the demanded rate of return for instrument j should only be a function of the risk-free rate r_f and the excess returns on risk factors $(X - r_f)$:

$$k_j = r_f + \sum_i \beta_{i,j}(X_i - r_f). \tag{13.57}$$

Typically, we estimate this with a model of the form:

$$E(r_j - r_f) = \hat{\alpha} + \sum_i \hat{\beta}_{i,j}(X_i - r_f), \tag{13.58}$$

$$\hat{k}_j = \sum_i \hat{\beta}_{i,j}(X_i - r_f). \tag{13.59}$$

This shift to modeling, however, raises a few questions.

13.12.1   Why Not Use the Average Excess Return?

The first question seems obvious: If we are never sure of the important risk factors, why use a risk factor model at all? Why not just use the average excess return for instrument j?

There are a few reasons for not using the average return:

1. *Average excess returns are noisier.* That affects the valuation in two ways: it makes the valuation less certain; and, it inflates the size of the Jensen correction.
2. *We can use long-run risk premia.* These may be smoother (*i.e.* less volatile) and easier to estimate.
3. *We should correct for spurious trends.* Any estimation period is likely to have some trend; we cannot expect that trend to continue. Therefore, we remove that trend from our pricing kernel by excluding $\hat{\alpha}$.
4. *We can allow for mispricings* if we exclude $\hat{\alpha}$. The resulting valuation will reflect a price target more in the direction of $\hat{\alpha}$. However, we must believe we have missed no risk factor: that the seeming mispricing does not reflect taking more risk. We should not assume this lightly.

13.12.2   Which Risk-Free Rate?

Suppose we use the pricing kernel to evaluate the return on a project that will take ten years. The risk-free rate we use in the pricing kernel to evaluate the project should be the ten-year rate. If the project were a two-year project, the two-year rate would be appropriate. In general, the risk-free rate varies with the length of the project being valued.

Unfortunately, when we look at pricing kernels used by research, the practice varies widely. Some researchers use one-month T-bill rates; others say to use "long-term government bond rates" with little more specificity; and, some will note that the risk-free rate should match the term of a project being valued. That is, of course, little help when valuing equities by discounting a perpetuity of risky cashflows. Worse still: some theories will claim that all investors should use the same risk-free rate.

In general, if you are trading over short time horizons, a short-term (overnight to three-month-bill) rate should be used. If you are running a portfolio rebalanced occasionally, perhaps use something between a six-month and two-year government bond rate. Pension funds and endowments would likely use somewhere from ten-year to thirty-year (or longer-dated) government bond rates.

13.12.3   Can We Beat the Market Cap Rate?

The simplest risk factor model would be some forward-looking measure of the macroeconomy. Typically, we (silently) admit defeat on finding such a macroeconomic measure and instead propose to use a measure of the overall market. Then, we often (again, silently) admit defeat on finding such a market measure and use (what might not be) the next-best thing: a stock index. This one-factor model is called the capital asset pricing model.

When we use such a model, we sometimes refer to the pricing kernel k as the **market cap rate**. Can we find a better pricing kernel? The answer is definitive: yes. However, most investments texts never stray beyond that pricing kernel. We will spend the next few chapters trying to develop better pricing kernels. I recommend reading Cochrane (2011) as you proceed on. The details might be a bit much, but the overarching message is clear: pricing kernels are more important than we thought years ago; thinking about them will yield dividends.

13.13   Quiz

Try to answer these questions in five minutes. For answers with equations, just write the equations; do not evaluate them.

1. Your friend can predict the future and tells you we are about to enter a recession.

   a) Name three types of investments you should buy.

   b) Name three types of investments you should sell or sell short.

2. Risk-free rates are 1% and a stock has an expected annual return k of 10% (s.e. 1%). If the stock pays an annual dividend of $3, what does a (corrected) dividend discount model suggest is a fair price?

3. If the preceding stock's dividend grows 1% annually (s.e. 0.5%), what does the Gordon-Shapiro model suggest is a fair stock price? (Assume a correlation between g and k of 0.6.)

4. The replacement cost of a firm is $70 mn. The market price of that firm is $100 mn. If this firm is in a highly-competitive industry (so minimal barriers to entry), what does Tobin suggest will happen?

5. A firm has free cashflow to the firm (FCFF) of $3,000,000/year. This cashflow grows at a rate g of 2%/year (s.e. 0.5%). The weighted average cost of capital is 6%/year (s.e. 0.5%). Assume a correlation between WACC and g of 0.4.

a) What is the value of the firm?

b) If the firm has debt outstanding of $3 mn and 3 mn shares of stock outstanding, what is your estimate of the proper stock price?

6. If the last five questions refer to the same firm, what is a reasonable price target — and why? (So do not just write down a number with no explanation.)

7. (BONUS) Amazon.com stock (AMZN) does not pay out a dividend. The stock is currently trading at $1025/share. If the stock has an expected annual return of 30% and risk-free rates are 1%, what can we expect in Amazon's future?

13.14   Exercises

Instructions

Consider the following defense conglomerate firms' financials as of 3 April 2018:

Firm Name	Boeing	General Dynamics	Honeywell	Lockheed Martin	Northrup Grumman	Raytheon	United. Tech.
Ticker	BA	GD	HON	LMT	NOC	RTN	UTX
Price/share	330.82	218.88	142.43	334.71	346.04	214.05	124.91
Shares Out mn	587.223	298.08	748.38	285.82	174.38	288.51	800.09
Debt bn	11.12	3.98	17.88	14.26	15.27	5.05	27.48
Book value bn	0.352	11.521	17.276	-0.683	7.048	9.963	29.61
EPS	13.43	9.56	2.14	6.89	11.47	6.95	5.70
Sales bn	93.40	30.98	40.53	51.05	25.80	25.35	59.84
E(Div)/share	6.84	3.72	2.98	8.00	4.40	3.47	2.80
Ret. earnings	58%	66%	0%	0%	66%	64%	52%
ROE	1272%	26.8%	9.2%	387%	32.7%	19.0%	16.1%
FCFF bn	9.74	2.08	3.86	1.23	1.15	2.12	3.95
Pr. kernel k	0.369	0.193	0.232	0.153	0.188	0.149	0.237
Std Error σ_k	0.05	0.030	0.02	0.025	0.031	0.027	0.018

1. Create R code to calculate as many of the models as we have covered without — and then with — the Jensen's Inequality correction.

2. Do some models not make sense for some firms? Why not? What should you do in those situations?

3. Do any of the data look unusual? Is there a good reason that those data might look unusual?

4. If profits are given by sales − variable costs − fixed costs and variable costs are linear in sales, prove the degree of operating leverage is given by 1+fixed costs/profits. (Hint: think of DOL as an elasticity.)

References

Ahrens, Dan. *Investing in Vice: The Recession-Proof Portfolio of Booze, Bets, Bombs, and Butts.* New York: St, Martin's Press, 2004.

Barbee Jr., William C., Sandip Mukherji, and Gary A. Raines. "Do Sales-Price and Debt-Equity Explain Stock Returns Better than Book-Market and Firm Size?" *Financial Analyst's Journal* 52.2 (1996), pp. 56–60. DOI: 10.2469/faj.v52.n2.1980.

Coase, Ronald H. *How Should Economists Choose?* G. Warren Nutter Lectures in Political Economy. American Enterprise Institute, 1982. URL: http://www.aei.org/wp-content/uploads/2016/03/NutterLectures03.pdf.

Cochrane, John H. "Presidential Address: Discount Rates". *Journal of Finance* 66.4 (2011), pp. 1047–1108. DOI: 10.1111/j.1540-6261.2011.01671.x.

Gordon, Myron J. and Eli Shapiro. "Capital Equipment Analysis: The Required Rate of Profit". *Management Science* 3.1 (1956), pp. 102–110. DOI: 10.1287/mnsc.3.1.102.

Harrison, Lauren R. "Your Cubicle Here?" *Chicago Tribune* (Mar. 10, 2009).

Meyer, Chris and Julia Kirby. "End the Religion of ROE". *Harvard Business Review* (Oct. 20, 2011). Retrieved on 31 July 2017. URL: http://hbr.org/2011/10/can-we-end-the-religion-of-roe.

Pástor, Ľuboš and Pietro Veronesi. "Stock Valuation and Learning about Profitability". *Journal of Finance* 58.5 (2003), pp. 1749–1789. DOI: 10.1111/1540-6261.00587.

Trueman, Brett, M. H. Franco Wong, and Xiao-Jun Zhang. "The Eyeballs Have It: Searching for the Value in Internet Stocks". *Journal of Accounting Research* 38.Supplement: Studies on Accounting Information and the Economics of the Firm (2000), pp. 137–162. DOI: 10.2307/2672912.

Williams, John Burr. *The Theory of Investment Value.* Cambridge, MA: Harvard University Press, 1938.

Chapter 14

Capital Asset Pricing Model

We discussed the idea of a pricing kernel in the prior chapter. It makes sense to start considering certain forms for that kernel. In particular, we need some model if we are going to value a business, a piece of property, a product line, or any other sort of capital asset.

The goal of this chapter is therefore to introduce our first factor model for a pricing kernel, the capital asset pricing model; to discuss its assumptions and critique its performance; and, to see how others have tried to extend and broaden the idea.

14.1 A Simple Factor Model

We can start off simply with a model where we have one risk factor. To think about this, realize that we can always decompose log-returns for asset i into expected and unexpected (*i.e.* risky) parts:

$$r_i = \underbrace{E(r_i)}_{\text{mean}} + \underbrace{\epsilon_i}_{\text{risk}} \qquad \epsilon_i \sim (0, \sigma_i^2). \tag{14.1}$$

Statisticians and econometricians think of **fixed effects** as modeling expectations and **random effects** as modeling what is unexpected or uncertain. For returns, we typically use risk factors to specify this decomposition. We also often sweep all of what we do not or cannot know into a randomness term. Thus we specify models like so:[1]

$$\underbrace{y_{it}}_{\substack{\text{response}}} = \underbrace{\mu}_{\substack{\text{overall} \\ \text{mean}}} + \underbrace{\delta_j}_{\substack{\text{group} \\ \text{mean}}} + \underbrace{\beta x_t}_{\substack{\text{risk} \\ \text{factor}}} + \underbrace{m_t}_{\substack{\text{overall} \\ \text{randomness}}} + \underbrace{g_j}_{\substack{\text{group} \\ \text{randomness}}} + \underbrace{e_{it}}_{\substack{\text{unexplained} \\ \text{randomness}}}, \tag{14.2}$$

$$m_t \overset{\perp}{\sim} (0, \sigma_m^2) \perp g_j \overset{\perp}{\sim} (0, \sigma_g^2) \perp e_{it} \overset{\perp}{\sim} (0, \sigma_{e_i}^2) \perp m_t. \tag{14.3}$$

[1]This is just an example. Note that statisticians tend to use Roman letters for random effects and Greek letters for fixed effects. We will not stick to this strictly since returns use r's and R's.

Many finance texts are unclear about which terms are random, fixed, or both (having a non-zero mean and a variance). This is needlessly confusing. It is also unfortunate because these are models for more than just returns, they are also correlation models. We will be explicit either by taking expectations and variances of both sides, specifying the mean and variance of the random effects (e.g. $m_t \overset{\perp}{\sim} (0, \sigma_m^2)$), or by discussing each term.

When we discuss random terms, we also need to stipulate if they are uncorrelated to each other $m_t \perp g_j$ or across time/categories $m_t \overset{\perp}{\sim} (0, \sigma_m^2)$. While we could assume independence $m_t \perp\!\!\!\perp e_{it}$, that is often a stronger assumption than necessary.

14.1.1 A Random Effects Model

To model a risk factor, we can *decompose the risk* of asset i's returns with a random effects model:

$$r_i = E(r_i) + m + \eta_i, \quad m \sim (0, \sigma_m^2) \perp \eta_i \overset{\perp}{\sim} (0, \sigma_\eta^2). \tag{14.4}$$

This decomposes the risk into m, the shared part of uncertainty which we call the **systematic risk**, and η_i which is unique to asset i and so is called the **specific** or **idiosyncratic risk**. This is very similar to the model we used to explore diversification in Section 9.7.

Note that this decomposition automatically leads to a decomposition of variance and induces a covariance:

$$\text{Var}(r_i) = E[(r_i - E(r_i))^2] = \sigma_i^2 = \sigma_m^2 + \sigma_\eta^2 \tag{14.5}$$

$$\text{Cov}(r_i, r_j) = E[(r_i - E(r_i))(r_j - E(r_j))] = \Sigma_{ij} = \sigma_m^2. \tag{14.6}$$

14.1.2 What is the Systematic Factor m?

We have yet to answer a simple question: what is m? I used m to be purposely vague. In general, m is some factor that captures the state of the macroeconomy. It could be the marginal return on risk or some economic multiplier on investment. Some people think that this is the market performance of all investments. However, the simple truth is this: *we do not know and never will know what m is.*

Unfortunately, this complicates modeling. Since we know markets are forward-looking, we often use something market-related. However, even measuring the performance of all investments is impossible: private firms need not report their returns or valuations; and, many investments in land and intellectual property are difficult to value and do not publicize their data. We need a measure which is observable.

Therefore, we typically make stronger assumptions and use a "broad-based market index" as a proxy for m. What does that mean? Usually, it means a market-capitalization-weighted stock index. Often times it means such an index which also has futures traded on it (for reasons we will discuss in Chapter 19). What about bonds, commodities, real estate, and foreign exchange? Some people will combine indices for each of these asset classes; that is sensible. More commonly, analysts just plug in a stock index because that was what they did in their introductory finance classes.[2]

14.2   The Single-Index Model

We can easily see a weakness of the preceding model: some instruments might have differing sensitivities to the macroeconomic factor m and different amounts of idiosyncratic variance. Sharpe (1963) was the first to propose making this model concrete with a proxy for market returns.[3] Finally, we thought that excess returns should be related to risk.

We can instead write a model of excess returns for firm i, R_{it}, as a function of excess returns on the market proxy, R_{mt}. Putting these together, we get the **single-index model** of Sharpe (1963):[4]

$$R_{it} = \alpha_i + \beta_i R_{mt} + \eta_{it}, \quad R_{mt} \sim (\bar{R}_m, \sigma_m^2) \perp \eta_{it} \overset{\perp}{\sim} (0, \sigma_{\eta_i}^2), \qquad (14.7)$$

where $R_{it} = r_{it} - r_{ft}$.

From here forward, we will write excess returns as capital R's. The difference between r and R is crucial. Do not mix up r's and R's.

Note that in subtracting off the risk-free rate r_f from r_i and r_m, we changed the expectation of r_i to include a part due to risk (the systematic premium) and a part not due to risk (the idiosyncratic premium):

$$\underbrace{E(R_i)}_{\substack{\text{risk} \\ \text{premium}}} = \underbrace{\alpha_i}_{\substack{\text{idiosyncratic} \\ \text{premium}}} + \underbrace{\beta_i E(R_m)}_{\substack{\text{systematic} \\ \text{premium}}}. \qquad (14.8)$$

If our model is correct, then the idiosyncratic premium (aka **alpha**) is a reward not due to risk. Often, it is attributed to market inefficiency; therefore, α may be the reward for imparting information to guide prices toward more correct values.

We also implied variances and covariances:

$$\sigma_i^2 = \beta_i^2 \sigma_m^2 + \sigma_{\eta_i}^2, \qquad (14.9)$$

$$\Sigma_{ij} = \beta_i \beta_j \sigma_m^2. \qquad (14.10)$$

Here we have assumed no volatility for the risk-free rate r_f. That is not likely to be true; however, for all but longer-term projects which use longer-tenor risk-free rates, this approximation is likely to be very good.

---

[2]This is often accompanied by a lack of thinking about what index is appropriate. While we often use the S&P 500 in the US, that is not what financiers use in the UK, Germany, China, Australia, or Brazil.

[3]Well... sort of. Sharpe's model was more vague and then assumed an index level.

[4]Some texts call this the **single factor model**, although that term is far from unique.

14.2.1 The Normality Lie

I said so before; but, it is a truth that bears repeating — because many texts perpetuate this lie: *None of these models require normality.* Our log-returns do not need to be normally-distributed; our risk factors do not need to be normally-distributed; and, the unexplained risk does not need to be normally-distributed.

Linear models still work when the data are non-normal. The ordinary least squares estimator is still the best linear unbiased estimator (BLUE). The coefficient estimates are still unbiased, even when the analyzed data are not normal. That is the key result of the **Gauss-Markov Theorem**.

Furthermore, the coefficient estimates are asymptotically normal under all but the most extreme assumptions. While asymptotically normal is not the same as normal, we can correct for that when we assess the coefficients for significance. One such way is to use the bootstrap first explained in Efron (1979).

It is important to remember that we do not need normality — because we do not think m and η_i are normally-distributed. Furthermore, evidence suggests that log-returns R_{it} and R_{mt} are not normally-distributed either.

If you believe that normality is required, re-read the above sections very carefully — because I have been very careful in writing them. All we have used so far is properties of variances and covariances and minimal assumptions of what is uncorrelated. We have not assumed independence nor any distributional form.

14.2.2 Escaping the Curse of Dimensionality

Another advantage of this model is that it helps us escape the curse of dimensionality that plagues modern portfolio theory. Specifically, to find the optimal risky portfolio for a universe of n instruments required $\frac{n(n+1)}{2} + n + 1$ inputs — most of which we needed to estimate the full covariance matrix.

You might remember that Sharpe (1963) and Elton and Gruber (1973) examined similar models to reduce the estimation problem. In this case, we need fewer inputs:

1. $1 \times$ risk-free return r_f;
2. $n \times$ idiosyncratic returns α_i for all instruments i;
3. $n \times$ "market" sensitivities β_{im} for all instruments i;
4. $n \times$ idiosyncratic variances $\sigma_{\eta_i}^2$;
5. $1 \times$ market risk premium $E(R_m)$; and,
6. $1 \times$ market variance σ_m^2.

While many optimizations use the risk-free rate r_f as an input, few texts consider that we really want to maximize the future Sharpe ratio of our portfolio. That implies that we would like to predict the portfolio return, portfolio risk, and the risk-free return. Why do so few texts discuss predicting the risk-free rate? The answer is because predicting interest rates is very difficult. Therefore many texts just use the current risk-free rate and do not mention that this is inherently a prediction.[5]

---

[5]Ernst & Young (2015) discusses many of these issues — although when it discusses differences

Despite these issues, this parameterization greatly reduces the number of inputs needed. Instead of estimating a full covariance matrix and needing $\frac{n(n+1)}{2} + n + 1$ inputs, we now only need $3n + 3$ inputs.

For a 50-instrument universe, the MPT full-covariance-matrix approach needs $50(50+1)/2+n+1 = 1,326$ estimates. Contrast this with the single index model which needs only $3 \times 50 + 3 = 153$ estimates. The single-index model requires much less data for estimation.

14.3   The Capital Asset Pricing Model

If we are willing to make a few more assumptions, it is a short jump from the single-index model to the capital asset pricing model (CAPM). The CAPM was published first in Sharpe (1964) and Sharpe received the Nobel Prize for this in 1990 (alongside Markowitz). However, Lintner (1965b) and Mossin (1966) seem to have made the discovery simultaneously:. If we look even more carefully, the discovery of the CAPM seems to be in (the unpublished) Treynor (1961).

14.3.1   An Equilibrium Model

The CAPM is an **equilibrium model**: it uses an economic equilibrium to derive insights about financial markets. In the case of the CAPM, we make the following assumptions:

1. There are many small, price-taking investors.
2. There are no transactions costs and no price impact.
3. There are no taxes.
4. Investors have no capital limits.
5. All investors plan for same (short) investment horizon.
6. Investors only invest in publicly-traded instruments.
7. Investors maximize mean-variance utility.
8. All investors have the same information (and expectations).

If these assumptions hold, then the CAPM posits an equilibrium that all investors hold the same optimal risky portfolio; and, all investments drift to offering the same ratio of excess return to risk. That will result in "the market" (*i.e.* all investments) being the optimal risky portfolio.

Our exploration of diversification also showed that idiosyncratic variance disappears in the limit when $n \to \infty$. Thus the asymptotic contribution of instrument i to the optimal risky portfolio variance is due to portfolio weight times the covariance: $w_i \Sigma_{iM}$.

The **market price of risk** is the ratio of market excess return to variance, $\frac{R_M}{\sigma_M^2}$.

---

in valuations, it does not separate the Jensen's Inequality effect from the effect of trying to predict a future risk-free rate.

For individual instruments in the optimal risky portfolio, the **marginal price of risk** is ratio of their marginal contribution to return to their marginal asymptotic contribution to portfolio variance:

$$\frac{w_i R_i}{w_i \Sigma_{iM}} = \frac{R_i}{\Sigma_{iM}}. \tag{14.11}$$

Knowing that variance is not a coherent risk measure, we can agree that these are poorly-named ratios. Nonetheless, these are the basis of the theory behind the CAPM so we will stick with them.

In equilibrium, all investments have the same ratio of excess return to risk (measured in variance) as the market; otherwise, we would reallocate our holdings to get a higher portfolio ratio of excess return to variance. Therefore, we have that:

$$\frac{R_i}{\Sigma_{iM}} = \frac{R_M}{\sigma_M^2} \implies R_i = \frac{\Sigma_{iM}}{\sigma_M^2} R_M. \tag{14.12}$$

This is the core of the **capital asset pricing model**: that returns are related to the overall market of all public investments.

We know from linear regression that a slope is given by $\frac{\text{Cov}(X,Y)}{\text{Var}(X)}$. This yields the **Sharpe-Lintner form** of the CAPM:

$$E(R_i) = \frac{\Sigma_{iM}}{\sigma_M^2} E(R_M) = \beta_i E(R_{Mt}), \text{ or,} \tag{14.13}$$

$$R_{it} = \underbrace{\alpha_i}_{=0} + \beta_i R_{Mt} + \epsilon_{it}. \tag{14.14}$$

This implies that $\text{Var}(R_i) = \beta_i^2 \sigma_M^2 + \sigma_{\epsilon_i}^2$ and $\text{Cov}(R_i, R_j) = \beta_i \beta_j \sigma_M^2$.

Note that the CAPM assumes that (1) the risk premium for instrument i is just β_i times the market risk premium, and (2) the idiosyncratic premium of the single-index model is zero (*i.e.* $\alpha_i = 0$). This suggests that we should not expect to "beat the market." These equilibrium results are what elevates the CAPM from just a statistical model to a model with theoretical economic justification. While the β's are the same in both models, the CAPM assumes the α_i's are all 0.

There is only one problem: We know that these assumptions are all wrong. However, all models are wrong; is the CAPM useful? The answer is yes, for a few reasons.

First, as a single-factor model, the CAPM is not a bad approximation. If the market index is up 50 bp and your portfolio has a beta of 1.2, guessing your portfolio is up 60 bp is not a bad first-order approximation. Second, the CAPM suggests that beating the market is hard. This is true. Third, the CAPM suggests the market is a pretty good investment. This is also true.

14.3.2 *We Are All Indexers Now*

If the market M is the optimal risky portfolio, we should invest in risk-free bonds and a market-representative risky portfolio — which *should* be the market index. Thus we should all be "indexers."

Unfortunately, there were lots of reasons we discussed in Chapter 9 for why investors do not all hold the same optimal risky portfolio. Despite that reality, a broad market portfolio will always be tending toward optimality. That yields another perspective. The market M may not be the optimal risky portfolio; however, it is not likely to be far from the optimal risky portfolio. So we can view M as a good first guess at (or first-order approximation to) the optimal risky portfolio.

Unfortunately, we must remember that this hypothetical market portfolio M may not be what we think of as the market "index." In the US, for example, M is surely not so limited as to be the S&P 500, nor that plus the Russell 2000, nor even the addition of non-S&P-500 members of the Russell 1000. Even if we were to add in the Bloomberg Barclays Aggregate Bond index, we would still not have the market portfolio. Even if we had the US market portfolio, we would then need to repeat that index creation for all the other countries with publicly-traded instruments.

So are the available stock, bond, commodity, and real estate indices a good first-approximation? Yes. However, we should remember that they are not the same as this hypothetical market portfolio M.

14.3.3   The Equilibrium Market Return?

Since we all hold the market and borrowing has to be balanced by lending, every lender who invests in F is balanced by an investor who is short F — and therefore must be long that much more of M. This suggests that the average weight of M must be $\bar{y} = 1$. Maybe.

The unclear assumption is that risk-free borrowers, such as the government, also invest in the market and that their borrowing allows them to leverage their market investment. That may be true, but it is not clearly true.

However, suppose we believe this. Then it would seem that:

$$\bar{y} = E\left(\frac{r_M - r_f}{\lambda \sigma_M^2}\right) \overset{?}{\Longrightarrow} \frac{E(r_M - r_f)}{E(\lambda \sigma_M^2)} \tag{14.15}$$

$$\Longrightarrow E(r_M - r_f) = E(\lambda \sigma_M^2) \tag{14.16}$$

$$\Longrightarrow E(r_M) - r_f = \bar{\lambda} \sigma_M^2. \tag{14.17}$$

Yet there is also a problem with the first implication. We want the expectation of a convex function but have replaced it with the convex function of the expectation. We must account for the uncertainty of the $\lambda \sigma_M^2$ in the denominator. This requires a correction due to Jensen's Inequality. Unfortunately, this correction is a bit more complicated.

The third implication assumes that there is no variation in the risk-free rate over the time period examined or that the risk-free rate is a martingale. We will revisit these issues when we make use of this implication in Chapter 24.

14.3.4 The Security Market Line

If we plot expected return versus beta, the CAPM implies we should get a straight line. The line should go through F ($\beta = 0$, return of r_f) and M ($\beta = 1$, return of $E(r_M)$). This line is called the **security market line** (SML). We can then overlay the expected returns for instruments and compare those points to the line.

Fairly-priced instruments will lie on the SML. Instruments with an expected return above that implied by the CAPM will lie above the SML; and, instruments with an expected return below that implied by the CAPM will lie below the SML. The distance above the SML is the same as α_i from the single-index model.

We can also use the SML to determine the proper pricing kernel for valuing a project. We determine the beta for our firm and that implies the required rate of return.

14.3.5 Input List Construction

The single-index model and CAPM allow a modular approach to model inputs. First, predict the market risk premium $\hat{R}_m$ and variance $\hat{\sigma}_m^2$ via historical estimation, macroeconomic analysis, or other models. Next, estimate betas via

$$R_{i,t} = \alpha_i + \beta_i R_{m,t} + \eta_{i,t} \tag{14.18}$$

to get $\hat{\beta}_i$'s and $\hat{\sigma}_{\eta_i}$'s; we may adjust these or try to predict future β_i's. (We will discuss that shortly.) Then multiply $\hat{R}_m$ and the $\hat{\beta}_i$'s to get $E(R_i|\text{common info})$. Finally, if we are using the single-index model, use security valuation models to predict α_i's.

14.4   Single-Index Model and CAPM Problems

The single-index model and the CAPM help us think of returns in terms of compensation for a risk factor; and, they greatly reduce the burden of estimating the covariance matrix needed to optimize a portfolio. Unfortunately, these models also have problems.

14.4.1 Theoretical Problems

While we gain statistical efficiency with these models, we lose flexibility. These pricing kernel models impose some strong assumptions:

1. There is *only one risk factor* to consider: the market;
2. The instruments' *market proxy relation determines correlations*;
3. That investors *are all mean-variance optimizers*;
4. An *equilibrium which may not exist*; and,
5. We *may earn risk-free excess returns* α_i.

Only One Risk Factor

First, most people believe (and most evidence suggests) that instruments are affected by more than one risk factor. The equilibrium argument for the CAPM is reassuring; but, it relies on the assumption that all risk not universally shared can be diversified away. However, if (1) a subset of the portfolio is exposed to some other factor and (2) that subset does not become a vanishingly small fraction of the portfolio as $n \to \infty$... well, then a single-factor model will not be adequate. Furthermore, the compensation for that other risk factor will bias those instruments to have an estimated $\hat{\alpha}_i > 0$ in the single-index model.

All Correlations Are Related to Market Correlations

Second, all correlations are determined by the sensitivity to the market proxy. That can prevent us from seeing unusual pairwise correlations.

For example, consider the ADRs UN and UL, both on Unilever stock. UN holds shares listed in the Netherlands; UL holds shares listed on the London Stock Exchange. They are both shares in the same firm with the same dividends and voting rights. Therefore, their log-returns are highly correlated — almost 1 exactly. However, if we use a single-factor model to parameterize the correlation matrix, the correlation between UN and UL is:

$$\hat{\rho}_{UN,UL} = \frac{\text{Cov}(R_{UN}, R_{UL})}{\sqrt{\text{Var}(R_{UN})}\sqrt{\text{Var}(R_{UL})}} \qquad (14.19)$$

$$= \frac{\beta_{UN}\beta_{UL}\sigma_M^2}{\sqrt{\beta_{UN}^2\sigma_M^2 + \sigma_{\epsilon_{UN}}^2}\sqrt{\beta_{UL}^2\sigma_M^2 + \sigma_{\epsilon_{UL}}^2}}. \qquad (14.20)$$

Since $\hat{\beta}_{UN}$ and $\hat{\beta}_{UL}$ are almost identical as would be $\hat{\sigma}_{\epsilon_{UN}}^2$ and $\hat{\sigma}_{\epsilon_{UL}}^2$, we can replace these with a single $\hat{\beta}_{\text{Unilever}}$ and $\hat{\sigma}_{\epsilon_{\text{Unilever}}}^2$ which yields:

$$\hat{\rho}_{UN,UL} = \frac{\beta_{\text{Unilever}}^2\sigma_M^2}{\beta_{\text{Unilever}}^2\sigma_M^2 + \sigma_{\epsilon_{\text{Unilever}}}^2} < 1. \qquad (14.21)$$

However, this is wholly unsatisfactory since we know that the correlation, especially after approximation, should basically be 1. The single-index model and the CAPM imply a correlation structure which misses such highly-correlated pairs.

Instruments Uncorrelated With the Market Look Safe

Third, instruments that are uncorrelated to the market proxy ($\beta_i = 0$) will look like they have minimal risk. For example, prices for ultra-low sulphur diesel fuel, Chinese tech stocks, and Brazilian bonds might well have a correlation of zero (or nearly zero) with some market proxies. However, we should never be so blinded by our model as to think that any of these contributes no risk (or even just no variance) when added to a portfolio.

Are Investors Really Mean-Variance Optimizers?

Fourth, the idea that investors are mean-variance optimizers disagrees with what we know about risk. Ross (1976) noted that log-returns are not normal and so investors being mean-variance optimizers was questionable. We will see more of the ideas in Ross (1976) in Chapter 15.

The CAPM Equilibrium May Be Different

Fifth, the CAPM proposes an equilibrium: that all firms will have the same marginal price of risk as the market price of risk. However, that assumes perfect competition and no frictions. Data analyses have shown that regulated firms tend to diverge from the CAPM. Furthermore, firms with strong economic moats may be able to sustain a marginal price of risk higher than that of other firms. Elton and Gruber (1987) have shown that different investor beliefs and knowledge sets lead to different optimal risky portfolios. Lewellen, Lease, and Schlarbaum (1977) show that investors have a **clientele effect**: different investors prefer different stocks with different dividend policies. (This is likely due to differences in investment horizons.) In the presence of these imperfections, the posited equilibrium may not exist.[6]

Money For Nothing?

Finally, the ability to earn money above the risk-free rate without taking risk bothers many theoreticians. That is why they prefer the CAPM to the single-index model. However, this is only disturbing if we believe the world should always be in steady-state. That is unlikely.

14.4.2 Empirical Problems

There are also a few well-known empirical issues with the CAPM. Lehmann (1990b) explores some of these. The biggest issues are:

1. The universe of publicly-traded assets;
2. Using proxies for the market portfolio;
3. Heteroskedasticity;
4. Serial correlations; and,
5. Poor performance of estimated betas.

An Unknowable Investment Universe

One key problem with the CAPM is that the universe of all publicly-traded assets is effectively unknowable. Gathering this information would take time; and, by the time the information had been gathered, the universe would have changed. This

---

[6]This is not to say that there is no equilibrium; however, what the equilibrium is can no longer be justified by symmetry.

might seem like a pedantic complaint; however, hundreds of millions of investors do not invest in countries merely because of language and cultural barriers. Contrast that with the large amount of Canadian investment in the US. Language differences matter.

Proxies Cause Problems

Using proxies for the market portfolio also causes problems. Roll (1977) notes that using proxies for the market portfolio means that any tests of the model using data and any performance issues are really only tests of those proxies. Furthermore, Roll notes that we can only test if the proxy is mean-variance efficient.

There is a small sub-industry of academics who have collectively spent years of their lives trying to "prove" or "disprove" the CAPM. These analyses are just as bound to fail as researchers attempting to prove or disprove the EMH. Proof of a theory is a mathematical argument of logic. Data analyses contain randomness and therefore can never prove or disprove anything. Why be so picky about semantics? Because these articles all use those semantics and argue as vehemently as if proof were possible. You should not be persuaded to join such fruitless wars.

However, it is educational to see why these tests are flawed so that you can see how to better test your own models. We will do this shortly.

Heteroskedasticity

Another problem with most of these tests is **heteroskedasticity**: that variance is not constant across time. This is very well-known and is the whole reason that there are models for time-varying volatility. One could model the volatility with the ARCH model of Engle (1982) or the (generalized) GARCH of Bollerslev (1986). However, there is an even simpler solution: reweighting the regression observations to downweight observations when volatility is high. This methodology was known and available long before the single-index model or CAPM.

Serial Correlations

Another problem is that the data may be autocorrelated. If that is the case, then we would need to correct for it. In the worst case, serial correlation could make coefficients seem (artificially) significant. Various corrections have been proposed for this such as the sandwich estimator discovered by all of Eicker (1967), Huber (1967), and White (1980) and the correction for two-pass regression on autocorrelated data of Shanken (1992).

Poor Performance of Betas

Estimated past betas may not be the best predictors of future betas. This may occur for a number of reasons (including heteroskedasticity affecting estimation).

However, instead of trying to estimate past betas, we should try to predict future betas. This can greatly improve the out-of-sample performance.

14.4.3 The Litany of Flawed CAPM Tests

It is very educational to go through the litany of flawed tests of the CAPM. Criticism might seem harsh; however, the tests that follow were all done by smart people. It is helpful to realize that smart people also make mistakes or do things imperfectly. That encourages us all to do better. Furthermore, many of these tests are flawed in ways that are subtle and which arise with many financial data analyses. Seeing these flaws will hopefully help you see how to better test your own models.

Finally, although these tests are flawed, they are not uninformative. Almost every test below offers some insight that can help us better analyze and model markets. Therefore, let me be clear that (1) a flawed test is often better than no test at all, and (2) a flawed answer to an important question may be better than a perfect answer to a minor question.

Mixing Trend, Under-Specification, and Proxies

Some tests claim that the CAPM "fails" because the single-index model $\hat{\alpha}_i$'s tend to be positive. While that does not make the CAPM look good, we have no way of knowing if this result is due to an under-specified model, the market proxy, or the random sample of data used. Sadly, academic studies rarely examine multiple sub-periods or random periods.

Basic Randomness

Even if the model were correct, the proxy were perfect, and the data sample were perfectly representative, we still need to remember that it is not a true model failure if the $\hat{\alpha}_i$'s are not uniformly zero. We should expect some of the $\hat{\alpha}_i$'s to appear to be statistically significant (*i.e.* non-zero) just due to randomness.

Errors in Variables

Other tests examine the expected return-beta relationship:

$$E(r_i) = r_f + \beta_{i,M}(E(r_M) - r_f). \tag{14.22}$$

Most of these tests use data to estimate $\hat{\beta}_i$'s, $\overline{r_i - r_f}$'s, $\overline{r_M - r_f}$, and σ_{ϵ_i}'s. They then use other data to see if the relationship holds, that is:

$$\overline{r_i - r_f} = \gamma_0 + \gamma_1 \hat{\beta}_i + \gamma_2 \hat{\sigma}_{\epsilon_i}^2 \stackrel{?}{=} 0 + (\overline{r_M - r_f})\hat{\beta}_i + 0\hat{\sigma}_{\epsilon_i}^2. \tag{14.23}$$

For example, Lintner (1965a) and Miller and Scholes (1972) (L and M-S below) estimate this model for 301 stocks over 1954–1963. They find that:

$$\overline{r_i - r_f} = 0.108 + \underbrace{0.064}_{t=6.9}\hat{\beta}_i + \underbrace{0.237}_{t=6.8}\hat{\sigma}^2_{\epsilon_i} \quad (\text{L}), \tag{14.24}$$

$$\overline{r_i - r_f} = \underbrace{0.13}_{t=21.3} + \underbrace{0.04}_{t=7.4}\hat{\beta}_i + \underbrace{0.31}_{t=11.8}\hat{\sigma}^2_{\epsilon_i} \quad (\text{M-S}). \tag{14.25}$$

There are a number of issues with this model. First, from both a risk and a linear algebra spanning perspective, the model should also have a $\hat{\sigma}_{\epsilon_i}$ term. It is not clear whether volatility or variance is a better expression of risk, so there is no reason for the model to preclude one over the other. Second, they analyzed this data over a period when $\overline{r_M - r_f} = 16.5\%$. A period with such a strong market trend is going to have results that are biased toward a large intercept term since that explains the overall average performance.

Third, the model uses estimated betas; estimated coefficients include random noise. Whenever the inputs to a model include random noise, we have a classic **errors-in-variables problem**. That setting biases the slope coefficients toward zero. Sure enough: the beta coefficients are not 0.165 but are closer to 0.

Kandel and Stambaugh (1987) tested the model with the zero-beta portfolio approach (which we will discuss shortly). They find the intercept $\hat{\gamma}_0$ and beta-slope $\hat{\gamma}_1$ coefficients are biased proportional to the market proxy statistical inefficiency.

Finally, we might wonder if we are forgetting about the error term. Perhaps we should look at idiosyncratic risk?

Sorting by Estimated Betas

Fama and MacBeth (1973) try testing the CAPM with portfolios having maximal beta-dispersion. They use data from 1935–1968 to estimate the model:

$$E(r_i) = \gamma_0 + \gamma_1\hat{\beta}_i + \gamma_2\hat{\beta}_i^2 + \gamma_3\sigma_{\epsilon_i} \tag{14.26}$$

over many sub-periods and many portfolios.

They find that the beta-squared and idiosyncratic volatility coefficients, $\hat{\gamma}_2$ and $\hat{\gamma}_3$, are statistically insignificant. While they find the beta coefficient $\hat{\gamma}_1$ is usually positive, it is also often insignificant and is not close to the market risk premium.

Unfortunately, in creating the maximal-beta-dispersion portfolios, Fama and MacBeth sorted on $\hat{\beta}_i$'s. Thus there will be some mechanical reversion. The effect of this will be to bias the beta and beta-squared slopes, $\hat{\gamma}_1$ and $\hat{\gamma}_2$, toward 0 — on top of the bias toward 0 due to the errors-in-variables problem. Furthermore, they are looking at data over a time period that includes World War 2 and the Korean War. Expecting betas to be constant over this period seems unlikely. Therefore, they made it harder on themselves to conclude significance; however, that also means that we cannot so readily accept that the other model terms are not significant. Finally, Heaton and Lucas (2000) tried adding investors in private firms. They found that this helps; but, the $\hat{\gamma}_1$ and $\hat{\gamma}_2$ coefficients were still insignificant.

14.5   Improving the CAPM

Clearly the CAPM is not perfect. However, it is useful so we should ask if we can improve upon it. This is usually done in one of a few ways:

1. Devising *better betas*;
2. *Conditioning* on the macroeconomy;
3. Adding *other investments* to the investment universe;
4. Considering *other risk factors*; or,
5. Building a *precursor model*.

14.5.1   Better Betas

We mentioned before that risk aversion, risk premia, and firm sensitivity to the macroeconomy change over time, whether due to the business cycle, crises, or changes to the economic structure of the firm or macroeconomy. Therefore, it should come as no surprise that Fama and French (1989) find betas change over the business cycle. Furthermore, betas do not seem to perform well out-of-sample. Instead of trying to estimate past betas, we should try to predict future betas. For example,

$$E(\beta_{i,t+1}) = a + b_1\beta_{i,t} + b_2\text{mktcap}_{i,t} + b_3\frac{\text{debt}_{i,t}}{\text{assets}_{i,t}}. \tag{14.27}$$

Rosenberg and Guy (1976b) examined this model and others like it. They found that the stock's market capitalization, the debt-assets ratio, and the stock's industry were all significant. Rosenberg and Guy (1976a) examined the effect of inflation and energy prices and how those might act to change beta over time.

Others have tried squeezing betas. Blume (1975) suggested using $\tilde{\beta}$ where:

$$\tilde{\beta}_i = \frac{1}{3} + \frac{2}{3}\hat{\beta}_i. \tag{14.28}$$

Obviously, this is a crude sort of James-Stein estimator.

Similarly, Vašíček (1973) suggested a relative-variance weighted squeezing that is a bit closer to a James-Stein estimator. The prediction, based on an analysis of n different stocks for T time periods, is:

$$\tilde{\beta}_i = \frac{\hat{\beta}_i/\hat{\sigma}^2_{\hat{\beta}_i} + \bar{\beta}/\hat{\sigma}^2_{\bar{\beta}}}{\frac{1}{\hat{\sigma}^2_{\hat{\beta}_i}} + \frac{1}{\hat{\sigma}^2_{\bar{\beta}}}} = \frac{\hat{\beta}_i\hat{\sigma}^2_{\bar{\beta}} + \bar{\beta}\hat{\sigma}^2_{\hat{\beta}_i}}{\hat{\sigma}^2_{\hat{\beta}_i} + \hat{\sigma}^2_{\bar{\beta}}}, \quad \text{where} \tag{14.29}$$

$$\hat{\sigma}^2_{\hat{\beta}_i} = \frac{\frac{1}{T-2}\sum_{t=1}^{T}(R_{it} - \hat{\alpha} - \hat{\beta}_iR_{Mt})^2}{\sum_{t=1}^{T}(R_{Mt} - \bar{R}_M)^2}, \tag{14.30}$$

$$\hat{\sigma}^2_{\bar{\beta}} = \frac{1}{n-1}\sum_{i=1}^{n}(\hat{\beta}_i - \bar{\beta})^2. \tag{14.31}$$

Elton, Gruber, and Urich (1978) studied these and found that Blume (1975) and Vašíček (1973) betas both outperform estimated betas; however, there was no clear winner between those two.

Finally, we could consider a true James-Stein estimator. We might suspect that the average of all betas should be 1. Based on Stein (1956), James and Stein (1961), Sclove (1968), and Bock (1975), we can then construct a James-Stein beta estimate $\tilde{\beta}_{i,JS}$ if we have $\hat{\beta}_i$'s for n instruments:

$$\tilde{\beta}_{i,JS} = \left(1 - \frac{(n-3)\hat{\sigma}^2}{\sum_{i=1}^{n}(\hat{\beta}_i - 1)^2}\right)^{+} (\hat{\beta} - 1) + 1, \tag{14.32}$$

$$\hat{\sigma}^2 = \frac{1}{n(T-2)} \sum_{i=1}^{n} \sum_{t=1}^{T} (R_{it} - \hat{\alpha}_i - \hat{\beta}_i R_{Mt})^2. \tag{14.33}$$

14.5.2   Conditional CAPM

Another possibility to improve the CAPM is to condition on more information instead of trying to find a model that works all of the time with minimal information about the state of the world. This was the idea of Rothschild (1985) and Harvey (1989), the latter of which focused on the business cycle. This conditioning yields the **conditional capital asset pricing model**.

The idea of the conditional CAPM is that betas may change in a way that is less desirable to investors. For example, if firms become more sensitive to the economy in recessions or crises (when losses are more painful) and less sensitive to the economy during expansions, then investors will demand compensation for that more painful beta variation. Petkova and Zhang (2005) find that the conditional CAPM helps explain the premium earned by value stocks.

14.5.3   Other Investments

Another possible way to improve the CAPM is to expand the "market" portfolio to consider all possible investments. I mentioned before that Heaton and Lucas (2000) added private firms and that this improved the CAPM performance. However, one of the biggest omissions from the CAPM is an investment you are making right now: **human capital** — a fancy way of saying knowledge, education, and skills.

Duflo (2001) shows that Indonesian investment in school construction yielded returns of 6.8%–10.6% and internal rates of return of 8.8%–12% — greater than Indonesian interest payments on their sovereign bonds at the time. Schultz (2004) shows about an 8% internal rate of return to Mexican subsidies to education. Hanushek et al. (2015) show large returns to educational outcomes (based on standardized tests); and, Squicciarini and Voigtländer (2015) show that increased knowledge in certain French cities led to greater economic growth in the Industrial Revolution.

Given these returns, Mayers (1972) sought to add human capital to the CAPM. He found that this can lead investors to hold differing portfolios due to their difference in human capital uncertainty. Jagannathan and Wang (1996) added human capital to the CAPM, using the monthly growth rate in labor income as their measure of human capital growth. They find that this improves the performance of the CAPM and the conditional CAPM.

Palacios-Huerta (2003) notes that various measures of human capital all subsume the explanatory power of multiple risk factors. Furthermore, he finds that an increase in financial returns may decrease the return on human capital. (This may explain why some high-beta stocks have negative alphas.) Palacios (2015) examines a human capital model in an equilibrium model and find that the risk of human capital is lower than the market while the fraction of wealth in human capital is much higher than previously estimated: about 93% of total wealth.

Apparently, a model with an investment universe which better matches investors' actual investment universe yields a better CAPM.

14.5.4 Other Risk Factors

Since CAPM betas vary over time, it might make sense to add other risk factors. In particular, we know that different investors have different investment horizons, it makes sense to allow for multiple time periods. However, with multiple time periods, the risk is no longer just moves in the market; the possibility of changing sensitivities to the market becomes another risk. In practice, that means finding a risk factor to capture the variation in the state of the macroeconomy.

The Intertemporal CAPM

Merton (1973a) explored this possibility and the result was the **intertemporal capital asset pricing model** (ICAPM). Merton's Three Fund Theorem states that all investments are equivalent to some combination of three funds: the risk-free portfolio F, the market M, and a state-capturing portfolio S. Therefore, the ICAPM modifies the CAPM to add a term that varies with the state of the macroeconomy:

$$R_{it} = \alpha_i = \beta_{iM} R_{Mt} + \beta_{iS} R_{St} + \epsilon_{it}. \tag{14.34}$$

The last term allows the market beta to remain constant. However, this does mean that some instruments with no market sensitivity may still have an expected return above the risk-free rate — due to their sensitivity to the macroeconomic state.

Since investors may have different investment horizons, they may hold different optimal risky portfolios. Merton also noted that the ICAPM could be generalized to a number of risk factors. That yields the more commonly-known form of the ICAPM even though that form was only briefly mentioned.

A Multi-Index CAPM

Another possibility is that the CAPM proxy cannot describe all of the instruments we are considering. In linear algebra terms, the proxy we have is one dimension and does not span the investment space. We have mentioned trying to build a complete index including stocks, bonds, commodities, real estate, and FX; however, there is a simple approximation to improve upon the single-stock-index form of the CAPM: use multiple stock indices. This **multi-index capital asset pricing model** can be very useful in practice.

In the US, the S&P 500 is often used as a CAPM proxy because it is somewhat broad-based and has futures traded on the index. However, it only covers large-cap stocks. Adding the Russell 2000 (which also has traded index futures) may yield a much better fit:

$$R_{it} = \alpha_i + \beta_{i,SPX} R_{SPX,t} + \beta_{i,RUT} R_{RUT,t} + \epsilon_{it}. \tag{14.35}$$

Interpreting the coefficients of the model requires some thought, however. Some economists believe that both coefficients should be positive, however this is both unlikely and unrepresentative. Often, the coefficients will be of a different sign. Small cap stocks may have a positive Russell 2000 coefficient and a negative S&P 500 coefficient; this essentially says that the stock's performance is related to the outperformance of small stocks versus big stocks.

An imbalance in those coefficients may represent the layering of that outperformance on a positive exposure. For example, if $\hat{\beta}_{i,SPX} = -0.5$ and $\hat{\beta}_{i,RUT} = 1.2$, we can think of this stock as being long 0.7 units of Russell 2000 exposure and long 0.5 units of small-stock versus large-stock outperformance. This might seem strange; however, we will see a model with both of these risk factors in the next chapter.

14.5.5   A CAPM Precursor?

If we want to improve the CAPM, another way to attempt this is by developing a model that is a precursor: a model for the market returns. One theory that has been tried extensively is the **consumption capital asset pricing model**. This approach was first tried by Rubinstein (1976), Lucas (1978), and Breeden (1979). The idea comes from Keynes's formula for aggregate demand:

$$\underbrace{Y}_{\substack{\text{aggregate} \\ \text{demand}}} = \underbrace{C}_{\text{consumption}} + \underbrace{I}_{\text{investment}} + \underbrace{G}_{\substack{\text{government} \\ \text{spending}}} + \underbrace{X}_{\text{exports}} - \underbrace{M}_{\text{imports}}. \tag{14.36}$$

Since we can measure personal consumption, that should imply revenues (and thus profits) for firms. Therefore, measuring consumption changes should help us predict returns. Then, the consumption CAPM is given by one of:

$$R_M = \alpha_M + \beta_{MC} E(R_C); \text{ or,} \tag{14.37}$$

$$R_i = \alpha_i + \beta_{iC} E(R_C). \tag{14.38}$$

where R_C is excess consumption growth and $\beta_{MC} > 1$ usually.

The consumption CAPM *should* do well at explaining market returns. Unfortunately, it does not. Many have tried to fix the model and failed. Liu, Luo, and Zhao (2016) show that accounting for transactions costs help; but, the model just does not perform well.

Going back to the components of aggregate demand, Cochrane (1991) used investment to create a **production capital asset pricing model** which he finds promising and has some predictive power. Asprem (1989) looked at exports and imports and found they too had some predictive power.

That said, there seems to be a flaw with these approaches. Consumers spend money on products produced worldwide. That spending may flow to domestic firms, foreign firms, or both. Investment and exports are both other forms of spending; why ignore them when they seem to have predictive power?

Finally, what about imports? Keynes's equation views imports as reducing demand; however, that narrow view of trade is not supported by the data. Imports extend a country's production possibilities frontier, increasing productivity and yielding savings for consumers; there is economic benefit to imports. Maybe $1 of imports reduces aggregate demand by $1 but also yields a $0.05 benefit which shows up later in consumption and investment?

One reason these are ignored may be that their impact on firms is unclear. Or, as noted by Cochrane (1991), there may be a lag before these affect the economy. We may also be using the wrong risk measures for the ratio of excess return to risk, as suggested by Martin (2013). Finally, Kroencke (2017) suggests researchers have worked with a filtered version of consumption — and that unfiltering recovers informative variation.

In general, consumption-based models have done poorly at explaining the data without strong assumptions to justify the mismatch — such as consumers being far more risk-averse than other data suggest. The Kroencke work may fix this, but we will see how it holds up over time.

14.6 Hedging

Perhaps the greatest gift of the single-index model and the CAPM is that they extended the idea of **hedging**: that we can identify risk factors and reduce or eliminate those risks with positions in other instruments. Before these models, farmers and food processors hedged agricultural risks with futures and forward agreements; and, many businesses used forward agreements with their suppliers. However, it was not clear how to hedge a portfolio of stocks. These models also revealed other benefits of hedging.

14.6.1 Tracking Portfolios

When the single-index model was first discovered, investors did not have instruments allowing them to easily hedge their market exposure. The single-index model and the CAPM led to thinking about ways to hedge risk factors. One way is to use a **tracking portfolio**: a portfolio designed to replicate the movement of a risk factor.[7] Thus an investor long a portfolio P with a market $\beta = 0.9$ could sell short a tracking portfolio T worth 90% of P.

Suppose we hold a portfolio P with returns described by:

$$R_P = 0.02 + 1.3 R_M + \eta_P. \tag{14.39}$$

What if we can find a tracking portfolio T which mirrors the performance of M: T has a β of 1 with respect to M and minimal idiosyncratic variance? In that case, we can hedge $1 of portfolio P against the market risk factor by shorting $1.3 of T. We might also decide to buy $0.3 units of the risk-free portfolio F. Why? We would be long the $\hat{\alpha}_P = 0.02$ at zero cost and we earn interest on the excess $0.3. We can rearrange the returns equation to see this:

$$r_P = r_f + 0.02 + 1.3(r_M - r_f) + \eta_P = 0.02 + 1.3 r_M - 0.3 r_f + \eta_P. \tag{14.40}$$

Is it crucial to short 0.3 units of F? No; however, it will be useful — as we will see in the next chapter.

The net result of this hedging is to eliminate the portfolio's risks as much as possible. When that elimination is complete, we say that the resulting portfolio (long P and short T) is **market-neutral**. If we eliminated other risk factors as well, we would say that the hedged portfolio is **factor-neutral**.

In theory, we could build a tracking portfolio for all sorts of economic variables. Those interested in this idea should consult Breeden, Gibbons, and Litzenberger (1989) and Lamont (2001).

> **Potable   Alpha?   A   market-neutral** or factor-neutral portfolio with alpha may seem to earn risk-free returns beyond the risk-free rate.   Why not add it to other portfolios?   This is idea behind **alpha transport** or **portable alpha**.   However, this also adds model risk: if the factor model is wrong or factor exposures change, the other portfolios are at risk. Sure enough: Gilbert (2009) and Smith (2010) note how pension funds which swallowed the promise of portable alpha lost (USD) billions.

14.6.2   The Zero-Beta Portfolio

The excess returns R_i and R_M assume we have a risk-free rate. What if we do not have a risk-free rate or we cannot borrow? Black (1972) suggests using the return from a portfolio that is long portfolio P and short β_P of M or a portfolio uncorrelated with M. This **zero-beta portfolio** has no risk, according to the CAPM, and an average return of r_z. We can then use r_z in place of a risk-free rate.

---

[7]For a strict definition, we can say $R_T \overset{a.e.}{=} R_M$.

To find the zero-beta portfolio graphically, we take where the tangent line to the efficient frontier at P intersects the $E(r)$ axis at Z having $E(r) = r_z$. Since the frontier is a hyperbola, we know that the zero-beta rate will always be below the expected return of the minimum variance portfolio.

The zero-beta companion P_Z for portfolio P is then the portfolio on the inefficient frontier having $E(r) = r_z$. P_Z has zero beta and thus earns r_z. Figure 14.1 shows this for two portfolios, P_1 and P_2.

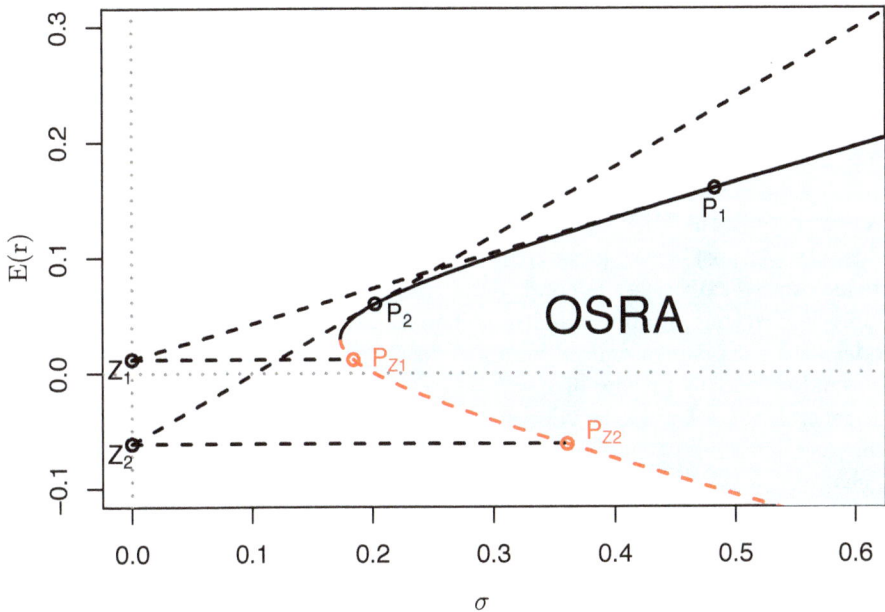

Figure 14.1: The opportunity set of risky assets with two risky portfolios P_1 and P_2 and their tangent lines indicating zero-beta portfolio returns at Z_1 and Z_2. The horizontal lines from those points show the zero-beta companion portfolios, P_{Z1} and P_{Z2}.

This approach gives us the **Black form** of the CAPM:

$$E(r_{it}) = r_z + \beta_i E(r_{Mt} - r_z), \text{ or,} \qquad (14.41)$$

$$r_{it} = r_z + \beta_i(r_{Mt} - r_z) + \epsilon_{it}. \qquad (14.42)$$

So what is our optimal risky portfolio P (since we do not have an F and thus cannot find the capital allocation line)? P could be the portfolio where the highest-utility indifference curve is just tangent to the efficient frontier. Typically, academics have assumed $P = M$. For most portfolios on the nearly-flat part of the efficient frontier, however, the difference in the implied zero-beta rate r_z is minimal.

14.6.3   The Value of Speculators

The other benefit of the single-index model, CAPM, and ICAPM is that they demonstrate how speculators add value. If investors demand higher returns to bear risk, then this means that people would pay somebody to take that risk from them. The fact that risk factors have a risk premium mean that speculators are providing a service. If that were not the case, speculators would compete and the risk premium for certain risk factors would vanish.

14.7   Summary

The CAPM is a major step in our progression to being quantitatively-aware financiers. It is the first step in seeing that we can model the pricing kernel. Furthermore, even though the assumptions of the CAPM do not hold, and we can pick apart most proxies for "the market," we still talk about the CAPM and many firms and portfolio managers still use the CAPM.

Ultimately, the CAPM joins three great ideas. First, investors will demand compensation to take risks. Second, linear modeling is a powerful tool even when it is only uncovering an approximation. Third, we like the CAPM because we like a model with simple economic dynamics. In short, the CAPM is a parsimonious approximation for the pricing of risk.

In general, these key ideas will serve you well throughout your life. The trick is finding good and useful factor models. We will see more about risk factors in the next chapter.

14.8   Quiz

Try to answer these questions in ten minutes. For answers with equations, just write the equations; do not evaluate them.

1. For a 7-stock universe, how many inputs including variances, covariances, and expected returns are required for MPT (Markowitz/Roy) portfolio construction?

2. How many inputs would you need for the 7 stocks in question 1 if you instead used a single-index model?

3. If a 1.1-beta stock's idiosyncratic variance is 0.15 and the market variance is 0.1, what is the stock's variance?

4. Suppose we estimate betas, $\hat{\beta}_i$'s, using past data. We take those past betas and predict future betas, $\tilde{\beta}_i$'s, as being:

$$\tilde{\beta}_i = \hat{\beta}_i \cdot \frac{2}{3} + 1 \cdot \frac{1}{3}. \tag{14.43}$$

Why is this a bad idea or a good idea?

5. In the single-factor model:

$$r_i = E(r_i) + \beta_i m + \eta_i, \tag{14.44}$$

what is m?

6. If returns disturbances η_i in the above equation are not normal, what happens to the single-factor model?

7. If we have a portfolio P and a tracking portfolio T which mimics the systematic part of P, what is the term for being long P and short T?

8. If we hold a stock with a $\hat{\beta}$ of 1.1, risk-free rate of r_f is 1%, and expected "market" return of $E(r_M) = 13\%$, what is the expected return of the stock?

9. What does positive risk premium for risk facotrs and the macroeconomic state (like in the conditional and intertemporal CAPMs) imply about shifting risks to speculators?

10. (2 points) How can you use the single-index model to figure out if there are correlated instruments which are not well-captured by the model/chosen index? (*e.g.* corn and wheat)

14.9   Exercises

Instructions

We will download data for a few stocks and indices to explore the CAPM.

- Risk-free rate: we will use the 3M CMT UST (Quandl: FRED/DGS3MO)
- Indices: S&P 500, Russell 2000 (getSymbols from Yahoo: ^GSPC, ^RUT)
- Stocks (getSymbols from Yahoo: BA, GD, HON, LMT, NOC, QCOM, RTN, UTX)

The risk-free rate needs to be rescaled (divided by 100) to get it on the same scale as log-returns. Ensure the index and equity prices you download are corrected for splits and dividends by using the adjusted close field.

I have said many times that we often use the S&P 500 as a proxy for the market here in the US; however, people outside the US do not use the SPX. Furthermore, the SPX is a large-cap index: it doesn't represent the entire market. Therefore, we will explore another index, the Russell 2000, to see if it is informative or better.

1. Modify the sample code below, as needed, to create log-returns for the indices and your stocks. Then create excess returns by subtracting off the 3-month T-bill yield scaled to a daily yield. Use those excess returns to compute the following correlations: SPX vs RUT, SPX vs each stock, and RUT vs each stock. Also compute volatilities for each of the excess return series.

2. We can try scaling those correlations for the variability of the stock and index excess returns. Do the following for each stock.

Using your answers from the previous question: multiply (1) the correlation of each index with a stock times (2) the standard deviation of a stock's excess returns, and divide that by (3) the standard deviation of the index's excess returns. Do this for both indices and each stock. (You should get 16 numbers.) Report the scaled correlations you get.[8]

3. Now we can explore the CAPM. Estimate the CAPM using the excess log-returns for the SPX and each stock. To build a linear model, use the `lm` command as shown in the example code. Report the intercept and slope estimates as well as their *t*-statistics. Are any of the S&P 500 betas significant? Which coefficients and their significance make sense? Which do not make sense?

4. Perhaps the S&P 500 is not the most representative index for some stocks. The other most actively-used equity index in the US is the Russell 2000, a small-cap equity index. Estimate the CAPM using the Russell 2000 index instead of the S&P 500. Report the intercept and slope estimates as well as their *t*-statistics. Are any of the Russell 2000 betas significant? Which coefficients and their significance make sense? Which do not make sense?

5. Which index better captures the behavior of each stock? Provide multiple pieces of evidence for that conclusion.

6. Perhaps no single index accurately captures the behavior of some stocks. To explore this possibility, we will look at multi-index betas. Estimate the multi-index CAPM for each stock using the excess log-returns for both SPX and RUT. Report the intercept and slope estimates as well as their *t*-statistics. Which S&P 500 betas are significant? What about the Russell 2000 betas? Are both significant for any stocks? Can you conclude anything about any of the stocks based on the betas?

R **Code**

```
library(xts)
library(Quandl)
library(quantmod)

# Get risk-free rate
```

---

[8]Note that when we say "the correlation of the SPX with your stock" we mean the correlation of returns or excess returns. (In this case, we mean excess returns.)

```
rf.raw <- Quandl("FRED/DGS3MO", type="xts")/100
colnames(rf.raw) <- c("T3M")

# Get S&P 500, Russell 2000, and stock returns
adj.close <- 6  # 6th field is adjusted close
equity.tickers <- c("^GSPC","^RUT","BA","GD","HON","LMT","NOC","QCOM","RTN","UTX")
prices <- getSymbols(equity.tickers[1], source="yahoo", auto.assign=FALSE,
                     return.class="xts")[,adj.close]
for (i in 2:length(equity.tickers)) {
  prices.tmp <- getSymbols(equity.tickers[i], source="yahoo",
                      auto.assign=FALSE, return.class="xts")[,adj.close]
  prices <- cbind(prices, prices.tmp)
}
equity.names <- c("SPX","RUT","BA","GD","HON","LMT","NOC","QCOM","RTN","UTX")
colnames(prices) <- equity.names
returns <- diff(log(prices))

# Now we join all of the datasets together and trim to recent
alldata <- cbind(rf.raw, returns)["2010/"]

# create excess returns
equity.names.xs <- paste(equity.names, ".xs", sep="")
# now in a for loop subtract off a daily risk-free rate, for example:
alldata$SPX.xs <- alldata$SPX - alldata$T3M/250

# If your ticker were DAL and you wanted to model returns
# (not excess returns) using ESTOX and SMI, you would do like so:
simple.wrong.model <- lm(DAL ~ ESTOX + SMI, data=alldata)
summary(simple.wrong.model)
# NOTE that this is not the model you are supposed to do
```

References

Asprem, Mads. "Stock Prices, Asset Portfolios and Macroeconomic Variables in Ten European Countries". *Journal of Banking and Finance* 13.4–5 (1989), pp. 589–612. DOI: 10.1016/0378-4266(89)90032-0.

Black, Fischer. "Capital Market Equilibrium with Restricted Borrowing". *Journal of Business* 45.3 (1972), pp. 444–455. DOI: 10.1086/295472.

Blume, Marshall E. "Betas and Their Regression Tendencies". *Journal of Finance* 30.3 (1975), pp. 785–795. DOI: 10.1111/j.1540-6261.1975.tb01850.x.

Bock, M. E. "Minimax Estimators of the Mean of a Multivariate Normal Distribution". *Annals of Statistics* 3.1 (1975), pp. 209–218. DOI: 10.1214/aos/1176343009.

Bollerslev, Tim. "Generalized Autoregressive Conditional Heteroskedasticity". *Journal of Econometrics* 31.3 (1986), pp. 307–327. DOI: 10.1016/0304-4076(86)90063-1.

Breeden, Douglas T. "An Intertemporal Asset Pricing Model with Stochastic Consumption and Investment Opportunities". *Journal of Financial Economics* 7.3 (1979), pp. 265–296. DOI: 10.1016/0304-405X(79)90016-3.

Breeden, Douglas T., Michael R. Gibbons, and Robert H. Litzenberger. "Empirical Test of the Consumption-Oriented CAPM". *Journal of Finance* 44.2 (1989), pp. 231–262. DOI: 10.2307/2328589.

Cochrane, John H. "Production-Based Asset Pricing and the Link Between Stock Returns and Economic Fluctuations". *Journal of Finance* 46.1 (1991), pp. 209–237. DOI: 10.1111/j.1540-6261.1991.tb03750.x.

Duflo, Esther. "Schooling and Labor Market Consequences of School Construction in Indonesia: Evidence from an Unusual Policy Experiment". *American Economic Review* 91.4 (2001), pp. 795–813. DOI: 10.1257/aer.91.4.795.

Efron, Bradley. "Bootstrap Methods: Another Look at the Jackknife". *Annals of Statistics* 7.1 (1979), pp. 1–26. DOI: 10.1214/aos/1176344552.

Eicker, Friedhelm. "Limit Theorems for Regressions with Unequal and Dependent Errors". *Proceedings of the 5th Berkeley Symposium on Mathematical Statistics and Probability* 1 (1967), pp. 59–82. URL: https://projecteuclid.org/euclid.bsmsp/1200512981.

Elton, Edwin J. and Martin J. Gruber. "Estimating the Dependence Structure of Share Prices – Implications for Portfolio Selection". *Journal of Finance* 28.5 (1973), pp. 1203–1232. DOI: 10.1111/j.1540-6261.1973.tb01451.x.

— "Portfolio Analysis with Partial Information: The Case of Grouped Data". *Management Science* 33.10 (1987), pp. 1238–1246. DOI: 10.1287/mnsc.33.10.1238.

Elton, Edwin J., Martin J. Gruber, and Thomas J. Urich. ""Are Betas Best?"". *Journal of Finance* 33.5 (1978), pp. 1375–1384. DOI: 10.2307/2327272.

Engle, Robert F. "Autoregressive Conditional Heteroscedasticity with Estimates of Variance of United Kingdom Inflation". *Econometrica* 50.4 (1982), pp. 987–1008. DOI: 10.2307/1912773.

Ernst & Young. *Estimating Risk-Free Rates for Valuations.* Publication. Ernst & Young Global Limited, 2015. URL: http://www.ey.com/Publication/vwLUAssets/EY-estimating-risk-free-rates-for-valuations/$FILE/EY-estimating-risk-free-rates-for-valuations.pdf.

Fama, Eugene F. and Kenneth R. French. "Business Conditions and Expected Returns on Stocks and Bonds". *Journal of Financial Economics* 25.1 (1989), pp. 23–49. DOI: 10.1016/0304-405X(89)90095-0.

Fama, Eugene F. and James D. MacBeth. "Risk, Return, and Equilibrium: Empirical Tests". *Journal of Political Economy* 81.3 (1973), pp. 607–636. DOI: 10.1086/260061.

Gilbert, Katie. "Portable Alpha Pothole: Colorado Fire and Police moves into absolute return vehicles". *Institutional Investor* (Sept. 23, 2009). URL: http://www.institutionalinvestor.com/Article/2302030/Research/4368/Overview.html?ArticleId=2302030#/.WZ4tfbQRC2x.

Hanushek, Eric A. et al. "Returns to Skills Around the World: Evidence from PIAAC". *European Economic Review* 73 (2015), pp. 103–130. DOI: 10.1016/j.euroecorev.2014.10.006.

Harvey, Campbell R. "Time-Varying Conditional Covariances in Tests of Asset Pricing Models". *Journal of Financial Economics* 24.2 (1989), pp. 289–317. DOI: 10.1016/0304-405X(89)90049-4.

Heaton, John and Deborah Lucas. "Portfolio Choice and Asset Prices: The Importance of Entrepreneurial Risk". *Journal of Finance* 55.3 (2000), pp. 1163–1198. DOI: 10.1111/0022-1082.00244.

Huber, Peter J. "The Behavior of Maximum Likelihood Estimates Under Nonstandard Conditions". *Proceedings of the 5th Berkeley Symposium on Mathematical Statistics and Probability* 1 (1967), pp. 221–233. URL: ttps://projecteuclid.org/euclid.bsmsp/1200512988.

Jagannathan, Ravi and Zhenyu Wang. "The Conditional CAPM and the Cross-Section of Expected Returns". *Journal of Finance* 51.1 (1996), pp. 3–53. DOI: 10.2307/2329301.

James, Willard and Charles Stein. "Estimation with Quadratic Loss". *Proceedings of the 4th Berkeley Symposium on Mathematical Statistics and Probability* 1 (1961), pp. 361–379. URL: https://projecteuclid.org/euclid.bsmsp/1200512173.

Kandel, Shmuel and Robert F. Stambaugh. "On Correlations and Inferences About Mean-Variance Efficiency". *Journal of Financial Economics* 18.1 (1987), pp. 61–90. DOI: 10.1016/0304-405X(87)90061-4.

Kroencke, Tim A. "Asset Pricing without Garbage". *Journal of Finance* 72.1 (2017), pp. 47–98. DOI: 10.1111/jofi.12438.

Lamont, Owen A. "Economic Tracking Portfolios". *Journal of Econometrics* 105.1 (2001), pp. 161–184. DOI: 10.1016/S0304-4076(01)00074-4.

Lehmann, Bruce N. "Residual Risk Revisited". *Journal of Econometrics* 45.1–2 (1990), pp. 71–97. DOI: 10.1016/0304-4076(90)90094-A.

Lewellen, Wilbur G., Ronald C. Lease, and Gary G. Schlarbaum. "Patterns of Investment Strategy and Behavior Among Individual Investors". *Journal of Business* 50.3 (1977), pp. 296–333. DOI: 10.1086/295947.

Lintner, John. "Security Prices, Risk, and Maximal Gains From Diversification". *Journal of Finance* 20.4 (1965), pp. 587–615. DOI: 10.1111/j.1540-6261.1965.tb02930.x.

— "The Valuation of Risk Assets and the Selection of Risky Investments in Stock Portfolios and Capital Budgets". *Review of Economics and Statistics* 47.1 (1965), pp. 13–37. DOI: 10.2307/1924119.

Liu, Weimin, Di Luo, and Huainan Zhao. "Transaction Costs, Liquidity Risk, and the CCAPM". *Journal of Banking and Finance* 63.C (2016), pp. 126–145. DOI: 10.1016/j.jbankfin.2015.11.011.

Lucas Jr., Robert E. "Asset Prices in an Exchange Economy". *Econometrica* 46.6 (1978), pp. 1429–1445. DOI: 10.2307/1913837.

Martin, Ian W. R. "Consumption-Based Asset Pricing with Higher Cumulants". *Review of Economic Studies* 80.2 (2013), pp. 745–773. DOI: 10.1093/restud/rds029.

Mayers, David. "Nonmarketable Assets and Capital Market Equilibrium under Uncertainty". In: *Studies in the Theory of Capital Markets*. Ed. by Michael C. Jensen. New York: Praeger, 1972, pp. 223–48.

Merton, Robert C. "An Intertemporal Capital Asset Pricing Model". *Econometrica* 41.5 (1973), pp. 867–887. DOI: 10.2307/1913811.

Miller, Merton H. and Myron Scholes. "Rates of Return in Relation to Risk: A Re-examination of Some Recent Findings". In: *Studies in the Theory of Capital Markets*. New York: Praeger, 1972, pp. 47–78.

Mossin, Jan. "Equilibrium in a Capital Asset Market". *Econometrica* 34.4 (1966), pp. 768–783. DOI: 10.2307/1910098.

Palacios, Miguel. "Human Capital as an Asset Class Implications from a General Equilibrium Model". *Review of Financial Studies* 28.4 (2015), pp. 978–1023. DOI: 10.1093/rfs/hhu073.

Palacios-Huerta, Ignacio. "The Robustness of the Conditional CAPM with Human Capital". *Journal of Financial Econometrics* 1.2 (2003), pp. 272–289. DOI: 10.1093/jjfinec/nbg012.

Petkova, Ralitsa and Lu Zhang. "Is Value Riskier Than Growth?" *Journal of Financial Economics* 78.1 (2005), pp. 187–202. DOI: 10.1016/j.jfineco.2004.12.001.

Roll, Richard. "A Critique of the Asset Pricing Theory's Tests Part I: On Past and Potential Testability of the Theory". *Journal of Financial Economics* 4.2 (1977), pp. 129–176. DOI: 10.1016/0304-405X(77)90009-5.

Rosenberg, Barr and James Guy. "Prediction of Beta from Investment Fundamentals: Part One, Prediction Criteria". *Financial Analyst's Journal* 32.3 (1976), pp. 60–72. DOI: 10.2469/faj.v32.n3.60.

— "Prediction of Beta from Investment Fundamentals: Part Two, Alternative Prediction Methods". *Financial Analyst's Journal* 32.4 (1976), pp. 62–70. DOI: 10.2469/faj.v32.n4.62.

Ross, Stephen A. "The Arbitrage Theory of Capital Asset Pricing". *Journal of Economic Theory* 13.3 (1976), pp. 341–360. DOI: 10.1016/0022-0531(76)90046-6.

Rothschild, Michael. *Asset Pricing Theories*. Technical Working Paper 44. NBER, 1985.

Rubinstein, Mark. "The Valuation of Uncertain Income Streams and the Pricing of Options". *The Bell Journal of Economics* 7.2 (1976), pp. 407–425. DOI: 10.2307/3003264.

Schultz, T. Paul. "School Subsidies for the Poor: Evaluating the Mexican Progresa Poverty Program". *Journal of Development Economics* 74.1 (2004), pp. 199–250. DOI: 10.1016/j.jdeveco.2003.12.009.

Sclove, Stanley L. "Improved Estimators for Coefficients in Linear Regression". *Journal of the American Statistical Association* 63.322 (1968), pp. 596–606. DOI: 10.1080/01621459.1968.11009278.

Shanken, Jay. "On the Estimation of Beta-Pricing Models". *Review of Financial Studies* 5.1 (1992), pp. 1–33. DOI: 10.1093/rfs/5.1.1.

Sharpe, William F. "A Simplified Model for Portfolio Analysis". *Management Science* 9.2 (1963), pp. 277–293. DOI: 10.1287/mnsc.9.2.277.

— "Capital Asset Prices: A Theory of Market Equilibrium under Conditions of Risk". *Journal of Finance* 19.3 (1964), pp. 425–442. DOI: 10.1111/j.1540-6261.1964.tb02865.x.

Smith, Imogen Rose. "Easy Money". *Institutional Investor* (Feb. 2010), pp. 62–65,90–91.

Squicciarini, Mara P. and Nico Voigtländer. "Human Capital and Industrialization: Evidence from the Age of Enlightenment". *Quarterly Journal of Economics* 130.4 (2015), pp. 1825–1883. DOI: 10.1093/qje/qjv025.

Stein, Charles. "Inadmissibility of the Usual Estimator for the Mean of a Multivariate Normal Distribution". *Proceedings of the 3rd Berkeley Symposium on Mathematical Statistics and Probability* 1 (1956), pp. 197–206. URL: https://projecteuclid.org/euclid.bsmsp/1200501656.

Treynor, Jack L. *Market Value, Time, and Risk.* Working Paper 2600356. SSRN, Aug. 8, 1961. DOI: 10.2139/ssrn.2600356. URL: http://ssrn.com/abstract=2600356.

Vašíček, Oldřich A. "A Note on Using Cross-Sectional Information in Bayesian Estimation of Security Betas". *Journal of Finance* 28.5 (1973), pp. 1233–1239. DOI: 10.2307/2978759.

White, Halbert. "A Heteroskedasticity-Consistent Covariance Matrix Estimator and a Direct Test for Heteroskedasticity". *Econometrica* 48.4 (1980), pp. 817–838. DOI: 10.2307/1912934.

Chapter 15

Factor Models and the Arbitrage Pricing Theory

After seeing our first factor model and hinting at more risk factors, we might have a few questions: Can we economically justify more factors? Do the models behave like the CAPM? And what are some other risk factors? We could devote an entire text to just this last question. However, there are a few factor models that are believed or considered by both academics and practitioners. We will investigate some of these. Furthermore, we will consider another argument to justify our pricing kernels.

The goal of this chapter is to explain the idea of arbitrage pricing, to discuss some commonly-used factor models, and to critique possible sources of alpha.

⚠️ 경고! *When we discuss specific factor models, the writing may seem to get a little... "cookbooky." This is because I am not shielding you from a sad fact: some of the literature has become a bit* ad hoc *and poorly justified. While we will see useful factor models, this perhaps-jarring exposition will reveal some problems in the literature and build skepticism in you.*

15.1 Introduction

The conditional CAPM and the ICAPM both showed that a model with only one risk factor is insufficient to capture the pricing kernel. Thus we allow for multiple risk factors, for example:

$$R_i = \alpha_i + \beta_{i,GDP}(\Delta GDP - r_f) + \beta_{i,r_f}\Delta r_f + \eta_i. \tag{15.1}$$

We call the β_i's **factor sensitivities** or **factor loadings** when we want to be specific (or sound fancy); but, usually, we just call them betas.

The truth is, however, that you have already seen a multiple **factor model**, in a way. When we discussed yield curves, we found that changes in the yield curve's level were analogous to DV01 (which is related to duration); and, we saw that changes in the level, slope, and curvature explained most curve movements. This defined, in a way, a factor model. If I asked you to concisely describe the factors affecting a bond's price, a natural guess would be: the level, slope, and curvature of the yield curve.

Obviously, we will have to modify a few concepts as we move to multiple risk factors. For example, the security market line becomes a **multifactor security market hyperplane** (which some texts incorrectly call a "line"). However, visualization is difficult for planes and very hard for hyperplanes — so we often skip this concept and just remember that $\hat{\alpha}_i$'s are distances from the hyperplane defined by the estimated risk factors.

As with the multi-index CAPM, we will increasingly find that some of our coefficient estimates are negative. This may happen for a few reasons:

1. The negative coefficient may be one part of a spread between risk factors;
2. The negative coefficient may represent that the instrument is a **hedge instrument** for that risk factor; or,
3. The risk factors may be multicollinear.

15.2 Arbitrage Pricing

Recall that arbitrage is the possibility of making a profit with no risk and no capital. Arbitrage is a rare phenomenon; and, most trading strategies which are called arbitrage are not: they require capital, have some risks, or both.

However, the idea of arbitrage and market efficiency is useful: the possibility of arbitrage often holds many prices together. This can let us make some strong assertions.

15.2.1 Arbitrage Pricing Theory (APT)

The **arbitrage pricing theory** (APT) was developed by Ross (1976) and has three assumptions:

1. Returns may be described by a factor model:

$$r_i = \nu_i + \beta_{i1}f_1 + \beta_{i2}f_2 + \cdots + \beta_{ik}f_k + \epsilon_i; \tag{15.2}$$

2. We can diversify away idiosyncratic variance (the effect of ϵ_i); and,
3. Markets do not allow persistence of arbitrage.

If these hold, the APT asserts that:

$$R_i \approx \beta_{i1}F_1 + \beta_{i2}F_2 + \cdots + \beta_{ik}F_k, \tag{15.3}$$

where R_i and $F_1, \ldots, F_k$ are the excess returns $r_i - r_f$ and $f_1 - r_f, \ldots, f_k - r_f$ if there is a risk-free asset and, if not, r_f is replaced by the zero-beta rate r_z.

This equation is unusual. We usually write a model with returns equal to the sum of model coefficients times the data plus an error term. Sometimes we write that the expected return equals the sum of model coefficients times the expected data — and the error term falls out since it has mean zero.

Here, we assert that returns are (approximately) the sum of the factor loadings times the factor excess returns. There is no error term. This is one of the few models to make such a strong assertion. While stated by Ross (1976) as an approximation ($\approx$), to drop the error term implies that the approximation is very good. This makes the APT different from the CAPM.

In fact, this is so good that we need to ask: Is it too good to be true?

15.2.2   Corrections and Connections to the APT

A weakness of Ross's APT is that despite some strong claims, it used unclear definitions... and that approximation. Dropping the error term but using an approximation sign makes a bold assertion and then qualifies it. However, subsequent work has shown what assumptions would justify equality.

Huberman (1982) strengthened the definitions of arbitrage and clarified that the assumptions lead to a linear model of risk factors. Chamberlain (1983) showed equality will hold if there is a risky, well-diversified portfolio (*i.e.* without idiosyncratic risk) on the efficient frontier. Chamberlain also states that if there are k risk factors, then k eigenvalues of the X covariance matrix are unbounded and the other eigenvalues must be positive but bounded (and thus vanishingly small as the number of instruments $n \to \infty$). Note that this allows us to diversify away idiosyncratic risk without $n \to \infty$.

Connor (1984) showed the CAPM equilibrium argument could also justify the APT; thus the betas are the same and the number of portfolio assets need not grow to infinity to eliminate idiosyncratic risk.

Bansal and Viswanathan (1993) offer convincing evidence that the pricing kernel must be nonlinear in risk factors to hold for nonlinear derivative instruments. This can be seen as extending the first APT assumption to include a wider class of instruments.

Lehmann and Modest (1988) discuss the assumptions needed for APT to hold exactly (*i.e.* without an error term) and, in data analyses, show convincingly that the APT does not hold exactly and that tracking portfolios for the k risks do not span the mean-variance efficient frontier. Despite the APT's strong claims, risk management is not yet trivial.

15.2.3   The Law of One Price and Convergence

The idea that drives the APT is the **Law of One Price** (LOOP): the belief that economically equivalent instruments will be priced the same. If prices diverged, arbitrageurs would rush in and take large positions, pushing the prices of economically-equivalent instruments back together until their prices were the same (or within transactions costs).

This implies a far stronger form of convergence than the CAPM. The CAPM suggests that many investors, gradually adjusting their optimal risky portfolio, will guide prices toward similar excess-return-to-risk ratios — a **dominance argument**. The APT, on the other hand, says that it only takes one person to spot the mispricing and quickly smash the prices back together — an **arbitrage argument**. If you are looking for an analogy: the CAPM is like a river, slowly carving out a path through the soil — while the APT is like using TNT to move a lot of soil immediately.

> **Chips and Guarbitrage** I once saw an arbitrage at a taco chain: chips cost \$1.12 and guacamole \$1.79, but chips and guacamole cost \$3.14. I watched like a hawk for different sizes of chips or guacamole to justify the mispricing. Seeing none, I ordered chips and, once that was entered, guacamole. The cashier canceled the chips and hit the chips+guacamole button, charging me \$3.14. "No, cancel that. I want an order of chips... <cashier presses button> ...and an order of guacamole." The cashier canceled the chips again and hit chips+guacamole. "No," I said, "I want an order of chips and an order of guacamole. Separately. It's cheaper that way." The cashier smirked. "Yes it is," she said, and finally rang them up separately.

15.2.4 An Equivalence Between Pricing Methods

Given the power of APT convergence, we should ask: when do arbitrage arguments hold? We will get to this, but to understand part of the answer we need to learn (just a little!) about a different approach to pricing.

There are two ways of pricing assets; and, there is an equivalence between them in many circumstances. The way we have discussed so far uses "physical" probabilities, *i.e.* those we can estimate as real-world event frequencies, often called $\mathbb{P}$-measure. However, we then need a discount rate (pricing kernel) above the risk-free rate since the outcomes are risky.

An alternate pricing method creates a different distribution of probabilities which compensate for the risky outcomes so that the pricing kernel is the risk-free rate. Since there is no penalty for risk, we call this **risk-neutral pricing** and the alternate probability measure the **risk-neutral density** or $\mathbb{Q}$-measure.[1] Note that the $\mathbb{Q}$-measure depends on our choice of **numéraire** (risk-free money).

---

[1] Without getting into the details of Girsanov's Theorem or the Radon-Nikodym derivative, you can imagine how the $\mathbb{Q}$-measure is created. If we increase the discounting above the risk-free rate when we use $\mathbb{P}$-measure, could we just shift the $\mathbb{P}$-measure downward (so negative returns are more

15.2.5   Fundamental Theorems

The **First Fundamental Theorem of Asset Pricing** of Harrison and Pliska (1981) states that a market with a finite number of assets and a discrete probability space does not allow the persistence of arbitrage if and only if there is a risk-neutral probability density $\mathbb{Q}$ with the same support as the physical probability density $\mathbb{P}$. This implies the LOOP.

Delbaen and Schachermayer (1994) loosens this to allow for a **semimartingale** price process: a martingale (possibly up to some expiry time) plus a càdlàg process with finite variance.[2]   That yields a result that there is **no free lunch with vanishing risk**, *i.e.* that there is no sequence of strategies which converge to arbitrage and eliminate risk.

The **Second Fundamental Theorem of Asset Pricing** of Harrison and Pliska (1981) states that a market with stocks and risk-free bonds is **complete** (can price all assets over all outcomes with zero transactions costs) if and only if the $\mathbb{Q}$-measure (for a numèraire of risk-free bonds) is unique.

What is the upshot of these theorems? They provide a bit of an all-or-nothing justification to arbitrage pricing. Hence why the APT makes the assumption that returns must be described by a factor model. However, while the CAPM claims an equilibrium for all instruments, the APT has nothing to say about instruments where these assumptions do not hold. Even the fundamental theorems are unaffected: such instruments fall outside of their assumed "market."

15.2.6   When the APT Breaks Down

As we will see in Chapter 21, the risk-neutral pricing framework is used to price options. This framework is often backed up by assumptions of markets functioning in continuous time so that we can trade dynamically to replicate all sorts of payoffs.

However, if we cannot uniquely price the underliers with risk factors, we cannot price derivatives either — even though derivatives just use the market prices of their underlying instruments. This plus Bansal and Viswanathan (1993) raises the possibility that the risk pricing for non-derivative instruments may be nonlinear. Furthermore, the results of Lehmann and Modest (1988) foreshadow that we might be able to break arbitrage pricing under certain circumstances. We will see more of that later.

Following Lehmann and Modest (1988), a number of researchers sought to provide sharper tests of factor models and the APT.

---

likely) to get the $\mathbb{Q}$-measure we use when discounting at the risk-free rate? The answer is: Yes. We will see more of this in Chapter 21.

[2]**Càdlàg** is a mathematical term from a French acronym for *continu à droite, limite à gauche* or "continuous on the right, limit on the left." This essentially means a process that is piecewise continuous and, when it jumps, assumes the right-side values at the jumps. Càdlàg processes are useful because they encapsulate that we may not be able to anticipate a value at some arbitrary time t... which is useful for developing the mathematical theory of finance. Some probabilists instead write rcll for "right continuous, left limit."

Gibbons, Ross, and Shanken (1989) propose a test of a factor model's efficiency across all economic states $s \in \mathcal{S}$. They show that three conditions are equivalent:

1. $\alpha_i = 0$ for all instruments i and all macroeconomic states $s \in \mathcal{S}$;
2. each factor portfolio is **multifactor-minimum-variance**: minimum-variance for its expected return and factor sensitivities in each state $s \in \mathcal{S}$; and,
3. A convex combination of factor portfolios are multifactor-minimum-variance in each state $s \in \mathcal{S}$.[3]

The Gibbons, Ross, and Shanken (1989) test allows us to easily test factor models to see if we are likely to have uncovered a true structure of risk factors or not — if you are willing to believe the APT assumptions. Even when we cannot clearly break the APT, this test can tell us if it applies and if we are close to a model of the efficient market. Interestingly, the second condition mirrors the construction of the optimal hedge outlined in Johnson (1960) years before the APT or the use of cointegration in finance.

Finally, another set of tests has related the variation in the pricing kernel to the Sharpe ratio of investment portfolios. Hansen and Jagannathan (1997) was the first such work and bounds the Sharpe ratio by the coefficient of variation for a stochastic discount factor d.[4] Specifically:

$$\frac{\text{Var}(d)}{E(d)} \geq \frac{E(R_P)}{\sigma_P}. \tag{15.4}$$

The Hansen-Jagannathan bound can help us determine when a factor model is not admissible. For example, if the optimal risky portfolio has a Sharpe ratio of 0.8 and the stochastic discount factor has an expectation of 0.9, then the standard deviation of the stochastic discount factor must be at least 0.72 — and any model with a lower standard deviation is rejected as not likely to be a correct model. Jagannathan and Wang (1996) has an example of using this bound to compute how much a factor model is mispricing assets.

Finally, Kan and Zhou (2006) derive an even tighter bound that works in most circumstances.[5] Their bound uses the correlation between a linearly-modeled stochastic discount factor d_0 and inputs X:

$$\text{Var}(d) \geq \frac{1}{\rho_{d_0,x}^2} \text{Var}(d_0), \quad \text{where} \tag{15.5}$$

$$d_0 = \alpha + X^T \beta + \eta, \quad \text{and} \tag{15.6}$$

$$\rho_{d_0,x}^2 = \frac{\beta^T \Sigma_{xx} \beta}{\text{Var}(d_0)}. \tag{15.7}$$

---

[3]Recall from linear algebra that a **convex combination** of x's is a weighted sum $w^T x$ where $w \in [0, 1]$ and $\sum_j w_j = 1$.

[4]Recall that if we know d exactly, the pricing kernel k is $k = 1/d - 1$.

[5]We must assume the distribution of returns and inputs are in the elliptical family.

15.3   Arbitraging Mispriced Instruments

If we find two instruments which should be equally priced, there is a potential for arbitrage. If the two instruments are trading at different prices, we may be able to make money. We call the less expensive/higher-yielding instrument **cheap** and the more expensive/lower-yielding instrument **rich** or **dear**. The price/yield difference between the instruments is the **mispricing**.

The rule for arbitrage is simple: Buy the cheap; sell the rich.[6,7]

The trick is what proportions to do this in. First, we need to cancel out all the risk factors; otherwise we are taking risk and the trade is not an arbitrage. Second, we need to cancel out costs by lending or borrowing using risk-free bonds.

If we do this, we should earn the mispricing.

15.3.1   Examples of APT Arbitrage

The idea of arbitrage pricing may seem clear; however, the bookkeeping can be fussy and confusing. This is one of the few times when clarity demands that we work out a few short examples.

For thinking about arbitrage, it helps to remember another way we can write returns given by a factor model: the *factor-surprise form*. This expresses returns in terms of expected returns and surprises (differences from expected returns):

$$r_i = E(r_i) + \beta_{i1}(f_1 - E(f_1)). \qquad (15.8)$$

With that, we can now see a few examples:

1. **Relative mispricing.** We analyze some instruments with APT factor model regressions. We find two instruments with the same risk exposures, but different $\hat{\alpha}_i$ estimates:

$$E(r_A) = 0.1 + 1.2F, \text{ and} \qquad (15.9)$$
$$E(r_B) = 0.09 + 1.2F. \qquad (15.10)$$

   Here, A is cheap, B is rich, and we can easily cancel out the risk. We buy \$1 of instrument A and short \$1 of instrument B. This cancels out all the risks and we pocket the 1% difference in expected returns: \$0.01. This also costs us nothing since the short of B pays for the purchase of A.[8] Not big money, you say? Well, size it up then! Instead, we trade \$1 mn a side and pocket 1% of \$1 mn = \$10,000. We might trade more or less; it all depends on how much trading closes the gap in prices.

---

[6]If this sounds like the title of a heavy metal or punk song, congratulations to you for finding a clever way to remember it.

[7]If you think I just mentioned punk and heavy metal to help you remember "Buy the cheap? Sell the rich!" then congratulations to you for seeing through me.

[8]This is only true in theory. Any market will insist that you post money or collateral to trade; and, some markets will not credit you the full value of your short sale.

2. **Multi-factor absolute mispricing.** Suppose we have tracking portfolios T_1, T_2 for factors 1, 2 such that $T_1 \stackrel{a.e.}{=} f_1$ and $T_2 \stackrel{a.e.}{=} f_2$. Suppose $E(f_1) = 5\%$, $E(f_2) = 8\%$, and portfolio A's returns are described by:

$$r_A = r_f + 1F_1 + 0.5F_2, \tag{15.11}$$

where $r_f = 0.02$. The no-arbitrage expected return on A is:

$$E(r_A)^* = 0.02 + 1(0.05 - 0.02) + 0.5(0.08 - 0.02) = 0.08. \tag{15.12}$$

What if $E(r_A) = 0.10$? Then A is cheap and we build an arbitrage portfolio G: we buy \$1 of A, short \$1 of T_1, short \$0.5 of T_2, and buy \$0.5 of risk-free bonds. The return for portfolio G is then, in factor-surprise form:

$$
\begin{aligned}
r_G &= E(r_A) + 1(f_1 - E(f_1)) + 0.5(f_2 - E(f_2)) \\
&\quad - T_1 - 0.5T_2 + 0.5r_f
\end{aligned} \tag{15.13}
$$

$$= E(r_A) - E(f_1) - 0.5E(f_2) + 0.5r_f \tag{15.14}$$

$$= 0.10 - 0.05 - 0.5 \cdot 0.08 + 0.01 = 0.02. \tag{15.15}$$

Notice that this is exactly the A mispricing: $0.10 - 0.08$.

3. **Multi-factor relative mispricing.** Suppose the same setup as above, except we add portfolio B:

$$r_A = r_f + 1F_1 + 0.5F_2, \tag{15.16}$$

$$r_B = r_f + 0.8F_1 + 2F_2. \tag{15.17}$$

The no-arbitrage expected return on B is:

$$E(r_B)^* = 0.02 + 0.8(0.05 - 0.02) + 2(0.08 - 0.02) = 0.164. \tag{15.18}$$

What if $E(r_B) = 0.14$? Then A is cheap and B is rich. We build an arbitrage portfolio G: we buy \$1 of A, short \$1 of B, short \$0.2 of T_1, buy \$1.5 of T_2, and short \$1.3 of risk-free bonds. The return for portfolio G is then, in factor-surprise form:

$$
\begin{aligned}
r_G &= E(r_A) + 1(f_1 - E(f_1)) + 0.5(f_2 - E(f_2)) \\
&\quad - E(r_B) - 0.8(f_1 - E(f_1)) - 2(f_2 - E(f_2)) \\
&\quad - 0.2T_1 + 1.5T_2 - 1.3r_f
\end{aligned} \tag{15.19}
$$

$$= E(r_A) - E(r_B) + 0.2E(f_1) - 1.5E(f_2) - 1.3r_f \tag{15.20}$$

$$= 0.10 - 0.14 - 0.2 \cdot 0.05 + 1.5 \cdot 0.08 - 0.026 \tag{15.21}$$

$$= 0.10 - 0.14 - 0.01 + 0.12 - 0.026 = 0.044 \tag{15.22}$$

$$= \underbrace{0.10 - 0.08}_{\text{A mispricing}} + \underbrace{0.164 - 0.14}_{\text{B mispricing}}. \tag{15.23}$$

From those examples, we can see how we can combine many mispricings into a portfolio of mispricings. This is especially attractive if the collected mispricings help cancel out factor exposures.

15.4   Macro Factors

Now that we have an idea how to trade on mispricings, you might want to know what are useful risk factors. One set of useful risk factors are **macro factors**: factors having to do with the macroeconomy. Here, we broaden that to include certain asset classes or potential state variables.

In general, what distinguishes these models from other (micro) factor models is that nothing in the model is a function of the instrument being modeled. That means these models use no accounting measures or characteristics of instrument j.

15.4.1   Litterman-Scheinkman Three-Factor Model

We mentioned before that Litterman and Scheinkman (1991) decomposed the yield curve into movements of level, slope, and curvature. That itself implies a macro factor model for bonds:

$$r_{jt} = \alpha_j + \beta_{j,DV01}\Delta \text{Level}_t + \beta_{j,slope}\Delta \text{Slope}_t + \beta_{j,curv}\Delta \text{Curv}_t + \eta_{jt}. \quad (15.24)$$

Fama and French (1993) confirm that duration/DV01 is a significant risk factor for bonds and note the significance of a credit-related factor. Recently, Kim and Wright (2005) note that the term premium (LMS, like Slope) has fallen, probably due to a fall in inflation.

15.4.2   Chen-Roll-Ross Five-Factor Model

The Chen, Roll, and Ross (1986) model is a five-factor model which uses macro-based factors:

$$
\begin{aligned}
r_{jt} = \alpha_j &+ \beta_{j,IP}\ \overbrace{\Delta\%IP_t}^{\substack{\text{industrial} \\ \text{production} \\ \text{growth}}} + \beta_{j,Ei}\ \overbrace{\Delta E(i_t)}^{\substack{\text{change in} \\ \text{expected} \\ \text{inflation}}} + \beta_{j,ei}\ \overbrace{\epsilon_{it}}^{\substack{\text{inflation} \\ \text{surprise}}} \\
&+ \beta_{j,CMG}\ \underbrace{CMG_t}_{\substack{\text{credit} \\ \text{spread}}} + \beta_{j,LMS}\ \underbrace{LMS_t}_{\substack{\text{yield} \\ \text{curve} \\ \text{slope}}} + \eta_{jt}.
\end{aligned}
\quad (15.25)
$$

where $\Delta\%IP_t = \log(IP_t/IP_{t-1})$ is the industrial production growth rate;
$\Delta E(i_t) = E(i_{t+1}|\mathcal{F}_t) - E(i_t|\mathcal{F}_{t-1})$ is change in expected inflation,
$\epsilon_{it} = i_t - E(i_t|\mathcal{F}_{t-1})$ is the surprise in inflation,
$CMG_t = $ BAA-rated corp. $-$ long-term govt. bond yields, and
$LMS_t = $ long-term $-$ short-term govt. bond yields.

Interestingly, most analyses find that the growth rate of industrial production is the least informative factor. However, the other factors are often significant and demonstrate the importance of inflation, credit spreads, and the slope of the yield curve.

15.4.3   Hasanhodzic and Lo Six-Factor Model

The Hasanhodzic and Lo (2007) six-factor model also incorporates some macro-economic variables. As originally written, the model was used as a factor model for hedge funds and was not written in terms of excess returns. The model was also very US-oriented: it used the S&P 500, a US dollar index, and the S&P 500 volatility index (VIX).

If we fix up some of this, we get:

$$
\begin{aligned}
R_{jt} = \alpha_j + \beta_{j,M} \overbrace{R_{Mt}}^{\text{market}} + \beta_{j,AAC} \overbrace{R_{AAC,t}}^{\substack{\text{AA corporate}\\\text{bond index}}} + \beta_{j,curr} \overbrace{r_{curr,t}}^{\substack{\text{currency}\\\text{index}}} \\
+ \beta_{j,CMG} \underbrace{CMG_t}_{\substack{\text{credit}\\\text{spread}}} + \beta_{j,vol} \underbrace{\Delta\tilde{\sigma}_t^{\text{implied}}}_{\substack{\text{implied}\\\text{volatility}\\\text{index}}} + \beta_{j,GSCI} \underbrace{r_{GSCI,t}}_{\substack{\text{commodity}\\\text{index}}} + \eta_{jt}.
\end{aligned} \tag{15.26}
$$

where $R_{AAC,T}$ is a high-credit (AA) corporate bond index excess return,
   $r_{curr,t}$ is the return on a local currency index,
   CMG_t is a corporate-minus-government yield spread (as above),
   $\Delta\tilde{\sigma}_t^{\text{implied}}$ is the change in index implied volatility (*e.g.* VIX), and
   $r_{comm,t}$ is the return on the GSCI commodity index.

While this model has a reassuring spread among asset classes and types of risks (volatility and credit spreads), the exposition is a little confusing. Froot (1995) implies that the GSCI factor is related to the Chen-Roll-Ross unexpected inflation factor. Disappointing (for determining risk factors) but intriguing is that in their analysis, the fund manager's alpha $\hat{\alpha}_j$ had the most explanatory power.

15.4.4   Fung and Hsieh Seven-Factor Model

Fung and Hsieh (2004) created a seven-factor model to also help explain hedge fund returns:

$$
\begin{aligned}
r_{jt} = \alpha_j + \beta_{SP,j} \overbrace{R_{SP,t}}^{\text{S\&P 500}} + \beta_{SML,j} \overbrace{SML_t}^{\substack{\text{small-cap}\\\text{minus}\\\text{large-cap}}} + \beta_{10Y,j} \overbrace{\Delta Y_{10Y}}^{\substack{\text{UST 10Y}\\\text{yield change}}} \\
+ \beta_{CMG,j} \underbrace{CMG_t}_{\substack{\text{credit}\\\text{spread}}} + \beta_{BT,j} \underbrace{TF_{B,t}}_{\substack{\text{bond}\\\text{trend}\\\text{factor}}} + \beta_{FXT,j} \underbrace{TF_{FX,t}}_{\substack{\text{FX trend}\\\text{factor}}} \\
+ \beta_{CT,j} \underbrace{TF_{C,t}}_{\substack{\text{commodity}\\\text{trend}\\\text{factor}}} + \eta_{jt}.
\end{aligned} \tag{15.27}
$$

Most of these factors are self-explanatory. However, the trend-following variables are unusual. They are lookback straddles (combinations of options) on futures contracts. These are contracts which pay out the largest move away from a specified price. Thus if a fund has some trend-following (and market-timing) ability, their returns should be related to those factors.

15.4.5   Fung and Hsieh Eight-Factor Model

However, Fung and Hsieh (1997) first created an eight-factor model to help explain hedge fund returns:

$$
\begin{aligned}
r_{jt} = \alpha_j &+ \beta_{USE,j} \overbrace{R_{USE,t}}^{\substack{\text{MSCI US}\\\text{equities}}} + \beta_{NUSE,j} \overbrace{R_{NUSE,t}}^{\substack{\text{MSCI non-}\\\text{US equities}}} + \beta_{EME,j} \overbrace{R_{EME,t}}^{\substack{\text{IFC emerging}\\\text{mkt equities}}} \\
&+ \beta_{USG,j} \underbrace{r_{USG,t}}_{\substack{\text{US govt}\\\text{bonds}}} + \beta_{NUSG,j} \underbrace{r_{NUSG,t}}_{\substack{\text{non-US}\\\text{govt bonds}}} + \beta_{ED1M,j} \underbrace{r_{ED1M,t}}_{\substack{\text{one-month}\\\text{eurodollars}}} \\
&+ \beta_{Au,j} \underbrace{r_{Au,t}}_{\text{gold}} + \beta_{USD,j} \underbrace{r_{USD,t}}_{\substack{\text{Fed trade-}\\\text{weighted}\\\text{USD index}}} + \eta_{jt},
\end{aligned}
\tag{15.28}
$$

where the *USE*, *NUSE*, and *EME* factors are US, non-US developed-economy, and emerging market equities; the *USG* and *NUSG* factors are for US and non-US developed-economy government bonds; the *ED1M* factor is one-month Eurodollars; the *Au* factor is gold; and, the *USD* factor is the Federal Reserve's trade-weighted US dollar index.

Obviously, this corresponds to much more of an asset-class and US-versus-the-world breakdown than their later seven-factor model. In a way, however, this can be seen as just a more complete version of the CAPM.

15.5   Micro Factors

15.5.1   Dynamic Factors

We first noticed that factor loadings are not constant across time or the business cycle with the CAPM. The conditional and intertemporal CAPM models proposed to fix that by incorporating more information or a state variable for the economy. However, none of these considered just giving the CAPM a dynamic form so that it made the most use of the data.

That is the idea behind two factor models which incorporate volatility models to see if changing volatility can help explain the varying coefficients and improve model performance. Both use **autoregressive conditional heteroskedasticity** (ARCH): models in which a large prediction error increases the volatility (hence the conditioning and heteroskedasticity) and volatility is autoregressive.

Engle, Lilien, and Robins ARCH-in-Mean Model

Engle, Lilien, and Robins (1987) developed the **ARCH-in-mean** model to incorporate dynamic volatility as a potential factor in determining interest rates. The model has a mean that is a constant plus a factor for instantaneous volatility:

$$R_{30Y,t} = \alpha + \beta h_t + \epsilon_t \quad \epsilon_t \sim (0, h_t^2), \tag{15.29}$$

$$h_t^2 = \alpha_0 + \alpha_1 \sum_{i=1}^{p} w_i \epsilon_{t-i}^2. \tag{15.30}$$

where the excess return R_{30Y} is the return on a long-term government bond minus the return on short-term government bills.

The model reveals that instantaneous volatility is significant. This suggests that more models should incorporate volatility dynamics. It also suggests that the expectations hypothesis that we saw in Chapter 12 does not hold.

Bollerslev, Engle, and Wooldridge GARCH-in-Mean Model

Bollerslev, Engle, and Wooldridge (1988) developed the **GARCH-in-mean** model to handle multiple assets (which might have dynamic covariances) and to reduce the time-variation of coefficients. Their model looked at three instruments (indexed by i): a US stock index, a US government bond, and a US Treasury bill.

The model is very similar to the ARCH model except that it also allows for cross-correlations through the $\epsilon_{i,t-1}\epsilon_{j,t-1}$ term. This allows a volatility increase in one instrument to cause a volatility increase in the other instruments:

$$r_{it} = \alpha + \beta \alpha_1 \sum_{i=1}^{p} w_i h_{ijt} + \epsilon_{it} \quad \epsilon_t \sim (0, H_t), \tag{15.31}$$

$$h_{ijt} = \gamma_{ij} + \alpha_{ij}\epsilon_{i,t-i}\epsilon_{j,t-1} + \beta_{ij}h_{ij,t-1}. \tag{15.32}$$

where H_t is a covariance matrix with $H_{tij} = h_{ijt} = h_{jit}$.

This greatly reduced the variance in the implied risk premium for stocks. It also reduced the estimation variability in the implied risk premium for bonds and bills — until the Fed changed policy abruptly to fight stagflation. This abrupt change, known as Volcker's "Saturday Night Special," was a shift to combating inflation in addition to unemployment. To do that most effectively, Volcker increased Fed Funds on 6 October 1979 more than typically, from 11% to 12%, at an unusual time: a Saturday night. He also committed the Fed to fighting inflation.

15.5.2 *Liquidity Factors*

Liquidity is the ability to trade anything, anytime, at any size. Illiquid instruments tend to have higher returns — in large part because they are riskier and thus investors demand compensation to hold those instruments.

Kindelberger and Aliber (2005) note that many financial crises have their roots in illiquidity.[9] Therefore, we have a strong prior that liquidity should be a priced factor. Sure enough, these models find that liquidity has a lot of explanatory power. We will see more of these ideas in Chapter 26.

Amihud and Mendelson Liquidity CAPM

Amihud and Mendelson (1986) create a liquidity CAPM to study the effect of changes in bid-ask spreads on asset prices. While they tested various model forms, we can consider their model to be of the form:

$$r_{jt} = \alpha_j + \beta_{M,j}R_{Mt} + \beta_{S,j}(S_{jt} - E(S_j)) + \eta_{jt}, \qquad (15.33)$$

where $S_{jt} = \log(\text{Ask}_{jt}) - \log(\text{Bid}_{jt})$ is the relative bid-ask spread.[10]

They find a strong relationship between liquidity and asset prices: a stock moving from a 3.2% spread to a 0.5% bid-ask spread would increase firm value by 50%.

Acharya and Pedersen Liquidity CAPM

Acharya and Pedersen (2005) consider **liquidity risk** to be the possibility that market liquidity may change. To study this, they looked at liquidity costs for instrument j and the market: essentially S_j and S_M as defined previously.

They formulated an equilibrium argument which states that investors will demand a higher return for having to pay a greater bid-ask spread. That led them to propose a model with three liquidity betas as well as the CAPM beta:

$$E(R_{jt} - S_{jt}) = \beta_{all}E(R_{Mt} - S_{Mt}) \qquad (15.34)$$

$$= (\beta_{jM} + \beta_{L1} + \beta_{L2} + \beta_{L3})E(R_M - S_{Mt}), \qquad (15.35)$$

$$\text{where } \beta_{L1} = \frac{\text{Cov}(S_{jt}, S_{Mt})}{\text{Var}(r_{Mt} - S_{Mt})}, \qquad (15.36)$$

$$\beta_{L2} = \frac{\text{Cov}(r_{jt}, S_{Mt})}{\text{Var}(r_{Mt} - S_{Mt})}, \qquad (15.37)$$

$$\beta_{L2} = \frac{\text{Cov}(S_{jt}, r_{Mt})}{\text{Var}(r_{Mt} - S_{Mt})}. \qquad (15.38)$$

In case covariances are not intuitive for you, we can clarify this in English: β_{L1} is instrument j's illiquidity sensitivity to systematic illiquidity; β_{L2} is instrument j's return sensitivity to market illiquidity; and, β_{L3} is instrument j's illiquidity sensitivity to market return.

---

[9]If you have not read Kindelberger and Aliber (2005), you should. The introduction, written decades ago, always sounds current in a financial crisis — a truly sobering fact.

[10]Amihud and Mendelson define this as $1 - \frac{\text{Bid}}{\text{Ask}}$, but the two are nearly identical.

Pastor and Stambaugh Liquidity Risk Model

Pástor and Stambaugh (2003) study an implied market-wide liquidity surprise factor. They build this from an average of individual stock measures. Looking over thirty-four years, they find that stocks with high versus low sensitivities to liquidity have an abnormal return 7.5%/year higher, The liquidity risk factor accounts for half of the profits to a momentum strategy over the same 34-year period.

To find this, however, is a bit complicated. They first run a regression to find the signed dollar-volume effect for each month τ. They then average these to get a marketwide dollar-volume effect; and, they use the total monthly dollar volume in month τ, m_τ, to scale versus the baseline in August 1964 dollars m_0:

$$
\underbrace{r_{i,t+1,\tau} - r_{M,t+1,\tau}}_{\substack{\text{market-relative} \\ \text{outperformance}}} = \underbrace{\theta_{i\tau}}_{\substack{\text{average daily} \\ \text{outperformance}}} + \underbrace{\phi_{i\tau}\, r_{it\tau}}_{\substack{\text{AR(1)} \\ \text{effect}}}
$$
$$
+ \gamma_{i\tau} \underbrace{\operatorname{sgn}(r_{it\tau} - r_{Mt\tau})v_{it\tau}}_{\substack{\text{outperformance-signed} \\ \text{dollar volume}}} + \eta_{it\tau}. \tag{15.39}
$$

$$
\hat{\gamma}_{M\tau} = \frac{1}{n}\sum_{i=1}^{n}\hat{\gamma}_{i\tau}, \quad \Delta\hat{\gamma}_{M\tau} = \frac{m_\tau}{m_0}(\hat{\gamma}_{M\tau} - \hat{\gamma}_{M,\tau-1}). \tag{15.40}
$$

This seems complicated, but it is just an estimator of price impact parameters. The model is, admittedly, crude which is why they need such a long period of data. The irony of this is that practitioners were building better and simpler estimators using intraday data at least five years earlier.[11]

With this, they can then estimate the liquidity surprise u_τ. While this model looks unusual, it has the same effect as an AR(2) model of $\Delta\hat{\gamma}_{M\tau}$:

$$
\Delta\hat{\gamma}_{M\tau} = a + b\Delta\hat{\gamma}_{M,\tau-1} + c\frac{m_\tau}{m_0}\hat{\gamma}_{M,\tau-1} + u_\tau, \tag{15.41}
$$

$$
L_\tau = \hat{u}_\tau/100. \tag{15.42}
$$

With the surprise in liquidity, we can finally see if the innovation is priced. Intuitively, we see if unexpected lower (or higher) liquidity is associated with higher (or lower) returns:

$$
r_{it} = \alpha_i + \beta_{iM}R_{Mt} + \beta_{SMB}SMB_t + \beta_{HML}HML_t + \beta_{iL}L_t + \eta_{it} \tag{15.43}
$$

where SMB and HML are factors we will discuss later when we talk about the Fama-French 3-factor model.

They also look at returns for portfolios sorted on β_{iL}, but that would seem to be circling back to the first regression — in addition to the problems induced by sorting on fitted betas.

---

[11]If you sense some impatience with this model, I will admit to being biased since I myself was one of those practitioners.

The drawback of this model is obvious: it is complicated. The approach is fine for estimating liquidity surprises. However, it is not clear why the model uses the surprises (or innovations) when some measure of the risk of these surprises (standard deviation?) might better correspond to the definition of liquidity risk.[12]

The model could also adjust price impact for each stock's size or typical dollar volume. The model should also look at abnormal returns instead of just outperformance versus the market. This last idea might have required iterating to get a stable model. However, since complexity does not seem to be a concern here, why not try for a more accurate model?

While the Pástor and Stambaugh model shows liquidity risk is priced, the model could undoubtedly achieve that in a simpler way.

15.5.3   Firm Risks

Finally, we could look at models with factors relating to idiosyncratic volatility, assets versus liabilities, incoming versus outgoing cashflows, or cashflow variability. We will see some models like this when we examine credit in Chapter 22.

15.6   Style Factors

The preceding models largely dealt with factors which were obviously risk-related or were returns for instruments with risk premia. However, there is a controversial set of models which look at firm characteristics to form **style factors**: portfolios which are used in factor models. It is not clear whether these portfolios are risk factors, relate to risk factors, or are just correlation-capturing factors. This is why some researchers call these **firm-characteristic models** or **style models**.

15.6.1   Opacity and Relevance of Factors

Creation of these models starts with sorting securities on one or more characteristics. The analyst then forms portfolios based on quantiles, *e.g.* decile or tercile portfolios, with a goal of creating equal-sized groupings. (I mention this is the claimed goal because many of the groupings do not end up equally-sized.) The factor returns are then differences in returns between quantile portfolios; for example, the tenth versus first decile portfolios. With those factor portfolios, the analyst can estimate a model for various instruments.

The controversy with these models arises for many reasons:

1. unclear interpretation;
2. intertemporal instability;

---

[12]For those who think the standard deviation would use up too much data, there is no reason why these could not be done weekly or daily with week or day effects. There is also no reason they could not have made a GARCH model for the liquidity innovations since liquidity probably has periods when it is more and less volatile.

3. ignored transactions costs;

4. potential sorting issues;

5. a curse of dimensionality; and,

6. unclear risk implications.

First, it is not obvious what these factors mean. Even if the cross-sectional models were built using understood risk factors, it is not so clear what the effects of the sorting are. Why not just create a model with the characteristics as a covariate?

Second, the definition of these quantile groupings is not stable over time; they change. Thus a stock which has a high characteristic value this month may not in the future. However, that means that the composition of the factor portfolios changes.

The changing nature of the factors leads to a third issue: a changing portfolio incurs transactions costs. Comparisons that ignore this are unachievable; however, comparisons that include transactions costs will, by construction, be correlated with liquidity-based factors. This leads to a choice between evils: either do not update the factor portfolios and have their meaning drift over time; change the factor portfolios and ignore transactions costs (yielding an illusory benchmark); or, include transactions costs which makes the factor correlated with liquidity.

Fourth, it is easy for a misspecified cross-sectional regression to sweep other risks into the sort portfolios. Related to that is the fact that while we start with a multivariate regression which controls for other factors, we can easily lose that control unless we make sure to sort portfolios on the Cartesian product of all factors and percentile buckets. For example, if we control for liquidity but ignore that in the portfolio sorts, we might find that the quantile portfolios are biased or unequal in their exposure to liquidity.

Fifth, this can get complicated when there are many variables since those multi-dimensional portfolio sorts can quickly cause the portfolios to cease being well-diversified due to the curse of dimensionality. If we are splitting our universe into deciles of deciles of deciles... we quickly get quantile portfolios which are not well-diversified. Also, looking at the most extreme portfolios throws away a lot of information.

Finally, the driving motivation for our factor models has been risk which is priced by amount (*e.g.* expected inflation) or by surprise (*e.g.* unexpected inflation). We can easily formulate models for how these factors might affect an investor's wealth. Models with firm characteristics or investment styles have no such clear wealth effect. This is a problem because risk management is crucial for firms to perform well across states of the economy. Risk managers need guidance about whether or not they should pay money to reduce certain exposures.

An example is illuminating: consider exposure to the technology sector. Tech stocks and bonds are very likely to be correlated since they share exposures to similar macroeconomic and industry risks. However, very few portfolio managers would have a default perspective that they might willingly earn less to eliminate their tech exposure. That clarifies that these models are not uncovering risk factors. Indeed,

Daniel and Titman (1997) present considerable evidence that these characteristics are unrelated to risk factors. Petkova and Zhang (2005) find that the average value beta varies across the business cycle: from -0.15 in an expansion and -0.33 at peak growth to +0.05 in recession and +0.40 in the trough; and, Houge and Loughran (2006) find no average value premium across time. This also explains why many practitioners report seeing size and value exposures which seem counter to a stock's book-to-market or size.

These issues, coupled with their proponents' influence, is why these models have received a lot of attention. A literature search will show that many critical articles in top journals are followed by swift rebuttals (often using different datasets). This is not scientific or even close to impartial, evidence-based scholarship. That is one of the reasons for assessments and tests like Lehmann and Modest (1988) and Gibbons, Ross, and Shanken (1989). Sadly, it is also one of the reasons that "asset pricing" has developed a bad reputation among some finance academics lately.

That is not to say these models are worthless; there is value to finding correlating variables so that we limit our exposure to them. While no portfolio manager would gladly pay money to eliminate their exposure to the tech sector, many portfolio managers want to limit how much of their portfolio is exposed to the tech sector.

However, these models have been over-promoted and over-defended. At best, we think some of these style factors are associated with unknown risks. More likely is that they proxy for differing sensitivities to unspecified and unknown macroeconomic factors. Thus the search for the driving risk factors continues.

15.6.2   The Fama-French Three-Factor Model

The ultimate example of all of these issues is the Fama and French (1992) three-factor model. The model looks at the market excess return and two characteristic-implied sort portfolio differences for firm size and firm book-to-market (aka value):

$$r_{it} = \alpha_i + \beta_{i,M} R_{M,t} + \beta_{i,SMB} SMB_t + \beta_{i,HML} HML_t + \eta_{it}, \qquad (15.44)$$

where SMB_t is the return on a small-minus-big market capitalization sort portfolio and HML_t is the return on a high-minus-low book-to-market sort portfolio.

Incidentally, the Fama-French three-factor model has a few additional problems. The authors note that there is a high correlation between the market beta and firm size: -0.988. Thus multicollinearity is a problem for the Fama-French model.

Second, the size sorts are done for NYSE stocks and then other stocks are added with the size boundaries staying intact. The NYSE has historically had a higher threshold for listing on their market. Therefore, the Fama-French methodology over-allocates Nasdaq stocks to the lower-size portfolios, unbalancing the size portfolios. That almost guarantees a problem with heteroskedasticity among the portfolios. Since the Nasdaq has historically attracted more technology startups, this also induces a correlation between the SMB and HML factors.

Finally, the model uses the S&P 500 as the market proxy — and then notes that adding small firms (via the SMB factor) to the model improves its performance. This is vacuous and nearly assured by construction. It would be more surprising if small firms did *not* improve performance after restricting the model to use the S&P 500. A poor choice of market proxy should not yield a claim of finding a new risk factor when all it does is better complete the proxy to be closer to that proposed in the CAPM.

15.6.3 Momentum Factors

One of the details noticed early on about returns was **momentum**: the tendency for performance or outperformance to persist. There are two forms we consider.

Time series momentum is the persistence of positive or negative returns: stocks which went up keep going up; stocks which went down keep going down. Thus time series momentum is like positive autocorrelation.

Cross-sectional momentum is the persistence of outperformance: stocks which were relative winners keep winning; stocks which were relative losers keep losing.

Jegadeesh and Titman (1993) studied stocks and the persistence of their performance over 3–12-month horizons — time series momentum. They also noted that portfolios of "winners" versus "losers" (cross-sectional momentum) had even stronger results. Since then, Moskowitz, Ooi, and Pedersen (2012) also studied time series momentum and found the effect across asset classes.

Carhart (1997) used the Fama-French model as a base to explore cross-sectional momentum. He noted that quantile portfolios based on sorting over the past year's returns generated significant outperformance. This factor is sometimes referred to as MOM (monthly momentum) or in a manner similar to the Fama-French factors: UMD (up-minus-down) or WML (winners-minus-losers):

$$r_{it} = \alpha_i + \beta_{i,M} R_{M,t} + \beta_{i,SMB} SMB_t + \beta_{i,HML} HML_t$$
$$+ \beta_{i,WML} WML_t + \eta_{it}. \tag{15.45}$$

Cross-sectional momentum is likely stronger than the academic literature indicates because most papers use the wrong null hypothesis: no persistence. In fact, the correct null hypothesis should account for the mechanical regression to the mean due to sorting based on a variable containing randomness. This suggests that stocks should move in the opposite direction from momentum. For this reason, cross-sectional momentum is very likely significant.

We should note that cross-sectional momentum goes against some commonly-known trading strategies such as the "Dogs of the Dow" which every year buys the lagging ten stocks in the Dow 30 and shorts the leading ten stocks. Domian, Louton, and Mossman (1998) discuss this strategy and attribute its rise in profile to Dorfman (1998) discussing research on the strategy by analyst John Slatter.

15.6.4   Fama-French Works Well?

One of the factors complicating discussion of the Fama and French and Carhart (1997) models is that many people claim they "work well" at explaining returns in practice. Yes, it is true that these models deliver great in-sample R^2. However, any econometrician or statistician will tell you that is not necessarily informative. Furthermore, these models only "work" if we redefine what we are trying to accomplish.

As mentioned before, the Fama-French model starts with a flawed proxy. Reducing the misfit of that proxy to the theory by adding small-cap stocks should not be seen as an improvement when better proxies were always available.

More troubling is that these sort portfolios explain little about returns. We still do not know what risks are associated with these portfolios. Furthermore, when the factors do not return a premium (as HML/value has failed to do for extended periods of time), we do not know why that is and we certainly do not know what economic forces suggest when these portfolios will resume returning a premium.

Also, the justification for saying that these models work is often simplistic: in-sample R^2. We can get a high R^2 by adding any number of covariates to a model; and, if we do this enough, we might even find covariates associated with the unknown risk factor which is actually driving returns. While those would seem to hold up over time, there is no justification other than past historical performance.

Even if the covariates continue to provide good out-of-sample performance, that does not mean they are causal. An analogy is instructive: Suppose we looked at weather data and sunlight. We would probably find that a good indicator for rain is unusual darkness for the time of day. The in-sample R^2 would certainly be good. However, this does not explain what leads to rain; and, it can lead to very poor advice. Telling farmers to block out the sun over their fields or to relocate to areas with less sunlight would not lead to more rain or more crop production.

Finally, the claim that we need not worry what these factors represent is belied by the advice people give: hold some small-cap firms and some value firms. The former is certainly good advice; the CAPM suggests everyone should start by holding the complete market portfolio and adding small cap stocks gets you closer to holding the complete market portfolio. However, holding value firms is not clearly good advice, as the evidence from Houge and Loughran (2006) confirms.

15.6.5   The Fama-French Five-Factor Model

It is ironic that after decades of defending and promoting their three-factor model, Fama and French began promoting a five-factor model. This gave the lie to the idea that the three-factor model was as infallible as they had claimed.

The Fama and French (2016) five-factor model is an extension of the three-factor model but adds a profitability and an investment factor:

$$r_{it} = \alpha_i + \beta_{i,M} R_{M,t} + \beta_{i,SMB} SMB_t + \beta_{i,HML} HML_t \\ + \beta_{i,RMW} RMW_t + \beta_{i,CMA} CMA_t + \eta_{it},$$

(15.46)

where RMW_t is a factor reflecting the return on a robust-minus-weak profitability sort portfolio and CMA_t is a factor reflecting the return on a conservative-minus-aggressive investment sort portfolio.

This agrees with earlier work by Novy-Marx (2013) on the profit margin premium. He found that portfolios sorted by profit margins produced a large spread in returns. The RMW and CMA factors would also seem to separate out two dimensions of the QMJ (quality-minus-junk) factor in Asness, Frazzini, and Pedersen (2017). Despite this, Fama and French concede that the model does not pass the Gibbons, Ross, and Shanken (1989) test. In other words: these are still not risk models and we still do not know what is really behind these variables. However, we are starting to get some ideas — as we will see shortly.

15.6.6 Morningstar's Style Box

I previously said that finding correlating variables is a benefit — perhaps the greatest benefit — of the Fama-French three-factor model. This has given rise to a related innovation: the **style box** created by fund investment research agency Morningstar. The box is divided into 3×3 cells as seen in Figure 15.1.[13] Funds are then assigned to one of the 9 boxes based on characteristics of their holdings.

	Value	Blend	Growth
Large			
Medium			
Small	X		

Figure 15.1: The equity style box created by Morningstar. Comparing only funds within a cell cancels out past trends to reduce the noise in fund comparisons. This shows the benefits of the correlation-finding Fama and French (1992) model. In this case, the box indicates that a fund holds more small value stocks than large or growth stocks.

In comparing funds, we would not say they were all great because they all had

---

[13]Morningstar also has a style box for fixed income funds with groupings by interest rate sensitivity and credit risk, the risk factors found in Fama and French (1993).

positive returns if the market overall were also up — nor would we say they all were poorly-performing if they all had negative returns when the market overall was down. The key is that we want to assess their performance relative to similar funds. Hence why we often remove the overall market trend when comparing investment funds.

A more sophisticated way to do this is to account for movement that is unique to certain groupings of funds. Fama and French (1992) suggests that these groupings should be two-dimensional: by size and value/growth. Fund comparisons are thus made only against other funds in the same cell — a more-similar set of peer funds. This greatly reduces the noise of comparing funds. Thus the style box (and Fama-French factors) are really useful ways of removing overall trends.

15.6.7   What Exactly Are the Style Factors?

One of the frustrations of the style factors is not knowing what drives them. That causes us to continually ask if they are really the right factors or if we can instead find some better explanatory factors. Ideally, we might even find risk or information-based drivers that are the true sources or risk and variation.

Palacios-Huerta (2003) builds a more complete market proxy by accounting for human capital — and finds that the more complete market (including human capital) subsumes the explanatory power of the Chen-Roll-Ross and Fama-French three-factor models.

Chan, Chen, and Hsieh (1985) show that the outperformance of small versus large stocks is related to a credit spread. This is often claimed as supporting that SMB is driven by a risk factor. However, the study looks at actual firm sizes and not SMB, since it predates Fama and French (1992). It is not clear that a credit spread would explain SMB if a more complete index were used for the proxy.

Das, King, and Sinha (2015) show that the HML premium is only positive on a few days for a given stock. Specifically: if they remove the days near each stock's earnings announcement, the HML effect disappears: there is no longer any premium to the HML factor. Thus a "value" investor could merely invest in a few stocks at a time, around their particular earnings announcements, and the rest of the time do nothing.

Sinha (2016) studies **news sentiment**, the positive or negative content of news stories. He finds that after subtracting out momentum, there is still news sentiment left; but, after subtracting out news sentiment, there is no momentum left. The effect he finds is pervasive; it is not restricted to small, low-analyst-coverage, less-held, or losing stocks. A long-short strategy constructed from news sentiment yields 8.6%/year. Thus momentum would seem to be related to the diffusion of information.

Similarly, Wang (2015) looked at macroeconomic news releases to see if any had predictive power.[14] She found that most (monthly) releases had only limited power,

---

[14]Full disclosure: Fan was my PhD advisee. However, she came upon this topic completely by herself; and, I was very pleased with what she did on an independently-conceived research project.

but that surprises to the (weekly) US initial jobless claims did have predictive power. The effect persisted for several months and yielded an 8.4%/year abnormal return. Her news momentum strategy was also highly correlated with time series momentum and cross-sectional momentum. Finally, this drift even helped explain momentum in some non-US markets.

Finally, some of these may be related to Ball and Brown (1968) finding **post-earnings announcement drift** (PEAD): that positive or negative returns persist for months after a positive or negative earnings surprise. Thus there is earnings surprise momentum. Sadka (2006) finds that momentum and PEAD are likely related to variations in the ratio of informed to uninformed traders. This suggests that PEAD, momentum, and news may all be related.

All of these studies suggest that the meaning of these style factors is unclear. SMB may be credit, a symptom of a poor proxy choice, or both. HML may be earnings risk; and, UMD may be the diffusion of information from news and macroeconomic announcements.

15.7 Modeling Issues

As the preceding makes clear, researchers are not all in agreement on what these factors mean, if they correspond to risks, or even how to incorporate them in analyses. Thus a modeler faces a number of questions when analyzing instruments.

15.7.1 Levels or Changes?

One of the issues which often goes unmentioned is whether models should use the levels, changes, or shocks: differences from the expectation. The typical econometric advice is to only use variables which are stationary; hence why we analyze log-returns and not prices. However, this gives us little guidance if a variable is stationary or seems potentially stationary.

The truth is that this issue is much more nuanced (and controversial) than a pure methodological debate. While I cannot do these issues justice, I will summarize the perspectives to help clarify the implied meaning of using each.

The Case for Levels

Some models use levels, for example the slope of the yield curve or a credit spread. If these variables are stationary, we can think of these variables as implying certain macroeconomic states. This brings us back to the ideas of the conditional and intertemporal CAPM. Furthermore, there is evidence to confirm these ideas: upward-sloping yield curves indicate that we are likely in the recovery or expansion part of a business cycle and not the peak or contraction. Boudt, Paulus, and Rosenthal (2017) find that the market seems to change state when a credit spread crosses a threshold.

Furthermore, to the extent that levels correspond to risk, we should not expect a one-time return for taking a certain amount of risk. For example, a higher level of volatility should imply that stocks will return more. This is the whole idea of a risk premium.

Another reason to use levels might be because the analyst does not believe that prices or returns adjust immediately to changes. This implies some doubt that the market is efficient. However, this belief need not require using levels; it could instead be accommodated using multiple lags of changes.

The Case for Changes

Many economists suggest that we should instead look at changes: returns are changes in price and prices should not change unless other variables change. In effect, we view changes in variables as implying changes in information. We also assume prices have adjusted to previous levels and so only changes need be considered to explain returns.

This perspective implies some belief in market efficiency. This perspective may also make sense when we are looking at traded instruments or variables that can be derived from traded instruments. For example, the change in the slope of the yield curve results from bond returns. The case for using changes is, therefore, very strong.

The Case for Shocks

Related to the case for changes is the case for shocks: divergences from what was expected. (If a variable is a martingale, then these cases are the same.) In particular, including a shock in a model implies a response to an unanticipated change. This can even be extended to an unanticipated and real change. For example: if returns and inflation increase, perhaps the change is ignorable because real returns did not increase.

This perspective also implies a belief in market efficiency. It is also closest to the perspective of real business cycle theory: that the only relevant information are real (not nominal) changes and that business cycle fluctuations are optimal.[15]

Summary

Thus an analyst is faced with competing choices. A belief in the EMH or real business cycles suggests changes or shocks should be used. This might even require modeling to find the expected value of a variable to produce its shocks. A belief that markets are always trending toward efficiency as in the Lo (2004) adaptive market hypothesis implies using lagged variables or levels. And a belief in the primacy of economic state variables would definitely suggest using levels.

---

[15]For more on real business cycles, you can read Kydland and Prescott (1982) and Long and Plosser (1983).

On the other hand, a good analyst might prefer to allow for multiple perspectives and let the data speak.

15.7.2 Excess Returns, Returns, or Surprises?

It can also seem confusing whether to use models with excess returns, returns, or shocks. We typically use excess returns for tradable instruments that have a risk premium; returns for stationary and mean-zero/martingale factors; and, surprises for macroeconomic factors.

Note that many macro models use factors in the factor-surprise form:

$$r_{jt} = E(r_j) + \beta_1(f_{1t} - E(f_1)) + \cdots + \beta_k(f_{kt} - E(f_k)) + \eta_{jt} \tag{15.47}$$

How do we integrate these factors with excess-return factors? Since they are mean-zero, they may just be added to the model since $E(r_j)$ is the average of $r_f + \sum_{i=1}^{k'} \beta_{k+i} F_{k+i}$:

$$R_{jt} = r_f + \overbrace{\beta_1(f_{1t} - E(f_1)) + \cdots + \beta_k(f_{kt} - E(f_k))}^{\text{mean-zero (surprise) factors}}$$
$$+ \underbrace{\beta_{k+1}F_{k+1,t} + \cdots + \beta_{k+k'}F_{k+k',t}}_{\text{priced risk factors}} + \eta_{jt}. \tag{15.48}$$

Finally, it may be that the best way to capture the pricing of surprise factors is to use their volatilities in a model.

15.7.3 What Do We Want from Factor Models?

If we seem to be much more introspective in this chapter, it is because researchers have not been clear about what we want from factor models.

Just a Pricing Kernel?

If all we want are pricing kernels, then we can use models like Jurek and Stafford (2015) which find an implied cost of capital through an arbitrage argument unrelated to the particular risk exposures. However, this approach says nothing about the instruments being priced. We get a pricing kernel but no intuition on actual factors.

Do Factor Models Have Meaning?

One telling fact is how much ink has been used discussing the meaning of factor models. What we often want from factor models is not just a pricing kernel but also an explanation of which risks are implicit to an investment or drive its value.

Do We Want a Performance Benchmark?

Sometimes we are not looking for a pricing kernel at all; we just want a benchmark for an investment's performance. Often this means relating the performance to various investment styles. While we may not know what these models mean, we know they reveal correlations along common dimensions. Thus we would expect an investment manager to do better than the model to justify fees higher than competitors. However, even in these cases we often comment on and debate if the styles and estimated loadings are relevant for the instrument in question.[16]

While we have discussed models for hedge fund performance, researchers should be highly suspicious of hedge fund data. Since these funds are not publicly-traded, their returns may not be the prices at which the fund shares would trade; the market price could be different due to illiquidity. Furthermore, some funds find ways to game which returns they report. This can make funds look artificially good.

Are We Replicating?

Finally, in finance we frequently find practitioners who propose to replicate the returns of high-cost investments using factor models and lower-cost investments related to significant factors. Do all of these replicators worry about whether the factors they use are true risk factors which should imply risk premia? No. Do they ignore transactions costs? They should not, but many do. This is foolish since many investment funds have failed due to illiquidity and transactions costs.

15.7.4   How Many Factors?

Finally, we need to be a bit skeptical. Harvey, Liu, and Zhu (2016) note that 313 papers have proposed over 316 factors since 1967. It seems doubtful that we live in a world where 300+ different risk factors are priced. The alternative, believed by many academics, is that most factors are spurious, arise out of a self-serving lack of skepticism, or are even manufactured out of disdain for honesty.

Harvey, Liu, and Zhu consider that finding factors implies a multiple-hypothesis testing setup and find which factors seem to pass the stricter hurdle implied by how many hypotheses were tested over time. They find that the most believable factors are the CAPM market factor, the HML "value" factor, momentum, durable consumption, short-term volatility, and liquidity.[17]

The one aspect lacking from this analysis is the market angle. If there is an active market in a hedging instrument and investors have shown themselves willing to pay

---

[16]The most extreme case of this is Sharpe (1992) which builds a twelve-factor US-oriented model to decompose investment fund returns. He also finds that the results are more informative if he constrains the betas to sum to 1 and, sometimes, to all lie between 0 and 1.

[17]Durable consumption is the consumption CAPM using only consumption of durable goods — expensive goods with purchases known to be volatile and sensitive to the business cycle. This was proposed by Yogo (2006) and may be effectively undoing some of the filtering as discussed in Kroencke (2017).

to eliminate a risk factor with an instrument, that is a strong indicator that the variable in question is a true risk factor. Thus while they do not find credit spreads to pass their higher hurdle, the active market for credit default swaps suggests that default is a true priced risk factor.

15.8 How Arbitrage Pricing Can Fail

While arbitrage pricing is useful, it can fail. This is not a trivial or academic concern: investors have lost billions of dollars, Euros, and pounds due to arbitrage pricing failing.

15.8.1 The Absence of Quasi-Arbitrage

One of the strongest criticisms of the APT comes from the work of Huberman and Stanzl (2004). Their work comes from the field of microstructure which studies liquidity and transactions costs. They find that markets preclude **quasi-arbitrage**: there is no sequence of buys and sells which are expected to make money just from trading. In other words, you cannot trade so as to expect to move prices more when buying versus selling.

What this means for the APT is devastating. The APT says that when there is a violation of the LOOP, that traders will rush in; buy the cheap; sell the rich; and, do this in such size as to smash prices together and reap a profit. The problem with this is in how the traders extract their profit: they must sell what was cheap and buy what was rich. This will, in expectation, move the prices back to their prior levels of mispricing. Furthermore, the expected prices for entering the position are the same for exiting the position: the trader cannot even recover fees.

The only way in which the APT can work in these scenarios is if exiting the position can be done without trading.

Separating Siamese Twins Economically identical stocks which are not fungible are called **Siamese twin shares**. Examples of such shares are dual listings like the London and Amsterdam listings of Unilever and RELX Group; the London and Hong Kong listings of HSBC; and, the London and Sydney listings of BHP Billiton. These shares have typically traded at prices close to economically equivalent — except during financial crises. In 1998 and during the 2008 financial crisis, prices of such stocks diverged from economic equivalence for long periods of time. Maymin (2011) suggests these divergences may relate to self-imposed risk limits. Either way, the divergences greatly challenge the LOOP and APT. They also continue to disillusion investors seeking easy arbitrage profits.

This can happen if one instrument can be converted into the other or if the instruments are hedges for another process. For example, index arbitrageurs can turn futures into stocks via an **exchange for physical** (EFP) and a position that is long soybeans and short soy meal and oil can be exited by taking delivery of soybeans; crushing them into meal and oil; and, then delivering the meal and oil into the short futures contracts.

This is why when we look at prices for commodity futures, they tend to stay in line with the underlying physical goods. On the other hand, prices for Siamese twin shares can diverge for long periods of time if one stock cannot be converted into the other.

15.8.2   Model Risk and Fundamental Risk

The mispricing implied by the APT is only arbitrage if the factor model return relationships hold. This means that relying on the APT exposes us to **model risk**: the risk that our model may be wrong now or in the future.

The possibility of model risk coupled with the absence of quasi-arbitrage is very troubling to a potential arbitrageur. These mean that they might not make money and, even if they do, the timeline for making money is not known. Thus APT-based trades are subject to **fundamental risk**: the risk that the trade may not make money over the arbitrageur's investment horizon.

15.8.3   Credit and Trust

The APT can fail in real life due to credit issues. Very few venues will allow a person to trade without passing a basic credit check and often without also posting some amount of money to an account. Even if the venue does not require this, counterparties may require it. In some markets (as we saw before), trust is also an issue. While you might be able to provide an economic equivalent, if nobody trusts you they will not purchase it from you.

15.8.4   Market Segmentation

Finally, the APT can fail due to market segmentation. Specifically Kamara et al. (2016) find that risk factors are priced differently by investors with differing investment horizons. This means that our goal of finding a single pricing kernel is destined to fail. Rather, our pricing kernel is likely to be a curve. While this creates an almost beautiful parallelism with yield curves, it greatly complicates the search for risk factors and pricing kernels as well as valuation.

15.9 Quiz

Try to answer these questions in five minutes. For answers with equations, just write the equations; do not evaluate them.

1. How do securities converge to fair value via APT versus the CAPM?

2. (2 points!) Suppose $E(r_M) = 0.10$, $r_f = 0.06$, and $r_P = 0.06 + 1.5(r_M - 0.06)$. If $E(r_P) = 0.10$, is there an arbitrage opportunity? If not, show why not; if so, show why and how to make money using it.

3. What risks might stop an arbitrageur from trading APT-based strategies?

4. What are the three factors in the Fama-French 3-factor model? What is the sometimes-added fourth factor?

5. The Chen, Roll, and Ross (1986) factor model features a factor which is the yield difference between long-term government bonds and T-bills. Why is this informative?

6. Can the APT be proven true or false? What if we use a proxy?

7. You are considering investing in a hedge fund. The fees are fairly high, but the returns seem good. When you analyze the returns, they are almost perfectly described by the Fung and Hsieh (1997) eight-factor model. Is investing in this hedge fund worthwhile; or, if not, how would you achieve similar returns?

8. You are considering investing in a mutual fund. The fees are high, but the returns seem good. When you analyze the returns, they are almost perfectly described by the Fama and French (1992) three-factor model. How would you see if investing in this mutual fund is worthwhile?

9. Which are more likely to obey the Law of One Price: West Texas Intermediate versus Brent North Sea crude oils (which are largely interchangeable) or Unilever's London-listed versus Amsterdam-listed shares? Why?

15.10 Exercises

Instructions

We will download data for a few stocks and some risk factors to explore factor models.

- CMT USTs: 3M, 2Y, 10Y, and 30Y (FRED/DGS3MO, FRED/DGS2, FRED/DGS10, FRED/DGS30)
- Data for Chen, Roll, Ross factors:
  - Industrial production (FRED/INDPRO)
  - Expected inflation (FRBC/EXIN)

- Inflation (Quandl ticker `FRBC/USINFL`)
- Long-term BAA corporate bond yields (`FED/RIMLPBAAR_N_B`)

- Indices: S&P 500, Russell 2000 (getSymbols from Yahoo: `^GSPC`, `^RUT`)
- Stocks (getSymbols from Yahoo: `BA, GD, HON, LMT, NOC, QCOM, RTN, UTX`)
- Fama-French factors: these used to be available from Quandl, now they are much more difficult to work with. We will have to do some work to get them from Ken French's website: `http://mba.tuck.dartmouth.edu/pages/faculty/ken.french/ftp/F-F_Research_Data_Factors_daily_CSV.zip`
- The Carhart momentum factor is also available for download from Ken French's website: `http://mba.tuck.dartmouth.edu/pages/faculty/ken.french/ftp/F-F_Momentum_Factor_daily_CSV.zip`

The risk-free rate, Fama-French, and Carhart returns need to be rescaled (divided by 100) to get them on the same scale as log-returns. Ensure the index and equity prices you download are corrected for splits and dividends by using the adjusted close field.

Since the Fama-French data are now harder to download into R, we will skip looking at the five-factor model. Then again, since the Fama-French factors are not clearly related to risk factors, this is not a major omission.

1. Chen, Roll, and Ross (1986) introduced a macro factor model with five macro-conomic factors: the percent change in industrial production, expected inflation, the surprise to inflation (expected versus actual), the yield of long-term corporate bonds over treasuries, and the yield of long-term government bonds over T-bills. We will explore how well these explain stock returns.

We have all of these from the example code except for the last two. For the credit spread, subtract the 10-year yields from the long-term corporate bond yields; for the yield curve factor, subtract the yield on 3M T-bills from the yield on 30Y USTs.

a) We always start by checking our data. What are the min, max, average, and standard deviation of each of the five factors.
b) Fit the Chen, Roll, and Ross model for the excess returns of the SPX, RUT, and the stocks. What are the intercept and slope estimates and their t-statistics?
c) Which factors seem to be more significant across these equity instruments? Discuss why these would be informative.
d) Which factors were not significant? Were any of these surprising?

2. Next we will work with a dynamic microeconomic model: the GARCH-in-mean model. To estimate this, we will use the `rugarch` package and the sample code.

Estimate the GARCH-in-mean model for the indices and the stocks. Do the coefficients make sense? Do they seem to align with what we might expect from what we know so far about risk-aversion?

3. Finally, we will work with two style factor models: the Fama-French three-factor model and the added Carhart, four-factor model. For the market we will use (yawn!) the S&P 500 index.

a) We always start by checking our data. Over this time period, what are the min, max, average, and standard deviation of excess SPX returns and returns for HML, and SMB?

b) Fit the Fama and French model to excess returns for the stocks. What are the intercept and slope estimates and their t-statistics?

c) Are any of the coefficients or their significances surprising? Why might this be?

d) Carhart (1997) added a fourth factor: momentum (aka UMD). Fit the four factor model for excess returns of the stocks. What are the intercept and slope estimates and their t-statistics?

e) Do any of the coefficient estimates change a lot between the three- and four-factor models?

f) Are any of the coefficient estimates or their significances surprising? Can you explain those?

R **Code**

```
library(xts)
library(quantmod)
library(Quandl)
library(rugarch)

# get CMT USTs: 3M, 2Y, 10Y, 30Y

## Download Fama-French data
french.base <- "http://mba.tuck.dartmouth.edu/pages/faculty/ken.french/ftp"
factor.file <- "F-F_Research_Data_Factors_daily_CSV.zip"
french.url <- paste(french.base, factor.file, sep="/")
temp.file <- tempfile()
download.file(french.url, destfile=temp.file)
ff.tmp <- read.csv(unz(temp.file, "F-F_Research_Data_Factors_daily.CSV"),
                   header = TRUE, skip = 3)
unlink(temp.file)
# remove obnoxious last line, scale percentages, create xts object
ff.tmp <- ff.tmp[-length(ff.tmp[,1]),]
ff.data <- as.xts(ff.tmp[,c("SMB","HML")],
                  order.by=as.POSIXct(ff.tmp[[1]], format="%Y%m%d"))

## Download Carhart (momentum) data; skip absurd number of comment lines
factor.file <- "F-F_Momentum_Factor_daily_CSV.zip"
french.url <- paste(french.base, factor.file, sep="/")
temp.file <- tempfile()
download.file(french.url, destfile=temp.file)
umd.tmp <- read.csv(unz(temp.file, "F-F_Momentum_Factor_daily.CSV"),
                    header = TRUE, skip = 13)
unlink(temp.file)
# remove obnoxious last line, scale percentages, create xts object
umd.tmp <- umd.tmp[-length(umd.tmp[,1]),]
umd.data <- as.xts(umd.tmp[,c("Mom")], order.by=as.POSIXct(umd.tmp[[1]], format="%Y%m%d"))
colnames(umd.data) <- c("UMD")
```

```
### Handle monthly data
# For expected CPI and realized CPI, only get the first column of
# data... like so:
exinfl <- Quandl("FRBC/EXIN", type="xts")[,1]
colnames(exinfl) <- c("EXINFL")

cpi <- Quandl("FRBC/USINFL", type="xts")[,1]
colnames(cpi) <- c("CPI")

excpi <- cpi*(1+exinfl)  # expected CPI in twelve months
cpi.surprise <- log(cpi) - log(lag(excpi, 12))  # % CPI surprise
colnames(cpi.surprise) <- c("INFLSURP")

# For industrial production, compute log-returns (% changes)
indprod <- Quandl("FRED/INDPRO", type="xts")
colnames(indprod) <- c("INDPROD")
indprod.logret <- diff(log(indprod))

# Get index and stock prices; create returns

# Now we join all of the datasets together
alldata.full <- cbind(ust, exinfl, cpi.surprise, ltcorpbond, indprod, ff.data, umd.data, returns)

# For monthly data: Last Observation Carried Forward (until new number)
alldata <- na.locf(alldata.full)["2010/"]

# create excess returns for indices, stocks

# Handy way to compute a function for each column
apply(alldata, 2, mean, na.rm=TRUE)  # "2" = by columns; "1" = by rows

# If your ticker were DAL and you wanted to model returns (not excess
# returns) using HML and SMB, you would do like so:
hml.wrong.model <- lm(DAL ~ HML + SMB, data=alldata)
summary(hml.wrong.model)
# NOTE that this is not a model you are supposed to do for the homework

# Now do GARCH-in-mean models
gim.spec <- ugarchspec(variance.model=list(model="sGARCH", archm=TRUE, archpow=2),
                       mean.model=list(armaOrder=c(0,0), include.mean=TRUE))
garch.in.mean.spx <- ugarchfit(data=alldata$SPX.xs, spec=gim.spec)
show(garch.in.mean.spx)
```

References

Acharya, Viral V. and Lasse H. Pedersen. "Asset Pricing with Liquidity Risk". *Journal of Financial Economics* 77.2 (2005), pp. 375–410. DOI: 10.1016/j.jfineco.2004.06.007.

Amihud, Yakov and Haim Mendelson. "Asset Pricing and the Bid-Ask Spread". *Journal of Financial Economics* 17.2 (1986), pp. 223–249. DOI: 10.1016/0304-405X(86)90065-6.

Asness, Clifford S., Andrea Frazzini, and Lasse Heje Pedersen. *Quality Minus Junk*. Working Paper 2312432. SSRN, 2017. DOI: 10.2139/ssrn.2312432.

Ball, Ray and Philip Brown. "An Empirical Evaluation of Accounting Income Numbers". *Journal of Accounting Research* 6.2 (1968), pp. 159–178. DOI: 10.2307/2490232.

Bansal, Ravi and S. Viswanathan. "No Arbitrage and Arbitrage Pricing: A New Approach". *Journal of Finance* 48.4 (1993), pp. 1231–1262. DOI: 10.1111/j.1540-6261.1993.tb04753.x.

Bollerslev, Tim, Robert F. Engle, and Jeffrey M. Wooldridge. "A Capital Asset Pricing Model with Time-Varying Covariances". *Journal of Political Economy* 96.1 (1988), pp. 116–131. DOI: 10.1086/261527.

Boudt, Kris, Ellen C. S. Paulus, and Dale W. R. Rosenthal. "Funding Liquidity, Market Liquidity and TED Spread: A Two-Regime Model". *Journal of Empirical Finance* 43 (2017), pp. 143–158. DOI: 10.1016/j.jempfin.2017.06.002.

Carhart, Mark M. "On Persistence in Mutual Fund Performance". *Journal of Finance* 52.1 (1997), pp. 57–82. DOI: 10.1111/j.1540-6261.1997.tb03808.x.

Chamberlain, Gary. "Funds, Factors, and Diversification in Arbitrage Pricing Models". *Econometrica* 51.5 (1983), pp. 1305–1323. DOI: 10.2307/1912276.

Chan, K.C., Nai fu Chen, and David A. Hsieh. "An Exploratory Investigation of the Firm Size Effect". *Journal of Financial Economics* 14.3 (1985), pp. 451–471. DOI: 10.1016/0304-405X(85)90008-X.

Chen, Nai-Fu, Richard Roll, and Stephen A. Ross. "Economic Forces and the Stock Market". *Journal of Business* 59.3 (1986), pp. 383–403. DOI: 10.1086/296344.

Connor, Gregory. "A Unified Beta Pricing Theory". *Journal of Economic Theory* 34.1 (1984), pp. 13–31. DOI: 10.1016/0022-0531(84)90159-5.

Daniel, Kent and Sheridan Titman. "Evidence on the Characteristics of Cross Sectional Variation in Stock Returns". *Journal of Finance* 52.1 (1997), pp. 1–33. DOI: 10.1111/j.1540-6261.1997.tb03806.x.

Das, Somnath, Alexander King, and Nitish Sinha. *Earnings Information and the Value in Value Premium.* Working Paper. University of Illinois at Chicago, 2015.

Delbaen, Freddy and Walter Schachermayer. "A General Version of the Fundamental Theorem of Asset Pricing". *Mathematische Annalen* 300.1 (1994), pp. 463–520. DOI: 10.1007/BF01450498.

Domian, Dale L., David A. Louton, and Charles E. Mossman. "The Rise and Fall of the "Dogs of the Dow"". *Financial Services Review* 7.3 (1998), pp. 145–159. DOI: 10.1016/S1057-0810(99)00007-4.

Dorfman, John R. "Study of Industrial Averages Finds Stocks with High Dividends Are Big Winners". *Wall Street Journal* (Aug. 11, 1998).

Engle, Robert F., David M. Lilien, and Russell P. Robins. "Estimating Time Varying Risk Premia in the Term Structure: The ARCH-M Model". *Econometrica* 55.2 (1987), pp. 391–407. DOI: 10.2307/1913242.

Fama, Eugene F. and Kenneth R. French. "The Cross-Section of Expected Stock Returns". *Journal of Finance* 47.2 (1992), pp. 427–465. DOI: 10.1111/j.1540-6261.1992.tb04398.x.

Fama, Eugene F. and Kenneth R. French. "Common Risk Factors in the Returns on

Stocks and Bonds". *Journal of Financial Economics* 33.1 (1993), pp. 3–56. DOI: 10.1016/0304-405X(93)90023-5.

— "Dissecting Anomalies with a Five-Factor Model". *Review of Financial Studies* 29.1 (2016), pp. 69–103. DOI: 10.1093/rfs/hhv043.

Froot, Kenneth A. "Hedging Portfolios with Real Assets". *Journal of Portfolio Management* 21.4 (1995), pp. 60–77. DOI: 10.3905/jpm.1995.409527.

Fung, William and David A. Hsieh. "Empirical Characteristics of Dynamic Trading Strategies: The Case of Hedge Funds". *Review of Financial Studies* 10.2 (1997), pp. 275–302. DOI: 10.1093/rfs/10.2.275.

— "Hedge Fund Benchmarks: A Risk-Based Approach". *Financial Analyst's Journal* 60.5 (2004), pp. 65–80. DOI: 10.2469/faj.v60.n5.2657.

Ghalanos, Alexios. *rugarch: Univariate GARCH models*. R package version 1.3-8. 2017. URL: https://CRAN.R-project.org/package=rugarch.

Gibbons, Michael R., Stephen A. Ross, and Jay Shanken. "A Test of the Efficiency of a Given Portfolio". *Econometrica* 57.5 (1989), pp. 1121–1152. DOI: 10.2307/1913625.

Hansen, Lars Peter and Ravi Jagannathan. "Assessing Specification Errors in Stochastic Discount Factor Models". *Journal of Finance* 52.2 (1997), pp. 557–590. DOI: 10.1111/j.1540-6261.1997.tb04813.x.

Harrison, J. Michael and Stanley R. Pliska. "Martingales and Stochastic Integrals in the Theory of Continuous Trading". *Stochastic Processes and their Applications* 11.3 (1981), pp. 215–260. DOI: 10.1016/0304-4149(81)90026-0.

Harvey, Campbell R., Yan Liu, and Heqing Zhu. "...and the Cross-Section of Expected Returns". *Review of Financial Studies* 29.1 (2016), pp. 5–68. DOI: 10.1093/rfs/hhv059.

Hasanhodzic, Jasmina and Andrew W. Lo. "Can Hedge-Fund Returns Be Replicated?: The Linear Case". *Journal of Investment Management* 5.2 (2007), pp. 5–45.

Houge, Todd and Tim Loughran. "Do Investors Capture the Value Premium?" *Financial Management* 35.2 (2006), pp. 5–19. DOI: 10.1111/j.1755-053X.2006.tb00139.x.

Huberman, Greg and Werner Stanzl. "Price Manipulation and Quasi-Arbitrage". *Econometrica* 74.4 (2004), pp. 1247–1276. DOI: 10.1111/j.1468-0262.2004.00531.x.

Huberman, Gur. "A Simple Approach to Arbitrage Pricing Theory". *Journal of Economic Theory* 28.1 (1982), pp. 183–191. DOI: 10.1016/0022-0531(82)90098-9.

Jagannathan, Ravi and Zhenyu Wang. "The Conditional CAPM and the Cross-Section of Expected Returns". *Journal of Finance* 51.1 (1996), pp. 3–53. DOI: 10.2307/2329301.

Jegadeesh, Narasimhan and Sheridan Titman. "Returns to Buying Winners and Selling Losers: Implications for Stock Market Efficiency". *Journal of Finance* 48.1 (1993), pp. 65–91. DOI: 10.1111/j.1540-6261.1993.tb04702.x.

Johnson, Leland L. "The Theory of Hedging and Speculation in Commodity Futures". *Review of Economic Studies* 27.3 (1960), pp. 139–151. DOI: 10.2307/2296076.

Jurek, Jakub W. and Erik Stafford. "The Cost of Capital for Alternative Investments". *Journal of Finance* 70.5 (2015), pp. 2185–2226. DOI: 10.1111/jofi.12269.

Kamara, Avraham et al. "Horizon Pricing". *Journal of Financial and Quantitative Analysis* 51.6 (2016), pp. 1769–1793. DOI: 10.1017/S0022109016000685.

Kan, Raymond and Guofu Zhou. "A New Variance Bound on the Stochastic Discount Factor". *Journal of Business* 79.2 (2006), pp. 941–961. DOI: 10.1086/499144.

Kim, Don H. and Jonathan H. Wright. *An Arbitrage-Free Three-Factor Term Structure Model and the Recent Behavior of Long-Term Yields and Distant-Horizon Forward Rates*. Finance and Economics Discussion Paper 2005-33. Board of Governors of the Federal Reserve System, 2005. URL: https://www.federalreserve.gov/pubs/feds/2005/200533/200533abs.html.

Kindelberger, Charles P. and Robert Aliber. *Manias, Panics, and Crashes: A History of Financial Crises*. 5th ed. New York: Wiley, 2005.

Kroencke, Tim A. "Asset Pricing without Garbage". *Journal of Finance* 72.1 (2017), pp. 47–98. DOI: 10.1111/jofi.12438.

Kydland, Finn E. and Edward C. Prescott. "Time to Build and Aggregate Fluctuations". *Econometrica* 50.6 (1982), pp. 1345–1370. DOI: 10.2307/1913386.

Lehmann, Bruce N. and David M. Modest. "The Empirical Foundations of the Arbitrage Pricing Theory". *Journal of Financial Economics* 21.2 (1988), pp. 213–254. DOI: 10.1016/0304-405X(88)90061-X.

Litterman, Robert and José Scheinkman. "Common Factors Affecting Bond Returns". *Journal of Fixed Income* 1.1 (1991), pp. 54–61. DOI: 10.3905/jfi.1991.692347.

Lo, Andrew W. "The Adaptive Markets Hypothesis". *Journal of Portfolio Management* 30.5 (2004), pp. 15–29. DOI: 10.3905/jpm.2004.442611.

Long Jr., John B. and Charles I. Plosser. "Real Business Cycles". *Journal of Political Economy* 91.1 (1983), pp. 39–69. DOI: 10.1086/261128.

Maymin, Philip Z. "Self-Imposed Limits of Arbitrage". *Journal of Applied Finance* 21.2 (2011), pp. 88–105.

Moskowitz, Tobias J., Yao Hua Ooi, and Lasse Heje Pedersen. "Time Series Momentum". *Journal of Financial Economics* 104.2 (2012), pp. 228–250. DOI: 10.1016/j.jfineco.2011.11.003.

Novy-Marx, Robert. "The Other Side of Value: The Gross Profitability Premium". *Journal of Financial Economics* 108.1 (2013), pp. 1–28. DOI: 10.1016/j.jfineco.2013.01.003.

Palacios-Huerta, Ignacio. "The Robustness of the Conditional CAPM with Human Capital". *Journal of Financial Econometrics* 1.2 (2003), pp. 272–289. DOI: 10.1093/jjfinec/nbg012.

Pástor, Ľuboš and Robert F. Stambaugh. "Liquidity Risk and Expected Stock Returns". *Journal of Political Economy* 111.3 (2003), pp. 642–685. DOI: 10.1086/374184.

Petkova, Ralitsa and Lu Zhang. "Is Value Riskier Than Growth?" *Journal of Financial Economics* 78.1 (2005), pp. 187–202. DOI: 10.1016/j.jfineco.2004.12.001.

Ross, Stephen A. "The Arbitrage Theory of Capital Asset Pricing". *Journal of Economic Theory* 13.3 (1976), pp. 341–360. DOI: 10.1016/0022-0531(76)90046-6.

Sadka, Ronnie. "Momentum and Post-Earnings-Announcement Drift Anomalies: The Role of Liquidity Risk". *Journal of Financial Economics* 80.2 (2006), pp. 309–349. DOI: 10.1016/j.jfineco.2005.04.005.

Sharpe, William F. "Asset Allocation: Management Style and Performance Measurement". *Journal of Portfolio Management* 18.2 (1992), pp. 7–19. DOI: 10.3905/jpm.1992.409394.

Sinha, Nitish Ranjan. "Underreaction to News in the US Stock Market". *Quarterly Journal of Finance* 6.2 (2016), pp. 1–46. DOI: 10.1142/S2010139216500051.

Wang, Fan. *Post Macro Announcement Drift*. Working Paper. University of Illinois at Chicago, 2015.

Yogo, Motohiro. "A Consumption-Based Explanation of Expected Stock Returns". *Journal of Finance* 61.2 (2006), pp. 539–580. DOI: 10.1111/j.1540-6261.2006.00848.x.

Chapter 16

Examining Microfoundations

The CAPM suggests that investment performance should be related to the overall market and that all investments should drift toward the same ratio of return to risk. The APT suggests that investment performance should be strongly related to some (unknown) risk factors — and that they should revert quickly to the pricing implied by those factors. However, we also found that the APT can break for a number of reasons including the preclusion of quasi-arbitrage. It is therefore typical to follow a discussion of the CAPM and APT with a discussion of results which may challenge them.

Up to now, we have assumed that the market should behave according to rationally-optimizing equilibrium models — either in aggregate (CAPM and APT with an error term) or down to the individual level (exact equality form of the APT). However, we have also seen results which challenge the CAPM and APT. We should wonder: when do these models tend to break and how do investors depart from our assumptions? This means examining the **microfoundations** of our models: the behavior of individual economic agents.

The purpose of this chapter is to examine the microfoundations of our models based on insights from psychology, neuroscience, and limits to arbitrage — and to consider the implications of these insights.

16.1   Introduction

In the last two chapters, we saw a few results which seem like they should always hold but do not.

First, the market proxies we looked at were not always efficient in terms of excess return per unit of risk.. That could be a flaw in our choice of proxy, choice of risk measure, or both. It could also be a flaw in the equilibrium argument, akin to the adaptive market hypothesis: maybe instruments are not always at the same ratio of excess return to risk but are always trending toward the same ratio?

Second, the risk factor models we found would seem to imply perfect pricing, but we do not know which risk factors matter. Further complicating the search for risk factors is that we can only come up with bounds which tell us if certain models are wrong.

Third, the violations of the LOOP for Siamese twin shares suggests that factor models can never yield perfect pricing. We can find perfect economic substitutes and yet still have pricing not hold with equality. In fact, there are times when the LOOP violations are large and persistent. This suggests that we have missed some important details.

The question then is why do these models fail? Are there circumstances which help explain when they will fail and how? Thankfully, we do have some ideas, some results from psychology and neuroscience, and even some answers. Some of these are collected in a grab bag of contradictory ideas and theories often called, collectively, **behavioral finance**. However, that term increasingly implies a rejection of all forms of the EMH and even of rational pricing models. The literature from the intersection of neuroscience and finance often does not take so strong a view. The literature on limits to arbitrage is the least extreme; it often merely requires that models accommodate certain variables to account for market state and imperfections. Since these areas are so different, we will discuss behavioral finance, neurofinance, and limits to arbitrage separately.

16.1.1   The Danger of Irrationality

The basic idea behind all of these ideas is that economic theory ignores how real people make decisions and that this difference can explain the model failings we see. This can quickly lead us down a slippery slope, however. Assuming people behave irrationally is very problematic.

It is common at this point for students to tell stories of people they know who behaved "irrationally." However, this is often a fallacy. What may appear to be irrational from a distance is often rational upon closer inspection. In fact, we often instead speak of an idea proposed by Simon (1955): **bounded rationality**. Bounded rationality is the idea that people are rational within the constraints of what they know, what they can reason out, and the time or money needed to improve upon either of these.

For example: suppose you are driving somewhere and your navigation system tells you a certain route is faster. You might not know that there is a school about to let out along your route which could delay you for an average of a half hour.[1] If you spent money to hire analysts or time searching the web, you might discover that your route is not optimal. However, the cost of these might not be worth the savings versus just starting to drive without doing deeper research.

However, we assume in economic models that investors behave rationally given

---

[1]This is far from hypothetical, as I once discovered in Vancouver. Stay away from Point Grey Secondary around 3 PM.

what they know.[2] This is important: if investors did not behave rationally, we would be ignoring a vital trait of their intelligence: the ability to choose. **Strategic choice** is the economic belief that people will make the choices they believe to be best for themselves. Even people who do things which harm themselves are often doing it because they get pleasure from the action or believe it will benefit others whom they value. How else would we explain extreme drunkenness or a soldier leaping upon a bomb to save others?

If economic actors do not exercise strategic choice or choose irrationally, we reduce our economic actors to automatons who make unthinking decisions; they might as well have these "decisions" forced upon them by fiat or the roll of the dice. Furthermore, it is very easy for models which lack strategic choice to imply absurd conclusions. Often, people exercise choice to avoid such extreme irrationality.

If only a few small investors are irrational, we should probably not worry about ill large effects on pricing. Either way, the presence of rational investors with capital is a powerful force. If some investors are irrational, the rational investors will take advantage of them to make profits — so long as the rational investors have capital. In doing so, they will push the market to efficient pricing and take money from the irrational investors. As the rational investors acquire more capital, they will be increasingly able to trade in more markets and thus bring rational pricing to those markets.

Irrational investors who lose money in this way might invest less or stop investing altogether due to their lowered returns. Alternately, they might invest their money in a professionally-managed fund after realizing that they are not good at investing. Either way, the presence of some irrational investors may add some noise to the market but it should not push valuations away from what is sensible and rational.

However, there are certain situations in which strategic choice is curtailed. For example, we required the rational investors to have access to sufficient capital. The situations where choice is curtailed are cases in which the actions of arbitrageurs are limited. Thus **limits to arbitrage** can sometimes explain some of the more extreme situations we observe in the world.

Irrationality, it seems, is not the path to explaining the world around us. Bounded rationality and limits to arbitrage, however, are more hopeful approaches.

16.1.2 *Does the Decision Process Matter?*

Even if there were irrational traders and investors, would it matter? We have discussed how rational investors might exploit irrational investors for profit. What about the nature of the decision process? Does it matter if we are wrong about how investors make decisions? It may not.

Friedman and Savage (1948) discuss the example of a good billiards player making a shot. They note that we might model how that person plays by analyzing

---

[2]In statistical terms, many of these issues come down to clarifying what is in the sigma field you condition on for calculating expectations.

angles and considering momentum and resistance. These formulas could easily be complicated since rolling resistance is likely related to ball velocity, collisions with a bumper are not perfectly elastic, and ball spin plays a role in all of these interactions. However, a good billiards player does not compute all of these; rather, he or she intuits these and can find an approximation which achieves the necessary result (or close). Similarly, our models might be approximations which are sufficiently close.

Does it matter that these processes are not the same? It might, but it also might not. So while investors do not constantly run optimization software when making investing decisions, they may use heuristics and approximations which achieve largely the same result. Therefore, we cannot assume that ignorance or apathy of how decisions are actually made is necessarily a problem.

As Miller (1986) noted: "That we abstract from all these stories in building our models is not because the stories are uninteresting but because they may be too interesting and thereby distract us from the pervasive market forces that should be our principal concern." In other words, the burden of proof is on those who would have us believe that irrationality matters and that we need to know the details of how decisions are made. However, we may well find surprises about the fundamentals of how decisions are made.

16.2 Behavioral Finance

Many of the critiques of rational actors (aka **homo economicus**) are based on theories of behavior from psychology. Unfortunately, the search for novel insights has not yet led to clear extensions of financial theory.

16.2.1 Conflicting Theories of Individual Behavior

One of the most troubling aspects of much "behavioral" research is that it posits certain aspects of individuals' decision-making and then uses a subset of data to justify this proposition. If that does not sound like thorough and defensible social science, you are correct. Apart from torturing the data, however, certain terms get used a lot; so it makes sense to cover them. This will also make clear the inherent conflicts in the literature.

First, a number of behavioralists claim that people handle information incorrectly. Some researchers say that people make **forecasting errors** by overweighting recent experience or **representativeness errors** by inferring patterns from small amounts of data. Other researchers say that people are likely to exhibit **conservatism** by overweighting older experience too much. Which is it? That depends on which paper, dataset, or time period you look at. If this sounds like the fact that models sometimes over- and under-predict when they are correct on average. . . then you too have hit on a common criticism of behavioral research.

Second, there are certain biases which behavioralists claim lead to inconsistent decision making. One of these is **framing**: the idea that people give different answers when the same economic question is posed differently. This is just a restatement of what survey statisticians have long known: that people respond differently to different wordings of questions. (Zaller and Feldman (1992) review some of the literature on such survey response effects.) Given the rich nuances and connotations versus denotations of language, this should not be a surprise. Also, when a person might not know the answer, it is not surprising that a leading question could encourage some to answer in a way guided by the question. Thus framing does not clearly suggest any weakness in financial theory.

Another claimed bias is **mental accounting**: the idea that people segregate certain decisions from others and do not consider their exchangeability. The classic example to show this is the following setup:

> You have a date and spent $200 for tickets to an event you know your date will like a lot. (Students often have many questions at this point: Is the date "hot?" Does this evening seem "hopeful?" etc.) We will assume the date is "hot" and the evening is "hopeful."
>
> You arrive at the performance venue, open your wallet, and find that the tickets are gone: you have lost them. However, the ticket window is open and you can purchase two new tickets with identical views for $200. Do you re-buy the tickets?
>
> Alternately, suppose you arrive at the performance venue, open your wallet, and realize you just lost two $100 bills — but still have the tickets. Do you still go in, or do you sell the tickets?

The fact that people often give different answers is seen as evidence of mental accounting: people have a separate budget for entertainment versus cash. Why? Because the two situations are "economically identical." However, is that true?

Re-buying the tickets sends a signal to your date that you want them to be happy; however, with $200 less you might not have bought the tickets in the first place. Therefore, the loss gives you an excuse to choose another activity for your date without sending a very negative signal. On the other hand, selling the tickets sends a more negative signal to your date and requires that people outside the venue trust you as much as the box office (an unlikely proposition). Furthermore, finding the tickets at home later (a possibility) has no value while finding the cash at home later would restore its full value. The question is an interesting one to consider; however, the economics of the different choices are not equal.

Which of these effects — forecasting errors, representativeness errors, conservatism, framing, or mental accounting — are true or not? That is a source of continuing debate. Therefore, until these areas can resolve divergent implications which may well stem from differences in datasets and meanings, there is little to recommend further focus on these ideas.

I know I am being a bit harsh here; however, my perspective is inherently skeptical (as yours should be). A theory needs to be consistent and overcome some threshold of doubt before we embrace it. The inconsistency of the aforementioned bias claims have not yet met that threshold.

16.2.2 Effects We See Consistently

There are some effects we observe unequivocally in investors and these are worth considering. One effect we often observe is **loss avoidance**, also known as the **disposition effect**: the tendency of investors to sell winning positions but not losing positions as documented in Odean (1998). This is suboptimal according to both theory and empirical studies. Given what we now know about momentum, it is also not very sensible.

We mostly see this effect for individual investors. Many people seeking to become traders work on overcoming this bias. Sometimes, convincing people is simple: get them to consider that cutting losses lets them redeploy their diminished funds into better investments which will be more profitable than if their current position recovered. For individual investors, the superior returns of professional money managers (versus individuals engaging in stock picking) often coaxes individual investors into funds which eliminate their exposure to the disposition effect.

Another consistent effect we see is **overconfidence**: some traders overestimate their ability or their forecast precisions. Benos (1998) considers the effects of overconfident traders; and, Odean (1999) shows that retail investors tend to overtrade — in that they do not cover their trading costs and stock positions they trade into perform worse than those they had previously.[3] This is the trading equivalent of the **Dunning-Kruger effect**: fools and bunglers think they have superior intellect and capabilities.

Barber and Odean (2001) show that more trading is associated with lower returns. Furthermore, they show that the tendency to overtrade is stronger in men than women: men reduce their returns by 2.7%/year due to (more) overtrading versus 1.7%/year for women. Barber et al. (2009) find that individual investors in Taiwan reduce their returns by 3.8%/year while institutional traders and intermediaries profit from their own trading. Gervais and Odean (2001) develop theory which suggests less-experienced traders should be more overconfident.

Another behavior we see is **regret avoidance**: that investors who fail are reluctant for that failure to be seen as an unconventional failure. One of the classic manifestations of this is **window dressing**: when funds lose money overall, they sell out of their losing investments and replace them with investments which did well historically. Thus while they cannot hide their losses, they can make the fund appear to have sensible holdings and not holdings known *ex post* to be losing positions. Lakonishok et al. (1991) document window dressing by pension funds; and, Khorana (2001) documents mutual funds engaging in window dressing.

---

[3]The motivation for Odean (1999), however, is flawed. He tries to relate investment with stock market turnover yet neglects that intermediation increases volume as it increases market efficiency. While total transaction costs and net investment are certainly related to economic growth, there is no reason absolute volume in a multi-venue intermediated market should be related to investment.

16.2.3 Nudges to Mitigate Bounded Rationality

Finally, it makes sense to consider one of the more intriguing and hopeful policy suggestions from the behavioral literature: the idea of a nudge. A **nudge** is a change to policies or default choices which does not eliminate individual choice but encourages people to make more rational decisions. Sometimes, this is done by making default choices be those which would be optimal for most people.

For example: Cronqvist and Thaler (2004) discuss this idea with respect to the conversion of the Swedish pension system from a state-run system to an individually-managed retirement account. The enrollment page for individually-managed accounts had a staggering multiplicity of choices. Cronqvist and Thaler documented that many participants just chose whatever the default setting was on the webpage — even when it was a poor choice for them. Thus it would make sense for the default to be a sensible choice such as a low-cost all-market index fund.

The idea of a nudge is best developed in Thaler and Sunstein (2008). They note that we need not remove choice from individuals, but that bounded rationality matters: finding a better choice may take a lot of time and require some education. So, they ask: why not offer better defaults? There must be some default choice anyway; why make it arbitrary or the safest? Why not make it what would be optimal for the most people?

The idea was so influential that the UK created the Behavioral Insights Team (the "Nudge Unit") in 2010 to help shape government policy and implementation; and, the US created the Social and Behavioral Sciences Team in 2015.[4] In 2017, these ideas led to Thaler receiving the Nobel Prize.

16.2.4 Summaries

For those interested in reading more about behavioral finance, a good place to start is Shleifer (2012). For greater depth, Shleifer (2000) and Burton and Shah (2013) are excellent introductions.

16.3 Neurofinance

One of the more surprising areas of research is **neurofinance**: the study of how brain behavior relates to financial decision making. Neurofinance uses tools from neuroscience and genetics to explain differing investor behavior. These studies often look at brain imaging, genetic polymorphism (variations in genes which persist and are not just due to mutations), and genetic mutations. Many studies examine traders since trading can be very stressful and involves constant decision-making under uncertainty.

Some of these studies use functional magnetic resonance imaging (fMRI) for brain imaging. Recently, some work such as Eklund, Nichols, and Knutsson (2006)

---

[4]The SBST has since dissolved.

has challenged the statistical significance of fMRI results. They note that corrections for multiple hypothesis testing are not always straightforward and that some fMRI analysis software had bugs. Despite their initial claims, however, few fMRI-based studies were affected.

16.3.1 *Experimental Testing of Financial Theories*

A number of neurofinance researchers have been able to use their tools in laboratory settings to test financial ideas which are otherwise difficult to resolve with only observational (non-causal) data.

For example, we might wonder if people can correctly assess variance. Behrens et al. (2007) show that people can indeed assess variance. Furthermore, Payzan-LeNestour et al. (2013) find that people perceive three types of uncertainty: known uncertainty (risk), uncertainty about known uncertainty (estimation uncertainty), and unknown uncertainty (Knightian uncertainty). Intuitively, this is akin to people being able to assess the mean risk (*e.g.* $\hat{\sigma}$), the uncertainty of that mean estimate (*e.g.* sd($\hat{\sigma}$)), and the idea that maybe the assumptions are wrong and another parameter or measure is needed or that there are other scenarios which may need to be considered. Preuschoff, Quartz, and Bossaerts (2008) show that people are also good at updating their beliefs about risk when they make prediction errors.

In market microstructure, there are two large classes of dynamic models. Bayesian Nash equilibrium models, such as Kyle (1985), consider strategic traders who optimize trading size in light of its effect on pricing to maximize their profit and minimize information leakage to the market. Noisy rational expectations equilibrium models, such as Glosten and Milgrom (1985), consider markets where some traders are informed, some are not (and add only noise), and no one trader has a large impact on prices. In noisy rational expectations equilibrium models, prices tend toward the valuation known by informed traders. (This class of models includes sequential trader models.)

Bossaerts, Frydman, and Ledyard (2014) examined the question of which model dynamics we see in real markets. They used simulated markets to test these theories and found results suggesting pricing appears to be based on Bayesian Nash equilibrium models; however, prices do tend toward the noisy rational expectations equilibrium equilibrium. (This agrees with Back and Baruch (2004) who find convergence between Kyle (1985) and Glosten and Milgrom (1985) as trade sizes become smaller and more frequent.) They also find that volatility increases as information is impounded into prices.

Finally, Frydman et al. (2014) use fMRI data and experiments to test the **realization effect**: that investors gain or lose utility when they realize profits or losses. This is a possible explanation for the disposition effect. They find evidence supporting the realization and disposition effects.

16.3.2   Hormonal Effects on Financial Decision Making

One of the more unusual traits observed by scientists is the ratio of second-digit to fourth-digit lengths. While most people have a shorter index than ring finger, the ratio of second-to-fourth digit lengths (aka the **2D:4D digit ratio**) is typically higher for men. The ratio is a rough proxy for in-utero exposure to androgenizing hormones (*e.g.* testosterone versus estrogen).

Coates, Gurnell, and Rustichini (2009) studied if there was a relationship between the 2D:4D digit ratio and financial decision making. They found that the 2D:4D ratio predicted success among high-frequency traders in London. Later research in Coates and Page (2009) found that the 2D:4D digit ratio was related to risk taking (and thus earning a risk premium) but not to Sharpe ratios — and that Sharpe ratios increased with a trader's experience.

Coates and Herbert (2008) studied traders in London and found that their morning testosterone levels predicted daily profitability. They also found that cortisol rose with the variance of both profitability and the market. In particular, their results suggested that testosterone levels were related to returns while cortisol levels were related to risk. Since these hormones are known to relate to changes in cognition and behavior, they posited that longer-term elevation of these hormones could shift risk preferences and affect a trader's ability to make rational choices.

Coates, Gurnell, and Sarnyai (2010) find that production of cortisol is related to risk and testosterone to reward. They also note a difference between acute and chronic exposure to these hormones: acute elevations might improve performance on some tasks; but, chronic elevation seems to encourage suboptimal risk-taking. They posit that the irrational exuberance and revulsion observed during bubbles and crashes may result from hormones. That suggests the age and sex distribution of traders and investors may affect the instability of financial markets.

One might wonder if these hormonal changes were causal or endogenous. Cueva et al. (2015) tested this in two ways. First, they recorded levels of testosterone and cortisol of traders in a simulated market. The researchers found that individual and overall levels of cortisol predicted risk-taking and price volatility. Then they administered cortisol or testosterone to the traders (young males) before the traders traded in a simulated market. The researchers found that both hormones shifted the traders to invest in riskier assets. Cortisol affected risk preferences while testosterone seemed to increase optimism. Thus both hormones could affect market volatility and the creation and destruction of bubbles.

Finally, Preuschoff, 't Hart, and Einhäuser (2011) add to the literature on types of uncertainty which people can perceive by showing that noradrenaline increases (as measured by pupil dilation) when people are surprised, *i.e.* when they see a difference from expected uncertainty.

16.3.3   The Genetics of Balancing Risk and Reward

Other works find that areas of the brain related to pain and pleasure are activated in, and affect, financial decision making. For example, the insula (aka insular cortex) is an area which registers pain while the nucleus accumbens is associated with pleasure.

Kuhnen and Knutson (2005) find that increased activity in the insula area of the brain reduced financial risk-taking, often to a sub-optimal level, while increased activity in the nucleus accumbens increased financial risk-taking. They also find that losses and gains increase activity in the insula and nucleus accumbens. Thus there is an autoregressive effect in the brains of financial decision makers. Fung, Bode, and Murawski (2017) discuss this persistence effect and note that it decreases with increasing financial rewards. Page and Coates (2017) also find autoregressive performance — in their case, among closely-matched tennis players.

Nucleus accumbens activity is particularly associated with increases in dopamine, a neurotransmitter related to signaling rewards in the brain. Knutson et al. (2008) show that elevated levels of activity in the nucleus accumbens (and thus elevated levels of dopamine) are present before people make financial decisions. Most unusually, they find that men anticipating seeing pornography take more risk when making financial decisions.

Sapra, Beavin, and Zak (2012) find that successful traders in New York City tend to have certain genetic polymorphisms in their dopamine receptor 4 promoter (DRD4P) and catechol-O-methyl transferase (COMT) coding gene — both of which affect dopamine levels. In particular, successful traders had alleles (genetic variations in chromosomes) which were associated with *moderate* levels of dopamine; they had neither too much nor too little dopamine. (Since dopamine levels are also associated with addiction, this suggests that the stereotypes of drug-taking traders is unlikely to hold for traders who are successful over the long-term.)

Frydman et al. (2011) study how decision making relates to monoamine oxidase-A (MAOA), an enzyme which breaks down dopamine and serotonin. They find that polymorphism in genes encoding for MAOA has an effect on financial decision making, while polymorphisms in the genes coding for serotonin transporter 5-HTT and dopamine receptor DRD4 do not have a significant effect.[5] In particular, individuals with the polymorphism (MAOA-L) which produces less MAOA were more likely to take financial risks. However, the authors claim this is because those individuals performed better at assessing those risks, not because they were more impulsive.

Unfortunately, this polymorphism has also been referred to as the "psycho gene" for its effects on counterproductive behaviors. Williams et al. (2009) find the MAOA-L polymorphism is associated with antisocial personality traits; and, Buckholtz and Meyer-Lindenberg (2008) note an increased likelihood of psychopathy for those with the MAOA-L polymorphism. In particular, they find the strongest associations for males and especially those exposed to persistent abuse in early childhood.

---

[5]Note that DRD4 is not the same as DRD4P.

16.3.4   Mental States for Success

Finally, there are studies which look at mental state or abilities and relate these to success in financial decision making.

Kandasamy et al. (2016) study **interoception**, sensing physiological signals from inside the body (such as hunger, pain or heart rate). Typically, people with better interoception make better risk-taking decisions in laboratory settings. They find that London-based traders were better than otherwise-similar individuals at detecting their own heart beats, and that traders' interoceptive ability predicted their relative profitability and how long they survived in the financial markets.

This might seem to be at odds with the prior studies which suggest successful traders are worse at empathy. However, that would be extending the interoception results too far. De Martino et al. (2013) show that traders who better empathize with and understand the motivations of other traders... do *worse* in simulated financial markets and that their (more societally-aware) actions can lead to bubbles. Introversion is more profitable than extroversion, it seems.

16.3.5   Summaries

Neurofinance seems to support Keynes's claim that "animal spirits" drive markets — which justifies central bank intervention in crises. To learn more about neurofinance, I recommend reading Kirman, Livet, and Teschl (2010), the special issue of *Philosophical Transactions of the Royal Society B* on "Rationality and Emotions," and O'Doherty and Camerer (2015), the special issue of *Current Opinion in Behavioral Sciences* on "Neuroeconomics" which includes a review article: Bossaerts and Murawski (2015).

Finally, there is John Coates's book. Coates is an unusual researcher on the intersection of neuroscience and finance. He was a Wall Street derivatives trader at Goldman Sachs and Merrill Lynch and headed a trading desk at Deutsche Bank — before switching to study neuroscience and financial decision making. His book, *The Hour Between Dog and Wolf: How Risk Taking Transforms Us, Body and Mind*, discusses neurofinance research and even offers ideas on performance targets for finance professionals.

16.4   Prospect Theory

One of the most troubling and unresolved areas of finance is that of Prospect Theory, proposed by Kahneman and Tversky (1979) and refined by Tversky and Kahneman (1992).[6] The theory came from psychology experiments on real people faced with

---

[6]This modification addressed some problems with the initial theory and is known as Cumulative Prospect Theory. This is the form we will discuss.

financial decisions and led to Kahneman winning the Nobel Prize in 2002.[7] Barberis (2013) has an excellent overview of the theory.

16.4.1 Assumptions

There are four key assumptions underlying **Prospect Theory**:

1. (Framing) Decisions are evaluated in terms of gains and losses versus a reference point, often current wealth or outcomes common across all decisions (and thus certain).
2. (Loss aversion) People are more sensitive to losses than they are to gains of the same magnitude.
3. (Diminishing sensitivity) People have diminished sensitivity to gains and losses. Thus they are risk averse when evaluating gains and risk-loving when evaluating losses. This means that the value function is concave for gains and convex for losses.
4. (Probability shrinkage) People's decisions place higher weight on small probabilities and less weight on large probabilities. This is like squeezing these probabilities toward some risk-averse average.[8]

These properties are very different than those of the utility functions most economists use. The value function estimated in Tversky and Kahneman (1992) is shown in Figure 16.1.

16.4.2 Implications

What this means is that the utility functions most economists use are wrong. Most economists build models using a utility function that involves the log of wealth. That sort of function implies that the wealthy are happier and less risk averse. Thus Bill Gates (who has a lot of money) is much happier and less risk averse than Joe Hobo (who has very little money). It also means that a 10% gain on Bill Gates's wealth (a very big number to add to his total) makes him equally *happier* as a 10% increase to Joe Hobo's wealth makes him *happier*.

Note that I said the change made them happier, not happy. This is where Prospect Theory diverges from most economic models. Prospect Theory says that Bill Gates and Joe Hobo start off neither happy nor sad – but that a 10% gain makes them happy — not *happier* but happy. In Prospect Theory, your utility is a function of wealth *change*, not wealth; and, your change in utility (getting happier) would be the second derivative of wealth: the acceleration of your wealth.

On the one hand, this is troubling: it disagrees with much of economic theory. On the other hand, this is not radically different from how we look at problems in finance. Up to now, our utility functions have often looked at log-returns less some

---

[7]Tversky did not win since he had already passed away.
[8]Tversky and Kahneman (1992) find people shrink probabilities toward about 0.36.

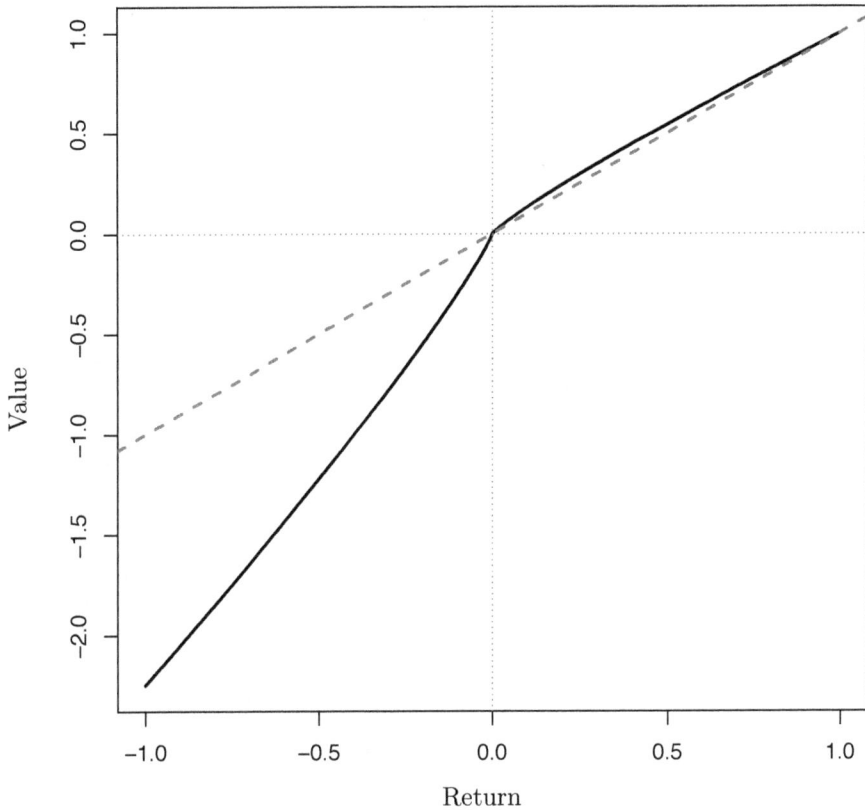

Figure 16.1: The value function estimated by Tversky and Kahneman (1992): $x^{0.88}$ for $x \geq 0$; $-2.25(-x)^{0.88}$ for $x < 0$. The 45° gray line shows the utility function normally assumed. Note that the value function is concave for $x \geq 0$ and convex for $x < 0$.

risk penalty. Thus changes in wealth (log-returns) are in our utility function. Maybe Prospect Theory is not such a revolution!

Prospect theory also says that utility is given by an S-shaped curve versus the change in wealth — not a straight-line function of log-returns. Furthermore, the utility S-curve is not symmetric and odd; a loss yields more sadness than the happiness yielded by an equal-sized gain. However, apart from the kink at the origin, the value function in Figure 16.1 is not markedly different from a linear function with different slopes across the origin.

The diminishing sensitivity and asymmetry implies loss aversion. This can also explain why investors become risk-seeking after losses. However, we do not need Prospect Theory for this last behavior to be true. A simple exercise in stochastic programming of saving for retirement at a certain age will yield the same result. The reason is because retirement is like an option: Sometimes your only chance of having enough money is to take more risk.

16.4.3 Applications of Prospect Theory

Unfortunately, these aspects of Prospect Theory are difficult to incorporate into economic and financial models. There have been a few attempts. For example, Barberis, Huang, and Santos (2001) looked at asset prices using a Prospect Theory-implied utility function. They found that Prospect Theory might help explain the higher return, volatility, and predictability of prices than would otherwise be expected.

Also, if we step back from taking Prospect Theory so literally, it does mesh well with some aspects of financial practice. First, we look at log-returns, so we also work often with wealth changes.

Second, we might analyze investments and build models with an asymmetric loss function:

$$\arg\min_{\alpha,\beta} \Psi(r_{it} - (\alpha + \beta r_{Mt})), \tag{16.1}$$

where Ψ is an asymmetric function instead of the typical OLS $\Psi(d) = d^2$.

Finally, the focus many finance professionals have on risk management and eliminating downside risk implies an asymmetric focus on risk much like the value function in Prospect Theory.

While Prospect Theory has not formally made its way into mainstream economics and finance, many of its implications are in keeping with common practice — and so we see its implications throughout the world of finance.

16.5   Limits to Arbitrage

Markets may stay inefficient due to **limits to arbitrage**. This idea has been around for a long time. It is referred to off-handedly as access to credit or capital in Lefèvre (1923) and was surely mentioned long before that. One of the earlier academic studies of the idea is in Tuckman and Vila (1992) which considers how the cost of holding a position affects divergences from the "fundamental" value. The idea was popularized by Shleifer and Vishny (1997) who examined how a number of mispricings could arise.

16.5.1   External and Self-Imposed Limits to Arbitrage

While arbitrageurs are always looking to make money, sometimes they cannot do so. Their actions may be limited by a number of forces. These limits may be externally-imposed or self-imposed.

External limits are common but sometimes may be circumvented. Trading has **implementation costs**: explicit fees and implicit expenses due to liquidity (for example) which make some mispricings unprofitable to arbitrage. Any security or physical asset may be affected by **finite supply** issues. For example, short selling a stock requires borrowing shares and there are only so many shares available for borrowing. (We will discuss ways around this later.) **Credit limits** exist because lenders will not offer unlimited capital to arbitrageurs and what capital they do offer is based on an assessment of the likelihood that the capital will be repaid. Regulators may also impose **restrictions** such as the US and UK banning shorting financial stocks during the 2008 financial crisis. Sometimes, investors impose **mandates** such as funds only being able to hold stocks in an index or bonds of a certain credit quality. These externally-imposed limits may preclude arbitrage or they may force a suboptimal, even unprofitable, early exit from positions.

Self-imposed limits would seem to be minor; however, these are some of the more powerful effects because they are not easily circumvented.

Fundamental risk is the risk that an arbitrage portfolio may not converge by the arbitrageur's investment horizon. For example, you might see the possibility to make big money trading Siamese twin shares; but, if you will need the investment capital back to pay your monthly rent, you are not likely to enter a position in the first place. You might also worry about **model risk**: the uncertainty of how correct your model is. While many investors and traders overcome model risk, it can still arise if a model yields a valuation far from market prices. In that case, a rational response may be to doubt the model. Many arbitrageurs have **risk limits**: restrictions on how much of an instrument they will hold or how much economic exposure they will have to any one sector or industry. Maymin (2011) shows that price divergences in Siamese twin shares seem to be related to traders limiting their holdings to some multiple of average daily volume. Finally, uncertainties about possible restrictions or mandates may lead arbitrageurs to opt-out of taking arbitrage positions. (See the sidebar "Maybe Means No" for more on this.)

> **Maybe Means No** Early in the 2008 financial crisis, the US banned short sales of financial stocks. The US also discussed, but did not ban options on those stocks (which give upside or downside exposure) or short sales used by options market makers to hedge their positions. A student who worked at a top options market maker was late to class one evening because the firm had just ceased making markets in all options on financial stocks. The reason? The discussion of a possible ban. They could not accept the risk of waking up one morning to find that the government would no longer let them hedge their positions — since that would leave them stuck in those positions and exposed to their (nonlinear) risk exposures. Uncertainties about a mandate deprived the market of downside protection for those troubled stocks.

16.5.2   The Effects of Limits to Arbitrage

We previously mentioned Siamese twin shares and how they may break the LOOP. This could be due to fundamental risk or self-imposed risk limits. We also discussed short-selling constraints and Diamond and Verrecchia (1987) who showed that such constraints affect market efficiency and valuation.

Another set of mispricings occurs with **equity carve outs**: separating a division from a company and selling it ("spinning it off") to shareholders. In these cases, a share of the parent firm splits into the spin-off and the remainder (aka **stub**): Parent = Stub + Spin-off.

Sometimes, this split is done partially or in stages resulting in parent shares trading alongside the spin-off (and maybe the stub also). Even if the terms are set, the stub+spin-off may imply a different price than the market price of the parent. The classic case of this was the spin-off of Palm Computing from 3Com in 2000.

In 2000, mobile phones and pocket-sized computers were starting to become popular. Networking equipment manufacturer 3Com was spinning off their Palm Computing division, then one of the dominant firms in the small computer space. Palm had even just released a pocket computer which could also be used as a phone. Investors were very excited by the prospects for Palm. 3Com decided to first hold a Palm IPO and sell 5% of Palm shares to investors; then, later, 95% of the shares would be given to 3Com investors: 1.5 Palm shares for each share of 3Com held.

Since the Palm IPO was popular, the share price of Palm shot up to close on the IPO day at $95 per share. That same day, 3Com stock closed at $81 13/16 per share. This valued the remainder of 3Com at:

$$\text{Stub} = \$81.81 - 1.5 \times \$95 = -\$60.69. \tag{16.2}$$

Clearly this was an arbitrage. However, because so few Palm shares were sold in the IPO, there were very few shares to borrow.

Another set of mispricings occur in closed-end funds. These are funds which raise a fixed amount of capital and then trade on an exchange. However, since the fund has expenses and holds stocks which are often illiquid, the share price can differ substantially from the net asset value (NAV) of their holdings. Ross (2002) theorizes that the deviations from net asset value are larger in funds which are more difficult to arbitrage. He also notes that the discount may be rational:

$$\text{Discount} = \frac{\text{NAV} - \text{Price}}{\text{NAV}} = \frac{\mu}{\mu + \epsilon + \delta + \gamma} \tag{16.3}$$

where μ is management fees (in percent), ϵ is the expense ratio, δ is the dividend yield, and γ is the capital gains yield.

However, this finding raises an alternate question: If closed-end funds holding illiquid assets should trade at a discount, then are open-end funds, which trade at net asset value, mispriced if they hold illiquid assets?

Limits to arbitrage can also affect corporate takeovers. Mangeldorf (2009) discusses how Porsche tried to takeover Volkswagen in late 2008. This created a short squeeze which caused wild variations in Volkswagen's stock price. The financial crisis, however, led to credit constraints which caused the takeover to collapse and backfire: Volkswagen acquired Porsche. Allen et al. (2017) study how this incident affected market efficiency and increased risk.

Taxes can also create limits to arbitrage. Banz (1981) notes that US small-cap firms tend to outperform large-cap firms. Roll (1981) notes that the effect is overstated due to infrequent trading of smaller firms. Most convincing, however, is the explanation in Reinganum (1983): that the effect is largely concentrated in the beginning of January and in stocks which did poorly the previous year. These stocks also underperform in the preceding December. This suggests these stocks did poorly which led investors to harvest tax losses in December. When the selling pressure subsides in January, the stocks do well.

> **Poorsche?** Over 2005–2008, Porsche sought to stealthily amass Volkswagen stock to acquire the much-larger Volkswagen. Once Porsche's holdings were revealed to be 43% (with options to reach 74%), short sellers of VW quickly exited their short positions. Since there were many short sellers, this drove Volkswagen to briefly become the most valuable company in the world. Porsche was almost able to grab €8 bn of cash from Volkswagen when the unfolding financial crisis led their lenders to curtail the additional credit needed to complete the deal. Porsche and Volkswagen attempted to woo rich investors and Volkswagen succeeded. They not only repelled Porsche's takeover but were able to instead takeover Porsche. The Porsche and Piëche families, which controlled Porsche's voting shares, also had to pay money in to reduce Porsche's debt burden.

Finally, Brunnermeier and Pedersen (2009) discuss how limits to arbitrage at a microstructure level leads to financial crises with macroeconomic effects. We will see more of this in Chapter 26.

16.5.3 Home Bias

We should discuss one last limit to arbitrage that affects most investors. **Home bias** is the tendency of most investors to over-invest in assets of their home country and under-invest in assets of other countries. Stulz (1981) is one of the first works to consider this bias. He studies how costs of holding foreign assets lead investors to demand a higher beta on foreign stocks and lead to under-investment in foreign stocks, even when the investor would increase their expected return.

French and Poterba (1991) show that investors in the US, UK, Japan, France, Canada, and Germany strongly over-invest in their domestic stocks. One might argue that holding more domestic assets is a way to hedge inflation; however, Cooper and

Kaplanis (1994) document that this would only explain under-investment in foreign assets if investors were unbelievably risk averse. In fact, Tesar and Werner (1995) show that foreign holdings tend to be unrelated to diversification of financial risk and that transactions costs do not seem to explain home bias. Kang and Stulz (1997) study foreign holdings of Japanese stocks (which have no restrictions on foreign holdings). They find that foreign investors tend to hold larger firms; manufacturing firms; liquid export-focused firms; firms with ADRs; and, firms with good accounting performance, low idiosyncratic risk, and low leverage.

We might wonder then: will lower transactions costs reduce home bias? Or, are there other reasons that home bias persists? Mishra and Ratti (2013) find that introducing foreign tax credits reduces (but does not eliminate) home bias. Unfortunately, Levy and Levy (2014) show that correlations between markets inflates the effect of foreign holding costs and that correlations have been increasing between markets. Therefore, home bias may well continue.

Coeurdacier and Gourinchas (2016) consider that investors can also hold foreign bonds which allows them to (mostly) hedge foreign exchange risk. They show that home bias is rational if non-financial returns are negatively correlated with domestic equity returns more than with foreign equity returns — conditional on bond returns (*i.e.* post-hedging FX). When they examine the data, they find that investors do use bonds to hedge FX risk but also that this negative correlation is often present. This explains most (but not all) of home bias. Thus home bias persists because domestic financial instruments provide investors with a better hedge for non-financial (*e.g.* income) risk than foreign financial instruments. Will home bias persist as correlations between domestic and foreign markets increase, as noted in Levy and Levy (2014)? Increasing correlations suggest foreign assets are becoming better substitutes for domestic assets. However, domestic equities may still offer a better hedge.

Even apart from these considerations, home bias is not so surprising. Different countries have differences in accounting standards (which investors may not be able to easily assess to determine their trust in foreign standards). Most financial reports and news are published in the local language and not translated. Furthermore, countries differ in legal systems, property rights, and fairness of treatment for foreign entities. Even when investors want to invest in foreign assets, few brokers provide easy access to all (or even many) foreign markets. This is precisely why there is demand for depository receipts and international investment funds.

Finally, Coval and Moskowitz (1999) find that there is even home bias within a country: investors tend to over-invest in local firms and especially in small local firms.

16.6   Lies, Damned Lies, and Voodoo Finance

So far, we have discussed a number of effects which might be valid, effects we are pretty sure are valid, and effects which result from limits to arbitrage. However, whenever we discuss these areas, there are always a few topics which some people try to push as plausible. These are largely garbage. Hence my riff on an old quote from Mark Twain (who attributed it to Benjamin Disraeli): "There are three kinds of lies: lies, damned lies, and statistics." In this case, these garbage financial theories might as well be voodoo or some other religion — for they are not based on any sound analysis.[9]

Perhaps the most widely-believed and least-suspect theory is **technical analysis**: the drawing of lines on price charts which are supposed to reveal bounds on prices or show where prices are going. The truth is that we all are a little guilty of this thinking: the first response to hearing of an investment is often to pull up its price chart. Why is just seeing the current price not sufficient? So much for the weak form of the EMH!

Lo, Mamaysky, and Wang (2000) were able to train a computer to do technical analysis in agreement with human technical analysts. They then analyzed 31 years of data and found a few patterns were significant: particularly the "head and shoulders" pattern and inferred lines of resistance. However, most patterns were found to be bogus. Similar to the quote in the movie *Anchorman: The Legend of Ron Burgundy*: "60% of the time, they work every time."

Much more skepticism should be taken when discussing various "wave" theories which purport to offer predictions or guidance about when investors should expect markets to revert. Many of these are either vapid or unfalsifiable — they make claims which cannot be disproven.

Dow theory posits that there are three horizons of trends which affect prices. The primary trend plays out over months to years and is responsible for the tops and bottoms of long-term trends. The secondary trend is responsible for short deviations from the primary trend which are ended by "corrections." Finally, tertiary trends are daily fluctuations of little importance. How would an investor know these trends without hindsight? That is not clear. Furthermore, why split movements into three groups? Anybody familiar with Fourier transforms or frequency analysis can see this this is an arbitrary classification.

Elliott wave theory is the idea, popularized by accountant Ralph Nelson Elliott, that there are short- and long-term oscillations about trends — because life moves in cycles and thus optimism and pessimism are also periodic. There are numerous systems purporting to infer these waves and help investors make money. However, the LOOP, their prevalence in late-night television advertising, and the number of professionals proclaiming the theory to be bogus would all suggest that these systems are not reliable or valuable.

The most extreme version of wave theory is that of Kondratieff waves. This theory posits that there are very long-term waves having periods on the order of 48–60 years which create long-term bull and bear markets. This idea sometimes goes by other names like supercycles. However, the problem is always the same: these theories are largely untestable because there are few periods of data available

---

[9]The "voodoo" reference recalls George H.W. Bush's disbelief in supply-side economics: he dubbed it "voodoo economics."

historically. To confirm such an idea, we would need a few hundred years of data. Furthermore, there is no economic basis for fluctuation and ample evidence against such mechanical periodicity.

16.7   The Equity Premium

A number of academics get very excited about the **equity premium puzzle**: the idea that stock markets have outperformed compared to what we would expect given normal levels of risk aversion and the volatility of markets.

Shiller (1982) first mentioned and Mehra and Prescott (1985) first documented the puzzle in looking at US stock and bond data over 1889–1978. Fama and French (2002) then examined US stock returns over 1872–1999. They note that the equity premium increases post-1949, after World War 2. Given the war-time destruction of Europe and Japan; China's descent into civil war; and, the rise of Marxist influence after the war, outperformance of the US equity market is not so surprising. Goetzmann and Ibbotson (2006) gather data for the period 1792–1999 and find the same outperformance; however, they also note the effects of world wars and Marxism.

Constantinides (2008) summarizes a number of his earlier approaches to explain the equity risk premium with income shocks (Constantinides and Duffie (1996)); life-cycle issues and borrowing constraints: the young should borrow to save for retirement but cannot while retirees get most of their income from investments funded in middle age (Constantinides, Donaldson, and Mehra (2002)); and, habit formation: the autocorrelation of consumption (Constantinides (1990)).[10] Barberis and Huang (2008) show they may explain the premium if they consider loss aversion.

However, one of the most powerful explanations comes from a consideration of sampling bias. Jorion and Goetzmann (1999) suggest the equity premium is not a puzzle but arises out of survivorship bias. In particular, we investigate equity premia for active markets and thus ignore dead and sleepy markets. This may even occur without thinking — because we lack data for those markets.

Thus it seems the premium is not quite the puzzle many claim it to be; however, there is still no shortage of researchers chasing this idea.

16.8   Quiz

Try to answer these questions in five minutes. For answers with equations, just write the equations; do not evaluate them.

---

[10]The best intuitive description of habit formation comes from Schmitt-Grohé and Uribe (2008): "the more the consumer eats today, the hungrier he wakes up tomorrow."

1. (2 points) I see ADRs for Unilever's London and Amsterdam stocks trading at different prices in the US. Since these are economically the same, I should be able to make money. Suppose credit or access to capital is not an issue. Give two reasons why you might not try to arbitrage these.

2. Suppose Sears is considering spinning off Lands' End. They propose to grant 10% of the company to employees and managers now and plan to spin off the remaining 90% in three months. If the 10% (10 million shares) of Lands' End shares are trading at \$20 now and Sears has a market cap of \$1.5 billion:

    a) Prove that there is not (or is) a violation of the Law of One Price.

    b) Why might this situation occur?

3. How is survivorship bias relevant to the equity premium puzzle?

4. The equity premium puzzle studies why stock market returns tend to outpace what we would expect given market volatility and reasonable levels of risk-aversion λ. Jorion and Goetzmann (1999) suggest survivorship bias plays a role.

    a) How would this be so?

    b) Jorion and Goetzmann criticized the equity premium puzzle because it ignores counterexamples: countries where survivorship bias was an issue. Name two countries that (currently or historically) would be such counterexamples. If historically, give dates.

5. What is fundamental risk?

6. What does fundamental risk mean for arbitrageurs?

7. Limits to arbitrage occur because investors may behave irrationally: T F.

8. Which humans do better at trading: those who are emotional and excitable or those who are less emotional? What does this imply are the effects of the increasing prevalence of computerized trading?

9. What are three types of uncertainty humans perceive?

16.9   Exercises

Instruction

We will download data for a few stocks to explore limits to arbitrage.

- "Siamese Twin" ADRs: Unilever[11], Reed/Elsevier, BHP Billiton
  (`UN, UL, RELX, RENX, BHP, BBL`)

---

[11]Unilever has announced that they are moving their headquarters to Rotterdam; however, they have (so far) said they intend to keep the dual-listing of shares.

- Indices: S&P 500, Russell 2000 (getSymbols from Yahoo: ^GSPC, ^RUT)
- ETFs (getSymbols from Yahoo: SPY, IWM)
- TED Spread (Quandl: FRED/TEDRATE)

1. To explore limits to arbitrage, we will look at ADRs for "Siamese Twin" shares — stocks which are listed on different exchanges and are not convertible into one another but are economically identical.

a) The shares are not always equivalent on a 1:1 basis. Given the following ratios, compute the average weighted price difference for each of the twin pairs: UN vs UL, RELX vs RENX, and BHP vs BBL.

Ticker	UN	UL	RELX	RENX	BHP	BBL
Ownership	50%	50%	52.9%	47.1%	50%	50%
Ratio (weights)	1:	1	1.12:	1	1:	1

b) Compute the average absolute value of those price differences. How does it differ from the preceding answer; and, what does that tell you?
c) Plot the price differences together using R like so: plot(w.un*un-w.ul*ul).
d) How often do the price differences cross zero for each of the twin pairs? What does that imply for an average time between crossings?
e) Do the crossings occur more frequently in certain states of the macroeconomy?

2. We can further explore limits to arbitrage by looking at ETFs versus the indices on stocks underlying the ETF — specifically SPX vs SPY and RUT vs IWM. In both these cases, the ratio is 1:1.

a) Compute the average absolute value of those price differences. How does it differ from the preceding answer; and, what does that tell you?
b) Plot the price differences together using R like so: plot(spx-spy).
c) How often do the price differences cross zero for each of the twin pairs? What does that imply for an average time between crossings?
d) Do the crossings occur more frequently in certain states of the macroeconomy?

3. Do mispricings/divergences tend to happen at the same time? Why might this be?

4. Are these differences tradeable? When might they not be? How would you assess the tradeability of a discrepancy?

R Code

```
library(xts)
library(quantmod)
library(Quandl)

# Get TED spread
ted <- Quandl("FRED/TEDRATE", type="xts")/100
```

```
colnames(ted) <- c("TED")

# Get S&P 500, Russell 2000, and ETF returns
adj.close <- 6   # 6th field is adjusted close
equity.tickers <- c("^GSPC","^RUT","SPY","IWM","UN","UL","RELX","RENX","BHP","BBL")
prices <- getSymbols(equity.tickers[1], source="yahoo", auto.assign=FALSE,
                     return.class="xts")[,adj.close]
for (i in 2:length(equity.tickers)) {
  prices.tmp <- getSymbols(equity.tickers[i], source="yahoo",
                     auto.assign=FALSE, return.class="xts")[,adj.close]
  prices <- cbind(prices, prices.tmp)
}
equity.names <- c("SPX","RUT","SPY","IWM","UN","UL","RELX","RENX","BHP","BBL")
colnames(prices) <- equity.names

# compute differences

# Now we join all of the datasets together
alldata.full <- cbind(ted, differences)["2007/"]
```

References

Allen, Franklin et al. *Market Efficiency and Limits to Arbitrage: Evidence from the Biggest Short Squeeze in History.* Working Paper 2977019. SSRN, May 29, 2017. DOI: 10.2139/ssrn.2977019.

Back, Kerry and Shmuel Baruch. "Information in Securities Markets: Kyle Meets Glosten and Milgrom". *Econometrica* 72.2 (2004), pp. 433–465. DOI: 10.1111/j.1468-0262.2004.00497.x.

Banz, Rolf W. "The Relationship Between Return and Market Value of Common Stocks". *Journal of Financial Economics* 9.1 (1981), pp. 3–18. DOI: 10.1016/0304-405X(81)90018-0.

Barber, Brad M. and Terrance Odean. "Boys Will Be Boys: Gender, Overconfidence, and Common Stock Investment". *Quarterly Journal of Economics* 116.1 (2001), pp. 261–292. DOI: 10.1162/003355301556400.

Barber, Brad M. et al. "Just How Much Do Individual Investors Lose by Trading?" *Review of Financial Studies* 22.2 (2009), pp. 609–632. DOI: 10.1093/rfs/hhn046.

Barberis, Nicholas and Ming Huang. "The Loss Aversion/Narrow Framing Approach to the Equity Premium Puzzle". In: *Handbook of the Equity Risk Premium.* Ed. by Rajnish Mehra. Amsterdam: Elsevier Science, 2008, pp. 199–229.

Barberis, Nicholas, Ming Huang, and Tano Santos. "Prospect Theory and Asset Prices". *Quarterly Journal of Economics* 116.1 (2001), pp. 1–53. DOI: 10.1162/003355301556310.

Barberis, Nicholas C. "Thirty Years of Prospect Theory in Economics: A Review and Assessment". *Journal of Economic Perspectives* 27.1 (2013), pp. 173–196. DOI: 10.1257/jep.27.1.173.

Behrens, Timothy E.J. et al. "Learning the Value of Information in an Uncertain World". *Nature Neuroscience* 10.9 (2007), pp. 1214–1221. DOI: 10.1038/nn1954.

Benos, Alexandros V. "Aggressiveness and Survival of Overconfident Traders". *Journal of Financial Markets* 1.3–4 (1998), pp. 353–383. DOI: 10.1016/S1386-4181(97)00010-4.

Bossaerts, Peter, Cary Frydman, and John Ledyard. "The Speed of Information Revelation and Eventual Price Quality in Markets with Insiders: Comparing Two Theories". *Review of Finance* 18.1 (2014), pp. 1–22. DOI: 10.1093/rof/rfs049.

Bossaerts, Peter and Carsten Murawski. "From Behavioral Economics To Neuroeconomics To Decision Neuroscience: The Ascent of Biology in Research on Human Decision Making". *Current Opinion in Behavioral Sciences* 5 (2015), pp. 37–42. DOI: 10.1016/j.cobeha.2015.07.001.

Brunnermeier, Markus K. and Lasse Heje Pedersen. "Market Liquidity and Funding Liquidity". *Review of Financial Studies* 22.6 (2009), pp. 2201–2238. DOI: 10.1093/rfs/hhn098.

Buckholtz, Joshua W. and Andreas Meyer-Lindenberg. "MAOA and the Neurogenetic Architecture of Human Aggression". *Trends in Neurosciences* 31.3 (2008), pp. 120–129. DOI: 10.1016/j.tins.2007.12.006.

Burton, Edwin and Sunit N. Shah. *Behavioral Finance: Understanding the Social, Cognitive, and Economic Debates.* New York: Wiley, 2013.

Coates, John. *The Hour Between Dog and Wolf: How Risk Taking Transforms Us, Body and Mind.* New York: Penguin, 2013.

Coates, John M., Mark Gurnell, and Aldo Rustichini. "Second-to-Fourth Digit Ratio Predicts Success Among High-Frequency Financial Traders". *Proceedings of the National Academy of Sciences of the United States of America* 106.2 (2009), pp. 623–628. DOI: 10.1073/pnas.0810907106.

Coates, John M., Mark Gurnell, and Zoltan Sarnyai. "From Molecule to Market: Steroid Hormones and Financial Risk-Taking". *Philosophical Transactions of the Royal Society B* 365.1538 (2010), pp. 331–343. DOI: 10.1098/rstb.2009.0193.

Coates, John M. and Joe Herbert. "Endogenous Steroids and Financial Risk Taking on a London Trading Floor". *Proceedings of the National Academy of Sciences of the United States of America* 105.16 (2008), pp. 6167–6172. DOI: 10.1073/pnas.0704025105.

Coates, John M. and Lionel Page. "A Note on Trader Sharpe Ratios". *PLoS ONE* 4.11 (2009), e8036. DOI: 10.1371/journal.pone.0008036.

Coeurdacier, Nicolas and Pierre-Olivier Gourinchas. "When Bonds Matter: Home Bias in Goods and Assets". *Journal of Monetary Economics* 82 (2016), pp. 119–137. DOI: 10.1016/j.jmoneco.2016.07.005.

Constantinides, George M. "Habit Formation: A Resolution of the Equity Premium Puzzle". *Journal of Political Economy* 98.3 (1990), pp. 519–543. DOI: 10.1086/261693.

— "Understanding the Equity Risk Premium Puzzle". In: *Handbook of the Equity Risk Premium.* Ed. by Rajnish Mehra. Amsterdam: Elsevier Science, 2008, pp. 331–359.

Constantinides, George M., John B. Donaldson, and Rajnish Mehra. "Junior Can't

Borrow: A New Perspective on the Equity Premium Puzzle". *Quarterly Journal of Economics* 117.1 (2002), pp. 269–296. DOI: 10.1162/003355302753399508.

Constantinides, George M. and Darrell Duffie. "Asset Pricing with Heterogeneous Consumers". *Journal of Political Economy* 104.2 (1996), pp. 219–240. DOI: 10.1086/262023.

Cooper, Ian and Evi Kaplanis. "Home Bias in Equity Portfolios, Inflation Hedging, and International Capital Market Equilibrium". *Review of Financial Studies* 7.1 (1994), pp. 45–60. DOI: 10.1093/rfs/7.1.45.

Coval, Joshua D. and Tobias J. Moskowitz. "Home Bias at Home: Local Equity Preference in Domestic Portfolios". *Journal of Finance* 54.6 (1999), pp. 2045–2073. DOI: 10.1111/0022-1082.00181.

Cronqvist, Henrik and Richard H. Thaler. "Design Choices in Privatized Social-Security Systems: Learning from the Swedish Experience". *American Economic Review: Papers and Proceedings* 94.2 (2004), pp. 424–428. DOI: 10.1257/0002828041301632.

Cueva, Carlos et al. "Cortisol and Testosterone Increase Financial Risk Taking and May Destabilize Markets". *Scientific Reports* 5 (2015), p. 11206. DOI: 10.1038/srep11206.

De Martino, Benedetto et al. "In the Mind of the Market: Theory of Mind Biases Value Computation during Financial Bubbles". *Neuron* 79.6 (2013), pp. 122–1231. DOI: 10.1016/j.neuron.2013.07.003.

Diamond, Douglas W. and Robert E. Verrecchia. "Constraints on Short-selling and Asset Price Adjustment to Private Information". *Journal of Financial Economics* 18 (1987), pp. 277–311. DOI: 10.1016/0304-405X(87)90042-0.

Eklund, Anders, Thomas E. Nichols, and Hans Knutsson. "Cluster Failure: Why fMRI Inferences for Spatial Extent Have Inflated False-Positive Rates". *Proceedings of the National Academy of Sciences of the United States of America* 113.28 (2006), pp. 7900–7905. DOI: 10.1073/pnas.1602413113.

Fama, Eugene F. and Kenneth R. French. "The Equity Premium". *Journal of Finance* 57.2 (2002), pp. 637–659. DOI: 10.1111/1540-6261.00437.

French, Kenneth R. and James M. Poterba. "Investor Diversification and International Equity Markets". *American Economic Review: Papers and Proceedings* 81.2 (1991), pp. 222–226. URL: http://www.jstor.org/stable/2006858.

Friedman, Milton and Leonard J. Savage. "The Utility Analysis of Choices Involving Risk". *Journal of Political Economy* 56.4 (1948), pp. 279–304. DOI: 10.1086/256692.

Frydman, Cary et al. "MAOA-L Carriers Are Better at Making Optimal Financial Decisions under Risk". *Proceedings of the Royal Society B* 278.1714 (2011), pp. 2053–2059. DOI: 10.1098/rspb.2010.2304.

Frydman, Cary et al. "Using Neural Data to Test a Theory of Investor Behavior: An Application to Realization Utility". *Journal of Finance* 69.2 (2014), pp. 907–946. DOI: 10.1111/jofi.12126.

Fung, Bowen J., Stefan Bode, and Carsten Murawski. "High Monetary Reward Rates and Caloric Rewards Decrease Temporal Persistence". *Proceedings of the Royal Society B* 284.1849 (2017), p. 20162759. DOI: 10.1098/rspb.2016.2759.

Gervais, Simon and Terrance Odean. "Learning to Be Overconfident". *Review of Financial Studies* 14.1 (2001), pp. 1–27. DOI: 10.1093/rfs/14.1.1.

Glosten, Lawrence R. and Paul R. Milgrom. "Ask and Transaction Prices in a Specialist Market with Heterogeneously Informed Traders". *Journal of Financial Economics* 14 (1985), pp. 71–100. DOI: 10.1016/0304-405X(85)90044-3.

Goetzmann, William N. and Roger G. Ibbotson. "History and the Equity Risk Premium". In: *The Equity Risk Premium: Essays and Explorations*. Ed. by William N. Goetzmann and Roger G. Ibbotson. Oxford: Oxford University Press, 2006, pp. 25–40.

Jorion, Philippe and William N. Goetzmann. "Global Stock Markets in the Twentieth Century". *Journal of Finance* 54.3 (1999), pp. 953–980. DOI: 10.1111/0022-1082.00133.

Kahneman, Daniel and Amos Tversky. "Prospect Theory: An Analysis of Decision under Risk". *Econometrica* 47.2 (1979), pp. 263–292. DOI: 10.2307/1914185.

Kandasamy, Narayanan et al. "Interoceptive Ability Predicts Survival on a London Trading Floor". *Scientific Reports* 6 (2016), p. 32986. DOI: 10.1038/srep32986.

Kang, Jun-Koo and René M. Stulz. "Why Is There a Home Bias? An Analysis of Foreign Portfolio Equity Ownership in Japan". *Journal of Financial Economics* 46.1 (1997), pp. 3–28. DOI: 10.1016/S0304-405X(97)00023-8.

Khorana, Ajay. "Performance Changes Following Top Management Turnover: Evidence from Open-End Mutual Funds". *Journal of Financial and Quantitative Analysis* 36.3 (2001), pp. 371–393. DOI: 10.2307/2676288.

Kirman, Alan, Pierre Livet, and Miriam Teschl, eds. *Philosophical Transactions of the Royal Society B* 365.1538 (Jan. 27, 2010): *Rationality and Emotions*.

Knutson, Brian et al. "Nucleus Accumbens Activation Mediates the Influence of Reward Cues on Financial Risk Taking". *Neuroreport* 19.5 (2008), pp. 509–513. DOI: 10.1097/WNR.0b013e3282f85c01.

Kruger, Justin and David Dunning. "Unskilled and Unaware of It: How Difficulties in Recognizing One's Own Incompetence Lead to Inflated Self-Assessments". *Journal of Personality and Social Psychology* 77.6 (1999), pp. 1121–1134. DOI: 10.1037/0022-3514.77.6.1121.

Kuhnen, Camelia M. and Brian Knutson. "The Neural Basis of Financial Risk Taking". *Neuron* 47.5 (2005), pp. 763–770. DOI: 10.1016/j.neuron.2005.08.008.

Kyle, Albert S. "Continuous Auctions and Insider Trading". *Econometrica* 53.6 (1985), pp. 1315–1336. DOI: 10.2307/1913210.

Lakonishok, Josef et al. "Window Dressing by Pension Fund Managers". *American Economic Review: Papers and Proceedings* 81.2 (1991), pp. 227–231. DOI: 10.3386/w3617.

Lefèvre, Edwin. *Reminiscences of a Stock Operator*. New York: Doubleday, Doran & Company, 1923.

Levy, Haim and Moshe Levy. "The Home Bias is Here to Stay". *Journal of Banking and Finance* 47 (2014), pp. 29–40. DOI: 10.1016/j.jbankfin.2014.06.020.

Lo, Andrew W., Harry Mamaysky, and Jiang Wang. "Foundations of Technical Analysis: Computational Algorithms, Statistical Inference, and Empirical Implementation". *Journal of Finance Papers and Proceedings* 55.4 (2000), pp. 1705–1765. DOI: 10.1111/0022-1082.00265.

Mangeldorf, Tyson. "Porsche and VW: What the Hell Happened?" *Automobile Magazine* (Oct. 26, 2009). Retrieved on 9 October 2017 from http://www.automobilemag.com/news/porsche-and-volkswagen-what-happened/.

Maymin, Philip Z. "Self-Imposed Limits of Arbitrage". *Journal of Applied Finance* 21.2 (2011), pp. 88–105.

McKay, Adam. *Anchorman: The Legend of Ron Burgundy.* Produced by Judd Apatow. 2004.

Mehra, Rajnish and Edward C. Prescott. "The Equity Premium: A Puzzle". *Journal of Monetary Economics* 15.2 (1985), pp. 145–161. DOI: 10.1016/0304-3932(85)90061-3.

Miller, Merton H. "Behavioral Rationality in Finance: The Case of Dividends". *Journal of Business* 59.4, Part 2: The Behavioral Foundations of Economic Theory (1986), S451–S468. DOI: 10.1086/296380.

Mishra, Anil V. and Ronald A. Ratti. "Home Bias and Cross Border Taxation". *Journal of International Money and Finance* 32.1 (2013), pp. 169–193. DOI: 10.1016/j.jimonfin.2012.04.004.

Odean, Terrance. "Are Investors Reluctant to Realize Their Losses?" *Journal of Finance* 53.5 (1998), pp. 1775–1798. DOI: 10.1111/0022-1082.00072.

— "Do Investors Trade Too Much?" *American Economic Review* 89.5 (1999), pp. 1279–1298. DOI: 10.1257/aer.89.5.1279.

O'Doherty, John P. and Colin C. Camerer, eds. *Current Opinion in Behavioral Sciences* 5 (2015): *Neuroeconomics.*

Page, Lionel and John M. Coates. "Winner and Loser Effects in Human Competitions. Evidence from Equally Matched Tennis Players". *Evolution and Human Behavior* 38 (4 2017), pp. 530–535. DOI: 10.1016/j.evolhumbehav.2017.02.003.

Payzan-LeNestour, Elise et al. "The Neural Representation of Unexpected Uncertainty during Value-Based Decision Making". *Neuron* 79.1 (2013), pp. 191–201. DOI: 10.1016/j.neuron.2013.04.037.

Preuschoff, Kerstin, Steven R. Quartz, and Peter Bossaerts. "Human Insula Activation Reflects Risk Prediction Errors As Well As Risk". *Journal of Neuroscience* 28.11 (2008), pp. 2745–2752. DOI: 10.1523/jneurosci.4286-07.2008.

Preuschoff, Kerstin, Bernard Marius 't Hart, and Wolfgang Einhäuser. "Pupil Dilation Signals Surprise: Evidence for Noradrenaline's Role in Decision Making". *Frontiers in Neuroscience* 5 (2011), p. 115. DOI: 10.3389/fnins.2011.00115.

Reinganum, Marc R. "The Anomalous Stock Market Behavior of Small Firms in January: Empirical Tests for Tax-Loss Selling Effects". *Journal of Financial Economics* 12.1 (1983), pp. 89–104. DOI: 10.1016/0304-405X(83)90029-6.

Roll, Richard. "A Possible Explanation of the Small Firm Effect". *Journal of Finance* 36.4 (1981), pp. 879–888. DOI: 10.1111/j.1540-6261.1981.tb04890.x.

Ross, Stephen A. "Neoclassical Finance, Alternative Finance and the Closed End Fund Puzzle". *European Financial Management* 8.2 (2002), pp. 129–137. DOI: 10.1111/1468-036X.00181.

Sapra, Steve, Laura E. Beavin, and Paul J. Zak. "A Combination of Dopamine Genes Predicts Success by Professional Wall Street Traders". *PLoS ONE* 7.1 (2012), e30844. DOI: 10.1371/journal.pone.0030844.

Schmitt-Grohé, Stephanie and Martin Uribe. "Habit Persistence". In: *New Palgrave Dictionary of Economics*. Ed. by Steven Durlauf and Lawrence E. Blume. 2nd ed. New York: Palgrave Macmillan, 2008. DOI: 10.1007/978-1-349-58802-2.

Shiller, Robert J. "Consumption, Asset Markets and Macroeconomic Fluctuations". *Carnegie-Rochester Conference Series on Public Policy* 17 (1982), pp. 203–238. DOI: 10.1016/0167-2231(82)90046-X.

Shleifer, Andrei. *Inefficient Markets: A Introduction to Behavioral Finance*. Oxford: Oxford University Press, 2000.

— "Psychologists at the Gate: A Review of Daniel Kahneman's *Thinking, Fast and Slow*". *Journal of Economic Literature* 50.4 (2012), pp. 1080–1091. DOI: 10.1257/jel.50.4.1080.

Shleifer, Andrei and Robert W. Vishny. "The Limits of Arbitrage". *Journal of Finance* 52.1 (1997), pp. 35–55. DOI: 10.2307/2329555.

Simon, Herbert A. "A Behavioral Model of Rational Choice". *Quarterly Journal of Economics* 69.1 (1955), pp. 99–118. DOI: 10.2307/1884852.

Stulz, René M. "On the Effects of Barriers to International Investment". *Journal of Finance* 36.4 (1981), pp. 923–934. DOI: 10.2307/2327556.

Tesar, Linda L. and Ingrid M. Werner. "Home Bias and High Turnover". *Journal of International Money and Finance* 14.4 (1995), pp. 467–492. DOI: 10.1016/0261-5606(95)00023-8.

Thaler, Richard H. and Cass R. Sunstein. *Nudge: Improving Decisions about Health, Wealth, and Happiness*. New Haven, CT: Yale University Press, 2008.

Tuckman, Bruce and Jean-Luc Vila. "Arbitrage With Holding Costs: A Utility-Based Approach". *Journal of Finance* 47.4 (1992), pp. 1283–1302. DOI: 10.2307/2328940.

Tversky, Amos and Daniel Kahneman. "Advances in Prospect Theory: Cumulative Representation of Uncertainty". *Journal of Risk and Uncertainty* 5.4 (1992), pp. 297–323. DOI: 10.1007/BF00122574.

Williams, Leanne M. et al. "A Polymorphism of the MAOA Gene is Associated with Emotional Brain Markers and Personality Traits on an Antisocial Index". *Neuropsychopharmacology* 34.7 (2009), pp. 1797–1809. DOI: 10.1038/npp.2009.1.

Zaller, John and Stanley Feldman. "A Simple Theory of the Survey Response: Answering Questions versus Revealing Preferences". *American Journal of Political Science* 36.3 (1992), pp. 579–616. DOI: 10.2307/2111583.

Chapter 17

Global Investing

We have spent a lot of time discussing problems with the CAPM and factor models. One of the most persistent sources of criticism is that researchers are not looking at the complete market portfolio. In discussing microfoundations, we even saw that investors are subject to home bias and that this may make sense to some extent. However, even with some sensible explanations, we find that investors should be investing more beyond their home country.

Therefore, we should discuss investing globally. The purpose of this chapter is to discuss global investing, explore risk factors, and consider some models for less-easily-modeled risks.

As a side note: we are going to be referring to many countries and this could get unwieldy at times. Therefore, we will sometimes use "country codes" such as AU, CA, CH, CN, DE, GB, ID, IE, IN, JP, NZ, US, and ZA.[1] Section 0.5 (at the front) has a helpful reference list of common codes.

17.1   Introduction

Obviously, the US is not the only place you can invest. If you are reading this in Canada or Mexico, South America, Asia, Europe, Africa, or Oceania, you know this. You have also probably read scores of books discussing investments which only focus on the US. While I have tried to avoid a US-centric focus, it makes sense to specifically have a non-US focus in this chapter to highlight opportunities available outside of the world's largest equity market.[2]

---

[1]These are properly ISO 3166-1 alpha-2 codes and not technically country codes since there are codes for some territories, autonomous regions, and disputed areas. The codes listed are, if you do not know: Australia, Canada, Switzerland, China, Germany, the UK, Indonesia, Ireland, India, Japan, New Zealand, the US, and South Africa.

[2]For those interested in foreign stocks: stock tickers in Asia and parts of the Middle East are often numbers or, in a few cases, mixes of letters and numbers.

17.1.1   Global Brands

You probably unwittingly know many well-run international companies already. Table 17.1 lists a number of globally-known international brands. Due to trade, much of our world involves brands from around the globe. This should also make clear that well-run companies exist worldwide. In that case, why not invest in them?

While some of these firms are private, private firms still borrow from banks or issue bonds. Therefore, the possibilities for investment still exist. Furthermore, many other well-run global firms have names that are not so well-recognized.

17.2   Global Markets

Having firms organized enough to develop well-known brands is not sufficient for investment. The natural question after seeing there are well-run companies abroad is: are the markets sufficiently large and liquid to make investing sensible?

17.2.1   Global Financing

Globally, firms are not all equally likely to finance their operations with equity or bonds. For example, firms in Germany have traditionally been more likely to use bank financing than capital market financing. Nonetheless, it is informative to look at the sizes of stock, corporate bond, and bank corporate lending markets. Figures 17.1–17.3 show the sizes of these markets.[3]

There are a few details we can note from these figures. Most obvious is the rapid growth of Chinese capital markets: While the stock and corporate bond markets seem to have evolved at similar speeds, bank lending to firms has grown even faster. Hong Kong's stock market has also grown quickly, likely due to trade with and outsourcing to China. We can also see that the US and Canadian firms tend to have more stock market financing versus bond or loan financing. British, German, Italian, Japanese, Korean, and Australian firms tend to use more debt financing with a preference for bank loans; and, this preference is especially strong in Germany and Japan. French and Dutch firms also prefer debt financing, but they get more financing from bonds than loans. Taiwanese and South African firms use far more equity financing than bonds or bank loans.

Finally, we might notice that while the Swiss stock market is about 50% larger than the bank loan market, their corporate bond market is very small. However, the corporate bond market is unusually large in Luxembourg and the Cayman Islands. Many Swiss firms (which are outside the EU) access the bond markets by selling bonds to European investors via Luxembourg (which is in the EU). According to

---

[3]The BIS data for corporate bonds require some cleaning. Based on Gruić and Wooldridge (2012), I used the totals for financial and non-financial firms if they are all that is available; the domestic and international numbers if they were all that was available; and, if all figures were available, I used the maximum of the totals or domestic+international figures before 2013 and the totals from 2013 onward.

Canada (CA) Circle K, On the Run (Couche-Tard) • Bombardier • Fairmont, Raffles, Swissôtel • Four Seasons Hotels • Lululemon • Burger King, Popeye's, Tim Horton's (Restaurant Brands) • TD Ameritrade
Mexico (MX) StraightTalk (América Móvil) • Arnold, Sara Lee, Thomas (Grupo Bimbo) • Borden Milk (Grupo Lala) • TracFone
Brazil (BR) Embraer • Chiquita (Safra) • Vale
Austria (AT) Red Bull • Swarovski
Denmark (DK) ECCO • LEGO • Maersk
Finland (FI) Arc'teryx, Atomic, Salomon, Wilson (Amer Sports) • Fiskars • Nokia • Rovio
France (FR) Dannon, Evian (Danone) • Hermès • Gucci, Puma (Kering) • Chanel • Hennessey, Louis Vuitton, Moët & Chandon (LVMH) • Lancôme, Maybelline, NYX (L'Oréal) • Citroën, Peugeot (PSA Group)
Germany (DE) Adidas • Hofer, Trader Joe's (Aldi) • Bayer • Mini, Rolls Royce (BMW) • Mercedes Benz, Smart (Daimler) • DHL (Deutsche Post) • T-Mobile (Deutsche Telekom) • Audi, Bentley, Bugatti, Ducati, Lamborghini, MAN, SEAT, Škoda, Porsche (Volkswagen)
Italy (IT) Benetton • De'Longhi • Ferrari • Moleskine
Netherlands (NL) Heineken • KPMG • Philips • Randstad
Spain (ES) Pull & Bear, Zara (Inditex) • MANGO (Punto Fa)
Sweden (SE) Electrolux • Elfa • H&M • IKEA • Saab
Switzerland (CH) Nestlé • Cartier, Dunhill, Montblanc (Richemont) • Roche • Omega, Longines, Tissot (Swatch) • TetraPak
Turkey (TR) Beko, Grundig (Koç) • Carr's, Godiva, McVities (Yıldız)
UK (GB) Aon • AstraZeneca • BP • Body Shop • Dyson • Fiat Chrysler • HSBC • Kangol • Pret a Manger • PWC • Tesco • Virgin
China (CN) AMC (Dalian Wanda) • Lotus, Volvo (Geely) • GE Appliances, Haier, Hotpoint (Haier) • Huawei • Motorola Mobility (Lenovo)
Hong Kong (HK) 3, Watson's (CK Hutchison) • HSBC • Mandarin Oriental Hotel (Jardine Matheson) • Peninsula Hotel
India (IN) Jaguar, Land Rover (Tata)
Japan (JP) Asics • Bridgestone • Helmut Lang, Theory, Uniqlo (Fast Retailing) • 7-11 (Ito Yokado) • Acura (Honda) • Mazda • Infiniti (Nissan) • Shiseido • Sony • Subaru • Daihatsu, Hino, Lexus (Toyota)
Korea (KR) Fila • Guylian (Lotte) • Kia (Hyundai) • LG • Samsung
Malaysia (MY) Shangri-La Hotels
Taiwan (TW) Acer • ASUS • Giant Bicycles • HTC
Australia (AU) Billabong • Breville • Coogi

Table 17.1: List of economies with ISO code and some globally-known brands (with parent firm in parentheses for multiple brands).

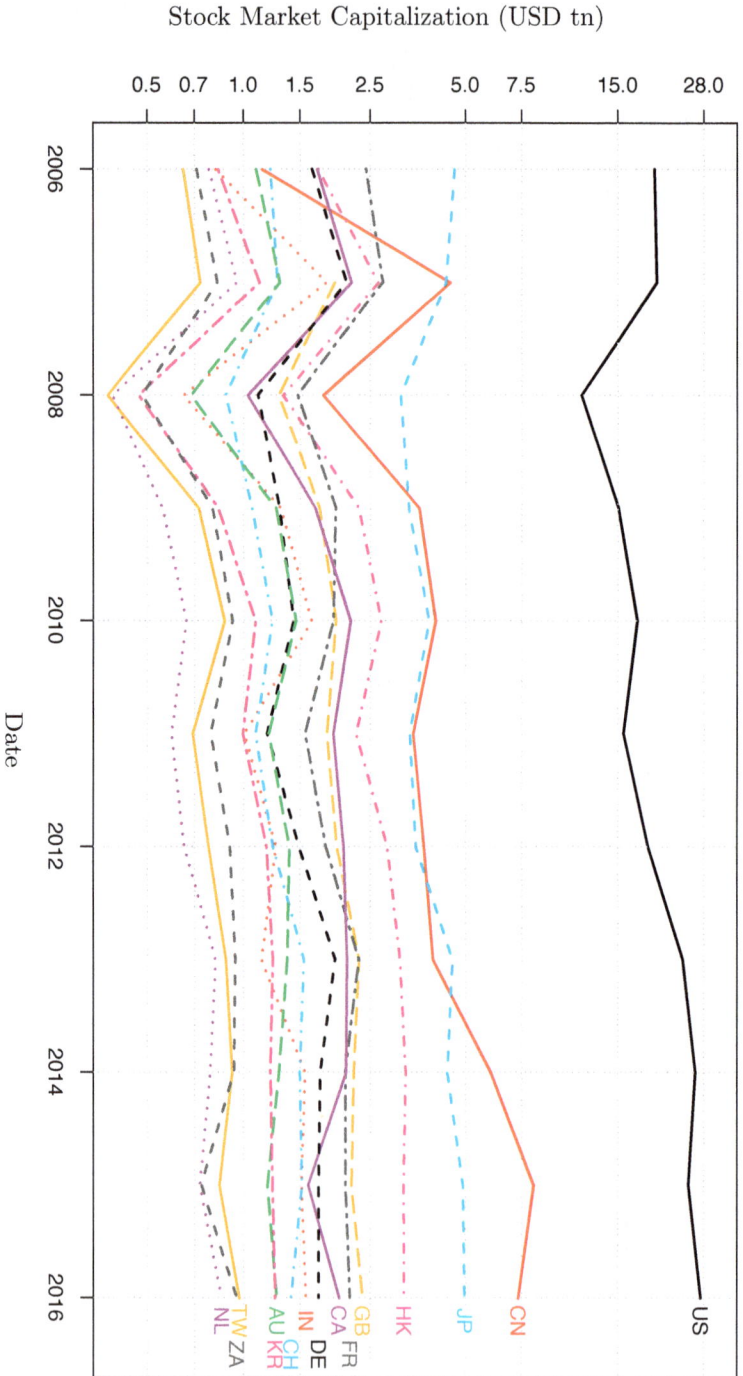

Figure 17.1: Top fifteen global stock markets (as of 2016) by capitalization of domestic listings in trillions of USD over time. Data from World Federation of Exchanges (Table 1.1), LSE Group, Nasdaq OMX, Taiwan and Taipei stock exchanges.

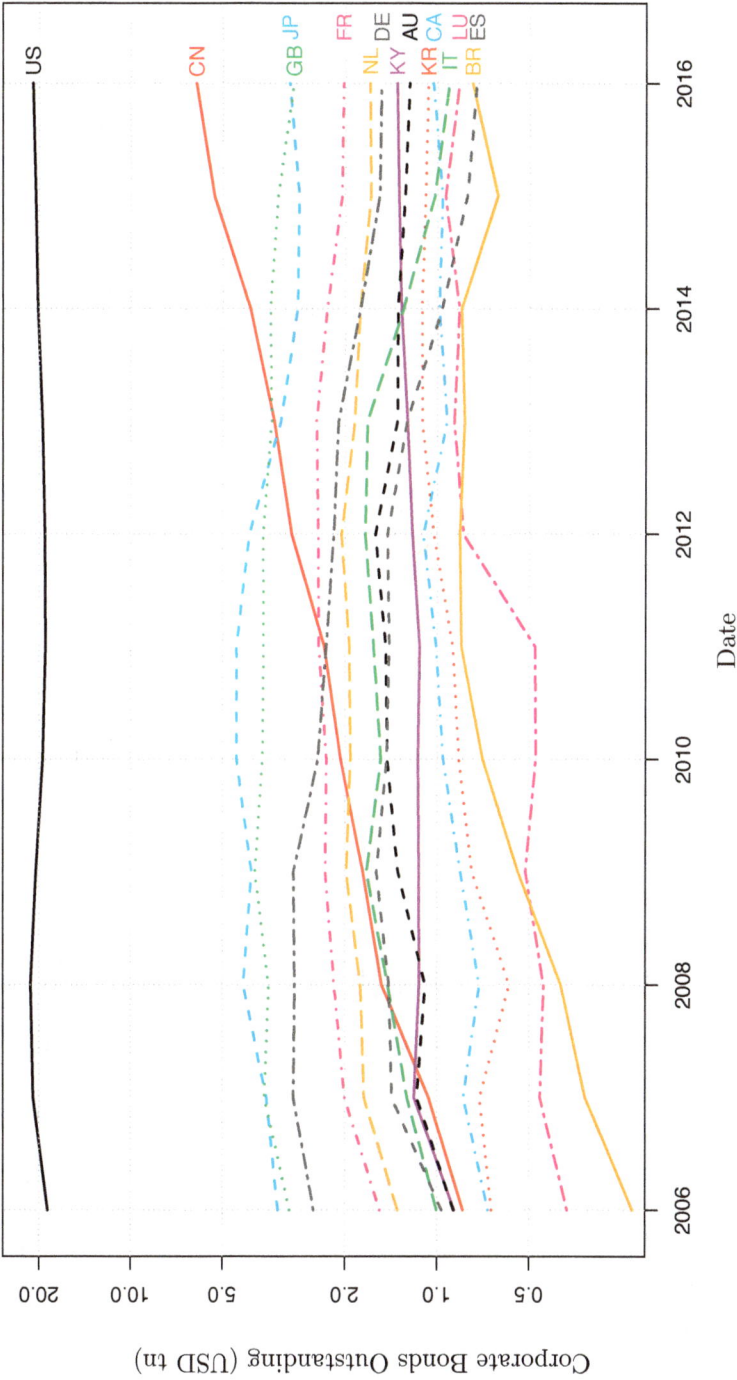

Figure 17.2: Top fifteen global corporate bond markets (as of 2016) by outstanding notional in trillions of USD over time. Outstanding notional includes financial and non-financial firms. Data from Bank for International Settlements (Table C1) and author's calculations.

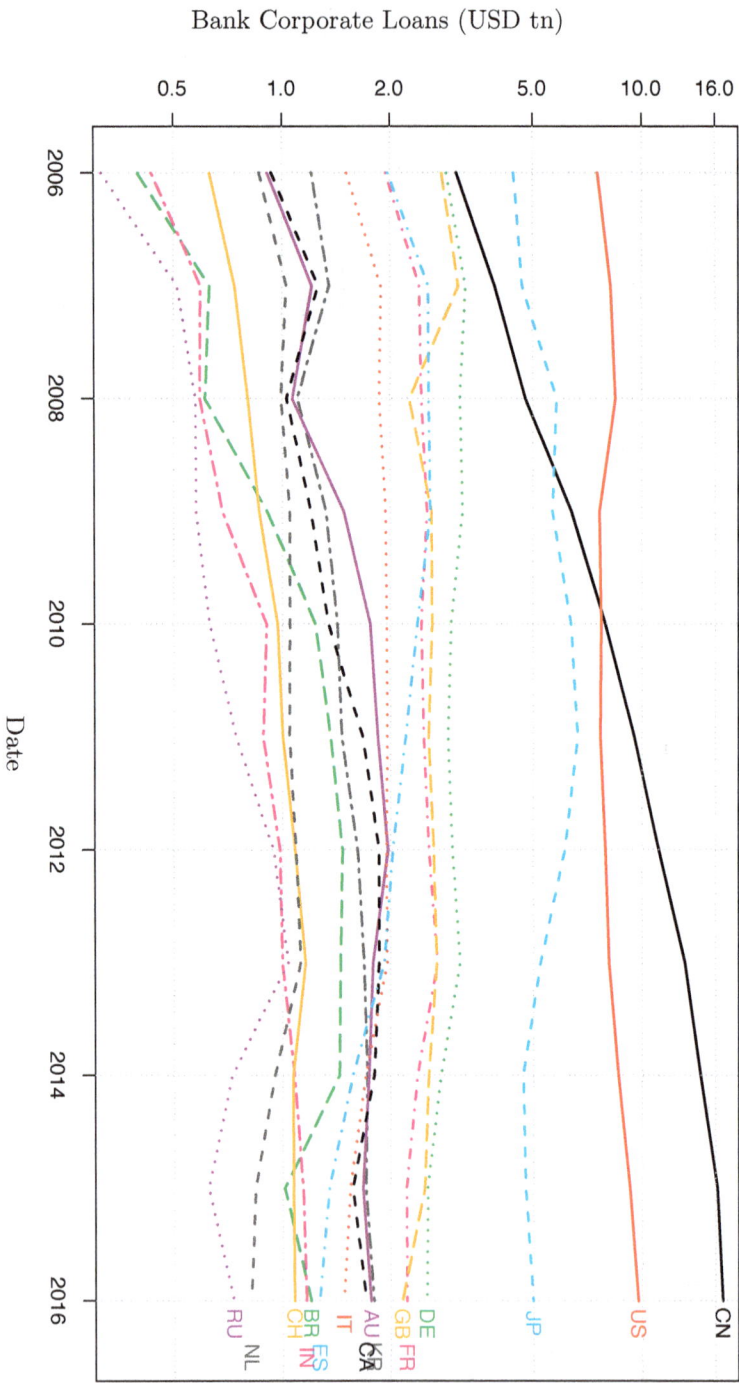

Figure 17.3: Top fifteen global bank corporate lending markets by loans outstanding in trillions of USD over time. Loans outstanding excludes financial firms since interbank lending is large, fluid, and highly variable. Data from Bank for International Settlements (Table F2.5).

FDFA (2017), 10% of Luxembourg's trade in services is with Switzerland; and, Swiss banks have 14% of the Luxembourg fund market. As for the Cayman Islands: many Swiss insurers and re-insurers run captive insurers which issue bonds (including catastrophe bonds) in the Cayman Islands.

17.2.2   Global Equity Indices

One of the repeated messages from many financial models is that passive investing in a market index is a good start to an investment strategy. Are there global or international indices we can invest in?

There are no currency indices which have attracted significant investment: different investors have different FX exposures and many funds just hedge their FX exposure. Bond indices are also rare due to numerous problems building bond indices. As discussed in Grene (2010), few bond indices have historically been built with investibility in mind. Furthermore, the large fraction of bonds which are bought and held to maturity complicates the construction of an index which is investible and representative. Commodities are sufficiently international that we probably do not need more than the few indices which are already targets for investment. Finally, while real estate might seem ripe for indexing, there are not many active indices even within the US; and, investibility is again an issue.

This leaves one asset class for which we do have many indices: equities. How do we know which index is a good benchmark? A common rule is to choose the index with the most active index futures — because institutional money managers use futures as hedging tools. We also should prefer indices with a weighting scheme close to market capitalization-weighted. See Table 17.2 for a recap of non-US indices.

17.3   Global Risks

While home bias implies investors invest sub-optimally abroad, there are real risks for would-be global investors.[4] We can categorize these risks as:

- Foreign exchange;
- Informational;
- Reporting and governance;
- Governmental and monetary policy; and,
- Political instability.

Corruption, while not a risk factor *per se*, tends to exacerbate these risks and complicate mitigating or reducing them. Investors in developed economies mostly need only worry about the first two or three risks; however, as one invests more broadly, the other risks become less ignorable.

---

[4]Home bias is like the **Feldstein-Horioka puzzle**: that investors do not invest in the highest-return economy leading all economies to similar returns.

Index	Locale	Comments
S&P GSCI	Global	Production-weighted futures
Bloomberg Commodity	Global	Volume-weighted futures
MSCI EAFE	Global	Float-weighted; 21 economies
MSCI Emerging Markets	Global	Float-weighted; 24 economies
MSCI ACWI	Global	Float-weighted; 47 economies
S&P/TSX 60	Canada	60 large-cap stocks
Ibovespa	Brazil	c. 50 large-/mid-cap stocks
IPC	Mexico	35 large-cap stocks
Nikkei 225	Japan	Price-weighted; 225 large stocks
Topix	Japan	Composite of stocks
CSI 300	China	300 large-cap stocks
Hang Seng	Hong Kong	50 large-cap stocks
Straits Times	Singapore	30 large-cap stocks
ASX All Ordinaries	Australia	500 largest stocks
KOSPI	Korea	Composite of stocks
JSE Top 40	South Africa	40 large-cap stocks
Euro Stoxx 50	Eurozone	50 mega-cap stocks
Stoxx Europe 600	Eurozone	600 large-/mid-cap stocks
FTSE 100	UK	100 large-cap stocks
SMI	Switzerland	20 large-cap stocks
DAX	Germany	30 large-cap stocks
CAC 40	France	40 large-cap stocks
MIB 30	Italy	30 large-cap stocks

Table 17.2: Non-US indices commonly used by institutional investors. All have active futures traded on them, easing hedging of market exposure. Most are large-cap indices while a few capture more of the market. The MSCI All Country World Index (ACWI) includes the US; Canada; Europe, Australasia, and Far East (EAFE); and, Emerging Markets economies with some hurdles for equities based on floating shares.

The risk of changing FX rates is the most tractable of all these risks — which is why USD 5 tn worth of currencies trade every day, according to Graham (2016).

Informational risks are one of the most obvious barriers to investment: access to information from outside the country may be tough; and, even when the internet has made this information more available, it may not be translated or easily searchable without knowing the language.

Reporting and **governance risks** are the next barrier. Firms may not produce regular financial reports; the reporting standards may differ from those in other countries; and, standards of corporate governance may differ. For example: It is illegal for US firms to pay bribes to foreign officials; it is not illegal for Swiss firms to do so. On the other hand, US firms are much more aggressive about incentivizing CEOs to increase the firm's stock price. When that incentive is based on one day's price, however, there is an incentive for the CEO to push the stock price up on that day to trigger a (possibly large) bonus payout. That is not sound management.

These differences in governance are relatively minor compared to the governance issues of business practices common to some parts of the world. In one large economy, many factories pay employees in cash, underreport earnings, and selectively repatriate profits from shell companies abroad. How can one invest in a firm when the actual expenses and revenues are hidden?

Governmental policy can be an extreme source of risk. **Expropriation risk**, the risk of having firm assets seized by the government, was once a major concern. However, Minor (1994) shows this risk has declined and is likely to remain low. Henisz and Zelner (2010) discuss how policy and regulatory risk is increasingly a concern since it can be used to extract even more value than expropriation.

In many countries, **monetary policy** may not be sensible or free of political interference. History shows us that when politicians gain control of the mint, they often run the presses or set rates to enrich themselves and their friends. This has led to inflation or worse: hyperinflation, economic ruin, and a descent into chaos.

Political instability is another risk. Negotiations firms make with one government may be canceled by another. Furthermore, it is difficult for an economy to grow when businesses are uncertain what policies they might face over time. That reluctance to deploy capital reduces economic growth.

Ultimately, these risks are greatly affected by political leadership. While financiers often note how powerless politicians are to direct markets, Jones and Olken (2005) show clearly that political leadership matters for economic growth. For sobering accounts of when political leadership fails and these risks run amok, I recommend reading Godwin (2010) and Rogers (2010) on the decline of Zimbabwe and Gallegos (2016) on the decline of Venezuela.

17.4 Assessing and Managing Global Risks

Before we can manage these risks, we must assess them. That may mean measuring, looking at rankings, or modeling. Sometimes the problem is so nebulous that all we can do is gather data and use the most powerful modeling tool of all: our human ability to subjectively reason and discern.

Foreign exchange risk is the easiest to assess and manage. Investors may hedge FX exposure with futures and other derivatives. We will discuss this in Chapter 18.

Handling informational risks is often straightforward: hire people fluent in the languages and familiar with the culture where we invest to follow the news. Ideally, they would also know accounting and governance standards to identify superior performance or possible trouble. This can be especially important in large countries such as China, India, and Indonesia where whole lexicons of nuanced language, allusion, and slang develop.

Reporting and governance risks are very difficult to assess. You cannot just ask firms if they are reporting different financial figures to the government; and, many governance issues are also management issues. If you are a shareholder, you have delegated running your firm to the managers. If you are a creditor, you have even less say over how the firm is run. . . so long as your loan is not in default.

Recall the factory owner who pays salaries in cash, keeps two sets of financial statements, and repatriates overseas profits selectively. The firm owner might use that overseas capital to invest abroad. This creates difficulties for investment managers who must, in many countries, adhere to **KYC** ("Know Your Customer") practices: the investment manager must verify investor funds do not come from illegal actions. Thus an investment fund might not be able to accept an investor as a client when it is (unwittingly) investing in the potential investor's firm.

Policy risk is the risk of value-destroying policies and regulations. Mauro (1995) shows bureaucratic efficiency is significantly related to investment in an economy; and, Young and Findley (2011) show better political governance and civil society (democracy, free and fair elections, defense of human rights) reduce the likelihood of terrorism. Investors worried about policy risk can reduce liquidity in those markets. Handling this is partly informational and partly communicating with political leaders. However, the risk cannot be completely hedged.

In most economies, dialogue is more likely on monetary and economic policy. No good central banker would tell you if they were about to raise or lower interest rates, but many will listen to you explain your investments and how certain policies might increase or reduce those investments. If the central bank has been politicized, however, dialogue is pointless. While it is easy to hedge interest-rate risk, there are no easy ways to hedge the effects of politicizing central bank decisions.

Political instability risk is very difficult to assess but also very destructive. Mo (2001) shows that political instability is the main channel through which corruption reduces economic growth. Wei (2000) shows that corruption acts like a high tax: increasing a country's corruption from the level of Singapore to that of Mexico would affect inbound investment similar to raising taxes by fifty percentage points.

One of the more surprising effects that Young and Findley (2011) show is that aid to education and health also reduces terrorism. Thus it may make sense for some firms to give to charitable causes in places they invest.

For many of these risks, the best risk management tool is simply diversification.

17.5   Quantifying Global Risks

It might seem that we have done as much as possible to manage global risks. However, over the past few years, a number of research and market developments have given us new tools and data to help quantify global risks.

17.5.1   Global Risk Indices

Our risk assessments may be aided by the development of a number of indices of global risks. Some of these are shown in Table 17.3. *The Economist* Intelligence Unit is particularly useful since they follow operational risk issues and examine situations as they arise. No corporate governance indices are listed since most are created by different camps of academics arguing about the problems of each others' indices and few indices are ever compared to actual measures of governance.

Risk	Publisher: Index
	URL
Info.	Reporters Without Borders: World Press Freedom
	http://rsf.org/en/ranking
Info.	Freedom House: Freedom of the Press
	http://freedomhouse.org/report-types/freedom-press
Policy	The Fraser Institute: Economic Freedom
	http://www.freetheworld.com
Policy	Cato Institute: Economic Freedom of the World
	http://www.cato.org/economic-freedom-world
Policy	Heritage Institute: Economic Freedom
	http://www.heritage.org/index/ranking/
Policy/	*The Economist* Intelligence Unit: Democracy
Stability	http://www.eiu.com/topic/democracy-index
Policy/	Freedom House: Freedom in the World
Stability	http://freedomhouse.org/report-types/freedom-world
Corruption	Transparency International: Global Corruption Barometer
	http://www.transparency.org/research/gcb/
Multiple	World Bank: Worldwide Governance Indicators
	http://info.worldbank.org/governance/wgi/

Table 17.3: Indices which assess various dimensions of global risk.

Many of these indices attempt to measure institution quality. As mentioned in Chapters 1 and 3, institution quality and trade have been shown to relate strongly to economic growth. For more on this, read Acemoğlu and Robinson (2013) and Dollar and Kraay (2003).

17.5.2   Data for Modeling Extreme Risks

A more recent innovation is the creation of databases tracking global sentiment, unrest, political instability, and terrorism. Some of these are developed by political scientists while others are developed by economic historians or **cliometricians**: statistical/econometric historians.

The Global Database of Events, Location, and Tone (GDELT) tracks incidents of unrest back to 1979 as well as evolutions in the tone of news and books back to 1800 (in some cases). The database originated from a project at the University of Illinois at Urbana-Champaign's National Center for Supercomputing Applications and is now supported by Google Jigsaw. GDELT is described in Leetaru and Schrodt (2013) and Leetaru (2014) and can be accessed at `http://www.gdeltproject.org`.

The Center for Systemic Peace was borne out of the Center for Global Policy at George Mason University and has many useful datasets, including: Major Episodes of Political Violence (since 1946), PITF State Failure (since 1955), Polity IV (on political regimes, since 1800), and the State Fragility Index and Matrix (since 1995). These datasets may be accessed at `http://www.systemicpeace.org/inscrdata.html`.

The Global Terrorism Database (GTD) tracks incidents of terrorism since 1970 and is a project of the National Consortium for the Study of Terrorism and Responses to Terrorism housed at the University of Maryland, College Park and supported by the US Department of Homeland Security. The GTD is described in LaFree and Dugan (2007) and can be accessed at `http://www.start.umd.edu/gtd`.

Collaborative Research Center 700 in Germany studies governance in areas of limited statehood and is supported by the German Research Foundation. They offer some data online: Event Data on Armed Conflict and Security (EDACS) and the Private Security Database (PSD) which details state use of private security and military companies. The data are described in Chojnacki et al. (2012) and Branović (2011) and may be accessed at `http://www.conflict-data.org`.

Finally, there are three sources of data on conflict among both state and non-state actors. Uppsala University maintains the Uppsala Conflict Data Program (UCDP) which is described in Kreutz (2010); Sundberg, Eck, and Kreutz (2012); and, Sundberg and Melander (2013) and is available at `http://ucdp.uu.se`. The Center for Global Economic History at Utrecht University maintains a number of datasets, including Peter Brecke's Conflict Catalog with data on violent conflicts as far back as 1400. The data are described in Brecke (1999) and are available at `http://www.cgeh.nl/data`. The International Institute for Strategic Studies maintains the Armed Conflict Database which has weekly data back to 1997 and is available at `https://acd.iiss.org`.

These data sources offer substantial promise for assessing risks that may affect global investments. For example, Chang and Zeng (2011) show the effect of terrorism on hospitality stocks is greater than on the rest of the market — and that after an event (and devaluation), hospitality stocks beat the market index by 10%–15% per annum. Greenbaum, Dugan, and LaFree (2007) show the effect of terrorism on economic growth in Italy and show that terrorism especially reduces business formation and expansion.

17.5.3 *Prediction Markets*

Perhaps the most unusual development in assessing these sorts of risk over the past few years has been the development of **prediction markets**: markets which trade Arrow-Debreu securities with payoffs related to political outcomes and other events. These markets can be used both to assess risks and even to possibly insure against those risks. (Many of these markets, however, are not very liquid.)

While Rhode and Strumpf (2004) show that betting on political outcomes has a long history, the first organized prediction market was the Iowa Political Stock Market at the University of Iowa and discussed in Forsythe et al. (1992). This market is now known as the Iowa Electronic Markets.

Many prediction markets have had trouble with politicians and regulators. Intrade, in the US, and iPredict, in New Zealand, are both shuttered exchanges which ran afoul of regulators. The Policy Analysis Market (PAM) fared worse. PAM was proposed by the US Defense Advanced Research Projects Agency as a means to reveal the probabilities of events such as unrest, terrorism, and regime change. The US Congress was outraged by the idea and killed PAM before its completion. This led Roth (2007) to note that repugnance is itself a constraint on markets. That repugnance backlash is still a threat to prediction markets.

Current markets include Nadex, PredictIt, Smarkets, and FAZ.NET-Orakel in Germany. There is also Augur which is decentralized and uses cryptocurrencies. While that avoids the risk of closure due to regulation, it has KYC issues since one cannot verify the origin of cryptocurrency funds.

17.6 Differing Levels of Development

When investing, most money focuses on **developed markets**: the economies with the highest GDP/capita and most advanced infrastructure and rule of law. We also typically assume that these economies have a free press, low corruption, stable politics, and are highly urbanized.

The exact membership of such a group is unclear, but most economists would at least include the IMF (2017) group of advanced economies in Table 17.4.[5] The more expansive list of World Bank (2017) is defined strictly by GDP/capita and adds a number of small island nations and territories, more European and Middle Eastern countries, and two South American countries (Chile and Uruguay).

The difference between these is where many analysts draw the line between developed and developing economies. For a thought experiment: how might you classify The Bahamas, Bermuda, Cayman Islands, Greece, Hungary, Oman, Poland, Qatar, Saudi Arabia, or the United Arab Emirates?

Other countries are often referred to by a number of poorly-defined terms. The IMF calls these countries "emerging markets and developing economies" — although they note which are "heavily indebted poor countries" and which are "low income developing countries." Most analysts and researchers refer to the next income tier as **developing economies** or **emerging markets**.

These economies are typically distinguished by clearly rising GDP/capita, an increasingly-developed financial system, and a move toward the rule of law. This is often accompanied by a move from labor-intensive farming to urbanization and

---

[5]While IMF (2017) included Puerto Rico in their list, it remains unclear if this will continue given the destruction wrought by Hurricane Maria.

Australia	Germany	Luxembourg	Slovakia
Austria	Greece	Macao	Slovenia
Belgium	Hong Kong	Malta	South Korea
Canada	Iceland	Netherlands	Spain
Cyprus	Ireland	New Zealand	Sweden
Czech Republic	Israel	Norway	Switzerland
Denmark	Italy	Portugal	Taiwan
Estonia	Japan	Puerto Rico	United Kingdom
Finland	Latvia	San Marino	United States
France	Lithuania	Singapore	

Table 17.4: IMF group of 39 advanced economies. As of May 2018, there was no guidance on how extensive damage from Hurricane Maria might affect Puerto Rico's classification.

decreasing corruption. Less common, but positive indicators, are stable political transitions, more representative government, and a freer press. Often included in this group are the **BRICS**, five large and quickly-growing economies: Brazil, Russia, India, China, and South Africa. Other economies often in this group include those not in the IMF advanced economy group but in the World Bank high-income group as well as Argentina, Bulgaria, Croatia, Mexico, Romania, and Vietnam.

Riskier still are the **frontier markets** characterized by low GDP/capita, a nascent financial system, and often unequally-applied laws, more corruption, labor-intensive farming, and lower education.

17.6.1   Why Invest Outside Developed Markets?

Why would people invest outside of developed markets? The answer is simple: reward versus risk and diversification. Some people think that they can earn an outsized reward while taking less risk than typically associated with that expected reward, especially in light of how that investment diversifies their portfolio.

Countries which clean up their laws and politics help business to flourish. If a finance industry develops, that also eases business growth. Emerging market economies doing this may yield much higher returns while diversifying your portfolio. However, lurking in the background is always a potential Peso problem: politicians might reverse reforms, new leaders might seize power, or corruption might grow.

This is similar to how high-yield bonds initially offered attractive investment potential but were soon close to fairly-priced; how these investments often hold out the promise of better governance; and, how they are still included in most diversified bond funds' holdings. Hence many emerging market analysts think about countries similar to how debt analysts think about high-yield instruments.

Furthermore, some countries have transitioned from lower- to higher-income.

- Portugal, Slovenia, and Slovakia all transitioned from lower-income in the 1980s and 1990s to high-income EU members now.
- Singapore, the only country created against its will when expelled from Malaysia in 1965, was then poor and is now one of the richest economies in the world.
- South Korea was a military dictatorship until 1987, when it had one-fifth the GDP/capita of the US and Japan. South Korea's GDP/capita is now two-thirds that of the US and over 90% of Japan's. South Korea is the only OECD member to move from receiving aid to being an aid donor.
- Taiwan only revoked martial law in 1987 and held free elections in 1991. Taiwan's GDP/capita was half that of Japan's in 1987, surpassed Japan's in 2009, and is now 17% higher than Japan's and over four-fifths that of the US.

17.6.2 Why Not Invest Outside Developed Markets?

Why might we not invest outside of developed economies? The most compelling response is an appeal to the EMH: There is a reason these economies have not developed and, barring changes to structural issues, these economies are probably already fairly-priced.

It is fine to ask why some markets have not developed; and, sometimes economies pursue foolish policies and later realize that fact. However, the scariest four words in finance are those invoked to make you less skeptical: "This time it's different." The response to this claim should *always* be an emphatic "Really? Why? What has changed? And why is this different than prior changes?"

Furthermore, without the rule of law politicians may roll back reforms or impose extractive policies. Courts may also overlook seizing of private property. As a creditor, the last thing you want to learn is that your collateral was seized and you now hold debentures in a firm with less capital. Politicians may break contracts if other firms bribe them. All of these risks can destroy your investments in an economy.

Fiji versus FIJI In 1996, FIJI Water negotiated a 12-year deal to bottle and export water from a pure aquifer on Fiji for FJD 0.0033/L. In 2006, the head of the military seized power. When FIJI Water's deal expired in 2008, Fiji proposed a FJD 0.2/L export tax — which would only affect FIJI Water. The company protested and threatened to close. FIJI Water is Fiji's #1 export; the government backed down.

In 2010, Fiji expelled a FIJI Water executive which led to the defence and immigration minister resigning. Fiji proposed a lower FJD 0.15/L tax. FIJI Water shut down and laid off 400 employees; Fiji proposed leasing the aquifer to other firms; and, FIJI Water then decided to reopen, pay the tax, and help local communities access clean water. For more information read McDonald (2010).

From a risk perspective, developing economies are also scary. They typically perform far worse than more-developed economies in times of crisis. In a crisis, developing economy investments may be harder to justify leading many investors to exit those markets. This causes further price drops and reduces liquidity. Thus you reduce your holdings at a time when others also do so and when exiting the market is expensive.

17.7   Quiz

Try to answer these questions in five minutes. For answers with equations, just write the equations; do not evaluate them.

1. What does KYC mean and what does it require of investment managers?

2. The US has the world's largest equity market by market capitalization. Name three other of the top ten largest (by market cap) equity markets.

3. The US also has the world's largest corporate debt market. Name three other of the top ten largest (by amount outstanding) corporate debt markets.

4. The US has the world's second-largest corporate bank lending by loan amounts outstanding. Name three other of the top ten largest (by amount outstanding) corporate bank lending markets.

5. You are considering investing in two countries: South Korea and the People's Republic of China.

   a) What are two risks to managing investments in South Korea?
   b) What are two *additional* risks to investing in China? (In other words: two risks you are very unlikely to face with Korean investments but more likely to face with Chinese investments.)

6. You are investing globally and your auditor wants to know about the risk of tail events — specifically political turmoil, unrest, violence, armed conflict, and terrorism — for the markets you invest in. how would you assess these risks quantitatively?

7. What are three of the big success stories in global investing and economic development over the past fifty years?

8. Suppose you are invested in an economy where a very business-hostile candidate is running for election. If you needed to assess the risk of that candidate winning the election, how would you do so?

9. What are the equity indices most commonly-used by investment managers for two of the following: the Eurozone, China, Japan, Hong Kong, and the UK?

17.8 Exercises

Instructions

We will download data for a few global stocks and indices to explore the CAPM in an international context. Be careful, however! Trade and other issues may mean that what you think is the obvious index is not the best fit. Careful sleuthing can sometimes resolve these seeming puzzles, so this is no time to turn off your brain.

When we learned about the CAPM, we talked about excess returns: the asset's returns less the risk-free rate. However, there are many risk-free rates — depending on how long you are willing to lock your money up. The rate we should use is dictated by what investment we want to compare — essentially our investment horizon. We will pretend like we would be looking at risk given quarterly rebalancing, even though we do not have a 3-month EUR risk-free rate. (One exists, but downloading the data is not straightforward.)

- *Short-term risk-Free Rates:* USD (3M T-bill), CAD (3M T bill), EUR (6M German bond), CHF (1Y Confederation bond), AUD (3M yield), JPY (1Y JGB), SGD (1Y TBill) (`FRED/DGS3MO`, `BOC/V39065`, `BUNDESBANK/BBK01_WT3210`, `SNB/RENDOBLID` column 1, `RBA/F17_0` column 2, `MOFJ/INTEREST_RATE_JAPAN` column 1)
- *Indices:* S&P 500, TSX Composite, EuroStoxx 50, SMI, All Ordinaries, Hang Seng, Nikkei 225 (`^GSPC`, `^GSPTSE`, `^STOXX50E`, `^SSMI`, `^AORD`, `^HSI`, `^N225`)
- *US and Canadian Stocks:* Canadian Tire, Ford, Pfizer, Seven and i, and the Toyota ADR (`CTC-A.TO`, `F`, `PFE`, `SVNDY`, `TM`)
- *European Stocks:* Electricité de France, Novartis, Siemens, Volkswagen (`EDF.PA`, `NOVN.VX`, `SIE.DE`, `VOW.DE`)
- *Asian/Oceanian Stocks:* Breville, Jardine Matheson, Macquarie, and Swire Pacific ("A" share) (`BRG.AX`, `MQG.AX`, `J36.SI`, `0019.HK`)

The risk-free rates need to be rescaled (divided by 100) to get them on the same scale as log-returns. Ensure the index and equity prices you download are corrected for splits and dividends by using the adjusted close field.

Compute excess returns by subtracting off the short-term risk-free rate (divided by 252) from both the stock and the index. Make sure you use the the appropriate rates for each index and stock — for example, the EUR rate for Eurozone stocks and the EuroStoxx 50.

1. Using your excess returns, calculate the correlations between the indices. Are any of the correlations much higher than the others? Why would that be; or, is it just spurious?

2. Using the excess returns, calculate the correlations between the indices. Did anything change in the correlations? What does that imply about the relationship between monetary policy and financial markets?

3. For each foreign stock, do the following:

- Fit and report the resulting coefficients, standard errors, and t-stats for a multi-beta CAPM. Do this by regressing the stock's excess returns on excess returns for the seven indices.
- Eliminate the least-significant index, re-run, and repeat this process until all of the indices are significant. This is called backward selection and, while not ideal, it is a crude start to finding which indices best match each stock.
- Report the estimated intercept and slope coefficient and their t-stats.

4. Discuss why each of these selected indices does (or does not) make sense for that stock. You may need to think hard about this; consider relationships between each stock and the various index countries. There should be a few surprises. . . by design.

R Code

```
library(xts)
library(Quandl)
library(quantmod)

## Get risk-free rates
rf.tickers <- c("FRED/DGS3MO", "BOC/V39065", "BUNDESBANK/BBK01_WT3210",
                "SNB/RENDOBLID", "RBA/F17_0", "MOFJ/INTEREST_RATE_JAPAN")
rf.columns <- c(1,1,1,1,2,1)
rf.ids <- c("USD3M", "CAD3M","EUR6M","CHF1Y","AUD3M","JPY1Y","HKD3M")
## loop through tickers and columns
rf <- Quandl(rf.tickers[1], type="xts")[,rf.columns[1]]/100
for (i in 2:length(rf.tickers)) {
    rf.tmp <- Quandl(rf.tickers[i], type="xts")[,rf.columns[i]]/100
    rf <- cbind(rf, rf.tmp)
}

## Getting HKMA data is not straightforward, so...
## ...these are from the Hong Kong Monetary Authority
hkma.exfund.3M.rates <-
    c(0.09,0.10,0.10,0.11,0.26,0.62,0.27,0.18,0.24,0.25,0.30,0.28, # 2010
      0.16,0.19,0.20,0.11,0.13,0.06,0.07,0.10,0.11,0.10,0.17,0.22, # 2011
      0.18,0.11,0.10,0.12,0.10,0.08,0.15,0.17,0.23,0.09,0.07,0.05, # 2012
      0.11,0.08,0.06,0.08,0.09,0.15,0.16,0.15,0.17,0.13,0.12,0.11, # 2013
      0.14,0.14,0.14,0.10,0.07,0.09,0.07,0.04,0.09,0.03,0.03,0.04, # 2014
      0.03,0.01,0.02,0.01,0.01,0.00,0.01,-0.01,-0.01,0.00,-0.01,0.04, # 2015
      0.24,0.07,0.07,0.06,0.20,0.17,0.28,0.30,0.31,0.30,0.28,0.67, # 2016
      0.54,0.41,0.27,0.40,0.29,0.31,0.35,0.28,0.45,0.85,0.75,1.02, # 2017
      0.66,0.56) # 2018
rf.subset <- rf["201001/201802"]
hkma.3M <- xts(hkma.exfund.3M.rates,
               order.by = index(rf.subset[xts:::startof(rf.subset, "months")]))
rf <- cbind(rf, hkma.3M)
rf <- na.locf(rf)
colnames(rf) <- rf.ids

# Get indices and stock prices
adj.close <- 6  # 6th field is adjusted close
equity.tickers <- c("^GSPC","^GSPTSE","^STOXX50E","^SSMI","^AORD","^HSI","^N225",
                    "CTC-A.TO","F","HSBC","PFE","SVNDY","TM","EDF.PA","NOVN.VX",
                    "SIE.DE","VOW.DE","BRG.AX","MQG.AX","J36.SI","0019.HK")
equity.ids <- c("SPX","TSXCOMP","ESX50","SMI","AORD","HS","N225",
```

```
               "CATIRE","FORD","HSBC","PFIZER","SEVENANDI","TOY","EDF","NOVARTIS",
               "SIEMENS","VW","BREVILLE","MACQUARIE","JARDINES","SWIRE")
prices <- getSymbols(equity.tickers[1], source="yahoo", auto.assign=FALSE,
                     return.class="xts")[,adj.close]
for (i in 2:length(equity.tickers)) {
  prices.tmp <- getSymbols(equity.tickers[i], source="yahoo",
                     auto.assign=FALSE, return.class="xts")[,adj.close]
  prices <- cbind(prices, prices.tmp)
}
## We often get errors here since international stocks are not always
## traded on our home days, so there are some NAs. No worries; fill
## forward and returns will be zero on non-trading days.  (Might be a
## minor bias on volatility estimates; we will probably survive.
prices <- na.locf(prices)
colnames(prices) <- equity.ids
returns <- diff(log(prices))

## Now we join all of the datasets together and trim to recent
alldata <- cbind(rf, returns)["2010/"]

## create excess returns
equity.names.xs <- paste(equity.names, ".xs", sep="")
## now in a for loop subtract off a daily risk-free rate, FOR EXAMPLE:
alldata$SPX.xs <- alldata$SPX - alldata$T3M/250
## Only oddity: use HKD rf for Jardines.

# If your ticker were DAL and you wanted to model returns
# (not excess returns) using ESTOX and SMI, you would do like so:
simple.wrong.model <- lm(DAL ~ ESTOX + SMI, data=alldata)
summary(simple.wrong.model)
# NOTE that this is not the model you are supposed to do
```

References

Acemoğlu, Daron and James Robinson. *Why Nations Fail: The Origins of Power, Prosperity, and Poverty*. New York: Crown Business, 2013.

Arrow, Kenneth J. and Gerard Debreu. "Existence of an Equilibrium for a Competitive Economy". *Econometrica* 22.3 (1954), pp. 265–290. DOI: 10.2307/1907353.

Branović, Željko. *The Privatisation of Security in Failing States: A Quantitative Assessment*. Occasional Paper 24. Geneva Centre for the Democratic Control of Armed Forces (DCAF), 2011. URL: http://www.operationspaix.net/DATA/DOCUMENT/4194~v~The_Privatisation_of_Security_in_Failing_States__A_Quantitative_Assessment.pdf.

Brecke, Peter. *Violent Conflicts 1400 AD to the Present in Different Regions of the World*. Paper prepared for the 1999 Meeting of the Peace Science Society, Ann Arbor, Michigan. Oct. 8, 1999. URL: http://pwp.gatech.edu/brecke/wp-content/uploads/sites/19/2014/11/PSS99_paper.pdf.

Chang, Charles and Ying Ying Zeng. "Impact of Terrorism on Hospitality Stocks and the Role of Investor Sentiment". *Cornell Hospitality Quarterly* 52.2 (2011), pp. 165–175. DOI: 10.1177/1938965510392915.

Chojnacki, Sven et al. "Event Data on Armed Conflict and Security: New Perspectives, Old Challenges, and Some Solutions". *International Interactions* (2012), pp. 382–401. DOI: 10.1080/03050629.2012.696981.

Dollar, David and Aart Kraay. "Institutions, Trade, and Growth". *Journal of Monetary Economics* 50.1 (2003), pp. 133–162. DOI: 10.1016/S0304-3932(02)00206-4.

FDFA, Swiss. *Bilateral relations Switzerland-Luxembourg*. Retrieved on 15 October 2017 from https://www.eda.admin.ch/eda/en/home/representations-and-travel-advice/luxembourg/switzerland-luxembourg.html. 2017.

Forsythe, Robert et al. "Anatomy of an Experimental Political Stock Market". *American Economic Review* 82.5 (1992), pp. 1142–1161. URL: http://www.jstor.org/stable/2117471.

Gallegos, Raúl. *Crude Nation: How Oil Riches Ruined Venezuela*. Lincoln, NE: Potomac Books, 2016.

Godwin, Peter. *The Fear: Robert Mugabe and the Martyrdom of Zimbabwe*. New York: Little, Brown and Company, 2010.

Graham, Patrick. "Daily FX volumes rise to $4.84 trillion in Jan - CLS". *Reuters* (May 11, 2016). Retrieved 11 May 2017 from: http://www.reuters.com/article/global-forex-volumes-idUSL8N15P2VA.

Greenbaum, Robert, Laura Dugan, and Gary LaFree. "The Impact of Terrorism on Italian Employment and Business Activity". *Urban Studies* 44.5–6 (2007), pp. 1093–1108. DOI: 10.1080/00420980701255999.

Grene, Sophia. "The Challenge of Building Fixed Income Indices". *Financial Times* (Mar. 7, 2010). Retrieved on 16 October 2017 from https://www.ft.com/content/23409022-289a-11df-a0b1-00144feabdc0?mhq5j=e5.

Gruić, Branimir and Philip D. Wooldridge. "Enhancements to the BIS Debt Securities Statistics". *BIS Quarterly Review* December (2012). URL: https://www.bis.org/publ/qtrpdf/r_qt1212h.htm.

Henisz, Witold J. and Bennet A. Zelner. "The Hidden Risks in Emerging Markets". *Harvard Business Review* April (2010). Retrieved on 16 October 2017. URL: https://hbr.org/2010/04/the-hidden-risks-in-emerging-markets.

IMF. *World Economic Outlook, October 2017*. International Monetary Fund, 2017. URL: http://www.imf.org/en/Publications/WEO/Issues/2017/09/19/world-economic-outlook-october-2017.

Jones, Benjamin F. and Benjamin A. Olken. "Do Leaders Matter? National Leadership and Growth Since World War II". *Quarterly Journal of Economics* 120.3 (2005), pp. 835–864. DOI: 10.1093/qje/120.3.835.

Kreutz, Joakim. "How and When Armed Conflicts End: Introducing the UCDP Conflict Termination Dataset". *Journal of Peace Research* 47.2 (2010), pp. 243–250. DOI: 10.1177/0022343309353108.

LaFree, Gary and Laura Dugan. "Introducing the Global Terrorism Database". *Terrorism and Political Violence* 19.2 (2007), pp. 181–204. DOI: 10.1080/09546550701246817.

Leetaru, Kalev. "Half a Billion Clicks Can't Be Wrong: What Big Data Tells Us About Next Year's Crisis Zones". *Foreign Policy* (Jan. 3, 2014). URL: http://foreignpolicy.com/2014/01/03/half-a-billion-clicks-cant-be-wrong/.

Leetaru, Kalev and Philip A. Schrodt. "GDELT: Global Data on Events, Location, and Tone, 1979–2012". *Proceedings of the International Studies Association Annual Convention* 2.4 (2013). URL: http://data.gdeltproject.org/documentation/ISA.2013.GDELT.pdf.

Mauro, Paolo. "Corruption and Growth". *Quarterly Journal of Economics* 110.3 (1995), pp. 681–712. DOI: 10.2307/2946696.

McDonald, Hamish. "Bainimarama Shows He's the Full Bottle, But Challenges Await". *The Sydney Morning Herald* (Dec. 4, 2010). URL: http://www.smh.com.au/world/bainimarama-shows-hes-the-full-bottle-but-challenges-await-20101203-18jvg.html.

Minor, Michael S. "The Demise of Expropriation as an Instrument of LDC Policy, 1980–1992". *Journal of International Business Studies* 25.1 (1994), pp. 177–188. DOI: 10.1057/palgrave.jibs.8490850.

Mo, Pak Hung. "Corruption and Economic Growth". *Journal of Comparative Economics* 29.1 (2001), pp. 66–79. DOI: 10.1006/jcec.2000.1703.

Rhode, Paul W. and Koleman S. Strumpf. "Historical Presidential Betting Markets". *Journal of Economic Perspectives* 18.2 (2004), pp. 127–141. DOI: 10.1257/0895330041371277.

Rogers, Douglas. *The Last Resort: A Memoir of Mischief and Mayhem on a Family Farm in Africa*. New York: Three Rivers Press, 2010.

Roth, Alvin E. "Repugnance as a Constraint on Markets". *Journal of Economic Perspectives* 21.3 (2007), pp. 37–58. DOI: 10.1257/jep.21.3.37.

Sundberg, Ralph, Kristine Eck, and Joakim Kreutz. "Introducing the UCDP Non-State Conflict Dataset". *Journal of Peace Research* 49.2 (2012), pp. 351–362. DOI: 10.1177/0022343311431598.

Sundberg, Ralph and Erik Melander. "Introducing the UCDP Georeferenced Event Dataset". *Journal of Peace Research* 50.4 (2013), pp. 523–532. DOI: 10.1177/0022343313484347.

Wei, Shang-Jin. "How Taxing is Corruption on International Investors?" *Review of Economics and Statistics* 82 (1 2000), pp. 1–11. DOI: 10.1162/003465300558533.

World Bank. *World Bank Country and Lending Groups*. July 1, 2017. URL: https://datahelpdesk.worldbank.org/knowledgebase/articles/906519-world-bank-country-and-lending-groups.

Young, Joseph K. and Michael G. Findley. "Can Peace Be Purchased? A Sectoral-Level Analysis of Aid's Influence on Transnational Terrorism". *Public Choice* 149.3–4 (2011), pp. 365–381. DOI: 10.1007/s11127-011-9875-y.

Chapter 18

Foreign Exchange

Investing globally invariably requires dealing with foreign exchange and exchange rate risk. Thinking about differences between economies also gives us other tools for comparing costs and exchange rates. Thankfully, FX markets are less complicated than they seem. Once you get used to a few conventions, you will likely find foreign exchange very approachable. Beware, however: the currency market never sleeps!

The purpose of this chapter is to introduce foreign exchange conventions, discuss some models for exchange rates, and consider how rates relate to economic growth.

⚠️ **Varoitus!** *Many currency names overlap. "The dollar" is unclear in an international context: do you mean the US dollar... or the dollar from Australia, Canada, New Zealand, Hong Kong, Singapore, Taiwan, Cayman Islands, Bermuda, or The Bahamas (among others)? The "dollar sign," $, is even less clear: that symbol is also used to write Mexican and Argentinian pesos, and the similar cifrão, $, is used to write Brazilian reals. The Japanese yen and Chinese yuan both use ¥; and 元 may be used for Chinese yuan, Hong Kong and Taiwanese dollars, or Macanese Patacas. Hence we will use ISO 4217 currency codes such as MXN, ARS, and BRL. Section 0.4 (at the front) has a helpful reference list of common codes.*

18.1   Global Currencies

You may remember the major currencies: USD, EUR, JPY, GBP, AUD, CAD, and CHF. However, many other currencies trade in significant volume. Figure 18.1 shows the top 15 currencies by daily turnover. This plot shows clearly the rapid growth of trade in the Chinese yuan (CNY), aka the *renminbi* (RMB) or "people's money." This is despite strict **capital controls**, restrictions on money leaving China, which make CNY not **freely-convertible**.[1] The plot also shows the dominance of USD in currency trading. We will say more about that shortly.

18.1.1 Exchange Rate Quoting Conventions

Currencies are quoted in pairs: to buy some amount of one currency, you must do so with some amount of another currency. On many web interfaces, this is easy and intuitive: You enter two currencies and it tells you currency ABC is worth x of currency DEF and currency DEF is worth y of currency ABC. Generally, $y = 1/x$ or very close to that — with the difference due to using a bid or ask quote.

However, you will often see currencies quoted in newspapers, on scrolling quotes, or in other places. You might hear quotes from a market maker; or, you might request the exchange rate (aka a **cross rate**) from market data software. Often, these quotes have a certain convention which is known by the market but not specified.

Base and Quoting Currencies

The first convention is that currency pairs are quoted in terms of a **base currency** and a **quoting currency**. The base currency is listed first and the quoting currency is listed second as: BaseQuoting or Base/Quoting. For "ABC/DEF," this would seem to show the amount of ABC per unit of DEF. That makes sense from a mathematical notation perspective, and... it is completely wrong. The **currency quoting convention** is that a quote of x for ABC/DEF tells you that 1 unit of ABC (the base currency) is worth x units of DEF (the quoting currency).

Currency Precedence

The second convention is that there is a **currency precedence convention**. When a currency is quoted for conversion from an implied home currency (*e.g.* quotes for the EUR, GBP, and JPY in your local newspaper), the base currency is the higher-ranking currency, not the home currency. Thus the exchange rate between EUR and USD is quoted as EUR/USD while the rate between USD and JPY is quoted as USD/JPY. A precedence list would be long, but the following ordering takes care of most currency trades: EUR>GBP>AUD>NZD>USD>CAD>CHF>NOK>SEK>JPY.

Beyond that list, there are a few guidelines: the base currency is often (but not always) that which makes the cross rate greater than 1; and, currencies for less-developed economies tend to have lower priorities. If you look for a complete list of priorities, however, you will probably not find one. The reason is simple: currencies for less-developed-economies are often only actively quoted against USD. If we look back at Figure 18.1, we can see (since each currency trade involves two currencies) that USD is involved in 88% of FX trades (by notional). Many currencies outside of less-developed economies are also traded through USD.

---

[1]Those looking to trade CNY for profit will also be disappointed that China maintains a fixed USD/CNY exchange rate.

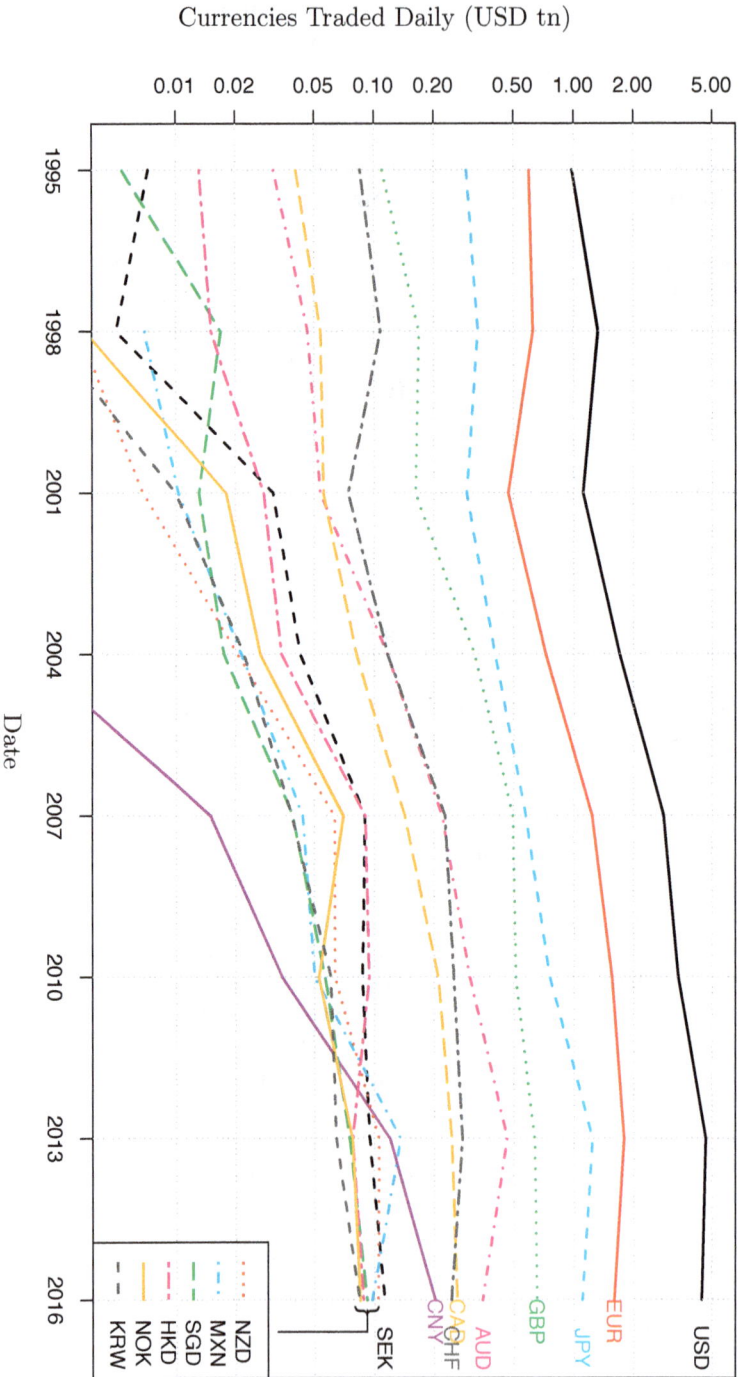

Figure 18.1: Top fifteen global currencies by daily amount traded in trillions of USD over time. EUR data before 1999 are the total of European currency unit (XEU), DEM, FRF, ITL, NLG, BEF, ESP, GRD, IEP, ATS, PTE, FIM, and LUF. Data from Bank for International Settlements (Table D11.3).

There is history behind the precedence of currencies. When the first (lasting) transatlantic cable was laid in 1866, the exchange rate between USD and GBP began to be regularly published. However, the pound was not decimalized then: it had 20 schillings/pound and 10 pence/schilling. Quoting dollars in terms of fractional pounds would have taken more bandwidth than quoting pounds in decimal dollars. Furthermore, the pound was a stronger currency then. This led to the cross rate between USD and GBP being called "cable" and being quoted as GBP/USD.

Other British Empire/Commonwealth countries used GBP or their own similar currencies. When these countries created their own currencies, some went with a decimal system, like the Canadian dollar in 1858, while others continued with a pound-schillings-pence system, like the Australian pound in 1910 and New Zealand pound in 1933. For this reason, CAD was quoted as USD/CAD while the others were "quoted cable," *i.e.* AUP/USD and NZP/USD. When these became decimalized as dollars, the quoting convention persisted as AUD/USD and NZD/USD. This also explains why many other ex-British Empire currencies are "quoted cable," including BHD, BMD, BWP, FJD, KYD, PGK, and TOP.

Finally: Why is the Euro the highest priority? When the European Central Bank premiered the Euro, they wanted it to be the highest-priority currency. While the UK disliked this idea, the market chose to stick with it.

18.1.2 Position Conventions

Another confusing convention in FX is the use of "long" and "short." In every FX transaction, you sell one currency to buy another, *e.g.* you sell CAD to buy EUR.

What if you have a contract with a payoff in terms of the exchange rate? For example, you might be long a futures contract on USD/JPY. If you are long USD/JPY, you are long the base currency (USD) and short the quoting currency (JPY). If the exchange rate increases, you make more money. In other words: you make more money when the number of Japanese yen per US dollar increases, *i.e.* when the yen price of dollars increases.

What if you are short JPY/USD? Then you are short JPY and long USD and you make money when the US dollar price of Japanese yen declines. While this may seem different from the preceding paragraph, it is not. Being long USD/JPY is the same as being short JPY/USD: one is long USD (and thus short JPY) while the other is short JPY (and thus long USD).

Sometimes, traders will say something like "I am long the Swissy." This means they are long Swiss Francs and short their home currency (or many others).

18.2 Handling Currency Risks

How do we hedge FX risk? Many businesses trade currencies through their bank. Some banks are better than others at this. That matters because currencies are typically traded over a dealer network. The top banks do a lot of trading in currencies for their clients and so some large banks are very active currency dealers.

We can often anticipate cash flows, *e.g.* interest, dividends, receivables, and payables. How do you lock in an FX rate for a cash flow one year from now? We will explore hedging in detail in the following chapters but cover it here briefly.

You could arrange a forward agreement: you agree to exchange USD X for EUR Y on a date one year from now. Or you could trade an FX futures contract: you deposit a small amount of money, and the change in the FX rate accrues in your account. A year from now, you exit the contract and collect the accrued P&L. Finally, you could trade an FX swap or trade in FX options to protect yourself against FX rate upside or downside.

18.2.1   An Example FX Hedge

Suppose I decide to invest USD 30 mn in the Euro Stoxx 50. To do this I sell USD 30 mn and buy EUR. Once that is done, I can make the investment.

My returns will be affected by the market index returns and by changes in the exchange rate. If I do not want to be exposed to FX rate changes, I must hedge my Euro exposure. To do this, I lock in the FX rate.

After I sell my Euro Stoxx 50 investment, I will sell EUR and buy USD. To lock that in now, I sell CME 6E (Euro FX) futures.[2] If EUR/USD is at 1.179, USD 30 mn is equal to EUR 30/1.179=25.445 mn. Since each contract is for EUR 125,000, this is 203.56 contracts of exposure — so we sell 204 contracts.

18.2.2   How the Hedge Works

If EUR appreciates versus USD, we get less USD per EUR. Had we not hedged, we could lose money even if the Euro Stoxx 50 had risen. If we hedged, however, 6E futures will decline in value. Our short position in 6E will therefore accrue a profit. This counterbalances the loss we will have when we convert EUR back into USD.

There is one other detail we have neglected: As the Euro Stoxx 50 rises or falls, the amount of EUR we will need to convert back to USD increases or decreases. We sold about EUR 25 mn of 6E futures. If the index rises, we are unhedged on the gains or **underhedged**. Had the index fallen in value, we would have hedged the losses — but in the wrong direction: we are **overhedged**. To avoid this situation, we can adjust the FX hedge daily.

18.2.3   Why Hedge FX Rates?

Some people might wonder why we hedged the FX rate. This gets to a fundamental question: When you invest in the Euro Stoxx 50, what are you investing in? Are you

---

[2]Many CME contracts have multiple identifiers from when they were traded in-person in trading pits and electronically in Globex. "EC" was the pit symbol and is still used for clearing while "6E" is the symbol used for Globex.

investing in just those firms or, more generally, economic growth in the Eurozone? If so, it makes sense to hedge your EUR exposure. Or, are you also investing in the Eurozone economy versus the rest of the world? In that case, you may want to be simultaneously long the Euro Stoxx 50 and long the Euro; you would not want to hedge your EUR exposure.

Neither of these perspectives are wrong; however, they are different perspectives and your hedge (or lack thereof) should match your intended investment objective.

18.3 Uncovered Interest Rate Parity

We hinted at one of the drivers of exchange rates: opportunities. If we expect high returns on EUR-denominated investments, we will convert other currencies into EUR. When we exit our investment, we will convert (probably more) EUR back to the other currencies. That will make EUR more expensive now and cheaper later — and the other currencies cheaper now and more expensive later. This acts to counter the larger returns on our EUR investments.

A common way to explore this idea is through interest rate differentials. Given interest rates and FX rates, we should not be able to make easy money. Interest rate differences now should imply expected FX rates in the future. This is the idea behind **uncovered interest rate parity**.

This gives us a model for later exchange rates. Suppose we are at time t. Let $r_{\tau,CAD}$ be the CAD risk-free (short) rate from t to $t+\tau$ and $r_{\tau,EUR}$ be the EUR risk-free (short) rate from t to $t+\tau$. We will also write the exchange rate of 1 EUR into CAD at time t as $X_{t,EUR/CAD}$. Uncovered interest rate parity then states that:

$$1 + r_{\tau,CAD} \overset{\text{should}}{=} \frac{E(X_{t+\tau,EUR/CAD})}{X_{t,EUR/CAD}}(1 + r_{\tau,EUR}). \tag{18.1}$$

Since we know the risk-free rates and the current EUR/CAD FX rate, we can rearrange these to get an implied future exchange rate $\tilde{X}$:

$$\tilde{X}_{t+\tau,EUR/CAD} = \frac{1 + r_{\tau,CAD}}{1 + r_{\tau,EUR}} X_{t,EUR/CAD}. \tag{18.2}$$

Or we can rearrange these and take logs to see that:

$$\%\Delta\tilde{X}_{t\to t+\tau,EUR/CAD} \approx r_{\tau,CAD} - r_{\tau,EUR}, \tag{18.3}$$

which is a good approximation for low interest rates (typical of developed economies). If EUR interest rates are 1% higher than CAD rates over the next year, we should expect the EUR/CAD rate to fall by about 1% — eliminating the interest rate gain.

Similarly, for a currency pair that is not quoted cable like CAD/JPY:

$$\tilde{X}_{t+\tau,CAD/JPY} = \frac{1 + r_{\tau,JPY}}{1 + r_{\tau,CAD}} X_{t,CAD/JPY}, \tag{18.4}$$

$$\%\Delta\tilde{X}_{t\to t+\tau,CAD/JPY} \approx r_{\tau,JPY} - r_{\tau,CAD}. \tag{18.5}$$

What this means is that yield curves and current exchange rates imply whole curves of expected exchange rates in the future... or do they?

18.3.1 *Carry Trades and a Puzzle*

Uncovered interest rate parity implies later exchange rates: higher-interest-rate economies should find their currencies depreciating. However, the data often differ.

Fama (1984) found the **forward premium puzzle** (aka the **uncovered interest rate parity puzzle**), that economies with higher interest rates tend to see their currency appreciate.

This has lead to a common trading strategy: the **carry trade**. A carry trade is what we discussed in uncovered interest rate parity — except often with expectations of currency appreciation. An investor borrows money in a low-interest-rate economy, exchanges for a higher-interest-rate currency, and invests it at those higher interest rates. The assumption is that the currency will not depreciate and may appreciate.

How could this be? Backus et al. (2013) find that differences in monetary policy may help explain the puzzle, especially if monetary policy in the high-interest-rate economy is sensitive to exchange rate fluctuations. Bilson (1981) shows that an investor could reliably profit from an FX strategy using forward premia.

You might also wonder about Peso Problems. This is a reasonable concern because any economy with high interest rates and an appreciating currency cannot keep growing forever. As we discussed with currency defenses, high interest rates may just be a stopgap to paper over the need for structural reforms in an economy. Once investors realize reform is not coming, devaluation can be swift. Sure enough, Burnside et al. (2011) argue convincingly that these trades are not arbitrage or a mispricing but

---

Fire and Iced Accounts In 2003, Iceland had 290,000 people and a GDP of USD 9.7 bn. In the mid-2000s, banks expanded with easy borrowing from European debt markets. They also attracted (foreign) online depositors, offering rates near 8% in 2005, 10% in 2006, and 13% in 2007. At that time, European rates were mostly in the 4%–6% range.

This yielded large inflows of money to ISK. The banks, holding large deposits, offered easy (even foolish) loans at higher interest rates. By 2007, Iceland had 312,000 people and a GDP of USD 21 bn. Over 2007–2008, Icelandic inflation hit 14% — above the target of 2.5%.

In September 2008, the central bank raised rates over 15% to stem inflation. The banks could not replace their maturing debt and began failing. Iceland imposed capital controls, effectively freezing accounts. Ultimately, the government fell, bank executives were imprisoned, and capital controls remained until March of 2017. For more on the crisis, read Economist (2008); Darvas (2011); and, BBC (2017).

fairly-priced given lurking Peso Problems. Similarly, Fama and Bliss (1987) implies carry trades earn a devaluation risk premium; and, Lee and Wang (2018?) show the return on a carry trade is positively related with jump risk. Yet again, there is "no free lunch."

18.4   Covered Interest Rate Parity

What if we could lock in future FX rates? The LOOP tells us there should not be easy money; otherwise, we would arbitrage it away. Furthermore, unlike the (erroneous) APT assumptions that we can exit a trade without price impact, here we implicitly account for the price of exiting the trade.

The idea of locking in the later exchange rate (and thus locking in a profit) is the idea behind **covered interest rate parity**.

We take the setup from before; however, we now also know the later FX rate $X_{t+\tau, EUR/CAD}$. Then we have that:

$$\underbrace{X_{t,EUR/CAD}(1 + r_{\tau,CAD})}_{\text{EUR 1}\to\text{CAD, earn CAD interest}} \overset{\text{should}}{=} \underbrace{(1 + r_{\tau,EUR})X_{t+\tau,EUR/CAD}}_{\text{EUR 1 earns EUR interest, }\to\text{CAD}} . \tag{18.6}$$

FX rates should compensate for different interest rates. If this does not hold, within the bid-ask spread costs of entering and exiting the trade, we would seem to have an arbitrage. (Note that this differs from a carry trade in that we lock in the conversion back to our home currency.)

Suppose rates were 4% (CAD) and 3% (EUR) with a flat FX rate curve of $X_{t,EUR/CAD} = X_{t+\tau,EUR/CAD} = 1.5$. We would then borrow EUR at 3%, convert EUR to CAD, and lock in the later conversion from CAD back to EUR. Then, we invest the CAD at 4%. At time $t+\tau$ we convert our CAD back to EUR. We have 4% more EUR and we use 3/4 of that to pay off the 3% loan. We pocket the remaining 1% of interest.

In this situation, we might think we have finally found easy money. All we have to do is fire up the money machine and make cash! However, even when covered interest rate parity breaks, there are still risks that may explain the divergence. First, the risk of default on the high-interest rate bonds may be non-ignorable. If a bond promises you 8% but then defaults, having exchange rates locked in will only ensure that you get back your (reduced) capital — without having to also endure the pain of a likely devaluation of the foreign currency. The situation is worse if the interest rates were from bank accounts. In that case, the possibility of bank failure is even higher than the possibility of government bonds defaulting.

There are other risks as well. Foreign depositors in Icelandic banks recently learned this when capital controls prevented them from converting ISK back into their home currencies. (See the sidebar "Fire and Iced Accounts.")

18.5   Purchasing Power Parity

After talking about exchange rates, it would seem like we know enough to compare investments across the globe. However, just as we consider real versus nominal rates, so we must also consider how much goods and services we can buy for equivalent units of currency, aka **purchasing power**.

Often, we look at a **market basket** (aka **commodity bundle**): a representative collection, of goods that consumers would purchase. The changing price of this basket lets us assess changes in the **cost of living**. If EUR/CAD is 1.5, comparing purchasing power means looking at how much of a basket can be purchased for EUR 1 (in the Eurozone) and 1.5 CAD (in Canada).

Market baskets vary depending on the type of consumer we consider; this is the difference between the consumer price index and the producer price index.[3]

18.5.1   Comparing Purchasing Power

If we are going to compare the output of economies, it makes sense to consider the real output and not just nominal output. We need to adjust for inflation and equivalent purchasing power in different economies. For example, adjusting GDPs for relative purchasing power yields comparable GDPs. We say that these GDPs are at **purchasing power parity** (PPP). Typically, we refer to PPP with respect to some baseline, *e.g.* in 1990 US dollars.

There are two problems with comparing purchasing power and calculating PPP: basket differences and non-tradable goods.

The first problem is that different economies use different representative baskets of goods and services. This reflects the reality that different cultures consume different goods and services: North Americans drive more and so have more motor vehicle fuel in their representative basket; the European basket excludes owner-occupied housing; and, some Asian economies feature less childcare in their basket since grandparents live closer or in an extended-family home and may care for children. This also explains much of the difference between the CPI and HICP; the HICP is much closer to the US **consumer price index for urban consumers**, CPI-U, which has a lower weight on motor vehicle fuel.

Dryden, Reut, and Slater (1987) is an excellent example of comparing market baskets. They show, for example, that in 1987 Canadians purchased more alcohol and tobacco than Americans but far less non-hospital medical services.

The second problem is that some goods and services consumed are **non-tradable**: they cannot be transported to other locales easily, willingly, or without greatly increasing the price. Services like massages, haircuts, home cleaning, and even prostitution cannot be transported and may not even be legal in some jurisdictions. People choose where they work; we cannot just load them into a truck. Some goods

---

[3]In Europe, the European Central Bank uses the Harmonised Indices of Consumer Prices, or HICP, like the consumer price index. In Canada, the equivalent of the producer price index is the Industrial Product Price Index.

are non-tradable as well. We cannot easily ship electricity from Australia to South Africa or natural gas from Canada to Korea.[4] We also cannot export productivity or access to information. We will see shortly that non-tradable goods complicate comparing purchasing power.

18.5.2   The Big Mac Index

One of the simplest indices of purchasing power is one designed by McDonald's Hong Kong joint venture partner Daniel Ng Yat-chiu and first published by Pam Woodall in *The Economist*.[5] Woodall (1986) debuted the **Big Mac Index** as a humorous way to compare purchasing power.

While the index seems frivolous, a Big Mac actually represents a sensible basket of goods that is largely the same across economies. A Big Mac "market basket" contains bread (a sesame seed bun), beef, vegetables (tomato, lettuce, pickles, and onion), and edible fats (in the secret sauce). However, the burger's price also includes transport to get its components to the restaurant, energy to cook the burger, labor to get the burger to the consumer, cleaning supplies, and real estate for the restaurant. Academics like Ong (1997) have noted that this unusual index performs well.

You can play with with the index yourself at `http://www.economist.com/content/big-mac-index`.

18.6   Other Models for Exchange Rates

There are a few other models for exchange rates. A number of economists have considered the relationship between purchasing power parity and exchange rates. Others have noted how consumption growth and exchange-rate-hedged contracts relate to exchange rates.

18.6.1   Purchasing Power Parity and Exchange Rates

The most common alternative model for exchange rates is that of comparing PPP. Balassa (1964) and Samuelson (1964) examine this, and Balassa notes two forms of this idea, both of which he attributes to Cassel (1918).

The first, absolute, form states that the exchange rate should be the ratio of two economies' price indices — based on identical market baskets. Continuing with the EUR/CAD and CAD/JPY examples, this would mean that the exchange rates

---

[4]There are companies pushing the limits of liquifying natural gas for transport because prices are much cheaper in North America than the rest of the world; however, this is still a small and expensive part of the natgas market.

[5]The history of the index is discussed in Economist (2017) and Cho (2013). Yat-chiu went on to be Chairman of McDonald's HK and serve on the McDonald's board.

should be $\tilde{X}_{t,EUR/CAD}$ and $\tilde{X}_{t,CAD/JPY}$ where:

$$\tilde{X}_{t,EUR/CAD} = \frac{CPI_{t,CAD}}{CPI_{t,EUR}}, \text{ and} \tag{18.7}$$

$$\tilde{X}_{t,CAD/JPY} = \frac{CPI_{t,JPY}}{CPI_{t,CAD}}. \tag{18.8}$$

The second, relative, form states that the change in PPP from when the exchange rate was at an equilibrium determines the change in the exchange rate. If rates were in equilibrium at time t, then the exchange rates at time $t + \tau$ should be:

$$\tilde{X}_{t+\tau,EUR/CAD} = \frac{\Delta CPI_{t\rightarrow t+\tau,CAD}}{\Delta CPI_{t\rightarrow t+\tau,EUR}} X_{t,EUR/CAD}, \text{ and} \tag{18.9}$$

$$\tilde{X}_{t+\tau,CAD/JPY} = \frac{\Delta CPI_{t\rightarrow t+\tau,JPY}}{\Delta CPI_{t\rightarrow t+\tau,CAD}} X_{t,CAD/JPY}. \tag{18.10}$$

One problem with this idea is we rarely know when exchange rates are at their equilibrium levels.

18.6.2   Productivity Biases in PPP

A problem with both of these ideas is noted by Balassa (1964) and Samuelson (1964): productivities differ. As hinted at earlier, non-tradable goods matter.

The idea is that higher productivities will result in higher wages; however, that will also elevate wages in labor-intensive jobs where productivity typically varies less. Thus the more-productive economy in a pair should have a higher equilibrium price index than the other economy. This is the **Balassa-Samuelson effect**. This suggests that the relationship between relative PPPs and exchange rates should not be equalities but inequalities: the more-productive economy's price index should be higher than what is implied by the exchange rate. This is supported by analysis in Officer (1976).

If we look at 2015 OECD data for GDP/hours worked, we see that the 2010-relative indices for Canada, the Eurozone, and Japan are 105.1, 105.2, and 104.8 (with the EU at 105.5 and the US at 102). This suggests that the relationship should instead be:[6]

$$\tilde{X}_{t,EUR/CAD} = \frac{CPI_{t,CAD}/Prod_{t,CA}}{CPI_{t,EUR}/Prod_{t,EU}} = \frac{CPI_{t,CAD}/105.1}{CPI_{t,EUR}/105.2}, \text{ and} \tag{18.11}$$

$$\tilde{X}_{t,CAD/JPY} = \frac{CPI_{t,JPY}/Prod_{t,JP}}{CPI_{t,CAD}/Prod_{t,CA}} = \frac{CPI_{t,JPY}/104.8}{CPI_{t,CAD}/105.1}. \tag{18.12}$$

For those interested in exploring this idea further, Hsieh (1982) builds a time series model of exchange rates using productivities.

---

[6]If you are curious, the OECD gives the September 2017 CPI (in 2010 USD) for Canada, the Eurozone, and Japan as 112.3, 109.5, and 103.9. Converting these with FX rates of 1.28 (USD/CAD), 1.17 (EUR/USD), and 113.19 (USD/JPY) implies FX rates of EUR/CAD=1.5374 and CAD/JPY=82.05. The current FX rates, for comparison, are EUR/CAD=1.50 and CAD/JPY=88.21.

18.6.3 Consumption Growth and Currency Appreciation

Another issue is the Backus and Smith (1993) puzzle: that consumption growth should imply rising prices and thus currency depreciation. Instead, they find that consumption growth is related to currency appreciation.

This may be because consumption growth implies better institutions, stability, and safety or better investment opportunities (*i.e.* is forward-looking). In the latter case, we might not quickly reconvert foreign currencies at position exit.

18.6.4 Information from Hedged Contracts

We mentioned before that we could try to hedge foreign exchange risk. One way to do this is to look at investment contracts with a built-in exchange rate hedge (aka quanto contracts). Mano (2013) and Kremens and Martin (2017) look at these and find evidence that they provide superior predictive power to the uncovered interest rate parity model.

18.7 What Exchange Rates Imply for Growth

We have seen productivity and consumption are related to exchange rates; and, economists have long tried to relate consumption and growth. We might therefore wonder if exchange rates could help us predict economic growth. The answer is: yes.

Dollar (1992) looks at production-based exchange-rate pricing and how it might relate to economic growth. First, he computes a relative price level for an economy i (with currency CUR_i) at time t:

$$RPL_{it} = 100 \frac{P_{i,t}}{P_{US,t}} X_{t,CUR_i/USD}. \tag{18.13}$$

Because of the Balassa-Samuelson effect, Dollar models the price level with a simple production function containing per-capita GDP, per-capita GDP^2, regional dummy variables for Africa and Latin America as well as time fixed effects to correct for global macroeconomic variation over time.[7] That model is used to create a measure of the distortion of an economy's relative price level versus (what is assumed

---

[7]The per-capita GDP^2 term allows for increasing or decreasing returns to scale like we discussed in Chapter 5.

to be) the equilibrium:

$$RPL_{it} = \alpha + \gamma_t + \beta_1 GDP_{it} + \beta_2 GDP_{it}^2 +$$
$$\beta_A \mathbf{1}_{\text{Africa}} + \beta_{LA} \mathbf{1}_{\text{Lat. Am.}} + \epsilon_{it}, \tag{18.14}$$

$$\text{Distort}_{it} = RPL_{it}/\widehat{RPL}_{it}, \tag{18.15}$$

$$\hat{\mu}_{\text{Distort},i} = \frac{1}{n} \sum_{t=1}^{n} \text{Distort}_{it}, \text{ and} \tag{18.16}$$

$$\hat{\sigma}_{\text{Distort},i} = \sqrt{\text{Var}(\text{Distort}_{it})}. \tag{18.17}$$

where the γ_t's are year dummy-variable controls and the **1**'s are regional dummy variables.

The idea of the growth model is that an outward orientation which encourages exports and trade, instead of autarky, encourages growth. The outward orientation is measured along two dimensions which encourage trade: (1) keeping price levels near equilibrium instead of keeping the exchange rate artificially high (which encourages import substitution), and (2) maintaining stable price levels.[8]

Dollar then computes an average distortion and a coefficient of variation for the distortion as the outward orientation measures and uses these, with investment, to model per-capita GDP growth for 95 developing economies:

$$\%\Delta GDP_i = \alpha + \beta_\mu \hat{\mu}_{\text{Distort},i} + \beta_{CV} \frac{\hat{\mu}_{\text{Distort},i}}{\hat{\sigma}_{\text{Distort},i}} + \beta_I \text{Invest}_i + \epsilon_i. \tag{18.18}$$

He finds that both distortion of relative prices and variation in that distortion are both significantly associated with reduced economic growth while investment is significantly associated with positive economic growth. Furthermore, he finds only four outliers with high distortion and significantly positive economic growth: Algeria, Cameroon, Congo, and Egypt. Adding a dummy variable for those four economies yields a better-fitting model but similar coefficients for the other effects.

The model reveals a few interesting features. Developing Asian economies had the lowest average distortion measure and variability of distortion equal to that of developed economies. Removing protections to reduce distortion in Africa and Latin America to Asian levels would increase GDP/capita growth by 1.8% and 0.7%. Reducing distortion variability in Africa and Latin America to Asian levels would increase GDP/capita growth by 0.3% and 0.8%. Finally, increasing investment in Africa and Latin America to Asian levels would increase GDP/capita growth by 0.5% and 0.1%.

This suggests that African growth has been hampered by protectionism and insufficient investment while Latin American growth has been hampered by variability in the real exchange rate. It also suggests that policy changes in Africa and Latin

---

[8]There is nothing magical about USD here; it is merely the baseline used for all economies. The baseline could just as easily be EUR or another reserve currency.

America could lead to 2.6% and 1.6% higher GDP/capita growth. Overall, these findings suggest that trade liberalization, devaluation of real exchange rates, stable real exchange rates, and investment lead to economic growth.

18.8 Current Issues

There are a few issues that are currently of heightened interest in the world of foreign exchange. One is the future of the European Union's economic and monetary union. The other is cryptocurrencies.

18.8.1 The Eurozone

With the multiple bailouts of Greece followed a few years later by **Brexit**, the exit of the United Kingdom from the European Union, many commentators have wondered about the stability of the EU and Eurozone.

This is really a questioning of the EU itself since the UK was never in the Eurozone nor engaged in any part of economic or monetary union. The Bank of England has maintained its independence throughout the emergence of the European Union. However, this questioning of the EU is based on many of the same concerns underlying the viability of the Eurozone. While few believe the Euro will go away, some analysts have wondered to what extent the Euro is effectively the wider adoption of a renamed version of the Deutschemark.[9] The seminal work on such thinking is Mundell (1961).

18.8.2 Cryptocurrencies

We should also discuss the latest fad: cryptocurrencies. A **cryptocurrency**, such as bitcoin, is a means of exchange with issuance tied to verifying a distributed ledger of trades.

The Blockchain

The ledger is called the **blockchain** because it is a chain of **blocks**: records of a group of verified value exchanges which point to prior such records. A difficult-to-invert mathematical function (*e.g.* a hash) of these records and the prior record are stored in each block. The blockchain is thus tamper-resistant because changing earlier trades would (1) alter the cascade of computed values in later blocks, and (2) require collusion by a majority of network ledger-holders.

Computing these functions is itself complicated, but checking if their value is correct is easy. Why would anyone do this work then? The answer is circular: solving the difficult problem is rewarded with some (newly-created) cryptocurrency.

---

[9]In the interest of discretion, I will only note that some of these analysts were at the European Central Bank.

The blockchain itself is an interesting technology. Economist (2015a) discusses a few other possible applications including maintaining property titles (since some countries lack land title systems), recording trades on exchanges, and tracking diamonds.

Cryptocurrency Exchanges

Some cryptocurrency exchanges have lost account records or had weak and sloppy controls which allowed theft and embezzlement. Probably the most infamous failure was of the then-largest exchange MtGOX — an acronym for Magic: the Gathering Online eXchange. The site had begun as a market for trading cards for the popular game. When the exchange filed for bankruptcy in 2014, it had lost USD 450 mn in bitcoin and USD 27 mn in cash. Adelstein and Stucky (2016) and Eichholz (2017) discuss the exchange's many problems.

Uses for Cryptocurrencies

A number of potential benefits have been claimed for cryptocurrencies. Some say cryptocurrencies could replace credit cards and cash for daily transactions; serve as electronic cash in developing countries; or, reduce the possibility of a central bank debasing the currency. Unfortunately for these proposals, the throughput is far too low currently for the first to be plausible; this and the existence of cheaper mobile money solutions make the second proposal unlikely; and, the failures of exchanges and occasional hacks are currently far more likely concerns than debasement of value by a central bank in any developed country.

Worse, this is not the first introduction of digital currencies. Digital currencies Flooz and Beenz debuted during the internet bubble; and, DigiCash appeared in the 1990s. However, as Higgins (2014) discusses, all three ultimately faltered. Research by Marchiori (2018) suggests that cryptocurrencies will also falter as the work to verify the blockchain becomes too much to justify the decreasing amount of coins received for the work. While some say verifying the blockchain (and thus the coins) has inherent value, this is just another version of the labor theory of value fallacy.

Why are cryptocurrencies popular then? There are a few reasons that may explain their popularity. First, the difficulty of tracing cryptocurrency usage back to an actual person makes them more enticing for use in purchasing illicit goods and services or funding oppressed causes. Second, cryptocurrencies may allow individuals to get around capital controls. When China announced they would be banning cryptocurrencies, bitcoin fell by 16%. Third, and most likely, is that cryptocurrencies may be experiencing a bubble.

Cryptocurrency Intermediation

The CME and CBOE have recently debuted bitcoin futures and a number of trading firms have begun trading across futures markets and bitcoin exchanges. Unlike the cryptocurrency users above, these traders are not interested in using bitcoin; rather, some like to make markets in a new product and many like that its volatility creates opportunities for cross-market arbitrage: they are getting paid to keep all the venues in synchrony.

The problem with this is that the exchanges are a weak link. The typical "risk management" advice is to not store cryptocurrencies at the exchange. However, for a trader to be ready to take advantage of an arbitrage opportunity, they cannot wait to send funds to the venue and then trade. Thus these arbitrageurs maintain some positions at many exchanges. Some arbitrageurs say that in a crash they would extract these funds. However, that is when the arbitrage opportunities may be the most attractive.

Furthermore, if the exchange operators are skimming funds or themselves invested in cryptocurrencies, they may then incur large losses and be unwilling or unable to return funds to clients in a timely manner (or at all). By the time a crisis hits, it may be too late to extract funds. Finally, if one venue does not return traders' funds, any traders who were arbitraging that venue are then unhedged and exposed to market movements. This would lead to a panic of rehedging which would move markets further. This is very similar to effects seen in OTC derivative market crises. (We will discuss those in Chapter 26.) Thus cross-market arbitrage of cryptocurrencies is a source of operational (and possibly systemic) risk.

The Prognosis for Cryptocurrencies

Ultimately, the inability of cryptocurrency transactions to pass KYC is a severely limiting factor. Furthermore, as governments restrict their use for evading capital controls, the quantity demanded will decrease. Finally, while arbitraging the various trading venues might seem profitable, in a crash multiple exchanges could become insolvent or seize clients' funds. That could easily erase prior gains made from arbitrage. Thus even many players claiming to be taking no risk are, in fact, shouldering unwise levels of operational risk.

For those seeking to learn more about cryptocurrencies, Velde (2013) and Brito and Castillo (2016) are good places to start and Barber et al. (2012) discusses some problems and potential solutions.

18.9   Quiz

Try to answer these questions in five minutes. For answers with equations, just write the equations; do not evaluate them.

1. (2 points) The risk-free USD interest rate for five years is 1.34% while in Japan the five-year (JPY) risk-free rate is 0.13%. The cash FX rate is 119.1 JPY/USD. What is a quick guess at how much this FX rate will change over the next five years? (Note: Make sure to get the sign right for how the FX rate was quoted.)

2. (To Live and Let Live) You recently read about the formation of Liberland, a low-tax, business-friendly micronation proposed by Vít Jedlička on *terra nullius* between Croatia and Serbia. Suppose it is a few years in the future and Liberland has joined Vatican City, and Monaco (both smaller) as well as San Marino, Liechtenstein, Malta, and Andorra (larger) as a recognized European microstate. Land has been cleared, banks are open, wealthy tourists are arriving via Danube ferries, casinos are making healthy profits, and real-estate development is progressing quickly.

You see that the AA-rated Bank of Liberland offers an internet bank account with interest of 8%/year while your local Bank of Enormica is lending (USD) at 4%/year.

   a) (2 points) Since FX rates are a concern, you lock in a forward rate to protect your 4% higher interest versus the BofE loan. Assuming Liberland does not get invaded, what other risks might you worry about?

   b) If Liberland sovereign debt is yielding 6%, are you more or less worried than if it were yielding 7.5%? Why?

   c) How might you hedge one of the big risks using a traded financial instrument?

3. You notice that AUD/BRL is at 2.5 but the Big Mac Index is at USD 4.53 for Australia and USD 5.10 for Brazil.

   a) According to Cassell — and ignoring the Balassa-Samuelson effect — what should the rate be for AUD/BRL?

   b) What does the difference between this rate and the market FX rate suggest?

4. Dollar (1992) suggests that investment encourages economic growth as does an outward orientation of the economy. He proposes two dimensions of outward orientation which relate to different policies. What are these dimensions or policies which encourage economic growth?

5. What are a few problems that (currently) stand in the way of wider adoption of cryptocurrencies?

18.10   Exercises

Instructions

You will need to download the following data; tickers for Quandl are in parentheses.

- *Spot FX rates:* EUR/USD, USD/JPY, USD/CHF FX rate
  (CURRFX/USDEUR, CURRFX/USDJPY, CURRFX/USDCHF)
- *FX futures:* EUR/USD, USD/JPY, USD/CHF
  (CHRIS/CME_EC1, CHRIS/CME_JY1, CHRIS/CME_SF1)

- *3-month interest rates from deposit futures:* Eurodollars (USD 3M LIBOR), EUR Euribor, Euroyen (JPY 3M TIBOR), Euroswiss (CHF 3M LIBOR) (CHRIS/CME_ED1, CHRIS/LIFFE_I1, CHRIS/CME_EY1, CHRIS/LIFFE_S1)

Deposit futures give the price of a zero-coupon bond; to convert this to a yield you subtract the price from 100. Dividing by 100 then gives numbers like we work with (i.e. "0.01" = 1%).

Make sure the index and equity prices you download are corrected for splits and dividends by using the adjusted close field if available. Note that for a few stocks there is only a close field available. I have picked stocks where the close field is equal to the adjusted close field (so stocks that have not had splits).

A Few Words on Foreign Exchange Rates

We know that FX markets traditionally quote currencies in certain ways. However, CME FX contracts are specified so that they are always "USD per unit of foreign currency."[10] This makes the contracts easy to use if you need to hedge FX exposure; however, if you try to check the data you get versus some sources, you could easily wind up confused. The spot rates in Quandl are also changed from their conventions to be consistent: they are quoted as foreign currency per unit of USD.

1. To see if USD-JPY interest rate parity holds, look at the difference between USD Eurodollar deposit rates and: converting USD to JPY in the spot market, investing in a Euroyen deposit, and locking in the conversion back to USD. Check that you have the FX conversions all correct and then plot the difference between these two rates (Eurodollars vs implied rate investing in JPY with hedged FX conversions).

2. To see if USD-EUR interest rate parity holds, look at the difference between USD Eurodollar deposit rates and: converting USD to EUR in the spot market, investing in a Euribor deposit, and locking in the conversion back to USD. Check that you have the FX conversions all correct and then plot the difference between these two rates.

3. To see if USD-CHF interest rate parity holds, look at the difference between USD Eurodollar deposit rates and: converting USD to CHF in the spot market, investing in a Euroswiss deposit, and locking in the conversion back to USD. Check that you have the FX conversions all correct and then plot the difference between these two rates.

4. Compute the average and standard deviation of all three parity differences: USD-JPY, USD-EUR, and USD-CHF.

5. Is there a consistent (economically significant) parity violation for any of these? Why would this be?

---

[10] In the case of the JPY futures, you must divide by 1,000,000.

Sample *R* Code

```
library(xts)
library(Quandl)

# Read in spot fx rates
fxspot.tickers <- c("CURRFX/USDEUR", "CURRFX/USDJPY", "CURRFX/USDCHF")
fxspot.raw <- Quandl(fxspot.tickers[1], type="xts")
for (i in 2:length(fxspot.tickers)) {
  fxspot.temp <- Quandl(fxspot.tickers[i], type="xts")
  fxspot.raw <- merge(fxspot.raw, fxspot.temp)
}
colnames(fxspot.raw) <- c("USDEUR.spot", "USDJPY.spot", "USDCHF.spot")

# Read in future fx rates
fxfut.tickers <- c("CHRIS/CME_EC1", "CHRIS/CME_JY1", "CHRIS/CME_SF1")
fxfut.raw <- Quandl(fxfut.tickers[1], type="xts")
for (i in 2:length(fxfut.tickers)) {
  fxfut.temp <- Quandl(fxfut.tickers[i], type="xts")
  fxfut.raw <- merge(fxfut.raw, fxfut.temp)
}
colnames(fxfut.raw) <- c("USDEUR.fut", "USDJPY.fut", "USDCHF.fut")

# Read in 3M USD deposit futures
usd.3m.raw <- Quandl("CHRIS/CME_ED1", type="xts")[,"Settle"]
eur.3m.raw <- Quandl("CHRIS/LIFFE_I1", type="xts")[,"Settle"]
jpy.3m.raw <- Quandl("CHRIS/CME_EY1", type="xts")[,"Settle"]
chf.3m.raw <- Quandl("CHRIS/LIFFE_S1", type="xts")[,"Settle"]
chf.3m.raw["20150122"] <- 101.08   # Fix 1st data error
chf.3m.raw["20150508"] <- 100.83   # Fix 2nd data error
deposits3m.raw <- cbind(usd.3m.raw, eur.3m.raw, jpy.3m.raw, chf.3m.raw)
deposits3m <- (100-deposits3m.raw)/100   # convert futures prices to yield
colnames(deposits3m) <- c("3MUSDLIBOR", "3MCHFLIBOR", "3MJPYTIBOR", "3MEURIBOR")

alldata.full <- cbind(fxspot.raw, deposits3m, fxfut.raw)
alldata <- alldata.full["2013/"]

# here some calculations have to happen...
```

References

Adelstein, Jake and Nathalie-Kyoko Stucky. "Behind the Biggest Bitcoin Heist in History: Inside the Implosion of Mt. Gox". *The Daily Beast* (May 19, 2016). Retrieved on 26 October 2017. URL: https://www.thedailybeast.com/behind-the-biggest-bitcoin-heist-in-history-inside-the-implosion-of-mt-gox.

Backus, David K. and Gregor W. Smith. "Consumption and Real Exchange Rates in Dynamic Economies with Non-Traded Goods". *Journal of International Economics* 35.3–4 (1993), pp. 297–316. DOI: 10.1016/0022-1996(93)90021-0.

Backus, David K. et al. *Monetary Policy and the Uncovered Interest Rate Parity Puzzle*. Working Paper 1634825. SSRN, 2013. DOI: 10.2139/ssrn.1634825.

Balassa, Bela. "The Purchasing-Power Parity Doctrine: A Reappraisal". *Journal of Political Economy* 72.6 (1964), pp. 584–596. DOI: 10.1086/258965.

Barber, Simon et al. "Bitter to Better: How to Make Bitcoin a Better Currency". In: *Financial Cryptography—FC 2012*. Vol. 7397. Lecture Notes in Computer Science. Retrieved from http://www.cs.stanford.edu/~xb/fc12/ on 28 November 2017. Berlin: Springer-Verlag, 2012, pp. 399–414. DOI: 10.1007/978-3-642-32946-3_29.

BBC. "Iceland to End Capital Controls from 2008 Financial Crisis". *BBC Business News* (Mar. 12, 2017). URL: http://www.bbc.co.uk/news/business-39248677.

Bilson, John F. O. "The "Speculative Efficiency" Hypothesis". *Journal of Business* 54.3 (1981), pp. 435–451. DOI: 10.1086/296139.

Brito, Jerry and Andrea Castillo. *Bitcoin: A Primer for Policymakers*. 2nd ed. Retrieved on 26 October 2017. Arlington, VA: Mercatus Center at George Mason University, 2016. URL: https://www.mercatus.org/system/files/GMU_Bitcoin_042516_WEBv2_0.pdf.

Burnside, Craig et al. "Do Peso Problems Explain the Returns to the Carry Trade?" *Review of Financial Studies* 24.3 (2011), pp. 853–891. DOI: 10.1093/rfs/hhq138.

Cassel, Gustav. "Abnormal Deviations in International Exchanges". *Economic Journal* 28.112 (1918), pp. 413–415. DOI: 10.2307/2223329.

Cho, Meeyoung. "South Korea's Spicy Kimchi Index to Rival Big Mac". *Reuters* (Nov. 8, 2013). Retrieved on 25 October 2017. URL: http://www.reuters.com/article/korea-kimchi/idUSL3N0IT1R520131108.

Darvas, Zsolt. *A Tale of Three Countries: Recovery after a Banking Crisis*. Policy Contribution 2011/19. Bruegel, 2011. URL: http://bruegel.org/wp-content/uploads/imported/publications/111229_zd_A_tale_of_three_countries.pdf.

Dollar, David. "Outward-Oriented Developing Economies Really Do Grow More Rapidly: Evidence from 95 LDCs, 1976–1985". *Economic Development and Cultural Change* 40.3 (1992), pp. 523–544. DOI: 10.1086/451959.

Dryden, John, Katrina Reut, and Barbara Slater. *Comparison of Purchasing Power Parity between the United States and Canada*. Dec. 1, 1987. URL: https://www.bls.gov/opub/mlr/1987/12/art2full.pdf.

Economist. "Cracks in the Crust". *The Economist* (Dec. 11, 2008). Retrieved on 23 October 2017. URL: http://www.economist.com/node/12762027.

— "The Great Chain of Being Sure about Things". *The Economist* (Oct. 31, 2015). Retrieved on 26 October 2017. URL: https://www.economist.com/news/briefing/21677228-technology-behind-bitcoin-lets-people-who-do-not-know-or-trust-each-other-build-dependable.

— "Economics A–Z Terms Beginning with B". *The Economist* (2017). Retrieved on 25 October 2017. URL: http://www.economist.com/economics-a-to-z/b.

Eichholz, Liesl. "MtGox, BTC-e, and the Missing Coins: A Living Timeline of the Greatest Cyber Crime Ever". *Brave New Coin* (Aug. 17, 2017). Retrieved on 26 October 2017. URL: https://bravenewcoin.com/news/mtgox-btc-e-and-the-missing-coins-a-living-timeline-of-the-greatest-cyber-crime-ever/.

Fama, Eugene F. "Forward and Spot Exchange Rates". *Journal of Monetary Economics* 14.3 (1984), pp. 319–338. DOI: 10.1016/0304-3932(84)90046-1.

Fama, Eugene F. and Robert R. Bliss. "The Information in Long-Maturity Forward Rates". *American Economic Review* 77.4 (1987), pp. 680–692. URL: http://www.jstor.org/stable/1814539.

Higgins, Stan. *3 Pre-Bitcoin Virtual Currencies That Bit the Dust.* Nov. 30, 2014. URL: https://www.coindesk.com/3-pre-bitcoin-virtual-currencies-bit-dust/.

Hsieh, David A. "The Determination of the Real Exchange Rate: The Productivity Approach". *Journal of International Economics* 12.3–4 (1982), pp. 355–362. DOI: 10.1016/0022-1996(82)90045-9.

Kremens, Luka and Ian Martin. *The Quanto Theory of Exchange Rates.* Working Paper 2952250. SSRN, 2017. DOI: 10.2139/ssrn.2952250.

Lee, Suzanne S. and Minho Wang. "The Impact of Jumps on Carry Trade Returns". *Journal of Financial Economics* Forthcoming.? (2018?), ??–?? DOI: ?/?.

Mano, Rui C. *Exchange Rates upon Sovereign Default.* Working Paper. University of Chicago, 2013.

Marchiori, Luca. *Monetary Theory Reversed: Virtual Currency Issuance and Miners' Remuneration.* Working Paper 115. Banque Centrale du Luxembourg, 2018. URL: http://www.bcl.lu/en/publications/Working-papers/115/BCLWP115.pdf.

Mundell, Robert A. "A Theory of Optimum Currency Areas". *American Economic Review* 51.4 (1961), pp. 657–665. URL: http://www.jstor.org/stable/1812792.

Officer, Lawrence H. "The Productivity Bias in Purchasing Power Parity: An Econometric Investigation". *Staff Papers (International Monetary Fund)* 23.3 (1976), pp. 545–579. DOI: 10.2307/3866641.

Ong, Li Lian. "Burgernomics: the Economics of the Big Mac Standard". *Journal of International Money and Finance* 16.6 (1997), pp. 865–878. DOI: 10.1016/S0261-5606(97)00032-6.

Samuelson, Paul A. "Theoretical Notes on Trade Problems". *Review of Economics and Statistics* 46.2 (1964), pp. 145–154. DOI: 10.2307/1928178.

Velde, François R. "Bitcoin: A Primer". *Chicago Fed Letter* 317.Dec (2013). Retrieved on 26 October 2017. URL: https://www.chicagofed.org/~/media/publications/chicago-fed-letter/2013/cfldecember2013-317-pdf.pdf.

Woodall, Pam. "On the Hamburger Standard". *The Economist* (Sept. 6, 1986), p. 83.

Part IV

Risk Alleviation

※◻◻

Chapter 19 explains forwards, futures, and swaps: linear hedging instruments.
Chapter 20 introduces options basics and arbitrage relationships.
Chapter 21 explores how to value options and extract useful information from their values.
Chapter 22 discusses credit models, including credit protection, and a model of the firm.
Chapter 23 shows how structured finance uses sorting to offer differing risk-return tradeoffs.

Chapter 19

Forwards, Futures, and Swaps

In Chapter 9 we mentioned how diversification is one of the two major risk-reduction technologies; and, in Chapter 14, we discussed tracking portfolios and how hedging is the other major risk-reduction technology. While tracking portfolios are useful, derivatives like forwards, futures, and swaps are the purest ways to hedge risk factors. They are also the oldest methods of hedging: futures were first seen in the 1700s and forwards can be traced back to Babylonian times over 3500 years ago.

The purpose of this chapter is to introduce these derivative contracts, show how they work, and explain their differences.

19.1 The Specialization of Prices

The earliest concept in trade was likely that of a **spot price**, the paid for a good delivered now at the buyer's location ("on the spot"). Factored into this price are the location, the quality of the goods, and the immediacy with which the goods are delivered; these all affect the price.

However, finding a buyer is difficult, and considering a large number of spot prices is onerous for buyers and sellers alike. The first innovation is typically the rise of markets centered on certain locations — often ports, processing centers, or rail termini. That "or" often became an "and" as industry consolidated in key cities, for example: Chicago, NYC, London, or Tokyo.[1] Large cities like these offered economies of scale, specialized workers, deep labor pools, and interchange between modes of transport.

Once many people regularly came together in these places, these spot prices became more important than other spot prices. This was the first step in standardization. Soon, those spot prices were more liquid and reliable — so other prices were quoted relative to (aka **basis**) the big city prices. This basis is sometimes referred to

---

[1]For an amazing dissection of how such cities affect a nation's development, see Cronon's *Nature's Metropolis: Chicago and the Great West.*

as a **location differential**, the difference between a spot price and the cash price. For example, if the demand for coal to make steel in Gary, Indiana is high, the Gary location differential for coal will be high.

Often, these locations introduced quality grading to group liquidity into a few market segments. Thus these prices became **cash prices**: the price for a standardized amount and quality of a good, now, in a standard location. (People often use "spot" and "cash" interchangeably; however, this is wrong and regulators do distinguish between spot and cash prices.)

19.1.1   Standardization and Speculation

While standardized (cash) prices arise organically, they have other benefits which encourage them to persist. Standardized prices allow comparison across time and also across markets. That allows observers to assess prices in light of their historical levels and uncertainty. Standardized prices also attract buyers and sellers who know what they are getting. This effect has a positive feedback: as potential buyers and sellers see more activity (and thus a greater possibility to trade), they become more likely to enter the market. That makes markets more liquid.

Standardized prices and liquid markets attract speculators because they can assess if prices are unusually cheap or rich versus the variability of prices and see if the market is likely to be liquid enough to permit them to trade. Speculators seek to profit by betting on which way prices will move. In doing this, they take risk off of other peoples' hands (who are willing to sell it) at some price. If the speculators are successful, they will attract more speculators. This encourages competition which helps lower the cost for assuming these risks until it reaches an equilibrium.

Thus speculators offer three major benefits:

- **Risk Transfer**: they assume risk others do not want;
- **Risk Pricing**: they help determine costs of those risks; and,
- **Liquidity**: they trade when others will not and attract competition.

Over time, speculators who are good at assessing economic information and determining where prices will go make money and are able to remain in the market. Those unable to predict well lose money and must leave the market. Thus the market rewards those who can quickly assess information and incorporate it into better prices. If this sounds like we are back to price theory and prices being signals to the macro-economy... you are correct.

Speculators can profit significantly if there are supply constraints. If an asset has high demand and the supply has yet to adjust, the price will rise. If this rise is large, we might say there is a **squeeze** in the asset. Profiting from a squeeze is legal. However, if a speculator creates a squeeze (say, by amassing a large amount of supply and witholding it from the market), that is a **corner** and is not legal. You can profit from tight supply but you may not interfere with supply and demand.

We mentioned before that derivatives are contracts with a payoff depending on (derived from) some measure of an underlying instrument. Usually, this measure is a price or index level, but it may also be a yield or a realized volatility. The contracts are negotiated between two individuals, aka **counterparties**, and may be traded on-exchange or over-the-counter (OTC).

OTC trading is often done over the phone. The advantage of OTC contracts is that they are customized for the counterparties and allow for flexible terms. However, finding a price for such a contract requires contacting a dealer for a quote; and, trades are rarely reported publicly. This makes OTC markets less price-competitive.

19.2 Forwards

Some people cannot tolerate risking where prices will be. They must make expensive business decisions in advance. Often, they base these decisions on prices. This is the classic conundrum of a farmer. The farmer would like to be able to look at prices and, if those seem likely to be profitable, lock in sales at those prices and begin farming. Consumers of the farmer's crops, for example the local baker and brewer, might also like to lock in purchases at those prices. Then all of them can focus on what they do best: farming, baking, and brewing.

Early in history, farmers and those who used their crops devised ways to protect against changing prices. In 1750 BCE Babylonia, the Code of Hammurabi laid out rules for handling contracts in which a farmer sells the crop before harvest. These were the first **forward contracts**: agreements between two people to trade an asset later at a set price. The contract specifies the amount, quality, delivery location/process, and the date. Money changes hands at that later specified date.

19.3 Futures

The main inconvenience of forwards is that they are not traded in one place. Thus a common evolution was the development of an exchange to trade standardized versions of these contracts.

The main risk of forwards is that one of the counterparties may become impaired: they could die, go bankrupt, or run away. There are a few technologies which help mitigate this risk. Schaede (1989) discusses how these were first seen in 1730 in the Dōjima Rice Market.[2]

19.3.1 Marking to Market and Margin

The first technology we can use is **marking to market**, the regular paying or

---

[2]West (2000) discusses the Dōjima Rice Market's rules in detail.

receiving of payment for incremental changes in P&L. The second technology to reduce risk is the use of a **margin account**. Traders must post margin: fund the margin account to the level required for each contract in a position they hold. That account and the funds in it are then credited or debited when marking to market.

Suppose we buy 10 March CME corn contracts expiring in 2019. For these contracts, pricing is per bushel of corn, one contract is for 5,000 bushels (the **contract multiplier**), and the contract requires posting $2,000/contract. The timeline in Table 19.1 shows marking to market (MTM) as prices change.

Day 1	Buy 10 Mar CME corn (ZCH9) @ $4.0700.
	Post margin of $2,000/contract = $20,000.
	Mar corn (ZCH9) closes @ $4.0625.
	Pay MTM debit of $10 \times 5,000 \times \$0.0075 = \$375$.
Day 2	Mar corn (ZCH9) closes @ $4.1950.
	Receive MTM payment of $10 \times 5,000 \times \$0.1225 = \$6,625$.
Day 3	Mar corn (ZCH9) expires @ $4.1900.
	Pay MTM debit of $10 \times 5,000 \times \$0.005 = \$250$.

Table 19.1: Example of marking to market using a margin account.

There are a few key details to remember from this timeline. At expiry, most of the P&L had already been *previously* paid/debited. Therefore, when the contract expires and we close out our position, we get back our total margin posted plus the P&L: in this case, we get back $20,000+$6,000. At no time do we actually pay the purchase cost of $10\times5,000=50,000$ bushels worth of corn. Instead, we receive a payment to offset the change in value of those 50,000 bushels:

$$(\$4.19 - \$4.07) \times 50,000 = \$209,500 - \$203,500 = \$6,000. \qquad (19.1)$$

Without marking to market, we would realize all $6,000 of P&L on day 3 — and hope that the other person was still around and had $6,000 to pay us. With a forward contract, we would have bought 50,000 bushels for $203,500, a $6,000 savings off of the market price on day 3.

So far, our margin account seems to just be a place to hold money. However, margin accounts impose far more requirements on traders. As mentioned before, traders must post margin: fund the margin account to the level required for each contract in their position. The account can be funded with cash and, in some places, a bank letter of credit or government bonds. Those funds are kept in a segregated account; they are not commingled with the exchange's funds.

Margin works like collateral to ensure all monies owed can be paid when mark-to-market happens. There are four key terms to remember when working with a margin account. **Initial margin** is the initial deposit required to fund a margin account.[3] **Maintenance margin** is a minimum account level; falling below this

---

[3]This amount should, in theory, be related to the maximum expected loss at mark-to-market

requires posting more margin. If you fall below maintenance margin, there is a **margin call**: you need to post more margin. However, the exchange *will not* actually call to ask for funds.

Finally, **variation margin** is the amount of money you need to add to the margin account to satisfy a margin call. Usually, the account must be refilled to the initial margin level. This is just like when you share a car with someone: if the tank is low, you refill the tank. What you do *not* do is add just a little bit of fuel and then let the other person refill the tank; that is being a bad person. Similarly, when we need to refill a margin account, we refill it completely.

What do all of these numbers look like as a margin account changes? We can see this by looking at the margin account of somebody with the opposite position of ours in the last example. Table 19.2 shows how a margin account would work for a trader who was short corn in the previous example.

Day 1	Short 10 contracts of Mar CME corn (ZCH9) @ $4.0700.
	Initial margin = 10 × $2,000 = $20,000.
	Mar corn closes @ $4.0625
	Mark-to-market credit = $375; margin balance = $20,375.
Day 2	Mar corn closes @ $4.1950
	Mark-to-market debit = $6,625; margin balance = $13,750.
	Below maintenance margin (75% of $20,000 = $15,000).
	Margin call: must deposit variation margin of $6,250.
	After meeting margin call, margin balance = $20,000.
Day 3	Mar corn closes @ $4.1900
	Mark-to-market credit = $250; margin balance = $20,250.
	Withdraw $20,250 having deposited $26,250; $6,000 less.

Table 19.2: Example of margin account workings for marking to market and a margin call.

19.3.2   The Clearinghouse and Position Netting

Up to now, we pretended that all of these traders have money moving, effectively, just between one another. However, we often use another risk-reduction technique: We often interpose a **clearinghouse** or **central counterparty**, an entity that steps in between every buyer and seller and becomes *everyone's* counterparty. Often, we have only one clearinghouse, a setup known as **central clearing**.

The reason to use a clearinghouse is simple: I might trust a counterparty who posted margin and marks my account to market, but I trust a well-capitalized high-credit intermediary even more. Interposing a clearinghouse greatly reduces

---

time or the first-passage time for the margin amount set. See Telser (1981a), Figlewski (1984) and Longin (1999) for more on these ideas.

counterparties' concerns. Since these contracts hedge risks, trust and stability entices people to enter the market.

If a counterparty goes bankrupt, the bankrupted party only has contracts with the clearinghouse. As we will see in Chapter 26, this reduces chaos and panics. Hence why the US Dodd-Frank Act, EU European Market Infrastructure Regulation, and Swiss Financial Market Infrastructure Act (among others) mandate central clearing for standardized derivatives.

Onions Make You Cry   Onions are easily bruised and contain a lot of sugar, so they go bad quickly. This makes their price volatile. In 1955, two traders cornered the onion market on the CME. They took delivery on futures and stored the onions which led to shortages in parts of the US. They then went short futures and flooded the market. Prices for onions fell so far that the bags were more valuable and many onion farmers went bankrupt. Since onions decay quickly, storage was not an option and many of the excess onions were dumped into Lake Michigan.

In response, Congress passed the Onion Futures Act in 1958 which banned trading futures on onions. Sadly, Working (1960) and Gray (1963) showed that onion futures made the market less volatile and that banning onion futures likely hurt onion farmers. Surprisingly, the traders were not prosecuted and one even ran a restaurant for years: The Jolly Onion Inn. Even now, onion futures are banned in the US.

When we talk about trading and positions, there is some specialized language we use with derivatives. This is because they are agreements between entities: one side's loss is the other side's gain. Since each long is balanced by a short, we say these contracts are in **zero net supply**.

Suppose B sells A 10 contracts of March CME corn at $4.07. In that case, A's position is $+10$ and B's position is -10. If the price of March CME corn goes up $0.10, A makes $0.10 \times 10 \times 5,000 = \$5,000$ and B loses $5,000. Derivatives markets are **zero-sum games**. Furthermore, if we have a clearinghouse, then A would receive a credit from the clearinghouse, not from B; and, B would be debited by the clearinghouse and not by A.

Since there are 10 contracts of exposure exchanging P&L, we say that the **open interest** is 10 contracts. Open interest measures how much risk has been shifted between counterparties. Since 10 contracts were traded. the volume is also 10 contracts. If A were to sell 10 contracts, we would **net positions** and close out A's position. This is convenient: A only needs to hold a hedge so long as necessary.

If A sold the 10 contracts back to B, the open interest would fall to 0; no more risk is being shifted. However, the volume would increase to 20. On the other hand, if A had instead sold to C, C would just be taking over A's position; the open interest would remain at 10 contracts and the volume would increase to 20.

With short-term intermediation, volume can differ greatly from open interest.

19.3.3 Forward to the Futures

We have discussed some ways to reduce risk and increase liquidity. We can:

- *standardize* contracts along a number of dimensions: quality, size, expiry dates, and delivery location;
- trade contracts on an *exchange*;
- require traders to *post margin* in an account;
- *mark to market* (realize P&L) in traders' margin accounts;
- *net positions* regularly to ease exiting positions; and,
- use a well-capitalized *clearinghouse* as all contracts' counterparty.

The features are, together, what change a forward contract into a **futures contract**. These innovations are so useful that they have arisen multiple times, independently, throughout history. The first futures were traded at the Dōjima Rice Market in Osaka, Japan in 1730. They arose again in 1848 at the Chicago Board of Trade (CBOT). The first use of the term "futures" was in 1865 at the CBOT (now merged with the CME).

There are other features that are common but not necessary for futures markets. Among these are **price limits**, maximum price changes allowed before a market is closed for the day or session. Brennan (1986) notes price limits may substitute for margin requirements and are more common in markets with few outside information sources. Chowdhry and Nanda (1998) suggest that price limits increase market stability. Shanker and Balakrishnan (2005) develop theory for the optimal combination of margin, capital, and price limits that a clearinghouse should set.

19.3.4 What People Hedge with Futures

Since the days of rice and corn, futures are now traded on a wide range of underliers allowing us to hedge a number of business-specific risks as well as potential economic state variables. Table 19.3 list a number of types of underliers which are actively traded. Stock index and short-term interest-rate (STIRs) futures are *very* liquid. Some financial economists believe these are the most-liquid financial instruments on Earth (depending on whether one counts the FX market or not). FX futures are also very liquid.

19.4 Using Futures

To use futures to hedge, there are a few details we still need to understand. We should know how to exit a contract and how to not exit and (instead) hedge over an extended period of time. We should also know what opportunities futures make available.

Underlier Type	Underliers
Equity Indices	domestic and foreign, large- and small-cap, sectors.
Interest Rates	short-term (*e.g.* LIBOR), sovereign bonds.
Foreign Exchange	cross-rates with major currencies, others.
Agriculturals	grains, oilseeds/oil/meal, fibers, livestock, softs, ethanol.
Metals	ferrous, base, minor, strategic, precious.
Plastics	plastics, plastic precursors.
Petroleum	crude oil, refined products (*e.g.* jet), natgas, liquified petroleum gases.
Power-related	electric power (daily/monthly, on-/off-peak).
Emissions-related	coal, SO_2, NO_x, CO_2, greenhouse gases.
Other	shipping costs, real estate, weather (heating/cooling days), volatility.

Table 19.3: Actively-traded underliers for futures contracts.

19.4.1   Exiting a Contract

Typically, futures are used to hedge a risk that affects a business. The aforementioned farmer could sell futures to lock in current prices for a later crop sale; and, the baker and brewer could buy futures to lock in prices for later purchases of grain.

Thus producers and consumers use futures to hedge price changes by entering these contracts when they make a commitment to sell or buy later. The specific commodity they get via their supply chain may not be a perfect match with the hedging instrument; however, if the mismatch is compensated for with higher liquidity, then the hedging contract is beneficial.

Offsetting

These hedgers, and speculators, usually **offset** (exit) their position before their futures contracts expire. Hedgers are then free to use their supply chain to get the specific grade of commodity they use delivered to their place of business.

Taking Delivery

Many contracts, especially those for physical commodities, FX, and bonds allow participants to **take delivery**: at expiry, holders of the contract may receive the underlying instrument. The exchange will verify that they want to take delivery, match them with a delivering counterparty, and arrange the payment details. While once possible, the belief that a position at expiry will result in commodities being delivered to somebody's home is now a myth.

Payment happens at the cash price; the futures hedge compensates for how much prices have moved since position entry. Often, delivery is made at **seller's**

option: the counterparty delivering the underlying may have some choice as to which bond or grade of commodity they deliver and where it is delivered. Thus when you take delivery you should expect to receive the lowest-value deliverable in the least-valuable location.

Taking delivery is rare for physical commodities. Kolb and Overdahl (2006) suggests around 1% of metals and energy to 0.25% of grains and oilseeds contracts are delivered. For financial contracts like FX and bonds, delivery is more common: Bowen et al. (2016) show delivery being taken for 1–5% of CME US Treasury futures.

Exchange for Physical

A third option is related to taking delivery: holders may do an **exchange for physical** (EFP). This is like taking delivery except it may be done before expiry and it may be done for contracts which normally do not allow for taking delivery. The quality, location, and price are negotiated by the two parties agreeing to an EFP.

19.4.2 Extended Hedging: Not Exiting a Contract

If we want to maintain our position over an extended period of time, we run into some difficulties. Some exchanges, such as the London Metal Exchange, have longer-term hedging which is somewhat liquid. (This is because LME contracts are a hybrid between forwards and futures.) However, most futures contracts expire quarterly or even monthly.

The contract which expires soonest is typically called the **front month** or **near futures** contract. While spot prices are often quoted basis (relative to) cash prices, when futures traders refer to **the basis** they mean the difference between cash and the near futures: cash−near futures. The contract which expires after that is the **next futures contract**. The near contract is almost always the most-liquid. Apart from short-term interest-rate contracts, even the next contract has far less liquidity.

For this reason, most hedgers and speculators hold the near contract. A few days before the near contract expires, traders who want to keep their futures exposure will **roll** their contracts: they exit the soon-to-expire (near) futures position and transfer that position to the (soon-to-be-near) next futures. The cost of rolling contracts may be positive or negative. We typically state the price of the roll as:

$$\text{Roll}_t = \text{Near Futures}_t - \text{Next Futures}_t. \tag{19.2}$$

If the roll is EUR -5.3, you will pay EUR 5.3 to roll each long contract or will receive EUR 5.3 to roll each short contract. When do people usually roll contracts? Often, people roll when the volume or open interest in the next contract approaches that of the near contract. (These may or may not be the same day.)

19.4.3   What Hath Futures Wrought?

Futures have many benefits and enable some strategies and methods not otherwise possible. Some of these help make markets more fairly priced and some enable us to get around constraints.

Market-wide Benefits

Futures bestow a number of benefits on markets and the economy. As Gray (1963), Turnovsky and Campbell (1985), and Bessembinder and Seguin (1993) note, cash market volatility declines after futures are introduced; and, Bologna and Cavallo (2002) show that this reduction in cash market volatility is likely to be immediate. Telser and Higinbotham (1977) and Telser (1981b) both offer evidence that futures markets enable trade between strangers. This is supported by Bessembinder and Seguin (1992) who note that futures improve liquidity and depth in the underlying cash market.

Chang et al. (2013) show that speculators make futures prices more informative; and, they find little reason to support position limits. ap Gwilym and Ebrahim (2013) also find that position limits are detrimental to the informativeness of the market and do not constrain market manipulation. Turnovsky (1979) shows that futures markets improve the welfare of producers and consumers by helping to guide producers' decisions; and, Turnovsky and Campbell (1985) find that futures markets tend to reduce cash prices with the gains for consumers exceeding the losses for producers. (Thus one side could compensate the other and all would be equally-well- or better-off.)

> **Movies Make You Cry** In 2010, a few finance executives noted that many firms in the film industry had no ability to hedge the risks they took. The financiers thought that if firms could hedge their risk, they might be able to do more and find other sources of financing. They proposed futures contracts on movie box office receipts.
>
> The Motion Picture Association of America (MPAA) hated the idea and lobbied Congress to ban the futures. They claimed such futures were "not good" for their members and could hurt their "image and integrity." While the CFTC approved the futures, Congress banned them in the 2010 Dodd-Frank Act. Cynics claimed the MPAA attacked futures so studios would not have to face transparency and competition on financing. Either way, there are now two prohibited futures underliers in the US: onions and movie box office receipts. For more on this sad ending, read Johnson (2010), Fritz and Popper (2010), and Block (2010).

Gorton and Rouwenhorst (2006) show that commodities futures offer a risk premium with excellent diversification potential for portfolios. Ten years later, Bhardwaj, Gorton, and Rouwenhorst (2015) revisited this idea and confirmed that it holds up out-of-sample.

Thus futures reduce risk, market volatility, and prices for consumers; help send better signals to the economy; increase trade and economic growth; and, provide attractive diversifying investments.

Hedging

The most obvious use of futures is for hedging. Suppose our portfolio had a DV01 of USD 10,000 and we wanted to use the US Treasury ten-year note futures to hedge. The futures contract has a $1,000 face value (multiplier) and a duration of about 8.9 years for notes with about a 2% coupon, yielding a modified duration of about 8.7. If the futures are trading at 90, then:

$$\text{Futures DV01} = 8.7 \times 0.0001 \times \$1000 \times 90 = \$78.3. \tag{19.3}$$

Hedging the portfolio DV01 is easy: we find the DV01 of an interest rate futures contract and then sell the appropriate number of contracts (aka the **hedge ratio**):

$$\text{Hedge ratio} = \frac{\text{Portfolio DV01}}{\text{Futures DV01}} = \frac{\$10,000}{\$78.3} = 127.7 \approx 127. \tag{19.4}$$

Hedging a stock portfolio is even easier. Suppose we have an EUR 1 mn portfolio with a Euro Stoxx 50 beta of 1.1, and we want to eliminate all of our market exposure. Since each contract is for EUR 10 of exposure, we would sell 110,000 contracts.

Index Arbitrage

Stock index futures can be used to enforce the LOOP via **index arbitrage**. When this is done, traders watch the value of the index futures and the value of the stocks in the index multiplied by their weights (minus the present value of any pending dividends, since futures holders do not get dividends). When the ask price for one is below the bid price for the other, they can be traded for a profit.[4]

Index arb traders then have futures positions that are counterbalanced by stock positions. If these positions grow large enough, they can then do an EFP to convert the futures to opposite-way stock positions. Their prime broker will then "flatten" all positions to be 0. Thus index arbitrageurs avoid the Huberman and Stanzl (2004) quasi-arbitrage problems that price impact creates for the APT.[5]

Synthetic Shorting

We can also use the futures to **synthetically short** stocks. To do this, we first buy a stock index futures contract and do an EFP. That gives us the index portfolio of stocks which we hold long. We then short a stock index futures contract, leaving us

---

[4]Some texts will say it is prohibitive or impossible to trade all 500 stocks of the S&P 500, all 1,700 stocks of the Topix, or all 2,000 stocks of the Russell 2000. This is just not true. I know this is false: I have done this trade!

[5]This is not technically an arbitrage since traders might not get filled at those prices. However, this is much closer to true arbitrage than most claimed "arbitrage" strategies.

"flat" (market-neutral); the long stocks balance out the short futures. If we then sell some of our long stocks, we are effectively shorting these stocks — even though we sold them long.

If short sales are banned or only allowed under certain conditions, this is a way around such restrictions. This does, however, use up some of the trader's working capital — which means it is not costless. As we mentioned in Chapter 3, restricting short sales only hurts retail investors because institutions with enough capital have ways around such a ban.

19.5   Swaps

A **swap** is a negotiated agreement to exchange cashflows. Thus a swap is very similar to a futures contract — except with more potential for customization and, therefore, a slower and less-transparent market.

With a futures contract, you go long or short a number of contracts and post margin for each contract; in exchange, you get mark-to-market cashflows. With a swap, you agree to exchange cashflows based on some **notional** amount, but post no margin; in exchange, you pay financing flows and receive your desired cashflows (but do not exchange the notional amount).

The payment cashflows are called the **pay leg**; and, the reception cashflows are called the **receive leg**. One of the legs usually involves a floating interest rate and is often called the **financing leg**. The floating rate on the financing leg also often includes a credit spread specific to your creditworthiness. (The worse your credit is, the higher the spread is.) If the swap **resets** annually, then the floating rate changes every year. At every reset, the counterparties exchange cashflows.

Swaps come in as many different types as there are futures — and then some. Examples of the additional types of swaps include: equity and bond basket swaps, credit default swaps, and asset swaps. An example swap is shown in Figure 19.1.

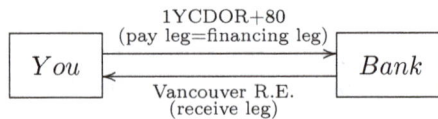

Notional = CAD 50 mn

Figure 19.1: Example swap where you pay floating-rate interest (1-year CDOR + 80 bp) and receive the returns on a Vancouver real estate index from Bank. This is a way to get the same returns as investing CAD 50 mn in the Vancouver real estate market underlying the receive leg.

Kapur, Lewis, and Webb (2011) discuss the first swap: a currency swap between IBM and the World Bank done in August 1981. IBM had obligations in CHF which had depreciated, so it wanted to realize the profits on those; and, IBM had been able to borrow at a better rate in CHF than the World Bank could. The World Bank, meanwhile, was better able to borrow in USD than in CHF.

To take advantage of this, the World Bank borrowed in USD and swapped that payment to IBM in exchange for paying IBM's CHF obligations. Thus each used the relative power of each others' credit.

Since IBM and the World Bank are respected institutions, this quickly lent legitimacy to the swap market. The most common swaps now, however, are interest-rate swaps and equity index swaps.

19.5.1 Interest Rate Swaps

Interest rate swaps are the most "plain-vanilla" swaps. The idea is that one side swaps a fixed-rate payment for a floating-rate payment. For example, you might be receiving interest at a floating rate and owe payments with a fixed interest rate. You could then protect yourself from a cashflow shortfall using an interest rate swap like that in Figure 19.2.

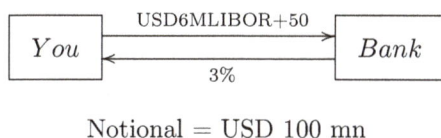

Notional = USD 100 mn

Figure 19.2: Interest rate swap; you pay floating-rate interest (6-month USD LIBOR + 50 bp) and receive fixed-rate interest of 3% from Bank.

A common question at this point is: what determines the fixed rate? The fixed rate is set based on market conditions when the swap is created. At that time, the net present values of expected cashflows should be equal. Interest rate swaps often reset semi-annually to match the coupon frequency of sovereign bonds. However, a swap leg has a lower DV01 than a bond of the same maturity — because the notional for a swap is never exchanged.

While people rarely use the terms "bought" or "sold" with swaps, it is sometimes heard. For an interest rate swap, the person who pays fixed is said to have "sold" the swap.

19.5.2 Other Swaps

Instead of "fixed-for-float" plain-vanilla interest-rate swaps, we might swap other types of cashflows.

In an equity index swap, we might pay USD 3M LIBOR + 35 bp and receive the return on the S&P 500 index. Why would a counterparty do this? It is low-risk: your counterparty need only borrow money, buy the S&P 500 index stocks (or index futures), and pass the returns on. For this reason, equity index swaps often reset quarterly to match the most liquid equity index futures.

In an equity basket swap, we might pay USD 1M LIBOR + 20 bp and receive returns on a portfolio P where both legs have a notional of USD 200 mn. At reset (which is often monthly) we might exchange cashflows and be able to alter the portfolio holdings for the following month. The idea of such a swap is that it works like a **prime brokerage agreement**: when a bank agrees to hold, service, and finance the securities you purchase. However, with a basket swap the financing is limited and transactional which may make it more competitive.

Credit default swaps and asset swaps allow you to hedge your exposure to a default. We will discuss those swaps more in Chapter 23.

19.5.3   Swaps versus Futures

While swaps sound exciting, they are remarkably boring and similar to futures. However, swaps differ from futures in a few key ways. They are:

- *not standardized*, may use any underlying price;
- *traded OTC*, mostly out of London;[6]
- have *no margin* ever posted;
- have *no position netting*; and,
- are often bilaterally-cleared, *not centrally-cleared*.

Standardization and OTC Trading

The lack of standardization and OTC trading go hand-in-hand: it is difficult to have exchange trading of customized products. Some swap counterparties agree to post collateral; however, this may not be involved in making payments at reset dates. The reset dates might seem like marking-to-market, but they are infrequent enough that significant risk can build up (unlike with marking to market).

Position Netting

The lack of position netting is problematic. First, a lack of position netting can enable **cherry picking**: In bankruptcy, counterparty A could choose to only enforce profitable swap contracts while defaulting on unprofitable swap contracts. These swaps might even all be with the same counterparty.

Second, if counterparties A and B enter into a swap and A later wants to exit the swap, it is unlikely that B is looking to exit at the same time. Instead, A will typically enter into another opposite-way swap with a third counterparty (C) to "exit" a trade. While A is no longer exposed to the underlying risk, both swaps still exist.

This accretion of swaps has three effects. First, outstanding notionals for many

---

[6]London may lose a large amount of the swap market when (if?) the UK exits the EU.

swaps are nearly meaningless; they are more like volume than open interest. Second, the countervailing A⇒B and A⇐C swaps make A responsible for the cashflows between B and C; A has become a conduit. Third, accretion of swaps exposes A to increasing amounts of **counterparty risk**: the risk that a counterparty (*e.g.* B or C) will fail to meet their obligations. If A needed the cash flows from B to pay C or vice versa, the failure of B or C could force A into bankruptcy.

While some point out that swap counterparties must have very good credit, swaps often last for years. During that time, a counterparty's credit can drift far from where it was at the start of the swap.

There are optional **compression** services which net out all swaps with a counterparty and even try to eliminate countervailing swaps and replace them with swaps between exposed counterparties (*e.g.* B⇐C).

Margin

Some swaps traders demand that their counterparty post margin into an escrow account. This is still unusual though.

Central Clearing

Central clearing can claim many successes. The events it has handled smoothly is impressive:

- 1987 stock market crash;
- 1991 Persian Gulf War;
- Refco bankruptcy (failure of #1 CME futures broker);
- Amaranth bankruptcy (failure of a large commodities hedge fund);
- Bear Stearns near-bankruptcy;
- Lehman Brothers bankruptcy.

The last two events are especially impressive. Before nearly failing, Melamed (2009) reveals that Bear Stearns held futures contracts with exposure equivalent to about USD 700 bn at the CME; and, Lehman held futures contracts with exposure equivalent to about USD 1.3 tn at the CME. The CME clearinghouse and Options Clearing Corporation (the central clearinghouse for options in the US) have never defaulted.

Before the 2008 financial crisis, a subset of the interest rate swaps market was centrally-cleared by the London Clearing House's SwapClear.[7] After 2008, regulations in many economies were changed to encourage central clearing of OTC products. The idea of this is to reduce the counterparty risk of these contracts. Centralized trading is also often encouraged.

You might then wonder: what would be the difference between centrally-cleared swaps and futures? Apart from not requiring margin or needing to roll contracts

---

[7]SwapClear now clears over half of the interest-rate swap market.

and far less-frequent marking to market (*i.e.* resets), the answer seems to be "not much."[8]

19.6   Pricing Forwards and Futures

We have already heard arguments that futures exist to help with price discovery. Therefore, it should not be surprising that Fama and French (1987) and Ma (1989) find futures are better predictors of later cash prices than some advanced econometric models.

Since forwards and futures effectively lock in the current price for later trade of an underlying instrument, we should be able to determine no-arbitrage prices for them.

If you were to borrow the money to pay the cash price and hold the underlier for the duration of the contract, you would owe the cash price plus interest from time t to T, $r_{t,T}$. Therefore, the valuation needs to include interest. Depending on how the loan charges interest, the value $f_{t,T}$ at time t of a forward contract maturing at time T (*i.e.* in $T - t$ years) would be:

$$f_{t,T} = S_t(1 + (T - t)r_{t,T}) \quad \text{(simple interest) or,} \qquad (19.5)$$

$$= S_t e^{r_{t,T}(T-t)} \quad \text{(continuous interest).} \qquad (19.6)$$

19.6.1   How Dividends Affect Pricing

If the underlier is a stock, stock portfolio, or stock index, however, holding a forward has another important difference: you do not get dividends. Therefore, the value calculation needs to exclude the present value of dividends. This gives us what is often called **fair value**:

$$f_{t,T} = (S_t - D_{t,T})(1 + (T - t)r_{t,T}) \quad \text{(simple rates) or,} \qquad (19.7)$$

$$= S_t e^{(r_{t,T} - d_{t,T})(T-t)} \quad \text{(continuous rates),} \qquad (19.8)$$

where $D_{t,T}$ is the present value of dividends payable during the period (t, T) scaled by the index weights and divided by the index divisor; and, $d_{t,T} = \frac{D_{t,T}}{S_t}$, is the **dividend yield**.

19.6.2   Convenience Yield and Cost of Carry

One of the earlier observations about forwards and futures was that they tended to trade at a discount to holding the underlier. This reason? If the underlier price is

---

[8]This comment is not of minor significance. In 1998, CFTC Chair Brooksley Born noted that many swaps seemed similar to futures and thus might be subject to CFTC oversight. In response, many banks migrated their swaps trading to London. History showed, however, that she was right.

volatile, holding the underlier allows a person to sell the underlier when prices spike. Holding the underlier gives the holder an option to take advantage of volatility.

Kaldor (1939) noted this and coined the term **convenience yield**: an offset to interest rates that accounts for the option value of being able to deliver into price spikes.[9] Weymar (1968) related convenience yield to the probability of inventory stockout: the higher the likelihood of running out of the commodity, the higher the convenience yield. Gorton, Hayashi, and Rouwenhorst (2013) also show the convenience yield is a decreasing (and nonlinear) function of inventories.

We also need to add in the **cost of carry**: the cost of storage, transport, and insurance. While we will not explore this topic, Working (1949) is a good place to start for those interested.

Note that convenience yield and cost-of-carry also apply to financial underliers. Borrowing currencies costs money; and, some bonds that underlie futures contracts can be involved in a squeeze if more futures holders want to take delivery than there are easily-available bonds to deliver.

If we let y_t and c_t be the convenience yield and cost of carry, we then have our final formulas for forward pricing:

$$f_{t,T} = (S_t - D_{t,T})(1 + (T - t)(r_{t,T} + c_t - y_t))) \quad \text{or,} \tag{19.9}$$
$$= S_t e^{(r_{t,T} + c_t - y_t - d_{t,T})(T-t)}. \tag{19.10}$$

For **full carry markets**, this relationship holds up well: the full cost-of-carry is priced in. Some markets trade below full carry. This may be due to mis-estimation of the convenience yield or because some market participants have access to lower-cost storage than the rest of the market.

19.6.3   The Effect of Marking to Market

Unfortunately, fair value is misleading because it gives the value of a forward contract not a futures contract. With a forward, we lock in a later trade price; there are no cashflows until the expiry and that is for an already-agreed-upon price. Interest rates are uncertain but we assume (due to market efficiency) that interest rates are semimartingales. Therefore, the fair value has only one source of randomness: the interest rate. Taking the expectation of that only requires plugging in the current interest rate.

With a futures contract, the cashflows are uncertain due to marking-to-market. We get interest on the capital we need not tie up by buying the underlier, on the money in our margin account, and on the money credited to our margin account. Thus we can write the random futures value $F_{t,T}$ at time t for a contract maturing

---

[9]Kaldor actually refers to a yield "that consists of 'convenience.'" That is close enough for a neologism.

at time T as:

$$F_{t,T} = (S_t - D_{t,T})(1 + (T - t)(r_{t,T} + c_t - y_t)) \quad \text{or,} \qquad (19.11)$$

$$= S_t e^{(r_{t,T} + c_t - y_t - d_{t,T})(T-t)}. \qquad (19.12)$$

While $T - t$ is deterministic and known, S_t, r_t, and $D_{t,T}$ are random. We need to find the expectation of the dynamics equation; however, futures are marked-to-market so we must consider the correlations to properly evaluate the expectation. Since dividends change slowly, we will ignore correlations between $D_{t,T}$ and S_t or $r_{t,T}$.

Using the identity $\text{Cov}(X, Y) = \rho_{XY}\sigma_X\sigma_Y = E(XY) - E(X)E(Y)$ and a first-order Taylor expansion, we have:

$$\tilde{F}_{t,T} = E(F_{t,T} | \mathcal{F}_t, D_{t,T}, y_t, c_t), \qquad (19.13)$$

$$= (S_t - D_{t,T})(1 + (T - t)(r_{t,T} + c_t - y_t)) +$$
$$(T - t)\rho_{S,r,t,T}\sigma_{S_t}\sigma_{r_{t,T}} \quad \text{or,} \qquad (19.14)$$

$$\approx S_t e^{(r_{t,T} + c_t - d_{t,T})(T-t)} + (T - t)\rho_{S,r,t,T}\sigma_{S_t}\sigma_{r_{t,T}}, \qquad (19.15)$$

where $\rho_{S,r,t,T} = \text{Corr}(S_t, r_{t,T})$.

This shows that if there is a positive correlation between interest rates and the underlier, the value of a futures contract will differ from fair value:

$$\tilde{F}_{t,T} > f_{t,T} \text{ if } \text{Corr}(S_t, r_{t,T}) > 0, \text{ and} \qquad (19.16)$$

$$\tilde{F}_{t,T} < f_{t,T} \text{ if } \text{Corr}(S_t, r_{t,T}) < 0. \qquad (19.17)$$

19.7   The Futures Curve

One of the more useful tools used by futures traders is the **futures curve**: the plot of cash and futures contract prices versus their expiry dates. This plot gives us some idea of relative supply and demand, including the cost of carry. Figure 19.3 shows two example futures curves. There are a few details we should note about these plots.

First, we should explain these plots: Figure 19.3 shows prices for cash and futures with increasing times to expiry. As time moves on, the futures time to expiry decreases — so all of the points (except cash) move to the left. However, they do not just move to the left; they also tend to move along the curve. Points on curve A will tend to move down and to the left as time goes on; points on curve B will tend to move up and to the left as time goes on. At the same time, cash and the near futures often have a mild tendency to move in the direction of later futures. If this sounds like mean-reverting behavior, hold that thought: we will talk about that shortly.

If the futures curve increases, like curve A, we say the market is in **contango**.

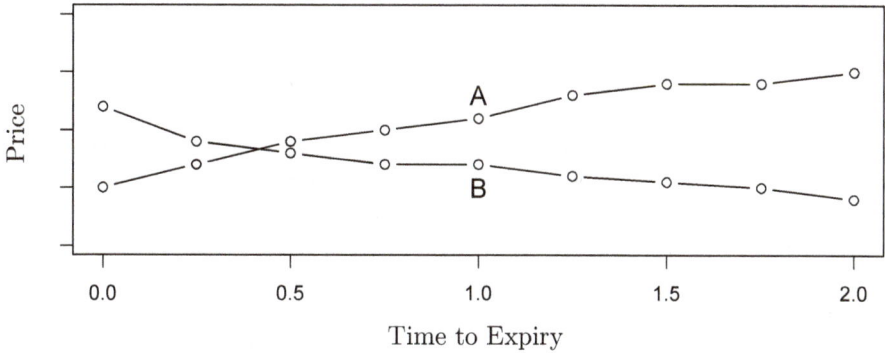

Figure 19.3: Futures curve showing cash price and prices of futures contracts for various expiries. Curve A is said to be in contango; curve B is said to be in backwardation.

Contango is sometimes defined as futures prices being above the cash price expected at expiry. Since prices tend to move along the curve, these two definitions agree. Contango markets often exhibit a rising futures curve due to the cost of carry.

If the futures curve decreases, like curve B, we say the market is in **backwardation**. This comes from the theory in Keynes (1930) that producers will seek to hedge and those seeking to hedge farther in the future are more risk-averse and thus will depress later-expiring futures prices more. While this sounds sensible, it completely ignores the reality that consumers also want to hedge.

Often, however, curves are neither clearly in backwardation or contango. This could be due to the direction of the macroeconomy, harvest season, earnings-reporting season, or other fluctuations in supply and demand for hedging.

Also, since cash and the near futures are the most liquid and active instruments, they tend to move around more. Thus most futures curve models focus on modeling the front of the futures curve and not the whole curve (as is done for yield curves).

19.7.1 Futures Curve Models

We have already mentioned the Keynes (1930) theory of "normal" backwardation. Hotelling (1931) suggests that the price of exhaustible resources should increase at the risk-free rate; however, he neglected short-term supply constraints, changes in extraction or usage technology, and tail risks.

Hence it should not be so surprising that these theories do not agree with the data. Instead, Telser and Higinbotham (1977) and Telser (1981b) suggest that the main driver of futures markets is that they enable trade between strangers, not merely the hedging needs of producers.

Stylized Facts

First, we should examine some **stylized facts**: generalities that tend to be true across many analyses (and often many time periods and economies).[10] Samuelson (1965a) noted that price volatility falls with increasing times to expiry. Unusual prices far in the future will affect production and storage and induce more holders to deviate from their preferred holdings to take advantage of that unusual price. Thus the cash price is often the most volatile. Fama and French (1988) note that this is generally true when inventory is low; however, when inventory is high they note that all expiries have similar (lower) volatility.

Fama and French (1987) proposed a proxy for inventory related to the slope of the future curve (via changes in the convenience yield). Geman and Nguyen (2005) showed that volatility was proportional to 1/inventory and added that to a curve model. However, it was unclear if the Fama and French (1987) curve slope proxy was accurate until Geman and Ohana (2009); they showed that the curve slope is a good proxy for inventory.

Curve Models

Bessembinder et al. (1995) showed that investors expect mean reversion of cash prices for commodities but only mildly for financial underliers. If we think about how slowly industry cost structures change, this makes sense for physical commodities; and, if we think about how the macroeconomy changes more quickly, it also makes sense for financial underliers to revert less and be more volatile.

Schwartz (1997) considers models with mean-reversion in the cash, the convenience yield, and even interest rates. Given that cost structures and the macroeconomy do change, we might wonder if a model should include a non-constant equilibrium to which cash prices revert. Schwartz and Smith (2000) model prices with a mean-reverting cash price toward an uncertain (*i.e.* stochastic) equilibrium. They note that this performs better than earlier models with a stochastic convenience yield.

These suggest a model something like the following model for log-returns $r_{F,t,T}$ of futures $F_{t,T}$ with underlier price X_t:

$$r_{F,t,T} = \alpha + \beta(\bar{X}_t - X_t)e^{-\gamma_1(T-t)} + \epsilon_{t,T}, \tag{19.18}$$

$$\epsilon_{t,T} \overset{\perp}{\sim} \left(0, \frac{\sigma_t}{\text{inventory}_t}e^{-\gamma_2(T-t)}\right), \tag{19.19}$$

$$\bar{X}_t = \frac{\sum_{i=1}^n \phi_i X_{t-i}}{\sum_{i=1}^n \phi_i}. \tag{19.20}$$

However, if cash prices revert to an equilibrium, that suggests they are stationary. In that case we need not work with log-returns; we can work with prices. (Obviously,

---

[10]This term, in addition to "convenience yield," was coined by Kaldor, a master of the brave new word.

the weak mean-reversion findings for financials would mean we cannot do this for financial underliers. Except, perhaps, for fixed income underliers which we found earlier might be mean-reverting.)

If we believe cash prices are stationary, we can just model the futures curve directly:

$$F_{t,T} = \alpha + \beta(\bar{X}_t - X_t)e^{-\gamma_1(T-t)} + \beta_2 X_t e^{r_{t,T}+\kappa c_t - d_{t,T} - \upsilon_{t,T}} + \epsilon_{t,T}, \qquad (19.21)$$

$$\epsilon_{t,T} \overset{\perp}{\sim} \left(0, \frac{\sigma_t}{\text{inventory}_t}e^{-\gamma_2(T-t)}\right), \qquad (19.22)$$

$$\bar{X}_t = \frac{\sum_{i=1}^n \phi_i X_{t-i}}{\sum_{i=1}^n \phi_i}, \qquad (19.23)$$

with the cost-of-carry coefficient κ and the convenience yield $\upsilon_{t,T}$ being estimated as well. How long of a window n should we use? Pesaran and Timmermann (2007) and Matteson et al. (2013) offer guidance on that.

Obviously, futures curve models can get a bit complicated. We will explore that a little in the exercises.

19.8 Quiz

Try to answer these questions in ten minutes. For answers with equations, just write the equations; do not evaluate them or use a calculator.

1. Name three differences that turn a forward contract into a futures contract.

2. Suppose you have a margin account. Initial margin is $8,000; maintenance margin is $6,000. You hold a futures contract for $100,000 of S&P 500 exposure. The S&P 500 drops by 3%.

   Your account balance was $7,500 before the S&P dropped.

   a) What is your account balance after the drop?
   b) What is your variation margin?

3. Many exchange-traded derivatives are "marked to market." What is marking to market?

4. What is one of the laws which have pushed many swaps to be centrally-cleared?

5. Abhi buys 20 S&P 500 index futures contracts from Sabrina. Who is on the other side of Abhi's position?

6. Abhi then sells the preceding 20 contracts to Catie.

   a) What is Abhi's exposure?
   b) What is Abhi's capital commitment?

7. If Abhi instead entered into a $10 mn notional S&P 500 index swap with Sabrina and then a similar opposite-way swap with Catie:

   a) What would Abhi's S&P 500 exposure be?
   b) What would Abhi's capital commitment be?
   c) What would be the notional value of contracts held by Abhi?
   d) What risks would Abhi be exposed to?

8. (Bonus!) Suppose the tech industry is having trouble; but, the government bans short selling and put options on tech firms — to stop speculators from driving prices down. How might we still gain short exposure to Motorola?

19.9   Exercises

Instructions

We have seen that the term structure matters for interest rates; and, we have mentioned the futures curve. Now it is time to see how the two might differ. We will be looking at the futures curve for two commodities that are strongly connected to economic activity: crude oil and natural gas.

Crude oil is refined to make naphtha, gasoline (petrol), middle distillates (diesel fuel, kerosene, gasoil, jet fuel), fuel oil, and coke — but also light aromatics which may be plastics precursors like benzene, toluene, ethylene, and xylene. Natural gas can be used to make methane, ethane, propane, and cracked to make light aromatics; natgas is also increasingly burned in North America to create electricity.

1. Using the code supplied, get prices for West Texas Intermediate crude oil. Create returns and then do a principle components. Looking at the eigenvectors, what two curve movements seem to dominate the way the term structure moves?

2. How has the way the curve moves changed since the introduction of hydraulic fracturing? Did the financial crisis induce any unusual curve movements?

3. Using the code supplied, get prices for Henry Hub natural gas. Create returns and then do a principle components analysis. Looking at the eigenvectors, what three curve movements seem to dominate the way the term structure moves?

4. How has the way the curve moves changed since the introduction of hydraulic fracturing? Did the financial crisis induce any unusual curve movements? Is there a trend in how the curve movements have changed?

R Code

```
library(xts)
library(Quandl)
```

```
## Get 6 contracts of the crude curve
crude.tickers <- c("CHRIS/CME_CL1", "CHRIS/CME_CL2", "CHRIS/CME_CL3",
                   "CHRIS/CME_CL4", "CHRIS/CME_CL5", "CHRIS/CME_CL6")
settle.field <- "Settle"
crude.prices <- Quandl(crude.tickers[1], type="xts")[,settle.field]
for (i in 2:length(crude.tickers)) {
    crude.tmp <- Quandl(crude.tickers[i], type="xts")[,settle.field]
    crude.prices <- cbind(crude.prices, crude.tmp)
}
colnames(crude.prices) <- paste("CL", 1:6, sep="")

crude.returns <- na.omit(diff(log(crude.prices)))
pc.crude <- princomp(crude.returns)
summary(pc.crude)
loadings(pc.crude)

## Get 6 contracts of the natgas curve
natgas.tickers <- c("CHRIS/CME_NG1", "CHRIS/CME_NG2", "CHRIS/CME_NG3",
                    "CHRIS/CME_NG4", "CHRIS/CME_NG5", "CHRIS/CME_NG6")
settle.field <- "Settle"
natgas.prices <- Quandl(natgas.tickers[1], type="xts")[,settle.field]
for (i in 2:length(natgas.tickers)) {
    natgas.tmp <- Quandl(natgas.tickers[i], type="xts")[,settle.field]
    natgas.prices <- cbind(natgas.prices, natgas.tmp)
}
colnames(natgas.prices) <- paste("NG", 1:6, sep="")

natgas.returns <- na.omit(diff(log(natgas.prices)))
pc.natgas <- princomp(natgas.returns)
summary(pc.natgas)
loadings(pc.natgas)
```

References

ap Gwilym, Rhys and M. Shahid Ebrahim. "Can Position Limits Restrain 'Rogue' Trading?" *Journal of Banking and Finance* 37.3 (2013), pp. 824–836. DOI: 10.1016/j.jbankfin.2012.10.025.

Bessembinder, Hendrik and Paul J. Seguin. "Futures-Trading Activity and Stock Price Volatility". *Journal of Finance* 47.5 (1992), pp. 2015–2034. DOI: 10.1111/j.1540-6261.1992.tb04695.x.

— "Price Volatility, Trading Volume, and Market Depth: Evidence from Futures Markets". 28.1 (1993), pp. 21–39. DOI: 10.2307/2331149.

Bessembinder, Hendrik et al. "Mean Reversion in Equilibrium Asset Prices: Evidence from the Futures Term Structure". *Journal of Finance* 50.1 (1995), pp. 361–375. DOI: 10.1111/j.1540-6261.1995.tb05178.x.

Bhardwaj, Geetesh, Gary Gorton, and K. Geert Rouwenhorst. *Facts and Fantasies about Commodity Futures Ten Years Later*. Working Paper 21243. NBER, 2015. DOI: 10.3386/w21243.

Block, Alex Ben. "Congress Bans Boxoffice Futures Trading". *The Hollywood Reporter* (July 15, 2010). URL: https://www.hollywoodreporter.com/news/congress-bans-boxoffice-futures-trading-25542.

Bologna, Pierluigi and Laura Cavallo. "Does the Introduction of Stock Index Futures Effectively Reduce Stock Market Volatility? Is the 'Futures Effect' Immediate? Evidence from the Italian Stock Exchange Using GARCH". *Applied Financial Economics* 12.3 (2002), pp. 183–192. DOI: 10.1080/09603100110088085.

Bowen, Christopher et al. *The Treasury Futures Delivery Process*. 6th ed. Chicago: Chicago Mercantile Exchange, 2016. URL: http://www.cmegroup.com/trading/interest-rates/files/us-treasury-futures-delivery-process.pdf.

Brennan, Michael J. "A Theory of Price Limits in Futures Markets". *Journal of Financial Economics* 16.2 (1986), pp. 213–233. DOI: 10.1016/0304-405X(86)90061-9.

Chang, Ya-Kai et al. "The Effectiveness of Position Limits: Evidence from the Foreign Exchange Futures Markets". *Journal of Banking and Finance* 37.11 (2013), pp. 4501–4509. DOI: 10.1016/j.jbankfin.2013.02.033.

Chowdhry, Bhagwan and Vikram Nanda. "Leverage and Market Stability: The Role of Margin Rules and Price Limits". *Journal of Business* 71.2 (1998), pp. 179–210. DOI: 10.1086/209742.

Cronon, William. *Nature's Metropolis: Chicago and the Great West*. New York: W.W. Norton & Co., 1991.

Fama, Eugene F. and Kenneth R. French. "Commodity Futures Prices: Some Evidence on Forecast Power, Premiums, and the Theory of Storage". *Journal of Business* 60.1 (1987), pp. 55–73. DOI: 10.1086/296385.

— "Business Cycles and the Behavior of Metals Prices". *Journal of Finance* 43.5 (1988), pp. 1075–1093. DOI: 10.1111/j.1540-6261.1988.tb03957.x.

Figlewski, Stephen. "Margins and Market Integrity: Margin Setting for Stock Index Futures and Options". *Journal of Futures Markets* 4.3 (1984), pp. 385–416. DOI: 10.1002/fut.3990040307.

Fritz, Ben and Nathaniel Popper. "Hollywood Wants Movie Bets off the Table". *Los Angeles Times* (Mar. 26, 2010). URL: articles.latimes.com/2010/mar/26/business/la-fi-ct-mpaa26-2010mar26.

Geman, Hélyette and Vu-Nhat Nguyen. "Soybean Inventory and Forward Curve Dynamics". *Management Science* 51.7 (2005), pp. 1076–1091. DOI: 10.1287/mnsc.1050.0361.

Geman, Hélyette and Steve Ohana. "Forward Curves, Scarcity and Price Volatility in Oil and Natural Gas Markets". *Energy Economics* 31.4 (2009), pp. 576–585. DOI: 10.1016/j.eneco.2009.01.014.

Gorton, Gary and K. Geert Rouwenhorst. "Facts and Fantasies about Commodity Futures". *Financial Analyst's Journal* 62.2 (2006), pp. 47–68. DOI: 10.2469/faj.v62.n2.4083.

Gorton, Gary B., Fumio Hayashi, and K. Geert Rouwenhorst. "The Fundamentals of Commodity Futures Returns". *Review of Finance* 17.1 (2013), pp. 35–105. DOI: 10.1093/rof/rfs019.

Gray, Roger W. "Onions Revisited". *American Journal of Agricultural Economics*

45.2 (1963). The journal was called the *Journal of Farm Economics* when this article was published, pp. 273–276. DOI: 10.2307/1235974.

Hotelling, Harold. "The Economics of Exhaustible Resources". *Journal of Political Economy* 39.2 (1931), pp. 137–175. DOI: 10.1086/254195.

Huberman, Greg and Werner Stanzl. "Price Manipulation and Quasi-Arbitrage". *Econometrica* 74.4 (2004), pp. 1247–1276. DOI: 10.1111/j.1468-0262.2004.00531.x.

Johnson, Ted. "Senate Snuffs out Film Futures' Future". *Variety* (July 15, 2010). URL: http://variety.com/2010/film/markets-festivals/senate-snuffs-out-film-futures-future-1118021839/.

Kaldor, Nicholas. "Speculation and Economic Stability". *Review of Economic Studies* 7.1 (1939), pp. 1–27. DOI: 10.2307/2967593.

Kapur, Devesh, John P. Lewis, and Richard C. Webb. *The World Bank: Its First Half Century*. Vol. 1. Washington, DC: Brookings Institution Press, 2011.

Keynes, John Maynard. *A Treatise on Money*. Vol. 2. New York: Harcourt, Brace and Company, 1930.

Kolb, Robert W. and James A. Overdahl. *Understanding Futures Markets*. 6th ed. New York: Wiley-Blackwell, 2006.

Longin, François M. "Optimal Margin Level in Futures Markets: Extreme Price Movements". *Journal of Futures Markets* 19.2 (1999), pp. 127–152. DOI: 10.1002/(sici)1096-9934(199904)19:2<127::aid-fut1>3.0.co;2-m.

Ma, Cindy W. "Forecasting Efficiency of Energy Futures Prices". *Journal of Futures Markets* 9.5 (1989), pp. 393–419. DOI: 10.1002/fut.3990090504.

Matteson, David S. et al. "Locally Stationary Vector Processes and Adaptive Multivariate Modeling". *2013 IEEE International Conference on Acoustics, Speech and Signal Processing* (2013), pp. 8722–8726. DOI: 10.1109/ICASSP.2013.6639369.

Melamed, Leo. *For Crying Out Loud: From Open Outcry to the Electronic Screen*. New York: Wiley, 2009.

Pesaran, M. Hashem and Allan Timmermann. "Selection of Estimation Window in the Presence of Breaks". *Journal of Econometrics* 137.1 (2007), pp. 134–161. DOI: 10.1016/j.jeconom.2006.03.010.

Samuelson, Paul A. "Proof That Properly Anticipated Prices Fluctuate Randomly". *Industrial Management Review* 6.2 (1965), pp. 41–49.

Schaede, Ulrike. "Forwards and Futures In Tokugawa-Period Japan: A New Perspective on the Dōjima Rice Market". *Journal of Banking and Finance* 13.4-5 (1989), pp. 487–513. DOI: 10.1016/0378-4266(89)90028-9.

Schwartz, Eduardo and James E. Smith. "Short-Term Variations and Long-Term Dynamics in Commodity Prices". *Management Science* 46.7 (2000), pp. 893–911. DOI: 10.1287/mnsc.46.7.893.12034.

Schwartz, Eduardo S. "The Stochastic Behavior of Commodity Prices: Implications for Valuation and Hedging". *Journal of Finance* 52.3 (1997), pp. 923–973. DOI: 10.1111/j.1540-6261.1997.tb02721.x.

Shanker, Latha and Narayanaswamy Balakrishnan. "Optimal Clearing Margin, Capital and Price Limits for Futures Clearinghouses". *Journal of Banking and Finance* 29.7 (2005), pp. 1611–1630. DOI: 10.1016/j.jbankfin.2004.06.037.

Telser, Lester G. "Margins and Futures Contracts". *Journal of Futures Markets* 1.2 (1981), pp. 225–253. DOI: 10.1002/fut.3990010213.

— "Why There Are Organized Futures Markets". *The Journal of Law & Economics* 24.1 (1981), pp. 1–22. DOI: 10.1086/466971.

Telser, Lester G. and Harlow N. Higinbotham. "Organized Futures Markets: Costs and Benefits". *Journal of Political Economy* 85.5 (1977), pp. 969–1000. DOI: 10.1086/260617.

Turnovsky, Stephen J. "Futures Markets, Private Storage, and Price Stabilization". *Journal of Public Economics* 12.3 (1979), pp. 301–327. DOI: 10.1016/0047-2727(79)90035-5.

Turnovsky, Stephen J. and Robert B. Campbell. "The Stabilizing and Welfare Properties of Futures Markets: A Simulation Approach". *International Economic Review* 26.2 (1985), pp. 277–303. DOI: 10.2307/2526584.

West, Mark D. "Private Ordering at the World's First Futures Exchange". *Michigan Law Review* 98.8 (2000): *Symposium: Empirical Research in Commercial Transactions*, pp. 2574–2615. DOI: 10.2307/1290356.

Weymar, Frank Helmut. *The Dynamics of the World Cocoa Market*. Cambridge, MA: MIT Press, 1968.

Working, Holbrook. "The Theory of Price of Storage". *American Economic Review* 39.6 (1949), pp. 1254–1262. URL: http://www.jstor.org/stable/1816601.

— "Price Effects of Futures Trading". *Food Research Institute Studies* 1.1 (1960), pp. 3–31.

Chapter 20

Options Basics

Once we begin to consider hedging, we often realize that we might want to only hedge downside or upside in prices. Alternately, we might wonder how to value choices we have in our lives or in business. This is where options come in.

The purpose of this chapter is to introduce options, discuss some relationships which hold, and illustrate how options exist in contracts and decisions all around us.

20.1 Fundamentals

An **option** is a contract which gives holder the right, but not the obligation, to buy or sell an underlying instrument.[1] As with futures, options also have an **expiry date**. The right to buy or sell is at a **strike price**, typically denoted as K. (Some options reference prices indirectly, such as those which reference yields.) Trading at the strike price might be a good deal at expiry, depending on the underlier price which we typically denote S_t. The option holder **exercises** that right if the price is a good deal.

Comparing the underlier price to the strike price determines option value. **Call options** allow the holder to buy the underlier at the strike price. **Put options** allow the holder to sell the underlier at the strike price. **Moneyness** refers to the value of immediately exercising an option. We say that an option which offers a good deal is **in-the-money** (ITM); one that is not a good deal is **out-of-the-money** (OOM); and, one with the underlying price at the strike price is **at-the-money** (ATM). Table 20.1 shows the cases where we use different terms for moneyness.

Since an option might offer a good deal, it is not free to purchase. The price to buy an option is called the **premium**. The seller, or **writer**, of an option gives up the ability to choose whether an option is exercised; the writer is obliged to provide the benefit if the holder exercises the option. (This benefit may be financial

---

[1]This phrase, "the right, but not the obligation," is another shibboleth in finance.

Option	$S_t < K$	$S_t = K$	$S_t > K$
Put	In the money	At the money	Out of the money
Call	Out of the money	At the money	In the money

Table 20.1: Moneyness for various cases of underlier price S_t versus strike price K.

compensation or the underlying instrument.) In exchange for giving up the ability to choose, options writers get paid premium.

Finally, some options may only be exercised on the expiry date; we say these options are **European**. Other options have... more freedom: they can be exercised at any time; we say these options are **American**.[2] Most stock, interest-rate, and futures options are American. Most index and many FX options are European.

20.2   Options Markets

While forwards are over 3500 years old, Knoll (2008) only finds evidence of using embedded options back about 2000 years ago. As for explicitly-traded options, de la Vega (1688) discusses options being traded in Amsterdam; and, Kohn (2017) notes options being sold in Italy in the 1400s.

However, organized exchanges devoted to options are a recent invention. The first options exchange was the Chicago Board Options Exchange (CBOE), formed by traders from the Chicago Board of Trade on 26 April 1973. The date was auspicious for two reasons: 1973 was the 125-th anniversary of the Chicago Board of Trade, and it was shortly before some innovations which would give a jolt to option trading. (We will get to those shortly.) At the time, however, options were considered so minor that an article about the CBOT's anniversary, Lee (1973a), did not even mention their new options exchange. (The author was not uninformed: he also wrote about the options exchange's first day in Lee (1973b).)

However, trading in options grew quickly. As with the competition among trading venues for equities and bonds, options venues are now competing vigorously in the US. While the CBOE is the biggest options exchange, there are many other exchanges competing with it including the International Securities Exchange (ISE), venues from the NYSE and Nasdaq, and even the Boston Options Exchange... which recently opened a trading floor in Chicago.

While popular in the US, options trading is not nearly as widespread globally as futures trading. However, it has taken off in a few places outside of the US. According to WFE (2016) and IOMA (2017), single-stock options are also heavily-traded in Brazil, the EU, India, Australia, and South Africa. Stock index options are more

---

[2]No, I am not making this up. I know it plays into every stereotype Europeans have about Americans obsessing about freedom and seeing the US as superior. However, I bet that now you will not forget which option can be exercised when.

widely-traded: they are heavily-traded in those countries as well as Korea, Taiwan, Israel, Japan, and Hong Kong. Interest-rate options are traded mostly in the US, Europe, Australia, and Canada. FX options are largely traded in the US (followed distantly by India and Israel). Finally, commodity options are almost exclusively traded in the US and the UK.

As with futures, options are a potential source of counterparty risk. For that reason, exchange-traded options use central clearing. Unlike futures, however, options markets have sometimes separated the clearinghouse from the exchange to allow for venue competition. For example, the clearinghouse for options in the US, the Options Clearing Corp, is not tied to any one exchange. This structure allows a person to buy an option on one venue and sell it on another.

20.3 Payoffs and Strategies

With what we know, we can determine the payoff at expiry for an option. Since the value involves strategic choice, we would exercise the option if it has positive value and otherwise not exercise it. Thus the value has a floor at zero. Since this choice is mechanical, we can write it like so:

$$X^+ = \begin{cases} 0 & \text{if } X \leq 0, \\ X & \text{if } X > 0. \end{cases} \tag{20.1}$$

20.3.1 *Payoff Diagrams and Intrinsic Value*

For a strike price of K, underlier price of S_t, and an option expiring at time T, the payoffs for a put P_T and call C_T are then:

$$C_T = (S_T - K)^+ \quad \text{and,} \quad P_T = (K - S_T)^+. \tag{20.2}$$

If we evaluate these before expiry, we get what is called **intrinsic value**:

$$C_t^{\text{intr}} = (S_t - K)^+ \quad \text{and,} \quad P_t^{\text{intr}} = (K - S_t)^+. \tag{20.3}$$

The **payoff diagram** is a plot of the payoff versus the underlier price. For puts and calls, we see the typical "hockey stick" payoffs shown in Figure 20.1.

20.3.2 *Option Strategies*

We can combine payoff diagrams to create basic strategies — since the range of underlier prices give us various states of the world at option expiry.

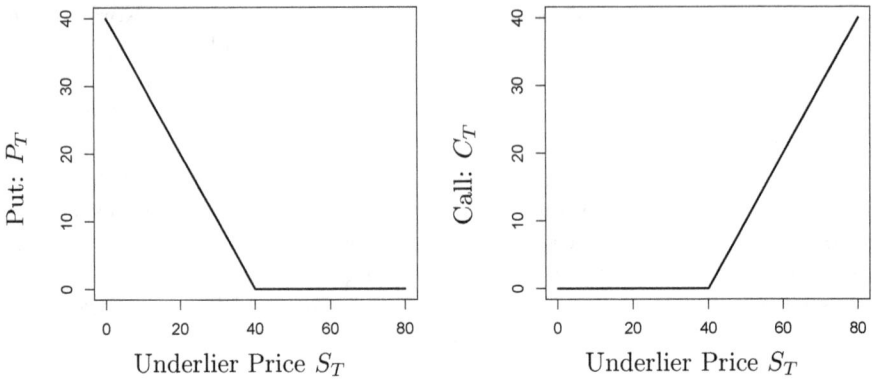

Figure 20.1: Payoffs versus underlier price S_T for a put P_T (left) and call C_T (right) and at expiry time T for a strike price of $K = 40$.

Eliminating Upside or Downside

Some of the earliest and easiest strategies involve modifying the payoff of holding the underlying. We can eliminate upside or downside from the underlier by adding or subtracting an option.

A **protective put** is the purchase of a put to eliminate downside (until expiry) below the strike price. A **covered call** is the writing of a call to eliminate upside (until expiry) above the strike price and generate income. Furthermore, if you had planned to rebalance your portfolio by reducing certain holdings as they increased in value, this automates that action — and pays you in the meantime. The payoff diagrams for these strategies are shown in Figure 20.2.

You might notice that these strategies change the economics of holding the underlying to something with a payoff like being long a call or short a put. We will use that fact when we talk about put-call parity.

Bull and Bear Spreads

We can also use options to express more complicated views about prices. A bear or bull spread bets on the direction of price changes without expressing much opinion on the magnitude of a future move. Figure 20.3 shows the payoffs for these spreads.

If we thought prices would decline, we could buy a **bear spread** by going long a high-strike put and short a low-strike put. We could also go short a low-strike call and long a high-strike call. These may be referred to as put and call bear spreads. Both construction methods should cost the same.

If we thought prices would increase, we could buy a (call) **bull spread** by going long a low-strike call and short a high-strike call. We could also go short a high-strike put and long a low-strike put — a put bull spread.

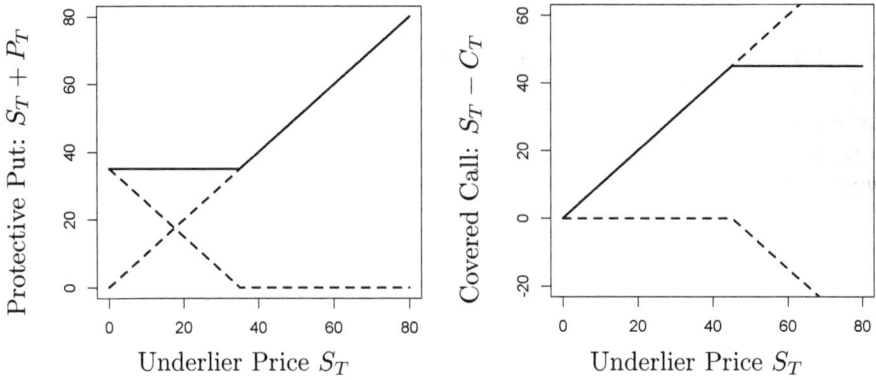

Figure 20.2: Payoffs versus underlier price S_T for a protective put strategy (left; long underlying and a put) and a covered call strategy (right; long underlying, short a call). The constituents (underlying and options) are shown with dashed lines.

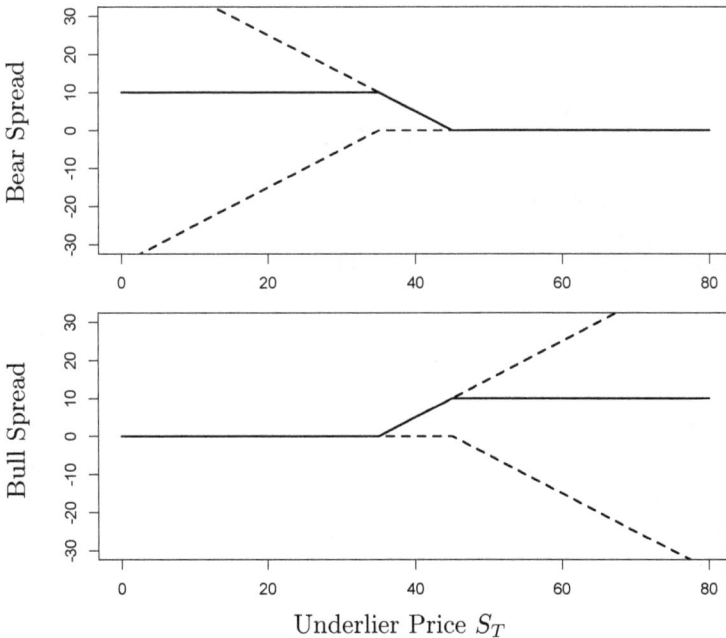

Figure 20.3: Payoffs versus underlier price S_T for a bear spread strategy (top) and a bull spread strategy (bottom), shown with solid lines. The constituent puts (for a put bear spread) and calls (for a call bull spread) are shown with dashed lines.

Collar

A **collar** usually refers to a combination of a protective put and a covered call. The idea is that you limit the downside of the underlying and pay for it by selling off some upside. However, collars also have another common use. When a merger occurs, the acquiring firm may pay for the target firm in stock. In this case, they may specify a fixed-price or fixed-ratio collar.

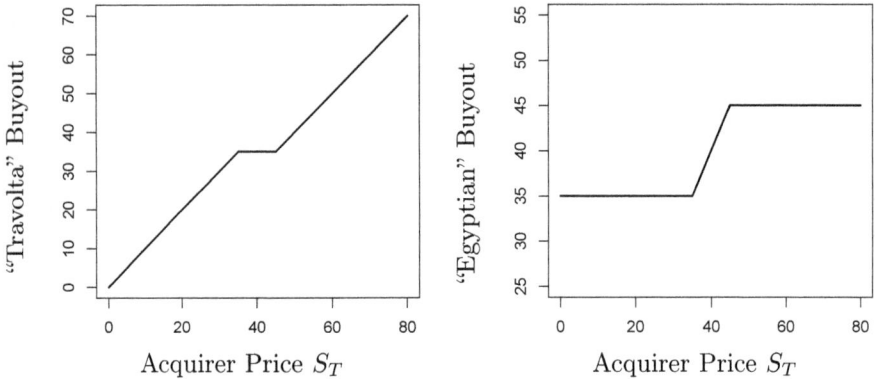

Figure 20.4: Buyout (payoff) to the target versus acquirer stock price S_T for a fixed-price ("Travolta," left) and a fixed-ratio ("Egyptian," right) merger collar.

A **fixed-price collar** states that the acquirer will pay some price per share of the target firm within a range of acquirer-to-target stock price ratios and less or more for ratios below or above that range. This gives the target a fixed price within a range and a price that increases or decreases with the acquirer's stock outside of that range. The payoff for this looks a lot like shares in the acquirer, short calls at a low strike and long calls at a higher strike. Officer (2004) calls this a "Travolta" because the payoff diagram looks like John Travolta's arms when disco dancing in *Saturday Night Fever*.

A **fixed-ratio collar** states that the acquiring firm will exchange a fixed number of shares per target share within some range of the acquirer's stock price — but more shares if the price is below that range and fewer shares if the price is above the range. This yields a payoff like that of a bull spread (and the typically option collar) strategy. Officer (2004) calls this an "Egyptian" for its similarity to stereotypical Ancient Egyptian poses.

Since target stock prices often become stable once bid upon, we can think of these buyout values in terms of the acquirer's stock price. The payoff diagrams are shown in Figure 20.4. Clearly, a target firm could use options to hedge against changes in the buyout value of a merger deal. For more on merger collars, read Officer (2004) and Adolph and Pettit (2007).

Volatility: Straddles, Strangles, Butterflies, and Condors

Finally, some strategies allow us to trade volatility. In fact, Carr and Madan (1998) showed that a variance swap may be replicated by a portfolio of straddles.

A **straddle** is a long position in a call and a put with the same strike price K. Thus if the underlier moves far from the strike price, the contract pays off significantly. A strangle is similar to a straddle except the put has a lower strike price than the call. These payoffs are shown in Figure 20.5.

A few contracts let us express a specific low-volatility view: that the underlier price will remain in a narrow range.

A **butterfly** has a payoff with a positive triangular shape. To build a butterfly with calls, we buy a call struck at K_1; short two calls struck at K_2; and, buy a call struck at K_3 with equally-spaced strikes: $K_3 - K_2 = K_2 - K_1 > 0$. Thus the terminal payoff is only positive if the underlier price is between K_1 and K_3. A butterfly can also be built from put options.

> **Baring Volatility** Barings Bank was historic: Founded in 1762, they helped finance the Louisiana Purchase and the British fight against Napoleon. However, in 1994, their Singapore head trader, Nick Leeson, was losing money and hiding his losses. To recover, he bet on low volatility by selling Nikkei 225 straddles struck at JPY 18,500–19,500.
>
> The Great Kobe earthquake on 17 January 1995 caused over 6,400 deaths and JPY 20 tn property damage. Leeson bought futures, but the market fell below JPY 17,500 within weeks. On 27 February 1995, Barings declared bankruptcy with ultimate losses over GBP 900 mn. Leeson fled Singapore but was later imprisoned for four years. Read Gapper and Denton (1996) for more on the collapse.

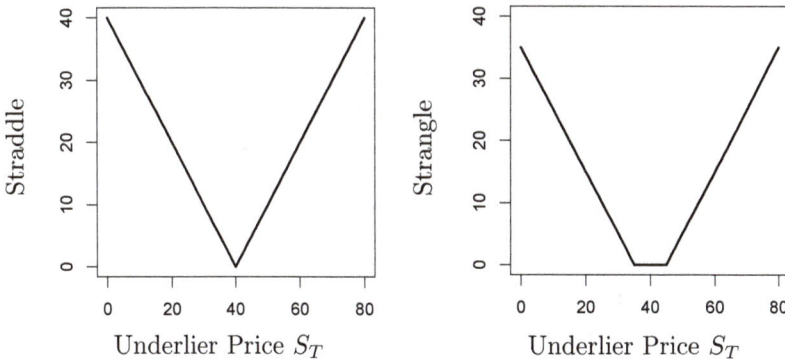

Figure 20.5: Payoffs versus underlier price S_T for a straddle (left) and a strangle (right). The constituent puts and calls are not shown.

A **condor** is much like a butterfly except with some width at the peak. (A condor is to a butterfly as a strangle is to a straddle.) A condor can also be built with either calls or puts. To build a condor with calls, we would go long a call struck at K_1, short a call struck at K_2, short a call struck at K_3, and long a call struck at K_4 with $K_1 < K_2 < K_3 < K_4$ and $K_2 - K_1 = K_4 - K_3 > 0$. Payoffs for a butterfly and condor are shown in Figure 20.6.

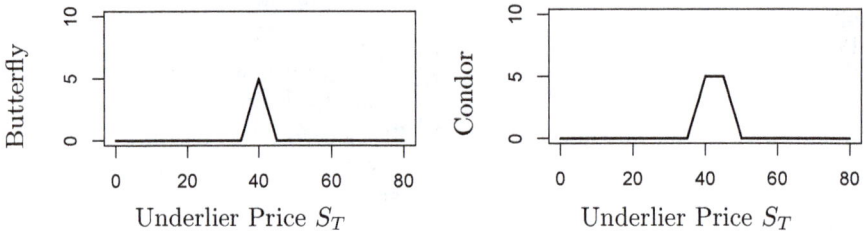

Figure 20.6: Payoffs versus underlier price S_T for a butterfly (left) and a condor (right). Constituent puts and calls are not shown.

20.3.3   Time Value

Hockey and Options An unusual idea of option theory is behind a common move in ice hockey. An ice hockey team may remove their goaltender from the ice and instead add a sixth attacker. Often, this is done in the last minutes of a game by a losing team. This leaves their goal unprotected but increases their probability of scoring a goal. "Pulling the goalie" essentially increases the volatility of the score — which increases the probability of tying the game and winning in overtime. Those interested in this should read Morrison and Wheat (1986), Erkut (1987), Nydick and Weiss (1989), and Washburn (1991).

Even without knowing how to price an option, we know that these payoffs (1) do not come for free, and (2) do not fully express the value of options.

For example, suppose we have a call struck at 30 that expires in a year and the underlier is priced at 29.99. We know that the call is not worthless; there is a possibility that in a year the underlier will be worth more than 30. If the underlier is more volatile, it has a greater possibility of being above 30 at expiry. Similarly, if the call expired in two years instead of one year, it would also have a greater possibility of expiring ITM. These changes both make the options more valuable.

The difference between what an option is worth and its intrinsic value is the option's **time value**. We could build a crude option pricer just by using a smoother (like a kernel estimator) on the payoff diagrams. While this would not be perfect, the intuition this idea yields is helpful.

There are some strategies which are wholly reliant on time value. For example, there is a strategy called a **calendar spread**. This involves buying a call or put and shorting a call or put with a sooner expiry date. This yields a payoff that, before either option expires, is like a butterfly but skewed depending on whether puts or calls were used to create the spread.

20.4 Put-Call Parity

Payoff diagrams can yield powerful insights. One insight is that we can combine options to get something like the performance of the underlier — but shifted lower. Specifically, if we buy a call and short a put, both struck at K, we have a terminal payoff that is the same as the underlier minus K. In other words, the call and put maturing at time T are worth, at time T:

$$C_{K,T,T} - P_{K,T,T} = (S_T - K)^+ - (K - S_T)^+ = S_T - K. \qquad (20.4)$$

This insight is the idea of **put-call parity**.

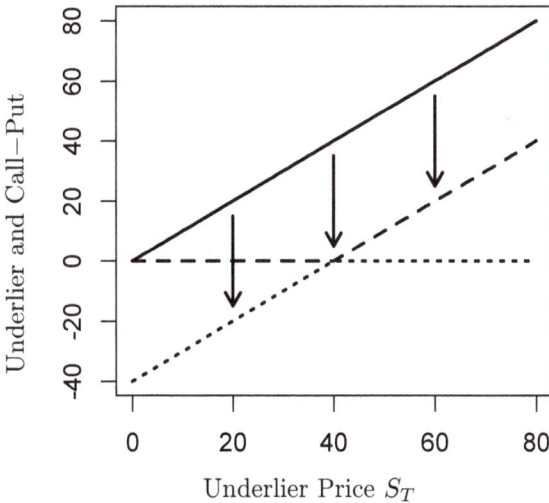

Figure 20.7: Put-call parity illustrated. Notice that the underlier price at expiry (S_T, solid line) is just K higher than the portfolio which is long a call (dashed line) and short a put (dotted line), both struck at K.

We can take our option position (long a call, short a put, both struck at K) and short the underlier. For European options, this yields a guaranteed payoff of K at time T — an arbitrage argument. We can see this illustrated in Figure 20.7. Therefore the five prices we use are related:

- Prices of European calls and puts struck at K, expiring at T $(C^E_{K,t,T}, P^E_{K,t,T})$;
- Price of the underlier and the strike (S_t, K); and,
- Price of money, *i.e.* the interest rate $t \to T$ (r_f).

This arbitrage argument is useful because it gives us a version of put-call parity that holds before option expiry:

$$C^E_{K,t,T} - P^E_{K,t,T} = S_t - Ke^{-r_f(T-t)}. \tag{20.5}$$

If we account for omitted dividends through a dividend yield d, we can modify this because the option portfolio would not earn the dividends:

$$C^E_{K,t,T} - P^E_{K,t,T} = S_t e^{-d(T-t)} - Ke^{-r_f(T-t)}. \tag{20.6}$$

You might wonder: what about American options — the ones with more freedom? Well, American options may be exercised early, so we need not wait to get a guaranteed payout of K. Therefore, the American option portfolio should be valued somewhere between the value of $S_t - K$ and the European option portfolio:

$$S_t - K \le C^A_{K,t,T} - P^A_{K,t,T} \le S_t e^{-d(T-t)} - Ke^{-r_f(T-t)}. \tag{20.7}$$

While put-call parity was first noted in the academic literature by Stoll (1969), it has been noted by practitioners much earlier. Higgins (1902) and Nelson (1904) both mentioned it in books on options; and, put-call parity was indirectly referred to in the classic book on markets: de la Vega (1688).

Put-call parity is useful in a number of ways. First, if we know the price of a call or put, parity will give us the price of a corresponding put or call. Second, put-call parity should hold (within transactions costs) at all times. We can measure how much stress markets are under and if limits to arbitrage are binding by how much put-call parity does not hold, *i.e.* by measuring the difference between the two sides of equation (20.6) or the distance from the range in equation (20.7). Finally, put-call parity has been used in some contexts to create what are effectively loans in markets that prohibit usury.

20.5   Embedded and Exotic Options

Many contracts have embedded options or option-like behavior. Sometimes the embedded option is explicit, sometimes it is subtle or not well-defined.

A **convertible bond** allows the bondholder to convert the bond to stock instead of receiving repayment at maturity. The conversion option specifies the **conversion ratio**, the number of firm shares to be received upon conversion. The **conversion price** is the strike price. If the share price is above the conversion price at maturity, conversion is a good deal. This lets investors participate in upside. If the capital raised from issuing the bond enables more growth for the firm (and its stock), this can be a very good deal. However, the stock investors receive is issued from the company treasury: there is dilution.

Bonds with **warrants** are much like convertible bonds. Often, these warrants are detachable which allows them to be traded separately from the bond. However, the warrants still counterbalance the repayment of the bond at maturity: if the warrants are ITM, the exercise and purchase of stock will fund the bond repayment. As with convertible bonds, exercising warrants results in shares being issued from the firm treasury (and thus dilution).

Callable bonds are bonds which include an interest rate call. Often this is specified via a **call price**: if the bond is above that price, the issuer may refund bondholders at the call price. Companies tend to be very aggressive about exercising this option if it is worthwhile, (For a strange counterexample, see the sidebar "Tokyo Calling?")

Often this call may be exercised on one or more **call dates** or even during a window of time. Thus bondholders are short a call at the call price. Since prices and yields move inversely, this is like holding a bond which is short a call on the bond's price.

Collateralized loans are loans backed by collateral. These can be considered to be like a risk-free bond that is short a collateral put: it is likely that the collateral is worth less than a risk-free bond. Worse: if the bond defaults, the holder gets the collateral — which may be impaired. This is especially true for bonds with defaults that are correlated with other defaults. (Read the sidebar "Take a Seat...Please" in Chapter 13 for an example of such effects.)

Tokyo Calling? In the 1990s, Ford acquired an increasingly large interest in Mazda Motors. The managers Ford sent to Japan were well-versed in financial matters and immediately set about reducing costs. The first thing they noticed was that some of the firm's debt was expensive with interest rates far above the market rate. Strangely, the bonds were callable. When they tried to call the bonds, however...the Ministry of Finance rejected the request: calling the bonds would frighten bondholders.

Thankfully, Mazda did eventually retire the bonds. We spend a lot of time on fancy math in this chapter. However, it pays to remember that interventionist government officials do not care about fancy math or even sound economics.

Finally, **real options** are the term coined by Myers (1977) for option-like decisions we face in business and in life. These choices may be embedded in contracts or in the freedom to make certain business decisions. Often, these decisions give us the possibility of starting, stopping, canceling, or abandoning a project; increasing or decreasing output; lengthening or shortening the output period; or, switching assets.

Examples of real options include decisions like: reactivating or leasing a gold mine; storing inventory for a busy business season ahead; starting and running a "peaker" plant to create electricity when prices are high; increasing factory capacity to create more high-margin product; or, purchasing more fuel in later months at an agreed-upon price.

20.5.1   Exotic Options

American and European puts and calls are often called **vanilla options**. In contrast, **exotic options** have payoffs that are calculated differently: they may involve extra optionality or price history or the payoffs may be on oddly-behaved underliers like spreads. (Spreads behave oddly because they can assume negative values.)

Asian options differ from American and European options not in when they can be exercised but in how we use the underlier price. Asian options typically evaluate the average underlier price versus the strike price. This is useful for commodity consumers who need to always process some input to run their business. This makes Asian options the most liquid options for certain underliers. For example, Asian options are often used to hedge upside or downside price risk for power, natural gas, jet fuel (for airlines), or even metals (for smelters and automakers).

Swing options are also popular in commodity markets because they allow for a number of deviations in volume from a straight average; the optionality is not on price. Thus a swing option might specify that A buys q kWh of power every day at the "strike" price of K; however, up to 10 times over a month, A can specify to buy more (up to $\bar{q}$) or less (down to $\underline{q}$) the next day.

Note that pairing an Asian and a swing option can approximate hedging both price and needed-quantity variation.

An **exchange option** gives the holder the right to choose between two or more underliers. For example: if I can turn natural gas into power (with a generator), then I am implicitly long an exchange call on some amount of natural gas and the corresponding amount of power I could make with that natural gas. Or if I am a portfolio manager, I might be able to purchase the cheaper of any bonds meeting certain criteria: I am long an exchange put on the bonds.

Similar to an exchange option is a **spread option** where the underlier is a long-short portfolio. The spread could be power $-$ αnatural gas, in which case the spread option is like the exchange option; or, the spread could be crude oil minus quantities of the major products refined from crude oil. The nice part about spreads is that they can (and often are) created to reflect the unit producer margin (sometimes called gross producer margin): the difference between revenue and cost of goods sold. Thus spreads can indicate the profitability of an industry and options on those spreads may help hedge firm losses.

Another exotic option which is often used is the **quanto option** — which is a normal option except that it also includes a fixed conversion rate from the underlier currency. Thus a quanto option includes an FX hedge. However, we then need to consider that the FX rate might be correlated with the underlier.

Barrier options are options which may either activate if the underlier goes beyond some barrier (a **knock-in option**) or deactivate if the underlier goes beyond that barrier (a **knock-out option**). These sometimes are referred to with the direction from the underlier to the barrier, *e.g.* "up-and-in," "up-and-out," "down-and-in," or "down-and-out." As with put-call parity, a combination of knock-in and knock-out options with the same barrier should be priced the same as a vanilla option without a barrier.

Finally, **lookback options** have a payoff that depends on the best or worse price over the option's lifetime.

20.6 Comparative Statics and Issues

To finish off our introduction to options, we now know enough to think about how various variables affect the value of optionality. Therefore, we will look at some **comparative statics** — comparisons of economic outcomes for differing inputs. This tells us how option valuations change in response to changes in one input variable. Table 20.2 shows how vanilla options respond to changes in certain key variables:

Variable	Call value	Put value
$S_t \uparrow$	↑	↓
$K \uparrow$	↓	↑
$\sigma \uparrow$	↑	↑
$T \uparrow$	↑	↑
$r_f \uparrow$	↑	↓
$d \uparrow$	↓	↑

Table 20.2: A list of comparative statics showing how vanilla calls and puts respond to increases in the input variables.

20.6.1 Early Exercise

Since we distinguished between European and American options, we might wonder how the difference in exercisability matters for pricing. The truth is that the difference is usually minor; however, there are certain cases where the difference is not ignorable. We can do some thought experiments to see intuitively how this is so.

In general, exercising options early is sub-optimal. This is why people wait until the last second to assess traffic before taking an early exit on the motorway or paying income taxes (if they owe money): people intuitively understand the value of "keeping your options open." Similarly, it usually makes no sense to exercise an option early: the underlier could move further ITM; or, by expiry, the underlier might be OOM — in which case you avoided selling for too little or buying for too much. Therefore, European and American options are often worth nearly the same.

However, if a stock were about to pay an unusually large dividend, often called a **special dividend**, we might want to exercise a call early so that we could hold the stock and receive the dividend. We might also want to do this if a call were deep ITM and a normal-sized dividend was about to be issued — so long as the value of the dividend was greater than the time value of the option. In these cases, the American call is worth more than the European call.[3]

On the other hand, suppose a stock has fallen far in price — perhaps due to bankruptcy. The likelihood of this stock recovering or even changing much in value is low. In that case, early exercise of a put lets us realize a large profit now rather than waiting for it. For example, if the stock has fallen to $S_t = 0.01$ and we hold a put struck at $K = 30$, a European put would be worth about $P^E_{30,t,T} \approx 30e^{-r_f(T-t)} - 0.01 < 29.99$. On the other hand, if we exercise early, we get 29.99 right away and can earn interest on the money; thus $P^A_{30,t,T} = 29.99$.

What this suggests is that below some threshold S^*, early exercise becomes optimal making the American put option more valuable than the European put option:

$$P^A_{K,t,T} = K - S_t > P^E_{K,t,T} > Ke^{-r_f(T-t)} - S_t \quad \forall S_t \leq S^*. \tag{20.8}$$

20.7   Quiz

Try to answer these questions in ten minutes. For answers with equations, just write the equations; do not evaluate them.

1. Draw the payoff diagram for a call, struck at K, at option expiry.

2. Draw the payoff diagram for a put, struck at K, at option expiry.

3. How does an American option differ from a European option?

4. I buy a butterfly.

   a) Draw the payoff diagram.
   b) What am I hoping for that will make this strategy profitable?

5. You apply for jobs and get an offer from Union Bank of Greater Liechtenstein. They tell you that your bonus has the following structure in the first year: On February 4th you will get the greater of $20,000 or 1000 shares of their ADR. You can decompose the bonus into a bond component and an option component.

   a) What is the bond component?

---

[3]This leads to an unusual strategy. Some options traders sell ITM American calls before a dividend and buy stock to hedge. For calls that are exercised, they deliver the stock; for those that are not exercised, they get to keep the dividend. They then close out the remaining options positions and sell the stock at a profit.

b) What is the option component? Make sure to specify as many details as you can determine about the option.

6. (2 points) Consider a stock with no dividends; and, assume a six-month discount factor of $e^{-r \cdot 0.5} = 0.98$. You also know that the stock price now is $S_t = \$52$. For a strike price of $K = 50$, calls are trading at $C_{t,0.5} = \$4.10$. From put-call parity, what price $P_{t,0.5}$ should puts trade at?

7. When might you exercise an American option early?

20.8 Exercises

Instructions

Use the supplied R code to download the put/call ratio data from the Chicago Board Options Exchange. We will focus on index options.

1. What is the standard deviation of how much the put/call ratio changes in a day?

2. Does there seem to be a significant day-of-week effect? What is the pattern that you observe?

3. Does there seem to be a significant day-of-month effect? What is the pattern that you observe? Why might you see a pattern — or not?

4. Some phenomena might be directional whereas others might not. Can you surmise which day-of-week or day-of-month patterns would be directional and which would be more conditional? Is there a way to clean up the conditional aspects of the above exploratory questions to get sharper results?

R Code

```
library(xts)

## get put/call ratio data from CBOE
## skip the first two lines
index.pcr.file <- "http://www.cboe.com/publish/scheduledtask/mktdata/datahouse/indexpc.csv"
putcall.tmp <- read.csv(index.pcr.file, skip=2)
putcall <- xts(putcall.tmp$P.C.Ratio,
               order.by=as.POSIXct(putcall.tmp$DATE, format="%m/%d/%Y"))
colnames(putcall) <- "ratio"
putcall$change <- diff(putcall$ratio)
putcall$dayofweek <- .indexwday(putcall)
putcall$dayofmonth <- day(putcall)
putcall$monday <- putcall$dayofweek == 1
putcall$friday <- putcall$dayofweek == 5
putcall$monthstart <- putcall$dayofmonth <= 3
putcall$monthend <- putcall$dayofmonth >= 28
```

References

Adolph, Gerald and Justin Pettit. *The M&A Collar Handbook: How to Manage Equity Risk*. Booz Allen Hamilton, 2007. DOI: 10.2139/ssrn.954612.

Badham, John. *Saturday Night Fever*. Produced by Robert Stigwood. 1977.

Carr, Peter and Dilip Madan. "Towards a Theory of Volatility Trading". In: *Volatility*. Ed. by Robert A. Jarrow. London: Risk Publications, 1998, pp. 417–427.

de la Vega, Joseph Penso. *Confusión de Confusiones*. Amsterdam, 1688.

Erkut, Erhan. "Note: More on Morrison and Wheat's "Pulling the Goalie Revisited"". *Interfaces* 17.5 (1987), pp. 121–123. DOI: 10.1287/inte.17.5.121.

Gapper, John and Nicholas Denton. *All That Glitters: The Fall of Barings*. New York: Penguin Books, 1996.

Higgins, Leonard R. *The Put-and-Call*. London: Effingham Wilson, 1902.

IOMA. *WFE IOMA 2016 Derivatives Report*. World Federation of Exchanges: International Options Market Association, 2017. URL: http://www.worldexchanges.org/home/index.php/files/53/IOMA-Derivatives-Market-Survey/448/2016-IOMA-Derivatives-Market-Survey.pdf.

Knoll, Michael S. "The Ancient Roots of Modern Financial Innovation: The Early History of Regulatory Arbitrage". *Oregon Law Review* 87.1 (2008), pp. 93–116. URL: https://scholarsbank.uoregon.edu/xmlui/handle/1794/8366.

Kohn, Meir. "Risk Instruments in the Medieval and Early Modern Economy". In: *The Origins of Western Economic Success: Commerce, Finance, and Government in Preindustrial Europe*. unpublished manuscript, 2017, Chapter 12.

Lee, Edward. "Ceres Flexes Worldwide Muscle". *Chicago Tribune* (Nov. 25, 1973), A17.

— "Lady Luck Frowns on Options Exchange". *Chicago Tribune* (Apr. 27, 1973), p. C13.

Maidenberg, H. J. "Trading in Options Opens On New Chicago Board". *New York Times* (Apr. 27, 1973), p. 47.

Morrison, Donald G. and Rita D. Wheat. "Misapplications Reviews: Pulling the Goalie Revisited". *Interfaces* 16.6 (1986), pp. 28–34. DOI: 10.1287/inte.16.6.28.

Myers, Stewart C. "Determinants of Corporate Borrowing". *Journal of Financial Economics* 5.2 (1977), pp. 147–175. DOI: 10.1016/0304-405X(77)90015-0.

Nelson, Samuel Armstrong. *The A B C of Options and Arbitrage*. New York: S. A. Nelson's Wall Street Library, 1904.

Nydick Jr., Robert L. and Howard J. Weiss. "More on Erkut's "More on Morrison and Wheat's 'Pulling the Goalie Revisited'"". *Interfaces* 19.5 (1989), pp. 45–48. DOI: 10.1287/inte.19.5.45.

Officer, Micah S. "Collars and Renegotiation in Mergers and Acquisitions". *Journal of Finance* 59.6 (2004), pp. 2719–2743. DOI: 10.1111/j.1540-6261.2004.00714.x.

Stoll, Hans R. "The Relationship between Put and Call Option Prices". *Journal of Finance* 24.5 (1969), pp. 801–824. DOI: 10.1111/j.1540-6261.1969.tb01694.x.

Washburn, Alan. "Still More on Pulling the Goalie". *Interfaces* 21.2 (1991), pp. 59–64. DOI: 10.1287/inte.21.2.59.

WFE. *WFE Annual Statistics Guide 2016*. 2016. URL: http://www.world-exchanges.org/home/index.php/files/52/Annual-Statistics-Guide/453/WFE-Annual-Statistics-Guide-2016.xlsx.

Chapter 21

Option Valuation

Pricing options is one of the more advanced tasks we will tackle in this text. The pricing largely avoids the complicated philosophical questions like "have we considered all the risk factors?" or "what is the stochastic discount factor?" or even "what is the proper risk measure and how do we calculate it?" (We will have more to say on that soon, however.)

> ⚠ **Awas!** *Pricing options is involved because the formulas and methods are more complicated than many of those we have dealt with up to now. My advice is to read this chapter with some strong tea or coffee; this material needs a bit more focus than usual.*

There are many approaches we can take to price options. We could *simulate* scenarios which is easier but slower. We could use a *binomial tree* which is flexible but can be slow. We might be able to use the closed-form *Black-Scholes-Merton* formulas which are fast to calculate. Three more advanced methods are not covered here: we could use a *measure-theoretic* approach, *partial differential equations*, or a *dynamic programming* approach.[1]

The goal of this chapter is to explore the first three solution methods, to look at how markets diverge from these theoretical models, and to see what options tell us about markets and business decisions.

21.1 Modern History of Options

---

[1]Measure theory applied to options is typically restricted to stochastic calculus. The tree method we discuss is a limited version of dynamic programming.

I said in the prior chapter that the opening of the first options exchange, the CBOE, in April of 1973 was auspiciously-timed because it preceded innovations which gave option pricing a jolt. One month after the CBOE opened, Black and Scholes (1973) was published which finally revealed the correct formula for pricing options.[2] Merton (1973b) followed which explored and developed more of the theory behind the pricing formula. Then, as Bernstein (1996) notes, the first handheld calculators became available a few months after that. Traders on the new exchange quickly began programming the Black-Scholes equation into their calculators; and, calculator makers advertised this capability in the *Wall Street Journal*. The rapid adoption of their work led to Scholes and Merton receiving the Nobel Prize in 1997.[3]

However, it turns out that Black and Scholes (1973) was not the first attempt at pricing options. Many earlier attempts had come close or very close. Sprenkle (1961) used log-returns instead of price as was common at the time. Boness (1964) had very similar formulas but the wrong value for the discount factor.

> **A Driver of Option Values**
>
> Myron Scholes once told a story about visiting Chicago. He grabbed a taxi in the Loop to go to the University of Chicago's business school. As they drove, the cab driver related how he used to trade options on the new CBOE. But right after he started, some professors came out with a formula for pricing options and a bunch of traders used calculators programmed with the formula.
>
> Did he use the formula, Myron asked? The driver explained that no, he had not used the formula because he did not believe it. He had relied on his gut for what prices should be. As they pulled up in front of the business school, the driver said "I'd probably still be trading options if I had used that formula."
>
> I asked Myron if he told the cab driver that he was one of those professors. He said "No way! I got out of that cab as fast as I could. I was worried he would blame me for him driving a cab all that time!"

About seventy years earlier, Bachelier (1900) used Brownian motion to model stock prices and price options. While his analysis use prices instead of log-returns, the analysis was remarkably advanced for its time. Unbeknownst to Bachelier, Bronzin (1908) derived similar formulas also with an assumption of normally-distributed prices. Sullivan and Weithers (1991) and Schachermayer and Teichmann (2007) discuss Bachelier's work; and, Zimmermann and Hafner (2007) and Hafner and Zimmermann (2009) have more background on Bronzin's work. Amazingly, after the publication of these they were almost completely forgotten until their recent rediscovery.

---

[2] I say "correct" since they found a way around estimating the underlier pricing kernel.

[3] Fisher Black did not receive the Nobel Prize as he had passed away earlier.

21.2   Simulation

Recall that simulation involves generating **random variates**: realizations of random variables drawn from the outcome distribution. We then find expected values of quantities of interest. This is often referred to as a **Monte Carlo approach** (for Monaco's Monte Carlo Casino) and was proposed for option pricing by Boyle (1977). If a Markov chain affects the simulation, we may mix simulations with the evolving Markov chain states. This is referred to as a **Markov chain Monte Carlo approach** (aka MCMC).

Simulation may be the easiest way to price an option. This is an advantage in that it often requires far less work to program. However, one of the drawbacks of simulation is that accuracy converges slowly: with the square root of the number of simulations. Simulation is popular, however, because programmer time is far more expensive than computer time.

The slow convergence rate of simulation can be especially troublesome if the option is exotic or has complicated optionality like knock-in or knock-out provisions. If the option depends on tail behavior or rare events, this difficulty may be surmountable with **importance sampling**: we oversample the region of interest and then downweight those observations to compensate for the oversampling. (See Siegmund (1976) for more information.)

The generation of random variates is often done using **pseudorandom numbers**: a deterministic sequence of numbers which passes tests of random-like behavior.[4] Different generators are used for generating uniform versus non-uniform random variates. For those interested in the methods of random variate generation, a good place to start is Devroye (1986).

21.2.1   *Process Considerations*

To simulate random variates, we choose an economically justified stochastic process which implies an outcome distribution. We have only a few closed-form processes implied by a system of stochastic differential equations:

1. *arithmetic Brownian motion,*

$$dS_t = \mu dt + \sigma_A dW_t, \tag{21.1}$$

$$S_t - S_0 \sim N(\mu t, \sigma_A^2 t); \tag{21.2}$$

2. *geometric Brownian motion,*

$$d\log(S_t) = \frac{dS_t}{S_t} = \mu dt + \sigma_G dW_t, \tag{21.3}$$

$$\log(S_t) - \log(S_0) \sim N((\mu - \sigma_G^2/2)t, \sigma_G^2 t); \tag{21.4}$$

---

[4]I know a senior economist who will not use pseudorandom numbers and only uses truly random numbers generated from natural entropy sources. This position is a bit extreme.

3. an *Ornstein-Uhlenbeck process,*

$$dS_t = \gamma(S_t - \bar{S})dt + \sigma_O dW_t, \tag{21.5}$$

$$S_t \sim N\left(\bar{S} + (S_0 - \bar{S})e^{-\gamma t}, \sigma_O^2 \frac{1 - e^{-2\gamma t}}{2\gamma}\right); \quad \text{or,} \tag{21.6}$$

4. a *Brownian bridge,*

$$\bar{B}_t = B_0 + (B_T - B_0)t/T, \tag{21.7}$$

$$dB_t = \frac{\bar{B}_t - B_t}{1 - t/T}dt + \sigma_B dW_t, \tag{21.8}$$

$$B_t - B_0 \sim N\left(\bar{B}_t, \sigma_B^2 \frac{t(T - t)}{T^2}\right). \tag{21.9}$$

The **Brownian bridge** is a process we have not yet seen. It is useful for modeling a risk-free bond issued at price B_0 and paying off face value B_T at maturity time T. We could also use it to model the price of a firm being acquired for a set price at a given time.

Note that the volatility varies among these forms. The volatilities for the arithmetic Brownian motion, Ornstein-Uhlenbeck, and Brownian bridge processes all use an annualized standard deviation of price changes while geometric Brownian motion uses the volatility we are more familiar with: the annualized standard deviation of log-returns. The conversion from the typical σ_G is typically done in simulations by multiplying a volatility by the initial price or the price expected at time t.

For these stochastic processes, we can easily generate random variates with these distributions for the underlier price at expiry (time T). However, if we need to simulate intermediate steps to check certain conditions (*e.g.* knock-out), the simulations for the remaining times must be conditional on the intermediate value. Using R code, this is fairly straightforward:

```
rf <- 0.02  # 2% interest rates
num.sims <- 100000 # 100,000 simulations
s0 <- 90  # underlier price at t=0
s.bar <- 95
K <- 102  # strike price
sigma <- 0.25  # volatility of underlier log-returns
T <- 2  # 2 years = option expiry
tau <- 1  # mid-life of one-year bond
lambda <- 2  # mean reversion rate; 2 => half-life = ln(2)/2 = 0.35 years

## arithmetic Brownian motion; normal underlier price
w1 <- rnorm(num.sims) # simulated W_T values
sigma.abm <- sigma*s0  # rescale volatility for initial prife level
s.sim.abm <- s0 + rf*T + sigma.abm*sqrt(T)*w1
opt.payoff.abm <- pmax(s.sim.abm - K, 0)
opt.value.abm <- mean(opt.payoff.abm)*exp(-rf*T)

## geometric Brownian motion; normal underlier log-returns
w2 <- rnorm(num.sims) # simulated W_T values
```

```
s.sim.gbm <- s0*exp((rf-sigma^2/2)*T + sigma*sqrt(T)*w2)
opt.payoff.gbm <- pmax(s.sim.gbm - K, 0)
opt.value.gbm <- mean(opt.payoff.gbm)*exp(-rf*T)

## Ornstein-Uhlenbeck process for underlier price
w3 <- rnorm(num.sims) # simulated W_T values
s.sim.ou <- s.bar + exp(-lambda*T)*(s0-s.bar) + sigma*s.bar*
        sqrt((1-exp(-2*lambda*T))/(2*lambda))*w3
opt.payoff.ou <- pmax(s.sim.ou - K, 0)
opt.value.ou <- mean(opt.payoff.ou)*exp(-rf*T)

## Brownian bridge; two-year bond maturing at 100
## option is struck at 102 in year 1
## FYI: vol of 0.25 is very high for a two-year bond
w4 <- rnorm(num.sims) # simulated W_tau values
s.bar.bb <- s0 + (100-s0)*tau/T
s.sim.bb <- s.bar.bb + sigma*s.bar.bb*sqrt(tau/T*(T-tau)/T)*w4
opt.payoff.bb <- pmax(s.sim.bb - K, 0)
opt.value.bb <- mean(opt.payoff.bb)*exp(-rf*tau)
```

Another option for simulating is to use the **sde** *R* package. This has more features and is useful for simulating intermediate values. The only feature it lacks is the exact form for the stopped Brownian bridge given above.

21.3   Binomial Trees

An intuitive way to price options is using a **binomial tree**, a method first proposed by Cox, Ross, and Rubinstein (1979). We map out future scenarios in discrete time and space steps. At discrete times, the underlier moves up or down some amount. Depending on how we build the tree, up-then-down may (or may not) be the same scenario as down-then-up. If it is the same, we also call the tree a **mesh** or **lattice**.

The tree ends at the time of option expiry. We then create another corresponding tree or lattice to hold option values for all of the different future scenarios. At expiry, we find what the option would be worth for the different underlier price scenarios. That is easy: it is just calculating the payoff diagram. (Note that this allows us to price all sorts of payoffs and handle early exercise or other unusual choices.)

For times before expiry, we find in each scenario a combination of underlier and risk-free bond yielding the option payoffs for up or down scenarios one time step ahead. By the LOOP, the value of this portfolio must equal the option value. Finally, we work backwards in time doing this repeatedly until we get to the current time.

Because the process is confusing, this is another time when we can really benefit from working out some examples. Once you see those, revisit the preceding paragraph. In the following examples, we will consider a call option on a stock which pays no dividends.

21.3.1   Example: One-Step Tree

For a simple example, consider a tree with one time step — so two possible future outcomes — for a year from now. In this world, the underlier moves up or down

+12.2% or -10%. Figure 21.1 shows the scenarios and what our option would be worth in those scenarios.

Figure 21.1: One-step trees for a stock with future states in one year shown on the left and an option with terminal payoffs shown on the right.

If the risk-free rate is $r_f = 3\%$, what is the value of the option C? It turns out we can replicate the option payouts at each time step with the stock and a risk-free bond. This implies a dynamic trading strategy — one that changes depending on the scenario. If we walk through this methodically, we can see the arbitrage argument.

At $t = 0$, we set up our arbitrage position. In the down state, we want to end up with 0. $PV(81) = 81/1.03 = 78.64$. To try replicating the option, we buy 1 share of stock for 90 and sell 78.64 worth of bonds.

At $t = T = 1$, we sell the stock and buy back the bond. In the up state, the stock is worth 101; the stock–bond P&L $= 101 - 81 = 20$. In the down state, the stock is worth 81; the stock–bond P&L $= 81 - 81 = 0$.

Finally, we correct the replicating portfolio to get the right payoffs. The cost of the stock–bond portfolio: $90 - 78.64 = 11.36$. This payoff is *almost* that of the option; we need only scale it up. To get the value of the option, scale the portfolio by 21/20. Thus the option C is worth $11.36 \times \frac{21}{20} = 11.93$.

For a one-step tree, valuation is straightforward. Note that this is the just a form of scenario analysis like we discussed in Chapter 10. If you are puzzled by the simple interest (lack of compounding) from the bond, do not worry: we will address that shortly.

21.3.2 Example: Two-Step Tree

What if we needed to price a two-year option? We can take the tree we have and extend it to allow for two time steps. Again, prices move up 12.2% or down 10% and up-then-down is the same as down-then-up. Figure 21.2 shows this evolution.

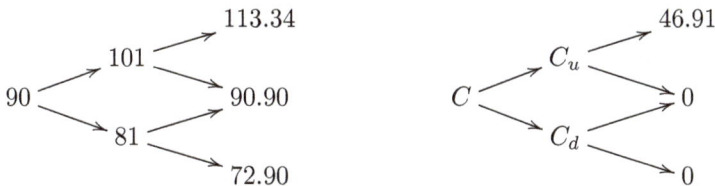

Figure 21.2: Two-step trees for a stock with future states in one and two years (left) and an option with terminal payoffs (right).

Now we can walk through the arbitrage arguments for this extended tree. While it seems more complicated, all we are doing is recursively doing the same thing we did for a one-step tree. First, we determine C_u and C_d. As before, interest rates are 3%.

At $t = 1$, we would set up an arbitrage position. From the down state, it is obvious that $C_d = 0$ since the up-down and down-down payoffs are both 0. From the up state, we want to end up with 0 in the up-down state; therefore, we want the bond and stock to cancel each other out. The one-year PV(90.90) = 88.25. Therefore, in the up state we buy the stock for 101 and sell 88.25 of bonds.

At $t = T = 2$ (from the up state), we sell the stock and buy back the bond traded at $t = 1$. In the up-up state, the stock is worth 113.34; the stock$-$bond P&L $= 113.34 - 90.90 = 22.44$. In the up-down state, the stock is worth 90.90; the stock$-$bond P&L $= 90.90 - 90.90 = 0$.

We then correct the replicating portfolio in the $t = 1$ up state. The cost of stock $-$ bond $= 101 - 88.25 = 12.75$ and pays off either 22.44 or 0. To get the value of C_u, we need to scale the portfolio by $46.91/22.44$. Thus C_u is worth $12.75 \times \frac{46.91}{22.44} = 26.65$.

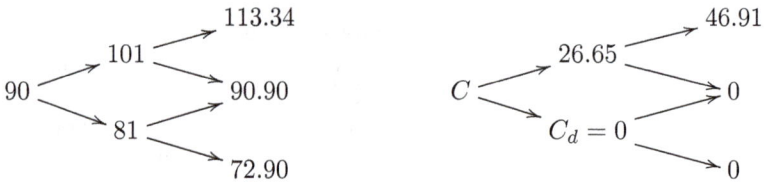

Figure 21.3: Two-step trees for a stock with future states in one and two years shown on the left and an option with terminal payoffs shown on the right. Here we have worked one step back from expiry.

This gives us the intermediate trees in Figure 21.3. Analyzing these is easier; notice that this is just a scaled version of the option we priced earlier. In the first example, the call paying off 21 or 0 for the given stock price scenarios and $r_f = 3\%$ was worth $11.93. Here the call pays off 26.65 or 0; we need to scale our original results. Thus $C = \frac{26.65}{21} \times 11.93 = 15.14$.

21.3.3   *Example: Interpolating the One-Step Tree*

By now, you should see the general way we handle trees: we find the value of the option in various scenarios one-step before expiry. These are a function of the underlier evolution and the risk-free rate. Once we have option values for one time step before expiry, we can price options for various scenarios two time steps before expiry.

We explored extending the tree; however, we can also interpolate in time and look at those scenarios. To do this, we revisit the tree from the first example. We first split up time: instead of just looking at $t = 0, 1 = T$ we look at times $t = 0, 0.5, 1 = T$. Splitting up time is the easy part.

To split up scenarios, we need to account for compounding. Thus instead of up movements being a 12.2% increase, they are now a $\sqrt{1.122} - 1 = 5.9\%$ increase; and, down movements are now a $\sqrt{0.9} - 1 = 5.1\%$ decrease.

What about the option payouts? While I did not specify a functional form, we know that one share versus a bond would have paid out 20 or 0 and that we needed to scale our portfolio by $21/20$ to get the specified option payouts. This implies our option has a strike price of $101 - 20 = 81$ and a multiplier of $21/20 = 1.05$.

Therefore, the underlier at $t = 0.5$ will either be at $90\sqrt{101/90} = 95.34$ or $90\sqrt{81/90} = 85.38$. The middle state at $t = 1$ is $90\sqrt{101/90}\sqrt{81/90} = 90.45$. That yields an option value in the up-down state of $1.05(90.45 - 81) = 9.92$. Putting all this together gives us the trees in Figure 21.4.

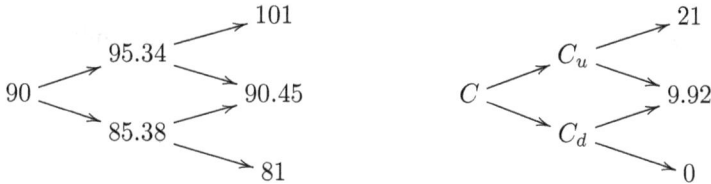

Figure 21.4: Two-step trees for a stock with future states in one-half and one year shown on the left and an option with terminal payoffs shown on the right. Here we have worked one step back from expiry.

Handling this pricing is a little more complicated: we no longer have easy 0-or-X outcomes which allow for easy scaling. We therefore need to find a general rule to create the replicating portfolio.

Suppose we have a stock priced at S which will be worth either Su or Sd in one time step. Also, suppose our option pays off C_u or C_d in these states. We want to find a number of shares to hold H and bonds to hold B so that:

$$C_u = HSu + FV(B) = HSu + B \cdot FV(1), \qquad (21.10)$$
$$C_d = HSd + FV(B) = HSd + B \cdot FV(1). \qquad (21.11)$$

If we solve these simultaneous equations, we get that:

$$H = \frac{C_u - C_d}{Su - Sd}, \quad \text{and,} \qquad (21.12)$$
$$B = \frac{SuC_d - SdC_u}{(Su - Sd)FV(1)} = \frac{uC_d - dC_u}{u - d}PV(1). \qquad (21.13)$$

Our replicating portfolio holds H shares of stock and B worth of bonds (at purchase time; $B \cdot FV(1)$ face value of bond). The portfolio replicates both possible outcomes which means that our stock position counterbalances the variation in option value. Thus we refer to H as the **hedge ratio**: the number of shares to hold to hedge the price risk of the option. The bond position is often referred to as the financing leg since $B < 0$ for a call option. The option price is just the cost of the replicating portfolio:

$$C = HS + B. \qquad (21.14)$$

If we apply this, we can now fill in the interpolated tree. We need to remember, however, that $PV(1) = \sqrt{1.03}$. Thus (using full precision, and not rounding as is done here):

$$C_d = \frac{9.92 - 0}{90.45 - 81} \times 85.38 + \frac{90.45 \cdot 0 - 81 \cdot 9.92}{(90.45 - 81)\sqrt{1.03}} = 5.8467, \tag{21.15}$$

$$C_u = \frac{21 - 9.92}{101 - 90.45} \times 95.34 + \frac{101 \cdot 9.92 - 90.45 \cdot 21}{(101 - 90.45)\sqrt{1.03}} = 16.3047, \tag{21.16}$$

$$C = \frac{16.30 - 5.85}{95.34 - 85.38} \times 90 + \frac{95.34 \cdot 5.85 - 85.38 \cdot 16.30}{(95.34 - 85.38)\sqrt{1.03}} = 11.9272. \tag{21.17}$$

Figure 21.5 shows the values filled in based on these general results.

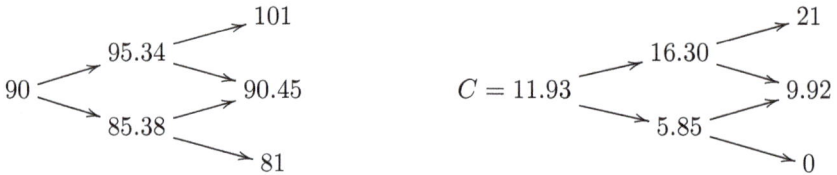

Figure 21.5: Two-step trees for a stock with future states in one-half and one year shown on the left and an option with terminal payoffs shown on the right. Here we have filled in all option values based on the general formulas we developed for tree pricing.

21.3.4   Recursive Pricing

The fact that this pricing is recursive means that we can split the problem into finer and finer sub-problems, solve those, and then work backwards to get the solution for the whole tree. This sort of recursion is something computers do very well. Thus we could fill out the option tree and price the option in R. Typically, this is done using a square matrix like a tree. You can visualize this if you rotate the matrix 45° anti-clockwise:

```
price.tree <- function(numsteps, under.tree, opt.payoffs,
                    rf, delta.t, ups=0, downs=0) {
    if (numsteps > 0) {
        up.value <- price.tree(numsteps-1, under.tree, opt.payoffs,
                         rf, delta.t, ups+1, downs)
        down.value <- price.tree(numsteps-1, under.tree, opt.payoffs,
                          rf, delta.t, ups, downs+1)
    } else {
        # We have reached a leaf; return the option payoff
        return(opt.payoffs[downs+1])
    }
    under.up.value <- under.tree[downs+1,ups+1+1]
    under.down.value <- under.tree[downs+1+1,ups+1]
    H <- (up.value-down.value)/(under.up.value-under.down.value)
    B <- (under.up.value*down.value - under.down.value*up.value)/
        (under.up.value - under.down.value)*exp(-rf*delta.t)
    H*under.tree[downs+1,ups+1] + B
```

```
}

rf <- 0.03  # 3% risk-free rates
sigma <- 0.45  # 45% volatility
T <- 1.25  # 15-month option
n.steps <- 16  # number of steps total
delta.t <- T/n.steps  # interpolated time step size
u <- exp(sigma*sqrt(delta.t))  # up move
d <- exp(-sigma*sqrt(delta.t))  # down move
s0 <- 100  # initial stock price
K <- 80  # strike price

## This creates a full matrix with the tree -- and steps beyond the tree
## in the lower-right triangle of the matrix.  Since this is an easy way
## to create the tree, we will just ignore the lower-right triangle.
underlier.tree <- s0*d^(0:n.steps)%*%t(u^(0:n.steps))
option.payoffs <- pmax(s0*u^(n.steps:0)*d^(0:n.steps) - K, 0)
price.tree(numsteps=n.steps, underlier.tree, option.payoffs, rf, delta.t)
```

You can see the recursive aspect: `price.tree()` splits the tree into sub-trees and then calls itself on those smaller trees. This continues until that iteration's tree is a leaf (when `numsteps = 0`), at which point the option payoff is returned.[5] Once the function has priced up and down trees, it can price the option and return that value to a function call one step back. The recursion causes values to percolate backward until we get back to the initial call and we get the option value at time $t = 0$. Those looking for a gentle yet eye-opening discussion of recursion would do well to read Hofstadter (1979).

21.3.5 Other Ways to Grow Option Trees

There are a few other issues which might affect the trees we use.

For American options, we need to make an additional evaluation at each step of the option tree: what would be the value of early exercise? Early exercise may allow us to receive an upcoming dividend (for a call) or intrinsic value now (for a put). Therefore, each step of the option tree computes these values and then takes the maximum of the arbitrage portfolio value or the early exercise value.

We might need to use a non-recombining tree in certain scenarios. Typically, these are scenarios which have **path dependency**: where the underlier can trigger situations which permanently affect the option value. Examples of such path dependency include a knock-out (down-and-out) barrier option or the prepayment option on a mortgage: if interest rates drop below a certain level, many homeowners will refinance their mortgages which results in the mortgages being repaid early.

21.3.6 How to Grow Underlier Trees

Up to this point, we have just seen an underlier tree which I made up. There is nothing wrong with that; the arbitrage arguments all still hold. However we typically

---

[5]This code is a little weird in that the underlier "tree" is actually a diamond since the tree is in the upper-left diagonal of the matrix and we also define steps beyond the tree (in the lower-right part of the matrix). We do this because it lets us easily define the tree with a matrix multiplication.

create the underlier tree to match certain characteristics of the underlier. Thus we break up time into steps of size Δt and then set the price up/down steps accordingly.

In general, all of these underlier tree creation approaches converge to a limit of log-returns being normally-distributed. We know this is wrong. However, as we will see shortly, we can correct for that.

Cox, Ross, and Rubinstein (1979) first proposed a parameterization using only the volatility to characterize the evolution of the underlier:

$$u = e^{\sigma\sqrt{\Delta t}}, \tag{21.18}$$

$$d = 1/u = e^{-\sigma\sqrt{\Delta t}}. \tag{21.19}$$

They also noted that the arbitrage portfolios implied probabilities of up and down moves. Since there is an arbitrage portfolio, the future scenarios are discounted at the risk-free rate making these probabilities **risk-neutral probabilities**, sometimes denoted as P_Q:

$$P_Q(\text{up}) = E_Q(1_{\text{up}}) = \frac{e^{r_f \Delta t} - d}{u - d}. \tag{21.20}$$

Some find this evolution less-than-appealing. If a stock is volatile, geometric Brownian motion has a negative component of drift: A stock which goes up 10% and then down 10% ends up at a lower price — because the second (decline) 10% is larger than first (increase) 10%. For trees with fewer time steps, this effect is more important. Therefore, Jarrow and Rudd (1983) included terms to capture this and the effect of dividends:

$$u = e^{(r_f - \delta - \sigma^2/2)\Delta t + \sigma\sqrt{\Delta t}}, \tag{21.21}$$

$$d = e^{(r_f - \delta - \sigma^2/2)\Delta t - \sigma\sqrt{\Delta t}}, \tag{21.22}$$

where δ is the dividend yield.

When Jarrow and Rudd first proposed this evolution, they used equal probabilities for an up and down move; however, we need not do that: we will stick with the arbitrage-free pricing we have developed so far. (This also implies sticking with the risk-neutral probabilities above.)

Tian (1993) proposed another evolution which also matches the skewness of the limiting log-normal return distribution.

$$u = \frac{e^{(r_f + \sigma^2)\Delta t}}{2}\left((e^{\sigma^2 \Delta t} + 1) + \sqrt{e^{2\sigma^2 \Delta t} + 2e^{\sigma^2 \Delta t} - 3}\right), \tag{21.23}$$

$$d = \frac{e^{(r_f + \sigma^2)\Delta t}}{2}\left((e^{\sigma^2 \Delta t} + 1) - \sqrt{e^{2\sigma^2 \Delta t} + 2e^{\sigma^2 \Delta t} - 3}\right). \tag{21.24}$$

Leisen and Reimer (1996) noted that all of these approaches have non-monotone convergence: sometimes increasing the number of steps produces a less accurate solution. They and Tian (1999) proposed methods which ensure monotone convergence; however, these are a bit more involved. Since the convergence often oscillates around the correct value, an easy approximation is to average or project from the last few solutions.

21.3.7 Whither Trees?

Trees give us an approximation which is crude but tractable. As we interpolate trees more finely, dividing time into lengths Δt and shrinking price space by $e^{1/\sqrt{\Delta t}}$ (or, equivalently, shrinking log-return space by $1/\sqrt{\Delta t}$), the approximation converges to the true option value. However, in some cases we need not even find this limit computationally. This leads to our next solution methodology: The Black-Scholes-Merton formula.

21.4 The Black-Scholes-Merton Formula

Before the binomial tree approach, Black and Scholes (1973) derived a closed-form solution to the option pricing problem. While others before them had gotten very close to the correct answer, they had all missed one crucial point: because there is an arbitrage portfolio that can combine stock and option to get a risk-free bond, the discounting must be at the risk-free rate.

However, we should review the dynamics which lead to the Black-Scholes-Merton formula because it will help us to interpret its meaning. Believe it or not: the formula is complicated but very intuitive.

21.4.1 Drift and Diffusion

We begin by assuming the underlier follows a simple drift and diffusion stochastic differential equation, also known as geometric Brownian motion:

$$dS_t = \underbrace{\mu S_t dt}_{\text{drift}} + \underbrace{\sigma S_t dW_t}_{\text{diffusion}}. \tag{21.25}$$

This causes the drift and diffusion terms to scale with the underlier price making them constant in terms of log-returns.[6] Note that log-returns are naturally implied by this setup since we can divide both sides by S_t and the derivative of $\log(S_t)$ is $1/S_t$.

You might then wonder: can we just plug in drift and diffusion for mean and standard deviation?

$$\log(S_T) - \log(S_t) \overset{?}{\sim} N(\mu(T-t), \sigma^2(T-t)). \tag{21.26}$$

The answer is: no. As hinted at earlier, the mean for geometric Brownian motion requires us to correct the drift by $-\sigma^2/2$. This means that

$$\log(S_T) \sim N(\log(S_t) + (\mu - \sigma^2/2)(T-t), \sigma^2(T-t)). \tag{21.27}$$

---

[6]The logs, we use are always natural logs, aka $\log_e$ or ℓn.

You may notice I moved $\log(S_t)$ to the LHS of the equation. The reason for doing this will make sense shortly. If we next subtract $\log(K)$ from each side, we get the distribution of log-returns above the strike price K:

$$\log(S_T/K) \sim N(\log(S_t/K) + (\mu - \sigma^2/2)(T - t), \sigma^2(T - t)). \qquad (21.28)$$

21.4.2   Risk-Neutral and Physical Probabilities

The preceding density is also known as the **risk-neutral density**. Recall that we can price assets in two ways. We can do as in Chapters 13–15: use a stochastic discount factor which is higher than the risk-free rate and **physical probabilities**, which we often call $\mathbb{P}$-measure. Alternately, we can use the risk-free rate for discounting with no penalty for risk, but then we have to adjust the probabilities we use to be risk-neutral probabilities which we often call $\mathbb{Q}$-measure.[7]

Consider the one-year risky bond mentioned in Section 11.7.1. That bond paid off \$1000 with probability 0.9 and \$400 with probability 0.1. If a one-year T-bill was yielding 5%, the corporate bond expected present value is \$895.24 which is a yield (to maturity) of 11.7%. However, that is not a market price we are likely to ever see: most traders would demand a return greater than 11.7% to compensate for the risk. Thus the pricing kernel would be above 11.7% and the risk-neutral probabilities would put more weight on the default scenario.

If the market demanded a 15% return for the bond — the pricing kernel, then the market price would be \$940/1.15=\$817.39. That implies risk-neutral probabilities of:

$$P_Q(\text{no default}) = \left\{ q : \frac{1000q + 400(1 - q)}{1.05} = 817.39 \right\} \qquad (21.29)$$
$$\implies q = 0.76.$$

Thankfully, working with $\mathbb{Q}$-measure is not as difficult as it sounds. The arbitrage arguments we have developed so far allowed us to find risk-neutral probabilities. Girsanov's Theorem tells us that we can get the risk-neutral probabilities from the physical probabilities by simply shifting the distribution to the left; the volatility does not change.

21.4.3   Black-Scholes-Merton (1973) Model

Since we can use underlier and option to replicate a risk-free bond, we can use the implied probabilities and discount by the risk-free rate; thus $\mu = r_f$. This realization was the breakthrough of Black and Scholes (1973).

---

[7]A third approach which is often done is to take payoffs that are promised, discount them using the risk-free rate, and then use the implied yield as a gauge of investment risk. This approach is not very rigorous.

To determine the value of a call option $C_{K,t,T}$ at time t, we need to find:

$$C_{K,t,T} = E_Q[(S_T - K)^+ | \mathcal{F}_t]. \tag{21.30}$$

We can separate this into finding two quantities under the $\mathbb{Q}$-measure:

1. the expected underlier value if above the strike price: $E_Q(S_T | S_T > K)$; and,
2. the present value of K multiplied by the probability that the underlier is above the strike price: $P_Q(S_T > K) = E_Q(1_{S_T > K})$.

Thus this is just a complicated (risk-neutral) DCF valuation.

Continuing with equation (21.28), we can integrate to get the expected value of the underlier if it is above the strike:

$$E_Q(S_T | S_T > K) = S_t \Phi(d_1), \tag{21.31}$$

$$d_1 = \frac{\log(\frac{S_t}{K}) + (r_f + \frac{\sigma^2}{2})(T-t)}{\sigma\sqrt{T-t}}, \tag{21.32}$$

where $\Phi(z)$ is the standard normal cdf which gives $P(Z < z)$ for $Z \sim N(0,1)$.

We find the probability of a call ending ITM easily (*i.e.* without integrating):

$$P_Q(S_T > K) = \Phi(d_2), \tag{21.33}$$

$$d_2 = \frac{\log(\frac{S_t}{K}) + (r_f - \frac{\sigma^2}{2})(T-t)}{\sigma\sqrt{T-t}}. \tag{21.34}$$

Putting these together, we get the Black and Scholes (1973) and Merton (1973b) formula for the value of a European call option:

$$C_{K,t,T} = \underbrace{S_t \Phi(d_1)}_{E_Q(S_T | S_T > K)} - \underbrace{K e^{-r_f(T-t)} \Phi(d_2)}_{PV(K) \cdot P_Q(S_T > K)}. \tag{21.35}$$

Similarly, the Black-Scholes-Merton value of a put option is:

$$P_{K,t,T} = K e^{-r_f(T-t)} \Phi(-d_2) - S_t \Phi(-d_1). \tag{21.36}$$

21.4.4 *Extensions to Other Underliers*

Merton (1973b) showed how to easily modify this formula to accommodate other underliers such as stocks with dividends or commodities. If the underlier is a stock paying a continuous dividend yield of δ, we instead use $\mu = r_f - \delta$. While no stocks pay continuous dividends, a *continuous dividend yield* is an easy approximation:

$$C_{K,t,T} = S_t e^{-\delta(T-t)} \Phi(d_1) - K e^{-r_f(T-t)} \Phi(d_2), \tag{21.37}$$

$$d_1 = \frac{\log(\frac{S_t}{K}) + (r_f - \delta + \frac{\sigma^2}{2})(T-t)}{\sigma\sqrt{T-t}}, \tag{21.38}$$

$$d_2 = \frac{\log(\frac{S_t}{K}) + (r_f - \delta - \frac{\sigma^2}{2})(T-t)}{\sigma\sqrt{T-t}} = d_1 - \sigma\sqrt{T-t}. \tag{21.39}$$

For *currencies*, assuming a continuous yield is much better. Garman and Kohlhagen (1983) valued a call to convert ABC to DEF (*i.e.* a call on ABC/DEF) as:

$$C_{K,t,T} = S_t e^{-r_{DEF}(T-t)} \Phi(d_1) - K e^{-r_{ABC}(T-t)} \Phi(d_2), \qquad (21.40)$$

$$d_1 = \frac{\log(S_t/K) + (r_{ABC} - r_{DEF} + \frac{\sigma^2}{2})(T-t)}{\sigma\sqrt{T-t}}, \qquad (21.41)$$

$$d_2 = d_1 - \sigma\sqrt{T-t}. \qquad (21.42)$$

For *commodities*, Black (1976) suggests to add the convenience yield $v_{t,T}$ over the time period and subtract the cost of carry $\kappa_{t,T}$ (as hinted at above):[8]

$$C_{K,t,T} = S_t e^{-(v_{t,T} - \kappa_{t,T})(T-t)} \Phi(d_1) - K e^{-r_f(T-t)} \Phi(d_2), \qquad (21.43)$$

$$d_1 = \frac{\log(S_t/K) + (r - v_{t,T} + \kappa_{t,T} + \frac{\sigma^2}{2})(T-t)}{\sigma\sqrt{T-t}}, \qquad (21.44)$$

$$d_2 = d_1 - \sigma\sqrt{T-t}. \qquad (21.45)$$

Black (1976) also showed how to price options expiring at time T on *futures* F_{t,T_F} maturing at time $T_F > T$:

$$C_{K,t,T} = e^{-r_f(T-t)} [F_{t,T_F} \Phi(d_1) - K \Phi(d_2)] \qquad (21.46)$$

$$d_1 = \frac{\log(F_{t,T_F}/K) + \frac{\sigma^2}{2}(T-t)}{\sigma\sqrt{T-t}}, \quad d_2 = d_1 - \sigma\sqrt{T-t}. \qquad (21.47)$$

21.4.5   *Sensitivities and Risk Factors*

We might trade options to eliminate upside or downside price risk. However, financial intermediaries are often market makers with options inventory from trading with buyers and sellers; and, speculators trade options because they think they are mispriced. For these traders, hedging an option's risk factors is crucial. Therefore, we often analyze the sensitivity of an option to risk factors such as model inputs.

These sensitivities allow us to calculate exposures to certain risk factors for a portfolio of options. We can then easily hedge the exposures with the underlier and futures. If we have options on many stocks, we might even hedge the underlier exposures with an equity index futures contract. While not a perfect hedge, this may be less expensive than trading more often for each of the underlying stocks.

We typically denote these sensitivities with Greek letters. Hence people often refer to them as **option Greeks**. In general, these are computed by taking the partial derivative $\frac{\partial V}{\partial F}$ of the option value V with respect to the risk factor F. While myriad Greeks may be calculated, most traders focus on a handful of factors which often have the largest effects.

---

[8]Note, however, that this is a wholly unsatisfying approach since the idea of convenience yield is the option value of being able to deliver into price spikes. If we are pricing options, it seems appropriate to also price that optionality. We will return to this idea later.

Delta

The most critical risk factor is **delta**, Δ, the sensitivity of the option to changes in the underlier. Delta is the same as the hedge ratio H we computed when working with binomial trees. From the Black-Scholes-Merton formula (for a call and put on a stock, in this case), we can see that delta is *usually* given by:

$$\Delta_C = \frac{\partial C}{\partial S} \overset{\text{usu.}}{=} \Phi(d_1)e^{-\delta(T-t)} \in (0,1), \tag{21.48}$$

$$\Delta_P = \frac{\partial P}{\partial S} \overset{\text{usu.}}{=} -\Phi(-d_1)e^{-\delta(T-t)} \in (-1,0). \tag{21.49}$$

Since $\Phi(d_1) = 1 - \Phi(-d_1)$, we can see that $\Delta_C - \Delta_P = e^{-\delta(T-t)}$ which is usually close to 1. This is what we found when we looked at put-call parity.

These formulas are incorrect, however, when we have an American option that we would exercise early. In that case, early exercise means the option value moves up 1:1 with the underlier: American call and puts in their early-exercise regimes would have $\Delta_C = 1$ and $\Delta_P = -1$.

Gamma

The next-most critical risk factor is **gamma**, Γ, the sensitivity of the option delta to changes in the underlier, *i.e.* the second derivative of the option value with respect to the underlier. Gamma effectively tells us how often a delta-hedger would need to adjust their hedging of underlier price risk. From the Black-Scholes-Merton formulas, we can see that gamma is *usually* given by:

$$\Gamma_C = \Gamma_P = \frac{\partial^2 V}{\partial S^2} = \frac{\partial \Delta}{\partial S} \overset{\text{usu.}}{=} \frac{e^{-\delta(T-t)}\phi(d_1)}{S_t\sigma\sqrt{T-t}}, \tag{21.50}$$

where $\phi(z)$ is the standard normal pdf. For an American option in the early-exercise regime, Δ does not change and so $\Gamma = 0$.

Vega

Probably the most critical risk factor after gamma is **vega**, the sensitivity of the option to changes in volatility σ.

This is the awkward moment when Spanish-speaking students furrow their brows. Clearly, when option traders went around the circle naming the Greeks, somebody was neither cosmopolitan nor familiar with Greek letters — because vega is not a Greek letter. It is not even *close* to the name of a Greek letter. Nonetheless, the name has stuck: the consonance of vega and volatility is just too appealing. If "vega" being claimed as a Greek letter is not maddening enough, it is often represented with a Greek letter nu, ν, which looks like a "v" but has an "n" sound.[9]

---

[9]Some purists try to substitute kappa, but this is not used nearly as often as nu. Furthermore, κ lacks even the slightly-redeeming feature of ν looking like "v."

From the Black-Scholes-Merton formulas, vega is *usually* given by:

$$\text{Vega} = \nu_C = \nu_P = \frac{\partial V}{\partial \sigma} \overset{\text{usu.}}{=} S_t e^{-\delta(T-t)} \phi(d_1)\sqrt{T-t}. \tag{21.51}$$

Typically, vega is divided by 100 to give the change in option value for a 1% increase in volatility (*e.g.* from 0.20 to 0.21). As with gamma, the vega for an American option in the early-exercise regime is 0.

Rho

Rho, denoted ρ, is the option sensitivity to the risk-free rate — or the domestic risk-free rate r_{ABC} in equation (21.40) for FX options. (The sensitivity of an FX option to the foreign risk-free rate r_{DEF} in equation (21.40) is often called "foreign rho.") Rho is not the most critical factor for options on underliers that are not interest-rate related. However, since rho does not tend to change quickly, it is easy to hedge and is not trivial for a decent-sized portfolio of options.

$$\rho_C = \frac{\partial C}{\partial r_f} \overset{\text{usu.}}{=} K e^{-r_f(T-t)}\Phi(d_2)(T-t), \tag{21.52}$$

$$\rho_P = \frac{\partial P}{\partial r_f} \overset{\text{usu.}}{=} -K e^{-r_f(T-t)}\Phi(-d_2)(T-t). \tag{21.53}$$

Typically, we scale rho by dividing it by 10000 which makes it scaled for a 1 bp move. Thus $\rho/10000 = DV01$.

Psi

Psi, denoted Ψ, is the option sensitivity to the dividend yield rate for stock options or, for commodity options, the convenience yield or the negative cost-of-carry. Like rho, psi is not the most critical factor for options on underliers that are not interest-rate related. Also like rho, psi does not tend to change quickly and is not trivial for a large portfolio of options.

$$\Psi_C = \frac{\partial C}{\partial d} \overset{\text{usu.}}{=} -S_t e^{-\delta(T-t)}\Phi(d_1)(T-t), \tag{21.54}$$

$$\Psi_P = \frac{\partial P}{\partial d} \overset{\text{usu.}}{=} S_t e^{-\delta(T-t)}\Phi(-d_1)(T-t). \tag{21.55}$$

Typically, we scale psi by dividing it by 100.

Theta

Theta, denoted Θ, is the change in option value for a change in time to expiry.

Since time to expiry always decreases, we usually multiply the derivative by -1:[10]

$$\Theta = -\frac{\partial V}{\partial (T - t)} = \frac{\partial V}{\partial t}. \tag{21.56}$$

Since time is in units of years, we often divide theta by the number of trading days in a year. Note that theta cannot be cleanly hedged.

21.4.6 Black-Scholes-Merton Complications

While these formulas work reasonably well for European options, there are problems we should anticipate. The first is that we started with flawed fundamentals: prices are not log-normally-distributed, *i.e.* log-returns are not normally-distributed. This seems like a minor point, but we will see that it makes a difference for equities and is even more important for commodities. If anything, for commodities the call formula should be a lower bound due to the possibility of short-term price spikes. (Adding in the convenience yield might help alleviate some of this issue.)

American Options and Early Exercise

As we have already seen, American options are more complicated to analyze since we need to value the possibility of early exercise. For an American put P^A, the valuation is not so difficult:

$$P^A_{K,t,T} = \max(K - S_t, P^E_{K,t,T}). \tag{21.57}$$

An American call on a dividend-free stock has the same value as a European call. An American call on a dividend-paying stock, however, is worth more but has no known closed-form (*i.e.* formula) for the price. When a stock pays a dividend, the firm records equity holders on a certain date (the **ex-dividend date**) and pays dividends to those holders a few days later. On the ex-dividend date, the stock drops by the present value of the dividend. Holders of call options do not get the dividend and the underlying price falls, making their call options worth a little less.

Holders of American call options, however, can avoid this with early exercise. An approximation for the value of an American call in this scenario was found by Black (1975). For a dividend of D_τ with ex-dividend date at time $t < \tau < T$, Black suggests the value of the American put is approximately the greater of (1) a European put expiring at time τ, or (2) a European put expiring at time T with the

---

[10]I have not given the explicit formula for theta because it is more involved and theta is not cleanly hedgeable.

underlying reduced by $PV(D_\tau)$:

$$P^A_{K,t,T} \approx \max(P^E_{K,t,\tau}, P^{E*}_{K,t,T}) \quad \text{where} \tag{21.58}$$

$$P^{E*}_{K,t,T} = (S_t - D_\tau e^{-r_f(\tau-t)})\Phi(d^*_1) - Ke^{-r_f(T-t)}\Phi(d^*_2), \tag{21.59}$$

$$d^*_1 = \frac{\log((S_t - D_\tau e^{-r_f(\tau-t)})/K) + (r_f - \sigma^2/2)(T-t)}{\sigma\sqrt{T-t}}, \tag{21.60}$$

$$d^*_2 = d^*_1 - \sigma\sqrt{T-t}. \tag{21.61}$$

Replication Complications

Everything we have done in trees and stochastic processes has rested on arbitrage arguments: the ability to replicate the option by continuously (in truth: continually) trading the underlier and a risk-free bond. What if these arbitrage pricing arguments do not hold? This is not hypothetical; this can happen a few ways.

One way for these arbitrage arguments to fail is simply if risk-free bonds default. In that case, everything becomes chaotic. This is why politicians who threaten to default for political purposes are very bad people.

However, the most common replication complication comes from jumps. Jumps in volatility are discussed in Eraker, Johannes, and Polson (2003); and, Naik (1993) shows how to create an arbitrage portfolio with another option to hedge volatility jumps. If we add jumps in price to equation (21.25), we get a **jump-diffusion process**. Jumps in price are discussed in Rosenberg (1972) and Merton (1976). Jarrow and Rosenfeld (1984) find that price jumps are not diversifiable and thus not ignorable; and, Naik and Lee (1990) find that price jumps create unavoidable losses. Föllmer and Schweizer (1991) find an approximate hedge for price jumps, but it does not eliminate all risk. This suggests that price jumps are a priced risk factor.

Portfolio Insurance and 1987

The concern about jumps might seem academic; it is not. In the 1980s many brokers began offering clients a service that seemed too good to be true. Since options can be replicated by trading stocks and bonds, a **dynamic trading strategy**, brokers proposed replicating put options on client portfolios. The portfolio would never fall below a certain level... or so they claimed. This was offered to clients as **portfolio insurance**. Apart from the higher trading fees, this seemed like sheer brilliance.

However, on 19 October 1987 (aka **Black Monday**), the replication complications became a very real and non-academic concern. On that day, markets across the globe declined precipitously, starting in Hong Kong and spreading across Europe to the US and back to New Zealand (known there as **Black Tuesday**). Declines ranged from over 45% in Hong Kong, to 22% in the US. The New Zealand market declined 15% on Black Tuesday. While most markets recovered most of the losses within a few months, New Zealand's market had been plagued by speculative IPOs and bubble-ish investment schemes; after the crash, the Reserve Bank did not lower interest rates. New Zealand's market eventually fell 60% from its 1987 peak.

In the US, the exchanges were so overloaded with trading that prices were delayed by hours (and fill reports were also very delayed). That made replicating a put option impossible. Clients who bought portfolio insurance sustained big losses. Worse: portfolio insurance was blamed for destabilizing the market since hedgers sold increasing numbers of shares as the market fell further. After the 1987 crash, portfolio insurance became much less popular.

Pin Risk

Finally, one of the stranger risks of options is that of **pin risk**: the unusually-high probability of options to expire at the strike price of an option.

Pin risk affects options which are near-ATM. Delta hedging by options holders causes price impact which tends to push underlying prices. As the options get closer to expiry, the change in delta as the underlier crosses the strike price can be very sharp: between -1 and 0 for puts and 0 and 1 for calls.

If the most-active delta hedgers are long calls and puts, their delta hedging will tend to push the underlier toward the option strike price: we say the underlier "pins" the strike price. On the other hand, if the most-active delta hedgers are short calls and puts, the underlier will be pushed away from the option strike price: we say the underlier "avoids" the strike price.

> **Pin Risk and Illiquidity** I once sat across from an option trader. One day, the head of the option desk began yelling at the option trader. Being hot-headed, the desk head yelled, gestured wildly, clutched his head, and made sure we all knew what had happened.
>
> The option trader had been delta hedging a long call position on an illiquid underlier. He saw that his calls were ITM, noted how many shares he needed to short, and then worked the order over an hour or two. He then saw the calls were OTM and needed to buy shares. Back he went to working a hedge order — now a buy. By the time the desk head was yelling, the option trader had pushed the underlying through the strike a few times. The desk head was no help either: he invested his energy in drama instead of discussing price impact and an equilibrium solution.

This effect has been documented in numerous sources. Anders (1982) first mentioned pin risk. Natenberg (1988) discussed it, but incorrectly attributed it to the risk of delivery of the underlying. While that is a concern, pin risk is still troublesome for cash-settled options. Patel and Koh (2002) noted the effect and the cause being the price impact of delta hedging in a Morgan Stanley research report. Academics took notice as well with Avellaneda and Lipkin (2003) and Ni, Pearson, and Poteshman (2005) studying the effect. This effect can be particularly pronounced near the expiry of warrants and convertible bonds — since all delta hedgers are long.[11]

21.5   Volatility Curves

We have made a big assumption: that we know the volatility. In reality, we never know the volatility. We can estimate it, but God never whispers to us from a bush to use a 19% volatility for KOSPI log-returns.[12] While that is probably for the better, it complicates our analyses.

21.5.1   Implied Volatility and the VIX

Even if we estimate the volatility using historical log-returns, that is still a backward-looking measure. That might be very different from what volatility will be going forward a few months or years. However, traded instrument prices are forward-looking. So what if we turned the option pricing upside-down? In that case, we could find an **implied volatility**, the volatility we would need to use to match market prices of options.

At this point, you might recall the results from Carr and Madan (1998) that we can replicate a variance swap with a portfolio of straddles. You might think we could then get a measure of market volatility by finding the implied volatility for a set of straddles on an equity index and then averaging those implied volatilities. This would be close but not totally correct.

Instead, we do something similar: we take a weighted sum of OOM puts and calls.[13] Demeterfi et al. (1999) develop this idea and show that the right weighting scheme yields a portfolio with a flat payoff related only to the level of variance. Dividing by time and taking the square root gives an estimate of the market index volatility. Indeed, this **volatility index** which debuted at the CBOE was given the better-known name of the **VIX**.

21.5.2   Volatility Curves

Also informative is to look at implied volatilities for options with different strike prices: there is a clear term structure. If we plot implied volatilities (averaged across puts and calls) versus various strikes K, we see the **volatility curve**. This was first noted by Macbeth and Merville (1979).

The volatility curve exists, in part, because our model started with flawed fundamentals: dynamics which tended toward normal log-returns. These curves correct for that flaw and often exhibit a **smile** (a U-shaped curve) or a **smirk** (a J-

---

[11]I first saw this effect in the 1990s with Japanese warrants and convertible bonds we traded.

[12]It is doubtful that divine intervention would extend to such mundane matters.

[13]Note that this uses a form of implied volatility without inverting the valuation formulas.

or L-shaped curve). This tendency for volatility to fall or rise with increases in the underlier price is referred to as the **leverage effect** or **reverse leverage effect**.[14]

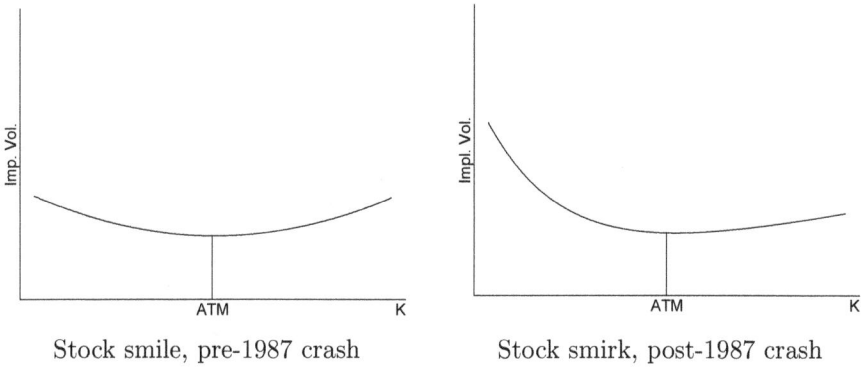

Stock smile, pre-1987 crash   Stock smirk, post-1987 crash

Figure 21.6: Volatility curves for US stocks pre- and post-1987 crash (left and right). Note the increasing concern about downside risk and the "leverage" effect for post-1987 stocks.

Figure 21.6 shows typical volatility curves for US stocks before and after the 1987 crash. We see from these curves that before the 1987 crash, investors viewed upside and downside risk similarly. Based on the 1987 crash, we might think investors underestimated the difficulty of providing portfolio insurance, delta hedging, and the general chaos of a crash. However, if we look at the volatility curve after 1987, we see that investors' perceptions changed.

These curves express where the log-normal distribution is lacking. The elevated parts of the volatility curve means that the market prices those options at a higher volatility — a higher price. This implies that OOM options, high-strike calls and especially low-strike puts, are more valuable than the log-normal assumption implies. This is a direct expression of the log-return distribution have negative skewness and kurtosis greater than 3. That puts are especially valued is an unusual fact first noted by Bondarenko (2014).[15]

After the 1987 crash, investors decided either that (1) downside crashes are more likely than upside spikes, (2) the damage caused by crashes is greater than the good caused by upward price spikes, or (3) both of these. While the Black-Scholes-Merton formula starts with a flawed log-normal assumption, one of the beautiful aspects of the model is that we can easily correct for this with a volatility curve.

Since I have claimed that volatility curves help correct for how log-returns depart

---

[14]Note that these leverage effects have no relation to funding leverage, *i.e.* assets to debt, as shown by Hasanhodzic and Lo (2013).

[15]The work generated so much commentary as a 2003 working paper that the published literature raced ahead. This complicated any literature review since related work grew quickly, but those works referred back to the working paper. This was resolved with publication in 2014.

from normality, you might wonder about how the volatility curves look for other asset classes. If we look at an asset class with skewness and high kurtosis, would we see a different shape? Figure 21.7 shows a typical volatility curve for commodities. Note the J-shaped (smirk) curve. This is because of a few stylized facts about commodity markets: prices can spike when short-term supply cannot adjust; and, volatility thus increases as prices rise (a "reverse leverage" effect).

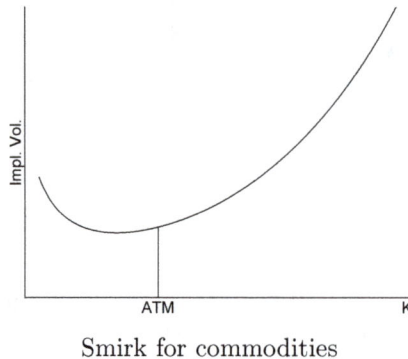

Smirk for commodities

Figure 21.7: Volatility curve for commodities. Note the reverse leverage effect due to the possibility of price spikes when short-term supply cannot adjust which also increases volatility.

If the log-return distribution were normal, we would see a volatility curve that was approximately a horizontal line. However, we know by now that log-returns are not normal; the true distribution is often skewed and with higher kurtosis — so it has a narrower peak and fatter tails. We also know that pricing is affected by unhedgeable jumps and, therefore, risk aversion enters into pricing.

We often fit volatility curves with a model so that we can use a smoother curve for pricing and, possibly, for inferring options which seem mispriced versus the volatility curve.

21.5.3   Beyond the Volatility Curve

If we want to model log-return dynamics, one place to start is with the fact that volatility is not constant. We could try fitting an ARCH model like Engle (1982) or a GARCH model like Bollerslev (1986). We could even fit these or something more complicated (which we will discuss shortly) using Aït-Sahalia and Kimmel (2007).

Stochastic Volatility

We can also estimate parameters for a dynamic volatility model which best fits the observed volatility curve. Since the dynamics are random, we call this a **stochastic**

volatility model. The exemplar of such models is the Heston (1993) model:

$$dS_t = (r_f - \delta)S_t dt + \sqrt{\Sigma_t}S_t dW_t^S, \tag{21.62}$$

$$d\Sigma_t = \underbrace{a(b - \Sigma_t)dt}_{\substack{\text{OU mean} \\ \text{reversion}}} + \gamma\sqrt{\Sigma_t}dW_t^\Sigma, \tag{21.63}$$

$$dW_t^\Sigma \cdot dW_t^S = \rho \qquad (\rho < 0 \Rightarrow \text{leverage effect}). \tag{21.64}$$

Equation (21.62) says that the underlier follows a geometric Brownian motion with the risk-free rate (less dividend yield) for the drift and volatility $\sqrt{\Sigma_t}$ which scales the diffusion. This is almost the same as the stochastic differential equation we used when finding the Black-Scholes-Merton formula — except here the variance Σ_t changes over time. Equation (21.63) says that the variance is a mean-reverting Ornstein-Uhlenbeck process with another source of randomness dW_t^Σ scaled by γ. Finally, equation (21.64) allows for the underlier and variance processes to be correlated (like how commodity volatility increases with prices).

Volatility Surfaces

Another way to explore volatility curves is to extend them into another dimension. If we plot implied volatilities against K and T, we get a **volatility surface**. As with the volatility curve, if we think the surface is stationary we can try to fit it with a parametric model.

In general, as we go further out in time, the volatility surface typically flattens. Furthermore, if we are going to price other instruments with the volatility surface, we might want the fitted curve to have smooth first and second derivatives.

21.6 Extracting Risk-Neutral Densities

If getting forward-looking estimates of volatility was not cool enough, volatility curves hint at something even cooler: the ability to extract an estimate of the risk-neutral density of future prices. Unlike so many areas of estimation where we try to estimate some moments, options allow us to see much more.

21.6.1 Butterflies, Second Derivatives, and Dirac

This idea was pioneered by Breeden and Litzenberger (1978) who noted that taking the second partial derivative of option prices with respect to the strike price yields the risk-neutral density. The proof is intuitive: They create a butterfly with strikes at $K - h$, K, and $K + h$. Thus the butterfly is a triangle with width $2h$ and height h. The area of that triangle, which you learned in primary school, is: $\frac{1}{2} \cdot 2h \cdot h = h^2$. Thus we divide the butterfly by h^2 — essentially holding a portfolio of $1/h^2$ butterflies.

If we write out the butterfly portfolio value, $V_{B,h}$,

$$V_{B,h} = \frac{C_{K-h,t,T} - 2C_{K,t,T} + C_{K+h,t,T}}{h^2} \tag{21.65}$$

$$= \frac{P_{K-h,t,T} - 2P_{K,t,T} + P_{K+h,t,T}}{h^2}, \tag{21.66}$$

we can see that this is the centered difference formula for the approximate second derivative of call $C_{K,t,T}$ or put $P_{K,t,T}$ prices with respect to strike K. Taking the limit of this as $h \downarrow 0$ yields the second derivative with respect to strike price K:

$$\frac{\partial^2 C_{K,t,T}}{\partial K^2} = \lim_{h \downarrow 0} \frac{C_{K-h,t,T} - 2C_{K,t,T} + C_{K+h,t,T}}{h^2} = \tag{21.67}$$

$$\frac{\partial^2 P_{K,t,T}}{\partial K^2} = \lim_{h \downarrow 0} \frac{P_{K-h,t,T} - 2P_{K,t,T} + P_{K+h,t,T}}{h^2} = \lim_{h \downarrow 0} V_{B,h}. \tag{21.68}$$

We can see what the butterfly, and the sequence of butterflies converging to the limit, look like in Figure 21.8.

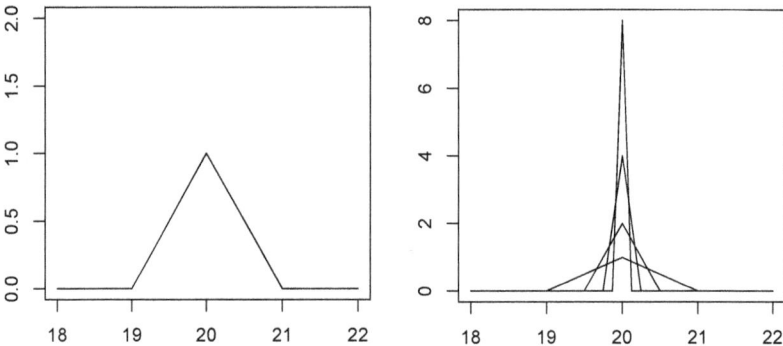

Figure 21.8: Butterfly portfolio payoffs for $h = 1$ (left) and for $h \in \{1, \frac{1}{2}, \frac{1}{4}, \frac{1}{8}\}$ (right). The butterflies on the right are converging to the Dirac delta function. The limit allows us to recover the risk-neutral density from option prices.

The limit of the butterfly portfolio payoffs $V_{B,h}$ is also the **Dirac delta function**, δ, shifted right to K. Because we are finding the price of $V_{B,h\downarrow 0}$, we are finding its expected present value. Thus this second derivative gives us the convolution:

$$V_{B,h} = e^{-r_f(T-t)} \int_0^\infty f(S_T)\delta(S_T - K)dS_T = e^{-r_f(T-t)}f(K), \tag{21.69}$$

where f is the risk-neutral density of S_T. Thus calculating $\frac{\partial^2 C_{K,t,T}}{\partial K^2}$ for all K from 0 to ∞ gives us f from 0 to ∞.

21.6.2 A Smooth Spectrum of Butterflies

The only problem is that we do not have option prices for all strike prices but only for a grid of strike prices. We could use this to find a histogram of the risk neutral density. However, Shimko (1993) shows an elegant way to do better: find the implied volatilities and interpolate or estimate a function for the volatility curve. This then allows computing option values for any strike price.

Often, people impose certain conditions on these forms: continuity, smoothness, or even thrice-differentiability — so that the extracted risk-neutral density is differentiable. However, none of these are required by the theory; and, in some industries where certain price levels may have economic meaning or even be limited by regulations, allowing for a discontinuous density may make sense.

Söderlind and Svensson (1997) has a very easy-to-understand walk-through of the process, including resolving some of the challenges typically encountered. Andersen and Wagener (2002) gives a fascinating tutorial on the process including extracting the risk-neutral densities of interest rates immediately before and after the 11 September 2001 terrorist attacks. For those looking to extract risk-neutral densities in R, the RND package implements many of these techniques.

21.6.3 So What about the Real World?

Finally, we might wonder: what about real-world densities? Risk-neutral densities are great for valuation but less helpful for policy makers worried about real-world probabilities. For example, Chan-Lau (2006) notes that regulators might set capital requirements for banks based on real-world probabilities of default; more pessimistic risk-neutral probabilities could lead to higher-than-optimal capital requirements.

Furthermore, while $\mathbb{Q}$-measure is useful for arbitrage pricing, those who believe in the possibility of mispricings care more about $\mathbb{P}$-measure. Meucci (2011) refers to this difference as splitting the quantitative finance world into $\mathbb{Q}$-quants and $\mathbb{P}$-quants.

For a sequence of risky cashflows X and a stochastic discount factor d_0:

$$E_P(d_0 X) = \frac{E_Q(X)}{1 + r_f}. \tag{21.70}$$

The conversion from $\mathbb{Q}$ to $\mathbb{P}$ is trickier than it seems though: for example, how do we disentangle $\mathbb{P}$ and d_0?

Few approaches attempt this conversion. The most theoretically-justified approach is in Ross (2015) and generalized (from an early working paper) by Carr and Yu (2012). This theory has a few key implications. First, interest rates must be random; otherwise, all pricing kernels would be the risk-free rate. Second, the underlier volatility process must be bounded and a function of the underlier state.

Unfortunately, some strong assumptions are needed. Least troubling is that we assume the absence of arbitrage; even for those who dispute this, we know our models should be internally consistent. More problematic is that we can only analyze underlying instruments which the "representative investor" would hold such as the "market" or long-term government debt — analyzed by Martin and Ross (2013). We cannot analyze instruments in zero net supply (*e.g.* futures) or those not held by all investors (*e.g.* Omani crude oil, Vancouver real estate, or ZAR).

Some doubt this approach is correct. Borovička, Hansen, and Scheinkman (2016) suggest the approach confuses long-run effects on risk-neutral pricing with investors' preferences and risk aversion. The difference is important even though investor preferences affect long-run equilibria. Their work suggests the pricing kernel recovered is misspecified and thus incorrect. Jackwerth and Menner (2017) find that the implied stochastic discount factor does not pass the Berkowitz (2001) test.

As an additional note: the Ross approach uses the Perron-Frobenius Theorem to invert implied prices of Arrow-Debreu securities to find physical probabilities. However, since there is inversion being done we can easily run into issues with Jensen's Inequality as we saw earlier in Chapter 13 since there is randomness in all of these prices. Even in small toy examples, this inversion is problematic.

While this debate has not yet been resolved, we can get less-disputable results for easier problems. Chan-Lau (2006) shows an easy approach for an analysis involving only two future bond states: default or not.

21.7   Valuing Real Options

In the prior chapter, we discussed option-like decisions we face in business which Myers (1977) called real options. He also noted that analyzing the present value of growth opportunities requires properly analyzing the optionality of corporate decisions. Mason and Merton (1985) gives an excellent tour of such an analysis.

In the prior chapter we did not have the tools to use option pricing techniques for valuing real options. However, we now have a few techniques at our disposal. We typically value real options in one of a handful of ways:

- *comparative* analysis;
- *Monte Carlo simulation* analysis;
- *binomial tree* analysis;
- *discounted cashflow* (DCF) analysis;
- *using option formulas* for similar options; or,
- *stochastic optimization.*

The comparative approach is much like valuing equities by comparables: you find similar decisions or opportunities which others have valued and then scale those valuations up or down. While this is lazy in a good way (reusing work) it is also lazy in a bad way (unlikely to be accurate). Furthermore, you will never pioneer a new type of business decision if you wait for others to analyze similar possibilities. While often used in casual discussions of valuation, comparative analysis is very limited.

The Monte Carlo simulation and binomial tree approaches value real options using approaches similar to what was done in Sections 21.2 and 21.3. These are valid approaches — and sometimes the only ones which can give an accurate answer;

however, they may be demanding of computational power or programmer time for complicated options.

DCF analysis is the most common valuation method. One need only estimate or predict future cashflows and then compute the net present value (NPV) of those cashflows, often using the weighted average cost of capital.[16] The DCF method can have trouble when the time horizon for the project/new business is uncertain. The biggest problem with a DCF analysis, however, is that it neglects volatility and strategic choice, *i.e.* that one would produce (or not) based on profit projections. For an approach to pricing option-like decisions, this is a serious flaw.

Stochastic optimization can be a useful and powerful method for analyzing real options; however, this is too advanced for a discussion here to do the subject merit. As mentioned before, those interested in such techniques should consult Birge and Louveaux (2011).

Finally, we could analyze real options using the Black-Scholes-Merton formula and related models. In a thoroughly confusing bit of semantics, doing this is called a **real options approach** to valuing real options. Thus "real options" and a "real options approach" are different; you might not use a real options approach to value real options.

Note that we have not even added in complications like the term structure of interest rates and how those might affect pricing kernels to different time horizons.

21.7.1   *Analyzing Real Options Using Option Formulas*

Geman (2005) points out that the real options approach requires certain regularity conditions be met:

1. the option must have starting and ending dates $t_0 < T \leq \infty$;
2. risk factors $S_1, S_2, \ldots$ must be clearly identified;
3. risk factors $S_1, S_2, \ldots$ must be continuously traded, for hedging and arbitrage valuation;
4. we need stochastic process models for $S_1, S_2, \ldots$;
5. we must know the exact option form (*e.g.* exercise type, payoff); and,
6. the option cannot violate market completeness or measurability.

Obviously, we rarely have all of these assumptions hold. However, she notes that assumptions 3 and 4 are the most critical. While the fifth condition rarely holds, we can try various model forms and guess which is closest or use a weighted average.

21.7.2   *Example: Value of a Gold Mine Lease*

To see how we can value real options, we will value leasing a gold mine for ten years. With a gold mine, we need to make extraction decisions and then sell the mined

---

[16]If we were analyzing the industry or competitors, we might use the CAPM or a factor model for our pricing kernel.

gold. When we create this example, we have to be very careful about when decisions are made and when we get paid for extraction.

Assumptions

In this case, we make the extraction decision at the start of a period based on prices which we lock in by hedging. We then invest firm capital (incurring one period of cost-of-capital charges) and collect the revenue at the end of the period. Since we make decisions at the start of each period, the first-period decision (and value) will be the same for any method; however, subsequent period valuations will differ.

As gold prices rise, extraction comes from increasingly expensive mines. Assume the mine we lease can produce 10,000 oz per year and extraction costs $1000/oz.[17] Also assume cash gold is $1300/oz and futures out to one year are $1300/oz before declining linearly to $1200/oz at two years out and beyond. Gold volatility is 30%, our weighted average cost of capital is 8%, and the risk-free rate r_f is 3%. Finally, for simplicity assume the convenience yield is equal to storage costs.

We also need to consider what process gold prices follow. We could assume they follow geometric Brownian motion. However, this choice is questionable for many commodities since competition pushes prices toward mean extraction costs: when prices rise above mean extraction costs, more firms extract for a profit. This drives prices down until enough firms cease profitable extraction. Thus we could also assume gold prices follow an autoregressive (aka mean-reverting or Ornstein-Uhlenbeck) process. The only trick: as prices rise, the average extraction costs rise. We will assume the short-term equilibrium is the futures price.

Extraction Process

The extraction process has a few steps governing how valuation is done. Therefore, we walk-through the extraction decisions and some ideas about their valuation.

At time $t = 0$ we see futures for delivery in a year at $1300/oz versus extraction costs of $1000/oz. We lock that price in and run the mine incurring the weighted average cost of capital which is used to discount the $300/oz profit. We assume no uncertainty in the amount of gold produced.[18] This value is the same for all methods.

The risk-neutral present-valued expected profit at time $t = 1$ is given by the one-year call option struck at $1000/oz with underlier at $1300/oz. That would lead us to lock in prices and incur extraction costs to realize the expected profit at $t = 2$, so we discount the option value back one period for the extraction over $t \in [1, 2)$ using the weighted average cost of capital. The DCF valuation assumes we

---

[17]Typical extraction costs are $600–$700/oz with more expensive mines in Asia and Africa.
[18]This is not accurate, but it would complicate this example.

will be able to lock in the $200/oz profit and incurs two periods of discounting at the weighted average cost of capital because we have committed to extraction.[19]

The decision at $t = 2$ and afterward is more complicated. We have a futures curve that suggests the underlier will be at $1200/oz. That would be our equilibrium price. So we price the decision with a one-year option over $t \in [1, 2)$ with the underlier assumed to be at $1200/oz and the strike again at $1000/oz. Is this realistic? We could enter into a forward contract on this option, so... yes. However, you can start to see how unclear the funding and valuation structures can be. We then run the mine, incur one period of capital costs, but we have a forward on the option — so we need to discount that at the risk-free rate. (We need not commit capital for the forward.) For the DCF valuation, we assume we will run the mine for a $200/oz profit. We commit to that and incur three periods of WACC discounting.

The decision at $t = 3$ is still based off of the futures curve. Since curves get illiquid as we go out farther, we will price this as an option with the underlier at $1200 and the strike at $1000. If we assume a geometric Brownian motion price process, this would be a two-year option over $t \in [1, 3)$; if we assume an Ornstein-Uhlenbeck price process, a one-year option will yield a more accurate price than the two-year option. We use either of these to get the risk-neutral expected profit present-valued to time $t = 1$. Then we lock in prices, run the mine, and incur a period of capital costs. Again, we have a forward that requires a period of risk-free discounting for $t = 1$ to $t = 0$. The periods from here on are similar except with more risk-free discounting if we use the one-year-option approximation.

DCF Gold Mine Lease Valuation

If we price the lease with a DCF approach and make extraction decisions annually or quarterly, we get that the mine lease is worth:

$$V_{DCF,ann} = \frac{\$1300 - \$1000}{1.08} + \sum_{t=2}^{10} \frac{\$1200 - \$1000}{1.08^t} = \$14.3 \text{ mn or,} \qquad (21.71)$$

$$V_{DCF,qtr} = \sum_{t=1}^{4} \frac{\$1300 - \$1000}{1.08^{t/4}} + \sum_{t=5}^{8} \frac{\$1300 - 25(i - 4) - \$1000}{1.08^{t/4}}$$

$$+ \sum_{t=9}^{40} \frac{\$1200 - \$1000}{1.08^{t/4}} = \$15.1 \text{ mn.} \qquad (21.72)$$

Simulated Gold Mine Lease Valuation

We can easily simulate the gold price process for either a geometric Brownian motion or an Ornstein-Uhlenbeck process. The code to do this is straightforward:

---

[19]Remember that the options are not discounted at the WACC because they are priced by arbitrage with the underlier and a risk-free bond.

```
oz.per.year <- 10000
rf <- 0.03  # 3% interest rates
wacc <- 0.08  # 8% weighted average cost of capital
num.sims <- 100000 # 100,000 simulations
s0 <- 1300  # gold price at t=0
K <- 1000  # cost of extraction
sigma <- 0.3  # volatility of gold log-returns
lambda <- 1  # rate of mean reversion; 1 => half-life = ln(2) = 0.69 years

## Annual extraction decisions at start of each year (t=0,...,9)
T.list <- 1:9  # 1--9 year options; years 2:8 are 1 year fwd
s.bar.list <- c(1300, rep(1200, 8))  # 1300/oz, then 1200/oz

# gold price follows geometric Brownian motion
sum.val <- (s0-K)/(1+wacc)  # time t=0 decision
for (i in 1:9) {
    T <- T.list[i]
    z <- rnorm(num.sims) # simulated Z_T values
    s.sim <- s0*exp((rf-sigma^2/2)*T+sigma*sqrt(T)*z)
    if (T>1) s.sim <- s.sim*s.bar.list[i]/s0
    opt.terminal.val.sim <- pmax(s.sim - K, 0)
    opt.value <- mean(opt.terminal.val.sim)*exp(-rf*T)
    sum.val <- sum.val + opt.value/(1+wacc)
}
print(sum.val*oz.per.year)

## gold price follows Ornstein-Uhlenbeck mean reversion
sum.val <- (s0-K)/(1+wacc)
for (i in 1:9) {
    T <- T.list[i]
    s.bar <- s.bar.list[i]
    s.meanrevert.sim <- s.bar + exp(-lambda*T)*(s0-s.bar) + sigma*s0*
        sqrt((1-exp(-2*lambda*T))/(2*lambda))*z
    opt.terminal.val.meanrevert.sim <- pmax(s.meanrevert.sim - K, 0)
    opt.meanrevert.value <- mean(opt.terminal.val.meanrevert.sim)*
        exp(-rf*T)
    sum.val <- sum.val + opt.meanrevert.value/(1+wacc)
}
print(sum.val*oz.per.year)

## Quarterly extract decisions at start of each quarter
T.list <- (1:39)/4 # 1--39 quarter options
s.bar.list <- c(rep(1300, 4), 1275, 1250, 1225, rep(1200, 32))

# gold price follows geometric Brownian motion
sum.val <- (s0-K)/(1+wacc)^0.25
for (i in 1:39) {
    T <- T.list[i]
    z <- rnorm(num.sims) # simulated Z_T values
    s.sim <- s0*exp(sigma*sqrt(T)*z)
    opt.terminal.val.sim <- pmax(s.sim - K, 0)
    opt.value <- mean(opt.terminal.val.sim)*exp(-rf*T)
    sum.val <- sum.val + opt.value/(1+wacc)^0.25
}
print(sum.val*oz.per.year/4)

# gold price follows Ornstein-Uhlenbeck mean reversion
sum.val <- (s0-K)/(1+wacc)^0.25
for (i in 1:39) {
    T <- T.list[i]
    s.bar <- s.bar.list[i]
    s.meanrevert.sim <- s.bar + exp(-lambda*T)*(s0-s.bar) + sigma*s0*
        sqrt((1-exp(-2*lambda*T))/(2*lambda))*z
    opt.terminal.val.meanrevert.sim <- pmax(s.meanrevert.sim - K, 0)
```

```
        opt.meanrevert.value <- mean(opt.terminal.val.meanrevert.sim)*exp(-rf*T)
        sum.val <- sum.val + opt.meanrevert.value/(1+wacc)^0.25
}
print(sum.val*oz.per.year/4)
```

If we run these simulations, we get some crazy prices for the geometric Brownian motion processes: \$41.7 mn for annual extraction decisions and \$60.5 mn for quarterly extraction decisions. The Ornstein-Uhlenbeck processes yield more reasonable and believable valuations: \$20.8 mn for annual extraction decisions and \$21.9 mn for quarterly extraction decisions.

Real Options Approach to Gold Mine Lease Valuation

If we price the mine lease with options, we again consider both the geometric Brownian motion-implied price and the approximation for a mean-reverting process. The code to do this is also easy:

```
bs.call <- function(S,K,rf,T,sigma) {
    d1 <- (log(S/K)+(rf+sigma^2/2)*T)/(sigma*sqrt(T))
    S*pnorm(d1)-K*exp(-rf*T)*pnorm(d1-sigma*sqrt(T))
}

oz.per.year <- 10000
rf <- 0.03  # 3% interest rates
wacc <- 0.08  # 8% weighted average cost of capital
s0 <- 1300
s0.lt <- 1200
K <- 1000
sigma <- 0.3

## annual real options approach, no mean reversion
oz.per.year*((s0-K)/(1+wacc) + bs.call(s0,K,rf,1,sigma)/(1+wacc) +
            sum(bs.call(s0.lt,K,rf,1:8,sigma)/(1+wacc)*exp(-rf)))

## annual real options, assuming mean reversion (approximation)
oz.per.year*((s0-K)/(1+wacc) + bs.call(s0,K,rf,1,sigma)/(1+wacc) +
            sum(bs.call(1200,1000,0.03,1,0.3)/(1+wacc)*exp(-rf*(1:8))))

## quarterly real options, no mean reversion
oz.per.year/4*((s0-K)/(1+wacc)^0.25
    + sum(bs.call(1300,1000,0.03,(1:4)/4,0.3)/(1+wacc)^0.25)
    + sum(bs.call(1300-25*(1:3),1000,0.03,0.25,0.3)/(1+wacc)^0.25*exp(-rf*(5:7)/4))
    + sum(bs.call(1200,1000,0.03,(1:32)/4,0.3)/(1+wacc)^0.25*exp(-rf*(8:39)/4)))

## quarterly real options, assuming mean reversion (approximation)
oz.per.year/4*((s0-K)/(1+wacc)^0.25
    + sum(bs.call(1300,1000,0.03,0.25,0.3)/(1+wacc)^0.25*exp(-rf*(0:3)/4))
    + sum(bs.call(1300-25*(1:4),1000,0.03,0.25,0.3)/(1+wacc)^0.25*exp(-rf*(4:7)/4))
    + sum(bs.call(1200,1000,0.03,0.25,0.3)/(1+wacc)^0.25*exp(-rf*(8:39)/4)))
```

For the real option approaches discussed, we (again) get crazy prices for the standard options formulas — although less so since some of the options are shorter-term or start from two years out. For the standard geometric Brownian motion real options approach, we get a value of \$37.7 mn for annual extraction decisions and \$33.3 mn for quarterly extraction decisions. The mean-reverting approximation real options approach again yields more reasonable and believable valuations: \$23.9 mn for annual extraction decisions and \$20.3 mn for quarterly extraction decisions.

Summary

Comparing these, we can get a better impression of how much we believe each and the uncertainty of valuation. Table 21.1 shows all of the different valuation results.

Methodology	Annual	Quarterly
DCF	$14.3	$15.1
Simulated, GBM	$41.7	$60.5
Simulated, OU	$20.8	$21.9
Real Options, GBM	$37.7	$33.3
Real Options, OU Approx.	$23.9	$20.3

Table 21.1: Comparison of valuations in millions from various methodologies for valuing a ten-year gold mine lease. The simulated Ornstein-Uhlenbeck and real options approach Ornstein-Uhlenbeck approximation results are the closer to what we believe given prior assumptions than the geometric Brownian motion and DCF approaches.

Given that the simulated Ornstein-Uhlenbeck and the real options approach with the Ornstein-Uhlenbeck approximation results are the closest to what we believe for the gold price process, these results are the most believable. Given that we would likely make quarterly extraction decisions instead of annually, this suggests the mine lease is worth about $22 mn. Note that this is almost 50% greater than the DCF valuation.

If we had production constraints or other complicated conditions on the lease, we would need to use simulation, a tree, or stochastic optimization. Also note that if gold were below $1000/oz at any point on the futures curve, the DCF valuation would be even more flawed.

21.8   Summary

For those interested in learning more about options, I highly recommend McDonald (2010) and Luenberger (2013). For information on commodity options, Geman (2005) is superb. Also, Derman and Miller (2016) is a good text covering volatility surfaces and recent modeling advances. To dig into the probability theory behind pricing contingent claims, Etheridge (2002) and Steele (2001) are delightful introductions.

For those wanting to be a full-blown $\mathbb{Q}$-quant, Wichura (2006) (if you can find a copy) is *by far* the best text on measure theory available.[20] If that is not available, Øksendahl (2013), Billingsley (1996) (the 3rd, not later editions), and Karatzas and Shreve (1991) are OK substitutes.

---

[20]Wichura's suggestions to Billingsley eliminated an entire chapter of unneeded development in the second edition of Billingsley (1996).

21.9   Quiz

Try to answer these questions in ten minutes. For answers with equations, just write the equations; do not evaluate them.

1. (2 points) Consider the following stock (left) and option (right) trees:

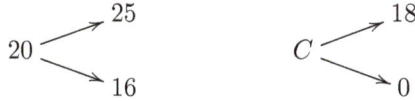

$$20 \nearrow 25 \searrow 16 \qquad C \nearrow 18 \searrow 0$$

If these trees are for one year's time; and, if PV($16, $25) = ($15.69, $24.51), what is the value of the option C?

2. Suppose we plotted volatilities implied by options versus the strike prices of those options.

   a) What would this plot look like?
   b) What does this mean — or is it random model noise?

3. (2 points) Suppose you are given a number of prices for puts and calls expiring in one year. How would you determine the risk-neutral density? If you know of a way to reduce the noise of estimation, mention how to do that.

4. Assume you want to price a call on an underlier which is at S_0 with volatility σ, the call is struck at K and matures in T years, and the risk-free rate is r_f.

   a) What is the Black-Scholes-Merton formula for the value of a call option in terms of d_1 and d_2?
   b) What are d_1 and d_2?
   c) What is the meaning of the first term in the formula?
   d) What is the meaning of the second term in the formula?

21.10   Exercises

Instructions

There is no R code supplied this time. You should know what to do based on code in the prior chapters.

1. For a vanilla European call option on one share of stock expiring at time T, show that $0 < \Delta < 1$ for all times $t < T$ using:

   a) The tree method
   b) The Black-Scholes-Merton formula

2. You observe the following volatility curve on the CBOE website for IBM options:

Percent ATMF	50	60	70	80	90	100	110	120	130
Implied σ %	80	62	44	31	26	22	21	27	39

Can you infer a reasonable shape for the curve?

3. Using the vol curve you inferred in the prior question, can you infer the risk-neutral density for IBM's stock price?

4. (Convertible Bond Pricing: Preparation) We can also price a convertible bond on IBM. A convertible bond can be thought of as a bond plus a call option. We will price a zero-coupon convertible bond maturing in two years as of now (the pricing date).

To do this we will need five quantities:

- the stock price on the pricing date S_0;
- the interest rate on the pricing date r_0;
- the conversion (option strike) price K (set so that the option component is 10% OOM, *i.e.* $K = 1.1 \cdot S_0$);
- the conversion ratio n, *i.e.* how many shares we receive: $n = \$1000/K$ shares;[21] and,
- the volatility estimated as of the pricing date σ.

To get those, we will need to answer the following:

a) Which UST should you use to determine the interest rate for pricing this bond?

b) What is the interest rate on the pricing date, r_0?

c) Price the zero coupon bond component. Note that while the bond face is $1000, we quote the price as a percentage: "100" means 100% of $1000. You should get a price less than 100.

d) What is the stock price of IBM on the pricing date, S_0?

e) What are the conversion price and ratio, K and n, for the convertible bond?

f) Estimate the historical volatility of IBM over the prior three years.

g) Estimate the historical volatility of the SPX over the prior three years.

h) Estimate the beta of IBM versus the SPX using data from the prior three years.

i) Using the CAPM estimation data, and the fact that $\sigma^2 = \beta^2 \sigma_{SPX}^2 + \sigma_\epsilon^2$, compute σ_ϵ.

j) What is the VIX on the pricing date? Make sure to convert it to the appropriate scale — so a 40% value is 0.40, not 40.

---

[21] The option gives us the right to receive shares of stock at the conversion price instead of the bond face. Thus the conversion ratio is just the face divided by the conversion price.

5. (Convertible Bond Pricing: Implementation) We now have enough data to price the option embedded in the convertible bond. Remember that we will compute the price for an options on one share and then multiply that to find out how much it adds to the option value.

   a) Price the call option on one share with the historical volatility for IBM using the Black-Scholes-Merton formula. Your code should show and compute the full formula; do not use a package or function that computes the option price for you. You will need the `pnorm()` function.

   b) We can instead use a forward-looking (*i.e.* best guess of the future) volatility. Since the VIX is forward-looking, estimate your forward-looking volatility. You may use the variance formula $\sigma_{fwd}^2 = \beta^2 VIX^2 + \sigma_\epsilon^2$.

   c) Price the call option on one share using the forward-looking volatility for your stock using the Black-Scholes-Merton formula. Your code should show and compute the full formula; do not use a package or function that computes the option price for you. You will need the `pnorm()` function.

   d) Now we will put these together. Your option prices C (for historical and beta-VIX volatilities) are for 1 share, so the conversion value for n shares is $C \cdot n$. However, the \$1000 face bond trades on a percentage basis, so we need to divide by 10 to get the option value on the same scale. Thus the option adds $Cn/10$ to the zero coupon bond value.

   Report the convertible bond value for historical and beta-VIX forward-looking volatility.

References

Aït-Sahalia, Yacine and Robert Kimmel. "Maximum Likelihood Estimation of Stochastic Volatility Models". *Journal of Financial Economics* 83.2 (2007), pp. 413–452. DOI: 10.1016/j.jfineco.2005.10.006.

Anders, George. "Options Trading at Expiration Might Influence Prices of Underlying Stocks, Studies Indicate". *Wall Street Journal* (Apr. 15, 1982), p. 55.

Andersen, Allan Bødskov and Tom Wagener. *Extracting Risk Neutral Probability Densities by Fitting Implied Volatility Smiles: Some Methodological Points and an Application to the 3M Euribor Futures Option Prices.* Working Paper 198. European Central Bank, 2002.

Avellaneda, Marco and Michael D. Lipkin. "A Market-Induced Mechanism for Stock Pinning". *Quantitative Finance* 3.6 (2003), pp. 417–425. DOI: 10.1088/1469-7688/3/6/301.

Bachelier, Louis Jean-Baptiste Alphonse. "Théorie de la Spéculation". *Annales Scientifiques de l'École Normale Supérieure* 3.17 (1900).

Berkowitz, Jeremy. "Testing Density Forecasts, With Applications to Risk Management". *Journal of Business and Economic Statistics* 19.4 (2001), pp. 465–474. DOI: 10.1198/07350010152596718.

Bernstein, Peter L. *Against the Gods: The Remarkable Story of Risk.* New York: John Wiley & Sons, 1996.

Billingsley, Patrick. *Probability and Measure.* 3rd ed. New York: Wiley, 1996.

Birge, John R. and François Louveaux. *Introduction to Stochastic Programming.* 2nd ed. New York: Springer-Verlag, 2011.

Black, Fischer. "Fact and Fantasy in the Use of Options". *Financial Analyst's Journal* 31.4 (1975), pp. 36–41+61–72. DOI: 10.2469/faj.v31.n4.36.

— "The Pricing of Commodity Contracts". *Journal of Financial Economics* 3.1–2 (1976), pp. 167–179. DOI: 10.1016/0304-405X(76)90024-6.

Black, Fischer and Myron Scholes. "The Pricing of Options and Corporate Liabilities". *Journal of Political Economy* 81.3 (1973), pp. 637–654. DOI: 10.1086/260062.

Bollerslev, Tim. "Generalized Autoregressive Conditional Heteroskedasticity". *Journal of Econometrics* 31.3 (1986), pp. 307–327. DOI: 10.1016/0304-4076(86)90063-1.

Bondarenko, Oleg. "Why Are Put Options So Expensive?" *Quarterly Journal of Finance* 4.3 (2014), pp. 1–50. DOI: 10.1142/S2010139214500153.

Boness, A. James. "Elements of a Theory of Stock-Option Value". *Journal of Political Economy* 72.2 (1964), pp. 163–175. DOI: 10.1086/258885.

Borovička, Jaroslav, Lars Peter Hansen, and José A. Scheinkman. "Misspecified Recovery". *Journal of Finance* 71.6 (2016), pp. 2493–2544. DOI: 10.1111/jofi.12404.

Boyle, Phelim P. "Options: A Monte Carlo approach". *Journal of Financial Economics* 4.3 (1977), pp. 323–338. DOI: 10.1016/0304-405X(77)90005-8.

Breeden, Douglas T. and Robert H. Litzenberger. "Prices of State-Contingent Claims Implicit in Option Prices". *Journal of Business* 51.4 (1978), pp. 621–651. DOI: 10.1086/296025.

Bronzin, Vincenz. *Theorie der Prämiengeschäfte.* Leipzig/Vienna: Franz Deuticke, 1908.

Carr, Peter and Dilip Madan. "Towards a Theory of Volatility Trading". In: *Volatility.* Ed. by Robert A. Jarrow. London: Risk Publications, 1998, pp. 417–427.

Carr, Peter and Jiming Yu. "Risk, Return, and Ross Recovery". *Journal of Derivatives* 20.1 (2012), pp. 38–59. DOI: 10.3905/jod.2012.20.1.038.

Chan-Lau, Jorge A. *Market-Based Estimation of Default Probabilities and Its Application to Financial Market Surveillance.* Working Paper 06/104. International Monetary Fund, 2006. URL: https://www.imf.org/external/pubs/ft/wp/2006/wp06104.pdf.

Cox, John C., Stephen A. Ross, and Mark Rubinstein. "Option Pricing: A Simplified Approach". *Journal of Financial Economics* 7.3 (1979), pp. 229–263. DOI: 10.1016/0304-405X(79)90015-1.

Demeterfi, Kresimir et al. *More Than You Ever Wanted To Know About Volatility Swaps.* Quantitative Strategies Research Notes. Goldman Sachs, Mar. 1999, pp. 1–52. URL: http://www.emanuelderman.com/media/gs-volatility_swaps.pdf.

Derman, Emanuel and Michael B. Miller. *The Volatility Smile*. New York: Wiley, 2016.

Devroye, Luc. *Non-uniform Random Variate Generation*. New York: Springer-Verlag, 1986. URL: http://luc.devroye.org/rnbookindex.html.

Engle, Robert F. "Autoregressive Conditional Heteroscedasticity with Estimates of Variance of United Kingdom Inflation". *Econometrica* 50.4 (1982), pp. 987–1008. DOI: 10.2307/1912773.

Eraker, Bjørn, Michael Johannes, and Nicholas Polson. "The Impact of Jumps in Volatility and Returns". *Journal of Finance* 58.3 (2003), pp. 1269–1300. DOI: 10.1111/1540-6261.00566.

Etheridge, Alison. *A Course in Financial Calculus*. Cambridge (UK): Cambridge University Press, 2002.

Föllmer, Hans and Martin Schweizer. "Hedging of Contingent Claims under Incomplete Information". In: *Applied Stochastic Analysis*. Ed. by M. H. A. Davis and R. J. Elliott. Vol. 5. Stochastics Monographs. London/New York: Gordon and Breach, 1991, pp. 389–414.

Garman, Mark B. and Steven W. Kohlhagen. "Foreign Currency Option Values". *Journal of International Money and Finance* 2.3 (1983), pp. 231–237. DOI: 10.1016/S0261-5606(83)80001-1.

Geman, Hélyette. *Commodities and Commodity Derivatives: Modeling and Pricing for Agriculturals, Metals and Energy*. New York: Wiley, 2005.

Hafner, Wolfgang and Heinz Zimmermann, eds. *Vinzenz Bronzin's Option Pricing Models: Exposition and Appraisal*. Berlin: Springer-Verlag, 2009. DOI: 10.1007/978-3-540-85711-2.

Hamidieh, Kam. *RND: Risk Neutral Density Extraction Package*. R package version 1.2. 2017. URL: https://CRAN.R-project.org/package=RND.

Hasanhodzic, Jasmina and Andrew W. Lo. *Black's Leverage Effect is Not Due to Leverage*. Working Paper. Babson College, 2013. URL: http://jasminah.com/Papers/leverage-web.pdf.

Heston, Steven L. "A Closed-Form Solution for Options with Stochastic Volatility with Applications to Bond and Currency Options". *Review of Financial Studies* 6.2 (1993), pp. 327–343. DOI: 10.1093/rfs/6.2.327.

Hofstadter, Douglas R. *Gödel, Escher, Bach: An Eternal Golden Braid*. New York: Basic Books, 1979.

Iacus, Stefano Maria. *sde: Simulation and Inference for Stochastic Differential Equations*. R package version 2.0.15. 2016. URL: https://CRAN.R-project.org/package=sde.

Jackwerth, Jens Carsten and Marco Menner. *Does the Ross Recovery Theorem Work Empirically?* Working Paper 2960733. SSRN, 2017. DOI: 10.2139/ssrn.2960733.

Jarrow, Robert and Andrew Rudd. *Option Pricing*. Homewood, IL: Dow Jones-Irwin, 1983.

Jarrow, Robert A. and Eric R. Rosenfeld. "Jump Risks and the Intertemporal

Capital Asset Pricing Model". *Journal of Business* 57.3 (1984), pp. 337–351. DOI: 10.1086/296267.

Karatzas, Ioannis and Steven E. Shreve. *Brownian Motion and Stochastic Calculus.* 2nd ed. New York: Springer-Verlag, 1991.

Leisen, Dietmar P. J. and Matthias Reimer. "Binomial Models for Option Valuation – Examining and Improving Convergence". *Applied Mathematical Finance* 3.4 (1996), pp. 319–346. DOI: 10.1080/13504869600000015.

Luenberger, David G. *Investment Science.* 2nd ed. Oxford: Oxford University Press, 2013.

Macbeth, James D. and Larry J. Merville. "An Empirical Examination of the Black-Scholes Call Option Pricing Model". *Journal of Finance* 34.5 (1979), pp. 1173–1186. DOI: 10.1111/j.1540-6261.1979.tb00063.x.

Martin, Ian and Steve Ross. *The Long Bond.* Working Paper. London School of Economics, 2013.

Mason, Scott P. and Robert C. Merton. "The Role of Contingent Claims Analysis in Corporate Finance". In: *Recent Advances in Corporate Finance.* Ed. by Edward I. Altman and Marti G. Subrahmanyam. Homewood, IL: Irwin, 1985, pp. 7–54.

McDonald, Hamish. "Bainimarama Shows He's the Full Bottle, But Challenges Await". *The Sydney Morning Herald* (Dec. 4, 2010). URL: http://www.smh.com.au/world/bainimarama-shows-hes-the-full-bottle-but-challenges-await-20101203-18jvg.html.

Merton, Robert C. "Theory of Rational Option Pricing". *The Bell Journal of Economics and Management Science* 4.1 (1973), pp. 141–183. DOI: 10.2307/3003143.

— "Option Pricing When Underlying Stock Returns Are Discontinuous". *Journal of Financial Economics* 3.1–2 (1976), pp. 125–144. DOI: 10.1016/0304-405X(76)90022-2.

Meucci, Attilio. ""P" versus "Q": Differences and Commonalities between the Two Areas of Quantitative Finance". *GARP Risk Professional* (Feb. 2011), pp. 47–50.

Myers, Stewart C. "Determinants of Corporate Borrowing". *Journal of Financial Economics* 5.2 (1977), pp. 147–175. DOI: 10.1016/0304-405X(77)90015-0.

Naik, Vasanttilak. "Option Valuation and Hedging Strategies with Jumps in the Volatility of Asset Returns". *Journal of Finance* 48.5 (1993), pp. 1969–1984. DOI: 10.2307/2329076.

Naik, Vasanttilak and Moon Lee. "General Equilibrium Pricing of Options on the Market Portfolio with Discontinuous Returns". *Review of Financial Studies* 3.4 (1990), pp. 493–521. DOI: 10.1093/rfs/3.4.493.

Natenberg, Sheldon. *Option Volatility and Pricing Strategies: Advanced Trading Techniques for Professionals.* Chicago: Probus, 1988.

Ni, Sophie Xiaoyan, Neil D. Pearson, and Allen M. Poteshman. "Stock Price Clustering on Option Expiration Dates". *Journal of Financial Economics* 78.1 (2005), pp. 49–87. DOI: 10.1016/j.jfineco.2004.08.005.

Øksendahl, Bernt. *Stochastic Differential Equations: An Introduction with Applications.* 6th ed. Springer-Verlag, 2013.

Patel, Sheila H. and Glenn Koh. "Anatomy of an Expiration". In: *Global Equity and Derivatives Markets*. New York: Morgan Stanley, Jan. 2002, pp. 1–7.

Rosenberg, Barr. *The Behavior of Random Variables with Nonstationary Variance and the Distribution of Security Prices*. Research Program in Finance Working Papers 11. University of California at Berkeley, 1972. URL: http://www.haas.berkeley.edu/groups/finance/WP/rpf011.pdf.

Ross, Steve. "The Recovery Theorem". *Journal of Finance* 70.2 (2015), pp. 615–648. DOI: 10.1111/jofi.12092.

Schachermayer, Walter and Josef Teichmann. "How Close Are the Option Pricing Formulas of Bachelier and Black-Merton-Scholes?" *Mathematical Finance* 18.1 (2007), pp. 155–170. DOI: 10.1111/j.1467-9965.2007.00326.x.

Shimko, David. "Bounds of Probability". *RISK* 6.4 (1993), pp. 33–37.

Siegmund, D. "Importance Sampling in the Monte Carlo Study of Sequential Tests". *Annals of Statistics* 4.4 (1976), pp. 673–684. DOI: 10.1214/aos/1176343541.

Söderlind, Paul and Lars Svensson. "New Techniques to Extract Market Expectations from Financial Instruments". *Journal of Monetary Economics* 40.2 (1997), pp. 383–429. DOI: 10.1016/S0304-3932(97)00047-0.

Sprenkle, Case. "Warrant Prices as Indicators of Expectations and Preferences". *Yale Economics Essays* 1 (1961), pp. 178–231.

Steele, J. Michael. *Stochastic Calculus and Financial Applications*. New York: Springer-Verlag, 2001.

Sullivan, Edward J. and Timothy M. Weithers. "Louis Bachelier: The Father of Modern Option Pricing Theory". *The Journal of Economic Education* 22.2 (1991), pp. 165–171. DOI: 10.2307/1182421.

Tian, Yisong. "A Modified Lattice Approach to Option Pricing". *Journal of Futures Markets* 13.5 (1993), pp. 563–577. DOI: 10.1002/fut.3990130509.

Tian, Yisong "Sam". "A Flexible Binomial Option Pricing Model". *Journal of Futures Markets* 19.7 (1999), pp. 817–843. DOI: 10.1002/(SICI)1096-9934(199910)19:7<817::AID-FUT5>3.0.CO;2-D.

Wichura, Michael J. *Lecture Notes on Measure Theory*. Chicago: unpublished manuscript, 2006.

Zimmermann, Heinz and Wolfgang Hafner. "Amazing Discovery: Vincenz Bronzin's Option Pricing Models". *Journal of Banking and Finance* 31.2 (2007), pp. 531–546. DOI: 10.1016/j.jbankfin.2006.07.003.

Chapter 22

Credit

One of the most powerful forces in financial markets is credit. Inflation, the price of money as a function of time (interest rates and the yield curve), and volatility are all key variables that affect the macroeconomy. Credit is another such variable. In fact, some economists argue convincingly that credit is the strongest variable affecting markets. Kindelberger and Aliber (2005) shows how illiquidity and credit concerns lead to financial crises.

Up to now we discussed credit obliquely: we referred to high yields on bonds and mentioned credit spreads. However, credit is central to many issues including proper modeling of a firm and equity. In this chapter we will discuss credit measures and issues, introduce credit derivatives, develop a new model of the firm which departs from earlier assumptions, and explore credit models. We will look at four types of credit models: those modeling firm structure, those based on accounting measures, models of default intensities, and market-based models.

The credit measures and issues we cover are relevant to any model; hence the reason for covering them first. The new model of a firm looks at its **capital structure**: the liabilities and equity and the preference ordering of who is repaid in default. This differs from the typical Modigliani and Miller (1958,1963) theorem of the irrelevance of capital structure — because we assume default can impose costs. It also yields a criticism of the typical "drift and diffusion" model for a firm's equity which helps explain some of the non-normality we see in log-returns.

Credit models have typically been characterized as either structural (modeling the firm) or reduced-form (statistically-based). We break from this for a few reasons. Accounting-based models are reduced-form models, but they try to assess aspects of the firm's structure. Default intensity models are reduced-form models which look more at risk factors, similar to factor models we saw earlier. Finally, models which use data on credit default swaps are almost model-free and completely ignore risk factors and firm structure. Thus the order we explore these models spans the spectrum, from structural to extremely agnostic of firm structure.

22.1 The Basics of Credit

The central idea of **credit** is the ability of an entity to borrow money (or something of value) from a lender. **Credit risk** is the risk of default — the lender not receiving all contractually promised cashflows. Cruces and Trebesch (2013) show that default hurts a borrower's reputation and reduces their ability to access credit later even though it sometimes seems like the punishment is weak.[1]

Credit has both a relative and an absolute aspect. In relative terms, some entities can borrow more or pay a lower cost for their borrowing than other entities; they have **better credit**. In absolute terms, sometimes credit is **loose** and everyone finds it easier and cheaper to borrow; and, sometimes credit is **tight** and everyone finds it harder and more costly to borrow.

Absolute credit conditions change with monetary policy. As mentioned in Section 5.10.3, when a central bank lowers interest rates, they loosen credit and make borrowing easier. The idea is that by increasing the supply of money, it will (hopefully) flow to the right places in the economy due to demand. However, absolute credit conditions also change with the market perception of crisis risk.

22.1.1 The Procyclical Nature of Credit

The problem is that credit rationing by the market is **procyclical**: it accentuates business cycles. When the economy does well, firms are more profitable and so lending to them is (relatively) low-risk. If a small "hiccup" arises — say a firm runs into some trouble or loans become expensive, competition and the prospect of profits encourages lenders to step in and loosen credit to help address this temporary problem. Thus as we often find from economic models, markets have a **self-healing** equilibrium.

However, if lenders think the economy is headed for trouble, a small "hiccup" is not seen as an opportunity but as a warning which leads lenders to withdraw loan offers and raise borrowing prices. While central banks may lower interest rates, market fears may be more powerful. Tighter credit makes it harder for firms to survive which leads to further tightening of credit and economic contraction. If lenders refuse to lend, we end up in a **credit crunch**. Thus markets also have a **self-harming** equilibrium.

These two equilibria — one of good times, loose credit, and growth versus one of bad times, tight credit, and contraction — can also be found in financial market liquidity effects. This duality of a self-healing and self-harming market is the central thesis of Brunnermeier and Pedersen (2009).

---

[1]They show that sovereign bond defaults with lower recovery rates predict longer exclusion times from capital markets and higher funding costs on returning to those markets. Cruces and Trebesch also published their default and recovery data.

22.2   Measures of Credit

There are a number of ways we measure and compare creditworthiness. While yields are an easy measure, they are a bit mechanical. Thus we also have ratings which take into account the circumstances of the firm and the economy. Finally, we might wonder how to map these to probabilities.

22.2.1   Yields as Credit Measures

In Section 21.4.2, we revisited a risky bond with an annual **probability of default** (PD) of 0.1 and a **loss given default** (LGD), the fraction of face value lost in default, of 0.6. (We sometimes discuss the **recovery rate** which is just $1 - LGD$.) When we suspect the cashflows are not guaranteed, we may consider the **expected yield** which accounts for expected (not promised) cashflows. However, this requires assuming a PD and LGD. Furthermore, lenders are not likely to be risk-neutral: the risk of default will lead them to discount uncertain cashflows more as a risk penalty. Since the measure the entire market can agree upon is the (promised) yield to maturity, we can decompose the promised yield into these two components:

$$\text{Promised YTM} = \text{Expected yield} + \text{Risk penalty.} \tag{22.1}$$

Another measure we often consider is the default premium, a credit spread versus a "risk-free" bond:

$$\text{Default premium} = \text{Promised YTM} - \text{Similar-tenor sovereign YTM.} \tag{22.2}$$

For the risky bond example, we had noted that the market was demanding a yield of 15% for a price of 817.39 while T-bills were yielding 5%. This suggests that the expected yield is $\frac{940/1.05}{817.39} - 1 = 9.5\%$ and implies a risk penalty of $15\% - 9.5\% = 5.5\%$. The default premium for the risky bond is $15\% - 5\% = 10\%$. Fons (1994) notes that this spread typically declines over a bond's life. Credit spreads also vary across maturities: Leland and Toft (1996) and Jarrow, Lando, and Turnbull (1997) discuss models for the term structure of credit spreads; and, Jarrow, Lando, and Yu (2005) discuss theory for a term structure of credit risk.

A credit spread between sovereign bonds (often considered risk-free) and that for the least-risky borrowers (often the interbank rate) is a measure of absolute credit risk. Boudt, Paulus, and Rosenthal (2017) show that the TED spread (Eurodollars versus T-bills) indicates which Brunnermeier and Pedersen (2009) equilibrium we are in: self-healing or self-harming.

Therefore, we often quote credit spreads relative to the yield for the highest-credit risky borrowers, an interbank rate. This leads to lending rates begin quoted as the interbank rate plus a credit spread, *e.g.* LIBOR+110.[2]

---

[2]This is technically not-fully specified since a proper LIBOR rate requires a currency and a tenor; however, these are often implied by context.

22.2.2 Credit Ratings

While the simplest measure of creditworthiness is a yield, we often need more nuanced measures. Thus many investors rely on assessments of credit from **rating agencies**, organizations which try to estimate the credit risk of bonds and issuers.[3] The largest rating agencies are Standard and Poor's (S&P), Fitch, and Moody's with over 90% of market share, depending on the survey. DBRS (formerly Dominion Bond Rating Service), a Canadian company, is a distant fourth. These four are the only agencies whose ratings are recognized by the European Central Bank for assessing collateral when borrowing from the bank.

There are a few other rating agencies you might encounter. Morningstar has recently been building their credit-rating business and seems to be aiming to compete with the top agencies. A.M. Best is a specialized agency which focuses on rating insurers and financial products they issue. There are also a few regional agencies which rate global issues. The biggest of these are Japan Credit Rating Agency (JCR), Rating and Investment Information (R&I, Japan), Rating Agency Malaysia (RAM), Dagong Global Credit Rating (China), and HR Ratings de México. Most other agencies are affiliates of one of the large rating agencies.

The most well-known credit ratings are long-term debt ratings. For most rating agencies, these ratings range from AAA (the best) to C or lower. Table 22.1 lists the various ratings assigned by the top four credit rating agencies. For these agencies, a bond rated BBB-/Baa3/BBL or higher is an **investment-grade bond** while those with lower ratings are **high-yield bonds** (also known as junk bonds).

	Investment Grade		Sub-Investment Grade	
Agency	Highest	High	Speculative	Very Poor
S&P	AAA,AA+→AA−	A+→BBB−	BB+→B−	CCC+→CCC−,CC,C,D
Moody's	Aaa,Aa1→Aa3	A1→Baa3	Ba1→B3	Caa1→Caa3,Ca,C
Fitch	AAA,AA+→AA−	A+→BBB−	BB+→B−	CCC,DDD,DD,D
DBRS	AAA,AAH→AAL	AH→BBBL	BBH→BL	CCCH→CL

Table 22.1: Long-term debt credit ratings from the top four rating agencies which are recognized by the ECB for assessing loan collateral. All have one prime rating (AAA or Aaa) and assign something akin to pluses and minuses until the lowest sub-investment-grade ratings.

Short-term debt ratings are much simpler: typically a letter followed by a number, 1–3 with lower being better, for investment-grade and a prime grade that may be denoted with a trailing plus: for example, "A-1+" is S&P's top rating for short-term debt. Sub-investment grade debt gets ratings like B, C, D, NP, or a trailing 4 or 5.

---

[3]The EU and ECB refer to these as **external credit assessment institutions** (ECAIs).

22.2.3 Probabilities of Default

Mapping long-term debt ratings to a PD is not easy.[4] If bond ratings were strictly relative, they might not change much in a crisis (apart from cyclical versus defensive industries), and after the 2008 financial crisis the US would probably have still have some AAA-rated banks. It would also be fruitless trying to estimate PDs from relative ratings since PDs are absolute measures. If bond ratings were strictly absolute, almost all ratings would decrease in a crisis and we would not see large spikes of defaults in higher credit ratings during a crisis — since ratings would change to account for that likelihood.

What we see, however, is a mixture of these phenomena. We see more downgrades in a crisis, but not enough to insulate the higher ratings from an increase in defaults. Furthermore, PDs do exhibit variation with the business cycle. Clearly, bond ratings are a mix of both relative and absolute ratings which complicates the mapping to a probability of default. This is implied by Kaplan and Urwitz (1979) who model bond ratings and find that while their model does OK at predicting ratings that it does a better job than ratings at assessing bond default risk.

Because borrowing is contingent on credit assessments, defaults on a portfolio of loans typically start out very low. This is different than we would expect if there were no credit assessment. This makes the exponential distribution an imperfect modeling choice.

A further complication is **seasoning**: PDs are higher earlier in bonds' lives before declining to a more stable level. We can see how this arises by simplifying. Suppose there are two types of borrowers in any rating category: "good bets" who are unlikely to default and "bad bets" who are risky. Lenders face adverse selection because bad bets try to hide their troubles and look like good bets. Bad bets are more likely to default sooner: their lack of organization or other troubles may catch up with them. Thus a bond portfolio sees more defaults early in its life as many bad bets default. A portfolio of bonds where this accelerated rate of default has passed is referred to as **seasoned**.

A final complication is that rating agencies do not like to look bad — so they may downgrade a bond shortly before it defaults so as not to make higher rating categories look risky. The problem is that this is similar to a lookback bias: If lenders had known the eventual rating would be lower, they might not have lent to that borrower. This can make higher ratings look unrealistically safe.

Table 22.2 lists default rates over 1983–2016 for various Moody's ratings from Liu, Duggar, and Ou (2017). The rates are cumulated to one, two, five, and ten years since those are close to equally-spaced in log-time and many model forms assume an exponentially-decaying number of defaults. Since these ratings are month-by-month, a Aaa-rated bond which was downgraded a month before default will not affect the statistics for Aaa ratings.

---

[4]Note that we are back to working with real-world probabilities, *i.e.* $\mathbb{P}$-measure.

	Sovereigns				Corporates			
Rating	Yr 1	Yr 2	Yr 5	Yr 10	Yr 1	Yr 2	Yr 5	Yr 10
Aaa	0.0%	0.0%	0.0%	0.0%	0.0%	0+%	0.1%	0.1%
Aa	0.0%	0.0%	0.9%	1.1%	0+%	0.1%	0.3%	0.7%
A	0.0%	0.1%	1.2%	4.9%	0.1%	0.2%	0.8%	2.3%
Baa	0.0%	0.4%	1.3%	1.6%	0.2%	0.5%	1.6%	3.7%
Ba	0.5%	1.4%	5.0%	10.9%	0.9%	2.7%	8.7%	16.2%
B	2.8%	5.8%	12.6%	21.4%	3.6%	8.5%	22.0%	36.2%
Caa–C	12.2%	19.1%	37.7%	50.6%	10.5%	18.6%	35.5%	50.4%

Table 22.2: A table showing cumulative default percentages over 1983–2016 by bond rating group and years since issuance with the ratings grouped monthly. The sovereign defaults are higher in year 10 for A- versus Baa-rated bonds due to the 2012 defaults by Greece.

22.2.4 *Bank Lending and Credit Scoring*

In Chapter 17, we saw that some economies use more bank-loan financing than bond-market financing. Bank loans have some credit advantages over bonds. Most obviously, banks may have the borrower as a customer for banking, payments, and other businesses. This can help the bank better assess the creditworthiness of the firm. Banks may even offer banking services at a discount to secure a borrower's business and thus gain better information about the state of a borrower.

Banks can insist on more restrictive loan covenants; for example, banks are more likely to require collateral for lending. They may also insist on the ability to use funds held at the bank as backup collateral. Bank loans often have a different repayment structure from bonds: typically the principal repayment is amortized so that the lender need not wait until maturity to receive some principal back. Bank loans are also more likely to use a floating interest rate.

In economies where bank-loan financing dominates, banks' **credit scoring** models, which assess the credit risk of a potential borrower, may be more important than credit ratings. Frame, Srinivasan, and Woosley (2001) show that the use of credit scoring increases lending to small businesses; and, Frame, Padhi, and Woosley (2004) show that credit scoring increases lending to firms in low- and moderate-income areas. Thus they posit that credit scoring models help reduce the adverse selection faced by lenders.

22.3 Credit Issues

We have already discussed how bond covenants help avoid strategic default and preserve the creditworthiness of bonds. However, bond creditworthiness is also affected by other issues like seniority, correlation of defaults, and correlations of defaults and recovery rates. Finally, while the economy affects credit, credit also affects the economy.

22.3.1   Seniority Effects

Another factor which affects a bond's or loan's creditworthiness is its **seniority** or (antonym) **subordination**: its location in the hierarchy of creditors' claims in the event of bankruptcy and liquidation. **Senior debt** is that which is supposed to be paid first in liquidation while **junior** or **subordinated debt** is paid after senior debt — and before preferred and then common shareholders. This is the legal idea known as the **absolute priority rule**.

Strangely, the absolute priority rule is frequently violated in bankruptcy proceedings, as noted by Longhofer (1997). Since all bondholders and shareholders must agree to a liquidation plan, junior claimants can disrupt the process and demand a payout (like ransom). Longhofer notes that these diversions may be non-trivial and reduce the efficiency of debt financing. However, Altman and Eberhart (1994) present evidence that lenders account for this when valuing bonds and so are not surprised (and harmed) by violations of the absolute priority rule.

Despite violations of the absolute priority rule, seniority is crucial to determining a bond's credit. Altman and Kishore (1996) find that after controlling for a bond's seniority, a bond's initial rating has no relationship to the recovery rate (*i.e.* $1-$ LGD).

> **Double-Cross Default?** Investors often finance holdings with repos — a form of collateralized loans. In 2014, metal bought by Mercuria from Decheng Mining and repoed to Citigroup was found to be backed by fraudulent documents. Decheng used duplicate receipts for metal in Qingdao and Penglai warehouses as collateral on multiple loans and even sold some receipts.
>
> While banks usually verify warehouse receipts when lending, the warehouses created the duplicates. Three years later, lenders' losses are *still* unclear but may be billions of USD. Commodity-backed financing has plummeted in China and many firms moved metal to warehouses in Korea and Malaysia.
>
> In 2017, forged warehouse receipts for nickel in Korea, Malaysia, and Singapore were found before major losses. For more info on these scandals, see Home (2014), Taylor and Hardaker (2015), and Bermingham (2017). For more on liens in China, read Tham (2017).

However, there is an overarching hierarchy of seniority apart from bonds and equity. Bonds are subordinate to bank loans with collateralized bank loans having the first **lien** (claim) on collateral in liquidation. (See the sidebar "Double-Cross Default" for a story of conflicting first liens.) Bank loans are, in turn, subordinate to derivatives which are marked to market. Since there might not be covenants between these different types of creditors, strategic gaming and manipulation can still occur between these groups. Why then do we have these groups?

Bolton and Freixas (2000) show that bank loans, bonds, and equity financing have different advantages and firms adopt different shares of these depending on the extent of potential information asymmetries between borrower and lender. They find that the riskiest firms mostly use bank loans, the safest firms mostly issue bonds, and firms in between use equities and bonds for financing. Similarly, Ayotte (2017) suggests these various capital and corporate structures exist to exploit differences in valuation so that the firm minimizes its cost of capital.[5]

What about derivatives? We know that hedging reduces risk. However, mark-to-market accounting has been shown to be destabilizing by Heaton, Lucas, and McDonald (2010) and accounts are updated less frequently than derivatives are marked to market. Can marking to market of derivatives positions be destabilizing? Bolton and Oehmke (2015) suggests that it can be since derivatives can increase the credit risk of debt holders. We will revisit this issue in Chapter 26.

22.3.2 Correlated Defaults

The possibility of correlated defaults is another concern when we analyze credit. If a portfolio of mortgage loans had 250 borrowers, you might think it is likely to be a well-diversified portfolio. However, if 60% of the loans were to borrowers in Wayne County, Michigan — where Detroit is — or Greece, you might be concerned. The problem is not with Detroit or Greece *per se*.[6] The problem is that borrowers in Detroit are likely to work in the auto industry. If the US auto industry were to have trouble, as it has in the past, you could find many borrowers defaulting at nearly the same times. This portfolio has a large latent exposure to the automaking industry. Similarly, many borrowers from Greece means a portfolio has a large exposure to the Greek macroeconomy.

We can model default in a time period (say, annually, for a PD) as a Bernoulli random variable with the single parameter p being the PD. For a Bernoulli random variable, the mean is p and the variance is $p(1-p)$. If we have two bonds, A and B, and denote their defaults as events D_A and D_B, their default correlation is given by:

$$\text{Corr}(D_A, D_B) = \frac{P(D_A \cap D_B) - P(D_A)P(D_B)}{\sqrt{\text{Var}(D_A)}\sqrt{\text{Var}(D_B)}} \tag{22.3}$$

$$= \frac{P(D_A \cap D_B) - p_A p_B}{\sqrt{p_A(1-p_A)}\sqrt{p_B(1-p_B)}}. \tag{22.4}$$

Thus default correlation is a measure of how often defaults occur in the same time period beyond what we would expect if defaults were independent. With this formula,

---

[5]Those with further interests in capital structure should read Rauh and Sufi (2010).

[6]For those outside the Midwest: Detroit is currently undergoing a renaissance. While perceptions of Detroit are bad, the current reality is better.

we can measure defaults for types of bonds and infer the default correlation among those types.

Lucas (1995a) does this analysis using default data over 1970–1993 for bonds broken into the larger categories (Aaa, Aa, etc.) from Moody's. To infer the probability of joint default on, say, two Aa-rated bonds $P(D_{Aa,i} \cap D_{Aa,j})$, he looks at the number of joint default pairs versus the number of possible Aa-rated pairs. If there are $n_{Aa,t}$ Aa-rated bonds and $d_{Aa,t}$ of them default in a year t:

$$\hat{P}(D_{Aa,i} \cap D_{Aa,j}) = \sum_t \frac{d_{Aa,t}(d_{Aa,t} - 1)/2}{n_{Aa,t}(n_{Aa,t} - 1)/2} \quad \forall i \neq j, \tag{22.5}$$

$$\hat{P}(D_{Aa}) = \sum_t \frac{d_{Aa,t}}{n_{Aa,t}}. \tag{22.6}$$

Between rating categories, say Aa and A (and canceling divisions by two):

$$\hat{P}(D_{Aa,i} \cap D_{A,j}) = \sum_t \frac{d_{Aa,t} d_{A,t}}{n_{Aa,t} n_{A,t}}. \tag{22.7}$$

Lucas finds default correlations are higher in and between lower rating categories with the highest correlation among the lowest rating category he studies: B-rated bonds exhibit a 7% correlation over a one-year time period.

Another approach is to study probability-of-default correlations. Das, Fong, and Geng (2001) and Das et al. (2006) model default probabilities and then measure the correlation of the modeled probabilities of default. They use data over 1987–2000 and find that the PDs are far more correlated than the realized defaults analyzed by Lucas (1995a). They find correlations within and between rating categories largely in the 20%–30% range. They also note that these correlations increase in crises.

This suggests that there are latent or unobserved factors affecting defaults. Both Das et al. (2007) and Duffie et al. (2009) find support for latent factors being necessary to explain observed correlations. Thus we should look for factors and consider how to build models that handle latent factors. However, until we find those factors, we need to be able to create models that work despite latent factors if we are to have any hope of capturing the dynamics we observe.

The upshot of this is that modeling correlated defaults is difficult. Furthermore, we observe different levels of correlation when we look at actual defaults versus model-implied PDs. The reason is because firms have many tools at their disposal and will work vigorously to avoid default.

Copulas

A common method to simulate correlated defaults before the financial crisis used a **copula**, a distribution on the n-dimensional [0,1] hypercube that maps marginal distributions to a joint distribution. With this approach, one creates correlated random variables, inverts them to get quantiles, and then remaps those quantiles to a new joint distribution. The result is correlated random variables from a new distribution; however, the correlation is not the same.

There are a few problems, however, The final correlation structure is unclear. Worse is that different joint distributions have different risk management implications. Finally, the most popular method starts with correlated normal random variates. Thus a distribution with no skew, too little kurtosis, and thin tails was the starting point for simulating correlated fat-tail events. Some have gone so far as to blame the Gaussian copula for the 2008 financial crisis due to opacity and understating tail risks.

If this method has so many problems, why did people use it? One reason was because there is no clear way of creating correlated variables for most distributions which model times to default. Most marginal distributions can be combined in multiple ways to create a joint distribution with a given correlation. (Devroye (1986) discusses this.) The copula method can, in theory, yield any joint distribution; however, a driving reason for its use was ease: it allowed for easily simulating correlated random variables.

While many practitioners have used copulas, I have yet to meet a statistician or econometrician who finds them intuitive. We prefer to build models where the dynamics act directly and the economics are clear. Even these simple models are difficult enough to fully understand. Therefore, we will not discuss copulas further.

22.3.3   Correlated Default and Recovery Rates

We mentioned another problem early in this text: the possibility that default and recovery rates may be correlated. When an industry has many defaults, creditors will sell similar assets and may find that their recovery rates are lower. You can read about such a story in the sidebar "Take a Seat... Please" in Chapter 13.

Hu and Perraudin (2006) (first in a 2002 working paper) and Altman et al. (2005) show this by fitting functional forms which corroborate the inverse relationship between default and recovery rates. Guo, Jarrow, and Zeng (2009) model recovery rates and find implications for default and bankruptcy rates.

22.3.4   Mandate Effects

Bond ratings are important: many investment funds, insurance companies, and endowments have mandates to hold much of their money in investment-grade bonds. A bond downgraded to below investment grade may be subject to heavy selling in a short period of time. Furthermore, many central banks require investment-grade bonds for loan or margin collateral.

Some counterparties and clearinghouses require **"safe" assets** as collateral. Before the 2008 financial crisis, that meant risk-free sovereign bonds, bonds from government-sponsored entities (with implicit government backing), municipal bonds, securitized loans, highly-rated financial-sector corporates, bank deposits, interbank loans, money market mutual funds, and commercial paper. After the 2008 financial crisis, however, many of these were downgraded or no longer deemed "safe." For example, many counterparties no longer see Italian and Greek bonds as safe. This also holds for the debt of many government-sponsored entities, some municipal bonds, securitized loans, and many financial-sector corporates.

Gorton, Lewellen, and Metrick (2012) note how after the crisis, many counterparties demanded more "safe" assets as collateral. Yet post-crisis we view far fewer assets as safe. Thus demand has risen as supply has fallen. The net result is, as discussed in Klein (2012) and Caballero, Farhi, and Gourinchas (2017), a shortage of safe assets. This has driven many assets still seen as safe to low or even negative yields. The effects of this shortage and how to address it are currently major focuses for policy makers.

Finally, the ratings of a bank's holdings affect capital adequacy requirements under EU directives as well as Basel II and Basel III accords. Credit scores also affect capital adequacy requirements under Basel II and III. Thus ratings downgrades can force banks to purchase other highly-rated debt or sell off the downgraded debt and replace it with higher-rated debt.

22.4   Credit Derivatives

There are now derivatives which protect bond holders from default. Those markets grew rapidly prior to the 2008 financial crisis. While many firms suffered losses from poor modeling of these derivatives in the crisis, the markets are useful and have persisted post-crisis.

One such derivative is an **asset swap**. You could swap a bond for most of its value plus an option to buy the bond back at par. This reduces the capital used in holding the bond and eliminates the downside of default — like a repo plus a put struck at the bond's face value.

Credit default swaps (CDSs) are the most liquid derivatives providing default protection and are traded on both individual bonds (single-name CDSs) and indices of sovereign, emerging market, investment-grade, and high-yield bonds. CDSs allow buyers of protection to receive the face value of a bond if it defaults: the buyer may tender the (impaired) bond to the seller and receive face value or the buyer may just receive the difference between the bond's market price and face value.

An oddity of single-name CDSs is that buyers may not own the underlying bond. CDSs on a bond have occasionally exceeded the amount of bond issued. Insurers do not sell fire insurance on a structure to non-tenants because it incentivizes arson. Similarly, researchers have wondered if "over-selling" CDSs incentivizes creating credit crises. (This is **moral hazard**: the problem that insurance can lead people to take *more* risks.)

The most common indices are the CDX (for North American and emerging market entities) and iTraxx (for European and Asian entities). These indices are equally-weighted and reconstituted every six months (since bonds mature). Most derivatives reference the latest **series** although "vintage" series are still traded, albeit with less liquidity. If a name in the index defaults, the buyer receives a payout for that bond proportional to its weight in the index. The index is then recreated with one fewer name in the index.[7]

22.5 The Value of Firm Equity

In the previous chapter, we posited a stochastic process for equity based on geometric Brownian motion given by the classic drift and diffusion stochastic differential equation:

$$dS_t = \mu S_t dt + \sigma S_t dW_t. \tag{22.8}$$

We also noted Bachelier (1900) and Bronzin (1908) as early-but-flawed work since they used arithmetic Brownian motion. The problem with this characterization is that Bachelier and Bronzin were not so wrong.

As Goetzmann (2016) notes, one of the innovations which allowed equity markets to flourish was limited liability. Limited liability prevents a stock from having negative value.[8] Sure enough, equation (22.8) implies that a zero stock price is not possible. However, zero (and nearly zero) stock prices are not only possible, they happen often.

The root of this problem is that we ignored how limited liability works. While assets are the sum of equity and liabilities, that does not mean that equity is the difference of assets and liabilities:

$$\text{Equity} \overset{?}{=} \text{Assets} - \text{Liabilities}. \tag{22.9}$$

Rather, limited liability means that if the assets are not sufficient to pay off the liabilities, the lenders take the loss. Thus the value of equity is:

$$\text{Equity} = (\text{Assets} - \text{Liabilities})^+. \tag{22.10}$$

With this formulation, we can finally see equity in its true form: equity is a call option on the firm struck at the value of debt. This is the revelation of Merton (1974). Thus we should really model equity S_t through the asset value process A_t in light of liabilities L_t at some terminal time τ:

$$dA_t = \mu A_t dt + \sigma_A A_t dW_t, \tag{22.11}$$

$$S_t = (A_\tau - L_\tau)^+. \tag{22.12}$$

This explains some of the unusual phenomena we see with stocks such as the leverage effect: The volatility of the asset price will decrease in proportion to the asset price while the equity price will decline faster (on a percentage basis) than the asset price. This leads to the volatility being larger (on a percentage basis) when the stock price falls. Geske (1979) also notes that this explains some of the skewness in equity log-returns.

---

[7]For more information on CDS indices, see Markit (2014).

[8]As a colleague once jokingly "predicted," stock prices have "strong support at zero."

22.6   Structural Credit Models

Structural credit models use the firm's capital structure to model the risk of default. In particular, structural models use the Merton (1974) idea that equity is a long call option on the firm struck at the total of liabilities. Thus when the firm's equity is out of the money, the firm is bankrupt.

> ⚠ **Aviso!** *For many finance firms, the regulatory mandate to meet some level of capital adequacy is a shadow liability. If the firm's capital (including equity) falls below the minimum mandated, they may sell assets to increase their capital. This reduces the value of equity and can drive the firm into a "death spiral" where the need for regulatory capital forces them into bankruptcy even though assets exceed liabilities. Regulations can have the opposite effect of what was intended.*

For the **Merton model**, we assume one issue of zero-coupon debt. (If not, we convert coupon bonds to equivalent-yielding zero-coupon bonds.) The firm's equity is then a call option on assets with the expiry date being the maturity date of the debt. At expiry, the firm then transitions to a new capital structure. We could handle multiple bond issues by modeling each bond as a bull spread with strikes implied by seniority.

How do we handle firms with callable bonds since calling a bond changes the capital structure? For b callable bonds, Jones, Mason, and Rosenfeld (1983,1984) consider all 2^b possible capital structures with varying stopping times (defined by the earliest maturity date of all un-called bonds). Each scenario requires solving a system of partial differential equations. The value of equity (and optimal call policy) is given by the scenario maximizing the net present value of equity.

Non-traded bonds are assumed to be valued at the same multiple of book value as traded bonds. Finally, they solve for σ_A from the asset value A_t, equity value S_t, and volatility σ_S:

$$\sigma_S S_t = \sigma_A A_t \frac{\partial S_t}{\partial A_t}. \tag{22.13}$$

The **Moody's KMV family of models** equate the value of equity with the option value and the volatility of equity with the equation above.[9] This yields a system of equations which can be solved for σ_A and A_t. If we use the Merton setup, these equations would be:

$$A_t e^{-\delta(\tau-t)}\Phi(d_1) - L_t e^{-r_f(\tau-t)}\Phi(d_2) - S_t = 0, \tag{22.14}$$

$$\sigma_A A_t \Phi(d_1) - \sigma_S S_t = 0. \tag{22.15}$$

The d_1 and d_2 are as in the Black-Scholes-Merton formula — except functions of σ_A.

---

[9]The Moody's KMV model is discussed extensively in Kealhofer (2003a, 2003b), Crosbie and Bohn (2003), and Vasicek (1984).

The option has a finite expiry date. However, equity is a perpetuity and, if debt is refinanced at maturity, the firm does not transition to a new capital structure. Thus we must handle the perpetual aspect of equity.

Before the Black-Scholes-Merton formula, Samuelson (1965b) and McKean (1965) jointly priced a perpetual American call option.[10] They find the optimal exercise boundary and show that for an underlier above that level, early exercise is optimal. Early exercise happens when $A_t > A_t^*$:

$$A_t^* = \frac{L_t \eta}{\eta - 1} \quad \text{(early exercise boundary)} \tag{22.16}$$

$$\eta = \frac{r_f - \delta + \frac{\sigma_A^2}{2} + \sqrt{(\delta - r_f - \frac{\sigma_A^2}{2})^2 + 2\delta\sigma_A^2}}{\sigma_A^2}, \tag{22.17}$$

$$S_t = C_{L_t, t, \infty} = \begin{cases} (A_t^* - L_t)(\frac{A_t}{A_t^*})^\eta & A_t \leq A_t^*, \\ A_t - L_t & A_t > A_t^*. \end{cases} \tag{22.18}$$

While equity might not seem to be an American option, at any time the equity holders can "exercise" their option by buying out the creditors and owning all of the assets, *i.e.* a debt-free firm.

Giesecke (2006) notes financial reports are infrequent so we rarely know L_t. Since Geske (1979) shows we expect skewness in equity log-returns, we could infer $\hat{L}_t$ by matching the skewness of stock log-returns to the skewness implied by a log-normal asset price process driving an option struck at an unknown strike $\hat{L}_t$. Alternately, we might be able to use information from the volatility curve of options on the stock.

An inferred $\hat{L}_t$ might include "shadow" liabilities for finance firms or impound market expectations of government bailouts or repos used to hide assets or liabilities — as mentioned at the end of Chapter 11. The Moody's KMV approach assumes a $\hat{L}_t$ called the default point which lies between total and current liabilities.

Finally, another modeling approach comes from Hull, Nelken, and White (2004). Since options on equity are options on options, they use the work of Geske (1979) on compound options. That allows them to infer σ_A from points on the volatility curve. This implicitly corrects for higher moments and the leverage effect of equity itself being a call option.

A key variable implicit in structural models is the **distance to default**, the number of standard deviations the firm is from default, *i.e.* a t-score. The simplest definition, mentioned by Crosbie and Bohn (2003), requires no options theory whatsoever; we merely use an annual volatility:

$$d_{\text{default}} = \frac{\log(A_t/L_t)}{\sigma_A}. \tag{22.19}$$

---

[10]Since Samuelson (1965b) and McKean (1965) can be a bit opaque, readers may find Gerber and Shiu (1994) more enlightening.

For the Merton model, the risk-neutral distance to default is:

$$d_{\text{default}}^{\mathbb{Q}} = d_2 = \frac{\log(A_t/L_t) + (r_f - \delta - \frac{\sigma_A^2}{2})(T-t)}{\sigma_A\sqrt{T-t}}. \tag{22.20}$$

Since A_t/L_t is an inverse leverage, leverage reduces the distance to default.

22.7   Accounting-Based Credit Models

Some of the earliest credit models were based on accounting measures. When analysts assess credit, they often look at certain accounting ratios. These fall into a few groups: coverage of fixed costs, liquidity to pay liabilities, cashflow to pay debts, leverage ratios, and profitability measures. The idea is that these measures give us information about the firm's capital structure.

Coverage ratios tell us how many times a firm could pay certain fixed costs from revenues. The **times-interest-earned** (TIE) ratio is the coverage ratio for interest payments. The **fixed-charge coverage ratio** (FCCR) adds leases and sinking funds to fixed costs:

$$\text{TIE} = \text{EBIT}/\text{interest}, \tag{22.21}$$

$$\text{FCCR} = \frac{\text{EBIT}}{\text{interest}+\text{leases}+\text{sinking funds}}. \tag{22.22}$$

Liquidity ratios measure how many times a firm could pay its bills using liquid assets on hand. Most ratios look at **current assets**, cash or assets convertible to cash within the next year, and **current liabilities**, liabilities which must be paid within the next year. The **current ratio** looks at the ratio of these two while the **quick ratio** eliminates inventory from current assets since inventory might not sell quickly at book value:

$$\text{current ratio} = \text{current assets}/\text{current liabilities}, \tag{22.23}$$

$$\text{quick ratio} = \frac{\text{current assets} - \text{inventory}}{\text{current liabilities}}. \tag{22.24}$$

The **cashflow-debt ratio** measures the need for short-term funding.

The purpose of coverage ratios, liquidity ratios, and cashflow-debt ratios is to assess how close the firm is to a potential cash crunch. This is important since short-term funding is often impaired early in a financial crisis.

Leverage ratios assess if the firm is excessively indebted. The most common example is the **debt-equity ratio**: debt/equity. However, we can also look at the **assets-equity** ratio. As a leveraged firm moves closer to bankruptcy, these ratios can grow very large as equity approaches zero.

Finally, **profitability ratios** measure earnings versus capital used to generate those earnings. If the firm were to find liquidity insufficient, these ratios help us gauge if the firm could successfully raise capital. We tend to look mostly at **return on assets** (ROA) and **return on equity** (ROE):

$$ROA = EBIT/\text{total assets}, \tag{22.25}$$

$$ROE = \text{net income}/\text{equity}. \tag{22.26}$$

For those who have forgotten accounting definitions: EBIT is earnings before interest and taxes, *i.e.* operative revenues minus operating expenses; and, net earnings is EBIT minus interest and taxes. Note that we could also break up ROE like the DuPont model does (as discussed in Chapter 13).

While these ratios were known for a long time, the first rigorous statistical analyses of their predictive power was by Beaver (1966) and Beaver (1968). Altman (1968) extended this with discriminant analysis, an early classification method to use the binary outcomes to find the most informative ratios.[11] Using data from 66 firms, he created **Altman's Z-score:**[12]

$$
Z = 1.2 \overbrace{\frac{\text{working capital}}{\text{total assets}} + 1.4 \frac{\text{retained earnings}}{\text{total assets}}}^{\text{liquidity ratios}} \\
+ \underbrace{3.3 ROA + \frac{\text{sales}}{\text{total assets}}}_{\text{profitability ratios}} + \underbrace{0.6 \frac{\text{equity value}}{\text{total liabilities}}}_{\text{(inverse) leverage}}. \tag{22.27}
$$

Based on the analysis, Altman suggests that $Z > 3$ is "safe," $Z \in [1.8, 3)$ is in a "grey area," and $Z < 1.8$ is "distressed."

While the accuracy of Altman's predictions fell quickly after the initial year, Beaver's predictions held up longer. Deakin (1972) found that using Beaver's ratios with Altman's discriminant analysis approach yielded a more accurate model over a longer time period.

Altman, Haldeman, and Narayanan (1977) then estimated a model for industrial firms which they called the **ZETA score**. They first fit a model for the time trend of ROA. ZETA is then a function of ROA, the uncertainty around the ROA time trend, the times-interest-earned ratio, retained earnings to total assets, the quick ratio, a time average of equity to liabilities, and the log of total assets. The ZETA analysis was done with a matched (by industry and year) sample of 53 bankrupted and 58 non-bankrupted firms. The model form and significance were unspecified since it is proprietary and owned by Altman's firm.

Ohlson (1980) notes a couple problems with these analyses. First, they use small datasets for estimation. Second, they are not careful about only looking at pre-bankruptcy data. Instead, Ohlson analyzed 105 bankrupted firms and 2058

---

[11]We would now use generalized linear models for this analysis.

[12]Altman (2013) estimated a score Z' for private firms, Z'' for non-manufacturing firms, and Z''_{EM} for emerging markets.

non-bankrupted firms using data with consistent times. He then estimated the
log-odds of bankruptcy, aka **Ohlson's O-score**:

$$O = -1.3 - \text{size} - \text{profitability} - \text{liquidity} + \text{leverage} \tag{22.28}$$

$$(\text{firm}) \text{ size} = 0.4 \frac{\text{total assets}}{\text{GNP}} \tag{22.29}$$

$$\text{profitability} = 2.3 \frac{\text{net income}}{\text{total assets}} - 0.29 \times \mathbf{1}(\text{net loss for 2 years})$$
$$+ 0.5 \frac{\text{change in net income}}{\text{sum of } |\text{net income}| \text{ over past 2 years}} \tag{22.30}$$

$$\text{liquidity} = 1.4 \frac{\text{working capital}}{\text{total assets}} - 0.08 \frac{1}{\text{current ratio}}$$
$$+ 1.8 \frac{\text{funds from operations}}{\text{total liabilities}} \tag{22.31}$$

$$\text{leverage} = 6 \frac{\text{total liabilities}}{\text{total assets}} - 1.7 \times \mathbf{1}\left(\frac{\text{total liabilities}}{\text{total assets}} > 1\right) \tag{22.32}$$

$$P(\text{Bankruptcy}) = \frac{1}{1 + e^{-O}} = \text{logistic}(O). \tag{22.33}$$

The negative sign for the indicator if total liabilities exceed total assets is unusual.
This just corrects the leverage slope for companies in bankruptcy. Ohlson's explanation is that bankruptcy is complicated (so perhaps leverage then matters less). No
model selection was done: the terms for the inverse current ratio, two losing years,
and intercept were all not significant.

Another well-known accounting-based measure is the **Piotroski's (2000) F-
score**. This approach looks at the sum of nine indicator variables, four assessing
profitability, three assessing financial performance, and two assessing operating
efficiency. The indicator variables are shown in Table 22.3.

Measure Type	Indicator
Profitability	$ROA > 0$
Profitability	growing ROA: $\Delta ROA > 0$
Profitability	cashflow from operations > 0
Profitability	accruals< 0: cashflow from operations $>$ EBIT
Financial Performance	falling leverage: Δ long term leverage < 0
Financial Performance	rising liquidity: Δ current ratio > 0
Financial Performance	no new shares issued?
Operating Efficiency	rising margins: Δ gross margin > 0
Operating Efficiency	rising turnover: Δ asset turnover > 0

Table 22.3: Performance measures used in calculating Piotroski's F-score. Each affirmative
test yields one point with F being the sum of all points.

Probably the most interesting aspect of the Piotroski F-score is that it penalizes firms which make more earnings from **accruals**: non-cash revenue recognition. This makes sense since Sloan (1996) notes the **accruals anomaly**: that firms with negative accruals tend to have persistent earnings performance and earn outsized returns. However, Piotroski shows that the performance of the F-score is not strictly driven by accruals.[13]

22.8 Default Intensity Credit Models

Another form of models are those which seek to model the default intensity (aka the hazard rate) or, equivalently, the PD.

An important difference from the prior model types is that the default intensity research tends not to promulgate particular models: there is no "Jarrow's J-score" or "Duffie's D." Rather, these models promote a modeling *approach*. Furthermore, in accepting ignorance of firm structure, they join a long literature of statistical models which sweep the unknown into the error term and then work, over time, to find factors and shrink the error variance. This makes these analogs of the risk-factor models like we explored in Chapters 14 and 15.

Most models in this family rely on classic statistical models for delays or arrival times of rare events. For this modeling approach, we often talk about the **time to default** — with the understanding that the time is random and may be censored if the loan matures before default would have "arrived."

If rare events depend on only one source of randomness, the number of events are often modeled as being Poisson-distributed with a rate parameter λ. This goes back to Bortkiewicz (1898) modeling deaths by horse kick in the Prussian army and Erlang (1909) modeling calls arriving at a call center. Poisson event counts mean times between events are exponentially-distributed with rate parameter λ. One of the earliest works on this approach in the finance literature was Jarrow and Turnbull (1995).

The simple assumption of exponential times to default often fails: there may be seasoning effects, as noted by Altman (1998); defaults may depend on multiple sources of risk; or, defaults may only happen after multiple rare events take place (*e.g.* having negative cashflow, exhausting credit, being no longer able to cut costs and shuffle cashflows). Furthermore, credit analysis implies that firms receiving a loan have already been screened to exclude those which would have defaulted early. Thus we might expect the distribution of default times to be low at first, rise, and then decay over time.

If default is a multi-step process with all m steps being Poisson events with the same arrival rate, the time-to-default is a gamma(m, λ)-distributed random variable with mean m/λ and variance m/λ^2. (We call m the shape parameter.) If each step has a different rate $\lambda_{i \in \{1,...,m\}}$ or some events cause defaults to accelerate,

---

[13]Those troubled by accruals and looking to measure earnings manipulation should read Beneish (1999).

Rosenthal (2008) shows that the resulting distribution is often approximately gamma-distributed.[14]

One approach in this case is to use a **compound exponential** model: the arrival rate is a function of other random variables. (The analog of the associated Poisson process is then called a **Cox process**.) This is sometimes called a hierarchical or **doubly-stochastic model** because arrivals are random and the arrival rate parameter is itself random (with models for each). One way to do this is with gamma generalized linear models:

$$\underbrace{E(Y|X) = \mu,}_{\text{response}} \quad \underbrace{\frac{1}{\mu} = \eta}_{\text{link function}} \ , \quad \underbrace{\eta = \alpha + \sum_{i=1}^{k} \beta_i X_i}_{\text{linear predictor}}. \tag{22.34}$$

McCullagh and Nelder (1989) discuss how to recover the shape parameter $\hat{m}$. One way is through the inverse of the dispersion parameter, another is as a moment estimator, and a third is through a maximum-likelihood estimator implemented in the MASS R package:

```
## example of gamma GLM fit
library(MASS)
types <- rbinom(100, 1, 0.6)  # create types (0 or 1)
times <- rgamma(100, 3, 0.2+0.1*types) # gamma r.v.s w/rate 0.2 (0.3 for types==1)
model.fit <- glm(times ~ types, family=Gamma())
summary(model.fit)  # show linear model for 1/mu = rate/m = rate/3
## moment estimator of m, preferred by McCullagh and Nelder
m.hat1 <- 1/summary(model.fit)$dispersion
## common estimator of m
m.hat2 <- summary(model.fit)$df.residual/summary(model.fit)$deviance
## MLE estimator of m, implemented in MASS
m.hat3 <- gamma.shape(model.fit)
```

While this can model default times, it is only modeling the mean. We cannot separately model the rate and shape parameters since we only model their ratio. Even when the model fits the data well, that inability prevents us from making conclusions about the data generating process.

While we could try to solve this problem, we still have to deal with a much larger problem: the fact that default data tend to be heavily censored. This is, in a way, good; most bonds do not default. However, it further complicates the analysis.

The proper way to analyze censored rate data comes from the epidemiology and biostatistics community where they must analyze treatments before everyone has died. The approach is called **survival analysis**. Thankfully, there are a few R packages which we can use for such analyses.

The survival R package is flexible and can provide inference on the data themselves (forecasting likelihoods of default on unmatured bonds with the survfit() function) as well as inferring distributional parameters (with the survreg() function). Unfortunately, survival does not work (by default) for the gamma distribution; the

---

[14]A better source for those interested in default modeling theory is Rosenthal (2018).

gamma is less useful in medical applications. However, the modeling can be extended for any distribution with d<dist>() and p<dist>() functions, *e.g.* dgamma() and pgamma(). An easier approach which allows for other flexible model types is to use the flexsurv *R* package. That even allows for separate modeling of the shape parameter (*i.e.* a compound gamma model):

```
## example of survival analysis
## suppose bonds mature at 15 years so times > 15 are censored
library(survival)
library(flexsurv)
defaulted <- times < 15    # TRUE => data not censored
times.censored <- pmin(times, 15)

## Fit gamma parameters
## Note that covariate coefficients are modeling rate
## anc (ancillary) parameter allows modeling shape parameter
model.fit <- flexsurvreg(Surv(times, defaulted) ~ types, dist="gamma")
model.fit  # show parameter estimates
```

Survival analysis is a well-developed field dating back to the 1660s when John Graunt studied London mortality and health statistics. As an example of the promise the field offers: one could use competing risks models to model not just default but the competing mechanisms for default. Nonetheless, the field's level of development means we cannot do it justice here. Interested readers should consult Kleinbaum and Klein (2012) and Crowder (2012).

The finance work on intensity-based credit models has yet to make the most of the available statistical tools. However, there are promising developments. Lando (1998) discussed modeling defaults as a Cox process; and, Banasik, Crook, and Thomas (1999) noted the connection to survival analysis and even discussed some fertile areas of possible research. Duffie, Saita, and Wang (2007) develop a compound exponential model with covariates that are outputs of time series models. The covariates make their approach act as a competing risks model. The doubly stochastic approach allows the two models to be decoupled. However, the separation of the default time and intensity models precludes defaults which affect one another.

Das et al. (2007) and Duffie et al. (2009) find evidence against doubly-stochastic models and in favor of latent factors. In particular, their work suggests models should incorporate "frailty" — the possibility of default clustering due to unknown factors.[15] Thus we cannot avoid the issue of correlated defaults. Much of the research into default correlation has been by researchers working on default intensity models. Jarrow and Yu (2001) looked at cross-holdings as a possible source or correlation of default intensities. Yu (2007) discusses theory for correlations, various correlation structures, and how those fit in an intensity-based modeling approach.

How would we proceed with a latent factor model? Theory in Rosenthal (2018) suggests that a latent factor which accelerates failure times generates correlated defaults and may also yield a portfolio seemingly composed of fewer (and larger)

---

[15]The use of "frailty" differs from earlier work by Marshall and Olkin (1967) which used the term for joint failure time distributions with a singular component. That gives a non-zero probability to bonds simultaneously defaulting.

independent bonds. In particular, the time to portfolio default is then approximately gamma-distributed. That means a gamma model implies a default-approximating portfolio. Another approach is using latent factors — random effects — in the gamma GLM. McNeil and Wendin (2007) explore this and find that the model performs well.

Recent work has used **Hawkes processes**, mutually-exciting processes, to model defaults which cascade or influence one another. This is similar to the ACD model of Engle and Russell (1998) extended to a vector approach to allow for cross-correlations, such as Russell (1999).

22.9   Market-Based Credit Models

Some call structural models market-based since they use the market value of equity. However, markets have moved on and that term is now a poor descriptor since markets trade liquid derivatives providing default protection.

Despite the financial crisis, CDSs *are* a useful innovation: they allow hedging a risk many do not want to shoulder. Houweling and Vorst (2005) and Ericsson, Jacobs, and Oviedo (2009) show that CDS spreads are more related to default risk factors than bond yield spreads. Longstaff, Mithal, and Neis (2005) use CDS spreads to show that liquidity explains part of bond yield spreads. Thus CDS data are cleaner measures of credit conditions than yield spreads. Pan and Singleton (2008) show CDSs provide a nearly-direct measure of the risk-neutral probability of default and recovery rate.

As forward-looking instruments, CDSs have great potential for credit modelers seeking to anticipate default. Hull, Predescu, and White (2004) show that CDSs anticipate ratings reviews and downgrades. Blanco, Brennan, and Marsh (2005) show that CDSs even lead credit spreads in anticipating bond price changes. Strangely, however, Forte and Peña (2009) suggest that stocks returns may even lead CDSs returns.

If CDSs are a direct measure of the market's assessment of default risk, one might wonder if it makes any sense to model credit default swaps. However, the market is based on pricing models: Duffie (1999) discusses pricing CDSs and Bielecki, Jeanblanc, and Rutkowski (2008) show CDSs can be priced with a default intensity (hazard) model. Carr and Wu (2011) show that CDSs are related to out-of-the-money American put options.

22.10   Modeling Summary

Out of all these approaches thus far, which work the best? Das, Hanouna, and Sarin (2009) show structural models perform similar to accounting-based models, but that combining the models performs better than either. Bharath and Shumway (2008) and Bauer and Agarwal (2014) both suggest that default intensity (aka hazard rate) models work better than either structural or accounting-based models.

Campbell, Hilscher, and Szilagyi (2008) finds that some firm-specific accounting and market variables, as well as time controls for the state of the macroeconomy, work better than most accounting- or intensity-based models. They also find evidence against the Fama-French SMB and HML factors being associated with risk

While CDS data would seem to obliviate the need for other models, that is not so. The story from all this research is thus consistent: hybrid models which use all of these information sources perform the best.

For more information on credit modeling, I recommend reading Altman and Hotchkiss (2005) and Duffie and Singleton (2012).

22.11   Letters of Credit

Finally, we should discuss one of the more under-appreciated issues in finance: how to handle financing and payments in risky situations. How do you buy factory equipment or a shipment of bauxite from people you do not know when a misstep could cost millions of USD? Bank guarantees of payments are often used for domestic trade; and, trade credit insurance is increasingly used to protect against defaults, failures, and breaches of contract.

However, trade credit insurance does not eliminate all loss: it still has a **deductible** (first loss amount covered by the insured). Furthermore, trade credit insurance works best for lower-risk transactions: those between repeat buyers and sellers in developed economies. We need a credit instrument for high-risk or one-off interactions so that people of wildly-varying credit with no history of mutual trade can still conduct commerce.

One solution is a **letter of credit** (sometimes called an LoC, LC, or L/C) which is a contractual promise by the **issuing (buyer's) bank** to pay promised funds for specified goods if certain conditions are met. This allows buyer and seller to worry less about each other's credit. Letters of credit are **self-liquidating** methods of secure payment; using an LoC extinguishes the contract upon fulfillment.

The rules for letters of credit are set by the International Chamber of Commerce, an organization which predates the United Nations.[16] The latest iteration of rules governing letters of credit is UCP600 — the sixth revision of the Uniform Customs and Practice for Documentary Credits. UCP600 uses **incoterms**, pre-defined terms governing trade obligations, costs, and risks (such as transport and liability). The first UCP rules premiered in 1933; UCP600 took effect in 2007 and has been agreed upon by more than 175 countries.

The process of using a letter of credit is diagrammed in Figure 22.1. The process generally proceeds as follows, although 8–9–10–11 may be replaced with 8–10–11–9:[17]

---

[16]For those who say we need politicians to get along, the ICC is a wonderful counterexample.

[17]Note that when the buyer and seller have a history of trade, these procedures may be relaxed or abbreviated.

1. Buyer and seller negotiate a deal and agree to trade.
2. The buyer (**applicant**) applies for a letter of credit from their (issuing) bank.
3. If the buyer has sufficient credit or funds, the issuing bank issues the LoC and sends it to the **advising (seller's) bank**.
4. The advising bank inspects the LoC and, if the details they know are correct, sends it to the seller (**beneficiary**)
5. The seller inspects the LoC and, if the details are as agreed, brings the goods they are selling to the **carrier** (transporter).
6. The carrier accepts the goods and issues the shipper a **bill of lading** (BoL): a receipt listing the shipper (seller), goods, consignee (buyer), carrier, shipping and due dates, and any special instructions.
7. The goods are now transported from shipper to consignee.
8. At the same time, the BoL and LoC start a parallel journey retracing the LoC's initial path. The seller presents their (advising) bank with the LoC and BoL.
9. If all details are in order and match, the advising bank will often send the funds to the shipper.
10. The advising bank sends the BoL and LoC to the issuing bank.
11. If the BoL and LoC pass the issuing bank's inspection, they send the money to the advising bank and debit the buyer's account.
12. The issuing bank then sends the BoL to the Buyer.
13. The buyer gives the BoL to the carrier.
14. The buyer may then claim the goods from the carrier.

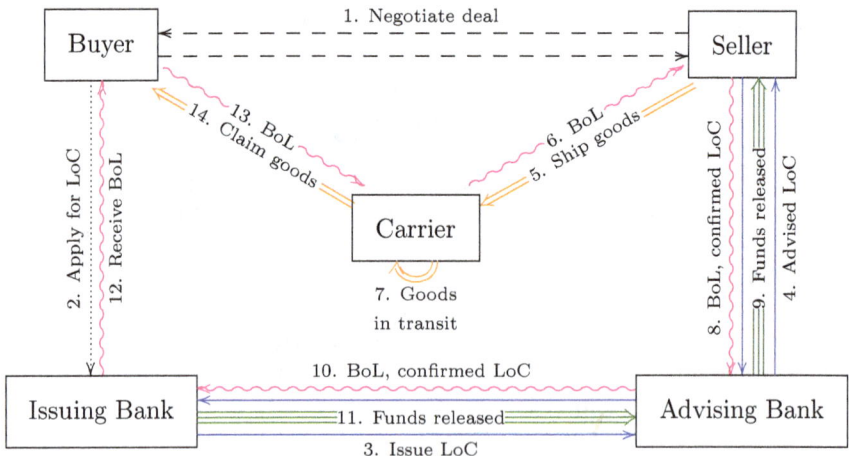

Figure 22.1: Process of buying goods with a letter of credit. The paths of various components of the trade are shown: LoC (—), bill of lading (∿), goods (═), and funds (≡). Standby LoC is not shown. For buyers and sellers with an ongoing relationship, these paths may vary or be simplified. In some cases, 8–9–10–11 may proceed as 8–10–11–9.

While this sounds complicated, this system has allowed people to do business in places where even the rule of law is tenuous. There are other details we could discuss like standby LoCs which act as insurance in case of any issues. However, we need not explore those issues to see how we can create creditworthy situations even when it might seem impossible.

22.12   Quiz

Try to answer these questions in five minutes. For your answers, just write the equations; do not evaluate them.

1. The default premium typically declines over a bond's life. | T   F

2. How are default rates and recovery rates related?

3. What are the top four bond rating agencies?

4. What is the lowest investment-grade long-term bond rating?

5. What is the meaning of "seasoning?"

6. What is new (compared to previous chapters) about the Merton model of the firm?

7. What (intuitively) is the "distance to default?"

8. Why do accounting models look at liquidity, coverage, and cashflow ratios?

9. What is the prediction from a default intensity model?

10. What is the cleanest market-based measure of probabilities of default and recovery rates?

11. (Bonus) What instrument helps counterparties of unknown credit conduct trade?

22.13   Exercises

Instructions

. . .

1. Suppose we have a firm with assets of EUR 20 bn and liabilities of EUR 12 bn. If asset volatility is 0.5, the firm pays out dividends at a yield of $\delta=1\%$, and the risk-free rate is 2%. Using the Samuelson (1965a)/McKean (1965) model, find the stock price and equity volatility for three scenarios: now (with assets of EUR 20 bn); if assets fell to EUR 16 bn; and, if assets fell to EUR 14 bn?

2. (Risky Business II) Suppose we are considering investing in a Venezuelan bond. The Venezuelans recently cast off *Chavismo*, but 17 years of rule by Chávez left the country in tatters: inflation and crime are high and debt owed is more than the reserves held. Furthermore, the country's main wealth (oil) has fallen greatly in value. Because of this, Venezuelan government bonds are trading at very high yields. If Venezuela is able to pay their debts, a bond will pay off $1000 in one year; if not, creditors will only get a partial recovery: a bond will pay off, say, $500. (This is hypothetical, but we will fix that shortly.)

a) If the bond is a zero-coupon bond and the probability of a default is $1/2$ — and an implied risk-free rate is 10% — what is the present value of the Venezuelan bond?

b) What is the yield of the Venezuelan bond?

c) Aswath Damodaran's country risk webpage (http://pages.stern.nyu.edu/~adamodar/New_Home_Page/dataarchived.html suggests that as of January 2017, Venezuelan debt had a default premium of 11.55%. (The 2018 data suggest a default premium of 10.25%, but you are trying to be more conservative.) What does that discount rate imply for the market price of the 1Y zero-coupon bond?

d) What does the difference between the risk-neutral price and market price suggest? Is this sensible? If yes, why; if not, how might this result?

e) Now suppose we can invest in a risky perpetuity. Each year we flip a coin. If the coin comes up heads, we get $15; otherwise, we get $30. What is the value of this perpetuity if we can invest in risk-free zero-coupon bonds yielding 10% annualized?

3. (The Land of Grace Exceeds the Grace Period) With what we know so far, we can see what financial markets say about the situation in Venezuela.[18]

Let p be the probability Venezuela defaults in a year and L be the loss given default (*i.e.* fraction of bond face not repaid). We assume defaulting in a year is independent of prior years; so, we get Bs.F.1000 back in t years if there are no defaults (probability $(1-p)^t$) and Bs.F.1000$\times(1-L)$ back otherwise.[19]

Below are the yields and implied prices of four Venezuelan government bonds as well as discount rates for investing over each time period. Prices are as of 25 January 2016:

---

[18]Yes, a new government came to power; but, the old problems have not yet been fixed.

[19]Bs.F. is the abbreviation for the Venezuelan currency VEF. The abbreviation comes from its name, *bolívares fuertes*... which is not so accurate a description of the currency.

t	Yield	B	r_f
1 year	49.90%	66.711	0.13%
5 years	38.56%	19.580	0.11%
15 years	35.37%	10.645	0.10%
20 years	28.63%	6.504	0.09%

Find the values of p and L that best explain these bond prices. Remember that your expected bond payoff will need to be scaled to get it in percentage of bond face ("1000" = "100"% of bond face); and, you need to compute the present value of the expected bond face percentage to match up with the current bond price. Finally, minimize the sum of squared differences between your predicted (modeled) bond price and the market price given.

a) Give the formula for the expected bond payoff.

b) Show how you modify that formula to get the present value of the expected percent of bond face.

c) Use that formula to find your estimated p and L. What are the estimates — and the sum of squared differences? (If you do not have a formula shown for the prior part, you cannot earn any points for this part.)

d) Are these findings reasonable? What are some weaknesses of the model, the data, or how the two relate?

e) Based on your model, which bond looks to be the most mispriced?

4. (Put Your Money Where Your Mouth Is) In the recent financial crisis, credit rating agencies were found to have been lackadaisical in the rigor of their rating process. Many economists and politicians attributed this to the fact that bond issuers pay the rating agencies to rate their bonds; thus, there is an incentive for rating agencies to give good ratings so issuers return with more business.

One remedy proposed by market participants was that rating agencies should have to write default protection (*i.e.* quote CDS prices) based on their ratings. With the potential to lose money if ratings are inaccurate or biased, rating agencies be incentivized to produce accurate ratings.

Comment on the pros and cons of this idea.

References

Altman, Edward I. "Financial Ratios, Discriminant Analysis and the Prediction of Corporate Bankruptcy". *Journal of Finance* 23.4 (1968), pp. 589–609. DOI: 10.1111/j.1540-6261.1968.tb00843.x.

Altman, Edward I. "The Importance and Subtlety of Credit Rating Migration". *Journal of Banking and Finance* 22.10–11 (1998), pp. 1231–1247. DOI: 10.1016/S0378-4266(98)00066-1.

— "Predicting Financial Distress of Companies: Revisiting the Z-Score and ZETA® Models". In: *Handbook of Research Methods and Applications in Empirical Finance*. Ed. by Adrian R. Bell, Chris Brooks, and Marcel Prokopczuk. Cheltenham, UK: Edward Elgar Publishing, 2013, pp. 428–456. DOI: 10.4337/9780857936097.00027.

Altman, Edward I. and Allan C. Eberhart. "Do Seniority Provisions Protect Bondholders' Investments?" *Journal of Portfolio Management* 20.4 (1994), pp. 67–75. DOI: 10.3905/jpm.1994.67.

Altman, Edward I., Robert G. Haldeman, and P. Narayanan. "ZETA™ Analysis: A New Model to Identify Bankruptcy Risk of Corporations". *Journal of Banking and Finance* 1.1 (1977), pp. 29–54. DOI: 10.1016/0378-4266(77)90017-6.

Altman, Edward I. and Edith Hotchkiss. *Corporate Financial Distress and Bankruptcy: Predict and Avoid Bankruptcy, Analyze and Invest in Distressed Debt*. 3rd ed. New York: Wiley, 2005. DOI: 10.1002/9781118267806.

Altman, Edward I. and Vellore M. Kishore. "Almost Everything You Wanted to Know about Recoveries on Defaulted Bonds". *Financial Analyst's Journal* 52.6 (1996). DOI: 10.2469/faj.v52.n6.2040.

Altman, Edward I. et al. "The Link Between Default and Recovery Rates: Theory, Empirical Evidence, and Implications". *Journal of Business* 78.6 (2005), pp. 2203–2228. DOI: 10.1086/497044.

Ayotte, Kenneth. *Disagreement and Capital Structure Complexity*. Working Paper. University of California-Berkeley School of Law, 2017.

Bachelier, Louis Jean-Baptiste Alphonse. "Théorie de la Spéculation". *Annales Scientifiques de l'École Normale Supérieure* 3.17 (1900).

Banasik, J., J. N. Crook, and L. C. Thomas. "Not if but When will Borrowers Default". *Journal of the Operational Research Society* 50.12 (1999), pp. 1185–1190. DOI: 10.2307/3010627.

Bauer, Julian and Vineet Agarwal. "Are Hazard Models Superior to Traditional Bankruptcy Prediction Approaches? A Comprehensive Test". *Journal of Banking and Finance* 40 (2014), pp. 432–442. DOI: 10.1016/j.jbankfin.2013.12.013.

Beaver, William H. "Financial Ratios As Predictors of Failure". *Journal of Accounting Research* 4.Empirical Research in Accounting: Selected Studies (1966), pp. 71–111. DOI: 10.2307/2490171.

— "Alternative Accounting Measures as Predictors of Failure". *The Accounting Review* 43.1 (1968), pp. 113–122. URL: http://www.jstor.org/stable/244122.

Beneish, Messod D. "The Detection of Earnings Manipulation". *Financial Analyst's Journal* 55.5 (1999), pp. 24–36. DOI: 10.2469/faj.v55.n5.2296.

Bermingham, Finbarr. "ANZ Stung by Nickel Fraud: What We Know". *Global Trade Review* (July 5, 2017). URL: https://www.gtreview.com/news/asia/anz-stung-by-nickel-fraud-what-we-know/.

Bharath, Sreedhar T. and Tyler Shumway. "Forecasting Default with the Merton Distance to Default Model". *Review of Financial Studies* 21.3 (2008), pp. 1339–1369. DOI: 10.1093/rfs/hhn044.

Bielecki, Tomasz R., Monique Jeanblanc, and Marek Rutkowski. "Pricing and Trading Credit Default Swaps in a Hazard Process Model". *Annals of Applied Probability* 18.6 (2008), pp. 2495–2529. DOI: 10.1214/00-AAP520.

Blanco, Roberto, Simon Brennan, and Ian W. Marsh. "An Empirical Analysis of the Dynamic Relation between Investment-Grade Bonds and Credit Default Swaps". *Journal of Finance* 60.5 (2005), pp. 2255–2281. DOI: 10.1111/j.1540-6261.2005.00798.x.

Bolton, Patrick and Xavier Freixas. "Equity, Bonds, and Bank Debt: Capital Structure and Financial Market Equilibrium under Asymmetric Information". *Journal of Political Economy* 108.2 (2000), pp. 324–351. DOI: 10.1086/262121.

Bolton, Patrick and Martin Oehmke. "Should Derivatives Be Privileged in Bankruptcy?" *Journal of Finance* 70.6 (2015), pp. 2353–2394. DOI: 10.1111/jofi.12201.

Bortkiewicz, Ladislaus. *Das Gesetz der kleinen Zahlen*. Leipzig: B.G. Teubner, 1898.

Boudt, Kris, Ellen C. S. Paulus, and Dale W. R. Rosenthal. "Funding Liquidity, Market Liquidity and TED Spread: A Two-Regime Model". *Journal of Empirical Finance* 43 (2017), pp. 143–158. DOI: 10.1016/j.jempfin.2017.06.002.

Bronzin, Vincenz. *Theorie der Prämiengeschäfte*. Leipzig/Vienna: Franz Deuticke, 1908.

Brunnermeier, Markus K. and Lasse Heje Pedersen. "Market Liquidity and Funding Liquidity". *Review of Financial Studies* 22.6 (2009), pp. 2201–2238. DOI: 10.1093/rfs/hhn098.

Caballero, Ricardo J., Emmanuel Farhi, and Pierre-Olivier Gourinchas. "The Safe Asset Shortage Conundrum". *Journal of Economic Perspectives* 31.3 (2017), pp. 29–46. DOI: 10.1257/jep.31.3.29.

Campbell, John Y., Jens Hilscher, and Jan Szilagyi. "In Search of Distress Risk". *Journal of Finance* 63.6 (2008), pp. 2899–2939. DOI: 10.1111/j.1540-6261.2008.01416.x.

Carr, Peter and Liuren Wu. "A Simple Robust Link Between American Puts and Credit Protection". *Review of Financial Studies* 24.2 (2011), pp. 473–505. DOI: 10.1093/rfs/hhq129.

Crosbie, Peter and Jeff Bohn. *Modeling Default Risk*. San Francisco: Moody's KMV, 2003.

Crowder, Martin J. *Multivariate Survival Analysis and Competing Risks*. Boca Raton, FL: Chapman & Hall/CRC, 2012. DOI: 10.1201/b11893. URL: https://www.crcpress.com/Multivariate-Survival-Analysis-and-Competing-Risks/Crowder/p/book/9781138199606.

Cruces, Juan J. and Christoph Trebesch. "Sovereign Defaults: The Price of Haircuts". *American Economic Journal: Macroeconomics* 5.3 (2013), pp. 85–117. DOI: 10.1257/mac.5.3.85.

Das, Sanjiv R., Gifford Fong, and Gary Geng. "Impact of Correlated Default Risk on Credit Portfolios". *Journal of Fixed Income* 11.3 (2001), pp. 9–19. DOI: 10.3905/jfi.2001.319301.

Das, Sanjiv R., Paul Hanouna, and Atulya Sarin. "Accounting-Based versus Market-Based Cross-Sectional Models of CDS Spreads". *Journal of Banking and Finance* 33.4 (2009), pp. 719–730. DOI: 10.1016/j.jbankfin.2008.11.003.

Das, Sanjiv R. et al. "Correlated Default Risk". *Journal of Fixed Income* 16.2 (2006), pp. 7–32. DOI: 10.3905/jfi.2006.656006.

Das, Sanjiv R. et al. "Common Failings: How Corporate Defaults Are Correlated". *Journal of Finance* 62.1 (2007), pp. 93–117. DOI: 10.1111/j.1540-6261.2007.01202.x.

Deakin, Edward B. "A Discriminant Analysis of Predictors of Business Failure". *Journal of Accounting Research* 10.1 (1972), pp. 167–179. DOI: 10.2307/2490225.

Devroye, Luc. *Non-uniform Random Variate Generation*. New York: Springer-Verlag, 1986. URL: http://luc.devroye.org/rnbookindex.html.

Duffie, Darrell. "Credit Swap Valuation". *Financial Analyst's Journal* 55.1 (1999), pp. 73–87. DOI: 10.2469/faj.v55.n1.2243.

Duffie, Darrell, Leandro Saita, and Ke Wang. "Multi-Period Corporate Default Prediction with Stochastic Covariates". *Journal of Financial Economics* 83.3 (2007), pp. 635–665. DOI: 10.1016/j.jfineco.2005.10.011.

Duffie, Darrell and Kenneth J. Singleton. *Credit Risk: Pricing, Measurement, and Management*. Princeton, NJ: Princeton University Press, 2012.

Duffie, Darrell et al. "Frailty Correlated Default". *Journal of Finance* 64.5 (2009), pp. 2089–2123. DOI: 10.1111/j.1540-6261.2009.01495.x.

Engle, Robert F. and Jeffrey R. Russell. "Autoregressive Conditional Duration: A New Model for Irregularly Spaced Transaction Data". *Econometrica* 66.5 (1998), pp. 1127–1162. DOI: 10.2307/2999632.

Ericsson, Jan, Kris Jacobs, and Rodolfo Oviedo. "The Determinants of Credit Default Swap Premia". *Journal of Financial and Quantitative Analysis* 44.1 (2009), pp. 109–132. DOI: 10.1017/S0022109009090061.

Erlang, A. K. "The Theory of Probabilities and Telephone Conversations". *Nyt Tidsskrift for Matematik* B.20 (1909), pp. 33–39.

Fons, Jerome S. "Using Default Rates to Model the Term Structure of Credit Risk". *Financial Analyst's Journal* 50.5 (1994), pp. 25–32. DOI: 10.2469/faj.v50.n5.25.

Forte, Santiago and Juan Ignacio Peña. "Credit Spreads: An Empirical Analysis on the Informational Content of Stocks, Bonds, and CDS". *Journal of Banking and Finance* 33.11 (2009), pp. 2013–2025. DOI: 10.1016/j.jbankfin.2009.04.015.

Frame, W. Scott, Michael Padhi, and Lynn Woosley. "Credit Scoring and the Availability of Small Business Credit in Low- and Moderate-Income Areas". *The Financial Review* 39.1 (2004), pp. 35–54. DOI: 10.1111/j.0732-8516.2004.00066.x.

Frame, W. Scott, Aruna Srinivasan, and Lynn Woosley. "The Effect of Credit Scoring on Small-Business Lending". *Journal of Money, Credit, and Banking* 33.3 (2001), pp. 813–825. DOI: 10.2307/2673896.

Gerber, Hans U. and Elias S.W. Shiu. "Martingale Approach to Pricing Perpetual American Options". *ASTIN Bulletin* 24.2 (1994), pp. 195–220. DOI: 10.2143/AST.24.2.2005065.

Geske, Robert. "The Valuation of Compound Options". *Journal of Financial Economics* 7.1 (1979), pp. 63–81. DOI: 10.1016/0304-405X(79)90022-9.

Giesecke, Kay. "Default and Information". *Journal of Economic Dynamics and Control* 30.11 (2006), pp. 2281–2303. DOI: 10.1016/j.jedc.2005.07.003.

Goetzmann, William N. *Money Changes Everything: How Finance Made Civilization Possible*. Princeton University Press, 2016.

Gorton, Gary, Stefan Lewellen, and Andrew Metrick. "The Safe-Asset Share". *American Economic Review: Papers and Proceedings* 102.3 (2012), pp. 101–106. DOI: 10.1257/aer.102.3.101.

Guo, Xin, Robert A. Jarrow, and Yan Zeng. "Modeling the Recovery Rate in a Reduced Form Model". *Mathematical Finance* 19.1 (2009), pp. 73–97. DOI: 10.1111/j.1467-9965.2008.00358.x.

Hawkes, Alan G. "Spectra of Some Self-Exciting and Mutually Exciting Point Processes". *Biometrika* 58.1 (1971), pp. 83–90. DOI: 10.1093/biomet/58.1.83.

Heaton, John C., Deborah Lucas, and Robert L. McDonald. "Is Mark-to-market Accounting Destabilizing? Analysis and Implications for Policy". *Journal of Monetary Economics* 57.1 (2010), pp. 64–75. DOI: 10.1016/j.jmoneco.2009.11.005.

Home, Andy. "Qingdao Scandal Casts a Long Shadow over Metal Markets". *Reuters* (Dec. 18, 2014). URL: https://www.reuters.com/article/us-qingdao-metals-ahome/qingdao-scandal-casts-a-long-shadow-over-metal-markets-andy-home-idUSKBN0JW18620141218.

Houweling, Patrick and Ton Vorst. "Pricing Default Swaps: Empirical Evidence". *Journal of International Money and Finance* 24.8 (2005), pp. 1200–1225. DOI: 10.1016/j.jimonfin.2005.08.009.

Hu, Yen-Ting and William Perraudin. *The Dependence of Recovery Rates and Defaults*. working paper 1961142. Risk Control working paper 6/1. SSRN, 2006. DOI: 10.2139/ssrn.1961142.

Hull, John, Mirela Predescu, and Alan White. "The Relationship between Credit Default Swap Spreads, Bond Yields, and Credit Rating Announcements". *Journal of Banking and Finance* 28.11 (2004), pp. 2789–2811. DOI: 10.1016/j.jbankfin.2004.06.010.

Hull, John C., Izzy Nelken, and Alan D. White. "Merton's Model, Credit Risk, and Volatility Skews". *Journal of Credit Risk* 1.1 (2004), pp. 3–27. DOI: 10.21314/JCR.2005.004.

Jackson, Christopher. "flexsurv: A Platform for Parametric Survival Modeling in R". *Journal of Statistical Software* 70.8 (2016). R package version 7.3-45, pp. 1–33.

DOI: 10.18637/jss.v070.i08. URL: https://CRAN.R-project.org/package=
flexsurv.

Jarrow, Robert A., David Lando, and Stuart M. Turnbull. "A Markov Model for the
Term Structure of Credit Risk Spreads". *Review of Financial Studies* 10.2 (1997),
pp. 481–523. DOI: 10.1093/rfs/10.2.481.

Jarrow, Robert A., David Lando, and Fan Yu. "Default Risk and Diversification:
Theory and Empirical Implications". *Mathematical Finance* 15.1 (2005), pp. 1–26.
DOI: 10.1111/j.0960-1627.2005.00208.x.

Jarrow, Robert A. and Stuart M. Turnbull. "Pricing Derivatives on Financial Securities Subject to Credit Risk". *Journal of Finance* 50.1 (1995), pp. 53–85. DOI:
10.1111/j.1540-6261.1995.tb05167.x.

Jarrow, Robert A. and Fan Yu. "Counterparty Risk and the Pricing of Defaultable
Securities". *Journal of Finance* 56.5 (2001), pp. 1765–1799. DOI: 10.1111/0022-
1082.00389.

Jones, E. Philip, Scott P. Mason, and Eric Rosenfeld. *Contingent Claims Valuation of
Corporate Liabilities: Theory and Empirical Tests.* Working Paper 1143. NBER,
1983. DOI: 10.3386/w1143.

— "Contingent Claims Analysis of Corporate Capital Structures: an Empirical
Investigation". *Journal of Finance Papers and Proceedings* 39.3 (1984), pp. 611–
625. DOI: 10.1111/j.1540-6261.1984.tb03649.x.

Kaplan, Robert S. and Gabriel Urwitz. "Statistical Models of Bond Ratings: A
Methodological Inquiry". *Journal of Business* 52.2 (1979), pp. 231–261. DOI:
10.1086/296045.

Kealhofer, Stephen. "Quantifying Credit Risk I: Default Prediction". *Financial
Analyst's Journal* 59.1 (2003), pp. 30–44. DOI: 10.2469/faj.v59.n1.2501.

— "Quantifying Credit Risk II: Debt Valuation". *Financial Analyst's Journal* 59.3
(2003), pp. 78–92. DOI: 10.2469/faj.v59.n3.2534.

Kindelberger, Charles P. and Robert Aliber. *Manias, Panics, and Crashes: A History
of Financial Crises.* 5th ed. New York: Wiley, 2005.

Klein, Matthew C. "The Safe Asset Shortage". *The Economist* (Dec. 17, 2012). URL:
https://www.economist.com/blogs/freeexchange/2012/12/finance.

Kleinbaum, David G. and Mitchel Klein. *Survival Analysis: A Self-Learning Text.*
3rd ed. New York: Springer, 2012. DOI: 10.1007/978-1-4419-6646-9.

Lando, David. "On Cox Processes and Credit Risky Securities". *Review of Derivatives
Research* 2.2–3 (1998), pp. 99–120. DOI: 10.1007/BF01531332.

Leland, Hayne E. and Klaus Bjerre Toft. "Optimal Capital Structure, Endogenous
Bankruptcy, and the Term Structure of Credit Spreads". *Journal of Finance* 51.3
(1996), pp. 987–1019. DOI: 10.1111/j.1540-6261.1996.tb02714.x.

Liu, Yang, Elena H. Duggar, and Sharon Ou. *Sovereign Default and Recovery Rates,
1983–2016.* Data Report. Moody's Investors Services, June 30, 2017.

Longhofer, Stanley D. "Absolute Priority Rule Violations, Credit Rationing, and
Efficiency". *Journal of Financial Intermediation* 6.3 (1997), pp. 249–267. DOI:
10.1006/jfin.1997.0220.

Longstaff, Francis A., Sanjay Mithal, and Eric Neis. "Corporate Yield Spreads: Default Risk or Liquidity? New Evidence from the Credit Default Swap Market". *Journal of Finance* 60.5 (2005), pp. 2213–2253. DOI: 10.1111/j.1540-6261. 2005.00797.x.

Lucas, Douglas J. "Default Correlation and Credit Analysis". *Journal of Fixed Income* 4.4 (1995), pp. 76–87. DOI: 10.3905/jfi.1995.408124.

Markit. *Markit Credit Indices: A Primer*. London: IHS Markit, July 2014. URL: http://content.markitcdn.com/corporate/Company/Files/DownloadFiles? CMSID=577e364482314b31b158ae2c2cecc89d.

Marshall, A. W. and Ingram Olkin. "A Multivariate Exponential Distribution". *Journal of the American Statistical Association* 62.317 (1967), pp. 30–44. DOI: 10.2307/2282907.

McCullagh, Peter and John A. Nelder. *Generalized Linear Models*. 2nd ed. London: Chapman and Hall, 1989.

McKean Jr., Henry P. "Appendix: A Free Boundary Problem for the Heat Equation Arising from a Problem in Mathematical Economics". *Industrial Management Review* 6.2 (1965), pp. 32–39.

McNeil, Alexander J. and Jonathan P. Wendin. "Bayesian Inference for Generalized Linear Mixed Models of Portfolio Credit Risk". *Journal of Empirical Finance* 14.2 (2007), pp. 131–149. DOI: 10.1016/j.jempfin.2006.05.002.

Merton, Robert C. "On the Pricing of Corporate Debt: The Risk Structure of Interest Rates". *Journal of Finance Papers and Proceedings* 29.2 (1974), pp. 449–470. DOI: 10.1111/j.1540-6261.1974.tb03058.x.

Modigliani, Franco and Merton H. Miller. "The Cost of Capital, Corporation Finance and the Theory of Investment". *American Economic Review* 48.3 (1958), pp. 261–297. DOI: 10.1257/aer.48.3.261.

— "Corporate Income Taxes and the Cost of Capital: A Correction". *American Economic Review* 53.3 (1963), pp. 433–443. DOI: 10.1257/aer.53.3.433.

Ohlson, James A. "Financial Ratios and the Probabilistic Prediction of Bankruptcy". *Journal of Accounting Research* 18.1 (1980), pp. 109–131. DOI: 10.2307/2490395.

Pan, Jun and Kenneth J. Singleton. "Default and Recovery Implicit in the Term Structure of Sovereign CDS Spreads". *Journal of Finance* 63.5 (2008), pp. 2345–2384. DOI: 10.1111/j.1540-6261.2008.01399.x.

Piotroski, Joseph D. "Value Investing: The Use of Historical Financial Statement Information to Separate Winners from Losers". *Journal of Accounting Research* 38.Supplement: Studies on Accounting Information and the Economics of the Firm (2000), pp. 1–41. DOI: 10.2307/2672906.

Rauh, Joshua D. and Amir Sufi. "Capital Structure and Debt Structure". *Review of Financial Studies* 23.12 (2010), pp. 4242–4280. DOI: 10.1093/rfs/hhq095.

Rosenthal, Dale W. R. "Trade Classification and Nearly-Gamma Random Variables". PhD dissertation. Department of Statistics: University of Chicago, 2008.

Rosenthal, Dale W.R. *Approximating Correlated Defaults*. Working Paper 1317865.

SSRN, 2018. DOI: 10.2139/ssrn.1317865. URL: http://ssrn.com/abstract=1317865.

Russell, Jeffrey R. *Econometric Modeling of Multivariate Irregularly-Spaced High-Frequency Data.* working paper. University of Chicago, Nov. 1999. URL: http://faculty.chicagobooth.edu/jeffrey.russell/research/multi.pdf.

Samuelson, Paul A. "Proof That Properly Anticipated Prices Fluctuate Randomly". *Industrial Management Review* 6.2 (1965), pp. 41–49.

— "Rational Theory of Warrant Pricing". *Industrial Management Review* 6.2 (1965), pp. 13–32.

Sloan, Richard G. "Do Stock Prices Fully Reflect Information in Accruals and Cash Flows about Future Earnings?" *The Accounting Review* 71.3 (1996), pp. 289–315. URL: http://www.jstor.org/stable/248290.

Taylor, Sarah and Guy Hardaker. *Qingdao: Judgment in* Mercuria v Citigroup *in London's Commercial Court.* Briefing. Holman Fenwick Willan, May 22, 2015. URL: http://www.hfw.com/downloads/HFW-Qingdao-judgment-in-Mercuria-v-Citigroup-May-2015.pdf.

Tham, Engen. "Special Report: 'Ghost Collateral' Haunts Loans across China's Banking System". *Reuters* (May 31, 2017). URL: http://www.reuters.com/article/us-china-collateral-fake-specialreport/special-report-ghost-collateral-haunts-loans-across-chinas-banking-system-idUSKBN18R1NP.

Therneau, Terry M. *survival: A Package for Survival Analysis in S.* R package version 2.38. 2015. URL: https://CRAN.R-project.org/package=survival.

Vasicek, Oldrich Alfons. *Credit Valuation.* Unpublished paper. KMV Corporation, 1984.

Venables, W. N. and B. D. Ripley. *Modern Applied Statistics with S.* 4th ed. R package version 7.3-45. New York: Springer-Verlag, 2002. DOI: 10.1007/978-0-387-21706-2. URL: http://www.stats.ox.ac.uk/pub/MASS4.

Yu, Fan. "Correlated Defaults in Intensity-Based Models". *Mathematical Finance* 17.2 (2007), pp. 155–173. DOI: 10.1111/j.1467-9965.2007.00298.x.

Chapter 23

Structured Products and Private Equity

One of the less-understood recent innovations in finance is structured finance. **Structured products** are derivatives, often customized, which package instruments together to deliver a product with desired cashflows.[1] These cashflows are typically structured to attract investors, shift risk, or enable certain investments. Structured products often aggregate, sort, and then disaggregate cashflows; however, this is not a strict requirement. **Private equity** is investment in private firms or in public firms with the intention of taking them private — often to restructure them and re-offer them to the public.

If it sounds like a structured product is a portfolio or portfolio derivative, you are correct. If the above definitions do not seem to be as clear about what is and is not a structured product...well, you are correct again. A number of financial instruments can considered to be structured products even if not always labeled so. Although private equity seems unrelated, the cashflow structures are similar.

The purpose of this chapter is to discuss a number of common structured products, explain some of the technologies used in structuring, briefly explore some of the modeling issues for these instruments, and discuss private equity.

23.1   Mortgages

Real estate is one of the most widely-held investments; however, each property is unique. A portfolio is an excellent technology for aggregating many disparate investments and making the (collective) analysis tractable. Therefore, it is natural that we begin by discussing **mortgages**: loans used to purchase real estate.

Payment terms are generally structured to have monthly payments for some

---

[1]For those outside the US, substitute the word "bespoke" for "customized."

fixed number of years with interest at a fixed or adjustable rate. Adjustable-rate mortgages (ARMs) have an initial period where the interest rate is fixed and then a period for how frequently the rate adjusts. For example, a "5/1" ARM has a fixed rate for the first five years which then adjusts every year after that until the mortgage is repaid.

Mortgages are either **open** or **closed** to **prepayments**: partial or full early repayment. Prepayment is commonly done to refinance a mortgage if lower interest rates are available, if the owner moves and sells the property, in some cases if the borrower defaults, or if the owner wants to cash out some of their equity. For lenders, prepayment is a negative feature: prepayments by borrowers seeking a lower interest rate leave lenders unable to re-lend at the same interest rate without taking more credit risk. Since ARMs have floating rates, most are open to prepayments.

The most-common terms vary by market. For example, 30-year open fixed-rate mortgages are typical in the US and Denmark; 5-year closed fixed-rate mortgages are typical in Canada; 25-year adjustable-rate mortgages are common in the UK; and, 20-year fixed rate mortgages with some refinancing penalties are common in Germany. In other parts of Europe, however, adjustable-rate mortgages are the most common. An excellent overview of cross-country variation in mortgages is given by Campbell (2013).

23.1.1   *Amortization*

Borrowers typically prefer payments which are **amortized**: payments are constant but the balance of principal versus interest in each payment varies. We can easily figure out the per-period payment π for a loan of principal P, interest rate r, term T in years, and n payments/year by finding the annuity with the same net present value. This is easily found as a difference of perpetuities:

$$P = \frac{\pi}{r/n} \left(1 - \frac{1}{(1 + r/n)^{nT}} \right) \tag{23.1}$$

$$\pi = \frac{Pr}{n \left(1 - \frac{1}{(1+r/n)^{nT}} \right)}. \tag{23.2}$$

However, since the payments are amortizing, a natural question is what the principal $\pi_{P,t}$ and interest $\pi_{i,t}$ is in a given payment at time $t = 1, \ldots, nT$. We can easily find this by finding $\pi_{P,t}$ as the difference of annuities from $t_1 \to t_{nT}$ and $t_2 \to t_{nT}$. This difference is just the present value of the current payment, since all of those present values sum to the loan principal:

$$\pi_{P,t} = \frac{\pi}{(1 + r/n)^{nT-t+1}}, \tag{23.3}$$

$$\pi_{i,t} = \pi - \pi_{P,t} = \pi \left(1 - \frac{1}{(1 + r/n)^{nT-t+1}} \right). \tag{23.4}$$

To see this (and many other behaviors) over time, we are going to use stacked area plots. These are implemented cleanly in the **areaplot** *R* package.

The stacked plot on the left side of Figure 23.1 shows us what payments look like. We can easily implement this in *R* for a ¤300000 mortgage at 6.25% fixed for 30 years:[2]

```
principal <- 300000  # mortgage principal
n.peryr <- 12  # monthly = 12 payments per year
T <- 30    # 30-year mortgage
r <- 0.0625  # 6.25%
t <- 1:(n.peryr*T)
pmt.level <- principal*r/(n.peryr*(1-1/(1+r/n.peryr)^(n.peryr*T)))
pmt.principal <- pmt.level/(1+r/n.peryr)^(n.peryr*T-t+1)
pmt.interest <- pmt.level-pmt.principal

areaplot(t, data.frame(pmt.interest, pmt.principal), col=c("red","blue"),
         ylim=c(0,pmt.level), border=FALSE)
```

23.1.2 Prepayments for a Single Mortgage

If a borrower prepays their mortgage, that reduces the principal outstanding. What does this do to the schedule of payments? Typically, prepayments made on a mortgage do not lower the per-period payment; instead, they shorten (**curtail**) the mortgage life. This affects the interest due in a given payment which means that the principal paid per period increases.

The right side of Figure 23.1 shows the effect of a borrower paying an extra 5% per payment toward the principal balance. The mortgage is finally repaid in the 316-th month ($26\frac{1}{3}$ years), a 12.2% reduction in the mortgage's life.

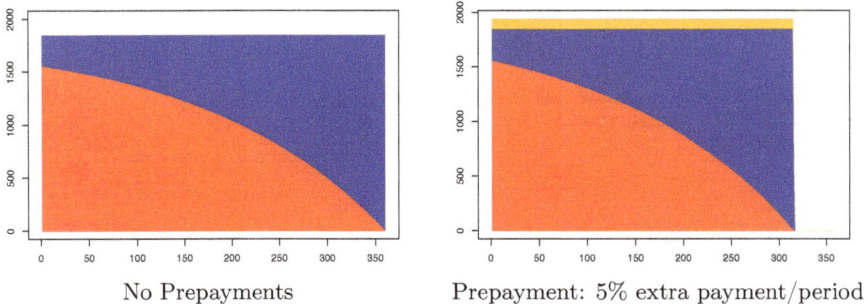

No Prepayments   Prepayment: 5% extra payment/period

Figure 23.1: Amortized payments for a ¤300000 30-year mortgage at 6.25% interest with no prepayments (left) and prepayments of 5% extra each payment (right). The interest component of each payment is in red; the principal component is in blue; and, the prepayment amount is in orange.

---

[2]The "¤" symbol is a generic currency symbol. You can find it throughout this text next to the reference mark "✱" (which indicates an aside). Since the two look like inversions of one another and the asides are about finance, they are apropos partners to help you navigate the text.

The R code to calculate interest and principal with prepayments and create the plot in Figure 23.1 is straightforward. While the `for` loop is not efficient, it does clarify the calculations.

```
principal.start <- 300e3  # mortgage principal
n.peryr <- 12  # monthly = 12 payments per year
T <- 30   # 30-year mortgage
r <- 0.0625  # 6.25%
t <- 1:(n.peryr*T)
## calculate level monthly payment
pmt.level <- principal.start*r/(n.peryr*(1-1/(1+r/n.peryr)^(n.peryr*T)))

## Prepay an extra 5\% each payment
pmt.prepay.plan <- 0.05*pmt.level

## In production code, this would be more elegant; however,
## a for loop shows the intuition better than other approaches
num.pmts <- n.peryr*T
principal.left <- c(principal.start, rep(0,num.pmts-1))
pmt.interest <- pmt.principal <- pmt.prepays <- rep(0, num.pmts)
for (i in 1:num.pmts) {
    pmt.interest[i] <- principal.left[i]*r/n.peryr
    pmt.principal[i] <- pmt.level - pmt.interest[i]
    if (pmt.principal[i] > principal.left[i]) {
        ## do not repay more than principal remaining
        pmt.principal[i] <- principal.left[i]
        ## stop the loop; mortgage is paid off
        break
    } else {
        ## do not prepay more than principal remaining after normal payment
        pmt.prepays[i] <- pmt.prepay.plan
        if ((pmt.principal[i] + pmt.prepays[i]) > principal.left[i]) {
            pmt.prepays[i] <- principal.left[i] - pmt.principal[i]
            ## stop the loop; mortgage is paid off
            break
        }
    }
    if (i < num.pmts) {
        principal.left[i+1] <- principal.left[i] - pmt.principal[i] - pmt.prepays[i]
    }
}

areaplot(t,data.frame(pmt.interest, pmt.principal, pmt.prepays),
        ylim=c(0,pmt.level+max(pmt.prepays)), col=c("red","blue","orange"),
        border=FALSE)
```

23.2 From Mortgages to Securities

Sometimes, mortgage loans made by banks are kept on their balance sheets. Increasingly, however, banks are **originators** who lend and then shift or sell the loan to another entity. Often, this shift or sale involves creating securities from mortgages. That enables borrowers to access the capital markets and not just local lenders, encourages competition in funding and pricing, and may free up the bank's balance sheet to make other loans. These processes lower interest rates for borrowers.[3]

---

[3]Bolton and Freixas (2000) discuss other reasons for banks to transform loans into securities and note that these explain the prevalence of the practice.

Typically, mortgages are aggregated together into collections called **pools**. Pools and pool shares are more attractive than investing in an individual mortgage; diversification gives the pool lower risk than its constituent mortgages. That makes lenders more comfortable lending, requires less invasive disclosure by borrowers, and makes more money available to lower the cost of borrowing.

Pools may be granted legal rights as pass-through entities so payments are not taxed at the pool level. Sometimes, pools are put into a **special purpose vehicle** (SPV) (aka **special purpose entity**, SPE): a portfolio held and administered by a company with its own assets and liabilities separate from the bank which created it.[4] Pools are often **ring-fenced**: beyond the reach of the bank's creditors. If the issuing/originating bank fails or goes bankrupt, the pools are safe. However, a key question is what **recourse** — avenues for legal remedies — are available to lenders in the event of a default.

We typically characterize a pool by a few measures of the mortgages it holds (often weighted by mortgage principal): the notional value, the **weighted average coupon** (WAC), the **weighted average maturity** (WAM, in years), and the **weighted average loan age** (WALA, often 30−WAM in the US).[5] Since mortgages require administration, the trust often charges fees for servicing the mortgages. Thus investors in a pool do not receive the WAC but the WAC less fees.

23.2.1 *Covered Bonds*

One type of security, **covered bonds**, have long been a hallmark of the German and Danish mortgage markets. There they are known as *Pfandbriefe* and *realkreditobligationer* and have existed since their creation in 1769 in Prussia by Frederick the Great (and shortly thereafter for Denmark). German *Pfandbriefe* are even used to fund ship and aircraft loans as well as state debt.[6] More recently, Spain and France have issued large amounts of covered bonds.

Covered bonds are issued by mortgage banks; however, they are collateralized by the properties in the funded mortgages. This means that holders of covered bonds have dual recourse: in default they can seek recourse from the issuing bank and the underlying property (collateral). That forces originating banks to be more careful about the credit quality of mortgages they originate. This also means that the cover pool underlying a covered bond is not an SPV/SPE.

Figure 23.2 illustrates how covered bonds are created, their cashflows, and recourse in the event of a default. On the left side of the figure, properties are mortgaged and become loan collateral. The originating mortgage bank then places the mortgages into the cover pool. The issuer issues covered bonds to investors,

---

[4]This is essentially an investment trust, which we will discuss in Chapter 25.

[5]While not often quoted, it would also be useful to know the weighted standard deviations of coupon, maturity, and average loan age.

[6]Further information about European covered bond markets may be found in Falch (2016), Platzer and Holbek (2016), and VDP (2017). ECBC (2017) has information on covered bond markets in many national markets.

who (effectively) become the lenders. On the right side of the figure, cashflows from mortgage payments go to the cover pool and then the issuing bank which allocates them to investors. In the event of a default, investors have dual recourse: to the issuing bank and the collateral property.

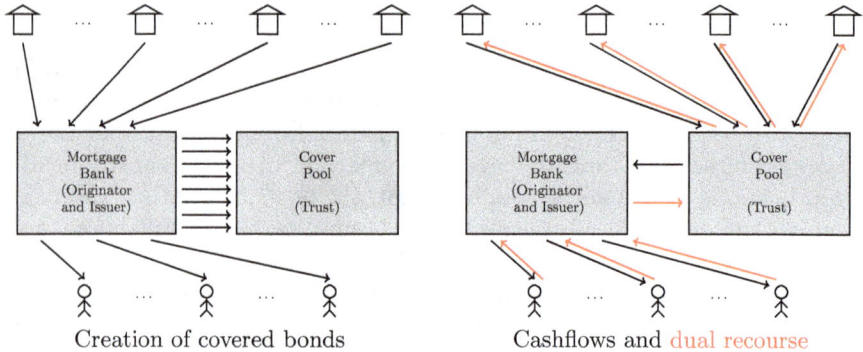

Creation of covered bonds   Cashflows and dual recourse

Figure 23.2: Diagrams showing the creation of covered bonds and cashflows with legal recourse. On the left, mortgages are originated by a mortgage bank which places the mortgages into a cover pool. The bank then issues covered bonds to investors. On the right, payment cashflows go to the cover pool and then the issuer which allocates them to investors. In a default, investors' recourse flows through the issuer and cover pool to the collateral (property); thus they have dual recourse.

Not shown is a common feature of covered bonds: **over-collateralization**. Since the originating bank issues the covered bonds, they often issue bonds for less notional than is in the cover pool. Thus they take the first losses from the cover pool to provide some level of protection to investors.

23.2.2   Mortgage-Backed Securities

A competing type of security is a **mortgage-backed security** (MBS), which is just like its name sounds: the security is backed solely by the mortgages in an SPV. Holders of mortgage pools — lenders — have no recourse to the originating bank. In some countries (*e.g.* the US), mortgages which meet certain criteria are called **conforming mortgages** and may be put into SPVs created by a government-sponsored entity; there is no issuing bank involved as there is with covered bonds.

Figure 23.3 illustrates how mortgage-backed securities are created, their cashflows, and recourse in the event of a default. On the left side of the figure, properties are mortgaged and become loan collateral. The originating mortgage bank then sells the mortgages into a pool in an SPV. The SPV issues mortgage-backed securities to investors, who become the lenders. On the right side of the figure, cashflows from mortgage payments go to the SPV which reapportions them to investors. In the event of a default, investors only have recourse to the collateral property since the SPV is a pass-through entity.

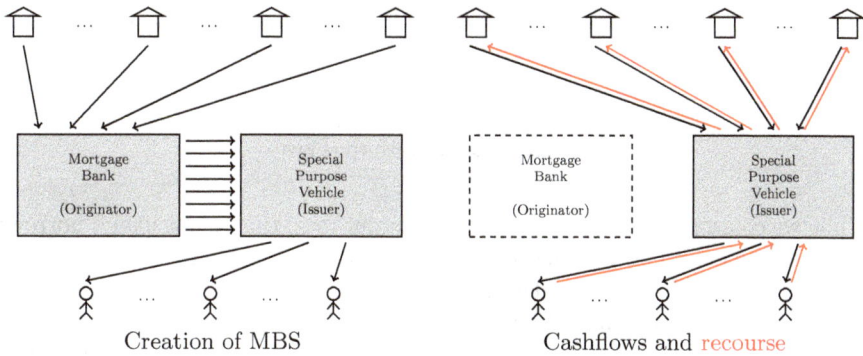

Figure 23.3: Diagrams showing the creation of mortgage-backed securities and cashflows with legal recourse. On the left, mortgages are originated by a mortgage bank which sells the mortgages into a pool in an SPV. The SPV issues mortgage-backed securities to investors. On the right, payment cashflows go to the SPV which allocates them to investors. In a default, investors' recourse flows through the SPV to the collateral (property).

Note that the originating bank has no obligations after forming the SPV, and investors have no recourse against the originating bank. Some economists believe this fueled the 2008 financial crisis since originating banks had little incentive to police the credit quality of their pools so long as they could sell the resulting MBSs.

The 2010 (US) Dodd-Frank Act was enacted to ameliorate future crises and it addresses this issue (in Section 941) by requiring originators to retain at least 5% of the credit risk of pools sold.[7] While this lacks dual recourse, it should better align the incentives of investors and originators.

23.2.3 *Prepayments in Pools*

When a single borrower prepays their mortgage, they shorten the mortgage life. In a pool, however, it is unlikely that all borrowers prepay: some may prepay early, some when it is advantageous (*e.g.* to refinance at lower interest rates), and some "dumbos" may never prepay. Thus prepayments do not similarly reduce the life of a pool. (They do reduce the *average* life of mortgages in the pool, however.)

With pools, we discuss prepayments in terms of the **conditional prepayment rate** (CPR), the equivalent of the mortality rate conditional on the remaining

---

[7]The 5% can be 5% of each tranche or a 5% first-loss (equity) tranche.

principal. For an annual prepayment rate ρ, the prepayment per period is:[8]

$$\pi_{\rho,t} = \underbrace{\left(P - \sum_{t'=1}^{t-1} \pi_{P,t'}\right)}_{\text{outstanding principal}} \underbrace{\left(1 - (1-\rho)^{1/n}\right)}_{\text{per-period prepay rate}} . \qquad (23.5)$$

While we could model prepayment as a constant rate, that is not likely; borrowers probably self-select to be less likely to prepay early in the life of the mortgage. A prepayment model commonly used as a benchmark is the **PSA prepayment model**, created in 1985 by the Public Securities Association (now a part of the US self regulatory organization SIFMA). The PSA model says that mortgage prepayments rise from 0 at time $t = 0$ to 6% at month 30 and are constant at 6% from then forward. (Thus the first month sees an annualized prepayment rate of $\frac{1}{5}$%.) At month 30, the mortgage is considered "seasoned."

Prepayment assumptions are often quoted at **prepayment speeds** like "PSA 100" (the PSA model), "PSA 50" (half the prepayment rates), or "PSA 200" (double the prepayment rates). Suppose we had a \$30 mn pool of 30-year fixed-rate open mortgages with a WAC of 6.6% and a servicing fee of 0.35% (yielding an effective WAC of 6.25%). The amortization of this mortgage pool under various PSA prepayment speeds is shown in Figure 23.4.

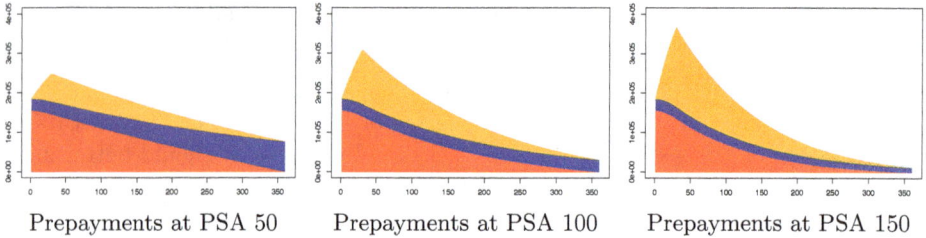

| Prepayments at PSA 50 | Prepayments at PSA 100 | Prepayments at PSA 150 |

Figure 23.4: Amortized payments for a \$30 mn pool of 30-year (360-month) mortgages with 6.25% WAC and prepayments at PSA 50 (left), PSA 100 (center), and PSA 150 (right). The interest component of each payment is in red; the principal component is in blue; and, the prepayment amount is in orange.

The R code to calculate interest, principal, and prepayment amounts for a mortgage pool is similar, but not identical, to the code for single mortgage prepayments. The code to create the plot in Figure 23.4 again uses a **for** loop for clarity.

```
principal.start <- 30e6  # pool principal
n.peryr <- 12  # monthly = 12 payments per year
T <- 30    # 30-year mortgage
r <- 0.0625  # 6.25%
t <- 1:(n.peryr*T)
```

---

[8]While rho (ρ) does not make a "p" sound in Greek, it looks "p-ish" and functions like an "r" — so you can think of ρ as the fraction of outstanding principal retired on an annualized basis.

```
## calculate level monthly payment
pmt.level <- principal.start*r/(n.peryr*(1-1/(1+r/n.peryr)^(n.peryr*T)))

## 100% PSA prepayment: rate up to 6% annual at 30 months
psa.speed <- 100   # 100% PSA
max.rate <- psa.speed/100*0.06
seasoned.month <- 30   # at 30 months, PSA says mortgages are seasoned
prepay.rate <- c(seq(max.rate/seasoned.month, max.rate, max.rate/seasoned.month),
                 rep(max.rate, n.peryr*T-seasoned.month))
prepay.monthly.survival <- (1-prepay.rate)^(1/n.peryr)
prepay.monthly.rate <- 1-prepay.monthly.survival

## In production code, this would be more elegant; however,
## a for loop shows the intuition better than other approaches
num.pmts <- n.peryr*T
principal.left <- c(principal.start, rep(0,num.pmts-1))
pmt.perperiod <- c(pmt.level, rep(0,num.pmts-1))
pmt.interest <- rep(0, num.pmts)
pmt.principal <- rep(0, num.pmts)
pmt.prepays <- rep(0, num.pmts)
for (i in 1:num.pmts) {
    pmt.interest[i] <- principal.left[i]*r/n.peryr
    pmt.principal[i] <- pmt.perperiod[i] - pmt.interest[i]
    if (pmt.principal[i] > principal.left[i]) {
        ## do not repay more than principal remaining
        pmt.principal[i] <- principal.left[i]
        ## stop the loop; pool is paid off!
        break
    } else {
        ## do not prepay more than principal remaining after normal payment
        pmt.prepays[i] <- (principal.left[i]-pmt.principal[i])*prepay.monthly.rate[i]
        if ((pmt.principal[i] + pmt.prepays[i]) > principal.left[i]) {
            pmt.prepays[i] <- principal.left[i] - pmt.principal[i]
            ## stop the loop; pool is paid off!
            break
        }
    }
    if (i < num.pmts) {
        principal.left[i+1] <- principal.left[i] - pmt.principal[i] - pmt.prepays[i]
        pmt.perperiod[i+1] <- pmt.perperiod[i]*prepay.monthly.survival[i]
    }
}

areaplot(t,data.frame(pmt.interest, pmt.principal, pmt.prepays),
         ylim=c(0,pmt.level+max(pmt.prepays)), col=c("red","blue","orange"),
         border=FALSE)
```

As with credit modeling, prepayment modeling should use survival analysis and linear modeling to create models that respond to the state of the economy and the yield curve. For example, prepayments increase when interest rates fall, since borrowers refinance fixed-rate mortgages; when housing turnover is high, because people move and repay the mortgage after selling their home; and, when defaults are high if the mortgage is guaranteed by the government or a government-sponsored entity.[9] We might also expect people to be less likely to move in winter; and, we might expect some of these effects to be related to borrowers' credit scores. Finally, there is the issue of **burnout** to consider: while prepayments rise when interest

---

[9]Lewis (1989) mentions early mortgage traders looking for properties likely to default soon to get the principal repaid quickly and earn a high rate of return.

rates fall, they tend to decline after a while as the pool becomes increasingly full of borrowers who will not or cannot prepay.

23.3   Securitization

While the above are effectively forms of securitization, we typically reserve the term **securitization** for the reallocation of principal, interest, prepayments, and losses among investors in SPV-issued securities (and not covered bonds). This is done by the SPV issuing different securities against the debt in its pool.

23.3.1   Terminology

When an SPV creates a number of different securities from mortgages, we often refer to it as a **collateralized mortgage obligation** (CMO). The birth and flowering of this market was largely driven by Salomon Brothers and is discussed in the amusing classic *Liar's Poker*.

A CMO might do something simple like separate the interest and principal to offer investors interest-only and principal-only instruments. However, a CMO might also offer some investors more protection from prepayments or defaults by shifting that risk to other investors willing to bear it for the potential of high returns.

The main technologies a CMO uses for reducing and shifting risk are diversification, **tranching** — a way of slicing up the portfolio and reapportioning risks and cashflows to different slices, and subordination of tranches.

We define a tranche by an **attachment point** (the fraction of debt subordinate to that tranche) and **detachment point** (which defines the subordination for the tranche and its subordinates. The difference between the detachment and attachment points also defines the "thickness" or fraction of notional impairment that the tranche can absorb. Together, the tranche definitions define the CMO's capital structure.

According to Chaudhary (2006), CMOs have five common structure archetypes:

1. **pass-through**: send shares of payments out to all investors;
2. **sequential**: tranches are paid principal sequentially;
3. **amortization classes**: tranches receive principal according to assumed prepayment rates;
4. **IO/PO**: tranches receive interest- or principal-only; and,
5. **indexed**: tranches receive interest based on an index, often a floating rate.

Obviously, these can be combined. In many of these cases, creating one type of desired tranche requires creating another **support tranche** which may have the opposite risk or which absorbs risk to protect the desired tranche. The division of these tranches is largely dictated by market demand. For example, there is a lot of demand for short- to intermediate-term debt yielding more than government bonds at low risk, less demand for longer-term debt at risk of prepayment, and little demand for risky debt which may pay off handsomely or receive little interest at all if interest rates drop over the life of the pool. An example is illuminating.

23.3.2 Example CMO

Suppose we have a sequential CMO funded with the previously-mentioned $30 mn pool of 30-year fixed-rate US mortgages — and that they are conforming mortgages securitized by a government-sponsored entity. Since they are backed by that entity and, implicitly, by the US government, we (for this example) ignore default risk.

We create a set of tranches A, B, C, and Z with seniority in that order: A is senior to B is senior to C is senior to Z: $A > B > C > Z$. The tranche structure is given in Table 23.1. Typically, the thinner tranches between A and Z are referred to as **mezzanine** tranches; and, the senior tranches sacrifice interest to fund the Z tranche which provides protection against prepayments.

Tranche	Attach	Detach	Principal Owed	Claims Interest On
A	22%	100%	$24.0 mn	$23.4 mn
B	14%	22%	$3.0 mn	$2.4 mn
C	5%	14%	$3.0 mn	$2.7 mn
Z	0%	5%	$0.0 mn	$1.5 mn

Table 23.1: Tranche structure for example sequential CMO. The senior tranches sacrifice some interest to fund the Z tranche which protects senior tranches from prepayments.

Typically, tranche names mirror bond ratings (as above); however, the names should not be conflated with ratings.[10] Furthermore, the naming of the Z tranche (aka "toxic waste") is puzzling. Some say it is because it does not get paid until near the end of its life making it like a zero-coupon bond; others say the Z tranche is named because the Z tranche absorbs the first prepayments (giving it the highest prepayment risk) and Z is as far from A as possible (connoting the worst rating).

The payment structure is often defined by the **waterfall**: the ordering and structure which dictates how tranches participate in principal and interest payments. A diagram showing the intuition for how tranches work and the cashflow waterfall is shown in Figure 23.5.

Figures 23.6 and 23.7 show the CMO at maturity with no prepayments and prepayment of some mortgages. Note that prepayments do not affect the cashflows received by senior tranches in this case; however, they do impose a loss on the Z tranche — since it loses out on curtailed interest payments. Prepayments normally hasten the repayment of senior tranches and, if they are severe enough, can affect the mezzanine or even A tranche.

There is another subtlety only hinted at in these diagrams: the Z tranche foregoes

---

[10]Credit rating documents even note that a "AAA" or "A" tranche rating is not equivalent to a "AAA" or "A" bond rating. This raises the question: why use the same rating names if the ratings should not be conflated?

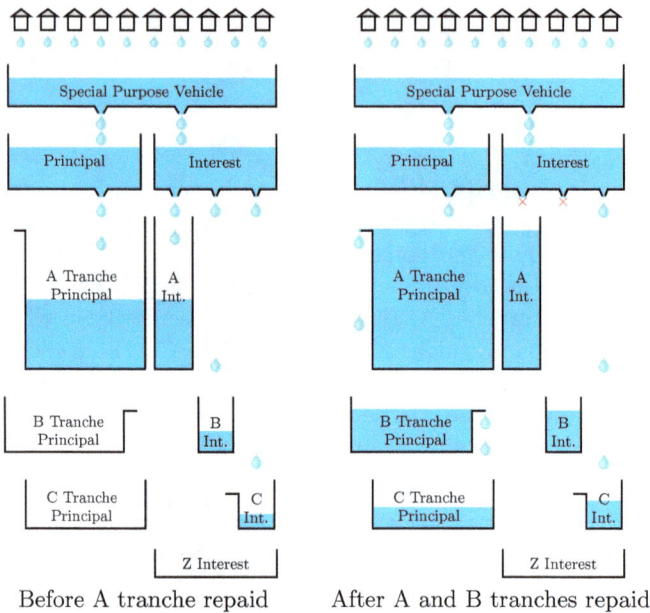

Figure 23.5: Cashflow "waterfall" as sequential CMO tranches are repaid in order.

interest until the senior tranches are repaid — but it then gets all of the remaining interest (if any). In effect, the Z tranche swaps its earlier interest payments for the later interest and principal payments of the senior tranches. Not only that, but those early interest payments are used to repay principal on the senior tranches.

While these colorful plots are intuitive, they are not how most structurers and mortgage analysts look at CMOs. When they discuss the waterfall, it is often defined in terms of a computer language that specifies the reapportionment and prioritization of cashflows for each tranche. Also typical is to show a **waterfall plot**: a plot of cashflows expected across time for each tranche under some assumption of prepayment rates. The plots use stacked areas versus time (as in Figure 23.4) to show when various tranches are paid off.

The code for allocating payments to tranches is a bit involved. Below is the *R* code for our example sequential CMO. The waterfall plot based on this code is shown in Figure 23.8. While waterfall plots typically show interest plotted on top, that is more confusing and so I have done otherwise here.

```
principal.start <- 30e6  # pool principal
n.peryr <- 12  # monthly = 12 payments per year
T <- 30   # 30-year mortgage
r <- 0.0625  # 6.25%
t <- 1:(n.peryr*T)

## tranche info
attach.pts <- list(a=0.22, b=0.14, c=0.05, z=0)
```

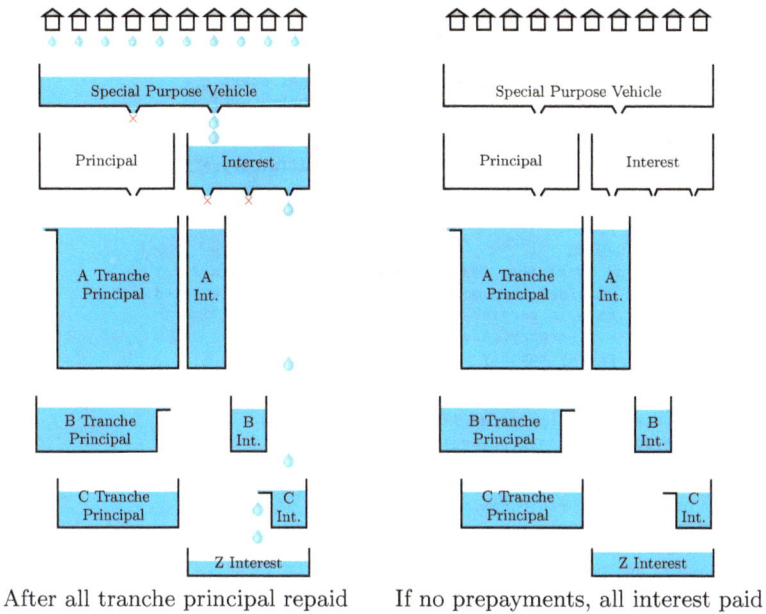

After all tranche principal repaid   If no prepayments, all interest paid

Figure 23.6: Cashflow "waterfall" for sequential CMO ending with no prepayments.

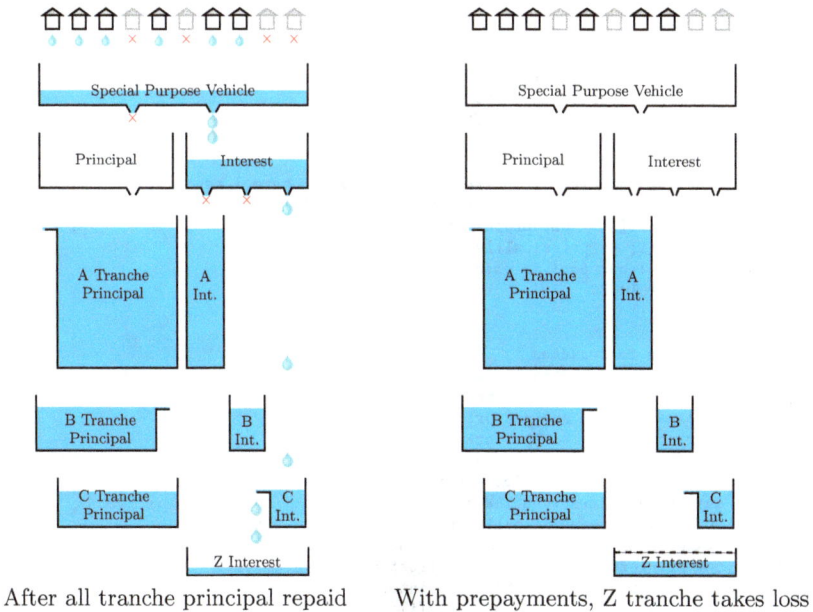

After all tranche principal repaid   With prepayments, Z tranche takes loss

Figure 23.7: Cashflow "waterfall" for sequential CMO ending with some prepayments.

```r
principal <- list(a=24e6,b=3e6,c=3e6,z=0)
interestbase <- list(a=(1-attach.pts$a)*principal.start,
                     b=(attach.pts$a-attach.pts$b)*principal.start,
                     c=(attach.pts$b-attach.pts$c)*principal.start,
                     z=(attach.pts$c-attach.pts$z)*principal.start)

## calculate level monthly payment
pmt.level <- principal.start*r/(n.peryr*(1-1/(1+r/n.peryr)^(n.peryr*T)))

## 100% PSA prepayment: rate up to 6% annual at 30 months
psa.speed <- 100  # 100% PSA
max.rate <- psa.speed/100*0.06
seasoned.month <- 30  # at 30 months, PSA says mortgages are seasoned
prepay.rate <- c(seq(max.rate/seasoned.month, max.rate, max.rate/seasoned.month),
                 rep(max.rate, n.peryr*T-seasoned.month))
prepay.monthly.survival <- (1-prepay.rate)^(1/n.peryr)
prepay.monthly.rate <- 1-prepay.monthly.survival

## In production code, this would be more elegant; however,
## a for loop shows the intuition better than other approaches
### Use fullword.variables for pool payments...
num.pmts <- n.peryr*T
principal.left <- c(principal.start, rep(0,num.pmts-1))
pmt.perperiod <- c(pmt.level, rep(0,num.pmts-1))
pmt.interest <- rep(0, num.pmts)
pmt.principal <- rep(0, num.pmts)
pmt.prepays <- rep(0, num.pmts)
### ... and use abbr.vars (abbreviated) for tranche payments
pmt.prin.a <- pmt.prin.b <- pmt.prin.c <- rep(0, num.pmts)
pmt.int.a <- pmt.int.b <- pmt.int.c <- pmt.int.z <- rep(0, num.pmts)
stop.loop <- FALSE
for (i in 1:num.pmts) {
    ## determine pool cashflows
    pmt.interest[i] <- principal.left[i]*r/n.peryr
    pmt.principal[i] <- pmt.perperiod[i] - pmt.interest[i]
    if (pmt.principal[i] > principal.left[i]) {
        ## do not repay more than principal remaining
        pmt.principal[i] <- principal.left[i]
        ## stop the loop; pool is paid off!
        stop.loop <- TRUE
    } else {
        ## do not prepay more than principal remaining after normal payment
        pmt.prepays[i] <- (principal.left[i]-pmt.principal[i])*prepay.monthly.rate[i]
        if ((pmt.principal[i] + pmt.prepays[i]) > principal.left[i]) {
            pmt.prepays[i] <- principal.left[i] - pmt.principal[i]
            ## stop the loop; pool is paid off!
            stop.loop <- TRUE
        }
    }
    ## allocate payments to tranches
    prin.to.allocate <- pmt.principal[i]+pmt.prepays[i]
    prinleft.a <- principal$a - sum(pmt.prin.a)
    prinleft.b <- principal$b - sum(pmt.prin.b)
    prinleft.c <- principal$c - sum(pmt.prin.c)
    ## Scale interest payments by fraction not repaid*interestbase
    ## Remaining interest will get allocated to principal repayment
    ## and then deferred interest on the z tranche
    pmt.int.a[i] <- prinleft.a/principal$a*interestbase$a*r/n.peryr
    pmt.int.b[i] <- prinleft.b/principal$b*interestbase$b*r/n.peryr
    pmt.int.c[i] <- prinleft.c/principal$c*interestbase$c*r/n.peryr
    prin.to.allocate <- prin.to.allocate + pmt.interest[i] -
        pmt.int.a[i] - pmt.int.b[i] - pmt.int.c[i]
    ## A is first in line for principal (Andropov is the name to say)
    if (prinleft.a > 0) {
        pmt.prin.a[i] <- min(prinleft.a, prin.to.allocate)
```

```
            prin.to.allocate <- prin.to.allocate - pmt.prin.a[i]
    }
    ## The letter B is next in line (for principal, Brezhnev's dead so he'll do just fine)
    if (prinleft.b > 0 & prin.to.allocate > 0) {
        pmt.prin.b[i] <- min(prinleft.b, prin.to.allocate)
        prin.to.allocate <- prin.to.allocate - pmt.prin.b[i]
    }
    ## The letter C is next for principal (C is for Chernenko)
    if (prinleft.c > 0 & prin.to.allocate > 0) {
        pmt.prin.c[i] <- min(prinleft.c, prin.to.allocate)
        prin.to.allocate <- prin.to.allocate - pmt.prin.c[i]
    }
    ## Finally, if any cashflows are left, they go to the Z tranche
    if (prin.to.allocate > 0)
        pmt.int.z[i] <- prin.to.allocate

    ## prepare for next iteration of loop
    if (i < num.pmts) {
        principal.left[i+1] <- principal.left[i] - pmt.principal[i] - pmt.prepays[i]
        pmt.perperiod[i+1] <- pmt.perperiod[i]*prepay.monthly.survival[i]
    }

    if (stop.loop)
        break
}

areaplot(t,data.frame(pmt.int.c,pmt.int.b,pmt.int.a,
                   pmt.prin.a,pmt.prin.b,pmt.prin.c,pmt.int.z),
        col=c("green","yellow","lightblue","blue","orange","darkgreen","red"),
        ylab="", border=FALSE)
text(100, 150000, "A", cex=2, col="white")
text(210, 60000, "B", cex=2)
text(255, 40000, "C", cex=2, col="white")
text(310, 20000, "Z", cex=2)
```

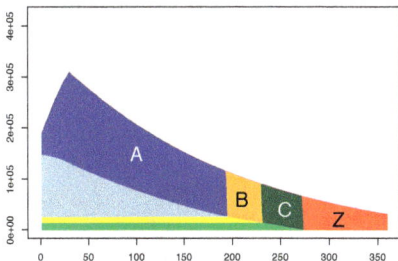

Prepayments at PSA 100   Prepayments at PSA 200

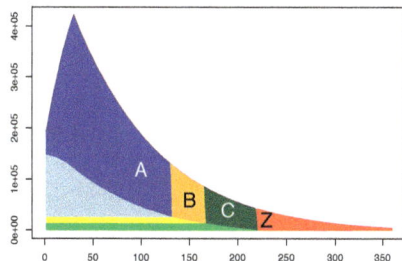

Figure 23.8: Waterfall plot for the example sequential CMO created from $30 mn of 30-year (360-month) fixed-rate mortgages with prepayments at PSA 100 (left) and PSA 200 (right). Tranche A is shown in blue colors; tranche B in orange colors; and tranche C in green colors. Dark colors are principal; light colors are interest. The Z tranche (all interest) is shown in red and is the last tranche to be repaid. Prepayments clearly shift the maturities of the senior tranches and diminish the value of the Z tranche.

We can see from looking at the waterfall plots that for prepayments at PSA 100, the A tranche is paid off after about 16 years; the B tranche is paid off a little more than 3 years after the A tranche; and, the C tranche is paid off about 4 years after the B tranche. If prepayments happen at PSA 200, the A tranche is paid off at 11–12 years. This yields a higher rate of return which helps counteract the reinvestment risk at what are probably lower interest rates. The C tranche lasts closer to 5 years at PSA 200. The Z tranche receives interest for the last 9 years or so at PSA 100 and the last 11 years or so at PSA 200. However, we can also see that the value of the Z tranche is greatly diminished by more prepayments while the value of the mezzanine tranches is slightly diminished.[11]

This illustrates the benefit of tranches. Investors who want a bond with low risk sacrifice a little bit of interest and accept some variation on the maturity to receive an intermediate-term bond that may look attractive compared to similar-maturity government bonds. Investors who are willing to take a bit more risk (including locking up their money for longer) may get a bargain on a mezzanine tranche — or not if there are many prepayments. Finally, the Z tranche offers potential for outsized returns in the future; however, investors must have a long time horizon and their ultimate payoff varies greatly.[12]

23.3.3   *The Option-Adjusted Spread*

The option of a homeowner to prepay their mortgage is valuable, especially if they refinance to lower their borrowing costs when interest rates fall. While the value gained by the homeowner is lost by mortgage lenders, valuing this option is difficult: the cost of refinancing, the coupon rate on a mortgage, and a borrower's economic state all affect the likelihood that a mortgage will be refinanced.[13]

Instead of valuing this option, we often look at a number of possible interest rate paths over the life of the mortgage, make some assumptions about prepayment behavior, and use that to infer prepayments and valuation for each interest rate path. We then determine the **option-adjusted spread** (OAS): the parallel shift of the yield curve in each of those states required to match current market prices. In this way, the OAS is similar to the implied volatility — the value of an unobserved parameter needed to agree with market prices.

The difficulty with this approach is path dependency: if interest rates fall and then recover to current levels, that has very different implications for prepayments than if rates stay flat or rise and then fall back to current levels. Path dependency means we cannot use a recombining tree as we did with options: each step in time doubles the number of states instead of merely adding one.[14] For this reason,

---

[11]While it is difficult to see in the plots, you can play with plotting order in the code to confirm that the interest payments to the B and C tranches are constant until they begin receiving principal payments.

[12]Many mortgage traders have stories of investors who bought Z tranches because the promised yields looked very high... and then "blew up" when prepayments eroded the value of their investments. Hence the Z tranche nickname of "toxic waste."

[13]Since moving usually results in prepayment, we might also consider modeling people moving as a function of the state of the economy.

[14]We could only use a splitting tree for interest rates below the level at the start of a mortgage or tranche life; however, this only (approximately) halves the computational workload.

simulation is a common method of sampling interest rate paths. Furthermore, we suspect interest rates are mean-reverting, *i.e.* following an Ornstein-Uhlenbeck process. This is easier to implement with simulation. We might even want to simulate the entire yield curve.[15]

23.3.4   *Tranche Warfare*

One problem with securitization and tranching is that tranches' interests may not be aligned. For example, consider the previously-mentioned strategy of buying government-guaranteed mortgages which are likely to default. Holders of the A tranche might want these mortgages to default and go to foreclosure since the government will return the lenders' principal sooner. That may increase the rate of return on the A tranche. On the other hand, holders of the Z tranche would much prefer a debt workout since foreclosure and prepayment (by the government) curtails some of their later interest.

This difference in incentives has been pointed out by one of the pioneers of mortgage securitization, Lewis Ranieri. He noted that traditionally, lenders who were fiduciaries almost always preferred a debt workout to foreclosure since it was ultimately less expensive for them and less traumatic to the borrower. With securitization, however, lenders may end up fighting or acting counter to how a fiduciary would act. Ranieri's comments can be found in more detail in Dungey (2007). Alloway (2010) discusses an actual instance of tranche warfare.

23.3.5   *Asset-Backed Securities*

With the development of mortgage-backed securities, it was natural to extend the ideas to other forms of debt. Many types of debt are typically securitized now and the securities are referred to as **asset-backed securities** (ABS).

Auto loans are another common form of debt and have a much shorter maturity (typically 5 years or less). They are also collateralized which explains why the first ABS issued were backed by auto loans (from Chrysler in 1985). *Student loans* are less common but have longer maturities. **Revolving lines of credit** are on-going loans which may be repeatedly used and repaid without maturing. *Home equity lines of credit* (HELOCs) and *credit card debt* are dominant in ABS issuance on revolving lines of credit.

Each of these presents its own idiosyncrasies. Auto loans are closer to mortgages in that they are also collateralized. Auto loan ABSs tend to sell tranches that form a standard coupon bond maturing early plus commercial paper which absorbs the remaining amortization.

HELOCs are also collateralized but are often second lien debt: they are subordinated to the original mortgage. Revolving lines of credit are different in that they

---

[15]For example: rates might tend to fall when the yield curve is flatter — but you already guessed that after reading Chapter 12!

do not naturally amortize; the principal fluctuates as new debt is incurred and paid off each month. Instead, these ABSs often have a fixed revolving period before a controlled amortization period where only old debts are paid down leading up to the maturity of the ABS.

23.4 Collateralized Debt Obligations

When CMOs were developed, they were largely created with conforming mortgages. Since these were backed implicitly or explicitly by a government guarantee of repayment, default risk was not a concern. In fact, defaults could increase the rate of return (as mentioned earlier).

As structured products incorporated more types of loans, default became another risk to worry about. In response, structurers created the **collateralized debt obligation** (CDO), a product to shift default risk.

Similar to MBSs, CMOs, and ABSs: debt instruments are collected and put in a trust which lives in a special purpose vehicle. The cashflows from the trust are tranched with the A tranche getting lower interest payments and the last tranche, the **equity tranche**, getting higher interest payments. However, the equity tranche absorbs the first defaults of debt in the trust.

As with our example CMO, the A tranche offers an intermediate-term bond — hopefully with lower risk but paying more than similarly-risky bonds. The equity tranche, on the other hand, offers handsome returns... if defaults are low; if defaults are high, the equity tranche can become worthless. Thus the equity tranche is more volatile than the Z tranche of a CMO. Demand for the A tranche is typically high; demand for mezzanine tranches is often lower; and, demand for equity tranches is the lowest. An example CDO capital structure is shown in Table 23.2.

Tranche	Attach	Detach	Principal	Interest
A	36%	100%	$256 mn	LIBOR + 30
B	22%	36%	$56 mn	LIBOR + 110
C	10%	22%	$48 mn	LIBOR + 250
Equity	0%	10%	$40 mn	Excess

Table 23.2: Tranche structure for example CDO. The senior tranches sacrifice some interest to fund the equity tranche which protects senior tranches from defaults.

While this would seem more complicated, we can return to our credit models. For example, suppose we have a CDO holding 100 equally-sized iid bonds with default times $\tau_i \overset{iid}{\sim} f(t|\theta)$ and $F(t|\theta) = \int_\Omega f(t|\theta)dt$ is the cdf of τ_i. Then, the density of the default time for a 10% equity tranche is when the CDO's 10-th loan defaults.[16] We

---

[16]It is more common for a CDO to hold 125 bonds; however, using 100 bonds makes the intuition more clear.

know this from the distribution of order statistics:

$$f_{\tau,\text{equity}}(t|\theta) = \frac{100!}{9!1!90!}F(t|\theta)^9 f(t|\theta)(1 - F(t|\theta))^{90}. \tag{23.6}$$

If defaults are correlated, we need a better model. One possibility is to find a default-replicating portfolio (which accounts for correlated defaults) and then estimate when 5% of that portfolio would default. This is explored in Rosenthal (2018).

23.4.1 Synthetic CDOs

While we can build a CDO with any form of debt or bonds — a **cash CDO**, we do not actually need those underliers. Since a CDO takes in cashflows and occasionally suffers a loss which eliminates some cashflows, we can build a **synthetic CDO** with credit default swaps. In that case, the CDO receives the financing cashflows and, in the event of default, trades the face value of defaulted bonds for the bonds themselves — and then proceeds through legal recourse (or a debt workout) to recover as much principal as possible. Note that in default this is the same as would occur with a loan-/bond-holding CDO.

One key difference between cash and synthetic CDOs is that CDS financing cashflows are smaller since they do not include any principal being repaid.

Finally, we should wonder if having many credit default swaps outstanding on a bond is innocuous. While it may seem harmless, having so many CDSs could create moral hazard (an incentive to be reckless or even cause problems). Even without malicious intent, it is reasonable to expect that bond and CDS holders will push the two instruments to be coherent in pricing. An excess of CDSs could therefore lead to something similar to pin risk with options: CDS hedging trades could become a dominant driver of movements in the underlying bond.

23.4.2 CDO²s: The Cream of the Crap

Some structurers who were not well-versed in statistics saw the tranching of CDOs as magic: risky debt goes in, less-risky debt comes out. This led to (I will be direct here) sheer idiocy in the form of CDO²s and worse. The idea is to take a bunch of CDO equity tranches; place those into a CDO; and, then harvest the A tranche yielding — $\mathcal{MAGIC}$! — high-quality debt. This is, of course, wrong.

Equity tranches are built from order statistics and the left tail of the distribution. Putting a bunch of these together does not yield an investment in the right tail of the distribution. The A tranche of a CDO² created from equity tranches is "the cream of the crap" as my high school history teacher punned.[17] The best of the worst is not the same as the best.

---

[17]For those unfamiliar with the idiom, the "cream of the crop" is considered the best. He used the pun to refer to criticisms of American immigrants not being descended from aristocracy.

However, the worst of the worst is wretched: equity tranches from a CDO^2 are highly toxic. Some were so toxic they blew up as the CDO^2 was being assembled — before the SPV could sell it.

23.4.3   Holds Water Like a SIV

Before the 2008 financial crisis, another innovation in structured products was used far more than CDO^2s. An upward-sloping yield curve offered the promise of easy profits: create an investment vehicle, have the vehicle issue (cheap) commercial paper, and use the capital raised to purchase higher-yielding bonds or CDO tranches. This is, effectively, going long the slope of the yield curve.

These **structured investment vehicle**s (SIVs) were designed to be perpetual: when the commercial paper funding the portfolio was about to mature, they would roll the trades by issuing more commercial paper. If the bonds or CDO tranches declined in value, the SIV would sell them. To do all of this, the SIV had a management team choosing what to invest in. This allowed the SIV to be funded with low-yielding short-term debt and to invest in higher-yielding bonds and tranches.

The claim was that this structure was very similar to a bank. However, short-term funding markets are far more likely to freeze in a crisis than a bank's deposits. Furthermore, the entire premise is flawed: In a crisis the yield curve will flatten and is likely to invert. Rolling short-term debt then would be expensive or impossible; and, rebalancing the portfolio then would lock in losses. That is also when holdings are likely to incur losses and be sold; therefore, the likelihood of trouble was high.

More clever SIV managers thought they could hedge this risk by buying credit default swaps. Unfortunately, some CDSs were written by undercapitalized SPVs or issuers. Furthermore, that did not protect SIVs from short-term funding risk.

The strangest outcome of all came when some SIVs were unable to roll their short-term debt and faced potentially catastrophic losses. SIVs were independent legal entities not on the balance sheets of the banks which created them. However, in the financial crisis, a number of banks — Citigroup most famously — brought the SIVs back onto their balance sheets at great loss to protect their reputations with customers. From a legal standpoint, this is truly shocking and called into question the entire independence of SPVs as well. Read Plumb and Wilchins (2007) and Wilchins (2008) for more on Citigroup moving their SIVs back on-balance-sheet.

23.4.4   Moral Hazard

Ultimately, these issues all came together to create the financial crisis of 2008. Regulations specifying VaR as a risk measure for these sorts of products did not help. The most destructive issue, however, was probably the aforementioned moral hazard. Originating banks saw no reason to police the credit quality of borrowers when they only had to sell the loan on to an SPV or SIV. Furthermore, CDOs and CDSs seemed to reduce and eliminate risk.

Was the market totally unaware of this risk? It is not clear. Longstaff and Myers

(2014) show that CDO equity tranches were more correlated with financial stocks than with any other industry. This suggests that some market players did know that CDO health was related to bank health. (The inversion of the yield curve in mid-2006, mentioned in Chapter 12, corroborates that hypothesis.)

In the end, the European covered bond system fared much better than the US-created securitization system. Despite all of the fancy structures, the issues we confronted early in this chapter — legal recourse and incentive compatibility — were still paramount.

23.5 Credit Enhancement

Many of the tools we have looked at are methods of **credit enhancement**: ways to improve borrowers' credit, reduce the frictions of dealing with individuals' credit, or remove obstacles to lenders providing credit. Therefore, it makes sense to review the methods we have for credit enhancement:

Diversification: If we spread our lending among multiple borrowers, we need not know more about each borrower (nor do we need to worry as much if *some* are deceitful). Furthermore, packaging debt into a portfolio yields an investment with lower risk which entices lenders. This was famously done by Alexander Hamilton aggregating all US states' debt from the Revolutionary War (in exchange for moving the capitol to Washington DC). The result was successful enough to allow the US to finance the Louisiana Purchase from France.

Tranching: Reapportioning cashflows allows for debt to be made the most appealing to the market of potential lenders. This yields competition to fund borrowers and better meets the needs of lenders. We saw this in Chapter 11 with stripping government coupon bonds into zero-coupon bonds.

Prepayment Subordination: Having some tranches incur most of the risk of prepayments limits other lenders' reinvestment risk.

Default Subordination: Having some tranches incur most of the risk of defaults limits other lenders' default risk. That eliminates lost principal and interest. Note that over-collateralization can be seen as a super-subordinated tranche.

Default Protection: Having government guarantees of full principal repayment, a credit default swap, or dual recourse all offer lenders some level of default protection. In short: somebody else covers the loss if there is a default. That may enable lending by firms with mandates to only hold higher-quality credit.

While some claim these are ways to lend to unfit borrowers, that is not the case. Risk alleviation and risk shifting are not mirages nor are they accounting tricks. However, we must remember that they do not always work: portfolios become more correlated in crises; investors may not want the support tranches needed to create the higher-quality senior tranches; subordination can lead to tranche warfare; and, default protection may fail if too much is demanded at the same time.

Despite these potential problems, credit enhancement has helped borrowers appeal to more lenders and pay less to fund homes, cars, revolving lines of credit, and business expansions. The resulting increase in credit card use has even reduced theft of cash and money laundering. Credit enhancement has clearly improved society's overall welfare. However, we can do better at aligning incentives and reducing risks.

23.6   Private Equity

Private equity (PE) might seem like an odd fit for this chapter; however, PE investments behave like a structured product. Investors commit to invest capital over time; the fund's manager finds, acquires, manages, and then divests investments in other firms; and, returns are then distributed according to a fund waterfall.

23.6.1   Timeline

A timeline clarifies the lifecycle and the processes involved:

1. In the **formation period**, a **general partner** (GP, fund manager) forms a new fund with a stated theme (often an industry or geographic area).
2. **Limited partners** (LPs, investors) commit to invest a maximum amount of capital C_0 over a time period $(0, T_L]$, often 10–14 years, in the fund — a **blind fund**, since it has no holdings yet.
3. The GP finds firms to invest in during the **investment period** $(0, T_I < T_L]$. As the GP invests at times $t \leq T_I$, LPs receive **drawdowns** on their capital commitments: they must invest capital ΔD_t where $\sum_{u<t} \Delta D_u = D_t \leq C_0$.
4. During the **harvest period** $(T_I, T_L]$, the GP manages the firms, possibly makes additional investments in those firms, and ultimately sells them. Often, funds are not allowed to invest in new firms during this period.
5. As invested capital and gains ΔR_t are returned to LPs at times $t \leq T_L$, the GP also extracts fees. Distributions are made according to the fund waterfall.
6. The GP may request an **extension period** to sell holdings in firms which were less successful. Otherwise, the GP liquidates the fund at a time $t \leq T_L$.

Though the investment period and harvesting period do not overlap, it is not unusual for LPs to receive drawdowns for follow-on investments during the harvesting period. This may happen even as returns are being distributed to LPs. Latta (2017) has more detail on these stages.

The resulting net cashflows are thus negative as money is invested before turning positive and then tapering off. The cumulated net cashflows yield the **J curve**, which is convex and then concave.

23.6.2   Fees

The fund imposes a management fee on the total capital committed (and not returned) after fund formation. Collecting management fees during an extension period is often a touchy subject: many LPs believe that a GP should not collect management fees during an extension period since that creates an incentive to maximize fees. As investments are harvested, they also collect a performance fee: a share of the profits known as **carried interest**. These fees may be applied across the fund or on a deal-by-deal basis. Proceeds are then distributed to the GP and LPs according to the fund's waterfall.

23.6.3   Types

PE funds tend to fall into six types:

1. **Leveraged buyouts** (LBOs) use debt to acquire underperforming firms, buy out shareholders, trim the firm and make it more efficient, and then resell the firm via a public offering.
2. **Growth capital** funds invest (often a minority stake) in mature firms seeking to expand or restructure.
3. **Mezzanine capital** funds issue subordinated debt, often high-coupon debt, to small highly-leveraged firms which cannot otherwise borrow.
4. **Distressed** funds invest in the debt of financially-troubled firms to convert it to equity and take them over.
5. **Special situation** funds invest in financially-troubled firms to provide funding and see them through the trouble.
6. **Venture capital** (VC) funds invest in startup and young firms which often need large amounts of capital to reach sustainability (and possibly an IPO).

While a focused fund type may be run by people who are specialists in that area, it does yield a portfolio that is less diversified.

23.6.4   Waterfall

The fund waterfall typically has a few layers. Suppose a fund earns χ (*e.g.* 20%) carried interest and offered LPs a **preferred return** (**hurdle rate**) η (*e.g.* 8% compounded annually). LPs have contributed capital of C_t up to time $t < L$.

First, LPs are repaid the capital C_t they have contributed thus far, including contributions to pay fees. Second, LPs are paid up to their **hurdle rate** or **preferred return** η on the capital contributed (*i.e.* a notional of $((1 + \eta)^t - 1)C_t$). Third, the GP is paid all cashflows until they reach χ of all payouts; this is referred to as **catch-up**. Finally, all remaining cashflows are split between the LPs and GP at a ratio of $1 - \chi$ to χ. Note that as investments are made and time passes, the size of some tranches may increase.

This still allows for some leeway: **European-style carry** calculates carried interest on an aggregated basis. **American-style carry** calculates carried interest on a deal-by-deal basis — so the GP still gets paid for profitable deals even if the unprofitable deals lose more than the profitable deals gain. Intuition-building diagrams of example waterfalls are shown in Figure 23.9.

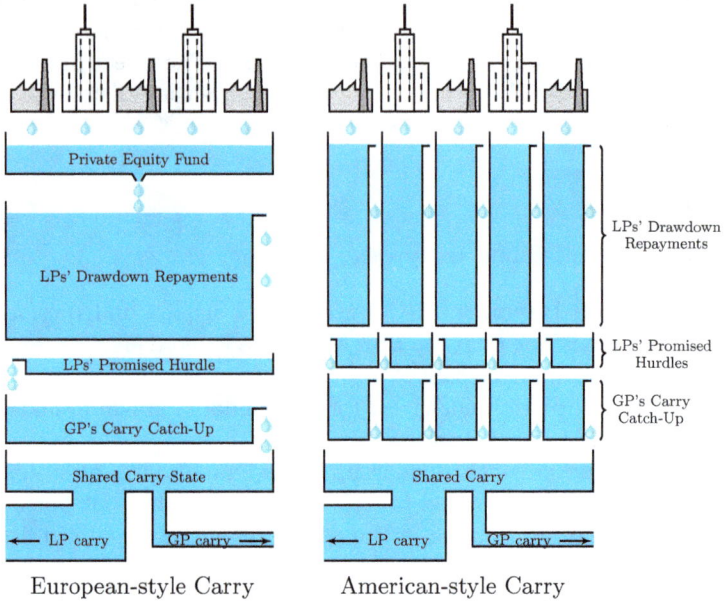

Figure 23.9: Payment "waterfall" for a private equity fund with European-style carry (left) and American-style carry (right). Note that with the American-style carry, the GP still receives some carried interest even if some portfolio companies are impaired or bankrupt; the carried interest is not a function of the aggregate fund return.

23.6.5   *Yale Model*

The Takahashi and Alexander (2002) model, also known as the Yale model because the authors managed Yale's endowment, is a system of difference equations for dynamics of drawdowns, received distributions, and fund value. (This is a fancy way of saying it has a simple deterministic structure.)

We assume LPs commit capital C_0 at time 0 and have had drawdowns of $D_t \leq C_0$ up to time t against that commitment. They have also received distributions of R_t up to time t. The model then requires specifying exogenous values for the drawdown rate δ_t, growth rate g, yield (of income-producing assets like real estate) y, fund life L in years, and a bowing exponent B which governs if the distribution rate is concave or convex.[18] These imply the distribution rate ν_t and the fund value V_t.

With these defined, the authors lay out dynamics for drawdowns of committed

---

[18]These are exogenous because they are not determined by the model's dynamics.

capital, received distributions and distribution rate, and the fund value:

$$\Delta D_t = \delta_t(C_0 - D_t) \qquad \text{(current capital drawdowns)}, \qquad (23.7)$$

$$\Delta R_t = \nu_t V_t(1 + g) \qquad \text{(current distribution received)}, \qquad (23.8)$$

$$\nu_t = \max(y, (t/L)^B) \qquad \text{(distribution rate)}, \qquad (23.9)$$

$$\Delta V_t = V_t g + \Delta D_t - \Delta R_t, \qquad \text{(change in fund value)}. \qquad (23.10)$$

The authors then show that the parameters can be specified to match the cashflows seen in many funds. As a nonlinear regression model, this might be OK. As a dynamic model for simulations and risk modeling, however, it leaves a lot to be desired.

23.6.6 *Buchner Model*

Buchner (2017) and Buchner and Wagner (2017) introduced a continuous-time model governed by a system of stochastic differential equations.[19] The model is concerned with three types of risk:

1. **Market risk**: losses from declining market prices of portfolio companies;
2. **Liquidity risk**: losses from sales occurring below the fund's NAV; and,
3. **Funding risk**: risks from the unknown timing of capital drawdowns; aka **cashflow risk**.[20]

Five sources of randomness, Brownian motions, drive the dynamics. These encapsulate the randomness in the CAPM, variation in the rates of drawdowns and received distributions, and uncertainty about price impact incurred when exiting the investment:

1. $B_{M,t}$ is systematic randomness (from the stock market) driving fund returns;
2. $B_{\epsilon,t}$ is idiosyncratic randomness driving fund returns;
3. $B_{\delta,t}$ drives the capital drawdown rate;
4. $B_{\nu,t}$ drives the received distribution rate; and,
5. $B_{\pi,t}$ drives the evolution of price impact.

Each of these has an associated volatility scaling, *e.g.* σ_M. Thus, as we are used to seeing, stock market log-returns evolve with a classic drift and diffusion:

$$r_{Mt} = \mu_M + \sigma_M dB_{M,t}. \qquad (23.11)$$

The correlation structure for these sources of randomness is that the drawdown

---

[19]In full disclosure, I was a discussant for Buchner (2017) at the 2016 NUS-RMI conference. While a math error I noted was not fixed, that does not affect the main results and I am still a fan of this paper. Those looking for a summary should consult Harte (2017).

[20]Funding risk is a concern because defaulting may result in losing prior drawdowns on the capital commitment.

rate, received distribution rate, and price impact are all correlated with the systematic (market) randomness: $dB_{\delta,t}dB_{M,t} = \rho_\delta$, $dB_{\nu,t}dB_{M,t} = \rho_\nu$, and $dB_{\pi,t}dB_{M,t} = \rho_\pi$. All other correlations are assumed to be 0.

This results in the stochastic differential equations governing fund dynamics:

$$dD_t = \delta_t(I_0 - D_t)\mathbf{1}_{0 \leq t \leq T_I}dt, \qquad \text{(drawdowns)} \qquad (23.12)$$
$$\delta_t = \delta + \sigma_\delta B_{\delta,t}, \qquad \text{(drawdown rate)} \qquad (23.13)$$
$$dR_t = \nu_t V_t \mathbf{1}_{0 \leq t < T_L}dt, \qquad \text{(received distributions)} \qquad (23.14)$$
$$\nu_t = \nu t + \sigma_\nu B_{\nu,t}, \qquad \text{(distribution rate)} \qquad (23.15)$$
$$d\pi_t = \kappa_\pi(\theta_\pi - \pi_t)dt + \sigma_\pi dB_{\pi,t}, \qquad \text{(price impact)} \qquad (23.16)$$
$$dC_t = C_t r_f dt - dD_t + dR_t \qquad \text{(change in cash)} \qquad (23.17)$$

where I_0 is C_0−fees and $\mu_V, \delta, \nu, \kappa_\pi, \theta_\pi > 0$. Note that the third equation allows for a discrete payoff at the end time T_L of the fund's life:

$$R_t = V_t \mathbf{1}_{t=T_L} + \int_0^{t<T_L} \nu_u V_u du. \qquad (23.18)$$

Putting these together, we get the dynamics for the fund value:

$$dV_t = V_t(\mu_V dt + \beta_V \sigma_M dB_{M,t} + \sigma_\epsilon dB_{\epsilon,t}) + dD_t - dR_t. \qquad (23.19)$$

This model is supposed to be implemented in the PE R package; however, that seems to be currently delayed.

23.7   Collateralized Fund Obligations

For publicly-traded securities, an **exchange fund** allows investors to exchange securities (which are often restricted and thus not sellable) for a share in a portfolio of other restricted securities. Thus investors diversify without breaking sales restrictions or triggering a taxable sale. A **collateralized fund obligation** (CFO) offers similar functionality for investors in hedge funds and private equity funds — alternative investments restricted to accredited investors.

Since CFOs are composed of equity instruments, they have a different structure (and different issues) from CMOs and CDOs. First, they cannot easily provide interest payments. As Forrester (2013) notes, this is why debt tranches are often structured as zero-coupon bonds. If this is not the case, the CFO must engage in a swap to receive cashflows needed to pay tranche coupons. Second, if they hold private equity investments, provisions must be made for funding drawdowns after the investment is transferred to the SPV. Third, as equity-holding investments CFOs attract more interest in an equity component than other structured products. Thus a typical tranche structure might be as we see in Table 23.3 with typical funds lasting 3–7 years.

Tranche	Attach	Detach	Principal	Interest
A	50%	100%	$500 mn	LIBOR+100
B	37.5%	50%	$125 mn	LIBOR+200
C	25%	37.5%	$125 mn	LIBOR+300
Equity	0%	25%	$250 mn	7.5% + excess

Table 23.3: Tranche structure for example CFO. The senior tranches are zero-coupon bonds. This example is from Niles (2010) — although there it is not clarified that the equity tranche receives all returns beyond the interest and principal repayments.

In addition to the diversification benefits, Niles (2010) suggests that CFOs may be a cheaper alternative to funds of funds. Missinhoun and Chacowry (2005) found that the equity tranche of hedge fund CFOs outperformed hedge fund of funds in 80% of the cases they studied — even though the equity tranches takes the first losses. CFOs may also allow some institutional investors to access alternative investments without breaking their investment mandates.

While there are few CFOs issued, this area could grow. Furthermore, with companies like Lumni providing student-equity education financing, a CFO would be an ideal structure to invest in a portfolio of such financings.

23.8 Structured Notes

One of the largest areas of structured products is structured note issuance — the creation of bonds with optionality in payoffs.

23.8.1 Insurance-Linked Notes

One of the biggest areas of structured note issuance is insurance-linked notes. In particular, **cat bonds** are insurance-linked securities which reduce their pay off to investors in an SPV if certain catastrophe-related event triggers occur. Many of these SPVs are located in the Cayman Islands. Careful readers may recall the unusual prevalence of fixed income issuance from the Cayman Islands shown in Figure 17.2. That is largely due to cat bond issuance.

Swiss Re (2011) mentions five types of triggers for cat bonds:

1. **Industry index** triggers reduce the principal repaid by a percentage of industry losses above an initial trigger level. This has the advantage of investors not worrying about adverse selection in the risks they are asked to insure; and, investors can clearly see the indices used to compute the principal impairment. However, these triggers may not match the insurance company's actual liabilities.

2. **Pure parametric**, aka physical, triggers depend solely on the location and measured severity of a risk event — for example, an earthquake of at least 8

on the moment magnitude scale occurring 200 km or lower and centered in a certain region. Pure parametric triggers are very transparent; but, they also may not match the insurance company's liabilities.

3. **Parametric index** triggers modify pure parametric triggers by computing weighted averages of multiple measurements at different locations with weightings which better reflect the insurance company's exposures. These triggers are also very transparent albeit slightly more involved to calculate.

4. **Modeled loss** triggers use a model which predicts losses and determines the principal impairment. Typically, the model is produced by a third party to ease verification and reduce concerns about gaming.

5. **Indemnity** triggers match the insurance company's risk because they pass on a share of actual losses. However, this can raise adverse selection issues since an insurer might choose to only issue securities for the worst risks.

Readers with more interest in insurance-linked securities should first consult Swiss Re (2011). That discusses everything here as well as some health- and life-insurance linked securities.

23.8.2   Exchange-Traded Notes

Finally, there have recently been a number of **exchange-traded notes** issued on unusual underliers. Many of these are marketed as being *like* ETFs which invest in oil, gold, and rare-earth metals. However, they are not ETFs. Rather, they are structured products — often with exorbitant fees and markets only made by the issuer (and exacting a heavy price on those selling the notes).

Worse, these fees have resulted in some funds not matching the performance of their underlying assets over time. This has been especially true for commodity-linked notes: their performance has been terrible overall. In fact, their performance is so bad that Henderson, Pearson, and Wang (2015) use them as a way to study uninformed investors.

23.9   Summary

Structured products are an excellent way of bringing competition and diversification to financing and investment in illiquid instruments. In that way, structured finance has been an overwhelming success for society. This also means that these markets are very large in most cases. There is no way a single book chapter can do justice to the wide range of different structured products. My hope is that I have shown you enough to raise your interest.

If I have done that, a good starting resource is Goldman Sachs (2004) followed by Hayre (2001). For an introduction to CDOs, I recommend Tavakoli (2008), Fender and Kiff (2004), and Lucas (2001). Those wanting more information on private equity and venture capital should read Metrick and Yasuda (2011). Based on quotes from numerous successful PE and VC investors, it sounds like the book has become a key resource for quantitatively-minded PE and VC investors.[21] The best resource I have seen on collateralized fund obligations is a PhD dissertation from the University of Bergamo: Tassinari (2009) is excellent, even though it focuses on hedge fund-backed CFOs.

23.10   Quiz

Try to answer these questions in five minutes. For answers with equations, just write the equations; do not evaluate them.

1. A CMO is created from mortgages originated by Fannie May (FNMA) and Freddie Mac (FHMLC). Because these are originated by Fannie and Freddie, the US government bears the default risk. The CMO has three tranches: A, mezzanine, and Z. The Z tranche is yielding 30%.

   a) What is the biggest risk to investing in the Z tranche?
   b) Interest rates fall below the WAC. What happens to the A tranche value?
   c) What are the reasons for the change in the A tranche's value?

2. What approaches to mortgages might have kept banks' incentives aligned with maintaining loan quality?

3. Suppose you hold a portfolio of mortgages and interest rates are fall to well below the weighted average coupon of the mortgages in the portfolio. Why might you not see all of the mortgages prepaying?

4. What is the term for the additional discounting needed to explain a mortgage's market price since it can be refinanced? (Hint: This is similar to implied volatility with options.)

5. You are considering investing in a collateralized debt obligation (CDO).

   a) What risk does a CDO shift?
   b) What makes synthetic CDOs different from cash CDOs?
   c) What additional risk to you incur when you hold a tranche of a synthetic CDO?

6. Private equity investments have cash promised and then provided over time. If we graph the net capital injected and then paid out, what graph do we see?

---

[21] There are also amusing reviews online from people who are not quantitatively-minded and engage in the classic nit-picking of quantitative analysis — the sort of criticism that suggests anything short of modeling everything is a failure. I would posit that such a perspective comes from people who have the most to lose if quantitative analysis grows in popularity.

23.11   Exercises

Instructions

We are going to try some simulation to get at the behavior of structured products and private equity. Modify the supplied R code to answer the following questions.

1. A CDO often has 125 loans in it. However, some of these might share common risk factors. For those loans, we expect that under adverse circumstances they will experience comovement in their default probabilities. We will try a few simulation approaches.

We will assume that these are twenty-year loans and that the conditional default rates are exponentially-distributed.[22] We will also assume that the base arrival rate of a default is 0.01 (so these are middling-credit borrowers); and, that there are 5 groups of ten loans which are each exposed to a common risk factor (*e.g.* the economy of their metropolitan area).

Suppose the CDO has a 5% equity tranch, a 15% mezzanine tranche, and an 80% A tranche.

a) If the equity tranche represents a 5% slice of notional losses and default incurs a 25% loss given default (*i.e.* a 75% recovery rate), how many defaults are needed to erode the equity tranche?

b) Simulate 125 independent defaults with arrival rates of $\lambda = 0.01$. Note that any defaults happening at time $t \geq 20$ are right-censored. How many loans defaulted? Try this a few times and see how often the equity tranche is eroded. How much is the mezzanine tranche typically impaired?

c) Now suppose that crises occurs in a large city at a rate of 0.01. Simulate crises each time you simulate the 125 loans. If a crisis occurs before $t = 20$ generate 10 integers in the range of 1–125. These will be the loans in the affected city. For the city's undefaulted loans, regenerate them with a default rate of $\lambda = 0.02$. Try this a few times. How much do the impairment levels change?

2. We can try implementing a crude version of the PE package by generating correlated multivariate normal random variates in the Buchner (2017)/Buchner and Wagner (2017) model. To make things easy, we will just simulate in discrete time for a fourteen-year fund.

a) Use the sample code provided to simulate the variables in the model. Note how we handle the Ornstein-Uhlenbeck process simulation — since that differs from simulating the O-U process at some end time, as was done in Chapter 21.

---

[22]This is not as severe an assumption as it seems. The unconditional default rates end up closer to being gamma-distributed because the conditions which change the default rates make default like a sum of processes.

b) Plot the sequences $(\delta, \nu, \pi, V, D, R)$ to see that they make sense. Then plot the J curve: $R - D$.

c) Run the code 100 times, averaging the sequences. Plot the average for V, D, and R.

R Code

```
library(MASS)

## simulation for PE exercise
## Values are from Harte (2017)
n.years <- 12
periods.per.year <- 4
dtime <- 1/periods.per.year
times <- seq(dtime, n.years, by=dtime)
mgmt.fee <- 0.02
invest.time.end <- max(times)
capital0 <- 100
fees <- capital0*mgmt.fee*dtime
investment0 <- capital0 - fees

rf <- 0.05

## drift/OU reversion parameters
#pe.alpha <- 0.04
mu.mkt <- 0.11
mu.delta <- 0.41
mu.nu <- 0.08
theta.pi <- 0.16; kappa.pi <- 0.42
pi0 <- theta.pi

## covariance parameters; some correlations differ from Harte (2017)
pe.beta <- 1.3
vol.delta <- 0.21*sqrt(dtime); vol.nu <- 0.11*sqrt(dtime); vol.pi <- 0.16*sqrt(dtime)
vol.mkt.sys <- 0.15*sqrt(dtime); vol.mkt.idio <- 0.35*sqrt(dtime)
corr.delta <- -0.3; corr.nu <- 0.8; corr.pi <- -0.3

cov.delta <- corr.delta*vol.delta*vol.mkt.sys
cov.nu    <- corr.nu*vol.nu*vol.mkt.sys
cov.pi    <- corr.pi*vol.pi*vol.mkt.sys
cov.mtx <- matrix(c(vol.delta^2,         0,        0,    cov.delta,      0,
                    0,           vol.nu^2,         0,       cov.nu,      0,
                    0,                   0, vol.pi^2,       cov.pi,      0,
                    cov.delta,      cov.nu,   cov.pi, vol.mkt.sys^2,     0,
                    0,                   0,        0,            0, vol.mkt.idio^2),
                nrow=5)

## generate random variates
B.rvs <- mvrnorm(mu=rep(0, 5), Sigma=cov.mtx, n=n.years*periods.per.year)
colnames(B.rvs) <- c("B.delta", "B.nu", "B.pi", "B.mkt", "B.epsilon")

delta <- pmin(pmax(mu.delta*dtime + B.rvs[,"B.delta"], 0), 1)
nu <- pmin(pmax(mu.nu*times + B.rvs[,"B.nu"], 0), 1)
pi.ou <- c(pi0)
for (i in 2:length(times)) {
    pi.ou[i] <- pi.ou[i-1] + kappa.pi*(theta.pi - pi.ou[i-1])*dtime + B.rvs[i-1,"B.pi"]
}
dmkt <- mu.mkt*dtime + pe.beta*B.rvs[,"B.mkt"] + B.rvs[,"B.epsilon"]

## simulate the cashflows and value
```

```
drawdowns <- c(delta[1]*investment0)
rcvd.distn <- c(0)
value <- c(0)
for (i in 2:length(times)) {
    d.drawdowns <- delta[i]*(investment0 - drawdowns[i-1])*(times[i] < invest.time.end)
    drawdowns[i] <- drawdowns[i-1] + d.drawdowns
    d.rcvd.distn <- nu[i]*value[i-1]
    if (i < length(times)) {
        rcvd.distn[i] <- rcvd.distn[i-1] + d.rcvd.distn
        dvalue <- value[i-1]*dmkt[i-1] + d.drawdowns - d.rcvd.distn
    } else {
        rcvd.distn[i] <- rcvd.distn[i-1] + value[i-1]
        dvalue <- -value[i-1]
    }
    value[i] <- value[i-1] + dvalue
}
```

References

Alloway, Tracy. "The mother of all (RMBS) tranche warfare". *FT Alphaville* (Oct. 11, 2010). URL: https://ftalphaville.ft.com/2010/10/11/364796/the-mother-of-all-rmbs-tranche-warfare/.

Bolton, Patrick and Xavier Freixas. "Equity, Bonds, and Bank Debt: Capital Structure and Financial Market Equilibrium under Asymmetric Information". *Journal of Political Economy* 108.2 (2000), pp. 324–351. DOI: 10.1086/262121.

Buchner, Axel. "Risk Management for Private Equity Funds". *Journal of Risk* 19.6 (2017), pp. 1–32. DOI: 10.21314/JOR.2017.363.

Buchner, Axel and Niklas F. Wagner. "Rewarding Risk-Taking or Skill? The Case of Private Equity Fund Managers". *Journal of Banking and Finance* 80 (2017), pp. 14–32. DOI: 10.1016/j.jbankfin.2017.03.014.

Campbell, John Y. "Mortgage Market Design". *Review of Finance* 17.1 (2013), pp. 1–33. DOI: 10.1093/rof/rfs030.

Chaudhary, Sharad. *Introduction to Agency CMO Structures*. New York, Oct. 16, 2006.

Dungey, Doris. "Ranieri on the MBS Market: It's Broke". *Calculated Risk (blog)* (Apr. 28, 2007). URL: http://www.calculatedriskblog.com/2007/04/ranieri-on-mbs-market-its-broke.html.

ECBC. *2017 ECBC European Covered Bond Fact Book*. Ed. by Wolfgang Kälberer et al. Brussels: European Covered Bond Council, 2017. URL: https://hypo.org/app/uploads/sites/3/2017/09/ECBC-Fact-Book-2017_Web.pdf.

Falch, Christina Emilia. *Danish Covered Bond Handbook*. Copenhagen: Danske Bank, Sept. 2016. URL: https://danskebank.com/da-dk/ir/Documents/Other/Danish-Covered-Bond-Handbook-2016.pdf.

Fender, Ingo and John Kiff. *CDO Rating Methodology: Some Thoughts on Model Risk and its Implications*. Working Paper 163. Bank for International Settlements, 2004. URL: https://www.bis.org/publ/work163.htm.

Forrester, J. Paul. "Collateralized Fund Obligations: A Primer". *Mayer Brown Newsletter* (July 29, 2013).

Goldman Sachs, Mortgage Strategies. *A Mortgage Product Primer*. New York: Goldman, Sachs & Co., 2004.

Harte, Thomas P. "The PE Package: Modeling Private Equity in the 21st Century". In: *R/Finance 2017 Presentation*. May 20, 2017. URL: http://past.rinfinance.com/agenda/2017/talk/ThomasHarte.pdf.

Harte, Thomas P. and Axel Buchner. *PE: R package for modeling private equity*. R package version 0.0? 2018. URL: https://github.com/tharte/PE.

Hayre, Lakhbir, ed. *Salomon Smith Barney Guide to Mortgage-Backed and Asset-Backed Securities*. New York: Wiley, 2001.

Henderson, Brian J., Neil D. Pearson, and Li Wang. "New Evidence on the Financialization of Commodity Markets". *Review of Financial Studies* 28.5 (2015), pp. 1285–1311. DOI: 10.1093/rfs/hhu091.

Latta, Allen. *LP Corner: The Four Phases in the Life of a Private Equity Fund*. June 24, 2017. URL: http://www.allenlatta.com/allens-blog/lp-corner-the-four-phases-in-the-life-of-a-private-equity-fund.

Lewis, Michael. *Liar's Poker: Rising through the Wreckage on Wall Street*. New York: W. W. Norton & Company, 1989.

Longstaff, Francis A. and Brett W. Myers. "How Does the Market Value Toxic Assets?" *Journal of Financial and Quantitative Analysis* 49.2 (2014), pp. 297–319. DOI: 10.1017/S0022109014000222.

Lucas, Douglas J. *CDO Handbook*. New York: JP Morgan Securities, 2001.

Magnusson, Arni. *areaplot: Title Plot Stacked Areas and Confidence Bands as Filled Polygons*. R package version 1.2-0. 2017. URL: https://CRAN.R-project.org/package=areaplot.

Metrick, Andrew and Ayako Yasuda. *Venture Capital and the Finance of Innovation*. 2nd ed. New York: Wiley, 2011.

Missinhoun, Jean and Leena Chacowry. "Collateralized Fund Obligations: The Value of Investing in the Equity Tranche". *Journal of Structured Finance* 10.4 (2005), pp. 32–37. DOI: 10.3905/jsf.2005.470596.

Niles, Philip. "Collateralized Fund Obligations: A Future Alternative to Fund of Funds?" *Canadian Hedgewatch* 10.2 (Feb. 2010). URL: http://www.philniles.com/images/pdf/745539081_CHW_Vol_10_Issue_2.pdf.

NYT. "Calculation Standard Set on C.M.O. Yields". *New York Times* (June 14, 1985), p. D13.

Platzer, Lukas and Sverre Holbek. *Nordic Covered Bond Handbook*. Copenhagen: Danske Bank, Sept. 2016. URL: http://danskeanalyse.danskebank.dk/abo/NordicCoveredBondHandbook2016/$file/NordicCoveredBondHandbook_2016.pdf.

Plumb, Christian and Dan Wilchins. "Citi to take $49 bln in SIVs onto balance sheet". *Reuters* (Dec. 13, 2007). URL: https://www.reuters.com/article/us-citigroup-sivs/citi-to-take-49-bln-in-sivs-onto-balance-sheet-idUSN1326316020071214.

Rosenthal, Dale W.R. *Approximating Correlated Defaults*. Working Paper 1317865. SSRN, 2018. DOI: 10.2139/ssrn.1317865. URL: http://ssrn.com/abstract=1317865.

Swiss Re, Insurance-Linked Securities Team. *The Fundamentals of Insurance-Linked Securities*. New York: Swiss Re, 2011. URL: http://www.swissre.com/library/archive/ILS__The_fundamentals_of_insurancelinked_securities.html.

Takahashi, Dean and Seth Alexander. "Illiquid Alternative Asset Fund Modeling". *Journal of Portfolio Management* 28.2 (2002), pp. 90–100. DOI: 10.3905/jpm.2002.319836.

Tassinari, Gian Luca. "Pricing Equity and Debt Tranches of Collateralized Fund of Hedge Funds Obligations". PhD dissertation. Department of Mathematics, Statistics, and Computer Applications: University of Bergamo, 2009. URL: https://aisberg.unibg.it/retrieve/handle/10446/64/1487/Tesi%20Phd%20Latex.pdf.

Tavakoli, Janet M. *Structured Finance and Collateralized Debt Obligations: New Developments in Cash and Synthetic Securitization*. 2nd ed. New York: Wiley, 2008.

VDP. *The Pfandbrief 2017 / 2018*. Berlin: Verband Deutscher Pfandbriefbanken / Association of German Pfandbrief Banks, 2017. URL: http://www.pfandbrief.de/cms/bcenter.nsf/0/8BB7C68DF142BC62C1258192004D91F0/$File/PFB_2017_2018_EN.pdf.

Wilchins, Dan. "Citigroup buying back remaining SIV assets". *Reuters* (Nov. 19, 2008). URL: https://www.reuters.com/article/citigroup-siv/update-2-citigroup-buying-back-remaining-siv-assets-idUSN1933094420081119.

Part V

All Together Now

Chapter 24

Active Portfolio Management

When we discussed portfolio theory in Chapter 9, we had yet to explore much about valuation, factor models, derivatives, microfoundations, or structural models of the firm. The irony is that once we explored the CAPM in Chapter 14, we concluded that all portfolios should be holding the market portfolio. We developed a framework for active management — and then quickly decided that framework was unnecessary.

However, as we explored beyond the CAPM, we found lots of facts and theories which break the assumptions of Markowitz (1952) and Roy (1952). Those breaks might have seemed like failures; rather, they are opportunities for superior returns. Thus despite modern portfolio theory and the CAPM implying we should all hold an unknowable "market," we can find many reasons to actively manage our portfolio.

If we are going to actively manage a portfolio, we need to decide how to do that and gauge our performance. The purpose of this chapter is to introduce ways to incorporate alpha and macroeconomic views into portfolio construction, offer a glimpse at how we might better accommodate the randomness of instrument returns, and discuss how to assess portfolio management performance,.

24.1 Introduction

Accommodating all of the potential breaks in our assumptions means handling expectations of abnormal returns and relative value assessments. We could just compute expected abnormal returns for all possible instruments, compute a covariance matrix (perhaps with some structure to ease the curse of dimensionality), and use the Markowitz-Roy approach. However, we also need to accommodate non-normality, better risk measures, and just plain randomness.

MPT maximizes the utility of a portfolio using the first two moments (*i.e.* expectations). However, like the Jensen's Inequality correction in Chapter 13, the maximum expected utility dominates the maximum utility of expectations. In mathematical terms, given data X and finding weights w:

$$\underbrace{\max_w E(U(w|X))}_{\text{stochastic optimization}} \geq \underbrace{\max_w U(w|E(X), \text{Var}(X))}_{\text{modern portfolio theory}}. \qquad (24.1)$$

Thus we should expect to be able to exceed the performance of MPT portfolios.

Brinson, Hood, and Beebower (1986) and Brinson et al. (1991) suggest that over 90% of the variation of pension portfolio returns is explained by asset allocation. However, Ibbotson (2010) and Xiong et al. (2010) note that explaining return variation is not the same as explaining returns. They suggest that 75% of those returns come from market exposure with the remaining 25% of returns being equally-determined by asset allocation and active portfolio management. Nonetheless, asset allocation and active portfolio management are clearly valuable additions to portfolio management. More recently, **smart beta** strategies, which mix passive indices with factor portfolios, have become popular. These factor portfolios may be passive but are often actively-managed.

There are a few approaches which can handle some of these issues and accommodate asset allocation and active management; however, they require modifying the portfolio construction process. We will look at a few portfolio construction methods: the Treynor-Black model, the Black-Litterman model, the Almgren-Chriss model, and the risk parity approach. We will also discuss ways in which these approaches still fall short of the ideal; and, we will finally see some ideas for how to extend these to do the best analysis currently possible. Then we will discuss practical issues and assess the value of active management.

24.2   The Treynor-Black Approach

If we assume MPT and the single-index model are largely correct, then we need only accommodate alpha. This is the underlying perspective of the Treynor-Black approach. Treynor and Black (1973) first proposed their method to decompose a portfolio into market and actively-managed components. (Pay attention, however: two different decompositions are used which can be confusing.)

24.2.1   Decomposing the Portfolio: Market versus Active

We start by decomposing a portfolio P into two parts: a portfolio invested in the market, M, and an actively-managed portfolio A with instruments indexed by $i \in \{1, \dots, n\}$. From the single-index model, the return on instrument i is:

$$r_i = r_f + \alpha_A + \beta_A(R_M + \epsilon_M) + \epsilon_i, \quad r_i \perp r_j, R_M \ \forall i, j, \qquad (24.2)$$

where R_M is the excess return we saw in Chapter 7, $r_M - r_f$.

The key assumption is that all instruments are related through their beta times the market excess return: even the "active" portfolio A has a market component. To ease computation, we then split A into a market-exposure component A_M and a market-neutral alpha component A_α. The end result is a new market-exposure portfolio $M^* = M + A_M$ and a new active, market-neutral alpha portfolio $A^* = A_\alpha$. This split is shown in Figure 24.1.

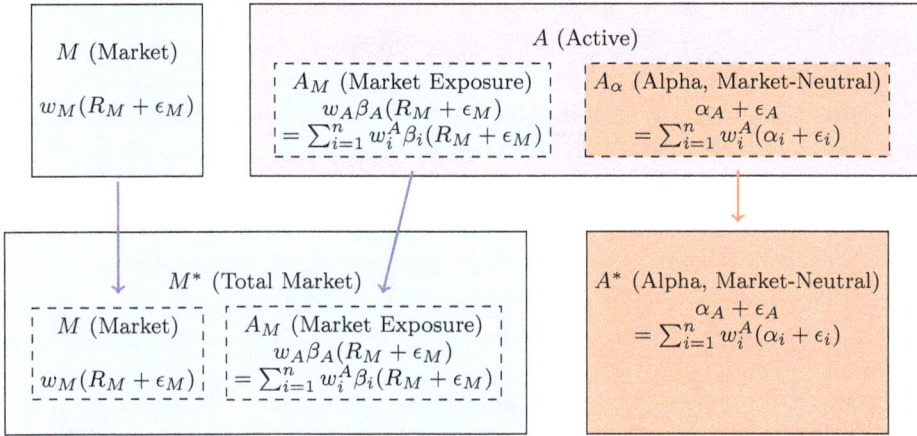

Figure 24.1: Decomposition of Treynor-Black portfolio. Note that the active part of the portfolio has a component with market exposure. Thus we separate that from the component with market-neutral alpha. The decision variables for a portfolio are then weights in A^* and the weight of M to get the desired weight for M^*.

24.2.2 Finding Active and Market Component Weights

This split lets us focus on the decision variables to optimize the portfolio: the portfolio weights. We find the weights for instruments in portfolio A^* and for the market portfolio M to achieve the desired weight for M^*.[1] Since portfolios A^* and M are uncorrelated, we can separately determine the A^* weights for each instrument i, $w_i^A = w_i^{A_M} = w_i^{A^*}$. We then find weights for A^* and M^* such that $w_{A^*} + w_{M^*} = 1$.

The utility of alpha portfolio A^* for weights within A^* is then:

$$U^{A^*}(w) = \sum_{i=1}^n w_i^A \alpha_i - \lambda/2 \sum_{i=1}^n (w_i^A)^2 \sigma_{\epsilon_i}^2. \tag{24.3}$$

---

[1]I have been explicit here about this split and whether we work with M or M^* in hopes of clarifying the approach — since it is easy to get confused.

We maximize this by differentiating, setting that to 0, and solving:

$$\frac{\partial U^{A^*}(w)}{\partial w_i^A} = \alpha_i - \lambda w_i^A \sigma_{\epsilon_i}^2. \tag{24.4}$$

$$\frac{\partial U^{A^*}(w)}{\partial w_i^A} = 0 \implies w_i^A = \frac{\alpha_i}{\lambda \sigma_{\epsilon_i}^2}. \tag{24.5}$$

However, the weights must sum to 1 so we rescale this to get:

$$w_i^A = \frac{\alpha_i/(\lambda \sigma_{\epsilon_i}^2)}{\sum_{j=1}^n \alpha_j/(\lambda \sigma_{\epsilon_j}^2)} = \frac{\alpha_i/\sigma_{\epsilon_i}^2}{\sum_{j=1}^n \alpha_j/\sigma_{\epsilon_j}^2}. \tag{24.6}$$

Similarly, we could find the weights for A^* and M^* in portfolio P:

$$w_{A^*} = \frac{\alpha_{A^*}/\sigma_{A^*}^2}{\alpha_{A^*}/\sigma_{A^*}^2 + E(R_{M^*})/\sigma_{M^*}^2}, \tag{24.7}$$

where $\alpha_{A^*} = \alpha_A = \sum_{i=1}^n w_i^A \alpha_i$ and $\sigma_{A^*}^2 = \sum_{i=1}^n \sigma_{\epsilon_i}^2$.

However, the market-exposure component from A affects the total market exposure; we cannot control the weight on M^* but only on M. We therefore need to subtract the market exposure of A from the total market weight w_{M^*} to get the explicit market weight w_M. This means that $w_M = w_{M^*} - w_{A^*}\beta_A$ and normalizing gives us:[2]

$$w_{A^*} = \frac{\alpha_{A^*}/\sigma_{A^*}^2}{E(R_M)/\sigma_M^2 + (1 - \beta_A)\alpha_{A^*}/\sigma_{A^*}^2}. \tag{24.8}$$

Two quantities govern the balance between investing in the market portfolio and in the actively-managed alpha portfolio: $E(R_M)/\sigma_M^2$ and $\alpha_{A^*}/\sigma_{A^*}^2$. These are the market price of risk, first encountered in Chapter 14, and what we can think of as the "idiosyncratic price of risk." The relative ratios of return to risk govern the balance of passive versus active management of the portfolio.[3]

The information ratio of the alpha portfolio A^* is then:

$$IR_{A^*} = \frac{\sum_{i=1}^n w_i^A \alpha_i}{\sqrt{\sum_{i=1}^n (w_i^A)^2 \sigma_{\epsilon_i}^2}} = \frac{\frac{\sum_{i=1}^n (\alpha_i/\sigma_{\epsilon_i}^2)\alpha_i}{\sum_{i=1}^n \alpha_i/\sigma_{\epsilon_i}^2}}{\sqrt{\frac{\sum_{i=1}^n (\alpha_i^2/\sigma_{\epsilon_i}^4)\sigma_{\epsilon_i}^2}{(\sum_{i=1}^n \alpha_i/\sigma_{\epsilon_i}^2)^2}}} \tag{24.9}$$

$$= \sqrt{\sum_{i=1}^n \frac{\alpha_i^2}{\sigma_{\epsilon_i}^2}} = \sqrt{\sum_{i=1}^n IR_i^2}. \tag{24.10}$$

---

[2]While $E(R_M) = E(R_{M^*})$ and $\sigma_M = \sigma_{M^*}$, I have switched subscripts to be clear which weights we sum in the denominator for normalization.

[3]Obviously, variance is not the best risk measure. We could modify this idea to use coherent risk measures. However, we would still need to believe that the market exposure is the only risk factor.

Since we can view portfolio P as a sum of uncorrelated terms based on the $M^* + A^*$ decomposition in Figure 24.1, we can use this to write the Sharpe ratio of P like we wrote the information ratio above:

$$S_P = \sqrt{\left(\frac{R_M}{\sigma_M}\right)^2 + \left(\frac{\alpha_A}{\sigma_{A^*}}\right)^2} = \sqrt{S_M^2 + IR_A^2} \qquad (24.11)$$

If our portfolio had no alpha, all of our investment would be in the market. Alpha, however, gives us an increased return (often at reduced risk).

24.2.3 Problems with Treynor-Black

One of the first problems we can see with the Treynor-Black approach is a common complaint: if $\alpha_A/\sigma_{A^*}^2$ is large and $\beta_A > 0$, we can easily find ourselves with an "optimal" portfolio that chooses weights like $w_A = 5$ and $w_M = -4$.

On the one hand, we get lots of alpha and and an excess of market exposure from the large investment in A; and, shorting M then corrects the market exposure. On the other hand, we are effectively taking a leveraged bet on alpha versus the market; and, the large sub-portfolios use more working capital and incur higher capital charges.

The large and opposing weights is a classic result of the fragility of optimized solutions when we work with expectations. Put simply: we bet big on alpha because the optimizer is unaware of the uncertainty of that alpha.[4] By using the estimated parameters, the optimizer also assumes ergodicity: it has no clue that the market might change states. As Black and Litterman (1992) note: "Mean-variance optimization ... is extremely sensitive to ... assumptions the investor must provide."

While these criticisms are valid, there are solutions. This situation is similar to linear regression when covariates are multicollinear. One solution is to limit the size of long and short portfolios, *e.g.* :

$$\text{Maximize } S_P - \kappa_L \max(w_A, w_M, 0)^2 - \kappa_S \min(w_A, w_M, 0)^2 \qquad (24.12)$$

where κ_L, κ_S are capital usage penalties. Thus we allow but discourage large weights. We might also use a factor model and constrain factor risks.

We could try shrinking our alphas; however, this does not guarantee we will not have large opposing weights for A and M.

24.3 Bayesian Statistics

We keep hitting problems due to input uncertainty. Worse is that we seem to have a problem with Knightian uncertainty: we rarely know how uncertain we are

---

[4]Yes, the optimizer has the σ_i's; however, we must also estimate those and so they too have uncertainty. Furthermore, there is no escaping Jensen's Inequality.

about these inputs. We might also want to incorporate alpha, other risk factors, or macroeconomics models — or even just unmodeled beliefs or biases. Bayesian statistics gives us a way to handle all of these issues.

Bayesian statistics is an approach that combines a **prior distribution** for inputs with the likelihood of the observed data according to another assumed distribution. Combining these generates a **posterior distribution** for inputs. The prior distribution expresses our beliefs prior to observing the data; and, we often use "loose" (aka "flat" or "weak") priors to let the data largely dictate the posterior. Tighter priors let our preconceived beliefs more strongly affect posterior. To illustrate these ideas, we can consider an example.[5]

⚠️ 注意！ *There is a philosophical difference between frequentists, who believe in a true-but-unknown parameter θ with a value we try to estimate, and Bayesians, who believe θ is random but that we can learn about its distribution. While this difference used to be the source of fervent disputes, most statisticians now see the benefits of both perspectives. Nonetheless, many statisticians still have philosophical beliefs which lean one way or the other.*

24.3.1   An Example of Bayesian Inference

Suppose we enter a coin-flipping contest, but are unsure if they use a fair coin. We could check the fairness by flipping the coin many times and estimating the probability of heads as the number of heads over the number of flips. However, we would rather estimate the probability that the coin is fair. We might even want to estimate the distribution of heads probabilities.

If you recall basic probability, you know that for n coin flips and a heads probability of p, the number of heads k is a binomially-distributed random variable: $k \sim \text{binomial}(n, p)$. For some Bayesian inferences, we can use a **conjugate prior** distribution: a prior which makes the math easier.

For the binomial distribution, the beta distribution is a conjugate prior. The beta has two parameters, α and β, with mean $\alpha/(\alpha+\beta)$ and variance $\frac{\alpha\beta}{(\alpha+\beta)^2(\alpha+\beta+1)}$. The beta also makes sense for inference on p since all of its probability mass lies on $[0, 1]$ and includes the uniform distribution — what we would guess for p if we had no idea of the coin's fairness:

$$\text{beta}(\alpha = 1, \beta = 1) = \text{unif}(0, 1). \tag{24.13}$$

The beta(1,1) (*i.e.* uniform) is a flat or weak prior: it has values spread out equally so as to allow the data to exert the most influence.

Suppose we flip the coin 50 times and get 20 heads. Is that unusual? The conjugate prior greatly eases the analysis; the posterior is just a beta distribution

---

[5]Those seeking a thorough guide to Bayesian analysis should read Gelman et al. (2013).

with new parameters $\alpha + k$ and $\beta + n - k$: beta$(21, 31)$. Thus our estimate of the mean and variance, after observing the data X, is:

$$E(p|X) = \frac{\alpha}{\alpha + \beta} = \frac{21}{52} = 0.404, \tag{24.14}$$

$$sd(p|X) = \sqrt{\frac{\alpha\beta}{(\alpha + \beta)^2(\alpha + \beta + 1)}} = \sqrt{\frac{21 \cdot 31}{52^2 \cdot 53}} = 0.07. \tag{24.15}$$

Note that instead of estimating $\hat{p} = 20/50 = 0.4$, our prior pushed the estimate of p toward the mean of the distribution (0.5). Thus Bayesian inference is a way of squeezing estimates toward a theoretical mean.

So is $k = 20$ heads unusual? The Bayesian analog of a 95% confidence interval, a 95% **credible interval**, can be found using R with `qbeta(0.025, 21,31)` and `qbeta(0.975, 21,31)`. The resulting credible interval, $[0.276, 0.539]$, includes 0.5 — so we should not doubt the coin's fairness.

If we had a strong prior belief that the coin was fair, we could have used a prior distribution of beta$(\alpha = \beta > 1)$. As you can see, Bayesian methods give us a lot of flexibility.

24.4 The Black-Litterman Approach

While the Treynor-Black approach departed only slightly from the MPT/CAPM perspective, Black and Litterman (1991, 1992) proposed an approach which is a greater departure from MPT. Their approach is also very flexible: it can be generalized to accommodate the non-normality of returns and even a Monte Carlo approach to stochastic optimization.

Where the Treynor-Black approach to portfolio construction is top-down, the Black-Litterman approach is bottom-up: they work with asset classes, not individual instruments, to determine asset allocation by combining multiple sources of information.

Their approach uses Bayesian statistics to combine data with distributional assumptions and get more informed estimation of the entire distribution of random parameters. Interestingly, the initial papers on this by Black and Litterman make little mention of Bayesian statistics.

The problem noted by Black and Litterman (1991, 1992) is precisely that we encountered with the Treynor-Black approach and even with the above coin flips: we want good inputs; but, handling them properly is difficult. Proper handling would require merging historical data, predictions from factor and equilibrium models, and client or personal views. We might even want to use macro and cyclical factors to forecast returns while using higher-frequency data to forecast covariances and other risk factors. Finally, we might want to squeeze our estimates toward some overall or theoretical mean.

The model consists of the following steps:

1. Estimate the covariance matrix Σ with recent data.
2. Determine the baseline (prior) forecast (expectation and variance).
3. Express your views quantitatively (expected return and volatility).
4. Add those views to get the revised (posterior) forecast and precision.
5. Optimize the portfolio using the posterior return distribution.

While a mean and variance might not seem sufficient to specify a distribution, the Black-Litterman approach implicitly uses a normal prior and normal data (views) likelihood. These combine to give a normal posterior.

24.4.1   Estimating the Covariance Matrix

To estimate the covariance matrix, we can use any of the intraday (high-frequency) estimation methods discussed in Section 7.2.6 and implemented in the `highfrequency` R package. Alternately, we could build a model for volatilities which uses lower-frequency estimates, overall and industry averages, economic state variables, and firm characteristics.

24.4.2   Computing the Prior Forecast

For the prior forecast, Black and Litterman propose using an equilibrium model. First, they consider excess returns R across a number of sub-markets — asset classes, in this case. They note that all investors maximize the same mean-variance utility:

$$\arg\max_w U_w = \arg\max_w (w^T E(R) - \frac{\bar{\lambda}}{2} w^T \hat{\Sigma} w), \qquad (24.16)$$

where $\bar{\lambda}$ is the market-wide average coefficient of risk aversion and $\hat{\Sigma}$ is the estimated covariance matrix of sub-market returns.

They differentiate to solve for the optimal weights; however, they do not actually find those weights. Instead, they use the resulting equilibrium first-order condition:

$$E(R_M) = \bar{\lambda}\hat{\Sigma} w. \qquad (24.17)$$

They assume that the total market is in equilibrium so the component weights for the market are the relative amounts invested in bonds and stocks, A_B and A_S.[6] This implies weights $w^T = (w_B, w_S) = \left(\frac{A_B}{A_B+A_S}, \frac{A_S}{A_B+A_S} \right)$. That also yields forecasts of the expected returns for the various asset classes:

$$E(R_B) = \bar{\lambda}(w_B \hat{\sigma}_B^2 + w_S \hat{\Sigma}_{BS}), \qquad (24.18)$$

$$E(R_S) = \bar{\lambda}(w_S \hat{\sigma}_S^2 + w_B \hat{\Sigma}_{BS}). \qquad (24.19)$$

---

[6]This ignores commodities, FX, real estate, and other investments. While wrong, we will just use stocks and bonds for now as an illustration. The weight we would use for FX is tough to determine, as Black and Litterman (1992) discuss.

While the forecasts may not be highly uncertain, the realized returns will be. Hence the difference between the variance of returns and the variance of the forecasts. To get the estimated forecast covariance matrix $\hat{\Sigma}_{\hat{R}}$, we divide the $\hat{\Sigma}$ entries by n, the number of observations used to estimate $\hat{\Sigma}$.[7] We then have that:

$$\text{Var}(\hat{R}) = \hat{\Sigma}/n. \tag{24.20}$$

Thus the prior distribution for our return *forecasts* is:

$$\hat{R}^{\text{prior}} \sim N(\bar{\lambda}\hat{\Sigma}w, \hat{\Sigma}/n). \tag{24.21}$$

24.4.3 *Expressing Views*

Black and Litterman also allow for an analyst to express views on the relative (or absolute) performance of asset classes. For example, the quantified view Q that bonds will outperform stocks by 1% is $Q = E(R_B) - E(R_S) = 0.01$. This view is derived from "picks" P, in this case $P = (1, -1)$. Therefore, our view is $Q = PE(R) = E(R_B) - E(R_S)$. If we also wanted to express the view that bonds will have excess returns of 3%, Q would be a vector of expectations and P would be a matrix:

$$\underbrace{\begin{bmatrix} 0.01 \\ 0.03 \end{bmatrix}}_{Q} = \underbrace{\begin{bmatrix} 1 & -1 \\ 1 & 0 \end{bmatrix}}_{P} \underbrace{\begin{bmatrix} \hat{R}_B \\ \hat{R}_S \end{bmatrix}}_{\hat{R}}. \tag{24.22}$$

The one truly *ad hoc* aspect of the Black-Litterman approach is to then assess the uncertainty of the views — via a covariance matrix Ω. Using linear algebra does not make this any less subjective. The problem, as anyone familiar with politicians knows, is that the ignorant rarely realize the uncertainty of their views while the wise may overestimate their own uncertainty. Nonetheless, we "guesstimate" the variance $\text{Var}(Q) = \Omega$ of our view. Thus we get our "data" (views) likelihood:

$$P\hat{R} \sim N(Q, \Omega). \tag{24.23}$$

If the view comes from another model, we may have a reasonable idea of the uncertainty Ω. However, this is certainly one place where a dishonest or inept analyst can bias the resulting portfolio.

24.4.4 *Determining the Posterior Distribution*

Once we have our prior distribution and have expressed our views, we can find the posterior distribution. As with the coin flip, this is merely a matter of Bayesian inference. If we did not use a conjugate prior, we could find the product of the

---

[7]Using $1/n$ presumes we have used independent observations or corrected $\hat{\Sigma}$ for persistence among observations. In Black and Litterman (1992), the $1/n$ is replaced by the more mysterious τ.

likelihood and data (or prior and views) and then normalize so that the inferred density integrated to unity.

In this case, however, a normal prior and normal views leads to a normal posterior distribution — which is easily calculated.

$$\hat{R}^{\text{post}} \sim N\left(\hat{\Sigma}^{\text{post}} \left[n\hat{\Sigma}^{-1}\bar{\lambda}\hat{\Sigma}w + P^T\Omega^{-1}Q\right], \hat{\Sigma}^{\text{post}}\right) \tag{24.24}$$

$$\hat{\Sigma}^{\text{post}} = \left[n\hat{\Sigma}^{-1} + P^T\Omega^{-1}P\right]^{-1}. \tag{24.25}$$

If you look at the posterior mean, you can see that it is just a precision-weighted (*i.e.* inverse-variance-weighted) average of the equilibrium forecasts and views.

Black and Litterman (1992) note that we can write this expectation as a sum of the market and view portfolios:

$$E(\hat{R}^{\text{post}}) = \bar{\lambda}\hat{\Sigma}w + \frac{1}{n}\hat{\Sigma}P^T\left(\frac{1}{n}P\hat{\Sigma}P^T + \Omega\right)^{-1}(Q - P\bar{\lambda}\hat{\Sigma}w). \tag{24.26}$$

Meucci (2010) notes that this form is more numerically stable and also provides a more stable form for the variance:

$$\text{Var}(\hat{R}^{\text{post}}) = \hat{\Sigma}^{\text{post}} = \frac{1}{n}\hat{\Sigma} - \frac{1}{n^2}\hat{\Sigma}P^T\left(\frac{1}{n}P\hat{\Sigma}P^T + \Omega\right)^{-1}P\hat{\Sigma}. \tag{24.27}$$

24.4.5 Optimizing the Black-Litterman Portfolio

With the posterior distribution of forecasts, we can easily get the posterior distribution of returns:

$$R^{\text{post}} \sim N(E(\hat{R}^{\text{post}}), \hat{\Sigma} + \text{Var}(\hat{R}^{\text{post}})). \tag{24.28}$$

We can then use Markowitz-Roy portfolio optimization to find new optimal weights for bonds and stocks, $w^{\text{post}} = (w_B^{\text{post}}, w_S^{\text{post}})$. However, we could do better — a point we will address in a few paragraphs.

24.4.6 Criticism of Black-Litterman Approach

Despite the Black-Litterman approach using more advanced machinery to handle a number of inputs, the approach still has potential problems. First, and most obvious, is that we need to use a better risk measure than variance.

A more subtle criticism is of the equilibrium model: not all countries are equally efficient. This is why total factor productivity (mentioned in Chapter 5) varies among countries. Therefore we should expect differing equilibria — perhaps with risk being more rewarded in developing countries since access to capital or information might be limited.

If we are going to use an equilibrium approach, we should probably also consider how FX rates might change if we (and others) invest more in more appealing markets.

Perhaps the most egregious step of the Black-Litterman approach is the most subjective: specifying the uncertainty of our views. While there are ways around this, it is a way for an analyst to bias the resulting posterior distribution.

Other criticisms, however, show the potential for the Black-Litterman approach. While the assumption of normal returns is wrong, nothing in the Bayesian framework prevents us from using non-normal distributions or even distribution estimates like those discussed in Chapter 8. We could also express views on sub-market volatilities and correlations with a Wishart prior, a conjugate prior for Σ^{-1}.

Finally, using Markowitz-Roy portfolio optimization after using machinery which gives us an estimate of the full return distribution is a bit of a fizzle for an ending — like building a sportscar and then using it only to fetch groceries from the store. We can and should do more. For example, we could sample from the posterior return distribution and use those samples to do stochastic optimization.

There are a few ways we could do this. We could take a number of samples from the joint distribution of returns and then optimize the portfolio to have the best average performance across all these samples. While this might seem computationally-intensive, modern optimizers are very fast and often used for far larger problems. Alternatively, we could **numerical quadrature**: choosing key quantiles from the posterior distribution to allow the optimizer to approximate the true optimal solution. Finally, we could compute moments from the posterior distribution and feed these higher moments into an optimization technique like Markowitz-Roy.

For more on stochastic optimization, I highly recommend consulting Birge and Louveaux (2011). An excellent discussion of other ways to extend the Black-Litterman framework is given by Meucci (2010).

24.5 The Almgren-Chriss Model

Another way to handle portfolio construction is to, in some ways, disregard the inputs. We can use **nonparametric statistics**, statistics that make no distributional assumptions, to possibly find an optimal portfolio. This is the approach developed by Almgren and Chriss (2006).[8]

As is common with nonparametric statistics, we think about **rank statistics**: the ranking which would order the data from lowest to highest. This preserves some information from the data but ignores information implying a particular distribution of observed values. The observed returns r for k instruments $r = (r_1, \ldots, r_k)$ then become the ranks $\rho(r) = (\rho_1, \ldots, \rho_k)$. If $r_i \geq r_j$ for $i \neq j$, then $\rho_i \geq \rho_j$. We call Q the set of all returns r' with the same ranking as r: $Q = \{r' : \rho(r') = \rho(r)\}$.

We also need to think about preferences. For example: given two portfolios A and B with weights w^A and w^B, we would say we (weakly) prefer A to B by writing $A \succeq B$, or $w^A \succeq w^B$, if $w^A \rho(r') \geq w^B \rho(r')$ for all $r' \in Q$. In other words: we weakly

---

[8]Some may find Almgren and Chriss (2005) a more approachable introduction to the model.

prefer portfolio A to portfolio B if A does not have worse returns than B for all return distributions with the same ordering of the data.

We may then impose **budget constraints**, *e.g.* that all weights sum to 1, that risk is at most X, or that short sales are limited or prohibited. An efficient portfolio P is then a portfolio meeting all these constraints and with weights such that $P \succeq P'$ for all P' also meeting the constraints.

It turns out that we can find the optimal portfolio by working with centroids. While not exactly correct, centroids are approximately the quantiles of the returns r. That would seem to require knowing the joint distribution of r, but Almgren and Chriss (2006) show that it is well-approximated in some cases by a function using the normal quantile function (*i.e.* inverse cdf).

The Almgren-Chriss method is implemented in the `PortfolioAnalytics` R package.

24.6   Risk Parity Portfolios

Budget constraints are common in practice. Many portfolio optimizers include constraints on the investment in an industry, short exposure, or risk of any one position. This is the idea of **risk budgeting**: constraining the risk contribution of any one portfolio investment, whether at the instrument or asset class level.

In Chapter 9, we discussed the equally-weighted or "$1/n$" portfolio. While simple, it offered a useful comparison. Like the $1/n$ portfolio, many practitioners have advocated a **risk parity** (equal risk contribution) approach to portfolio construction.

These ideas were first espoused in two practitioner papers: Dalio (2004), describing a principle used at Bridgewater since 1996, and Qian (2005), who coined the term "risk parity" for the same principle — used at PanAgora. Both firms (and others) have used the principle with great success.

Since then, some theory has helped explain the reasons why this approach might be valuable. Maillard, Roncalli, and Teïletche (2010) have shown that if volatility is the risk measure used, then the risk parity portfolio volatility is between that of the minimum-variance and equally-weighted portfolios. Thus a risk parity portfolio may be seen as a shrinkage of the $1/n$ portfolio.

More troubling is work such as Haugen and Heins (1975) which fails to find risk premia and suggests that lower-risk stocks outperform higher-risk stocks. This anomaly calls into question the whole idea of a risk premium: a risk-versus-return tradeoff. That is troubling to most academics and probably why the idea has been slow to win acceptance despite the evidence: Haugen and Baker (1991) and Baker and Haugen (2012) show that this outperformance has persisted over the period of 1972–1989 and 1990–2011.

Almost forty years after Haugen first discussed this anomaly, Frazzini and Pedersen (2014) documented that low-beta (*i.e.* low-risk) stocks outperformed high-beta stocks. They suggested this could be due to investors' aversion to leverage. Asness, Frazzini, and Pedersen (2017) (from AQR, which also uses risk parity) develop this theory further: they note that lower-risk assets are only attractive with leverage and therefore must provide higher returns. They also show that the outperformance of lower-risk instruments extends to bonds and commodities.

While the outperformance and theory all provide justification for investigating risk parity portfolios, these analyses still rely on variance as a risk measure. Pearson (2002) and Boudt, Carl, and Peterson (2013) provide depth on how to work with other risk measures and handle the non-normality of returns. Those portfolios also outperform; thus risk parity portfolios are not just trading on the imperfection of the risk measure.

The one problem we should consider with the risk parity approach is the bias of regression to the mean. Similar to the Noisy Market Hypothesis, we will over-invest in instruments which look overly low-risk — those which are actually higher-risk but due to randomness appeared lower-risk. We will also under-invest in instruments which look overly high-risk but are actually lower-risk. Those two errors do not cancel out. However, shrinkage estimators of whichever risk measures we choose to use can guard against the regression effect.

Risk parity methods are implemented in the **PortfolioAnalytics** R package.

24.7 Practical Issues

There are a number of practical issues we still might need to deal with before building the optimal portfolio. These range from work-arounds to the optimization process not properly accounting for randomness to handling more mundane issues like the illiquidity of bonds and adjusting estimated alphas.

24.7.1 Jensen's Inequality Correction

When we previously looked at splitting our complete portfolio C between a risk-free portfolio F and a risky portfolio P, we ignored the randomness in estimating the volatility of P. In Chapter 13, however, we saw that randomness which enters into a denominator biases the result and requires correcting. As noted in the introduction to this chapter, Jensen's Inequality means that $E(\max_w U(w|X)) \geq \max_w E(U(w|X))$. While using stochastic optimization is the optimal fix, we can develop a Jensen's Inequality correction as a work-around.

In Chapter 9, we found the weight y of the optimal risky portfolio P in creating the optimal complete portfolio C. If we account for the uncertainty of estimating portfolio P's volatility, we would instead use the weight $\hat{y}$:

$$y = \frac{\sigma_C}{\sigma_P}; \quad \hat{y} = \frac{\sigma_C}{\hat{\sigma}_P} + \frac{\sigma_C}{\hat{\sigma}_P^3}\sigma_{\hat{\sigma}_P}^2, \tag{24.29}$$

where $\sigma_{\hat{\sigma}_P}$ is the standard error for the estimated portfolio volatility $\hat{\sigma}_P$. We can then restate the expected return on C as:

$$E(r_C) = r_f + (E(r_P) - r_f) \left(\frac{\sigma_C}{\hat{\sigma}_P} + \frac{\sigma_C}{\hat{\sigma}_P^3} \sigma_{\hat{\sigma}_P}^2 \right). \qquad (24.30)$$

We might even use this with a GARCH or stochastic volatility model to actively manage the complete portfolio. Unfortunately, developing a correction for the randomness of potential instruments in the optimal risky portfolio would not be simple.

24.7.2 Bond Portfolio Idiosyncrasies

As mentioned early in this book, bonds are like puppies: most are purchased when new (at or shortly after issuance) and that initial purchase often determines the bond's "forever home" since most bonds are held to maturity. This makes managing bond portfolios different than managing equity portfolios: replicating indices may be difficult to impossible and liquidity is often lower.

Since forecasting interest rates is difficult, most bond portfolio managers instead focus on identifying relative valuation opportunities: times when they can exchange a bond they hold for another bond which appears more attractive. Homer et al. (2013) discuss four types of portfolio-rebalancing exchanges ("swaps" as they called them in their pre-interest-rate-swaps 1972 edition):

- *Substitution*: nearly-identical bonds are exchanged to capture a higher yield.
- *Intermarket spread*: bonds from different sectors or countries are exchanged to express a view on the yield spread of that sector or country.
- *Rate anticipation*: bonds are exchanged to (hopefully) benefit more from and express a view on future interest rates.
- *Pure yield pickup*: bonds, often with differing maturities, are exchanged to capture a higher liquidity-premium. In the US Treasury market, this might be a trade of on-the-run bonds for off-the-run bonds.

Bonds may also be exchanged to capture tax benefits which might be idiosyncratic to the portfolio holder.

Other analyses often done by active bond portfolio managers include forecasting the shape of the yield curve (which may imply relative valuations of bonds), immunization (mentioned in Chapter 11), and forecasting prepayments and defaults (discussed in the previous two chapters).

24.7.3 Rebalancing with Options

We mentioned earlier how selling covered calls earns premium. If you would rebalance your portfolio by selling appreciated investments in the future, you can get paid for locking in that decision by selling a covered call. If the option expires in-the-money, you sell the underlying (as you would have in rebalancing) but also earned option premium. If the option expires out-of-the-money, you received premium yet need not rebalance.

24.7.4 *Adjusting Alphas*

We have already mentioned a few ways to adjust or squeeze estimated alphas. Another approach is to use the Bayesian framework and use that to adjust (squeeze) alphas. One way to do this would be to use the historical standard error for estimated alphas, σ_{ϵ_A}, to get a prior:

$$\hat{\alpha}^{\text{prior}} \sim N(0, \sigma_{\epsilon_A}^2). \tag{24.31}$$

Suppose we estimated this variance as $\hat{\sigma}_{\epsilon_A}^2 = 0.02$ and our data analysis yielded an estimated alpha $E(\hat{\alpha}_i) = 0.01$ with $\text{Var}(\hat{\alpha}_i) = 0.001$. We can then combine these to get a posterior:

$$\hat{\alpha}_i^{\text{post}} \sim N\left(\frac{\frac{0}{\sigma_{\epsilon_A}^2} + \frac{\hat{\alpha}_i}{\text{Var}(\hat{\alpha}_i)}}{\frac{1}{\sigma_{\epsilon_A}^2} + \frac{1}{\text{Var}(\hat{\alpha}_i)}}, \frac{1}{\frac{1}{\sigma_{\epsilon_A}^2} + \frac{1}{\text{Var}(\hat{\alpha}_i)}} \right) \tag{24.32}$$

$$\sim N\left(\frac{0.01/0.001}{1/0.02 + 1/0.001}, \frac{1}{1/0.02 + 1/0.001} \right) \tag{24.33}$$

$$= N(10/1050, 1/1050) = N(0.0095, 0.00095). \tag{24.34}$$

We can see that this has squeezed our estimated $\hat{\alpha}_i$ toward the prior mean of 0. Thus the Bayesian approach gives us a shrinkage estimator.

We could even combine this with results from another analysis. If a second alpha model yielded $E(\hat{\alpha}_i) = 0.005$ and $\text{Var}(\hat{\alpha}_i) = 0.002$, we would then have the posterior distribution $\hat{\alpha}_i^{\text{post}} \sim N(\mu_{1+2}^{\text{post}}, \sigma_{1+2}^{2,\text{post}})$ where:

$$\mu_{1+2}^{\text{post}} = \frac{\frac{0}{0.02} + \frac{0.01}{0.001} + \frac{0.005}{0.002}}{\frac{1}{0.02} + \frac{1}{0.001} + \frac{1}{0.002}} = \frac{12.5}{1550} = 0.008, \tag{24.35}$$

$$\sigma_{1+2}^{2,\text{post}} = \frac{1}{\frac{1}{0.02} + \frac{1}{0.001} + \frac{1}{0.002}} = \frac{1}{1550} = 0.00065. \tag{24.36}$$

Another approach comes from Treynor and Black (1973): Model abnormal returns on predicted alphas. Suppose we have a set of predicted alphas $\tilde{\alpha}_{i,t}$. We can create abnormal returns $u_{i,t}$ for each instrument i using either the CAPM or a factor model:

$$u_{i,t} = R_{i,t} - \beta_i R_{M,t} = \alpha_{i,t} + e_{i,t}, \text{ or} \tag{24.37}$$

$$u_{i,t} = R_{i,t} - \beta_{i,M} R_{M,t} - \beta_{i,SMB} SMB_t - \beta_{i,HML} HML_t - \beta_{i,X} \text{XFactor}_t \tag{24.38}$$

$$= \alpha_{i,t} + \varepsilon_{i,t}. \tag{24.39}$$

We then model the u_i's with predicted alphas $\tilde{\alpha}_i$'s.

$$u_{i,t} = \gamma + \delta_i \tilde{\alpha}_{i,t} + \xi_{i,t}. \tag{24.40}$$

The only problem with this is as discussed in Chapter 14 when we tested CAPM betas: we have an errors-in-variables problem. However, this may not be too awful since that shrinks the predicted alphas $\tilde{\alpha}_{i,t}$ toward the estimated overall average $\hat{\gamma}$; this too is a shrinkage estimator.

24.8   Valuing Active Management

Finally, perhaps the most important question in this chapter is "What is the value of active management?" We typically try to answer this question in a number of ways: we build metrics of performance; we look at these metrics for our investments and our investing, *i.e.* investment performance given our changing exposure across time; and, we try to separate luck from skill.

In general, statistical analysis of manager performance is tough. For this reason, we often use measures we know are flawed because doing better is very difficult. While many measures are gameable, Lehmann (2003) makes the point that this is mostly a concern for an **external performance measure** used by an investor to decide if they will invest with a manager — whereas an **internal performance measure** is used by a manager to improve their performance. While a manager might game external measures to attract investment, there is no incentive to game an internal measure used for self-improvement (absent office politics).

⚠ **ध्यान!** *We quote performance measures on an annualized basis, even though we often use daily returns to get precise estimates. We generally scale the average daily return by the number of trading days d in a year and risk measures like daily volatility by $\sqrt{d}$. Also: Many of these measures vary depending on whether geometric, simple, or log-returns are used. Which is typically used? Sadly: the one which looks best. We must be skeptical when looking at external performance measures.*

24.8.1   Absolute Performance Metrics

If we actively managed a portfolio, we might ask:

- How successful was that management?
- How did individual strategies/decisions perform?
- Could management have been better?

The key to performance evaluation is disentangling risk, noise, and skill. Did we just take risk and get lucky? How much of our performance is unpredictable and uncontrollable noise? What part of our performance is skill and therefore reproducible?

We start with the simplest internal measure of investment performance by looking at *our* effective rate of return, also known as the **internal rate of return** (IRR):

$$IRR = \left\{ r : \underbrace{i_0 + \frac{i_1}{1+r} + \frac{i_2}{(1+r)^2} + \cdots}_{PV(\text{cashflows in})} = \underbrace{\frac{o_1}{1+r} + \frac{o_2}{(1+r)^2} + \cdots}_{PV(\text{cashflows out})} \right\}, \quad (24.41)$$

where i_t are the cash inflows to the investments and o_t are the cashflows taken out of the investments.

This is especially useful for investors with changing capital invested over time (for example, most people saving for retirement of their childrens' education). One caveat with this measure is that herding with other investors can make the IRR look very good but masks the potential problem of everyone trying to exit an investment at the same time. Finally, cash inflows should include the transactions costs and fees paid.

We could also look at the risk-adjusted metrics from Section 8.4:

- *Sharpe ratio*: $S_P = \frac{\bar{r}_P - \bar{r}_f}{\sigma_P}$;
- *Sortino ratio*: $So_P = \frac{\bar{r}_P - \bar{r}_f}{\theta_P}$; and,
- *conditional Sharpe ratio*: $CS_P = \frac{\bar{r}_P - \bar{r}_f}{ES_P}$,

where σ_P, θ_P, and ES_P are the volatility, semideviation, and expected shortfall of portfolio P.

If we have a large portfolio invested in the overall market and sufficiently diversified that we believe the only risk factor is the market, then β_P should encapsulate the portfolio's risk.[9] In that case, we could look at the **Treynor ratio**:

$$T_P = \frac{\bar{r}_P - \bar{r}_f}{\beta_P}. \quad (24.42)$$

We could also look at the abnormal return from the CAPM, also known as **Jensen's alpha** from Jensen (1968):[10]

$$\alpha_P = \bar{r}_P - (\bar{r}_f + \beta_P(\bar{r}_M - \bar{r}_f)). \quad (24.43)$$

Connor and Korajczyk (1986) generalize this to consider the alpha from any factor model:

$$r_P = r_f + \alpha_P + \sum_{j=1}^{k} \beta_{P,j} \bar{F}_j + \epsilon_P, \quad (24.44)$$

$$\hat{\alpha}_P = \bar{r}_P - \left(\bar{r}_f + \sum_{j=1}^{k} \beta_{P,j} \bar{F}_j \right). \quad (24.45)$$

---

[9]By now we should see that these are some tough assumptions to swallow — even if we come up with a better guess for "the market" than the S&P 500. Note that we do not annualize betas.

[10]Note that this is a different Jensen from the mathematician famous for Jensen's Inequality.

This can then feed into an information ratio as we have implicitly done up to now:

$$IR_P = \frac{\hat{\alpha}_P}{\hat{\sigma}_{\epsilon_P}}. \tag{24.46}$$

The information ratio is particularly useful for judging active management. What is a good value for an information ratio? Zephyr Associates (2013) notes that "an information ratio in the 0.40–0.60 range is considered quite good. Information ratios of 1.00 for long periods of time are rare."

A point often neglected about the Sharpe and information ratios is that they are basically t-statistics. Market efficiency, however, means that Sharpe or information ratios of 2 or higher are far rarer than 5% of portfolios.

The one metric we should never use is the R^2 from a factor model. We can artificially drive $R^2 \uparrow 1$ by just adding garbage to any model. While some claim that using adjusted-R^2 fixes this, it does not.

24.8.2   *Benchmark-Relative Performance Metrics*

Some managers are judged by comparing their performance to a target or benchmark B. For these managers, absolute performance is not as important as benchmark-relative performance.

One way to judge performance versus a benchmark (*e.g.* the market) is to compare portfolio P to the market. The $\mathbf{M}^2$ **measure** of Modigliani and Modigliani (1997) scales P to have the same volatility as the market, makes up the difference (or funds the leverage) with risk-free bonds F, and then looks at the outperformance of this portfolio P^*:

$$P^* = \frac{\sigma_M}{\sigma_P}P + \left(1 - \frac{\sigma_M}{\sigma_P}\right)F \tag{24.47}$$

$$M_P^2 = r_{P^*} - r_M. \tag{24.48}$$

Some funds will even shift their investments to the benchmark or cash once they surpass the benchmark or its projected performance for the year. These funds are concerned about **tracking error** which may be defined as divergence D from the benchmark, shortfalls D^- versus the benchmark, or the variability σ_D versus the benchmark:

$$D = R_P - R_B, \tag{24.49}$$

$$D^- = (R_P - R_B)^-, \quad \text{or} \tag{24.50}$$

$$\sigma_D = \sqrt{\text{Var}(R_P - R_B)}. \tag{24.51}$$

For example, in the Treynor-Black model with the market M as the benchmark, these would be defined as:

$$D_{\text{T-B}} = w_{A*}(\alpha_A + \epsilon_A) + [1 - w_{A*}(1 - \beta_A)](R_M + \epsilon_M) - (R_M + \epsilon_M) \quad (24.52)$$
$$= w_{A*}(\alpha_A + \epsilon_A) - w_{A*}(1 - \beta_A)(R_M + \epsilon_M) \quad (24.53)$$

$$\sigma_{\text{T-B},D} = w_{A*}\sqrt{\sigma_{\epsilon_A}^2 + (1 - \beta_A)^2\sigma_M^2}. \quad (24.54)$$

For managers who really care only about tracking error, they can scale w_{A*} to hit the desired level of σ_D.

Another common type of benchmark-relative performance assessment is **style analysis**, which allocates performance to style factors. This is the method used by the Morningstar style box mentioned in Chapter 15. However, this inherits all of the problems of style models discussed in that chapter.

24.8.3   Metrics for Alternative Investments

Another difficult question is how to evaluate alternative investments such as hedge funds, commodity trading advisors, and private equity firms?[11] We could use the Hasanhodzic and Lo (2007) six-factor, Fung and Hsieh (2004) seven-factor, or Fung and Hsieh (1997) eight-factor model and then search for firms with alpha after accounting for those factors.

We should also consider the factor model of Jurek and Stafford (2015). They use the finding by Bondarenko (2014) that put options are overly expensive and compare alternative investment performance to a put-writing strategy. For an investment i, there model is:

$$R_i = \alpha_i + \beta_{iM}R_M + \beta_{i,PW}PW + \epsilon_i. \quad (24.55)$$

Some versions of the model have lags of the market and put-writing factors.

As with active portfolio managers, information ratios are useful metrics — since we are ostensibly paying high fees for alpha and not (inexpensively-acquired) beta. However, many funds prefer not to report information ratios; or, they do so using alpha from a factor model that is inappropriate to assess if they add value.

Finally, since alternative investments are often highly illiquid or in opaque markets, we should be especially watchful for observability issues, potential Peso problems, survivorship bias, and **reporting bias**: the bias from funds selectively reporting their results.

For example, funds may start "fundlets" and only report successful results; or, they may only report results to a data gatherer while they are trying to attract investors. In general, hedge fund data is very hard to work with due to all of the potential biases. Fung and Hsieh (2000, 2002, 2009) discuss a number of potential

---

[11]We will discuss alternative investments in the following chapter.

problems with such data.[12] Brown et al. (1992) discuss how such problems can even affect mutual fund performance data.

24.8.4   Market Timing

One of the more controversial ideas is that some market participants may be able to time markets. It is controversial enough to claim that some investors can better discern value. However, adding the additional dimension that some of those investors also know how to time those investments (instead of having to wait for them to be realized) seems to be especially troubling.

Nonetheless, we can easily imagine how we might test for market timing skill. One way is to build a factor model with asymmetric exposures to risk factors: when risk factors are beneficial, the investor benefits; when risk factors incur losses, the investor suffers less or not at all.

The simplest test is to add a nonlinear (*e.g.* quadratic) term, an approach explored by Treynor and Mazuy (1966):

$$r_P - r_f = \alpha + \beta_P(r_M - r_f) + \gamma(r_M - r_f)^2 + \epsilon. \qquad (24.56)$$

To test market timing, we merely conduct a one-tailed test of the alternative hypothesis $\gamma > 0$ versus the null hypothesis $\gamma \leq 0$. Alternatively, we could use a discontinuity at the negative-versus-positive excess return threshold for the market, as done by Henriksson and Merton (1981):

$$r_P - r_f = \alpha + \beta_P(r_M - r_f) + \gamma(r_M - r_f)^+ + \epsilon. \qquad (24.57)$$

Another way to measure market timing ability is to look at a manager's semideviation versus volatility. If the manager has market timing ability, the downside risk should be much lower than the upside (or two-sided) risk: $\theta_P > \sigma_P$.[13]

Finally, another way we can value market timing is as an option, the approach considered by Merton (1981). He notes that market timing ability is similar to a call option (for long investors). Furthermore, if that is so, then we can easily value market-timing ability as the cost of a similarly-performing option.

24.8.5   Evidence from Investment Professionals

Armed with the above measures, we can assess if investment professionals add value. While the results are mixed, they make sense if we delve deeper.

---

[12]In the spirit of full disclosure: A hedge fund data provider once asked me to use their data for some analysis. They claimed they had resolved all the issues discussed here. When I pointed out how those issues (and others) were still present, they stopped returning my emails. *Plus ça change, plus c'est la même chose....*

[13]This is why it is important to define semideviation with n^- in the denominator. Otherwise, the semideviation could appear lower that the volatility even though most of the risk was downside risk.

Analysts

Some of the more derided professionals are the bank-employed analysts who assign "buy," "sell," or "hold" ratings on stocks — since the vast proportion of stocks rated are some form of "buy" and the ratings seem to be skewed so as not to scare away potential future clients for other bank services

To get around this, Womack (1996) looked at *changes* in analyst ratings. He found that ratings increases (*e.g.* "sell" to "hold") were associated with future positive returns while ratings decreases were associated with future negative returns.

Kane, Kim, and White (2011) studied analysts who produce alpha forecasts. They found that a random sample of those forecasts anticipated abnormal returns from the CAPM with an S&P 500 benchmark. That suggested these analysts had an overall M^2 of 2.1%, yielding a portfolio with a Sharpe ratio of 1.15 versus the market Sharpe ratio of 0.91. They also calculated that if they had used all of the stocks for which they had forecasts, they would have achieved an M^2 of 9.4% with a Sharpe ratio of 1.95. Some might be surprised by how low their R^2 was — about 0.1%. When they examined this setup in Kane, Kim, and White (2010), they found that even analysts whose predictions have a correlation of 0.03 (implying $R^2 = 0.03^2 = 0.0009$) can still add value to portfolio returns.

Mutual Funds

While the performance of analysts is interesting, we might not agree on how to map alpha to investment. However, the performance of mutual funds is completely germane to determining where we can find valuable active management

Carhart (1997) shows that the performance of most mutual funds can be explained by momentum — except the worst funds; their performance is persistently poor (perhaps due to transactions costs). It also appears that much of the momentum effect comes from lower-liquidity stocks.

Elton et al. (1993) used a multi-index CAPM model (S&P 500, small-cap index, bond index) to study mutual fund performance. After controlling for those factors, they find that funds had negative but insignificant alpha — with the exception of "balanced" funds which had significant negative alpha. Also, funds which charged higher fee funds performed worse.

Similarly, Henriksson (1984) analyzed 116 mutual funds with the market timing test of Henriksson and Merton (1981) and found an insignificant negative coefficient for the market-timing term. Allowing for a firm-specific market-timing coefficient, he found 11 funds with significantly positive coefficients and 8 funds with significantly negative coefficients — well within the range or randomness.

The most bleak findings come from Blake et al. (1993) who studied the performance of bond mutual funds. They find that bond funds have no persistence of performance; underperform the benchmark bond index overall; and, fully pass on higher expenses to investors via lower returns.

Why might mutual funds have such poor performance across time and no persistence yet some momentum? While many have interpreted these findings as meaning fund managers have no skill, Berk and Green (2004) show that many of these features can be replicated by a world with some skilled fund managers and investors who invest in funds with attractive past returns in their effort to find skilled fund managers.

Attractive past returns can attract fund inflows. Inflows can push up the prices of the funds' holdings (especially for less liquid stocks), leading to momentum. As a fund grows and attracts inflows, skill or alpha is eventually spread thinner: the alpha cannot support enough liquidity, other firms learn and compete for the same alpha, or costs of managing more investments rise. Finally, as inflows slow, the price pressure on the funds' specific holdings declines and returns may be reduced. Thus returns are not persistent.

While these findings do not mean there are no good fund managers, they do mean that we need to be careful about inferring poor management from historical fund performance.

Good management might seem implausible, but Wermers (2000) shows that mutual funds' stock picks would beat the market by 1.3% — except that their gains are overcome by underperformance of non-stock holdings (-0.7%) and transactions costs (-1.6%). Thus the changes in markets reducing transactions costs, discussed in Chapter 4, could greatly benefit investors.

Mutual Funds and Hedge Funds

A common criticism of this literature is that analysts and mutual fund portfolio managers might not be most-skilled investors. The reason behind this claim is Jensen and Meckling (1976) finding that agents perform better when their pay is linked to their performance. Mutual funds in many countries (including the US) do not allow such compensation structures while hedge funds and trading firms often use such structures. If mutual fund managers had skill, why would they not go to a trading firm or hedge fund where they could get paid much more — often a part or equity stake in their profits?

Nohel, Wang, and Zheng (2010) studied if pay-for-performance matters by looking at **side-by-side managers**, mutual fund managers who also manage a hedge fund. They find that side-by-side managers are superior mutual fund managers, outperforming similar mutual funds and generating alpha after controlling for the Fung and Hsieh (2004) factors. In particular, they find that side-by-side managers who started as mutual fund managers earn alpha of 1.1%/year in their mutual funds. Furthermore, they do not find that the hedge funds they run take advantage of the mutual funds. Deuskar et al. (2011) show that side-by-side management is used as a retention tool for the best mutual fund managers.

Interestingly, both articles find that these skills are similar but not the same. Nohel, Wang, and Zheng (2010) show that hedge fund managers who add a mutual fund on the side have average mutual fund performance — and mutual fund managers who add a hedge fund on the side have worse-than-average hedge fund performance.

Deuskar et al. (2011) show that mutual fund managers who depart for hedge funds subsequently underperform.

Thus it seems clear that there are superior fund managers and that incentive pay can help to attract and keep talent. Furthermore, there does seem to be some difference in the skills which make for a superior mutual fund versus hedge fund manager.

24.8.6 Time-Varying Measures

Many of the metrics we use change in unexpected ways if performance and risk vary over time. That might seem obvious, but we can easily create what seem like paradoxes.

Suppose our portfolio P has the same Sharpe ratio over two time periods, $t_0 \to t_1$ and $t_1 \to t_2$. The Sharpe ratio for the whole period, $t_0 \to t_2$, may not be the same:[14]

$$P_{t_0 \to t_1}: S_P = \frac{0.2}{0.3} = \frac{2}{3}; \tag{24.58}$$

$$P_{t_1 \to t_2}: S_P = \frac{0.1}{0.15} = \frac{2}{3}; \text{ but,} \tag{24.59}$$

$$P_{t_0 \to t_2}: S_P = \frac{(0.1 + 0.2)/2}{\sqrt{(0.3^2 + 0.15^2)/2 + 0.05^2}} = \frac{0.15}{0.24} < \frac{2}{3}. \tag{24.60}$$

Since the Sharpe ratio changes, the M^2 measure also changes.

To see the intuition behind this, consider modeling returns depending on the states $s \in \mathcal{S}$ of the economy: "bull" versus "bear" or even weak and strong versions of these. In this setup, returns vary around some mean μ_s with some volatility σ_s; and, the mean and volatility are different for each state of the economy $(\mu_s, \sigma_s) \neq (\mu_{s'}, \sigma_{s'}) \; \forall x, x' \in \mathcal{S}$.

However, if we observe returns for long enough, we will see multiple states of the economy. Thus we see the variation around state-specific means $\{\sigma_s\}_{s \in \mathcal{S}}$ as well as the variation of the state-specific means $\{\mu_s\}_{s \in \mathcal{S}}$ — what experiment-analyzing statisticians call the **within-group variation** and **between-group variation**.

We also expect successful market timers to adjust their positions over time. This would give them better performance when the market goes up and may give them better performance when the market goes down. Thus their profitability and its risk might be very different depending on if the market is trending up, down, or "sideways" (no trend).

24.8.7 Manipulation of Measures

Another concern is that it is possible (and even easy) to manipulate standard performance measures. Ingersoll et al. (2007) show that this can be done for a

---

[14]The variance in the denominator for $t_0 \to t_2$ is essentially a sum of squares within groups and a sum of squares between groups. This should be familiar to anyone who has used ANOVA.

number of risk measures such as the Sharpe ratio. They also define the properties that make for a better performance measure.[15]

They discuss three types of manipulations to performance measures:

1. *Static manipulation of underlying distribution*: *e.g.* write OOM options, deposit all money in risk-free bonds, and potentially earn positive returns with no realized volatility.
2. *Dynamic manipulation to induce time variation, non-stationarity*: *e.g.* increase or decrease leverage after poor or excellent returns.[16]
3. *Dynamic manipulation to induce measurement error*: *e.g.* smooth returns or hold illiquid investments which may have infrequently-updated prices.

To counteract such manipulations, they propose four properties of a manipulation-proof performance measure:

1. **Functionhood**: The measure must give a single score for each investment.
2. **Scale Invariance**: A score cannot depend on the investment notional value.
3. **Unbiasedness**: (a) An uninformed investor cannot improve the expected score by deviating from a benchmark investment; and, (b) an informed investor can improve the expected score via arbitrage opportunities.
4. **Economic Consistency**: The measure should be consistent with standard market equilibrium conditions.

They also explain the unbiasedness and economic consistency properties briefly: the measure must be increasing in returns; concave, to penalize leverage; time-separable, to prevent dynamic manipulation; and, a power form to be consistent with an equilibrium.

These properties suggest using an additively-separable power utility function for a **manipulation-proof performance measure** $\hat{\Theta}$:

$$\hat{\Theta} = \frac{1}{(1-\rho)\Delta t} \log \left(\frac{1}{T} \sum_{t=1}^{T} \left[\frac{1+r_t}{1+r_{f,t}} \right]^{1-\rho} \right), \tag{24.61}$$

where ρ is the coefficient of relative risk aversion (usually close to 3) and r_t is the geometric investment return (*i.e.* $1 + r_t = v_t/v_{t-1}$ where v is the investment value). The value of $\hat{\Theta}$ is the certainty equivalent return in excess of the risk-free rate r_f.

24.8.8   *What Fee is Fair?*

Finally, one of the questions frequently asked by both investors and investment managers is: what is a fair fee for a given level of investment performance?

---

[15]If you look at the citation, you will see this is another "Gang of Four" that has proposed properties of a good measure — like Artzner, Delbaen, Eber, and Heath.

[16]Note that this may also reduce time variation as shown by Kyle (1985) which adaptively trades to reduce information leaked to the market.

An early attempt to find such a fee was made by Kane, Marcus, and Trippi (1999); their approach is best thought of from the Treynor-Black perspective. They found that the value of active management value could be expressed by S_P and S_M. This implies a fractional one-time fee of:[17]

$$\% \text{ fee} = f_{\text{one-time}} = \frac{S_P^2 - S_M^2}{2\bar{\lambda}} = \frac{IR_A^2}{2\bar{\lambda}} = \frac{\sum_{i=1}^{n} IR_i^2}{2\bar{\lambda}}. \tag{24.62}$$

This says that an actively-managed fund with a Sharpe ratio of $S_P = 1.0$ when the market Sharpe ratio is $S_M = 0.8$ can charge investors having mean risk aversion of $\bar{\lambda} = 3$ a one-time fee of $\frac{0.36}{6} = 0.06 = 6\%$ (plus the cost of an index fund).

On the other hand, Berk and Green (2004) suggest that investment managers' annual fees would consume all of the expected alpha:

$$f_{\text{annual}} = E(\alpha_A). \tag{24.63}$$

This seems unlikely unless investors are somehow being provided with other services. That is the idea of Glode (2011) who suggests investors will pay that and more if the fund provides alpha in bad states of the economy (when stock prices fall and their expected future return becomes larger):

$$f_{\text{annual}} = E(\alpha_A) + r_f \operatorname{Cov}(R_M, \alpha_A) \tag{24.64}$$

This is *not* like Treynor-Black where portfolio A contains a market component and A_α excludes the market component; in that setup $\operatorname{Cov}(R_M, \alpha_A) = 0$. Rather, we assume the active management is dynamic: it is more intense (and valuable) in bad economic times.

We might instead think that investors will pay a fee above that of an index fund based on the (abnormal) returns they receive $(\alpha - f)$ minus a penalty for the uncertainty of the alpha. While we think log-returns are not normal, the Gauss-Markov Theorem makes $\hat{\alpha}$ much closer to normality than the estimation data. Thus we can use mean-variance utility to find the optimal fee f^*:

$$f = \alpha - f - \frac{\bar{\lambda}}{2}\hat{\sigma}_\alpha^2, \tag{24.65}$$

$$\implies f_{\text{annual}}^* = \frac{\alpha}{2} - \frac{\bar{\lambda}\sigma_\alpha^2}{4}; \quad \text{or} \quad \frac{f_{\text{annual}}^*}{\alpha} = \frac{1}{2} - \frac{\bar{\lambda}\alpha}{4IR_A^2}. \tag{24.66}$$

The nice part of this solution is that it does not presume the manager will claim all the alpha in fees; what rational investor would deviate from the market (or the market and a put option) and pay higher fees to a manager of unknown quality

---

[17]This article suggests that R^2 should factor into fees since predicted alphas are more variable. Unfortunately, that confuses the variability of future averages with the variability of one future return. Furthermore, even if that perspective were correct, the analysis should then use a prediction interval — which does not depend on R^2.

without getting some alpha? Furthermore, as the manager has an increasingly high information ratio, the solution approaches splitting the alpha with the investor.

We might even try to find a fee based on the Ingersoll et al. manipulation-proof performance measure. While that might be useful, it turns out that we should not expect to find a clearly superior fee structure: Foster and Young (2010) show that there is no manipulation-proof fee structure. Thus even if we can find the best managers, we cannot find a compensation scheme which they cannot expect to manipulate for their benefit. At best, we can only appeal to their desire to maintain a good reputation.

Finally, the fee models which lack an effect due to investors' risk aversion are troubling. We expect that a fund with more risk-averse investors would have a demanded lower fee. If risk aversion increases in a crisis, we would also expect investors to demand a fee reduction. (We see this often in crises.) Similarly, if more risk-averse investors invest in a fund, they will also demand a fee reduction. The effects also work the other way: when investors become more risk-averse, the fees for active managers fall and so we should see active managers exiting the market.

24.9 Performance Attribution

If we are a manager with skill for some parts of our investment process, we might want to determine in what ways our skills adds value. This can help us focus internal improvement efforts on the areas which need improvement and not on areas already adding the most value. That way we can find how to add more value to investors and attract capital.

We would also like to be more sophisticated so that we can try to distinguish different types of skill — since we might be able to hire people or buy software to handle different tasks. This sort of a decomposition of skill can be difficult and subject to manipulation; however, the idea is incredibly useful and manipulation is not a concern if we use the decomposition as an internal measure.

One excellent decomposition is suggested by Brinson, Hood, and Beebower (1986). Suppose we want to assess our skill at asset allocation and sector/instrument selection compared to a benchmark B. The benchmark is allocated among K asset classes, yielding the benchmark asset allocation weights $\{w_{B_k}\}_{k=1}^K$. Our portfolio has different asset allocation weights $\{w_{P_k}\}_{k=1}^K$. To assess our performance, we then need the returns for the benchmark's asset allocations r_{B_k} and our portfolio's asset allocations r_{P_k}.

With this setup, we can see that the benchmark B and our portfolio P have performance broken down by asset class as:

$$r_B = \sum_{k=1}^K w_{B_k} r_{B_k} \qquad r_P = \sum_{k=1}^K w_{P_k} r_{P_k}. \qquad (24.67)$$

To decompose our performance, we need to think in terms of a **counterfactual**:

a decision we might have made. In this case, we consider what would have happened had we invested our portfolio's asset allocation in the benchmark's asset class sub-portfolios, creating counterfactual portfolio P':

$$r_{P'} = \sum_{k=1}^{K} w_{P_k} r_{B_k}. \tag{24.68}$$

We start with the difference between the performance of our portfolio P and the benchmark portfolio B:

$$r_P - r_B = \sum_{k=1}^{K} (w_{P_k} r_{P_k} - w_{B_k} r_{B_k}). \tag{24.69}$$

Adding and subtracting the counterfactual performance, we get:

$$r_P - r_{P'} + r_{P'} - r_B = \sum_{k=1}^{K} (w_{P_k} r_{P_k} - w_{P_k} r_{B_k} + w_{P_k} r_{B_k} - w_{B_k} r_{B_k}) \tag{24.70}$$

$$= \sum_{k=1}^{K} [\underbrace{w_{P_k}(r_{P_k} - r_{B_k})}_{\substack{\text{instrument/sector} \\ \text{selection}}} + \underbrace{(w_{P_k} - w_{B_k}) r_{B_k}}_{\substack{\text{asset} \\ \text{allocation}}}]. \tag{24.71}$$

We can take this idea further.[18] For each asset class in B and P, we have sub-portfolios B_k and P_k. Imagine another counterfactual portfolio P'' which invests with our portfolio's asset allocation w_{P_k} and instruments within a sector $r_{P_{k,s}}$ but the benchmark portfolio's sector allocations within an asset class $\frac{\{w_{B_k,s}\}_{s=1}^{S}}{w_{B_k}}$:

$$r_{P_k''} = \sum_{s=1}^{S} \frac{w_{B_k,s}}{w_{B_k}} r_{P_{k,s}}, \quad w_{B_k} = \sum_{s=1}^{S} w_{B_k,s}. \tag{24.72}$$

We can then use the counterfactual P'' to separate the effects of sector and instrument selection:

$$r_{P_k} - r_{P_k''} + r_{P_k''} - r_{B_k} = \overbrace{\sum_{s=1}^{S} \left(\frac{w_{P_{k,s}}}{w_{P_k}} - \frac{w_{B_k,s}}{w_{B_k}} \right) r_{P_{k,s}}}^{\text{sector selection}} \tag{24.73}$$

$$+ \underbrace{\sum_{s=1}^{S} \frac{w_{B_k,s}}{w_{B_k}} (r_{P_{k,s}} - r_{B_{k,s}})}_{\text{instrument selection}}. \tag{24.74}$$

---

[18]The following breakdown is not from Brinson, Hood, and Beebower (1986); however, it is an application of their ideas with some conditioning.

The last term looks different than we started with; but, it is equal because
$$r_{B_k} = \sum_{s=1}^{S} \frac{w_{B_{k,s}}}{w_{B_k}} r_{B_{k,s}}.$$
There are also decompositions of trading performance, such as the split between market timing, trade scheduling, and execution skill in Rosenthal (2012b); however, those are more suited to a course in market microstructure.

24.10   Quiz

Try to answer these questions in fifteen minutes. If the math is difficult, leave your answer in the form of a fraction. However, work through as much of the math as you can. Also, do not use a calculator; it will only slow you down.

1. At the start of year 0 you invest $10 which grows to $12. At the start of year 1 you invest another $10. At the end of year 1 (start of year 2) you sell your investments for $24.20.

(a) What is the time-weighted average return?
(b) What is the dollar-weighted average return (IRR)?

2. Portfolio P has the following characteristics: $\sigma_P = 30\%$, $\theta_P = 50\%$, $\alpha_P = 3\%$, $E(R_P) = 10\%$. The "market portfolio" (yes, I know...) has the following characteristics: $\sigma_M = 15\%$ and $E(R_M) = 5\%$. The risk-free rate is $r_f = 2\%$. Compute the following performance metrics:

(a) Sharpe ratio $S_P = ?$
(b) Sortino ratio $So_P = ?$
(c) Market beta of P, $\beta_P = ?$
(d) Modigliani^2 $M^2 = ?$
(e) Treynor ratio $T_P = ?$
(f) (BONUS 2!) Information ratio $IR_P = ?$

3. Give a few reasons why the manager of the preceding portfolio P is or is not a good market timer.

4. For a portfolio P, you note that $r_P = 10\%$ while for the benchmark portfolio B, $r_B = 8\%$. If the technology sector weightings and returns are $w_{B_{tech}} = 10\%$, $w_{P_{tech}} = 20\%$, $r_{B_{tech}} = 10\%$, and $r_{P_{tech}} = 15\%$. Both P and B are fully invested in equities, so there are no asset allocation effects.

(a) What return is due to portfolio P being overweight technology stocks relative to the benchmark portfolio B?
(b) What return is due to portfolio P doing a better job at picking technology stocks relative to the benchmark portfolio B?

5. Name a serious problem with the Treynor-Black model and one way to (hopefully) fix that problem.

6. What is unusual about how the Black-Litterman model predicts asset class returns?

7. Name a serious problem with the Black-Litterman model and one way to (hopefully) fix it?

8. For each of the Treynor-Black and Black-Litterman models, is each top-down or bottom-up? Be clear!

9. You run a hedge fund with $\alpha = 0.10$, $\sigma_\alpha = 0.10$, and $\text{Cov}(R_M, \alpha) = 0.0075$. If $r_f = 2\%$ and the average risk aversion of your investors is $\bar{\lambda} = 1$, what percentage fee should you charge? What happens if $\bar{\lambda}$ increases to 3?

24.11   Exercises

1. Suppose you build two portfolios. One is like that discussed in the fees section: It was built using the Treynor-Black model and has a Sharpe ratio of $S_{p_1} = 1.0$ while the market has a Sharpe ratio of $S_M = 0.8$. The other portfolio has the same excess return and volatility (and therefore the same Sharpe ratio $S_{P_2} = S_{P_1}$) but achieves all of its returns from market-neutral alpha.

   a) Explain why you must charge a higher fee for P_1 and P_2.
   b) Discuss what assumptions would need to change to justify charging different fees for P_1 and P_2 in the above scenario. (Thus the portfolios having different excess returns is not a reason.)

2. Using the R code from Chapter 9, construct and compare portfolios. You will need to get data for an investment universe of 9 ETFs: SPY (S&P 500), IWM (Russell 2000), FEZ (Euro Stoxx 50), ACWI (MSCI All-Country World), AGG (Barclays Aggregate US Bond), IAGG (iShares Core International Aggregate Bond), IYR (Dow Jones US Real Estate), REET (iShares Global REIT), and GSG (iShares GSCI Commodity Index).

   a) Create Markowitz and equal-risk contribution portfolios.
   b) Construct expected returns by finding the sizes of these markets (or amounts indexed to those indices) and using those in an equilibrium model. Then find the optimal Black-Litterman portfolio.
   c) Find the optimal Treynor-Black portfolio using a CAPM model with an index comprised of each of the ETFs weighted by the amount indexed to each index.
   d) Find the optimal ETF portfolio using the Almgren-Chriss method.
   e) How do the results of these approaches differ?

References

Almgren, Robert and Neil Chriss. *Portfolios from Sorts*. Working Paper 720041. SSRN, 2005. DOI: 10.2139/ssrn.720041.

— "Optimal Portfolios from Ordering Information". *Journal of Risk* 9.1 (2006), pp. 1–47. DOI: 10.21314/jor.2006.143.

Asness, Clifford S., Andrea Frazzini, and Lasse Heje Pedersen. *Quality Minus Junk*. Working Paper 2312432. SSRN, 2017. DOI: 10.2139/ssrn.2312432.

Baker, Nardin L. and Robert A. Haugen. "Low Risk Stocks Outperform within All Observable Markets of the World". 2055431 (2012). DOI: 10.2139/ssrn.2055431.

Berk, Jonathan B. and Richard C. Green. "Mutual Fund Flows and Performance in Rational Markets". *Journal of Political Economy* 112.6 (2004), pp. 1269–1295. DOI: 10.1086/424739.

Birge, John R. and François Louveaux. *Introduction to Stochastic Programming*. 2nd ed. New York: Springer-Verlag, 2011.

Black, Fischer and Robert Litterman. "Global Portfolio Optimization". *Financial Analyst's Journal* 48.5 (1992), pp. 28–43. DOI: 10.2469/faj.v48.n5.28.

Black, Fischer and Robert B. Litterman. "Asset Allocation: Combining Investor Views with Market Equilibrium". *Journal of Fixed Income* 1.2 (1991), pp. 7–18. DOI: 10.3905/jfi.1991.408013.

Blake, Christopher R. et al. "The Performance of Bond Mutual Funds". *Journal of Business* 66.3 (1993), pp. 371–404. DOI: 10.1086/296609.

Bondarenko, Oleg. "Why Are Put Options So Expensive?" *Quarterly Journal of Finance* 4.3 (2014), pp. 1–50. DOI: 10.1142/S2010139214500153.

Boudt, Kris, Peter Carl, and Brian G. Peterson. "Asset Allocation with Conditional Value-at-Risk Budgets". *Journal of Risk* 15.3 (2013), pp. 39–68. DOI: 10.21314/jor.2013.258.

Boudt, Kris, Jonathan Cornelissen, and Scott Payseur. *highfrequency: Tools for Highfrequency Data Analysis*. R package version 0.5.2. 2017. URL: https://CRAN.R-project.org/package=highfrequency.

Brinson, Gary P., L. Randolph Hood, and Gilbert L. Beebower. "Determinants of Portfolio Performance". *Financial Analyst's Journal* 42.4 (1986), pp. 39–44. DOI: 10.2469/faj.v42.n4.39.

Brinson, Gary P. et al. "Determinants of Portfolio Performance II: An Update". *Financial Analyst's Journal* 47.3 (1991), pp. 40–48. DOI: 10.2469/faj.v47.n3.40.

Brown, Stephen J. et al. "Survivorship Bias in Performance Studies". *Review of Financial Studies* 5.4 (1992), pp. 553–580. DOI: 10.1093/rfs/5.4.553.

Carhart, Mark M. "On Persistence in Mutual Fund Performance". *Journal of Finance* 52.1 (1997), pp. 57–82. DOI: 10.1111/j.1540-6261.1997.tb03808.x.

Connor, Gregory and Robert A. Korajczyk. "Performance Measurement with the Arbitrage Pricing Theory: A New Framework for Analysis". *Journal of Financial Economics* 15.3 (1986), pp. 373–394. DOI: 10.1016/0304-405X(86)90027-9.

Dalio, Ray. *Engineering Targeted Returns & Risks*. Research Paper. Available in reprinted form at https://www.bridgewater.com/resources/engineering-targeted-returns-and-risks.pdf. Bridgewater Associates, 2004.

Deuskar, Prachi et al. "The Good or the Bad? Which Mutual Fund Managers Join Hedge Funds?" *Review of Financial Studies* 24.9 (2011), pp. 3008–3024. DOI: 10.1093/rfs/hhr057.

Elton, Edwin J. et al. "Efficiency with Costly Information: A Reinterpretation of Evidence from Managed Portfolios". *Review of Financial Studies* 6.1 (1993), pp. 1–22. DOI: 10.1093/rfs/6.1.1.

Foster, Dean P. and H. Peyton Young. "Gaming Performance Fees By Portfolio Managers". *Quarterly Journal of Economics* 125.4 (2010), pp. 1435–1458. DOI: 10.1162/qjec.2010.125.4.1435.

Frazzini, Andrea and Lasse Heje Pedersen. "Betting against Beta". *Journal of Financial Economics* 111.1 (2014), pp. 1–25. DOI: 10.1016/j.jfineco.2013.10.005.

Fung, William and David A. Hsieh. "Empirical Characteristics of Dynamic Trading Strategies: The Case of Hedge Funds". *Review of Financial Studies* 10.2 (1997), pp. 275–302. DOI: 10.1093/rfs/10.2.275.

— "Performance Characteristics of Hedge Funds and Commodity Funds: Natural vs. Spurious Biases". *Journal of Financial and Quantitative Analysis* 35.3 (2000), pp. 291–307. DOI: 10.2307/2676205.

— "Hedge-Fund Benchmarks: Information Content and Biases". *Financial Analyst's Journal* 58.1 (2002), pp. 6–14. DOI: 10.2469/faj.v58.n1.2507.

— "Hedge Fund Benchmarks: A Risk-Based Approach". *Financial Analyst's Journal* 60.5 (2004), pp. 65–80. DOI: 10.2469/faj.v60.n5.2657.

— "Measurement Biases in Hedge Fund Performance Data: An Update". *Financial Analyst's Journal* 65.3 (2009), pp. 36–38. DOI: 10.2469/faj.v65.n3.6.

Gelman, Andrew et al. *Bayesian Data Analysis*. 3rd ed. Boca Raton, FL: Chapman & Hall/CRC, 2013.

Glode, Vincent. "Why Mutual Funds "Underperform"". *Journal of Financial Economics* 99.3 (2011), pp. 546–559. DOI: 10.1016/j.jfineco.2010.10.008.

Hasanhodzic, Jasmina and Andrew W. Lo. "Can Hedge-Fund Returns Be Replicated?: The Linear Case". *Journal of Investment Management* 5.2 (2007), pp. 5–45.

Haugen, Robert A. and Nardin L. Baker. "The Efficient Market Inefficiency of Capitalization-Weighted Stock Portfolios". *Journal of Portfolio Management* 17.1 (1991), pp. 35–40. DOI: 10.3905/jpm.1991.409335.

Haugen, Robert A. and A. James Heins. "Risk and the Rate of Return on Financial Assets: Some Old Wine in New Bottles". *Journal of Financial and Quantitative Analysis* 10.5 (1975), pp. 775–784. DOI: 10.2307/2330270.

Henriksson, Roy D. "Market Timing and Mutual Fund Performance: An Empirical Investigation". *Journal of Business* 57.1 (1984), pp. 73–96. DOI: 10.1086/296225.

Henriksson, Roy D. and Robert C. Merton. "On Market Timing and Investment

Performance. II. Statistical Procedures for Evaluating Forecast Skills". *Journal of Business* 54.4 (1981), pp. 513–533. DOI: 10.1086/296144.

Homer, Sidney et al. "Inside the Yield Book: The Classic That Created the Science of Bond Analysis" (2013).

Ibbotson, Roger G. "The Importance of Asset Allocation". *Financial Analyst's Journal* 66.2 (2010), pp. 18–20. DOI: 10.2469/faj.v66.n2.4.

Ingersoll, Jonathan et al. "Portfolio Performance Manipulation and Manipulation-proof Performance Measures". *Review of Financial Studies* 20.5 (2007), pp. 1503–1546. DOI: 10.1093/rfs/hhm025.

Jensen, Michael C. "The Performance of Mutual Funds in the Period 1945–1964". *Journal of Finance Papers and Proceedings* 23.2 (1968), pp. 389–416. DOI: 10.1111/j.1540-6261.1968.tb00815.x.

Jensen, Michael C. and William H. Meckling. "Theory of the Firm: Managerial Behavior, Agency Costs and Ownership Structure". *Journal of Financial Economics* 3.4 (1976), pp. 305–360. DOI: 10.1016/0304-405X(76)90026-X.

Jurek, Jakub W. and Erik Stafford. "The Cost of Capital for Alternative Investments". *Journal of Finance* 70.5 (2015), pp. 2185–2226. DOI: 10.1111/jofi.12269.

Kane, Alex, Tae-Hwan Kim, and Halbert White. "Forecast Precision and Portfolio Performance". *Journal of Financial Econometrics* 8.3 (2010), pp. 265–304. DOI: 10.1093/jjfinec/nbq018.

— "Active Portfolio Management: The Power of the Treynor-Black Model". In: *Progress in Financial Markets Research*. Ed. by Catherine Kyrtsou and Costas Vorlow. New York: Nova Science, 2011, pp. 311–332.

Kane, Alex, Alan J. Marcus, and Robert R. Trippi. "The Valuation of Security Analysis". *Journal of Portfolio Management* 25.3 (1999), pp. 25–37. DOI: 10.3905/jpm.1999.319712.

Kyle, Albert S. "Continuous Auctions and Insider Trading". *Econometrica* 53.6 (1985), pp. 1315–1336. DOI: 10.2307/1913210.

Lehmann, Bruce N. "What We Measure in Execution Cost Measurement". *Journal of Financial Markets* 6.3 (2003), pp. 227–231. DOI: 10.1016/S1386-4181(03)00005-3.

Maillard, Sébastian, Thierry Roncalli, and Jérôme Teïletche. "The Properties of Equally Weighted Risk Contribution Portfolios". *Journal of Portfolio Management* 36.4 (2010), pp. 60–70. DOI: 10.3905/jpm.2010.36.4.060.

Markowitz, Harry. "Portfolio Selection". *Journal of Finance* 7.1 (1952), pp. 77–91. DOI: 10.1111/j.1540-6261.1952.tb01525.x.

Merton, Robert C. "On Market Timing and Investment Performance. I. An Equilibrium Theory of Value for Market Forecasts". *Journal of Business* 54.3 (1981), pp. 363–406. DOI: 10.1086/296137.

Meucci, Attilio. *The Black-Litterman Approach: Original Model and Extensions*. Working Paper 1117574. SSRN, 2010. DOI: 10.2139/ssrn.1117574.

Modigliani, Franco and Leah Modigliani. "Risk-Adjusted Performance". *Journal of Portfolio Management* 23.2 (1997), pp. 45–54. DOI: 10.3905/jpm.23.2.45.

Nohel, Tom, Z. Jay Wang, and Lu Zheng. "Side-by-Side Management of Hedge Funds and Mutual Funds". *Review of Financial Studies* 23.6 (2010), pp. 2342–2373. DOI: 10.1093/rfs/hhq008.

Pearson, Neil D. *Risk Budgeting: Portfolio Problem Solving with Value-at-Risk.* New York: Wiley, 2002.

Peterson, Brian G. and Peter Carl. *PortfolioAnalytics: Portfolio Analysis, Including Numerical Methods for Optimization of Portfolios.* R package version 1.0.3636. 2015. URL: https://CRAN.R-project.org/package=PortfolioAnalytics.

Qian, Edward. *Risk Parity Portfolios: Efficient Portfolios through True Diversification.* Report. Available from https://www.panagora.com/assets/PanAgora-Risk-Parity-Portfolios-Efficient-Portfolios-Through-True-Diversification.pdf. Panagora Asset Management, 2005.

Rosenthal, Dale W.R. *Performance Metrics for Algorithmic Traders.* Working Paper 1439902. SSRN, 2012. DOI: 10.2139/ssrn.1439902.

Roy, A.D. "Safety First and the Holding of Assets". *Econometrica* 20.3 (1952), pp. 431–449. DOI: 10.2307/1907413.

Sharpe, William F. "Mutual Fund Performance". *Journal of Business* 39.1 (1966), pp. 119–138. DOI: 10.1086/294846.

Sortino, Frank A. and Lee N. Price. "Performance Measurement in a Downside Risk Framework". *Journal of Investing* 3.3 (1994), pp. 59–64. DOI: 10.3905/joi.3.3.59.

Treynor, Jack L. and Fischer Black. "How to Use Security Analysis to Improve Portfolio Selection". *Journal of Business* 46.1 (1973), pp. 66–86. DOI: 10.1086/295508.

Treynor, Jack L. and Kay Mazuy. "Can Mutual Funds Outguess the Market?" *Harvard Business Review* 44.4 (1966), pp. 131–136.

Wermers, Russ. "Mutual Fund Performance: An Empirical Decomposition into Stock-Picking Talent, Style, Transactions Costs, and Expenses". *Journal of Finance Papers and Proceedings* 55.4 (2000), pp. 1655–1695. DOI: 10.1111/0022-1082.00263.

Womack, Kent L. "Do Brokerage Analysts' Recommendations Have Investment Value?" *Journal of Finance* 51.1 (1996), pp. 137–167. DOI: 10.1111/j.1540-6261.1996.tb05205.x.

Xiong, James et al. "The Equal Importance of Asset Allocation and Active Management". *Financial Analyst's Journal* 66.2 (2010), pp. 22–30. DOI: 10.2469/faj.v66.n4.13.

Zephyr Associates. *StatFacts: Information Ratio.* 2013. URL: http://www.styleadvisor.com/sites/default/files/StatFacts_Information_Ratio.pdf.

Chapter 25

Investment Management Companies

> ⚠ **Atenção!** *Some readers or instructors may want to discuss investment companies well before discussing investment management. This is particularly germane when introducing investments to an audience with some less finance-oriented members. Knowing some basics about investment companies is crucial for people to begin investing for their future. If that is your goal, you can read the first six sections and return later to the following sections.*

An **investment company** pools client funds, possibly commingling those funds, and invests them. Most investors will invest in an investment company. Investment companies remove the hassle of investing: they record cashflows in and out of the fund, corporate actions, and interest; they track cost basis and the tax status of investors' gains (*i.e.* short- vs long-term); and, they report results to investors.

Investment companies may also offer better management. Their size may help them negotiate better prices and trade more cheaply. They (hopefully) offer economies of scale benefits by sharing fixed costs and employing specialists. Finally, they manage the portfolio professionally, all day. That is not something most investors can do while they are working.

Learning about investment management companies is some of the most directly useful information for students of investments. Almost every discussion of investment management (outside of this text) is with someone *who is trying to sell you something*. The purpose of this chapter is to review the different types of investment management companies, discuss the different performance of various investment strategy types, and examine some issues with investment managers.

25.1 Terminology

If we are going to discuss investment companies, we will need a few terms.

An investment company takes in client monies. These monies may then be **pooled** if they are commingled. In that case, a legal entity called a **trust** is created to hold assets and monies. The entities who operate the trust are called **trustees** and are expected to exercise fiduciary duty. On the other hand, monies might not be commingled; in that case, they are kept in **segregated accounts**. This offers a higher level of assurance that client funds are not mixed with company funds nor used for company cash management.

The **assets under management**, often abbreviated as AUM, is the amount of money a firm's clients have invested with the firm. That is not a historical number, it is current and reflects gains on prior AUM (as well as inflows and outflows); however, AUM does not include leverage. Suppose I take in $100 mn of client funds; take out $100 mn in loans; and, then invest in a $200×$200 mn long-short portfolio. If, in a quarter, that is worth $220×$175 mn, I gained $20 mn on the long side and $25 mn on the short side. Ignoring transaction costs (something we should never do), that means our clients' funds are now worth the AUM of $145 mn. The AUM is *not* $200 mn, $395 mn, nor $400 mn. Related to AUM is the **net asset value (NAV)**, defined as $\text{NAV} = \frac{\text{market value of assets} - \text{liabilities}}{\text{shares outstanding}}$. Mapping the AUM calculation to this accounting-speak is trickier than it seems: Figure 25.1 works it out for the long-short fund above. (Side note: I hate accounting because it seems arbitrary and gameable. However, this is basic accounting and is useful.)

Assets	Liabilities		
$220 mn long stock	$100 mn loan		
$200 mn stock borrowed	$175 mn short		
solve for:	$145 mn shareholder equity	= AUM	
	200 shares	$\implies$	$725k/share NAV

Figure 25.1: NAV calculations for what was initially a $100 mn AUM long-short fund which took out a loan and had gains on both the long and short sides of the portfolio.

Many funds maintain **pass-through tax status**: no corporate taxes are assessed on investor payouts. This avoids double- or triple-taxation: only the final investor pays taxes on gains in the investment portfolio. If this were not so, using professional investment managers would be at a disadvantage to managing your own money.

Finally, one of the important metrics to think about is **turnover**: the ratio of portfolio sales to value. Intuitively, this is like the fraction of the portfolio "replaced" in a year.

25.2 Types of Investment Companies

The most common investment funds are of a handful of types:

- Open-End Funds;
- Closed-End Funds;
- Real Estate Investment Trusts;
- Unit Investment Trusts;
- Royalty Trusts and Master Limited Partnerships;
- Managed Futures/Commodity Trading Advisors; and,
- Hedge Funds.

The last three or four are often called **alternative investments** since they are more unusual investments: the latter two can short more and invest in ways most funds cannot (by law). This is not as secretive as it sounds; many mutual funds are prohibited from shorting stocks or trading in derivatives. Other alternative investments include real estate, infrastructure, pure commodities, private equity, and venture capital.

The Investment Company Act (1940) first defined mutual funds as well as distinguishing between unmanaged and managed funds.

25.2.1 *Mutual Funds*

A **mutual fund** is an **open ended** investment fund: a fund which increases the shares outstanding as money flows in or out of the fund. Thus open-ended funds see daily inflows and outflows of investment; and, the fund size changes with these flows. Investors buy and sell their shares at the end-of-day NAV (less fees). Although mutual funds often have ticker symbols, these are merely for reference or to access data; they are not exchange-listed.

Some funds are unusual in that they try to preserve a fixed NAV. Money market funds try to hold their NAV at $1 and pay out interest to investors by granting fractional shares to investors.

Mutual funds are a gigantic part of the financial ecosystem: they collectively have about $16 tn in AUM in the US and about $15 tn in AUM outside of the US.[1] Furthermore, mutual fund AUMs are increasing as more people turn to professional money management.

25.2.2 *Exchange-Traded Funds (ETFs)*

An **exchange-traded fund (ETF)** is another open-ended fund and is very similar to mutual fund. Unlike mutual funds, however, ETFs are listed and traded on-exchange. The advantage for investors is that this makes them shortable. ETFs are commonly used for index funds which lowers their portfolio trading, marketing, and

---

[1]Unless otherwise noted, the AUM figures that follow are from ICI (2016).

(thus) expenses. Unlike a mutual fund, however, purchasers have to pay brokerage commissions and may have to pay the bid-ask spread. What keeps an ETF market price connected to its NAV? Index arbitrageurs and the managers of the fund who can issue new shares to the market or remove them to ensure that the market price and NAV stay together.

The best-known ETFs in the US are the SPY (aka "spiders"), and S&P 500 index fund; the IWM, a Russell 2000 index fund; and, the QQQQ (Q's), a Nasdaq 100 index fund. There are also sector-specific ETFs like XLE and XLF (which invest in the energy and financial sectors).

At this point, I often hear about "ETFs" which invest in all sorts of things like oil, gold, and rare-earth metals. There's nothing wrong with investing in those assets, but caution is advisable: some funds have not matched the performance of those assets over time. In particular, some exchange-traded *notes* and commodity-linked notes have had terrible performance. Henderson, Pearson, and Wang (2015) discusses the suboptimality of commodity-linked notes as a way to study uninformed investors.

Exchange-traded funds are not a gigantic part of the financial ecosystem, but they are big: $2.1 tn in AUM with much of that in index ETFs. ETF AUMs are also growing quickly.

25.2.3   Closed-End Funds

A **closed-end fund** is more like a stock: they issue a fixed ("closed") number of shares to raise capital for the portfolio. Like ETFs, closed-end funds are listed and traded on-exchange. That makes them shortable. What makes closed-end funds different is that investors buy and sell them at the market price — which may (and often does) diverge from NAV. Funds often trade at a discount to NAV and some investors see this as free money. Unfortunately, discounts can persist for months or years.

These facts are not unrelated. Closed-end funds are well-suited for investing in illiquid assets. If you are going to buy shares in a Sri Lankan tea blender or a Turkish engineering firm, you might not want to be constantly crossing the spread as investors move in or out. The investment could even be a strategic private placement — in which case buying and selling would not likely be possible. However, that illiquidity is a risk: if the fund had to quickly sell off assets, they would likely get prices far worse than the last-measured market value of their investments.

However, closed-end funds are sometimes the only way to easily invest in a certain country or region. For example, investors who wanted to bet on the resurgent economies of the Vyšehrad Group (Poland, Czech Republic, Slovak Republic, and Hungary) before their accession to the EU had no other option than a closed-end fund. Furthermore, closed-end funds sometimes have a break-up clause that states the shareholders can elect to break up the fund and receive (or sell off) the assets if the discount persists below some level (say, 25%). Some investment managers look for such closed-end funds, estimate the cost of selling assets, and then may invest and agitate for break up to realize more value.

Closed-end funds were popular in the 1920s, but they are now a small part of the financial ecosystem: about \$261 bn in AUM in the US.

25.2.4   Real Estate Investment Trusts (REITs)

A real estate investment trust (REIT, pronounced "reet") is a closed-end fund which invests in real estate. While a closed-end fund (per se) may diverge from NAV, just determining NAV for a REIT can be difficult. Many REITs are leveraged: debt ratios of half to three-quarters are not unusual. As mentioned before, REITs invest in property (equity REITs), in mortgages and construction loans (mortgage REITs), or in both (hybrid REITs).

REITs typically focus on a type of property: offices, hotels, condos, apartments, shopping malls, mobile home parks, or even timberland. To maintain their pass-through status, they must pay out over 90% of their earnings. REITs are neither huge nor small: US REITs have about \$1 tn in AUM according to National Association of Real Estate Investment Trusts (2016).

25.2.5   Unit Investment Trusts

A **unit investment trust** invests in a fixed portfolio. The fund sponsor buys the portfolio and deposits it into trust. The sponsor then sells public shares ("units") of the trust[2]. From then on, the income, gains, and principal payments are paid to shareholders. However, the trust is unmanaged: the portfolio composition is not directed. No changes are made to the portfolio. This can make expenses very low; however, if an investment turns out to be an obvious loser, it still will not be sold. The sponsor earns money by selling units at a premium to NAV. Investors exit the investment by selling their units back to the trustees at NAV, often minus a hefty fee. For these reasons, unit investment trusts are a small part of the financial ecosystem about \$94 bn in AUM (insofar as the assets are managed).

25.2.6   Master Limited Partnerships and Royalty Trusts

Master limited partnerships and royalty trusts are two ways of commodity-linked investing; however, their potential upside and role in a portfolio are very different.

A **master limited partnership (MLP)** is a US-traded limited partnership interest. These interests are mostly in firms that explore, produce, process, or transport resources (like oil or natural gas). MLPs have stringent quarterly-minimum distributions that they must meet to maintain their pass-through status. Thus MLPs are used to invest in businesses with stable payouts: less volatile firms like pipelines (which are not volatile because many are price-capped by FERC). That means

---

[2]These units are properly called **redeemable trust certificates**.

that although they are commodity-linked, they do not move around much with commodities. A few things to watch out for: some MLPs have high fees, many are illiquid, and the distributions are taxed like income.

A **royalty trust** holds the rights to commodity-related income. Typically, that means holding assets like oil or gas wells, but it could also hold mines or power generation. Royalty trusts have volatile payouts: they represent a perpetuity of real options to produce from a depleting asset. However, that means they may (or may not) produce revenue in a quarter, depending on prices. Royalty trusts pass-through almost all earnings and are mostly used in the US and Canada. In the US, royalty trusts are closed-end investments; in Canada, royalty trusts can (and do) manage their asset portfolio. Many Canadian royalty trusts converted to companies after the 2006 "Hallowe'en Massacre" when the government announced the end of preferential tax treatment. (The announcement shaved about one-third off many valuations.)

You can buy a US royalty trust and receive income while it depletes; and, the yield may be high (because of depletion and other risks). The endgame is what varies. If the trust is structured to sell off the assets after a certain number of non-performing years, the fund will eventually fall down near zero; then the trust sells off the assets and you get a final payment and may be able to take a nice tax loss. If the trust is structured to participate in a certain amount of extraction, you may hit that early and be done. How long will these take? That is not clear although extraction-to-reserves ratios may offer some guidance.[3]

However, some trusts have an aggressive target, and some have stranger termination clauses (say, 21 years after the last of a group of people dies).[4] In those cases, the trust may decline significantly in value without terminating. If that happens, you then sell it to your kids, take a tax loss, and wait. When prices and/or technology improve so extraction is again economically viable, they get a big gain. Distributions from a royalty trust are usually taxed as capital gains, and they may include tax credits. However, you may need to file taxes in the state where the assets are.

MLPs and royalty trusts are not big parts of the investment landscape: Alerian (2016) puts MLPs at about $400 bn in AUM. Royalty trusts are tiny: old figures from Zweig (2012) put AUM at about $12 bn in the US.

25.2.7 Managed Futures/Commodity Trading Advisors (CTAs)

A **managed futures** account is like a mutual fund of futures. The fund is managed by a **commodity trading advisor (CTA)**. The CTA invests long or short in futures and futures options. Also different from most funds: customer funds are often segregated, not pooled. Thus customers see every trade and bookkeeping action on their statements. Managed futures accounts are very transparent.

Managed futures investments tend to be valued for their low correlation with

---

[3]One *caveat* with this is that proven reserves are a measure of economically-viable reserves — and so they increase and decreases as prices rise and fall.

[4]This is the actual termination clause for the Mesabi Trust.

bond and equity returns — even though most funds invest in bond and equity index futures. Managed futures often have performance that is better than similar ETFs because futures can be more liquid than stocks. Furthermore, managed futures can have significant tax advantages over mutual funds due to futures being taxed partially at long-term gains rates.

Managed futures and CTAs are regulated by the CFTC and, according to Barclay Hedge (2016), manage about $348 bn in AUM in the US.

25.2.8   Hedge Funds

A **hedge fund** invests money for accredited investors only. For a long time, they were defined by omission: they were structured to fall into one of the exemption categories of the Investment Company Act (1940) and are exempt under the Investment Advisors Act (1940) because most advisors have only one client: the fund itself. That omitted the need for registration and regulation. The term itself originates from Loomis (1966) to describe some of the earliest funds run by Alfred Winslow Jones.

Many journalists like to refer to hedge funds as "unregulated" investment vehicles; however, that is dishonest: funds have to obey the rules and regulations of any markets they trade in; however, they often do not need to be regulated beyond that. That is not, however, unregulated.

Why do people invest in hedge funds? Because their restriction to accredited investors allows the fund much more freedom. They may invest long and short, with or without leverage, and in just about anything. For example, they can invest in viaticals, rhodium, art, timberland, and cat bonds — as well as stocks, bonds, futures, and options. Because hedge funds may invest in illiquid assets, they often restrict redemptions until after a lock-up period (which we will discuss shortly).

Another reason to invest in hedge funds is because of their incentive structure: Hedge funds typically charge fees on the AUM and also on the excess profits. Most investment companies are not allowed to pay the manager based on returns; not so with hedge funds. That means the investment manager does well when investors do well. Unfortunately, this can also lead to perverse incentives like taking too much risk.[5] Nohel, Wang, and Zheng (2010) and Chen and Chen (2009) both provide evidence that hedge funds attract superior managers. (Unfortunately, they can also attract inferior managers; there is no separating equilibrium.)

Hedge funds have been growing quickly and are now a large part of the financial ecosystem. Preqin (2017) puts global hedge fund AUM at about $3.2 tn.

25.3   Manager versus Portfolio

In the world of investment management, people often conflate the investment

---

[5]The joke on a trading desk is you are long an option. Take risk and make money: you get a big bonus. Take risk and lose money: you get fired and go to work elsewhere. Lather, rinse, repeat.

managers or advisors with the investment fund. It is important to clear up this confusion because the fund manager or advisor may not be employed by the fund (aka portfolio company).

This distinction exists among many investment companies. Some Vanguard mutual funds are managed by Wellington. The previously-mentioned Central European Equity closed-end fund was managed by Deutsche Asset Management; however, in 2002 a shareholder proposal sought to terminate the management agreement and seek a new fund manager.

Hedge funds also often adopt this separation, but that is because they often locate the portfolio company in a stable, low-tax, light-regulation location. That way, clients from multiple countries need not deal with foreign taxes and regulations. For example, hedge fund "LTCM" had managers/advisors in Greenwich, CT (LTCM), London (LTCM (UK)), and Tokyo (LTCMJ); all three advised the portfolio company LTCP (Cayman) — which was the holder of the Fund. Often, the fund also has local funds which then feed into the portfolio company. This can make taxes, investing, and legal issues easier for investors. An example of this structure is shown in Figure 25.2 and is often referred to as a **master-feeder structure** for the master fund and the local funds which feed into the master.

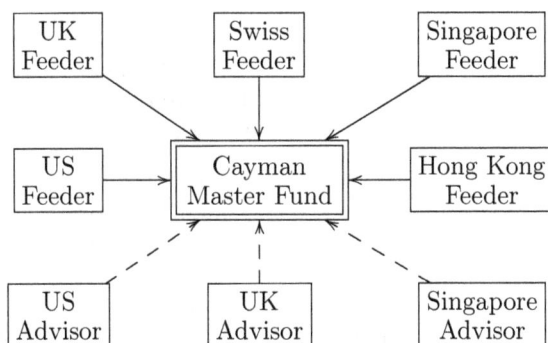

Figure 25.2: Master-feeder structure for a large fund with investors in many locales. The feeders are created in many locales to ease investment by investors in those locations. Advisors hold no assets but provide advice to the master fund.

This legalese is important because when people talk about "hedge funds," they often are imprecise about whether they are referring to the manager, master fund, or feeder fund. Furthermore, the fact that the master fund is in another country (aka "offshore") makes it hard for politicians to add on additional regulation. US politicians can regulate US businesses and onshore investments, but they cannot regulate investment funds in another country; that is a breach of national sovereignty. Furthermore, it would be onerous to regulate advisors or consultants offering advice to a foreign entity.

This hints at another reason many funds locate the portfolio offshore: they do not trust politicians to leave them alone if they are successful. To protect their investors and the fund, they locate it somewhere beyond the reach of politicians. That way they are regulated by the rules and laws of the markets they trade in but are not regulated in other ways.

25.4   Investment Fund Types

Investment funds often specialize. Publicly-available funds tend to be organized around the asset class or region they invest in. Common publicly-accessible fund types and their typical holdings include:

- Money market: money market bills, commercial paper, CDs, and repos;
- Bond funds: corporates, munis, USTs; may target short- or long-term bonds;
- Equity funds of many types: index, sector, growth, value, and income;
- International funds: global/regional/emerging markets bonds or shares;
- Balanced, asset allocation, or target date funds: stocks, bonds, and cash in proportions dictated by a schedule; and,
- Specialty funds: real estate, commodities, mergers, convertible bonds, and even vice.[6]

Interestingly, Brown and Goetzmann (1997) find that instead of trusting a fund's claimed "style," they get better predictions of future performance by using fund performance data to assign funds to a data-derived number of cohesive clusters. Their analysis suggests eight clusters of funds with similar typical holdings:

1. *Growth and income*: large-cap stocks and indices;
2. *Growth*: mostly large-cap stocks, some small-cap stocks;
3. *Income*: high dividend-yield and utility stocks and debt;
4. *Value*: small-cap stocks with low P/B and P/E;
5. *Global timing*: non-US stocks, more US stock exposure as US market rises;
6. *Glamour*: small-cap stocks with high P/B and P/E; trend-chasers;
7. *International*: non-US stocks, may vary Asian/European stock exposure; and,
8. *Metal*: metal (commodity) funds, *e.g.* gold.

Alternative investment funds tend to be organized around the particular skills of the management company and their perspective on analysis. Common alternative investment fund types include:

- Common hedge fund types:
    - Directional: short bias; equity long/short; macro; emerging markets; volatility.[7]
    - Convergence: event-driven; tax arbitrage; capital structure arbitrage
    - Relative Value: convertible bonds; equity market-neutral; fixed income arbitrage; statistical arbitrage.

---

[6]See the sidebar "Guns, Buns, Butts, Bets, and Booze" in Chapter 13 if you forgot about vice.
[7]Macro funds are increasingly quantitative and not exclusively directional.

- – Other: multistrategy; fund of funds.
- Commodity Trading Advisors (aka managed futures): macro, asset allocation.
- Venture capital (usually related to technology in some form).
- Private equity funds (often reforming lower-tech industries).

LTCM (1997) suggested looking at investments as being one of five types (in terms of increasing exposure to risk factors):

Arbitrage: self-funding long and short exposure to economically-identical instruments which may yield a profit or, at worst, no loss.
Example: buying an option and simultaneously selling it for more than the purchase price (which is nearly impossible to do with certainty).

Convergence trades: long and short exposure to instruments which are economically identical or will become so at a later date.
Example: selling index futures and buying the index stocks at a lower implied index price. Later, the stocks may be converted to an offsetting futures position via an EFP.

Conditional convergence trades: long and short exposure to instruments which may become economically-identical at a later date or some unknown date (possibly never) if certain conditions are met.
Example: buying Polish bonds and selling German bonds in the belief that Poland might later enter the Eurozone and their bonds would then yield similarly to German bonds.

Relative value trades: long and short exposure to instruments which should be or historically have been related but which may not be related in the future if the modeling is incorrect or the economic fundamentals change.
Example: buying GM stock and shorting Ford stock because GM stock seems to be temporarily undervalued to the typical Ford-GM relationship.

Directional trades: long- or short-only exposure or long and short exposure which is designed to create a long- or short-only exposure to a known risk factor.
Example: buying Apple stock or shorting puts and calls as a way to short volatility.

You might hear many hedge funds (or other traders) refer to their strategies as arbitrage. While people often say that, such trades are rarely true arbitrage. True arbitrage is exceedingly rare: I only saw it once in nine years. (Some would argue that high-frequency trading uses arbitrage, however that is not true: they can find themselves exiting a trade at a loss if the markets they trade in are increasingly efficient and rebates are small.

25.5 Costs

If there is one topic you should always consider in investing, it is costs. People talk a lot about returns, but returns are uncertain; and, even after you collect them, you still pay taxes on them. However, costs are often more certain and might not be fully deductible.

25.5.1 Fees

Fees are one of the obvious costs we need to think about. Some fees are implicit: we may not be able to directly measure them, but we should not forget they are there.

The one explicit fee charged by every fund is the **operating fee** or **management fee**. Management fees are quoted as a fraction of AUM per year and often range over 0.2%–2%. Some index funds are very cheap: 0.05%; some hedge funds are very expensive: 5%.

Mutual funds charge other fees. Before the internet, getting information on mutual funds was difficult. To promote themselves, many funds charged a **load**: a sales fee, part of which went to the broker as a reward for getting you to invest in the fund. The load could be paid at purchase (front-load), sale (back-load), or over time (even-load). The load could also be waived for repeat purchases or long-term holders of fund shares. In this age of the internet, a fund would have to have great performance to justify the expense of a load. Mutual funds can also charge a **marketing fee** (often called a 12b-1 fee in the US). Unlike the load, these fees are charged every year as a percentage of AUM. Some funds quote a low management fee or no load but then recoup their costs through marketing fees. In general, you should pay less fees for comparable mutual funds. Most research shows that funds with lower fees perform better over time.

Hedge funds, CTAs, venture capitalists, and private equity managers earn an **incentive fee**: often 10%–20% of profits (sometimes with other qualifiers). Some people refer to the incentive fee as carried interest. When people discuss hedge fund fees, they often quote numbers like "1 and 10" or "2 and 20." A "1 and 10" fund is just one that earns a 1% management fee and a 10% incentive fee.

Finally, there are the implicit costs. **Soft dollars** cost investors money but are rarely reported. Here is how soft dollars work.

Johnny Mudmarket is not a competitive market maker; he attracts few people with his quotes. Johnny comes to you and offers to pay for your market data. All you have to do is route 5% of your orders to him. You can then show a lower expense ratio on paper; but, your investors will get worse prices. What about best execution? In some situations, best-execution is not guaranteed; perhaps that is where Johnny makes his money. Or maybe Johnny has good quotes but wants greater market share to attract other liquidity. Maybe he gets a bonus if he increases his firm's market share.[8]

Sometimes the agreement is less explicit. Maybe one year you happen to route a bunch of orders to Tommy Trashbid. Tommy then invites you to their investment conference in Las Vegas held to reward their best customers. They have some

---

[8]Isn't Johnny taking advantage of his firm then? Maybe it's "turtles all the way down!" (It is not.)

speakers talk about investing, so it's educational. The big steaks, endless glasses of red wine, and cocktails around the rooftop pool would surely never influence your routing decisions next year... would they?

Just like with the eagles and the flags: If the attention is not on the economics, the economics are probably not in your favor.

Finally, **turnover** is akin to the fraction of the portfolio replaced every year. For example, a $100 mn fund which traded $30 mn during the year would be said to have a 30% turnover. What if the fund changed value over the year? Well, then that formula can be defined in many ways and I am sure a marketing person might prefer one definition to another. Nonetheless, turnover is important because all trading incurs explicit and implicit transactions costs.

25.5.2 Taxation

Any bluesman will tell you: there is no escaping the "tax man." Taxes are a major consideration for investment funds. Taxes may alter what we sell and when. If you wanted to sell an instrument but waiting one day would lower your tax bill (perhaps by classifying the gain as long-term instead of short-term), you might be willing to wait a day to sell.

Funds have to separate interest, dividends, and capital gains (short-term versus long-term) for their investors. If short-term gains are taxed at a much higher rate, high turnover is also likely to lead to paying higher taxes on any gains. Thus lower-turnover funds are more likely to be **tax-efficient**, *i.e.* they can achieve similar economic exposure while incurring a lower tax bill.

Some investments incur other taxes: foreign investments may incur foreign taxes; sometimes, you can file extra forms to recover those taxes. Investors holding physical precious metals (*e.g.* gold or silver) will see their long-term capital gains taxed at the 28% collectibles rate, not the 20% used for other investments.

On the other hand, futures gains are taxed as 60% long-term gains, 40% short-term gains — no matter how long the investment was held.[9] This split is because marking to market realizes profits and losses before a position is exited and forcing short-term gains taxation on hedging would discourage investors from hedging. Hold your futures for one day? Sixty percent of your gains are taxed at the lower long-term rate. Hold your futures for two years? Too bad; 40% of your gains will be taxed at the short-term rate. Nonetheless, this can lead to significant tax advantages compared to investing in equities, bonds, and physical commodities. This is another advantage of managed futures investing: it can be tax-efficient.

---

[9]Section 1256 of the US tax code lists the details of this beneficial tax treatment. Although I like to joke that Congress was unable to understand marking to market (and that may be true), the section was enacted in 1981 after widespread use of straddles in the 1970s as tax shelters. To eliminate this they moved to mark-to-market taxation and "split the baby" on whether gains were short- or long-term.

25.6   Investment Management Company Problems

Investment management companies sometimes have problems. Below are some ongoing and historic problems to illustrate the sort of situations to watch for.

25.6.1   Late Trading

In 2003, the mutual fund industry was rocked by the revelation that a number of mutual funds had let some customers trade after the market had closed. Preferred investors could trade at the NAV, even (especially) after news emerged which was likely to affect the next day's NAV. This meant the fund and other investors would have to cover the difference between that day's NAV and the price paid for additional shares the next day; the late traders were effectively stealing from other fund investors. McCabe (2009) discusses the **late trading scandal** and notes that the violations did not even earn the fund managers more money than if they had behaved properly. Worse, the scandal resulted in $3.7 bn in fines and fee reductions by funds.

We should be careful here, though, because there is a similar strategy that is legal. **Mutual fund market timing** involves investing in a regional or country fund after those markets close but before investors' markets close. For example, suppose we know of a mutual fund investing in Europe. At 3 PM New York time, a scandal breaks about the European Central Bank. That is likely to send European shares down; but, we can sell out of the mutual fund at the old (inflated) NAV. Similarly, late-emerging news about a big EU trade deal and agreement to reduce taxes would allow us to buy into the fund at an old (undervalued) NAV. This is legal even though it pushes the mismatch of NAVs back onto the fund at large. Other fundholders pay for your taking advantage of stale NAVs.

25.6.2   Window Dressing

Window dressing is another major problem with mutual funds: funds temporarily change their holdings for when the holdings are recorded. A few days before the holdings are recorded, they sell out of investments they are embarrassed to be holding and buy investments which have done well or are more sensible. Then, after holdings are recorded, they sell out of those respectable shares and repurchase the shares that embarrassed them. This is like swapping out your embarrassing relatives for cool people in a family photo: sad and a sign of larger problems.

Lakonishok et al. (1991) first documented this phenomenon for pension funds; and, Khorana (2001) provides evidence of mutual fund window dressing and its drag on performance. If you speak with mutual fund managers, most claim to know about window dressing; that it is common; but, that they do not do it. (This is like all the kids in Lake Wobegon being above average; it just cannot be true.)

Similarly, Kacperczyk, Sialm, and Zheng (2008) look at mutual fund returns versus what fund returns would have been had they invested in their reported holdings. However, their findings are not universally negative. They find that this return gap persists and is positively related to the fund performance and hidden benefits. Thus some window dressing might disguise fund alpha.

25.6.3 Hedge Fund Opacity and Lock-Ups

Hedge funds are not without their problems either, especially given that they are opaque by regulation and choice. Regulations in many countries stipulate that hedge funds can only discuss their investments with accredited investors. (See the sidebar "Are You 'Sophisticated?'" in Chapter 3 for more on this.) Secrecy also makes sense if you are long or short illiquid assets. Furthermore, if you have an analytical advantage, you might reasonably worry about others inferring your model based on the data. On the other hand, that opacity is appealing to managers who do not have superior skills.

Hedge fund databases do not resolve this issue since their data is often imperfect to bias-ridden (as mentioned in the previous chapter). There are numerous games which funds can play to make their data look better or to report it strategically. When funds give out information on strategies or their holdings, it is often limited.

Finally, many hedge funds have six-month to multi-year **lock-ups**: minimum periods of time before investors can redeem their investments. When a fund does poorly, investors may only be able to watch in horror instead of exiting the fund.

25.6.4 Funds of Funds, Fees on Fees

You may also hear about funds of funds: often hedge funds which hold other hedge funds although there are also mutual fund and CTA funds of funds. At first, a fund of funds seems like an absurd idea: why pay two levels of fees to invest in funds you could otherwise invest in? However, funds of funds have some powerful benefits. Fund-of-funds managers may make large investments in a hedge fund in exchange for more information about the funds they invest in. They also may offer advice on better business practices. Thus fund-of-funds managers are better-informed, wield outsized influence, and can advocate for better management. Those are all benefits to fund-of-funds investors.

However, funds of funds also have some major drawbacks. As mentioned, there are two levels of fees — both management fees and (for CTA and hedge funds of funds) incentive fees. Furthermore, investors may pay incentive fees to some of the underlying funds even if fund of funds itself is net down. For these reasons, investors in funds of funds should proceed with caution.

25.6.5 Model Risk

Finally, one of the hardest risks to grasp is model risk.

While models give us insight, they are always wrong: they always have assumptions which may be close-to-true to wildly improbable. Experience helps us see the failings of models; and, seeing that makes us a better modeler, analyst, investor, and trader. Ultimately, disagreeing with your model can be the ultimate responsible act — the point at which you intervene because you know the model's weaknesses. That may even be a highly profitable bit of wisdom: avoiding blind obedience to a model may prevent you from making mistakes others make or may help you profit from their mistakes.

Even for models which are well-researched as criticized, we need to worry about **strategy rot** — the fact that even successful strategies eventually fail or have trouble. Patel, Suri, and Weisman (2007) and Till (2008) discuss this and refer to it as "periodic market efficiency." Typically, they note, the severity of that failure also increases over time. Some may think of these as "dry spells" — periods of model unprofitability due to the market learning part of the strategy and competing away its returns, randomness, or unknown changes in the market. Because of those root causes, strategy rot can happen even with continual research.

25.7   Investment Company Information

To find investment fund information, there are a few key sources. Information about a particular fund can be found in the fund prospectus; that lists the manager, policies, fees, and risks. The prospectus Statement of Additional Information (Part B) can also be very informative. Often, websites like Yahoo and Google summarize this information. There are also firms which specialize in rating funds. However, remember that highly-rated funds can and do perform poorly.

One of the more useful but overlooked sources of information is the investor communication from the fund itself. These communications range from the awful (poor reasoning or meaningless platitudes) to brilliant (clear, concise, and honest). Good fund managers can admit to their mistakes and will even show them to you so you can see why they made the decision they did. This is why people circulate Warren Buffett's letters to Berkshire Hathaway shareholders. This is not just idle speculating: Li (2008) finds that the equity market responds positively to companies with more readable annual reports; and, Lee (2012) finds that more readable investor communications make market prices more efficient.

Finally, for information about a type of investment vehicle, there are many groups and trade associations with information. In the US, useful sources of information include the Investment Company Institute, Managed Funds Association, National Association of REITs, and Alerian.

25.8 Quiz

Try answering the following questions in five minutes.

1. You would like to invest in two strategies: You want to sell short the S&P 500; and, you want to go long illiquid Brazilian equities. What investment fund type would you use for each of these strategies? (Be clear which is which!)

2. What tax status do most investment management companies have? What is done by some hard-asset-holding firms to maintain that status?

    What is the major difference between a closed- and an open-ended fund? (Be clear which fund type has which feature!)

3. (3 points!) Sen. Zephyrus of Oregon "knows" the stock market is manipulated by hedge funds. He proposes regulation that states "any hedge fund domiciled in the United States and with non-operational assets of greater than $10 MM shall report all positions to the Securities and Exchange Commission." List the problems with the proposed regulation.

4. What qualifies an individual to be a "sophisticated" investor — and thus eligible to invest in a hedge fund?

5. You are trying to save for a condo near the Loop; but, you worry that the market is increasing faster than you can save. What is one way you could help hedge your exposure to the risk of condo prices running away from you?

6. Name three fees which can affect mutual fund holders' returns?

7. How much should one trust overall data on hedge fund returns? Give reasons for why or why not.

25.9 Exercises

Instructions

Download data for the following funds using the sample code provided in prior chapters. You will want to use `quantmod` to download the fund and index data and `Quandl` to download the bond and futures data.

We will then analyze the funds with some factor models to see if you can discern the main risk factors for each fund.

Download the following data. Tickers are in parentheses.

- CMT USTs: 3M, 2Y, 10Y, and 30Y (FRED/DGS3MO, FRED/DGS2, FRED/DGS10, FRED/DGS30)
- Assorted investment funds:

- Vanguard 500 Index (VFINX)
- Vanguard 500 Index ETF (VOO)
- S&P 500 Depository Receipts (SPDR) ETF (SPY)
- American Century Fundamental Equity (AFDAX)
- Prudential Large Cap Core Equity (PTMAX)
- Putnam Investors (PINVX)
- Rydex S&P 500 Index (RYSOX)
- SA US Core Market (SAMKX)
- Spirit of America Large Cap Value (SOAVX)
- Wells Fargo Advantage Index C (WFINX)
- Annaly Capital Management REIT (NLY)
- Eaton Vance Large Cap Core Research A (EAERX)
- The Arbitrage Fund (ARBFX)
- T. Rowe Price New Era (PRNEX)
- Goldman Sachs Commodity Index near futures (CHRIS/CME_GI1)
- Teucrium ETFs (CORN, WEAT, SOYB)

- Indices:

  - S&P 500, Russell 2000 (^GSPC, ^RUT)
  - TED Spread (FRED/TEDRATE)
  - VIX (^VIX)

- Commodities:

  - WTI Crude Oil near futures (CHRIS/CME_CL1)
  - Natural Gas near futures (CHRIS/CME_NG1)
  - Copper near futures (CHRIS/CME_HG1)
  - Corn near futures (CHRIS/CME_C1)
  - Wheat near futures (CHRIS/CME_W1)
  - Soybeans near futures (CHRIS/CME_S1)

Remember to divide CMT UST yields by 100. For funds, indices, and equities, use the adjusted close field. For futures, use the settle field. For each fund and index, create excess returns as done before.

1. (Indexpensive?) Download data for the Vanguard index funds and the S&P 500 Depository Receipts (SPDR) ETF (VFINX, VOO, SPY) as well as the next six funds (AFDAX, PTMAX, PINVX, RYSOX, SAMKX, SOAVX). You will want to save the adjusted close and the volume. Create log-returns from the adjusted close field.

Try fitting an S&P 500 CAPM and a Russell 2000 CAPM for each fund. What do the results suggest? Look at the estimated alphas, betas, t-stats, and R^2 of the regression.

Next, look at the expense ratios and the volume of each fund. Why might these differences exist? Which seems most appealing? (This answer may vary, so justify your answer.) Is there a relationship between expenses and alpha?

2. (What's in the Box?) Next we will step up our game a bit and see if we can infer the risk factors for other funds.

For each of the following funds, regress the fund's excess returns on a multivariate factor model containing: S&P 500 excess returns; Russell 2000 excess returns; the TED spread; VIX; 3M UST yield; and, the difference between the 30Y and 3M yields (a rough proxy for the yield curve slope). In some cases, we may add another factor.

Report which seem to be the significant factors. Try to find a smaller model with only significant terms. Report the coefficient estimates and t-stats. While not normally useful, a high R^2 is also worth noting. Note which factors make sense and why — and which do not make sense.

Report the Sharpe ratio, Sortino ratio, and information ratio for the fund.

a) WFINX
b) NLY (add copper returns)
c) EAERX
d) ARBFX
e) GSCI returns, not excess returns (add oil, natgas, copper, and corn returns)
f) PRNEX (add oil, natgas, copper, and corn returns)

3. (Commodities or Posh Spice?) Regress excess returns for the Teucrium ETFs (CORN, WEAT, SOYB) on commodity returns. See if you can find which commodity futures they perform like. How close is the performance? Look at the expense ratios of the funds. How do those compare to the cost of holding futures? Why might these be attractive to some investors?

References

Alerian. *Figures and Tables*. Retrieved 25 May 2017 from: `https://www.alerian.com/education/figures-and-tables/`. 2016.

Barclay Hedge. *Managed Futures (CTA) Money Under Management*. Retrieved on 24 May 2017 from: `https://www.barclayhedge.com/research/indices/cta/Money_Under_Management.html`. 2016.

Brown, Stephen J. and William N. Goetzmann. "Mutual Fund Styles". *Journal of Financial Economics* 43.3 (1997), pp. 373–399. DOI: `10.1016/S0304-405X(96)00898-7`.

Chen, Li-Wen and Fan Chen. "Does Concurrent Management of Mutual and Hedge Funds Create Conflicts of Interest?" *Journal of Banking and Finance* 33.8 (2009), pp. 1423–1433. DOI: `10.1016/j.jbankfin.2009.02.006`.

Henderson, Brian J., Neil D. Pearson, and Li Wang. "New Evidence on the Financialization of Commodity Markets". *Review of Financial Studies* 28.5 (2015), pp. 1285–1311. DOI: `10.1093/rfs/hhu091`.

ICI. *ICI Fact Book*. Investment Company Institute, 2016.

Kacperczyk, Marcin, Clemens Sialm, and Lu Zheng. "Unobserved Actions of Mutual Funds". *Review of Financial Studies* 21.6 (2008), pp. 2379–2416. DOI: 10.1093/rfs/hhl041.

Khorana, Ajay. "Performance Changes Following Top Management Turnover: Evidence from Open-End Mutual Funds". *Journal of Financial and Quantitative Analysis* 36.3 (2001), pp. 371–393. DOI: 10.2307/2676288.

Lakonishok, Josef et al. "Window Dressing by Pension Fund Managers". *American Economic Review: Papers and Proceedings* 81.2 (1991), pp. 227–231. DOI: 10.3386/w3617.

Lee, Yen-Jung. "The Effect of Quarterly Report Readability on Information Efficiency of Stock Prices". *Contemporary Accounting Research* 29.4 (2012), pp. 1137–1170. DOI: 10.1111/j.1911-3846.2011.01152.x.

Li, Feng. "Annual Report Readability, Current Earnings, and Earnings Persistence". *Journal of Accounting and Economics* 45.2–3 (2008), pp. 221–247. DOI: 10.1016/j.jacceco.2008.02.003.

Loomis, Carol. "The Jones Nobody Keeps Up With". *Fortune* (Apr. 1966), pp. 237–247.

LTCM. *Executive Summary of Long-Term Capital Management, L.P.* recruitment material. Greenwich, CT, Oct. 1997.

McCabe, Patrick. *The Economics of the Mutual Fund Trading Scandal.* Working Paper 2009-06. Board of Governors of the Federal Reserve System, 2009.

McTaggart, Raymond, Gergely Daroczi, and Clement Leung. *Quandl: API Wrapper for Quandl.com.* R package version 2.8.0. 2016. URL: https://CRAN.R-project.org/package=Quandl.

National Association of Real Estate Investment Trusts. *US REIT Industry Equity Market Cap.* Retrieved on 24 May 2017 from: https://www.reit.com/data-research/data/us-reit-industry-equity-market-cap. 2016.

Nohel, Tom, Z. Jay Wang, and Lu Zheng. "Side-by-Side Management of Hedge Funds and Mutual Funds". *Review of Financial Studies* 23.6 (2010), pp. 2342–2373. DOI: 10.1093/rfs/hhq008.

Patel, Sandeep, Anil Suri, and Andrew Weisman. *Chasing Your Tail.* Presentation to the Q-Group. Mar. 28, 2007. URL: http://www.q-group.org/wp-content/uploads/2014/01/Slides-Weisman.pdf.

Preqin. *2017 Preqin Global Hedge Fund Report.* Preqin Ltd., 2017.

Ryan, Jeffrey A. *quantmod: Quantitative Financial Modelling Framework.* R package version 0.4-8. 2017. URL: https://CRAN.R-project.org/package=quantmod.

Till, Hilary. "Case Studies and Risk Management Lessons in Commodity Derivatives Trading". In: *Risk Management in Commodity Markets: From Shipping to Agriculturals and Energy.* Ed. by Hélyette Geman. Chichester (UK): John Wiley & Sons Ltd., 2008, pp. 255–291.

Zweig, Jason. "Will These Royal Yields Rule?" *Wall Street Journal* (Aug. 24, 2012).

Chapter 26

Crises

Throughout this text, we have talked about recessions, economic contractions, and crises. The reason these are so important comes from an idea in statistics: an **absorbing state** is a state in a Markov chain that cannot be exited once it is entered. Dissolution of a firm and death are absorbing states. Being laid off from a job may be an absorbing state since those workers are rarely recalled.

Absorbing states greatly alter our utility calculations and our objective function: we have to err on the side of caution because those states "end the game." Aggregated to the macroeconomy, many people and firms hitting absorbing states reduces economic growth and can lead to a recession.

Studying crises is, therefore, very important. The purpose of this chapter is to discuss some theory of the forces at play in crises; examine some crises to see how they match with the theory; and, to discuss the particular issues in recent crises.

26.1 Bubbles

A **bubble** is a growth in prices of an instrument beyond its fundamental value. There are, however, many other phenomena we typically associate with a bubble:

- rapid price appreciation;
- speculation based on continued price appreciation and not fundamental value;
- widespread acknowledgment that prices are high;
- claims that "this time it's different;" and,
- hype like "you can't afford *not* to hold this instrument!"

All of these are symptoms of a bubble. While the hype is patently absurd, "this time it's different" is the classic rejoinder used to brush aside comparisons to past bubbles. I believe it is the most dangerous claim in finance, both in its plea for unthinking acceptance and in its prevalence as a symptom of impending trouble.

Bubbles also tend to attract over-investment in industries which are overvalued.

That is suboptimal or inefficient; and, some economists (especially Austrian-school economists like Hayek) would say that malinvestment sows the seeds of a bubble's destruction. That is another phenomenon associated with bubbles: they eventually "pop," *i.e.* prices eventually crash. If bubbles attracted little investment, this would not be a grave concern; however, some attract large amounts of investment and so a popping bubble can cause heavy losses and even a recession.

26.1.1 Detecting a Bubble

Recessions alone are a reason to detect bubbles as early as possible. However, what is "fundamental value?" Complicating valuation is that a bubble may be for a new technology that has a very uncertain value. The value may depend on if the technology permanently lowers costs or enables new businesses.

This is why some economists even claim that there are no bubbles. Their opinion is that the market has a very uncertain valuation of the new technology. More unfortunate is that even with new technologies, early "pioneering" companies are often not the most successful investments. Take, for example, the poor performance of early railroad stocks and early internet companies like Netscape or Napster.

If determining fundamental value is so difficult, how then do we detect bubbles? We often proceed by trying to detect the symptoms of a bubble. While one could write a chapter entirely on bubble tests, we will consider a few approaches to show the diversity of tests.

Divergence from Fundamental Value. The most obvious approach is the hardest: comparing the market price to fundamental value. Jarrow (2016b) states this as:

$$\beta_t = S_t - E_{\mathbb{Q}}\left(\frac{X_T}{B_T} + \int_t^T \frac{dD_u}{B_u}\bigg|\mathcal{F}_t\right) B_t, \qquad (26.1)$$

where β_t captures the bubble-induced overvaluation, S_t is the instrument's market price at time t and X_T is its fundamental value at horizon T, B_t is the price of a discount bond maturing at time t, and D_t is the instrument's payout process.

Strict Local Martingale Test. Cox and Hobson (2005) and Jarrow, Kchia, and Protter (2011) estimate local volatility to see if the price process is a strict local martingale, *i.e.* a martingale only on intervals ending at a finite random time (and so having a drift that is eventually unbounded). We can test for this by checking if

$$\int_t^\infty \frac{p}{\sigma^2(p)}dp < \infty. \qquad (26.2)$$

If $\sigma^2(p)$ grows faster than p then the integral is finite, p is a strictly local martingale, and there is a bubble. Often, this is obvious from inspecting a plot of estimated variance versus price: bubbles typically have the variance increasing superlinearly versus price.

Bubble Component of Call Prices. Jarrow, Protter, and Shimbo (2010) suggest to look at option prices. They show that put prices in a bubble $\mathring{P}_t$ (which we will pronounce "P-bubble") will not contain a bubble component.[1] Call prices in a bubble $\mathring{C}_t$, however, do contain a bubble component:

$$\mathring{P}_t = P_t = E_{\mathbb{Q}} \left(\frac{(K - S_u)^+}{B_u} \middle| \mathcal{F}_t \right) B_t, \tag{26.3}$$

$$\mathring{C}_t = \underbrace{E_{\mathbb{Q}} \left(\frac{(S_u - K)^+}{B_u} \middle| \mathcal{F}_t \right) B_t}_{=C_t} + \beta_t - E_{\mathbb{Q}} \left(\frac{\beta_u}{B_u} \middle| \mathcal{F}_t \right). \tag{26.4}$$

Therefore, one can use violations of put-call parity to estimate β_t.

Super-Unit-Root Price Growth. Phillips, Wu, and Yu (2011) suggest looking at returns instead of prices. Normally, we believe that asset prices follow a unit-root process: that they are autoregressive with $p_t = p_{t-1} + \epsilon_t$ (where the unit root is implied by the multiplier of 1 for p_{t-1}). If a bubble involves explosive growth, this should be exhibited in prices being autoregressive with a multiplier greater than 1. Thus we examine the model

$$p_t = \mu + \phi p_{t-1} + \sum_{j=1}^{J} \Delta p_{t-j} + \epsilon_t. \tag{26.5}$$

Normally, we test for a unit-root process with the unit-root test of Dickey and Fuller (1979) and the null hypothesis $H_0 : \phi < 1$ versus the alternative $H_A : \phi = 1$. In this case, however, we suspect that $\phi = 1$ and may even be greater. Thus we conduct what they call an SADF (sup-augmented Dickey-Fuller) test: We test $H_0 : \phi \leq 1$ versus $H_A : \phi > 1$.[2]

Bubble Component in a Factor Model. Jarrow (2016a) looks at a factor model which allows us to see if there is a systematic component to the bubble. We first need the excess returns for the instrument R_t, excess returns for the bubble component $R_{\beta,t}$, and excess returns for factor components $R_{j,t}$. Then we can decompose instrument excess returns with a set of risk factors Φ as:

$$R_t = \theta_t R_{\beta,t} + \sum_{j \in \Phi} \delta_j R_{j,t} - \sum_{j \in \Phi} \theta_{j,t} \gamma_{j,t} (\mu_{j,t} - r_{f,t}) + \epsilon_t, \tag{26.6}$$

where $\mu_{j,t}$ are the bubble components correlated with risk factors.

Campbell-Shiller Decomposition. A different approach is to use Campbell and Shiller's (1988a,1988b) **Campbell-Shiller decomposition** of sources of price

---

[1] The put prices may incorporate a higher volatility and the potential for a crash, however.

[2] The article actually tests $H_0 : \phi = 1$, but anyone familiar with the Neyman-Pearson lemma should know these are equivalent tests.

volatility. If we look at prices P_t and dividends/payouts D_t, we have that:

$$\log\left(\frac{P_{t+1} + D_{t+1}}{P_t}\right) = \log\left(\frac{P_{t+1} + D_{t+1}}{P_{t+1}} P_{t+1}\right) - \log(P_t) \tag{26.7}$$

$$= \log(1 + \exp(\log(D_{t+1}) - \log(P_{t+1})))$$
$$+ \underbrace{\log(P_{t+1}) - \log(P_t)}_{\text{log-return}}. \tag{26.8}$$

We then expand around the average of $\log(D)$ and $\log(P)$. This is typically used as a test for excess volatility in market prices. When we use it to test for bubbles, it ends up as a joint test of the fundamental valuation model *and* the bubble hypothesis. Unfortunately, that complicates determining if a bubble is present.

Tracing Uncertainty in the Gordon-Shapiro Model. Another approach to something like the Campbell-Shiller decomposition is to go back to the discounted cashflow models of Chapter 13. There, we used the delta method to correct for the Jensen's Inequality effect on the expectation of firm value. Here, we can use the delta method to get a better second moment expectation, *i.e.* a better estimate of variance.

We start with the Gordon-Shapiro model of valuation, $V = \frac{d}{k-g}$. We then find the first partial derivative of V with respect to the parameter vector θ containing dividends d, the pricing kernel k, and the dividend growth rate g. That gives us the variance of the security value σ_V^2:

$$\sigma_V^2 = V'^T \Sigma_{\text{G-S}} V', \quad \text{where} \tag{26.9}$$

$$\theta = \begin{pmatrix} d \\ k \\ g \end{pmatrix} \text{ and } V' = \frac{\partial V}{\partial \theta} = \begin{pmatrix} \frac{1}{k-g} \\ \frac{-d}{(k-g)^2} \\ \frac{d}{(k-g)^2} \end{pmatrix}, \tag{26.10}$$

$$\Sigma_{\text{G-S}} = \begin{pmatrix} \sigma_d^2 & \rho_{dk}\sigma_d\sigma_k & \rho_{dg}\sigma_d\sigma_g \\ \rho_{dk}\sigma_d\sigma_k & \sigma_k^2 & \rho_{kg}\sigma_k\sigma_g \\ \rho_{dg}\sigma_d\sigma_g & \rho_{kg}\sigma_k\sigma_g & \sigma_g^2 \end{pmatrix}, \tag{26.11}$$

and the ρ terms capture the correlations among d, k, and g.

We then have two options. We can either test if the implied price variance σ_V^2 is statistically different from that measured empirically; or, we can simulate V using the covariance matrix and test the difference of that from market prices. This second approach would allow us to see the higher kurtosis of V from when $k - g$ is close to 0. This may be preferable since the assumptions behind the delta method can break down as $k - g$ approaches 0. However, simulation might allow $k - g$ to be negative which no firm would choose for an extended period of time.

26.1.2   Types of Bubbles

Not all bubbles are the same: some are financial instrument bubbles and some are hard asset bubbles. These different types of bubbles leave the macroeconomy in different states when they pop.

A bubble in stock prices may lead stocks to great heights; however, when the bubble pops the economy is not left with a large inventory of stocks which then affect other firms' attempts to start a business. The failure of those firms may lead to an excess of labor from laid-off workers; however, this is a benefit to other firms starting up or which previously had to pay higher wages to similar workers.

A bubble in hard assets, however, leaves a physical scar. Overproduction of homes, for example, leaves a large inventory of homes. That excess in supply hampers the ability of the housing market to recover quickly. While some might argue that cheap homes (like cheap labor) are a benefit to the economy, there are only so many homes needed in a given location. People and firms are usually able to make use of cheaper labor, but a finite population of people cannot do much with an excess of homes — apart from maybe offering them as a substitute for hotel rooms.[3]

Finally, one concern with both types of bubbles is the **wealth effect**, the tendency of consumers to spend as though they will shortly realize their unrealized gains in overpriced instruments or assets. While malinvestment is a concern with bubbles, the wealth effect causes further damage when households take on too much debt and make purchases that they might not otherwise make.

Case, Quigley, and Shiller (2005) find a barely significant stock market wealth effect but a significant housing market wealth effect for 14 developed European and North American countries *prior to* economic and monetary union. On the other hand, Sousa (2009) finds that the wealth effect is present with stock market rises but not property market rises in the Eurozone over 1980–2007.

26.1.3 *Popping a Bubble*

Policy makers often try to find and eliminate bubbles before they become large and redirect significant parts of the economy into malinvestment. The tools used to do this are varied and often weak. This is not a reflection of policy makers' failings; rather, it is difficult to disenchant investors who insist on viewing an investment as a source of almost-sure profits.

Sometimes, policy makers try to talk down bubbles. Thus we heard Alan Greenspan, then Chair of the Federal Reserve, talking about "irrational exuberance" in internet stocks in late 1996; and, we heard Janet Yellen talk about "frothy" markets for leveraged loans in 2014 when she was Chair of the Federal Reserve.[4]

Talk by policy makers implies possible monetary or fiscal policy action. If talk fails, however, central bankers are often willing to raise interest rates to slow down all investing. That, however, can cause a lot of collateral damage. Many investors see bubbles as "get-rich-quick" schemes: easy ways to instant riches. As Bivens and

---

[3]Perhaps with the rise of firms like Airbnb, we will be able to test this hypothesis when the next housing bubble bursts.

[4]A weekly briefing by Nitish Sinha, whose work we saw in Chapter 15, was the origin of the term "frothy."

Baker (2016) point out, raising rates high enough to pop a bubble can cause damage to other sectors and the labor market.

Since fiscal policy is more targeted, it may be better suited to popping a bubble. While fiscal policy is slow to implement (since politicians must come to an agreement), it is less likely to cause collateral damage. Pearson (2018) discusses how the province of British Columbia has recently tried to cool the Vancouver-area property market by taxing foreign buyers as well as property transfers. Jang (2018) notes that these taxes are starting to have some effects a year after first being enacted and shortly after they were increased. It remains to be seen, however, if popping this bubble will help or hurt overall growth in the Canadian economy.

Some governments have reduced lending limits on purchasing assets or instruments perceived to be "bubbly." Shen (2015) discusses how, in June 2015, the China Securities Regulatory Commission capped margin lending at four times net capital (when it was previously uncapped). This helped pop the bubble in Chinese stocks.

In the most extreme cases, governments or regulators can restrict trading in markets thought to be subject to a bubble. The short-term equivalent of a bubble in commodity markets is a squeeze or a corner. In those cases, supply and demand constraints (real or artificial, respectively) cause prices to diverge from fundamental value. In these cases, as Birger (2008) discusses, the CFTC can (and has, rarely) dictated liquidation-only trading for a futures contract. That almost certainly prevents any further support for a bubble. In the case of the Hunt brothers trying to manipulate silver markets, this resulted in the markets crashing and returning quickly to the equilibrium implied by real supply and demand.

However, such a result leads to the next concern with bubbles.

26.1.4   Controlling Bubble Deflation

One of the things most policy makers do not want is for bubbles to deflate quickly since that can cause a panic.[5] Furthermore, once regulators or governments have intervened to pop a bubble, they are rarely content to stop their interventions.

Thus we see governments instituting rules in an attempt to prop up or prevent rapid declines in prices. One simple measure is banning short sales, as was done in the US and UK during the 2008 financial crisis. China's 2015 stock market meltdown showcased other approaches: they restricted position sizes in financial futures and suspended institutional trading accounts which they said were related to activity depressing the market. (The latter is discussed in Lu and Sweeney (2015).)

More extreme measures may even be used although these can shake investors' confidence in markets. Central banks may buy assets at elevated prices, as done by Fed programs like the Term Asset-Backed Securities Loan Facility, or allow risky

---

[5]The CFTC allowed the silver to market crash after the Hunt Brothers' actions since that imposed large losses on them and reminded all participants that markets must stay connected to real supply and demand. While some traders might joke that this difference in perspective is due to the CFTC employing more economists and fewer lawyers than the SEC, I suspect the more limited size of the market was also a factor.

securities to be used as collateral for loans. The US is not alone in this: as admitted in Kodaira (2015), Japan's Price Keeping Operation used government money to prop up the Japanese market in the 1990s. More recently, the PBoC and state-owned firms (the "National Team") intervened in China's markets in 2015. Wildau (2015) suggests they bought up to 6% of the market. Surely the most extreme intervention is canceling trades as was done by Nasdaq after some traders bought at low prices during the 2010 Flash Crash. (Readers wanting to reread about the Flash Crash can revisit it in Chapter 4.)

Ultimately, controlling the deflation of a bubble is very difficult; and, for a government that wants to keep a pristine reputation for not intervening in markets, it may well be impossible.

26.2 A Taxonomy of Trouble Transmuters

While bubbles are an obvious concern, trouble can arise in other ways as well. Sometimes trouble seems to come "out of a clear blue sky." However, there is usually an ultimate force at work. These forces take trouble — sometimes idiosyncratic trouble — and transmute it into something that can affect the market at large. Thus these forces are all sources of **systemic risk**, risk that threatens enough economic actors to present a risk to the well-functioning of the financial system. Often, systemic risk is entwined with **contagion**: risk that spreads from impaired to previously-unimpaired economic actors, like the spreading of disease.

Most of these forces are externalities or have externalities. That means that risk reduction may sometimes target seemingly-unrelated metrics or practices. The most common forces we see are:

- hoarding;
- fire sales;
- runs;
- crowded trades and herding;
- network effects;
- liquidity and intermediation; and,
- capital structure.

Related to many of these is observations of unusual correlations during crises.

26.2.1 Hoarding

Hoarding cash is a natural response to certain conditions. For example, Pinkowitz and Williamson (2001) show that Japanese firms hoard cash when banks have monopoly power. Thus hoarding cash means that firms increasingly self-finance their projects. This is inefficient from an economic growth perspective. Furthermore, hoarding cash means that it sits in a bank and is likely only used for short-term lending. If the cash sits in short-term government bonds, it may generate even less economic activity. If the banks are worried about losses and greatly concerned about risk, they may not even lend out the cash they have — in which case the cash generates no economic activity.

Hoarding cash is also a natural response when the world looks unusually risky. Unfortunately, moving funds into cash reduces the liquidity of other markets. As Malherbe (2014) points out, that leaves those markets *more* subject to adverse selection as the only traders remaining in those markets are those with private information. Thus a crisis can become self-fulfilling: money is withdrawn from some markets and not made available for risky ventures; this lowers economic growth; and, the reason for withdrawing money from risky markets looks more certain (with some actors withdrawing even more funds). The combination of these reduces liquidity in the short-term and economic growth (needed for a recovery) in the medium-term.

Worse still is that we live in a full equilibrium world: people take action based on the actions they think others will take in anticipation of their actions which anticipate.... Thus we might expect to see economic actors who anticipate a possible crisis beginning to hoard cash. The problem is that this then makes a crisis more likely; sometimes, trying to protect yourself makes the worst scenario more likely and that protection all the more necessary. Sadly, as Berrospide (2013) finds, this is not hypothetical: he shows that banks before the 2008 financial crisis engaged in **precautionary hoarding** of cash. Acharya and Merrouche (2013) show that banks hoarded liquidity during the crisis. Furthermore, Duchin and Sosyura (2014) show that even after the 2008 financial crisis, banks hoarded cash given to them from the government despite political pressure to use that cash to resume lending.

However, as the salesperson says on late-night TV: "Wait: there's more!" If economic actors hoard cash in sufficient quantities, economic activity can fall enough that prices start to decline. **Deflation** is not, by itself, bad; if prices are adjusting to shifts in supply and demand, that is a healthy market reaction. The problem, however, is that the economy can get stuck in a vicious cycle of falling prices and cash hoarding, what Hicks (1937) dubbed a **liquidity trap**.

In a liquidity trap, economic actors hoard cash so economic activity and prices fall. The actors, seeing falling prices, choose to wait for even better deals. This depresses economic activity and prices further. While this seems hypothetical, observers of the Japanese economy over the past few decades would agree with Krugman, Dominquez, and Rogoff (1998) that Japan has suffered under a liquidity trap.

26.2.2 Fire Sales

Trouble may also creep into one market from another market. One way this can happen is if an economic actor has exposure to the two markets. In that case, a large loss in one market may lead the actor to sell investments in both markets to raise cash. This is the idea of a **fire sale**: losses in one area lead to sales at low prices in another area. This can transmit a crisis in one market to a crisis in another market.

In its purest form, a fire sale need not be industry-wide. For example, Pulvino

(1998) studies financially-troubled airlines selling assets at prices below fundamental value. However, if the entire industry is in crisis, there is an additional discount since many firms are trying to simultaneously sell assets which are substitutes. This more severe scenario is considered by Shleifer and Vishny (1992). (This is also the scenario discussed in the Chapter 13 sidebar "Take a Seat... Please.")

As with cash hoarding, however, full equilibrium can yield truly catastrophic effects. Diamond and Rajan (2011) show that if buyers anticipate a fire sale, they may hold off on purchasing and refuse to lend cash which makes the fire sale larger and more destructive. This happens whether buyers are malevolent or precautionary about interacting with firms likely to fail soon.

26.2.3 Runs

The preceding situation where anticipation of a fire sale makes the crisis worse is a perfect lead-in to the idea of a **run**.

A bank run is a situation in which fear of a bank failing leads its depositors to withdraw their funds. This saps the bank's liquidity, forces it to sell investments quickly (and often at a loss), and leads to these effects spiraling in a vicious circle. Diamond and Dybvig (1983) discuss this scenario and their insight is that it occurs because banks transform illiquid assets like loans into liquid liabilities like deposits.

Diamond and Dybvig's depositors panic and their actions seal the bank's doom. Jacklin and Bhattacharya (1988) note that there is also an information-driven type of run when depositors do not know the quality of the bank's assets and the bank does not know the true liquidity needs of depositors. The solution in both cases is either a well-capitalized investor intervening publicly or deposit insurance that protects deposits up to some amount.

Runs are not limited to banks, however. He and Xiong (2012) discuss how staggered maturities of debt can lead bondholders to anticipate credit problems before they would roll over their debt. In this case, lenders may make a run on the firm, forcing it into premature receivership so as to receive more principal back than other bondholders. Note that this is like tranche warfare discussed in Chapter 23.

26.2.4 Crowded Trades and Herding

Often, market participants hold similar exposures to risk factors. In extreme cases, however, some participants may hold the same exposures or even the same instruments. In this case, if some commonly-held investments experience a shock which reduces their expected value or a loss forces some participants to exit their positions, then all of these participants may find themselves racing to be the first to exit their positions while prices are still high. These trades have what Clunie (2009) termed **crowded exits**. The effect is similar to a run albeit a "run" on the market.

Because of their fears, investors behave like they are **herding** — trading together as though they were coordinated. While crowded exits sound esoteric, short squeezes are a classic example of crowded exit. Furthermore, Hwang and Salmon (2004) find

evidence that investors herd toward the market portfolio and risk factors. A review
of herding theories can be found in Bikhchandani and Sharma (2000). These effects
are worthy of attention: crowding and herding are so strong that Chincarini (2012)
charges them with making the financial system more fragile.

26.2.5   Network Effects

All of the preceding effects can be seen as monolithic: some or all economic actors
behave in a way that exacerbates a crisis. Network effects are more complicated
and explicitly live in the realm of **complex systems**: systems of many interacting
parts which cannot be understood by examining the individual parts.

In financial markets, we have numerous networks; however, most of these are not
troublesome in crises. Networks of market data or trading venues are merely sources
of information or liquidity. While interbank networks involve short-term lending,
the *network* rarely has an affect on crises since credit analysis and the maturation
of the loan occur days to weeks apart; any borrower sufficiently unlikely to repay
would be excluded from the network.

Troublesome networks are those which persist long after the initial assessment of
an entity's creditworthiness. Two types of networks exhibit these sorts of concerns:
supply chain networks and derivatives networks. Recent work on supply chains such
as Scheibe and Blackhurst (2018) are just starting to look at issues like systemic risk.
Far more relevant for our concerns are derivatives networks since they are marked
to market; ongoing exposures result in regularly-realized profits and losses. Gai and
Kapadia (2010) showed these can transmute counterparty risk into systemic risk.

Zawadowski (2013) examines a ring of banks which borrow to invest in a project.
Each bank can trade derivatives with its neighbor to hedge the project outcome and
buy insurance against the counterparty risk of that neighbor. He finds an effect like a
run, that banks choose not to self-insure, and that taxing bilaterally-cleared contracts
to fund later bailouts is beneficial. While a ring topology of bank interactions is not
realistic, it is interesting that even this simple topology yields contagion.

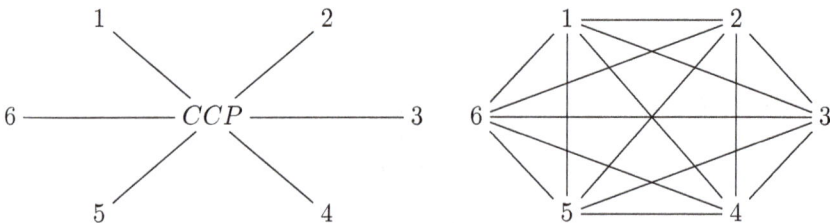

Figure 26.1: Centrally-cleared (left) and bilaterally-cleared (right) derivatives networks.
Each node is a counterparty (including the central counterparty, CCP) and each edge is
one or more contracts which create mark-to-market cashflows.

With derivatives contracts, exposures may go through central clearing (as mentioned in Chapters 19 and 20) or they may use bilateral clearing. The difference between these is best illustrated by Figure 26.1.

In this example, we can assume that each node is a counterparty i with some amount of capital and risk aversion. Each edge represents one or more swap or futures contracts with a directed exposure $q_{ij} = -q_{ij}$ which hedges either an underlying instrument or (more generally) a business risk factor. We can then find the net exposure of a counterparty $Q_i = \sum_{j \neq i} q_{ij}$. Since the contracts hedge a business risk, the net exposures Q_i are not related to capital and risk aversion.

Rosenthal (2014) compares the bilaterally-cleared network with a centrally-cleared market when the most-exposed counterparty fails. That forces all other counterparties to recreate the hedge eliminated by the initial failure as well as anticipated subsequent failures. I find that the bilaterally-cleared market has an equilibrium where all counterparties rehedge together and one where one side waits for the best prices which causes the maximum damage — as in Diamond and Rajan (2011). Furthermore, the switch to this maximally-damaging equilibrium, where rehedging buyers and sellers trade at separate times, occurs slightly *before* we would anticipate contagion. The centrally-cleared market still has systemic risk, but for a large initial failure the number of firm failures and the exposure to rehedge are not maximized. Finally, this work shows that some market participants may profit by forcing others into bankruptcy and that this may be an equilibrium or even inevitable.

> **Appetite for Destruction** In 2010, I presented the work in Rosenthal (2014) at a conference at NYU. At lunch, a man from ISDA, the International Swap Dealers Association, insisted on sitting next to me. He was curious why I did not focus on the costs of posting margin for central clearing or the resulting decrease in derivatives trading volume.
>
> I said that while bilaterally-cleared bespoke swaps are where innovation happens, for standardized contracts people should have money to trade, put it in a margin account, and be marked to market; that not doing so was effectively a subsidy to trading and encouraged destructive crises; and, that the amount of trade should be commensurate with capital requirements needed to trade and ensure payment to a counterparty. I then joked that our responsibility is not to subsidize the trading of swaps or futures so that young guys (like myself) can afford sports cars.
>
> The man from ISDA did not smile. He glared at me, turned his back, and talked only to his other neighbor for the rest of lunch. So much for dialogue!

The findings that central clearing may mitigate systemic risk are not without controversy. When regulations in many countries encouraged central clearing of derivatives, some counterparties complained that being forced to post margin would reduce trading volumes. Others suggested that requiring market participants to post margin is capital inefficient. Biais, Heider, and Hoerova (2016) suggest that central clearing (*i.e.* the use of a central counterparty) is capital efficient. Duffie and Zhu (2011) suggested that a central counterparty could not be viable without monopolizing all central clearing; however, Cont and Kokholm (2014) showed that for typical correlations this was not true — and that competing central counterparties could be viable.

26.2.6   Liquidity and Intermediation

Liquidity is behind many crises, as Kindelberger and Aliber (2005) note. However, defining liquidity is tough. In some ways, it is like Winston Churchill's characterization of the Soviet Union: "A mystery in a riddle inside an enigma." It is also a lot like obscenity: we know it when we see it.[6] It can also be fleeting. Michael Milken is credited with saying "Liquidity is an illusion. It's always there when you don't need it, and rarely there when you do." Thus the ability to trade what we want, when we want, and cheaply is not easily quantified.

Further complicating matters is that there are different types of liquidity. **Funding liquidity** is the ability to easily and cheaply borrow money. As we have mentioned before, funding liquidity and especially short-term funding liquidity is often the source of financial crises. On the other hand, **market liquidity** refers to the ease and cost of trading assets and financial instruments. In general, we are concerned with both of these; however, one must be careful because macroeconomists and microeconomists/financiers typically use "liquidity" to refer to funding or market liquidity without considering the other meaning.

Effects on Intermediaries

Brunnermeier and Pedersen (2009) consider the interaction (endogeneity) of funding liquidity when intermediaries' loans are collateralized by risky securities with varying market liquidity. They note that the value of the collateral will fluctuate, which may affect loan terms; but, loan terms may affect margin buys and short sales.

They propose two equilibria. If financiers think an increase in volatility or illiquidity is temporary, they will lower loan costs to encourage speculation which will lower volatility and increase market liquidity. However, if financiers think extra volatility or illiquidity will last, they raise loan costs to account for more risky collateral. That lowers funding and market liquidity and increases volatility. These

---

[6]For those unfamiliar with US law, obscenity has never been clearly defined. While many justices have tried to define obscenity, none has yet succeeded and most fall back to Justice Potter Stewart's 1964 declaration that "I know it when I see it." Silver (2001) discusses "movie days" at the US Supreme Court where justices and staffers would make popcorn and watch pornography related to cases they were going to hear. The idea of justices watching pornography for their jobs has been the subject of jokes by multiple comedians.

equilibria imply virtuous and vicious cycles of liquidity which helps explain why distress may occur quickly.

Boudt, Paulus, and Rosenthal (2017) study the Brunnermeier and Pedersen theory by looking at stock loan fees as a measure of funding liquidity and bid-ask spreads as a measure of market liquidity. They find empirical support for both virtuous and vicious cycles of market and funding liquidity — and show that these regimes are separated by a TED spread threshold of 48 basis points. When the TED spread is below 48 bp, an increase in bid-ask spreads leads to a decline in loan fees; however, when the TED spread is above 48 bp, an increase in bid-ask spreads leads to an increase in loan rates. This reveals one of the economic state variables mentioned when we discussed the intertemporal capital asset pricing model.

Similarly, He and Krishnamurthy (2012) build a theoretical model of financial intermediaries which experience a shock to their capital. This increases conditional volatility and correlation of assets held by intermediaries. He and Krishnamurthy (2013) find that capital-constrained financial intermediaries in a crisis are associated with a rise in risk premia. They also find that injecting capital into intermediaries is particularly effective at alleviating the crisis while purchasing troubled assets or reducing intermediary borrowing costs are less effective.

Effects on Market Function

Apart from the effects on intermediaries, liquidity effects can lead to problems in how markets function. Bernardo and Welch (2004) show how fear of funding/market liquidity shocks can lead to "runs" on financial markets; and, Dow and Han (2018) discuss how a lack of funding liquidity for arbitrageurs allows fire sales to happen. Krishnamurthy (2010) discusses amplifying factors in liquidity crises: how a shock leads to fire sales; and, how unusual shocks to untested financial innovations can cause market participants to retreat from those new markets making the crisis worse. In both cases, central bank intervention may help alleviate the crisis.

Brunnermeier and Sannikov (2014) find that market illiquidity and leverage lead to endogenous risk that can persist beyond an initial driving risk event. This leads to an unstable economy with occasional crises. Furthermore, securitization and derivatives may increase the frequency of crises even though they help share risk.

Effects on Securitized Lending and Repos

Finally, a number of papers look at securitized lending and repos.

Krishnamurthy, Nagel, and Orlov (2014) find that repo volumes for asset-backed securities plummeted to near zero during the 2008 financial crisis. While that only affected $182 bn of securities — small compared to the size of the ABS market, it disproportionately affected a few large financial intermediaries. Thus market liquidity (which reduced funding liquidity) affected intermediation and market liquidity for other markets.

Gorton and Metrick (2012) analyze MBS repos conditioning on the LIBOR-OIS spread, the difference between 3MUSDLIBOR and the overnight-lending indexed swap rate. (The LIBOR-OIS spread is a combination of a credit spread and the slope of the front end of the yield curve.) They find higher LIBOR-OIS spreads imply more uncertainty about bank solvency and lower values of repo collateral — and thus higher repo rates. Concerns about bond market liquidity also increased haircuts. Declining bond values and increasing haircuts led to a run on repo markets.

Finally, Shleifer and Vishny (2010) model banks which make, securitize, and trade loans; hold cash; or, borrow using held securities as collateral. They find bank credit and investment is volatile when loan market prices are volatile, banks' provision of market liquidity is less stable with increasing leverage, and profit maximization creates systemic risk.

26.2.7 Capital Structure

While capital structure seems to be a firm-specific issue, there are capital structure issues that can crop up in a crisis and make it worse. As mentioned before, tranche warfare can lead to different tranches of structured products having opposing interests in resolving defaults in a low-cost and minimally-damaging manner.

Much more destructive is the priority of derivatives contracts in bankruptcy. In most countries, the bankruptcy code gives first priority to the counterparties of derivatives contracts because that is thought to reduce instability in derivatives markets. Derivatives counterparties may even be able to terminate contracts and seize assets when other creditors cannot do so. Edwards and Morrison (2005) notes that this can be destabilizing and a source of systemic risk. If the bankruptcy-inducing force is a temporary market dislocation, the right to terminate contracts can let a counterparty exit contracts at prices far from fundamental value.

This is the idea behind Rosenthal (2014) which has firms fail purely due to mark to market cashflows. However, those problems would be largely mitigated with centrally-cleared derivatives contracts. While Lucas (1995b) suggested that firms could hedge counterparty risk, Zawadowski (2013) suggests that firms would not do so and we do not see firms doing so in the data.

Roe (2011) notes how derivatives counterparties have no incentive to mitigate the damage they cause in bankruptcy or to behave in a manner aligned with the fiduciary duty of a bankruptcy trustee. Bolton and Oehmke (2015) affirms that by noting how derivatives and mark to market cashflows can hurt bond creditors and may raise the cost of borrowing.

Worse: in a crisis, counterparties may use illiquid markets to push prices and exact mark-to-market payoffs as a way of stepping to the front of the line of all creditors. Details of one such example are in the sidebar "The Dogs of War," coming up in two sections. Wiggins and Metrick (2014) details a more recent example with the failure of Lehman Brothers — including the effects of **novation**, replacing a counterparty's obligations, which was used to exit contracts. They show how these contributed to Lehman's failure and the chaos of the 2008 financial crisis.

26.2.8 Correlations

One of the common observations of phenomena seen in a crisis is the presence of unusual correlations across typically-unrelated instruments, asset classes, and markets. This is even sometimes expressed as the squishy adage that "the correlations all go to 1."

While inaccurate, there is some truth to correlations increasing during crises. Longin and Solnik (1995) find that correlations between markets in different countries increase in periods of elevated volatility. Longin and Solnik (2001) use extreme value theory to study the correlation at times of extreme returns. They find higher correlations are associated with the market *trend* and not volatility — specifically that correlations increase during bear markets but not bull markets.

26.3 A Parade of Pre-Modern Problems

Looking at past problems can help us see commonalities so we can (hopefully!) prevent them in the future. For reasons that will soon be clear (in one section!), however, I will separate the crises into pre-modern and modern problems. That way we can examine more recent problems in greater detail since we just experienced a rather serious crisis.

The *Panic of 1857* was the first world-wide economic crisis. Calomiris and Schweikart (1991) note how, at the time, the cause was uncertain and much-debated but that it can be traced to the declines in the fortunes of (what were then) Western US railroads and prices of Western land as well as an over-concentration of those assets being held by New York City banks.

Riddiough and Thompson (2012) find, with new information, that the precipitating cause was the failure of the New York City-based Ohio Life Insurance and Trust Company (OLITC). OLITC had effectively become a bank and financed railroad expansion by securitizing **railroad farm mortgages**: mortgages of farms done in exchange for an equity stake in a railroad. It had also tried to prop up a railroad run by OLITC's former Cashier (similar to a CFO) — who was also mentor to the current OLITC Cashier. Because OLITC was seen as very safe, its failure was taken as a signal of financial weakness of all banks.

The *Long Depression* that stretched from 1873–1896 was begun by the *Panic of 1873* when the US switched from a gold- and silver-backed currency to one backed only by gold. That and increased silver mining caused silver prices to plummet — essentially forcing a currency devaluation on a number of countries. This led to a panic in Europe which later returned to the US with banks failing due to fraud and waste in their railroad investments. This is a recurring theme in crises: A crisis in one location causes enough stress to unveil fraud or mismanagement in other places. As Warren Buffet has said in his letters to shareholders: "only when the tide goes out do you discover who has been swimming naked."

The *Panic of 1907* is notable not for how widespread it was but for how it was ended. What started as a run on New York City banks nearly toppled the New York Stock Exchange — until John Pierpont Morgan (the J.P. Morgan who gave the bank its name) personally organized a rescue, largely using his own wealth. This avoided a much greater crisis and spurred the creation of the US Federal Reserve system.[7]

The *Stock Market Crash of 1929* on 20 September in the UK and then 29 October in the US and Canada (aka **Black Tuesday**) after 24 October (**Black Thursday**) resulted from a speculative bubble in stocks and investment trusts including closed-end funds. De Long and Shleifer (1991) show that closed-end funds were trading at premiums with a median around +30% — after excluding funds with a premium of more than 75%; thus it seems reasonable to conclude there was a bubble.

The subsequent *Great Depression* is largely thought to have resulted from inaction by the Federal Reserve and other central banks with the effective policy (due to currencies being backed by gold and/or silver) being mildly to severely contractionary.

The *Stock Market Crash of 1987* on 19 and 20 October is mentioned in Chapter 21 since some blamed derivatives. However, the root cause is still a mystery. On the one hand, there was a speculative bubble in Oceania, fears of a US war with Iran, and growing troubles with US savings and loan associations ("building societies," for those in the UK). On the other hand, the savings and loan crisis did not then seem likely to lead to severe economic troubles. Ultimately, concerted loosening of monetary policy by the Federal Reserve and other central banks (with the exception of the Reserve Bank of New Zealand) led to a rapid recovery in most countries — except New Zealand.

Economist (2014) has an excellent survey of major crises prior to 1929 and more background than is presented here.

26.4   Mini-Case: Long-Term Capital Management

More recently, there have been fund failures that portended trouble. It makes sense to examine these since they are relevant to the 2008 financial crisis. In particular, many investments courses cover the case of Long-Term Capital Management (LTCM). The topic leads to a valuable set of discussions and thought experiments, so we will also cover LTCM. Since we will approach this like a case, this section has a slightly different tone from the rest of the text.

Another reason for the difference in tone is that, in full disclosure, I am writing from experience. My first job after my undergraduate studies was as a strategist working with Japanese equities and derivatives in David Modest's group at Long-Term Capital Management. What follows is a combination of external references, recollections, and internal communications.

---

[7]Those interested can spend a few weeks reading about this and more in Chernow's *The House of Morgan* — which is *de rigueur* for employees of Morgan Stanley and J.P. Morgan.

26.4.1 The Beginning: 1994

In 1994, hedge fund manager David Askin's Granite Corporation, Granite Partners, and Quartz funds experienced losses of $600 mn trading principal-only tranches of CMOs. As Hansell (1994) discusses, the failure was a surprise because of how quickly it unfolded — and how quickly market liquidity dried up. The losses were, at the time, one of the larger investment fund failures in Wall Street history. Askin was forced to quickly sell his holdings at a loss which ended the funds. One of the largest purchasers of Askin's mortgage-backed securities was a new hedge fund with the boring name of Long-Term Capital Management (LTCM).

While LTCM had a boring name, the firm was very hot in the world of quantitative finance. The fund started with just over $1 bn — a record starting amount at that time. The firm's founders, listed in Table 26.1, were experienced quantitative traders and researchers who had made billions of dollars for Salomon Brothers in its fixed income arbitrage group. Many had PhDs in economics, econometrics, or finance from top universities and some partners had been professors at MIT, Stanford, Chicago, Harvard, Berkeley, Columbia, Yale, and Michigan. Myron Scholes and Bob Merton were considered likely candidates for the economics Nobel Prize. Eric Rosenfeld had even helped Mitch Kapor write early spreadsheet code that led to the founding of Lotus 1-2-3.[8]

The world at-large had also noticed them. The arb group and LTCM head partner John Meriwether had been mentioned reverently in *Liar's Poker* and Spiro (1994) even referred to them as the "dream team." A friend at Salomon Brothers reported that some colleagues referred to LTCM as "Salomon North" and believed that "Meriwether would return and shepherd Salomon back to greatness!" Everyone, it seemed, wanted John's "arb boys" on their team.

Take a look at the partners' backgrounds in Table 26.1. Given what you have read, consider these questions:

- *Do the partners' backgrounds influence how successful the fund will be?*
- *Would you trust these guys with your money?*
- *Is 2-and-25 reasonable?*

Since this is a mini-case, really think about these questions before moving to the next section. Consider what influences your answers. In this section — and those that follow — I highly recommend writing your answers on a piece of paper.

Part of the value of a case is seeing your own prior analyses as the case unfolds and being forced to confront your opinions. You could just read the case through, but you would lose the opportunity to learn about your own thinking.

---

[8]Eric helped Mitch create an analysis and plotting program called Tiny Troll which was then modified to create VisiTrend and VisiPlot. Those were sold to VisiCorp which marketed the Apple II spreadsheet program VisiCalc. The money seeded the development of the spreadsheet Lotus 1-2-3. For more on this fascinating aside, check out Rose (1984).

Name	Partnered	Brief Bio
Victor Haghani	1994	Member of arb group at Salomon. BS, LSE.
Greg Hawkins	1994	Member of arb group at Salomon; was head of Bill Clinton's campaign for Arkansas attorney general. PhD, MIT; was Professor at Berkeley.
Larry Hilibrand	1994	Youngest Managing Director at Salomon; member of Risk and Credit Committees; co-head of arb group. MS, MIT.
Hans Hufschmid	1994	Head of Global FX Sales and Trading at Salomon. MBA, UCLA.
Bill Krasker	1994	Member of arb group at Salomon; PhD, MIT; was Professor at Harvard, Michigan.
Dick Leahy	1994	Co-Head of the Mortgage Department at Salomon. BS, Boston State.
Jim McEntee	1994	Self-made entrepreneur millionaire, aka "The Sheikh" for his panache. Parlayed success into intuitive ("gut feel") bond trading.
John Meriwether	1994	Head partner. Was vice chair and head of bond trading at Salomon Brothers; created the arb group. MBA, U. Chicago.
Robert Merton	1994	Author of the Merton model and continuous-time pricing of contingent claims. PhD, MIT; Professor at Harvard, was Professor at MIT.
David Mullins	1994	Was Vice Chairman of the Federal Reserve Board and Assistant Treasury Secretary. PhD, MIT; was Professor at Harvard.
Eric Rosenfeld	1994	Member of Executive, Risk, and Asset Allocation Committees at Salomon; co-head of the arb group; helped found precursor of Lotus 1-2-3. PhD, MIT; was Professor at Harvard.
Myron Scholes	1994	Co-author of Black-Scholes model. PhD, U. Chicago; Professor at Stanford, was Professor at Chicago, MIT.
Chi-fu Huang	1997	Head of Fixed Income Derivatives Research at Goldman. PhD, Stanford; was Professor at MIT, Yale.
Arjun Krishnamachar	1997	Head of Fixed Income Structured Products desk at Salomon. MS, Berkeley; MBA, UPenn.
Robert Shustak	1997	Vice President, Group Manager of accounting and operations for fixed income trading and arbitrage at Salomon. BA, Queens.
David Modest	1998	PhD, MIT; was Professor at Berkeley, Columbia, and Stanford.

Table 26.1: Long-Term Capital Management partners, the year they became a partner, and their brief biographical details. Details from LTCM (1997).

26.4.2   From Strength to Strength: 1994–Late 1997

After LTCM's founding, the firm did well. By late 1997, the firm had three offices: LTCM LP in Greenwich, CT; LTCM (UK) in London; and, LTCMJ in Tokyo. Our locales had become trendier: more funds were moving to Greenwich; and, then-quiet Mayfair in London was starting to attract some hedge funds. Even the main office in Greenwich had improved; it had moved from a concrete bunker-like building to a glass-and-steel mid-rise with a gym — and a room with a pool table for relaxing and casually talking through work projects.

The returns were even more appealing. Figure 26.2 shows the growth in AUM, cumulative growth of investments, and monthly returns.

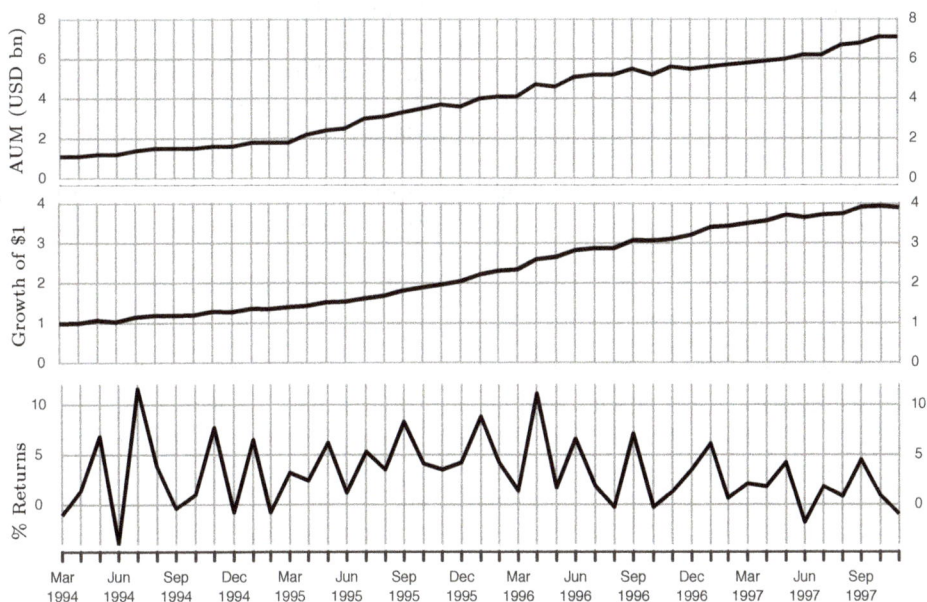

Figure 26.2: LTCP assets under management (top), growth of $1 invested at the start of the fund, and monthly returns from fund start in March 1994 to November 1997.

The firm had added three new partners: Chi-fu Huang and Arjun Krishnamachar, who co-ran the Tokyo office, and Robert Shustak, the CFO. The firm had averaged a return of about 44% per year and capital had grown to $7.1 bn. After the first few months, returns typically followed the pattern of a small gain or loss followed by a large return of around 6% or so. Given that the firm invested in some illiquid assets, autocorrelations and lag effects in returns were not seen as a large surprise.

At the time, the firm was looking to automate more and grow to eventually become a new kind of investment bank. The firm had many aspects that were appealing: a flat structure, a casual environment, regular research seminars with paper presentations, interaction with the partners, and an entrepreneurial spirit: new employees could find themselves suggesting and even heading up firm-wide projects. With less than 150 employees managing $7 bn, the atmosphere was welcoming but very high-performing.

Seeing how the early stages of this startup have gone, we should stop again to reflect on further questions:

- *Does this sound like a good place to work? Would you work there?*
- *Is "2-and-25" reasonable for fees in light of the returns?*
- *How do hedge funds manage that much money with so few people?* Other hedge funds often employ few people to manage a lot of money. How can this be given that large banks worth $80 bn might employ 30000 people or more?
- *What would you do with all that capital?* I ask this question because this was a legitimate concern inside the firm. $7 bn is a lot of money and many of the partners felt that they had sufficient funds for the investments they saw available. Some said the firm was a victim of its own success: LTCM had eliminated many of the attractive mispricings.

This last question is often a bit unsettling, especially when I say that opportunities in markets looked unattractive. We do not often find ourselves with a lot of capital just looking for a productive use. The obvious question to follow those above is what they might do with all that capital. Popular possibilities include:

- *Invest in new strategies.*
- *Pursue new lines of business.* Less strategy-driven lines of business like consumer or commercial lending, venture capital, or private equity could diversify the fund's portfolio. This might also fit with the vision of becoming a new kind of investment bank.
- *Put more money into current strategies.*
- *Invest in other funds.* What comparative advantage would LTCM have versus investors finding hedge funds on their own?
- *Close the fund to new investors.*
- *Hold the cash to be safe/be ready for new opportunities.* If you do choose to hold some cash, is it ethical to charge the same management fees on that cash? How do we align managers' and investors incentives when there is a fee charged on cash?
- *Refund some money to get smaller.*

The hard part is that none of the answers about what to do is obviously wrong. There are good arguments for each action and that makes the best action unclear.

26.4.3   *Realignment: Late 1997–Mid-1998*

On 5 December 1997, employees received the memo in Figure 26.3 — along with a local supplement which reiterated that fees would be charged and which limited annual contributions to the fund and rollovers of past contributions. (The latter action could prevent the firm from being forced to make someone a partner merely because they had a large fund investment: the contribution limits were small.)

LTCM's partners decided to return \$2.7 bn of capital. They returned capital mostly to newer investors to preference "strategic investors," those who had believed in the fund early on, and employees.[9] However, they also decided to impose fees on all investments — including the partners' investments.

These actions gave remaining investors and the partners more of the gains. This was a non-trivial consideration since they had just added three (soon four) new partners: David Modest was made partner early in 1998. These actions also made the investor base more aligned with the fund's interests and equalized the treatment of remaining investors. Just as a firm should focus on the "right" customers, in the words of Jones and Sasser (1995), a hedge fund needs the right investors. Finally, some would argue that it does not make sense to share profits with idle capital. (Others might argue that cash reduces risk which is a job worthy of reward.)

We can see the fund's performance after the refund of capital in Figure 26.4. The fund had a negative-return in January 1998, right after the refund. This should not be surprising since moving a lot of money out of a portfolio can have spillover effects. February–April had a mildly-positive, flat, and then more positive return; the fund seemed to have resumed the return pattern mentioned earlier. May and June, however, had large negative returns of -6.7% and -10.1%; July reverted with a small positive return of +0.5%. (Remember: that would be a good month for most investment funds.) Some observers wondered if reallocating capital among illiquid investments also had some delayed costs.

An action like returning capital and turning away customers is difficult and can anger those customers. The jitter in returns also suggests that the act of returning capital is not trivial: moving around that much money can rock the boat a bit.

At this point it makes sense to consider how you would have handled the situation (in hindsight) and what you think of the after-effects of the return of capital.

- *Did the fund refund too little or too much?*
- *Do fund managers want diversified investor types — or investors with similar comfort levels/worldviews?* This is a tough balancing act: we want to be challenged but we do not want investors who are unhappy being in the fund.
- *Would you be pleased or angry as an investor who had your investment refunded?*
- *Should LTCM have refunded some employee money?* Would that have hurt employee morale or reduced their incentives?
- *Is the early 1998 dip commensurate with returning idle capital and moving to a smaller capital base?*
- *Who should pay the costs of reallocation: old or new investors?* Should remaining investors pay since they were not ejected? Or should the refunded investors pay as a cost of getting cash? Many professionals are divided on this

---

[9]Since these details were reported by the press, including Jereski (1997), the market was aware of LTCM's actions. In game-theoretic terms, the refund was thus common knowledge.

LTCM Internal Memorandum

To: All Employees of LTCM, LTCM (UK) and LTCMJ

From: The Management Committee

Date: December 5, 1997

Re: Changes in Deferred Compensation Plans and Direct Investments

---

All employees of LTCM affiliated companies are eligible to participate in one of several deferred compensation plans. While these plans have some differences related to tax and regulatory considerations, they are substantially the same in providing employees an opportunity to participate in the growth of the Fund managed by LTCM. This announcement is to advise you in general terms of changes which will affect the plans beginning January 1, 1998. You will be receiving specific information pertaining to the plan in which you participate, however, the Management Committee wished to make this summary available to all employees uniformly.

Since 1994, the Management Committee has wanted to align the interests of Principals and employees with those of the investors whose funds we manage and provide a tax-efficient way of creating personal wealth in line with the growth of those funds. Employees have been able to achieve this through voluntary participation in the plans and, subject to regulatory conditions, by direct investments in the Fund. All participants have benefited from this arrangement because of the high returns produced by the Fund.

However, the Fund now has excess capital relative to its needs. As a result, steps have been completed in 1997 to return some amount of outside investor capital and to impose fees on Principals' investments in the Fund, both for the first time. Under these circumstances, it seems reasonable to revise the deferred compensation plans at this time as well. This means that there will be some new limitations on the size and period of deferral available and the deferral itself will be indexed to a Fund return calculated net of the impact of 2% per annum management fees and 25% of profit incentive fees. In particular, beginning in 1998 the deferred compensation plans will (i) compute the growth of certain previously deferred amounts net of fees, (ii) limit the size of future plan contributions and (iii) change the length of available deferral. Despite these changes, we trust that all employees will continue to view the deferred compensation plans as a valuable benefit which allows substantial participation on a tax-favored basis in a Fund which has produced superior returns. Although this past performance is not necessarily indicative of future results, the Management Committee expects the Fund to continue to be an attractive medium for wealth creation. As always, participation in the deferred compensation plans is voluntary.

In addition to the foregoing, all current and prospective direct investments by any employee will be subject to management and incentive fees beginning January 1, 1998 (except as may be noted in the attached supplement). Attached to this memorandum is a detailed explanation of these changes customized to your participation via LTCM, LTCM (UK) or LTCMJ. Questions regarding this announcement may be directed to Robert Shustak in the US, Dushy Selvaratanam in London or Masayoshi Nawa in Tokyo.

Figure 26.3: The 5 December 1997 memo informing employees that capital would be refunded and fees charged to all investors.

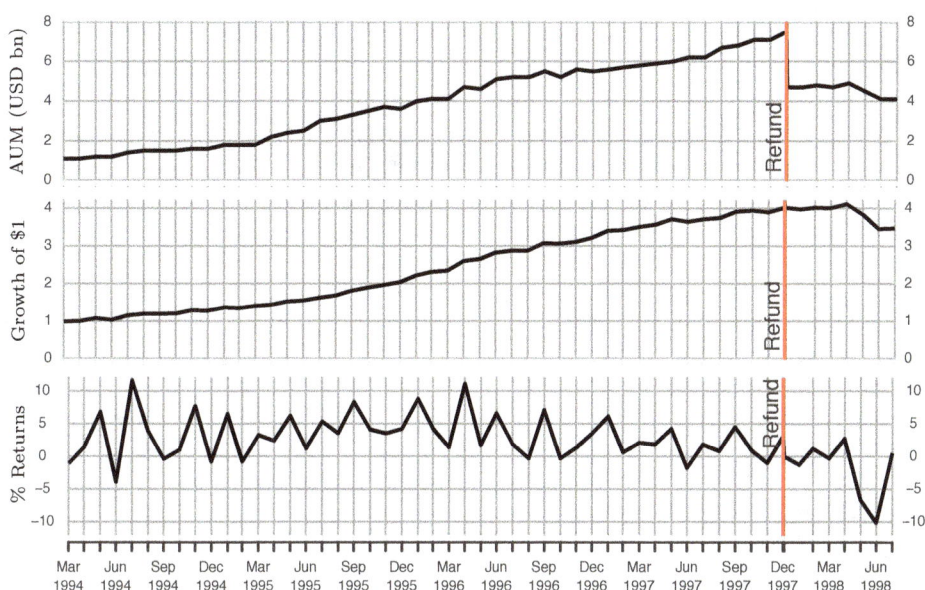

Figure 26.4: LTCP assets under management (top), growth of $1 invested at the start of the fund, and monthly returns from fund start in March 1994 to July 1998.

question. Even mutual funds face this issue: an outflow of funds often sticks remaining investors with temporarily-depressed holdings or costs of paying out departing investors.

Spend some time thinking about these questions. The questions about finding the right customers and who pays the costs of firm realignment come up repeatedly in business. Even if we do not have perfect answers, we should not shrink from asking or thinking about these issues. Again, I recommend writing down your thoughts on each question.

Now that the adjustment period is over, it makes sense to look ahead about how to run the new smaller fund. LTCM had heard a few months earlier that Salomon was going to close the fixed income arbitrage group; and, on 7 July it was reported in the *Wall Street Journal*. Inside LTCM, an early algorithmic trader was going to turn his system on any day now. We were excited about this and the prospect of less competition for more attractive opportunities.

26.4.4 A New Equilibrium? August and September 1998

August and September was all about reaching a new equilibrium of running a smaller fund. Running a smaller fund is usually easier although there is an adjustment from running a larger fund.

I set you up.[10] Reaching an equilibrium of running a smaller fund was *not at all* what happened in August and September, except maybe in a game-theoretic sense and it was a *bad* equilibrium.

In August, LTCM started experiencing large single-day losses. The outside world could not see this. Employees had most of their savings in the fund, but could not see the firm-wide daily P&L. However, we had heard rumors and started to wonder what was happening. Was the bad P&L in one group balanced out in another? To find out, one employee volunteered to be an aggregator. We sent our figures to the aggregator and the aggregator sent us back the best guess of that day's P&L. We saw days with movements of 2%-5% — 3–6 times larger than what we had seen in the past. (Before then, Rosenfeld (2009) notes the daily P&L standard deviation was $45 mn, about 0.85%.)

On Monday, the 17th, the Russian government defaulted on their government bonds rather than devalue their currency. This led to (surprise) a devaluation of their currency. LTCM had minimal exposure to Russia: someone noted that if we lost everything in our Russian trades, it would only be 3% of the fund.

Friday, the 21st, was therefore a big shock: the fund lost about $550 mn, or 15%. We first thought somebody made a calculation error and then that this was completely absurd. The Asian Currency Crisis of 1997 had been larger and yet had no large effect on the fund nor even on the Japanese/Asian equities and derivatives group where I worked. However, the effect of this new chaos on the firm was large. One of the firm's large trades was US **swap spreads**: a bet that the difference between swap fixed rates and US Treasury yields, credit spreads like the TED spread, would decline. Ten-year swap spreads had looked expensive at 35 bp, but were now at 75 bp.[11]

August ended up being very upsetting. One trader's dentist asked him "What is happening at your company? All of you are suddenly grinding your teeth a lot." LTCM lost 44% in August and was down 52% from January. Numerous strategies saw liquidity shocks: markets dried up and in some cases volumes were nearly nil. Many seemingly-unrelated strategies became correlated.

The equity derivatives group was a bright spot in August: while many other groups experienced large losses, we still made money. However, we were small compared to the rest of the firm. Furthermore, while my group did not trade volatility, we ran the risk and P&L reports for two of the firm's fixed income partners. . . who had decided (despite advice to the contrary) to short long-dated equity index volatility. Those trades were among the largest losses.

August was very unusual. Was it the Russian default? Or Salomon unwinding the fixed income arb group? That could explain the losses across fixed income books and not in the equity derivative books. . . except that the equity index volatility trades lost money. Had Salomon also been trading equity index volatility?

On the other hand, attractive possibilities pop up unexpectedly and many of the

---

[10]I even made sure this paragraph started on a new page.

[11]One friend joked morbidly: "If you liked swap spreads at 35, you're gonna *love* them at 75!"

firm's strategies were suddenly at levels that looked very attractive. Perhaps the firm could again pick up some investments cheaply, as in 1994?

In response to these opportunities, the partners drafted a letter (Figures 26.5–26.7) to current investors. They also spoke with employees which led some to invest more and a few to invest heavily. The money machine looked primed to restart.

At this point, it makes sense to ask yourself a few questions:

- *Given that LTCM has minor exposure to Russian debt, is this just a temporary dislocation?* You may struggle with this question. Imagine you were an employee who had invested more in the fund. Would that affect your ability to evaluate this question?
- *What if other people have major Russian debt exposure?*
- *The letter says this a good time to invest. Would you invest?* Remember that good opportunities rarely last long.

It turns out that at the end of August, John called Vinny Mattone at our clearing firm, Bear Stearns. Vinny had a long-time association with the firm. Vinny also knew markets. When John told him the fund was down by half, Vinny told him he was f——d: that once you go down by 50%, the market realizes they can push you the rest of the way; and, that no counterparties will "roll" (refinance) your repos or short-term loans. Trading with a firm that is about to die creates risk; and, not trading with them hastens their demise — and perhaps creates good deals as they "puke" out their positions. This was precisely the situation Askin's funds had found themselves in. The response to the letter would show if Vinny was right.

September was a whirlwind. As Rosenfeld (2009) notes: "Whereas August kind of was this economic crisis triggered by Russia, September was another beast. September really was an LTCM crisis: were we going to fail?" The partners were talking to various banks and investors; and, the P&L was mostly "L." Stern strangers in suits swept in and out. Right after one potential buyer saw my group's equity derivatives holdings, we finally lost money: a week of five-sigma losses each day. While we had been mindful of liquidity, seeing that was. . . disgusting.

Late in September, Goldman and AIG with backing from Warren Buffett looked at the firm's positions but, according to multiple accounts, did not tell other banks — who asked if anyone was bidding on the portfolio. (Their silence is not surprising; traders with alpha should not advertise their intentions.)

21 September

As the Goldman-AIG-Buffett crew looked at the firm, we had another shocking day: 21 September the fund again lost $550 mn. You read about revolving lines of credit in Chapter 23, and these are common products offered to businesses for emergency financing. Many have clauses that exempt the bank from lending if the would-be borrower has experienced a material adverse change (MAC). LTCM had a $900 mn revolver from Chase with no MAC clause; and, legal counsel advised that the fund would be failing in its duty to investors if it did not use every means to survive —

LONG-TERM CAPITAL MANAGEMENT, L.P.
ONE EAST WEAVER STREET
GREENWICH, CONNECTICUT 06831-5146 USA

JOHN MERIWETHER
CHIEF EXECUTIVE OFFICER

DIRECT 203-552-5590
FAX 203-552-5424

September 2, 1998

By Telefacsimile

To Investors in the
Investment Vehicles of
Long-Term Capital Portfolio, L. P.

Re: Impact on Net Asset Value of August Market Conditions

Dear Investor:

As you are all too aware, events surrounding the collapse in Russia caused large and dramatically increasing volatility in global markets throughout August, capped by a last-day decline in the Dow Jones Industrial Average of 513 points. The resulting dislocations in markets and greatly increased uncertainty have driven investors to safer and more liquid assets. With increases in both risk and liquidity premia, investment funds widely, many Wall Street firms, and money-center banks have reported large trading losses with resulting sharp declines in their share prices. Investors everywhere have experienced large declines in their wealth.

Unfortunately, Long-Term Capital Portfolio ("Fund") has also experienced a sharp decline in net asset value. As you know our formal procedure for releasing our official net asset value normally takes about ten days after month-end. Following our usual practice to give you an early estimate of the Fund's performance, it is down 44 percent for the month of August, and 52 percent for the year-to-date. Losses of this magnitude are a shock to us as they surely are to you, especially in light of the historical volatility of the Fund. The losses arising from the event-driven major increase in volatility and the flight to liquidity were magnified by the time of year when markets were seasonally thin.

The losses in August occurred in a wide variety of strategies, distributed approximately 82 percent in relative-value trades and 18 percent in directional trades. Emerging markets across both trade categories accounted for 16 percent of the month's total losses in the Fund. Within emerging markets, holdings involving Russia accounted for less than 10 percent of total losses.

A distinguishing characteristic of the Fund's investment philosophy has always been that its returns are generally expected not to exhibit systematic correlation with the returns on global bond, stock, and currency markets. August saw an accelerating increase in the demand for liquidity in nearly every market around the world. Consequently, Government bonds have been the best performers, while small-cap common stocks and other relatively illiquid and risky instruments such as high-yield bonds have performed poorly. Many of the Fund's investment strategies involve providing liquidity to the market. Hence, our losses across strategies were correlated after-the-fact from a sharp increase in the liquidity premium.

Figure 26.5: Page 1 of the 2 September 1998 letter informing investors and employees about August losses and seeking capital.

The majority of the Fund's risks are in our core investment strategies; that is, convergence, relative-value and conditional convergence trades in the U.S., Japan and the larger markets of Europe. Although we have hedged risk-exposure components that were not expected to add incremental value to performance, large divergences in August occurred in many of our key trading strategies that resulted in large losses. The use of leverage has accentuated these losses.

With the large and rapid fall in our capital, steps have been taken to reduce risks now, commensurate with our level of capital. We have raised the risk-return tradeoff requirements for positions. Risk and position reduction is occurring in some strategies that do not meet the new standard. This is a prudent step given the level of capital and uncertainties in the market place.

On the other hand, we see great opportunities in a number of our best strategies and these are being held by the Fund. As it happens, the best strategies are the ones we have worked on over many years. We will focus on these high expected return-to-risk positions and, thereby we can manage them more aggressively.

A cornerstone of our investment management philosophy is the availability and efficiency of financing to support the long horizon for many of our investment strategies. Our capital base is over $2.3 billion, and it is quite liquid. Our financing is in place, including secured and unsecured term debt and long-dated contractual arrangements. These term arrangements provide time to reduce our positions, if needed, as markets become more settled. We continue to work closely with counterparts.

Investors in the Fund provide long-term equity capital that can only be withdrawn in multi-year stages at each year-end. This capital allows the Fund to secure stronger term financing and contractual agreements. It also provides greater flexibility to adjust positions, given changes in the level of its capital. The first date that any investors can withdraw capital is year-end 1998 and that potential withdrawal is less than 12 percent of the capital of the Fund. The principals of LTCM represent over a third of the capital of the Fund. To provide a solid foundation for the Fund and to capitalize on the materially richer investment-opportunity set, LTCM is in the process of seeking to raise additional capital.

The poor performance of the Fund, year-to-date and especially in August, has been very disappointing to us all. However, I would ask in assessing performance going forward, that you keep in mind that the Fund's relative-value strategies may require a relatively long convergence horizon. The expected horizon for convergence on our trades can range from six months to two years, or even longer. Implementation of these strategies involves large positions that take significant time to accumulate and to reduce efficiently. The convergence return pattern of these core strategies normally implies that the day-to-day volatility is much greater in proportion to time than the month-to-month or year-to-year volatility of their performance. This does not imply, however, that the reported short-term performance of the Fund is in any way an inaccurate or invalid measure of actual returns. The mark-to-market valuations on positions in the Fund reported to you are always derived from actual dealer and broker quotations.

Figure 26.6: Page 2 of the 2 September 1998 letter informing investors and employees about August losses and seeking capital.

The Fund returned approximately $2.7 billion of its capital at year-end 1997 when it appeared that the existing investment opportunities were not large and attractive enough to warrant its retention. Many of the trades had converged producing profits and were being unwound. Over the past several months, however, those trades that had converged once again diverged. The Fund added to its positions in anticipation of convergence, yet largely because of last month's market events, the trades diverged dramatically. As a result, the opportunity set in these trades at this time is believed to be among the best that LTCM has ever seen. But, as we have seen, good convergence trades can diverge further. In August, many of them diverged at a speed and to an extent that had not been seen before. LTCM thus believes that it is prudent and opportunistic to increase the level of the Fund's capital to take full advantage of this unusually attractive environment.

With limited exceptions, the Fund has been closed to new investment since July 1995. Many of you have asked to add to your investment in the Fund. Since it is prudent to raise additional capital, the Fund is offering you the opportunity to invest in the Fund on special terms related to LTCM fees. If you have an interest in investing, please contact Richard Leahy at Long-Term Capital Management (203-552-5511) for further information.

I cannot close without telling you about the remarkable performance of the LTCM employees during this particularly difficult month. Over the first four years of the Fund, we had the great good fortune of consistent return performance resulting in larger-than-expected returns with lower-than-expected volatility. We expected that sooner or later that this good fortune could not continue uninterrupted and that we as a firm would be tested. I did not anticipate, however, how severe the test would be. I am happy to report the magnificent performance of our employees operating as a team - administration, technology, operations, legal and strategists – coordinated across our Greenwich, London, and Tokyo offices during this extreme period. August has been very painful for all of us, but I believe that as a consequence, LTCM will emerge a stronger and better firm.

Sincerely,

John W. Meriwether
Chief Executive Officer &
Chairman of the Management Committee

Figure 26.7: Page 3 of the 2 September 1998 letter informing investors and employees about August losses and seeking capital.

so the CFO fired $470 mn of the Chase revolver. (It would have been $500 mn, but some of the loan syndicate balked.)

That evening, the NY Fed ordered the heads of 16 banks to their offices; 13 banks showed up. The rumor I have heard is that the NY Fed President locked them in a conference room and ordered them to clean up the mess their client, LTCM, had created — or face punitive action.

That evening we also heard a rumor that a bid for the fund was coming.

22 September

The next morning, the Goldman-AIG-Buffett triumvirate offered $250 mn to buy out LTCM, inject $4 bn, and merge it into Goldman; however, they would need an answer in less than an hour. The offer should have been for LTCP, the portfolio company; and, contacting major investors would have taken longer than an hour. Without consulting any investors, the partners would be open to lawsuits. (The NY Fed President later agreed with this assessment.) However, Rosenfeld (2009) notes a larger issue: the portfolio could not just be transferred. OTC derivative contracts are not like stocks; a transfer would mean modifying over 15,000 contracts.

The partners proposed that the trio instead inject $4 bn into the fund, pay the partners the $250 mn and fire them, and then remove the outside investors. Unfortunately, Buffett was unreachable to modify the bid. The Goldman-AIG-Buffett bid failed. When the other banks found out about the bid, they were furious.[12] The fund's equity capital fell yet again, down to $600 mn.

23 September

On 23 September, the NY Fed succeeded in brokering a deal with a consortium of 13 (later 14) banks. They created Oversight Partners I LP to recapitalize the fund with $3.625 bn in exchange for 90% equity of the fund.

Bankers Trust, Barclays, Chase, Credit Suisse First Boston, Deutsche Bank, Goldman Sachs, Merrill Lynch, J.P. Morgan, Morgan Stanley, Salomon Smith Barney, and UBS each contributed $300 mn. Société Général contributed $125 mn and Paribas contributed $100 mn. Lehman Brothers declined at first, but later contributed $100 mn. Bear Stearns refused to participate on the grounds that, as LTCM's prime broker, they already had too much risk clearing the firm's trades.

26.4.5   A Return to Normalcy: Post-September 1998

Figure 26.8 shows how unusual the months of August and September were and the results of the recapitalization of the fund by the Consortium.

In the end, the trades in swap spreads and equity index volatility alone were responsible for about 35% and 30% of the losses. The losses in either of those trades

---

[12]I find this anger surprising since multiple investors and banks, in addition to Goldman, had looked at the fund's positions and considered buying some or all of the portfolio.

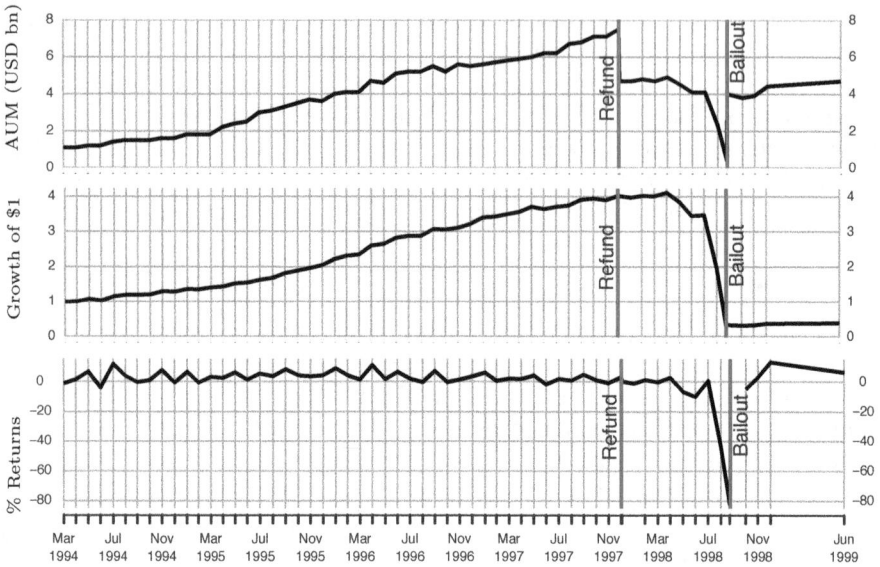

Figure 26.8: LTCP assets under management (top), growth of $1 invested at the start of the fund, and monthly returns from fund start in March 1994 to June 1999.

alone would have been difficult to survive. While these were large trades, they were only two of dozens of strategies traded by LTCM.

The fallout from the crisis was severe for many banks. UBS had sold a call option to LTCM struck at $800 mn for premium of about $290 mn. Then they realized they could lose money if the fund did well, so they "hedged" by investing in the fund. That transformed the short call to a short put. In the third quarter of 1998, UBS took a charge of $700 mn, and the chairman and three top executives resigned.

Dresdner Bank took a third quarter charge of $145 mn; and, Credit Suisse took a charge of $55 mn. At Merrill Lynch, the global head of risk and credit management resigned. At Goldman, Jon Corzine was forced out of the CEO position.

The Consortium dispatched a number of people to work on-site. Their first job was to assess risk and then decide how to pare it back. (This included creating tools for swap compression, the first time any of us had seen such a process.) I ran a report on equity index volatility which showed the firm had $40 mn of vega in five-year S&P 500 volatility and nearly as much in volatility for European and Asian indices. The Consortium members at my desk stepped back, conferred for five minutes, and did not come back to me for weeks. I later heard that Goldman had large vega tolerance — and their desk was limited to about $40 k of vega total.

The Consortium soon laid off employees in certain groups and roles. Due to mutual distrust, they made a "gentlemen's agreement" not to hire anyone who remained until the Consortium was repaid in full.

In the end, the Consortium was repaid in June, September, and December 1999 — and made about 10% on their investment. (While better than zero or a loss, that is not a great return in light of the risk.) In early 2000, LTCM effectively ceased and the gentlemen's agreement on hiring its employees was lifted.

I, many employees, and some of the partners left. Those who remained, and a few new partners, raised money for a new fund called JWM Partners. JWM was intended to run at a lower 10:1 leverage and be more conservative.

After all of this, you should consider the following questions and comments.

- *Could LTCM have accepted the Goldman offer? Should they have?* To what extent can managers make major, capital-structure-altering decisions without consulting investors? Rosenfeld (2009) notes that Buffett later said he would have taken the modified deal to inject $4 bn into the portfolio and pay the partners $250 mn to depart — instead of trying to transfer the portfolio.
- *Did the various banks act ethically?* The difference between pushing a firm into the grave and hedging to best ensure survival is often nil. However, this means that it may be sensible for government to step in — even if only to allow the situation to cool off without any bailouts.
- *Did the NY Fed do the right thing?* Maybe the crisis would have been worse had LTCM failed. Or maybe much of the damage was already done by the time the bailout was arranged.
- *Should employees invest in their employer given that they are already exposed to the firm by their employment?* Or, more provocatively: should employees hedge their exposure to their employer?

26.4.6 Coda: Late 1999

I am often asked "Was LTCM just like in the book?" which usually means either Lowenstein (2000) or Dunbar (1999). I think Lowenstein (2000) is stunningly accurate about the experience and emotions of the crisis. The economics are sometimes elided, but I cannot think of anything which stands out as grossly wrong. (I have not read the book in over 15 years, probably out of avoidance; perhaps that says something about how accurate it is?) Dunbar (1999) is more accurate about the economics but seems to occasionally confuse who was responsible for a project or trade.

There are a few nagging memories. Well before 2008, the fixed income partners who wanted to trade equity index volatility met with my group. For us, illiquidity had been a constant source of problems and we had slowly learned some rules of thumb for avoiding trouble. When we talked with these partners and a researcher, they did not seem to understand how illiquid equities and derivatives could be compared to a 30-year US Treasury bond.

At one point, one of my group's traders challenged them: "For that size, if you are 10% of the daily volume — which is moving things a bit — it would take you five years to exit the position! And you don't want to be 10% for that long!" The researcher replied with "Well, that's one point of view, but we just plan to hold on." The lack of sensitivity to one of their major risk factors (and the only one which cannot be hedged) was stunning. After the meeting, I asked someone about our trader's concerns. "He is right, isn't he? We've seen this." The response was resigned yet diplomatic and pragmatic: "Well, that's what they want to do, so we should help them so they can at least see their risk."

The Dogs of War   During the LTCM crisis, a few phenomena were unusual for their perfidy.

Some derivatives counterparties had also lent money to the fund. As markets became illiquid, some of those counterparties cooperated to push prices and trigger mark-to-market cashflows. These further imperiled the firm and roiled markets... but also put them at the head of the line of creditors.

A colleague helped create a spreadsheet of holdings for firms considering bidding on the fund. Months later, he met a guy who claimed his firm had pushed markets against LTCM. My colleague insisted this was bluster... until the guy named columns from the spreadsheet. He claimed this was to help them bid less for a weakened fund.

Cai (2003) examined a dataset of intraday trades and concludes that other firms front-ran LTCM's trades during the crisis. He also finds that the profitability of this front-running evaporated after the consortium bailout.

Angry people may overlook skulduggery against the crisis "source." However, we will not make crises better until we rein in these destabilizing behaviors.

I also remember a partner who was an excellent trader, after hearing about the new Greenwich office in 1997, saying "That building sounds expensive. If it were any firm — other than this one, I would be shorting that firm."

Finally, think back to the return patterns we saw early on. Returns typically alternated between large up and small flat returns. Some thought this might be due to illiquid investments converging at the same time. However, that should be troubling. Autocorrelations showing up at the portfolio level would mean that illiquidity and lag effects were correlated across disparate strategies and markets. We should be concerned by any portfolio-wide movements.

These three memories suggest that maybe we should be wary when we make an exception to our own rules and that we should probably be more aggressive about looking for signs of trouble.

Another risk is mysticism or ascribing unusual powers to people. Some people ascribe unusual power to LTCM and its employees. The truth is more humbling: we are less in control of markets than we think — so we must consider game-theoretic risks (which can be very nasty). We should all be more cautious and seek to make markets more robust.

Some employees left for the stability of big banks; some moved to servicing finance firms; and, a few embraced index investing. My LTCM experience made me want to learn all I could about market liquidity — so I went to a new group at Morgan Stanley called the Equity Trading Lab. I finally got to see (and help build) an algorithmic trading system; however, I also learned about liquidity and market microstructure. That perspective is woven throughout this book.

I later wondered why exchange-traded derivatives were not destructive to the firm while bilaterally-cleared (OTC) derivatives were. This led to the research in Rosenthal (2014), an attempt to understand what led to market failure. One former LTCM colleague characterized the paper as "an attempt to explain what happened to LTCM" and I suppose it is to an extent.

For those looking for an excellent retrospective beyond the two books mentioned, I highly recommend Rosenfeld (2009), Eric's presentation on video at MIT.

26.5   The Great Financial Crisis of 2008

It would seem that the LTCM tale is cautionary but singular. However, as Shakespeare wrote: "what's past is prologue." Most of the major forces in the Great Financial Crisis were on display in the LTCM crisis: fire sales, runs, crowded trades, and network effects with counterparty risk. There were issues with market liquidity which eventually bled over to funding liquidity; and, there were games played with the capital structure to jump to the front of the queue of creditors.

The US crisis first manifested itself as a credit crunch followed by financial crises as banks failed and counterparty risk spread the disease. For an excellent timeline of the US crisis, see Guillén (2015).

26.5.1   The Events of the Great Financial Crisis

The summary of what happened is a whirlwind of factors. We can, sadly, view it as a three-act tragedy.

Act I

Low interest rates make investors hungry for higher yields but also encourage investment in housing. Refinancings and new mortgages generate new MBSs with higher-yields than government securities. New structured products allow mitigating some of the default risk (with CDOs) and hedging what remained (with CDSs). Refinancings begin to taper off but low rates remain.

Banks make lots of money from selling mortgages into securitization. To keep this going, they lend increasingly to low-credit borrowers. The banks also lend more at floating rates with low initial "teaser" rates — to generate more fees from refinancings later. Banks also hide or lie about some details of unqualified borrowers. Poor risk measures do not even capture the risk of the fictitious details. Rating agencies know the risk measures are poor but want fees (paid by issuers) in exchange for stamping high ratings on the MBSs and CDO tranches. The high ratings allow investors mandated to hold only "safe" securities to buy these new securities.

Act II

As demand for higher-yielding securities outstrips the supply of shaky mortgages, investors purchase synthetic CDOs made of CDSs. Since CDSs have counterparty risk, some CDOs are now long counterparty risk. A group in AIG's London office is particularly active in writing CDSs. Many CDSs try to mitigate counterparty risk by demanding more collateral if counterparties' credit worsens. Property speculation is in full swing. The Fed emerges from the shadows and raises interest rates to tame speculation. Higher rates end refinancing for fixed-rate mortgages and ARMs with expiring initial teaser rates. The higher rates also slow the economy. This makes it harder for some borrowers to meet their mortgage payments.

Defaults rise, impairing the lower tranches of CDOs and triggering some CDSs. New mark-to-market accounting rules make banks and investors write down the value of their holdings, triggering demands for more collateral for derivatives like CDSs. Banks sell lower-quality assets to meet the collateral calls, further depressing prices and leading to an even greater need for collateral. As banks incur losses, they reduce lending which further slows the economy and a credit crunch ensues. That increases defaults on business and mortgage loans. The vicious circle is now closed: credit concerns and collateral calls rage.

Act III

Bear Stearns teeters on the brink of failure before the NY Fed arranges a takeover by JPMorgan Chase. Rating agencies' business has dried up; they repent and begin downgrading ratings on MBSs and CDO tranches. Many mortgage originators fail or are taken over by large banks. Lehman Brothers reports $4 bn in losses and seeks a buyer; but, the NY Fed cannot help them and Lehman enters bankruptcy. Lehman was a major derivatives counterparty and its death voids contracts with most global banks; counterparty risk spreads the disease and many banks panic to replace voided contracts. The US government bails out AIG with $85 bn — despite Lehman having been larger. As the crisis rages, large banks are pushed to buy smaller banks: Bank of America buys Merrill Lynch; Wells Fargo buys Wachovia; JPMorgan Chase buys Washington Mutual. Barclays and Nomura buy parts of Lehman's carcass.

The US government plans to bail out the financial system for $700 bn and bans shorting financial stocks. Warren Buffett injects $5 bn into Goldman; and, Goldman and Morgan Stanley become normal banks to qualify for a government bailout. Congress rejects the $700 bn bailout plan but reconsiders a week later and passes the bailout bill. The US government eventually buys troubled assets, forces money on banks, accepts high-risk assets as collateral for Fed loans, lowers short-term and raises long-term interest rates, and takes over Fannie Mae, Freddie Mac, and Citigroup. The economy crashes and firms cut costs, lay off and fire workers, automate, and outsource production. As the curtain falls, many of the lost jobs no longer exist — leaving lingering questions about what a recovery will look like.

26.5.2   The Factors of the Great Financial Crisis

While we could surely go into great depth about the Great Financial Crisis, the sad truth is we do not need to. Many of the issues on display in the LTCM crisis were also in full display leading up to 2008. The difference, however, was that the 2008 crisis was triggered by an asset bubble.

The proximate cause was rising interest rates in 2005–2006 which deflated a housing bubble in the US; however, there have been interest rate rises and housing bubbles before. A number of factors interacted to make the financial crisis far worse:

- initially low interest rates;
- hunger for yield;
- increase in subprime lending;
- rise in use of adjustable-rate mortgages;
- control fraud;
- growth of new structured products;
- poor risk measures;
- lax rating agencies;
- fair value accounting rules;
- network effects; and,
- technology-induced shifts in the workforce.

We will examine each of these; however, as Lo (2012) notes, we are faced with a set of somewhat inconsistent stories much like Akira Kurosawa's *Rashomon*. Finding the ultimate cause of the crisis is challenging.

Initially Low Interest Rates

Over 2000–2003, the US Federal Reserve lowered their target Fed Funds rate from 6.5% in late 2000 down to 1.75% in early 2002 after the collapse of the internet bubble to 1% from mid-2003 to mid-2004. From then the Fed engaged in a steady (i.e. regular) program of tightening to a high of 5.25% in mid-2006. From all accounts, this was done in hopes of deflating the housing bubble.

Lowering rates made sense after the internet bubble burst and the terrorist attacks of 11 September 2001. Economic growth resumed in early 2002, but measured inflation remained low. This is why Fed Chair Alan Greenspan encouraged rates to be kept so low for so long after growth had resumed. Could the inflation measures have missed the increasing use of the internet lowering prices of goods and services? In Fisher (2006), the President of the Dallas Federal Reserve Bank makes clear that he was concerned about where inflation was headed and that we do not measure inflation versus other countries (as done at, say, the Bank of Canada). Or perhaps Greenspan was blithe about rising overinvestment in housing?

A more strategic criticism of US monetary policy comes from University of Chicago economist and former Governor of the Reserve Bank of India Raghuram Rajan who warned about a coming financial crisis in 2005. He notes in Rajan (2010) that excessively low interest rates were partly driven by the "weak safety nets" in the US which (even still) make politics very sensitive to the economy and implicitly politicize monetary policy. He notes how Europe, in contrast, has weathered higher unemployment without the political or financial crises seen in the US. While you may not be familiar with Rajan's work, he is very much a free markets, supply-side economist — so to hear this critique from him should be sobering and cause us to truly reconsider monetary, fiscal, and even social policy.

Hunger for Yield

Low interest rates may have increased economic growth, but they also made many fixed income securities less attractive to investors. Higher-yielding securities increased in price and newly-issued securities carried lower interest rates. For insurance companies and endowments, fixed income is a large part of their portfolio which needs to be continually replaced as bonds mature. For pension funds faced with a looming wave of Baby Boomer retirements, bonds are especially sensible since they cannot risk having too little cash for later payouts.

If somebody could find a way to create investment-grade bonds with higher yields than low US Treasury yields, they would have many eager customers. As FCIC (2011) notes:

> Many investors preferred securities highly rated by the rating agencies — or were encouraged or restricted by regulations to buy them. And with yields low on other highly rated assets, investors hungered for Wall Street mortgage securities backed by higher-yield mortgages....

Increased Subprime Lending

Subprime lending is lending to consumers who are seen as more risky, the consumer equivalent of high yield borrowers. Lo (2012) notes that in the US this has usually been defined as borrowers with a Fair and Isaac Company credit score below 600.

In 1999, the government-sponsored entities of Fannie Mae and Freddie Mac faced pressure from the Clinton administration to increase lending to underserved areas in accordance with the Community Reinvestment Act. However, while lending increased to CRA-eligible areas, that does not seem to have distorted the market. Over 1996–2003, the subprime share of the mortgage market drifted between roughly 7.5% and 10.5%.

The internet lowered the cost to borrowers by making it easier for them to find the lowest interest rates through online comparison websites that effectively automated the role of a mortgage broker. However, FCIC (2011) notes a few other features which seem to have increased subprime lending. Increased use of credit scoring enabled automation of underwriting and determining which borrowers and mortgages would be conforming. That lowered the costs of origination. Placing those credit scoring algorithms in desktop applications also made it easy for mortgage originators to map out the models and look for loopholes or how to most easily game the algorithms. Finally, low interest rates had set off a wave of refinancings which generated new MBS and CMO offerings... but tapered off in 2003.

Subprime mortgages jumped from 8.3% of originations in 2003 to 20.9% of originations in 2004, then 22.7% in 2005, and peaking at 23.5% of mortgage originations in 2006. As the subprime mortgage market grew, most of the increase was securitized. The originators had not greatly increased their appetite for risk; they merely passed more risk along to others. This might explain the rise in non-conforming subprime loans like "No Doc" loans which lacked documentation for income, assets, or employment; "Alt A" loans to high-credit borrowers with other troubling factors; or, the truly absurd "NINJA" loans made to people with no income, no job, and no assets. Perhaps it is not surprising that, in 2007, almost no subprime mortgages were held by their originators.

Rise in the Use of Adjustable-Rate Mortgages

While low interest rates and automation lowered the cost for mortgage borrowers, another product made their initial costs even lower. Adjustable-rate mortgages (ARMs) became increasingly popular by offering low "teaser" rates for the first few years before the rate transitioned to a much more expensive floating rate. Many mortgage brokers openly stated that they pushed ARMs to drive people to refinance when the low teaser rates expired — so that, hopefully, they could create an annuity of refinancing fees.

ARMs have historically been far less popular with US borrowers; and, while banks like ARMs they do shift the risk of changing interest rates onto borrowers instead of lenders. In 2001, only 4% of prime borrowers took out an ARM which rose to 10% in 2003. However, as with subprime lending, the use of ARMs increased as refinancings dried up and interest rates rose. In 2004, 12% of prime borrowers used an ARM. Subprime borrowers have historically been heavier users of ARMs, a troubling fact in itself. However, as subprime lending ramped up in 2004, so did their use of ARMs. Whereas 60% of subprime borrowers had used an ARM in 2003, 76% used an ARM in 2004. An increasing use of ARMs when the Fed had said they would raise interest rates as needed to deflate the housing bubble is... well, it suggests that the borrowers were not educated about how ARMs work.

Control Fraud

Another factor is what Black (2014) calls **control fraud**: looting a company for personal profit. Both executives and loan officers earned bonuses and benefits from processing more business — even if the loans underwritten were problematic. FCIC (2011) has a number of details which suggest control fraud was a factor in the crisis.

The CEO of subprime lender Countrywide called one of the firm's products "poison" in an internal email and said "I have never seen a more toxic [product]." He even went so far as to compare his bank to those in the savings-and-loan crisis of the 1980s.

Another subprime lender, Ameriquest, sent loan documents on request to a Minnesota Assistant Attorney General. The official pulled a few documents at random and immediately found inconsistencies. Many people were listed as antiques dealers; and, a disabled man in his 80s was claimed to work in light construction.

Gordon (2010) and OSHA (2011) noted how loan officers at subprime lenders Washington Mutual and Countrywide cut-and-pasted fraudulent information onto loan applications to make them acceptable for underwriting.

Some elderly homeowners were sold home renovations that were funded with home equity lines of credit using renovation application details and generating fees for the agents and affiliates. Many homeowners were not told that this was the source of financing; and, the "home renovators" often ran off with the money leaving homeowners to pay for renovations they never received.

A fraud detection firm analyzed a sample of mortgages originated over 2005–2007 and found 13% of them contained material lies or omissions which would make the loan eligible for cancelation. Ashcraft and Schuermann (2008) discuss the various places where adverse selection and fraud can enter into mortgage underwriting.

Growth of New Structured Products

In Chapter 22 we discussed credit default swaps (CDSs); and, in Chapter 23 we discussed collateralized debt obligations (CDOs). CDSs had been around since the 1990s and CDOs since their introduction in 1987 by Drexel Burnham Lambert. However, as Greenspan (2005) notes, the CDS market was hampered until ISDA was able to create a standard contract form in 1999.

CDOs are computationally difficult to analyze; however, in 2000, Li (2000) showed an easy way to simulate correlated defaults using a Gaussian copula. As mentioned in Chapter 22, a copula is not intuitive. To simulate correlated defaults, you generate correlated normal random variables $z_1, \ldots, z_n$; map these through the inverse normal cdf Φ^{-1} to get correlated uniform random variates $u_1, \ldots, u_n$; and, then map these to the distribution you actually desire using that cdf F_v to get correlated variables $v_1, \ldots, v_n$.

This has many problems: the correlation of the u's, z's, and v's are all different; the dependence structures (*i.e.* higher cross-moments) are all different; and, the tail risk is completely wrong since we start from a thin-tailed distribution. Furthermore, even "default correlation" can be defined in a few ways: correlation of default events is often lower than the correlation of default times.

Despite all my statistical training and having played with copulas, I do not find them to be intuitive. I have no economic intuition for how the clustered defaults should look in the space of u's or z's. While the Gaussian copula approach is clearly incorrect, it has two advantages: it is fast to compute and easily coded.

CDSs and CDOs grew, but not rapidly until 2003 or 2004. Then, as subprime mortgage lending rose, CDOs also grew. FCIC (2011) notes that many subprime

CMO tranches were not easily sold; however, if they were collected in a CDO, the higher tranches would receive ratings allowing them to be easily sold.

Eventually, the hunger for yield outstripped what cash CDOs could supply and synthetic CDOs using CDSs as underliers also grew.

Some investors realized that the assumptions about defaults might be wrong and so also bought CDSs to hedge their risks. However, unlike CDOs which largely involve cashflows from borrowers to purchasers of tranches, CDSs are swaps with financial intermediaries. Worse, CDSs are much more likely to have triggering events (where protection is called on) during a crisis. Thus counterparty risk is a serious concern with CDSs (and synthetic CDOs).

Poor Risk Measures

We have repeatedly talked about the need to use better risk measures. The Basel I banking accords, adopted by regulators and banking supervisors globally, did not use risk measures so much as they used rules. A portfolio of mortgages was considered low-risk. Unfortunately, there was room for "regulatory arbitrage" as putting those mortgages into a CMO or CDO and holding all of the tranches lowered the capital the bank was required to hold.

Many banks, however, had adopted the framework created by JP Morgan's RiskMetrics group and mandated by the Basel II accords — and used value-at-risk (VaR) to measure their risk. Unfortunately, as mentioned in Chapter 8, VaR is a flawed measure and especially problematic when used to measure portfolios of bonds with default risk. The fact that VaR can penalize more diversified fixed income portfolios is especially troubling.

Finally, the Gaussian copula was used to simulate correlated defaults — often without a structural or even reduced-form model for defaults. Thus while defaults were correlated, they were not necessarily clustered due to some economic state variable. That made it difficult to watch for forces that could imperil a particular CDO or portfolio.

Lax Rating Agencies

The demand for higher-yielding CDO tranches would not have existed if they were not also higher rated. While the risk measures in use were insufficient, there was nothing to stop credit analysts at rating agencies from using better risk measures or subjective judgment. The ultimate modeling tool is, after all, not a computer program but the human brain.

Unfortunately, the rating agencies worked (and still work) under a strange model: they are paid by the issuers to supply a rating. Thus the incentive of the rating agency is to keep the issuers happy and returning with more business. As Scannell and Lucchetti (2008) first reported, rating agency analysts knew these incentives led to them understating risks. One infamous text chat between Standard & Poor's analysts was blunt:

Btw that deal is ridiculous.

I know right... model def does not capture half the risk.

We should not be rating it.

We rate every deal.

It could be structured by cows and we would rate it.

More confusing is that the ratings on CDO tranches were given the same letters as bond ratings; however, footnotes in research documents sometimes said those ratings should not be construed as equivalent to bond ratings.

While the rating agencies had their reputations at risk, they had no financial stake in the correctness of their ratings. Thus the ratings issued might imply one level of risk and CDS prices might imply a very different level of risk. On the other hand, if the rating agencies were making markets in CDSs, they would have incentives to manipulate their ratings or time their trading around announcements of ratings changes.[13]

Fair Value Accounting Rules

Accounting rules, while arbitrary, matter since contracts may depend on accounting statements. The Financial Accounting Standards Board's release of Statement of Financial Accounting Standards 157: Fair Value Measurements moved securitized assets to being marked not at cost but at the price which would be received in the market, aka **mark-to-market accounting**.

While this required companies to recognize losses even if they were not realized, the more serious problem is that these losses could trigger **collateral calls**. A collateral call forces a counterparty to pledge more assets to maintain the derivative contract. Faquiryan and Rodriguez (2014) discuss how this happened frequently during the crisis and how the demand for high-quality assets or cash to meet collateral calls led to fire sales.

Thus mark-to-market accounting coupled with derivative contracts with collateral calls became a force for vicious cycles of declining asset values.

Network Effects

While Bear Stearns did not fail, it got about as close as a bank could to failure without failing. Bear was a counterparty to numerous bilaterally-cleared OTC derivative contracts, so their failure would have spread losses and created the possibility of counterparty risk and contagion transmuting into systemic risk. As it was, many

---

[13]The best free market solution might be to eliminate rating agencies altogether and base classifications of "investment grade" on CDS prices.

counterparties had already been seeking to replace their contracts with Bear so some of the damage was done despite their "rescue" by JPMorgan Chase.

A feature often missed, however, is that Bear Stearns was also one of the largest prime brokerage banks in the world. Many hedge funds used Bear as the firm which maintained their payments, clearing for derivatives, and settlements. Bear's failure could have caused the failure of many hedge funds — a counterparty risk network effect of a second type.

Lehman's failure on 15 September 2008 was, truly, devastating. While counterparties might have started replacing their contracts as Bear teetered near collapse, there was no rescue in the end for Lehman — nor for Lehman's counterparties. Lehman failed in a spectacularly messy way with money being grabbed by various offices around the globe and legal proceedings in different countries fighting against each other.

Shortly after Lehman failed, AIG was bailed out. The claim was that AIG was so involved with credit default swaps that allowing them to fail would have further traumatized the market. Saving AIG after allowing Lehman to fail is puzzling since Lehman's failure would seem to ensure the financial crisis was maximally damaging.

Why was Bear allowed to come so close to failure and Lehman allowed to fail while AIG, which was smaller, was saved? It is hard not to notice that Bear refused to help recapitalize LTCM and Lehman initially refused. More than one senior banker I have mentioned this to have smiled tightly and said "Yes, well, they got theirs didn't they? They probably should have helped in 1998." Furthermore, AIG had long been cozy with Goldman and Treasury Secretary Hank Paulson had become the CEO of Goldman by pushing out Jon Corzine after LTCM was recapitalized. While it is unlikely these facts fully explain the differing fates of Bear and Lehman versus AIG, memories in the finance world *are* long-lived.

Technology-Induced Shifts in the Workforce

A factor in the recovery from the financial crisis was the ongoing changes wrought by the internet and the ability to easily outsource work. As the financial crisis impacted non-financial companies (aka the **real economy**), those firms laid off workers, closed offices and plants (as in the sidebar "Yoga Studio Down" in Chapter 1), or ceased operations. When firms suddenly needed to cut costs, the internet made outsourcing to countries with cheap labor easy. Some workers were faced with the choice of working harder and/or for less pay; other workers did not even get that choice.[14]

Once some competitors are using cheaper labor, it becomes difficult to compete on cost unless they also adopt cheaper labor.[15] That meant that the crisis also induced shifts in the workforce and in industrial processes. This made the recovery from the crisis unusual: as firms regained profitability, employment did not rise commensurately in all industries and jobs.

---

[14]It is not clear if this overwork led to the demand for analgesics which eventually became the opioid crisis; however, Case and Deaton (2015) note that it is possible.

[15]Here I mean "cheaper" in the sense of cost per unit for some acceptable quality level.

26.5.3   Plotting a Crisis

To help see these phenomena evolve across time, Figures 26.9 and 26.10 show a number of variables over 2002–2012.

In Figure 26.9, we see risk factors and indicators. As the effective Fed Funds rate rises, we see subprime mortgages become a much larger part of the mortgage market. Securitization increases, suggesting banks' inability or unwillingness to hold those loans. Returns on homes begin to fall in early 2005, the *first warning sign*. The TED spread pops above the 48 bp warning threshold twice in late 2005, the *second warning sign*. The yield curve then inverts briefly in early 2006, the *third warning sign*. Finally, in mid-2006, home returns go negative until 2009 and the yield curve inverts until mid-2007 (a very strong signal). The TED spread goes above the warning threshold from mid-2007 to mid-2009.

In Figure 26.10, we see the fallout of the US housing market crisis. Inflation measured year-over-year and month-over-month annualized show deflation from late-2008 to late-2009. Home mortgage delinquencies begin climbing in early 2007 until plateauing in late 2010. Business loan delinquencies peak in mid-2009. Employment begins falling in late 2007 for construction/extraction and routine jobs — which are easily outsourced and automated. Employment in cognitive non-routine jobs falls from 2009 to mid-2010, but then recovers. Employment in manual non-routine jobs (*e.g.* personal services) shows seasonality but continue to rise. The lack of a recovery for routine jobs suggests a shift in the makeup of the US job market.

26.6   The European Sovereign Debt Crisis

The European Sovereign Debt Crisis was a direct follow-on from the Great Financial Crisis. The crisis which built up in the US and parts of Europe first manifested as a credit crunch in the US followed by financial crises as banks failed and counterparty risk spread the disease. Some European banks failed, and that spread the credit crunch. The economic stresses then tore at the divisions in the Eurozone. However, the seeds of trouble were sown long before then. (For more details and references, the interested reader should consult Guillén (2015) and BBC (2012).)

26.6.1   A Fiscal Factor

The European crisis has one additional factor which was (and continues to be) important: the difference between fiscal and monetary policy. Prior to economic and monetary union (EMU), there was no single currency or central bank. There was, however, the **European Currency Unit** (ECU, ISO code XEU) and the European Monetary Institute. The Maastricht Treaty in 1992 set EMU as the final goal for all EU member states that met the convergence criteria of low inflation, deficits/GDP below 3%, debt/GDP below 60%, stable exchange rates, and low long-term interest rates — with Denmark and the UK being given an opt-out. On 1

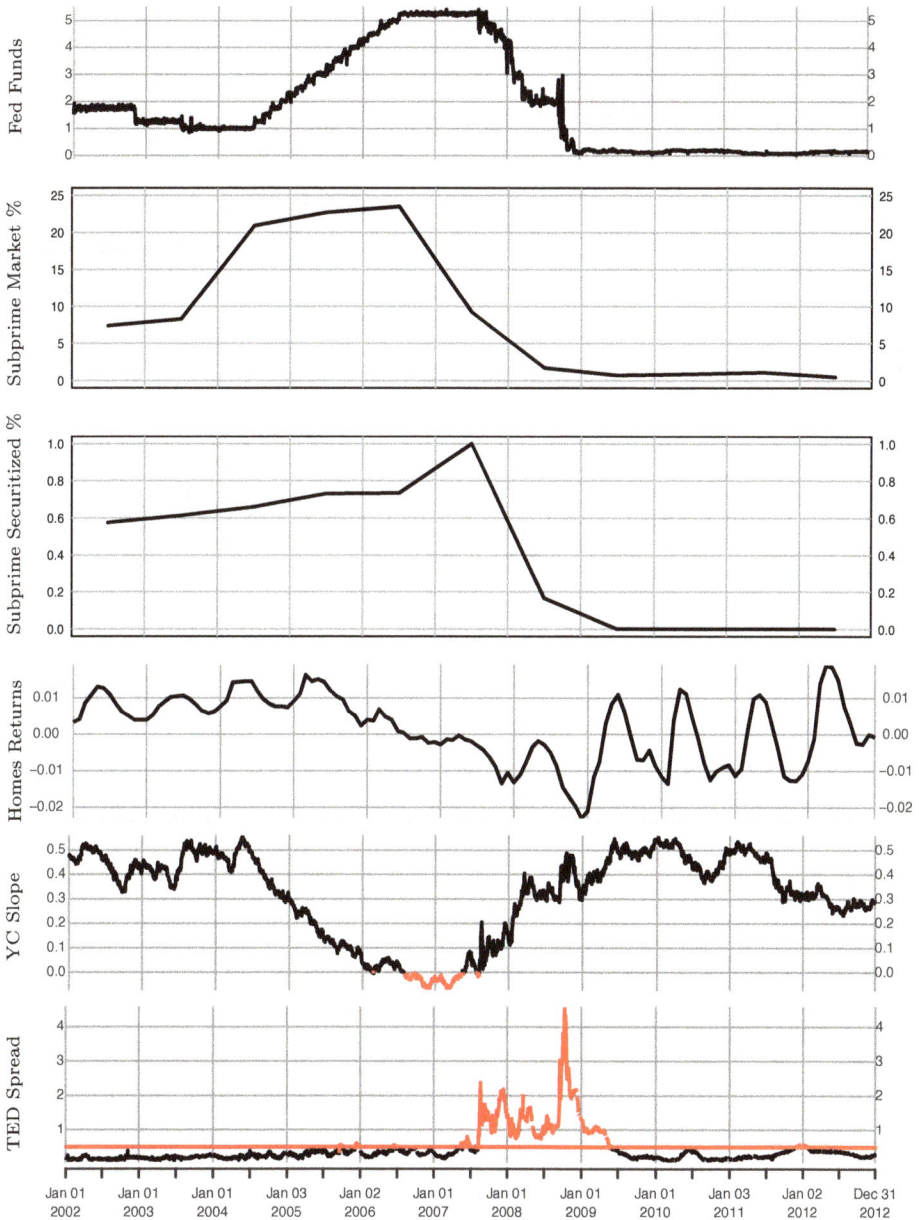

Figure 26.9: US housing market risk factors and indicators over 2002–2012. As Fed Funds, the effective target rate of monetary policy, increases in Nov 2004, subprime mortgages come to dominate the market. Securitization rises, suggesting lower-quality subprime lending. In Q1 2005, Case-Shiller returns on repeat home sales begin falling. The yield curve inverts (in red) in 2006Q1 and then over 2006Q2–2007Q2. The TED spread climbs over the (red) warning threshold of 48 bp in 2005H2, 2006Q2, and then 2007Q2–2009Q2.

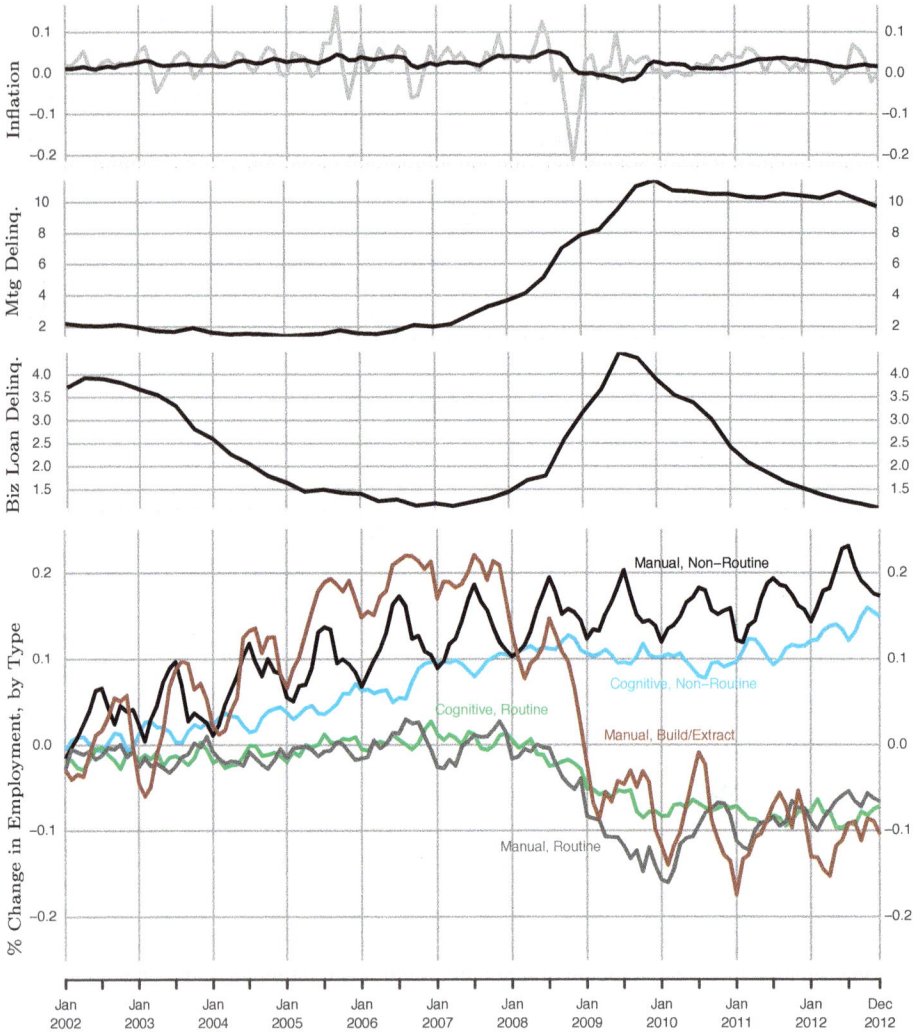

Figure 26.10: Fallout of the US housing market meltdown. Inflation measured year-over-year (in black) and month-over-month annualized (in gray) goes negative over late-2008–late-2009. Home mortgage delinquencies begin climbing in 2007Q1 until plateauing in late 2010. Business loan delinquencies peak in mid-2009. Employment in construction/extraction and routine (easily outsourced/automated) jobs begin falling in late 2007. Employment in cognitive non-routine jobs falls over 2009-mid-2010, but then recovers. Employment in manual non-routine jobs (*e.g.* personal services) shows seasonality but continues to rise.

January 1999, EMU began with the Euro introduced for financial transactions in Eurozone countries and the European Central Bank overseeing monetary policy.

The problem is in the very term "EMU." There is economic union in the free flow of goods and services and harmonized economic policy; and, there is monetary union in the use of a single currency and an overarching central bank overseeing monetary policy with help applying that policy from the Eurosystem national central banks.[16] However, while the convergence criteria mention some fiscal hurdles and Eurozone members are bound by the Stability and Growth Pact... the truth is that there is not *fiscal union* of Eurozone members.

What this means is that Eurozone members may squeeze through the convergence criteria and then be lax on controlling their spending and revenue collection. Rumors abounded before the start of EMU about Italy "massaging" their statistics; and, before Greece entered EMU, rumors were even stronger that accounting tricks or sleight-of-hand had been used to meet the convergence criteria. Later reports such as Story, Thomas, and Schwartz (2010) confirmed these rumors. As for post-EMU fiscal policy, Artavanis, Morse, and Tsoutsoura (2016) estimates that in 2009 in Greece, EUR 28 bn went untaxed — which would have covered 30% of their deficit.

26.6.2   The Fallout from the US

As the credit crunch raged in the US, stress began to show in Europe. In September 2007, the Bank of England helped prop up building society Northern Rock and sought buyers. (Shin (2009) notes how the run on Northern Rock differed from traditional bank runs and related to the credit crunch.) This was unsuccessful and five months later the bank was nationalized. Other banks suffered under rumors of credit problems and mortgage lending in the UK and Europe dried up.

As the US credit crunch became a financial crisis in 2008, European banks incurred losses and raised more equity capital. The Bank of England and European Central Bank pumped money into the banking system with emergency loans and lower interest rates. Irish banks which had underwritten large amounts of US commercial real estate started to incur major losses. Banking and insurance firm Fortis was partly nationalized, Franco-Belgian bank Dexia was bailed out, and Ireland guaranteed all Irish bank deposits. Icelandic banks, with many European depositors, began blocking withdrawals and failing. The Bank of England and European Central Bank promised bailouts in the hundreds of billions as more banks were bailed out.

In 2009, as the US crisis came under control, European banks were still being nationalized partly (Commerzbank in Germany; HBOS, Lloyd's TSB, and Royal Bank of Scotland in the UK) or fully (Anglo Irish Bank); Iceland's government fell

---

[16]We will ignore, for now, the ECB's single mandate of price stability with secondary mandates of financial stability and integration. The lack of employment in their mandate makes one wonder if something like stagflation will eventually stalk the Eurozone.

over their banking crisis; unemployment reached high levels throughout Europe; and, deflation even crept in.

26.6.3   A Gloom of One's Own

As bank lending dried up, loans from large established Eurozone countries to those on the periphery declined. This made it more expensive for businesses and consumers to roll their debt. This caused the economy to slow, particularly in the "PIGS" countries: Portugal, Italy, Greece, and Spain.[17] However, the crisis in Europe was different: longer, slower, and more anodyne. With a financial crisis, we have identifiable risks, clear sources of loss, and lots of daily or intraday data to monitor and study. With a governmental debt crisis brought on by policy failures, nothing happens quickly. For this reason, I have an abbreviated timeline below.

2009

In October 2009, the European crisis began to take on its own life. A new party won a snap election in Greece by promising to reduce corruption and weather the recession. Eurostat had complained regularly about Greek statistics being suspect; and, the new administration began to clean up the economic statistics: in December they admitted to debt of EUR 300 bn, the highest in modern history and about 113% of GDP. The world was shocked but Greece insisted they were not about to default.

2010

An EU report in January 2010 noted that the Greek deficit/GDP had also been understated: it was 12.7% and not 3.7%. Greece was far out of compliance with the Stability and Growth Pact. Greece imposed austerity measures and the citizens responded with strikes and riots. EUR fell versus USD and GBP. Further revisions showed the deficit/GDP was actually 13.6% and not 12.7%. Borrowing costs for Greece reached record highs.

On 2 May, the Eurozone and IMF agreed to an EUR 110 bn *bailout of Greece*. In November, they agreed on an EUR 85 bn *bailout of Ireland* — but insisted that Portugal would not need a bailout. Greek and Portuguese debt were downgraded.

2011

In May 2011, the Eurozone and IMF agreed on an EUR 78 bn *bailout of Portugal*. The Eurozone said Greece must continue with austerity to receive the last parts of their bailout. After much complaining, Greek debt was downgraded to one notch

---

[17]The PIGS (or PIIGS if Ireland is included) acronym is an obvious insult to those economies and an allusion to their inability to control spending; however, its usage has stuck and so it is included here.

above Pakistan's — but austerity was continued; and, the public continued to protest. In June, Greek debt was downgraded further to CCC.

In July, rumors swirled that Greece might have to leave the Euro.[18] However, the Maastricht Treaty stated that a country leaving the Euro must also leave the EU.[19] Such a severe penalty resulted in **regulatory capture**: leverage the regulated have because of what regulators want. In this case, Greece had negotiating leverage because the EU did not actually want to eject Greece. The Eurozone agreed to a second bailout of Greece for EUR 109 bn — conditional on austerity and a debt workout. Greek politicians dithered, protested, and even considered putting the second bailout to a referendum.

By August, the cost of borrowing had increased for Spain and Italy and fallen for Germany — a clear sign of a flight to quality. Italy passed austerity measures but still had its debt downgraded in September. The Greek Finance Minister complained that Greece had been treated poorly and suffered because of EU incompetence. In October, Franco-Belgian bank Dexia was bailed out — this time for its exposure to Greek debt. Spanish debt was downgraded. After long negotiations, some private banks agreed to a 50% loss on Greek debt; banks were also mandated to increase their capital reserves to protect against further losses. In November, Hungarian debt was cut to junk and Belgian debt was downgraded.

2012

In January 2012, France and Austria were downgraded from below AAA and Italy, Spain, Portugal, Slovakia, Slovenia, Cyprus, and Malta were also downgraded — with Portugal's debt dropped to junk status. The Eurozone bailout loan facilities were also downgraded. Finally, in March, a *second bailout of Greece* for EUR 130 bn was agreed. In May, the crisis spread to Spain with bank Bankia being bailed out. Further bailouts and an increase in Spanish borrowing costs led to the Eurozone providing an EUR 100 bn *support fund for Spain*. Since many Cypriot banks had held Greek debt, they were hurt by the debt workout and so in June 2012 Cyprus requested a bail out. However, they also argued over terms.

2013 and Beyond

Cyprus was finally able to agree to terms with the Eurozone. In late March 2013, *Cyprus was bailed out.*

The effects of the debt crisis were strong: interest rates in the Eurozone went negative in mid-2014; and, in 2015 Greece negotiated for a third bailout. The Greek

---

[18]At this time, I heard two morbid jokes from European economists. One proposed allowing for currency devaluation by creating a "Greek Euro" ... pronounced "drachma." The other suggested letting Turkey bail out Greece in exchange for EU accession — since Greek shame over being bailed out by their long-time rival would ensure they never again neglected their finances. The anger at Greek fiscal mismanagement ran very deep.

[19]The EU could ignore their own treaty — though that would signal even less teeth in their rules.

government did not like the proposed terms, so they broke off negotiations and decided to put the decision to a referendum. On 5 July 2015, a large majority rejected the bailout's terms in the referendum. Markets worldwide fell and it looked very likely that Greece would leave the Eurozone and possibly the EU. Finally, on 13 July 2015, the Eurozone agreed to a *third bailout of Greece* for EUR 86 bn. As of this writing, Greece is still promising to make changes to become fiscally responsible and to enact structural reforms.

26.6.4   *Three Pillars Pooh-Poohed*

Economic policy in the EU is based on the **Three Pillars** of investment, fiscal responsibility, and structural reforms. The common thread running through the debt crisis is the failure of countries to show fiscal responsibility and undertake structural reforms. These then affected investment.

Why were countries fiscally irresponsible? Surely politicians' need for adulation is a factor; even in isolated countries this can weigh on their finances. However, being in a union can generate perverse incentives. Perhaps some countries saw fiscal discipline in the Eurozone like the Prisoners' Dilemma: being responsible when others are not was a painful choice. This is where moral hazard creeps in: why not be reckless and let others pick up the bill?

More troubling is countries eschewing **structural reforms**: changes in policies and processes to make an economy more competitive and robust. Structural reforms include privatizing state-owned enterprises, removing regulations and red tape which reduce competition and retard business creation, encouraging innovation, making tax policy fair and tax collection effective, and trimming overly-generous social benefits. Structural reform often requires reining in corruption. Thus structural reforms are not flashy and may have political costs; however, they lay the foundation for future success.

The lesson many countries seemed to have learned was that they could bluff or lie about fiscal responsibility and structural reforms — and the EU would not punish them. Maybe the hope was that a little lying could yield investment which would make it easier to be fiscally responsible and make structural reforms "later." The problem is that "later" rarely arrives.

Another lesson of the crisis cuts the other way. Slovakia adopted low taxes, reined in social spending, adopted business-friendly laws, and pushed through other structural reforms to grow their economy. Their success led them to adopt the Euro in January of 2009. A year-and-a-half later, they were asked to help bail out a country with a higher GDP/capita which did not make similar hard choices. After a second Greek bailout, Slovaks were so angry that their government fell in 2012. What lesson would another middle-income country take from this? Surely not that fiscal responsibility and structural reforms will protect them or earn them the protection of the EU or Eurozone.

26.7   The Chinese Stock Market Mayhem of 2015

It makes sense to mention the most recent turmoil: the near-meltdown of the Chinese stock market. While not yet clarified by distant hindsight, the episode shows a different take on intervention in a crisis.

26.7.1   Europe, Ευρος, and Fēngfù de Fēngzi (丰富的疯子)[20]

The big trouble in China was a follow-on from the Great Financial Crisis and the European Sovereign Debt Crisis. Economic chaos in China's top trading partners had seriously threatened the economy and social stability. In response, China debuted a large infrastructure spending program in 2008. When a credit crunch arose in June of 2013, the government reined that in by demanding that banks lend. (The consequences would seem to be dire for banks not heeding the demand.)

Protective stimuli from the Chinese government may have stopped the crises from spreading to China, but the effects of those interventions built up over time. Furthermore, Bailey, Huang, and Yang (2011) show that lending in a state-controlled economy which targets low unemployment and social instability tends to produce lower-performing borrowers. By 2015, growth had fallen closer to 7% annually; and, some property and municipal investments were patent failures.

However, China was still enacting structural reforms and growing and the populace was still getting richer. This increased stock market participation, albeit slowly. To accelerate this, the government began a new campaign to increase share ownership. On 21 April 2015, the Communist Party-run *People's Daily* proclaimed that stocks hitting record highs were "the start of a bull market." Many citizens interpreted this as government backing of stocks and, as Economist (2015b) notes, piled into the stock market. Nearly two-thirds of these new traders had not even finished high school; thus they were often uneducated about investment risks. One Chinese academic I met told me his university was dirty because janitors were busy trading stocks on their phones instead of cleaning.

China's stock market regulator, the China Securities Regulatory Commission (CSRC), had loosened restrictions in good ways, such as allowing short selling and helping introduce CSI 300 index futures and (soon!) options. However, the CSRC had also ignored some other duties: it had failed to delist failing firms, overlooked loans being used for speculation, and even loosened margin trading rules despite rampant speculation. Li and Zhou (2016) note that the government may have wanted to pump up the market to unload state-owned enterprises at high prices.

The CSI 300 index peaked in mid-June around 5300 and then began falling. On 27 June, the People's Bank of China (PBoC) made a surprise interest rate cut. On 1 July, the CSRC eased collateral rules and allowed margin loans to be extended; and, stock exchanges lowered trading fees. Shares which fell significantly were suspended

---

[20]Fēngfù de fēngzi, or 丰富的疯子, is "a wealth of madmen" but also a play on 风 (fēng = wind) to power the Eastern wind Ευρος.

from trading. By July 3, the CSI 300 had fallen to just under 3900 and IPOs were canceled. The China Financial Futures Exchange suspended 19 accounts for shorting futures, began to limit position sizes, and put the introduction of index options on hold.[21]

The government then assembled the **National Team**, a group of brokerages, asset managers, and insurance companies who pledged to support share prices and, the PBoC provided liquidity to assist them. Asset managers and large shareholders were told not to sell shares. Criminal proceedings were begun against those seen as having manipulated share prices to drive them lower.

However, China quickly gave up on propping up the market and shares purchased in the mayhem were pledged to be transferred to the state sovereign wealth fund. In late August, the CSI 300 index fell from just under 4100 to around 3350. The PBoC cut interest rates for a fifth time in nine months.

For those seeking more detailed timelines, Rapoza (2015) and SCMP (2015) offer detailed timelines of the mayhem.

26.7.2   Black Cat, White Cat?

The legacy of the Chinese intervention is unclear. On the one hand, the Chinese government seemed to quickly learn that they could not prop up shares — something the Japanese Price Keeping Operation (or the US and UK authorities who banned shorting financial stocks in 2008) could have learned as quickly.

On the other hand, the trust in a market system was not yet fully developed as evidenced by both exhorting investors to take risks and then suspending shares. Capitalism requires that winners benefit and losers fail; otherwise incentives are distorted and undermined. However, it also requires that people realize this so that they do not take risk unduly. As Gao (2017) notes, the China Financial Futures Exchange still has small position limits. These make it difficult for institutional clients to hedge with futures; and, the exchange has yet to introduce index options.

In the end, the political concerns highlighted by Bailey, Huang, and Yang (2011) and Li and Zhou (2016) may have dominated economic concerns. Perhaps authorities applied Deng's famous "black cat, white cat" attitude to social stability and concluded that economic purity was less important.[22]

26.8   The Dogs That Did Not Bark

It is also informative to look at crises which could have been — but were not.

---

[21]With futures, every buy is paired with a short... so it is not clear what behavior triggered the suspensions.

[22]Deng Xiaoping's famous saying was 不管黑猫白猫。能抓到老鼠就是好猫。 In Pinyin, this is: Bùguǎn hēi māo bái māo. Néng zhuā dào lǎoshǔ jiùshì hǎo māo. The English version seems a bit opaque: "No matter if a black cat or white cat. If it can catch mice, it is a good cat." The meaning — which Mr. Deng was exiled for — was that socialist dogmatism was less important than improving the lives of Chinese citizens.

As Sherlock Holmes realizes in "The Adventure of Silver Blaze:" the "dog that didn't bark" is useful information. Similarly, the fact that these were not crises is informative about which differences can help make markets more robust.

26.8.1 Central Clearing Non-Failures

Refco, mentioned in Chapters 3 and 19, was the top futures broker at the Chicago Mercantile Exchange in 2005. Refco went public, despite accounting irregularities, in August of that year and was defunct by 17 October. A number of futures traders in Chicago were convinced that the day after Refco failed would be a market holiday. Instead, the market opened and trading continued.

Commodity hedge fund Amaranth went bankrupt in 2006 with large positions in natural gas futures; again, the market was not disrupted.

According to Melamed (2009), in March 2008, Bear Stearns held contracts with exposure equivalent to $700 bn at the CME when collapse appeared imminent. In September, Lehman Brothers held contracts with exposure equivalent to $1.3 tn at the CME when they went bankrupt. Note that none of the CME, ICE, Options Clearing Corporation, Singapore Exchange, Eurex, or other derivatives exchanges had disruptions.

Furthermore, during the Great Financial Crisis, no proprietary trading firms were bailed out for their futures positions. While these crises looked scary, in the liquid exchange-traded, centrally-cleared derivatives markets...the fear was much less. Prices moved, but trading still happened. If we are going to have crises, that is a better way to have crises.

26.8.2 The Quant Quake of 2007

In August 2007, an event some have called the **Quant Quake** occurred. As documented by Khandani and Lo (2007,2011), a number of quantitative firms experienced rapid and large losses in their investment portfolios. What is unusual about the losses, however, is they were concentrated along risk factors (similar to trades in Lehmann (1990a)) — but did not manifest themselves in the larger market. The S&P 500 did not move significantly; but, risk factors had very large moves. They attribute the cause to a quant fund deleveraging on 1 August and again on 6 August and lasting for 45 minutes and 3.5 hours.

Yet again, crowded trades and market liquidity seemed to have played an issue. Thankfully, this did not blow up to be a larger event; however, it does show that as trading gets more complicated, the sources of risk also become more complicated. It also suggests that a purely financial crisis without fire sales or counterparty risk might be far less incendiary and maybe less destructive.

26.8.3 Citadel Survives

The hedge fund arm of Citadel LLC incurred large losses in 2008. Their debt rating was cut to BBB in November of that year; and, their Kensington and Wellington funds had lost 55% by year end. In full disclosure, I was quoted in Boak (2008) as saying that I had never seen a fund lose more than 30% and survive. Citadel *did* survive: their investor agreement let them reallocate capital to more liquid and more promising investments; and, they suspended collecting management fees. Clients stayed, the firm stemmed the losses, and by 2012 the funds had recovered past their high-water marks. I hope more funds can show such durability when faced with losses — because post-2008 much more of the risk-bearing capacity of the world's economies is in hedge funds like Citadel.

26.8.4   Flash Crash of 2010

We have already mentioned the 2010 Flash Crash in Chapter 4. We also mentioned how Gao and Mizrach (2016) show that flash crashes are not unusual. It does not help economic growth or allocative efficiency to have price excursions which trigger limit orders and change people's positions. However, since such events are not new, it would seem that most of the damage was reputational — and that education could reduce that impact.

26.9   Recovery and Reform

The crises of the past few decades have been needlessly destructive. While the data are clear that free market economics are the surest path to improving people's lot in society, how we traverse crises is also important. Avoiding absorbing states is crucial since it allows countries, firms, and people to enter recovery with less damage to fix and still having the tools to fix that damage. To that end, some reforms have been used and proposed to recover from the recent crises and mitigate or avoid future crises.

26.9.1   Risk Retention

The Dodd-Frank Act mandates that originators hold a piece of the credit risk of each pool of mortgages sold — either all from the equity tranche or an equal slice of each tranche. That should help maintain some incentive compatibility of originators and lenders. We saw in Chapter 23 how covered bonds can also maintain incentive compatibility. We will have to see if the risk retention mandate is as effective as using covered bonds. However, we know that covered bonds require originators to hold more risk since over-collateralization is equivalent to the full risk retention being in the most subordinated tranche.

26.9.2   A New Mandate?

After 2010, many central banks seem to have taken on another mandate, often unspoken: financial stability. For a number of years after 2008 or so, the only topic of central banks conferences was financial stability and related issues: central clearing, funding liquidity, systemic risk, and so on.

The newness of this material to central bankers was also stunning: I recall one European central banker asking me in late 2011, "You really think we should be looking at credit spreads and maybe funding markets? Interesting.... The bond traders have been saying this as well, but your work gives us some evidence to support that idea." I had been expecting questions about my analysis or the data, not about the fundamental utility of looking at a credit spread.

However, while central bankers may have needed to play catch-up, they have done so and taken these ideas to heart. The unspoken mandate of protecting financial stability seemed a strong guide to monetary policy at times after 2010. For example, while the Fed wanted to raise interest rates in 2015, they held off because of concerns that the Chinese stock market mayhem could spread and destabilize the global financial system.

26.9.3 Non-Standard Monetary Policy

The US Federal Reserve did something unusual in 2011. With short-term rates at zero, they felt that they needed more tools. Thus they began Operation Twist, sales of long-term bonds to drive their yields higher and steepen the yield curve. This was one of the many **non-standard monetary policy** tools used and had not been used since the 1960s. The Fed has also paid variable interest on bank reserves to encourage banks to hold reserves instead of lending. Fed Board Governor Brainard (2014) stated, at a conference in Washington DC, that the Fed would continue to consider non-standard policy tools. In response to a question, she said that included action in repo and credit markets.[23]

26.9.4 Quantitative Easing

The Fed also performed multiple rounds of **quantitative easing** where they bought non-government instruments to reduce their yields. We could even consider this as just more non-standard monetary policy. However, there are two differences. On the one hand, this can be focused on certain areas of lending markets. That allows central banks to be more targeted in how they implement monetary policy. On the other hand, this involves the central bank buying risky assets. It would also seem to be inferior to buying similar-tenor government bonds. Quantitative easing has been heavily criticized and its use by Japan seemed to do nothing to improve their economy over the 1990s-2010s period. However, that seeming ineffectuality may have had as much to do with Japan not undertaking structural reforms and firms carrying defaulted loans at cost rather than writing off losses.

---

[23]In full disclosure, I asked a less open-ended question — and did not expect that answer.

26.9.5   Central Clearing

We have already mentioned central clearing — which the Dodd-Frank Act, European Market Infrastructure Regulation, and similar laws promoted. Others have proposed taxes on leverage or an institution's marginal contribution to systemic risk.

26.9.6   Bail-Ins

Another promising idea is **bail-ins**: automatic creation of equity capital in crises. Adler (1993) first proposed "chameleon equity," now known as **contingent convertible** (CoCo) securities: bonds which convert to equity when a certain event occurs. This can be used to allow a firm to keep their leverage low and receive a cash infusion when it is needed but when raising capital might prove difficult.

The Dodd-Frank Act encouraged banks to use CoCos to enable bail-ins and (hopefully) reduce the need for government bailouts. Consequently, a number of studies examined CoCos — in particular Pazarbasioglu et al. (2011), Calomiris and Herring (2013), and Albul, Jaffee, and Tchistyi (2015). Wilkens and Bethke (2014) compared pricing methods. However, many studies note that the trigger event must be carefully designed to avoid manipulation. McDonald (2013) suggests a two-dimensional trigger based on both the firm and the state of the economy — so that firms which are merely poorly-performing can still fail. Pennacchi, Vermaelen, and Wolff (2014) suggests allowing equity holders to participate in bail-ins to ensure that the bail-in price is not gamed. Finally, Avdjiev et al. (2017) studies recent CoCo issuance and notes that they lower firms' CDS spreads.

26.9.7   How to Recover

Cerra and Saxena (2008) suggests that economies often do not recover from output lost due to crises. (It could be, however, that those economies earn a risk premium between crises.) Which policies helped speed recovery? Reinhart and Rogoff (2014) study over 100 crisis recoveries and note that speeding up recovery reduces the damage. Furthermore, they suggest that imposing capital controls and engaging in debt restructurings — typically used only by emerging economies — might be wise policy tools for developed economies as well.

Darvas (2011) compares the banking crises in Iceland, Ireland, and Latvia. All three economies saw swells in banking and booms in property with large foreign investment. All three also addressed their problems with austerity, structural reforms, restructuring of private debt, and strengthening the banking systems. Iceland moved domestic activity to "good banks" making the problem banks into "bad banks" with international obligations.

He notes a few features which did (and did not) work:

- *Currency devaluation,* used by Iceland, was successful at preserving employment and speeding recovery. *Internal devaluation,* done by Ireland and Latvia through wage cuts, was not successful since the government was only able to devalue public-sector wages.

- *Failure* of banks in Iceland seemed to speed recovery. In Ireland, banks were bailed out; and, most Latvian banks were foreign-owned which made their owners the lenders of last resort (although those banks might have also been bailed out).
- *Increasing fiscal responsibility* was helpful in all three countries.
- *Preserving the finance sector* also helped speed recovery. Ironically, the financial sector was best preserved in Iceland, despite their allowing banks to fail.

Imposing capital controls as Iceland did is not addressed; however, that may have also helped hasten recovery.

The US and other countries have also created orderly liquidation authorities for financial firms; however, we have yet to see how those perform. That said, if they function similar to how Oversight Partners I did with LTCM, these authorities might be very prudent.

26.9.8 Escaping Liquidity Traps

Finally, if these economies had entered a liquidity trap, Svensson (2003) suggests that currency devaluation followed by a moving peg and inflation targeting would be the fastest way to recover. This seems to agree with the findings above.

26.9.9 History

For those interested in crises, I highly recommend reading the usual suspects: Minsky (1986), Kindelberger and Aliber (2005), Chancellor (1999), and MacKay (1841)

26.10 Quiz

Try answering the following questions in ten minutes.

1. You examine the market for stocks of electric car manufacturers wondering if there is a bubble. You estimate the following model of firm i's monthly excess returns considering the market excess returns R_{mt}, some macroeconomic information x_t, and lagged excess returns:

$$R_{it} = \underbrace{\alpha}_{\substack{\hat{\alpha}=0.001 \\ s.e.=0.0005}} + \underbrace{\beta}_{\substack{\hat{\beta}=1.7 \\ s.e.=0.2}} R_{mt} + \underbrace{\gamma}_{\substack{\hat{\gamma}=2.5 \\ s.e.=1.8}} x_t + \underbrace{\phi}_{\substack{\hat{\phi}=1.03 \\ s.e.=0.01}} R_{i,t-1} + \epsilon_{it} \qquad (26.12)$$

What evidence do you have for or against a bubble in electric car manufacturers?

2. Which would we expect to cause more economic damage: a stock market bubble or a real estate bubble? Why?

3. Suppose we see a crisis in the market for bitcoin: prices crash, exchanges close and do not return money owed, and trading firms incur large bitcoin losses. Could that be a systemic risk concern? What effect should worry us?

4. It turns out that many financial firms have decided to make markets on bitcoin. They leave some money at each exchange so that they can trade quickly trade on price discrepancies between venues. What effect and associated risk does this incur?

5. How do funding liquidity and market liquidity relate?

6. What are a few indicators of a crisis?

7. List at least three policies which might have mitigated the financial crisis in 2008?

8. Eurozone economies has economic and monetary union. So what did they lack which allowed for problems?

9. What type of security might allow for providing cash infusions to "bail in" firms instead of bailing them out?

26.11   Exercises

Instructions

Using the sample R code, we will explore bubbles and crises a bit.

1. Using the R code, download some cryptocurrency (bitcoin) data and some SPX data. Use the code to run a rolling window of AR models on prices. Then answer the following:

   a) What do we expect to find for a time series like the SPX?
   b) How do the bitcoin and SPX plots differ?
   c) Does this suggest there has been a bubble in bitcoin? Why or why not?

2. Download a basic USD yield curve (3M, 2Y, 10Y, 30Y), a basic German bond EUR yield curve (6M, 2Y, 10Y, 30Y), the TED spread, and 6M EURIBOR. Create an analog of the TED spread: 6MEURIBOR − 6MBuBills. (We can say we have made a BED: BuBills vs EURIBOR deposits.)

   a) Plot the TED spread, BED spread, and slopes of the yield curves across time.
   b) Do they agree with what you expect knowing about recent crises?
   c) What might explain some spikes in credit spreads not associated with recent financial/debt crises?

d) Can you use these to predit crises or falls in the index?

R Code

```
library(xts)
library(Quandl)
library(quantmod)

fit.bubblear1 <- function(prcs) {
    coef(lm.fit(cbind(Intercept = 1, prcs[,-1]), prcs[,1]))[2]
}

btc.prices <- Quandl("BITFINEX/BTCUSD", type="xts")[,"Mid"]
btc.prices$lagMid <- lag(btc.prices$Mid)
fits.btc.ar <- rollapply(na.omit(btc.prices), 90, fit.bubblear1, align="right", by.column=FALSE)

spx.prices <- Quandl("CHRIS/CME_SP1", type="xts")[,"Settle"]
spx.prices$lagSettle <- lag(spx.prices$Settle)
fits.spx.ar <- rollapply(na.omit(spx.prices), 90, fit.bubblear1, align="right", by.column=FALSE)

ust.tickers <- c("FRED/DGS3MO", "FRED/DGS2", "FRED/DGS10", "FRED/DGS30")
ust <- Quandl(ust.tickers, type="xts")/100
colnames(ust) <- c("UST3M", "UST2Y", "UST10Y", "UST30Y")

eugb.tickers <-c("BUNDESBANK/BBK01_WT3210", # 6M
                 "BUNDESBANK/BBK01_WT3213", # 2Y
                 "BUNDESBANK/BBK01_WT3229", # 10Y
                 "BUNDESBANK/BBK01_WT3500") # 30Y
eugb <- Quandl(eugb.tickers, type="xts")/100
colnames(eugb) <- c("EUGB6M", "EUGB2Y", "EUGB10Y", "EUGB30Y")

eonia.6m <- Quandl("BUNDESBANK/BBK01_ST0304", type="xts")/100

ted <- Quandl("FRED/TEDRATE", type="xts")/100
bed <- eonia.6m - eugb$EUGB6M

index.tickers <- c("^SPX", "^STOXX50E")
adj.close <- 6  # 6th field is adjusted close
spx.prices <- getSymbols("^SPX", source="yahoo", auto.assign=FALSE,
                         return.class="xts")[,adj.close]
estox.prices <- getSymbols("^STOXX50E", source="yahoo", auto.assign=FALSE,
                           return.class="xts")[,adj.close]
spx.rets <- diff(log(spx.prices))
estox.rets <- diff(log(estox.prices))
```

References

Acharya, Viral V. and Ouarda Merrouche. "Precautionary Hoarding of Liquidity and Interbank Markets: Evidence from the Subprime Crisis". *Review of Finance* 17.1 (2013), pp. 107–160. DOI: 10.1093/rof/rfs022.

Adler, Barry E. "Financial and Political Theories of American Corporate Bankruptcy". *Stanford Law Review* 45.2 (1993), pp. 311–346. DOI: 10.2307/1228953.

Albul, Boris, Dwight M. Jaffee, and Alexei Tchistyi. *Contingent Convertible Bonds and Capital Structure Decisions*. Working Paper 2772612. SSRN, 2015. DOI: 10.2139/ssrn.2772612. URL: https://ssrn.com/abstract=2772612.

Artavanis, Nikolaos, Adair Morse, and Margarita Tsoutsoura. "Measuring Income Tax Evasion Using Bank Credit: Evidence from Greece". *Quarterly Journal of Economics* 131.2 (2016), pp. 739–798. DOI: 10.1093/qje/qjw009.

Ashcraft, Adam B. and Til Schuermann. *Understanding the Securitization of Subprime Mortgage Credit*. Staff Report 318. Federal Reserve Bank of New York, 2008. URL: https://www.newyorkfed.org/medialibrary/media/research/staff_reports/sr318.pdf.

Avdjiev, Stefan et al. *CoCo Issuance and Bank Fragility*. Working Paper 678. Bank for International Settlements, 2017. URL: https://www.bis.org/publ/work678.pdf.

Bailey, Warren, Wei Huang, and Zhishu Yang. "Bank Loans with Chinese Characteristics: Some Evidence on Inside Debt in a State-Controlled Banking System". *Journal of Financial and Quantitative Analysis* 46.6 (2011), pp. 1795–1830. DOI: 10.1017/S0022109011000433.

BBC. "Timeline: The Unfolding Eurozone Crisis". *BBC News* (June 13, 2012). URL: http://www.bbc.com/news/business-13856580.

Bernardo, Antonio E. and Ivo Welch. "Liquidity and Financial Market Runs". *Quarterly Journal of Economics* 119.1 (2004), pp. 135–158. DOI: 10.1162/003355304772839542.

Berrospide, Jose. *Bank Liquidity Hoarding and the Financial Crisis: An Empirical Evaluation*. Finance and Economics Discussion Series working paper 2013-03. Board of Governors of the Federal Reserve System, 2013. URL: https://www.federalreserve.gov/Pubs/feds/2013/201303/201303pap.pdf.

Biais, Bruno, Florian Heider, and Marie Hoerova. *Risk-Sharing or Risk-Taking? Counterparty Risk, Incentives and Margins*. Tech. rep. 4. 2016. DOI: 10.1111/jofi.12396.

Bikhchandani, Sushil and Sunil Sharma. "Herd Behavior in Financial Markets". *IMF Staff Papers* 47.3 (2000), pp. 279–310. DOI: 10.2307/3867650.

Birger, Jon. "Hunting for Oil Villains". *Fortune* (July 5, 2008). URL: http://archive.fortune.com/2008/07/01/magazines/fortune/birger_hunt.fortune/index.htm.

Bivens, Josh and Dean Baker. "The Wrong Tool for the Right Job: The Fed Shouldn't Raise Interest Rates to Manage Asset Bubbles" (2016). URL: http://www.epi.org/files/pdf/106055.

Black, William K. *The Best Way to Rob a Bank is to Own One: How Corporate Executives and Politicians Looted the S&L Industry*. 2nd ed. Austin, TX: University of Texas Press, 2014.

Boak, Joshua. "Citadel to Cover Operating Expenses". *Chicago Tribune* (Dec. 12, 2008). URL: http://articles.chicagotribune.com/2008-12-12/news/0812110630_1_citadel-investment-group-hedge-fund.

Bolton, Patrick and Martin Oehmke. "Should Derivatives Be Privileged in Bankruptcy?" *Journal of Finance* 70.6 (2015), pp. 2353–2394. DOI: 10.1111/jofi.12201.

Boudt, Kris, Ellen C. S. Paulus, and Dale W. R. Rosenthal. "Funding Liquidity, Market Liquidity and TED Spread: A Two-Regime Model". *Journal of Empirical Finance* 43 (2017), pp. 143–158. DOI: 10.1016/j.jempfin.2017.06.002.

Brainard, Lael. *The Federal Reserve's Financial Stability Agenda*. Washington, DC, Dec. 4, 2014. URL: https://www.federalreserve.gov/newsevents/speech/brainard20141203a.htm.

Brunnermeier, Markus K. and Lasse Heje Pedersen. "Market Liquidity and Funding Liquidity". *Review of Financial Studies* 22.6 (2009), pp. 2201–2238. DOI: 10.1093/rfs/hhn098.

Brunnermeier, Markus K. and Yuliy Sannikov. "A Macroeconomic Model with a Financial Sector". *American Economic Review* 104.2 (2014), pp. 379–421. DOI: 10.1257/aer.104.2.379.

Cai, Fang. *Was there front running during the LTCM crisis?* International Finance Discussion Papers 758. Board of Governors of the Federal Reserve System, 2003. URL: https://www.federalreserve.gov/PubS/ifdp/2003/758/ifdp758.pdf.

Calomiris, Charles W. and Richard J. Herring. "How to Design a Contingent Convertible Debt Requirement That Helps Solve Our Too-Big-to-Fail Problem". *Journal of Applied Corporate Finance* 25.2 (2013), pp. 39–62. DOI: 10.1111/jacf.12015.

Calomiris, Charles W. and Larry Schweikart. "The Panic of 1857: Origins, Transmission, and Containment". *Journal of Economic History* 51.4 (1991), pp. 807–834. DOI: 10.1017/S0022050700040122.

Campbell, John Y. and Robert J. Shiller. "Stock Prices, Earnings, and Expected Dividends". *Journal of Finance* 43.3 (1988), pp. 661–676. DOI: 10.1111/j.1540-6261.1988.tb04598.x.

— "The Dividend-Price Ratio and Expectations of Future Dividends and Discount Factors". *Review of Financial Studies* 1.3 (1988), pp. 195–228. DOI: 10.1093/rfs/1.3.195.

Case, Anne and Angus Deaton. "Rising Morbidity and Mortality in Midlife among White Non-Hispanic Americans in the 21st Century". *Proceedings of the National Academy of Sciences of the United States of America* 112.49 (2015), pp. 15078–15083. DOI: 10.1073/pnas.1518393112.

Case, Karl E., John M. Quigley, and Robert J. Shiller. "Comparing Wealth Effects: The Stock Market versus the Housing Market". *B.E. Journal of Macroeconomics* 5.1 (2005), pp. 1–34. DOI: 10.2202/1534-6013.1235.

Cerra, Valerie and Sweta Chaman Saxena. "Growth Dynamics: The Myth of Economic Recovery". *American Economic Review* 98.1 (2008), pp. 439–457. DOI: 10.1257/aer.98.1.439.

Chancellor, Edward. *Devil Take the Hindmost: A History of Financial Speculation*. New York: Farrar, Straus and Giroux, 1999.

Chernow, Ron. *The House of Morgan*. New York: Atlantic Monthly Press, 1990.

Chincarini, Ludwig B. *The Crisis of Crowding: Quant Copycats, Ugly Models, and the New Crash Normal*. New York: Wiley/Bloomberg, 2012.

Clunie, James Bruce. "Indirect Short-Selling Constraints". PhD Dissertation. Accounting and Finance Group: University of Edinburgh, 2009. URL: https://core.ac.uk/download/pdf/280110.pdf.

Cont, Rama and Thomas Kokholm. "Central Clearing of OTC Derivatives: Bilateral vs Multilateral Netting". *Statistics & Risk Modeling* 31.1 (2014), pp. 3–22. DOI: 10.1515/strm-2013-1161.

Cox, Alexander M. G. and David G. Hobson. "Local Martingales, Bubbles and Option Prices". *Finance and Stochastics* 9.4 (2005), pp. 477–492. DOI: 10.1007/s00780-005-0162-y.

Darvas, Zsolt. *A Tale of Three Countries: Recovery after a Banking Crisis*. Policy Contribution 2011/19. Bruegel, 2011. URL: http://bruegel.org/wp-content/uploads/imported/publications/111229_zd_A_tale_of_three_countries.pdf.

De Long, J. Bradford and Andrei Shleifer. "The Stock Market Bubble of 1929: Evidence from Closed-End Mutual Funds". *Journal of Economic History* 51.3 (1991), pp. 675–700. DOI: 10.1017/S0022050700039619.

Diamond, Douglas W. and Philip H. Dybvig. "Bank Runs, Deposit Insurance, and Liquidity". *Journal of Political Economy* 91.3 (1983), pp. 401–419. DOI: 10.1086/261155.

Diamond, Douglas W. and Raghuram G. Rajan. "Fear of Fire Sales, Illiquidity Seeking, and Credit Freezes". *Quarterly Journal of Economics* 126.2 (2011), pp. 557–591. DOI: 10.1093/qje/qjr012.

Dickey, David A. and Wayne A. Fuller. "Distribution of the Estimators for Autoregressive Time Series With a Unit Root". *Journal of the American Statistical Association* 74.366 (1979), pp. 427–431. DOI: 10.2307/2286348.

Dow, James and Jungsuk Han. "The Paradox of Financial Fire Sales: The Role of Arbitrage Capital in Determining Liquidity". *Journal of Finance* 73.1 (2018), pp. 229–274. DOI: 10.1111/jofi.12584.

Duchin, Ran and Denis Sosyura. "Safer Ratios, Riskier Portfolios: Banks' Response to Government Aid". *Journal of Financial Economics* 113.1 (2014), pp. 1–28. DOI: 10.1016/j.jfineco.2014.03.005.

Duffie, Darrell and Haoxiang Zhu. "Does a Central Clearing Counterparty Reduce Counterparty Risk?" *Review of Asset Pricing Studies* 1.1 (2011), pp. 74–95. DOI: 10.1093/rapstu/rar001.

Dunbar, Nicholas. *Inventing Money: The Story of Long-Term Capital Management and the Legends Behind It*. New York: Wiley, 1999.

Economist. "The Slumps That Shaped Modern Finance". *The Economist* 8882 (Apr. 12, 2014), pp. 51–56. URL: https://www.economist.com/news/essays/21600451-finance-not-merely-prone-crises-it-shaped-them-five-historical-crises-show-how-aspects-today-s-fina.

— "Uncle Xi's Bear Market". *The Economist* (July 11, 2015). Retrieved on 20 March 2018. URL: https://www.economist.com/news/finance-and-economics/21657345-china-learns-stocks-are-beyond-communist-partys-control-uncle-xis-bear.

Edwards, Franklin R. and Edward R. Morrison. "Derivatives and the Bankruptcy Code: Why the Special Treatment?" *Yale Journal on Regulation* 22.1 (2005), pp. 94–122. DOI: `10.2139/ssrn.589261`.

Faquiryan, Hamed and Marius Rodriguez. *Bank Counterparties and Collateral Usage.* FRBSF Economic Letter 2014-21. Federal Reserve Bank of San Francisco, July 14, 2014. URL: `https://www.frbsf.org/economic-research/publications/economic-letter/2014/july/bank-counterparty-collateral-bhc-risk/el2014-21.pdf`.

FCIC. *The Financial Crisis Inquiry Report.* Washington, DC: US Goverment Printing Office, 2011. URL: `https://www.gpo.gov/fdsys/pkg/GPO-FCIC/pdf/GPO-FCIC.pdf`.

Fisher, Richard W. *Confessions of a Data Dependent.* Dallas, TX, Nov. 2, 2006. URL: `https://www.dallasfed.org/news/speeches/fisher/2006/fs061102.cfm`.

Gai, Prasanna and Sujit Kapadia. "Contagion in Financial Networks". *Proceedings of the Royal Society A* 466.2120 (2010), pp. 2401–2423. DOI: `10.1098/rspa.2009.0410`.

Gao, Cheng and Bruce Mizrach. "Market Quality Breakdowns in Equities". *Journal of Financial Markets* 28.C (2016), pp. 1–23. DOI: `10.1016/j.finmar.2016.03.002`.

Gao, Gary. "China Futures Volume Surges as Brokers Climb on Looser Curbs". *Bloomberg News* (Feb. 19, 2017). URL: `https://www.bloombergquint.com/markets/2017/02/17/chinese-futures-volume-doubles-as-brokers-jump-on-relaxed-curbs`.

Gordon, Marcy. "Ex-WaMu CEO Defends Bank's Actions before Failure". *The San Diego Union-Tribune* (Apr. 13, 2010). URL: `http://www.sandiegouniontribune.com/sdut-ex-wamu-ceo-defends-banks-actions-before-failure-2010apr13-story.html`.

Gorton, Gary and Andrew Metrick. "Securitized Banking and the Run on Repo". *Journal of Financial Economics* 104.3 (2012), pp. 425–451. DOI: `10.1016/j.jfineco.2011.03.016`.

Greenspan, Alan. *The Challenge of Central Banking in a Democratic Society.* Speech at the Annual Dinner and Francis Boyer Lecture of The American Enterprise Institute for Public Policy Research. Washington, DC, Dec. 5, 1996. URL: `https://www.federalreserve.gov/boarddocs/speeches/1996/19961205.htm`.

— *Risk Transfer and Financial Stability.* Washington, DC, May 5, 2005. URL: `https://www.federalreserve.gov/boarddocs/speeches/2005/20050505/default.htm`.

Guillén, Mauro F. *The Global Economic & Financial Crisis: A Timeline.* 2015. URL: `https://lauder.wharton.upenn.edu/wp-content/uploads/2015/06/Chronology_Economic_Financial_Crisis.pdf`.

Hansell, Saul. "Fund Manager Caught Short By Crude and Brutal Market". *New York Times* (Apr. 5, 1994), A1,D8.

He, Zhigu and Arvind Krishnamurthy. "A Model of Capital and Crises". *Review of Economic Studies* 79.2 (2012), pp. 735–777. DOI: `10.1093/restud/rdr036`.

He, Zhiguo and Arvind Krishnamurthy. "Intermediary Asset Pricing". *American Economic Review* 103.2 (2013), pp. 732–770. DOI: 10.1257/aer.103.2.732.

He, Zhiguo and Wei Xiong. "Dynamic Debt Runs". *Review of Financial Studies* 25.6 (2012), pp. 1799–1843. DOI: 10.1093/rfs/hhs004.

Hicks, J. R. "Mr. Keynes and the "Classics"; A Suggested Interpretation". *Econometrica* 5.2 (1937), pp. 147–159. DOI: 10.2307/1907242.

Hwang, Soosung and Mark Salmon. "Market Stress and Herding". *Journal of Empirical Finance* 11.4 (2004), pp. 585–616. DOI: 10.1016/j.jempfin.2004.04.003.

Jacklin, Charles J. and Sudipto Bhattacharya. "Distinguishing Panics and Information-based Bank Runs: Welfare and Policy Implications". *Journal of Political Economy* 96.3 (1988), pp. 568–592. DOI: 10.1086/261552.

Jang, Brent. "Vancouver Housing Sales Slump As Market Braces for Tax Impact". *The Globe and Mail* (Mar. 2, 2018). URL: https://www.theglobeandmail.com/real-estate/vancouver/vancouver-housing-sales-slump-as-market-braces-for-tax-impact/article38195805/.

Jarrow, Robert. "Bubbles and Multiple-Factor Asset Pricing Models". *International Journal of Theoretical and Applied Finance* 19.1 (2016), pp. 1650007–1–19. DOI: 10.1142/S0219024916500072.

— "Testing for Asset Price Bubbles: Three New Approaches". *Quantitative Finance Letters* 4.1 (2016), pp. 4–9. DOI: 10.1080/21649502.2015.1165838.

Jarrow, Robert, Younes Kchia, and Philip Protter. "How to Detect an Asset Bubble". *SIAM Journal on Financial Mathematics* 2.1 (2011), pp. 839–865. DOI: 10.1137/10079673X.

Jarrow, Robert A., Philip Protter, and Kazuhiro Shimbo. "Asset Price Bubbles in Incomplete Markets". *Mathematical Finance* 20.2 (2010), pp. 145–185. DOI: 10.1111/j.1467-9965.2010.00394.x.

Jereski, Laura. "Hedge Fund to Shrink Capital Of $6 Billion by Nearly Half". *Wall Street Journal* (Sept. 22, 1997), p. C1.

Jones, Thomas O. and W. Earl Sasser Jr. "Why Satisified Customers Defect". *Harvard Business Review* 73.6 (1995). URL: https://hbr.org/1995/11/why-satisfied-customers-defect.

Khandani, Amir E. and Andrew W. Lo. "What Happened To the Quants in August 2007?" *Journal of Investment Management* 5.4 (2007), pp. 29–78. URL: https://www.joim.com/happened-quants-august-2007/.

— "What Happened to the Quants in August 2007? Evidence from Factors and Transactions Data". *Journal of Financial Markets* 14.1 (2011), pp. 1–46. DOI: 10.1016/j.finmar.2010.07.005.

Kindelberger, Charles P. and Robert Aliber. *Manias, Panics, and Crashes: A History of Financial Crises.* 5th ed. New York: Wiley, 2005.

Kodaira, Ryushiro. "China Can Learn from Japan's Price-Keeping Operations in the 1990s". *Nikkei Asian Review* (July 14, 2015). URL: https://asia.nikkei.com/Features-archive/Market-Turmoil/China-can-learn-from-Japan-s-price-keeping-operations-in-the-1990s.

Krishnamurthy, Arvind. "Amplification Mechanisms in Liquidity Crises". *American Economic Journal: Macroeconomics* 2.3 (2010), pp. 1–30. DOI: 10.1257/mac.2.3.1.

Krishnamurthy, Arvind, Stefan Nagel, and Dmitry Orlov. "Sizing Up Repo". *Journal of Finance* 69.6 (2014), pp. 2381–2417. DOI: 10.1111/jofi.12168.

Krugman, Paul R., Kathryn M. Dominquez, and Kenneth Rogoff. "It's Baaack: Japan's Slump and the Return of the Liquidity Trap". *Brookings Papers on Economic Activity* 1998.2 (1998), pp. 137–205. DOI: 10.2307/2534694.

Lehmann, Bruce N. "Fads, Martingales, and Market Efficiency". *Quarterly Journal of Economics* 105.1 (1990), pp. 1–28. DOI: 10.2307/2937816.

Lewis, Michael. *Liar's Poker: Rising through the Wreckage on Wall Street*. New York: W. W. Norton & Company, 1989.

Li, David X. "On Default Correlation: A Copula Function Approach". *Journal of Fixed Income* 9.4 (2000), pp. 43–54. DOI: 10.3905/jfi.2000.319253.

Li, Guoping and Hong Zhou. "The Systematic Politicization of China's Stock Markets". *Journal of Contemporary China* 25.99 (2016), pp. 422–437. DOI: 10.1080/10670564.2015.1104909.

Lo, Andrew W. "Reading about the Financial Crisis: A Twenty-One-Book Review". *Journal of Economic Literature* 50.1 (2012), pp. 151–178. DOI: 10.1257/jel.50.1.151.

Longin, François and Bruno Solnik. "Is the Correlation in International Equity Returns Constant: 1960–1990?" *Journal of International Money and Finance* 14.1 (1995), pp. 3–26. DOI: 10.1016/0261-5606(94)00001-H.

— "Extreme Correlation of International Equity Markets". *Journal of Finance* 56.2 (2001), pp. 649–676. DOI: 10.1111/0022-1082.00340.

Lowenstein, Roger. *When Genius Failed: The Rise and Fall of Long-Term Capital Management*. New York: Random House, 2000.

LTCM. *Executive Summary of Long-Term Capital Management, L.P.* recruitment material. Greenwich, CT, Oct. 1997.

Lu, Jianxin and Pete Sweeney. "Timeline of China's Attempts to Prevent Stock Market Meltdown". *Reuters* (July 8, 2015). URL: https://www.reuters.com/article/us-china-stocks-factbox/timeline-of-chinas-attempts-to-prevent-stock-market-meltdown-idUSKCN0PI0RC20150708.

Lucas, Douglas J. "The Effectiveness of Downgrade Provision in Reducing Counterparty Credit Risk". *Journal of Fixed Income* 5.1 (1995), pp. 32–41. DOI: 10.3905/jfi.1995.408134.

MacKay, Charles. *Extraordinary Popular Delusions and the Madness of Crowds*. London: Richard Bentley, 1841.

Malherbe, Frederic. "Self-Fulfilling Liquidity Dry-Ups". *Journal of Finance* 69.2 (2014), pp. 947–970. DOI: 10.1111/jofi.12063.

McDonald, Robert L. "Contingent Capital with a Dual Price Trigger". *Journal of Financial Stability* 9.2 (2013), pp. 230–241. DOI: 10.1016/j.jfs.2011.11.001.

Melamed, Leo. *For Crying Out Loud: From Open Outcry to the Electronic Screen*. New York: Wiley, 2009.

Minsky, Hyman. *Stabilizing an Unstable Economy*. New York: McGraw-Hill, 1986.

Muehring, Kevin. "John Meriwether by the Numbers". *Institutional Investor* 30.11 (Nov. 1, 1996), pp. 68–81.

OSHA. *Re: Bank of America Corporation, et al. / Foster / 9-3290-01-013*. San Francisco, CA, Sept. 13, 2011.

Pazarbasioglu, Ceyla et al. *Contingent Capital: Economic Rationale and Design Features*. Staff Discussion Note 11/01. International Monetary Fund, 2011. DOI: 10.5089/9781462304141.006.

Pearson, Natalie Obiko. "Vancouver's Hot Housing Market Just Got Tougher for Wealthy Chinese". *Bloomberg News* (Feb. 21, 2018). URL: https://www.bloomberg.com/news/articles/2018-02-20/british-columbia-extends-housing-crackdown-with-tax-increases.

Pennacchi, George, Theo Vermaelen, and Christian C. P. Wolff. "Contingent Capital: The Case of COERCs". *Journal of Financial and Quantitative Analysis* 49.3 (2014), pp. 541–574. DOI: 10.1017/S0022109014000398.

Phillips, Peter C. B., Yangru Wu, and Jun Yu. "Explosive Behavior in the 1990s NASDAQ: When Did Exuberance Escalate Asset Values?" *International Economic Review* 52.1 (2011), pp. 201–226. DOI: 10.2139/ssrn.1091830.

Pinkowitz, Lee and Rohan Williamson. "Bank Power and Cash Holdings: Evidence from Japan". *Review of Financial Studies* 14.4 (2001), pp. 1059–1082. DOI: 10.1093/rfs/14.4.1059.

Pulvino, Todd C. "Do Asset Fire Sales Exist? An Empirical Investigation of Commercial Aircraft Transactions". *Journal of Finance* 53.3 (1998), pp. 939–978. DOI: 10.1111/0022-1082.00040.

Raghavan, Anita. "Salomon Shuts Down A Bond Unit: Arbitrage Group's End Aimed at Cutting Risk". *Wall Street Journal* (July 7, 1998), pp. C1,C15.

Rajan, Raghuram G. *Fault Lines: How Hidden Fractures Still Threaten the World Economy*. Princeton, NJ: Princeton University Press, 2010.

Rapoza, Kenneth. "A Timeline Of What China's Gov't Did To Save Stock Market". *Forbes* (July 13, 2015). URL: https://www.forbes.com/sites/kenrapoza/2015/07/13/a-timeline-of-what-chinas-govt-did-to-save-stock-market/.

Reinhart, Carmen M. and Kenneth S. Rogoff. "Recovery from Financial Crises: Evidence from 100 Episodes". *American Economic Review: Papers and Proceedings* 104.5 (2014), pp. 50–55. DOI: 10.1257/aer.104.5.50.

Riddiough, Timothy J. and Howard E. Thompson. *Deja vu All Over Again: Agency, Uncertainty, Leverage and the Panic of 1857*. Working Paper 10/2012. Hong Kong Institute for Monetary Research, 2012. URL: http://www.hkimr.org/uploads/publication/15/ub_full_0_2_317_wp-no-10_2012-final-.pdf.

Roe, Mark J. "The Derivatives Market's Payment Priorities As Financial Crisis Accelerator". *Stanford Law Review* 63.3 (2011), pp. 539–590. DOI: 10.2139/ssrn.

1567075. URL: http://www.stanfordlawreview.org/wp-content/uploads/sites/3/2011/03/Roe-63-Stan-L-Rev-539.pdf.

Rose, Frank. "Mitch Kapor and the Lotus Factor". *Esquire* (Dec. 1984), pp. 355–362. URL: http://www.frankrose.com/Mitch_Kapor_and_the_Lotus_Factor.pdf.

Rosenfeld, Eric. *Long-Term Capital Management: 10 Years Later / What Happened and Lessons Learned*. Video presentation to MIT 15.437 class. Feb. 19, 2009. URL: http://techtv.mit.edu/videos/2450-eric-rosenfeld-15437-presentation-21909.

Rosenthal, Dale W.R. *Market Structure, Counterparty Risk, and Systemic Risk*. Working Paper 1571552. SSRN, 2014. DOI: 10.2139/ssrn.1571552. URL: http://ssrn.com/abstract=1571552.

Saft, James. "Who's afraid of Janet Yellen?" *Reuters* (July 16, 2014). URL: https://www.reuters.com/article/us-saft-on-wealth-column/whos-afraid-of-janet-yellen-idUSKBN0FL2N720140716.

Scannell, Kara and Aaron Lucchetti. "SEC Says Debt-Rating Firms Sacrificed Quality for Profit". *Wall Street Journal* (July 9, 2008), p. C1.

Scheibe, Kevin P. and Jennifer Blackhurst. "Supply Chain Disruption Propagation: A Systemic Risk and Normal Accident Theory Perspective". *International Journal of Production Research* 56.1–2 (2018), pp. 43–59. DOI: 10.1080/00207543.2017.1355123.

SCMP. "Timeline of Decline: Key Dates in China's Stock Market Slide". *South China Morning Post* (Aug. 27, 2015). URL: http://www.scmp.com/news/china/economy/article/1852783/timeline-decline-key-dates-chinas-stock-market-slide.

Shen, Samuel. "UPDATE 1-China Market Regulator Seeks to Cap Margin Trading, Short Selling". *Reuters* (June 12, 2015). URL: https://www.reuters.com/article/china-margin-financing/update-1-china-market-regulator-seeks-to-cap-margin-trading-short-selling-idUSL3N0YY3H620150612.

Shin, Hyun Song. "Reflections on Northern Rock: The Bank Run That Heralded the Global Financial Crisis". *Journal of Economic Perspectives* 23.1 (2009), pp. 101–119. DOI: 10.1257/jep.23.1.101.

Shleifer, Andrei and Robert W. Vishny. "Liquidation Values and Debt Capacity: A Market Equilibrium Approach". *Journal of Finance* 47.4 (1992), pp. 1343–1366. DOI: 10.1111/j.1540-6261.1992.tb04661.x.

— "Unstable Banking". *Journal of Financial Economics* 97.3 (2010), pp. 306–318. DOI: 10.1016/j.jfineco.2009.10.007.

Silver, Judith. "Movie Day at the Supreme Court or "I Know It When I See It": A History of the Definition of Obscenity". *CoolLawyer.com* (2001). URL: https://www.coollawyer.com/uploads/7/1/6/8/71686999/obscenity_article.pdf.

Sousa, Ricardo M. *Wealth Effects on Consumption: Evidence from the Euro Area*. Working Paper 1050. European Central Bank, 2009. URL: https://www.ecb.europa.eu/pub/pdf/scpwps/ecbwp1050.pdf.

Spiro, Leah Nathans. "Dream Team". *Business Week* 3387 (Aug. 29, 1994), 50–?

Story, Louise, Jr. Thomas Landon, and Nelson D. Schwartz. "Wall St. Helped to Mask Debt Fueling Europe's Crisis". *New York Times* (Feb. 13, 2010). URL: http://www.nytimes.com/2010/02/14/business/global/14debt.html.

Svensson, Lars E.O. "Escaping from a Liquidity Trap and Deflation: The Foolproof Way and Others". *Journal of Economic Perspectives* 17.4 (2003), pp. 145–166. DOI: 10.1257/089533003772034934.

Wiggins, Rosalind Z. and Andrew Metrick. *The Lehman Brothers Bankruptcy G: The Special Case of Derivatives*. Case Study 2014-3G-V1. Yale Program on Financial Stability, 2014. DOI: 10.2139/ssrn.2593080. URL: https://ssrn.com/abstract=2593080.

Wildau, Gabriel. "China's 'National Team' Owns 6% of Stock Market". *Financial Times* (Nov. 25, 2015). URL: https://www.ft.com/content/7515f06c-939d-11e5-9e3e-eb48769cecab.

Wilkens, Sascha and Nastja Bethke. "Contingent Convertible (CoCo) Bonds: A First Empirical Assessment of Selected Pricing Models". *Financial Analyst's Journal* 70.2 (2014), pp. 59–77. DOI: 10.2469/faj.v70.n2.3.

Zawadowski, Adam. "Entangled Financial Systems". *Review of Financial Studies* 26.5 (2013), pp. 1291–1323. DOI: 10.1093/rfs/hht008.

Chapter 27

Coda

I hope that you have enjoyed learning about investments in 26 chapters — one for each letter of the English alphabet or (more practically) one for each week in a half-year of study.[1]

I think that one of the hardest tasks is to look forward. By that I do not just mean forecasting in the most literal sense but also in a larger philosophical sense.

The Key Takeaway

My high school track coach (who also taught me precalculus and calculus) liked to tell the story of the old prospector. I think it is a useful metaphor:

> An old prospector was asleep one day when he was awoken by a voice: "Get up! Put all the rocks around you into your saddle bags!"
>
> The prospector woke up and started putting rocks in his bags. As he did that, he started to question why he was grabbing all these rocks and he got weary. The prospector decided this was foolish and went back to sleep.
>
> The next day the old prospector went into town to get supplies for mining. Coming out of the store, he realized his bags were full of rocks. He was embarrassed because the people in town would now surely think he was a crazy old man. However, he needed to bring back his supplies so he opened the bags.
>
> Lo and behold: gold! The prospector's bags were full of gold!

At this point, my coach would stop and ask us to consider the feelings of the old prospector. "Bittersweet" was always his conclusion. The old prospector was

---

[1]If we include this chapter, I suppose we can appeal to the English alphabet once including the ampersand, &. Really.

undoubtedly pleased to have gold; however, with more hard work and less laziness he could have easily had more treasure.

Learning about investments is like being the old prospector. Early on, it seems like we are pulling together disparate and unusual pieces. It can be a lot of work and it is easy to get discouraged. However, the knowledge has value. The work is worth the reward.

Why do I mention this at the end of the book? Because if you remember anything from this book, I hope it is the economic forces behind why finance exists, why we invest, and how we invest. The world *will* change: the underlying theme of the *I'Ching* (易经) is that everything is subject to constant change. That is why I mention concerns about stationarity and ergodicity; the world *will* change in ways that shake up what we know and how we do business.

If you focus on the fundamentals, you may anticipate when those big changes will come and how they are likely to play out. Furthermore, remembering the economics forces us to acknowledge that finance is not an idiosyncratic aspect of our world; finance is a fundamental building block of civilization — the point that Will Goetzmann makes in *Money Changes Everything*. Societies that have tried to eliminate finance only showed its durability and power: finance just moved underground and became less fair.

The Big Concerns

The big concerns that I would hope you care about after reading this is that we need to do a better job dealing with crises and creative destruction.

We are not getting rid of crises. When I interned at Goldman, one of the managing directors was famous for a quote:[2]

> We model, analyze, shift, and manage risk — and that is all important. However, we cannot forget that the fundamental nature of business is to take risk. We need to be smart, but we can never lose sight of that purpose or think that we will eliminate risk.

Indeed, many theoretical finance models show that profit maximization with competition puts firms on the edge of failure and makes crises a recurring feature.

The split of cognitive versus manual and routine versus non-routine jobs (shown in the preceding chapter) is an insight from Autor, Levy, and Murnane (2003). Figure 27.1 shows that plot over a longer time period of 1983–2018. The plot is both breathtaking and sobering. Around the time of the internet bubble, the employment trajectories for different job types changed. The financial crisis only exacerbated this split. If you still wonder where the wave of populism and anger at "global elites" comes from, this plot explains a lot. It shows that different groups in our society have had very different fortunes and susceptibilities to misfortune.

---

[2]This is not a direct quote. I have searched for years trying to find the name of the female partner who said this in hopes of getting the exact quote.

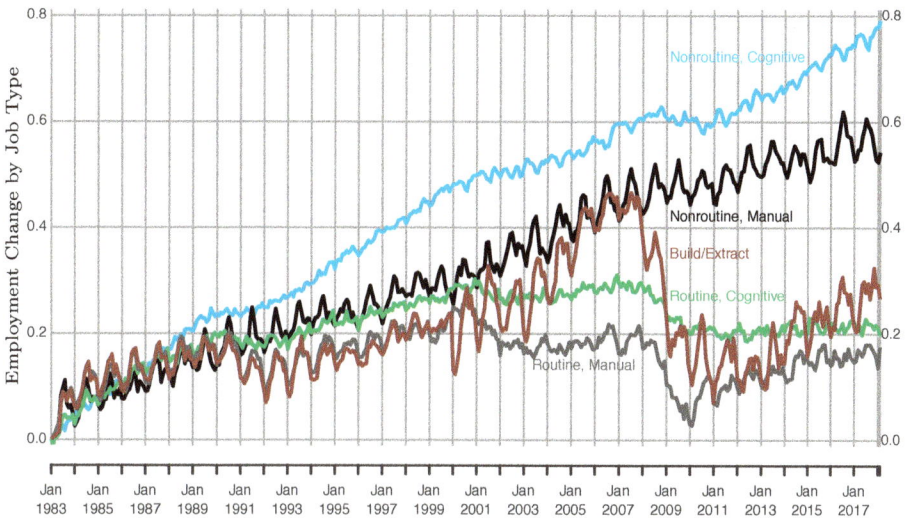

Figure 27.1: Employment by job types for the US over 1983–2018.

It is tempting to think of this phenomenon as unique to the US; however, that view is not accurate. We can easily produce a cruder version of this plot using United Nations International Labour Organisation data.[3] The plot for World Bank high-income economies is shown in Figure 27.2. Here we see a similar trend — except that cognitive routine jobs seem to have suffered less in other high-income countries. Lewandowski (2017) notes that routine cognitive employment also declined in Western Europe. He shows that some of the non-decline we see is explained by those jobs shifting from richer to poorer high-income countries, especially Central and Eastern European countries in the EU. Either way, the trend and the effect of the crises in 2008 and 2010 are present in this plot as well.

That the crises in the US and Europe predominantly affected the large number of "baby boomers" who were about to retire is tragic. Whether that wave of impending retirements made the financial system more fragile or made people more desperate to invest in risky high-yield investments is unclear; however, it is a possibility we should not shy away from considering.

Given all this, it is not so surprising that the despised "global elites" often seem to be those with cognitive non-routine jobs. However, we should be wary. This sort of social unrest often brings other ugliness with it: old religious, ethnic, and racial

---

[3]The non-US data are annual from the ILO and use ISCO job codes to (roughly) map to job types. Here, code groups 1 (managers) and 2 (professionals) are assigned to cognitive non-routine; groups 3 (technicians, paraprofessionals) and 4 (clerks) are assigned to routine cognitive; group 5 (service and sales) is assigned to manual non-routine; and, groups 7 (crafts and trades) and 8 (machine operators and assemblers) are assigned to manual routine.

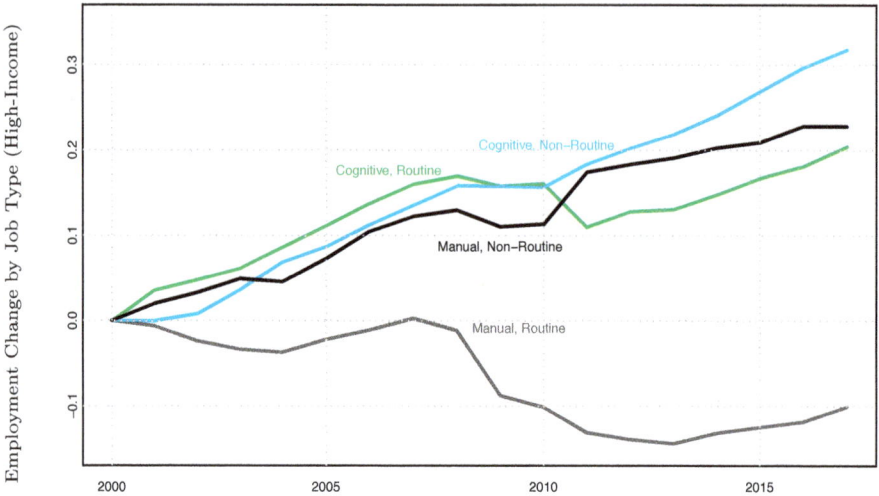

Figure 27.2: Employment by job types for the World Bank high-income economies. Annual ILO data was used with ISCO job codes.

hatreds that make it easy to blame others for society's troubles. It is nice to live in a society where we can use equations and data to make more money with less risk for our clients. However, these high-minded pleasures are pointless if people need to fear somebody bashing their brains in due to resentment. Sadly, we have seen a rise in such tragedies.

We cannot run away from this problem either. Figure 27.3 shows a similar pattern for upper-middle-income economies and shows that only in lower-middle-income economies are routine jobs growing. This may be evidence of outsourcing or merely a sign of economic growth in those countries unrelated to trade. However, even lower-middle-income economies were affected by the 2008 financial crisis: manual routine jobs declined precipitously and have made almost no recovery. It seems likely that many of those jobs were automated and no longer exist.

When I toured a friend-of-a-friend's factory in Dongguan (just north of Shenzhen) in 2016, he said that labor costs had risen enough that the firm was unprofitable. His plan was to plow more money into the firm and invest in robots from a Shenzhen firm. Once he does that, his firm's assembly and machining jobs will largely go away and he will make more more products for less money with fewer workers. Those workers will work with robots, design, or business planning: non-routine jobs. That story is the same across much of the world.

In the Industrial Revolution, Luddites in the UK smashed machines that threatened to eliminate their jobs. In response, the government used the military to

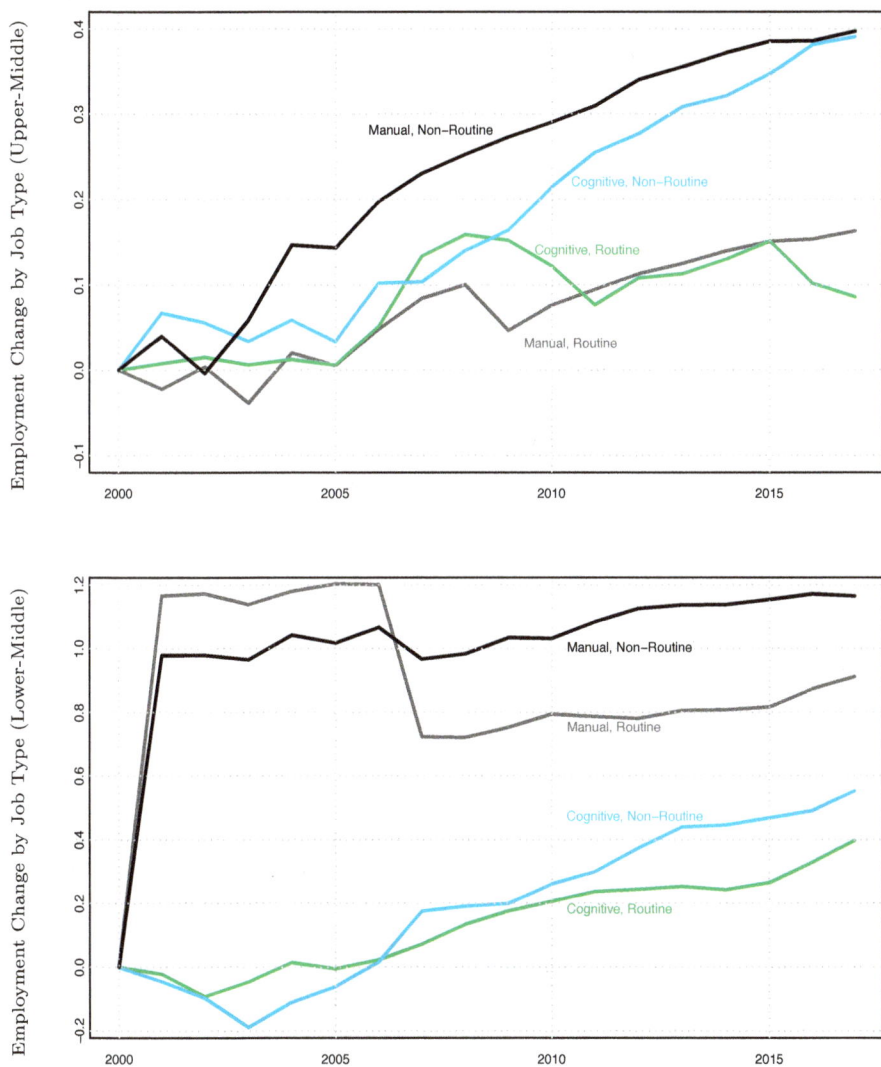

Figure 27.3: Employment by job types for World Bank upper-middle-income economies (top) and lower-middle-income economies (bottom). Annual ILO data was used with ISCO job codes.

violently suppress the Luddite movement. That response is unacceptable in a civilized society; however, electing politicians who ignore facts and economics and play on hatred is also a poor solution. We need to find out how to best handle creative destruction. Do we use some of the savings to re-train workers? Do we provide a benefit to workers whose jobs were rendered outmoded by technology?

The Big Hope

These larger questions bring us back to the beginning: what is an investment and why do we invest? Despite all of the pains — crises and creative destruction leading to social unrest — we *are* better off with capitalism and trade. Centuries of data are resoundingly clear about that.

However, we must answer these larger questions. Avoiding answering is not an option and it denies us the nuanced understanding that leads to wisdom. Nobody captures this idea better than T.S. Eliot:

> We shall not cease from exploration
> And the end of all our exploring
> Will be to arrive where we started
> And know the place for the first time.
> — T.S. Eliot, "Little Gidding"

The benefit is that if we answer these questions well, finance will be there to help us make the most of those solutions. I hope you will be able to invest to help make that better world happen.

References

Autor, David H., Frank Levy, and Richard J. Murnane. "The Skill Content of Recent Technological Change: An Empirical Exploration". *Quarterly Journal of Economics* 118.4 (2003), pp. 1279–1333. DOI: 10.1162/003355303322552801.

Goetzmann, William N. *Money Changes Everything: How Finance Made Civilization Possible*. Princeton University Press, 2016.

Lewandowski, Piotr. *The Changing Nature of Jobs in Central and Eastern Europe*. World of Labor paper 351. IZA, 2017. DOI: 10.15185/izawol.351.

※⛶⛶※⛶⛶

Appendix A

How to Get *R*

To make life easy, we will use *R* with a number of packages for our analyses. You may download *R* from www.r-project.org. Some people prefer to use the IDE environment provided by RStudio, available from www.rstudio.com. To get working with *R*, you may take the intro *R* course at DataCamp (www.datacamp.com). Alternately, you can just follow the text and slowly get the Gestalt of the language.

To install a package: go to the Package Manager in *R*; get the list of packages from CRAN; and, find the package by name. Highlight the package name, check the box for "Install dependencies," and click install. Alternately, you can use the install.packages function. Some packages are available from r-forge.r-project.org instead of cran.r-project.org. You will want to get these packages:

areaplot to make waterfall plots.
corrplot to make correlation heatmap plots.
EQL to use Edgeworth expansions.
evir to do extreme-value theory estimation.
flexsurv to do more flexible survival analysis in credit modeling.
highfrequency for estimating volatility models using intraday data.
lmtest for hypothesis tests of linear models (such as the Durbin-Watson test).
MASS for many useful statistical methods (such as the gamma shape estimation).
PE to simulate private equity funds.
PerformanceAnalytics to estimate higher moments and other risk measures.
PortfolioAnalytics to handle different portfolio optimization methods.
quadprog to solve quadratic programming problems.
Quandl to download data from Quandl.
quantmod to download prices from free online sources.
RND to extract risk-neutral densities from options.
rneos to use the NEOS (network-enabled optimization system) solvers.
rugarch to fit a univariate GARCH model.
sandwich to create sandwich estimators of standard errors.

sde to simulate from various stochastic differential equations.

survival to do survival analysis in credit modeling.

systemfit to fit simultaneous equations and two-stage least squares models.

termstrc to fit yield curves.

xts to take care of time series date/time alignment.

Appendix B

Further Reading (and Viewing)

Students often ask which books are most helpful as references and which are best to help understand the culture of finance.

For learning about your finance cultural heritage: you could read Adam Smith, John Locke, David Hume, David Ricardo, or Frédéric Bastiat — all fine philosophers whose work I would recommend. However, I typically recommend a list of shorter books to whet the appetite.

Below, I list some excellent reference books and then some finance books which are more entertaining, *i.e.* they do not focus on equations or methodology. Finally, I recommend some videos (ordered by title). These are more light-hearted ways to get to know the world of finance.

B.1   Reference Books

Data Analysis

Statistics and Data Analysis for Financial Engineering: with R examples, 2nd Ed., David Ruppert and David S. Mattesson.
This text was why we asked David Ruppert to be a keynote speaker at the first R/Finance conference in 2009. The second edition in 2015 added David Mattesson and more data analysis examples. Of all the books below, this is the closest in spirit to this text and is an excellent companion text.
Applied Linear Regression, 4th Ed., Sanford Weisberg.
There are lots of statistics and econometrics texts on linear modeling. Weisberg's book is intuitive, clear, and does not neglect model diagnostics. I used it to learn linear modeling and I still find it a useful reference.
Time Series Analysis: Forecasting and Control, 5th Ed., George E.P. Box, Gwilym M. Jenkins, Gregory C. Reinsel, and Greta Ljung.
This is my favorite time series book: it is lucid and covers some topics

other books omit (like transfer function models). The latest edition has
added material on multivariate time series.

Causality: Models, Reasoning, and Inference, 2nd Ed., Judea Pearl.

Probably the clearest writing on causal inference. While you could get
some of this material in an econometrics text, that would involve buying
a book that largely overlaps with a solid (and probably better) book on
linear modeling like Weisberg.

Data Analysis Using Regression and Multilevel/Hierarchical Models, Andrew
Gelman and Jennifer Hill.

An excellent book on regression and hierarchical models using R. Also
has nice insights on causal inference and handling endogeneity (*e.g.* via
instrumental variables). For a sneak peek, read his blog post on causal
inference and regression here: `http://andrewgelman.com/2007/12/08/`
`causal_inferenc_2/`.

Economic Dynamics

Economic Dynamics: Theory and Computation, John Stachurski.

If you wanted to get into game theory and modeling economic dynamics,
this is the best hands-on book I know. It uses python for modeling economic
systems. Much more readable (and fun!) than the typical dynamics texts.

Optimization

Numerical Optimization, Jorge Nocedal and Stephen J. Wright.

This is the book I used to learn optimization and I still find it useful
as a reference. I especially like the breakdown by chapter of various
methodologies.

Convex Optimization, Stephen Boyd and Lieven Vandenberghe.

This is the other optimization book I use as a reference. It is a bit more
focused on theory than Nocedal and Wright.

Introduction to Stochastic Programming, 2nd Ed., John Birge and François
Louveaux.

One of the great failings of MPT is optimizing using moments instead of
doing a stochastic optimization. If you want to do better than MPT and
actually optimize a portfolio in light of the randomness of future returns,
this is probably the first book you should consult.

Financial Risk Modelling and Portfolio Optimization with R, 2nd Ed., Bernhard
Pfaff.

The other book on stochastic optimization I would recommend is more
about robust optimization — techniques used when we do not know the
distribution of returns. If you want to do better than MPT and actually
optimize a portfolio in light of the randomness of future returns, this is
probably the second book you should consult.

Computing

A Gentle Introduction to Effective Computing in Quantitative Research: What
Every Research Assistant Should Know, Harry J. Paarsch and Konstantin
Golyaev.
 If computation, programming, and working with an operating system like
 UNIX is scary to you, this is the ideal text for getting comfortable with
 those tasks.

Security Analysis

Security Analysis, Benjamin Graham and David Dodd.
 Often referred to as "the bible" of value investing. If that interests you,
 you can also follow up with Graham's *The Intelligent Investor* (with recent
 updates after Graham's death by Jason Zweig as a co-author).
A Random Walk Down Wall Street, Burton G. Malkiel.
 Probably the best popular defense and explication of the efficient market
 hypothesis. Also, an excellent justification fo why most people should at
 least start by holding index funds.

B.2   Entertaining Books

Economics

Why Nations Fail, Daron Acemoğlu and James Robinson.
 Very clear and thoroughly-researched explanation of what drives economic
 and financial development. A true modern classic of political economy.
 Probably the best book I have read in years.
Economics in One Lesson, Henry Hazlitt.
 A beautifully clear explanation of the Austrian/Chicago School view that
 unfettered markets work best and that government intervention has a cost
 which we always need to consider. (If you like this, then follow up with
 Friedrich Hayek's *The Road to Serfdom* or Frédéric Bastiat's *Economic
 Sophisms*.)

Financial History

Money Changes Everything, William Goetzmann.
 Wonderful history of money and finance that explains *why* we need finance
 and how it has arisen and eveloped in different parts of the world. Amazing
 to see the parallels drawn between centuries-old contracts and recent
 instruments and structured products.

Finance Culture

Liar's Poker, Michael Lewis.
> A humorous view of life at Salomon Brothers, the dominant bond market firm of the 1980s. Also has information about the mortgage market, CMOs, John Meriwether, and the arb desk.

When Genius Failed, Roger Lowenstein.
> Perfectly captures the culture of Long-Term Capital Management and the emotional roller-coaster of its implosion. Also entertaining because of the personalities involved.

Reminiscences of a Stock Operator, Edwin Lefèvre.
> Possibly the best book yet written about trading — how its done, why many people do it, and the midset of a successful trader. (If you like this, follow up with Josef de la Vega's *Confusion de Confusiones*.)

The Smartest Guys in the Room, Bethany McLean and Peter Elkind.
> A bit churlish and pulpy in places; and, the authors occasionally denigrate legitimate practices with sound economic rationales. Nonetheless, this book evokes the rugged individualist culture of Enron and explores markets (natural gas, electricity) which Enron largely created by themselves.

Where Are the Customers' Yachts?, Fred Schwed.
> Humorously skewers all the major players in the finance industry; dryly notes the conflicts of interest between investors and brokers; and, makes fun of forecasters whose predictions are useless.

Barbarians at the Gate: The Fall of RJR Nabisco, Bryan Burrough and John Helyar.
> Probably the best book yet about a corporate takeover. While not as much about investments, it is very entertaining.

Financial Crises

Manias, Panics, and Crashes, Charles Kindleberger (and Robert Aliber).
> An examination of the history of financial bubbles and their implosions. If you had to read no other books on crises, it would be a tough decision between this book and Minsky's.

Stabilizing an Unstable Economy, Hyman Minsky.
> Probably the other supreme book on bubbles and economic crises.

Extraordinary Popular Delusions and the Madness of Crowds, Charles Mackay.
> Over 150 years old and still relevant as to how bubbles and financial crises occur.

Lombard Street, Walter Bagehot.
> Describes London's bond market in the late 1800s. Remarkably clear-headed on why panics can occur and what can (and cannot) be done.

B.3 News

The Economist is superb: a weekly magazine that treats you as though you were truly intelligent. It is probably the most international new source you will read. Their analyses are often insightful and can show remarkable nuance. They are the creators of the famed Big Mac Index; and, their weekly news summary and data roundup are *tours de force*. However, *The Economist* can also be wickedly humorous. (One color piece on historical re-enactment showed a man dressed as a Roman Centurion leering at a lady passing by. The photo was captioned simply: "Maximus Decimus admires gluteus maximus.")

Far East Economic Review has, sadly, ceased as of 2009. However, in its time it was the source of biting and trenchant criticism and also often hilarious. For those looking for historical sources about Asian economies, I highly recommend it.

Financial Times is an excellent newspaper if a bit terse. It is more international than US papers and has kept some of their in-depth special coverage.

Nihon Keizai Shimbun, aka the *Nikkei* is the top financial newspaper of Japan. Although published in Japanese, there is the English-language *Nikkei Weekly* for those with an interest in Japanese markets.

South China Morning Post, though not a business newspaper, is Hong Kong's paper of record. It is also often the clearest and most-informed view of what is going on in mainland China.

Wall Street Journal is, despite having occasionally veered into maddeningly political territory, a solid newspaper with excellent coverage of North American markets and, to a lesser extent, global markets.

B.4 Finance and Quantitative Analysis Videos

The Fog of War: Eleven Lessons from the Life of Robert S. McNamara is a documentary interview with McNamara who brought quantitative analysis to the fore as US Secretary of Defense. The movie is a superb tour of quantitative decision making in an environment of uncertainty with extreme costs of being wrong.

Free to Choose is a television mini-series that was hosted by Milton Friedman. It is perhaps the most lucid and entertaining defense of free markets and trade I have ever seen. Even if you disagree with "Uncle Milt," you will not be able to watch this series without thinking hard about your own beliefs. You can find these (legally) online.

The Big Short is a concise explanation of some aspects of the 2008 financial crisis. Furthermore, the shockingly direct and hyper-rational personalities are very true to the world of finance.

Trading Places, with Eddie Murphy and Dan Aykroyd as commodity traders.

While a little dated (and awkward) in a few places, the movie is still a fun picture of markets and trading.

Floored is an excellent-if-depressing documentary about the closing of futures trading pits in Chicago as machines replace human traders.

Appendix C

Quiz Answers

> ⚠️**Figyelem!** *While I had hoped to provide answers for exercises as well, this has proved difficult for a few reasons. Furthermore, I have heard from some people that they* emphatically *do not want me to provide answers to the exercises. Therefore, I present here answers to the quiz questions and I will defer exercise answers to (possibly) a solutions manual to be made available later.*

Chapter 1

1. resources; benefits

2. opportunity costs

3. financial; real

4. True

5. Agency

6. capital/money; economy

7. buyers; sellers; money; demands/opportunities for money.

8. Allow them to shift risk to others willing to bear that risk

9. Allow them to bet against firms and profit from revealed problems

10. Taking risk

Chapter 2

1. USD, EUR, GBP, JPY, CHF

2. A new asset class behaves differently which increases your ability to diversify. You also might be able to find some bargains in this newly-discovered asset class.

3. S&P 500, Russell 2000. If you said the Dow, double shame on you.

4. Because a larger firm has more effect on the economy.

5. False. Derivatives aren't really an asset class; and, this neglects foreign currencies (aka FX) and commodities. There might also be asset classes which are distinct but too small to concern most investores. A good general rule: any supposedly canonical list probably isn't.

6. False; an index ETF is a portfolio derivative one. We don't usually think of them as derivatives but they are. Furthermore, we might even consider indices to be derivatives even though they are untradeable. There is a good reason to think of ETFs (and even indices) indices as derivatives: it clarifies that derivatives need not be scary or complicated.

7. Real estate

8. LIBOR: the London Interbank Offered Rate.

9. The coupon rate would be even higher. (Much higher, perhaps 8%.) Many people try to find an exact answer for this. Don't let the form of the question guide you to not answering what you do know.

10. Florida has no state income tax, so their municipal bonds were not attractive for potential state tax savings.

Chapter 3

1. Primary: where securities are issued; secondary: where issued (or soon-to-be-issued) securities are traded.

2. False; auctions are used to begin and end continuous trading.

3. market; limit

4. An intermediary buys at the bid and sells at the ask/offer. (one-half point for each)

5. A retail investor sending market buys will buy at the offer and market sells will sell at the bid. (one-half point for each)

6.

 a) Asset prices would fall.
 b) Being unable to trade at any time means taking on more risk.

7. False. Bookbuilding is when investment bankers collect indications of interest in an IPO; collecting buy and sell limit orders is just maintaining a limit order book.

8. Split by Glass-Steagall (1933; aka Banking Act).

9. Lightest touch; incorporates nuanced understanding of how market works; being regulated by competitors helps level the playing field.

10. I must "get" locates, *i.e.* believe I can borrow the shares.

Chapter 4

1. True; electronic markets do offer more pre- and post-trade transparency.

2. True; electronic markets also have higher fixed or startup costs.

3. Fast executions, visible order book, just acts as a broker? That's an ECN!

4. First, these rules were passed to punish market maker collusion. Second, they were passed to promote competition among market venues so that the market would better police itself with respect to collusion. I suppose one could even see a third reason: to bring extreme savings quickly to the market as a reward for past overcharging. From an economics perspective, it is also interesting in that there seems to have been no *regulatory capture*: the affected firms had little influence over the reforms.

5. Effective spreads (the difference between the average buy and sell price) dropped by a factor of 6. Average quoted spreads dropped by a factor of 16.

6. Program trading is *not* computerized or automated trading. (Yes, yes: I know you might read otherwise in the paper. Trust a trader, not a journalist, to know about trading.) Program trading is the meticulous, pre-planned trading of a large portfolio. In the US, a program trade is defined trading a portfolio of 15+ names worth $1+MM.

7. First: No, you should not be concerned. Second: You should not be overly concerned because index arbitrageurs will ensure that all of these are (almost always) trading at the same price. It makes more sense to think about which is the appropriate vehicle. (That means thinking about expected length of holding and taxes. More on that later.)

8. False. Most high-frequency traders need to act quickly. Optimization might take 30 seconds and even a multiply takes more operations than a sinple conditional test.

9. Because the data are easier for anyone to see now. Trading glitches happened in 2005 (Mizuho), 2001 (Nasdaq Russell rebalance outage), and many in 2000 and back into the 1990s — as shown in Gao and Mizrach (2016). What changed was the availability of free intraday data and charting.

10. Commercial and investment banks were split by Glass-Steagall (1933, aka Banking Act). They were then reunited by Gramm-Leach-Bliley (1999). Prop trading and other forms of risk-taking were limited by Dodd-Frank (2010). (Well... Gramm-Leach-Bliley didn't reunite them *per se*; the House of Morgan remains, to this day, divided.)

Chapter 5

1. Market efficiency is unlikely to be affected: none of this money affects the workings of the markets *per se*.

Allocative efficiency will decrease. Market prices will reflect these firms having more cash, making them look more valuable than they should be. That encourages excess investment into automobile manufacturing when that industry is evidently not highly profitable. This comes at the cost of investing in an industry which would have been more profitable.

X-efficiency will stay depressed. Less efficient firms in the industry could have gone out of business. That would have reallocated capital and labor to more efficient firms — which would have increased X-efficiency. Instead, X-efficiency will stay low and might even decrease since management now knows their jobs are completely secure.

2. Cap-weighted indices make errors: they over-invest in overvalued companies and under-invest in undervalued companies. Indexes should instead use fundamental value and/or shrinkage.

3. 1/2 point for the names, 1/2 point for each definition.

- Weak: all previous trade info is impounded in the price;
- Semi-strong: all public info is impounded in the price;
- Strong: all public and private info impounded in the price.

4. As a passive investor, you are not going to be agitating for change; you merely want to choose the best-run firm that should (over the long-run) be more profitable, better weather trouble, and grow. Therefore, you would want the firm operating at the highest technical efficiency. Mötörhaus produces 9 motors/person-day versus $7\frac{11}{12}$ motors/person-day at PowerFab and $7\frac{1}{3}$ motors/person-day at Engine & Tonic.

As an activist investor, Engine & Tonic shows the most potential for improvement; therefore, your efforts might be best rewarded by investing there and then agitating for better management, automation, and processes.

What about PowerFab? With a capacity utilization of 95%, they might seem to be better than Mötörhaus (180/200=90%) or Engine & Tonic (110/140=78.6%). However, they use more employees to reach that higher level. Thus they are not the most efficient firm.

5.

    a) It means that prices more quickly reflect information about the prospects of an investment. We would look at changes in average spreads (quoted and effective) as well as changes in the autocorrelation of quote changes.

    b) We want allocative and X-efficiency: we want our economy to produce the optimal balance of goods at the least cost.

6. Peak-to-peak, the average business cycle lasts 6–7 years.

7. No. And no.

8. Fiscal policy is slower to enact and political: it requires politicians to compromise and act. Monetary policy, on the other hand, is not politicized and is decided by economists (non-politicians) at the central bank.

Also a valid answer: In Europe, fiscal policy rests at the national level while monetary policy is controlled at the Eurozone (super-national) level.

9.

    a) Defensive, vice stocks; long-dated Treasury bonds; TIPS; gold; commodities; CHF
    b) Cyclical stocks (car, appliance makers; home builders); non-defensive stocks; high-yield debt.

10. If the country has a lot of political corruption, it is likely that politician's family members and relatives are in cushy state jobs, possibly running state-owned firms. The government ticket kiosks are likely to be one such firm, especially with all the cash business they do. If the government is planning on privatizing firms, it might want to spin off that firm to enrich a family member running the firm and so it doesn't have to provide for all those employees' retirement and healthcare.

Therefore, one big risk is that the government will obstruct or prevent the start-up from undercutting the government kiosks. Schumpeter's Gale may not blow away the inefficiency.

Chapter 6

1. Consider real rate, inflation, and taxes (τ). Since i is low, we can approximate: $(r+i)(1-\tau)-i = r(1-\tau)-i\tau = 3\%(0.7)-2\% = 1\%(0.7)-2\%(0.3) = 0.7\%-0.6\% = 0.1\%$.
Compare this to $1\%(0.7) = 0.7\%$. The $i\tau$ term is taxed inflation.

2. EAR=$1.2\times1.5 = 2.25 = 125\%$; APR $= 50\%\times2 = 100\%$

3. False; all models are wrong. If the government defaults, even time value of money calculations will fail.

4. $1.03

5. It tracks a portfolio of goods: meat, vegetables, dairy, grains, transport of these, plus energy and labor to cook them.

6.
$$\log(p_2/p_1) = \log(27.18/10) = \log(2.718) = 1 = 100\%$$

Chapter 7

1.

$$\bar{x} = \frac{1}{n}\sum x = \frac{24}{12} = 2 \tag{C.1}$$

$$\hat{s}^2 = \frac{1}{n-1}\sum(x-\bar{x})^2 = \frac{72}{12-1} = 6.545 \tag{C.2}$$

$$\hat{s} = \sqrt{s^2} = 2.56 \tag{C.3}$$

$$\hat{\gamma} = \frac{1}{n-2}\sum\left(\frac{x-\bar{x}}{s}\right)^3 = \frac{-4.3}{12-2} = -0.43 \tag{C.4}$$

$$\hat{\kappa} = \frac{1}{n-3}\sum\left(\frac{x-\bar{x}}{s}\right)^4 = \frac{22.97}{12-3} = 2.55 \tag{C.5}$$

If you only have the equations, take full points (if you have the degrees of freedom) or half points otherwise.

2. Log-returns add, so the cumulative log-return is 18%.

3. Mathematically, if we model returns as coming from geometric Brownian motion, then log-returns should be normally-distributed.

4. False. Financial asset returns sometimes display positive or negative skewness and often display kurtoses greater than 3.

5. The average excess return is known as the risk premium.

6. $0.03\sqrt{250} = 0.47 = 47\% \approx 0.03 \times 15 = 0.45 = 45\%$

7. First, there is a "peakedness:" an exaggerated clustering near the center. Second, there are "fat tails:" thicker tails with much higher likelihoods of extreme observations.

8. The correlation of X and Z is zero. Correlation is just scaled covariance. Futhermore, $\text{Cov}(X,Z) = E(XZ) - E(X)E(Z) = E(X(X^2 + Y)) - E(X)E(X^2 + Y) = E(X^3 + XY) - 0 \times (16 + 0) = E(X^3) + E(XY) = 0 + 0 = 0$. An easier way to see this: Z is just X^2 plus noise (Y). $X \perp\!\!\!\perp Y$ and X is uncorrelated with X^2; thus X and Z must be uncorrelated.

Chapter 8

1. False: Value-at-risk does not explain how bad extreme losses can be.

2.

   a) To see how excess returns look adjusted for a downside risk measure.
   b) There are some periods with big drawdowns/losses.

3. coherent

4. a) decreases b) has k times the risk c) $\leq$

5. 5% VaR (value-at-risk); is not a good risk measure

6. expected shortfall or conditional value at risk (CVaR) or tail conditional expectation; it IS a good risk measure.

7. That there is little we can do to protect ourselves.

8. Use multiple models and be suspicious or critical of all of them.

9. semideviation or lower partial standard deviation; is not a good risk measure. (Semideviation is a better risk measure than volatility, but it is still not coherent).

Chapter 9

1.

a) $U_{\text{T-bill}} = 2\%$, $U_{\text{Stock}} = 14\% - \frac{4}{2}0.3^2 = 0.14 - 0.18 = -0.04 = -4\%$

b) $U_{\text{T-bill}} = 2\%$, $U_{\text{Stock}} = 14\% - \frac{2}{2}0.3^2 = 0.14 - 0.09 = 0.05 = 5\%$

2. For a gambler, risk aversion is $\lambda < 0$; for a speculator, risk aversion $\lambda \geq 0$.

3.

a) Bond market index; stock market index; industry; general credit risk (*e.g.* TED spread)

b) Firm is "cooking the books;" CEO's health; HQ swallowed by giant sinkhole.

4.

a) P_4 is the optimal risky portfolio.

b) For P_1, the Sharpe ratio is $\frac{0.20-0.01}{0.35}$ (=0.543).

c) You would not prefer P_3 to P_1 because it offers the least return for the same amount of volatility as P_1.

d) The OSRA would shift down and to the right. This would change what is the optimal risky portfolio.

5.

a) Yes, because Laszlo is more risk-averse.

b) Yes; just because Laszlo is more risk-averse does not mean he should choose a suboptimal risky portfolio.

c) Ellen may have: self-imposed constraints such as wanting to invest in "socially-responsible" investments; used different inputs; measured/estimated at differing times; have a different total portfolio; or, manage risk with different risk measures.

Chapter 10

1. a) $\$1000 \times \frac{1}{2} + \$800 \times \frac{1}{2} = \$900$. b) PV $= \$900/1.02$.

2. That the future of the random process depends on its past.

3. An autoregressive/AR/AR(1) process.

4. $|\phi| < 1$.

5. Corr $= \frac{0.07}{\sqrt{0.09+0.07}\sqrt{0.09+0.07}} = \frac{0.07}{0.16} = 0.4375$.

6. True: we often do not work with the full data to maintain tractability.

7. $E(Y_{t+1}|\mathcal{F}_t) = \alpha + \phi Y_t$

8. That the student is an egghead or did the modeling wrong — because the $\phi > 1$ yields a process which will explode.

Chapter 11

1. a) 70 days b) 71 days

2. Value $= \frac{\$1}{0.001} = \$1000$.

3.

a) $P_0 = \$98.70 + \$4.85 + \$4.95 = \$108.50$.
b) $D = \frac{4.95 \times 1 + 4.85 \times 2 + 98.7 \times 3}{108.5} = \frac{4.95 + 9.7 + 296.1}{108.5} = \frac{310.75}{108.5} = 2.86$
c) Most likely below 5% because a 5% bond is trading at a premium (above $100).

4.

a) Both 1 bp differences in the table show a price change of $-\$0.04 = DV01$. Therefore, their average is also $-\$0.04$.
b) Zero — since both DV01's are the same.
c) No, because rates are currently 2.8% and the bond is trading at a premium.
d) Can determine the modified duration D^*: $DV01 = -D^* P \times 0.0001 \Rightarrow D^* = \frac{10,000 \times \$0.04}{\$105.01} = \frac{\$400}{\$105.01} (= 3.81)$ Guess that the bond matures in 10 years because of modified duration being greater than 3.

5.

a) If firm is not bankrupt and selling assets would incur a large cost.
b) Cross-default: bond investors cannot be played against each other.
c) Limits on dividend payouts exceeding revenues.

6. You should hedge the 30Y zero first, the 30Y coupon bond next, and the 2Y coupon bond last — because you should hedge bonds in the order of their interest-rate sensitivity (most-sensitive first).

7. $P = 1.5 \sum_{i=1}^{4} \frac{1}{(1+0.02/2)^i} + \frac{100}{(1.01)^4}$

8. Tax-free interest

9. BB+, Ba1, or BBH

10. Investment fund mandates often preclude holding sub-investment-grade debt.

Chapter 12

1.

a) Aproximate rate would average with 0.4% to be 0.6%. Thus approximately, $\frac{0.004+y}{2} = 0.006 \rightarrow y = 0.8\%$.

b) $\sqrt{1.004}\sqrt{1+y} = 1.006 \Rightarrow y = \frac{1.006^2}{1.004} - 1 = 0.8\%$. Note that the approximation and exact answer will differ by more than rounding error when rates increase.

2.

a) Sell short 1Y bond; invest proceeds in 2Y bond. Agree now to sell short (what will then be a) 1Y bond one year from now in an amount sufficient to pay off the shorted 1Y bond. Pay that off when 2Y bond matures; keep difference as free money.

b) Approximately 1.2%-0.7% = 0.5% of face value.

3.

a) Slowing growth/economic downturn.

b) Equities not attractive/look scary, so people buy long-dated USTs for safety — which pushes down long-dated UST yields.

4. A healthy economy usually has an upward-sloping yield curve.

5. The yield curve will look humped — yields wil be elevated in the "belly" of the curve.

6. The most common movement is a shift of the average level up or down. The next-most common movement is an increase or decrease in the slope (aka a twist).

Chapter 13

1.

   a) Defensive, vice stocks; long-dated Treasury bonds; TIPS; gold; commodities; CHF

   b) Cyclical stocks (car, appliance makers; home builders); non-defensive stocks; high-yield debt.

2. $P = \frac{\$3}{0.1} + \frac{\$3}{0.1^3} 0.01^2 = \$30 + \$0.30 = \$30.30.$

3. $P = \frac{\$3}{0.10-0.01} + \frac{\$3}{(0.10-0.01)^3}(0.01^2 + 0.005^2 - 2 \cdot 0.01 \cdot 0.005 \cdot 0.6) = \frac{\$3}{0.09} + \frac{\$3}{0.09^3} 0.000065 = \$33.33 + \$0.03 = \$33.36$

4. $q = 1.43$. The firm will be replicated, and its value will fall to $\approx \$70$ mn.

5.

   a) $\hat{F} = \frac{\$3 \text{ mn}}{0.06-0.02} + \frac{\$3 \text{ mn}}{(0.06-0.02)^3}(0.005^2 + 0.005^2 - 2 \cdot 0.005 \cdot 0.005 \cdot 0.4) = \frac{\$3 \text{ mn}}{0.04} + \frac{\$3 \text{ mn}}{0.04^3} 0.00003 = \$76.41mn$

   b) $\frac{\$76.41 \text{ mn} - \$3 \text{ mn}}{3 \text{ mn}} = \$24.47$

6. Somewhere near \$40. Tobin's q suggests a current market price of $\$160/3 = \$53$ is too high; and, only the Gordon model suggests a price nearly that high. Other models suggest \$40, \$43, and \$50 — so \$40 seems like a good price expectation.

7. Amazon will eventually pay out a dividend when growth slows.

Chapter 14

1. 7 variances, $7(7-1)/2 = 21$ covariances, 7 expected returns, 1 risk-free rate $= 36$ parameters.

2. 7 vars, 7 betas, 7 expected returns, 1 market expected return, 1 market variance, 1 risk-free rate $= 24$ inputs.

3. Var $= 0.15 + 1.1^2 \times 0.1 = 0.15 + 0.121 = 0.271.$

4. Good idea; a crude form of squeezing that outperforms just using $\hat{\beta}_i$'s estimated using historical data.

5. The market? Marginal return on risk? Some economic multiplier? A macroeconomic factor? The meaning of m is unknown.

6. Nothing. It still holds. Non-normality does not invalidate the model.

7. Market neutral

8. $E(r) = r_f + \hat{\beta}E(r_M - r_f) = 1\% + 1.1 \times (13\% - 1\%) = 1\% + 13.2\% = 14.2\%$.

9. That speculators add value by absorbing risks, including the risk that economic sensitivites may change in adverse ways.

10. One hint is that these instrumented are likely to have large estimated alphas. Much better, however, is to look at the residuals from estimating betas. Find which residuals are highly correlated with each other — meaning that there is comovement that the model did not capture. A check of those models will also likely show that they had poor descriptive ability.

Chapter 15

1. APT: rapidly; one huge trader forces convergence; CAPM: "dominance" = slowly; many small adjustments to investors' portfolios guide valuations to correct levels.

2. Yes, because $E(r_P) = 0.10 \neq E(r_P|E(r_M)) = 0.06 + 1.5(0.10\text{-}0.06) = 0.06 + 1.5(0.04) = 0.12$. To make money, sell short 1 unit of P and buy 1.5 units of M, then finance the balance by shorting 0.5 units of risk-free bond.

3. Fundamental risk, the risk that the trade might not converge by the arbitageur's horizon; model risk, the risk that the APT model may be wrong or may drift; liquidity risk and the preclusion of quasi-arbitrage — because if the arbitrageur tries to exit prematurely or quickly, the trade may not be profitable and may even lose money.

4. SMB = small-minus-big market cap aka "size"; HML = high-minus-low book/-market aka "value"; and, the market. Carhart's fourth factor is momentum, aka UMD (up-minus-down) or WML (winners-minus-lowers).

5. Because this is related to the slope of the yield curve, which we earlier saw was informative about the state of (and prospects for) the economy.

6. No and no. There is no mathematical proof of a regression model. The randomness of data makes this impossible.

7. The fees are not likely to be worthwhile since we can replicate the fund with the eight Fung-Hsieh factors (which are largely cheaply-available assets/indexes.. While these might not perfectly mimic the fund returns due to drifts in the factor loadings, this mismatch is likely to be less than the (high) fund fees.

8. The fees may not be worthwhile. We would determine the replicating portfolios for the SMB and HML factors. We can see how much it would cost (on a percentage basis) to purchase these in the right quantity. These might not perfectly mimic the fund returns due to drifts in the portfolio composition and factor loadings; therefore, we would also want to assess the cost of tracking error and rebalancing.

9. The crudes are more likely to obey the Law of One Price because if there is a price difference that can cover transportation, you just ship one and deliver it to capture the mispricing. The shares are subject to fundamental risk as well as price impact and the preclusion of quasi-arbitrage, so they can drift apart and stay that way.

Chapter 16

1. Fundamental risk, preclusion of quasi-arbitrage, risk limits

2.

a) Lands' End is implied to be worth $20/share$\times$100 mn shares $=$ $2 bn. The part remaining inside Sears is worth $1.8 bn; however, Sears has a market cap of $1.5 bn. $1.8 bn $>$ $1.5 billion; so, there is a violation of the LOOP.

b) Lands' End shares are probably hard to borrow, especially since only 10% are circulating.

3. When we analyze data looking backwards, we may only have data for companies/markets which survived. Thus we omit those that failed — which biases our analysis. This suggests the "puzzle" may not be such a puzzle.

4.

a) We tend to study markets which have done well — the winners. This is both because those markets attract researchers investigating their success and because we lack data for markets which failed. Thus asking why these markets did so well compared to others has an implicit observation bias.

b) We need to consider countries where equities did terribly or where we lacked data. Examples include: Rhodesia/Zimbabwe (especially in the post-UDI–Mugabe 1961–2010s period; Venezuela from Chavez to the present; Cuba from Castro to the present; Myanmar under military rule: 1962–2011... though post-military-dictatorship violence against Rohingya Muslims, Kachins, the Shan, the Lahu, and the Karen looks similar to campaigns active under the

military dictatorship; Argentina since Peron and perhaps earlier; Côte d'Ivoire
for much of its existence; Congo during their civil war; Uganda under Idi Amin;
Weimar Republic Germany; Cambodia under the Khmer Rouge; and possibly
Malaysia and Indonesia during periods of anti-Chinese ethnic strife.

5. Fundamental risk is the risk that a trade may not converge by the end of a
trader's investment horizon.

6. It means a trade might not converge by the time they need to exit. So, they
might be hesitant to enter an arbitrage trade.

7. False. Limits to arbitrage often exist for rational reasons.

8. Humans do better at trading when they are less emotional. This suggests that
as computers trade more, markets will be less prone to bubbles and more likely to
be fairly priced.

9. Expected uncertainty, aka risk; uncertainty about that expectation, aka estimation error; and, unknown uncertainty, aka Knightian uncertainty.

Chapter 17

1. KYC stands for "Know Your Customer" and it means you need to be able to
vouch for the provenance of the funds they invest with you. You need to verify that
the funds did not result from illegal activities or terrorism.

2. 1–2=1/2 point, 3=1 points: CN, JP, HK, GB, FR, CA, DE, IN, CH

3. 1–2=1/2 point, 3=1 point: CN, JP, GB, FR, NL, DE, KY, AU, KR

4. 1–2=1/2 point, 3=1 point: CN, JP, DE, FR, GB, KR, AU, CA, IT

5.

  a) Informational and reporting risks, a changing FX rate.
  b) Governance risks (*e.g.* fraud), governmental and monetary policy risks, politi-
     cal/social instability. Also, different informational risks if you are inside the
     country: media censorship. Also, another type of FX risk: capital controls.

6. You would use data from one of the databases with records of such issues, such
as GDELT, the Center for Systemic Peace's Major Episodes of Political Violence, or
the GTD.

7. Korea, Taiwan, Singapore, Portugal, Slovakia, and Slovenia are all excellent examples. Behind these would likely be Chile, Uruguay, and Peru.

8. Your best bet would be to find a prediction market trading that election as a contract. That might help you estimate the probability of victory for the business-hostile candidate. If the market were liquid, you could even use it as a hedge.

9. The Euro Stoxx 50, CSI 300, Nikkei 225 and/or Topix, Hang Seng, and FTSE 100.

Chapter 18

1. Approximate change will negate the interest rate difference, so JPY/USD rate would change by $0.13\% - 1.34\% = -1.21\%$.

2.

  a) BofL going bust; Liberlandia default; taxes going up; capital controls; FX controls
  b) More, because where is the bank getting that 2% extra? Or, is their credit that bad?
  c) Buy CDS of BofL, and maybe Liberland

3.

  a) The Cassell absolute valuation hypothesis suggests AUD/BRL should be 5.10/4.53. (You need not compute this, but it is 1.1258 if you are curious.)
  b) The big difference between the market FX rate and the PPP-implied rate suggests Australia is much more productive than Brazil.

4. The two outward orientation dimensions are low distortion of the relative price level (versus its equilibrium given an economy's factor endowments) and low variability in the real exchange rate.

5. Operational risk/poor controls at exchanges; cannot pass KYC; slow throughput of transactions; governmental restrictions on their use (in some jurisdictions).

Chapter 19

1. Standardization of price and location, quantity, and quality; central clearing; margin and marking to market; trading on an exchange.

2.

  a) $7,500 -$100,000×0.03 = $4,500.
  b) Variation margin = $8,000 -$4,500 = $3,500.

3. *Realizing* P&L daily (or more often)

4. One of: the US Dodd-Frank Act; the EU European Market Infrastructure Regulation; and, the Swiss Financial Market infrastructure Act.

5. The CCP: central counterparty

6.

  a) Abhi has zero exposure.
  b) Abhi has zero capital committed.

7.

  a) Abhi's S&P 500 exposure is zero.
  b) Abhi's capital commitment is zero.
  c) Abhi holds contracts with notional of $10 mn + $10 mn = $20 mn.
  d) Abhi would be exposed to counterparty risk: the risk that either Sabrina or Catie went bankrupt and stopped making payments.

8. Sell futures and buy all index stocks except Motorola.

Chapter 20

1. Call: $\overline{}\diagup_{K}$

2. Put: $\diagdown_{K}\overline{}$

3. European options may only be exercised at expiry; American options may be exercised at any time.

4.

  a) Butterfly payoff: $\underset{K_1\ K_3}{\overline{\underset{}{\overset{K_2}{\wedge}}}}$
  b) I am hoping for prices to stay near K_2 (low volatility).

5.

   a) Bond component: \$20,000 zero-coupon-bond maturing on 4 Feb.

   b) European call struck at \$10 on 1000 shares expiring on 4 Feb.

6. $S_t - Ke^{-0.5r} = \$52 - \$49 = \$3 = C_{50,t,0.5} - P_{50,t,0.5}$.
$C_{50,t,0.5} - P_{50,t,0.5} = \$4.10 - P_{t,0.5} \Rightarrow P_{t,0.5} = \$1.10$.

7. For an American call: right before a dividend. For an American put: when it is deep out of the money.

Chapter 21

1. Note that we can sell \$16 worth of bond and buy the stock. This has values of

$$25 - 16 = 9$$
$$20 - 15.69 = 4.31$$
$$16 - 16 = 0$$

This has half the value of our option; therefore, a fair price for the option is half the initial investment cost: $\$4.31 \times 2 = \$8.62$.

2.

   a) We would see the volatility curve: a curve that (for stocks) is often shaped like the e^{-x} function (aka a "smirk" or U-shaped (aka a "smile").

   b) The volatility curve suggests ways in which the Black-Scholes-Merton formula is inaccurate.

3. To get the risk-neutral density, we need to find the second partial derivative of the option prices with respect to strike price:

$$\frac{\partial^2 V}{\partial K^2} = e^{-r_f \cdot 1} f(K), \tag{C.6}$$

where f is the risk-neutral density.

   To make this less noisy, we would likely fit a smooth volatility curve and then use that to price a range of options to get the second derivatives with respect to the strike prices.

4.

   a) Black-Scholes-Merton call formula:

$$S_0 \Phi(d_1) - Ke^{-r_f T} \Phi(d_2) \tag{C.7}$$

b) d_1 and d_2:

$$d_1 = \frac{\log(S_0/K) + (r_f + \sigma^2/2)T}{\sigma\sqrt{T}} \qquad \text{(C.8)}$$

$$d_1 = \frac{\log(S_0/K) + (r_f - \sigma^2/2)T}{\sigma\sqrt{T}} = d_1 - \sigma\sqrt{T} \qquad \text{(C.9)}$$

c) The first term gives the expected value of the underlier (using risk-neutral probabilities) given that the option is in-the-money.

d) The second term gives the present value of the probability that the option is in-the-money (using risk-neutral probabilities).

Chapter 22

1. True.

2. They are negatively correlated; they are inversely related.

3. Standard & Poor's (S&P), Moody's, Fitch, and DBRS.

4. BBB-, BBBL, or Baa3

5. Seasoning means that probabilities of defaults are higher earlier in a bond's life before settling down — ostensibly after the "bad bets" in the portfolio have mostly defaulted.

6. Before, we modeled equity as a geometric Brownian motion. The Merton approach models the firm's assets as a geometric Brownian motion with equity being a call option on the firm with the strike price being the firm's liabilities.

7. The number of standard deviations the asset value is above liabilities.

8. Because cashflow and short-term funding issues often arise early in a financial crisis, those ratios express potential risk in a crisis.

9. The time to default

10. Data from credit default swaps are the cleanest data — cleaner than yield spreads or stock prices.

11. A letter of credit

Chapter 23

1.

a) Prepayments/refinancing could greatly reduce the value of the Z tranche.
b) As interest rates fall below the weighted average coupon, the A tranche will become more valuable.
c) The value of the tranche increases because the bond will be trading at a premium (since it receives a higher interest rate) and because the maturity has decreased which reduces the discounting of future cashflows.

2. We could have banks hold part of the risk of each loan they originate; or, we could have banks issue covered bonds.

3. Some borrowers are not aware that they can refinance. Others are aware but cannot afford the fees involved in refinancing.

4. The option-adjusted spread

5.

a) A CDO shifts default risk.
b) Synthetic CDOs hold credit default swaps (CDSs) instead of the underlying bonds.
c) A synthetic CDO, since it holds CDSs, also exposes the investor to counterparty risk. If the writer of the CDSs fails, the synthetic CDO investor may not get the payments promised.

6. We see the "J curve."

Chapter 24

1.

a) $\sqrt{1.1 \times 1.2} = \sqrt{1.32} = 1.149 \Rightarrow 14.9\%$
b) r such that $\$10 + \frac{\$10}{1+r} = \frac{\$24.20}{(1+r)^2} = 13.4\%$

2.

a) $S_P = \frac{E(R_P)}{\sigma_P} = \frac{10\%}{30\%} = 1/3.$
b) $So_P = \frac{E(R_P)}{\theta_P} = \frac{10\%}{50\%} = 1/5.$
c) $E(R_P) = \alpha_P + \beta_M(E(R_M)) \Rightarrow 10\% = 3\% + \beta_P(5\%) \Rightarrow \beta_P = 7/5.$
d) $M_P^2 = \frac{\sigma_M}{\sigma_P}E(R_P) + \frac{\sigma_P - \sigma_M}{\sigma_P}r_f - E(R_M) = \frac{15\%}{30\%}10\% + \frac{30\% - 15\%}{15\%}2\% - 5\% = 1\%.$

e) $T_P = \frac{E(R_P)}{\beta_P} = \frac{10\%}{7/5} = 0.0714$

f)

$$\sigma_{\epsilon_P} = \sigma_\alpha = ?$$
$$\sigma_P^2 = \sigma_\alpha^2 + \beta_M \sigma_M^2$$
$$\Rightarrow 0.3^2 = \sigma_\alpha^2 + (7/5)^2 \times 0.15^2$$
$$\sigma_\alpha^2 = 0.3^2 - 0.21^2 = 0.0459 \Rightarrow \sigma_\alpha = 0.214$$
$$\Rightarrow IR_P = \frac{\alpha_P}{\sigma_\alpha} = \frac{3\%}{21.4\%} = 0.14$$

Why not use $S_{P*}^2 = S_M^2 + IR_P^2$? that only holds for portfolios constructed with an investor-optimal (e.g. TB) balance of M and A.

3. Not likely a good market timer: $S_{OP} \ll S_P$ implies semideviation is higher than volatility ($\theta_P > \sigma_P$) and so the manager does not avoid downside; and, IR_P is small.

4.

a) $r_P - r_B = 10\% - 8\% = 2\%$ $(w_P - w_B)r_B = (20\% - 10\%)10\% = 0.1 \times 10\% = 1\%$

b) $r_P - r_B = 10\% - 8\% = 2\%$ $w_P(r_P - r_B) = 20\%(15\% - 10\%) = 0.2 \times 5\% = 1\%$

5. The weights of the active and market portfolio can get large. Fixes: we can limit position sizes, constrain risks, or penalize the weights on M and A.

6. Uses market covariance matrix and λ to estimate $E(R_M)$ and then $E(R)$ of each asset class.

7. Must guesstimate standard errors of views; can impose strong views and push model to (largely) justify action you desired. Fix: use models to get views and standard errors.

8. TB: bottom-up; BL: top-down

9. As a one-time fee, Kane, Marcus, and Trippi (1999) say to charge:

$$\%\text{fee} = \frac{S_P^2 - S_M^2}{2\bar{\lambda}} = \frac{1}{2\bar{\lambda}} IR_P^2 = \frac{1}{2}1 = 50\%(\bar{\lambda} = 1); = \frac{1}{6}1 = 16.7\%(\bar{\lambda} = 3). \quad \text{(C.10)}$$

Best and Grauer (1991) would say to charge an annual fee of 10% while Glode (2011) says to charge $0.10 + 0.02 \cdot 0.0075 = 0.1015 = 10.15\%$. Finally, the solution we came up with suggests charging annual fees of:

$$\begin{cases} \frac{0.10}{2} + \frac{1 \cdot 0.01}{4} = 4.75\% & \bar{\lambda} = 1, \\ \frac{0.10}{2} + \frac{3 \cdot 0.01}{4} = 4.25\% & \bar{\lambda} = 3. \end{cases} \quad \text{(C.11)}$$

Chapter 25

1. Sell short an ETF; go long a closed-end fund

2. Closed-end funds do not issue or redeem shares as investment money flows in or out; their shares outstanding are fixed and the price, therefore, may differ from NAV. CEFs also trade intra-day whereas open-end (mutual) funds do not.

3.

- Portfolio company may be offshore with only management company (having minimal assets) in US;
- definition of "hedge fund" unclear: mgmt co or portfolio co?;
- assets = AUM or leveraged assets?;
- when must they report all positions?; How often?;
- what are "non-operational" assets? are investments operational given that the fund produces returns? or not?
- danger of data being exposed and thus destabilizing that fund or the market;
- hedge fund may trade in securities that the SEC does not regulate (*e.g.* CFTC or FERC regulates) = regulatory fight+nightmare;
- regulating investments in other countries could touch upon issues of national sovereignty.

4. Net worth of more than $1 million; or, $200,000 in annual salary for three years (two years + expectation of more, $300,000 if married)

5. Invest in a REIT focused on Chicago and/or urban condo residences.

6. management/operating fees; marketing fees; sales load; transactions costs; soft dollars

7. Almost not at all. Plagued with survivorship bias, reporting bias, and backfill bias.

Chapter 26

1. First, the positive and significant $\hat{\alpha}$ is a little concerning; but, that could be just due to the risk of new technology companies. The higher beta also suggests higher risk than is usual. However, most troubling is the AR(1) coefficient $\hat{\phi} > 1$. Furthermore, the coefficient is significantly different that 1: $\hat{\rho} - 1$ has a t-stat of 3. Finally, the lack of relaton to the macroeconomy is a bit troubling and also weakly indicative of a possible bubble.

2. A real estate bubble is usually more damaging since it leaves an overhang of inventory that is not quickly reduced.

3. There is absolutely a potential for systemic risk. If trading firms, hedge funds, or banks all lose a lot of money, they may engage in fire sales — selling assets in other markets. The bitcoin crisis would then be tranferred to seemingly unrelated markets. This is what we saw in 1998 with the Russian default leading to the LTCM crisis.

4. This creates an ongoing financial relationship. Thus the financial firms are exposed to the credit of the bitcoin venues. In the event of a fire sale or crisis, they might find some venues not returning their money. Worse: if they traded on mispricings, one side might cancel the trade leaving the intermediaries unhedged and long or short the market. This could result in firms needing to trade elsewhere. Thus bitcoin venues and financial intermediaries who leave monies at those venues are exposed to counterparty risk and network effects. This too points to a potential for systemic risk.

5. In peaceful times, a reduction in market liquidity is self-healing and results in a rise in funding liquidity. In crisis times, a reduction in market liquidity results in lower funding liquidity and the market and funding liquidity spiral downward.

6. The slope of the yield curve is one strong indicator. Another is a credit spread; in particular, a TED spread over 48 bp indicates a crisis. Some people look at the LIBOR-OIS spread which combines the very front-end yield curve slope with a credit spread.

7. Aggressively punishing fraud at mortgage lenders; securitization being done via covered bonds or making the banks hold on to some of the risk of the loans they originate; making bonuses contingent on longer-term performance; central clearing of standardized derivatives; and, revisiting how to prevent mark-to-market accounting from interacting with collateral calls in a destabilizing manner.

8. Eurozone members were not given believable incentives for punishment of not meeting fiscal criteria; and, ultimately, the lack of fiscal union produced bad incentives.

9. Contingent convertible bonds — which become equity when certain stress triggers are met — could allow for "bail ins."

Index

Definitions of terms are found at bolded page numbers. Where exercises touch upon a concept, those are given italicized page numbers.

Praise for *A Quantitative Primer on Investments with R*

A unique and comprehensive book for learning to invest with R; packed full of intuition, theory, and R code to let readers get their hands dirty with the ideas. Dale's passion for teaching and finance offers a wealth of insights on risk management, statistics, and economics.
— Kris Boudt, Professor of Finance & Econometrics, Vrije Universiteit Brussel / Amsterdam

This is the book I wish I had when I was starting my career.
— Justin Klosek, Portfolio Manager, Cambridge Square Capital

This book does for investments what John Hull's book did for derivatives: provides a clear, objective, formal treatment of a fundamental financial topic for quantitative readers with a practical inclination.
— Philip Maymin, Associate Professor of Analytics and Finance, University of Bridgeport; hedge fund portfolio manager; author of *Financial Hacking*

---

www.q36llc.com/think/investments
Chicago